Peterson's® Two-Year Colleges 2020

About Peterson's®

Peterson's® has been your trusted educational publisher for over 50 years. It's a milestone we're quite proud of, as we continue to offer the most accurate, dependable, high-quality educational content in the field, providing you with everything you need to succeed. No matter where you are on your academic or professional path, you can rely on Peterson's for its books, online information, expert test-prep tools, the most up-to-date education exploration data, and the highest quality career success resources—everything you need to achieve your education goals. For our complete line of products, visit **www.petersons.com**.

For more information about Peterson's range of educational products, contact Peterson's, 8740 Lucent Blvd., Suite 400, Highlands Ranch, CO 80129, or find us online at **www.petersons.com**.

Previous editions published as *Peterson's Annual Guide to Undergraduate Study* © 1970, 1971, 1972, 1973, 1974, 1975, 1976, 1977, 1978, 1979, 1980, 1981, 1982 and as *Peterson's Two-Year Colleges* © 1983, 1984, 1985, 1986, 1987, 1988, 1989, 1990, 1991, 1992, 1993, 1994, 1995, 1996, 1997, 1998, 1999, 2000, 2001, 2002, 2003, 2004, 2005, 2006, 2007, 2008, 2009, 2010, 2011, 2012, 2013, 2014, 2015, 2016, 2017, 2018

ISSN 0894-9328
ISBN: 978-0-7689-4328-3

Printed in the United States of America

10 9 8 7 6 5 4 3 2 21 20 19

Fiftieth Edition

Contents

A Note from the Peterson's® Editors

For more than 50 years, Peterson's has given students and parents the most comprehensive, up-to-date information on undergraduate institutions in the United States. Peterson's researches the data published in *Peterson's Two-Year Colleges* each year. The information is furnished by the colleges and is accurate at the time of publishing.

This guide also features advice and tips on the college search and selection process, such as how to decide if a two-year college is right for you, how to approach transferring to another college, and what's in store for adults returning to college. If you seem to be getting more, not less, anxious about choosing and getting into the right college, *Peterson's Two-Year Colleges* provides just the right help, giving you the information you need to make important college decisions and ace the admission process.

Opportunities abound for students, and this guide can help you find what you want in a number of ways:

"What You Need to Know About Two-Year Colleges" outlines the basic features and advantages of two-year colleges. "Surviving Standardized Tests" gives an overview of the common examinations students take prior to attending college. "Who's Paying for This? Financial Aid Basics" provides guidelines for financing your college education. "Frequently Asked Questions About Transferring" takes a look at the two-year college scene from the perspective of a student who is looking toward the day when he or she may pursue additional education at a four-year institution. "Returning to School: Advice for Adult Students" is an analysis of the pros and cons (mostly pros) of returning to college after already having begun a professional career. "Coming to America: Tips for International Students Considering Study in the U.S." is an article written particularly for students overseas who are considering a U.S. college education. "Community Colleges and the Green Economy" offers information on some exciting "green" programs at community colleges throughout the United States, as well as two insightful essays by Mary F. T. Spilde, President, Lane Community College and Tom Sutton, Director of Wind Energy and Technical Services, Kalamazoo Valley Community College. Finally, "How to Use This Guide" gives details on the data in this guide: what terms mean and why they're here.

- If you already have specifics in mind, such as a particular institution or major, turn to the easy-to-use **Two-Year Colleges At-a-Glance Chart** or **Indexes.** You can look up a particular feature—location and programs offered—or use the alphabetical index and immediately find the colleges that meet your criteria.
- For information about particular colleges, turn to the **Profiles of Two-Year Colleges** section. Here, our comprehensive college profiles are arranged alphabetically by state. They provide a complete picture of need-to-know information about every accredited two-year college—from admission to graduation, including expenses, financial aid, majors, and campus safety. All the information you need to apply is placed together at the conclusion of each college **Profile.** Display ads, which appear near some of the institutions' profiles, have been provided and paid for by those colleges or universities that wished to supplement their profile data with additional information about their institution.
- In addition, two-page narrative descriptions, which appear in the **Featured Two-Year Colleges** section, are paid for and written by college officials and offer great detail about each college. They are edited to provide a consistent format across entries for your ease of comparison.

Peterson's publishes a full line of books—education exploration, test prep, financial aid, and career preparation. Peterson's publications can be found at high school guidance offices, college libraries and career centers, and your local bookstore and library. Peterson's books are also available at www.petersonsbooks.com.

We welcome any comments or suggestions you may have about this publication. Your feedback will help us make educational dreams possible for you—and others like you.

Colleges will be pleased to know that Peterson's helped you in your selection. Admissions staff members are more than happy to answer questions, address specific problems and help in any way they can. The editors at Peterson's wish you great success in your college search.

The College Admissions Process: An Overview

What You Need to Know About Two-Year Colleges

David R. Pierce

Two-year colleges—better known as community colleges—are often called "the people's colleges." With their open-door policies (admission is open to individuals with a high school diploma or its equivalent), community colleges provide access to higher education for millions of Americans who might otherwise be excluded from higher education. Community college students are diverse and of all ages, races, and economic backgrounds. While many community college students enroll full-time, an equally large number attend on a part-time basis so they can fulfill employment and family commitments as they advance their education.

Community colleges can also be referred to as either technical or junior colleges, and they may either be under public or independent control. What unites two-year colleges is that they are regionally accredited, postsecondary institutions, whose highest credential is the associate degree. With few exceptions, community colleges offer a comprehensive curriculum, which includes transfer, technical, and continuing education programs.

IMPORTANT FACTORS IN A COMMUNITY COLLEGE EDUCATION

The student who attends a community college can count on receiving high-quality instruction in a supportive learning community. This setting frees the student to pursue his or her own goals, nurture special talents, explore new fields of learning, and develop the capacity for lifelong learning.

From the student's perspective, four characteristics capture the essence of community colleges:

1. They are community-based institutions that work in close partnership with high schools, community groups, and employers in extending high-quality programs at convenient times and places.
2. Community colleges are cost effective. Annual tuition and fees at public community colleges average approximately half those at public four-year colleges and less than 15 percent of private four-year institutions. In addition, since most community colleges are generally close to their students' homes, these students can also save a significant amount of money on the room, board, and transportation expenses traditionally associated with a college education.
3. Community colleges provide a caring environment, with faculty members who are expert instructors, known for excellent teaching and meeting students at the point of their individual needs, regardless of age, sex, race, current job status, or previous academic preparation. Community colleges join a strong curriculum with a broad range of counseling and career services that are intended to assist students in making the most of their educational opportunities.
4. Many offer comprehensive programs, including transfer curricula in such liberal arts programs as chemistry, psychology, and business management, that lead directly to a baccalaureate degree and career programs that prepare students for employment or assist those already employed in upgrading their skills. For those students who need to strengthen their academic skills, community colleges also offer a wide range of developmental programs in mathematics, languages, and learning skills, designed to prepare the student for success in college studies.

GETTING TO KNOW YOUR TWO-YEAR COLLEGE

The first step in determining the quality of a community college is to check the status of its accreditation. Once you have established that a community college is appropriately accredited, find out as much as you can about the programs and services it has to offer. Much of that information can be found in materials the college provides. However, the best way to learn about a college is to visit in person.

During a campus visit, be prepared to ask a lot of questions. Talk to students, faculty members, administrators, and counselors about the college and its programs, particularly those in which you have a special interest. Ask about available certificates and associate degrees. Don't be shy. Do what you can to dig below the surface. Ask college officials about the transfer rate to four-year colleges. If a college emphasizes student services, find out what particular assistance is offered, such as educational or career guidance. Colleges are eager to provide you with the information you need to make informed decisions.

COMMUNITY COLLEGES CAN SAVE YOU MONEY

If you are able to live at home while you attend college, you will certainly save money on room and board, but it does cost something to commute. Many two-year colleges offer you instruction in your own home through online learning programs or through home study courses that can save both time and money. Look into all the options, and be sure to add up all the costs of attending various colleges before deciding which is best for you.

FINANCIAL AID

Many students who attend community colleges are eligible for a range of federal financial aid programs, state aid, and on-campus jobs. Your high school counselor or the financial aid officer at a community college will also be able to help you. It is in your interest to apply for financial aid months in advance of the date you intend to start your college program, so find out early what assistance is available to you. While many community colleges are able to help students who make a last-minute decision to attend college, either through short-term loans or emergency grants, if you are considering entering college and think you might need financial aid, it is best to find out as much as you can as early as you can.

WORKING AND GOING TO SCHOOL

Many two-year college students maintain full-time or part-time employment while they earn their degrees. Over the years, a steadily growing number of students have chosen to attend community colleges while they fulfill family and employment responsibilities. To enable these students to balance the demands of home, work, and school, most community colleges offer classes at night and on weekends.

For the full-time student, the usual length of time it takes to obtain an associate degree is two years. However, your length of study will depend on the course load you take: the fewer credits you earn each term, the longer it will take you to earn a degree. To assist you in moving more quickly toward earning your degree, many community colleges now award credit through examination or for equivalent knowledge gained through relevant life experiences. Be certain to find out the credit options that are available to you at the college in which you are interested. You may discover that it will take less time to earn a degree than you first thought.

PREPARATION FOR TRANSFER

Studies have repeatedly shown that students who first attend a community college and then transfer to a four-year college or university do at least as well academically as the students who entered the four-year institutions as freshmen. Most community colleges have agreements with nearby four-year institutions to make transfer of credits easier. If you are thinking of transferring, be sure to meet with a counselor or faculty adviser before choosing your courses. You will want to map out a course of study with transfer in mind. Make sure you also find out the credit-transfer requirements of the four-year institution you might want to attend.

ATTENDING A TWO-YEAR COLLEGE IN ANOTHER REGION

Although many community colleges serve a specific county or district, they are committed (to the extent of their ability) to the goal of equal educational opportunity without regard to economic status, race, creed, color, sex, or national origin. Independent two-year colleges recruit from a much broader geographical area—throughout the United States and, increasingly, around the world.

Although some community colleges do provide on-campus housing for their students, most do not. However, even if on-campus housing is not available, most colleges do have housing referral services.

NEW CAREER OPPORTUNITIES

Community colleges realize that many entering students are not sure about the field in which they want to focus their studies or the career they would like to pursue. Often, students discover fields and careers they never knew existed. Community colleges have the resources to help students identify areas of career interest and to set challenging occupational goals.

Once a career goal is set, you can be confident that a community college will provide job-relevant, technical education. About half of the students who take courses for credit at community colleges do so to prepare for employment or to acquire or upgrade skills for their current job. Especially helpful in charting a career path is the assistance of a counselor or a faculty adviser, who can discuss job opportunities in your chosen field and help you map out your course of study.

In addition, since community colleges have close ties to their communities, they are in constant contact with leaders in business, industry, organized labor, and public life. Community colleges work with these individuals and their organizations to prepare students for direct entry into the world of work. For example, some community colleges have established partnerships with local businesses and industries to provide specialized training programs. Some also provide the academic portion of apprenticeship training, while others offer extensive job-shadowing and cooperative education opportunities. Be sure to examine all of the career-preparation opportunities offered by the community colleges in which you are interested.

David R. Pierce is the former President of the American Association of Community Colleges.

Surviving Standardized Tests

WHAT ARE STANDARDIZED TESTS?

Colleges and universities in the United States use tests to help evaluate applicants' readiness for admission or to place them in appropriate courses. The tests that are most frequently used by colleges are the ACT® of American College Testing, Inc., and the College Board's SAT®. In addition, the Educational Testing Service (ETS) offers the TOEFL® test, which evaluates the English-language proficiency of nonnative speakers. The tests are offered at designated testing centers located at high schools and colleges throughout the United States and U.S. territories and at testing centers in various countries throughout the world.

Upon request, special accommodations for students with documented visual, hearing, physical, or learning disabilities are available. Examples of special accommodations include tests in Braille or large print and such aids as a reader, recorder, magnifying glass, or sign language interpreter. Additional testing time may be allowed in some instances. Contact the appropriate testing program or your guidance counselor for details on how to request special accommodations.

THE ACT®

The ACT® is a standardized college entrance examination that measures knowledge and skills in English, mathematics, reading comprehension, and science reasoning and the application of these skills to future academic tasks. The ACT® consists of four multiple-choice tests.

Test 1: English

- 75 questions, 45 minutes
- Usage and mechanics
- Rhetorical skills

Test 2: Mathematics

- 60 questions, 60 minutes
- Pre-algebra
- Elementary algebra
- Intermediate algebra
- Coordinate geometry
- Plane geometry
- Trigonometry

Test 3: Reading

- 40 questions, 35 minutes
- Prose fiction
- Humanities
- Social studies
- Natural sciences

Test 4: Science

- 40 questions, 35 minutes
- Data representation
- Research summary
- Conflicting viewpoints

Each section is scored from 1 to 36 and is scaled for slight variations in difficulty. Students are not penalized for incorrect responses. The composite score is the average of the four scaled scores. The ACT® Plus Writing includes the four multiple-choice tests and a writing test, which measures writing skills emphasized in high school English classes and in entry-level college composition courses.

To prepare for the ACT®, ask your guidance counselor for a free guidebook, "Preparing for the ACT®," or download it at www.act.org/content/dam/act/unsecured/documents/Preparing-for-the-ACT.pdf. Besides providing general test-preparation information and additional test-taking strategies, this guidebook provides full-length practice tests, including a Writing test, information about the optional Writing Test, strategies to prepare for the tests, and what to expect on test day.

DON'T FORGET TO . . .

- ❑ Take the SAT® or ACT® before application deadlines.
- ❑ Note that test registration deadlines precede test dates by about six weeks.
- ❑ Register to take the TOEFL® test if English is not your native language and you are planning on studying at a North American college.
- ❑ Contact the College Board or American College Testing, Inc., in advance if you need special accommodations when taking tests.

THE SAT®

The redesigned SAT®, which saw its first test-takers in the spring of 2016, has these sections: Evidence-Based Reading and Writing, Math, and the Essay. It is based on 1,600 points—the top scores for the Math section and the Evidence-Based Reading and Writing section will be 800, and the Essay score is reported separately.

Evidence-based Reading Test

- 52 questions; 65 minutes
- Passages in U.S. and world literature, history/social studies, and science
- Paired passages
- Lower and higher text complexities
- Words in context, command of evidence, and analysis

Writing and Language Test

- 44 questions; 35 minutes
- Passages in careers, history/social studies, humanities, and science
- Argument, informative/explanatory, and nonfiction narrative passages

- Words in context, grammar, expression of ideas, and analysis

Mathematics Test

- One no-calculator section (25 minutes)
- One calculator section (55 minutes)
- Content includes algebra, problem solving and data analysis, advanced math, area and volume calculations, trigonometric functions, and lines, triangles, and circles using theorems.

Essay (Optional)

- 50 minutes
- Argument passage written for a general audience
- Analysis of argument in passage using text evidence
- Score: 3–12 (Reading: 1–4 scale, Analysis: 1–4 scale, Writing: 1–4 scale)

According to the College Board's website, the "Eight Key Changes" are the following:

- **Relevant Words in Context:** Students need to interpret the meaning of words based on the context of the passage in which they appear. The focus is on "relevant" words—not obscure ones.
- **Command of Evidence:** In addition to demonstrating writing skills, students need to show that they're able to interpret, synthesize, and use evidence found in a wide range of sources.
- **Essay Analyzing a Source:** Students read a passage and explain how the author builds an argument, supporting support their claims with actual data from the passage.
- **Math Focused on Three Key Areas:** Problem Solving and Data Analysis (using ratios, percentages, and proportional reasoning to solve problems in science, social science, and career contexts), the Heart of Algebra (mastery of linear equations and systems), and Passport to Advanced Math (more complex equations and the manipulation they require).
- **Problems Grounded in Real-World Contexts:** All of the questions are grounded in the real world, directly related to work performed in college.
- **Analysis in Science and in Social Studies:** Students need to apply reading, writing, language, and math skills to answer questions in contexts of science, history, and social studies.
- **Founding Documents and Great Global Conversation:** Students will find an excerpt from one of the Founding Documents—such as the Declaration of Independence, the Constitution, and the Bill of Rights—or a text from the "Great Global Conversation" about freedom, justice, and human dignity.
- **No Penalty for Wrong Answers:** Students earn points for the questions they answer correctly.

Check out the College Board's website at https://collegereadiness.collegeboard.org for the most up-to-date information.

Top 10 Ways Not to Take the Test

1. Cramming the night before the test.
2. Not becoming familiar with the directions before you take the test.
3. Not becoming familiar with the format of the test before you take it.
4. Not knowing how the test is graded.
5. Spending too much time on any one question.
6. Second-guessing yourself.
7. Not checking spelling, grammar, and sentence structure in essays.
8. Writing a one-paragraph essay.
9. Forgetting to take a deep breath—
10. and finally—Don't lose it!

SAT SUBJECT TESTS™

Subject Tests are required by some institutions for admission and/or placement in freshman-level courses. Each Subject Test measures one's knowledge of a specific subject and the ability to apply that knowledge. Students should check with each institution for its specific requirements. In general, students are required to take three Subject Tests (one English, one mathematics, and one of their choice).

Subject Tests are given in the following areas: biology, chemistry, Chinese, French, German, Italian, Japanese, Korean, Latin, literature, mathematics, modern Hebrew, physics, Spanish, U.S. history, and world history. These tests are one hour long and are primarily multiple-choice tests. Three Subject Tests may be taken on one test date.

Scored like the current SAT®, students gain a point for each correct answer and lose a fraction of a point for each incorrect answer. The raw scores are then converted to scaled scores that range from 200 to 800.

THE TOEFL® INTERNET-BASED TEST (IBT)

The Test of English as a Foreign Language Internet-Based Test (TOEFL® iBT) is designed to help assess a student's grasp of English if it is not the student's first language. Performance on the TOEFL® test may help interpret scores on the critical reading sections of the SAT®. The test consists of four integrated sections: speaking, listening, reading, and writing. The TOEFL® iBT emphasizes integrated skills. The paper-based versions of the TOEFL® will continue to be administered in certain countries where the Internet-based version has not yet been introduced. For further information, visit www.toefl.org.

WHAT OTHER TESTS SHOULD I KNOW ABOUT?

The AP® Program

This program allows high school students to try college-level work and build valuable skills and study habits in the process. Subject matter is explored in more depth in AP courses than in other high school classes. A qualifying score on an AP test—which varies from school to school—can earn you college credit or advanced placement. Getting qualifying grades on enough exams can even earn you a full year's credit and sophomore standing at more than 1,500 higher-education institutions. There are more than thirty AP courses across multiple subject areas, including art history, biology, and computer science. Speak to your guidance counselor for information about your school's offerings.

College-Level Examination Program (CLEP®)

The CLEP enables students to earn college credit for what they already know, whether it was learned in school, through independent study, or through other experiences outside of the classroom. More than 2,900 colleges and universities now award credit for qualifying scores on one or more of the 33 CLEP exams. The exams, which are 90 minutes in length and are primarily multiple choice, are administered at participating colleges and universities. For more information, check out the website at www.collegeboard.com/clep.

WHAT CAN I DO TO PREPARE FOR THESE TESTS?

Know what to expect. Get familiar with how the tests are structured, how much time is allowed, and the directions for each type of question. Get plenty of rest the night before the test and eat breakfast that morning.

There are a variety of products, from books to software to videos, available to help you prepare for most standardized tests. Find the learning style that suits you best. As for which products to buy, there are two major categories— those created by the test-makers and those created by private companies. The best approach is to talk to someone who has been through the process and find out which product or products he or she recommends.

Some students report significant increases in scores after participating in coaching programs. Longer-term programs (40 hours) seem to raise scores more than short-term programs (20 hours), but beyond 40 hours, score gains are minor. Math scores appear to benefit more from coaching than critical reading scores.

Resources

There is a variety of ways to prepare for standardized tests—find a method that fits your schedule and your budget. But you should definitely prepare. Far too many students walk into these tests cold, either because they find standardized tests frightening or annoying or they just haven't found the time to study. The key is that these exams are standardized. That means these tests are largely the same from administration to administration; they always test the same concepts. They have to, or else you couldn't compare the scores of people who took the tests on different dates. The numbers or words may change, but the underlying content doesn't.

So how do you prepare? At the very least, you should review relevant material, such as math formulas and commonly used vocabulary words, and know the directions for each question type or test section. You should take at least one practice test and review your mistakes so you don't make them again on the test day. Beyond that, you know best how much preparation you need. You'll also find lots of material in libraries or bookstores to help you: books and software from the test- makers and from other publishers (including Peterson's) or live courses that range from national test-preparation companies to teachers at your high school who offer classes.

Who's Paying for This? Financial Aid Basics

A college education can be expensive—costing more than $150,000 for four years at some of the higher priced private colleges and universities. Even at the lower-cost state colleges and universities, the cost of a four-year education can approach $60,000. Determining how you and your family will come up with the necessary funds to pay for your education requires planning, perseverance, and learning as much as you can about the options that are available to you. But before you get discouraged, College Board statistics show that 53 percent of full-time students attend four-year public and private colleges with tuition and fees less than $9,000, while 20 percent attend colleges that have tuition and fees more than $36,000. College costs tend to be less in the western states and higher in New England.

Paying for college should not be looked at as a four-year financial commitment. For many families, paying the total cost of a student's college education out of current income and savings is usually not realistic. For families that have planned ahead and have financial savings established for higher education, the burden is a lot easier. But for most, meeting the cost of college requires the pooling of current income and assets and investing in longer-term loan options. These family resources, together with financial assistance from state, federal, and institutional sources, enable millions of students each year to attend the institution of their choice.

FINANCIAL AID PROGRAMS

There are three types of financial aid:

1. Gift-aid—Scholarships and grants are funds that do not have to be repaid.
2. Loans—Loans must be repaid, usually after graduation; the amount you have to pay back is the total you've borrowed plus any accrued interest. This is considered a source of self-help aid.
3. Student employment—Student employment is a job arranged for you by the financial aid office. This is another source of self-help aid.

The federal government has four major grant programs—the Federal Pell Grant, the Federal Supplemental Educational Opportunity Grant, Academic Competitiveness Grants (ACG), and National SMART (Science and Mathematics Access to Retain Talent) grants. ACG and SMART grants are limited to students who qualify for a Pell Grant and are awarded to a select group of students. Overall, these grants are targeted to low-to-moderate income families with significant financial need. The federal government also sponsors a student employment program called the Federal Work-Study Program, which offers jobs both on and off campus, and several loan programs, including those for students and for parents of undergraduate students.

There are two types of student loan programs: subsidized and unsubsidized. The subsidized Federal Direct Loan and the Federal Perkins Loan are need-based, government-subsidized loans. Students who borrow through these programs do not have to pay interest on the loan until after they graduate or leave school. The unsubsidized Federal Direct Loan and the Federal Direct PLUS Loan Program are not based on need, and borrowers are responsible for the interest while the student is in school. These loans are administered by different methods. Once you choose your college, the financial aid office will guide you through this process.

After you've submitted your financial aid application and you've been accepted for admission, each college will send you a letter describing your financial aid award. Most award letters show estimated college costs, how much you and your family are expected to contribute, and the amount and types of aid you have been awarded. Most students are awarded aid from a combination of sources and programs. Hence, your award is often called a financial aid "package."

SOURCES OF FINANCIAL AID

Millions of students and families apply for financial aid each year. Financial aid from all sources exceeds $143 billion per year. The largest single source of aid is the federal government, which will award more than $100 billion this year.

The next largest source of financial aid is found in the college and university community. Most of this aid is awarded to students who have a demonstrated need based on the Federal Methodology. Some institutions use a different formula, the Institutional Methodology (IM), to award their own funds in conjunction with other forms of aid. Institutional aid may be either need-based or non-need based. Aid that is not based on need is usually awarded for a student's academic performance (merit awards), specific talents or abilities, or to attract the type of students a college seeks to enroll.

Another source of financial aid is from state government. All states offer grant and/or scholarship aid, most of which is need-based. However, more and more states are offering substantial merit-based aid programs. Most state programs award aid only to students attending college in their home state.

Other sources of financial aid include:

- Private agencies
- Foundations
- Corporations
- Clubs
- Fraternal and service organizations

- Civic associations
- Unions
- Religious groups that award grants, scholarships, and low-interest loans
- Employers that provide tuition reimbursement benefits for employees and their children

More information about these different sources of aid is available from high school guidance offices, public libraries, college financial aid offices, directly from the sponsoring organizations, and online at www.petersons.com/college-search/scholarship-search.aspx.

HOW NEED-BASED FINANCIAL AID IS AWARDED

When you apply for aid, your family's financial situation is analyzed using a government-approved formula called the Federal Methodology. This formula looks at five items:

1. Demographic information of the family
2. Income of the parents
3. Assets of the parents
4. Income of the student
5. Assets of the student

This analysis determines the amount you and your family are expected to contribute toward your college expenses, called your Expected Family Contribution, or EFC. If the EFC is equal to or more than the cost of attendance at a particular college, then you do not demonstrate financial need. However, even if you don't have financial need, you may still qualify for aid, as there are grants, scholarships, and loan programs that are not need-based.

If the cost of your education is greater than your EFC, then you do demonstrate financial need and qualify for assistance. The amount of your financial need that can be met varies from school to school. Some are able to meet your full need, while others can only cover a certain percentage of need. Here's the formula:

Cost of Attendance
<u>– Expected Family Contribution</u>
= Financial Need

The EFC remains constant, but your need will vary according to the costs of attendance at a particular college. In general, the higher the tuition and fees at a particular college, the higher the cost of attendance will be. Expenses for books and supplies, room and board, transportation, and other miscellaneous items are included in the overall cost of attendance. It is important to remember that you do not have to be low-income to qualify for financial aid. Many middle and upper-middle income families qualify for need-based financial aid.

APPLYING FOR FINANCIAL AID

Every student must complete the Free Application for Federal Student Aid (FAFSA®) to be considered for financial aid. The FAFSA® is available from your high school guidance office, many public libraries, colleges in your area, or directly from the U.S. Department of Education.

Students are encouraged to apply for federal student aid on the Web. The electronic version of the FAFSA® can be accessed at http://www.fafsa.ed.gov.

The NEW Federal Student Aid ID

In order for a student to complete the online FAFSA®, he or she will need a Federal Student Aid (FSA) ID. You can get this online at https://fsaid.ed.gov/npas/index.htm. Since May 2015, the FSA ID has replaced the previously used PIN system. Parents of dependent students also need to obtain their own FSA ID in order to sign their child's FAFSA® electronically online.

The FSA ID can be used to access several federal aid-related websites, including FAFSA.gov and StudentLoans.gov. It consists of a username and password and can be used to electronically sign Federal Student Aid documents, access your personal records, and make binding legal obligations. The FSA ID is beneficial in several ways:

- It removes your personal identifiable information (PII), such as your Social Security number, from your log-in credentials.
- It creates a more secure and efficient way to verify your information when you log in to access to your federal student aid information online.
- It gives you the ability to easily update your personal information.
- It allows you to easily retrieve your username and password by requesting a secure code be sent to your e-mail address or by answering challenge questions.

It's relatively simple to create an FSA ID and should only take a few minutes. In addition, you will have an opportunity to link your current Federal Student Aid PIN (if you already have one) to your FSA ID. The final step is to confirm your e-mail address. You will receive a secure code to the e-mail address you provided when you set up your FSA ID. Once you retrieve the code from your e-mail account and enter it—to confirm your e-mail address is valid—you will be able to use this e-mail address instead of your username to log in to any of the federal aid-related websites, making the log-in process EVEN simpler for you and your parents.

When you initially create your FSA ID, your information will need to be verified with the Social Security Administration. This process can take anywhere from one to three days. For that reason, it's a good idea to take care of setting up your FSA ID as early as possible, so it will be all set when you are ready to begin completing your FAFSA®.

<u>IMPORTANT NOTE:</u> Since your FSA ID provides access to your personal information and is used to sign online documents, it's imperative that you protect this ID. Don't share it with *anyone* or write it down in an insecure location—you could place yourself at great risk for identify theft.

If Every College You're Applying to for Fall 2019 Requires the FAFSA®

. . . then it's pretty simple: Complete the FAFSA® after October 1, 2018, being certain to send it in before any college-imposed deadlines. (Students will now be permitted to send in the 2019–20 FAFSA® before January 1, 2018.) Students (and parents, as appropriate) are required to report income for an earlier tax year, so for the 2019–20 school year, you would report 2017 income information.

After you send in your FAFSA®, you'll receive a Student Aid Report (SAR) that includes all of the information you reported and shows your EFC. If you provided an e-mail address, the SAR is sent to you electronically; otherwise, you will receive a SAR or SAR Acknowledgment in the mail, which lists your FAFSA® information but may require you to make any corrections on the FAFSA® website. Be sure to review the SAR, checking to see if the information you reported is accurately represented. If you used estimated numbers to complete the FAFSA®, you may have to resubmit the SAR with any corrections to the data. The college(s) you have designated on the FAFSA® will receive the information you reported and will use that data to make their decision.

The CSS/Financial Aid PROFILE®

To award their own funds, some colleges require an additional application, the CSS/Financial Aid PROFILE® form. The PROFILE asks supplemental questions that some colleges and awarding agencies feel provide a more accurate assessment of the family's ability to pay for college. It is up to the college to decide whether it will use only the FAFSA® or both the FAFSA® and the PROFILE. PROFILE applications are available from the high school guidance office and on the Web. Both the paper application and the website list those colleges and programs that require the PROFILE application.

If a College Requires the PROFILE

Step 1: Register for the CSS/Financial Aid PROFILE in the fall of your senior year in high school. You can apply for the PROFILE online at http://profileonline.collegeboard.com/prf/index.jsp. Registration information with a list of the colleges that require the PROFILE is available in most high school guidance offices. There is a fee for using the Financial Aid PROFILE application ($25 for the first college, which includes the $9 application fee, and $16 for each additional college). You must pay for the service by credit card when you register. If you do not have a credit card, you will be billed. A limited number of fee waivers are automatically granted to first-time applicants based on the financial information provided on the PROFILE.

Step 2: Fill out your customized CSS/Financial Aid PROFILE. Once you register, your application will be immediately available online and will have questions that all students must complete, questions which must be completed by the student's parents (unless the student is independent and the colleges or programs selected do not require parental information), and *may* have supplemental questions needed by one or more of your schools or programs. If required, those will be found in Section Q of the application.

In addition to the PROFILE application you complete online, you may also be required to complete a Business/ Farm Supplement via traditional paper format. Completion of this form is not a part of the online process. If this form is required, instructions on how to download and print the supplemental form are provided. If your biological or adoptive parents are separated or divorced and your colleges and programs require it, your noncustodial parent may be asked to complete the Noncustodial PROFILE.

Once you complete and submit your PROFILE application, it will be processed and sent directly to your requested colleges and programs.

IF YOU DON'T QUALIFY FOR NEED-BASED AID

If you are not eligible for need-based aid, you can still find ways to lessen your burden.

Here are some suggestions:

- Search for merit scholarships. You can start at the initial stages of your application process. College merit awards are increasingly important as more and more colleges award these to students they especially want to attract. As a result, applying to a college at which your qualifications put you at the top of the entering class may give you a larger merit award. Another source of aid to look for is private scholarships that are given for special skills and talents. Additional information can be found at www.finaid.org.
- Seek employment during the summer and the academic year. The student employment office at your college can help you locate a school-year job. Many colleges and local businesses have vacancies remaining after they have hired students who are receiving Federal Work-Study Program financial aid.
- Borrow through the unsubsidized Federal Direct Loan program. This is generally available to all students. The terms and conditions are similar to the subsidized loans. The biggest difference is that the borrower is responsible for the interest while still in college, although the government permits students to delay paying the interest right away and add the accrued interest to the total amount owed. You must file the FAFSA® to be considered.
- After you've secured what you can through scholarships, working, and borrowing, you and your parents will be expected to meet your share of the college bill (the Expected Family Contribution). Many colleges offer monthly payment plans that spread the cost over the academic year. If the monthly payments are too high, parents can borrow through the Federal Direct PLUS Loan Program, through one of the many private education loan programs available, or through home equity loans and lines of credit. Families seeking assistance in financing college expenses should inquire at the financial aid office about what programs are available at the college. Some families seek the advice of professional financial advisers and tax consultants.

Frequently Asked Questions About Transferring

Muriel M. Shishkoff

Among the students attending two-year colleges are a large number who began their higher education knowing they would eventually transfer to a four-year school to obtain their bachelor's degree. There are many reasons why students go this route. Upon graduating from high school, some simply do not have definite career goals. Although they don't want to put their education on hold, they prefer not to pay exorbitant amounts in tuition while trying to "find themselves." As the cost of a university education escalates—even in public institutions—the option of spending the freshman and sophomore years at a two-year college looks attractive to many students. Others attend a two-year college because they are unable to meet the initial entrance standards—a specified grade point average (GPA), standardized test scores, or knowledge of specific academic subjects—required by the four-year school of their choice. Many such students praise the community college system for giving them the chance to be, academically speaking, "born again." In addition, students from other countries often find that they can adapt more easily to language and cultural changes at a two-year school before transferring to a larger, more diverse four-year college.

If your plan is to attend a two-year college with the ultimate goal of transferring to a four-year school, you will be pleased to know that the increased importance of the community college route to a bachelor's degree is recognized by all segments of higher education. As a result, many two-year schools have revised their course outlines and established new courses in order to comply with the programs and curricular offerings of the universities. Institutional improvements to make transferring easier have also proliferated at both the two-and four-year levels. The generous transfer policies of the Pennsylvania, New York, and Florida state university systems, among others, reflect this attitude; these systems accept all credits from students who have graduated from accredited community colleges.

If you are interested in moving from a two-year college to a four-year school, the sooner you make up your mind that you are going to make the switch, the better position you will be to transfer successfully (that is, without having wasted valuable time and credits). The ideal point at which to make such a decision is **before** you register for classes at your two-year school; a counselor can help you plan your course work with an eye toward fulfilling the requirements needed for your major course of study.

Naturally, it is not always possible to plan your transferring strategy that far in advance, but keep in mind that the key to a successful transfer is **preparation,** and preparation takes time—time to think through your objectives and time to plan the right classes to take.

As students face the prospect of transferring from a two-year to a four-year school, many thoughts and concerns about this complicated and often frustrating process race through their minds. Here are answers to the questions that are most frequently asked by transferring students.

Q Does every college and university accept transfer students?

A Most four-year institutions accept transfer students, but some do so more enthusiastically than others. Graduating from a community college is an advantage at, for example, Arizona State University and the University of Massachusetts Boston; both accept more community college transfer students than traditional freshmen. At the University at Albany, SUNY, graduates of two-year transfer programs within the State University of New York System are given priority for upper-division (i.e., junior-and senior-level) vacancies.

Schools offering undergraduate work at the upper division only are especially receptive to transfer applications. On the other hand, some schools accept only a few transfer students; others refuse entrance to sophomores or those in their final year. Princeton University requires an "excellent academic record and particularly compelling reasons to transfer." Check the catalogs of several colleges for their transfer requirements before you make your final choice.

Q Do students who go directly from high school to a four-year college do better academically than transfer students from community colleges?

A On the contrary: some institutions report that transfers from two-year schools who persevere until graduation do *better* than those who started as freshmen in a four-year college.

Q Why is it so important that my two-year college be accredited?

A Four-year colleges and universities accept transfer credits only from schools formally recognized by a regional, national, or professional educational agency. This accreditation signifies that an institution or program of study meets or exceeds a minimum level of educational quality necessary for meeting stated educational objectives.

Q After enrolling at a four-year school, may I still make up necessary courses at a community college?

A Some institutions restrict credit after transfer to their own facilities. Others allow students to take a limited number of transfer courses after matriculation, depending on the subject matter. A few provide opportunities for cross-registration or dual enrollment, which means taking classes on more than one campus.

Q What do I need to do to transfer?

A First, send for your high school and college transcripts. Having chosen the school you wish to transfer to, check its admission requirements against your transcripts. If you find that you are admissible, file an application as early as possible before the deadline. Part of the process will be asking your former schools to send official transcripts to the admission office, i.e., not the copies you used in determining your admissibility.

Plan your transfer program with the head of your new department as soon as you have decided to transfer. Determine the recommended general education pattern and necessary preparation for your major. At your present school, take the courses you will need to meet transfer requirements for the new school.

Q What qualifies me for admission as a transfer student?

A Admission requirements for most four-year institutions vary. Depending on the reputation or popularity of the school and program you wish to enter, requirements may be quite selective and competitive. Usually, you will need to show satisfactory test scores, an academic record up to a certain standard, and completion of specific subject matter.

Transfer students can be eligible to enter a four-year school in a number of ways: by having been eligible for admission directly upon graduation from high school, by making up shortcomings in grades (or in subject matter not covered in high school) at a community college, or by satisfactory completion of necessary courses or credit hours at another postsecondary institution. Ordinarily, students coming from a community college or from another four-year institution must meet or exceed the receiving institution's standards for freshmen and show appropriate college-level course work taken since high school. Students who did not graduate from high school can present proof of proficiency through results on the the GED® Test, the HiSET® Exam, or another state-approved high school equivalency test.

Q Are exceptions ever made for students who don't meet all the requirements for transfer?

A Extenuating circumstances, such as disability, low family income, refugee or veteran status, or athletic talent, may permit the special enrollment of students who would not otherwise be eligible but who demonstrate the potential for academic success. Consult the appropriate office—the Educational Opportunity Program, the disabled students' office, the athletic department, or the academic dean—to see whether an exception can be made in your case.

Q How far in advance do I need to apply for transfer?

A Some schools have a rolling admission policy, which means that they process transfer applications as they are received, all year long. With other schools, you must apply during the priority filing period, which can be up to a year before you wish to enter. Check the date with the admission office at your prospective campus.

Q Is it possible to transfer courses from several different institutions?

A Institutions ordinarily accept the courses that they consider transferable, regardless of the number of accredited schools involved. However, there is the danger of exceeding the maximum number of credit hours that can be transferred from all other schools or earned through credit by examination, extension courses, or correspondence courses. The limit placed on transfer credits varies from school to school, so read the catalog carefully to avoid taking courses you won't be able to use. To avoid duplicating courses, keep attendance at different campuses to a minimum.

Q What is involved in transferring from a semester system to a quarter or trimester system?

A In the semester system, the academic calendar is divided into two equal parts. The quarter system is more aptly named trimester, since the academic calendar is divided into three equal terms (not counting a summer session). To convert semester units into quarter units or credit hours, simply multiply the semester units by one and a half. Conversely, multiply quarter units by two thirds to come up with semester units. If you are used to a semester system of fifteen- to sixteen-week courses, the ten-week courses of the quarter system may seem to fly by.

Q Why might a course be approved for transfer credit by one four-year school but not by another?

A The beauty of postsecondary education in the United States lies in its variety. Entrance policies and graduation requirements are designed to reflect and serve each institution's mission. Because institutional policies vary so widely, schools may interpret the subject matter of a course from quite different points of view. Given that the granting of transfer credit indicates that a course is viewed as being, in effect, parallel to one offered by the receiving institution, it is easy to see how this might be the case at one university and not another.

Q Must I take a foreign language to transfer?

A Foreign language proficiency is often required for admission to a four-year institution; such proficiency also often figures in certain majors or in the general education pattern. Often, two or three years of a single language in high school will do the trick. Find out if scores received on Advanced Placement (AP®) examinations, placement examinations given by the foreign language department, or SAT Subject Tests™ will be accepted in lieu of college course work.

Q Will the school to which I'm transferring accept pass/no pass, pass/fail, or credit/no credit grades in lieu of letter grades?

A Usually, a limit is placed on the number of these courses you can transfer, and there may be other restrictions as well. If you want to use other-than-letter grades for the fulfillment of general education requirements or lower-division (freshman and sophomore) preparation for the major, check with the receiving institution.

Q Which is more important for transfer—my grade point average or my course completion pattern?

A Some schools believe that your past grades indicate academic potential and overshadow prior preparation for a specific degree program. Others require completion of certain introductory courses before transfer to prepare you for upper-division work in your major. In any case, appropriate course selection will cut down the time to graduation and increase your chances of making a successful transfer.

Q What happens to my credits if I change majors?

A If you change majors after admission, your transferable course credit should remain fairly intact. However, because you may need extra or different preparation for your new major, some of the courses you've taken may now be useful only as electives. The need for additional lower-level preparation may mean you're staying longer at your new school than you originally planned. On the other hand, you may already have taken courses that count toward your new major as part of the university's general education pattern.

Excerpted (and updated) from *Transferring Made Easy: A Guide to Changing Colleges Successfully,* by Muriel M. Shishkoff, © 1991 by Muriel M. Shishkoff (published by Peterson's).

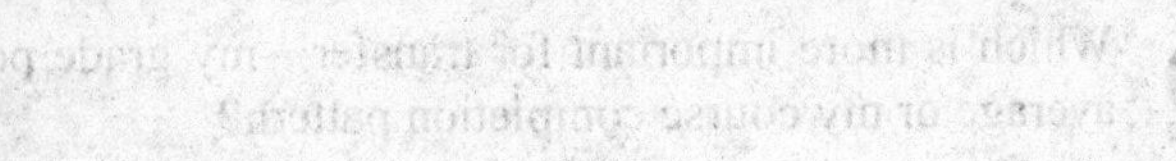

Returning to School: Advice for Adult Students

Sandra Cook, Ph.D.
Associate Vice President for Enrollment Management, San Diego State University

Many adults think for a long time about returning to school without taking any action. One purpose of this article is to help the "thinkers" finally make some decisions by examining what is keeping them from action. Another purpose is to describe not only some of the difficulties and obstacles that adult students may face when returning to school but also tactics for coping with them.

If you have been thinking about going back to college, and believing that you are the only person your age contemplating college, you should know that approximately 7 million adult students are currently enrolled in higher education institutions. This number represents 50 percent of total higher education enrollments. The majority of adult students are enrolled at two-year colleges.

There are many reasons why adult students choose to attend a two-year college. Studies have shown that the three most important criteria that adult students consider when choosing a college are location, cost, and availability of the major or program desired. Most two-year colleges are public institutions that serve a geographic district, making them readily accessible to the community. Costs at most two-year colleges are far less than at other types of higher education institutions. For many students who plan to pursue a bachelor's degree, completing their first two years of college at a community college is an affordable means to that end. If you are interested in an academic program that will transfer to a four-year institution, most two-year colleges offer the "general education" courses that compose most freshman and sophomore years. If you are interested in a vocational or technical program, two-year colleges excel in providing this type of training.

SETTING THE STAGE

There are three different "stages" in the process of adults returning to school. The first stage is uncertainty. Do I really want to go back to school? What will my friends or family think? Can I compete with those 18-year-old whiz kids? Am I too old? The second stage is choice. Once the decision to return has been made, you must choose where you will attend. There are many criteria to use in making this decision. The third stage is support. You have just added another role to your already-too-busy life. There are, however, strategies that will help you accomplish your goals—perhaps not without struggle, but with grace and humor nonetheless. Let's look at each of these stages.

UNCERTAINTY

Why are you thinking about returning to school? Is it to

- fulfill a dream that had to be delayed?
- become more educationally well-rounded?
- fill an intellectual void in your life?

These reasons focus on personal growth.

If you are returning to school to

- meet people and make friends
- attain and enjoy higher social status and prestige among friends, relatives, and associates
- understand/study a cultural heritage
- have a medium in which to exchange ideas

You are interested in social and cultural opportunities.

If you are like most adult students, you want to

- qualify for a new occupation
- enter or reenter the job market
- increase earnings potential
- qualify for a more challenging position in the same field of work

You are seeking career growth.

Understanding the reasons why you want to go back to school is an important step in setting your educational goals and will help you to establish some criteria for selecting a college. However, don't delay your decision because you have not been able to clearly define your motives. Many times, these aren't clear until you have already begun the process, and they may change as you move through your college experience.

Assuming you agree that additional education will benefit you, what is it that keeps you from returning to school? You may have a litany of excuses running through your mind:

- I don't have time.
- I can't afford it.
- I'm too old to learn.
- My friends will think I'm crazy.

- I'll be older than the teachers and other students.
- My family can't survive without me to take care of them every minute.
- I'll be X years old when I finish.
- I'm afraid.
- I don't know what to expect.

And that is just what these are—excuses. You can make school, like anything else in your life, a priority or not. If you really want to return, you can. The more you understand your motivation for returning to school and the more you understand what excuses are keeping you from taking action, the easier your task will be.

If you think you don't have time: The best way to decide how attending class and studying can fit into your schedule is to keep track of what you do with your time each day for several weeks. Completing a standard time-management grid (each day is plotted out by the half hour) is helpful for visualizing how your time is spent. For each 3-credit-hour class you take, you will need to find 3 hours for class plus 6 to 9 hours for reading-studying-library time. This study time should be spaced evenly throughout the week, not loaded up on one day. It is not possible to learn or retain the material that way. When you examine your grid, see where there are activities that could be replaced with school and study time. You may decide to give up your bowling league or some time in front of the TV. Try not to give up sleeping, and don't cut out every moment of free time. Here are some suggestions that have come from adults who have returned to school:

- Enroll in a time-management workshop. It helps you rethink how you use your time.
- Don't think you have to take more than one course at a time. You may eventually want to work up to taking more, but consider starting with one. (It is more than you are taking now!)
- If you have a family, start assigning to them those household chores that you usually do—and don't redo what they do.
- Use your lunch hour or commuting time for reading.

If you think you cannot afford it: As mentioned earlier, two-year colleges are extremely affordable. If you cannot afford the tuition, look into the various financial aid options. Most federal and state funds are available to full- and part-time students. Loans are also available. While many people prefer not to accumulate a debt for school, these same people will think nothing of taking out a loan to buy a car. After five or six years, which is the better investment? Adult students who work should look into whether their company has a tuition-reimbursement policy. There are also private scholarships, available through foundations, service organizations, and clubs, that are focused on adult learners. Your public library, the Web, and a college financial aid adviser are three excellent sources for reference materials regarding financial aid.

If you think you are too old to learn: This is pure myth. A number of studies have shown that adult learners perform as well as, or better than, traditional-age students.

If you are afraid your friends will think you're crazy: Who cares? Maybe they will, maybe they won't. Usually, they will admire your courage and be just a little jealous of your ambition (although they'll never tell you that). Follow your dreams, not theirs.

If you are concerned because the teachers or students will be younger than you: Don't be. The age differences that may be apparent in other settings evaporate in the classroom. If anything, an adult in the classroom strikes fear into the hearts of some 18-year-olds because adults have been known to be prepared, ask questions, be truly motivated, and be there to learn!

If you think your family will have a difficult time surviving while you are in school: If you have done everything for them up to now, they might struggle. Consider this an opportunity to help them become independent and self-sufficient. Your family can only make you feel guilty if you let them. You are not abandoning them; you are becoming an educational role model. When you are happy and working toward your goals, everyone benefits. Admittedly, it sometimes takes time for them to realize this. For single parents, there are schools that offer support groups, child care, and cooperative babysitting.

If you're appalled at the thought of being X years old when you graduate in Y years: How old will you be in Y years if you don't go back to school?

If you are afraid or don't know what to expect: Know that these are natural feelings when one encounters any new situation. Adult students find that their fears usually dissipate once they begin classes. Fear of trying is usually the biggest roadblock to the reentry process.

No doubt you have dreamed up a few more reasons for not making the decision to return to school. Keep in mind that what you are doing is making up excuses, and you are using these excuses to release you from the obligation to make a decision about your life. The thought of returning to college can be scary. Anytime anyone ventures into unknown territory, there is a risk, but taking risks is a necessary component of personal and professional growth. It is your life, and you alone are responsible for making the decisions that determine its course. Education is an investment in your future.

CHOICE

Once you have decided to go back to school, your next task is to decide where to go. If your educational goals are well defined (e.g., you want to pursue a degree in order to change careers), then your task is a bit easier. But even if your educational goals are still evolving, do not defer your return. Many students who enter higher education with a specific major in mind change that major at least once.

Most students who attend a public two-year college choose the community college in the district in which they live. This is generally the closest and least expensive option if the school offers the programs you want. If you are planning to begin your education at a two-year college and then transfer to a four-year school, there are distinct advantages to choosing your four-year school early. Many community and four-year colleges have "articulation" agreements that designate what credits from the two-year school will transfer to the four-year college and how. Some four-year institutions accept an associate degree as equivalent to the freshman and sophomore years, regardless of the courses you have taken. Some four-year schools accept two-year college work only on a course-by-course basis. If you can identify which school you will transfer to, you can know in advance exactly how your two-year credits will apply, preventing an unexpected loss of credit or time.

Each institution of higher education is distinctive. Your goal in choosing a college is to come up with the best student-institution fit—matching your needs with the offerings and characteristics of the school. The first step in choosing a college is to determine what criteria are most important to you in attaining your educational goals. Location, cost, and program availability are the three main factors that influence an adult student's college choice. In considering location, don't forget that some colleges have conveniently located branch campuses. In considering cost, remember to explore your financial aid options before ruling out an institution because of its tuition. Program availability should include not only the major in which you are interested, but also whether or not classes in that major are available when you can take them.

Some additional considerations beyond location, cost, and programs are:

- Does the school have a commitment to adult students and offer appropriate services, such as child care, tutoring, and advising?
- Are classes offered at times when you can take them?
- Are there academic options for adults, such as credit for life or work experience, credit by examination (including CLEP), credit for military service, or accelerated programs?
- Is the faculty sensitive to the needs of adult learners?

Once you determine which criteria are vital in your choice of an institution, you can begin to narrow your choices. There are myriad ways for you to locate the information you desire. Many newspapers publish a "School Guide" several times a year in which colleges and universities advertise to an adult student market. In addition, schools themselves publish catalogs, class schedules, and promotional materials that contain much of the information you need, and they are yours for the asking. Many colleges sponsor information sessions and open houses that allow you to visit the campus and ask questions. An appointment with an adviser is a good way to assess the fit between you and the institution. Be sure to bring your questions with you to your interview.

SUPPORT

Once you have made the decision to return to school and have chosen the institution that best meets your needs, take some additional steps to ensure your success during your crucial first semester. Take advantage of institutional support and build some social support systems of your own. Here are some ways of doing just that:

- Plan to participate in any orientation programs. These serve the threefold purpose of providing you with a great deal of important information, familiarizing you with the campus and its facilities, and giving you the opportunity to meet and begin networking with other students.
- Take steps to deal with any academic weaknesses. Take mathematics and writing placement tests if you have reason to believe you may need some extra help in these areas. It is not uncommon for adult students to need a math refresher course or a program to help alleviate math anxiety. Ignoring a weakness won't make it go away.
- Look into adult reentry programs. Many institutions offer adults workshops focusing on ways to improve study skills, textbook reading, test-taking, and time-management skills.
- Build new support networks by joining an adult student organization, making a point of meeting other adult students through workshops, or actively seeking out a "study buddy" in each class—that invaluable friend who shares and understands your experience.
- Incorporate your new status as "student" into your family life. Doing your homework with your children at a designated "homework time" is a valuable family activity and reinforces the importance of education.
- Make sure you take a reasonable course load in your first semester. It is far better to have some extra time on your hands and to succeed magnificently than to spend the entire semester on the brink of a breakdown. Also, whenever possible, try to focus your first courses not only on requirements, but also on areas of personal interest.
- Faculty members, advisers, and student affairs personnel are there to help you during difficult times—let them assist you as often as necessary.

After completing your first semester, you will probably look back in wonder at why you thought going back to school was so imposing. Certainly, it's not without its occasional exasperations. But, as with life, keeping things in perspective and maintaining your sense of humor make the difference between just coping and succeeding brilliantly.

Coming to America: Tips for International Students Considering Study in the U.S.

Introduction: Why Study in the United States?

Are you thinking about going to a college or university in the United States? If you're looking at this book, you probably are! All around the world, students like you, pursuing higher education, are considering that possibility. They envision themselves on modern, high-tech campuses in well-known cities, surrounded by American students, taking classes and having fun. A degree from a U.S. school would certainly lead to success and fortune, either back in your home country or perhaps even in the United States, wouldn't it?

It can be done—but becoming a student at a college or university in the U.S. requires academic talent, planning, time, effort, and money. While there may be only a small number of institutions of higher learning in your country, there are more than 2,900 four-year colleges and universities in the United States. Choosing one, being accepted, and then traveling and becoming a student in America is a big undertaking.

If this is your dream, here is some helpful information and expert tips from professionals who work with international students at colleges and universities throughout the United States.

Timing and Planning

The journey to a college or university in the U.S. often starts years in advance. Most international students choose to study in the U.S. because of the high quality of academics. Your family may also have a lot of input on this decision, too.

"We always tell students they should be looking in the sophomore year, visiting in the junior year, and applying in the senior year," says Father Francis E. Chambers, OSA, D.Min., Associate Director of International Admission at Villanova University. He stresses that prospective students need to be taking challenging courses in the years leading up to college. "We want to see academic rigor. Most admission decisions are based on the first six semesters—senior year is too late."

Heidi Gregori-Gahan, Assistant Provost for International Programs at the University of Southern Indiana agrees that it's important to start early. "Plan ahead and do your homework. There is so much to choose from—so many schools, programs, degrees, and experiences. It can be overwhelming."

While students in some countries may pay an agent to help them get into a school in the United States, Gregori-Gahan often directs potential international students to EducationUSA (http://educationusa.state.gov), a U.S. State Department network of over 400 international student advising centers in more than 170 countries. "They are there to provide unbiased information about studying in the United States and help you understand the process and what you need to do."

Two to three years of advance planning is also recommended by Daphne Durham, who has been an international student adviser at Harvard, Suffolk University, Valdosta State University, and the University of Georgia. She points out that the academic schedule in other countries is often different than that of the United States, so you need to synchronize your calendar accordingly.

You will have to take several tests in order to gain admission to a U.S. school, so it's important to know when those tests are given in your country, then register and take them so your scores will be available when you apply. Even if you have taken English in school, you will probably have to take The Test of English as a Foreign Language (TOEFL®), but some schools also accept the International English Language Testing Sytem (IELTS). You will probably also have to take the SAT® or ACT® tests, which are achievement or aptitude tests, and are usually required of all students applying for admission, not just international students.

"Make sure you understand how the international admissions process works at the school or schools you want to attend," says Durham. "What test scores are needed and when? Does the school have a fixed calendar or rolling admissions?" Those are just some of the many factors that can impact your application and could make a difference in when you are able to start school.

"Every university is unique in what's required and what they need to do. Even navigating each school's different website can be challenging," explains Gregori-Gahan.

Searching for Schools

This book contains information on thousands of four-year colleges and universities, and it will be a valuable resource for you in your search and application process. But with so many options, how do you decide which school you should attend?

"Where I find a big difference with international students is if their parents don't recognize the school, they don't apply to the school," says Fr. Chambers. "They could be overlooking a lot of great schools. They have to look outside the box."

The school Gregori-Gahan represents is in Evansville, Indiana, and it probably isn't familiar to students abroad. "Not many people have heard of anything beyond New York and California and maybe Florida. I like to tell students that this is 'real America.' But happy international students on our campus have recruited others to come here."

She points out that Internet technology has made a huge difference in the search process for international students. Websites full of information, live chat, webinars, virtual tours, and admission interviews via Skype have made it easier for potential students to connect with U.S. institutions, get more information, and be better able to visualize the campus.

One thing than will help narrow your search for a school is knowing specifically what you want to study. You need to know what the course of study is called in the United States, what it means, and what is required in order to study that subject. You also need to consider your future plans. What are your goals and objectives? What do you plan to do after earning your degree?

"If you're going to overcome the hurdles and get to a U.S. school, you have to have a directed path chosen," says Durham.

The other thing that could help your search process is finding a school that is a good fit.

Fit Is Important

You want your clothing and shoes to fit you properly and be comfortable, so a place where you will spend four or more years of your life studying should also be comfortable and appropriate for you. So how can you determine if a particular school is a good fit?

"We really recommend international students visit first. Yes, there are websites and virtual tours, but there's still nothing that beats an in-person visit," says Fr. Chambers. He estimates that 50 to 60 percent of Villanova's international students visited the campus before enrolling.

"It can be hard to get a sense of a place—you're so far away and you're probably not going to set foot on campus until you arrive," says Gregori-Gahan. "There is a high potential for culture shock."

You need to ask yourself what is important to you in a campus environment, then do some homework to ensure that the schools you are considering meet those needs. Here are some things to consider when it comes to fit:

- **Location:** Is it important for you to be in a well-known city or is a part of the United States that is unfamiliar a possibility? "Look at geographic areas, but also cost of living," recommends Durham. "Be sure to factor in transportation costs also, especially if you plan to return to your home country regularly."
- **Student population:** Some small schools have just 1,000 students while larger ones may have 30,000 students or more.
- **Familiar faces:** Is it important for you to be at a school with others from your home nation or region?
- **Climate:** Some students want a climate similar to where they live now, but others are open and curious about seasons and weather conditions they may not have ever experienced. "We do have four seasons here," says Gregori-Gahan. "Sometimes students who come here from tropical regions are concerned about the winters. The first snow is so exciting, but after that, students may not be aware of how cold it really is."
- **Amenities:** Do you want to find your own housing or choose a school where the majority of students live on campus? Is there public transportation available or is it necessary to walk or have a bicycle or car? Does the school or community have access to things that are important to you culturally and meet the traditions you want to follow?
- **Campus size:** Some campuses are tightly compacted into a few city blocks, but others cover hundreds of acres of land. "International students are amazed by how green and spacious our campus is, with blooming flowers, trees, and lots of grass," says Gregori-Gahan.
- **Academic offerings:** Does this school offer the program you want to study? Can you complete it in four years or perhaps sooner? What sort of internship and career services are available?
- **Finances:** Can you afford to attend this school? Is there any sort of financial assistance available for international students?
- **Support services:** Durham suggests students look carefully at each school's offerings for international students. "Does the school have online guidance for getting your visa? Is ESL tutoring available? Does the school offer host family or community friend programs?" She also suggests you look for campus support groups for students from your country or region.

Looking at the listings and reading the in-depth descriptions in this book can help you search for a school that is a good fit for you.

Government Requirements

The one thing that every international student must have in order to study in the United States is a student visa. Having accurate advice and following all the necessary steps regarding the visa process is essential to being able to enter this country and start school.

As you schedule your tests and application deadlines, you must also consider how long it will take to get your visa. This varies depending on where you live; in some countries, extensive background checks are required. The subject you plan to study can also impact your visa status; it does help to have a major rather than be undeclared. The U.S. State Department website, http://travel.state.gov/content/visas/english/study-exchange.html, can give you an idea of how long it will take.

In addition to the visa, you will also need a Form I-20, which is a U.S. government immigration form. You must have that form when you get to the United States.

"It's very different from being a tourist. You need to be prepared to meet with an immigration officer and be interviewed about your college," explains Durham. "Where you are going, why you are going, where the school is located, what you are studying, and so on."

You also need to keep in mind that there are reporting requirements once you are a student in the U.S. Every semester, your adviser has to report to the government to confirm that you are enrolled in and attending school in order for you to stay in the United States.

Finances

Part of the visa process includes having the funds to pay for the cost of your schooling and support yourself. Finances are a huge hurdle in the process of becoming a college student in the United States.

"It's crucial. So many foreign systems offer 'free' higher education to students. How is your family going to handle the ongoing expense of attending college for four years or longer in the United States?" Durham reiterates that planning ahead is key because there are so many details. Student loans require a U.S.-based cosigner. Each school has its own financial aid deadlines. You have to factor in your own government's requirements, such currency exchange and fund transfers.

The notion that abundant funds are available to assist international students is not true. Sometimes state schools may offer diversity waivers or there may be special scholarship opportunities for international students. But attending school in the U.S. is still a costly venture.

"We do offer financial aid to international students, but they still have to be able to handle a large portion of the costs. Full-need scholarships are not likely," explained Fr. Chambers. "Sometimes students think that once they get here, it will all work out and the funds will be there. But the scenario for the first year has to be repeated each year they are on campus.

Once You Arrive...

You've taken your tests, researched schools, found a good fit, applied, got accepted, arranged the financing, gotten your visa and I-20, and made it to the campus in the United States. Now what?

You can expect the school where you have enrolled to be welcoming and helpful, but within reason. If you arrive on a weekend, or at a time outside of the time when international students are scheduled to arrive, the assistance you need may not be available to you.

Every school offers different levels of assistance to international students. For instance, Villanova offers a full-service office that can assist students with everything from visas, to employment, to finding a place for students to stay over breaks.

Fr. Chambers attends the international student orientation session to greet the students he's worked with through the recruitment and application process. "But I rarely see an international student after that. I think that bodes well for them being integrated into the entire university."

"Those of us who work with international students are really working to help them adjust," says Gregori-Gahan. "International students get here well before school starts so they can get over jet lag. We have orientation sessions and pair them with peer advisers who help them navigate the first few days, and we assure them that we are there for them."

Students should be open to their new setting, but they should be prepared that things may not be at all how they had envisioned during their planning and searching process. "While you may think you'll meet lots of Americans, don't underestimate the importance of community with your traditional home culture and people," says Durham.

Don't Make These Mistakes

The journey to college attendance in the United States is a long one, with many steps. The experts warn about mistakes to avoid along the way.

"Not reading through everything thoroughly and not understanding what the program of study really is and what will it cost. You have to be really clear on the important details," says Gregori-Gahan.

"Every school does things differently," cautions Fr. Chambers. "International students must be aware of that as they are applying."

Durham stresses that going to school in the United States is too big a decision to leave to someone else. "Students need to know about their school—they have to be in charge of their application."

"It involves a lot of work to be successful and happy and not surprised by too many things," Gregori-Gahan says.

Hopefully now, you are more informed and better prepared to pursue your dream of studying at a college or university in the United States.

Community Colleges and the Green Economy

Community colleges are a focal point for state and national efforts to create a green economy and workforce. As the United States transforms its economy into a "green" one, community colleges are leading the way—filling the need for both educated technicians whose skills can cross industry lines as well as those technicians who are able to learn new skills as technologies evolve.

President Obama extolled community colleges as "the unsung heroes of America's education system," essential to our country's success in the "global competition to lead in the growth of industries of the twenty-first century." With the support of state governments, and, more importantly, local and international business partners, America's community colleges are rising to meet the demands of the new green economy. Community colleges are training individuals to work in fields such as renewable energy, energy efficiency, wind energy, green building, and sustainability. The programs are as diverse as the campuses housing them.

Here is a quick look at just some of the exciting "green" programs available at community colleges throughout the United States.

At Mesalands Community College in Tucumcari, New Mexico, the North American Wind Research and Training Center provides state-of-the-art facilities for research and training qualified technicians in wind energy technology to help meet the need for an estimated 170,000 new positions in the industry by 2030. The Center includes a facility for applied research in collaboration with Sandia National Laboratories—the first-ever such partnership between a national laboratory and a community college. It also provides associate degree training for wind energy technicians, meeting the fast-growing demand for "windsmiths" in the western part of the country—jobs that pay $45,000–$60,000 per year. For more information, visit http://www.mesalands.edu.

Cape Cod Community College (CCCC) in Massachusetts has become one of the nation's leading colleges in promoting and integrating sustainability and green practices throughout all campus operations and technical training programs. Ten years ago, Cape Wind Associates, Cape Cod's first wind farm, provided $50,000 to jumpstart CCCC's wind technician program—considered a state model for community-based clean energy workforce development and education. In addition, hundreds of CCCC students have earned associate degrees in environmental technology and environmental studies, as well as certificate programs in coastal zone management, environmental site assessment, solar thermal technology, and more. Visit http://www.capecod.edu/web/natsci/env/programs for more information.

At Oakland Community College in Michigan, more than 350 students are enrolled in the college's Renewable Energies and Sustainable Living program and its related courses. Students gain field experience refurbishing public buildings with renewable materials, performing energy audits for the government, and working with small businesses and hospitals to reduce waste and pollution. To learn more, visit http://www.oaklandcc.edu/est/.

Portland Community College (PCC) in Portland, Oregon, offers associate degree and certificate options in Renewable Energy Systems (RES) training, preparing technicians for solar power, wind power, fuel cell, and other renewable energy fields. Students can earn an Associate in Applied Science (A.A.S.) degree or a One-Year Certificate in EET: Renewable Energy Systems. PCC's Microelectronic Technology Department offers an A.A.S. degree and a Certificate of Completion (COC) in Solar Voltaic Manufacturing Technology. The COC provides an orientation in solar manufacturing for those who have no prior education or experience in the field, which enables students to obtain entry-level jobs in this industry and eventually complete their A.A.S. degree.

Central Carolina Community College (CCCC) in Pittsboro, North Carolina, has been leading the way in "green" programs for more than a decade. It offered a sustainable agriculture class at its Chatham campus in 1996 and soon became the first community college in the nation to offer an Associate in Applied Science degree in sustainable agriculture and the first in North Carolina to offer an associate degree in biofuels. In addition, it was the first North Carolina community college to offer a North American Board of Certified Energy Practitioners (NABCEP)–approved solar PV panel installation course as part of its green building/renewable energy program. CCC also offers an associate degree in sustainable technology, a Natural Chef culinary arts program, an ecotourism certificate, and certificates in other green programs. For more information about Central Carolina Community College's green programs, visit http://www.cccc.edu/green.

At Metropolitan Community College in Omaha, Nebraska, the Continuing Education Department in partnership with Pro-Train is offering green/renewable energy/sustainability online training courses. The courses are designed to provide students with the workforce skills necessary for many in-demand green-collar occupations. Green/Renewable Energy courses include Building Energy Efficient Level, Fundamentals of Solar Hot Water Heating, Green Building Sales (or Technical) Professional, and more. Sustainability Green Supply Chain Training courses include Alternative Energy Operations, Carbon Strategies, Green Building for Contractors, and Sustainability 101. Visit www.theknowledgebase.org/metropolitan/.

At Cascadia Community College in Bothell, Washington, thanks to a grant from Puget Sound Energy (PSE), students in the Energy Informatics class designed a kiosk screen that shows the energy usage and solar generation at the local 21 Acres Center for Local Food and Sustainable Living. The PSE grant supports the classroom materials for renewable energy education and the Web-based monitoring software that allows students and interested community members to track how much energy is being generated as the weather changes. For more information, visit http://www.cascadia.edu/Default.aspx.

At Grand Rapids Community College, the federally funded Pathways to Prosperity program has successfully prepared low-income residents for jobs in fields such as renewable energy. More than 200 people have completed the program, which began in 2010 thanks to a $4-million grant from the Department of Labor, and found jobs in industries ranging from energy-efficient building construction to alternative energy and sustainable manufacturing. For additional information, check out http://cms.grcc.edu/workforce-training/pathways-prosperity.

Established in 2008, the Green Institute at Heartland Community College in Normal, Illinois, supports a wide range of campus initiatives, educational programs, and community activities that are related to sustainability, energy conservation, renewable energy, recycling, retro-commissioning, and other environmental technologies. For more information, visit http://www.heartland.edu/greenInstitute/.

Most of California's 112 community colleges offer some type of green-tech classes. These include photovoltaic panel installation and repair, green construction practices, and biotechnology courses leading to careers in agriculture, medicine, and environmental forensics. Visit http://www.californiacommunitycolleges.cccco.edu/ProgramstoWatch/MoreProgramstoWatch/GreenTechnology.aspx.

Linn-Benton Community College (LBCC) in Albany, Oregon, is now offering training for the Oregon Green Technology Certificate. Oregon Green Tech is a federally funded program that is designed to prepare entry-level workers with foundational skills for a variety of industries associated with or in support of green jobs. Students learn skills in green occupations that include green energy production; manufacturing, construction, installation, monitoring, and repair of equipment for solar, wind, wave, and bio-energy; building retro-fitting; process recycling; hazardous materials removal work; and more. LBCC is one of ten Oregon community colleges to provide training for the Green Technology Certificate, offered through the Oregon Consortium and Oregon Workforce Alliance. Visit http://www.linnbenton.edu for additional information.

The Santa Fe Community College Sustainable Technology Center in New Mexico offers several green jobs training programs along with various noncredit courses. It also provides credit programs from certificates in green building systems, environmental technology training, and solar energy training as well as an Associate in Applied Science (A.A.S.) degree in environmental technology. For more information, go online to http://www.sfcc.edu/sustainable_technologies_center.

In Colorado, Red Rocks Community College (RRCC) offers degree and certificate programs in renewable energy (solar photovoltaic, solar thermal, and wind energy technology), energy and industrial maintenance, energy operations and process technology, environmental technology, water quality management, and energy audit. RRCC has made a commitment to the national challenge of creating and sustaining a green workforce and instructs students about the issues of energy, environmental stewardship, and renewable resources across the college curriculum. For more information, visit http://www.rrcc.edu/green/.

At GateWay Community College in Phoenix, Arizona, graduates of the Environmental Science program now work for the U.S. Geological Survey (USGS), the Arizona Department of Environmental Quality (ADEQ), the Occupational Safety and Health Administration (OSHA), and municipalities across the state and region, as well as private consultants and environmental organizations. For additional information, check out http://www.gatewaycc.edu/environment.

During the past 4.5 years, 17 Illinois community colleges and their partners have created 35 certificate and degree programs to prepare students for careers in green industry sectors. Over 185 courses were created and piloted, online and on-site, in communities across Illinois. The courses were created using open-source materials, with the intent to be shared with other colleges and universities through the Department of Labor's Trade Adjustment Assistance Community College and Career Training (TAACCCT) Grant Program repository.

Next you'll find two essays about other green community college programs. The first essay was written by the president of Lane Community College in Eugene, Oregon, about the role Lane and other community colleges are playing in creating a workforce for the green economy. Then, read a first-hand account of the new Wind Turbine Training Program at Kalamazoo Valley Community College in Kalamazoo, Michigan—a program that has more applicants than spaces and one whose students are being hired BEFORE they even graduate. It's clear that there are exciting "green" programs at community colleges throughout the United States.

The Role of Community Colleges in Creating a Workforce for the Green Economy

by Mary F.T. Spilde, President
Lane Community College

Community colleges are expected to play a leadership role in educating and training the workforce for the green economy. Due to close connections with local and regional labor markets, colleges assure a steady supply of skilled workers by developing and adapting programs to respond to the needs of business and industry. Further, instead of waiting for employers to create job openings, many colleges are actively engaged in local economic development to help educate potential employers to grow their green business opportunities and to participate in the creation of the green economy.

As the green movement emerges there has been confusion about what constitutes a green job. It is now clear that many of the green jobs span several economic sectors such as renewable energy, construction, manufacturing, transportation and agriculture. It is predicted that there will be many middle skill jobs requiring more than a high school diploma but less than a bachelor's degree. This is precisely the unique role that community colleges play. Community colleges develop training programs, including pre-apprenticeship, that ladder the curriculum to take lower skilled workers through a relevant and sequenced course of study that provides a clear pathway to career track jobs. As noted in *Going Green: The Vital Role of Community Colleges in Building a Sustainable Future and Green Workforce* by the National Council for Workforce Education and the Academy for Educational Development, community colleges are strategically positioned to work with employers to redefine skills and competencies needed by the green workforce and to create the framework for new and expanded green career pathways.

While there will be new occupations such as solar and wind technologists, the majority of the jobs will be in the energy management sector—retrofitting the built environment. For example, President Obama called for retrofitting more than 75 percent of federal buildings and more than 2 million homes to make them more energy-efficient. The second major area for growth will be the "greening" of existing jobs as they evolve to incorporate green practices. Both will require new knowledge, skills and abilities. For community colleges, this means developing new programs that meet newly created industry standards and adapting existing programs and courses to integrate green skills. The key is to create a new talent pool of environmentally conscious, highly skilled workers.

These two areas show remarkable promise for education and training leading to high wage/high demand jobs:

- Efficiency and energy management: There is a need for auditors and energy efficiency experts to retrofit existing buildings. Consider how much built environment we have in this country, and it's not difficult to see that this is where the vast amount of jobs are now and will be in the future.
- Greening of existing jobs: There are few currently available jobs that environmental sustainability will not impact. Whether it is jobs in construction, such as plumbers, electricians, heating and cooling technicians, painters, and building supervisors, or chefs, farmers, custodians, architects, automotive technicians and interior designers, all will need to understand how to lessen their impact on the environment.

Lane Community College offers a variety of degree and certificate programs to prepare students to enter the energy efficiency fields. Lane has offered an Energy Management program since the late 1980s—before it was hip to be green! Students in this program learn to apply basic principles of physics and analysis techniques to the description and measurement of energy in today's building systems, with the goal of evaluating and recommending alternative energy solutions that will result in greater energy efficiency and energy cost savings. Students gain a working understanding of energy systems in today's built environment and the tools to analyze and quantify energy efficiency efforts. The program began with an emphasis in residential energy efficiency/solar energy systems and has evolved to include commercial energy efficiency and renewable energy system installation technology.

The Renewable Energy Technician program is offered as a second-year option within the Energy Management program. Course work prepares students for employment designing and installing solar electric and domestic hot water systems. Renewable Energy students, along with Energy Management students, take a first-year curriculum in commercial energy efficiency giving them a solid background that includes residential energy efficiency, HVAC systems, lighting, and physics and math. In the second year, Renewable Energy students diverge from the Energy Management curriculum and take course work that starts with two courses in electricity fundamentals and one course in energy economics. In the following terms, students learn to design, install, and develop a thorough understanding of photovoltaics and domestic hot water systems.

Recent additions to Lane's offerings are Sustainability Coordinator and Water Conservation Technician degrees. Both programs were added to meet workforce demand.

Lane graduates find employment in a wide variety of disciplines and may work as facility managers, energy auditors, energy program coordinators, or control system specialists, for such diverse employers as engineering firms, public and private utilities, energy equipment companies, and departments of energy and as sustainability leaders within public and private sector organizations.

Lane Community College also provides continuing education for working professionals. The Sustainable Building Advisor (SBA) Certificate Program is a nine-month, specialized training program for working professionals. Graduate are able to advise employers or clients on strategies and tools for implementing sustainable building practices. Benefits from participating in the SBA program often include saving long-term building operating costs; improving the environmental, social, and economic viability of the region; and reducing environmental impacts and owner liability—not to mention the chance to improve one's job skills in a rapidly growing field.

The Building Operators Certificate is a professional development program created by The Northwest Energy Efficiency Council. It is offered through the Northwest Energy Education

Institute at Lane. The certificate is designed for operations and maintenance staff working in public or private commercial buildings. It certifies individuals in energy and resource-efficient operation of building systems at two levels: Level I–Building System Maintenance and Level II–Equipment Troubleshooting and Maintenance.

Lane Community College constantly scans the environment to assess workforce needs and develop programs that provide highly skilled employees. Lane, like most colleges, publishes information in its catalog on workforce demand and wages so that students can make informed decisions about program choice.

Green jobs will be a large part of a healthy economy. Opportunities will abound for those who take advantage of programs with a proven record of connecting with employers and successfully educating students to meet high skills standards.

Establishing a World-Class Wind Turbine Technician Academy

by Thomas Sutton, Director of Wind Energy and Technical Services
Kalamazoo Valley Community College

When Kalamazoo Valley Community College (KVCC) decided it wanted to become involved in the training of utility-grade technicians for wind-energy jobs, early on the choice was made to avoid another "me too" training course.

Our program here in Southwest Michigan, 30 miles from Lake Michigan, had to meet industry needs and industry standards.

It was also obvious from the start that the utility-grade or large wind industry had not yet adopted any uniform training standards in the United States.

Of course, these would come, but why should the college wait when European standards were solidly established and working well in Germany, France, Denmark and Great Britain?

As a result, in 2009, KVCC launched its Wind Turbine Technician Academy, the first of its kind in the United States. The noncredit academy runs 8 hours a day, five days a week, for twenty-four weeks of intense training in electricity, mechanics, wind dynamics, safety, and climbing. The college developed this program rather quickly—in eight months—to fast-track individuals into this emerging field.

KVCC based its program on the training standards forged by the Bildungszentrum fur Erneuerebare Energien (BZEE)—the Renewable Energy Education Center. Located in Husum, Germany, the BZEE was created and supported by major wind-turbine manufacturers, component makers, and enterprises that provide operation and maintenance services.

As wind-energy production increased throughout Europe, the need for high-quality, industry-driven, international standards emerged. The BZEE has become the leading trainer for wind-turbine technicians across Europe and now in Asia.

With the exception of one college in Canada, the standards were not yet available in North America. When Kalamazoo Valley realized it could be the first college or university in the United States to offer this training program—that was enough motivation to move forward.

For the College to become certified by the BZEE, it needed to hire and send an electrical instructor and a mechanical instructor to Germany for six weeks of "train the trainer." The instructors not only had to excel in their respective fields, they also needed to be able to climb the skyscraper towers supporting megawatt-class turbines—a unique combination of skills to possess. Truly, individuals who fit this job description don't walk through the door everyday—but we found them! Amazingly, we found a top mechanical instructor who was a part-time fireman and comfortable with tall ladder rescues and a skilled electrical instructor who used to teach rappelling off the Rockies to the Marine Corps.

In addition to employing new instructors, the College needed a working utility-grade nacelle that could fit in its training lab that would be located in the KVCC Michigan Technical Education Center. So one of the instructors traveled to Denmark and purchased a 300-kilowatt turbine.

Once their own training was behind them and the turbine was on its way from the North Sea, the instructors quickly turned to crafting the curriculum necessary for our graduates to earn both an academy certificate from KVCC and a certification from the BZEE.

Promoting the innovative program to qualified potential students across the country was the next step. News releases were published throughout Michigan, and they were also picked up on the Internet. Rather quickly, KVCC found itself with more than 500 requests for applications for a program built for 16 students.

Acceptance into the academy includes a medical release, a climbing test, reading and math tests, relevant work experience, and, finally, an interview. Students in the academy's pioneer class, which graduated in spring 2010, ranged in age from their late teens to early 50s. They hailed from throughout Michigan, Indiana, Ohio, and Illinois as well as from Puerto Rico and Great Britain.

The students brought with them degrees in marketing, law, business, science, and architecture, as well as entrepreneurial experiences in several businesses, knowledge of other languages, military service, extensive travel, and electrical, computer, artistic, and technical/mechanical skills.

Kalamazoo Valley's academy has provided some high-value work experiences for the students in the form of two collaborations with industry that has allowed them to maintain and/or repair actual utility-grade turbines, including those at the 2.5 megawatt size. This hands-on experience will add to the attractiveness of the graduates in the market place. Potential employers were recently invited to an open house where they could see the lab and meet members of this pioneer class.

The College's Turbine Technician Academy has also attracted a federal grant for $550,000 to expand its program through additional equipment purchases. The plan is to erect our own climbing tower. Climbing is a vital part of any valid program, and yet wind farms cannot afford to shut turbines down just for climb-training. The funds were put to use engineering, fabricating, and erecting a wind training tower that incorporated all of the necessary components to teach competency-based work at heights safety training.

When the students are asked what best distinguishes the Kalamazoo Valley program, their answers point to the experienced instructors and the working lab, which is constantly changing to offer the best training experiences. Students also consistently report that the hands-on field experience operating and maintaining the five large turbines during the course has set them apart at companies where they work.

Industry continues to tell us that community colleges need to offer fast-track training programs of this caliber if the nation is to reach the U.S. Department of Energy's goal of 20 percent renewable energy by 2030. This would require more than 1,500 new technicians each year.

The Wind Turbine Technician Academy continues the process improvements as directed by industry input. The academy not only holds the BZEE certification, it is also one of the few American Wind Energy Association (AWEA) Seal of Approval schools in the nation.

With that in mind, KVCC plans to host several BZEE orientation programs for other community colleges in order to encourage them to consider adopting the European training standards and start their own programs.

Meanwhile, applications are continuing to stream in from across the country for the next Wind Turbine Technician Academy program at Kalamazoo Valley Community College. For more information about the program, visit http://www.kvccgrovescenter.com/career/wtta.

How to Use This Guide

Peterson's *Two-Year Colleges 2019* contains a wealth of information for anyone interested in colleges offering associate degrees. This section details the criteria that institutions must meet to be included in this guide and provides information about research procedures used by Peterson's.

QUICK-REFERENCE CHART

The **Two-Year Colleges At-a-Glance Chart** is a geographically arranged table that lists colleges by name and city within the state, or country in which they are located. Areas listed include the United States, Canada, and other countries; the institutions are included because they are accredited by recognized U.S. accrediting bodies (see **Criteria for Inclusion** section).

The At-a-Glance chart contains basic information that enables you to compare institutions quickly according to broad characteristics such as degrees awarded, enrollment, application requirements, financial aid availability, and numbers of sports and majors offered. A dagger (†) after the institution's name indicates that an institution has an entry in the **Featured Two-Year Colleges** section.

Column 1: Degrees Awarded

C= *college transfer associate degree:* the degree awarded after a "university-parallel" program, equivalent to the first two years of a bachelor's degree.

T= *terminal associate degree:* the degree resulting from a one- to three-year program providing training for a specific occupation.

B= *bachelor's degree (baccalaureate):* the degree resulting from a liberal arts, science, professional, or preprofessional program normally lasting four years, although in some cases an accelerated program can be completed in three years.

M= *master's degree:* the first graduate (postbaccalaureate) degree in the liberal arts and sciences and certain professional fields, usually requiring one to two years of full-time study.

D= *doctoral degree* (research/scholarship, professional practice, or other)

Column 2: Institutional Control

Private institutions are designated as one of the following:

Ind = *independent* (nonprofit)

I-R = *independent-religious:* nonprofit; sponsored by or affiliated with a particular religious group or having a nondenominational or interdenominational religious orientation.

Prop = *proprietary* (profit-making)

Public institutions are designated by the source of funding, as follows:

Fed = *federal*

St = *state*

Comm = *commonwealth* (Puerto Rico)

Terr = *territory* (U.S. territories)

Cou = *county*

Dist = *district:* an administrative unit of public education, often having boundaries different from units of local government.

City = *city*

St-L = *state and local:* local may refer to county, district, or city.

St-R = *state-related:* funded primarily by the state but administratively autonomous.

Column 3: Student Body

M= *men only* (100% of student body)

PM = *coed, primarily men*

W= *women only* (100% of student body)

PW = *coed, primarily women*

M/W = *coeducational*

Column 4: Undergraduate Enrollment

The figure shown represents the number of full-time and part-time students enrolled in undergraduate degree programs as of fall 2017.

Columns 5–7: Enrollment Percentages

Figures are shown for the percentages of the fall 2017 undergraduate enrollment made up of students attending part-time (column 5) and students 25 years of age or older (column 6). Also listed is the percentage of students in the last graduating class who completed a college-transfer associate program and went directly on to four-year colleges (column 7).

For columns 8 through 15, the following letter codes are used: Y = yes; N = no; R = recommended; S = for some.

Columns 8–10: Admission Policies

The information in these columns shows whether the college has an open admission policy (column 8) whereby virtually all applicants are accepted without regard to standardized test scores, grade average, or class rank; whether a high school equivalency certificate is accepted in place of a high school diploma for admission consideration (column 9); and whether a high school transcript (column 10) is required as part of the application process. In column 10, the combination of the codes R and S indicates that a high school transcript is recommended for all applicants (R) or required for some (S).

Columns 11–12: Financial Aid

These columns show which colleges offer the following types of financial aid: need-based aid (column 11) and part-time jobs (column 12), including those offered through the federal government's Federal Work-Study program.

Columns 13–15: Services and Facilities

These columns show which colleges offer the following: career counseling (column 13) on either an individual or group basis, job placement services (column 14) for individual students, and college-owned or -operated housing facilities (column 16) for noncommuting students.

Column 16: Sports

This figure indicates the number of sports that a college offers at the intramural and/or intercollegiate levels.

Column 17: Majors

This figure indicates the number of major fields of study in which a college offers degree programs.

PROFILES OF TWO-YEAR COLLEGES AND SPECIAL MESSAGES

The **Profiles of Two-Year Colleges** contain basic data in capsule form for quick review and comparison. The following outline of the **Profile** format shows the section headings and the items that each section covers. Any item that does not apply to a particular college or for which no information was supplied is omitted from that college's **Profile.** Display ads, which appear near some of the institution's profiles, have been provided and paid for by those colleges that chose to supplement their profile with additional information. A star ★ next to the name of a school signifies that the school is one of the "Featured Two-Year Colleges," with a two-page in-depth description in that section of this guide and may also have an expanded profile on Peterson's website at www.petersons/com.

Bulleted Highlights

The bulleted highlights section features important information, for quick reference and comparison. The number of possible bulleted highlights that an ideal **Profile** would have if all questions were answered in a timely manner follow. However, not every institution provides all of the information necessary to fill out every bulleted line. In such instances, the line will not appear.

First Bullet

Institutional control: Private institutions are designated as independent (nonprofit), proprietary (profit-making), or independent, with a specific religious denomination or affiliation. Nondenominational or interdenominational religious orientation is possible and would be indicated.

Public institutions are designated by the source of funding. Designations include federal, state, province, commonwealth (Puerto Rico), territory (U.S. territories), county, district (an administrative unit of public education, often having boundaries different from units of local government), city, state and local (local may refer to county, district, or city), or state-related (funded primarily by the state but administratively autonomous).

Religious affiliation is also noted here.

Institutional type: Each institution is classified as one of the following:

> ***Primarily two-year college:*** Awards baccalaureate degrees, but the vast majority of students are enrolled in two-year programs.
>
> ***Four-year college:*** Awards baccalaureate degrees; may also award associate degrees; does not award graduate (postbaccalaureate) degrees.
>
> ***Upper-level institution:*** Awards baccalaureate degrees, but entering students must have at least two years of previous college-level credit; may also offer graduate degrees.
>
> ***Comprehensive institution:*** Awards baccalaureate degrees; may also award associate degrees; offers graduate degree programs, primarily at the master's, specialist's, or professional level, although one or two doctoral programs may be offered.
>
> ***University:*** Offers four years of undergraduate work plus graduate degrees through the doctorate in more than two academic or professional fields.

Founding date: If the year an institution was chartered differs from the year when instruction actually began, the earlier date is given.

System or administrative affiliation: Any coordinate institutions or system affiliations are indicated. An institution that has separate colleges or campuses for men and women but shares facilities and courses is termed a coordinate institution. A formal administrative grouping of institutions, either private or public, of which the college is a part, or the name of a single institution with which the college is administratively affiliated, is a system.

Second Bullet

Setting: Schools are designated as urban (located within a major city), suburban (a residential area within commuting distance of a major city), small-town (a small but compactly settled area not within commuting distance of a major city), or rural (a remote and sparsely populated area). The phrase *easy access to...* indicates that the campus is within an hour's drive of the nearest major metropolitan area that has a population greater than 500,000.

Third Bullet

Endowment: The total dollar value of funds and/or property donated to the institution or the multicampus educational system of which the institution is a part.

Fourth Bullet

Student body: An institution is coed (coeducational—admits men and women), primarily (80 percent or more) women, primarily men, women only, or men only.

Undergraduate students: Represents the number of full-time and part-time students enrolled in undergraduate degree programs as of fall 2017. The percentage of full-time undergraduates and the percentages of men and women are given.

Category Overviews

Undergraduates

For fall 2017, the number of full- and part-time undergraduate students is listed. This list provides the number of states and U.S. territories, including the District of Columbia and Puerto Rico (or for Canadian institutions, provinces and territories), and other countries from which undergraduates come. Percentages of undergraduates who are part-time or full-time students; transfers in; live on campus; out-of-state; Black or African American, non-Hispanic/Latino; Hispanic/Latino; Asian, non-Hispanic/Latino; Native Hawaiian or other Pacific Islander, non-Hispanic/Latino; American Indian or Alaska Native, non-Hispanic/Latino are given.

Retention: The percentage of freshmen (or, for upper-level institutions, entering students) who returned the following year for the fall term.

Freshmen

Admission: Figures are given for the number of students who applied for fall 2017 admission, the number of those who were admitted, and the number who enrolled. Freshman statistics include the average high school GPA; the percentage of freshmen who took the SAT® and received critical reading, writing, and math scores above 500, above 600, and above 700; as well as the percentage of freshmen taking the ACT® who received a composite score of 18 or higher.

Faculty

Total: The total number of faculty members; the percentage of full-time faculty members as of fall 2017; and the percentage of full-time faculty members who hold doctoral/first professional/ terminal degrees.

Student-faculty ratio: The school's estimate of the ratio of matriculated undergraduate students to faculty members teaching undergraduate courses.

Majors

This section lists the major fields of study offered by the college.

Academics

Calendar: Most colleges indicate one of the following: 4-1-4, 4-4-1, or a similar arrangement (two terms of equal length plus an abbreviated winter or spring term, with the numbers referring to months); semesters; trimesters; quarters; 3-3 (three courses for each of three terms); modular (the academic year is divided into small blocks of time; courses of varying lengths are assembled according to individual programs); or standard year (for most Canadian institutions).

Degrees: This names the full range of levels of certificates, diplomas, and degrees, including prebaccalaureate, graduate, and professional, that are offered by this institution:

Associate degree: Normally requires at least two but fewer than four years of full-time college work or its equivalent.

Bachelor's degree (baccalaureate): Requires at least four years but not more than five years of full-time college-level work or its equivalent. This includes all bachelor's degrees in which the normal four years of work are completed in three years and bachelor's degrees conferred in a five-year cooperative (work-study plan) program. A cooperative plan provides for alternate class attendance and employment in business, industry, or government. This allows students to combine actual work experience with their college studies.

Master's degree: Requires the successful completion of a program of study of at least the full-time equivalent of one but not more than two years of work beyond the bachelor's degree.

Doctoral degree (doctorate; research/scholarship, professional, or other): The highest degree in graduate study. The doctoral degree classification includes Doctor of Education, Doctor of Juridical Science, Doctor of Public Health, Doctor of Philosophy, Doctor of Podiatry, Doctor of Veterinary Medicine, and many more.

Post-master's certificate: Requires completion of an organized program of study of 24 credit hours beyond the master's degree but does not meet the requirements of academic degrees at the doctoral level.

Special study options: Details are next given here on study options available at each college:

Accelerated degree program: Students may earn a bachelor's degree in three academic years.

Academic remediation for entering students: Instructional courses designed for students deficient in the general competencies necessary for a regular postsecondary curriculum and educational setting.

Adult/continuing education programs: Courses offered for nontraditional students who are currently working or are returning to formal education.

Advanced placement: Credit toward a degree awarded for acceptable scores on College Board Advanced Placement (AP®) tests.

Cooperative (co-op) education programs: Formal arrangements with off-campus employers allowing students to combine work and study in order to gain degree-related experience, usually extending the time required to complete a degree.

Distance learning: For-credit courses that can be accessed off-campus via cable television, the Internet, satellite, DVD, correspondence course, or other media.

Double major: A program of study in which a student concurrently completes the requirements of two majors.

English as a second language (ESL): A course of study designed specifically for students whose native language is not English.

External degree programs: A program of study in which students earn credits toward a degree through a combination of independent study, college courses, proficiency examinations, and personal experience. External degree programs require minimal or no classroom attendance.

Freshmen honors college: A separate academic program for talented freshmen.

Honors programs: Any special program for very able students offering the opportunity for educational enrichment, independent study, acceleration, or some combination of these.

Independent study: Academic work, usually undertaken outside the regular classroom structure, chosen or designed by the student with departmental approval and instructor supervision.

Internships: Any short-term, supervised work experience usually related to a student's major field, for which the student earns academic credit. The work can be full-or part-time, on or off-campus, paid or unpaid.

Off-campus study: A formal arrangement with one or more domestic institutions under which students may take courses at the other institution(s) for credit.

Part-time degree program: Students may earn a degree through part-time enrollment in regular session (daytime) classes or evening, weekend, or summer classes.

Self-designed major: Program of study based on individual interests, designed by the student with the assistance of an adviser.

Services for LD students: Special help for learning-disabled students with resolvable difficulties, such as dyslexia.

Study abroad: An arrangement by which a student completes part of the academic program studying in another country. A college may operate a campus abroad or it may have a cooperative agreement with other U.S. institutions or institutions in other countries.

Summer session for credit: Summer courses through which students may make up degree work or accelerate their program.

Tutorials: Undergraduates can arrange for special in-depth academic assignments (not for remediation) working with faculty members one-on-one or in small groups.

ROTC: Army, Naval, or Air Force Reserve Officers' Training Corps programs offered either on campus, at a branch campus [designated by a (b)], or at a cooperating host institution [designated by (c)].

Unusual degree programs: Nontraditional programs such as a 3-2 degree program, in which three years of liberal arts study is followed by two years of study in a professional field at another institution (or in a professional division of the same institution), resulting in two bachelor's degrees or a bachelor's and a master's degree.

Library

The name of the college's main library, plus the number of other libraries on campus will appear followed by: *Books:* number of physical and digital/electronic books; *Serial titles:* number of physical and digital/electronic serial titles; and the number of *Databases.* Also included here (if provided by the school) are the number of "Weekly public service hours" and study area information—the number of hours and days of the week open and if students can reserve study rooms.

Student Life

Housing options: The institution's policy about whether students are permitted to live off-campus or are required to live on campus for a specified period; whether freshmen-only, coed, single-sex, cooperative, and disabled student housing options are available; whether campus housing is leased by the school and/or provided by a third party; whether freshman applicants are given priority for college housing. The phrase *college housing not available* indicates that no college-owned or -operated housing facilities are provided for undergraduates and that noncommuting students must arrange for their own accommodations.

Activities and organizations: Lists information on drama-theater groups, choral groups, marching bands, student-run campus newspapers, student-run radio stations, and social organizations (sororities, fraternities, eating clubs, etc.) and how many are represented on campus.

Campus security: Campus safety measures including 24-hour emergency response devices (telephones and alarms) and patrols by trained security personnel, student patrols, late-night transport-escort service, and controlled dormitory access (key, security card, etc.).

Student services: Information provided indicates services offered to students by the college, such as legal services, health clinics, personal-psychological counseling, and women's centers.

Athletics

Membership in one or more of the following athletic associations is indicated by initials.

NCAA: National Collegiate Athletic Association

NAIA: National Association of Intercollegiate Athletics

NCCAA: National Christian College Athletic Association

NJCAA: National Junior College Athletic Association

USCAA: United States Collegiate Athletic Association

CIS: Canadian Interuniversity Sports

The overall NCAA division in which all or most intercollegiate teams compete is designated by a roman numeral I, II, or III. All teams that do not compete in this division are listed as exceptions.

Sports offered by the college are divided into two groups: intercollegiate (**M** or **W** following the name of each sport indicates that it is offered for men or women or **M/W** if the sport is offered for both men and women) and intramural. An **s** in parentheses following an **M, W or M/W** for an intercollegiate sport indicates that athletic scholarships (or grants-in-aid) are offered for men and/or women in that sport, and a c indicates a club team as opposed to a varsity team.

Standardized Tests

The most commonly required standardized tests are the ACT®, SAT®, and SAT Subject Tests™. These and other standardized tests may be used for selective admission, as a basis for counseling or course placement, or for both purposes. This section notes if a test is used for admission or placement and whether it is required, required for some, or recommended.

In addition to the ACT and SAT, the following standardized entrance and placement examinations are referred to by their initials:

ABLE: Adult Basic Learning Examination

ACT ASSET: ACT Assessment of Skills for Successful Entry and Transfer

ACT PEP: ACT Proficiency Examination Program

CAT: California Achievement Tests

CELT: Comprehensive English Language Test

CPAt: Career Programs Assessment

CPT: Computerized Placement Test

DAT: Differential Aptitude Test

LSAT: Law School Admission Test

MAPS: Multiple Assessment Program Service

MCAT: Medical College Admission Test

MMPI: Minnesota Multiphasic Personality Inventory

OAT: Optometry Admission Test

PAA: Prueba de Aptitude Académica (Spanish-language version of the SAT)

PCAT: Pharmacy College Admission Test

PSAT/NMSQT: Preliminary SAT National Merit Scholarship Qualifying Test

SCAT: Scholastic College Aptitude Test

SRA: Scientific Research Association (administers verbal, arithmetical, and achievement tests)

TABE: Test of Adult Basic Education

TASP: Texas Academic Skills Program

TOEFL: Test of English as a Foreign Language (for international students whose native language is not English)

WPCT: Washington Pre-College Test

Costs

Costs are given for the 2018–19 academic year or for the 2017–18 academic year if 2018–19 figures were not yet available. Annual expenses may be expressed as a comprehensive fee (including full-time tuition, mandatory fees, and college room and board) or as separate figures for full-time tuition, fees, room and board, or room only. For public institutions where tuition differs according to residence, separate figures are given for area or state residents and for nonresidents. Part-time tuition is expressed in terms of a per-unit rate (per credit, per semester hour, etc.) as specified by the institution.

The tuition structure at some institutions is complex in that freshmen and sophomores may be charged a different rate from that for juniors and seniors, a professional or vocational division may have a different fee structure from the liberal arts division of the same institution, or part-time tuition may be prorated on a sliding scale according to the number of credit hours taken. Tuition and fees may vary according to academic program, campus/location, class time (day, evening, weekend), course/credit load, course level, degree level, reciprocity agreements, and student level. Room and board charges are reported as an average for one academic year and may vary according to the board plan selected, campus/location, type of housing facility, or student level. If no college-owned or college-operated housing facilities are offered, the phrase *college housing not available* will appear in the Housing section of the Student Life paragraph.

Tuition payment plans that may be offered to undergraduates include tuition prepayment, installment payments, and deferred payment. A tuition prepayment plan gives a student the option of locking in the current tuition rate for the entire term of enrollment by paying the full amount in advance rather than year by year. Colleges that offer such a prepayment plan may also help the student to arrange financing.

The availability of full or partial undergraduate tuition waivers to minority students, children of alumni, employees or their children, adult students, and senior citizens may be listed.

Financial Aid

The number of Federal Work Study and/or part-time jobs and average earnings are listed. Financial aid deadlines are given as well.

Applying

Application and admission options include the following:

Early admission: Highly qualified students may matriculate before graduating from high school.

Early action plan: An admission plan that allows students to apply and be notified of an admission decision well in advance of the regular notification dates. If accepted, the candidate is not committed to enroll; students may reply to the offer under the college's regular reply policy.

Early decision plan: A plan that permits students to apply and be notified of an admission decision (and financial aid offer, if applicable) well in advance of the regular notification date. Applicants agree to accept an offer of admission and to withdraw their applications from other colleges. Candidates who are not accepted under early decision are automatically considered with the regular applicant pool, without prejudice.

Deferred entrance: The practice of permitting accepted students to postpone enrollment, usually for a period of one academic term or year.

Application fee: The fee required with an application is noted. This is typically nonrefundable, although under certain specified conditions it may be waived or returned.

Requirements: Other application requirements are grouped into three categories: required for all, required for some, and recommended. They may include an essay, standardized test scores, a high school transcript, a minimum high school grade point average (expressed as a number on a scale of 0 to 4.0, where 4.0 equals A, 3.0 equals B, etc.), letters of recommendation, an interview on campus or with local alumni, and, for certain types of schools or programs, special requirements such as a musical audition or an art portfolio.

Application deadlines and notification dates: Admission application deadlines and dates for notification of acceptance or rejection are given either as specific dates or as **rolling** and **continuous.** Rolling means that applications are processed as they are received, and qualified students are accepted as long as there are openings. Continuous means that applicants are notified of acceptance or rejection as applications are processed up until the date indicated or the actual beginning of classes. The application deadline and the notification date for transfers are given if they differ from the dates for freshmen. Early decision and early action application deadlines and notification dates are also indicated when relevant.

Admissions Contact

The name, title, and phone number of the person to contact for application information are given at the end of the Profile. The admission office address is listed in most cases. Toll-free phone numbers may also be included. The admission office fax number and e-mail address, if available, are listed, provided the school wanted them printed for use by prospective students. Finally, the URL of the institution's Web site is provided.

Additional Information

Each college that has a **Featured Two-Year College Close-Up** in the guide will have a cross-reference appended to the Profile, referring you directly to the page number of that **Featured Two-Year College Close-Up.**

Institutional Changes Since *Peterson's® Two-Year Colleges 2018*

Here you will find an alphabetical listing of institutions that have recently closed, merged with other institutions, or changed their name or status.

FEATURED TWO-YEAR COLLEGES

These narrative descriptions provide an inside look at certain colleges, shifting the focus to a variety of other factors that should also be considered. The descriptions provide a wealth of information that is crucial in the college decision-making equation—such as tuition, financial aid, academic programs, and life on campus. Prepared exclusively by college officials, the descriptions are designed to help give students a better sense of the individuality of each institution, in terms that include campus environment, student activities, and lifestyle. Such quality-of-life intangibles can be the deciding factors in the college selection process. The absence of any college or university does not constitute an editorial decision on the part of Peterson's. In essence, these descriptions are an open forum for colleges, on a voluntary basis, to communicate their particular message to prospective students. The colleges included have paid a fee to Peterson's to provide this information. The Close-Ups in the **Featured Two-Year Colleges** section are edited to provide a generally consistent format across entries for your ease of comparison.

INDEXES

Associate Degree Programs at Two- and Four-Year Colleges

These indexes present hundreds of undergraduate fields of study that are currently offered most widely according to the colleges' responses on *Peterson's Annual Survey of Undergraduate Institutions*. The majors appear in alphabetical order, each followed by an alphabetical list of the schools that offer an associate-level program in that field. Liberal Arts and Studies indicates a general program with no specified major. The terms used for the majors are those of the U.S. Department of Education Classification of Instructional Programs (CIPs). Many institutions, however, use different terms. Readers should refer to the **Featured Two-Year Colleges** two-page descriptions in this book for the school's exact terminology. In addition, although the term "major" is used in this guide, some colleges may use other terms, such as "concentration," "program of study," or "field."

DATA COLLECTION PROCEDURES

The data contained in the **Profiles** of Two-Year Colleges and **Indexes** were researched in winter and spring 2018 through *Peterson's Annual Survey of Undergraduate Institutions.* Questionnaires were sent to the more than 1,700 colleges that meet the outlined inclusion criteria. All data included in this edition have been submitted by officials (usually admission and financial aid officers, registrars, or institutional research personnel) at the colleges themselves. All usable information received in time for publication has been included. The omission of any particular item from the **Profiles** of Two-Year Colleges and **Indexes** listing signifies either that the item is not applicable to that institution or that data were not available. Because of the comprehensive editorial review that takes place in our offices and because all material comes directly from college officials, Peterson's has every reason to believe that the information presented in this guide is accurate at the time of printing. However, students should check with a specific college or university at the time of application to verify such figures as tuition and fees, which may have changed since the publication of this volume.

CRITERIA FOR INCLUSION IN THIS BOOK

Peterson's Two-Year Colleges 2019 covers accredited institutions in the United States, U.S. territories, and other countries that award the associate degree as their most popular undergraduate offering (a few also offer bachelor's, master's, or doctoral degrees). The term two-year college is the commonly used designation for institutions that grant the associate degree, since two years is the normal duration of the traditional associate degree program. However, some programs may be completed in one year, others require three years, and, of course, part-time programs may take a considerably longer period. Therefore, "two-year college" should be understood as a conventional term that accurately describes most of the institutions included in this guide but which should not be taken literally in all cases. Also included are some non-degree-granting institutions, usually branch campuses of a multicampus system, which offer the equivalent of the first two years of a bachelor's degree, transferable to a bachelor's degree–granting institution.

To be included in this guide, an institution must have full accreditation or be a candidate for accreditation (preaccreditation) status by an institutional or specialized accrediting body recognized by the U.S. Department of Education or the Council for Higher Education Accreditation (CHEA). Institutional accrediting bodies, which review each institution as a whole, include the six regional associations of schools and colleges (Middle States, New England, North Central, Northwest, Southern, and Western), each of which is responsible for a specified portion of the United States and its territories. Other institutional accrediting bodies are national in scope and accredit specific kinds of institutions (e.g., Bible colleges, independent colleges, and rabbinical and Talmudic schools). Program registration by the New York State Board of Regents is considered to be the equivalent of institutional accreditation, since the board requires that all programs offered by an institution meet its standards before recognition is granted. This guide also includes institutions outside the United States that are accredited by these U.S. accrediting bodies. There are recognized specialized or professional accrediting bodies in more than forty different fields, each of which is authorized to accredit institutions or specific programs in its particular field. For specialized institutions that offer programs in one field only, we designate this to be the equivalent of institutional accreditation. A full explanation of the accrediting process and complete information on recognized, institutional (regional and national), and specialized accrediting bodies can be found online at www.chea.org or at www.ed.gov/admins/finaid/accred/index.html.

Quick-Reference Chart

Two-Year Colleges At-a-Glance

This chart includes the names and locations of accredited two-year colleges in the United States, Canada, and other countries and shows institutions' responses to the *Peterson's Annual Survey of Undergraduate Institutions.* If an institution submitted incomplete data, one or more columns opposite the institution's name is blank. A dagger after the school name indicates that the institution has one or more entries in the *Featured Two-Year Colleges* section. If a school does not appear, it did not report any of the information.

Y—Yes; N—No; R—Recommended; S—For Some

		Degrees Awarded: College Transfer Associate (C), Terminal Associate (T), Bachelor's (B), Master's (M), Doctoral (D)	Institutional Control: County, District, City, State and Local, State-Related, Federal, State, Commonwealth, Territory, Independent, Independent-Religious, Proprietary	Student Body: Men, Primarily Men, Women, Primarily Women, Coed	Undergraduate Enrollment	Percent Attending Part-Time	Percent 25 Years of Age or Older	Percent of Grads Going on to Four-Year Colleges	Open Admissions	High School Equivalency Certificate Accepted	High School Transcript Required	Need-Based Aid Available	Part-Time Jobs Available	Career Counseling Available	Job Placement Services Available	College Housing Available	Number of Sports Offered	Number of Majors Offered
UNITED STATES																		
Alabama																		
Bevill State Community College	Jasper	C,T	St	M/W	3,872	59												
George C. Wallace Community College	Dothan	C,T	St	M/W	4,645	58												
H. Councill Trenholm State Community College	Montgomery	C	St	M/W	1,845													
Jefferson State Community College	Birmingham	C,T	St	M/W	8,840	70												
Lurleen B. Wallace Community College	Andalusia	C,T	St	M/W	1,784	51	23		Y	Y	Y	Y	Y	Y		N	3	11
Marion Military Institute	Marion	C	St	M/W	446	1												
Northwest-Shoals Community College	Muscle Shoals	C	St	M/W	3,440	58												
Reid State Technical College	Evergreen	T	St	M/W	392	54												
American Samoa																		
American Samoa Community College	Pago Pago	C,T,B	Terr	M/W	1,095	44												
Arizona																		
Arizona Western College	Yuma	C,T	St-L	M/W	7,557	71												
Chandler-Gilbert Community College	Chandler	C,T	St-L	M/W	14,906	72												
Cochise County Community College District	Sierra Vista	C,T	St-L	M/W	3,918	61												
Eastern Arizona College	Thatcher	C,T	St-L	M/W	6,365	69												
Mesa Community College	Mesa	C	St-L	M/W	20,424													
Mohave Community College	Kingman	C	St	M/W	4,071	80	47		Y			Y	Y			N		31
Scottsdale Community College	Scottsdale	C,T	St-L	M/W	9,458													
Tohono O'odham Community College	Sells	C,T	Pub	M/W	462	69	58	41	Y	Y	Y			Y		Y	1	13
Arkansas																		
Arkansas State University Mid-South	West Memphis	C,T	St	M/W	1,423	75	22		Y	Y		Y	Y	Y		N	2	10
Arkansas State University–Newport	Newport	C,T	St	M/W	2,270	54	46		Y	Y	Y	Y	Y			N		16
College of the Ouachitas	Malvern	C,T	St	M/W	1,272	70												
National Park College	Hot Springs	C,T	St-L	M/W	2,996	59												
NorthWest Arkansas Community College	Bentonville	C,T	St	M/W	7,715													
Southeast Arkansas College	Pine Bluff	C,T	St	M/W	1,304	55												
University of Arkansas Community College at Morrilton	Morrilton	C,T	St	M/W	1,902	46	33			Y	Y	Y	Y	Y	Y	N		17
University of Arkansas Rich Mountain	Mena	C,T	St-L	M/W	938	51												
California																		
American Academy of Dramatic Arts–Los Angeles	Hollywood	C	Ind	M/W	303													
Antelope Valley College	Lancaster	C,T,B	Dist	M/W	14,125	71												
Coastline Community College	Fountain Valley	C	Dist	M/W	11,431	78	72		Y		R	Y	Y	Y	Y	N		1
College of Marin	Kentfield	C,T	Dist	M/W	5,026				Y			Y	Y	Y	Y	N	8	54
College of the Canyons	Santa Clarita	C,T	Dist	M/W	19,865	68	24		Y		R	Y	Y	Y	Y	N	10	62
College of the Desert	Palm Desert	C,T	Dist	M/W	11,146	60												
De Anza College	Cupertino	C,T	Dist	M/W	20,808	52												
Feather River College	Quincy	C,T,B	Dist	M/W	2,079													
FIDM/Fashion Institute of Design & Merchandising, Orange County Campus	Irvine	C,T	Prop	PW	71	6												
FIDM/Fashion Institute of Design & Merchandising, San Diego Campus	San Diego	C,T	Prop	PW	66	8												
Fullerton College	Fullerton	C,T	Dist	M/W	24,588													
Gurnick Academy of Medical Arts	San Mateo	C,T,B	Prop	M/W														
Los Angeles City College	Los Angeles	C,T	Dist	M/W	16,556	72												
Merced College	Merced	C,T	Dist	M/W	11,552													
Mission College	Santa Clara	C,T	Dist	M/W	7,868													
Mt. San Antonio College	Walnut	C,T	Dist	M/W	4,568	43												
Orange Coast College	Costa Mesa	C,T	Dist	M/W	21,731	61												
Palomar College	San Marcos	C	Dist	M/W	25,244													
Pasadena City College	Pasadena	C,T	Dist	M/W	27,324	62												
Rio Hondo College	Whittier	C,T	Dist	M/W														
The Salvation Army College for Officer Training at Crestmont	Rancho Palos Verdes	C,T	I-R	M/W	59													
San Joaquin Delta College	Stockton	C,T	Dist	M/W	18,102													
Santa Rosa Junior College	Santa Rosa	C,T	Dist	M/W	26,800													
Sierra College	Rocklin	C,T	Dist	M/W	18,796	66	35		Y			Y	Y	Y	Y	Y	13	60
Southwestern College	Chula Vista	C,T	Dist	M/W	18,413	60												
Colorado																		
Arapahoe Community College	Littleton	C,T,B	St	M/W	10,697	83	43		Y			Y	Y	Y	Y	N		30
CollegeAmerica–Denver	Denver	T	Ind	M/W	110													
Colorado Northwestern Community College	Rangely	C,T	St	M/W	1,154	58	33		Y	Y	Y	Y	Y	Y		Y	11	16
Community College of Aurora	Aurora	C,T	St	M/W	7,982	77	27				S	Y	Y	Y	Y	N		14
Community College of Denver	Denver	C,T	St	M/W	8,556	71	35		Y			Y	Y	Y	Y	N	23	21
Front Range Community College	Westminster	C,T	St	M/W	18,880	74	34		Y			Y	Y	Y	Y	N		33
Lamar Community College	Lamar	C,T	St	M/W	791	49												
Northeastern Junior College	Sterling	C,T	St	M/W	1,547	42												
Otero Junior College	La Junta	C,T	St	M/W	1,449													

This chart includes the names and locations of accredited two-year colleges in the United States, Canada, and other countries and shows institutions' responses to the *Peterson's Annual Survey of Undergraduate Institutions.* If an institution submitted incomplete data, one or more columns opposite the institution's name is blank. A dagger after the school name indicates that the institution has one or more entries in the *Featured Two-Year Colleges* section. If a school does not appear, it did not report any of the information.

Y—Yes; N—No; R—Recommended; S—For Some

Institution	Location	Degrees Awarded: College Transfer Associate (C), Terminal Associate (T), Bachelor's (B), Master's (M), Doctoral (D)	Institutional Control: Independent (Ind), Independent-Religious (I-R), Proprietary (Prop), Federal, State, Commonwealth, Territory, County, District, City, State and Local, State-Related	Student Body: Men, Primarily Men, Women, Primarily Women, Coed	Undergraduate Enrollment	Percent Attending Part-Time	Percent 25 Years of Age or Older	Percent of Grads Going on to Four-Year Colleges	Open Admissions	High School Equivalency Certificate Accepted	High School Transcript Required	Need-Based Aid Available	Part-Time Jobs Available	Career Counseling Available	Job Placement Services Available	College Housing Available	Number of Sports Offered	Number of Majors Offered
Pueblo Community College	Pueblo	C,T,B	St	M/W	5,650	69	49	21	Y			Y	Y	Y	Y	N		35
Connecticut																		
Housatonic Community College	Bridgeport	C,T	St	M/W	5,138	66												
Manchester Community College	Manchester	C,T	St	M/W	6,003	67	31		Y	Y	Y	Y	Y			N	4	31
Naugatuck Valley Community College	Waterbury	C,T	St	M/W	6,378	66												
Three Rivers Community College	Norwich	C,T	St	M/W	4,187	68												
Florida																		
Chipola College	Marianna	C,T,B	St	M/W	2,104	59												
College of Business and Technology–Cutler Bay Campus	Cutler Bay	C	Prop	M/W	137													
College of Business and Technology–Flagler Campus	Miami	C	Prop	M/W	256													
College of Business and Technology–Hialeah Campus	Hialeah	C	Prop	PM	200													
College of Business and Technology–Main Campus	Miami	C,B	Prop	M/W	10													
College of Business and Technology–Miami Gardens	Miami Gardens	C,B	Prop	M/W	91													
College of Central Florida	Ocala	C,T,B	St-L	M/W	6,820	56	20		Y	Y	Y	Y	Y	Y	Y	N	5	74
Daytona State College	Daytona Beach	C,B	St	M/W	19,530	60	40		Y	Y	Y	Y	Y	Y	Y	N	9	45
Florida Keys Community College	Key West	C,T,B	St	M/W	1,030	65												
Gulf Coast State College	Panama City	C,T,B	St	M/W	5,379	66												
Miami Dade College	Miami	C,T,B	St-L	M/W	56,001	58												
Pensacola State College	Pensacola	C,B	St	M/W	9,655	63												
Seminole State College of Florida	Sanford	C,T,B	St-L	M/W	17,706	65												
Southeastern College–West Palm Beach	West Palm Beach	T	Prop	M/W	558	52												
South Florida State College	Avon Park	C,T,B	St	M/W	2,885	66												
Tallahassee Community College	Tallahassee	C,T,B	St-L	M/W	11,782	51												
Georgia																		
Georgia Highlands College	Rome	C,T,B	St	M/W	6,184	53	21		N	Y	Y	Y	Y	Y		N	12	6
Georgia Military College	Milledgeville	C,B	Pub	M/W	8,595	50												
Gordon State College	Barnesville	C,T,B	St	M/W	3,986													
Gupton-Jones College of Funeral Service	Decatur	T	Ind	M/W	232													
Hawaii																		
Hawaii Tokai International College	Kapolei	C,T	Ind	M/W	85													
Idaho																		
College of Eastern Idaho	Idaho Falls	C,T	St	M/W	791													
Illinois																		
Black Hawk College	Moline	C,T	St-L	M/W	4,333	62	28	68	Y		R	Y	Y	Y	Y	N	6	29
City Colleges of Chicago, Olive-Harvey College	Chicago	C,T	St-L	M/W	2,882													
Danville Area Community College	Danville	C,T	St-L	M/W	2,645	62												
Harper College	Palatine	C,T	St-L	M/W	13,530	66	29		Y		Y	Y	Y	Y		N	12	65
Heartland Community College	Normal	C,T	St-L	M/W	4,722	62	27	67	Y		R	Y	Y	Y	Y	N	3	11
Highland Community College	Freeport	C,T	St-L	M/W	1,678	51												
Illinois Central College	East Peoria	C,T	St-L	M/W	9,266	66												
Illinois Eastern Community Colleges, Frontier Community College	Fairfield	C,T	St-L	M/W	1,791	84												
Illinois Eastern Community Colleges, Lincoln Trail College	Robinson	C,T	St-L	M/W	933	57												
Illinois Eastern Community Colleges, Olney Central College	Olney	C,T	St-L	M/W	1,142	54												
Illinois Eastern Community Colleges, Wabash Valley College	Mount Carmel	C,T	St-L	M/W	3,662	87												
Illinois Valley Community College	Oglesby	C,T	Dist	M/W	3,241	61												
Kaskaskia College	Centralia	C,T	St-L	M/W	3,164	61	21		Y	Y	Y	Y	Y	Y	Y	N	8	41
Kishwaukee College	Malta	C,T	St-L	M/W	3,775	57												
McHenry County College	Crystal Lake	C,T	St-L	M/W	6,843	69	27		Y		R	Y	Y	Y	Y	N	6	26
Morrison Institute of Technology	Morrison	C,T	Ind	PM	144	1												
Morton College	Cicero	C,T	St-L	M/W	4,387	69												
Oakton Community College	Des Plaines	C,T	Dist	M/W	7,942		36		Y	Y	R	Y	Y	Y		N	10	29
Rend Lake College	Ina	C,T	St	M/W	2,486	51	25		Y	Y	Y	Y	Y	Y	Y	N	5	33
Rock Valley College	Rockford	C	Dist	M/W	6,244	56	27		Y		Y	Y	Y	Y	Y	N	6	31
Sauk Valley Community College	Dixon	C,T	Dist	M/W	2,220	55												
Shawnee Community College	Ullin	C,T	St-L	M/W	1,505	55												
South Suburban College	South Holland	C,T	St-L	M/W	4,115													
Southwestern Illinois College	Belleville	C,T	Dist	M/W														
Indiana																		
Ancilla College	Donaldson	C,T	I-R	M/W	548	18												
Ivy Tech Community College–Bloomington	Bloomington	C,T	St	M/W	6,198	73												
Ivy Tech Community College–Central Indiana	Indianapolis	C,T	St	M/W	18,062	75												
Ivy Tech Community College–Columbus	Columbus	C,T	St	M/W	2,653	75												
Ivy Tech Community College–East Central	Muncie	C,T	St	M/W	5,462	63												
Ivy Tech Community College–Kokomo	Kokomo	C,T	St	M/W	2,422	67												
Ivy Tech Community College–Lafayette	Lafayette	C,T	St	M/W	4,517	62												
Ivy Tech Community College–North Central	South Bend	C,T	St	M/W	4,805	71												
Ivy Tech Community College–Northeast	Fort Wayne	C,T	St	M/W	6,795	72												
Ivy Tech Community College–Northwest	Gary	C,T	St	M/W	8,314	71												
Ivy Tech Community College–Richmond	Richmond	C,T	St	M/W	1,527	73												
Ivy Tech Community College–Sellersburg	Sellersburg	C,T	St	M/W	4,684	81												
Ivy Tech Community College–Southeast	Madison	C,T	St	M/W	2,334	73												

This chart includes the names and locations of accredited two-year colleges in the United States, Canada, and other countries and shows institutions' responses to the *Peterson's Annual Survey of Undergraduate Institutions*. If an institution submitted incomplete data, one or more columns opposite the institution's name is blank. A dagger after the school name indicates that the institution has one or more entries in the *Featured Two-Year Colleges* section. If a school does not appear, it did not report any of the information.

Y—Yes; N—No; R—Recommended; S—For Some

Institution	Location	Degrees Awarded: College Transfer Associate (C), Terminal Associate (T), Bachelor's (B), Master's (M), Doctoral (D)	Institutional Control: Independent, Independent-Religious, Proprietary, Federal, State, Commonwealth, Territory, County, District, City, State and Local, State-Related	Student Body: Men, Primarily Men, Women, Primarily Women, Coed	Undergraduate Enrollment	Percent Attending Part-Time	Percent 25 Years of Age or Older	Percent of Grads Going on to Four-Year Colleges	Open Admissions	High School Equivalency Certificate Accepted	High School Transcript Required	Need-Based Aid Available	Part-Time Jobs Available	Career Counseling Available	Job Placement Services Available	College Housing Available	Number of Sports Offered	Number of Majors Offered
Ivy Tech Community College–Southwest	Evansville	C,T	St	M/W	4,076	77												
Ivy Tech Community College–Wabash Valley	Terre Haute	C,T	St	M/W	3,637	67												
Vincennes University	Vincennes	C,B	St	M/W	17,481	72	32		Y	Y	Y	Y	Y			Y	4	95
Iowa																		
Des Moines Area Community College	Ankeny	C,T	St-L	M/W	22,982	72												
Hawkeye Community College	Waterloo	C,T	St-L	M/W	5,259	57	25		Y	Y	Y	Y	Y	Y	Y	N	11	38
Iowa Central Community College	Fort Dodge	C,T	St-L	M/W	5,489													
Northeast Iowa Community College	Calmar	C,T	St-L	M/W	4,545	73												
North Iowa Area Community College	Mason City	C	St-L	M/W	2,947	54												
St. Luke's College	Sioux City	C,T,B	Ind	M/W	270	53	53	60	N	Y	Y	Y	Y	Y	Y	N		4
Southwestern Community College	Creston	C,T	St	M/W	1,547	56	29		Y	Y	Y	Y	Y	Y	Y	Y	8	15
Western Iowa Tech Community College	Sioux City	C,T	St	M/W	6,152	63												
Kansas																		
Barton County Community College	Great Bend	C,T	St-L	M/W	4,131	79												
Cloud County Community College	Concordia	C,T	St-L	M/W	1,873	57												
Donnelly College	Kansas City	C,T,B	I-R	M/W	294	39												
Hesston College	Hesston	C,T,B	I-R	M/W	442	9												
Hutchinson Community College	Hutchinson	C,T	St-L	M/W	5,574	63	25	80	Y	Y	Y	Y	Y	Y		Y	11	58
Independence Community College	Independence	C,T	St	M/W	897	43												
Kentucky																		
Gateway Community and Technical College	Florence	C,T	St	M/W	4,215													
Henderson Community College	Henderson	C,T	St	M/W	1,586	68	41		Y	Y	Y	Y	Y	Y	Y	N		9
Hopkinsville Community College	Hopkinsville	C,T	St	M/W	3,120	60												
Maysville Community and Technical College	Maysville	C,T	St	M/W	3,495													
Owensboro Community and Technical College	Owensboro	C,T	St	M/W	3,947	62	37	11	Y	Y	Y	Y	Y	Y	Y	N		26
Somerset Community College	Somerset	C,T	St	M/W	5,900													
Southcentral Kentucky Community and Technical College	Bowling Green	C,T	St	M/W	4,953													
Southeast Kentucky Community and Technical College	Cumberland	C,T	St	M/W	3,125	53												
West Kentucky Community and Technical College	Paducah	C,T	St	M/W	6,043		35		Y	Y	Y	Y	Y	Y	Y	N	1	26
Louisiana																		
Bossier Parish Community College	Bossier City	C	St	M/W	6,042	62												
Central Louisiana Technical Community College	Alexandria	C	St	M/W	2,432	54												
ITI Technical College	Baton Rouge	T	Prop	M/W	622													
Louisiana State University at Eunice	Eunice	C,T	St	M/W	2,906	52												
Nunez Community College	Chalmette	C,T	St	M/W	2,599	62												
Southern University at Shreveport	Shreveport	C,T	St	M/W	2,651	43	35		Y	Y	R	Y	Y	Y	Y	Y	3	19
Sowela Technical Community College	Lake Charles	C,T	St	M/W	3,459	48	29	100	Y	Y	S	Y		Y	Y	N		18
Maine																		
Beal College	Bangor	T	Prop	M/W	464	22												
Central Maine Community College	Auburn	C,T	St	M/W	2,900	62												
Kennebec Valley Community College	Fairfield	C,T	St	M/W	2,554	78												
Maine College of Health Professions	Lewiston	T,B	Ind	M/W	188	77												
Northern Maine Community College	Presque Isle	C,T	St	M/W	955													
Southern Maine Community College	South Portland	C,T	St	M/W	8,491	60			Y	Y	Y	Y	Y	Y		Y	5	36
York County Community College	Wells	C,T	St	M/W	1,708	77												
Maryland																		
Anne Arundel Community College	Arnold	C,T	St-L	M/W	13,354	71												
Carroll Community College	Westminster	C,T	St-L	M/W	3,020	67												
Cecil College	North East	C,B	Cou	M/W	2,468	65												
Chesapeake College	Wye Mills	C,T	St-L	M/W	2,189													
Community College of Baltimore County	Baltimore	C,T	Cou	M/W	18,833	73			Y	Y	Y			Y		N	9	59
Frederick Community College	Frederick	C,T	St-L	M/W	6,220	67												
Hagerstown Community College	Hagerstown	C,T	St-L	M/W	4,069	75												
Harford Community College	Bel Air	C,T	St-L	M/W	6,100													
Howard Community College	Columbia	C,T	St-L	M/W	9,726													
Montgomery College	Rockville	C,T	St-L	M/W	22,875	65												
Wor-Wic Community College	Salisbury	C,T	St-L	M/W	3,025	74	42		Y		R		Y	Y		N		19
Massachusetts																		
Bristol Community College	Fall River	C,T	St	M/W	7,637													
Bunker Hill Community College	Boston	C	St	M/W	12,657	67			Y	Y	Y	Y	Y	Y	Y	N	4	58
FINE Mortuary College, LLC	Norwood	T	Prop	M/W	99	85												
Holyoke Community College	Holyoke	C,T	St	M/W	5,565	55												
Massachusetts Bay Community College	Wellesley Hills	C,T	St	M/W	4,368	66	37	59	Y	Y	S	Y	Y	Y	Y	N	5	33
Mount Wachusett Community College	Gardner	C,T	St	M/W	3,854	65												
Northern Essex Community College	Haverhill	C,T	St	M/W	5,726	66												
North Shore Community College	Danvers	C,T	St	M/W	6,087													
Quinsigamond Community College	Worcester	C,T	St	M/W	7,265	65	39		Y	Y	Y	Y	Y	Y	Y	N	7	53
Springfield Technical Community College	Springfield	C,T	St	M/W	5,343	57												
Urban College of Boston	Boston	T	Ind	PW	812	93												
Michigan																		
Grand Rapids Community College	Grand Rapids	C,T	Dist	M/W	13,767	70	30		Y	Y	Y	Y	Y	Y		N	6	35
Kellogg Community College	Battle Creek	C,T	St-L	M/W	4,814	76												
Kirtland Community College	Roscommon	C,T	Dist	M/W	1,528	67												
Macomb Community College	Warren	C,T	Dist	M/W	21,014	71												

This chart includes the names and locations of accredited two-year colleges in the United States, Canada, and other countries and shows institutions' responses to the *Peterson's Annual Survey of Undergraduate Institutions.* If an institution submitted incomplete data, one or more columns opposite the institution's name is blank. A dagger after the school name indicates that the institution has one or more entries in the *Featured Two-Year Colleges* section. If a school does not appear, it did not report any of the information.

Y—Yes; N—No; R—Recommended; S—For Some

Institution	Location	Degrees Awarded: College Transfer Associate (C), Terminal Associate (T), Bachelor's (B), Master's (M), Doctoral (D)	Institutional Control: Independent, Independent-Religious, Proprietary, Federal, State, Commonwealth, Territory, County, District, City, State and Local, State-Related	Student Body: Men, Primarily Men, Women, Primarily Women, Coed	Undergraduate Enrollment	Percent Attending Part-Time	Percent 25 Years of Age or Older	Percent of Grads Going on to Four-Year Colleges	Open Admissions	High School Equivalency Certificate Accepted	High School Transcript Required	Need-Based Aid Available	Part-Time Jobs Available	Career Counseling Available	Job Placement Services Available	College Housing Available	Number of Sports Offered	Number of Majors Offered
Monroe County Community College	Monroe	C,T	Cou	M/W	3,144													
Mott Community College	Flint	C,T	Dist	M/W	7,689	74												
Muskegon Community College	Muskegon	C,T	St-L	M/W	4,506	67												
Saginaw Chippewa Tribal College	Mount Pleasant	C,T	Ind	M/W	140	74												
Schoolcraft College	Livonia	C,T,B	Dist	M/W	10,558	72												
Southwestern Michigan College	Dowagiac	C,T	St-L	M/W	2,130	59	22		Y	Y	Y	Y	Y			Y	8	21
Wayne County Community College District	Detroit	C,T	St-L	M/W	14,957	87	57		Y	Y	Y	Y	Y	Y	Y	N	5	42
Minnesota																		
Alexandria Technical and Community College	Alexandria	C,T	St	M/W	2,483		17		Y	Y	S	Y	Y	Y		N	4	25
Central Lakes College	Brainerd	C,T	St	M/W	3,715													
Century College	White Bear Lake	C,T	St	M/W	8,442	57												
Dunwoody College of Technology	Minneapolis	T,B	Ind	PM	1,305	19	42		N	Y		Y	Y	Y	Y	N		27
Lake Superior College	Duluth	C,T	St	M/W	4,690	61	36		Y		Y	Y	Y	Y	Y	N	5	37
Mesabi Range College	Virginia	C,T	St	M/W	1,089													
Minnesota State College–Southeast Technical	Winona	C,T	St	M/W	1,814	61	45		Y	Y	Y	Y	Y			N		26
Minnesota State Community and Technical College	Fergus Falls	C,T	St	M/W	6,303													
Minnesota West Community and Technical College	Pipestone	C,T	St	M/W	3,182													
North Hennepin Community College	Brooklyn Park	C,T	St	M/W	6,509													
Northland Community and Technical College	Thief River Falls	C,T	St	M/W	3,599	62												
Rainy River Community College	International Falls	C,T	St	M/W	241													
Ridgewater College	Willmar	C,T	St	M/W					Y	Y	Y	Y	Y			N	5	50
Mississippi																		
Copiah-Lincoln Community College	Wesson	C,T	St-L	M/W	3,100	31												
Hinds Community College	Raymond	C,T	St-L	M/W	12,061	40												
Meridian Community College	Meridian	C,T	St-L	M/W	3,555													
Northwest Mississippi Community College	Senatobia	C,T	St-L	M/W	7,700													
Missouri																		
Cottey College	Nevada	C,B	Ind	CW	265	2												
Crowder College	Neosho	C,T	St-L	M/W	4,960													
East Central College	Union	C,T	Dist	M/W	2,629	54			Y	Y	Y	Y	Y	Y		N	3	24
Missouri State University–West Plains	West Plains	C,T	St	M/W	1,909	58	28		Y	Y	S	Y	Y	Y	Y	Y	2	15
Ozarks Technical Community College	Springfield	C,T	Dist	M/W	13,260													
St. Charles Community College	Cottleville	C,T	St	M/W	6,269	49	23		Y	Y	S	Y	Y	Y	Y		5	26
St. Louis Community College	St. Louis	C,T	Pub	M/W	18,157	64	38		Y	Y	S			Y	Y	N	5	29
State Technical College of Missouri	Linn	T	St	PM	1,256	17												
Three Rivers College	Poplar Bluff	C,T	St-L	M/W	3,226	45												
Montana																		
Dawson Community College	Glendive	C,T	St-L	M/W	329	38												
Great Falls College Montana State University	Great Falls	C,T	St	M/W	1,690	62												
Nebraska																		
CHI Health School of Radiologic Technology	Omaha	T	Ind	M/W	15													
Mid-Plains Community College	North Platte	C,T	Dist	M/W	2,222													
Nebraska Indian Community College	Macy	C,T	Fed	M/W	180	74												
Northeast Community College	Norfolk	C,T	St-L	M/W	5,075	58												
Nevada																		
Career College of Northern Nevada	Sparks	T	Prop	M/W	342													
Truckee Meadows Community College	Reno	C,T,B	St	M/W	10,861	73	36	47	Y			Y	Y	Y		N		54
New Hampshire																		
Lakes Region Community College	Laconia	C,T	St	M/W	1,179	58												
St. Joseph School of Nursing	Nashua	C,T	Ind	M/W	144	56												
White Mountains Community College	Berlin	C,T	St	M/W	802	63												
New Jersey																		
Camden County College	Blackwood	C,T	St-L	M/W	10,492	52												
County College of Morris	Randolph	C,T	Cou	M/W	7,949	52												
Eastern International College	Belleville	C,T,B	Prop	M/W														
Hudson County Community College	Jersey City	C,T	St-L	M/W	8,864	42												
Raritan Valley Community College	Branchburg	C,T	St-L	M/W	7,887	61	26	65	Y			Y	Y	Y		N	6	49
Union County College	Cranford	C,T	St-L	M/W	9,412	55	41		Y	Y	Y	Y	Y	Y	Y	N	8	34
New Mexico																		
Central New Mexico Community College	Albuquerque	C,T	St	M/W	23,717	72	39		Y			Y	Y	Y	Y	N		58
Mesalands Community College	Tucumcari	C,T	St	M/W	1,005													
New Mexico State University–Alamogordo	Alamogordo	C,T	St	M/W	1,710	75												
San Juan College	Farmington	C,T	St	M/W	4,790	54	45		Y	Y	Y	Y	Y	Y	Y	N	2	49
Southwestern Indian Polytechnic Institute	Albuquerque	C,T	Fed	M/W	402	14												
New York																		
Adirondack Community College	Queensbury	C,T	St-L	M/W	3,973	45												
American Academy of Dramatic Arts–New York	New York	T	Ind	M/W	310													
The Belanger School of Nursing	Schenectady	C,T	Ind	M/W	114	68												
Borough of Manhattan Community College of the City University of New York	New York	C,T	St-L	M/W	26,506	32	26		Y	Y	Y	Y	Y	Y	Y		4	44
Cayuga County Community College	Auburn	C,T	St-L	M/W	4,921	68	40		Y		Y	Y	Y	Y		N	7	24
Cochran School of Nursing	Yonkers	T	Ind	PW	120	78												

This chart includes the names and locations of accredited two-year colleges in the United States, Canada, and other countries and shows institutions' responses to the *Peterson's Annual Survey of Undergraduate Institutions*. If an institution submitted incomplete data, one or more columns opposite the institution's name is blank. A dagger after the school name indicates that the institution has one or more entries in the *Featured Two-Year Colleges* section. If a school does not appear, it did not report any of the information.

Y—Yes; N—No; R—Recommended; S—For Some

College	City	**Degrees Awarded** College Transfer Associate (C), Terminal Associate (T), Bachelor's (B), Master's (M), Doctoral (D)	**Institutional Control** Independent (Ind), Independent-Religious, Proprietary (Prop), Federal, State, Commonwealth, Territory, County, District, City, State and Local, State-Related	**Student Body** Men, Primarily Men, Women, Primarily Women, Coed	Undergraduate Enrollment	Percent Attending Part-Time	Percent 25 Years of Age or Older	Percent of Grads Going on to Four-Year Colleges	Open Admissions	High School Equivalency Certificate Accepted	High School Transcript Required	Need-Based Aid Available	Part-Time Jobs Available	Career Counseling Available	Job Placement Services Available	College Housing Available	Number of Sports Offered	Number of Majors Offered
The College of Westchester	White Plains	C,T,B	Prop	M/W	915	21												
Columbia-Greene Community College	Hudson	C,T	St-L	M/W	1,584	61	4		Y	Y	Y	Y	Y	Y	Y	N	3	16
Dutchess Community College	Poughkeepsie	C,T	St-L	M/W	9,061	58												
Erie Community College	Buffalo	C,T	St-L	M/W	2,417	24												
Erie Community College, North Campus	Williamsville	C,T	St-L	M/W	4,929	33												
Erie Community College, South Campus	Orchard Park	C,T	St-L	M/W	3,789	44												
Fiorello H. LaGuardia Community College of the City University of New York	Long Island City	C,T	St-L	M/W	19,356	44												
Genesee Community College	Batavia	C,T	St-L	M/W	5,906													
Jamestown Community College	Jamestown	C,T	St-L	M/W	4,463	54												
Jefferson Community College	Watertown	C,T	St-L	M/W	3,632	43												
Kingsborough Community College of the City University of New York	Brooklyn	C,T	St-L	M/W	15,280	46												
Mohawk Valley Community College	Utica	C,T	St-L	M/W	6,506	49												
Monroe Community College	Rochester	C,T	St-L	M/W	12,907	39												
Nassau Community College	Garden City	C,T	St-L	M/W	17,278	43			Y	Y	Y	Y	Y	Y	Y	N	17	53
Niagara County Community College	Sanborn	C,T	St-L	M/W	5,466	41												
Queensborough Community College of the City University of New York	Bayside	C,T	St-L	M/W	15,411	40	24	75	Y	Y	Y	Y	Y	Y	Y	N	11	34
Schenectady County Community College	Schenectady	C,T	St-L	M/W	6,634	67												
State University of New York College of Technology at Alfred	Alfred	C,T,B	St	M/W	3,737	8	12		N	Y	Y	Y	Y	Y	Y	Y	19	59
Sullivan County Community College	Loch Sheldrake	C,T	St-L	M/W	1,538	49	18	26	Y	Y	Y	Y	Y	Y	Y	Y	13	37
Tompkins Cortland Community College	Dryden	C,T	St-L	M/W	2,632	30												
Westchester Community College	Valhalla	C,T	St-L	M/W	11,535	47	28		Y	Y	Y	Y	Y	Y	Y	N	11	50
North Carolina																		
Alamance Community College	Graham	C,T	St	M/W	4,233	39	48		Y	Y	Y	Y	Y	Y	Y	N		28
Asheville-Buncombe Technical Community College	Asheville	C,T	St	M/W	7,542													
Caldwell Community College and Technical Institute	Hudson	C,T	St	M/W	3,514	65												
Carteret Community College	Morehead City	C,T	St	M/W	1,363	58												
Cleveland Community College	Shelby	C,T	St	M/W	2,700	63												
College of The Albemarle	Elizabeth City	C,T	St	M/W	2,557	61	24		Y	Y	Y	Y	Y	Y	Y	N	13	27
Craven Community College	New Bern	C,T	St	M/W	3,021	63												
Fayetteville Technical Community College	Fayetteville	C,T	St	M/W	11,534	61	54	20	Y	Y	Y	Y	Y	Y	Y	N	5	47
Halifax Community College	Weldon	C,T	St-L	M/W	1,083	62	29		Y	Y	Y	Y	Y			N		21
Haywood Community College	Clyde	C,T	St-L	M/W	1,627	65	36	44	Y	Y	Y	Y	Y	Y	Y	N		31
James Sprunt Community College	Kenansville	C,T	St	M/W	1,219	65												
Johnston Community College	Smithfield	C,T	St	M/W	4,152	63			Y	Y	Y	Y	Y	Y	Y	N	1	14
Lenoir Community College	Kinston	C,T	St	M/W	2,664	62												
Mitchell Community College	Statesville	C,T	St	M/W	3,164	69	33	59	Y	Y	Y	Y	Y	Y		N		34
Montgomery Community College	Troy	C,T	St	M/W	925													
Piedmont Community College	Roxboro	C,T	St	M/W	1,311													
Randolph Community College	Asheboro	C,T	St	M/W	2,647	65												
Richmond Community College	Hamlet	C,T	St	M/W	2,555	59	32		Y	Y	Y	Y	Y	Y	Y	N		21
Rowan-Cabarrus Community College	Salisbury	C,T	St	M/W	7,579													
Southwestern Community College	Sylva	C	St	M/W	2,353	65					Y	Y	Y	Y		N		31
Tri-County Community College	Murphy	C,T	St	M/W	1,160													
Wayne Community College	Goldsboro	C,T	St-L	M/W	3,837	53												
North Dakota																		
Dakota College at Bottineau	Bottineau	C,T	St	M/W	996				Y	Y	Y	Y	Y	Y	Y	Y	10	70
Lake Region State College	Devils Lake	C,T	St	M/W	2,072	74	20		Y	Y	S	Y	Y	Y		Y	7	14
North Dakota State College of Science	Wahpeton	C,T	St	M/W	2,985	43												
Williston State College	Williston	C,T	St	M/W	1,098	44												
Ohio																		
AIC College of Design	Cincinnati	T,B	Ind	M/W	34	12												
Bowling Green State University–Firelands College	Huron	C,T,B	St	M/W	1,970	52												
Central Ohio Technical College	Newark	T	St	M/W	3,442	79	28		Y	Y	S	Y	Y	Y	Y	N	8	28
Eastern Gateway Community College	Steubenville	C,T	St-L	M/W	8,546	79												
Edison State Community College	Piqua	C,T	St	M/W	3,248	77												
Kent State University at Ashtabula	Ashtabula	C,T,B	St	M/W	1,971	48												
Kent State University at East Liverpool	East Liverpool	C,T,B	St	M/W	1,174	46												
Kent State University at Salem	Salem	C,B	St	M/W	1,694	37												
Kent State University at Trumbull	Warren	C,B	St	M/W	2,277													
Kent State University at Tuscarawas	New Philadelphia	C,B	St	M/W	2,131	39												
Lakeland Community College	Kirtland	C,T	St-L	M/W	7,581	71												
Lorain County Community College	Elyria	C,T	St-L	M/W	11,042	73												
The Modern College of Design	Kettering	T	Prop	M/W	194	2												
The Ohio State University Agricultural Technical Institute	Wooster	C,T	St	M/W	757	7												
Ohio Technical College	Cleveland	T	Prop	M/W	905		18		Y	Y	Y			Y	Y			8
Stark State College	North Canton	C,T	St-R	M/W	11,028	72												
Oklahoma																		
Carl Albert State College	Poteau	C,T	St	M/W	2,194	40												
Oklahoma City Community College	Oklahoma City	C,T	St	M/W	12,314	65												
Oklahoma State University Institute of Technology	Okmulgee	C,T,B	St	M/W	2,502	30												
Oklahoma State University–Oklahoma City	Oklahoma City	C,T,B	St	M/W	5,839	70												
Seminole State College	Seminole	C,T	St	M/W	1,633	41												
Tulsa Community College	Tulsa	C,T	St	M/W	16,391	71	35		Y		Y	Y	Y	Y	Y	N	5	54

This chart includes the names and locations of accredited two-year colleges in the United States, Canada, and other countries and shows institutions' responses to the *Peterson's Annual Survey of Undergraduate Institutions.* If an institution submitted incomplete data, one or more columns opposite the institution's name is blank. A dagger after the school name indicates that the institution has one or more entries in the *Featured Two-Year Colleges* section. If a school does not appear, it did not report any of the information.

Y—Yes; N—No; R—Recommended; S—For Some

Institution	Location	Degrees Awarded: College Transfer Associate (C), Terminal Associate (T), Bachelor's (B), Master's (M), Doctoral (D)	Institutional Control: Independent, Independent-Religious, Proprietary, Federal, State, Commonwealth, Territory, County, District, City, State and Local, State-Related	Student Body: Men, Primarily Men, Women, Primarily Women, Coed	Undergraduate Enrollment	Percent Attending Part-Time	Percent 25 Years of Age or Older	Percent of Grads Going on to Four-Year Colleges	Open Admissions	High School Equivalency Certificate Accepted	High School Transcript Required	Need-Based Aid Available	Part-Time Jobs Available	Career Counseling Available	Job Placement Services Available	College Housing Available	Number of Sports Offered	Number of Majors Offered
Oregon																		
Central Oregon Community College	Bend	C,T	Dist	M/W	4,871	53			Y	Y		Y	Y	Y		Y	12	55
Sumner College	Portland	T	Prop	PW	261		65				Y			Y	Y	N		1
Tillamook Bay Community College	Tillamook	C,T	Dist	M/W	261	51												
Treasure Valley Community College	Ontario	C,T	St-L	M/W	1,866	57	46		Y			Y	Y	Y		Y	9	33
Pennsylvania																		
Bucks County Community College	Newtown	C,T	Cou	M/W	7,761	63	27	51	Y	Y	Y	Y	Y	Y	Y	N	12	58
Community College of Allegheny County	Pittsburgh	C,T	Cou	M/W	16,086	67				Y	R	Y	Y	Y	Y	N	13	139
Community College of Philadelphia	Philadelphia	C,T	St-L	M/W	30,194													
Harrisburg Area Community College	Harrisburg	C,T	St-L	M/W	18,081	71	42		Y		S	Y	Y	Y		N	4	61
Johnson College	Scranton	T	Ind	M/W	376	3												
Lackawanna College	Scranton	C,T,B	Ind	M/W	1,604	27												
Lehigh Carbon Community College	Schnecksville	C,T	St-L	M/W	6,953	64												
Luzerne County Community College	Nanticoke	C,T	Cou	M/W	4,984	59			Y	Y	R	Y	Y	Y	Y	N	6	67
Manor College	Jenkintown	C,T,B	I-R	M/W	740	35	21	60	N	Y	Y	Y	Y	Y		Y	6	22
Montgomery County Community College	Blue Bell	C,T	Cou	M/W	10,392	66												
New Castle School of Trades	New Castle	T	Ind	PM	503													
Northampton Community College	Bethlehem	C,T	St-L	M/W	9,769	56	34		Y	Y	S	Y	Y	Y	Y	Y	10	63
Penn State DuBois	DuBois	C,T,B	St-R	M/W	585	21												
Penn State Fayette, The Eberly Campus	Lemont Furnace	C,T,B	St-R	M/W	652	10												
Penn State Mont Alto	Mont Alto	C,T,B	St-R	M/W	917	29												
Pennsylvania Highlands Community College	Johnstown	C,T	St-L	M/W	2,784													
Pennsylvania Institute of Technology	Media	C,T	Ind	M/W	447													
Pittsburgh Technical College	Oakdale	T,B	Prop	M/W	1,835													
Thaddeus Stevens College of Technology	Lancaster	C,T	St	M/W	1,142	1												
Puerto Rico																		
Humacao Community College	Humacao	T,B	Ind	M/W	467	23												
South Carolina																		
Greenville Technical College	Greenville	C,T	St	M/W	11,745	59			Y	Y	Y	Y	Y	Y		Y	7	34
Northeastern Technical College	Cheraw	C,T	St-L	M/W	976	54												
Spartanburg Methodist College	Spartanburg	C,T	I-R	M/W	790	1												
Trident Technical College	Charleston	C,T	St-L	M/W	13,271	58												
University of South Carolina Lancaster	Lancaster	C,T	St	M/W	1,593													
University of South Carolina Union	Union	C,B	St	M/W	905		7	50	N	Y	Y	Y	Y			N	3	2
Williamsburg Technical College	Kingstree	C,T	St	M/W	732	73												
South Dakota																		
Lake Area Technical Institute	Watertown	T	St	M/W	2,055	26												
Mitchell Technical Institute	Mitchell	T	St	M/W	1,198	30	21		Y	Y	Y	Y	Y	Y	Y	N	2	25
Sisseton-Wahpeton College	Sisseton	C,T	Fed	M/W	175	27												
Southeast Technical Institute	Sioux Falls	T	St	M/W	2,244	36												
Western Dakota Technical Institute	Rapid City	T	St	M/W	1,049	42												
Tennessee																		
Cleveland State Community College	Cleveland	C,T	St	M/W	3,264	49	24	16	Y	Y	Y	Y	Y	Y	Y	N	10	22
Dyersburg State Community College	Dyersburg	C,T	St	M/W	2,816	56												
Motlow State Community College	Tullahoma	C,T	St	M/W	6,886	42	21		Y	Y	Y	Y		Y	Y	N	4	11
North Central Institute	Clarksville	T	Prop	PM	88													
Northeast State Community College	Blountville	C,T	St	M/W	6,088	44												
Volunteer State Community College	Gallatin	C,T	St	M/W	8,838	44												
Walters State Community College	Morristown	C,T	St	M/W	6,075	46												
Texas																		
Alvin Community College	Alvin	C,T	St-L	M/W	5,785	76												
Amarillo College	Amarillo	C,T	St-L	M/W														
Austin Community College District	Austin	C,T,B	St-L	M/W	40,799		38		Y	Y	Y	Y	Y	Y		N	3	103
Brookhaven College	Farmers Branch	C,T	Cou	M/W	13,284	83												
Cedar Valley College	Lancaster	C,T	St	M/W	7,249													
Central Texas College	Killeen	C,T	St-L	M/W	16,073	73	59		Y	Y	Y	Y	Y	Y		Y	5	48
Collin County Community College District	McKinney	C,T	St-L	M/W	31,619	68												
Culinary Institute LeNotre	Houston	T	Prop	M/W	320													
Dallas Institute of Funeral Service	Dallas	C,T	Ind	M/W	95													
Del Mar College	Corpus Christi	C,T	St-L	M/W	11,833	77												
El Paso Community College	El Paso	C,T	Cou	M/W	28,750	70												
Galveston College	Galveston	C,T	St-L	M/W	2,208	74												
Hill College	Hillsboro	C,T	Dist	M/W	4,075													
Houston Community College	Houston	C,T	St-L	M/W	57,120	70												
KD Conservatory College of Film and Dramatic Arts	Dallas	C,T	Prop	M/W	236													
Lamar Institute of Technology	Beaumont	T	St	M/W	3,565	62	23			Y		Y	Y	Y	Y	Y	4	25
McLennan Community College	Waco	C,T	Cou	M/W	8,799													
Navarro College	Corsicana	C,T	St-L	M/W	8,968	66												
North Central Texas College	Gainesville	C,T	St-L	M/W	10,327	74												
Northwest Vista College	San Antonio	C,T	Dist	M/W	13,115	69												
Odessa College	Odessa	C,T	St-L	M/W	6,308	64												
Panola College	Carthage	C,T	St-L	M/W	2,646	50												
Paris Junior College	Paris	C,T	St-L	M/W	4,835	62												
Richland College	Dallas	C,T	St-L	M/W	19,736													
St. Philip's College	San Antonio	C,T	Dist	M/W	12,050	87												

This chart includes the names and locations of accredited two-year colleges in the United States, Canada, and other countries and shows institutions' responses to the *Peterson's Annual Survey of Undergraduate Institutions*. If an institution submitted incomplete data, one or more columns opposite the institution's name is blank. A dagger after the school name indicates that the institution has one or more entries in the *Featured Two-Year Colleges* section. If a school does not appear, it did not report any of the information.

Y—Yes; N—No; R—Recommended; S—For Some

College	Location	Degrees Awarded: College Transfer Associate (C), Terminal Associate (T), Bachelor's (B), Master's (M), Doctoral (D)	Institutional Control: Independent (Ind), Independent-Religious (I-R), Proprietary (Prop), Federal, State, Commonwealth, Territory (St), County, District, City, State and Local, State-Related	Student Body: Men, Primarily Men, Women, Primarily Women, Coed	Undergraduate Enrollment	Percent Attending Part-Time	Percent 25 Years of Age or Older	Percent of Grads Going on to Four-Year Colleges	Open Admissions	High School Equivalency Certificate Accepted	High School Transcript Required	Need-Based Aid Available	Part-Time Jobs Available	Career Counseling Available	Job Placement Services Available	College Housing Available	Number of Sports Offered	Number of Majors Offered
San Jacinto College District	Pasadena	C	St-L	M/W	32,137	77	29	41	Y	Y	Y			Y	Y	N	8	80
Southwest Texas Junior College	Uvalde	C,T	St-L	M/W														
Tarrant County College District	Fort Worth	C,T	Cou	M/W	51,350	71												
Texarkana College	Texarkana	C,T	St-L	M/W	4,239	64	27		Y	Y	Y	Y	Y	Y	Y	Y	5	39
Texas State Technical College	Waco	C,T	St	M/W	12,717	61												
Trinity Valley Community College	Athens	C,T	St-L	M/W	4,449		44	20	Y	Y	Y	Y	Y	Y	Y	Y	6	54
Tyler Junior College	Tyler	C,T,B	St-L	M/W	10,106	40	24		Y	Y	Y	Y	Y	Y	Y	Y	11	66
Victoria College	Victoria	C,T	Cou	M/W	4,000	74												
Wade College	Dallas	C,T,B	Prop	M/W	238													
Western Texas College	Snyder	C,T	St-L	M/W	2,250	74												
Utah																		
LDS Business College	Salt Lake City	C,T	I-R	M/W														
Salt Lake Community College	Salt Lake City	C,T	St	M/W	29,620	74												
Snow College	Ephraim	C,T	St	M/W	5,574	42	9	70	Y	Y	Y	Y	Y	Y	Y	Y	17	57
Virginia																		
Central Virginia Community College	Lynchburg	C,T	St	M/W	4,128													
Dabney S. Lancaster Community College	Clifton Forge	C,T	St	M/W	1,186	64												
Eastern Shore Community College	Melfa	C,T	St	M/W	857													
John Tyler Community College	Chester	C,T	St	M/W	10,144	76	24		Y		R	Y	Y	Y	Y	N	3	20
J. Sargeant Reynolds Community College	Richmond	C,T	St	M/W	9,334	72												
New River Community College	Dublin	C,T	St	M/W	4,400													
Piedmont Virginia Community College	Charlottesville	C,T	St	M/W	5,608													
Rappahannock Community College	Glenns	C,T	St-L	M/W	3,463													
Southwest Virginia Community College	Richlands	C,T	St	M/W	2,304													
Tidewater Community College	Norfolk	C,T	St	M/W	20,941		45		Y			Y	Y	Y	Y	N		25
Wytheville Community College	Wytheville	C,T	St	M/W	2,745													
Washington																		
Clark College	Vancouver	C,T,B	St	M/W	10,477	52												
Renton Technical College	Renton	C,T,B	St	M/W	3,546						S	Y	Y	Y	Y	N		30
West Virginia																		
Blue Ridge Community and Technical College	Martinsburg	C,T	St	M/W	6,273	82	73		Y	Y	Y			Y	Y	N		24
Potomac State College of West Virginia University	Keyser	C,T,B	St	M/W	1,340	24	8		Y	Y	Y	Y	Y			Y	10	54
Wisconsin																		
Chippewa Valley Technical College	Eau Claire	C,T	Dist	M/W	7,134	70												
Fox Valley Technical College	Appleton	T	St-L	M/W	11,658	81												
Gateway Technical College	Kenosha	T	St-L	M/W	8,722	84												
Lakeshore Technical College	Cleveland	C,T	St-L	M/W														
Mid-State Technical College	Wisconsin Rapids	C,T	St-L	M/W	2,636	64												
Northcentral Technical College	Wausau	C,T	Dist	M/W	5,167	74												
Southwest Wisconsin Technical College	Fennimore	T	St-L	M/W	2,009	64	40		Y		Y	Y	Y	Y	Y	Y	2	19
University of Wisconsin–Baraboo/Sauk County	Baraboo	C,T,B	St	M/W	512													
University of Wisconsin–Barron County	Rice Lake	C,T,B	St	M/W	505													
University of Wisconsin–Fond du Lac	Fond du Lac	C,T	St	M/W	519													
University of Wisconsin–Fox Valley	Menasha	C,T	St	M/W	1,364													
University of Wisconsin–Manitowoc	Manitowoc	C,T	St	M/W	354													
University of Wisconsin–Marathon County	Wausau	C,T	St	M/W	838													
University of Wisconsin–Marinette	Marinette	C,T	St	M/W	286													
University of Wisconsin–Marshfield/Wood County	Marshfield	C,T,B	St	M/W	535													
University of Wisconsin–Richland	Richland Center	C,T,B	St	M/W	259													
University of Wisconsin–Rock County	Janesville	C,T,B	St	M/W	970													
University of Wisconsin–Sheboygan	Sheboygan	C,T	St	M/W	602													
University of Wisconsin–Washington County	West Bend	C,T	St	M/W	544													
University of Wisconsin–Waukesha	Waukesha	C,B	St	M/W	1,782													
Waukesha County Technical College	Pewaukee	T	St-L	M/W	7,696	80												
Wisconsin Indianhead Technical College	Shell Lake	C,T	Dist	M/W	3,021	64												
Wyoming																		
Laramie County Community College	Cheyenne	C,T	Dist	M/W	4,226	61												
Northwest College	Powell	C,T	St-L	M/W	1,654	42												
Western Wyoming Community College	Rock Springs	C,T	St-L	M/W	3,183	66	36	8	Y	Y	R	Y	Y	Y	Y	Y	4	83

Profiles of Two-Year Colleges

NOTICE: Certain portions of or information contained in this book have been submitted and paid for by the educational institution identified, and such institutions take full responsibility for the accuracy, timeliness, completeness and functionality of such content. Such portions or information include (i) each display ad in the "Profiles" section from pages 53 through 318 that comprises a half or full page of information covering a single educational institution, and (ii) each two-page description in the "Featured Two-Year Colleges" section from pages 322 through 327.

U.S. AND U.S. TERRITORIES

ALABAMA

Bevill State Community College

Jasper, Alabama

- **State-supported** 2-year, founded 1969, part of Alabama Community College System
- **Rural** 245-acre campus with easy access to Birmingham
- **Coed**

Undergraduates 1,583 full-time, 2,289 part-time. Students come from 10 states and territories; 2% are from out of state; 15% Black or African American, non-Hispanic/Latino; 2% Hispanic/Latino; 0.3% Asian, non-Hispanic/Latino; 0.1% American Indian or Alaska Native, non-Hispanic/Latino; 1% Two or more races, non-Hispanic/Latino; 0.9% Race/ethnicity unknown; 7% transferred in. *Retention:* 59% of full-time freshmen returned.

Faculty *Student/faculty ratio:* 17:1.

Academics *Calendar:* semesters. *Degree:* certificates and associate. *Special study options:* academic remediation for entering students, adult/continuing education programs, advanced placement credit, cooperative education, distance learning, honors programs, off-campus study, part-time degree program, services for LD students, summer session for credit.

Library Main Library plus 5 others. *Books:* 113,246 (physical); *Serial titles:* 3,563 (physical); *Databases:* 15. Weekly public service hours: 56.

Athletics Member NJCAA.

Financial Aid Of all full-time matriculated undergraduates who enrolled in 2016, 2,711 applied for aid, 2,568 were judged to have need, 45 had their need fully met. 41 Federal Work-Study jobs (averaging $3494). In 2016, 62. *Average percent of need met:* 42. *Average financial aid package:* $5291. *Average need-based gift aid:* $6235. *Average non-need-based aid:* $1937.

Applying *Options:* electronic application, early admission. *Required:* high school transcript.

Freshman Application Contact Ms. Melissa Stowe, Dean of Students, Bevill State Community College, 1411 Indiana Avenue, Jasper, AL 35501. *Phone:* 205-387-0511 Ext. 5813. *E-mail:* melissa.stowe@bscc.edu. *Website:* http://www.bscc.edu/.

Bishop State Community College

Mobile, Alabama

Freshman Application Contact Bishop State Community College, 351 North Broad Street, Mobile, AL 36603-5898. *Phone:* 251-405-7000. *Toll-free phone:* 800-523-7235. *Website:* http://www.bishop.edu/.

Calhoun Community College

Decatur, Alabama

Freshman Application Contact Admissions Office, Calhoun Community College, PO Box 2216, Decatur, AL 35609-2216. *Phone:* 256-306-2593. *Toll-free phone:* 800-626-3628. *Fax:* 256-306-2941. *E-mail:* admissions@calhoun.edu. *Website:* http://www.calhoun.edu/.

Central Alabama Community College

Alexander City, Alabama

Freshman Application Contact Ms. Donna Whaley, Central Alabama Community College, 1675 Cherokee Road, Alexander City, AL 35011-0699. *Phone:* 256-234-6346 Ext. 6232. *Toll-free phone:* 800-634-2657. *Website:* http://www.cacc.edu/.

Chattahoochee Valley Community College

Phenix City, Alabama

Freshman Application Contact Chattahoochee Valley Community College, 2602 College Drive, Phenix City, AL 36869-7928. *Phone:* 334-291-4929. *Website:* http://www.cv.edu/.

Coastal Alabama Community College

Bay Minette, Alabama

Freshman Application Contact Ms. Carmelita Mikkelsen, Director of Admissions and High School Relations, Coastal Alabama Community College, 1900 Highway 31 South, Bay Minette, AL 36507. *Phone:* 251-580-2213. *Toll-free phone:* 800-381-3722. *Fax:* 251-580-2285. *E-mail:* cmikkelsen@faulknerstate.edu. *Website:* http://www.coastalalabama.edu/.

Community College of the Air Force

Maxwell Gunter Air Force Base, Alabama

Freshman Application Contact Ms. Gwendolyn Ford, Chief of Admissions Flight, Community College of the Air Force, 100 South Turner Boulevard, Maxwell Air Force Base, Maxwell - Gunter AFB, AL 36114-3011. *Phone:* 334-649-5081. *Fax:* 334-649-5015. *E-mail:* gwendolyn.ford@us.af.mil. *Website:* http://www.airuniversity.af.mil/Barnes/CCAF/.

Enterprise State Community College

Enterprise, Alabama

Director of Admissions Mr. Gary Deas, Associate Dean of Students/Registrar, Enterprise State Community College, 600 Plaza Drive, Enterprise, AL 36330. *Phone:* 334-347-2623 Ext. 2233. *E-mail:* gdeas@eocc.edu. *Website:* http://www.escc.edu/.

Fortis College

Mobile, Alabama

Admissions Office Contact Fortis College, 7033 Airport Boulevard, Mobile, AL 36608. *Toll-free phone:* 855-4-FORTIS. *Website:* http://www.fortis.edu/.

Fortis College

Montgomery, Alabama

Admissions Office Contact Fortis College, 3470 Eastdale Circle, Montgomery, AL 36117. *Toll-free phone:* 855-4-FORTIS. *Website:* http://www.fortis.edu/.

Fortis College

Montgomery, Alabama

Admissions Office Contact Fortis College, 3736 Atlanta Highway, Montgomery, AL 36109. *Toll-free phone:* 855-4-FORTIS. *Website:* http://www.fortis.edu/.

Fortis Institute

Birmingham, Alabama

Admissions Office Contact Fortis Institute, 100 London Parkway, Suite 150, Birmingham, AL 35211. *Toll-free phone:* 855-4-FORTIS. *Website:* http://www.fortis.edu/.

Gadsden State Community College

Gadsden, Alabama

Freshman Application Contact Mrs. Jennie Dobson, Admissions and Records, Gadsden State Community College, PO Box 227, 1001 George Wallace Drive, Gadsden, AL 35902-0227. *Phone:* 256-549-8210. *Toll-free phone:* 800-226-5563. *Fax:* 256-549-8205. *E-mail:* info@gadsdenstate.edu. *Website:* http://www.gadsdenstate.edu/.

George Corley Wallace State Community College

Selma, Alabama

Director of Admissions Ms. Sunette Newman, Registrar, George Corley Wallace State Community College, PO Box 2530, Selma, AL 36702. *Phone:* 334-876-9305. *Website:* http://www.wccs.edu/.

George C. Wallace Community College

Dothan, Alabama

- **State-supported** 2-year, founded 1949, part of The Alabama Community College System
- **Rural** 258-acre campus
- **Coed**

Undergraduates 1,929 full-time, 2,716 part-time. Students come from 7 states and territories; 0.7% are from out of state; 28% Black or African American, non-Hispanic/Latino; 3% Hispanic/Latino; 0.8% Asian, non-Hispanic/Latino; 0.1% Native Hawaiian or other Pacific Islander, non-Hispanic/Latino; 0.4% American Indian or Alaska Native, non-Hispanic/Latino; 2% Two or more races, non-Hispanic/Latino; 0.3% Race/ethnicity unknown; 7% transferred in.
Faculty *Student/faculty ratio:* 17:1.
Academics *Calendar:* semesters. *Degree:* certificates, diplomas, and associate. *Special study options:* academic remediation for entering students, adult/continuing education programs, advanced placement credit, cooperative education, distance learning, English as a second language, independent study, off-campus study, part-time degree program.
Library Learning Resources Centers. *Books:* 35,060 (physical), 659 (digital/electronic); *Serial titles:* 50 (physical), 8 (digital/electronic); *Databases:* 9.
Student Life *Campus security:* 24-hour patrols.
Athletics Member NJCAA.
Standardized Tests *Recommended:* SAT or ACT (for admission).
Financial Aid Of all full-time matriculated undergraduates who enrolled in 2016, 36 Federal Work-Study jobs (averaging $1391).
Applying *Options:* electronic application, early admission. *Required:* high school transcript.
Freshman Application Contact Mr. Keith Saulsberry, Director, Enrollment Services/Registrar, George C. Wallace Community College, 1141 Wallace Drive, Dothan, AL 36303. *Phone:* 334-983-3521 Ext. 2470. *Toll-free phone:* 800-543-2426. *Fax:* 334-983-3600. *E-mail:* ksaulsberry@wallace.edu. *Website:* http://www.wallace.edu/.

H. Councill Trenholm State Community College

Montgomery, Alabama

- **State-supported** 2-year, founded 1966, part of Alabama Community College System
- **Urban** 83-acre campus with easy access to Montgomery
- **Coed**
- 31% of applicants were admitted

Undergraduates Students come from 2 states and territories; 68% Black or African American, non-Hispanic/Latino; 2% Hispanic/Latino; 1% Asian, non-Hispanic/Latino; 0.1% American Indian or Alaska Native, non-Hispanic/Latino; 0.2% Two or more races, non-Hispanic/Latino; 0.2% Race/ethnicity unknown; 0.1% international. *Retention:* 60% of full-time freshmen returned.
Faculty *Student/faculty ratio:* 15:1.
Academics *Calendar:* semesters. *Degree:* certificates, diplomas, and associate. *Special study options:* academic remediation for entering students, adult/continuing education programs, advanced placement credit, cooperative education, distance learning, English as a second language, external degree program, independent study, internships, part-time degree program, services for LD students, summer session for credit.
Library Trenholm State Learning Resources plus 2 others. *Books:* 10,315 (physical), 36,943 (digital/electronic); *Serial titles:* 91 (physical), 59 (digital/electronic); *Databases:* 18. Weekly public service hours: 108.
Student Life *Campus security:* 24-hour patrols.
Standardized Tests *Required for some:* SAT or ACT (for admission).
Applying *Options:* electronic application, early admission. *Required:* high school transcript.
Freshman Application Contact Dr. Tennie McBryde, Director of Admissions/Records, H. Councill Trenholm State Community College, Montgomery, AL 36108. *Phone:* 334-420-4306. *Toll-free phone:* 866-753-4544. *Fax:* 334-420-4201. *E-mail:* tmcbryde@trenholmstate.edu. *Website:* http://www.trenholmstate.edu/.

Jefferson State Community College

Birmingham, Alabama

- **State-supported** 2-year, founded 1965, part of Alabama Community College System
- **Suburban** 351-acre campus with easy access to Birmingham
- **Endowment** $1.3 million
- **Coed**

Undergraduates 2,647 full-time, 6,193 part-time. Students come from 30 states and territories; 52 other countries; 2% are from out of state; 25% Black or African American, non-Hispanic/Latino; 5% Hispanic/Latino; 2% Asian, non-Hispanic/Latino; 0.1% Native Hawaiian or other Pacific Islander, non-Hispanic/Latino; 0.3% American Indian or Alaska Native, non-Hispanic/Latino; 3% Two or more races, non-Hispanic/Latino; 3% international; 10% transferred in. *Retention:* 53% of full-time freshmen returned.
Faculty *Student/faculty ratio:* 19:1.
Academics *Calendar:* semesters. *Degree:* certificates and associate. *Special study options:* academic remediation for entering students, adult/continuing education programs, advanced placement credit, distance learning, English as a second language, honors programs, independent study, internships, part-time degree program, services for LD students, summer session for credit. *ROTC:* Army (c), Air Force (c).
Library Jefferson State Libraries plus 4 others. *Books:* 63,660 (physical), 193,910 (digital/electronic); *Serial titles:* 234 (physical), 296,861 (digital/electronic); *Databases:* 52. Weekly public service hours: 62.
Student Life *Campus security:* 24-hour patrols.
Athletics Member NJCAA.
Applying *Options:* electronic application, early admission, deferred entrance. *Required for some:* high school transcript.
Freshman Application Contact Mrs. Lillian Owens, Director of Admissions and Retention, Jefferson State Community College, 2601 Carson Road, Birmingham, AL 35215-3098. *Phone:* 205-853-1200 Ext. 7990. *Toll-free phone:* 800-239-5900. *Fax:* 205-856-6070. *E-mail:* lowens@jeffstateonline.com. *Website:* http://www.jeffersonstate.edu/.

J. F. Drake State Community and Technical College

Huntsville, Alabama

Freshman Application Contact Mrs. Kristin Treadway, Assistant Director of Admissions, J. F. Drake State Community and Technical College, Huntsville, AL 35811. *Phone:* 256-551-3111. *Toll-free phone:* 888-413-7253. *E-mail:* kristin.treadway@drakestate.edu. *Website:* http://www.drakestate.edu/.

J F Ingram State Technical College

Deatsville, Alabama

Admissions Office Contact J F Ingram State Technical College, 5375 Ingram Rd, Deatsville, AL 36022. *Website:* http://www.istc.edu/.

Lawson State Community College

Birmingham, Alabama

Freshman Application Contact Mr. Jeff Shelley, Director of Admissions and Records, Lawson State Community College, 3060 Wilson Road, SW, Birmingham, AL 35221-1798. *Phone:* 205-929-6361. *Fax:* 205-923-7106. *E-mail:* jshelley@lawsonstate.edu. *Website:* http://www.lawsonstate.edu/.

Lurleen B. Wallace Community College

Andalusia, Alabama

- **State-supported** 2-year, founded 2003, part of Alabama Community College System
- **Small-town** 200-acre campus
- **Coed,** 1,784 undergraduate students, 49% full-time, 57% women, 43% men

Undergraduates 880 full-time, 904 part-time. Students come from 9 states and territories; 8 other countries; 4% are from out of state; 25% Black or African American, non-Hispanic/Latino; 1% Hispanic/Latino; 0.6% Asian, non-Hispanic/Latino; 0.6% American Indian or Alaska Native, non-Hispanic/Latino; 3% Two or more races, non-Hispanic/Latino; 0.6% Race/ethnicity unknown; 0.3% international; 6% transferred in.
Freshmen *Admission:* 417 enrolled.
Faculty *Total:* 105, 53% full-time. *Student/faculty ratio:* 17:1.
Majors Administrative assistant and secretarial science; child-care and support services management; computer and information sciences; diagnostic

medical sonography and ultrasound technology; diesel mechanics technology; emergency medical technology (EMT paramedic); forest technology; general studies; industrial electronics technology; liberal arts and sciences/liberal studies; registered nursing/registered nurse.

Academics *Calendar:* semesters. *Degree:* certificates and associate. *Special study options:* academic remediation for entering students, cooperative education, distance learning, honors programs, independent study, part-time degree program, summer session for credit.

Library Lurleen B. Wallace Library plus 3 others. Students can reserve study rooms.

Student Life *Housing:* college housing not available. *Activities and Organizations:* drama/theater group, choral group, Student Government Association, Student Ambassadors, Campus Civitan, Christian Student Ministries, Saints Angels. *Student services:* personal/psychological counseling.

Athletics Member NJCAA.

Applying *Options:* electronic application. *Required:* high school transcript. *Application deadlines:* rolling (freshmen), rolling (out-of-state freshmen), rolling (transfers).

Director of Admissions Ms. Jan Riley, Director of Admission and Records, Lurleen B. Wallace Community College, PO Box 1418, Andalusia, AL 36420-1418. *Phone:* 334-881-2273. *Fax:* 334-881-2201. *E-mail:* jriley@lbwcc.edu. *Website:* http://www.lbwcc.edu/.

Marion Military Institute
Marion, Alabama

- **State-supported** 2-year, founded 1842, part of Alabama Community College System
- **Rural** 130-acre campus with easy access to Birmingham
- **Coed**

Undergraduates 442 full-time, 4 part-time. Students come from 45 states and territories; 51% are from out of state; 17% Black or African American, non-Hispanic/Latino; 6% Hispanic/Latino; 3% Asian, non-Hispanic/Latino; 0.7% Native Hawaiian or other Pacific Islander, non-Hispanic/Latino; 1% American Indian or Alaska Native, non-Hispanic/Latino; 6% Two or more races, non-Hispanic/Latino; 4% transferred in; 100% live on campus. *Retention:* 40% of full-time freshmen returned.

Faculty *Student/faculty ratio:* 16:1.

Academics *Calendar:* semesters. *Degree:* associate. *Special study options:* academic remediation for entering students, English as a second language, honors programs, services for LD students, study abroad. *ROTC:* Army (b), Air Force (c).

Library Baer Memorial Library. Weekly public service hours: 65; study areas open 24 hours, 5–7 days a week.

Student Life *Campus security:* 24-hour patrols.

Athletics Member NJCAA.

Standardized Tests *Required:* SAT or ACT (for admission).

Financial Aid Of all full-time matriculated undergraduates who enrolled in 2017, 29 Federal Work-Study jobs (averaging $210).

Applying *Options:* electronic application, deferred entrance. *Application fee:* $30. *Required:* high school transcript, minimum 2.0 GPA.

Freshman Application Contact Mrs. Brittany Crawford, Director of Admissions, Marion Military Institute, 1101 Washington Street, Marion, AL 36756. *Phone:* 800-664-1842. *Toll-free phone:* 800-664-1842. *Fax:* 334-683-2383. *E-mail:* bcrawford@marionmilitary.edu. *Website:* http://www.marionmilitary.edu/.

Northeast Alabama Community College
Rainsville, Alabama

Freshman Application Contact Northeast Alabama Community College, PO Box 159, Rainsville, AL 35986-0159. *Phone:* 256-228-6001 Ext. 2325. *Website:* http://www.nacc.edu/.

Northwest-Shoals Community College
Muscle Shoals, Alabama

- **State-supported** 2-year, founded 1963, part of Alabama Community College System
- **Small-town** 210-acre campus
- **Endowment** $733,034
- **Coed**

Undergraduates 1,436 full-time, 2,004 part-time. Students come from 3 states and territories; 2 other countries; 8% Black or African American, non-Hispanic/Latino; 6% Hispanic/Latino; 0.5% Asian, non-Hispanic/Latino; 0.9% American Indian or Alaska Native, non-Hispanic/Latino; 0.2% Two or more races, non-Hispanic/Latino; 2% Race/ethnicity unknown; 1% international; 3% transferred in.

Faculty *Student/faculty ratio:* 20:1.

Academics *Calendar:* semesters. *Degree:* certificates and associate. *Special study options:* academic remediation for entering students, accelerated degree program, adult/continuing education programs, advanced placement credit, cooperative education, distance learning, double majors, honors programs, independent study, internships, off-campus study, part-time degree program, services for LD students, summer session for credit.

Library Larry W. McCoy Learning Resource Center. *Books:* 65,800 (physical), 27,000 (digital/electronic); *Databases:* 2. Weekly public service hours: 62.

Student Life *Campus security:* 24-hour emergency response devices.

Financial Aid Of all full-time matriculated undergraduates who enrolled in 2017, 19 Federal Work-Study jobs (averaging $1033). *Financial aid deadline:* 6/1.

Applying *Options:* electronic application. *Required:* high school transcript.

Freshman Application Contact Mr. Tom Carter, Assistant Dean of Recruitment, Admissions and Financial Aid, Northwest-Shoals Community College, PO Box 2545, Muscle Shoals, AL 35662. *Phone:* 256-331-5263. *Fax:* 256-331-5366. *E-mail:* tom.carter@nwscc.edu. *Website:* http://www.nwscc.edu/.

Reid State Technical College
Evergreen, Alabama

- **State-supported** 2-year, founded 1966, part of Alabama Community College System
- **Rural** 26-acre campus
- **Coed**

Undergraduates 181 full-time, 211 part-time. Students come from 3 states and territories; 1% are from out of state; 49% Black or African American, non-Hispanic/Latino; 0.8% Hispanic/Latino; 0.3% Native Hawaiian or other Pacific Islander, non-Hispanic/Latino; 0.3% American Indian or Alaska Native, non-Hispanic/Latino; 1% Two or more races, non-Hispanic/Latino.

Faculty *Student/faculty ratio:* 12:1.

Academics *Calendar:* semesters. *Degree:* certificates and associate. *Special study options:* academic remediation for entering students, adult/continuing education programs, double majors, independent study, internships, part-time degree program, services for LD students, summer session for credit.

Library Edith A. Gray Library. *Books:* 6,392 (physical), 150,480 (digital/electronic); *Databases:* 2.

Student Life *Campus security:* 24-hour emergency response devices, day and evening security guard.

Financial Aid Of all full-time matriculated undergraduates who enrolled in 2017, 35 Federal Work-Study jobs (averaging $1500).

Applying *Options:* electronic application, early admission. *Required:* high school transcript.

Freshman Application Contact Ms. Mandy Godwin, Assistant to the Registrar, Reid State Technical College, Evergreen, AL 36401-0588. *Phone:* 251-578-1313 Ext. 148. *E-mail:* mwilson@rstc.edu. *Website:* http://www.rstc.edu/.

Remington College–Mobile Campus
Mobile, Alabama

Freshman Application Contact Remington College–Mobile Campus, 828 Downtowner Loop West, Mobile, AL 36609. *Phone:* 251-343-8200. *Toll-free phone:* 800-323-8122. *Website:* http://www.remingtoncollege.edu/.

Shelton State Community College
Tuscaloosa, Alabama

Freshman Application Contact Ms. Sharon Chastine, Secretary to the Associate Dean of Student Services Enrollment, Shelton State Community College, 9500 Old Greensboro Road, Tuscaloosa, AL 35405. *Phone:* 205-391-2309. *Fax:* 205-391-3910. *E-mail:* schastine@sheltonstate.edu. *Website:* http://www.sheltonstate.edu/.

Snead State Community College
Boaz, Alabama

Freshman Application Contact Mr. Jason Cannon, Vice President Student Services, Snead State Community College, PO Box 734, Boaz, AL 35957-0734. *Phone:* 256-840-4150. *Fax:* 256-593-7180. *E-mail:* jcannon@snead.edu. *Website:* http://www.snead.edu/.

Southern Union State Community College
Wadley, Alabama

Freshman Application Contact Admissions Office, Southern Union State Community College, PO Box 1000, Roberts Street, Wadley, AL 36276. *Phone:* 256-395-5157. *E-mail:* info@suscc.edu. *Website:* http://www.suscc.edu/.

Wallace State Community College
Hanceville, Alabama

Director of Admissions Ms. Jennifer Hill, Director of Admissions, Wallace State Community College, PO Box 2000, 801 Main Street, Hanceville, AL 35077-2000. *Phone:* 256-352-8278. *Toll-free phone:* 866-350-9722. *Website:* http://www.wallacestate.edu/.

ALASKA

Alaska Career College
Anchorage, Alaska

Freshman Application Contact Alaska Career College, 1415 East Tudor Road, Anchorage, AK 99507. *Website:* http://www.alaskacareercollege.edu/.

Alaska Christian College
Soldotna, Alaska

Admissions Office Contact Alaska Christian College, 35109 Royal Place, Soldotna, AK 99669. *Website:* http://www.alaskacc.edu/.

Charter College
Anchorage, Alaska

Director of Admissions Ms. Lily Sirianni, Vice President, Charter College, 2221 East Northern Lights Boulevard, Suite 120, Anchorage, AK 99508. *Phone:* 907-277-1000. *Toll-free phone:* 888-200-9942. *Website:* http://www.chartercollege.edu/.

Ilisagvik College
Barrow, Alaska

Freshman Application Contact Tennessee Judkins, Recruiter, Ilisagvik College, PO Box 749, Barrow, AK 99723. *Phone:* 907-852-1772. *Toll-free phone:* 800-478-7337. *Fax:* 907-852-1789. *E-mail:* tennessee.judkins@ilisagvik.edu. *Website:* http://www.ilisagvik.edu/.

University of Alaska Anchorage, Kenai Peninsula College
Soldotna, Alaska

Freshman Application Contact Mrs. Julie Cotterell, Admission and Student Records Coordinator, University of Alaska Anchorage, Kenai Peninsula College, 156 College Road, Soldotna, AK 99669-9798. *Phone:* 907-262-0311. *Toll-free phone:* 877-262-0330. *E-mail:* jmcotterell@kpc.alaska.edu. *Website:* http://www.kpc.alaska.edu/.

University of Alaska Anchorage, Kodiak College
Kodiak, Alaska

Freshman Application Contact University of Alaska Anchorage, Kodiak College, 117 Benny Benson Drive, Kodiak, AK 99615-6643. *Phone:* 907-486-1235. *Toll-free phone:* 800-486-7660. *Website:* http://www.koc.alaska.edu/.

University of Alaska Anchorage, Matanuska-Susitna College
Palmer, Alaska

Freshman Application Contact Ms. Sandra Gravley, Student Services Director, University of Alaska Anchorage, Matanuska-Susitna College, PO Box 2889, Palmer, AK 99645-2889. *Phone:* 907-745-9712. *Fax:* 907-745-9747. *E-mail:* info@matsu.alaska.edu. *Website:* http://www.matsu.alaska.edu/.

University of Alaska, Prince William Sound College
Valdez, Alaska

Freshman Application Contact Dr. Denise Runge, Academic Affairs, University of Alaska, Prince William Sound College, PO Box 97, Valdez, AK 99686-0097. *Phone:* 907-834-1600. *Toll-free phone:* 800-478-8800. *Fax:* 907-834-1691. *E-mail:* drunge@pwscc.edu. *Website:* http://www.pwsc.alaska.edu/.

University of Alaska Southeast, Ketchikan Campus
Ketchikan, Alaska

Freshman Application Contact Admissions Office, University of Alaska Southeast, Ketchikan Campus, 2600 7th Avenue, Ketchikan, AK 99901-5798. *Phone:* 907-225-6177. *Toll-free phone:* 888-550-6177. *Fax:* 907-225-3895. *E-mail:* ketch.info@uas.alaska.edu. *Website:* http://www.ketch.alaska.edu/.

University of Alaska Southeast, Sitka Campus
Sitka, Alaska

Freshman Application Contact Ms. Teal Gordon, Admissions Representative, University of Alaska Southeast, Sitka Campus, UAS Sitka, 1332 Seward Avenue, Sitka, AK 99835. *Phone:* 907-747-7726. *Toll-free phone:* 800-478-6653. *Fax:* 907-747-7731. *E-mail:* ktgordon@uas.alaska.edu. *Website:* http://www.uas.alaska.edu/sitka/.

AMERICAN SAMOA

American Samoa Community College
Pago Pago, American Samoa

- **Territory-supported** primarily 2-year, founded 1969
- **Rural** 20-acre campus
- **Endowment** $3.1 million
- **Coed**

Undergraduates 615 full-time, 480 part-time. Students come from 3 other countries; 0.8% Asian, non-Hispanic/Latino; 90% Native Hawaiian or other Pacific Islander, non-Hispanic/Latino; 9% international; 0.5% transferred in. *Retention:* 100% of full-time freshmen returned.

Faculty *Student/faculty ratio:* 20:1.

Academics *Calendar:* semesters. *Degrees:* certificates, associate, and bachelor's. *Special study options:* academic remediation for entering students, adult/continuing education programs, cooperative education, double majors, independent study, internships, part-time degree program, services for LD students, summer session for credit. *ROTC:* Army (b).

Library ASCC Learning Resource Center/Library plus 1 other. *Books:* 33,000 (physical); *Serial titles:* 330 (physical). Weekly public service hours: 43.

Student Life *Campus security:* 24-hour emergency response devices and patrols.

Standardized Tests *Recommended:* SAT and SAT Subject Tests or ACT (for admission).

Financial Aid Of all full-time matriculated undergraduates who enrolled in 2017, 532 applied for aid, 532 were judged to have need. 110 Federal Work-Study jobs (averaging $60,937). *Average percent of need met:* 54. *Average financial aid package:* $2726. *Average need-based gift aid:* $2726.

Applying *Options:* electronic application, early admission, deferred entrance.

Freshman Application Contact Elizabeth Leuma, Admissions Officer, American Samoa Community College, PO Box 2609, Pago Pago 96799, American Samoa. *Phone:* 684-699-9155 Ext. 411. *Fax:* 684-699-1083. *Website:* http://www.amsamoa.edu/.

ARIZONA

Arizona College
Glendale, Arizona

Freshman Application Contact Admissions Department, Arizona College, 4425 West Olive Avenue, Suite 300, Glendale, AZ 85302-3843. *Phone:* 602-222-9300. *E-mail:* lhicks@arizonacollege.edu. *Website:* http://www.arizonacollege.edu/.

Arizona Western College
Yuma, Arizona

- **State and locally supported** 2-year, founded 1962, part of Arizona State Community College System
- **Rural** 640-acre campus
- **Coed**

Undergraduates 2,221 full-time, 5,336 part-time. Students come from 32 states and territories; 29 other countries; 3% are from out of state; 2% Black or African American, non-Hispanic/Latino; 72% Hispanic/Latino; 0.9% Asian, non-Hispanic/Latino; 0.4% Native Hawaiian or other Pacific Islander, non-Hispanic/Latino; 1% American Indian or Alaska Native, non-Hispanic/Latino; 2% Two or more races, non-Hispanic/Latino; 4% Race/ethnicity unknown; 2% international; 6% live on campus.
Faculty *Student/faculty ratio:* 19:1.
Academics *Calendar:* semesters. *Degree:* certificates and associate. *Special study options:* academic remediation for entering students, adult/continuing education programs, advanced placement credit, cooperative education, distance learning, English as a second language, honors programs, independent study, part-time degree program, services for LD students, summer session for credit.
Library Arizona Western College and NAU-Yuma Library. *Books:* 58,607 (physical), 207,815 (digital/electronic); *Serial titles:* 406 (physical), 13,815 (digital/electronic); *Databases:* 49. Weekly public service hours: 68; students can reserve study rooms.
Student Life *Campus security:* 24-hour emergency response devices and patrols, student patrols, late-night transport/escort service, controlled dormitory access.
Athletics Member NJCAA.
Standardized Tests *Required for some:* SAT or ACT (for admission).
Financial Aid Of all full-time matriculated undergraduates who enrolled in 2017, 350 Federal Work-Study jobs (averaging $1500). 100 state and other part-time jobs (averaging $1800).
Applying *Options:* electronic application, early admission, deferred entrance.
Freshman Application Contact Nicole D. Harral, Director of Admissions/Registrar, Arizona Western College, PO Box 929, Yuma, AZ 85366. *Phone:* 928-344-7600. *Toll-free phone:* 888-293-0392. *Fax:* 928-344-7543. *E-mail:* nicole.harral@azwestern.edu. *Website:* http://www.azwestern.edu/.

Carrington College–Mesa
Mesa, Arizona

Freshman Application Contact Carrington College–Mesa, 1001 West Southern Avenue, Suite 130, Mesa, AZ 85210. *Website:* http://www.carrington.edu/.

Carrington College–Phoenix East
Phoenix, Arizona

Freshman Application Contact Carrington College–Phoenix East, 2149 West Dunlap Avenue, Suite 100, Phoenix, AZ 85021. *Website:* http://www.carrington.edu/.

Carrington College–Phoenix North
Phoenix, Arizona

Freshman Application Contact Carrington College–Phoenix North, 8503 North 27th Avenue, Phoenix, AZ 85051. *Website:* http://www.carrington.edu/.

Central Arizona College
Coolidge, Arizona

Freshman Application Contact Dr. James Moore, Dean of Records and Admissions, Central Arizona College, 8470 North Overfield Road, Coolidge, AZ 85128. *Phone:* 520-494-5261. *Toll-free phone:* 800-237-9814. *Fax:* 520-426-5083. *E-mail:* james.moore@centralaz.edu. *Website:* http://www.centralaz.edu/.

Chandler-Gilbert Community College
Chandler, Arizona

- **State and locally supported** 2-year, founded 1985, part of Maricopa County Community College District System
- **Suburban** 188-acre campus with easy access to Phoenix
- **Coed**

Undergraduates 4,178 full-time, 10,728 part-time. Students come from 20 states and territories; 2% are from out of state; 4% Black or African American, non-Hispanic/Latino; 24% Hispanic/Latino; 6% Asian, non-Hispanic/Latino; 0.3% Native Hawaiian or other Pacific Islander, non-Hispanic/Latino; 2% American Indian or Alaska Native, non-Hispanic/Latino; 4% Two or more races, non-Hispanic/Latino; 9% Race/ethnicity unknown.
Faculty *Student/faculty ratio:* 27:1.
Academics *Calendar:* semesters. *Degree:* certificates, diplomas, and associate. *Special study options:* academic remediation for entering students, advanced placement credit, English as a second language, freshman honors college, honors programs, independent study, part-time degree program, services for LD students, study abroad, summer session for credit.
Library Chandler-Gilbert Community College Library.
Student Life *Campus security:* 24-hour emergency response devices and patrols, late-night transport/escort service.
Athletics Member NJCAA.
Applying *Options:* electronic application.
Freshman Application Contact Alex Gadberry, Coordinator of Student Recruitment, Chandler-Gilbert Community College, 2626 East Pecos Road, Chandler, AZ 85225-2479. *Phone:* 480-726-4228. *E-mail:* alexander.gadberry@cgc.edu. *Website:* http://www.cgc.maricopa.edu/.

Cochise County Community College District
Sierra Vista, Arizona

- **State and locally supported** 2-year, founded 1962
- **Rural** 732-acre campus with easy access to Tucson
- **Coed**

Undergraduates 1,519 full-time, 2,399 part-time. Students come from 17 states and territories; 2 other countries; 8% are from out of state; 5% Black or African American, non-Hispanic/Latino; 46% Hispanic/Latino; 2% Asian, non-Hispanic/Latino; 0.3% Native Hawaiian or other Pacific Islander, non-Hispanic/Latino; 0.7% American Indian or Alaska Native, non-Hispanic/Latino; 4% Two or more races, non-Hispanic/Latino; 1% Race/ethnicity unknown; 1% international; 3% transferred in; 2% live on campus. *Retention:* 63% of full-time freshmen returned.
Faculty *Student/faculty ratio:* 16:1.
Academics *Calendar:* semesters. *Degrees:* certificates and associate (profile includes campuses in Douglas and Sierra Vista, AZ). *Special study options:* academic remediation for entering students, adult/continuing education programs, advanced placement credit, cooperative education, distance learning, English as a second language, honors programs, independent study, internships, part-time degree program, services for LD students, summer session for credit.
Library Andrea Cracchiolo plus 1 other. *Books:* 55,145 (physical), 40,945 (digital/electronic); *Serial titles:* 22 (physical), 7,401 (digital/electronic); *Databases:* 16. Weekly public service hours: 45.
Student Life *Campus security:* 24-hour emergency response devices and patrols, late-night transport/escort service.
Athletics Member NJCAA.
Financial Aid Of all full-time matriculated undergraduates who enrolled in 2014, 1,300 applied for aid, 1,121 were judged to have need. 72 Federal Work-Study jobs (averaging $5437). In 2014, 22. *Average financial aid package:* $5876. *Average need-based loan:* $3658. *Average need-based gift aid:* $3730. *Average non-need-based aid:* $1666. *Financial aid deadline:* 6/15.
Applying *Options:* electronic application, deferred entrance. *Required for some:* high school transcript. *Recommended:* high school transcript.
Freshman Application Contact Ms. Debbie Quick, Director of Admissions and Records, Cochise County Community College District, 901 North Colombo Avenue, Sierra Vista, AZ 85635-2317. *Phone:* 520-515-3640. *Toll-free phone:* 800-593-9567. *Fax:* 520-515-5452. *E-mail:* quickd@cochise.edu. *Website:* http://www.cochise.edu/.

Coconino Community College
Flagstaff, Arizona

Freshman Application Contact Veronica Hipolito, Director of Student Services, Coconino Community College, 2800 South Lone Tree Road, Flagstaff, AZ 86001. *Phone:* 928-226-4334 Ext. 4334. *Toll-free phone:* 800-350-7122. *Fax:* 928-226-4114. *E-mail:* veronica.hipolito@coconino.edu. *Website:* http://www.coconino.edu/.

CollegeAmerica–Flagstaff
Flagstaff, Arizona

Freshman Application Contact CollegeAmerica–Flagstaff, 399 South Malpais Lane, Flagstaff, AZ 86001. *Phone:* 928-213-6060 Ext. 1402. *Toll-free phone:* 800-622-2894. *Website:* http://www.collegeamerica.edu/.

CollegeAmerica–Phoenix
Phoenix, Arizona

Admissions Office Contact CollegeAmerica–Phoenix, 9801 North Metro Parkway East, Phoenix, AZ 85051. *Toll-free phone:* 800-622-2894. *Website:* http://www.collegeamerica.edu/.

Diné College
Tsaile, Arizona

Freshman Application Contact Mrs. Louise Litzin, Registrar, Diné College, PO Box 67, Tsaile, AZ 86556. *Phone:* 928-724-6633. *Toll-free phone:* 877-988-DINE. *Fax:* 928-724-3349. *E-mail:* louise@dinecollege.edu. *Website:* http://www.dinecollege.edu/.

Eastern Arizona College
Thatcher, Arizona

- **State and locally supported** 2-year, founded 1888, part of Arizona State Community College System
- **Small-town** campus
- **Endowment** $5.3 million
- **Coed**

Undergraduates 1,957 full-time, 4,408 part-time. Students come from 25 states and territories; 24 other countries; 3% are from out of state; 3% Black or African American, non-Hispanic/Latino; 20% Hispanic/Latino; 0.9% Asian, non-Hispanic/Latino; 0.8% Native Hawaiian or other Pacific Islander, non-Hispanic/Latino; 6% American Indian or Alaska Native, non-Hispanic/Latino; 1% Two or more races, non-Hispanic/Latino; 3% Race/ethnicity unknown; 1% international; 1% transferred in; 3% live on campus.
Faculty *Student/faculty ratio:* 19:1.
Academics *Calendar:* semesters. *Degree:* certificates and associate. *Special study options:* academic remediation for entering students, adult/continuing education programs, advanced placement credit, cooperative education, distance learning, double majors, independent study, internships, part-time degree program, services for LD students, study abroad, summer session for credit.
Library Alumni Library plus 1 other. *Books:* 37,902 (physical), 968 (digital/electronic); *Serial titles:* 637 (physical); *Databases:* 41. Weekly public service hours: 80; students can reserve study rooms.
Student Life *Campus security:* 24-hour emergency response devices, late-night transport/escort service, controlled dormitory access, 20-hour patrols by trained security personnel.
Athletics Member NJCAA.
Financial Aid Of all full-time matriculated undergraduates who enrolled in 2016, 1,105 applied for aid, 994 were judged to have need, 45 had their need fully met. In 2016, 99. *Average percent of need met:* 42. *Average financial aid package:* $6372. *Average need-based gift aid:* $6122. *Average non-need-based aid:* $2635.
Applying *Options:* electronic application, early admission, deferred entrance. *Recommended:* high school transcript.
Freshman Application Contact Suzette Udall, Records Assistant, Eastern Arizona College, 615 North Stadium Avenue, Thatcher, AZ 85552-0769. *Phone:* 928-428-8904. *Toll-free phone:* 800-678-3808. *Fax:* 928-428-3729. *E-mail:* admissions@eac.edu. *Website:* http://www.eac.edu/.

Estrella Mountain Community College
Avondale, Arizona

Freshman Application Contact Estrella Mountain Community College, 3000 North Dysart Road, Avondale, AZ 85392. *Phone:* 623-935-8812. *Website:* http://www.estrellamountain.edu/.

Fortis College
Phoenix, Arizona

Admissions Office Contact Fortis College, 555 North 18th Street, Suite 110, Phoenix, AZ 85006. *Toll-free phone:* 855-4-FORTIS. *Website:* http://www.fortis.edu/.

GateWay Community College
Phoenix, Arizona

Freshman Application Contact Director of Admissions and Records, GateWay Community College, 108 North 40th Street, Phoenix, AZ 85034. *Phone:* 602-286-8200. *Fax:* 602-286-8200. *E-mail:* enroll@gatewaycc.edu. *Website:* http://www.gatewaycc.edu/.

Glendale Community College
Glendale, Arizona

Freshman Application Contact Ms. Mary Blackwell, Dean of Enrollment Services, Glendale Community College, 6000 West Olive Avenue, Glendale, AZ 85302. *Phone:* 623-435-3305. *Fax:* 623-845-3303. *E-mail:* admissions.recruitment@gccaz.edu. *Website:* http://www.gccaz.edu/.

Mesa Community College
Mesa, Arizona

- **State and locally supported** 2-year, founded 1965, part of Maricopa County Community College District System
- **Urban** 160-acre campus with easy access to Phoenix
- **Coed**

Undergraduates 6,237 full-time, 14,187 part-time. 6% Black or African American, non-Hispanic/Latino; 28% Hispanic/Latino; 4% Asian, non-Hispanic/Latino; 0.4% Native Hawaiian or other Pacific Islander, non-Hispanic/Latino; 4% American Indian or Alaska Native, non-Hispanic/Latino; 3% Two or more races, non-Hispanic/Latino; 6% Race/ethnicity unknown; 2% international.
Faculty *Student/faculty ratio:* 21:1.
Academics *Calendar:* semesters. *Degree:* certificates and associate. *Special study options:* academic remediation for entering students, adult/continuing education programs, advanced placement credit, cooperative education, distance learning, English as a second language, freshman honors college, honors programs, independent study, off-campus study, part-time degree program, services for LD students, student-designed majors, study abroad, summer session for credit. *ROTC:* Army (c), Air Force (c).
Library Information Commons. Students can reserve study rooms.
Student Life *Campus security:* 24-hour emergency response devices and patrols, student patrols.
Athletics Member NJCAA.
Applying *Options:* electronic application, early admission, deferred entrance.
Freshman Application Contact Carmen Newland, Dean, Enrollment Services, Mesa Community College, 1833 West Southern Avenue, Mesa, AZ 85202-4866. *Phone:* 480-461-7600. *Toll-free phone:* 866-532-4983. *Fax:* 480-844-3117. *E-mail:* admissionsandrecords@mesacc.edu. *Website:* http://www.mesacc.edu/.

Mohave Community College
Kingman, Arizona

- **State-supported** 2-year, founded 1971
- **Small-town** 160-acre campus
- **Coed,** 4,071 undergraduate students, 20% full-time, 66% women, 34% men

Undergraduates 809 full-time, 3,262 part-time. Students come from 19 states and territories; 5% are from out of state; 1% Black or African American, non-Hispanic/Latino; 25% Hispanic/Latino; 2% Asian, non-Hispanic/Latino; 0.4% Native Hawaiian or other Pacific Islander, non-Hispanic/Latino; 2% American Indian or Alaska Native, non-Hispanic/Latino; 3% Two or more races, non-Hispanic/Latino; 0.8% Race/ethnicity unknown; 0.7% international.
Freshmen *Admission:* 404 enrolled.
Faculty *Total:* 282, 27% full-time. *Student/faculty ratio:* 13:1.
Majors Accounting; air and space operations technology; art; automobile/automotive mechanics technology; behavioral sciences; chemistry; computer and information sciences; computer science; criminal justice/police science; criminal justice/safety; culinary arts; dental assisting; dental hygiene; education; engineering; English; fire science/firefighting; geology/earth science; heating, air conditioning, ventilation and refrigeration maintenance technology; history related; homeland security, law enforcement, firefighting and protective services related; interdisciplinary studies; legal assistant/paralegal; liberal arts and sciences/liberal studies; mathematics; physical therapy technology; registered nursing/registered nurse; substance

abuse/addiction counseling; surgical technology; truck and bus driver/commercial vehicle operation/instruction; welding technology.
Academics *Calendar:* semesters. *Degree:* certificates, diplomas, and associate. *Special study options:* academic remediation for entering students, adult/continuing education programs, cooperative education, distance learning, English as a second language, independent study, part-time degree program, summer session for credit.
Library Mohave Community College Library.
Student Life *Housing:* college housing not available. *Activities and Organizations:* Art Club, Phi Theta Kappa, Computer Club (MC4), Science Club, Student Government. *Campus security:* late-night transport/escort service.
Applying *Options:* electronic application, early admission, deferred entrance. *Application deadlines:* rolling (freshmen), rolling (transfers). *Notification:* continuous (freshmen), continuous (transfers).
Freshman Application Contact Ana Masterson, Chief Student Services Officer, Mohave Community College, 1971 Jagerson Avenue, Kingman, AZ 86409. *Phone:* 928-757-0803. *Toll-free phone:* 888-664-2832. *Fax:* 928-757-0808. *E-mail:* amasterson@mohave.edu.
Website: http://www.mohave.edu/.

Northland Pioneer College
Holbrook, Arizona

Freshman Application Contact Ms. Suzette Willis, Coordinator of Admissions, Northland Pioneer College, PO Box 610, Holbrook, AZ 86025. *Phone:* 928-536-6271. *Toll-free phone:* 800-266-7845. *Fax:* 928-536-6212. *Website:* http://www.npc.edu/.

Paradise Valley Community College
Phoenix, Arizona

Freshman Application Contact Paradise Valley Community College, 18401 North 32nd Street, Phoenix, AZ 85032-1200. *Phone:* 602-787-7020. *Website:* http://www.pvc.maricopa.edu/.

The Paralegal Institute at Brighton College
Scottsdale, Arizona

Freshman Application Contact Patricia Yancy, Director of Admissions, The Paralegal Institute at Brighton College, 2933 West Indian School Road, Drawer 11408, Phoenix, AZ 85061-1408. *Phone:* 602-212-0501. *Toll-free phone:* 800-354-1254. *Fax:* 602-212-0502. *E-mail:* paralegalinst@mindspring.com. *Website:* http://www.theparalegalinstitute.edu/.

Penn Foster College
Scottsdale, Arizona

Freshman Application Contact Admissions, Penn Foster College, 14300 North Northsight Boulevard, Suite 120, Scottsdale, AZ 85260. *Phone:* 888-427-1000. *Toll-free phone:* 800-471-3232. *Website:* http://www.pennfostercollege.edu/.

Phoenix College
Phoenix, Arizona

Freshman Application Contact Ms. Brenda Stark, Director of Admissions, Registration, and Records, Phoenix College, 1202 West Thomas Road, Phoenix, AZ 85013. *Phone:* 602-285-7503. *Fax:* 602-285-7813. *E-mail:* kathy.french@pcmail.maricopa.edu. *Website:* http://www.phoenixcollege.edu/.

Pima Community College
Tucson, Arizona

Freshman Application Contact Terra Benson, Director of Admissions and Registrar, Pima Community College, 4905B East Broadway Boulevard, Tucson, AZ 85709-1120. *Phone:* 520-206-4640. *Fax:* 520-206-4790. *E-mail:* tbenson@pima.edu. *Website:* http://www.pima.edu/.

Pima Medical Institute
Mesa, Arizona

Freshman Application Contact Pima Medical Institute, 2160 South Power Road, Mesa, AZ 85209. *Phone:* 480-898-9898. *Toll-free phone:* 800-477-PIMA. *Website:* http://www.pmi.edu/.

Pima Medical Institute
Mesa, Arizona

Freshman Application Contact Admissions Office, Pima Medical Institute, 957 South Dobson Road, Mesa, AZ 85202. *Phone:* 480-644-0267 Ext. 225. *Toll-free phone:* 800-477-PIMA. *Website:* http://www.pmi.edu/.

Pima Medical Institute
Phoenix, Arizona

Admissions Office Contact Pima Medical Institute, 13610 North Black Canyon Highway, Phoenix, AZ 85029. *Website:* http://www.pmi.edu/.

Pima Medical Institute
Tucson, Arizona

Freshman Application Contact Admissions Office, Pima Medical Institute, 3350 East Grant Road, Tucson, AZ 85716. *Phone:* 520-326-1600 Ext. 5112. *Toll-free phone:* 800-477-PIMA. *Website:* http://www.pmi.edu/.

The Refrigeration School
Phoenix, Arizona

Freshman Application Contact Mr. John Palumbo, Regional Director of Admissions, The Refrigeration School, 4210 East Washington Street. *Phone:* 602-275-7133. *Toll-free phone:* 888-943-4822. *Fax:* 602-267-4811. *E-mail:* info@rsiaz.edu. *Website:* http://www.refrigerationschool.com/.

Rio Salado College
Tempe, Arizona

Freshman Application Contact Laurel Redman, Director of Admissions, Records and Registration, Rio Salado College, 2323 West 14th Street, Tempe 85281. *Phone:* 480-517-8563. *Toll-free phone:* 800-729-1197. *Fax:* 480-517-8199. *Website:* http://www.riosalado.edu/.

Scottsdale Community College
Scottsdale, Arizona

- **State and locally supported** 2-year, founded 1969, part of Maricopa County Community College District System
- **Urban** 160-acre campus with easy access to Phoenix
- **Coed**

Undergraduates Students come from 50 states and territories; 1% are from out of state; 4% Black or African American, non-Hispanic/Latino; 19% Hispanic/Latino; 3% Asian, non-Hispanic/Latino; 0.4% Native Hawaiian or other Pacific Islander, non-Hispanic/Latino; 5% American Indian or Alaska Native, non-Hispanic/Latino; 3% Two or more races, non-Hispanic/Latino; 6% Race/ethnicity unknown; 1% international.
Faculty *Student/faculty ratio:* 18:1.
Academics *Calendar:* semesters. *Degree:* certificates, diplomas, and associate. *Special study options:* academic remediation for entering students, adult/continuing education programs, advanced placement credit, cooperative education, English as a second language, honors programs, internships, off-campus study, part-time degree program, services for LD students, study abroad, summer session for credit.
Library Scottsdale Community College Library. *Books:* 44,599 (physical), 163,245 (digital/electronic); *Serial titles:* 608 (physical), 14 (digital/electronic); *Databases:* 66. Weekly public service hours: 62; students can reserve study rooms.
Student Life *Campus security:* 24-hour emergency response devices and patrols, student patrols, late-night transport/escort service, 24-hour automatic surveillance cameras.
Athletics Member NCAA, NJCAA. All NCAA Division II.
Financial Aid Of all full-time matriculated undergraduates who enrolled in 2017, 75 Federal Work-Study jobs (averaging $2000). *Financial aid deadline:* 7/15.
Applying *Options:* electronic application, early admission.
Freshman Application Contact Ms. Laura Krueger, Director of Admissions and Records, Scottsdale Community College, 9000 East Chaparral Road, Scottsdale, AZ 85256. *Phone:* 480-423-6133. *Fax:* 480-423-6200. *E-mail:* laura.krueger@scottsdalecc.edu. *Website:* http://www.scottsdalecc.edu/.

Sessions College for Professional Design
Tempe, Arizona
Freshman Application Contact Ms. Mhelanie Hernandez, Director of Admissions, Sessions College for Professional Design, 350 South Mill Avenue, Suite B-104, Tempe, AZ 85281. *Phone:* 480-212-1704. *Toll-free phone:* 800-258-4115. *E-mail:* admissions@sessions.edu. *Website:* http://www.sessions.edu/.

South Mountain Community College
Phoenix, Arizona
Director of Admissions Dean of Enrollment Services, South Mountain Community College, 7050 South Twenty-fourth Street, Phoenix, AZ 85040. *Phone:* 602-243-8120. *Website:* http://www.southmountaincc.edu/.

Southwest Institute of Healing Arts
Tempe, Arizona
Director of Admissions Katie Yearous, Student Advisor, Southwest Institute of Healing Arts, 1100 East Apache Boulevard, Tempe, AZ 85281. *Phone:* 480-994-9244. *Toll-free phone:* 888-504-9106. *E-mail:* joannl@swiha.net. *Website:* http://www.swiha.org/.

Tohono O'odham Community College
Sells, Arizona
- **Public** 2-year, founded 1998
- **Rural** 42-acre campus
- **Endowment** $362,851
- **Coed,** 462 undergraduate students, 31% full-time, 62% women, 38% men

Undergraduates 144 full-time, 318 part-time. Students come from 11 states and territories; 5% are from out of state; 3% Black or African American, non-Hispanic/Latino; 1% Hispanic/Latino; 90% American Indian or Alaska Native, non-Hispanic/Latino; 0.6% Two or more races, non-Hispanic/Latino; 0.6% Race/ethnicity unknown; 21% transferred in; 10% live on campus. *Retention:* 27% of full-time freshmen returned.
Freshmen *Admission:* 107 enrolled.
Faculty *Total:* 47, 32% full-time, 21% with terminal degrees. *Student/faculty ratio:* 10:1.
Majors Biology/biological sciences; business administration and management; carpentry; early childhood education; electrician; elementary education; fine/studio arts; health services/allied health/health sciences; interdisciplinary studies; liberal arts and sciences/liberal studies; painting and wall covering; plumbing technology; social sciences.
Academics *Calendar:* semesters. *Degree:* certificates, diplomas, and associate. *Special study options:* academic remediation for entering students, adult/continuing education programs, cooperative education, double majors, part-time degree program, services for LD students, summer session for credit.
Library Tohono O'odham Community College Library plus 1 other. *Books:* 13,355 (physical); *Serial titles:* 210 (physical); *Databases:* 8. Weekly public service hours: 44.
Student Life *Housing Options:* coed, men-only, women-only. Campus housing is university owned. *Activities and Organizations:* Student Senate, AISES, Archery Club. *Campus security:* 24-hour patrols. *Student services:* personal/psychological counseling.
Athletics Member NJCAA. *Intercollegiate sports:* basketball W(s).
Applying *Options:* electronic application. *Required:* high school transcript. *Application deadlines:* rolling (freshmen), rolling (transfers). *Notification:* continuous (freshmen), continuous (transfers), rolling (early decision).
Freshman Application Contact Gloria Benevidez, Student Support Specialist, Tohono O'odham Community College, PO Box 3129, Sells, AZ 85634. *Phone:* 520-383-8401. *E-mail:* gbenevidez@tocc.edu. *Website:* http://www.tocc.edu/.

Universal Technical Institute
Avondale, Arizona
Freshman Application Contact Director of Admission, Universal Technical Institute, 10695 West Pierce Street, Avondale, AZ 85323. *Phone:* 623-245-4600. *Toll-free phone:* 800-510-5072. *Fax:* 623-245-4601. *Website:* http://www.uti.edu/.

Yavapai College
Prescott, Arizona
Freshman Application Contact Mrs. Sheila Jarrell, Admissions, Registration, and Records Manager, Yavapai College, 1100 East Sheldon Street, Prescott, AZ 86301-3297. *Phone:* 928-776-2107. *Toll-free phone:* 800-922-6787. *Fax:* 928-776-2151. *E-mail:* registration@yc.edu. *Website:* http://www.yc.edu/.

ARKANSAS

Arkansas Northeastern College
Blytheville, Arkansas
Freshman Application Contact Arkansas Northeastern College, PO Box 1109, Blytheville, AR 72316. *Phone:* 870-762-1020. *Fax:* 870-763-1654. *Website:* http://www.anc.edu/.

Arkansas State University–Beebe
Beebe, Arkansas
Freshman Application Contact Mr. Ronald Hudson, Coordinator of Student Recruitment, Arkansas State University–Beebe, PO Box 1000, Beebe, AR 72012. *Phone:* 501-882-8860. *Toll-free phone:* 800-632-9985. *E-mail:* rdhudson@asub.edu. *Website:* http://www.asub.edu/.

Arkansas State University Mid-South
West Memphis, Arkansas
- **State-supported** 2-year, founded 1993, part of Arkansas State University System
- **Suburban** 80-acre campus with easy access to Memphis
- **Endowment** $967,261
- **Coed,** 1,423 undergraduate students, 25% full-time, 63% women, 37% men

Undergraduates 356 full-time, 1,067 part-time. Students come from 5 states and territories; 2 other countries; 1% are from out of state; 56% Black or African American, non-Hispanic/Latino; 4% Hispanic/Latino; 0.7% Asian, non-Hispanic/Latino; 0.1% Native Hawaiian or other Pacific Islander, non-Hispanic/Latino; 0.6% American Indian or Alaska Native, non-Hispanic/Latino; 3% Two or more races, non-Hispanic/Latino; 0.7% international; 3% transferred in. *Retention:* 40% of full-time freshmen returned.
Freshmen *Admission:* 492 applied, 492 admitted, 164 enrolled.
Faculty *Total:* 104, 34% full-time, 6% with terminal degrees. *Student/faculty ratio:* 14:1.
Majors Airframe mechanics and aircraft maintenance technology; business administration and management; business/commerce; computer and information sciences; digital communication and media/multimedia; hospitality administration; liberal arts and sciences/liberal studies; medical/clinical assistant; multi/interdisciplinary studies related; respiratory care therapy.
Academics *Calendar:* semesters. *Degree:* certificates and associate. *Special study options:* academic remediation for entering students, adult/continuing education programs, advanced placement credit, distance learning, independent study, internships, part-time degree program, services for LD students, summer session for credit.
Library Sandra C. Goldsby Library.
Student Life *Housing:* college housing not available. *Activities and Organizations:* Phi Theta Kappa, Baptist Collegiate Ministry, SkillsUSA–VICA. *Campus security:* 24-hour emergency response devices, security during class hours. *Student services:* health clinic, personal/psychological counseling.
Athletics Member NJCAA. *Intercollegiate sports:* basketball W(s). *Intramural sports:* football M.
Standardized Tests *Required:* SAT, ACT or ACT Compass (for admission).
Financial Aid Of all full-time matriculated undergraduates who enrolled in 2017, 39 Federal Work-Study jobs (averaging $1676).
Applying *Options:* early admission. *Application deadlines:* rolling (freshmen), rolling (transfers). *Notification:* continuous (freshmen), continuous (transfers).
Freshman Application Contact Leslie D Anderson, Registrar, Arkansas State University Mid-South, 2000 West Broadway, West Memphis, AR 72301. *Phone:* 870-733-6732. *Toll-free phone:* 866-733-6722. *Fax:* 870-733-6710. *E-mail:* landerson@asumidsouth.edu. *Website:* http://www.asumidsouth.edu/.

Arkansas State University–Mountain Home

Mountain Home, Arkansas

Freshman Application Contact Ms. Delba Parrish, Admissions Coordinator, Arkansas State University–Mountain Home, 1600 South College Street, Mountain Home, AR 72653. *Phone:* 870-508-6180. *Fax:* 870-508-6287. *E-mail:* dparrish@asumh.edu. *Website:* http://www.asumh.edu/.

Arkansas State University–Newport

Newport, Arkansas

- **State-supported** 2-year, founded 1989, part of Arkansas State University System
- **Rural** 189-acre campus
- **Endowment** $2.0 million
- **Coed,** 2,270 undergraduate students, 46% full-time, 60% women, 40% men

Undergraduates 1,039 full-time, 1,231 part-time. Students come from 8 states and territories; 1 other country; 5% are from out of state; 14% Black or African American, non-Hispanic/Latino; 3% Hispanic/Latino; 0.6% Asian, non-Hispanic/Latino; 0.5% American Indian or Alaska Native, non-Hispanic/Latino; 1% Two or more races, non-Hispanic/Latino; 4% Race/ethnicity unknown; 0.2% international; 4% transferred in.

Freshmen *Admission:* 354 applied, 354 admitted, 354 enrolled. *Average high school GPA:* 3.1.

Faculty *Total:* 157, 45% full-time, 4% with terminal degrees. *Student/faculty ratio:* 17:1.

Majors Agriculture and agriculture operations related; autobody/collision and repair technology; automobile/automotive mechanics technology; business/commerce; computer technology/computer systems technology; criminal justice/law enforcement administration; emergency medical technology (EMT paramedic); forensic science and technology; general studies; heating, air conditioning, ventilation and refrigeration maintenance technology; liberal arts and sciences/liberal studies; middle school education; multi/interdisciplinary studies related; natural sciences; registered nursing/registered nurse; surgical technology.

Academics *Calendar:* semesters. *Degree:* certificates, diplomas, and associate. *Special study options:* academic remediation for entering students, adult/continuing education programs, advanced placement credit, cooperative education, distance learning, double majors, external degree program, independent study, internships, off-campus study, part-time degree program, services for LD students, summer session for credit.

Library Harryette M. Hodges and Kaneaster Hodges, Sr. Library plus 2 others. *Books:* 11,653 (physical), 27 (digital/electronic); *Databases:* 6. Weekly public service hours: 40.

Student Life *Housing:* college housing not available. *Activities and Organizations:* Phi Theta Kappa, Phi Beta Lambda, Service Veterans Organization. *Campus security:* text-based alert system; campus police 8-5 on-site. *Student services:* veterans affairs office.

Standardized Tests *Required:* SAT or ACT or ACT Compass (for admission). *Recommended:* SAT or ACT (for admission), SAT and SAT Subject Tests or ACT (for admission), SAT Subject Tests (for admission).

Financial Aid Of all full-time matriculated undergraduates who enrolled in 2017, 19 Federal Work-Study jobs (averaging $4500).

Applying *Options:* electronic application. *Required:* high school transcript. *Application deadlines:* rolling (freshmen), rolling (transfers), rolling (early action). *Early decision deadline:* rolling (for plan 1), rolling (for plan 2). *Notification:* continuous (freshmen), continuous (transfers), rolling (early decision plan 1), rolling (early decision plan 2), rolling (early action).

Director of Admissions Candace L. Gross, Dean of Enrollment Services, Arkansas State University–Newport, 7648 Victory Boulevard, Newport, AR 72112. *Phone:* 870-512-7800. *Toll-free phone:* 800-976-1676. *Fax:* 870-512-7825. *E-mail:* candace_gross@asun.edu. *Website:* http://www.asun.edu/.

Baptist Health College Little Rock

Little Rock, Arkansas

Admissions Office Contact Baptist Health College Little Rock, 11900 Colonel Glenn Road, Suite 100, Little Rock, AR 72210-2820. *Website:* http://www.bhclr.edu/.

Black River Technical College

Pocahontas, Arkansas

Director of Admissions Director of Admissions, Black River Technical College, 1410 Highway 304 East, Pocahontas, AR 72455. *Phone:* 870-892-4565. *Website:* http://www.blackrivertech.edu/.

Bryan University

Rogers, Arkansas

Admissions Office Contact Bryan University, 3704 West Walnut Street, Rogers, AR 72756. *Website:* http://www.bryanu.edu/.

College of the Ouachitas

Malvern, Arkansas

- **State-supported** 2-year, founded 1972
- **Small-town** 11-acre campus with easy access to Little Rock
- **Coed**

Undergraduates 384 full-time, 888 part-time. Students come from 3 states and territories; 1% are from out of state; 14% Black or African American, non-Hispanic/Latino; 5% Hispanic/Latino; 0.5% Asian, non-Hispanic/Latino; 0.2% Native Hawaiian or other Pacific Islander, non-Hispanic/Latino; 0.6% American Indian or Alaska Native, non-Hispanic/Latino; 4% Two or more races, non-Hispanic/Latino; 0.6% Race/ethnicity unknown; 0.1% international; 22% transferred in.

Academics *Calendar:* semesters. *Degree:* certificates and associate. *Special study options:* academic remediation for entering students, accelerated degree program, advanced placement credit, cooperative education, distance learning, double majors, freshman honors college, honors programs, independent study, internships, part-time degree program, services for LD students, summer session for credit.

Library College of the Ouachitas Library/Learning Resource Center. Students can reserve study rooms.

Student Life *Campus security:* 24-hour emergency response devices and patrols.

Financial Aid Of all full-time matriculated undergraduates who enrolled in 2017, 18 Federal Work-Study jobs (averaging $2400).

Applying *Options:* electronic application, early admission, deferred entrance. *Required:* high school transcript, immunizations.

Freshman Application Contact Janet Hunt, Student Success Coordinator, College of the Ouachitas, One College Circle, Malvern, AR 72104. *Phone:* 501-337-5000 Ext. 1194. *Toll-free phone:* 800-337-0266. *Fax:* 501-337-9382. *E-mail:* jhunt@coto.edu. *Website:* http://www.coto.edu/.

Cossatot Community College of the University of Arkansas

De Queen, Arkansas

Freshman Application Contact Mrs. Tommi Cobb, Admissions Coordinator, Cossatot Community College of the University of Arkansas, 183 College Drive, DeQueen, AR 71832. *Phone:* 870-584-4471 Ext. 1158. *Toll-free phone:* 800-844-4471. *Fax:* 870-642-5088. *E-mail:* tcobb@cccua.edu. *Website:* http://www.cccua.edu/.

East Arkansas Community College

Forrest City, Arkansas

Freshman Application Contact Ms. Sharon Collier, Director of Enrollment Management/Institutional Research, East Arkansas Community College, 1700 Newcastle Road, Forrest City, AR 72335-2204. *Phone:* 870-633-4480. *Toll-free phone:* 877-797-3222. *Fax:* 870-633-3840. *E-mail:* dadams@eacc.edu. *Website:* http://www.eacc.edu/.

Jefferson Regional Medical Center School of Nursing

Pine Bluff, Arkansas

Admissions Office Contact Jefferson Regional Medical Center School of Nursing, 1600 West 40th Avenue, Pine Bluff, AR 71603. *Website:* http://www.jrmc.org/school-of-nursing/.

National Park College
Hot Springs, Arkansas

- **State and locally supported** 2-year, founded 1973, part of Arkansas Department of Higher Education
- **Suburban** 50-acre campus with easy access to Little Rock
- **Endowment** $11.3 million
- **Coed**

Undergraduates 1,237 full-time, 1,759 part-time. Students come from 1 other state; 2% are from out of state; 17% transferred in. *Retention:* 100% of full-time freshmen returned.
Faculty *Student/faculty ratio:* 18:1.
Academics *Calendar:* semesters. *Degree:* certificates, diplomas, and associate. *Special study options:* academic remediation for entering students, adult/continuing education programs, advanced placement credit, cooperative education, distance learning, double majors, external degree program, honors programs, independent study, internships, part-time degree program, services for LD students, student-designed majors, study abroad, summer session for credit.
Library NATIONAL PARK COLLEGE LIBRARY.
Student Life *Campus security:* 24-hour emergency response devices, Campus Resource Officer.
Athletics Member NJCAA.
Standardized Tests *Required:* ACT (for admission), SAT and SAT Subject Tests or ACT (for admission), ACCUPLACER (for admission).
Applying *Options:* early admission, deferred entrance. *Required:* high school transcript.
Freshman Application Contact National Park College, 101 College Drive, Hot Springs, AR 71913. *Phone:* 501-760-4202. *Website:* http://www.np.edu/.

North Arkansas College
Harrison, Arkansas

Freshman Application Contact Mrs. Charla Jennings, Director of Admissions, North Arkansas College, 1515 Pioneer Drive, Harrison, AR 72601. *Phone:* 870-391-3221. *Toll-free phone:* 800-679-6622. *Fax:* 870-391-3339. *E-mail:* charlam@northark.edu. *Website:* http://www.northark.edu/.

NorthWest Arkansas Community College
Bentonville, Arkansas

- **State-supported** 2-year, founded 1989
- **Suburban** 77-acre campus
- **Coed**

Undergraduates 2% Black or African American, non-Hispanic/Latino; 16% Hispanic/Latino; 3% Asian, non-Hispanic/Latino; 0.3% Native Hawaiian or other Pacific Islander, non-Hispanic/Latino; 2% American Indian or Alaska Native, non-Hispanic/Latino; 3% Two or more races, non-Hispanic/Latino; 3% Race/ethnicity unknown; 2% international. *Retention:* 59% of full-time freshmen returned.
Faculty *Student/faculty ratio:* 18:1.
Academics *Calendar:* semesters. *Degree:* certificates and associate. *Special study options:* academic remediation for entering students, accelerated degree program, adult/continuing education programs, advanced placement credit, cooperative education, distance learning, double majors, English as a second language, honors programs, independent study, internships, part-time degree program, services for LD students, student-designed majors, study abroad, summer session for credit. *ROTC:* Army (c), Air Force (c).
Library Pauline Whitaker Library plus 1 other.
Student Life *Campus security:* 24-hour emergency response devices and patrols.
Applying *Options:* electronic application. *Required:* high school transcript.
Freshman Application Contact NorthWest Arkansas Community College, One College Drive, Bentonville, AR 72712. *Phone:* 479-636-9222. *Toll-free phone:* 800-995-6922. *Fax:* 479-619-4116. *E-mail:* admissions@nwacc.edu. *Website:* http://www.nwacc.edu/.

Ozarka College
Melbourne, Arkansas

Freshman Application Contact Ms. Dylan Mowery, Director of Admissions, Ozarka College, PO Box 10, Melbourne, AR 72556. *Phone:* 870-368-7371 Ext. 2013. *Toll-free phone:* 800-821-4335. *E-mail:* dmmowery@ozarka.edu. *Website:* http://www.ozarka.edu/.

Phillips Community College of the University of Arkansas
Helena, Arkansas

Director of Admissions Mr. Lynn Boone, Registrar, Phillips Community College of the University of Arkansas, PO Box 785, Helena, AR 72342-0785. *Phone:* 870-338-6474. *Website:* http://www.pccua.edu/.

Remington College–Little Rock Campus
Little Rock, Arkansas

Director of Admissions Brian Maggio, Director of Recruitment, Remington College–Little Rock Campus, 10600 Colonel Glenn Road, Suite 100, Little Rock, AR 72204. *Phone:* 501-312-0007. *Toll-free phone:* 800-323-8122. *Fax:* 501-225-3819. *E-mail:* brian.maggio@remingtoncollege.edu. *Website:* http://www.remingtoncollege.edu/.

Shorter College
North Little Rock, Arkansas

Director of Admissions Mr. Keith Hunter, Director of Admissions, Shorter College, 604 Locust Street, North Little Rock, AR 72114-4885. *Phone:* 501-374-6305. *Website:* http://www.shortercollege.edu/.

South Arkansas Community College
El Dorado, Arkansas

Freshman Application Contact Dr. Stephanie Tully-Dartez, Director of Enrollment Services, South Arkansas Community College, PO Box 7010, El Dorado, AR 71731-7010. *Phone:* 870-864-7142. *Toll-free phone:* 800-955-2289. *Fax:* 870-864-7109. *E-mail:* dinman@southark.edu. *Website:* http://www.southark.edu/.

Southeast Arkansas College
Pine Bluff, Arkansas

- **State-supported** 2-year, founded 1991
- **Urban** 42-acre campus with easy access to Little Rock
- **Endowment** $559,963
- **Coed**

Undergraduates 582 full-time, 722 part-time. Students come from 3 states and territories; 1 other country; 57% Black or African American, non-Hispanic/Latino; 2% Hispanic/Latino; 0.9% Asian, non-Hispanic/Latino; 0.1% Native Hawaiian or other Pacific Islander, non-Hispanic/Latino; 0.1% American Indian or Alaska Native, non-Hispanic/Latino; 0.8% Two or more races, non-Hispanic/Latino; 0.1% Race/ethnicity unknown; 0.1% international; 5% transferred in. *Retention:* 63% of full-time freshmen returned.
Faculty *Student/faculty ratio:* 13:1.
Academics *Calendar:* semesters. *Degree:* certificates and associate. *Special study options:* academic remediation for entering students, accelerated degree program, advanced placement credit, cooperative education, distance learning, double majors, honors programs, independent study, internships, part-time degree program, services for LD students, summer session for credit.
Library Southeast Arkansas College Library. *Books:* 11,605 (physical), 94 (digital/electronic); *Serial titles:* 164 (physical), 8 (digital/electronic); *Databases:* 6.
Student Life *Campus security:* 24-hour patrols.
Standardized Tests *Required for some:* ACCUPLACER (if no other test scores are available, or test scores are older than 3 years). *Recommended:* SAT and SAT Subject Tests or ACT (for admission).
Financial Aid Of all full-time matriculated undergraduates who enrolled in 2016, 704 applied for aid, 670 were judged to have need, 19 had their need fully met. 23 Federal Work-Study jobs (averaging $3071). In 2016, 9. *Average percent of need met:* 50. *Average financial aid package:* $6296. *Average need-based loan:* $2991. *Average need-based gift aid:* $4668. *Average non-need-based aid:* $4721.
Applying *Options:* electronic application, early admission. *Required:* high school transcript.
Admissions Office Contact Southeast Arkansas College, 1900 Hazel Street, Pine Bluff, AR 71603. *Toll-free phone:* 888-SEARK TC (in-state); 888-SEARC TC (out-of-state). *Website:* http://www.seark.edu/.

Southern Arkansas University Tech
Camden, Arkansas

Freshman Application Contact Mrs. Lisa Smith, Admissions Analyst, Southern Arkansas University Tech, PO Box 3499, Camden, AR 71711-1599. *Phone:* 870-574-4558. *Fax:* 870-574-4442. *E-mail:* lsmith@sautech.edu. *Website:* http://www.sautech.edu/.

University of Arkansas Community College at Batesville

Batesville, Arkansas

Freshman Application Contact Ms. Amy Foree, Enrollment Specialist, University of Arkansas Community College at Batesville, PO Box 3350, Batesville, AR 72503. *Phone:* 870-612-2113. *Toll-free phone:* 800-508-7878. *Fax:* 870-612-2129. *E-mail:* amy.foree@uaccb.edu. *Website:* http://www.uaccb.edu/.

University of Arkansas Community College at Hope

Hope, Arkansas

Freshman Application Contact University of Arkansas Community College at Hope, PO Box 140, Hope, AR 71802. *Phone:* 870-772-8174. *Website:* http://www.uacch.edu/.

University of Arkansas Community College at Morrilton

Morrilton, Arkansas

- **State-supported** 2-year, founded 1961, part of University of Arkansas System
- **Rural** 89-acre campus
- **Coed,** 1,902 undergraduate students, 54% full-time, 63% women, 37% men

Undergraduates 1,033 full-time, 869 part-time. Students come from 4 states and territories; 3 other countries; 8% Black or African American, non-Hispanic/Latino; 8% Hispanic/Latino; 0.7% Asian, non-Hispanic/Latino; 0.1% Native Hawaiian or other Pacific Islander, non-Hispanic/Latino; 0.3% American Indian or Alaska Native, non-Hispanic/Latino; 6% Two or more races, non-Hispanic/Latino; 0.6% Race/ethnicity unknown; 2% international; 9% transferred in.
Freshmen *Admission:* 1,234 applied, 915 admitted, 469 enrolled. *Average high school GPA:* 3.0. *Test scores:* ACT scores over 18: 71%; ACT scores over 24: 14%.
Faculty *Total:* 73, 73% full-time, 10% with terminal degrees. *Student/faculty ratio:* 22:1.
Majors Autobody/collision and repair technology; automobile/automotive mechanics technology; business/commerce; child development; computer and information sciences; computer technology/computer systems technology; criminal justice/law enforcement administration; drafting and design technology; forensic science and technology; general studies; heating, air conditioning, ventilation and refrigeration maintenance technology; industrial mechanics and maintenance technology; liberal arts and sciences/liberal studies; machine shop technology; middle school education; registered nursing/registered nurse; surveying technology.
Academics *Calendar:* semesters. *Degree:* certificates and associate. *Special study options:* academic remediation for entering students, advanced placement credit, cooperative education, distance learning, double majors, independent study, internships, part-time degree program, services for LD students, summer session for credit.
Library E. Allen Gordon Library. *Books:* 27,196 (physical), 177,896 (digital/electronic); *Serial titles:* 81 (physical); *Databases:* 35. Weekly public service hours: 66; students can reserve study rooms.
Student Life *Housing:* college housing not available. *Activities and Organizations:* Phi Theta Kappa, Student Activities Board, National Technical Honors Society, Thrive Student Ministries, Computer Information Systems Club. *Campus security:* 24-hour emergency response devices, late-night transport/escort service. *Student services:* personal/psychological counseling.
Standardized Tests *Recommended:* SAT or ACT (for admission), ACT Compass, ACCUPLACER.
Financial Aid Of all full-time matriculated undergraduates who enrolled in 2015, 1,178 applied for aid, 1,028 were judged to have need, 31 had their need fully met. In 2015, 45 non-need-based awards were made. *Average percent of need met:* 44%. *Average financial aid package:* $6082. *Average need-based loan:* $1686. *Average need-based gift aid:* $3161. *Average non-need-based aid:* $1033.
Applying *Options:* electronic application, early admission, deferred entrance. *Required:* high school transcript. *Required for some:* immunization records, prior college transcript(s). *Application deadlines:* rolling (freshmen), rolling (transfers). *Notification:* continuous (freshmen), continuous (transfers).
Freshman Application Contact Ms. Lindsey Grier, Administrative Specialist, University of Arkansas Community College at Morrilton, 1537 University Boulevard, Morrilton, AR 72110. *Phone:* 501-977-2053. *Toll-free phone:* 800-264-1094. *Fax:* 501-977-2123. *E-mail:* grierlindsey@uaccm.edu. *Website:* http://www.uaccm.edu/.

University of Arkansas–Pulaski Technical College

North Little Rock, Arkansas

Freshman Application Contact Mr. Clark Atkins, Director of Admissions, University of Arkansas–Pulaski Technical College, 3000 West Scenic Drive, North Little Rock, AR 72118. *Phone:* 501-812-2734. *Fax:* 501-812-2316. *E-mail:* catkins@pulaskitech.edu. *Website:* http://www.pulaskitech.edu/.

University of Arkansas Rich Mountain

Mena, Arkansas

- **State and locally supported** 2-year, founded 1983, part of University of Arkansas System
- **Small-town** 40-acre campus
- **Coed**
- 100% of applicants were admitted

Undergraduates 456 full-time, 482 part-time. 0.3% Black or African American, non-Hispanic/Latino; 4% Hispanic/Latino; 1% Asian, non-Hispanic/Latino; 0.2% Native Hawaiian or other Pacific Islander, non-Hispanic/Latino; 2% American Indian or Alaska Native, non-Hispanic/Latino; 1% Two or more races, non-Hispanic/Latino; 1% Race/ethnicity unknown; 1% international. *Retention:* 61% of full-time freshmen returned.
Academics *Calendar:* semesters. *Degree:* certificates and associate. *Special study options:* academic remediation for entering students, adult/continuing education programs, advanced placement credit, distance learning, double majors, English as a second language, part-time degree program, services for LD students, summer session for credit.
Library St. John Library. *Books:* 14,668 (physical), 13,747 (digital/electronic); *Databases:* 27. Students can reserve study rooms.
Student Life *Campus security:* campus security on duty during college hours.
Financial Aid Of all full-time matriculated undergraduates who enrolled in 2017, 12 Federal Work-Study jobs (averaging $1500).
Applying *Options:* electronic application, early admission. *Required:* high school transcript.
Freshman Application Contact Wendy McDaniel, Director of Admissions, University of Arkansas Rich Mountain, 1100 College Drive, Mena, AR 71953. *Phone:* 479-394-7622 Ext. 1440. *E-mail:* wmcdaniel@uarichmountain.edu. *Website:* http://www.uarichmountain.edu/.

CALIFORNIA

Advanced College

South Gate, California

Admissions Office Contact Advanced College, 13180 Paramount Boulevard, South Gate, CA 90280. *Website:* http://www.advancedcollege.edu/.

Advanced College

Stockton, California

Admissions Office Contact Advanced College, 8838 North West Lane, Stockton, CA 95120. *Website:* http://www.advancedcollege.edu/.

Advanced Computing Institute

Los Angeles, California

Admissions Office Contact Advanced Computing Institute, 3470 Wilshire Boulevard 11th Floor, Los Angeles, CA 90010-3911. *Website:* http://www.advancedcomputinginstitute.edu/.

Advanced Training Associates

El Cajon, California

Admissions Office Contact Advanced Training Associates, 1810 Gillespie Way, Suite 104, El Cajon, CA 92020. *Toll-free phone:* 800-720-2125. *Website:* http://www.advancedtraining.edu/.

Allan Hancock College

Santa Maria, California

Freshman Application Contact Ms. Adela Esquivel Swinson, Director of Admissions and Records, Allan Hancock College, 800 South College Drive, Santa Maria, CA 93454-6399. *Phone:* 805-922-6966 Ext. 3272. *Toll-free phone:* 866-342-5242. *Fax:* 805-922-3477. *Website:* http://www.hancockcollege.edu/.

★ American Academy of Dramatic Arts–Los Angeles

Hollywood, California

- **Independent** 2-year, founded 1974
- **Urban** 4-acre campus with easy access to Los Angeles
- **Endowment** $1.7 million
- **Coed**

Undergraduates 303 full-time. Students come from 27 states and territories; 37 other countries; 53% are from out of state; 10% Black or African American, non-Hispanic/Latino; 8% Hispanic/Latino; 1% Asian, non-Hispanic/Latino; 0.3% Native Hawaiian or other Pacific Islander, non-Hispanic/Latino; 0.3% American Indian or Alaska Native, non-Hispanic/Latino; 6% Two or more races, non-Hispanic/Latino; 0.7% Race/ethnicity unknown; 33% international; 0.7% transferred in.
Faculty *Student/faculty ratio:* 12:1.
Academics *Calendar:* semesters. *Degree:* certificates, diplomas, and associate. *Special study options:* internships, services for LD students.
Library Bryn Morgan Library. *Books:* 15,000 (physical); *Serial titles:* 1,000 (physical). Weekly public service hours: 53.
Student Life *Campus security:* 24-hour emergency response devices and patrols, controlled dormitory access.
Financial Aid Of all full-time matriculated undergraduates who enrolled in 2017, 15 Federal Work-Study jobs (averaging $2000).
Applying *Options:* electronic application, deferred entrance. *Application fee:* $50. *Required:* essay or personal statement, high school transcript, 2 letters of recommendation, interview, audition. *Recommended:* minimum 2.0 GPA.
Freshman Application Contact Steven Hong, Director of Admissions, American Academy of Dramatic Arts–Los Angeles, 1336 North La Brea Avenue, Los Angeles, CA 90028. *Phone:* 323-464-2777 Ext. 103. *Toll-free phone:* 800-222-2867. *E-mail:* shong@aada.edu. *Website:* http://www.aada.edu/.

American Career College

Anaheim, California

Director of Admissions Susan Pailet, Senior Executive Director of Admission, American Career College, 1200 North Magnolia Avenue, Anaheim, CA 92801. *Phone:* 714-952-9066. *Toll-free phone:* 877-832-0790. *E-mail:* info@americancareer.com. *Website:* http://americancareercollege.edu/.

American Career College

Los Angeles, California

Director of Admissions Tamra Adams, Director of Admissions, American Career College, 4021 Rosewood Avenue, Los Angeles, CA 90004. *Phone:* 323-668-7555. *Toll-free phone:* 877-832-0790. *E-mail:* info@americancareer.com. *Website:* http://americancareercollege.edu/.

American Career College

Ontario, California

Director of Admissions Juan Tellez, Director of Admissions, American Career College, 3130 East Sedona Court, Ontario, CA 91764. *Phone:* 951-739-0788. *Toll-free phone:* 877-832-0790. *E-mail:* info@americiancareer.com. *Website:* http://americancareercollege.edu/.

American Medical Sciences Center

Glendale, California

Admissions Office Contact American Medical Sciences Center, 225 West Broadway, Suite 115, Glendale, CA 91204-5108. *Website:* http://www.amsc.edu/.

American River College

Sacramento, California

Freshman Application Contact American River College, 4700 College Oak Drive, Sacramento, CA 95841-4286. *Phone:* 916-484-8171. *Website:* http://www.arc.losrios.edu/.

Antelope Valley College

Lancaster, California

- **District-supported** primarily 2-year, founded 1929, part of California Community College System
- **Suburban** 135-acre campus with easy access to Los Angeles
- **Endowment** $4.6 million
- **Coed**

Undergraduates 4,031 full-time, 10,094 part-time. Students come from 10 states and territories; 1 other country; 16% Black or African American, non-Hispanic/Latino; 53% Hispanic/Latino; 4% Asian, non-Hispanic/Latino; 0.2% Native Hawaiian or other Pacific Islander, non-Hispanic/Latino; 0.3% American Indian or Alaska Native, non-Hispanic/Latino; 5% Two or more races, non-Hispanic/Latino; 0.8% Race/ethnicity unknown; 0.1% international.
Faculty *Student/faculty ratio:* 24:1.
Academics *Calendar:* semesters. *Degrees:* certificates, associate, and bachelor's. *Special study options:* academic remediation for entering students, advanced placement credit, cooperative education, distance learning, English as a second language, external degree program, honors programs, independent study, part-time degree program, services for LD students, study abroad, summer session for credit. *ROTC:* Army (c), Navy (c), Air Force (c).
Library Antelope Valley College Library. *Books:* 54,721 (physical), 8,152 (digital/electronic); *Serial titles:* 10 (physical); *Databases:* 65. Weekly public service hours: 58; students can reserve study rooms.
Student Life *Campus security:* 24-hour emergency response devices and patrols, late-night transport/escort service.
Applying *Options:* electronic application, early admission.
Freshman Application Contact Welcome Center, Antelope Valley College, 3041 West Avenue K, SSV Building, Lancaster, CA 93536. *Phone:* 661-722-6300 Ext. 6331. *Website:* http://www.avc.edu/.

APT College

Carlsbad, California

Director of Admissions Monica Hoffman, Director of Admissions/Registrar, APT College, 1939 Palomar Oaks Way, Suite A, Carlsbad, CA 92011. *Phone:* 800-431-8488. *Toll-free phone:* 800-431-8488. *Fax:* 888-431-8588. *E-mail:* aptc@aptc.com. *Website:* http://www.aptc.edu/.

Bakersfield College

Bakersfield, California

Freshman Application Contact Bakersfield College, 1801 Panorama Drive, Bakersfield, CA 93305-1299. *Phone:* 661-395-4301. *Website:* http://www.bakersfieldcollege.edu/.

Barstow Community College

Barstow, California

Freshman Application Contact Barstow Community College, 2700 Barstow Road, Barstow, CA 92311-6699. *Phone:* 760-252-2411 Ext. 7236. *Website:* http://www.barstow.edu/.

Berkeley City College

Berkeley, California

Freshman Application Contact Dr. May Kuang-chi Chen, Vice President of Student Services, Berkeley City College, 2050 Center Street, Berkeley, CA 94704. *Phone:* 510-981-2820. *Fax:* 510-841-7333. *E-mail:* mrivas@peralta.edu. *Website:* http://www.berkeleycitycollege.edu/.

Beverly Hills Design Institute

Beverly Hills, California

Freshman Application Contact Beverly Hills Design Institute, 8484 Wilshire Boulevard, Suite 730, Beverly Hills, CA 90211. *Phone:* 310-360-8888. *Website:* http://www.bhdi.edu/.

Bryan College

El Cajon, California

Freshman Application Contact Bryan College, 2065 North Marshall Avenue, El Cajon, CA 92020. *Phone:* 916-649-2400. *Toll-free phone:* 866-649-2400. *Website:* http://www.bryancollege.edu/.

Bryan University
Los Angeles, California

Admissions Office Contact Bryan University, 3580 Wilshire Boulevard, Los Angeles, CA 90010. *Website:* http://losangeles.bryanuniversity.edu/.

Butte College
Oroville, California

Freshman Application Contact Mr. Brad Zuniga, Director of Recruitment, Outreach and New Student Orientation, Butte College, 3536 Butte Campus Drive, Oroville, CA 95965-8399. *Phone:* 530-895-2948. *Website:* http://www.butte.edu/.

Cabrillo College
Aptos, California

Freshman Application Contact Tama Bolton, Director of Admissions and Records, Cabrillo College, 6500 Soquel Drive, Aptos, CA 95003-3194. *Phone:* 831-477-3548. *Fax:* 831-479-5782. *E-mail:* tabolton@cabrillo.edu. *Website:* http://www.cabrillo.edu/.

California Institute of Arts & Technology
San Diego, California

Admissions Office Contact California Institute of Arts & Technology, 2820 Camino Del Rio South, Suite 100, San Diego, CA 92108. *Website:* http://www.ciat.edu/.

Cambridge Junior College
Yuba City, California

Freshman Application Contact Admissions Office, Cambridge Junior College, 990-A Klamath Lane, Yuba City, CA 95993. *Phone:* 530-674-9199. *Fax:* 530-671-7319. *Website:* http://www.cambridge.edu/.

Cañada College
Redwood City, California

Freshman Application Contact Cañada College, 4200 Farm Hill Boulevard, Redwood City, CA 94061-1099. *Phone:* 650-306-3125. *Website:* http://www.canadacollege.edu/.

Carrington College–Citrus Heights
Citrus Heights, California

Freshman Application Contact Carrington College–Citrus Heights, 7301 Greenback Lane, Suite A, Citrus Heights, CA 95621. *Website:* http://www.carrington.edu/.

Carrington College–Pleasant Hill
Pleasant Hill, California

Freshman Application Contact Carrington College–Pleasant Hill, 380 Civic Drive, Suite 300, Pleasant Hill, CA 94523. *Website:* http://www.carrington.edu/.

Carrington College–Pomona
Pomona, California

Freshman Application Contact Carrington College–Pomona, 901 Corporate Center Drive, Suite 300, Pomona, CA 91768. *Toll-free phone:* 877-206-2106. *Website:* http://www.carrington.edu/.

Carrington College–Sacramento
Sacramento, California

Freshman Application Contact Carrington College–Sacramento, 8909 Folsom Boulevard, Sacramento, CA 95826. *Website:* http://www.carrington.edu/.

Carrington College–San Jose
San Jose, California

Freshman Application Contact Carrington College–San Jose, 5883 Rue Ferrari, Suite 125, San Jose, CA 95138. *Website:* http://www.carrington.edu/.

Carrington College–San Leandro
San Leandro, California

Freshman Application Contact Carrington College–San Leandro, 15555 East 14th Street, Suite 500, San Leandro, CA 94578. *Website:* http://www.carrington.edu/.

Carrington College–Stockton
Stockton, California

Freshman Application Contact Carrington College–Stockton, 1313 West Robinhood Drive, Suite B, Stockton, CA 95207. *Website:* http://www.carrington.edu/.

Casa Loma College–Van Nuys
Los Angeles, California

Admissions Office Contact Casa Loma College–Van Nuys, 6725 Kester Avenue, Los Angeles, CA 91405. *Website:* http://www.casalomacollege.edu/.

CBD College
Los Angeles, California

Admissions Office Contact CBD College, 3699 Wilshire Boulevard, 4th Floor, Los Angeles, CA 90010. *Website:* http://www.cbd.edu/.

Cerritos College
Norwalk, California

Freshman Application Contact Cerritos College, 11110 Alondra Boulevard, Norwalk, CA 90650-6298. *Phone:* 562-860-2451 Ext. 2102. *Website:* http://www.cerritos.edu/.

Cerro Coso Community College
Ridgecrest, California

Freshman Application Contact Mrs. Heather Ootash, Counseling/Matriculation Coordinator, Cerro Coso Community College, 3000 College Heights Boulevard, Ridgecrest, CA 93555. *Phone:* 760-384-6291. *Fax:* 760-375-4776. *E-mail:* hostash@cerrocoso.edu. *Website:* http://www.cerrocoso.edu/.

Chabot College
Hayward, California

Director of Admissions Paulette Lino, Director of Admissions and Records, Chabot College, 25555 Hesperian Boulevard, Hayward, CA 94545-5001. *Phone:* 510-723-6700. *Website:* http://www.chabotcollege.edu/.

Chaffey College
Rancho Cucamonga, California

Freshman Application Contact Erlinda Martinez, Coordinator of Admissions, Chaffey College, 5885 Haven Avenue, Rancho Cucamonga, CA 91737-3002. *Phone:* 909-652-6610. *E-mail:* erlinda.martinez@chaffey.edu. *Website:* http://www.chaffey.edu/.

Citrus College
Glendora, California

Freshman Application Contact Admissions and Records, Citrus College, Glendora, CA 91741-1899. *Phone:* 626-914-8511. *Fax:* 626-914-8613. *E-mail:* admissions@citruscollege.edu. *Website:* http://www.citruscollege.edu/.

City College of San Francisco
San Francisco, California

Freshman Application Contact Ms. Mary Lou Leyba-Frank, Dean of Admissions and Records, City College of San Francisco, 50 Phelan Avenue, San Francisco, CA 94112-1821. *Phone:* 415-239-3291. *Fax:* 415-239-3936. *E-mail:* mleyba@ccsf.edu. *Website:* http://www.ccsf.edu/.

Clovis Community College
Fresno, California

Admissions Office Contact Clovis Community College, 10309 North Willow Avenue, Fresno, CA 93730. *Website:* http://www.cloviscollege.edu/.

Coastline Community College
Fountain Valley, California

- **District-supported** 2-year, founded 1976, part of Coast Community College District System
- **Urban** campus with easy access to Orange County
- **Coed,** 11,431 undergraduate students, 22% full-time, 41% women, 59% men

Undergraduates 2,488 full-time, 8,943 part-time. 12% Black or African American, non-Hispanic/Latino; 28% Hispanic/Latino; 22% Asian, non-Hispanic/Latino; 0.5% Native Hawaiian or other Pacific Islander, non-Hispanic/Latino; 0.8% American Indian or Alaska Native, non-Hispanic/Latino; 4% Two or more races, non-Hispanic/Latino; 2% Race/ethnicity unknown.
Freshmen *Admission:* 900 enrolled.
Faculty *Total:* 296, 19% full-time. *Student/faculty ratio:* 32:1.
Majors Liberal arts and sciences/liberal studies.
Academics *Calendar:* semesters. *Degree:* certificates and associate. *Special study options:* academic remediation for entering students, accelerated degree program, adult/continuing education programs, advanced placement credit, cooperative education, distance learning, double majors, English as a second language, external degree program, honors programs, independent study, internships, off-campus study, part-time degree program, services for LD students, study abroad, summer session for credit.
Library Coastline Virtual Library plus 1 other.
Student Life *Housing:* college housing not available. *Campus security:* 24-hour emergency response devices. *Student services:* health clinic, personal/psychological counseling, veterans affairs office.
Financial Aid Of all full-time matriculated undergraduates who enrolled in 2015, 12,392 applied for aid, 11,568 were judged to have need, 12 had their need fully met. *Average percent of need met:* 15%. *Average financial aid package:* $3819. *Average need-based loan:* $3290. *Average need-based gift aid:* $3714. *Average indebtedness upon graduation:* $10,514. *Financial aid deadline:* 8/15.
Applying *Options:* electronic application, early admission. *Recommended:* high school transcript. *Application deadlines:* rolling (freshmen), rolling (transfers).
Freshman Application Contact Jennifer McDonald, Director of Admissions and Records, Coastline Community College, 11460 Warner Avenue, Fountain Valley, CA 92708. *Phone:* 714-241-6163.
Website: http://www.coastline.edu/.

College of Alameda
Alameda, California

Freshman Application Contact College of Alameda, 555 Ralph Appezzato Memorial Parkway, Alameda, CA 94501-2109. *Phone:* 510-748-2204. *Website:* http://alameda.peralta.edu/.

College of Marin
Kentfield, California

- **District-supported** 2-year, founded 1926, part of California Community College System
- **Suburban** 410-acre campus with easy access to San Francisco
- **Coed,** 5,026 undergraduate students, 27% full-time, 58% women, 42% men

Undergraduates 1,345 full-time, 3,681 part-time. 3% Black or African American, non-Hispanic/Latino; 31% Hispanic/Latino; 8% Asian, non-Hispanic/Latino; 0.3% Native Hawaiian or other Pacific Islander, non-Hispanic/Latino; 0.2% American Indian or Alaska Native, non-Hispanic/Latino; 6% Two or more races, non-Hispanic/Latino; 1% Race/ethnicity unknown; 1% international.
Faculty *Total:* 312, 37% full-time.
Majors Accounting technology and bookkeeping; animation, interactive technology, video graphics and special effects; architectural technology; art; autobody/collision and repair technology; automobile/automotive mechanics technology; biological and physical sciences; biology/biological sciences; business administration and management; business/commerce; chemistry; child-care provision; cinematography and film/video production; computer science; computer systems networking and telecommunications; court reporting; criminal justice/police science; dance; data modeling/warehousing and database administration; dental assisting; design and visual communications; dramatic/theater arts; engineering; engineering technology; ethnic, cultural minority, gender, and group studies related; film/cinema/video studies; foreign languages and literatures; French; geography; geology/earth science; health and physical education/fitness; history; humanities; interior design; international relations and affairs; landscaping and groundskeeping; liberal arts and sciences/liberal studies; machine tool technology; mass communication/media; mathematics; medical administrative assistant and medical secretary; medical/clinical assistant; music; office management; physical sciences; physics; plant nursery management; political science and government; psychology; real estate; registered nursing/registered nurse; social sciences; Spanish; speech communication and rhetoric.
Academics *Calendar:* semesters. *Degree:* certificates and associate. *Special study options:* academic remediation for entering students, advanced placement credit, cooperative education, distance learning, double majors, English as a second language, part-time degree program, services for LD students, summer session for credit.
Library Main Library plus 1 other.
Student Life *Housing:* college housing not available. *Activities and Organizations:* drama/theater group, student-run newspaper, choral group. *Campus security:* 24-hour emergency response devices and patrols, security cameras. *Student services:* health clinic, personal/psychological counseling, veterans affairs office.
Athletics *Intercollegiate sports:* basketball W, soccer W, softball W, swimming and diving W, track and field W, volleyball W, water polo W.
Applying *Options:* electronic application. *Application deadlines:* rolling (freshmen), rolling (transfers).
Admissions Office Contact College of Marin, 835 College Avenue, Kentfield, CA 94904.
Website: http://www.marin.edu/.

College of San Mateo
San Mateo, California

Director of Admissions Mr. Henry Villareal, Dean of Admissions and Records, College of San Mateo, 1700 West Hillsdale Boulevard, San Mateo, CA 94402-3784. *Phone:* 650-574-6590. *E-mail:* csmadmission@smccd.edu. *Website:* http://www.collegeofsanmateo.edu/.

College of the Canyons
Santa Clarita, California

- **District-supported** 2-year, founded 1969, part of California Community College System
- **Suburban** 224-acre campus with easy access to Los Angeles
- **Coed,** 20,489 undergraduate students, 31% full-time, 45% women, 52% men

Undergraduates 6,445 full-time, 13,420 part-time. Students come from 49 other countries; 3% are from out of state; 5% Black or African American, non-Hispanic/Latino; 47% Hispanic/Latino; 10% Asian, non-Hispanic/Latino; 0.3% Native Hawaiian or other Pacific Islander, non-Hispanic/Latino; 0.2% American Indian or Alaska Native, non-Hispanic/Latino; 2% Two or more races, non-Hispanic/Latino; 3% Race/ethnicity unknown; 0.9% international; 41% transferred in.
Freshmen *Admission:* 2,467 enrolled.
Faculty *Total:* 737, 25% full-time. *Student/faculty ratio:* 17:1.
Majors Accounting technology and bookkeeping; administrative assistant and secretarial science; animation, interactive technology, video graphics and special effects; architectural drafting and CAD/CADD; art; athletic training; automobile/automotive mechanics technology; biological and physical sciences; building/construction site management; building construction technology; business administration and management; child-care provision; cinematography and film/video production; clinical/medical laboratory technology; computer science; computer systems networking and telecommunications; criminal justice/police science; dramatic/theater arts; English; environmental science; fire prevention and safety technology; French; geography; geology/earth science; graphic design; health and physical education/fitness; history; hotel/motel administration; humanities; interior design; journalism; kinesiology and exercise science; legal assistant/paralegal; liberal arts and sciences/liberal studies; library and archives assisting; mathematics; music; musical theater; parks, recreation and leisure; parks, recreation, leisure, and fitness studies related; philosophy; photography; physics; political science and government; pre-engineering; psychology; real estate; registered nursing/registered nurse; restaurant, culinary, and catering management; sales, distribution, and marketing operations; sign language interpretation and translation; small business administration; social sciences; social sciences related; sociology; Spanish; speech communication and rhetoric; surveying technology; theater design and technology; water quality

and wastewater treatment management and recycling technology; web page, digital/multimedia and information resources design; welding technology.
Academics *Calendar:* semesters. *Degree:* certificates and associate. *Special study options:* academic remediation for entering students, accelerated degree program, adult/continuing education programs, advanced placement credit, cooperative education, distance learning, double majors, English as a second language, honors programs, internships, part-time degree program, services for LD students, study abroad, summer session for credit.
Library College of the Canyons Library. *Books:* 59,059 (physical), 138,941 (digital/electronic); *Serial titles:* 58 (physical), 2 (digital/electronic); *Databases:* 53. Weekly public service hours: 116; students can reserve study rooms.
Student Life *Housing:* college housing not available. *Activities and Organizations:* drama/theater group, student-run newspaper, choral group. *Campus security:* 24-hour emergency response devices, late-night transport/escort service. *Student services:* health clinic, personal/psychological counseling, women's center, veterans affairs office.
Athletics *Intercollegiate sports:* basketball W, cross-country running W, soccer W, softball W, swimming and diving W, track and field W, volleyball W.
Applying *Options:* electronic application. *Recommended:* high school transcript. *Application deadlines:* rolling (freshmen), rolling (out-of-state freshmen), rolling (transfers). *Notification:* continuous (freshmen), continuous (transfers).
Freshman Application Contact Dr. Jasmine Ruys, Dean, Enrollment Services, College of the Canyons, 26455 Rockwell Canyon Road, Santa Clarita, CA 91355. *Phone:* 661-362-3280. *Fax:* 661-254-7996. *E-mail:* jasmine.ruys@canyons.edu.
Website: http://www.canyons.edu/.

College of the Desert
Palm Desert, California

- **District-supported** 2-year, founded 1958, part of California Community College System
- **Small-town** 160-acre campus
- **Coed**

Undergraduates 4,434 full-time, 6,712 part-time. Students come from 20 states and territories; 1% are from out of state; 3% Black or African American, non-Hispanic/Latino; 72% Hispanic/Latino; 3% Asian, non-Hispanic/Latino; 0.1% Native Hawaiian or other Pacific Islander, non-Hispanic/Latino; 0.4% American Indian or Alaska Native, non-Hispanic/Latino; 3% Two or more races, non-Hispanic/Latino; 0.6% Race/ethnicity unknown; 1% international; 3% transferred in. *Retention:* 71% of full-time freshmen returned.
Faculty *Student/faculty ratio:* 23:1.
Academics *Calendar:* semesters. *Degree:* certificates, diplomas, and associate. *Special study options:* academic remediation for entering students, adult/continuing education programs, cooperative education, distance learning, double majors, English as a second language, part-time degree program, services for LD students, study abroad, summer session for credit.
Library College of the Desert Library. Weekly public service hours: 56; students can reserve study rooms.
Student Life *Campus security:* 24-hour emergency response devices and patrols.
Athletics Member NJCAA.
Applying *Options:* electronic application. *Recommended:* high school transcript.
Freshman Application Contact College of the Desert, 43-500 Monterey Avenue, Palm Desert, CA 92260-9305. *Phone:* 760-776-7441 Ext. 7441. *Website:* http://www.collegeofthedesert.edu/.

College of the Redwoods
Eureka, California

Freshman Application Contact Director of Enrollment Management, College of the Redwoods, 7351 Tompkins Hill Road, Eureka, CA 95501-9300. *Phone:* 707-476-4100. *Toll-free phone:* 800-641-0400. *Fax:* 707-476-4400. *Website:* http://www.redwoods.edu/.

College of the Sequoias
Visalia, California

Freshman Application Contact Ms. Lisa Hott, Director for Admissions, College of the Sequoias, 915 South Mooney Boulevard, Visalia, CA 93277-2234. *Phone:* 559-737-4844. *Fax:* 559-737-4820. *Website:* http://www.cos.edu/.

College of the Siskiyous
Weed, California

Freshman Application Contact Recruitment and Admissions, College of the Siskiyous, 800 College Avenue, Weed, CA 96094-2899. *Phone:* 530-938-5555. *Toll-free phone:* 888-397-4339. *E-mail:* admissions-weed@siskyous.edu. *Website:* http://www.siskiyous.edu/.

Columbia College
Sonora, California

Freshman Application Contact Admissions Office, Columbia College, 11600 Columbia College Drive, Sonora, CA 95370. *Phone:* 209-588-5231. *Fax:* 209-588-5337. *E-mail:* ccadmissions@yosemite.edu. *Website:* http://www.gocolumbia.edu/.

Community Christian College
Redlands, California

Freshman Application Contact Mr. Enrique D. Melendez, Assistant Director of Admissions, Community Christian College, 251 Tennessee Street, Redlands, CA 92373. *Phone:* 909-222-9556. *Fax:* 909-335-9101. *E-mail:* emelendez@cccollege.edu. *Website:* http://www.cccollege.edu/.

Compton College
Compton, California

Director of Admissions Ms. Stephanie Atkinson-Alston, Interim Associate Dean, Admissions and Records, Compton College, 1111 East Artesia Boulevard, Compton, CA 90221-5393. *Phone:* 310-900-1600 Ext. 2047. *Website:* http://www.compton.edu/.

Concorde Career College
Garden Grove, California

Freshman Application Contact Chris Becker, Director, Concorde Career College, 12951 South Euclid Street, Suite 101, Garden Grove, CA 92840. *Phone:* 714-703-1900. *Fax:* 714-530-4737. *E-mail:* cbecker@concorde.edu. *Website:* http://www.concorde.edu/.

Concorde Career College
North Hollywood, California

Freshman Application Contact Madeline Volker, Director, Concorde Career College, 12412 Victory Boulevard, North Hollywood, CA 91606. *Phone:* 818-766-8151. *Fax:* 818-766-1587. *E-mail:* mvolker@concorde.edu. *Website:* http://www.concorde.edu/.

Concorde Career College
San Bernardino, California

Admissions Office Contact Concorde Career College, 201 East Airport Drive, San Bernardino, CA 92408. *Website:* http://www.concorde.edu/.

Concorde Career College
San Diego, California

Admissions Office Contact Concorde Career College, 4393 Imperial Avenue, Suite 100, San Diego, CA 92113. *Website:* http://www.concorde.edu/.

Contra Costa College
San Pablo, California

Freshman Application Contact Admissions and Records Office, Contra Costa College, San Pablo, CA 94806. *Phone:* 510-235-7800 Ext. 7500. *Fax:* 510-412-0769. *E-mail:* ar@contracosta.edu. *Website:* http://www.contracosta.edu/.

Copper Mountain College
Joshua Tree, California

Freshman Application Contact Greg Brown, Executive Vice President for Academic and Student Affairs, Copper Mountain College, 6162 Rotary Way, Joshua Tree, CA 92252. *Phone:* 760-366-3791. *Toll-free phone:* 866-366-3791. *Fax:* 760-366-5257. *E-mail:* gbrown@cmccd.edu. *Website:* http://www.cmccd.edu/.

Cosumnes River College
Sacramento, California

Freshman Application Contact Admissions and Records, Cosumnes River College, 8401 Center Parkway, Sacramento, CA 95823-5799. *Phone:* 916-691-7411. *Website:* http://www.crc.losrios.edu/.

Crafton Hills College
Yucaipa, California

Director of Admissions Larry Aycock, Admissions and Records Coordinator, Crafton Hills College, 11711 Sand Canyon Road, Yucaipa, CA 92399-1799. *Phone:* 909-389-3663. *E-mail:* laycock@craftonhills.edu. *Website:* http://www.craftonhills.edu/.

Cuesta College
San Luis Obispo, California

Freshman Application Contact Cuesta College, PO Box 8106, San Luis Obispo, CA 93403-8106. *Phone:* 805-546-3130 Ext. 2262. *Website:* http://www.cuesta.edu/.

Cuyamaca College
El Cajon, California

Freshman Application Contact Ms. Susan Topham, Dean of Admissions and Records, Cuyamaca College, 900 Rancho San Diego Parkway, El Cajon, CA 92019-4304. *Phone:* 619-660-4302. *Fax:* 619-660-4575. *E-mail:* susan.topham@gcccd.edu. *Website:* http://www.cuyamaca.edu/.

Cypress College
Cypress, California

Freshman Application Contact Admissions Office, Cypress College, 9200 Valley View, Cypress, CA 90630-5897. *Phone:* 714-484-7346. *Fax:* 714-484-7446. *E-mail:* admissions@cypresscollege.edu. *Website:* http://www.cypresscollege.edu/.

De Anza College
Cupertino, California

- **District-supported** 2-year, founded 1967, part of California Community College System
- **Suburban** 112-acre campus with easy access to San Francisco, San Jose
- **Coed**

Undergraduates 9,940 full-time, 10,868 part-time. 4% Black or African American, non-Hispanic/Latino; 28% Hispanic/Latino; 46% Asian, non-Hispanic/Latino; 0.8% Native Hawaiian or other Pacific Islander, non-Hispanic/Latino; 0.5% American Indian or Alaska Native, non-Hispanic/Latino; 1% Race/ethnicity unknown.
Faculty *Student/faculty ratio:* 25:1.
Academics *Calendar:* quarters. *Degree:* certificates, diplomas, and associate. *Special study options:* academic remediation for entering students, adult/continuing education programs, distance learning, English as a second language, honors programs, independent study, internships, part-time degree program, services for LD students, student-designed majors, study abroad, summer session for credit. *ROTC:* Army (c), Air Force (c).
Library A. Robert DeHart Learning Center. Study areas open 24 hours, 5–7 days a week; students can reserve study rooms.
Student Life *Campus security:* 24-hour emergency response devices, student patrols, late-night transport/escort service.
Athletics Member NCAA. All Division II.
Freshman Application Contact De Anza College, 21250 Stevens Creek Boulevard, Cupertino, CA 95014-5793. *Phone:* 408-864-8292. *Website:* http://www.deanza.fhda.edu/.

Deep Springs College
Deep Springs, California

Freshman Application Contact Jack Davis, Chair, Applications Committee, Deep Springs College, HC 72, Box 45001, Dyer, NV 89010-9803. *Phone:* 760-872-2000. *Fax:* 760-874-0314. *E-mail:* apcom@deepsprings.edu. *Website:* http://www.deepsprings.edu/.

Diablo Valley College
Pleasant Hill, California

Freshman Application Contact Ileana Dorn, Director of Admissions and Records, Diablo Valley College, Pleasant Hill, CA 94523-1529. *Phone:* 925-685-1230 Ext. 2330. *Fax:* 925-609-8085. *E-mail:* idorn@dvc.edu. *Website:* http://www.dvc.edu/.

East Los Angeles College
Monterey Park, California

Freshman Application Contact Mr. Jeremy Allred, Associate Dean of Admissions, East Los Angeles College, 1301 Avenida Cesar Chavez, Monterey Park, CA 91754. *Phone:* 323-265-8801. *Fax:* 323-265-8688. *E-mail:* allredjp@elac.edu. *Website:* http://www.elac.edu/.

East San Gabriel Valley Regional Occupational Program & Technical Center
West Covina, California

Admissions Office Contact East San Gabriel Valley Regional Occupational Program & Technical Center, 1501 West Del Norte Avenue, West Covina, CA 91790. *Website:* http://www.esgvrop.org/.

El Camino College
Torrance, California

Director of Admissions Mr. William Mulrooney, Director of Admissions, El Camino College, 16007 Crenshaw Boulevard, Torrance, CA 90506-0001. *Phone:* 310-660-3418. *Toll-free phone:* 866-ELCAMINO. *Fax:* 310-660-6779. *E-mail:* wmulrooney@elcamino.edu. *Website:* http://www.elcamino.edu/.

Empire College
Santa Rosa, California

Freshman Application Contact Ms. Dahnja Barker, Admissions Officer, Empire College, 3035 Cleveland Avenue, Santa Rosa, CA 95403. *Phone:* 707-546-4000. *Toll-free phone:* 877-395-8535. *Website:* http://www.empcol.edu/.

Evergreen Valley College
San Jose, California

Freshman Application Contact Evergreen Valley College, 3095 Yerba Buena Road, San Jose, CA 95135-1598. *Phone:* 408-270-6423. *Website:* http://www.evc.edu/.

Feather River College
Quincy, California

- **District-supported** primarily 2-year, founded 1968, part of California Community College System
- **Rural** 420-acre campus
- **Endowment** $48,167
- **Coed**

Undergraduates Students come from 30 states and territories; 7 other countries; 8% are from out of state; 11% Black or African American, non-Hispanic/Latino; 30% Hispanic/Latino; 6% Asian, non-Hispanic/Latino; 1% Native Hawaiian or other Pacific Islander, non-Hispanic/Latino; 2% American Indian or Alaska Native, non-Hispanic/Latino; 6% Race/ethnicity unknown; 0.9% international.
Faculty *Student/faculty ratio:* 21:1.
Academics *Calendar:* semesters plus summer and winter terms. *Degrees:* certificates, diplomas, associate, and bachelor's. *Special study options:* academic remediation for entering students, adult/continuing education programs, advanced placement credit, cooperative education, distance learning, double majors, English as a second language, independent study, part-time degree program, services for LD students, summer session for credit.
Library Feather River College Library. *Books:* 24,291 (physical), 350,000 (digital/electronic); *Serial titles:* 98 (physical), 28,376 (digital/electronic); *Databases:* 35. Weekly public service hours: 61; students can reserve study rooms.
Student Life *Campus security:* student patrols, part-time private security company patrols.
Standardized Tests *Recommended:* ACCUPLACER.

Financial Aid Of all full-time matriculated undergraduates who enrolled in 2017, 22 Federal Work-Study jobs (averaging $750). 103 state and other part-time jobs (averaging $1504).
Applying *Options:* electronic application.
Freshman Application Contact Mrs. Leslie Mikesell, Director of Admissions and Records, Feather River College, 570 Golden Eagle Avenue, Quincy, CA 95971. *Phone:* 530-283-0202 Ext. 285. *Toll-free phone:* 800-442-9799. *E-mail:* info@frc.edu. *Website:* http://www.frc.edu/.

FIDM/Fashion Institute of Design & Merchandising, Orange County Campus
Irvine, California

- **Proprietary** 2-year, founded 1981, part of FIDM/Fashion Institute of Design & Merchandising
- **Urban** campus with easy access to Los Angeles
- **Coed, primarily women**

Undergraduates 67 full-time, 4 part-time. Students come from 11 states and territories; 5 other countries; 12% are from out of state; 24% transferred in.
Faculty *Student/faculty ratio:* 7:1.
Academics *Calendar:* quarters. *Degree:* associate. *Special study options:* academic remediation for entering students, accelerated degree program, adult/continuing education programs, advanced placement credit, cooperative education, distance learning, English as a second language, independent study, internships, part-time degree program, services for LD students, study abroad, summer session for credit.
Library FIDM Orange County Campus Library. Students can reserve study rooms.
Student Life *Campus security:* 24-hour emergency response devices, late-night transport/escort service, security guard escort.
Standardized Tests *Recommended:* SAT or ACT (for admission).
Applying *Options:* electronic application, deferred entrance. *Application fee:* $225. *Required:* essay or personal statement, high school transcript, minimum 2.5 GPA, 3 letters of recommendation, interview, entrance project.
Freshman Application Contact Mr. Michael Mirabella, Admissions, FIDM/Fashion Institute of Design & Merchandising, Orange County Campus, 919 So Grand Avenue, Los Angeles, CA 90015. *Phone:* 213-624-1200. *Toll-free phone:* 888-974-3436. *Website:* http://www.fidm.edu/.

FIDM/Fashion Institute of Design & Merchandising, San Diego Campus
San Diego, California

- **Proprietary** 2-year, founded 1985, part of FIDM/Fashion Institute of Design & Merchandising
- **Urban** campus with easy access to San Diego
- **Coed, primarily women**

Undergraduates 61 full-time, 5 part-time. Students come from 17 states and territories; 4 other countries; 23% are from out of state; 50% transferred in. *Retention:* 82% of full-time freshmen returned.
Faculty *Student/faculty ratio:* 5:1.
Academics *Calendar:* quarters. *Degree:* associate. *Special study options:* academic remediation for entering students, accelerated degree program, adult/continuing education programs, advanced placement credit, cooperative education, distance learning, English as a second language, independent study, internships, part-time degree program, services for LD students, study abroad, summer session for credit.
Library FIDM San Diego Campus Library. Students can reserve study rooms.
Student Life *Campus security:* 24-hour emergency response devices and patrols.
Standardized Tests *Recommended:* SAT or ACT (for admission).
Applying *Options:* electronic application, deferred entrance. *Application fee:* $225. *Required:* essay or personal statement, high school transcript, minimum 2.5 GPA, 3 letters of recommendation, interview, major-determined project.
Freshman Application Contact Ms. Denise Baca, Campus Director, FIDM/Fashion Institute of Design & Merchandising, San Diego Campus, 350 Tenth Avenue, San Diego, CA 92101. *Phone:* 619-235-2049. *Toll-free phone:* 800-243-3436. *E-mail:* dbaca@fidm.edu. *Website:* http://www.fidm.edu/.

Folsom Lake College
Folsom, California

Freshman Application Contact Admissions Office, Folsom Lake College, 10 College Parkway, Folsom, CA 95630. *Phone:* 916-608-6500. *Website:* http://www.flc.losrios.edu/.

Foothill College
Los Altos Hills, California

Freshman Application Contact Ms. Shawna Aced, Registrar, Foothill College, Admissions and Records, 12345 El Monte Road, Los Altos Hills, CA 94022. *Phone:* 650-949-7771. *E-mail:* acedshawna@hda.edu. *Website:* http://www.foothill.edu/.

Fremont College
Cerritos, California

Freshman Application Contact Natasha Dawson, Director of Admissions, Fremont College, 18000 Studebaker Road, Suite 900A, Cerritos, CA 90703. *Phone:* 562-809-5100. *Toll-free phone:* 800-373-6668. *Fax:* 562-809-5100. *E-mail:* info@fremont.edu. *Website:* http://www.fremont.edu/.

Fresno City College
Fresno, California

Freshman Application Contact Office Assistant, Fresno City College, 1101 East University Avenue, Fresno, CA 93741-0002. *Phone:* 559-442-4600 Ext. 8604. *Fax:* 559-237-4232. *E-mail:* fcc.admissions@fresnocitycollege.edu. *Website:* http://www.fresnocitycollege.edu/.

Fullerton College
Fullerton, California

- **District-supported** 2-year, founded 1913, part of California Community College System
- **Suburban** 79-acre campus with easy access to Los Angeles
- **Coed**

Undergraduates Students come from 28 states and territories; 1% are from out of state; 4% Black or African American, non-Hispanic/Latino; 57% Hispanic/Latino; 17% Asian, non-Hispanic/Latino; 0.6% American Indian or Alaska Native, non-Hispanic/Latino; 1% Race/ethnicity unknown. *Retention:* 61% of full-time freshmen returned.
Faculty *Student/faculty ratio:* 26:1.
Academics *Calendar:* semesters. *Degree:* certificates and associate. *Special study options:* academic remediation for entering students, adult/continuing education programs, advanced placement credit, cooperative education, English as a second language, honors programs, part-time degree program, services for LD students, study abroad, summer session for credit. *ROTC:* Army (c), Navy (c), Air Force (c).
Library William T. Boyce Library.
Financial Aid ***Financial aid deadline:*** 6/30.
Applying *Options:* electronic application, early admission.
Freshman Application Contact Fullerton College, 321 East Chapman Avenue, Fullerton, CA 92832-2095. *Phone:* 714-992-7076. *Website:* http://www.fullcoll.edu/.

Gavilan College
Gilroy, California

Freshman Application Contact Gavilan College, 5055 Santa Teresa Boulevard, Gilroy, CA 95020-9599. *Phone:* 408-848-4754. *Website:* http://www.gavilan.edu/.

Glendale Career College
Glendale, California

Admissions Office Contact Glendale Career College, 240 North Brand Boulevard, Lower Level, Glendale, CA 91203. *Website:* http://www.glendalecareer.com/.

Glendale Community College
Glendale, California

Freshman Application Contact Ms. Sharon Combs, Dean, Admissions, and Records, Glendale Community College, 1500 North Verdugo Road, Glendale, CA 91208. *Phone:* 818-240-1000 Ext. 5910. *E-mail:* scombs@glendale.edu. *Website:* http://www.glendale.edu/.

Golden West College
Huntington Beach, California

Freshman Application Contact Golden West College, PO Box 2748, 15744 Golden West Street, Huntington Beach, CA 92647-2748. *Phone:* 714-892-7711 Ext. 58965. *Website:* http://www.goldenwestcollege.edu/.

Grossmont College
El Cajon, California

Freshman Application Contact Admissions Office, Grossmont College, 8800 Grossmont College Drive, El Cajon, CA 92020-1799. *Phone:* 619-644-7186. *Website:* http://www.grossmont.edu/.

Gurnick Academy of Medical Arts
San Mateo, California

- **Proprietary** primarily 2-year
- **Coed**

Academics *Degrees:* certificates, diplomas, associate, and bachelor's.
Freshman Application Contact Gurnick Academy of Medical Arts, 2121 South El Camino Real, Building C 2000, San Mateo, CA 94403. *Website:* http://www.gurnick.edu/.

Hartnell College
Salinas, California

Director of Admissions Director of Admissions, Hartnell College, 411 Central Avenue, Salinas, CA 93901. *Phone:* 831-755-6711. *Fax:* 831-759-6014. *Website:* http://www.hartnell.edu/.

Healthcare Career College
Paramount, California

Admissions Office Contact Healthcare Career College, 8527 Alondra Boulevard, #174, Paramount, CA 90723. *Website:* http://www.healthcarecareercollege.edu/.

Imperial Valley College
Imperial, California

Freshman Application Contact Imperial Valley College, 380 East Aten Road, PO Box 158, Imperial, CA 92251-0158. *Phone:* 760-355-6244. *Website:* http://www.imperial.edu/.

Institute of Technology
Clovis, California

Admissions Office Contact Institute of Technology, 564 West Herndon Avenue, Clovis, CA 93612. *Website:* http://www.iot.edu/.

International Sports Sciences Association
Carpinteria, California

Admissions Office Contact International Sports Sciences Association, 1015 Mark Avenue, Carpinteria, CA 93013. *Website:* http://www.college.issaonline.edu/.

Irvine Valley College
Irvine, California

Director of Admissions Mr. John Edwards, Director of Admissions, Records, and Enrollment Services, Irvine Valley College, 5500 Irvine Center Drive, Irvine, CA 92618. *Phone:* 949-451-5416. *Website:* http://www.ivc.edu/.

Lake Tahoe Community College
South Lake Tahoe, California

Freshman Application Contact Office of Admissions and Records, Lake Tahoe Community College, One College Drive, South Lake Tahoe, CA 96150. *Phone:* 530-541-4660 Ext. 211. *Fax:* 530-541-7852. *E-mail:* admissions@ltcc.edu. *Website:* http://www.ltcc.edu/.

Laney College
Oakland, California

Freshman Application Contact Mrs. Barbara Simmons, District Admissions Officer, Laney College, 900 Fallon Street, Oakland, CA 94607-4893. *Phone:* 510-466-7369. *Website:* http://www.laney.edu/.

Las Positas College
Livermore, California

Director of Admissions Mrs. Sylvia R. Rodriguez, Director of Admissions and Records, Las Positas College, 3000 Campus Hill Drive, Livermore, CA 94551. *Phone:* 925-373-4942. *Website:* http://www.laspositascollege.edu/.

Lassen Community College
Susanville, California

Freshman Application Contact Mr. Chris J. Alberico, Registrar, Lassen Community College, Highway 139, PO Box 3000, Susanville, CA 96130. *Phone:* 530-257-6181. *Website:* http://www.lassencollege.edu/.

Laurus College
San Luis Obispo, California

Admissions Office Contact Laurus College, 81 Higuera Street, Suite 110, San Luis Obispo, CA 93401. *Website:* http://www.lauruscollege.edu/.

Learnet Academy
Los Angeles, California

Admissions Office Contact Learnet Academy, 3251 West 6th Street, 2nd Floor, Los Angeles, CA 90020. *Website:* http://www.learnet.edu/.

Long Beach City College
Long Beach, California

Director of Admissions Mr. Ross Miyashiro, Dean of Admissions and Records, Long Beach City College, 4901 East Carson Street, Long Beach, CA 90808-1780. *Phone:* 562-938-4130. *Website:* http://www.lbcc.edu/.

Los Angeles City College
Los Angeles, California

- **District-supported** 2-year, founded 1929, part of Los Angeles Community College District (LACCD)
- **Urban** 42-acre campus
- **Coed**

Undergraduates 4,671 full-time, 11,885 part-time. 9% Black or African American, non-Hispanic/Latino; 50% Hispanic/Latino; 15% Asian, non-Hispanic/Latino; 2% American Indian or Alaska Native, non-Hispanic/Latino; 3% Race/ethnicity unknown; 4% international; 6% transferred in.
Academics *Calendar:* semesters. *Degree:* certificates, diplomas, and associate. *Special study options:* academic remediation for entering students, accelerated degree program, adult/continuing education programs, advanced placement credit, cooperative education, distance learning, double majors, English as a second language, freshman honors college, honors programs, internships, part-time degree program, services for LD students, study abroad, summer session for credit. *ROTC:* Army (c), Navy (c), Air Force (c).
Library Martin Luther King Jr. Library. *Books:* 155,954 (physical), 195,000 (digital/electronic); *Serial titles:* 87 (physical); *Databases:* 60. Weekly public service hours: 77; students can reserve study rooms.
Student Life *Campus security:* 24-hour emergency response devices and patrols, student patrols, late-night transport/escort service.
Applying *Options:* electronic application. *Recommended:* high school transcript.
Freshman Application Contact Dr. Terri Anderson, Office of Outreach and Recruitment, Los Angeles City College, 855 N. Vermont Avenue, Los Angeles, CA 90029. *Phone:* 323-953-4000 Ext. 2598. *E-mail:* anderst@lacitycollege.edu. *Website:* http://www.lacitycollege.edu/.

Los Angeles County College of Nursing and Allied Health
Los Angeles, California

Freshman Application Contact Admissions Office, Los Angeles County College of Nursing and Allied Health, 1237 North Mission Road, Los Angeles, CA 90033. *Phone:* 323-226-4911. *Website:* http://www.dhs.lacounty.gov/wps/portal/dhs/conah/.

Los Angeles Harbor College

Wilmington, California

Freshman Application Contact Los Angeles Harbor College, 1111 Figueroa Place, Wilmington, CA 90744-2397. *Phone:* 310-233-4091. *Website:* http://www.lahc.edu/.

Los Angeles Mission College

Sylmar, California

Freshman Application Contact Los Angeles Mission College, 13356 Eldridge Avenue, Sylmar, CA 91342-3245. *Website:* http://www.lamission.edu/.

Los Angeles ORT College–Los Angeles

Los Angeles, California

Admissions Office Contact Los Angeles ORT College–Los Angeles, 6435 Wilshire Boulevard, Los Angeles, CA 90048. *Website:* http://www.laort.edu/.

Los Angeles Pierce College

Woodland Hills, California

Director of Admissions Ms. Shelley L. Gerstl, Dean of Admissions and Records, Los Angeles Pierce College, 6201 Winnetka Avenue, Woodland Hills, CA 91371-0001. *Phone:* 818-719-6448. *Website:* http://www.piercecollege.edu/.

Los Angeles Southwest College

Los Angeles, California

Director of Admissions Dan W. Walden, Dean of Academic Affairs, Los Angeles Southwest College, 1600 West Imperial Highway, Los Angeles, CA 90047-4810. *Phone:* 323-242-5511. *Website:* http://www.lasc.edu/.

Los Angeles Trade-Technical College

Los Angeles, California

Freshman Application Contact Los Angeles Trade-Technical College, 400 West Washington Boulevard, Los Angeles, CA 90015-4108. *Phone:* 213-763-7127. *Website:* http://www.lattc.edu/.

Los Angeles Valley College

Valley Glen, California

Freshman Application Contact Los Angeles Valley College, 5800 Fulton Avenue, Valley Glen, CA 91401. *Phone:* 818-947-5518. *Website:* http://www.lavc.edu/.

Los Medanos College

Pittsburg, California

Freshman Application Contact Ms. Gail Newman, Director of Admissions and Records, Los Medanos College, 2700 East Leland Road, Pittsburg, CA 94565-5197. *Phone:* 925-439-2181 Ext. 7500. *Website:* http://www.losmedanos.net/.

Mendocino College

Ukiah, California

Freshman Application Contact Mendocino College, 1000 Hensley Creek Road, Ukiah, CA 95482-0300. *Phone:* 707-468-3103. *Website:* http://www.mendocino.edu/.

Merced College

Merced, California

- **District-supported** 2-year, founded 1962, part of California Community College System
- **Small-town** 653-acre campus
- **Endowment** $3.2 million
- **Coed**

Undergraduates 2% are from out of state.
Faculty *Student/faculty ratio:* 26:1.
Academics *Calendar:* semesters. *Degree:* certificates and associate. *Special study options:* academic remediation for entering students, accelerated degree program, adult/continuing education programs, advanced placement credit, cooperative education, distance learning, double majors, English as a second language, honors programs, independent study, off-campus study, part-time degree program, services for LD students, student-designed majors, summer session for credit.
Library Lesher Library plus 1 other. *Databases:* 76. Weekly public service hours: 56; students can reserve study rooms.
Student Life *Campus security:* 24-hour patrols.
Athletics Member NAIA.
Financial Aid Of all full-time matriculated undergraduates who enrolled in 2014, 319 Federal Work-Study jobs (averaging $3456). 131 state and other part-time jobs (averaging $3456). *Financial aid deadline:* 7/15.
Applying *Options:* electronic application, early admission. *Recommended:* high school transcript.
Admissions Office Contact Merced College, 3600 M Street, Merced, CA 95348-2898. *Website:* http://www.mccd.edu/.

Merritt College

Oakland, California

Freshman Application Contact Ms. Barbara Simmons, District Admissions Officer, Merritt College, 12500 Campus Drive, Oakland, CA 94619-3196. *Phone:* 510-466-7369. *E-mail:* hperdue@peralta.cc.ca.us. *Website:* http://www.merritt.edu/.

MiraCosta College

Oceanside, California

Freshman Application Contact Jane Sparks, Interim Director of Admissions and Records, MiraCosta College, One Barnard Drive, Oceanside, CA 92057. *Phone:* 760-795-6620. *Toll-free phone:* 888-201-8480. *E-mail:* admissions@miracosta.edu. *Website:* http://www.miracosta.edu/.

Mission College

Santa Clara, California

- **District-supported** 2-year, founded 1977, part of California Community College System
- **Urban** 167-acre campus with easy access to San Francisco, San Jose
- **Endowment** $6.8 million
- **Coed**

Undergraduates Students come from 18 other countries; 0.3% are from out of state. *Retention:* 77% of full-time freshmen returned.
Faculty *Student/faculty ratio:* 22:1.
Academics *Calendar:* semesters. *Degree:* certificates, diplomas, and associate. *Special study options:* academic remediation for entering students, adult/continuing education programs, advanced placement credit, cooperative education, distance learning, double majors, English as a second language, honors programs, independent study, internships, part-time degree program, services for LD students, summer session for credit. *ROTC:* Army (c), Air Force (c).
Library Mission College Library. *Books:* 65,071 (physical); *Serial titles:* 19,025 (digital/electronic); *Databases:* 59. Weekly public service hours: 55; students can reserve study rooms.
Student Life *Campus security:* 24-hour emergency response devices, late-night transport/escort service, district police department, evening administrators.
Applying *Options:* electronic application.
Admissions Office Contact Mission College, 3000 Mission College Boulevard, Santa Clara, CA 95054-1897. *Website:* http://www.missioncollege.edu/.

Modesto Junior College

Modesto, California

Freshman Application Contact Ms. Martha Robles, Dean of Student Services and Support, Modesto Junior College, 435 College Avenue, Modesto, CA 95350. *Phone:* 209-575-6470. *Fax:* 209-575-6859. *E-mail:* mjcadmissions@mail.yosemite.cc.ca.us. *Website:* http://www.mjc.edu/.

Monterey Peninsula College

Monterey, California

Director of Admissions Ms. Vera Coleman, Registrar, Monterey Peninsula College, 980 Fremont Street, Monterey, CA 93940-4799. *Phone:* 831-646-4007. *E-mail:* vcoleman@mpc.edu. *Website:* http://www.mpc.edu/.

Moorpark College
Moorpark, California

Freshman Application Contact Ms. Katherine Colborn, Registrar, Moorpark College, 7075 Campus Road, Moorpark, CA 93021-2899. *Phone:* 805-378-1415. *Website:* http://www.moorparkcollege.edu/.

Moreno Valley College
Moreno Valley, California

Freshman Application Contact Jamie Clifton, Director, Enrollment Services, Moreno Valley College, 16130 Lasselle Street, Moreno Valley, CA 92551. *Phone:* 951-571-6293. *E-mail:* admissions@mvc.edu. *Website:* http://www.mvc.edu/.

Mt. San Antonio College
Walnut, California

- **District-supported** 2-year, founded 1946, part of California Community College System
- **Suburban** 421-acre campus with easy access to Los Angeles
- **Coed**

Undergraduates 2,581 full-time, 1,987 part-time. 4% Black or African American, non-Hispanic/Latino; 63% Hispanic/Latino; 17% Asian, non-Hispanic/Latino; 0.3% Native Hawaiian or other Pacific Islander, non-Hispanic/Latino; 0.1% American Indian or Alaska Native, non-Hispanic/Latino; 3% Two or more races, non-Hispanic/Latino; 0.4% Race/ethnicity unknown; 2% international. *Retention:* 79% of full-time freshmen returned.
Faculty *Student/faculty ratio:* 24:1.
Academics *Calendar:* semesters. *Degree:* certificates, diplomas, and associate. *Special study options:* academic remediation for entering students, adult/continuing education programs, advanced placement credit, cooperative education, distance learning, double majors, English as a second language, honors programs, independent study, part-time degree program, services for LD students, study abroad, summer session for credit. *ROTC:* Army (b), Air Force (b).
Library Learning Resources Center. *Books:* 75,587 (physical), 82,336 (digital/electronic); *Databases:* 113. Students can reserve study rooms.
Student Life *Campus security:* 24-hour emergency response devices and patrols, late-night transport/escort service.
Applying *Options:* electronic application, early admission, deferred entrance. *Required for some:* high school transcript.
Admissions Office Contact Mt. San Antonio College, 1100 North Grand Avenue, Walnut, CA 91789-1399. *Website:* http://www.mtsac.edu/.

Mt. San Jacinto College
San Jacinto, California

Freshman Application Contact Mt. San Jacinto College, 1499 North State Street, San Jacinto, CA 92583-2399. *Phone:* 951-639-5212. *Website:* http://www.msjc.edu/.

MTI College
Sacramento, California

Freshman Application Contact Director of Admissions, MTI College, 5221 Madison Avenue, Sacramento, CA 95841. *Phone:* 916-339-1500. *Fax:* 916-339-0305. *Website:* http://www.mticollege.edu/.

Napa Valley College
Napa, California

Director of Admissions Mr. Oscar De Haro, Vice President of Student Services, Napa Valley College, 2277 Napa-Vallejo Highway, Napa, CA 94558-6236. *Phone:* 707-253-3000. *Toll-free phone:* 800-826-1077. *E-mail:* odeharo@napavalley.edu. *Website:* http://www.napavalley.edu/.

National Career College
Panorama City, California

Admissions Office Contact National Career College, 14355 Roscoe Boulevard, Panorama City, CA 91402. *Website:* http://www.nccusa.edu/.

National Polytechnic College
Commerce, California

Admissions Office Contact National Polytechnic College, 6630 Telegraph Road, Commerce, CA 90040. *Website:* http://www.npcollege.edu/.

Norco College
Norco, California

Freshman Application Contact Mark DeAsis, Director, Enrollment Services, Norco College, 2001 Third Street, Norco, CA 92860. *E-mail:* admissionsnorco@norcocollege.edu. *Website:* http://www.norcocollege.edu/.

North-West College
West Covina, California

Admissions Office Contact North-West College, 2121 West Garvey Avenue, West Covina, CA 91790. *Toll-free phone:* 888-408-4211. *Website:* http://www.nw.edu/.

Ohlone College
Fremont, California

Freshman Application Contact Ohlone College, 43600 Mission Boulevard, Fremont, CA 94539-5884. *Phone:* 510-659-6107. *Website:* http://www.ohlone.edu/.

Orange Coast College
Costa Mesa, California

- **District-supported** 2-year, founded 1947, part of Coast Community College District System
- **Suburban** 164-acre campus with easy access to Los Angeles
- **Endowment** $18.2 million
- **Coed**

Undergraduates 8,561 full-time, 13,170 part-time. Students come from 75 other countries; 2% are from out of state; 2% Black or African American, non-Hispanic/Latino; 34% Hispanic/Latino; 20% Asian, non-Hispanic/Latino; 0.2% American Indian or Alaska Native, non-Hispanic/Latino; 4% Two or more races, non-Hispanic/Latino; 1% Race/ethnicity unknown; 5% international; 10% transferred in.
Faculty *Student/faculty ratio:* 32:1.
Academics *Calendar:* semesters plus summer session. *Degree:* certificates and associate. *Special study options:* academic remediation for entering students, adult/continuing education programs, advanced placement credit, cooperative education, distance learning, double majors, English as a second language, external degree program, freshman honors college, honors programs, internships, off-campus study, part-time degree program, services for LD students, student-designed majors, study abroad, summer session for credit. *ROTC:* Army (c), Air Force (c).
Library Main Library plus 1 other. *Books:* 108,078 (physical), 24,666 (digital/electronic); *Serial titles:* 91 (physical), 4 (digital/electronic); *Databases:* 59. Weekly public service hours: 64; students can reserve study rooms.
Student Life *Campus security:* 24-hour emergency response devices and patrols, student patrols, late-night transport/escort service.
Financial Aid Of all full-time matriculated undergraduates who enrolled in 2017, 108 Federal Work-Study jobs (averaging $3000). *Financial aid deadline:* 5/28.
Applying *Options:* electronic application.
Admissions Office Contact Orange Coast College, 2701 Fairview Road, Costa Mesa, CA 92626. *Website:* http://www.orangecoastcollege.edu/.

Oxnard College
Oxnard, California

Freshman Application Contact Mr. Joel Diaz, Registrar, Oxnard College, 4000 South Rose Avenue, Oxnard, CA 93033-6699. *Phone:* 805-986-5843. *Fax:* 805-986-5943. *E-mail:* jdiaz@vcccd.edu. *Website:* http://www.oxnardcollege.edu/.

Palomar College
San Marcos, California

- **District-supported** 2-year, founded 1946, part of California Community College System
- **Suburban** 156-acre campus with easy access to San Diego
- **Coed**

Undergraduates 25,244 full-time.
Faculty *Student/faculty ratio:* 21:1.
Academics *Calendar:* semesters. *Degree:* certificates and associate. *Special study options:* academic remediation for entering students, advanced placement credit, cooperative education, distance learning, English as a second language, internships, part-time degree program, services for LD students, summer session for credit. *ROTC:* Air Force (c).
Library Palomar College Library plus 1 other. *Books:* 100,000 (physical); *Serial titles:* 689 (physical). Weekly public service hours: 64.
Student Life *Campus security:* 24-hour emergency response devices and patrols, late-night transport/escort service.
Applying *Options:* electronic application.
Freshman Application Contact Dr. Kendyl Magnuson, Senior Director of Enrollment Services, Palomar College, 1140 W Mission Road, San Marcos, CA 92069. *Phone:* 760-744-1150 Ext. 2171. *Fax:* 760-744-2932. *E-mail:* kmagnuson@palomar.edu. *Website:* http://www.palomar.edu/.

Palo Verde College
Blythe, California

Freshman Application Contact Diana Rodriguez, Vice President of Student Services, Palo Verde College, 1 College Drive, Blythe, CA 92225. *Phone:* 760-921-5428. *Fax:* 760-921-3608. *E-mail:* diana.rodriguez@paloverde.edu. *Website:* http://www.paloverde.edu/.

Pasadena City College
Pasadena, California

- **District-supported** 2-year, founded 1924, part of California Community College System
- **Urban** 55-acre campus with easy access to Los Angeles
- **Coed**

Undergraduates 10,422 full-time, 16,902 part-time. Students come from 28 states and territories; 20 other countries; 2% are from out of state; 4% Black or African American, non-Hispanic/Latino; 51% Hispanic/Latino; 23% Asian, non-Hispanic/Latino; 0.1% Native Hawaiian or other Pacific Islander, non-Hispanic/Latino; 0.1% American Indian or Alaska Native, non-Hispanic/Latino; 3% Two or more races, non-Hispanic/Latino; 0.9% Race/ethnicity unknown; 3% international; 92% transferred in. *Retention:* 74% of full-time freshmen returned.
Faculty *Student/faculty ratio:* 25:1.
Academics *Calendar:* semesters. *Degree:* certificates, diplomas, and associate. *Special study options:* academic remediation for entering students, adult/continuing education programs, advanced placement credit, distance learning, double majors, English as a second language, honors programs, independent study, internships, part-time degree program, services for LD students, study abroad, summer session for credit.
Library Pasadena City College Library plus 1 other. *Books:* 133,975 (physical), 35,619 (digital/electronic); *Databases:* 56. Weekly public service hours: 54; students can reserve study rooms.
Student Life *Campus security:* 24-hour emergency response devices and patrols, late-night transport/escort service, cadet patrols.
Applying *Options:* electronic application.
Admissions Office Contact Pasadena City College, 1570 East Colorado Boulevard, Pasadena, CA 91106-2041. *Website:* http://www.pasadena.edu/.

PCI College
Cerritos, California

Admissions Office Contact PCI College, 17215 Studebaker Road #310, Cerritos, CA 90703. *Website:* http://www.pci-ed.com/.

Pima Medical Institute
Chula Vista, California

Freshman Application Contact Admissions Office, Pima Medical Institute, 780 Bay Boulevard, Chula Vista, CA 91910. *Phone:* 619-425-3200. *Toll-free phone:* 800-477-PIMA. *Website:* http://www.pmi.edu/.

Platt College
Alhambra, California

Director of Admissions Mr. Detroit Whiteside, Director of Admissions, Platt College, 1000 South Fremont A9W, Alhambra, CA 91803. *Phone:* 323-258-8050. *Toll-free phone:* 888-866-6697 (in-state); 888-80-PLATT (out-of-state). *Website:* http://www.plattcollege.edu/.

Platt College
Anaheim, California

Admissions Office Contact Platt College, 1551 South Douglass Road, Anaheim, CA 92806. *Website:* http://www.plattcollege.edu/.

Platt College
Ontario, California

Director of Admissions Ms. Jennifer Abandonato, Director of Admissions, Platt College, 3700 Inland Empire Boulevard, Ontario, CA 91764. *Phone:* 909-941-9410. *Toll-free phone:* 888-80-PLATT. *Website:* http://www.plattcollege.edu/.

Porterville College
Porterville, California

Director of Admissions Ms. Judy Pope, Director of Admissions and Records/Registrar, Porterville College, 100 East College Avenue, Porterville, CA 93257-6058. *Phone:* 559-791-2222. *Website:* http://www.portervillecollege.edu/.

Professional Golfers Career College
Temecula, California

Freshman Application Contact Mr. Gary Gilleon, Professional Golfers Career College, 26109 Ynez Road, Temecula, CA 92591. *Phone:* 951-719-2994 Ext. 1021. *Toll-free phone:* 800-877-4380. *Fax:* 951-719-1643. *E-mail:* garygilleon@golfcollege.edu. *Website:* http://www.golfcollege.edu/.

Reedley College
Reedley, California

Freshman Application Contact Admissions and Records Office, Reedley College, 995 North Reed Avenue, Reedley, CA 93654. *Phone:* 559-638-0323. *Fax:* 559-637-2523. *Website:* http://www.reedleycollege.edu/.

Rio Hondo College
Whittier, California

- **District-supported** 2-year, founded 1960, part of California Community College System
- **Suburban** 128-acre campus with easy access to Los Angeles
- **Coed**

Undergraduates Students come from 5 states and territories; 0.2% are from out of state; 2% Black or African American, non-Hispanic/Latino; 77% Hispanic/Latino; 6% Asian, non-Hispanic/Latino; 0.1% Native Hawaiian or other Pacific Islander, non-Hispanic/Latino; 0.2% American Indian or Alaska Native, non-Hispanic/Latino; 0.9% Two or more races, non-Hispanic/Latino; 5% Race/ethnicity unknown; 0.3% international.
Faculty *Student/faculty ratio:* 34:1.
Academics *Calendar:* semesters. *Degree:* certificates and associate. *Special study options:* academic remediation for entering students, adult/continuing education programs, advanced placement credit, distance learning, English as a second language, honors programs, part-time degree program, services for LD students, study abroad, summer session for credit. *ROTC:* Army (c), Navy (c), Air Force (c).
Library Library and Learning Resource Center plus 1 other. *Books:* 88,245 (physical); *Serial titles:* 104 (physical); *Databases:* 12. Weekly public service hours: 68; students can reserve study rooms.
Student Life *Campus security:* 24-hour patrols, late-night transport/escort service.
Financial Aid Of all full-time matriculated undergraduates who enrolled in 2017, 150 Federal Work-Study jobs (averaging $3200). 35 state and other part-time jobs (averaging $3200). *Financial aid deadline:* 5/1.
Freshman Application Contact Rio Hondo College, 3600 Workman Mill Road, Whittier, CA 90601-1699. *Phone:* 562-692-0921 Ext. 3415. *Website:* http://www.riohondo.edu/.

Riverside City College
Riverside, California

Freshman Application Contact Joy Chambers, Dean of Enrollment Services, Riverside City College, Riverside, CA 92506. *Phone:* 951-222-8600. *Fax:* 951-222-8037. *E-mail:* admissionsriverside@rcc.edu. *Website:* http://www.rcc.edu/.

Sacramento City College
Sacramento, California

Director of Admissions Mr. Sam T. Sandusky, Dean, Student Services, Sacramento City College, 3835 Freeport Boulevard, Sacramento, CA 95822-1386. *Phone:* 916-558-2438. *Website:* http://www.scc.losrios.edu/.

Saddleback College
Mission Viejo, California

Freshman Application Contact Admissions Office, Saddleback College, 28000 Marguerite Parkway, Mission Viejo, CA 92692. *Phone:* 949-582-4555. *Fax:* 949-347-8315. *E-mail:* earaiza@saddleback.edu. *Website:* http://www.saddleback.edu/.

The Salvation Army College for Officer Training at Crestmont
Rancho Palos Verdes, California

- **Independent Salvation Army** 2-year, founded 1921
- **Suburban** 44-acre campus with easy access to Los Angeles
- **Coed**

Undergraduates 59 full-time. Students come from 14 states and territories; 67% are from out of state; 7% Black or African American, non-Hispanic/Latino; 20% Hispanic/Latino; 5% Asian, non-Hispanic/Latino; 2% Native Hawaiian or other Pacific Islander, non-Hispanic/Latino; 8% Two or more races, non-Hispanic/Latino; 100% live on campus. *Retention:* 98% of full-time freshmen returned.

Faculty *Student/faculty ratio:* 3:1.

Academics *Calendar:* quarters. *Degree:* associate. *Special study options:* academic remediation for entering students, accelerated degree program, cooperative education, distance learning, English as a second language, external degree program, independent study, internships, off-campus study, student-designed majors.

Library The Salvation Army Elfman Memorial Library plus 1 other. *Books:* 45,000 (physical).

Student Life *Campus security:* 24-hour emergency response devices and patrols.

Applying *Application fee:* $15. *Required:* essay or personal statement, high school transcript, 2 letters of recommendation, interview.

Freshman Application Contact Capt. Brian Jones, Director of Curriculum, The Salvation Army College for Officer Training at Crestmont, 30840 Hawthorne Boulevard, Rancho Palos Verdes, CA 90275. *Phone:* 310-544-6442. *Fax:* 310-265-6520. *Website:* http://www.crestmont.edu/.

San Bernardino Valley College
San Bernardino, California

Director of Admissions Ms. Helena Johnson, Director of Admissions and Records, San Bernardino Valley College, 701 South Mount Vernon Avenue, San Bernardino, CA 92410-2748. *Phone:* 909-384-4401. *Website:* http://www.valleycollege.edu/.

San Diego City College
San Diego, California

Freshman Application Contact Ms. Lou Humphries, Registrar/Supervisor of Admissions, Records, Evaluations and Veterans, San Diego City College, 1313 Park Boulevard, San Diego, CA 92101-4787. *Phone:* 619-388-3474. *Fax:* 619-388-3505. *E-mail:* lhumphri@sdccd.edu. *Website:* http://www.sdcity.edu/.

San Diego Mesa College
San Diego, California

Freshman Application Contact Ms. Cheri Sawyer, Admissions Supervisor, San Diego Mesa College, 7250 Mesa College Drive, San Diego, CA 92111. *Phone:* 619-388-2686. *Fax:* 619-388-2960. *E-mail:* csawyer@sdccd.edu. *Website:* http://www.sdmesa.edu/.

San Diego Miramar College
San Diego, California

Freshman Application Contact Ms. Dana Stack, Admissions Supervisor, San Diego Miramar College, 10440 Black Mountain Road, San Diego, CA 92126-2999. *Phone:* 619-536-7854. *E-mail:* dstack@sdccd.edu. *Website:* http://www.sdmiramar.edu/.

San Joaquin Delta College
Stockton, California

- **District-supported** 2-year, founded 1935, part of California Community College System
- **Urban** 165-acre campus with easy access to Sacramento
- **Coed**

Undergraduates Students come from 20 states and territories; 0.2% are from out of state; 13% Black or African American, non-Hispanic/Latino; 44% Hispanic/Latino; 17% Asian, non-Hispanic/Latino; 0.5% Native Hawaiian or other Pacific Islander, non-Hispanic/Latino; 0.3% American Indian or Alaska Native, non-Hispanic/Latino; 5% Two or more races, non-Hispanic/Latino; 0.5% Race/ethnicity unknown; 0.3% international. *Retention:* 77% of full-time freshmen returned.

Faculty *Student/faculty ratio:* 27:1.

Academics *Calendar:* semesters. *Degree:* certificates and associate. *Special study options:* academic remediation for entering students, adult/continuing education programs, advanced placement credit, cooperative education, distance learning, English as a second language, honors programs, independent study, part-time degree program, services for LD students, summer session for credit.

Library Goleman Library plus 1 other.

Student Life *Campus security:* 24-hour emergency response devices and patrols, late-night transport/escort service.

Athletics Member NJCAA.

Financial Aid Of all full-time matriculated undergraduates who enrolled in 2017, 10,605 applied for aid, 9,514 were judged to have need, 37 had their need fully met. 162 Federal Work-Study jobs (averaging $3450). In 2017, 4. *Average percent of need met:* 31. *Average financial aid package:* $5872. *Average need-based loan:* $2548. *Average need-based gift aid:* $5647. *Average non-need-based aid:* $235. *Average indebtedness upon graduation:* $11,340.

Applying *Options:* electronic application, early admission.

Freshman Application Contact Ms. Karen Sea, Registrar, San Joaquin Delta College, 5151 Pacific Avenue, Stockton, CA 95207. *Phone:* 209-954-6127. *E-mail:* ksea@deltacollege.edu. *Website:* http://www.deltacollege.edu/.

San Joaquin Valley College
Bakersfield, California

Freshman Application Contact Enrollment Services Director, San Joaquin Valley College, 201 New Stine Road, Bakersfield, CA 93309. *Phone:* 661-834-0126. *Toll-free phone:* 866-544-7898. *Fax:* 661-834-8124. *E-mail:* admissions@sjvc.edu. *Website:* http://www.sjvc.edu/campuses/central-california/bakersfield.

San Joaquin Valley College
Fresno, California

Freshman Application Contact Enrollment Services Director, San Joaquin Valley College, 295 East Sierra Avenue, Fresno, CA 93710. *Phone:* 559-448-8282. *Toll-free phone:* 866-544-7898. *Fax:* 559-448-8250. *E-mail:* admissions@sjvc.edu. *Website:* http://www.sjvc.edu/campuses/central-california/fresno/.

San Joaquin Valley College
Hanford, California

Freshman Application Contact San Joaquin Valley College, 215 West 7th Street, Hanford, CA 93230. *Toll-free phone:* 866-544-7898. *Website:* http://www.sjvc.edu/campuses/central-california/hanford/.

San Joaquin Valley College
Hesperia, California

Freshman Application Contact San Joaquin Valley College, 9331 Mariposa Road, Hesperia, CA 92344. *Toll-free phone:* 866-544-7898. *Website:* http://www.sjvc.edu/campuses/southern-california/victor-valley/.

San Joaquin Valley College

Lancaster, California

Freshman Application Contact San Joaquin Valley College, 42135 10th Street West, Suite 147, Lancaster, CA 93534. *Toll-free phone:* 866-544-7898. *Website:* http://www.sjvc.edu/campuses/southern-california/antelope-valley/.

San Joaquin Valley College

Ontario, California

Freshman Application Contact Enrollment Services Director, San Joaquin Valley College, 4580 Ontario Mills Parkway, Ontario, CA 91764. *Phone:* 909-948-7582. *Toll-free phone:* 866-544-7898. *Fax:* 909-948-3860. *E-mail:* admissions@sjvc.edu. *Website:* http://www.sjvc.edu/campuses/southern-california/ontario/.

San Joaquin Valley College

Rancho Cordova, California

Freshman Application Contact Enrollment Services Director, San Joaquin Valley College, 11050 Olson Drive, Suite 210, Rancho Cordova, CA 95670. *Phone:* 916-638-7582. *Toll-free phone:* 866-544-7898. *Fax:* 916-638-7553. *E-mail:* admissions@sjvc.edu. *Website:* http://www.sjvc.edu/campuses/northern-california/rancho-cordova/.

San Joaquin Valley College

Salida, California

Freshman Application Contact Enrollment Services Director, San Joaquin Valley College, 5380 Pirrone Road, Salida, CA 95368. *Phone:* 209-543-8800. *Toll-free phone:* 866-544-7898. *Fax:* 209-543-8320. *E-mail:* admissions@sjvc.edu. *Website:* http://www.sjvc.edu/campuses/northern-california/modesto/.

San Joaquin Valley College

Temecula, California

Freshman Application Contact Ms. Robyn Whiles, Enrollment Services Director, San Joaquin Valley College, 27270 Madison Avenue, Suite 103, Temecula, CA 92590. *Phone:* 559-651-2500. *Toll-free phone:* 866-544-7898. *E-mail:* admissions@sjvc.edu. *Website:* http://www.sjvc.edu/campuses/southern-california/temecula/.

San Joaquin Valley College

Visalia, California

Freshman Application Contact Susie Topjian, Enrollment Services Director, San Joaquin Valley College, 8400 West Mineral King Boulevard, Visalia, CA 93291. *Phone:* 559-651-2500. *Toll-free phone:* 866-544-7898. *Fax:* 559-734-9048. *E-mail:* admissions@sjvc.edu. *Website:* http://www.sjvc.edu/campuses/central-california/visalia/.

San Joaquin Valley College–Fresno Aviation Campus

Fresno, California

Freshman Application Contact Enrollment Services Coordinator, San Joaquin Valley College–Fresno Aviation Campus, 4985 East Anderson Avenue, Fresno, CA 93727. *Phone:* 559-453-0123. *Toll-free phone:* 866-544-7898. *Fax:* 599-453-0133. *E-mail:* admissions@sjvc.edu. *Website:* http://www.sjvc.edu/campuses/central-california/fresno-aviation/.

San Joaquin Valley College–Online

Visalia, California

Freshman Application Contact Enrollment Services Director, San Joaquin Valley College–Online, 8344 West Mineral King Avenue, Visalia, CA 93291. *Toll-free phone:* 866-544-7898. *E-mail:* admissions@sjvc.edu. *Website:* http://www.sjvc.edu/online-programs/.

San Jose City College

San Jose, California

Freshman Application Contact Mr. Carlo Santos, Director of Admissions/Registrar, San Jose City College, 2100 Moorpark Avenue, San Jose, CA 95128-2799. *Phone:* 408-288-3707. *Fax:* 408-298-1935. *Website:* http://www.sjcc.edu/.

Santa Ana College

Santa Ana, California

Freshman Application Contact Mrs. Christie Steward, Admissions Clerk, Santa Ana College, 1530 West 17th Street, Santa Ana, CA 92706-3398. *Phone:* 714-564-6053. *Website:* http://www.sac.edu/.

Santa Barbara Business College

Bakersfield, California

Admissions Office Contact Santa Barbara Business College, 5300 California Avenue, Bakersfield, CA 93309. *Website:* http://www.sbbcollege.edu/.

Santa Barbara Business College

Santa Maria, California

Admissions Office Contact Santa Barbara Business College, 303 East Plaza Drive, Santa Maria, CA 93454. *Website:* http://www.sbbcollege.edu/.

Santa Barbara City College

Santa Barbara, California

Freshman Application Contact Ms. Allison Curtis, Director of Admissions and Records, Santa Barbara City College, Santa Barbara, CA 93109. *Phone:* 805-965-0581 Ext. 2352. *Fax:* 805-962-0497. *E-mail:* admissions@sbcc.edu. *Website:* http://www.sbcc.edu/.

Santa Monica College

Santa Monica, California

Freshman Application Contact Santa Monica College, 1900 Pico Boulevard, Santa Monica, CA 90405-1628. *Phone:* 310-434-4774. *Website:* http://www.smc.edu/.

Santa Rosa Junior College

Santa Rosa, California

- **District-supported** 2-year, founded 1918, part of California Community College System
- **Urban** 100-acre campus with easy access to San Francisco
- **Endowment** $41.3 million
- **Coed**

Undergraduates Students come from 36 other countries; 3% are from out of state; 2% Black or African American, non-Hispanic/Latino; 34% Hispanic/Latino; 5% Asian, non-Hispanic/Latino; 0.3% Native Hawaiian or other Pacific Islander, non-Hispanic/Latino; 0.7% American Indian or Alaska Native, non-Hispanic/Latino; 4% Two or more races, non-Hispanic/Latino; 7% Race/ethnicity unknown.

Academics *Calendar:* semesters. *Degree:* certificates and associate. *Special study options:* academic remediation for entering students, adult/continuing education programs, advanced placement credit, cooperative education, distance learning, English as a second language, independent study, internships, off-campus study, part-time degree program, services for LD students, study abroad, summer session for credit.

Library Doyle Library plus 1 other. Students can reserve study rooms.

Student Life *Campus security:* 24-hour emergency response devices and patrols, student patrols.

Financial Aid Of all full-time matriculated undergraduates who enrolled in 2009, 135 Federal Work-Study jobs (averaging $2210). 43 state and other part-time jobs (averaging $7396).

Applying *Options:* electronic application, early admission.

Admissions Office Contact Santa Rosa Junior College, 1501 Mendocino Avenue, Santa Rosa, CA 95401-4395. *Website:* http://www.santarosa.edu/.

Santiago Canyon College

Orange, California

Freshman Application Contact Tuyen Nguyen, Admissions and Records, Santiago Canyon College, 8045 East Chapman Avenue, Orange, CA 92869. *Phone:* 714-628-4902. *Website:* http://www.sccollege.edu/.

Shasta College

Redding, California

Director of Admissions Dr. Kevin O'Rorke, Dean of Enrollment Services, Shasta College, PO Box 496006, 11555 Old Oregon Trail, Redding, CA 96049-6006. *Phone:* 530-242-7669. *Website:* http://www.shastacollege.edu/.

Sierra College
Rocklin, California

- **District-supported** 2-year, founded 1936, part of California Community College System
- **Suburban** 327-acre campus with easy access to Sacramento
- **Coed,** 19,165 undergraduate students, 34% full-time, 54% women, 44% men

Undergraduates 6,477 full-time, 12,319 part-time. Students come from 22 states and territories; 8 other countries; 0.7% are from out of state; 4% Black or African American, non-Hispanic/Latino; 8% Hispanic/Latino; 9% Asian, non-Hispanic/Latino; 0.8% Native Hawaiian or other Pacific Islander, non-Hispanic/Latino; 1% American Indian or Alaska Native, non-Hispanic/Latino; 0.4% Race/ethnicity unknown; 0.5% international; 1% live on campus. *Retention:* 68% of full-time freshmen returned.
Freshmen *Admission:* 24,000 applied, 24,000 admitted, 3,914 enrolled.
Faculty *Total:* 870, 18% full-time. *Student/faculty ratio:* 25:1.
Majors Accounting; administrative assistant and secretarial science; agriculture; American Sign Language (ASL); animal/livestock husbandry and production; apparel and textile manufacturing; apparel and textile marketing management; applied horticulture/horticulture operations; architectural drafting and CAD/CADD; art; automobile/automotive mechanics technology; biological and physical sciences; biology/biological sciences; business administration and management; business/commerce; cabinetmaking and millwork; chemistry; child development; commercial photography; computer and information sciences and support services related; computer installation and repair technology; computer programming; computer systems networking and telecommunications; construction trades; criminal justice/police science; data entry/microcomputer applications; digital communication and media/multimedia; electrical/electronics equipment installation and repair; engineering; English; equestrian studies; fire science/firefighting; forestry; general studies; geology/earth science; graphic design; hazardous materials management and waste technology; health and physical education/fitness; industrial electronics technology; information technology; liberal arts and sciences/liberal studies; licensed practical/vocational nurse training; manufacturing engineering technology; mathematics; mechanical drafting and CAD/CADD; music; network and system administration; parks, recreation and leisure; philosophy; physics; psychology; real estate; registered nursing/registered nurse; rhetoric and composition; sales, distribution, and marketing operations; small business administration; social sciences; visual and performing arts; web page, digital/multimedia and information resources design; women's studies.
Academics *Calendar:* semesters. *Degree:* certificates and associate. *Special study options:* academic remediation for entering students, accelerated degree program, advanced placement credit, distance learning, double majors, English as a second language, honors programs, independent study, internships, off-campus study, part-time degree program, services for LD students, study abroad, summer session for credit.
Library Leary Resource Center plus 1 other.
Student Life *Housing Options:* coed. Campus housing is university owned. *Activities and Organizations:* drama/theater group, student-run newspaper, choral group, Drama Club, Student Government, Art Club, Band, Aggie Club. *Campus security:* 24-hour emergency response devices and patrols, late-night transport/escort service. *Student services:* health clinic, personal/psychological counseling.
Athletics *Intercollegiate sports:* basketball W, soccer W, softball W, swimming and diving W, tennis W, volleyball W, water polo W. *Intramural sports:* archery M, badminton M, basketball M, tennis M, volleyball M.
Applying *Options:* electronic application, early admission. *Application deadline:* rolling (freshmen). *Notification:* continuous (freshmen), continuous (transfers).
Director of Admissions Ms. Gail Modder, Program Manager, Admissions and Records, Sierra College, 5100 Sierra College Boulevard, Rocklin, CA 95677. *Phone:* 916-660-7341.
Website: http://www.sierracollege.edu/.

Skyline College
San Bruno, California

Freshman Application Contact Terry Stats, Admissions Office, Skyline College, 3300 College Drive, San Bruno, CA 94066-1698. *Phone:* 650-738-4251. *E-mail:* stats@smccd.net. *Website:* http://skylinecollege.edu/.

Solano Community College
Fairfield, California

Freshman Application Contact Solano Community College, 4000 Suisun Valley Road, Fairfield, CA 94534. *Phone:* 707-864-7000 Ext. 4313. *Website:* http://www.solano.edu/.

South Coast College
Orange, California

Director of Admissions South Coast College, 2011 West Chapman Avenue, Orange, CA 92868. *Toll-free phone:* 877-568-6130. *Website:* http://www.southcoastcollege.edu/.

Southwestern College
Chula Vista, California

- **District-supported** 2-year, founded 1961, part of California Community College system
- **Suburban** 158-acre campus with easy access to City of San Diego
- **Endowment** $1.2 million
- **Coed**

Undergraduates 7,405 full-time, 11,008 part-time. 5% transferred in. *Retention:* 74% of full-time freshmen returned.
Faculty *Student/faculty ratio:* 22:1.
Academics *Calendar:* semesters. *Degree:* certificates and associate. *Special study options:* academic remediation for entering students, adult/continuing education programs, advanced placement credit, cooperative education, distance learning, English as a second language, external degree program, honors programs, independent study, internships, part-time degree program, services for LD students, study abroad, summer session for credit.
Library Southwestern College Library/Learning Resource Center plus 3 others. *Books:* 104,784 (physical), 26,161 (digital/electronic); *Serial titles:* 191 (physical), 18 (digital/electronic); *Databases:* 58. Weekly public service hours: 126; students can reserve study rooms.
Student Life *Campus security:* 24-hour emergency response devices and patrols, late-night transport/escort service.
Financial Aid ***Average financial aid package:*** $5625. *Average need-based gift aid:* $810.
Applying *Options:* electronic application, early admission. *Required for some:* high school transcript.
Freshman Application Contact Admissions, Southwestern College, 900 Otay Lakes Road, Chula Vista, CA 91910-7299. *Phone:* 619-421-6700 Ext. 5215. *Fax:* 619-482-6489. *Website:* http://www.swccd.edu/.

Spartan College of Aeronautics and Technology
Inglewood, California

Freshman Application Contact Admissions Office, Spartan College of Aeronautics and Technology, 8911 Aviation Boulevard, Inglewood, CA 90301. *Phone:* 866-451-0818. *Toll-free phone:* 800-879-0554. *Website:* http://www.spartan.edu/.

Taft College
Taft, California

Freshman Application Contact Nichole Cook, Admissions/Counseling Technician, Taft College, 29 Cougar Court, Taft, CA 93268. *Phone:* 661-763-7790. *Fax:* 661-763-7758. *E-mail:* ncook@taftcollege.edu. *Website:* http://www.taftcollege.edu/.

Theatre of Arts
Hollywood, California

Admissions Office Contact Theatre of Arts, 1536 North Highland Avenue, Hollywood, CA 90028. *Website:* http://www.toa.edu/.

Unitek College
Fremont, California

Admissions Office Contact Unitek College, 4670 Auto Mall Parkway, Fremont, CA 94538. *Website:* http://www.unitekcollege.edu/.

Valley College of Medical Careers
West Hills, California

Admissions Office Contact Valley College of Medical Careers, 8399 Topanga Canyon Boulevard, Suite 200, West Hills, CA 91304. *Website:* http://www.vcmc.edu/.

Ventura College
Ventura, California

Freshman Application Contact Ms. Susan Bricker, Registrar, Ventura College, 4667 Telegraph Road, Ventura, CA 93003-3899. *Phone:* 805-654-6456. *Fax:* 805-654-6357. *E-mail:* sbricker@vcccd.net. *Website:* http://www.venturacollege.edu/.

Victor Valley College
Victorville, California

Freshman Application Contact Ms. Greta Moon, Interim Director of Admissions and Records, Victor Valley College, 18422 Bear Valley Road, Victorville, CA 92395. *Phone:* 760-245-4271. *Fax:* 760-843-7707. *E-mail:* moong@vvc.edu. *Website:* http://www.vvc.edu/.

West Coast Ultrasound Institute
Beverly Hills, California

Admissions Office Contact West Coast Ultrasound Institute, 291 S. La Cienega Boulevard, Suite 500, Beverly Hills, CA 90211. *Website:* http://wcui.edu/.

West Hills College Coalinga
Coalinga, California

Freshman Application Contact Sandra Dagnino, West Hills College Coalinga, 300 Cherry Lane, Coalinga, CA 93210-1399. *Phone:* 559-934-3203. *Toll-free phone:* 800-266-1114. *Fax:* 559-934-2830. *E-mail:* sandradagnino@westhillscollege.com. *Website:* http://www.westhillscollege.com/.

West Hills College Lemoore
Lemoore, California

Admissions Office Contact West Hills College Lemoore, 555 College Avenue, Lemoore, CA 93245. *Website:* http://www.westhillscollege.com/.

West Los Angeles College
Culver City, California

Director of Admissions Mr. Len Isaksen, Director of Admissions, West Los Angeles College, 9000 Overland Avenue, Culver City, CA 90230-3519. *Phone:* 310-287-4255. *Website:* http://www.lacolleges.net/.

West Valley College
Saratoga, California

Freshman Application Contact Ms. Barbara Ogilive, Supervisor, Admissions and Records, West Valley College, 14000 Fruitvale Avenue, Saratoga, CA 95070-5698. *Phone:* 408-741-4630. *E-mail:* barbara_ogilvie@westvalley.edu. *Website:* http://www.westvalley.edu/.

Woodland Community College
Woodland, California

Admissions Office Contact Woodland Community College, 2300 East Gibson Road, Woodland, CA 95776. *Website:* http://wcc.yccd.edu/.

Yuba College
Marysville, California

Director of Admissions Dr. David Farrell, Dean of Student Development, Yuba College, 2088 North Beale Road, Marysville, CA 95901-7699. *Phone:* 530-741-6705. *Website:* http://yc.yccd.edu/.

COLORADO

Aims Community College
Greeley, Colorado

Freshman Application Contact Ms. Susie Gallardo, Admissions Technician, Aims Community College, Box 69, 5401 West 20th Street, Greeley, CO 80632-0069. *Phone:* 970-330-8008 Ext. 6624. *E-mail:* wgreen@chiron.aims.edu. *Website:* http://www.aims.edu/.

Arapahoe Community College
Littleton, Colorado

- **State-supported** primarily 2-year, founded 1965, part of Colorado Community College and Occupational Education System
- **Suburban** 52-acre campus with easy access to Denver
- **Coed,** 10,697 undergraduate students, 17% full-time, 59% women, 41% men

Undergraduates 1,860 full-time, 8,837 part-time. Students come from 47 states and territories; 2 other countries; 15% are from out of state; 2% Black or African American, non-Hispanic/Latino; 14% Hispanic/Latino; 4% Asian, non-Hispanic/Latino; 0.3% Native Hawaiian or other Pacific Islander, non-Hispanic/Latino; 0.4% American Indian or Alaska Native, non-Hispanic/Latino; 4% Two or more races, non-Hispanic/Latino; 9% Race/ethnicity unknown; 1% international; 5% transferred in.

Freshmen *Admission:* 3,851 applied, 3,851 admitted, 997 enrolled.

Faculty *Total:* 489, 21% full-time. *Student/faculty ratio:* 23:1.

Majors Accounting technology and bookkeeping; architectural engineering technology; automobile/automotive mechanics technology; building/construction site management; business administration and management; clinical/medical laboratory technology; commercial photography; computer and information sciences; computer systems networking and telecommunications; cosmetology; criminal justice/law enforcement administration; crisis/emergency/disaster management; emergency medical technology (EMT paramedic); funeral service and mortuary science; game and interactive media design; general studies; graphic design; health and physical education/fitness; health information/medical records technology; interior design; journalism; legal assistant/paralegal; liberal arts and sciences and humanities related; liberal arts and sciences/liberal studies; mechanical engineering/mechanical technology; music technology; registered nursing/registered nurse; retailing; science technologies related; telecommunications technology.

Academics *Calendar:* semesters. *Degrees:* certificates, diplomas, associate, and bachelor's. *Special study options:* academic remediation for entering students, accelerated degree program, adult/continuing education programs, advanced placement credit, cooperative education, distance learning, double majors, English as a second language, external degree program, independent study, internships, off-campus study, part-time degree program, services for LD students, study abroad, summer session for credit. *ROTC:* Army (c), Air Force (c).

Library Weber Center for Learning Resources plus 1 other. *Books:* 28,076 (physical), 442 (digital/electronic).

Student Life *Housing:* college housing not available. *Activities and Organizations:* drama/theater group, student-run newspaper, choral group, American Society of Interior Designers, National Society of Leadership and Success, Phi Theta Kappa, Student Veterans of America, Transfer Club. *Campus security:* 24-hour emergency response devices and patrols, late-night transport/escort service. *Student services:* personal/psychological counseling, veterans affairs office.

Applying *Options:* electronic application, early admission, deferred entrance. *Application deadlines:* rolling (freshmen), rolling (out-of-state freshmen), rolling (transfers). *Notification:* continuous (freshmen), continuous (out-of-state freshmen), continuous (transfers).

Director of Admissions Darcy Briggs, Director of Enrollment Services, Arapahoe Community College, 5900 South Santa Fe Drive, PO Box 9002, Littleton, CO 80160-9002. *Phone:* 303-797-5623. *E-mail:* darcy.briggs@arapahoe.edu.
Website: http://www.arapahoe.edu/.

Bel–Rea Institute of Animal Technology
Denver, Colorado

Freshman Application Contact Bel–Rea Institute of Animal Technology, 1681 South Dayton Street, Denver, CO 80247. *Phone:* 303-751-8700. *Toll-free phone:* 800-950-8001. *Website:* http://www.belrea.edu/.

CollegeAmerica–Colorado Springs
Colorado Springs, Colorado

Freshman Application Contact CollegeAmerica–Colorado Springs, 2020 North Academy Boulevard, Colorado Springs, CO 80909. *Phone:* 719-637-0600. *Toll-free phone:* 800-622-2894. *Website:* http://www.collegeamerica.edu/.

CollegeAmerica–Denver
Denver, Colorado

• **Independent** 2-year, founded 1962
• **Urban** campus
• **Coed**

Faculty *Student/faculty ratio:* 10:1.
Academics *Calendar:* continuous. *Degree:* associate. *Special study options:* academic remediation for entering students, accelerated degree program, cooperative education, distance learning.
Freshman Application Contact Admissions Office, CollegeAmerica–Denver, 1385 South Colorado Boulevard, Denver, CO 80222. *Phone:* 303-300-8740 Ext. 7020. *Toll-free phone:* 800-622-2894. *Website:* http://www.collegeamerica.edu/.

CollegeAmerica–Fort Collins
Fort Collins, Colorado

Freshman Application Contact CollegeAmerica–Fort Collins, 4601 South Mason Street, Fort Collins, CO 80525. *Phone:* 970-223-6060 Ext. 8002. *Toll-free phone:* 800-622-2894. *Website:* http://www.collegeamerica.edu/.

Colorado Academy of Veterinary Technology
Colorado Springs, Colorado

Admissions Office Contact Colorado Academy of Veterinary Technology, 2766 Janitell Road, Colorado Springs, CO 80906. *Website:* http://www.cavt.edu/.

Colorado Northwestern Community College
Rangely, Colorado

• **State-supported** 2-year, founded 1962, part of Colorado Community College and Occupational Education System
• **Rural** 150-acre campus
• **Coed,** 1,154 undergraduate students, 42% full-time, 61% women, 39% men

Undergraduates 484 full-time, 670 part-time. 21% are from out of state; 3% Black or African American, non-Hispanic/Latino; 13% Hispanic/Latino; 1% Asian, non-Hispanic/Latino; 0.3% Native Hawaiian or other Pacific Islander, non-Hispanic/Latino; 0.4% American Indian or Alaska Native, non-Hispanic/Latino; 3% Two or more races, non-Hispanic/Latino; 9% Race/ethnicity unknown; 2% international; 10% transferred in; 45% live on campus. *Retention:* 46% of full-time freshmen returned.
Freshmen *Admission:* 863 applied, 863 admitted, 196 enrolled.
Faculty *Total:* 93, 41% full-time, 6% with terminal degrees. *Student/faculty ratio:* 13:1.
Majors Accounting; aircraft powerplant technology; airline pilot and flight crew; automobile/automotive mechanics technology; business/commerce; cosmetology; dental hygiene; early childhood education; emergency medical technology (EMT paramedic); equestrian studies; general studies; liberal arts and sciences and humanities related; liberal arts and sciences/liberal studies; medical/clinical assistant; registered nursing/registered nurse; small business administration.
Academics *Calendar:* semesters. *Degree:* certificates and associate. *Special study options:* academic remediation for entering students, adult/continuing education programs, advanced placement credit, distance learning, double majors, independent study, internships, part-time degree program, services for LD students, student-designed majors, summer session for credit.
Library Colorado Northwestern Community College Library plus 1 other. *Books:* 19,000 (physical), 10,524 (digital/electronic); *Serial titles:* 137 (physical); *Databases:* 47. Students can reserve study rooms.
Student Life *Housing:* on-campus residence required for freshman year. *Options:* coed. Campus housing is university owned. Freshman campus housing is guaranteed. *Campus security:* student patrols, late-night transport/escort service, controlled dormitory access. *Student services:* health clinic, personal/psychological counseling.
Athletics Member NJCAA. *Intercollegiate sports:* basketball W(s), soccer W(s), softball W(s), volleyball W(s). *Intramural sports:* basketball M, racquetball M, rock climbing M, skiing (cross-country) M, skiing (downhill) M, softball M, swimming and diving M, table tennis M, volleyball M.
Financial Aid Of all full-time matriculated undergraduates who enrolled in 2017, 382 applied for aid, 322 were judged to have need, 20 had their need fully met. In 2017, 29 non-need-based awards were made. *Average percent of need met:* 46%. *Average financial aid package:* $7954. *Average need-based loan:* $4254. *Average need-based gift aid:* $5373. *Average non-need-based aid:* $1376.
Applying *Options:* electronic application, early admission, deferred entrance. *Required:* high school transcript. *Required for some:* 3 letters of recommendation. *Application deadlines:* rolling (freshmen), rolling (out-of-state freshmen), rolling (transfers). *Notification:* continuous (freshmen), continuous (out-of-state freshmen), continuous (transfers).
Director of Admissions John Anderson, Director of Enrollment Services/Registrar, Colorado Northwestern Community College, 500 Kennedy Drive, Rangely, CO 81648-3598. *Phone:* 970-675-3217. *Toll-free phone:* 800-562-1105. *Fax:* 970-675-3343. *E-mail:* John.Anderson@cncc.edu. *Website:* http://www.cncc.edu/.

Colorado School of Trades
Lakewood, Colorado

Freshman Application Contact Colorado School of Trades, 1575 Hoyt Street, Lakewood, CO 80215-2996. *Phone:* 303-233-4697 Ext. 44. *Toll-free phone:* 800-234-4594. *Website:* http://www.schooloftrades.edu/.

Community College of Aurora
Aurora, Colorado

• **State-supported** 2-year, founded 1983, part of Colorado Community College System
• **Suburban** campus with easy access to Denver
• **Coed,** 7,982 undergraduate students, 23% full-time, 58% women, 42% men

Undergraduates 1,867 full-time, 6,115 part-time. Students come from 60 other countries; 2% are from out of state; 18% Black or African American, non-Hispanic/Latino; 30% Hispanic/Latino; 6% Asian, non-Hispanic/Latino; 0.4% Native Hawaiian or other Pacific Islander, non-Hispanic/Latino; 0.5% American Indian or Alaska Native, non-Hispanic/Latino; 5% Two or more races, non-Hispanic/Latino; 6% Race/ethnicity unknown; 4% international; 5% transferred in. *Retention:* 54% of full-time freshmen returned.
Freshmen *Admission:* 823 enrolled.
Faculty *Total:* 371, 19% full-time. *Student/faculty ratio:* 20:1.
Majors Accounting technology and bookkeeping; cinematography and film/video production; computer and information sciences; computer systems networking and telecommunications; criminal justice/law enforcement administration; emergency medical technology (EMT paramedic); fire science/firefighting; general studies; heavy equipment maintenance technology; liberal arts and sciences and humanities related; liberal arts and sciences/liberal studies; respiratory care therapy; science technologies related; web page, digital/multimedia and information resources design.
Academics *Calendar:* semesters. *Degree:* certificates and associate. *Special study options:* academic remediation for entering students, adult/continuing education programs, cooperative education, distance learning, English as a second language, external degree program, independent study, internships, off-campus study, part-time degree program, services for LD students, summer session for credit.
Library Community College of Aurora Learning Resource Center. *Books:* 3,374 (physical), 252,009 (digital/electronic); *Serial titles:* 11 (physical), 22,725 (digital/electronic); *Databases:* 84. Weekly public service hours: 63.
Student Life *Housing:* college housing not available. *Activities and Organizations:* drama/theater group. *Campus security:* late-night transport/escort service. *Student services:* women's center, veterans affairs office.
Applying *Required for some:* high school transcript.
Director of Admissions Kristen Cusack, Director, Admissions and Records, Community College of Aurora, 16000 East CentreTech Parkway, Aurora, CO 80011-9036. *Phone:* 303-360-4701. *Fax:* 303-361-7432. *E-mail:* kristen.cusack@ccaurora.edu. *Website:* http://www.ccaurora.edu/.

Community College of Denver
Denver, Colorado

• **State-supported** 2-year, founded 1970, part of Colorado Community College System
• **Urban** 124-acre campus
• **Coed,** 8,556 undergraduate students, 29% full-time, 58% women, 42% men

Undergraduates 2,441 full-time, 6,115 part-time. 2% are from out of state; 11% Black or African American, non-Hispanic/Latino; 33% Hispanic/Latino; 5% Asian, non-Hispanic/Latino; 0.2% Native Hawaiian or other Pacific Islander, non-Hispanic/Latino; 0.8% American Indian or Alaska Native, non-

Hispanic/Latino; 4% Two or more races, non-Hispanic/Latino; 7% Race/ethnicity unknown; 7% international.
Freshmen *Admission:* 3,829 applied, 3,829 admitted, 1,443 enrolled.
Faculty *Total:* 393, 27% full-time, 16% with terminal degrees. *Student/faculty ratio:* 25:1.
Majors Accounting technology and bookkeeping; administrative assistant and secretarial science; business administration and management; computer and information sciences; dental hygiene; drafting and design technology; electroneurodiagnostic/electroencephalographic technology; general studies; graphic design; human services; legal assistant/paralegal; liberal arts and sciences/liberal studies; licensed practical/vocational nurse training; machine shop technology; management information systems; office management; quality control and safety technologies related; radiologic technology/science; science technologies related; veterinary/animal health technology; welding technology.
Academics *Calendar:* semesters. *Degree:* certificates and associate. *Special study options:* academic remediation for entering students, accelerated degree program, adult/continuing education programs, advanced placement credit, cooperative education, distance learning, double majors, English as a second language, external degree program, freshman honors college, honors programs, independent study, internships, off-campus study, part-time degree program, services for LD students, study abroad, summer session for credit. *ROTC:* Army (b).
Library Auraria Library.
Student Life *Housing:* college housing not available. *Activities and Organizations:* student-run newspaper, choral group, Phi Theta Kappa, Black Student Alliance, La Mision, SAFI, Chinese Culture Club. *Campus security:* 24-hour emergency response devices and patrols, late-night transport/escort service. *Student services:* health clinic, personal/psychological counseling.
Athletics *Intramural sports:* archery M/W, badminton M/W, basketball M/W, bowling M/W, cross-country running M/W, equestrian sports M/W, fencing M/W, field hockey M/W, football M/W, golf M/W, gymnastics M/W, racquetball M/W, riflery M/W, rugby M/W, skiing (cross-country) M/W, skiing (downhill) M/W, soccer M/W, swimming and diving M/W, table tennis M/W, tennis M/W, track and field M/W, volleyball M/W, weight lifting M/W.
Applying *Options:* electronic application, early admission, deferred entrance.
Freshman Application Contact Andrew Garcia, Director of Admissions, Recruitment and Outreach, Community College of Denver, PO Box 173363, Campus Box 215, Denver, CO 80217-3363. *Phone:* 303-352-3079. *Fax:* 303-556-2431. *E-mail:* andrew.garcia@ccd.edu.
Website: http://www.ccd.edu/.

Concorde Career College
Aurora, Colorado

Admissions Office Contact Concorde Career College, 111 North Havana Street, Aurora, CO 80010. *Website:* http://www.concorde.edu/.

Front Range Community College
Westminster, Colorado

- **State-supported** 2-year, founded 1968, part of Community Colleges of Colorado System
- **Suburban** 90-acre campus with easy access to Denver
- **Endowment** $550,411
- **Coed,** 18,880 undergraduate students, 26% full-time, 56% women, 44% men

Undergraduates 4,999 full-time, 13,881 part-time. Students come from 43 states and territories; 85 other countries; 2% are from out of state; 2% Black or African American, non-Hispanic/Latino; 19% Hispanic/Latino; 3% Asian, non-Hispanic/Latino; 0.2% Native Hawaiian or other Pacific Islander, non-Hispanic/Latino; 0.7% American Indian or Alaska Native, non-Hispanic/Latino; 4% Two or more races, non-Hispanic/Latino; 4% Race/ethnicity unknown; 3% international; 10% transferred in. *Retention:* 59% of full-time freshmen returned.
Freshmen *Admission:* 5,106 applied, 5,106 admitted, 2,265 enrolled.
Faculty *Total:* 970, 25% full-time. *Student/faculty ratio:* 19:1.
Majors Accounting technology and bookkeeping; animation, interactive technology, video graphics and special effects; applied horticulture/horticulture operations; architectural engineering technology; automation engineer technology; automobile/automotive mechanics technology; business administration and management; CAD/CADD drafting/design technology; computer and information sciences; computer systems networking and telecommunications; criminal justice/police science; early childhood education; electrical, electronic and communications engineering technology; energy management and systems technology; general studies; geographic information science and cartography; health information/medical records technology; heating, ventilation, air conditioning and refrigeration engineering technology; holistic health; hospitality administration; interior design; legal assistant/paralegal; liberal arts and sciences and humanities related; liberal arts and sciences/liberal studies; medical office assistant; recording arts technology; registered nursing/registered nurse; science technologies related; sign language interpretation and translation; surgical technology; veterinary/animal health technology; welding technology; wildlife, fish and wildlands science and management.
Academics *Calendar:* semesters. *Degree:* certificates and associate. *Special study options:* academic remediation for entering students, advanced placement credit, cooperative education, distance learning, double majors, English as a second language, freshman honors college, honors programs, independent study, internships, off-campus study, part-time degree program, services for LD students, student-designed majors, study abroad, summer session for credit. *ROTC:* Army (c), Air Force (c).
Library College Hill Library plus 2 others. *Books:* 32,801 (physical), 546 (digital/electronic); *Databases:* 12. Weekly public service hours: 54; students can reserve study rooms.
Student Life *Housing:* college housing not available. *Activities and Organizations:* drama/theater group, student-run newspaper, Student Government Association, Student Colorado Registry of Interpreters for the Deaf, Students in Free Enterprise (SIFE), Gay-Straight Alliance, Recycling Club. *Campus security:* 24-hour emergency response devices and patrols, late-night transport/escort service. *Student services:* personal/psychological counseling, veterans affairs office.
Applying *Options:* electronic application, early admission, deferred entrance.
Freshman Application Contact Ms. Miori Gidley, Registrar, Front Range Community College, Westminster, CO 80031. *Phone:* 303-404-5000. *Fax:* 303-439-2614. *E-mail:* miori.gidley@frontrange.edu.
Website: http://www.frontrange.edu/.

IBMC College
Fort Collins, Colorado

Freshman Application Contact Mr. Jeremy Shoup, Admissions and Marketing Coordinator, IBMC College, 3842 South Mason Street, Fort Collins, CO 80525. *Phone:* 970-223-2669. *Toll-free phone:* 800-495-2669. *E-mail:* jshoup@ibmc.edu. *Website:* http://www.ibmc.edu/.

IntelliTec College
Colorado Springs, Colorado

Director of Admissions Director of Admissions, IntelliTec College, 2315 East Pikes Peak Avenue, Colorado Springs, CO 80909. *Phone:* 719-632-7626. *Toll-free phone:* 800-748-2282. *Website:* http://www.intelliteccollege.edu/.

IntelliTec College
Grand Junction, Colorado

Freshman Application Contact Admissions, IntelliTec College, 772 Horizon Drive, Grand Junction, CO 81506. *Phone:* 970-245-8101. *Toll-free phone:* 800-748-2282. *Fax:* 970-243-8074. *Website:* http://www.intelliteccollege.edu/.

Lamar Community College
Lamar, Colorado

- **State-supported** 2-year, founded 1937, part of Colorado Community College and Occupational Education System
- **Small-town** 125-acre campus
- **Coed**

Undergraduates 404 full-time, 387 part-time. Students come from 29 states and territories; 9 other countries; 10% are from out of state; 5% Black or African American, non-Hispanic/Latino; 23% Hispanic/Latino; 0.1% Asian, non-Hispanic/Latino; 0.1% Native Hawaiian or other Pacific Islander, non-Hispanic/Latino; 0.9% American Indian or Alaska Native, non-Hispanic/Latino; 3% Two or more races, non-Hispanic/Latino; 2% Race/ethnicity unknown; 6% international; 5% transferred in; 20% live on campus. *Retention:* 49% of full-time freshmen returned.
Faculty *Student/faculty ratio:* 21:1.
Academics *Calendar:* semesters. *Degree:* certificates, diplomas, and associate. *Special study options:* academic remediation for entering students, adult/continuing education programs, advanced placement credit, cooperative education, distance learning, double majors, English as a second language, independent study, internships, part-time degree program, services for LD students, student-designed majors, summer session for credit.
Library Learning Resources Center. *Books:* 10,825 (physical); *Serial titles:* 23 (physical). Weekly public service hours: 53.

Student Life *Campus security:* 24-hour emergency response devices and patrols, student patrols, late-night transport/escort service, controlled dormitory access.
Athletics Member NJCAA.
Applying *Options:* electronic application, early admission.
Freshman Application Contact Director of Admissions, Lamar Community College, 2401 South Main Street, Lamar, CO 81052-3999. *Phone:* 719-336-1592. *Toll-free phone:* 800-968-6920. *E-mail:* admissions@lamarcc.edu. *Website:* http://www.lamarcc.edu/.

Lincoln College of Technology
Denver, Colorado

Freshman Application Contact Lincoln College of Technology, 11194 East 45th Avenue, Denver, CO 80239. *Phone:* 800-347-3232 Ext. 43032. *Toll-free phone:* 844-215-1513. *Website:* http://www.lincolntech.edu/.

Morgan Community College
Fort Morgan, Colorado

Freshman Application Contact Ms. Kim Maxwell, Morgan Community College, 920 Barlow Road, Fort Morgan, CO 80701-4399. *Phone:* 970-542-3111. *Toll-free phone:* 800-622-0216. *Fax:* 970-867-6608. *E-mail:* kim.maxwell@morgancc.edu. *Website:* http://www.morgancc.edu/.

Northeastern Junior College
Sterling, Colorado

- **State-supported** 2-year, founded 1941, part of Colorado Community College and Occupational Education System
- **Small-town** 65-acre campus
- **Coed**

Undergraduates 896 full-time, 651 part-time. Students come from 29 states and territories; 11 other countries; 7% are from out of state; 4% Black or African American, non-Hispanic/Latino; 14% Hispanic/Latino; 1% Asian, non-Hispanic/Latino; 0.1% Native Hawaiian or other Pacific Islander, non-Hispanic/Latino; 1% American Indian or Alaska Native, non-Hispanic/Latino; 3% Two or more races, non-Hispanic/Latino; 4% Race/ethnicity unknown; 5% international; 5% transferred in; 40% live on campus.
Faculty *Student/faculty ratio:* 16:1.
Academics *Calendar:* semesters. *Degree:* certificates and associate. *Special study options:* academic remediation for entering students, accelerated degree program, adult/continuing education programs, advanced placement credit, cooperative education, distance learning, double majors, English as a second language, honors programs, internships, part-time degree program, services for LD students, summer session for credit.
Library Monahan Library. *Books:* 24,184 (physical), 105,876 (digital/electronic); *Serial titles:* 104 (physical), 86 (digital/electronic); *Databases:* 8. Weekly public service hours: 71.
Student Life *Campus security:* 24-hour emergency response devices, late-night transport/escort service, controlled dormitory access.
Athletics Member NJCAA.
Financial Aid Of all full-time matriculated undergraduates who enrolled in 2017, 55 Federal Work-Study jobs (averaging $1885). 108 state and other part-time jobs (averaging $1927).
Applying *Options:* electronic application. *Recommended:* high school transcript.
Freshman Application Contact Adam Kunkel, Director of Admission, Northeastern Junior College, Sterling, CO 80751. *Phone:* 970-521-7000. *Toll-free phone:* 800-626-4637. *Fax:* 970-521-6715. *E-mail:* adam.kunkel@njc.edu. *Website:* http://www.njc.edu/.

Otero Junior College
La Junta, Colorado

- **State-supported** 2-year, founded 1941, part of Colorado Community College System
- **Rural** 40-acre campus
- **Endowment** $1.5 million
- **Coed**

Undergraduates Students come from 20 states and territories; 15 other countries; 10% are from out of state; 3% Black or African American, non-Hispanic/Latino; 32% Hispanic/Latino; 0.8% Asian, non-Hispanic/Latino; 0.5% Native Hawaiian or other Pacific Islander, non-Hispanic/Latino; 1% American Indian or Alaska Native, non-Hispanic/Latino; 6% Race/ethnicity unknown; 3% international. *Retention:* 53% of full-time freshmen returned.
Faculty *Student/faculty ratio:* 19:1.
Academics *Calendar:* semesters. *Degree:* certificates and associate. *Special study options:* academic remediation for entering students, adult/continuing education programs, advanced placement credit, distance learning, external degree program, honors programs, internships, part-time degree program, summer session for credit.
Library Wheeler Library.
Student Life *Campus security:* 24-hour patrols, late-night transport/escort service, controlled dormitory access.
Athletics Member NJCAA.
Financial Aid Of all full-time matriculated undergraduates who enrolled in 2017, 30 Federal Work-Study jobs (averaging $2000). 100 state and other part-time jobs (averaging $2000).
Applying *Options:* electronic application, early admission. *Recommended:* high school transcript.
Freshman Application Contact Mrs. Lauren Berg, Registrar, Otero Junior College, 1802 Colorado Avenue, La Junta, CO 81050. *Phone:* 719-384-6831. *Fax:* 719-384-6933. *E-mail:* lauren.berg@ojc.edu. *Website:* http://www.ojc.edu/.

Pikes Peak Community College
Colorado Springs, Colorado

Freshman Application Contact Pikes Peak Community College, 5675 South Academy Boulevard, Colorado Springs, CO 80906-5498. *Phone:* 719-540-7041. *Toll-free phone:* 866-411-7722. *Website:* http://www.ppcc.edu/.

Pima Medical Institute
Aurora, Colorado

Admissions Office Contact Pima Medical Institute, 13750 East Mississippi Avenue, Aurora, CO 80012. *Toll-free phone:* 800-477-PIMA. *Website:* http://www.pmi.edu/.

Pima Medical Institute
Colorado Springs, Colorado

Freshman Application Contact Pima Medical Institute, 5725 Mark Dabling Boulevard, Colorado Springs, CO 80919. *Phone:* 719-482-7462. *Toll-free phone:* 800-477-PIMA. *Website:* http://www.pmi.edu/.

Pima Medical Institute
Denver, Colorado

Freshman Application Contact Admissions Office, Pima Medical Institute, 7475 Dakin Street, Denver, CO 80221. *Phone:* 303-426-1800. *Toll-free phone:* 800-477-PIMA. *Website:* http://www.pmi.edu/.

Pueblo Community College
Pueblo, Colorado

- **State-supported** primarily 2-year, founded 1933, part of Colorado Community College System
- **Urban** 35-acre campus
- **Endowment** $1.1 million
- **Coed,** 5,650 undergraduate students, 31% full-time, 55% women, 45% men

Undergraduates 1,770 full-time, 3,880 part-time. Students come from 23 states and territories; 0.8% are from out of state; 5% Black or African American, non-Hispanic/Latino; 32% Hispanic/Latino; 5% Asian, non-Hispanic/Latino; 0.2% Native Hawaiian or other Pacific Islander, non-Hispanic/Latino; 2% American Indian or Alaska Native, non-Hispanic/Latino; 3% Two or more races, non-Hispanic/Latino; 3% Race/ethnicity unknown; 0.6% international; 9% transferred in. *Retention:* 10% of full-time freshmen returned.
Freshmen *Admission:* 1,186 applied, 1,186 admitted, 470 enrolled.
Faculty *Total:* 349, 28% full-time. *Student/faculty ratio:* 16:1.
Majors Accounting technology and bookkeeping; animation, interactive technology, video graphics and special effects; autobody/collision and repair technology; automobile/automotive mechanics technology; business administration and management; business automation/technology/data entry; communications technology; computer and information sciences; cooking and related culinary arts; cosmetology; criminal justice/law enforcement administration; dental assisting; dental hygiene; early childhood education; electrical, electronic and communications engineering technology; electromechanical and instrumentation and maintenance technologies related; emergency medical technology (EMT paramedic); engineering technology; fire science/firefighting; general studies; liberal arts and sciences and humanities related; liberal arts and sciences/liberal studies; library and

archives assisting; machine shop technology; medical office management; occupational therapist assistant; physical therapy technology; psychiatric/mental health services technology; radiologic technology/science; registered nursing/registered nurse; respiratory care therapy; science technologies related; surgical technology; web page, digital/multimedia and information resources design; welding technology.
Academics *Calendar:* semesters. *Degrees:* certificates, associate, and bachelor's. *Special study options:* academic remediation for entering students, accelerated degree program, advanced placement credit, cooperative education, distance learning, double majors, English as a second language, honors programs, independent study, internships, part-time degree program, services for LD students, summer session for credit.
Library PCC Library. *Books:* 19,162 (physical), 33,004 (digital/electronic); *Serial titles:* 695 (physical), 7,707 (digital/electronic); *Databases:* 12. Weekly public service hours: 60.
Student Life *Housing:* college housing not available. *Activities and Organizations:* drama/theater group, choral group, Phi Theta Kappa, Welding Club, Culinary Arts Club, Performing Arts Club, Art Club. *Campus security:* 24-hour emergency response devices and patrols, late-night transport/escort service. *Student services:* health clinic, personal/psychological counseling, veterans affairs office.
Applying *Options:* electronic application, early admission, deferred entrance. *Application deadlines:* rolling (freshmen), rolling (transfers). *Notification:* continuous until 9/1 (freshmen), continuous until 9/1 (transfers).
Freshman Application Contact Mrs. Barbara Benedict, Director of Admissions and Records, Pueblo Community College, 900 West Orman Avenue, Pueblo, CO 81004. *Phone:* 719-549-3039. *Toll-free phone:* 888-642-6017. *Fax:* 719-549-3012. *E-mail:* barbara.benedict@pueblocc.edu. *Website:* http://www.pueblocc.edu/.

Red Rocks Community College
Lakewood, Colorado

Freshman Application Contact Admissions Office, Red Rocks Community College, 13300 West 6th Avenue, Lakewood, CO 80228-1255. *Phone:* 303-914-6360. *Fax:* 303-914-6919. *E-mail:* admissions@rrcc.edu. *Website:* http://www.rrcc.edu/.

Spartan College of Aeronautics and Technology
Broomfield, Colorado

Freshman Application Contact Spartan College of Aeronautics and Technology, 10851 West 120th Avenue, Broomfield, CO 80021. *Phone:* 303-466-7383. *Toll-free phone:* 800-510-3216. *Website:* http://www.spartan.edu/.

Trinidad State Junior College
Trinidad, Colorado

Freshman Application Contact Bernadine DeGarbo, Student Services Administrative Assistant, Trinidad State Junior College, 600 Prospect Street, Trinidad, CO 81082. *Phone:* 719-846-5621. *Toll-free phone:* 800-621-8752. *Fax:* 719-846-5620. *E-mail:* bernadine.degarbo@trinidadstate.edu. *Website:* http://www.trinidadstate.edu/.

CONNECTICUT

Asnuntuck Community College
Enfield, Connecticut

Freshman Application Contact Jennifer Anilowski, Interim Director of Admissions, Asnuntuck Community College, 170 Elm Street, Enfield, CT 06082. *Phone:* 860-253-3090. *Fax:* 860-253-3014. *E-mail:* janilowski@asnuntuck.edu. *Website:* http://www.asnuntuck.edu/.

Capital Community College
Hartford, Connecticut

Freshman Application Contact Ms. Jackie Phillips, Director of the Welcome and Advising Center, Capital Community College, 950 Main Street, Hartford, CT 06103. *Phone:* 860-906-5078. *Toll-free phone:* 800-894-6126. *E-mail:* jphillips@ccc.commnet.edu. *Website:* http://www.ccc.commnet.edu/.

Gateway Community College
New Haven, Connecticut

Freshman Application Contact Mr. Joseph Carberry, Director of Enrollment Management, Gateway Community College, 20 Church Street, New Haven, CT 06510. *Phone:* 203-285-2011. *Toll-free phone:* 800-390-7723. *Fax:* 203-285-2018. *E-mail:* jcarberry@gatewayct.edu. *Website:* http://www.gwcc.commnet.edu/.

Goodwin College
East Hartford, Connecticut

Freshman Application Contact Mr. Nicholas Lentino, Assistant Vice President for Admissions, Goodwin College, One Riverside Drive, East Hartford, CT 06118. *Phone:* 860-727-6765. *Toll-free phone:* 800-889-3282. *Fax:* 860-291-9550. *E-mail:* nlentino@goodwin.edu. *Website:* http://www.goodwin.edu/.

Housatonic Community College
Bridgeport, Connecticut

- **State-supported** 2-year, founded 1967, part of Connecticut State Colleges & Universities (CSCU)
- **Urban** 4-acre campus with easy access to New York City
- **Coed**

Undergraduates 1,729 full-time, 3,409 part-time. 31% Black or African American, non-Hispanic/Latino; 33% Hispanic/Latino; 3% Asian, non-Hispanic/Latino; 0.1% Native Hawaiian or other Pacific Islander, non-Hispanic/Latino; 0.2% American Indian or Alaska Native, non-Hispanic/Latino; 2% Two or more races, non-Hispanic/Latino; 1% Race/ethnicity unknown; 0.7% international; 7% transferred in. *Retention:* 57% of full-time freshmen returned.
Faculty *Student/faculty ratio:* 16:1.
Academics *Calendar:* semesters. *Degree:* certificates and associate. *Special study options:* academic remediation for entering students, adult/continuing education programs, advanced placement credit, cooperative education, distance learning, double majors, English as a second language, honors programs, independent study, internships, off-campus study, part-time degree program, services for LD students, summer session for credit.
Library Housatonic Community College Library. *Books:* 55,000 (physical), 45,290 (digital/electronic); *Serial titles:* 104 (physical); *Databases:* 99. Students can reserve study rooms.
Student Life *Campus security:* 24-hour emergency response devices, late-night transport/escort service.
Financial Aid Of all full-time matriculated undergraduates who enrolled in 2017, 70 Federal Work-Study jobs (averaging $2850).
Applying *Options:* electronic application, deferred entrance. *Application fee:* $20. *Required:* high school transcript.
Admissions Office Contact Housatonic Community College, 900 Lafayette Boulevard, Bridgeport, CT 06604-4704. *Website:* http://www.housatonic.edu/.

Manchester Community College
Manchester, Connecticut

- **State-supported** 2-year, founded 1963, part of Connecticut State Colleges & Universities (CSCU)
- **Small-town** campus
- **Coed,** 6,003 undergraduate students, 33% full-time, 55% women, 45% men

Undergraduates 2,004 full-time, 3,999 part-time. 19% Black or African American, non-Hispanic/Latino; 23% Hispanic/Latino; 6% Asian, non-Hispanic/Latino; 0.1% Native Hawaiian or other Pacific Islander, non-Hispanic/Latino; 0.2% American Indian or Alaska Native, non-Hispanic/Latino; 3% Two or more races, non-Hispanic/Latino; 3% Race/ethnicity unknown; 14% transferred in. *Retention:* 60% of full-time freshmen returned.
Freshmen *Admission:* 2,367 applied, 2,367 admitted, 1,215 enrolled.
Faculty *Total:* 421, 22% full-time. *Student/faculty ratio:* 16:1.
Majors Accounting; administrative assistant and secretarial science; business administration and management; clinical/medical laboratory technology; commercial and advertising art; criminal justice/law enforcement administration; dramatic/theater arts; engineering science; fine/studio arts; general studies; hotel/motel administration; human services; industrial engineering; industrial technology; information science/studies; journalism; kindergarten/preschool education; legal administrative assistant/secretary; legal assistant/paralegal; liberal arts and sciences/liberal studies; management information systems; marketing/marketing management; medical

assistant and medical secretary; music; occupational therapist assistant; physical therapy technology; respiratory care therapy; social work; speech communication and rhetoric; surgical technology; teacher assistant/aide.
Academics *Calendar:* semesters. *Degree:* certificates and associate. *Special study options:* adult/continuing education programs, part-time degree program.
Student Life *Housing:* college housing not available.
Athletics Member NJCAA. *Intercollegiate sports:* basketball W, soccer W, softball W.
Financial Aid ***Financial aid deadline:*** 8/13.
Applying *Options:* electronic application. *Application fee:* $20. *Required:* high school transcript.
Admissions Office Contact Manchester Community College, PO Box 1046, Manchester, CT 06045-1046.
Website: http://www.manchestercc.edu/.

Middlesex Community College

Middletown, Connecticut

Freshman Application Contact Mensimah Shabazz, Director of Admissions, Middlesex Community College, Middletown, CT 06457-4889. *Phone:* 860-343-5742. *Fax:* 860-344-3055. *E-mail:* mshabazz@mxcc.commnet.edu. *Website:* http://www.mxcc.commnet.edu/.

Naugatuck Valley Community College

Waterbury, Connecticut

- **State-supported** 2-year, founded 1992, part of Connecticut State Colleges & Universities (CSCU)
- **Urban** 110-acre campus
- **Coed**

Undergraduates 2,173 full-time, 4,205 part-time. Students come from 7 states and territories; 2 other countries; 0.3% are from out of state; 11% Black or African American, non-Hispanic/Latino; 30% Hispanic/Latino; 3% Asian, non-Hispanic/Latino; 0.2% Native Hawaiian or other Pacific Islander, non-Hispanic/Latino; 0.2% American Indian or Alaska Native, non-Hispanic/Latino; 3% Two or more races, non-Hispanic/Latino; 4% Race/ethnicity unknown; 0.3% international; 10% transferred in. *Retention:* 59% of full-time freshmen returned.
Faculty *Student/faculty ratio:* 17:1.
Academics *Calendar:* semesters. *Degree:* certificates and associate. *Special study options:* academic remediation for entering students, accelerated degree program, adult/continuing education programs, advanced placement credit, cooperative education, distance learning, English as a second language, external degree program, honors programs, independent study, internships, off-campus study, part-time degree program, services for LD students, summer session for credit.
Library Max R. Traurig Learning Resource Center. *Books:* 38,400 (physical); *Serial titles:* 108 (physical); *Databases:* 12. Weekly public service hours: 65; students can reserve study rooms.
Student Life *Campus security:* 24-hour emergency response devices and patrols, late-night transport/escort service, security escort service.
Standardized Tests *Required:* ACCUPLACER (for admission).
Financial Aid Of all full-time matriculated undergraduates who enrolled in 2017, 70 Federal Work-Study jobs (averaging $1942). 16 state and other part-time jobs (averaging $1660).
Applying *Options:* electronic application, deferred entrance. *Application fee:* $20. *Required:* high school transcript. *Required for some:* interview.
Freshman Application Contact Noel Rosamilio, Associate Dean of Enrollment Management, Naugatuck Valley Community College, Kinney Hall, K500, 750 Chase Parkway, Waterbury, CT 06708. *Phone:* 203-596-8780. *E-mail:* nrosamilio@nv.edu. *Website:* http://www.nvcc.commnet.edu/.

Northwestern Connecticut Community College

Winsted, Connecticut

Freshman Application Contact Admissions Office, Northwestern Connecticut Community College, Park Place East, Winsted, CT 06098-1798. *Phone:* 860-738-6330. *Fax:* 860-738-6437. *E-mail:* admissions@nwcc.commnet.edu. *Website:* http://www.nwcc.commnet.edu/.

Norwalk Community College

Norwalk, Connecticut

Freshman Application Contact Mr. Curtis Antrum, Admissions Counselor, Norwalk Community College, 188 Richards Avenue, Norwalk, CT 06854-1655. *Phone:* 203-857-7060. *Fax:* 203-857-3335. *E-mail:* admissions@ncc.commnet.edu. *Website:* http://www.ncc.commnet.edu/.

Quinebaug Valley Community College

Danielson, Connecticut

Freshman Application Contact Dr. Toni Moumouris, Director of Admissions, Quinebaug Valley Community College, 742 Upper Maple Street, Danielson, CT 06239. *Phone:* 860-774-1130 Ext. 318. *Fax:* 860-774-7768. *E-mail:* qu_isd@commnet.edu. *Website:* http://www.qvcc.edu/.

Three Rivers Community College

Norwich, Connecticut

- **State-supported** 2-year, founded 1963, part of Connecticut State Colleges & Universities (CSCU)
- **Suburban** 40-acre campus with easy access to Hartford
- **Coed**

Undergraduates 1,340 full-time, 2,847 part-time. Students come from 5 states and territories; 1% are from out of state; 8% Black or African American, non-Hispanic/Latino; 17% Hispanic/Latino; 4% Asian, non-Hispanic/Latino; 0.3% Native Hawaiian or other Pacific Islander, non-Hispanic/Latino; 0.7% American Indian or Alaska Native, non-Hispanic/Latino; 5% Two or more races, non-Hispanic/Latino; 3% Race/ethnicity unknown; 0.2% international; 9% transferred in. *Retention:* 63% of full-time freshmen returned.
Faculty *Student/faculty ratio:* 16:1.
Academics *Calendar:* semesters. *Degrees:* certificates and associate (engineering technology programs are offered on the Thames Valley Campus; liberal arts, transfer and career programs are offered on the Mohegan Campus). *Special study options:* adult/continuing education programs, part-time degree program.
Library Three Rivers Community College Learning Resource Center plus 1 other.
Student Life *Campus security:* 24-hour emergency response devices, late-night transport/escort service, 14-hour patrols by trained security personnel.
Financial Aid Of all full-time matriculated undergraduates who enrolled in 2010, 1,135 applied for aid, 967 were judged to have need, 266 had their need fully met. *Average percent of need met:* 48. *Average financial aid package:* $2631. *Average need-based loan:* $3308. *Average need-based gift aid:* $2409.
Applying *Options:* electronic application, early admission, deferred entrance. *Recommended:* high school transcript.
Freshman Application Contact Admissions Office, Three Rivers Community College, CT. *Phone:* 860-215-9296. *E-mail:* admissions@trcc.commnet.edu. *Website:* http://www.threerivers.edu/.

Tunxis Community College

Farmington, Connecticut

Freshman Application Contact Ms. Tamika Davis, Director of Admissions, Tunxis Community College, 271 Scott Swamp Road, Farmington, CT 06032. *Phone:* 860-773-1494. *Fax:* 860-606-9501. *E-mail:* pmccluskey@tunxis.edu. *Website:* http://www.tunxis.edu/.

DELAWARE

Delaware College of Art and Design

Wilmington, Delaware

Freshman Application Contact Ms. Allison Gullo, Delaware College of Art and Design, 600 North Market Street, Wilmington, DE 19801. *Phone:* 302-622-8867 Ext. 111. *Fax:* 302-622-8870. *E-mail:* agullo@dcad.edu. *Website:* http://www.dcad.edu/.

Delaware Technical & Community College, Jack F. Owens Campus

Georgetown, Delaware

Freshman Application Contact Ms. Claire McDonald, Admissions Counselor, Delaware Technical & Community College, Jack F. Owens Campus, PO Box 610, Georgetown, DE 19947. *Phone:* 302-856-5400. *Fax:* 302-856-9461. *Website:* http://www.dtcc.edu/.

Delaware Technical & Community College, Stanton/George Campus
Wilmington, Delaware

Freshman Application Contact Ms. Rebecca Bailey, Admissions Coordinator, Wilmington, Delaware Technical & Community College, Stanton/George Campus, 333 Shipley Street, Wilmington, DE 19713. *Phone:* 302-571-5343. *Fax:* 302-577-2548. *Website:* http://www.dtcc.edu/.

Delaware Technical & Community College, Terry Campus
Dover, Delaware

Freshman Application Contact Mrs. Maria Harris, Admissions Officer, Delaware Technical & Community College, Terry Campus, 100 Campus Drive, Dover, DE 19904. *Phone:* 302-857-1020. *Fax:* 302-857-1296. *E-mail:* terry-info@dtcc.edu. *Website:* http://www.dtcc.edu/.

FLORIDA

Academy for Nursing and Health Occupations
West Palm Beach, Florida

Admissions Office Contact Academy for Nursing and Health Occupations, 5154 Okeechobee Boulevard, Suite 201, West Palm Beach, FL 33417. *Website:* http://www.anho.edu/.

Advance Science College
Hialeah, Florida

Admissions Office Contact Advance Science College, 3750 W. 12 Avenue, Hialeah, FL 33012. *Website:* http://www.asicollege.edu/.

Altierus Career College
Tampa, Florida

Freshman Application Contact Altierus Career College, 3319 West Hillsborough Avenue, Tampa, FL 33614. *Phone:* 813-879-6000 Ext. 129. *Website:* http://www.altierus.edu/.

American Medical Academy
Miami, Florida

Admissions Office Contact American Medical Academy, 12215 SW 112 Street, Miami, FL 33186-4830. *Website:* http://www.ama.edu/.

ATA Career Education
Spring Hill, Florida

Admissions Office Contact ATA Career Education, 7351 Spring Hill Drive, Suite 11, Spring Hill, FL 34606. *Website:* http://www.atafl.edu/.

Aviator College of Aeronautical Science & Technology
Fort Pierce, Florida

Admissions Office Contact Aviator College of Aeronautical Science & Technology, 3800 St. Lucie Boulevard, Fort Pierce, FL 34946. *Website:* http://aviator.edu/FlightSchool/.

Broward College
Fort Lauderdale, Florida

Freshman Application Contact Mr. Willie J. Alexander, Associate Vice President for Student Affairs/College Registrar, Broward College, 225 East Las Olas Boulevard, Fort Lauderdale, FL 33301. *Phone:* 954-201-7471. *Fax:* 954-201-7466. *E-mail:* walexand@broward.edu. *Website:* http://www.broward.edu/.

Cambridge College of Healthcare & Technology
Delray Beach, Florida

Admissions Office Contact Cambridge College of Healthcare & Technology, 5150 Linton Boulevard, Suite 340, Delray Beach, FL 33484. *Website:* http://www.cambridgehealth.edu/.

Chipola College
Marianna, Florida

- **State-supported** primarily 2-year, founded 1947
- **Rural** 105-acre campus
- **Coed**

Undergraduates 859 full-time, 1,245 part-time. Students come from 7 states and territories; 6 other countries; 8% are from out of state; 15% Black or African American, non-Hispanic/Latino; 5% Hispanic/Latino; 0.7% Asian, non-Hispanic/Latino; 0.1% Native Hawaiian or other Pacific Islander, non-Hispanic/Latino; 1% American Indian or Alaska Native, non-Hispanic/Latino; 3% Two or more races, non-Hispanic/Latino; 1% Race/ethnicity unknown; 0.5% international; 7% transferred in.

Faculty *Student/faculty ratio:* 24:1.

Academics *Calendar:* semesters. *Degrees:* certificates, associate, and bachelor's. *Special study options:* academic remediation for entering students, adult/continuing education programs, advanced placement credit, distance learning, honors programs, independent study, part-time degree program, services for LD students, summer session for credit.

Library Chipola Library. *Books:* 30,000 (physical), 67,000 (digital/electronic); *Serial titles:* 150 (physical); *Databases:* 100. Weekly public service hours: 60; students can reserve study rooms.

Student Life *Campus security:* night security personnel.

Athletics Member NJCAA.

Applying *Options:* early admission. *Required:* high school transcript.

Freshman Application Contact Mrs. Kathy L. Rehberg, Registrar, Chipola College, 3094 Indian Circle, Marianna, FL 32446-3065. *Phone:* 850-718-2233. *Fax:* 850-718-2287. *E-mail:* rehbergk@chipola.edu. *Website:* http://www.chipola.edu/.

City College
Altamonte Springs, Florida

Director of Admissions Ms. Kimberly Bowden, Director of Admissions, City College, 177 Montgomery Road, Altamonte Springs, FL 32714. *Phone:* 352-335-4000. *Fax:* 352-335-4303. *E-mail:* kbowden@citycollege.edu. *Website:* http://www.citycollege.edu/.

City College
Fort Lauderdale, Florida

Freshman Application Contact City College, 2000 West Commercial Boulevard, Suite 200, Fort Lauderdale, FL 33309. *Phone:* 954-492-5353. *Toll-free phone:* 866-314-5681. *Website:* http://www.citycollege.edu/.

City College
Gainesville, Florida

Freshman Application Contact Admissions Office, City College, 7001 Northwest 4th Boulevard, Gainesville, FL 32607. *Phone:* 352-335-4000. *Website:* http://www.citycollege.edu/.

City College
Hollywood, Florida

Admissions Office Contact City College, 6565 Taft Street, Hollywood, FL 33024. *Toll-free phone:* 866-314-5681. *Website:* http://www.citycollege.edu/.

City College
Miami, Florida

Freshman Application Contact Admissions Office, City College, 9300 South Dadeland Boulevard, Suite PH, Miami, FL 33156. *Phone:* 305-666-9242. *Fax:* 305-666-9243. *Website:* http://www.citycollege.edu/.

College of Business and Technology–Cutler Bay Campus

Cutler Bay, Florida

- **Proprietary** 2-year, founded 2009
- **Urban** campus with easy access to Miami
- **Coed**

Undergraduates 137 full-time. Students come from 1 other state; 14% Black or African American, non-Hispanic/Latino; 79% Hispanic/Latino; 3% Asian, non-Hispanic/Latino; 1% Two or more races, non-Hispanic/Latino.
Faculty *Student/faculty ratio:* 13:1.
Academics *Calendar:* semesters. *Degree:* certificates, diplomas, and associate. *Special study options:* academic remediation for entering students, adult/continuing education programs, cooperative education, independent study, services for LD students.
Library CBT College–Cutler Bay Library. *Books:* 2,140 (physical); *Serial titles:* 20 (physical); *Databases:* 50.
Student Life *Campus security:* security guard patrol, local police department patrol.
Applying *Application fee:* $25. *Required:* high school transcript, interview.
Freshman Application Contact College of Business and Technology–Cutler Bay Campus, 19151 South Dixie Highway, Cutler Bay, FL 33157. *Phone:* 305-273-4499 Ext. 1100. *Website:* http://www.cbt.edu/.

College of Business and Technology–Flagler Campus

Miami, Florida

- **Proprietary** 2-year, founded 1988
- **Urban** campus
- **Coed**

Undergraduates 256 full-time. Students come from 1 other state; 0.4% Black or African American, non-Hispanic/Latino; 99% Hispanic/Latino.
Faculty *Student/faculty ratio:* 17:1.
Academics *Calendar:* semesters. *Degree:* certificates, diplomas, and associate. *Special study options:* academic remediation for entering students, adult/continuing education programs, cooperative education, English as a second language, independent study, services for LD students.
Library CBT College–Flagler Library. *Books:* 1,516 (physical); *Serial titles:* 6 (physical); *Databases:* 50.
Student Life *Campus security:* security guard patrol, local police department patrol.
Applying *Application fee:* $25. *Required:* high school transcript, interview.
Freshman Application Contact College of Business and Technology–Flagler Campus, 8230 West Flagler Street, Miami, FL 33144. *Phone:* 305-273-4499 Ext. 1100. *Website:* http://www.cbt.edu/.

College of Business and Technology–Hialeah Campus

Hialeah, Florida

- **Proprietary** 2-year, founded 1988
- **Urban** campus with easy access to Miami
- **Coed, primarily men**

Undergraduates 200 full-time. Students come from 1 other state; 0.5% Black or African American, non-Hispanic/Latino; 100% Hispanic/Latino.
Faculty *Student/faculty ratio:* 14:1.
Academics *Calendar:* semesters. *Degree:* certificates, diplomas, and associate. *Special study options:* academic remediation for entering students, adult/continuing education programs, cooperative education, English as a second language, independent study, services for LD students.
Library CBT College–Hialeah Library. *Books:* 897 (physical); *Serial titles:* 7 (physical); *Databases:* 50.
Student Life *Campus security:* local police department patrols.
Applying *Application fee:* $25. *Required:* high school transcript, interview.
Freshman Application Contact College of Business and Technology–Hialeah Campus, 935 West 49 Street, Hialeah, FL 33012. *Phone:* 305-273-4499 Ext. 1100. *Website:* http://www.cbt.edu/.

College of Business and Technology–Main Campus

Miami, Florida

- **Proprietary** primarily 2-year, founded 1988
- **Urban** campus
- **Coed**

Undergraduates 10 full-time. Students come from 1 other state; 100% Hispanic/Latino.
Faculty *Student/faculty ratio:* 10:1.
Academics *Calendar:* semesters. *Degrees:* certificates, diplomas, associate, and bachelor's. *Special study options:* academic remediation for entering students, adult/continuing education programs, cooperative education, English as a second language, independent study.
Library CBT College-Miami Branch Library (Use Flagler). *Books:* 590 (physical); *Serial titles:* 8 (physical); *Databases:* 50.
Student Life *Campus security:* security guard posted at main entrance, local police department.
Applying *Application fee:* $25. *Required:* high school transcript, interview.
Freshman Application Contact College of Business and Technology–Main Campus, 8700 West Flagler Street, Suite 420, Miami, FL 33174. *Phone:* 305-273-4499 Ext. 1100. *Website:* http://www.cbt.edu/.

College of Business and Technology–Miami Gardens

Miami Gardens, Florida

- **Proprietary** primarily 2-year, founded 2012
- **Urban** campus with easy access to Miami
- **Coed**

Undergraduates 91 full-time. Students come from 1 other state; 18% Black or African American, non-Hispanic/Latino; 81% Hispanic/Latino.
Faculty *Student/faculty ratio:* 15:1.
Academics *Calendar:* semesters. *Degrees:* certificates, diplomas, associate, and bachelor's. *Special study options:* academic remediation for entering students, adult/continuing education programs, cooperative education, independent study, services for LD students.
Library CBT College–Miami Gardens Library. *Books:* 1,085 (physical); *Serial titles:* 18 (physical); *Databases:* 50.
Student Life *Campus security:* local police department.
Applying *Application fee:* $25. *Required:* high school transcript, interview.
Freshman Application Contact College of Business and Technology–Miami Gardens, 5190 NW 167 Street, Miami Gardens, FL 33014. *Phone:* 305-273-4499 Ext. 1100. *Website:* http://www.cbt.edu/.

College of Central Florida

Ocala, Florida

- **State and locally supported** primarily 2-year, founded 1957, part of Florida College System
- **Small-town** 139-acre campus
- **Endowment** $65.4 million
- **Coed,** 6,820 undergraduate students, 44% full-time, 62% women, 38% men

Undergraduates 3,016 full-time, 3,804 part-time. 3% are from out of state; 14% Black or African American, non-Hispanic/Latino; 15% Hispanic/Latino; 2% Asian, non-Hispanic/Latino; 0.5% Native Hawaiian or other Pacific Islander, non-Hispanic/Latino; 0.4% American Indian or Alaska Native, non-Hispanic/Latino; 5% Two or more races, non-Hispanic/Latino; 1% Race/ethnicity unknown; 2% international; 6% transferred in.
Freshmen *Admission:* 4,090 applied, 1,593 admitted, 1,334 enrolled.
Majors Accounting technology and bookkeeping; advertising; agribusiness; agriculture; animal sciences; architecture; art; biology/biological sciences; business administration and management; business administration, management and operations related; business/commerce; chemistry; clinical laboratory science/medical technology; computer and information sciences; construction engineering technology; criminal justice/law enforcement administration; criminology; dental assisting; drafting and design technology; dramatic/theater arts; early childhood education; economics; elementary education; emergency medical technology (EMT paramedic); engineering technology; English; environmental studies; equestrian studies; family and consumer sciences/human sciences; fire science/firefighting; foreign languages and literatures; forestry; health information/medical records technology; health/medical preparatory programs related; health services/allied health/health sciences; history; humanities; human services; information technology; interior architecture; journalism; landscaping and groundskeeping; legal assistant/paralegal; liberal arts and sciences and

humanities related; liberal arts and sciences/liberal studies; library and information science; marketing/marketing management; mathematics; medical radiologic technology; music; music teacher education; occupational therapy; office management; parks, recreation and leisure; philosophy; physical education teaching and coaching; physical therapy; physical therapy technology; physics; pre-law studies; premedical studies; pre-pharmacy studies; pre-veterinary studies; psychology; registered nursing/registered nurse; religious studies; restaurant, culinary, and catering management; secondary education; social sciences; social work; sociology; special education; statistics; veterinary/animal health technology.

Academics *Calendar:* semesters. *Degrees:* certificates, diplomas, associate, and bachelor's. *Special study options:* academic remediation for entering students, adult/continuing education programs, advanced placement credit, cooperative education, distance learning, English as a second language, freshman honors college, honors programs, independent study, internships, part-time degree program, services for LD students, summer session for credit.

Library Clifford B. Stearns Learning Resources Center. *Books:* 75,935 (physical), 43,910 (digital/electronic); *Databases:* 152. Students can reserve study rooms.

Student Life *Housing:* college housing not available. *Activities and Organizations:* drama/theater group, student-run newspaper, choral group, Inspirational Choir, Model United Nations, Performing Arts, Phi Theta Kappa (PTK), Student Nurses Association. *Campus security:* 24-hour emergency response devices and patrols, student patrols, late-night transport/escort service. *Student services:* personal/psychological counseling.

Athletics Member NJCAA. *Intercollegiate sports:* basketball W(s), softball W(s), volleyball W(s). *Intramural sports:* bowling M.

Financial Aid Of all full-time matriculated undergraduates who enrolled in 2017, 1,184 applied for aid, 753 were judged to have need, 23 had their need fully met. In 2017, 38 non-need-based awards were made. *Average percent of need met:* 55%. *Average financial aid package:* $1744. *Average need-based loan:* $2164. *Average need-based gift aid:* $1731. *Average non-need-based aid:* $889.

Applying *Options:* electronic application, early admission. *Application fee:* $30. *Required:* high school transcript. *Application deadlines:* rolling (freshmen), rolling (transfers). *Notification:* continuous (freshmen), continuous (transfers).

Freshman Application Contact Mr. Alton Austin, Director of Enrollment Services/Registrar, College of Central Florida, 3001 SW College Road, Ocala, FL 34474. *Phone:* 352-237-2111 Ext. 1751. *Fax:* 352-873-5882. *E-mail:* austina@cf.edu.
Website: http://www.cf.edu/.

Concorde Career Institute
Jacksonville, Florida

Admissions Office Contact Concorde Career Institute, 7259 Salisbury Road, Jacksonville, FL 32256. *Website:* http://www.concorde.edu/.

Concorde Career Institute
Miramar, Florida

Admissions Office Contact Concorde Career Institute, 10933 Marks Way, Miramar, FL 33025. *Website:* http://www.concorde.edu/.

Concorde Career Institute
Orlando, Florida

Admissions Office Contact Concorde Career Institute, 3444 McCrory Place, Orlando, FL 32803. *Website:* http://www.concorde.edu/.

Concorde Career Institute
Tampa, Florida

Admissions Office Contact Concorde Career Institute, 4202 West Spruce Street, Tampa, FL 33607. *Website:* http://www.concorde.edu/.

Daytona College
Ormond Beach, Florida

Admissions Office Contact Daytona College, 469 South Nova Road, Ormond Beach, FL 32174-8445. *Website:* http://www.daytonacollege.edu/.

Daytona State College
Daytona Beach, Florida

- **State-supported** primarily 2-year, founded 1957, part of Florida College System
- **Suburban** 100-acre campus with easy access to Orlando
- **Endowment** $13.4 million
- **Coed,** 19,530 undergraduate students, 40% full-time, 62% women, 38% men

Undergraduates 7,848 full-time, 11,682 part-time. Students come from 26 other countries; 2% are from out of state; 13% Black or African American, non-Hispanic/Latino; 17% Hispanic/Latino; 2% Asian, non-Hispanic/Latino; 0.1% Native Hawaiian or other Pacific Islander, non-Hispanic/Latino; 0.2% American Indian or Alaska Native, non-Hispanic/Latino; 4% Two or more races, non-Hispanic/Latino; 2% Race/ethnicity unknown; 0.2% international.

Freshmen *Admission:* 1,417 enrolled.

Faculty *Total:* 913, 29% full-time, 17% with terminal degrees. *Student/faculty ratio:* 16:1.

Majors Accounting technology and bookkeeping; aeronautical/aerospace engineering technology; biology teacher education; business administration and management; business administration, management and operations related; chemistry teacher education; community health services counseling; computer engineering technology; computer programming; computer programming (specific applications); construction engineering technology; criminal justice/law enforcement administration; dental hygiene; digital communication and media/multimedia; drafting and design technology; early childhood education; electrical, electronic and communications engineering technology; elementary education; emergency medical technology (EMT paramedic); engineering technologies and engineering related; environmental science; fire prevention and safety technology; health information/medical records technology; hospitality administration; information technology; interior design; legal assistant/paralegal; liberal arts and sciences/liberal studies; mathematics teacher education; medical radiologic technology; music technology; network and system administration; occupational therapist assistant; office management; operations management; photographic and film/video technology; photography; physical therapy technology; physics teacher education; registered nursing/registered nurse; respiratory care therapy; restaurant, culinary, and catering management; science teacher education; special education; web page, digital/multimedia and information resources design.

Academics *Calendar:* semesters. *Degrees:* certificates, diplomas, associate, bachelor's, and postbachelor's certificates. *Special study options:* academic remediation for entering students, adult/continuing education programs, advanced placement credit, cooperative education, distance learning, English as a second language, external degree program, freshman honors college, honors programs, independent study, internships, off-campus study, part-time degree program, services for LD students, study abroad, summer session for credit. *ROTC:* Army (c), Air Force (c).

Library Mary Karl Memorial Learning Resources Center plus 1 other. *Books:* 36,000 (physical), 175,000 (digital/electronic); *Serial titles:* 164 (physical); *Databases:* 100. Weekly public service hours: 68; students can reserve study rooms.

Student Life *Housing:* college housing not available. *Activities and Organizations:* drama/theater group, student-run newspaper, choral group, Phi Theta Kappa International Honors Society, Student Government Association, Student Respiratory Therapy Club, Business Club, Student Paralegal Club, national fraternities, national sororities. *Campus security:* 24-hour emergency response devices and patrols, late-night transport/escort service, emergency alert system capable of delivering text messages, voice calls, and email messages to college email accounts. *Student services:* personal/psychological counseling, women's center, veterans affairs office.

Athletics Member NJCAA. *Intercollegiate sports:* basketball W(s), cross-country running W(s), soccer W(s), softball W(s), volleyball W(s). *Intramural sports:* basketball M, football M, soccer M, table tennis M, volleyball M.

Financial Aid Of all full-time matriculated undergraduates who enrolled in 2017, 2,424 applied for aid, 2,418 were judged to have need. 118 Federal Work-Study jobs (averaging $1585). In 2017, 82 non-need-based awards were made. *Average need-based loan:* $1517. *Average need-based gift aid:* $1815. *Average non-need-based aid:* $1878. *Average indebtedness upon graduation:* $2483.

Applying *Options:* electronic application, early admission, deferred entrance. *Required:* high school transcript. *Application deadlines:* rolling (freshmen), rolling (transfers). *Notification:* continuous (freshmen), continuous (transfers).

Freshman Application Contact Dr. Karen Sanders, Director of Admissions and Recruitment, Daytona State College, 1200 International Speedway Boulevard, Daytona Beach, FL 32114. *Phone:* 386-506-3050. *E-mail:* karen.sanders@daytonastate.edu.
Website: http://www.daytonastate.edu/.

Eastern Florida State College
Cocoa, Florida

Freshman Application Contact Ms. Stephanie Burnette, Registrar, Eastern Florida State College, 1519 Clearlake Road, Cocoa, FL 32922-6597. *Phone:* 321-433-7271. *Fax:* 321-433-7172. *E-mail:* cocoaadmissions@brevardcc.edu. *Website:* http://www.easternflorida.edu/.

Florida Career College
Boynton Beach, Florida

Admissions Office Contact Florida Career College, 1749 North Congress Avenue, Boynton Beach, FL 33426. *Website:* http://www.floridacareercollege.edu/.

Florida Career College
Hialeah, Florida

Admissions Office Contact Florida Career College, 3750 West 18th Avenue, Hialeah, FL 33012. *Toll-free phone:* 888-852-7272. *Website:* http://www.floridacareercollege.edu/.

Florida Career College
Jacksonville, Florida

Admissions Office Contact Florida Career College, 6600 Youngerman Circle, Jacksonville, FL 32244. *Website:* http://www.floridacareercollege.edu/.

Florida Career College
Lauderdale Lakes, Florida

Admissions Office Contact Florida Career College, 3383 North State Road 7, Lauderdale Lakes, FL 33319. *Website:* http://www.floridacareercollege.edu/.

Florida Career College
Margate, Florida

Admissions Office Contact Florida Career College, 3271 North State Road 7, Margate, FL 33063. *Website:* http://www.floridacareercollege.edu/.

Florida Career College
Miami, Florida

Director of Admissions Mr. David Knobel, President, Florida Career College, 1321 Southwest 107th Avenue, Suite 201B, Miami, FL 33174. *Phone:* 305-553-6065. *Toll-free phone:* 888-852-7272. *Website:* http://www.floridacareercollege.edu/.

Florida Career College
Orlando, Florida

Admissions Office Contact Florida Career College, 989 North Semoran Boulevard, Orlando, FL 32807. *Website:* http://www.floridacareercollege.edu/.

Florida Career College
Pembroke Pines, Florida

Admissions Office Contact Florida Career College, 7891 Pines Boulevard, Pembroke Pines, FL 33024. *Toll-free phone:* 888-852-7272. *Website:* http://www.floridacareercollege.edu/.

Florida Career College
Tampa, Florida

Admissions Office Contact Florida Career College, 9950 Princess Palm Avenue, Tampa, FL 33619. *Website:* http://www.floridacareercollege.edu/.

Florida Career College
West Palm Beach, Florida

Admissions Office Contact Florida Career College, 6058 Okeechobee Boulevard, West Palm Beach, FL 33417. *Toll-free phone:* 888-852-7272. *Website:* http://www.floridacareercollege.edu/.

Florida Gateway College
Lake City, Florida

Freshman Application Contact Admissions, Florida Gateway College, 149 SE College Place, Lake City, FL 32025-8703. *Phone:* 386-755-4236. *E-mail:* admissions@fgc.edu. *Website:* http://www.fgc.edu/.

Florida Keys Community College
Key West, Florida

- **State-supported** primarily 2-year, founded 1965, part of Florida College System
- **Small-town** 20-acre campus
- **Coed**

Undergraduates 363 full-time, 667 part-time. 9% Black or African American, non-Hispanic/Latino; 27% Hispanic/Latino; 2% Asian, non-Hispanic/Latino; 0.4% Native Hawaiian or other Pacific Islander, non-Hispanic/Latino; 0.3% American Indian or Alaska Native, non-Hispanic/Latino; 3% Two or more races, non-Hispanic/Latino; 4% Race/ethnicity unknown; 0.9% international; 10% transferred in.
Faculty *Student/faculty ratio:* 12:1.
Academics *Calendar:* semesters. *Degrees:* certificates, associate, and bachelor's. *Special study options:* academic remediation for entering students, adult/continuing education programs, advanced placement credit, cooperative education, distance learning, double majors, English as a second language, independent study, internships, part-time degree program, services for LD students, student-designed majors, summer session for credit.
Library Florida Keys Community College Library. Students can reserve study rooms.
Student Life *Campus security:* 24-hour patrols.
Financial Aid Of all full-time matriculated undergraduates who enrolled in 2017, 30 Federal Work-Study jobs (averaging $2000).
Applying *Options:* electronic application, early admission, deferred entrance. *Application fee:* $30. *Required for some:* essay or personal statement, high school transcript, letters of recommendation.
Freshman Application Contact Florida Keys Community College, 5901 College Road, Key West, FL 33040-4397. *Phone:* 305-296-9081 Ext. 237. *Website:* http://www.fkcc.edu/.

The Florida School of Traditional Midwifery
Gainseville, Florida

Freshman Application Contact Admissions Office, The Florida School of Traditional Midwifery, 810 East University Avenue, 2nd Floor, Gainseville, FL 32601. *Phone:* 352-338-0766. *Fax:* 352-338-2013. *E-mail:* info@midwiferyschool.org. *Website:* http://www.midwiferyschool.org/.

Florida SouthWestern State College
Fort Myers, Florida

Freshman Application Contact FSW Admissions, Florida SouthWestern State College, 8099 College Parkway, Fort Myers, FL 33919. *Phone:* 239-489-9054. *Fax:* 239-489-9094. *E-mail:* admissions@fsw.edu. *Website:* http://www.fsw.edu/.

Florida State College at Jacksonville
Jacksonville, Florida

Freshman Application Contact Dr. Peter Biegel, Registrar, Florida State College at Jacksonville, 501 West State Street, Jacksonville, FL 32202. *Phone:* 904-632-5112. *Toll-free phone:* 888-873-1145. *E-mail:* pbiegel@fscj.edu. *Website:* http://www.fscj.edu/.

Florida Technical College
Orlando, Florida

Director of Admissions Ms. Jeanette E. Muschlitz, Director of Admissions, Florida Technical College, 12900 Challenger Parkway, Orlando, FL 32826. *Phone:* 407-678-5600. *Toll-free phone:* 888-574-2082. *Website:* http://www.ftccollege.edu/.

Fortis College
Cutler Bay, Florida

Admissions Office Contact Fortis College, 19600 South Dixie Highway, Suite B, Cutler Bay, FL 33157. *Toll-free phone:* 855-4-FORTIS. *Website:* http://www.fortis.edu/.

Fortis College
Orange Park, Florida

Admissions Office Contact Fortis College, 700 Blanding Boulevard, Suite 16, Orange Park, FL 32065. *Toll-free phone:* 855-4-FORTIS. *Website:* http://www.fortis.edu/.

Fortis Institute
Pensacola, Florida

Admissions Office Contact Fortis Institute, 4081 East Olive Road, Suite B, Pensacola, FL 32514. *Toll-free phone:* 855-4-FORTIS. *Website:* http://www.fortis.edu/.

Fortis Institute
Port St. Lucie, Florida

Admissions Office Contact Fortis Institute, 9022 South US Highway 1, Port St. Lucie, FL 34952. *Toll-free phone:* 855-4-FORTIS. *Website:* http://www.fortis.edu/.

Galen College of Nursing
St. Petersburg, Florida

Admissions Office Contact Galen College of Nursing, 11101 Roosevelt Boulevard North, St. Petersburg, FL 33716. *Toll-free phone:* 877-223-7040. *Website:* http://www.galencollege.edu/.

Gulf Coast State College
Panama City, Florida

- **State-supported** primarily 2-year, founded 1957, part of Florida College System
- **Urban** 80-acre campus
- **Endowment** $30.5 million
- **Coed**

Undergraduates 1,840 full-time, 3,539 part-time. Students come from 13 states and territories; 3% are from out of state; 12% Black or African American, non-Hispanic/Latino; 7% Hispanic/Latino; 3% Asian, non-Hispanic/Latino; 0.9% American Indian or Alaska Native, non-Hispanic/Latino; 4% Two or more races, non-Hispanic/Latino; 3% Race/ethnicity unknown; 0.6% international; 3% transferred in.

Faculty *Student/faculty ratio:* 19:1.

Academics *Calendar:* semesters. *Degrees:* certificates, associate, and bachelor's. *Special study options:* academic remediation for entering students, accelerated degree program, adult/continuing education programs, advanced placement credit, cooperative education, distance learning, double majors, English as a second language, external degree program, honors programs, independent study, off-campus study, part-time degree program, services for LD students, study abroad, summer session for credit.

Library Gulf Coast State College Library. *Books:* 32,529 (physical), 57,578 (digital/electronic); *Serial titles:* 43 (physical), 55,302 (digital/electronic); *Databases:* 176.

Student Life *Campus security:* 24-hour patrols, late-night transport/escort service, patrols by trained security personnel during campus hours.

Athletics Member NJCAA.

Financial Aid Of all full-time matriculated undergraduates who enrolled in 2017, 145 Federal Work-Study jobs (averaging $3200). 60 state and other part-time jobs (averaging $2600).

Applying *Options:* electronic application, early admission, deferred entrance. *Application fee:* $20. *Required:* high school transcript.

Freshman Application Contact Mrs. Sam Wagner, Application Process Specialist, Gulf Coast State College, 5230 West U.S. Highway 98, Panama City, FL 32401. *Phone:* 850-769-1551 Ext. 2936. *Fax:* 850-913-3308. *E-mail:* swagner1@gulfcoast.edu. *Website:* http://www.gulfcoast.edu/.

Gwinnett Institute
Orlando, Florida

Admissions Office Contact Gwinnett Institute, 1900 North Alafaya Trail, Orlando, FL 32826. *Website:* http://www.gwinnettcollege.edu/locations/orlando/.

Health Career Institute
West Palm Beach, Florida

Admissions Office Contact Health Career Institute, 1764 North Congress Avenue, West Palm Beach, FL 33409. *Website:* http://www.hci.edu/.

Hillsborough Community College
Tampa, Florida

Freshman Application Contact Ms. Jennifer Young, College Registrar, Hillsborough Community College, PO Box 31127, Tampa, FL 33631-3127. *Phone:* 813-259-6565. *E-mail:* jyoung92@hccfl.edu. *Website:* http://www.hccfl.edu/.

Hope College of Arts and Sciences
Pompano Beach, Florida

Admissions Office Contact Hope College of Arts and Sciences, 1200 SW 3rd Street, Pompano Beach, FL 33069. *Website:* http://www.hcas.edu/.

Jones Technical Institute
Jacksonville, Florida

Admissions Office Contact Jones Technical Institute, 8813 Western Way, Jacksonville, FL 32256. *Website:* http://www.jtech.org/.

Lake-Sumter State College
Leesburg, Florida

Freshman Application Contact Ms. Bonnie Yanick, Enrollment Specialist, Lake-Sumter State College, 9501 U.S. Highway 441, Leesburg, FL 34788-8751. *Phone:* 352-365-3561. *Fax:* 352-365-3553. *E-mail:* admissinquiry@lscc.edu. *Website:* http://www.lssc.edu/.

Medical Prep Institute of Tampa Bay
Tampa, Florida

Admissions Office Contact Medical Prep Institute of Tampa Bay, 2304 East Busch Boulevard, Tampa, FL 33612. *Website:* http://www.medicalprepinstitute.org/.

Med-Life Institute
Kissimmee, Florida

Admissions Office Contact Med-Life Institute, 4727 West Irlo Bronson Memorial Highway, Kissimmee, FL 34746. *Website:* http://www.medlifeinstitute.com/.

Med-Life Institute
Lauderdale Lakes, Florida

Admissions Office Contact Med-Life Institute, 4000 North State Road 7, Lauderdale Lakes, FL 33319. *Website:* http://www.medlifeinstitute.com/.

Med-Life Institute
Naples, Florida

Admissions Office Contact Med-Life Institute, 4995 East Tamiami Trail, Naples, FL 34112. *Website:* http://www.medlifeinstitute.com/.

Meridian College
Sarasota, Florida

Admissions Office Contact Meridian College, 7020 Professional Parkway East, Sarasota, FL 34240. *Website:* http://www.meridian.edu/.

Miami Dade College

Miami, Florida

- **State and locally supported** primarily 2-year, founded 1960, part of Florida College System
- **Urban** campus
- **Endowment** $137.1 million
- **Coed**

Undergraduates 23,589 full-time, 32,412 part-time. Students come from 37 states and territories; 165 other countries; 0.4% are from out of state; 14% Black or African American, non-Hispanic/Latino; 70% Hispanic/Latino; 1% Asian, non-Hispanic/Latino; 0.1% Native Hawaiian or other Pacific Islander, non-Hispanic/Latino; 0.1% American Indian or Alaska Native, non-Hispanic/Latino; 0.6% Two or more races, non-Hispanic/Latino; 2% Race/ethnicity unknown; 6% international; 0.1% transferred in.
Faculty *Student/faculty ratio:* 26:1.
Academics *Calendar:* 16-16-6-6. *Degrees:* certificates, associate, bachelor's, and postbachelor's certificates. *Special study options:* academic remediation for entering students, accelerated degree program, adult/continuing education programs, advanced placement credit, cooperative education, distance learning, English as a second language, freshman honors college, honors programs, independent study, internships, off-campus study, part-time degree program, services for LD students, study abroad, summer session for credit. *ROTC:* Army (b), Air Force (c).
Library Miami Dade College Learning Resources plus 9 others. *Books:* 185,820 (physical), 60,221 (digital/electronic); *Serial titles:* 708 (physical), 46,482 (digital/electronic); *Databases:* 126. Weekly public service hours: 69; students can reserve study rooms.
Student Life *Campus security:* 24-hour emergency response devices and patrols, student patrols, late-night transport/escort service, Emergency Mass Notification System (EMNS), campus public address systems, LiveSafe mobile safety App for students/employees.
Athletics Member NCAA, NJCAA. All NCAA Division I.
Financial Aid Of all full-time matriculated undergraduates who enrolled in 2017, 800 Federal Work-Study jobs (averaging $5000). 125 state and other part-time jobs (averaging $5000).
Applying *Options:* electronic application, early admission. *Application fee:* $30. *Required:* high school transcript.
Freshman Application Contact Ms. Elisabet Vizoso, Interim College Registrar, Miami Dade College, 11011 SW 104th Street, Miami, FL 33176. *Phone:* 305-237-2206. *Fax:* 305-237-2532. *E-mail:* evizoso@mdc.edu. *Website:* http://www.mdc.edu/.

North Florida Community College

Madison, Florida

Freshman Application Contact Mr. Bobby Scott, North Florida Community College, 325 Northwest Turner Davis Drive, Madison, FL 32340. *Phone:* 850-973-9450. *Toll-free phone:* 866-937-6322. *Fax:* 850-973-1697. *Website:* http://www.nfcc.edu/.

Northwest Florida State College

Niceville, Florida

Freshman Application Contact Ms. Karen Cooper, Director of Admissions, Northwest Florida State College, 100 College Boulevard, Niceville, FL 32578. *Phone:* 850-729-4901. *Fax:* 850-729-5206. *E-mail:* cooperk@nwfsc.edu. *Website:* http://www.nwfsc.edu/.

NRI Institute of Health Sciences

Royal Palm Beach, Florida

Admissions Office Contact NRI Institute of Health Sciences, 500 Royal Palm Beach Boulevard, Royal Palm Beach, FL 33411. *Website:* http://www.nriinstitute.edu/.

Pasco-Hernando State College

New Port Richey, Florida

Freshman Application Contact Ms. Estela Carrion, Director of Admissions and Student Records, Pasco-Hernando State College, 10230 Ridge Road, New Port Richey, FL 34654-5199. *Phone:* 727-816-3261. *Toll-free phone:* 877-TRY-PHSC. *Fax:* 727-816-3389. *E-mail:* carrioe@phsc.edu. *Website:* http://www.phsc.edu/.

Pensacola State College

Pensacola, Florida

- **State-supported** primarily 2-year, founded 1948, part of Florida College System
- **Urban** 130-acre campus with easy access to Mobile, Alabama
- **Endowment** $11.3 million
- **Coed**

Undergraduates 3,583 full-time, 6,072 part-time. Students come from 37 states and territories; 5% are from out of state; 15% Black or African American, non-Hispanic/Latino; 7% Hispanic/Latino; 3% Asian, non-Hispanic/Latino; 0.4% Native Hawaiian or other Pacific Islander, non-Hispanic/Latino; 0.8% American Indian or Alaska Native, non-Hispanic/Latino; 6% Two or more races, non-Hispanic/Latino; 2% Race/ethnicity unknown; 0.4% international; 7% transferred in. *Retention:* 72% of full-time freshmen returned.
Faculty *Student/faculty ratio:* 19:1.
Academics *Calendar:* semesters. *Degrees:* certificates, diplomas, associate, and bachelor's. *Special study options:* academic remediation for entering students, adult/continuing education programs, advanced placement credit, cooperative education, distance learning, double majors, English as a second language, external degree program, honors programs, independent study, internships, part-time degree program, services for LD students, summer session for credit. *ROTC:* Army (b).
Library Edward M. Chadbourne Library plus 3 others. Students can reserve study rooms.
Student Life *Campus security:* 24-hour emergency response devices and patrols, late-night transport/escort service.
Athletics Member NJCAA.
Financial Aid Of all full-time matriculated undergraduates who enrolled in 2017, 120 Federal Work-Study jobs (averaging $3000).
Applying *Options:* electronic application, early admission. *Application fee:* $30. *Required:* high school transcript.
Freshman Application Contact Ms. Kathy Dutremble, Registrar, Pensacola State College, 1000 College Boulevard, Pensacola, FL 32504. *Phone:* 850-484-2076. *Fax:* 850-484-1020. *E-mail:* kdutremble@pensacolastate.edu. *Website:* http://www.pensacolastate.edu/.

Praxis Institute

Miami, Florida

Admissions Office Contact Praxis Institute, 1850 SW 8th Street, 4th Floor, Miami, FL 33135. *Website:* http://www.praxis.edu/.

Professional Hands Institute

Miami, Florida

Admissions Office Contact Professional Hands Institute, 10 NW 42 Avenue, Suite 200, Miami, FL 33126. *Website:* http://prohands.edu/.

Remington College–Heathrow Campus

Lake Mary, Florida

Admissions Office Contact Remington College–Heathrow Campus, 7131 Business Park Lane, Lake Mary, FL 32746. *Toll-free phone:* 800-323-8122. *Website:* http://www.remingtoncollege.edu/.

SABER College

Miami, Florida

Admissions Office Contact SABER College, 3990 W. Flagler Street, Suite 103, Miami, FL 33134. *Website:* http://www.sabercollege.edu/.

St. Johns River State College

Palatka, Florida

Director of Admissions Dean of Admissions and Records, St. Johns River State College, 5001 Saint Johns Avenue, Palatka, FL 32177-3897. *Phone:* 386-312-4032. *Fax:* 386-312-4289. *Website:* http://www.sjrstate.edu/.

Seminole State College of Florida
Sanford, Florida

- **State and locally supported** primarily 2-year, founded 1966, part of Florida College System
- **Small-town** 200-acre campus with easy access to Orlando
- **Endowment** $24.6 million
- **Coed**

Undergraduates 6,137 full-time, 11,569 part-time. Students come from 21 states and territories; 68 other countries; 3% are from out of state; 16% Black or African American, non-Hispanic/Latino; 24% Hispanic/Latino; 3% Asian, non-Hispanic/Latino; 0.3% Native Hawaiian or other Pacific Islander, non-Hispanic/Latino; 0.3% American Indian or Alaska Native, non-Hispanic/Latino; 3% Two or more races, non-Hispanic/Latino; 3% Race/ethnicity unknown; 2% international; 7% transferred in. *Retention:* 52% of full-time freshmen returned.
Faculty *Student/faculty ratio:* 26:1.
Academics *Calendar:* semesters. *Degrees:* certificates, diplomas, associate, bachelor's, and postbachelor's certificates. *Special study options:* academic remediation for entering students, accelerated degree program, adult/continuing education programs, advanced placement credit, cooperative education, distance learning, double majors, English as a second language, external degree program, honors programs, independent study, internships, part-time degree program, services for LD students, study abroad, summer session for credit. *ROTC:* Army (b).
Library Seminole State Library at Sanford Lake Mary plus 3 others. *Books:* 67,023 (physical), 145,374 (digital/electronic); *Serial titles:* 520 (physical), 18,003 (digital/electronic); *Databases:* 130. Weekly public service hours: 60; students can reserve study rooms.
Student Life *Campus security:* 24-hour emergency response devices and patrols, late-night transport/escort service.
Athletics Member NJCAA.
Applying *Options:* electronic application, early admission, deferred entrance. *Required:* high school transcript, minimum 2.0 GPA.
Admissions Office Contact Seminole State College of Florida, 100 Weldon Boulevard, Sanford, FL 32773-6199. *Website:* http://www.seminolestate.edu/.

Southeastern College–West Palm Beach
West Palm Beach, Florida

- **Proprietary** 2-year, founded 1988
- **Urban** campus
- **Coed**

Undergraduates 269 full-time, 289 part-time. Students come from 6 states and territories; 2% are from out of state; 36% Black or African American, non-Hispanic/Latino; 36% Hispanic/Latino; 2% Asian, non-Hispanic/Latino; 0.2% American Indian or Alaska Native, non-Hispanic/Latino; 1% Two or more races, non-Hispanic/Latino; 7% Race/ethnicity unknown.
Academics *Degree:* certificates, diplomas, and associate. *Special study options:* accelerated degree program, adult/continuing education programs, advanced placement credit, cooperative education, distance learning, English as a second language, internships, off-campus study, part-time degree program, services for LD students, summer session for credit.
Library Southeastern College Library. *Books:* 1,728 (physical); *Serial titles:* 26 (physical); *Databases:* 5. Weekly public service hours: 50.
Student Life *Campus security:* 24-hour patrols, late-night transport/escort service.
Standardized Tests *Required:* Wonderlic Assessment, TEAS (for admission).
Applying *Application fee:* $55. *Required:* high school transcript, interview. *Required for some:* essay or personal statement, letters of recommendation.
Freshman Application Contact Admissions Office, Southeastern College–West Palm Beach, 1756 North Congress Avenue, West Palm Beach, FL 33409. *Website:* http://www.sec.edu/.

Southern Technical College
Orlando, Florida

Freshman Application Contact Mr. Robinson Elie, Director of Admissions, Southern Technical College, 1485 Florida Mall Avenue, Orlando, FL 32809. *Phone:* 407-438-6000. *Toll-free phone:* 877-347-5492. *E-mail:* relie@southerntech.edu. *Website:* http://www.southerntech.edu/.

Southern Technical College
Tampa, Florida

Director of Admissions Admissions, Southern Technical College, 3910 Riga Boulevard, Tampa, FL 33619. *Phone:* 813-630-4401. *Toll-free phone:* 877-347-5492. *Website:* http://www.southerntech.edu/locations/tampa/.

South Florida State College
Avon Park, Florida

- **State-supported** primarily 2-year, founded 1965, part of Florida State College System
- **Rural** 228-acre campus with easy access to Tampa, St. Petersburg, Orlando
- **Endowment** $6.2 million
- **Coed**

Undergraduates 975 full-time, 1,910 part-time. 3% are from out of state; 11% Black or African American, non-Hispanic/Latino; 37% Hispanic/Latino; 2% Asian, non-Hispanic/Latino; 0.3% Native Hawaiian or other Pacific Islander, non-Hispanic/Latino; 0.2% American Indian or Alaska Native, non-Hispanic/Latino; 2% Two or more races, non-Hispanic/Latino; 2% Race/ethnicity unknown; 1% international; 4% transferred in.
Faculty *Student/faculty ratio:* 16:1.
Academics *Calendar:* semesters. *Degrees:* certificates, diplomas, associate, and bachelor's. *Special study options:* academic remediation for entering students, adult/continuing education programs, advanced placement credit, cooperative education, distance learning, English as a second language, independent study, internships, part-time degree program, services for LD students, summer session for credit.
Library Library Services.
Student Life *Campus security:* 24-hour emergency response devices and patrols, late-night transport/escort service.
Athletics Member NJCAA.
Financial Aid ***Average need-based gift aid:*** $4666. *Average indebtedness upon graduation:* $3083.
Applying *Options:* electronic application, early admission, deferred entrance. *Application fee:* $15. *Required:* high school transcript.
Freshman Application Contact Ms. Brenda Desantiago, Admissions, South Florida State College, 600 West College Drive, Avon Park, FL 33825. *Phone:* 863-784-7416. *Website:* http://www.southflorida.edu/.

Tallahassee Community College
Tallahassee, Florida

- **State and locally supported** primarily 2-year, founded 1966, part of Florida College System
- **Suburban** 214-acre campus
- **Endowment** $9.3 million
- **Coed**

Undergraduates 5,830 full-time, 5,952 part-time. Students come from 15 states and territories; 78 other countries; 6% are from out of state; 30% Black or African American, non-Hispanic/Latino; 13% Hispanic/Latino; 2% Asian, non-Hispanic/Latino; 0.1% Native Hawaiian or other Pacific Islander, non-Hispanic/Latino; 0.3% American Indian or Alaska Native, non-Hispanic/Latino; 3% Two or more races, non-Hispanic/Latino; 3% Race/ethnicity unknown; 1% international; 6% transferred in. *Retention:* 56% of full-time freshmen returned.
Faculty *Student/faculty ratio:* 22:1.
Academics *Calendar:* semesters. *Degrees:* certificates, associate, and bachelor's. *Special study options:* academic remediation for entering students, accelerated degree program, adult/continuing education programs, advanced placement credit, distance learning, English as a second language, external degree program, honors programs, independent study, off-campus study, part-time degree program, services for LD students, study abroad, summer session for credit. *ROTC:* Army (c), Navy (c), Air Force (c).
Library Tallahassee Community College Library. *Books:* 82,774 (physical), 53,129 (digital/electronic); *Serial titles:* 59 (physical), 42,687 (digital/electronic); *Databases:* 105. Weekly public service hours: 68; students can reserve study rooms.
Student Life *Campus security:* 24-hour emergency response devices and patrols, late-night transport/escort service.
Athletics Member NJCAA.
Financial Aid Of all full-time matriculated undergraduates who enrolled in 2017, 3,844 applied for aid, 2,633 were judged to have need. 107 Federal Work-Study jobs (averaging $1802). *Average financial aid package:* $3977. *Average need-based gift aid:* $3775.
Applying *Options:* electronic application, early admission, deferred entrance. *Required:* high school transcript.
Freshman Application Contact Student Success Center, Tallahassee Community College, 444 Appleyard Drive, Tallahassee, FL 32304-2895. *Phone:* 850-201-8555. *E-mail:* admissions@tcc.fl.edu. *Website:* http://www.tcc.fl.edu/.

Ultimate Medical Academy Clearwater

Clearwater, Florida

Freshman Application Contact Ultimate Medical Academy Clearwater, 1255 Cleveland Street, Clearwater, FL 33755. *Toll-free phone:* 888-205-2510. *Website:* http://www.ultimatemedical.edu/.

Ultimate Medical Academy Online

Tampa, Florida

Freshman Application Contact Online Admissions Department, Ultimate Medical Academy Online, 3101 West Dr. Martin Luther King Jr. Boulevard, Tampa, FL 33607. *Phone:* 888-209-8848. *Toll-free phone:* 888-205-2510. *E-mail:* onlineadmissions@ultimatemedical.edu. *Website:* http://www.ultimatemedical.edu/.

Universal Career School

Sweetwater, Florida

Admissions Office Contact Universal Career School, 10720 W. Flagler Street, Suite 21, Sweetwater, FL 33174. *Website:* http://www.ucs.edu/.

GEORGIA

Albany Technical College

Albany, Georgia

Freshman Application Contact Albany Technical College, 1704 South Slappey Boulevard, Albany, GA 31701. *Phone:* 229-430-3520. *Toll-free phone:* 877-261-3113. *Website:* http://www.albanytech.edu/.

Altierus Career College

Norcross, Georgia

Admissions Office Contact Altierus Career College, 1750 Beaver Ruin Road, Suite 500, Norcross, GA 30093. *Website:* http://www.altierus.edu/.

Andrew College

Cuthbert, Georgia

Freshman Application Contact Ms. Bridget Kurkowski, Director of Admission, Andrew College, 413 College Street, Cuthbert, GA 39840. *Phone:* 229-732-5986. *Toll-free phone:* 800-664-9250. *Fax:* 229-732-2176. *E-mail:* admissions@andrewcollege.edu. *Website:* http://www.andrewcollege.edu/.

Athens Technical College

Athens, Georgia

Freshman Application Contact Athens Technical College, 800 US Highway 29 North, Athens, GA 30601-1500. *Phone:* 706-355-5008. *Website:* http://www.athenstech.edu/.

Atlanta Metropolitan State College

Atlanta, Georgia

Freshman Application Contact Ms. Audrey Reid, Director, Office of Admissions, Atlanta Metropolitan State College, 1630 Metropolitan Parkway, SW, Atlanta, GA 30310-4498. *Phone:* 404-756-4004. *Fax:* 404-756-4407. *E-mail:* admissions@atlm.edu. *Website:* http://www.atlm.edu/.

Atlanta Technical College

Atlanta, Georgia

Freshman Application Contact Atlanta Technical College, 1560 Metropolitan Parkway, SW, Atlanta, GA 30310. *Phone:* 404-225-4455. *Website:* http://www.atlantatech.edu/.

Augusta Technical College

Augusta, Georgia

Freshman Application Contact Augusta Technical College, 3200 Augusta Tech Drive, Augusta, GA 30906. *Phone:* 706-771-4150. *Website:* http://www.augustatech.edu/.

Brown College of Court Reporting

Atlanta, Georgia

Admissions Office Contact Brown College of Court Reporting, 1900 Emery Street NW, Suite 200, Atlanta, GA 30318. *Website:* http://www.bccr.edu/.

Central Georgia Technical College

Warner Robins, Georgia

Freshman Application Contact Central Georgia Technical College, 80 Cohen Walker Drive, Warner Robins, GA 31088. *Phone:* 770-531-6332. *Toll-free phone:* 866-430-0135. *Website:* http://www.centralgatech.edu/.

Chattahoochee Technical College

Marietta, Georgia

Freshman Application Contact Chattahoochee Technical College, 980 South Cobb Drive, SE, Marietta, GA 30060. *Phone:* 770-757-3408. *Website:* http://www.chattahoocheetech.edu/.

Coastal Pines Technical College

Waycross, Georgia

Freshman Application Contact Coastal Pines Technical College, 1701 Carswell Avenue, Waycross, GA 31503. *Phone:* 912-338-5251. *Toll-free phone:* 877-ED-AT-OTC. *Website:* http://www.coastalpines.edu/.

Columbus Technical College

Columbus, Georgia

Freshman Application Contact Columbus Technical College, 928 Manchester Expressway, Columbus, GA 31904-6572. *Phone:* 706-649-1901. *Website:* http://www.columbustech.edu/.

East Georgia State College

Swainsboro, Georgia

Freshman Application Contact East Georgia State College, 131 College Circle, Swainsboro, GA 30401-2699. *Phone:* 478-289-2112. *Website:* http://www.ega.edu/.

Fortis College

Smyrna, Georgia

Admissions Office Contact Fortis College, 2140 South Cobb Drive, Smyrna, GA 30080. *Toll-free phone:* 855-4-FORTIS. *Website:* http://www.fortis.edu/.

Georgia Highlands College

Rome, Georgia

- **State-supported** primarily 2-year, founded 1970, part of University System of Georgia
- **Suburban** 226-acre campus with easy access to Atlanta
- **Endowment** $40,227
- **Coed**, 6,184 undergraduate students, 47% full-time, 62% women, 38% men

Undergraduates 2,885 full-time, 3,299 part-time. Students come from 23 states and territories; 1% are from out of state; 16% Black or African American, non-Hispanic/Latino; 15% Hispanic/Latino; 2% Asian, non-Hispanic/Latino; 0.1% Native Hawaiian or other Pacific Islander, non-Hispanic/Latino; 0.2% American Indian or Alaska Native, non-Hispanic/Latino; 4% Two or more races, non-Hispanic/Latino; 0.4% Race/ethnicity unknown; 6% transferred in. *Retention:* 67% of full-time freshmen returned.

Freshmen *Admission:* 1,308 enrolled. *Average high school GPA:* 3.0.

Faculty *Total:* 277, 47% full-time, 25% with terminal degrees. *Student/faculty ratio:* 21:1.

Majors Dental hygiene; health/health-care administration; human services; liberal arts and sciences and humanities related; logistics, materials, and supply chain management; registered nursing/registered nurse.

Academics *Calendar:* semesters. *Degrees:* associate and bachelor's. *Special study options:* academic remediation for entering students, advanced placement credit, cooperative education, distance learning, double majors, honors programs, independent study, part-time degree program, services for LD students, study abroad, summer session for credit.

Library Georgia Highlands College Library–Floyd Campus plus 4 others. *Books:* 79,592 (physical), 178,561 (digital/electronic); *Serial titles:* 48

(physical), 4,380 (digital/electronic); *Databases:* 382. Weekly public service hours: 58; students can reserve study rooms.
Student Life *Housing:* college housing not available. *Activities and Organizations:* student-run newspaper, Association of Nursing Students, Green Highlands, Brother 2 Brother, Student Government Association, Phi Theta Kappa. *Campus security:* 24-hour emergency response devices and patrols, emergency phone/email alert system. *Student services:* personal/psychological counseling, veterans affairs office.
Athletics Member NJCAA. *Intercollegiate sports:* basketball W(s), softball W(s). *Intramural sports:* basketball M, cheerleading M, football M, golf M, skiing (downhill) M, table tennis M, tennis M, ultimate Frisbee M, volleyball M, weight lifting M.
Standardized Tests *Required for some:* COMPASS. *Recommended:* SAT or ACT (for admission).
Financial Aid Of all full-time matriculated undergraduates who enrolled in 2017, 50 Federal Work-Study jobs (averaging $3500).
Applying *Options:* electronic application, deferred entrance. *Application fee:* $30. *Required:* high school transcript, minimum 2.0 GPA. *Application deadline:* 7/15 (transfers). *Notification:* continuous (freshmen), continuous (transfers).
Freshman Application Contact Charlene Graham, Assistant Director of Admissions, Georgia Highlands College, 3175 Cedartown Highway, Rome, GA 30161. *Phone:* 706-295-6339. *Toll-free phone:* 800-332-2406. *Fax:* 706-295-6341. *E-mail:* cgraham@highlands.edu.
Website: http://www.highlands.edu/.

Georgia Military College
Milledgeville, Georgia

- **Public** primarily 2-year, founded 1879
- **Small-town** campus
- **Endowment** $1.5 million
- **Coed**

Undergraduates 4,270 full-time, 4,325 part-time. Students come from 36 states and territories; 12 other countries; 4% are from out of state; 42% Black or African American, non-Hispanic/Latino; 7% Hispanic/Latino; 2% Asian, non-Hispanic/Latino; 0.4% Native Hawaiian or other Pacific Islander, non-Hispanic/Latino; 3% American Indian or Alaska Native, non-Hispanic/Latino; 0.2% Two or more races, non-Hispanic/Latino; 2% Race/ethnicity unknown; 0.2% international; 29% transferred in; 3% live on campus. *Retention:* 46% of full-time freshmen returned.
Faculty *Student/faculty ratio:* 15:1.
Academics *Calendar:* quarters. *Degrees:* associate and bachelor's. *Special study options:* academic remediation for entering students, advanced placement credit, cooperative education, distance learning, double majors, independent study, off-campus study, part-time degree program, services for LD students, student-designed majors, study abroad, summer session for credit. *ROTC:* Army (b).
Library Sibley Cone Library plus 1 other. *Books:* 38,125 (physical), 57,769 (digital/electronic); *Serial titles:* 52 (physical); *Databases:* 331. Weekly public service hours: 68.
Student Life *Campus security:* 24-hour emergency response devices and patrols, controlled dormitory access.
Athletics Member NJCAA.
Financial Aid Of all full-time matriculated undergraduates who enrolled in 2017, 5,060 applied for aid, 4,319 were judged to have need, 975 had their need fully met. In 2017, 685. *Average percent of need met:* 20. *Average financial aid package:* $10,096. *Average need-based loan:* $2253. *Average need-based gift aid:* $3845. *Average non-need-based aid:* $2222.
Applying *Options:* electronic application, early admission, deferred entrance. *Application fee:* $35. *Required for some:* high school transcript, interview.
Freshman Application Contact Georgia Military College, 201 East Greene Street, Old Capitol Building, Milledgeville, GA 31061-3398. *Phone:* 478-387-4890. *Toll-free phone:* 800-342-0413. *Website:* http://www.gmc.edu/.

Georgia Northwestern Technical College
Rome, Georgia

Freshman Application Contact Georgia Northwestern Technical College, One Maurice Culberson Drive, Rome, GA 30161. *Phone:* 706-295-6933. *Toll-free phone:* 866-983-GNTC. *Website:* http://www.gntc.edu/.

Georgia Piedmont Technical College
Clarkston, Georgia

Freshman Application Contact Georgia Piedmont Technical College, 495 North Indian Creek Drive, Clarkston, GA 30021-2397. *Phone:* 404-297-9522 Ext. 1229. *Website:* http://www.gptc.edu/.

Gordon State College
Barnesville, Georgia

- **State-supported** primarily 2-year, founded 1852, part of University System of Georgia
- **Small-town** 235-acre campus with easy access to Atlanta
- **Coed**
- 83% of applicants were admitted

Undergraduates 0.8% are from out of state; 38% Black or African American, non-Hispanic/Latino; 4% Hispanic/Latino; 1% Asian, non-Hispanic/Latino; 0.1% American Indian or Alaska Native, non-Hispanic/Latino; 4% Two or more races, non-Hispanic/Latino; 0.5% Race/ethnicity unknown.
Faculty *Student/faculty ratio:* 21:1.
Academics *Calendar:* semesters. *Degrees:* associate and bachelor's. *Special study options:* academic remediation for entering students, accelerated degree program, adult/continuing education programs, advanced placement credit, cooperative education, distance learning, double majors, honors programs, internships, off-campus study, part-time degree program, services for LD students, study abroad, summer session for credit.
Library Dorothy W. Hightower Collaborative Learning Center and Library. *Books:* 103,423 (physical), 35,999 (digital/electronic); *Serial titles:* 401 (physical), 87,985 (digital/electronic); *Databases:* 325. Weekly public service hours: 73.
Student Life *Campus security:* 24-hour emergency response devices and patrols, student patrols, controlled dormitory access, Resident Assistants and Resident Directors in housing, parking patrol.
Athletics Member NJCAA.
Standardized Tests *Required:* SAT or ACT (for admission).
Financial Aid Of all full-time matriculated undergraduates who enrolled in 2017, 75 Federal Work-Study jobs (averaging $1850).
Applying *Options:* electronic application, early admission. *Application fee:* $30. *Required:* high school transcript.
Freshman Application Contact Gordon State College, 419 College Drive, Barnesville, GA 30204-1762. *Phone:* 678-359-5021. *Toll-free phone:* 800-282-6504. *Website:* http://www.gordonstate.edu/.

Gupton-Jones College of Funeral Service
Decatur, Georgia

- **Independent** 2-year, founded 1920, part of Pierce Mortuary Colleges, Inc.
- **Suburban** 3-acre campus with easy access to Atlanta
- **Coed**

Undergraduates 232 full-time. Students come from 15 states and territories; 2 other countries; 86% are from out of state; 70% Black or African American, non-Hispanic/Latino; 0.9% Two or more races, non-Hispanic/Latino; 13% transferred in. *Retention:* 84% of full-time freshmen returned.
Faculty *Student/faculty ratio:* 28:1.
Academics *Calendar:* quarters. *Degree:* associate. *Special study options:* accelerated degree program, advanced placement credit, services for LD students.
Library Russell Millison Library. *Books:* 4,000 (physical).
Student Life *Campus security:* 24-hour emergency response devices.
Applying *Options:* electronic application. *Application fee:* $50. *Required:* high school transcript, health questionnaire.
Freshman Application Contact Gupton-Jones College of Funeral Service, 5141 Snapfinger Woods Drive, Decatur, GA 30035-4022. *Phone:* 770-593-2257. *Toll-free phone:* 800-848-5352. *Website:* http://www.gupton-jones.edu/.

Gwinnett College
Lilburn, Georgia

Admissions Office Contact Gwinnett College, 4230 Lawrenceville Highway, Suite 11, Lilburn, GA 30047. *Website:* http://www.gwinnettcollege.edu/.

Gwinnett College
Marietta, Georgia

Admissions Office Contact Gwinnett College, 1130 Northchase Parkway, Suite 100, Marietta, GA 30067. *Website:* http://www.gwinnettcollege.edu/locations/marietta/.

Gwinnett College
Sandy Springs, Georgia
Admissions Office Contact Gwinnett College, 6690 Roswell Road NE, Suite 2200, Sandy Springs, GA 30328. *Website:* http://www.gwinnettcollege.edu/locations/sandy-springs/.

Gwinnett Technical College
Lawrenceville, Georgia
Freshman Application Contact Gwinnett Technical College, 5150 Sugarloaf Parkway, Lawrenceville, GA 30043-5702. *Phone:* 678-762-7580 Ext. 434. *Website:* http://www.gwinnetttech.edu/.

Interactive College of Technology
Chamblee, Georgia
Freshman Application Contact Director of Admissions, Interactive College of Technology, 5303 New Peachtree Road, Chamblee, GA 30341. *Phone:* 770-216-2960. *Toll-free phone:* 800-447-2011. *Fax:* 770-216-2988. *Website:* http://ict.edu/.

Interactive College of Technology
Gainesville, Georgia
Freshman Application Contact Interactive College of Technology, 2323 Browns Bridge Road, Gainesville, GA 30504. *Website:* http://ict.edu/.

Interactive College of Technology
Morrow, Georgia
Admissions Office Contact Interactive College of Technology, 1580 Southlake Parkway, Suite C, Morrow, GA 30260. *Website:* http://ict.edu/.

Lanier Technical College
Oakwood, Georgia
Freshman Application Contact Lanier Technical College, 2990 Landrum Education Drive, PO Box 58, Oakwood, GA 30566. *Phone:* 770-531-6332. *Website:* http://www.laniertech.edu/.

Lincoln College of Technology
Marietta, Georgia
Admissions Office Contact Lincoln College of Technology, 2359 Windy Hill Road, Marietta, GA 30067. *Toll-free phone:* 844-215-1513. *Website:* http://www.lincolntech.edu/.

Miller-Motte Technical College
Augusta, Georgia
Admissions Office Contact Miller-Motte Technical College, 621 Frontage Road NW, Augusta, GA 30907. *Toll-free phone:* 800-705-9182. *Website:* http://www.miller-motte.edu/.

Miller-Motte Technical College
Columbus, Georgia
Admissions Office Contact Miller-Motte Technical College, 1800 Box Road, Columbus, GA 31907. *Toll-free phone:* 800-705-9182. *Website:* http://www.miller-motte.edu/.

Miller-Motte Technical College
Macon, Georgia
Admissions Office Contact Miller-Motte Technical College, 175 Tom Hill Sr. Boulevard, Macon, GA 31210. *Toll-free phone:* 800-705-9182. *Website:* http://www.miller-motte.edu/.

North Georgia Technical College
Clarkesville, Georgia
Freshman Application Contact North Georgia Technical College, 1500 Georgia Highway 197, North, PO Box 65, Clarkesville, GA 30523. *Phone:* 706-754-7724. *Website:* http://www.northgatech.edu/.

Oconee Fall Line Technical College
Sandersville, Georgia
Freshman Application Contact Oconee Fall Line Technical College, 1189 Deepstep Road, Sandersville, GA 31082. *Phone:* 478-553-2050. *Toll-free phone:* 877-399-8324. *Website:* http://www.oftc.edu/.

Ogeechee Technical College
Statesboro, Georgia
Freshman Application Contact Ogeechee Technical College, One Joe Kennedy Boulevard, Statesboro, GA 30458. *Phone:* 912-871-1600. *Toll-free phone:* 800-646-1316. *Website:* http://www.ogeecheetech.edu/.

SAE Institute Atlanta
Atlanta, Georgia
Admissions Office Contact SAE Institute Atlanta, 215 Peachtree Street NE, Atlanta, GA 30303. *Website:* http://www.sae.edu/.

Savannah Technical College
Savannah, Georgia
Freshman Application Contact Savannah Technical College, 5717 White Bluff Road, Savannah, GA 31405. *Phone:* 912-443-5711. *Toll-free phone:* 800-769-6362. *Website:* http://www.savannahtech.edu/.

Southeastern Technical College
Vidalia, Georgia
Freshman Application Contact Southeastern Technical College, 3001 East First Street, Vidalia, GA 30474. *Phone:* 912-538-3121. *Website:* http://www.southeasterntech.edu/.

Southern Crescent Technical College
Griffin, Georgia
Freshman Application Contact Southern Crescent Technical College, 501 Varsity Road, Griffin, GA 30223. *Phone:* 770-646-6160. *Website:* http://www.sctech.edu/.

Southern Regional Technical College
Thomasville, Georgia
Freshman Application Contact Southern Regional Technical College, 15689 US 19 North, Thomasville, GA 31792. *Phone:* 229-225-5089. *Website:* http://www.southwestgatech.edu/.

South Georgia State College
Douglas, Georgia
Freshman Application Contact South Georgia State College, 100 West College Park Drive, Douglas, GA 31533-5098. *Phone:* 912-260-4409. *Toll-free phone:* 800-342-6364. *Website:* http://www.sgc.edu/.

South Georgia Technical College
Americus, Georgia
Freshman Application Contact South Georgia Technical College, 900 South Georgia Tech Parkway, Americus, GA 31709. *Phone:* 229-931-2299. *Website:* http://www.southgatech.edu/.

West Georgia Technical College
Waco, Georgia
Freshman Application Contact West Georgia Technical College, 176 Murphy Campus Boulevard, Waco, GA 30182. *Phone:* 770-537-5719. *Website:* http://www.westgatech.edu/.

Wiregrass Georgia Technical College
Valdosta, Georgia
Freshman Application Contact Wiregrass Georgia Technical College, 4089 Val Tech Road, Valdosta, GA 31602. *Phone:* 229-468-2278. *Website:* http://www.wiregrass.edu/.

GUAM

Guam Community College

Mangilao, Guam

Freshman Application Contact Dr. Julie Ulloa-Heath, Registrar, Guam Community College, PO Box 23069 GMF, Barrigada, GU 96921. *Phone:* 671-735-5561. *Fax:* 671-735-5531. *E-mail:* julie.ulloaheath@guamcc.edu. *Website:* http://www.guamcc.edu/.

HAWAII

Hawaii Community College

Hilo, Hawaii

Director of Admissions Mrs. Tammy M. Tanaka, Admissions Specialist, Hawaii Community College, 1175 Manono Street, Hilo, HI 96720-5096. *Phone:* 808-974-7661. *Website:* http://www.hawcc.hawaii.edu/.

Hawaii Tokai International College

Kapolei, Hawaii

- **Independent** 2-year, founded 1992, part of Tokai University Educational System
- **Suburban** 7-acre campus with easy access to Honolulu
- **Coed**

Undergraduates 85 full-time. Students come from 2 states and territories; 2 other countries; 5% are from out of state; 2% Hispanic/Latino; 6% Asian, non-Hispanic/Latino; 4% Native Hawaiian or other Pacific Islander, non-Hispanic/Latino; 5% Two or more races, non-Hispanic/Latino; 81% international; 30% live on campus. *Retention:* 86% of full-time freshmen returned.
Faculty *Student/faculty ratio:* 7:1.
Academics *Calendar:* quarters. *Degree:* certificates, diplomas, and associate. *Special study options:* academic remediation for entering students, advanced placement credit, English as a second language, internships, part-time degree program, services for LD students, study abroad, summer session for credit.
Library Library and Learning Center plus 1 other. *Books:* 7,807 (physical); *Serial titles:* 30 (physical); *Databases:* 48. Weekly public service hours: 68; students can reserve study rooms.
Student Life *Campus security:* 24-hour emergency response devices and patrols, controlled dormitory access.
Applying *Options:* electronic application, deferred entrance. *Application fee:* $50. *Required:* essay or personal statement, high school transcript, minimum 2.5 GPA. *Required for some:* interview. *Recommended:* letters of recommendation.
Freshman Application Contact Mr. Darrell Kicker, Director of Admissions, Hawaii Tokai International College, 91-971 Farrington Highway, Kapolei, HI 96707. *Phone:* 808-983-4202. *Fax:* 808-983-4107. *E-mail:* admissions@tokai.edu. *Website:* http://www.htic.edu/.

Honolulu Community College

Honolulu, Hawaii

Freshman Application Contact Admissions Office, Honolulu Community College, 874 Dillingham Boulevard, Honolulu, HI 96817. *Phone:* 808-845-9129. *E-mail:* honcc@hawaii.edu. *Website:* http://www.honolulu.hawaii.edu/.

Kapiolani Community College

Honolulu, Hawaii

Freshman Application Contact Kapiolani Community College, 4303 Diamond Head Road, Honolulu, HI 96816-4421. *Phone:* 808-734-9555. *Website:* http://www.kapiolani.hawaii.edu/.

Kauai Community College

Lihue, Hawaii

Freshman Application Contact Mr. Leighton Oride, Admissions Officer and Registrar, Kauai Community College, 3-1901 Kaumualii Highway, Lihue, HI 96766. *Phone:* 808-245-8225. *Fax:* 808-245-8297. *E-mail:* arkauai@hawaii.edu. *Website:* http://kauai.hawaii.edu/.

Leeward Community College

Pearl City, Hawaii

Freshman Application Contact Ms. Sheryl Higa, Assistant Registrar, Leeward Community College, 96-045 Ala Ike, Pearl City, HI 96782-3393. *Phone:* 808-455-0643. *Website:* http://www.leeward.hawaii.edu/.

Remington College–Honolulu Campus

Honolulu, Hawaii

Director of Admissions Louis LaMair, Director of Recruitment, Remington College–Honolulu Campus, 1111 Bishop Street, Suite 400, Honolulu, HI 96813. *Phone:* 808-942-1000. *Toll-free phone:* 800-323-8122. *Fax:* 808-533-3064. *E-mail:* louis.lamair@remingtoncollege.edu. *Website:* http://www.remingtoncollege.edu/.

University of Hawaii Maui College

Kahului, Hawaii

Freshman Application Contact Mr. Stephen Kameda, Director of Admissions and Records, University of Hawaii Maui College, 310 Kaahumanu Avenue, Kahului, HI 96732. *Phone:* 808-984-3267. *Toll-free phone:* 800-479-6692. *Fax:* 808-984-3872. *E-mail:* skameda@hawaii.edu. *Website:* http://maui.hawaii.edu/.

Windward Community College

Kaneohe, Hawaii

Director of Admissions Geri Imai, Registrar, Windward Community College, 45-720 Keaahala Road, Kaneohe, HI 96744-3528. *Phone:* 808-235-7430. *E-mail:* gerii@hawaii.edu. *Website:* http://www.windward.hawaii.edu/.

IDAHO

Carrington College–Boise

Boise, Idaho

Freshman Application Contact Carrington College–Boise, 1122 North Liberty Street, Boise, ID 83704. *Website:* http://www.carrington.edu/.

College of Eastern Idaho

Idaho Falls, Idaho

- **State-supported** 2-year, founded 1969
- **Small-town** 60-acre campus
- **Coed**

Undergraduates 285 full-time, 506 part-time. Students come from 7 states and territories; 1% are from out of state; 0.1% Black or African American, non-Hispanic/Latino; 15% Hispanic/Latino; 0.6% Asian, non-Hispanic/Latino; 0.3% Native Hawaiian or other Pacific Islander, non-Hispanic/Latino; 0.6% American Indian or Alaska Native, non-Hispanic/Latino; 0.9% Two or more races, non-Hispanic/Latino; 1% Race/ethnicity unknown. *Retention:* 40% of full-time freshmen returned.
Faculty *Student/faculty ratio:* 8:1.
Academics *Calendar:* semesters. *Degree:* certificates and associate. *Special study options:* academic remediation for entering students, adult/continuing education programs, advanced placement credit, English as a second language, part-time degree program, services for LD students, summer session for credit.
Library Richard and Lila Jordan Library plus 1 other.
Student Life *Campus security:* 24-hour emergency response devices and patrols, late-night transport/escort service.
Standardized Tests *Required for some:* ACT Compass, ACT ASSET, or CPT.
Financial Aid Of all full-time matriculated undergraduates who enrolled in 2017, 37 Federal Work-Study jobs (averaging $1176). 11 state and other part-time jobs (averaging $1619).
Applying *Options:* electronic application, deferred entrance. *Required:* high school transcript. *Required for some:* essay or personal statement, interview.
Freshman Application Contact Hailey Mack, Career Placement and Recruiting Coordinator, College of Eastern Idaho, 1600 South 25th East, Idaho Falls, ID 83404. *Phone:* 208-524-5337 Ext. 35337. *Toll-free phone:* 800-662-0261. *Fax:* 208-524-0429. *E-mail:* hailey.mack@cei.edu. *Website:* http://www.eitc.edu/.

College of Southern Idaho
Twin Falls, Idaho

Freshman Application Contact Director of Admissions, Registration, and Records, College of Southern Idaho, PO Box 1238, Twin Falls, ID 83303-1238. *Phone:* 208-732-6232. *Toll-free phone:* 800-680-0274. *Fax:* 208-736-3014. *Website:* http://www.csi.edu/.

College of Western Idaho
Nampa, Idaho

Freshman Application Contact College of Western Idaho, 6056 Birch Lane, Nampa, ID 83687. *Website:* http://cwidaho.cc/.

North Idaho College
Coeur d'Alene, Idaho

Freshman Application Contact North Idaho College, 1000 West Garden Avenue, Coeur d Alene, ID 83814-2199. *Phone:* 208-769-3303. *Toll-free phone:* 877-404-4536 Ext. 3311. *E-mail:* admit@nic.edu. *Website:* http://www.nic.edu/.

ILLINOIS

Ambria College of Nursing
Hoffman Estates, Illinois

Admissions Office Contact Ambria College of Nursing, 5210 Trillium Boulevard, Hoffman Estates, IL 60192. *Website:* http://www.ambria.edu/.

Black Hawk College
Moline, Illinois

- **State and locally supported** 2-year, founded 1946
- **Urban** 232-acre campus
- **Coed,** 4,333 undergraduate students, 38% full-time, 61% women, 39% men

Undergraduates 1,625 full-time, 2,708 part-time. Students come from 9 states and territories; 10 other countries; 11% are from out of state; 11% Black or African American, non-Hispanic/Latino; 15% Hispanic/Latino; 2% Asian, non-Hispanic/Latino; 0.2% American Indian or Alaska Native, non-Hispanic/Latino; 4% Two or more races, non-Hispanic/Latino; 1% Race/ethnicity unknown; 4% transferred in.
Freshmen *Admission:* 859 applied, 859 admitted, 736 enrolled.
Faculty *Total:* 202, 50% full-time, 14% with terminal degrees. *Student/faculty ratio:* 20:1.
Majors Accounting; administrative assistant and secretarial science; agricultural business and management; agricultural mechanics and equipment technology; agricultural production; agriculture; applied horticulture/horticulture operations; art; automobile/automotive mechanics technology; biological and physical sciences; child-care provision; criminal justice/police science; crop production; design and visual communications; emergency medical technology (EMT paramedic); equestrian studies; fire services administration; general studies; health information/medical records technology; horse husbandry/equine science and management; information technology; liberal arts and sciences/liberal studies; manufacturing engineering technology; physical therapy technology; radiologic technology/science; retailing; small business administration; surgical technology; veterinary/animal health technology.
Academics *Calendar:* semesters. *Degree:* certificates and associate. *Special study options:* academic remediation for entering students, advanced placement credit, distance learning, English as a second language, independent study, internships, part-time degree program, services for LD students, summer session for credit.
Library Quad City Campus Library plus 1 other. *Books:* 28,441 (physical), 181,568 (digital/electronic); *Serial titles:* 136 (physical), 50,357 (digital/electronic); *Databases:* 39. Weekly public service hours: 51; students can reserve study rooms.
Student Life *Housing:* college housing not available. *Activities and Organizations:* drama/theater group, student-run newspaper, choral group, National Student Nurses Association, Wellness Club, Student Ambassadors, Association of Lation American Students, Clean Sphere. *Campus security:* 24-hour patrols. *Student services:* personal/psychological counseling, veterans affairs office.
Athletics Member NJCAA. *Intercollegiate sports:* baseball M(s), basketball M(s)/W(s), golf M(s), softball W(s), volleyball W(s). *Intramural sports:* soccer M.
Financial Aid Of all full-time matriculated undergraduates who enrolled in 2017, 157 Federal Work-Study jobs (averaging $1437). 176 state and other part-time jobs (averaging $1023).
Applying *Options:* electronic application, early admission, deferred entrance. *Application fee:* $20. *Recommended:* high school transcript. *Application deadlines:* rolling (freshmen), rolling (out-of-state freshmen), rolling (transfers), rolling (early action). *Early decision deadline:* rolling (for plan 1), rolling (for plan 2). *Notification:* continuous (freshmen), continuous (out-of-state freshmen), continuous (transfers), rolling (early decision plan 1), rolling (early decision plan 2), rolling (early action).
Freshman Application Contact Ms. Gabriella Hurtado, Recruitment Coordinator/Admissions Advisor, Black Hawk College, 6600-34th Avenue, Moline, IL 61265. *Phone:* 309-796-5341. *Toll-free phone:* 800-334-1311. *E-mail:* ghurtado@bhc.edu.
Website: http://www.bhc.edu/.

Carl Sandburg College
Galesburg, Illinois

Director of Admissions Ms. Carol Kreider, Dean of Student Support Services, Carl Sandburg College, 2400 Tom L. Wilson Boulevard, Galesburg, IL 61401-9576. *Phone:* 309-341-5234. *Website:* http://www.sandburg.edu/.

City Colleges of Chicago, Harold Washington College
Chicago, Illinois

Freshman Application Contact Admissions Office, City Colleges of Chicago, Harold Washington College, 30 East Lake Street, Chicago, IL 60601-2449. *Phone:* 312-553-6010. *Website:* http://hwashington.ccc.edu/.

City Colleges of Chicago, Harry S. Truman College
Chicago, Illinois

Freshman Application Contact City Colleges of Chicago, Harry S. Truman College, 1145 West Wilson Avenue, Chicago, IL 60640-5616. *Phone:* 773-907-4000 Ext. 1112. *Website:* http://www.trumancollege.edu/.

City Colleges of Chicago, Kennedy-King College
Chicago, Illinois

Freshman Application Contact Nicholas Ambrose, Assistant Registrar, City Colleges of Chicago, Kennedy-King College, 6301 South Halsted Street, W-110, Chicago, IL 60621. *Phone:* 773-602-5090. *Fax:* 773-602-5055. *E-mail:* nambrose1@ccc.edu. *Website:* http://www.ccc.edu/colleges/kennedy/.

City Colleges of Chicago, Malcolm X College
Chicago, Illinois

Freshman Application Contact Ms. Kimberly Hollingsworth, Dean of Student Services, City Colleges of Chicago, Malcolm X College, 1900 West Van Buren Street, Chicago, IL 60612-3145. *Phone:* 312-850-7120. *Fax:* 312-850-7119. *E-mail:* khollingsworth@ccc.edu. *Website:* http://malcolmx.ccc.edu/.

City Colleges of Chicago, Olive-Harvey College
Chicago, Illinois

- **State and locally supported** 2-year, founded 1970, part of City Colleges of Chicago
- **Urban** 67-acre campus with easy access to Chicago
- **Coed**

Undergraduates 1,013 full-time, 1,869 part-time. 69% Black or African American, non-Hispanic/Latino; 24% Hispanic/Latino; 1% Asian, non-Hispanic/Latino; 0.2% American Indian or Alaska Native, non-Hispanic/Latino; 2% Two or more races, non-Hispanic/Latino; 0.6%

Race/ethnicity unknown; 0.3% international. *Retention:* 52% of full-time freshmen returned.
Faculty *Student/faculty ratio:* 22:1.
Academics *Calendar:* semesters. *Degree:* certificates and associate. *Special study options:* academic remediation for entering students, accelerated degree program, adult/continuing education programs, advanced placement credit, cooperative education, distance learning, English as a second language, independent study, internships, part-time degree program, services for LD students, summer session for credit.
Library Olga-Haley Library-Learning Resource Center. *Books:* 70,820 (physical), 447,725 (digital/electronic); *Serial titles:* 50 (physical), 23,684 (digital/electronic); *Databases:* 81. Students can reserve study rooms.
Student Life *Campus security:* 24-hour emergency response devices and patrols.
Athletics Member NJCAA.
Financial Aid Of all full-time matriculated undergraduates who enrolled in 2017, 150 Federal Work-Study jobs (averaging $3900).
Applying *Options:* electronic application, early admission, deferred entrance. *Required for some:* high school transcript.
Freshman Application Contact Nailah Alexandar, Assistant Registrar, City Colleges of Chicago, Olive-Harvey College, 10001 South Woodlawn Avenue, Room 1405, Chicago, IL 60628. *Phone:* 773-291-6384. *E-mail:* nalexander17@ccc.edu. *Website:* http://oliveharvey.ccc.edu/.

City Colleges of Chicago, Richard J. Daley College

Chicago, Illinois

Freshman Application Contact City Colleges of Chicago, Richard J. Daley College, 7500 South Pulaski Road, Chicago, IL 60652-1242. *Phone:* 773-838-7606. *Website:* http://daley.ccc.edu/.

City Colleges of Chicago, Wilbur Wright College

Chicago, Illinois

Freshman Application Contact Ms. Amy Aiello, Assistant Dean of Student Services, City Colleges of Chicago, Wilbur Wright College, Chicago, IL 60634. *Phone:* 773-481-8207. *Fax:* 773-481-8185. *E-mail:* aaiello@ccc.edu. *Website:* http://wright.ccc.edu/.

College of DuPage

Glen Ellyn, Illinois

Freshman Application Contact College of DuPage, IL. *E-mail:* admissions@cod.edu. *Website:* http://www.cod.edu/.

College of Lake County

Grayslake, Illinois

Freshman Application Contact Director, Student Recruitment, College of Lake County, Grayslake, IL 60030-1198. *Phone:* 847-543-2383. *Fax:* 847-543-3061. *Website:* http://www.clcillinois.edu/.

Coyne College

Chicago, Illinois

Freshman Application Contact Coyne College, 1 North State Street, Suite 400, Chicago, IL 60602. *Phone:* 773-577-8100 Ext. 8102. *Toll-free phone:* 800-707-1922. *Website:* http://www.coynecollege.edu/.

Danville Area Community College

Danville, Illinois

- **State and locally supported** 2-year, founded 1946, part of Illinois Community College Board
- **Small-town** 50-acre campus
- **Endowment** $14.8 million
- **Coed**

Undergraduates 1,013 full-time, 1,632 part-time. Students come from 5 states and territories; 3 other countries; 7% are from out of state; 15% Black or African American, non-Hispanic/Latino; 5% Hispanic/Latino; 1% Asian, non-Hispanic/Latino; 0.1% Native Hawaiian or other Pacific Islander, non-Hispanic/Latino; 0.3% American Indian or Alaska Native, non-Hispanic/Latino; 9% Race/ethnicity unknown; 26% transferred in. *Retention:* 52% of full-time freshmen returned.
Faculty *Student/faculty ratio:* 18:1.
Academics *Calendar:* semesters. *Degree:* certificates and associate. *Special study options:* academic remediation for entering students, adult/continuing education programs, advanced placement credit, cooperative education, distance learning, double majors, English as a second language, independent study, internships, off-campus study, part-time degree program, services for LD students, summer session for credit.
Student Life *Campus security:* 24-hour emergency response devices and patrols.
Athletics Member NJCAA.
Financial Aid Of all full-time matriculated undergraduates who enrolled in 2016, 52 Federal Work-Study jobs (averaging $3000). 60 state and other part-time jobs (averaging $3000).
Applying *Options:* early admission, deferred entrance. *Required:* high school transcript.
Freshman Application Contact Mr. Nick Catlett, Coordinator of Recruitment, Danville Area Community College, 2000 East Main Street, Danville, IL 61832-5199. *Phone:* 217-443-8864. *Fax:* 217-443-8337. *E-mail:* ncatlett@dacc.edu. *Website:* http://www.dacc.edu/.

Elgin Community College

Elgin, Illinois

Freshman Application Contact Admissions, Recruitment, and Student Life, Elgin Community College, 1700 Spartan Drive, Elgin, IL 60123. *Phone:* 847-214-7414. *E-mail:* admissions@elgin.edu. *Website:* http://www.elgin.edu/.

Fox College

Bedford Park, Illinois

Freshman Application Contact Admissions Office, Fox College, 6640 South Cicero, Bedford Park, IL 60638. *Phone:* 708-444-4500. *Website:* http://www.foxcollege.edu/.

Harper College

Palatine, Illinois

- **State and locally supported** 2-year, founded 1965, part of Illinois Community College Board
- **Suburban** 200-acre campus with easy access to Chicago
- **Coed,** 13,530 undergraduate students, 34% full-time, 55% women, 45% men

Undergraduates 4,606 full-time, 8,924 part-time. 0.5% are from out of state; 4% Black or African American, non-Hispanic/Latino; 27% Hispanic/Latino; 13% Asian, non-Hispanic/Latino; 0.2% American Indian or Alaska Native, non-Hispanic/Latino; 2% Two or more races, non-Hispanic/Latino; 2% Race/ethnicity unknown; 0.7% international; 5% transferred in. *Retention:* 74% of full-time freshmen returned.
Freshmen *Admission:* 2,306 enrolled.
Faculty *Total:* 646, 32% full-time, 17% with terminal degrees. *Student/faculty ratio:* 19:1.
Majors Accounting; administrative assistant and secretarial science; architectural drafting and CAD/CADD; architectural engineering technology; art; banking and financial support services; biology/biological sciences; business administration and management; cardiovascular technology; chemistry; child-care provision; computer and information sciences; computer programming; computer programming (specific applications); computer science; criminal justice/law enforcement administration; cyber/computer forensics and counterterrorism; dental hygiene; diagnostic medical sonography and ultrasound technology; dietetics; dietetic technology; early childhood education; electrical, electronic and communications engineering technology; elementary education; engineering; English; environmental studies; fashion and fabric consulting; fashion/apparel design; fashion merchandising; finance; fine/studio arts; fire science/firefighting; food service systems administration; health teacher education; heating, air conditioning, ventilation and refrigeration maintenance technology; history; homeland security; hospitality administration; humanities; human services; interior design; international business/trade/commerce; legal administrative assistant/secretary; legal assistant/paralegal; liberal arts and sciences/liberal studies; marketing/marketing management; mathematics; medical administrative assistant and medical secretary; medical/clinical assistant; music; nanotechnology; philosophy; physical education teaching and coaching; physical sciences; psychology; public relations, advertising, and applied communication related; radiologic technology/science; registered nursing/registered nurse; sales, distribution, and marketing operations; small business administration; sociology and anthropology; speech communication and rhetoric; theater/theater arts management; web page, digital/multimedia and information resources design.

Academics *Calendar:* semesters. *Degree:* certificates and associate. *Special study options:* academic remediation for entering students, accelerated degree program, adult/continuing education programs, advanced placement credit, cooperative education, distance learning, English as a second language, freshman honors college, honors programs, independent study, internships, part-time degree program, services for LD students, study abroad, summer session for credit.
Library Harper College Library.
Student Life *Housing:* college housing not available. *Activities and Organizations:* drama/theater group, student-run newspaper, radio station, choral group, Student Radio Station, Program Board, Student Senate, Nursing Club, Phi Theta Kappa. *Campus security:* 24-hour emergency response devices and patrols, late-night transport/escort service. *Student services:* health clinic, personal/psychological counseling, women's center, legal services.
Athletics Member NJCAA. *Intercollegiate sports:* basketball W, cross-country running W, soccer W, softball W, track and field W, volleyball W. *Intramural sports:* baseball M, basketball M, football M, racquetball M, softball M, table tennis M, tennis M, volleyball M.
Financial Aid Of all full-time matriculated undergraduates who enrolled in 2017, 2,752 applied for aid, 2,247 were judged to have need, 60 had their need fully met. In 2017, 83 non-need-based awards were made. *Average percent of need met:* 47%. *Average financial aid package:* $5704. *Average need-based loan:* $3076. *Average need-based gift aid:* $5448. *Average non-need-based aid:* $2153.
Applying *Options:* electronic application. *Application fee:* $25. *Required:* high school transcript. *Application deadlines:* rolling (freshmen), rolling (transfers). *Notification:* continuous (freshmen), continuous (transfers).
Director of Admissions Robert Parzy, Director, Student Recruitment and Outreach, Harper College, 1200 West Algonquin Road, Palatine, IL 60067-7398. *Phone:* 847-925-6649. *Fax:* 847-925-6044. *E-mail:* rparzy@harpercollege.edu. *Website:* http://www.harpercollege.edu/.

Heartland Community College
Normal, Illinois

- **State and locally supported** 2-year, founded 1990, part of Illinois Community College Board
- **Urban** 145-acre campus
- **Coed,** 4,722 undergraduate students, 38% full-time, 55% women, 45% men

Undergraduates 1,816 full-time, 2,906 part-time. Students come from 27 states and territories; 13 other countries; 1% are from out of state; 9% Black or African American, non-Hispanic/Latino; 7% Hispanic/Latino; 2% Asian, non-Hispanic/Latino; 0.1% American Indian or Alaska Native, non-Hispanic/Latino; 5% Two or more races, non-Hispanic/Latino; 1% Race/ethnicity unknown; 1% international; 10% transferred in. *Retention:* 55% of full-time freshmen returned.
Freshmen *Admission:* 2,735 applied, 2,735 admitted, 679 enrolled.
Faculty *Total:* 299, 28% full-time, 17% with terminal degrees. *Student/faculty ratio:* 19:1.
Majors Administrative assistant and secretarial science; biological and physical sciences; child-care provision; computer systems networking and telecommunications; engineering; industrial technology; liberal arts and sciences/liberal studies; physical therapy technology; radiologic technology/science; registered nursing/registered nurse; web page, digital/multimedia and information resources design.
Academics *Calendar:* semesters. *Degree:* certificates and associate. *Special study options:* academic remediation for entering students, adult/continuing education programs, advanced placement credit, cooperative education, distance learning, double majors, English as a second language, honors programs, independent study, internships, part-time degree program, services for LD students, study abroad, summer session for credit.
Library Heartland Community College Library. *Books:* 19,860 (physical); *Serial titles:* 22,933 (physical), 99,327 (digital/electronic); *Databases:* 20. Weekly public service hours: 61.
Student Life *Housing:* college housing not available. *Activities and Organizations:* drama/theater group, student-run newspaper, choral group, Student Government, PRIDE, Game Club, Black Student Union, International Student Association. *Campus security:* 24-hour emergency response devices and patrols. *Student services:* personal/psychological counseling.
Athletics Member NJCAA. *Intercollegiate sports:* soccer W(s), softball W(s).
Financial Aid Of all full-time matriculated undergraduates who enrolled in 2016, 75 Federal Work-Study jobs (averaging $1500).
Applying *Options:* electronic application. *Recommended:* high school transcript. *Application deadlines:* rolling (freshmen), rolling (out-of-state freshmen), rolling (transfers). *Notification:* continuous (freshmen), continuous (out-of-state freshmen), continuous (transfers).
Freshman Application Contact Ms. Amanda Garard, Coordinator of Admissions, Heartland Community College, 1500 West Raab Road, Normal, IL 61761. *Phone:* 309-268-8010. *Fax:* 309-268-7992. *E-mail:* Amanda.Rambo@heartland.edu. *Website:* http://www.heartland.edu/.

Highland Community College
Freeport, Illinois

- **State and locally supported** 2-year, founded 1962, part of Illinois Community College Board
- **Rural** 240-acre campus
- **Coed**

Undergraduates 828 full-time, 850 part-time. 3% are from out of state; 8% Black or African American, non-Hispanic/Latino; 3% Hispanic/Latino; 1% Asian, non-Hispanic/Latino; 0.1% Native Hawaiian or other Pacific Islander, non-Hispanic/Latino; 0.7% American Indian or Alaska Native, non-Hispanic/Latino; 3% Two or more races, non-Hispanic/Latino; 3% Race/ethnicity unknown; 0.7% international; 3% transferred in.
Faculty *Student/faculty ratio:* 15:1.
Academics *Calendar:* semesters. *Degree:* certificates and associate. *Special study options:* academic remediation for entering students, adult/continuing education programs, advanced placement credit, cooperative education, distance learning, English as a second language, external degree program, honors programs, independent study, internships, part-time degree program, services for LD students, student-designed majors, summer session for credit.
Library Clarence Mitchell Library.
Student Life *Campus security:* 24-hour emergency response devices and patrols.
Athletics Member NJCAA.
Financial Aid Of all full-time matriculated undergraduates who enrolled in 2017, 634 applied for aid, 553 were judged to have need, 2 had their need fully met. 48 Federal Work-Study jobs (averaging $1673). 20 state and other part-time jobs (averaging $826). In 2017, 41. *Average percent of need met:* 37. *Average financial aid package:* $6281. *Average need-based loan:* $3337. *Average need-based gift aid:* $5790. *Average non-need-based aid:* $3734.
Applying *Options:* electronic application, early admission, deferred entrance. *Required for some:* high school transcript, 1 letter of recommendation. *Recommended:* high school transcript.
Freshman Application Contact Mr. Jeremy Bradt, Director, Enrollment and Records, Highland Community College, 2998 West Pearl City Road, Freeport, IL 61032. *Phone:* 815-235-6121 Ext. 3500. *Fax:* 815-235-6130. *E-mail:* jeremy.bradt@highland.edu. *Website:* http://www.highland.edu/.

Illinois Central College
East Peoria, Illinois

- **State and locally supported** 2-year, founded 1967, part of Illinois Community College Board
- **Suburban** 430-acre campus
- **Coed**

Undergraduates 3,115 full-time, 6,151 part-time. Students come from 20 states and territories; 13 other countries; 1% are from out of state; 12% Black or African American, non-Hispanic/Latino; 4% Hispanic/Latino; 2% Asian, non-Hispanic/Latino; 0.1% Native Hawaiian or other Pacific Islander, non-Hispanic/Latino; 0.3% American Indian or Alaska Native, non-Hispanic/Latino; 3% Two or more races, non-Hispanic/Latino; 0.2% Race/ethnicity unknown; 1% international; 2% transferred in; 3% live on campus. *Retention:* 66% of full-time freshmen returned.
Faculty *Student/faculty ratio:* 18:1.
Academics *Calendar:* semesters. *Degree:* certificates and associate. *Special study options:* academic remediation for entering students, adult/continuing education programs, advanced placement credit, distance learning, English as a second language, honors programs, independent study, internships, part-time degree program, services for LD students, study abroad, summer session for credit.
Library Illinois Central College Library plus 1 other. *Books:* 45,000 (physical), 67,809 (digital/electronic); *Serial titles:* 101 (physical), 11,251 (digital/electronic); *Databases:* 186. Weekly public service hours: 72.
Student Life *Campus security:* 24-hour emergency response devices and patrols, late-night transport/escort service, controlled dormitory access.
Athletics Member NJCAA.
Financial Aid Of all full-time matriculated undergraduates who enrolled in 2011, 6,521 applied for aid, 5,525 were judged to have need.
Applying *Options:* electronic application, early admission. *Required:* high school transcript.
Freshman Application Contact Emily Points, Dean of Students, Illinois Central College, 1 College Drive, East Peoria, IL 61635. *Phone:* 309-694-8501. *E-mail:* emily.points@icc.edu. *Website:* http://www.icc.edu/.

Illinois Eastern Community Colleges, Frontier Community College

Fairfield, Illinois

- **State and locally supported** 2-year, founded 1976, part of Illinois Eastern Community Colleges System
- **Rural** 8-acre campus
- **Coed**

Undergraduates 290 full-time, 1,501 part-time. 1% are from out of state; 1% Black or African American, non-Hispanic/Latino; 1% Hispanic/Latino; 0.3% Asian, non-Hispanic/Latino; 0.2% American Indian or Alaska Native, non-Hispanic/Latino; 0.1% Race/ethnicity unknown.
Faculty *Student/faculty ratio:* 27:1.
Academics *Calendar:* semesters. *Degree:* certificates and associate. *Special study options:* academic remediation for entering students, adult/continuing education programs, advanced placement credit, cooperative education, distance learning, double majors, English as a second language, external degree program, independent study, part-time degree program, services for LD students, student-designed majors, summer session for credit.
Library Learning Resource Center plus 1 other.
Athletics Member NJCAA.
Applying *Options:* electronic application, early admission, deferred entrance. *Required:* high school transcript.
Freshman Application Contact Ms. Amy Loss, Coordinator of Registration and Records, Illinois Eastern Community Colleges, Frontier Community College, 2 Frontier Drive, Fairfield, IL 62837. *Phone:* 618-842-3711 Ext. 4114. *Toll-free phone:* 877-464-3687. *Fax:* 618-842-6340. *E-mail:* lossa@iecc.edu. *Website:* http://www.iecc.edu/fcc/.

Illinois Eastern Community Colleges, Lincoln Trail College

Robinson, Illinois

- **State and locally supported** 2-year, founded 1969, part of Illinois Eastern Community Colleges System
- **Rural** 120-acre campus
- **Coed**

Undergraduates 399 full-time, 534 part-time. 6% are from out of state; 5% Black or African American, non-Hispanic/Latino; 1% Hispanic/Latino; 1% Asian, non-Hispanic/Latino; 0.1% Native Hawaiian or other Pacific Islander, non-Hispanic/Latino; 0.6% American Indian or Alaska Native, non-Hispanic/Latino; 0.5% Race/ethnicity unknown.
Faculty *Student/faculty ratio:* 19:1.
Academics *Calendar:* semesters. *Degree:* certificates and associate. *Special study options:* academic remediation for entering students, adult/continuing education programs, advanced placement credit, cooperative education, distance learning, double majors, English as a second language, external degree program, independent study, internships, part-time degree program, services for LD students, student-designed majors, summer session for credit.
Library Eagleton Learning Resource Center plus 1 other.
Athletics Member NJCAA.
Applying *Options:* electronic application, early admission, deferred entrance. *Required:* high school transcript.
Freshman Application Contact Ms. Megan Scott, Director of Admissions, Illinois Eastern Community Colleges, Lincoln Trail College, 11220 State Highway 1, Robinson, IL 62454. *Phone:* 618-544-8657 Ext. 1137. *Toll-free phone:* 866-582-4322. *Fax:* 618-544-7423. *E-mail:* scottm@iecc.edu. *Website:* http://www.iecc.edu/ltc/.

Illinois Eastern Community Colleges, Olney Central College

Olney, Illinois

- **State and locally supported** 2-year, founded 1962, part of Illinois Eastern Community Colleges System
- **Rural** 128-acre campus
- **Coed**

Undergraduates 522 full-time, 620 part-time. 2% Black or African American, non-Hispanic/Latino; 1% Hispanic/Latino; 1% Asian, non-Hispanic/Latino; 0.2% American Indian or Alaska Native, non-Hispanic/Latino.
Faculty *Student/faculty ratio:* 12:1.
Academics *Calendar:* semesters. *Degree:* certificates and associate. *Special study options:* academic remediation for entering students, adult/continuing education programs, advanced placement credit, cooperative education, distance learning, double majors, English as a second language, external degree program, independent study, internships, part-time degree program, services for LD students, student-designed majors, summer session for credit.
Library Anderson Learning Resources Center plus 1 other.
Athletics Member NJCAA.
Applying *Options:* electronic application, early admission, deferred entrance. *Required:* high school transcript.
Freshman Application Contact Ms. Andrea Pampe, Assistant Dean for Student Services, Illinois Eastern Community Colleges, Olney Central College, 305 North West Street, Olney, IL 62450. *Phone:* 618-395-7777 Ext. 2005. *Toll-free phone:* 866-622-4322. *Fax:* 618-392-5212. *E-mail:* pampea@iecc.edu. *Website:* http://www.iecc.edu/occ/.

Illinois Eastern Community Colleges, Wabash Valley College

Mount Carmel, Illinois

- **State and locally supported** 2-year, founded 1960, part of Illinois Eastern Community Colleges System
- **Rural** 40-acre campus
- **Coed**

Undergraduates 458 full-time, 3,204 part-time. 7% are from out of state; 5% Black or African American, non-Hispanic/Latino; 0.7% Hispanic/Latino; 1% Asian, non-Hispanic/Latino; 0.2% American Indian or Alaska Native, non-Hispanic/Latino.
Faculty *Student/faculty ratio:* 33:1.
Academics *Calendar:* semesters. *Degree:* certificates and associate. *Special study options:* academic remediation for entering students, adult/continuing education programs, advanced placement credit, cooperative education, distance learning, double majors, English as a second language, external degree program, independent study, internships, part-time degree program, services for LD students, student-designed majors, summer session for credit.
Library Bauer Media Center plus 1 other.
Athletics Member NJCAA.
Applying *Options:* electronic application, early admission, deferred entrance. *Required:* high school transcript.
Freshman Application Contact Mrs. Tiffany Cowger, Assistant Dean for Student Services, Illinois Eastern Community Colleges, Wabash Valley College, 2200 College Drive, Mt. Carmel, IL 62863. *Phone:* 618-262-8641 Ext. 3101. *Toll-free phone:* 866-982-4322. *Fax:* 618-262-8647. *E-mail:* cowgert@iecc.edu. *Website:* http://www.iecc.edu/wvc/.

Illinois Valley Community College

Oglesby, Illinois

- **District-supported** 2-year, founded 1924, part of Illinois Community College Board
- **Rural** 410-acre campus with easy access to Chicago
- **Endowment** $3.7 million
- **Coed**

Undergraduates 1,259 full-time, 1,982 part-time. Students come from 1 other state; 1 other country; 2% Black or African American, non-Hispanic/Latino; 5% Hispanic/Latino; 1% Asian, non-Hispanic/Latino; 0.3% American Indian or Alaska Native, non-Hispanic/Latino; 10% Race/ethnicity unknown; 3% transferred in. *Retention:* 59% of full-time freshmen returned.
Faculty *Student/faculty ratio:* 16:1.
Academics *Calendar:* semesters. *Degree:* certificates and associate. *Special study options:* academic remediation for entering students, advanced placement credit, distance learning, English as a second language, honors programs, independent study, internships, off-campus study, part-time degree program, services for LD students, student-designed majors, study abroad, summer session for credit.
Library Jacobs Library.
Student Life *Campus security:* 24-hour emergency response devices and patrols, late-night transport/escort service.
Athletics Member NJCAA.
Standardized Tests *Recommended:* ACT (for admission).
Financial Aid Of all full-time matriculated undergraduates who enrolled in 2017, 81 Federal Work-Study jobs (averaging $955).
Applying *Options:* electronic application, early admission, deferred entrance. *Required:* high school transcript.
Freshman Application Contact Mr. Quintin Overocker, Director of Admissions and Records, Illinois Valley Community College, Oglesby, IL 61348. *Phone:* 815-224-0437. *Fax:* 815-224-3033. *E-mail:* quintin_overocker@ivcc.edu. *Website:* http://www.ivcc.edu/.

John A. Logan College

Carterville, Illinois

Director of Admissions Mr. Terry Crain, Dean of Student Services, John A. Logan College, 700 Logan College Road, Carterville, IL 62918-9900. *Phone:* 618-985-3741 Ext. 8382. *Fax:* 618-985-4433. *E-mail:* terrycrain@jalc.edu. *Website:* http://www.jalc.edu/.

John Wood Community College

Quincy, Illinois

Freshman Application Contact Mr. Lee Wibbell, Director of Admissions, John Wood Community College, Quincy, IL 62305-8736. *Phone:* 217-641-4339. *Fax:* 217-224-4208. *E-mail:* admissions@jwcc.edu. *Website:* http://www.jwcc.edu/.

Joliet Junior College

Joliet, Illinois

Freshman Application Contact Ms. Jennifer Kloberdanz, Director of Admissions and Recruitment, Joliet Junior College, 1215 Houbolt Road, Joliet, IL 60431. *Phone:* 815-729-9020 Ext. 2414. *E-mail:* admission@jjc.edu. *Website:* http://www.jjc.edu/.

Kankakee Community College

Kankakee, Illinois

Freshman Application Contact Ms. Kim Harpin, Director of Support Services, Kankakee Community College, 100 College Drive, Kankakee, IL 60901. *Phone:* 815-802-8472. *Fax:* 815-802-8472. *E-mail:* kharpin@kcc.edu. *Website:* http://www.kcc.edu/.

Kaskaskia College

Centralia, Illinois

- **State and locally supported** 2-year, founded 1966, part of Illinois Community College Board
- **Rural** 195-acre campus with easy access to St. Louis
- **Endowment** $7.7 million
- **Coed,** 3,164 undergraduate students, 39% full-time, 61% women, 39% men

Undergraduates 1,229 full-time, 1,935 part-time. Students come from 12 states and territories; 0.4% are from out of state; 5% Black or African American, non-Hispanic/Latino; 2% Hispanic/Latino; 0.6% Asian, non-Hispanic/Latino; 0.3% American Indian or Alaska Native, non-Hispanic/Latino; 2% Two or more races, non-Hispanic/Latino; 0.1% Race/ethnicity unknown; 11% transferred in.

Freshmen *Admission:* 236 applied, 236 admitted, 247 enrolled.

Faculty *Total:* 158, 41% full-time, 7% with terminal degrees. *Student/faculty ratio:* 19:1.

Majors Accounting; agriculture; animal sciences; applied horticulture/horticulture operations; architectural drafting and CAD/CADD; automobile/automotive mechanics technology; biological and physical sciences; business automation/technology/data entry; business/commerce; carpentry; child-care provision; clinical/medical laboratory technology; construction management; cosmetology; criminal justice/law enforcement administration; culinary arts; dental assisting; electrical, electronic and communications engineering technology; emergency medical technology (EMT paramedic); engineering; executive assistant/executive secretary; food service and dining room management; general studies; health information/medical records technology; heating, air conditioning, ventilation and refrigeration maintenance technology; industrial mechanics and maintenance technology; juvenile corrections; liberal arts and sciences/liberal studies; library and archives assisting; music; network and system administration; occupational therapist assistant; physical therapy technology; radiologic technology/science; registered nursing/registered nurse; respiratory care therapy; robotics technology; teacher assistant/aide; veterinary/animal health technology; web/multimedia management and webmaster; welding technology.

Academics *Calendar:* semesters. *Degree:* certificates and associate. *Special study options:* academic remediation for entering students, accelerated degree program, adult/continuing education programs, cooperative education, distance learning, double majors, English as a second language, honors programs, independent study, internships, off-campus study, part-time degree program, services for LD students, summer session for credit. *ROTC:* Army (c).

Library Kaskaskia College Library. *Books:* 17,285 (physical), 24,433 (digital/electronic); *Serial titles:* 24 (physical); *Databases:* 86. Weekly public service hours: 47.

Student Life *Housing:* college housing not available. *Activities and Organizations:* drama/theater group, choral group, Phi Theta Kappa, Student Radiography Club, LPN Club, Physical Therapy Club, Fellowship of Christian Athletes. *Campus security:* 24-hour emergency response devices and patrols, late-night transport/escort service. *Student services:* personal/psychological counseling, veterans affairs office.

Athletics Member NJCAA. *Intercollegiate sports:* basketball W(s), cheerleading W(s), cross-country running W(s), soccer W(s), softball W(s), tennis W(s), volleyball W(s).

Standardized Tests *Recommended:* SAT or ACT (for admission).

Financial Aid Of all full-time matriculated undergraduates who enrolled in 2017, 328 applied for aid, 183 were judged to have need, 37 had their need fully met. 30 Federal Work-Study jobs (averaging $2625). 19 state and other part-time jobs (averaging $2592). In 2017, 41 non-need-based awards were made. *Average percent of need met:* 56%. *Average financial aid package:* $7424. *Average need-based gift aid:* $5118. *Average non-need-based aid:* $5002.

Applying *Options:* electronic application, early admission, deferred entrance. *Required:* high school transcript. *Required for some:* interview. *Application deadlines:* rolling (freshmen), rolling (transfers). *Notification:* continuous (freshmen), continuous (transfers).

Freshman Application Contact Jenna Lammers, Registrar, Kaskaskia College, 27210 College Road, Centralia, IL 62801. *Phone:* 618-545-3044. *Toll-free phone:* 800-642-0859. *Fax:* 618-532-1990. *E-mail:* jlammers@kaskaskia.edu. *Website:* http://www.kaskaskia.edu/.

Kishwaukee College

Malta, Illinois

- **State and locally supported** 2-year, founded 1967, part of Illinois Community College Board
- **Rural** 120-acre campus with easy access to Chicago
- **Coed**

Undergraduates 1,634 full-time, 2,141 part-time. 15% Black or African American, non-Hispanic/Latino; 15% Hispanic/Latino; 2% Asian, non-Hispanic/Latino; 0.1% Native Hawaiian or other Pacific Islander, non-Hispanic/Latino; 0.5% American Indian or Alaska Native, non-Hispanic/Latino; 3% Two or more races, non-Hispanic/Latino; 2% Race/ethnicity unknown. *Retention:* 59% of full-time freshmen returned.

Faculty *Student/faculty ratio:* 16:1.

Academics *Calendar:* semesters. *Degree:* certificates, diplomas, and associate. *Special study options:* academic remediation for entering students, adult/continuing education programs, advanced placement credit, cooperative education, distance learning, double majors, English as a second language, external degree program, freshman honors college, honors programs, independent study, internships, off-campus study, part-time degree program, services for LD students, study abroad, summer session for credit.

Library Kishwaukee College Library. Students can reserve study rooms.

Student Life *Campus security:* 24-hour emergency response devices and patrols.

Athletics Member NJCAA.

Financial Aid ***Average indebtedness upon graduation:*** $4375.

Applying *Options:* electronic application, early admission, deferred entrance. *Required for some:* high school transcript. *Recommended:* high school transcript, transcripts from all other colleges or universities previously attended.

Freshman Application Contact Ms. Graciela Horta, Coordinator, Student Outreach, Kishwaukee College, 21193 Malta Road, Malta, IL 60150. *Phone:* 815-825-1711. *E-mail:* ghorta@kish.edu. *Website:* http://www.kish.edu/.

Lake Land College

Mattoon, Illinois

Freshman Application Contact Mr. Jon VanDyke, Dean of Admissions Services, Lake Land College, Mattoon, IL 61938-9366. *Phone:* 217-234-5378. *E-mail:* admissions@lakeland.cc.il.us. *Website:* http://www.lakelandcollege.edu/.

Lewis and Clark Community College

Godfrey, Illinois

Freshman Application Contact Lewis and Clark Community College, 5800 Godfrey Road, Godfrey, IL 62035-2466. *Phone:* 618-468-5100. *Toll-free phone:* 800-YES-LCCC. *Website:* http://www.lc.edu/.

Lincoln College of Technology

Melrose Park, Illinois

Admissions Office Contact Lincoln College of Technology, 8317 West North Avenue, Melrose Park, IL 60160. *Toll-free phone:* 844-215-1513. *Website:* http://www.lincolntech.edu/.

Lincoln Land Community College
Springfield, Illinois

Freshman Application Contact Mr. Ron Gregoire, Executive Director of Admissions and Records, Lincoln Land Community College, 5250 Shepherd Road, PO Box 19256, Springfield, IL 62794-9256. *Phone:* 217-786-2243. *Toll-free phone:* 800-727-4161. *Fax:* 217-786-2492. *E-mail:* ron.gregoire@llcc.edu. *Website:* http://www.llcc.edu/.

MacCormac College
Chicago, Illinois

Director of Admissions Mr. David Grassi, Director of Admissions, MacCormac College, 506 South Wabash Avenue, Chicago, IL 60605-1667. *Phone:* 312-922-1884 Ext. 102. *Website:* http://www.maccormac.edu/.

McHenry County College
Crystal Lake, Illinois

- **State and locally supported** 2-year, founded 1967, part of Illinois Community College Board
- **Suburban** 168-acre campus with easy access to Chicago
- **Coed,** 6,843 undergraduate students, 31% full-time, 53% women, 47% men

Undergraduates 2,112 full-time, 4,731 part-time. 0.8% are from out of state; 2% Black or African American, non-Hispanic/Latino; 18% Hispanic/Latino; 2% Asian, non-Hispanic/Latino; 0.1% Native Hawaiian or other Pacific Islander, non-Hispanic/Latino; 0.1% American Indian or Alaska Native, non-Hispanic/Latino; 3% Two or more races, non-Hispanic/Latino; 5% Race/ethnicity unknown; 0.1% international; 9% transferred in.

Freshmen *Admission:* 1,739 applied, 1,739 admitted, 1,042 enrolled. *Average high school GPA:* 2.3.

Faculty *Total:* 338, 27% full-time, 67% with terminal degrees. *Student/faculty ratio:* 21:1.

Majors Accounting; administrative assistant and secretarial science; animation, interactive technology, video graphics and special effects; applied horticulture/horticulture operations; biological and physical sciences; business administration and management; child-care provision; commercial photography; computer systems networking and telecommunications; construction management; criminal justice/police science; emergency medical technology (EMT paramedic); engineering; fine/studio arts; fire science/firefighting; general studies; health and physical education/fitness; information technology; liberal arts and sciences/liberal studies; music; occupational therapist assistant; operations management; registered nursing/registered nurse; restaurant, culinary, and catering management; selling skills and sales; special education.

Academics *Calendar:* semesters. *Degree:* certificates and associate. *Special study options:* academic remediation for entering students, accelerated degree program, adult/continuing education programs, advanced placement credit, cooperative education, distance learning, English as a second language, independent study, internships, part-time degree program, services for LD students, study abroad, summer session for credit.

Library McHenry County College Library. *Books:* 38,157 (physical), 1,272 (digital/electronic); *Serial titles:* 52 (physical), 42,334 (digital/electronic); *Databases:* 113.

Student Life *Housing:* college housing not available. *Activities and Organizations:* drama/theater group, student-run newspaper, radio station, choral group, Phi Theta Kappa, Student Senate, Equality Club, Writer's Block, Latinos Unidos. *Campus security:* 24-hour emergency response devices and patrols, late-night transport/escort service.

Athletics Member NJCAA. *Intercollegiate sports:* basketball W(s), softball W(s), tennis W(s), volleyball W(s).

Financial Aid Of all full-time matriculated undergraduates who enrolled in 2017, 200 Federal Work-Study jobs (averaging $3700). 130 state and other part-time jobs (averaging $2000).

Applying *Options:* electronic application, early admission, deferred entrance. *Application fee:* $15. *Recommended:* high school transcript. *Application deadlines:* rolling (freshmen), rolling (out-of-state freshmen), rolling (transfers). *Notification:* continuous (freshmen), continuous (out-of-state freshmen), continuous (transfers).

Freshman Application Contact Kellie Carper-Sowiak, Manager of New Student Transitions, McHenry County College, 8900 US Highway 14, Crystal Lake, IL 60012-2761. *Phone:* 815-455-8670. *E-mail:* admissions@mchenry.edu. *Website:* http://www.mchenry.edu/.

Midwestern Career College
Chicago, Illinois

Admissions Office Contact Midwestern Career College, 20 North Wacker Drive #3800, Chicago, IL 60606. *Website:* http://www.mccollege.edu/.

Moraine Valley Community College
Palos Hills, Illinois

Freshman Application Contact Mr. Andrew Sarata, Director, Admissions and Recruitment, Moraine Valley Community College, 9000 West College Parkway, Palos Hills, IL 60465-0937. *Phone:* 708-974-5357. *Fax:* 708-974-0681. *E-mail:* sarataa@morainevalley.edu. *Website:* http://www.morainevalley.edu/.

Morrison Institute of Technology
Morrison, Illinois

- **Independent** 2-year, founded 1973
- **Small-town** 17-acre campus
- **Endowment** $76,000
- **Coed, primarily men**

Undergraduates 142 full-time, 2 part-time. Students come from 4 states and territories; 5% are from out of state; 7% transferred in; 55% live on campus.

Faculty *Student/faculty ratio:* 13:1.

Academics *Calendar:* semesters. *Degree:* associate. *Special study options:* academic remediation for entering students, double majors, internships, part-time degree program.

Library Morrison Tech Learning Center plus 1 other. Study areas open 24 hours, 5–7 days a week.

Student Life *Campus security:* late-night transport/escort service, controlled dormitory access.

Financial Aid Of all full-time matriculated undergraduates who enrolled in 2009, 20 Federal Work-Study jobs (averaging $2000).

Applying *Options:* deferred entrance. *Application fee:* $30. *Required:* high school transcript, proof of immunization.

Admissions Office Contact Morrison Institute of Technology, 701 Portland Avenue, Morrison, IL 61270-0410. *Website:* http://www.morrisontech.edu/.

Morton College
Cicero, Illinois

- **State and locally supported** 2-year, founded 1924, part of Illinois Community College Board
- **Suburban** 25-acre campus with easy access to Chicago
- **Coed**

Undergraduates 1,344 full-time, 3,043 part-time. Students come from 15 states and territories; 1% are from out of state; 3% Black or African American, non-Hispanic/Latino; 84% Hispanic/Latino; 1% Asian, non-Hispanic/Latino; 0.1% American Indian or Alaska Native, non-Hispanic/Latino; 0.7% Two or more races, non-Hispanic/Latino; 4% Race/ethnicity unknown; 36% transferred in.

Faculty *Student/faculty ratio:* 17:1.

Academics *Calendar:* semesters. *Degree:* certificates and associate. *Special study options:* academic remediation for entering students, adult/continuing education programs, advanced placement credit, distance learning, English as a second language, internships, part-time degree program, services for LD students, student-designed majors, summer session for credit.

Library Learning Resource Center. Students can reserve study rooms.

Student Life *Campus security:* 24-hour patrols, security cameras.

Athletics Member NJCAA.

Applying *Options:* electronic application. *Application fee:* $10. *Required:* high school transcript.

Admissions Office Contact Morton College, 3801 South Central Avenue, Cicero, IL 60804-4398. *Website:* http://www.morton.edu/.

Northwestern College–Bridgeview Campus
Bridgeview, Illinois

Admissions Office Contact Northwestern College–Bridgeview Campus, 7725 South Harlem Avenue, Bridgeview, IL 60645. *Toll-free phone:* 888-205-2283. *Website:* http://www.nc.edu/locations/bridgeview-campus/.

Northwestern College–Chicago Campus
Chicago, Illinois

Freshman Application Contact Northwestern College–Chicago Campus, 4829 North Lipps Avenue, Chicago, IL 60630. *Phone:* 708-233-5000. *Toll-free phone:* 888-205-2283. *Website:* http://www.nc.edu/locations/chicago-campus/.

Oakton Community College
Des Plaines, Illinois

- **District-supported** 2-year, founded 1969, part of Illinois Community College Board
- **Suburban** 193-acre campus with easy access to Chicago
- **Coed,** 7,942 undergraduate students

Undergraduates 8% Black or African American, non-Hispanic/Latino; 17% Hispanic/Latino; 23% Asian, non-Hispanic/Latino; 0.5% American Indian or Alaska Native, non-Hispanic/Latino; 6% Race/ethnicity unknown.

Majors Accounting technology and bookkeeping; administrative assistant and secretarial science; architectural drafting and CAD/CADD; automobile/automotive mechanics technology; banking and financial support services; biological and physical sciences; building/construction finishing, management, and inspection related; child-care provision; clinical/medical laboratory technology; computer programming; criminal justice/police science; electrical, electronic and communications engineering technology; engineering; fire science/firefighting; graphic design; health information/medical records administration; heating, ventilation, air conditioning and refrigeration engineering technology; information technology; liberal arts and sciences/liberal studies; manufacturing engineering technology; marketing/marketing management; mechanical engineering/mechanical technology; music; operations management; real estate; registered nursing/registered nurse; sales, distribution, and marketing operations; social work; substance abuse/addiction counseling.

Academics *Calendar:* semesters. *Degree:* certificates and associate. *Special study options:* academic remediation for entering students, adult/continuing education programs, advanced placement credit, distance learning, English as a second language, honors programs, independent study, internships, off-campus study, part-time degree program, services for LD students, study abroad, summer session for credit.

Library Oakton Community College Library plus 1 other.

Student Life *Housing:* college housing not available. *Activities and Organizations:* drama/theater group, student-run newspaper, choral group. *Campus security:* 24-hour emergency response devices and patrols, student patrols, late-night transport/escort service. *Student services:* health clinic, personal/psychological counseling, veterans affairs office.

Athletics Member NJCAA. *Intercollegiate sports:* basketball W, cross-country running W, soccer W, softball W, tennis W, track and field W, volleyball W. *Intramural sports:* basketball M, soccer M, table tennis M, volleyball M.

Applying *Options:* electronic application. *Application fee:* $25. *Required for some:* interview. *Recommended:* high school transcript. *Application deadlines:* rolling (freshmen), rolling (transfers). *Notification:* continuous (freshmen), continuous (transfers).

Freshman Application Contact Ms. Rebel Barber, Admissions Specialist, Oakton Community College, 1600 East Golf Road, Des Plaines, IL 60016-1268. *Phone:* 847-635-1703. *Fax:* 847-635-1890. *E-mail:* rcampbel@oakton.edu.
Website: http://www.oakton.edu/.

Parkland College
Champaign, Illinois

Freshman Application Contact Mr. Tim Wendt, Director of Enrollment Services, Parkland College, Champaign, IL 61821-1899. *Phone:* 217-351-2482. *Toll-free phone:* 800-346-8089. *Fax:* 217-353-2640. *E-mail:* admissions@parkland.edu. *Website:* http://www.parkland.edu/.

Prairie State College
Chicago Heights, Illinois

Freshman Application Contact Jaime Miller, Director of Admissions, Prairie State College, 202 South Halsted Street, Chicago Heights, IL 60411. *Phone:* 708-709-3513. *E-mail:* jmmiller@prairiestate.edu. *Website:* http://www.prairiestate.edu/.

Rend Lake College
Ina, Illinois

- **State-supported** 2-year, founded 1967, part of Illinois Community College Board
- **Rural** 350-acre campus
- **Coed,** 2,486 undergraduate students, 49% full-time, 53% women, 47% men

Undergraduates 1,213 full-time, 1,273 part-time. Students come from 5 states and territories; 7 other countries; 5% Black or African American, non-Hispanic/Latino; 1% Hispanic/Latino; 0.9% Asian, non-Hispanic/Latino; 0.1% Native Hawaiian or other Pacific Islander, non-Hispanic/Latino; 0.3% American Indian or Alaska Native, non-Hispanic/Latino; 0.6% Race/ethnicity unknown; 0.1% international; 3% transferred in.

Freshmen *Admission:* 549 admitted, 549 enrolled.

Faculty *Total:* 133, 44% full-time, 8% with terminal degrees. *Student/faculty ratio:* 18:1.

Majors Administrative assistant and secretarial science; agricultural business and management; agricultural mechanics and equipment technology; agricultural mechanization; agricultural production; architectural drafting and CAD/CADD; automobile/automotive mechanics technology; barbering; biological and physical sciences; biomedical technology; business/commerce; child-care provision; computer and information systems security; computer programming; computer technology/computer systems technology; cosmetology; criminal justice/police science; culinary arts; emergency medical technology (EMT paramedic); engineering; fine/studio arts; graphic design; health information/medical records technology; heavy equipment maintenance technology; industrial mechanics and maintenance technology; liberal arts and sciences/liberal studies; manufacturing engineering technology; medical/clinical assistant; medical radiologic technology; medical staff services technology; music; registered nursing/registered nurse; welding technology.

Academics *Calendar:* semesters. *Degree:* certificates and associate. *Special study options:* academic remediation for entering students, adult/continuing education programs, advanced placement credit, cooperative education, distance learning, double majors, English as a second language, honors programs, independent study, internships, off-campus study, part-time degree program, services for LD students, study abroad, summer session for credit.

Library Learning Resource Center. *Books:* 12,708 (physical), 36,511 (digital/electronic); *Serial titles:* 48 (physical), 24,174 (digital/electronic); *Databases:* 33. Weekly public service hours: 54; students can reserve study rooms.

Student Life *Housing:* college housing not available. *Activities and Organizations:* drama/theater group, choral group, Collegiate FFA, Automotive Club, Art League, Thespians Club, Phi Theta Kappa. *Campus security:* 24-hour emergency response devices and patrols, late-night transport/escort service. *Student services:* personal/psychological counseling, veterans affairs office.

Athletics Member NJCAA. *Intercollegiate sports:* baseball M(s), basketball M(s)/W(s), golf M(s)/W(s), softball W(s), volleyball W(s).

Financial Aid Of all full-time matriculated undergraduates who enrolled in 2017, 133 Federal Work-Study jobs (averaging $1000). 174 state and other part-time jobs (averaging $940).

Applying *Options:* electronic application, deferred entrance. *Required:* high school transcript. *Application deadlines:* 8/24 (freshmen), 8/24 (out-of-state freshmen), 8/24 (transfers).

Freshman Application Contact Mrs. Jena Jensik, Director of Academic Advisement, Rend Lake College, 468 North Ken Gray Parkway, Ina, IL 62846-9801. *Phone:* 618-437-5321 Ext. 1293. *Toll-free phone:* 800-369-5321. *Fax:* 618-437-5677. *E-mail:* jensikj@rlc.edu.
Website: http://www.rlc.edu/.

Richland Community College
Decatur, Illinois

Freshman Application Contact Ms. Catherine Sebok, Director of Admissions and Records, Richland Community College, Decatur, IL 62521. *Phone:* 217-875-7200 Ext. 558. *Fax:* 217-875-7783. *E-mail:* csebok@richland.edu. *Website:* http://www.richland.edu/.

Rockford Career College
Rockford, Illinois

Director of Admissions Ms. Barbara Holliman, Director of Admissions, Rockford Career College, 1130 South Alpine Road, Suite 100, Rockford, IL 61108. *Phone:* 815-965-8616 Ext. 16. *Website:* http://www.rockfordcareercollege.edu/.

Rock Valley College
Rockford, Illinois

- **District-supported** 2-year, founded 1964, part of Illinois Community College Board
- **Suburban** 217-acre campus with easy access to Chicago
- **Coed**, 6,244 undergraduate students, 44% full-time, 55% women, 45% men

Undergraduates 2,762 full-time, 3,482 part-time. 9% Black or African American, non-Hispanic/Latino; 21% Hispanic/Latino; 3% Asian, non-Hispanic/Latino; 0.1% Native Hawaiian or other Pacific Islander, non-Hispanic/Latino; 0.3% American Indian or Alaska Native, non-Hispanic/Latino; 3% Two or more races, non-Hispanic/Latino; 3% Race/ethnicity unknown; 0.4% international; 3% transferred in.
Freshmen *Admission:* 920 enrolled.
Faculty *Student/faculty ratio:* 17:1.
Majors Accounting; administrative assistant and secretarial science; automobile/automotive mechanics technology; avionics maintenance technology; business administration and management; child development; computer engineering technology; computer science; computer systems networking and telecommunications; construction engineering technology; criminal justice/law enforcement administration; dental hygiene; drafting/design engineering technologies related; electrical, electronic and communications engineering technology; electrician; energy management and systems technology; fire science/firefighting; graphic and printing equipment operation/production; human services; industrial and product design; industrial technology; liberal arts and sciences/liberal studies; marketing/marketing management; pre-engineering; registered nursing/registered nurse; respiratory care therapy; sheet metal technology; sport and fitness administration/management; surgical technology; tool and die technology; welding technology.
Academics *Calendar:* semesters. *Degree:* certificates, diplomas, and associate. *Special study options:* academic remediation for entering students, adult/continuing education programs, advanced placement credit, cooperative education, distance learning, English as a second language, honors programs, independent study, internships, part-time degree program, services for LD students, student-designed majors, study abroad, summer session for credit.
Library Educational Resource Center plus 1 other.
Student Life *Housing:* college housing not available. *Activities and Organizations:* drama/theater group, student-run newspaper, choral group, Black Student Alliance, Phi Theta Kappa, Adults on Campus, Inter-Varsity Club, Christian Fellowship. *Campus security:* 24-hour emergency response devices and patrols, late-night transport/escort service. *Student services:* personal/psychological counseling.
Athletics Member NJCAA. *Intercollegiate sports:* basketball W, bowling W, soccer W, softball W, volleyball W.
Financial Aid Of all full-time matriculated undergraduates who enrolled in 2017, 120 Federal Work-Study jobs (averaging $1800).
Applying *Required:* high school transcript.
Freshman Application Contact Sam Morgan, Dean of Enrollment and Retention, Rock Valley College, 3301 North Mulford Road, Rockford, IL 61008. *Phone:* -815-921-4262. *Toll-free phone:* 800-973-7821. *E-mail:* s.morgan@rockvalleycollege.edu.
Website: http://www.rockvalleycollege.edu/.

SAE Institute Chicago
Chicago, Illinois

Admissions Office Contact SAE Institute Chicago, 820 North Orleans Street #125, Chicago, IL 60610. *Website:* http://www.sae.edu/.

Sauk Valley Community College
Dixon, Illinois

- **District-supported** 2-year, founded 1965, part of Illinois Community College Board
- **Rural** 165-acre campus
- **Endowment** $2.0 million
- **Coed**

Undergraduates 998 full-time, 1,222 part-time. 4% Black or African American, non-Hispanic/Latino; 8% Hispanic/Latino; 0.7% Asian, non-Hispanic/Latino; 0.2% Native Hawaiian or other Pacific Islander, non-Hispanic/Latino; 0.3% American Indian or Alaska Native, non-Hispanic/Latino; 0.1% Two or more races, non-Hispanic/Latino; 2% Race/ethnicity unknown. *Retention:* 59% of full-time freshmen returned.
Faculty *Student/faculty ratio:* 21:1.
Academics *Calendar:* semesters. *Degree:* certificates and associate. *Special study options:* academic remediation for entering students, accelerated degree program, adult/continuing education programs, cooperative education, distance learning, English as a second language, honors programs, independent study, internships, off-campus study, part-time degree program, services for LD students, summer session for credit.
Library Learning Resource Center plus 1 other.
Student Life *Campus security:* 24-hour emergency response devices and patrols, late-night transport/escort service.
Athletics Member NJCAA.
Standardized Tests *Recommended:* ACT (for admission).
Financial Aid Of all full-time matriculated undergraduates who enrolled in 2017, 597 applied for aid, 402 were judged to have need, 1 had their need fully met. 49 Federal Work-Study jobs (averaging $2546). 12 state and other part-time jobs (averaging $1255). *Average percent of need met:* 32. *Average financial aid package:* $5704. *Average need-based loan:* $3417. *Average need-based gift aid:* $4925.
Applying *Options:* electronic application, early admission, deferred entrance. *Recommended:* high school transcript.
Freshman Application Contact Sauk Valley Community College, 173 Illinois Route 2, Dixon, IL 61021. *Phone:* 815-288-5511 Ext. 378. *Website:* http://www.svcc.edu/.

Shawnee Community College
Ullin, Illinois

- **State and locally supported** 2-year, founded 1967, part of Illinois Community College Board
- **Rural** 163-acre campus
- **Coed**

Undergraduates 680 full-time, 825 part-time. Students come from 3 states and territories; 2% are from out of state; 14% Black or African American, non-Hispanic/Latino; 4% Hispanic/Latino; 0.5% Asian, non-Hispanic/Latino; 0.1% Native Hawaiian or other Pacific Islander, non-Hispanic/Latino; 0.1% American Indian or Alaska Native, non-Hispanic/Latino; 2% Race/ethnicity unknown; 4% transferred in. *Retention:* 55% of full-time freshmen returned.
Faculty *Student/faculty ratio:* 19:1.
Academics *Calendar:* semesters. *Degree:* certificates, diplomas, and associate. *Special study options:* academic remediation for entering students, accelerated degree program, adult/continuing education programs, advanced placement credit, cooperative education, distance learning, double majors, English as a second language, external degree program, independent study, internships, off-campus study, part-time degree program, services for LD students, summer session for credit.
Library Shawnee Community College Library. Students can reserve study rooms.
Student Life *Campus security:* 24-hour patrols.
Athletics Member NJCAA.
Standardized Tests *Required for some:* SAT (for admission). *Recommended:* SAT (for admission).
Financial Aid Of all full-time matriculated undergraduates who enrolled in 2017, 60 Federal Work-Study jobs (averaging $2000). 50 state and other part-time jobs (averaging $2000).
Applying *Options:* electronic application, early admission, deferred entrance. *Required:* high school transcript.
Freshman Application Contact Mrs. Erin King, Recruiter/Advisor, Shawnee Community College, 8364 Shawnee College Road, Ullin, IL 62992. *Phone:* 618-634-3200. *Toll-free phone:* 800-481-2242. *Fax:* 618-634-3300. *E-mail:* erink@shawneecc.edu. *Website:* http://www.shawneecc.edu/.

Southeastern Illinois College
Harrisburg, Illinois

Freshman Application Contact Dr. David Nudo, Director of Counseling, Southeastern Illinois College, 3575 College Road, Harrisburg, IL 62946-4925. *Phone:* 618-252-5400 Ext. 2430. *Toll-free phone:* 866-338-2742. *Website:* http://www.sic.edu/.

South Suburban College
South Holland, Illinois

- **State and locally supported** 2-year, founded 1927, part of Illinois Community College Board
- **Suburban** 5-acre campus with easy access to Chicago
- **Coed**

Undergraduates 1,191 full-time, 2,924 part-time. 3% are from out of state; 54% Black or African American, non-Hispanic/Latino; 20% Hispanic/Latino; 1% Asian, non-Hispanic/Latino; 0.2% Native Hawaiian or other Pacific Islander, non-Hispanic/Latino; 0.3% American Indian or Alaska Native, non-Hispanic/Latino; 3% Two or more races, non-Hispanic/Latino; 0.8% Race/ethnicity unknown; 0.9% international. *Retention:* 20% of full-time freshmen returned.

Faculty *Student/faculty ratio:* 13:1.
Academics *Calendar:* semesters. *Degree:* certificates and associate. *Special study options:* academic remediation for entering students, adult/continuing education programs, advanced placement credit, cooperative education, distance learning, English as a second language, honors programs, internships, off-campus study, part-time degree program, services for LD students, study abroad, summer session for credit.
Library South Suburban College Library plus 1 other. *Books:* 25,563 (physical); *Serial titles:* 56 (physical); *Databases:* 25. Weekly public service hours: 60; students can reserve study rooms.
Student Life *Campus security:* 24-hour emergency response devices and patrols.
Athletics Member NJCAA.
Financial Aid Of all full-time matriculated undergraduates who enrolled in 2015, 4,111 applied for aid, 3,901 were judged to have need. 128 Federal Work-Study jobs (averaging $1678). In 2015, 59. *Average percent of need met:* 59. *Average financial aid package:* $4850. *Average need-based gift aid:* $2350. *Average non-need-based aid:* $611.
Applying *Options:* early admission, deferred entrance. *Required:* high school transcript. *Required for some:* essay or personal statement. *Recommended:* essay or personal statement, minimum 2.0 GPA.
Freshman Application Contact Ms. Tiffane Jones, Admissions, South Suburban College, 15800 South State Street, South Holland, IL 60473. *Phone:* 708-596-2000 Ext. 2158. *E-mail:* admissionsquestions@ssc.edu. *Website:* http://www.ssc.edu/.

Southwestern Illinois College
Belleville, Illinois

- **District-supported** 2-year, founded 1946, part of Illinois Community College Board
- **Suburban** campus with easy access to St. Louis
- **Coed**

Academics *Calendar:* semesters. *Degree:* certificates, diplomas, and associate.
Financial Aid Of all full-time matriculated undergraduates who enrolled in 2017, 170 Federal Work-Study jobs (averaging $1537). 179 state and other part-time jobs (averaging $1004).
Freshman Application Contact Southwestern Illinois College, 2500 Carlyle Avenue, Belleville, IL 62221-5899. *Toll-free phone:* 866-942-SWIC. *Website:* http://www.swic.edu/.

Spoon River College
Canton, Illinois

Freshman Application Contact Ms. Missy Wilkinson, Dean of Student Services, Spoon River College, 23235 North County 22, Canton, IL 61520-9801. *Phone:* 309-649-6305. *Toll-free phone:* 800-334-7337. *Fax:* 309-649-6235. *E-mail:* info@src.edu. *Website:* http://www.src.edu/.

Taylor Business Institute
Chicago, Illinois

Director of Admissions Mr. Rashed Jahangir, Taylor Business Institute, 318 West Adams, Chicago, IL 60606. *Website:* http://www.tbiil.edu/.

Tribeca Flashpoint College
Chicago, Illinois

Admissions Office Contact Tribeca Flashpoint College, 28 North Clark Street, Chicago, IL 60602. *Website:* http://www.tribecaflashpoint.edu/.

Triton College
River Grove, Illinois

Freshman Application Contact Ms. Mary-Rita Moore, Dean of Admissions, Triton College, 2000 Fifth Avenue, River Grove, IL 60171. *Phone:* 708-456-0300 Ext. 3679. *Fax:* 708-583-3162. *E-mail:* mpatrice@triton.edu. *Website:* http://www.triton.edu/.

Vet Tech Institute at Fox College
Tinley Park, Illinois

Freshman Application Contact Admissions Office, Vet Tech Institute at Fox College, 18020 South Oak Park Avenue, Tinley Park, IL 60477. *Phone:* 888-884-3694. *Toll-free phone:* 888-884-3694. *Website:* http://chicago.vettechinstitute.edu/.

Waubonsee Community College
Sugar Grove, Illinois

Freshman Application Contact Joy Sanders, Admissions Manager, Waubonsee Community College, Route 47 at Waubonsee Drive, Sugar Grove, IL 60554. *Phone:* 630-466-7900 Ext. 5756. *Fax:* 630-466-6663. *E-mail:* admissions@waubonsee.edu. *Website:* http://www.waubonsee.edu/.

Worsham College of Mortuary Science
Wheeling, Illinois

Director of Admissions President, Worsham College of Mortuary Science, 495 Northgate Parkway, Wheeling, IL 60090-2646. *Phone:* 847-808-8444. *Website:* http://www.worsham.edu/.

INDIANA

Ancilla College
Donaldson, Indiana

- **Independent Roman Catholic** 2-year, founded 1937
- **Rural** 63-acre campus
- **Endowment** $5.8 million
- **Coed**

Undergraduates 451 full-time, 97 part-time. Students come from 19 states and territories; 7 other countries; 12% are from out of state; 18% Black or African American, non-Hispanic/Latino; 10% Hispanic/Latino; 0.4% American Indian or Alaska Native, non-Hispanic/Latino; 5% Two or more races, non-Hispanic/Latino; 3% international; 11% transferred in; 35% live on campus. *Retention:* 41% of full-time freshmen returned.
Faculty *Student/faculty ratio:* 16:1.
Academics *Calendar:* semesters. *Degree:* associate. *Special study options:* academic remediation for entering students, adult/continuing education programs, advanced placement credit, cooperative education, distance learning, double majors, independent study, internships, part-time degree program, services for LD students, student-designed majors, summer session for credit.
Library Gerald J. Ball Library. *Books:* 15,692 (physical), 3,767 (digital/electronic); *Serial titles:* 39 (physical); *Databases:* 84. Weekly public service hours: 66.
Student Life *Campus security:* 24-hour emergency response devices and patrols, late-night transport/escort service, controlled dormitory access.
Athletics Member NJCAA.
Financial Aid Of all full-time matriculated undergraduates who enrolled in 2017, 22 Federal Work-Study jobs (averaging $1665). *Financial aid deadline:* 4/15.
Applying *Options:* electronic application. *Required:* high school transcript.
Freshman Application Contact Ms. Ericka Taylor-Joseph, Executive Director of Admissions, Ancilla College, PO Box 1, 9601 Union Road, Donaldson, IN 46513. *Phone:* 574-936-8898 Ext. 326. *Toll-free phone:* 866-ANCILLA. *Fax:* 574-935-1773. *E-mail:* admissions@ancilla.edu. *Website:* http://www.ancilla.edu/.

College of Court Reporting
Valparaiso, Indiana

Freshman Application Contact Ms. Nicky Rodriquez, Director of Admissions, College of Court Reporting, 455 West Lincolnway, Valparaiso, IN 46385. *Phone:* 219-942-1459 Ext. 222. *Toll-free phone:* 866-294-3974. *Fax:* 219-942-1631. *E-mail:* nrodriquez@ccr.edu. *Website:* http://www.ccr.edu/.

Fortis College
Indianapolis, Indiana

Freshman Application Contact Mr. Alex Teitelbaum, Vice President Systems and Administration, Fortis College, 9001 North Wesleyan Road, Suite 101, Indianapolis, IN 46268. *Phone:* 410-633-2929. *Toll-free phone:* 855-4-FORTIS. *E-mail:* kbennett@edaff.com. *Website:* http://www.fortis.edu/.

International Business College
Indianapolis, Indiana

Freshman Application Contact Admissions Office, International Business College, 7205 Shadeland Station, Indianapolis, IN 46256. *Phone:* 317-813-2300. *Toll-free phone:* 800-589-6500. *Website:* http://www.ibcindianapolis.edu/.

Ivy Tech Community College–Bloomington

Bloomington, Indiana

- **State-supported** 2-year, founded 2001, part of Ivy Tech Community College System
- **Coed**

Undergraduates 1,656 full-time, 4,542 part-time. 1% are from out of state; 3% Black or African American, non-Hispanic/Latino; 1% Hispanic/Latino; 2% Asian, non-Hispanic/Latino; 0.2% Native Hawaiian or other Pacific Islander, non-Hispanic/Latino; 0.2% American Indian or Alaska Native, non-Hispanic/Latino; 3% Two or more races, non-Hispanic/Latino; 19% Race/ethnicity unknown; 5% transferred in. *Retention:* 50% of full-time freshmen returned.

Faculty *Student/faculty ratio:* 19:1.

Academics *Calendar:* semesters. *Degree:* certificates and associate. *Special study options:* academic remediation for entering students, adult/continuing education programs, advanced placement credit, distance learning, external degree program, internships, part-time degree program, services for LD students, summer session for credit.

Student Life *Campus security:* late-night transport/escort service.

Financial Aid Of all full-time matriculated undergraduates who enrolled in 2017, 51 Federal Work-Study jobs (averaging $3259).

Applying *Options:* electronic application, deferred entrance. *Required:* high school transcript. *Required for some:* interview.

Freshman Application Contact Mr. Neil Frederick, Assistant Director of Admissions, Ivy Tech Community College–Bloomington, 200 Daniels Way, Bloomington, IN 47404. *Phone:* 812-330-6026. *Toll-free phone:* 888-IVY-LINE. *Fax:* 812-332-8147. *E-mail:* nfrederi@ivytech.edu. *Website:* http://www.ivytech.edu/.

Ivy Tech Community College–Central Indiana

Indianapolis, Indiana

- **State-supported** 2-year, founded 1963, part of Ivy Tech Community College System
- **Urban** 10-acre campus
- **Coed**

Undergraduates 4,604 full-time, 13,458 part-time. 1% are from out of state; 22% Black or African American, non-Hispanic/Latino; 5% Hispanic/Latino; 4% Asian, non-Hispanic/Latino; 0.2% Native Hawaiian or other Pacific Islander, non-Hispanic/Latino; 0.2% American Indian or Alaska Native, non-Hispanic/Latino; 4% Two or more races, non-Hispanic/Latino; 3% Race/ethnicity unknown; 7% transferred in. *Retention:* 46% of full-time freshmen returned.

Faculty *Student/faculty ratio:* 23:1.

Academics *Calendar:* semesters. *Degree:* certificates and associate. *Special study options:* academic remediation for entering students, adult/continuing education programs, advanced placement credit, cooperative education, distance learning, English as a second language, internships, off-campus study, part-time degree program, services for LD students, summer session for credit.

Student Life *Campus security:* 24-hour emergency response devices and patrols, late-night transport/escort service.

Financial Aid Of all full-time matriculated undergraduates who enrolled in 2017, 92 Federal Work-Study jobs (averaging $3766).

Applying *Options:* electronic application, early admission, deferred entrance. *Required:* high school transcript. *Required for some:* interview.

Freshman Application Contact Ms. Tracy Funk, Director of Admissions, Ivy Tech Community College–Central Indiana, 50 West Fall Creek Parkway North Drive, Indianapolis, IN 46208-4777. *Phone:* 317-921-4371. *Toll-free phone:* 888-IVYLINE. *Fax:* 317-917-5919. *E-mail:* tfunk@ivytech.edu. *Website:* http://www.ivytech.edu/.

Ivy Tech Community College–Columbus

Columbus, Indiana

- **State-supported** 2-year, founded 1963, part of Ivy Tech Community College System
- **Small-town** campus with easy access to Indianapolis
- **Coed**

Undergraduates 652 full-time, 2,001 part-time. 1% are from out of state; 2% Black or African American, non-Hispanic/Latino; 3% Hispanic/Latino; 1% Asian, non-Hispanic/Latino; 0.1% Native Hawaiian or other Pacific Islander, non-Hispanic/Latino; 0.2% American Indian or Alaska Native, non-Hispanic/Latino; 2% Two or more races, non-Hispanic/Latino; 9% Race/ethnicity unknown; 5% transferred in.

Faculty *Student/faculty ratio:* 15:1.

Academics *Calendar:* semesters. *Degree:* certificates and associate. *Special study options:* academic remediation for entering students, adult/continuing education programs, advanced placement credit, distance learning, internships, part-time degree program, services for LD students, summer session for credit.

Student Life *Campus security:* late-night transport/escort service, trained evening security personnel, escort service.

Financial Aid Of all full-time matriculated undergraduates who enrolled in 2017, 26 Federal Work-Study jobs (averaging $1694).

Applying *Options:* electronic application, early admission, deferred entrance. *Required:* high school transcript. *Required for some:* interview.

Freshman Application Contact Alisa Deck, Director of Admissions, Ivy Tech Community College–Columbus, 4475 Central Avenue, Columbus, IN 47203-1868. *Phone:* 812-374-5129. *Toll-free phone:* 888-IVY-LINE. *Fax:* 812-372-0331. *E-mail:* adeck@ivytech.edu. *Website:* http://www.ivytech.edu/.

Ivy Tech Community College–East Central

Muncie, Indiana

- **State-supported** 2-year, founded 1968, part of Ivy Tech Community College System
- **Suburban** 15-acre campus with easy access to Indianapolis
- **Coed**

Undergraduates 2,030 full-time, 3,432 part-time. 1% are from out of state; 7% Black or African American, non-Hispanic/Latino; 2% Hispanic/Latino; 0.7% Asian, non-Hispanic/Latino; 0.1% Native Hawaiian or other Pacific Islander, non-Hispanic/Latino; 0.3% American Indian or Alaska Native, non-Hispanic/Latino; 4% Two or more races, non-Hispanic/Latino; 4% Race/ethnicity unknown; 6% transferred in. *Retention:* 48% of full-time freshmen returned.

Faculty *Student/faculty ratio:* 15:1.

Academics *Calendar:* semesters. *Degree:* certificates and associate. *Special study options:* academic remediation for entering students, adult/continuing education programs, advanced placement credit, distance learning, internships, part-time degree program, services for LD students.

Financial Aid Of all full-time matriculated undergraduates who enrolled in 2017, 65 Federal Work-Study jobs (averaging $2666).

Applying *Options:* electronic application, early admission, deferred entrance. *Required:* high school transcript. *Required for some:* interview.

Freshman Application Contact Ms. Mary Lewellen, Ivy Tech Community College–East Central, 4301 South Cowan Road, Muncie, IN 47302-9448. *Phone:* 765-289-2291 Ext. 1391. *Toll-free phone:* 888-IVY-LINE. *Fax:* 765-289-2292. *E-mail:* mlewelle@ivytech.edu. *Website:* http://www.ivytech.edu/.

Ivy Tech Community College–Kokomo

Kokomo, Indiana

- **State-supported** 2-year, founded 1968, part of Ivy Tech Community College System
- **Small-town** 20-acre campus with easy access to Indianapolis
- **Coed**

Undergraduates 804 full-time, 1,618 part-time. 6% Black or African American, non-Hispanic/Latino; 4% Hispanic/Latino; 2% Asian, non-Hispanic/Latino; 0.7% American Indian or Alaska Native, non-Hispanic/Latino; 4% Two or more races, non-Hispanic/Latino; 2% Race/ethnicity unknown; 5% transferred in. *Retention:* 55% of full-time freshmen returned.

Faculty *Student/faculty ratio:* 12:1.

Academics *Calendar:* semesters. *Degree:* certificates and associate. *Special study options:* academic remediation for entering students, adult/continuing education programs, advanced placement credit, distance learning, internships, part-time degree program, services for LD students, summer session for credit.

Student Life *Campus security:* 24-hour emergency response devices, late-night transport/escort service.

Financial Aid Of all full-time matriculated undergraduates who enrolled in 2017, 45 Federal Work-Study jobs (averaging $1829).

Applying *Options:* electronic application, early admission. *Required:* high school transcript. *Required for some:* interview.

Freshman Application Contact Mr. Mike Federspill, Director of Admissions, Ivy Tech Community College–Kokomo, 1815 East Morgan Street, Kokomo, IN 46903-1373. *Phone:* 765-459-0561 Ext. 233. *Toll-free phone:* 888-IVY-LINE. *Fax:* 765-454-5111. *E-mail:* mfedersp@ivytech.edu. *Website:* http://www.ivytech.edu/.

Ivy Tech Community College–Lafayette

Lafayette, Indiana

- **State-supported** 2-year, founded 1968, part of Ivy Tech Community College System
- **Suburban** campus with easy access to Indianapolis
- **Coed**

Undergraduates 1,698 full-time, 2,819 part-time. 1% are from out of state; 5% Black or African American, non-Hispanic/Latino; 6% Hispanic/Latino; 2% Asian, non-Hispanic/Latino; 0.2% Native Hawaiian or other Pacific Islander, non-Hispanic/Latino; 0.4% American Indian or Alaska Native, non-Hispanic/Latino; 3% Two or more races, non-Hispanic/Latino; 9% Race/ethnicity unknown; 7% transferred in. *Retention:* 53% of full-time freshmen returned.
Faculty *Student/faculty ratio:* 15:1.
Academics *Calendar:* semesters. *Degree:* certificates and associate. *Special study options:* academic remediation for entering students, advanced placement credit, distance learning, internships, part-time degree program, services for LD students, summer session for credit.
Financial Aid Of all full-time matriculated undergraduates who enrolled in 2017, 65 Federal Work-Study jobs (averaging $2222). 1 state and other part-time job (averaging $2436).
Applying *Options:* electronic application. *Required:* high school transcript. *Required for some:* interview.
Freshman Application Contact Mr. Ivan Hernanadez, Director of Admissions, Ivy Tech Community College–Lafayette, 3101 South Creasy Lane, PO Box 6299, Lafayette, IN 47903. *Phone:* 765-269-5116. *Toll-free phone:* 888-IVY-LINE. *Fax:* 765-772-9293. *E-mail:* ihernand@ivytech.edu. *Website:* http://www.ivytech.edu/.

Ivy Tech Community College–North Central

South Bend, Indiana

- **State-supported** 2-year, founded 1968, part of Ivy Tech Community College System
- **Suburban** 4-acre campus
- **Coed**

Undergraduates 1,407 full-time, 3,398 part-time. 2% are from out of state; 14% Black or African American, non-Hispanic/Latino; 11% Hispanic/Latino; 1% Asian, non-Hispanic/Latino; 0.2% Native Hawaiian or other Pacific Islander, non-Hispanic/Latino; 0.4% American Indian or Alaska Native, non-Hispanic/Latino; 4% Two or more races, non-Hispanic/Latino; 3% Race/ethnicity unknown; 8% transferred in. *Retention:* 47% of full-time freshmen returned.
Faculty *Student/faculty ratio:* 14:1.
Academics *Calendar:* semesters. *Degree:* certificates and associate. *Special study options:* academic remediation for entering students, adult/continuing education programs, advanced placement credit, distance learning, English as a second language, internships, off-campus study, part-time degree program, services for LD students, summer session for credit.
Student Life *Campus security:* 24-hour emergency response devices and patrols, late-night transport/escort service, security during hours of operation.
Financial Aid Of all full-time matriculated undergraduates who enrolled in 2017, 100 Federal Work-Study jobs (averaging $1538).
Applying *Options:* electronic application, early admission, deferred entrance. *Required:* high school transcript. *Required for some:* interview.
Freshman Application Contact Darryl Williams, Bi-Regional Director of Admissions, Ivy Tech Community College–North Central, 220 Dean Johnson Boulevard, South Bend, IN 46601-3415. *Toll-free phone:* 888-IVY-LINE. *E-mail:* dwilliams770@ivytech.edu. *Website:* http://www.ivytech.edu/.

Ivy Tech Community College–Northeast

Fort Wayne, Indiana

- **State-supported** 2-year, founded 1969, part of Ivy Tech Community College System
- **Urban** 22-acre campus
- **Coed**

Undergraduates 1,869 full-time, 4,926 part-time. 1% are from out of state; 11% Black or African American, non-Hispanic/Latino; 5% Hispanic/Latino; 3% Asian, non-Hispanic/Latino; 0.2% Native Hawaiian or other Pacific Islander, non-Hispanic/Latino; 0.5% American Indian or Alaska Native, non-Hispanic/Latino; 4% Two or more races, non-Hispanic/Latino; 6% Race/ethnicity unknown; 7% transferred in. *Retention:* 50% of full-time freshmen returned.
Faculty *Student/faculty ratio:* 16:1.
Academics *Calendar:* semesters. *Degree:* certificates and associate. *Special study options:* adult/continuing education programs, advanced placement credit, distance learning, English as a second language, internships, part-time degree program, services for LD students, summer session for credit.
Student Life *Campus security:* 24-hour emergency response devices and patrols, late-night transport/escort service.
Financial Aid Of all full-time matriculated undergraduates who enrolled in 2017, 40 Federal Work-Study jobs (averaging $4041).
Applying *Options:* early admission. *Required:* high school transcript. *Required for some:* interview.
Freshman Application Contact Robyn Boss, Director of Admissions, Ivy Tech Community College–Northeast, 3800 North Anthony Boulevard, Ft. Wayne, IN 46805-1489. *Phone:* 260-480-4211. *Toll-free phone:* 888-IVY-LINE. *Fax:* 260-480-2053. *E-mail:* rboss1@ivytech.edu. *Website:* http://www.ivytech.edu/.

Ivy Tech Community College–Northwest

Gary, Indiana

- **State-supported** 2-year, founded 1963, part of Ivy Tech Community College System
- **Urban** 13-acre campus with easy access to Chicago
- **Coed**

Undergraduates 2,399 full-time, 5,915 part-time. 1% are from out of state; 21% Black or African American, non-Hispanic/Latino; 10% Hispanic/Latino; 0.9% Asian, non-Hispanic/Latino; 0.2% Native Hawaiian or other Pacific Islander, non-Hispanic/Latino; 0.4% American Indian or Alaska Native, non-Hispanic/Latino; 4% Two or more races, non-Hispanic/Latino; 5% Race/ethnicity unknown; 9% transferred in.
Faculty *Student/faculty ratio:* 18:1.
Academics *Calendar:* semesters. *Degree:* certificates and associate. *Special study options:* academic remediation for entering students, adult/continuing education programs, advanced placement credit, distance learning, internships, part-time degree program, services for LD students, summer session for credit.
Student Life *Campus security:* 24-hour emergency response devices, late-night transport/escort service.
Financial Aid Of all full-time matriculated undergraduates who enrolled in 2017, 74 Federal Work-Study jobs (averaging $2131).
Applying *Options:* electronic application, deferred entrance. *Required:* high school transcript. *Required for some:* interview.
Freshman Application Contact Darryl Williams, Bi-Regional Director of Admissions, Ivy Tech Community College–Northwest, 1440 East 35th Avenue, Gary, IN 46409-499. *Phone:* 219-981-1111. *Toll-free phone:* 888-IVY-LINE. *E-mail:* dwilliams770@ivytech.edu. *Website:* http://www.ivytech.edu/.

Ivy Tech Community College–Richmond

Richmond, Indiana

- **State-supported** 2-year, founded 1963, part of Ivy Tech Community College System
- **Small-town** 23-acre campus with easy access to Indianapolis
- **Coed**

Undergraduates 415 full-time, 1,112 part-time. 1% are from out of state; 4% Black or African American, non-Hispanic/Latino; 0.6% Hispanic/Latino; 0.5% Asian, non-Hispanic/Latino; 0.1% Native Hawaiian or other Pacific Islander, non-Hispanic/Latino; 0.6% American Indian or Alaska Native, non-Hispanic/Latino; 2% Two or more races, non-Hispanic/Latino; 3% Race/ethnicity unknown; 7% transferred in. *Retention:* 50% of full-time freshmen returned.
Faculty *Student/faculty ratio:* 13:1.
Academics *Calendar:* semesters. *Degree:* certificates and associate. *Special study options:* academic remediation for entering students, adult/continuing education programs, advanced placement credit, distance learning, independent study, internships, off-campus study, part-time degree program, services for LD students, summer session for credit.
Student Life *Campus security:* 24-hour emergency response devices, late-night transport/escort service.
Financial Aid Of all full-time matriculated undergraduates who enrolled in 2017, 14 Federal Work-Study jobs (averaging $3106). 1 state and other part-time job (averaging $3380).
Applying *Options:* electronic application, early admission. *Required:* high school transcript. *Required for some:* interview.
Freshman Application Contact Linda Przybysz, Director of Admissions, Ivy Tech Community College–Richmond, 2325 Chester Boulevard, Richmond, IN 47374-1298. *Phone:* 765-966-2656 Ext. 1246. *Toll-free phone:* 888-IVY-LINE. *E-mail:* lprzybys@ivytech.edu. *Website:* http://www.ivytech.edu/.

Ivy Tech Community College–Sellersburg

Sellersburg, Indiana

- **State-supported** 2-year, founded 1968, part of Ivy Tech Community College System
- **Small-town** 63-acre campus with easy access to Louisville
- **Coed**

Undergraduates 867 full-time, 3,817 part-time. 9% are from out of state; 7% Black or African American, non-Hispanic/Latino; 2% Hispanic/Latino; 0.8% Asian, non-Hispanic/Latino; 0.1% Native Hawaiian or other Pacific Islander, non-Hispanic/Latino; 0.3% American Indian or Alaska Native, non-Hispanic/Latino; 3% Two or more races, non-Hispanic/Latino; 14% Race/ethnicity unknown; 8% transferred in. *Retention:* 55% of full-time freshmen returned.
Faculty *Student/faculty ratio:* 20:1.
Academics *Calendar:* semesters. *Degree:* certificates and associate. *Special study options:* academic remediation for entering students, adult/continuing education programs, advanced placement credit, cooperative education, distance learning, internships, part-time degree program, services for LD students, summer session for credit.
Student Life *Campus security:* late-night transport/escort service.
Financial Aid Of all full-time matriculated undergraduates who enrolled in 2017, 20 Federal Work-Study jobs (averaging $5007). 1 state and other part-time job (averaging $6080).
Applying *Options:* electronic application, early admission, deferred entrance. *Required:* high school transcript. *Required for some:* interview.
Freshman Application Contact Ben Harris, Director of Admissions, Ivy Tech Community College–Sellersburg, 8204 Highway 311, Sellersburg, IN 47172-1897. *Phone:* 812-246-3301 Ext. 4137. *Toll-free phone:* 888-IVY-LINE. *Fax:* 812-246-9905. *E-mail:* bharris88@ivytech.edu. *Website:* http://www.ivytech.edu/.

Ivy Tech Community College–Southeast

Madison, Indiana

- **State-supported** 2-year, founded 1963, part of Ivy Tech Community College System
- **Small-town** 5-acre campus with easy access to Louisville
- **Coed**

Undergraduates 635 full-time, 1,699 part-time. 1% are from out of state; 1% Black or African American, non-Hispanic/Latino; 0.7% Hispanic/Latino; 0.5% Asian, non-Hispanic/Latino; 0.4% American Indian or Alaska Native, non-Hispanic/Latino; 2% Two or more races, non-Hispanic/Latino; 7% Race/ethnicity unknown; 5% transferred in. *Retention:* 63% of full-time freshmen returned.
Faculty *Student/faculty ratio:* 13:1.
Academics *Calendar:* semesters. *Degree:* certificates and associate. *Special study options:* academic remediation for entering students, advanced placement credit, distance learning, internships, part-time degree program, services for LD students, summer session for credit.
Student Life *Campus security:* 24-hour emergency response devices.
Financial Aid Of all full-time matriculated undergraduates who enrolled in 2017, 26 Federal Work-Study jobs (averaging $1696).
Applying *Options:* electronic application. *Required:* high school transcript. *Required for some:* interview.
Freshman Application Contact Shakira Grubbs, Director Express Enrollment Center, Ivy Tech Community College–Southeast, 590 Ivy Tech Drive, Madison, IN 47250-1881. *Phone:* 812-537-4010. *Toll-free phone:* 888-IVY-LINE. *E-mail:* sgrubbs5@ivytech.edu. *Website:* http://www.ivytech.edu/.

Ivy Tech Community College–Southwest

Evansville, Indiana

- **State-supported** 2-year, founded 1963, part of Ivy Tech Community College System
- **Suburban** 15-acre campus
- **Coed**

Undergraduates 928 full-time, 3,148 part-time. 1% are from out of state; 7% Black or African American, non-Hispanic/Latino; 0.9% Hispanic/Latino; 0.9% Asian, non-Hispanic/Latino; 0.1% Native Hawaiian or other Pacific Islander, non-Hispanic/Latino; 0.3% American Indian or Alaska Native, non-Hispanic/Latino; 3% Two or more races, non-Hispanic/Latino; 6% Race/ethnicity unknown; 7% transferred in. *Retention:* 52% of full-time freshmen returned.
Faculty *Student/faculty ratio:* 17:1.
Academics *Calendar:* semesters. *Degree:* certificates and associate. *Special study options:* academic remediation for entering students, advanced placement credit, cooperative education, distance learning, independent study, internships, part-time degree program, services for LD students, summer session for credit.
Student Life *Campus security:* late-night transport/escort service.
Financial Aid Of all full-time matriculated undergraduates who enrolled in 2017, 65 Federal Work-Study jobs (averaging $2264).
Applying *Options:* electronic application, early admission, deferred entrance. *Required:* high school transcript. *Required for some:* interview.
Freshman Application Contact Ms. Denise Johnson-Kincade, Director of Admissions, Ivy Tech Community College–Southwest, 3501 First Avenue, Evansville, IN 47710-3398. *Phone:* 812-429-1430. *Toll-free phone:* 888-IVY-LINE. *Fax:* 812-429-9878. *E-mail:* ajohnson@ivytech.edu. *Website:* http://www.ivytech.edu/.

Ivy Tech Community College–Wabash Valley

Terre Haute, Indiana

- **State-supported** 2-year, founded 1966, part of Ivy Tech Community College System
- **Suburban** 55-acre campus with easy access to Indianapolis
- **Coed**

Undergraduates 1,216 full-time, 2,421 part-time. 1% are from out of state; 4% Black or African American, non-Hispanic/Latino; 0.7% Hispanic/Latino; 0.5% Asian, non-Hispanic/Latino; 0.4% American Indian or Alaska Native, non-Hispanic/Latino; 2% Two or more races, non-Hispanic/Latino; 5% Race/ethnicity unknown; 7% transferred in. *Retention:* 55% of full-time freshmen returned.
Faculty *Student/faculty ratio:* 19:1.
Academics *Calendar:* semesters. *Degree:* certificates and associate. *Special study options:* academic remediation for entering students, adult/continuing education programs, advanced placement credit, distance learning, internships, part-time degree program, services for LD students, summer session for credit.
Student Life *Campus security:* 24-hour emergency response devices.
Financial Aid Of all full-time matriculated undergraduates who enrolled in 2017, 51 Federal Work-Study jobs (averaging $2110). 1 state and other part-time job (averaging $2963).
Applying *Options:* electronic application, early admission, deferred entrance. *Required:* high school transcript. *Required for some:* interview.
Freshman Application Contact Nina Storey, Director of Admissions, Ivy Tech Community College–Wabash Valley, 7999 U.S. Highway 41 South, Terre Haute, IN 47802-4898. *Phone:* 812-298-2288. *Toll-free phone:* 888-IVY-LINE. *E-mail:* nstorey@ivytech.edu. *Website:* http://www.ivytech.edu/.

Lincoln College of Technology

Indianapolis, Indiana

Director of Admissions Ms. Cindy Ryan, Director of Admissions, Lincoln College of Technology, 7225 Winton Drive, Building 128, Indianapolis, IN 46268. *Phone:* 317-632-5553. *Toll-free phone:* 844-215-1513. *Website:* http://www.lincolntech.edu/.

Mid-America College of Funeral Service

Jeffersonville, Indiana

Freshman Application Contact Mr. Richard Nelson, Dean of Students, Mid-America College of Funeral Service, 3111 Hamburg Pike, Jeffersonville, IN 47130-9630. *Phone:* 812-288-8878. *Toll-free phone:* 800-221-6158. *Fax:* 812-288-5942. *E-mail:* macfs@mindspring.com. *Website:* http://www.mid-america.edu/.

Vet Tech Institute at International Business College

Fort Wayne, Indiana

Freshman Application Contact Admissions Office, Vet Tech Institute at International Business College, 5699 Coventry Lane, Fort Wayne, IN 46804. *Phone:* 800-589-6363. *Toll-free phone:* 800-589-6363. *Website:* http://ftwayne.vettechinstitute.edu/.

Vet Tech Institute at International Business College

Indianapolis, Indiana

Freshman Application Contact Admissions Office, Vet Tech Institute at International Business College, 7205 Shadeland Station, Indianapolis, IN 46256. *Phone:* 800-589-6500. *Toll-free phone:* 800-589-6500. *Website:* http://indianapolis.vettechinstitute.edu/.

Vincennes University

Vincennes, Indiana

- **State-supported** primarily 2-year, founded 1801
- **Small-town** 160-acre campus
- **Coed,** 17,481 undergraduate students, 28% full-time, 46% women, 54% men

Undergraduates 4,970 full-time, 12,511 part-time. 17% are from out of state; 10% Black or African American, non-Hispanic/Latino; 15% Hispanic/Latino; 2% Asian, non-Hispanic/Latino; 0.2% Native Hawaiian or other Pacific Islander, non-Hispanic/Latino; 0.4% American Indian or Alaska Native, non-Hispanic/Latino; 2% Two or more races, non-Hispanic/Latino; 5% Race/ethnicity unknown; 0.2% international; 0.8% transferred in; 37% live on campus. *Retention:* 56% of full-time freshmen returned.

Freshmen *Admission:* 4,728 applied, 3,656 admitted, 2,193 enrolled.

Faculty *Total:* 817, 22% full-time. *Student/faculty ratio:* 16:1.

Majors Accounting technology and bookkeeping; agricultural business and management; aircraft powerplant technology; airline pilot and flight crew; American Sign Language (ASL); applied horticulture/horticulture operations; architectural drafting and CAD/CADD; art; art teacher education; autobody/collision and repair technology; automation engineer technology; automobile/automotive mechanics technology; behavioral sciences; biological and biomedical sciences related; building/construction finishing, management, and inspection related; business administration and management; business/commerce; business teacher education; carpentry; chemistry related; chemistry teacher education; child-care and support services management; commercial and advertising art; communications technologies and support services related; computer/information technology services administration related; computer programming; computer systems networking and telecommunications; cosmetology; criminal justice/police science; culinary arts; design and applied arts related; diesel mechanics technology; dietetics; dramatic/theater arts; early childhood education; electrical and power transmission installation related; electrical, electronic and communications engineering technology; electrician; elementary education; engineering science; English; environmental studies; family and consumer sciences/home economics teacher education; family and consumer sciences/human sciences; fashion merchandising; fire science/firefighting; foreign languages and literatures; funeral service and mortuary science; health and physical education/fitness; health information/medical records technology; health teacher education; heating, air conditioning, ventilation and refrigeration maintenance technology; history; hotel/motel administration; industrial technology; information technology; journalism; legal assistant/paralegal; liberal arts and sciences and humanities related; liberal arts and sciences/liberal studies; lineworker; logistics, materials, and supply chain management; manufacturing engineering technology; mathematics teacher education; mechanical drafting and CAD/CADD; medical radiologic technology; mining technology; music; natural resources/conservation; occupational therapy; pharmacy technician; philosophy; photojournalism; physical education teaching and coaching; physical therapy technology; pipefitting and sprinkler fitting; plumbing technology; pre-law studies; public relations/image management; radio and television broadcasting technology; recording arts technology; registered nursing, nursing administration, nursing research and clinical nursing related; registered nursing/registered nurse; restaurant, culinary, and catering management; science teacher education; secondary education; securities services administration; sheet metal technology; social work; special education; surgical technology; surveying technology; technology/industrial arts teacher education; tool and die technology; welding technology.

Academics *Calendar:* semesters. *Degrees:* certificates, associate, and bachelor's. *Special study options:* academic remediation for entering students, accelerated degree program, adult/continuing education programs, advanced placement credit, distance learning, double majors, English as a second language, external degree program, freshman honors college, honors programs, independent study, internships, off-campus study, part-time degree program, services for LD students, student-designed majors, summer session for credit. *ROTC:* Army (c).

Library Shake Learning Resource Center. *Books:* 85,614 (physical), 104,859 (digital/electronic); *Serial titles:* 1,377 (physical); *Databases:* 99.

Student Life *Housing:* on-campus residence required for freshman year. *Options:* coed, men-only, women-only, special housing for students with disabilities. Campus housing is university owned. Freshman campus housing is guaranteed. *Activities and Organizations:* drama/theater group, student-run newspaper, radio and television station, choral group, national fraternities, national sororities. *Campus security:* 24-hour emergency response devices and patrols, student patrols, late-night transport/escort service, controlled dormitory access. *Student services:* health clinic, personal/psychological counseling.

Athletics Member NJCAA. *Intercollegiate sports:* basketball W, cross-country running W, track and field W, volleyball W.

Applying *Options:* electronic application, deferred entrance. *Application fee:* $20. *Required:* high school transcript. *Required for some:* interview. *Application deadlines:* rolling (freshmen), rolling (transfers). *Notification:* continuous until 8/1 (freshmen), continuous (transfers).

Director of Admissions Heidi M. Whitehead, Director of Admissions, Vincennes University, 1002 North First Street, Vincennes, IN 47591. *Phone:* 812-888-4313. *Toll-free phone:* 800-742-9198. *Fax:* 812-888-5707. *Website:* http://www.vinu.edu/.

IOWA

Clinton Community College

Clinton, Iowa

Freshman Application Contact Mr. Gary Mohr, Executive Director of Enrollment Management and Marketing, Clinton Community College, 1000 Lincoln Boulevard, Clinton, IA 52732-6299. *Phone:* 563-336-3322. *Toll-free phone:* 800-462-3255. *Fax:* 563-336-3350. *E-mail:* gmohr@eicc.edu. *Website:* http://www.eicc.edu/about-eicc/colleges-and-centers/clinton-community-college.aspx.

Des Moines Area Community College

Ankeny, Iowa

- **State and locally supported** 2-year, founded 1966, part of Iowa Area Community Colleges System
- **Small-town** 362-acre campus
- **Endowment** $7.0 million
- **Coed**

Undergraduates 6,476 full-time, 16,506 part-time. Students come from 52 states and territories; 12 other countries; 7% are from out of state; 6% Black or African American, non-Hispanic/Latino; 8% Hispanic/Latino; 4% Asian, non-Hispanic/Latino; 0.1% Native Hawaiian or other Pacific Islander, non-Hispanic/Latino; 0.3% American Indian or Alaska Native, non-Hispanic/Latino; 2% Two or more races, non-Hispanic/Latino; 10% Race/ethnicity unknown; 0.9% international; 9% transferred in. *Retention:* 59% of full-time freshmen returned.

Faculty *Student/faculty ratio:* 20:1.

Academics *Calendar:* semesters. *Degrees:* certificates, diplomas, and associate (profile also includes information from the Boone, Carroll, Des Moines, and Newton campuses). *Special study options:* academic remediation for entering students, adult/continuing education programs, advanced placement credit, cooperative education, distance learning, English as a second language, honors programs, off-campus study, part-time degree program, services for LD students, student-designed majors, summer session for credit.

Library DMACC District Library plus 4 others.

Student Life *Campus security:* 24-hour emergency response devices and patrols, late-night transport/escort service.

Athletics Member NJCAA.

Standardized Tests *Required for some:* SAT or ACT (for admission), ACT Compass.

Financial Aid Of all full-time matriculated undergraduates who enrolled in 2017, 377 Federal Work-Study jobs (averaging $1055).

Applying *Options:* electronic application, early admission, deferred entrance. *Required for some:* high school transcript, interview.

Freshman Application Contact Mr. Michael Lentsch, Director of Program Development, Des Moines Area Community College, 2006 South Ankeny Boulevard, Ankeny, IA 50021-8995. *Phone:* 515-965-7086. *Toll-free phone:* 800-362-2127. *E-mail:* mjleutsch@dmacc.edu. *Website:* http://www.dmacc.edu/.

Ellsworth Community College

Iowa Falls, Iowa

Director of Admissions Mrs. Nancy Walters, Registrar, Ellsworth Community College, 1100 College Avenue, Iowa Falls, IA 50126-1199. *Phone:* 641-648-4611. *Toll-free phone:* 800-ECC-9235. *Website:* http://ecc.iavalley.edu/.

Hawkeye Community College
Waterloo, Iowa

- **State and locally supported** 2-year, founded 1966
- **Rural** 320-acre campus
- **Endowment** $2.3 million
- **Coed,** 5,259 undergraduate students, 43% full-time, 56% women, 44% men

Undergraduates 2,256 full-time, 3,003 part-time. Students come from 9 states and territories; 17 other countries; 1% are from out of state; 7% Black or African American, non-Hispanic/Latino; 4% Hispanic/Latino; 2% Asian, non-Hispanic/Latino; 0.3% Native Hawaiian or other Pacific Islander, non-Hispanic/Latino; 0.2% American Indian or Alaska Native, non-Hispanic/Latino; 3% Two or more races, non-Hispanic/Latino; 0.5% international; 5% transferred in.

Freshmen *Admission:* 1,562 applied, 1,485 admitted, 948 enrolled. *Test scores:* ACT scores over 18: 50%; ACT scores over 24: 14%; ACT scores over 30: 3%.

Faculty *Total:* 296, 37% full-time, 8% with terminal degrees. *Student/faculty ratio:* 17:1.

Majors Accounting; agricultural/farm supplies retailing and wholesaling; agricultural power machinery operation; animal/livestock husbandry and production; autobody/collision and repair technology; automation engineer technology; automobile/automotive mechanics technology; carpentry; child-care provision; civil engineering technology; clinical/medical laboratory technology; commercial photography; computer/information technology services administration related; computer systems networking and telecommunications; criminal justice/police science; dental hygiene; desktop publishing and digital imaging design; diesel mechanics technology; digital communication and media/multimedia; electrical, electronic and communications engineering technology; emergency medical technology (EMT paramedic); golf course operation and grounds management; hospitality administration; human resources management; landscaping and groundskeeping; liberal arts and sciences/liberal studies; machine tool technology; medical administrative assistant and medical secretary; medical insurance coding; multi/interdisciplinary studies related; natural resources management and policy; occupational therapist assistant; physical therapy technology; registered nursing/registered nurse; respiratory care therapy; sales, distribution, and marketing operations; web page, digital/multimedia and information resources design; welding technology.

Academics *Calendar:* semesters. *Degree:* certificates, diplomas, and associate. *Special study options:* academic remediation for entering students, accelerated degree program, adult/continuing education programs, advanced placement credit, cooperative education, distance learning, English as a second language, external degree program, part-time degree program, services for LD students, study abroad, summer session for credit. *ROTC:* Army (c).

Library Hawkeye Community College Library. *Books:* 29,911 (physical), 201,941 (digital/electronic); *Serial titles:* 85 (physical), 39 (digital/electronic); *Databases:* 62. Weekly public service hours: 70; students can reserve study rooms.

Student Life *Housing:* college housing not available. *Activities and Organizations:* drama/theater group, choral group, Student Leadership, Phi Theta Kappa, Student Ambassadors, Student American Dental Hygienist Association, Photography. *Campus security:* 24-hour patrols. *Student services:* health clinic, personal/psychological counseling, women's center, veterans affairs office.

Athletics Member NJCAA. *Intercollegiate sports:* cross-country running W(s), golf M(s), soccer M(s)/W(s), track and field M(s)/W(s), volleyball W(s). *Intramural sports:* badminton M/W, basketball M/W, bowling M/W, football M/W, softball M/W, table tennis M/W.

Standardized Tests *Required:* ACT ACCUPLACER or the equivalent from ACT or accredited college course(s) (for admission). *Required for some:* ACT (for admission).

Applying *Options:* electronic application, deferred entrance. *Required:* high school transcript. *Application deadlines:* rolling (freshmen), rolling (transfers). *Notification:* continuous (freshmen), continuous (transfers).

Freshman Application Contact Ms. Holly Grimm-See, Associate Director, Admissions and Recruitment, Hawkeye Community College, PO Box 8015, Waterloo, IA 50704-8015. *Phone:* 319-296-4277. *Toll-free phone:* 800-670-4769. *Fax:* 319-296-2505. *E-mail:* holly.grimm-see@hawkeyecollege.edu. *Website:* http://www.hawkeyecollege.edu/.

Indian Hills Community College
Ottumwa, Iowa

Freshman Application Contact Mrs. Jane Sapp, Admissions Officer, Indian Hills Community College, 525 Grandview Avenue, Building #1, Ottumwa, IA 52501-1398. *Phone:* 641-683-5155. *Toll-free phone:* 800-726-2585. *Website:* http://www.ihcc.cc.ia.us/.

Iowa Central Community College
Fort Dodge, Iowa

- **State and locally supported** 2-year, founded 1966
- **Small-town** 110-acre campus
- **Coed**

Undergraduates 2,774 full-time, 2,715 part-time. Students come from 40 states and territories; 34 other countries; 8% are from out of state; 9% Black or African American, non-Hispanic/Latino; 9% Hispanic/Latino; 2% Asian, non-Hispanic/Latino; 0.2% Native Hawaiian or other Pacific Islander, non-Hispanic/Latino; 1% American Indian or Alaska Native, non-Hispanic/Latino; 1% Two or more races, non-Hispanic/Latino; 6% Race/ethnicity unknown; 2% international; 18% live on campus.

Faculty *Student/faculty ratio:* 18:1.

Academics *Calendar:* semesters. *Degree:* certificates, diplomas, and associate. *Special study options:* academic remediation for entering students, adult/continuing education programs, advanced placement credit, cooperative education, English as a second language, independent study, internships, part-time degree program, services for LD students, study abroad, summer session for credit.

Library Iowa Central Community College Library plus 1 other. Students can reserve study rooms.

Student Life *Campus security:* 24-hour emergency response devices and patrols, student patrols, late-night transport/escort service, controlled dormitory access.

Athletics Member NJCAA.

Applying *Options:* electronic application, early admission, deferred entrance. *Required for some:* high school transcript, letters of recommendation, interview. *Recommended:* high school transcript.

Freshman Application Contact Mrs. Sue Flattery, Enrollment Management Secretary, Iowa Central Community College, One Triton Circle, Fort Dodge, IA 50501. *Phone:* 515-574-1010 Ext. 2402. *Toll-free phone:* 800-362-2793. *Fax:* 515-576-7207. *E-mail:* flattery@iowacentral.com. *Website:* http://www.iowacentral.edu/.

Iowa Lakes Community College
Estherville, Iowa

Freshman Application Contact Iowa Lakes Community College, IA. *Phone:* 712-362-7923 Ext. 7923. *Toll-free phone:* 800-521-5054. *E-mail:* info@iowalakes.edu. *Website:* http://www.iowalakes.edu/.

Iowa Western Community College
Council Bluffs, Iowa

Freshman Application Contact Ms. Tori Christie, Director of Admissions, Iowa Western Community College, 2700 College Road, Box 4-C, Council Bluffs, IA 51502. *Phone:* 712-325-3288. *Toll-free phone:* 800-432-5852. *E-mail:* admissions@iwcc.edu. *Website:* http://www.iwcc.edu/.

Kirkwood Community College
Cedar Rapids, Iowa

Freshman Application Contact Kirkwood Community College, PO Box 2068, Cedar Rapids, IA 52406-2068. *Phone:* 319-398-5517. *Toll-free phone:* 800-332-2055. *Website:* http://www.kirkwood.edu/.

Marshalltown Community College
Marshalltown, Iowa

Freshman Application Contact Ms. Deana Inman, Director of Admissions, Marshalltown Community College, 3700 South Center Street, Marshalltown, IA 50158-4760. *Phone:* 641-752-7106. *Toll-free phone:* 866-622-4748. *Fax:* 641-752-8149. *Website:* http://mcc.iavalley.edu/.

Muscatine Community College
Muscatine, Iowa

Freshman Application Contact Gary Mohr, Executive Director of Enrollment Management and Marketing, Muscatine Community College, 152 Colorado Street, Muscatine, IA 52761-5396. *Phone:* 563-336-3322. *Toll-free phone:* 800-351-4669. *Fax:* 563-336-3350. *E-mail:* gmohr@eicc.edu. *Website:* http://www.eicc.edu/about-eicc/colleges-and-centers/muscatine-community-college.aspx.

Northeast Iowa Community College

Calmar, Iowa

- **State and locally supported** 2-year, founded 1966, part of Iowa Area Community Colleges System
- **Rural** 210-acre campus
- **Coed**

Undergraduates 1,221 full-time, 3,324 part-time. 12% are from out of state; 5% Black or African American, non-Hispanic/Latino; 3% Hispanic/Latino; 0.7% Asian, non-Hispanic/Latino; 0.4% Native Hawaiian or other Pacific Islander, non-Hispanic/Latino; 0.4% American Indian or Alaska Native, non-Hispanic/Latino; 0.8% Two or more races, non-Hispanic/Latino; 3% Race/ethnicity unknown; 0.8% international; 4% transferred in. *Retention:* 52% of full-time freshmen returned.
Faculty *Student/faculty ratio:* 13:1.
Academics *Calendar:* semesters. *Degree:* certificates, diplomas, and associate. *Special study options:* academic remediation for entering students, adult/continuing education programs, advanced placement credit, cooperative education, distance learning, double majors, external degree program, honors programs, internships, off-campus study, part-time degree program, services for LD students, summer session for credit.
Library Wilder Resource Center and Burton Payne Library plus 2 others.
Student Life *Campus security:* security personnel on weeknights.
Financial Aid Of all full-time matriculated undergraduates who enrolled in 2017, 991 applied for aid, 877 were judged to have need, 32 had their need fully met. In 2017, 89. *Average percent of need met:* 49. *Average financial aid package:* $8335. *Average need-based loan:* $3470. *Average need-based gift aid:* $5421. *Average non-need-based aid:* $1760.
Applying *Options:* electronic application. *Recommended:* high school transcript.
Freshman Application Contact Ms. Brynn McConnell, Admissions Representative, Northeast Iowa Community College, Calmar, IA 52132. *Phone:* 563-562-3263 Ext. 307. *Toll-free phone:* 800-728-CALMAR. *Fax:* 563-562-4369. *E-mail:* mcconnellb@nicc.edu. *Website:* http://www.nicc.edu/.

North Iowa Area Community College

Mason City, Iowa

- **State and locally supported** 2-year, founded 1918, part of Iowa Community College System
- **Rural** 500-acre campus
- **Coed**

Undergraduates 1,346 full-time, 1,601 part-time. 4% Black or African American, non-Hispanic/Latino; 5% Hispanic/Latino; 1% Asian, non-Hispanic/Latino; 0.2% American Indian or Alaska Native, non-Hispanic/Latino; 1% Two or more races, non-Hispanic/Latino; 0.1% Race/ethnicity unknown; 2% international; 12% live on campus.
Faculty *Student/faculty ratio:* 10:1.
Academics *Calendar:* semesters. *Degree:* certificates, diplomas, and associate. *Special study options:* academic remediation for entering students, advanced placement credit, cooperative education, distance learning, English as a second language, honors programs, internships, part-time degree program, services for LD students, student-designed majors, summer session for credit.
Student Life *Campus security:* student patrols, late-night transport/escort service, controlled dormitory access.
Athletics Member NJCAA.
Financial Aid Of all full-time matriculated undergraduates who enrolled in 2017, 125 Federal Work-Study jobs (averaging $2000). 4 state and other part-time jobs (averaging $2000).
Applying *Options:* electronic application. *Required:* high school transcript.
Freshman Application Contact Ms. Rachel McGuire, Director of Enrollment Services, North Iowa Area Community College, 500 College Drive, Mason City, IA 50401. *Phone:* 641-422-4104. *Toll-free phone:* 888-GO NIACC Ext. 4245. *Fax:* 641-422-4385. *E-mail:* request@niacc.edu. *Website:* http://www.niacc.edu/.

Northwest Iowa Community College

Sheldon, Iowa

Director of Admissions Ms. Lisa Story, Director of Enrollment Management, Northwest Iowa Community College, 603 West Park Street, Sheldon, IA 51201-1046. *Phone:* 712-324-5061 Ext. 115. *Toll-free phone:* 800-352-4907. *E-mail:* lstory@nwicc.edu. *Website:* http://www.nwicc.edu/.

Ross College

Bettendorf, Iowa

Freshman Application Contact Ross College, 2119 East Kimberly Road, Bettendorf, IA 52722. *Phone:* 563-344-1500. *Toll-free phone:* 866-815-5578. *Website:* http://www.rosseducation.edu/.

St. Luke's College

Sioux City, Iowa

- **Independent** primarily 2-year, founded 1967
- **Rural** 3-acre campus with easy access to Omaha
- **Endowment** $1.2 million
- **Coed,** 270 undergraduate students, 47% full-time, 91% women, 9% men

Undergraduates 127 full-time, 143 part-time. Students come from 15 states and territories; 1 other country; 41% are from out of state; 3% Black or African American, non-Hispanic/Latino; 8% Hispanic/Latino; 3% Asian, non-Hispanic/Latino; 0.4% Native Hawaiian or other Pacific Islander, non-Hispanic/Latino; 2% American Indian or Alaska Native, non-Hispanic/Latino; 3% Two or more races, non-Hispanic/Latino; 0.4% Race/ethnicity unknown; 13% transferred in. *Retention:* 100% of full-time freshmen returned.
Freshmen *Admission:* 15 applied, 15 admitted, 10 enrolled. *Average high school GPA:* 3.5.
Faculty *Total:* 36, 61% full-time, 14% with terminal degrees. *Student/faculty ratio:* 6:1.
Majors Health services/allied health/health sciences; radiologic technology/science; registered nursing/registered nurse; respiratory care therapy.
Academics *Calendar:* semesters. *Degrees:* certificates, associate, and bachelor's. *Special study options:* advanced placement credit, distance learning, internships, services for LD students, summer session for credit.
Library St. Luke's College Library. *Books:* 2,205 (physical); *Serial titles:* 63 (physical); *Databases:* 5. Weekly public service hours: 56.
Student Life *Housing:* college housing not available. *Campus security:* 24-hour emergency response devices and patrols, late-night transport/escort service. *Student services:* health clinic, personal/psychological counseling.
Standardized Tests *Required:* SAT or ACT (for admission).
Financial Aid Of all full-time matriculated undergraduates who enrolled in 2017, 81 applied for aid, 81 were judged to have need. 5 Federal Work-Study jobs (averaging $900). *Average percent of need met:* 80%. *Average financial aid package:* $11,650. *Average need-based loan:* $6938. *Average need-based gift aid:* $4981. *Average indebtedness upon graduation:* $19,465.
Applying *Options:* electronic application. *Required:* essay or personal statement, high school transcript, minimum 2.5 GPA, interview. *Notification:* continuous (freshmen), continuous (out-of-state freshmen), continuous (transfers), rolling (early decision plan 1), rolling (early decision plan 2), rolling (early action).
Freshman Application Contact Ms. Sherry McCarthy, Admissions Coordinator, St. Luke's College, 2720 Stone Park Boulevard, Sioux City, IA 51104. *Phone:* 712-279-3149. *Toll-free phone:* 800-352-4660 Ext. 3149. *Fax:* 712-233-8017. *E-mail:* sherry.mccarthy@stlukescollege.edu. *Website:* http://stlukescollege.edu/.

Scott Community College

Bettendorf, Iowa

Freshman Application Contact Mr. Gary Mohr, Executive Director of Enrollment Management and Marketing, Scott Community College, 500 Belmont Road, Bettendorf, IA 52722-6804. *Phone:* 563-336-3322. *Toll-free phone:* 800-895-0811. *Fax:* 563-336-3350. *E-mail:* gmohr@eicc.edu. *Website:* http://www.eicc.edu/about-eicc/colleges-and-centers/scott-community-college.aspx.

Southeastern Community College

West Burlington, Iowa

Freshman Application Contact Ms. Stacy White, Admissions, Southeastern Community College, 1500 West Agency Road, West Burlington, IA 52655-0180. *Phone:* 319-752-2731 Ext. 8137. *Toll-free phone:* 866-722-4692. *E-mail:* admoff@scciowa.edu. *Website:* http://www.scciowa.edu/.

Southwestern Community College

Creston, Iowa

- **State-supported** 2-year, founded 1966, part of Iowa Department of Education Division of Community Colleges
- **Rural** 406-acre campus
- **Coed,** 1,547 undergraduate students, 44% full-time, 59% women, 41% men

Undergraduates 683 full-time, 864 part-time. Students come from 21 states and territories; 8 other countries; 5% are from out of state; 6% transferred in; 6% live on campus. *Retention:* 57% of full-time freshmen returned.
Freshmen *Admission:* 290 enrolled.
Faculty *Total:* 123, 35% full-time, 2% with terminal degrees. *Student/faculty ratio:* 16:1.
Majors Accounting technology and bookkeeping; agribusiness; autobody/collision and repair technology; automobile/automotive mechanics technology; business administration and management; carpentry; computer systems networking and telecommunications; electrician; industrial mechanics and maintenance technology; liberal arts and sciences/liberal studies; library and information science; music; registered nursing/registered nurse; web page, digital/multimedia and information resources design; welding technology.
Academics *Calendar:* semesters. *Degree:* certificates, diplomas, and associate. *Special study options:* academic remediation for entering students, adult/continuing education programs, advanced placement credit, distance learning, double majors, independent study, part-time degree program, summer session for credit.
Library Learning Resource Center. *Books:* 15,796 (physical), 28,886 (digital/electronic); *Databases:* 60. Weekly public service hours: 58.
Student Life *Housing Options:* coed, men-only, women-only. Campus housing is university owned. *Activities and Organizations:* drama/theater group, choral group. *Campus security:* 24-hour emergency response devices, controlled dormitory access. *Student services:* personal/psychological counseling.
Athletics Member NCAA, NJCAA. All NCAA Division II. *Intercollegiate sports:* basketball W(s), cross-country running W, softball W, track and field W, volleyball W. *Intramural sports:* basketball M, football M, volleyball M.
Standardized Tests *Required for some:* SAT or ACT (for admission), ACT Compass/ACCUPLACER.
Financial Aid Of all full-time matriculated undergraduates who enrolled in 2017, 84 Federal Work-Study jobs (averaging $1075). 42 state and other part-time jobs (averaging $1080).
Applying *Options:* electronic application, early admission. *Required:* high school transcript. *Application deadline:* 9/5 (transfers). *Notification:* continuous (freshmen), continuous (transfers).
Freshman Application Contact Ms. Cait Maitlen, Director of Admissions, Southwestern Community College, 1501 West Townline Street, Creston, IA 50801. *Phone:* 641-782-7081 Ext. 453. *Toll-free phone:* 800-247-4023. *Fax:* 641-782-3312. *E-mail:* maitlen@swcciowa.edu. *Website:* http://www.swcciowa.edu/.

Western Iowa Tech Community College

Sioux City, Iowa

- **State-supported** 2-year, founded 1966, part of Iowa Department of Education Division of Community Colleges
- **Suburban** 143-acre campus
- **Endowment** $1.7 million
- **Coed**

Undergraduates 2,292 full-time, 3,860 part-time. Students come from 30 states and territories; 8 other countries; 10% are from out of state; 3% Black or African American, non-Hispanic/Latino; 15% Hispanic/Latino; 2% Asian, non-Hispanic/Latino; 0.2% Native Hawaiian or other Pacific Islander, non-Hispanic/Latino; 2% American Indian or Alaska Native, non-Hispanic/Latino; 2% Two or more races, non-Hispanic/Latino; 11% Race/ethnicity unknown; 0.7% international; 4% transferred in; 5% live on campus. *Retention:* 52% of full-time freshmen returned.
Faculty *Student/faculty ratio:* 16:1.
Academics *Calendar:* semesters. *Degree:* certificates, diplomas, and associate. *Special study options:* academic remediation for entering students, accelerated degree program, advanced placement credit, cooperative education, distance learning, double majors, English as a second language, honors programs, independent study, internships, off-campus study, part-time degree program, services for LD students, student-designed majors, study abroad, summer session for credit.
Library Western Iowa Tech Community College Library Services plus 1 other. *Books:* 17,232 (physical), 12,438 (digital/electronic). Weekly public service hours: 60.
Student Life *Campus security:* 24-hour emergency response devices and patrols, controlled dormitory access.
Standardized Tests *Recommended:* ACT (for admission), SAT or ACT (for admission).
Financial Aid Of all full-time matriculated undergraduates who enrolled in 2017, 148 Federal Work-Study jobs (averaging $1000). 2 state and other part-time jobs (averaging $2500).
Applying *Options:* electronic application, early admission, deferred entrance. *Recommended:* high school transcript.
Admissions Office Contact Western Iowa Tech Community College, 4647 Stone Avenue, PO Box 5199, Sioux City, IA 51102-5199. *Toll-free phone:* 800-352-4649 Ext. 6403. *Website:* http://www.witcc.edu/.

KANSAS

Allen Community College

Iola, Kansas

Freshman Application Contact Rebecca Bilderback, Director of Admissions, Allen Community College, 1801 North Cottonwood, Iola, KS 66749. *Phone:* 620-365-5116 Ext. 267. *Fax:* 620-365-7406. *E-mail:* bilderback@allencc.edu. *Website:* http://www.allencc.edu/.

Barton County Community College

Great Bend, Kansas

- **State and locally supported** 2-year, founded 1969, part of Kansas Board of Regents
- **Rural** 140-acre campus
- **Coed**

Undergraduates 875 full-time, 3,256 part-time. 13% Black or African American, non-Hispanic/Latino; 12% Hispanic/Latino; 2% Asian, non-Hispanic/Latino; 0.7% Native Hawaiian or other Pacific Islander, non-Hispanic/Latino; 1% American Indian or Alaska Native, non-Hispanic/Latino; 3% Two or more races, non-Hispanic/Latino; 5% Race/ethnicity unknown; 0.3% international; 8% live on campus.
Faculty *Student/faculty ratio:* 20:1.
Academics *Calendar:* semesters. *Degree:* certificates and associate. *Special study options:* academic remediation for entering students, accelerated degree program, adult/continuing education programs, advanced placement credit, cooperative education, distance learning, double majors, English as a second language, external degree program, honors programs, independent study, internships, part-time degree program, services for LD students, summer session for credit. *ROTC:* Army (b).
Library Barton County Community College Library.
Student Life *Campus security:* 24-hour emergency response devices and patrols.
Athletics Member NJCAA.
Applying *Options:* electronic application, early admission. *Recommended:* high school transcript.
Freshman Application Contact Ms. Tana Cooper, Director of Admissions and Promotions, Barton County Community College, 245 Northeast 30th Road, Great Bend, KS 67530. *Phone:* 620-792-9241. *Toll-free phone:* 800-722-6842. *Fax:* 620-786-1160. *E-mail:* admissions@bartonccc.edu. *Website:* http://www.bartonccc.edu/.

Butler Community College

El Dorado, Kansas

Freshman Application Contact Mr. Glenn Lygrisse, Interim Director of Enrollment Management, Butler Community College, 901 South Haverhill Road, El Dorado, KS 67042. *Phone:* 316-321-2222. *Fax:* 316-322-3109. *E-mail:* admissions@butlercc.edu. *Website:* http://www.butlercc.edu/.

Cloud County Community College

Concordia, Kansas

- **State and locally supported** 2-year, founded 1965, part of Kansas Community College System
- **Rural** 35-acre campus
- **Coed**

Undergraduates 814 full-time, 1,059 part-time. Students come from 26 states and territories; 33 other countries; 7% are from out of state; 6% Black or African American, non-Hispanic/Latino; 7% Hispanic/Latino; 1% Asian, non-Hispanic/Latino; 0.2% Native Hawaiian or other Pacific Islander, non-Hispanic/Latino; 0.8% American Indian or Alaska Native, non-Hispanic/Latino; 4% Two or more races, non-Hispanic/Latino; 5%

Race/ethnicity unknown; 5% international; 7% transferred in. *Retention:* 64% of full-time freshmen returned.
Faculty *Student/faculty ratio:* 11:1.
Academics *Calendar:* semesters. *Degree:* certificates, diplomas, and associate. *Special study options:* academic remediation for entering students, adult/continuing education programs, advanced placement credit, cooperative education, distance learning, English as a second language, freshman honors college, honors programs, internships, part-time degree program, services for LD students, summer session for credit.
Library Cloud County Community College Library. *Books:* 16,807 (physical), 9,784 (digital/electronic); *Databases:* 45. Weekly public service hours: 40.
Student Life *Campus security:* 24-hour emergency response devices.
Athletics Member NJCAA.
Financial Aid Of all full-time matriculated undergraduates who enrolled in 2017, 122 Federal Work-Study jobs (averaging $800).
Applying *Options:* early admission, deferred entrance. *Required:* high school transcript.
Freshman Application Contact Shane Olson, Director of Admissions, Cloud County Community College, 2221 Campus Drive, PO Box 1002, Concordia, KS 66901-1002. *Phone:* 785-243-1435 Ext. 213. *Toll-free phone:* 800-729-5101. *E-mail:* solson@cloud.edu. *Website:* http://www.cloud.edu/.

Coffeyville Community College
Coffeyville, Kansas

Freshman Application Contact Stacia Meek, Admissions Counselor/Marketing Event Coordinator, Coffeyville Community College, 400 West 11th Street, Coffeyville, KS 67337-5063. *Phone:* 620-252-7100. *Toll-free phone:* 877-51-RAVEN. *E-mail:* staciam@coffeyville.edu. *Website:* http://www.coffeyville.edu/.

Colby Community College
Colby, Kansas

Freshman Application Contact Ms. Nikol Nolan, Admissions Director, Colby Community College, Colby, KS 67701-4099. *Phone:* 785-462-3984 Ext. 5496. *Toll-free phone:* 888-634-9350. *Fax:* 785-460-4691. *E-mail:* admissions@colbycc.edu. *Website:* http://www.colbycc.edu/.

Cowley County Community College and Area Vocational–Technical School
Arkansas City, Kansas

Freshman Application Contact Ms. Lory West, Director of Admissions, Cowley County Community College and Area Vocational–Technical School, PO Box 1147, Arkansas City, KS 67005. *Phone:* 620-441-5594. *Toll-free phone:* 800-593-CCCC. *Fax:* 620-441-5350. *E-mail:* admissions@cowley.edu. *Website:* http://www.cowley.edu/.

Dodge City Community College
Dodge City, Kansas

Freshman Application Contact Dodge City Community College, 2501 North 14th Avenue, Dodge City, KS 67801-2399. *Phone:* 620-225-1321. *Website:* http://www.dc3.edu/.

Donnelly College
Kansas City, Kansas

- **Independent Roman Catholic** primarily 2-year, founded 1949
- **Urban** 4-acre campus
- **Coed**

Undergraduates 179 full-time, 115 part-time. Students come from 2 states and territories; 24 other countries; 31% are from out of state; 33% Black or African American, non-Hispanic/Latino; 39% Hispanic/Latino; 6% Asian, non-Hispanic/Latino; 0.7% Native Hawaiian or other Pacific Islander, non-Hispanic/Latino; 2% American Indian or Alaska Native, non-Hispanic/Latino; 4% Two or more races, non-Hispanic/Latino; 1% international; 16% transferred in. *Retention:* 55% of full-time freshmen returned.
Faculty *Student/faculty ratio:* 11:1.
Academics *Calendar:* semesters. *Degrees:* certificates, associate, and bachelor's. *Special study options:* academic remediation for entering students, advanced placement credit, distance learning, English as a second language, external degree program, honors programs, independent study, part-time degree program, services for LD students, summer session for credit.
Library Trant Memorial Library plus 1 other.
Student Life *Campus security:* 24-hour emergency response devices.
Applying *Options:* electronic application, early admission, deferred entrance. *Recommended:* high school transcript.
Freshman Application Contact Ms. Kimkisha Stevenson, Director of Admissions, Donnelly College, 608 North 18th Street, Kansas City, KS 66102. *Phone:* 913-621-8762. *Fax:* 913-621-8719. *E-mail:* admissions@donnelly.edu. *Website:* http://www.donnelly.edu/.

Flint Hills Technical College
Emporia, Kansas

Freshman Application Contact Admissions Office, Flint Hills Technical College, 3301 West 18th Avenue, Emporia, KS 66801. *Phone:* 620-341-1325. *Toll-free phone:* 800-711-6947. *Website:* http://www.fhtc.edu/.

Fort Scott Community College
Fort Scott, Kansas

Director of Admissions Mrs. Mert Barrows, Director of Admissions, Fort Scott Community College, 2108 South Horton, Fort Scott, KS 66701. *Phone:* 620-223-2700 Ext. 353. *Toll-free phone:* 800-874-3722. *Website:* http://www.fortscott.edu/.

Garden City Community College
Garden City, Kansas

Freshman Application Contact Office of Admissions, Garden City Community College, 801 Campus Drive, Garden City, KS 67846. *Phone:* 620-276-9531. *Toll-free phone:* 800-658-1696. *Fax:* 620-276-9650. *E-mail:* admissions@gcccks.edu. *Website:* http://www.gcccks.edu/.

Hesston College
Hesston, Kansas

- **Independent Mennonite** primarily 2-year, founded 1909
- **Small-town** 50-acre campus with easy access to Wichita
- **Endowment** $12.9 million
- **Coed**

Undergraduates 403 full-time, 39 part-time. Students come from 29 states and territories; 15 other countries; 43% are from out of state; 5% Black or African American, non-Hispanic/Latino; 12% Hispanic/Latino; 2% Asian, non-Hispanic/Latino; 0.2% American Indian or Alaska Native, non-Hispanic/Latino; 3% Two or more races, non-Hispanic/Latino; 0.7% Race/ethnicity unknown; 13% international; 8% transferred in; 69% live on campus. *Retention:* 77% of full-time freshmen returned.
Faculty *Student/faculty ratio:* 8:1.
Academics *Calendar:* semesters. *Degrees:* associate and bachelor's. *Special study options:* academic remediation for entering students, adult/continuing education programs, advanced placement credit, cooperative education, double majors, English as a second language, independent study, internships, part-time degree program, services for LD students, summer session for credit.
Library Mary Miller Library. Students can reserve study rooms.
Student Life *Campus security:* 24-hour emergency response devices, controlled dormitory access.
Athletics Member NJCAA.
Standardized Tests *Required:* SAT or ACT (for admission).
Financial Aid Of all full-time matriculated undergraduates who enrolled in 2017, 120 Federal Work-Study jobs (averaging $800).
Applying *Options:* electronic application, early admission, deferred entrance. *Required:* high school transcript. *Required for some:* 2 letters of recommendation, interview.
Freshman Application Contact Rachel Swartzendruber-Miller, Vice President of Admissions, Hesston College, Hesston, KS 67062. *Phone:* 620-327-8206. *Toll-free phone:* 800-995-2757. *Fax:* 620-327-8300. *E-mail:* admissions@hesston.edu. *Website:* http://www.hesston.edu/.

Highland Community College
Highland, Kansas

Director of Admissions Ms. Cheryl Rasmussen, Vice President of Student Services, Highland Community College, 606 West Main Street, Highland, KS 66035. *Phone:* 785-442-6020. *Fax:* 785-442-6106. *Website:* http://www.highlandcc.edu/.

Hutchinson Community College

Hutchinson, Kansas

- **State and locally supported** 2-year, founded 1928, part of Kansas Board of Regents
- **Small-town** 47-acre campus with easy access to Wichita
- **Coed,** 5,574 undergraduate students, 37% full-time, 55% women, 45% men

Undergraduates 2,055 full-time, 3,519 part-time. Students come from 43 states and territories; 10 other countries; 8% are from out of state; 6% Black or African American, non-Hispanic/Latino; 12% Hispanic/Latino; 0.7% Asian, non-Hispanic/Latino; 0.1% Native Hawaiian or other Pacific Islander, non-Hispanic/Latino; 1% American Indian or Alaska Native, non-Hispanic/Latino; 3% Two or more races, non-Hispanic/Latino; 7% Race/ethnicity unknown; 0.6% international; 8% transferred in; 10% live on campus.

Freshmen *Admission:* 2,452 applied, 2,452 admitted, 943 enrolled. *Average high school GPA:* 3.1.

Faculty *Total:* 318, 34% full-time, 9% with terminal degrees. *Student/faculty ratio:* 18:1.

Majors Accounting technology and bookkeeping; administrative assistant and secretarial science; agricultural mechanics and equipment technology; agriculture; architectural drafting and CAD/CADD; autobody/collision and repair technology; automation engineer technology; automobile/automotive mechanics technology; biology/biological sciences; business and personal/financial services marketing; business/commerce; carpentry; child-care and support services management; clinical/medical laboratory technology; communications technology; computer and information sciences; computer support specialist; computer systems analysis; computer systems networking and telecommunications; cosmetology; criminal justice/police science; design and visual communications; education; electrical/electronics equipment installation and repair; electrician; emergency medical technology (EMT paramedic); engineering; English; family and consumer sciences/human sciences; farm and ranch management; fire science/firefighting; foreign languages and literatures; graphic communications; health information/medical records technology; legal assistant/paralegal; liberal arts and sciences/liberal studies; machine tool technology; manufacturing engineering technology; mathematics; mechanical drafting and CAD/CADD; natural resources management and policy; pharmacy technician; physical sciences; physical therapy technology; psychology; radio and television broadcasting technology; radiologic technology/science; registered nursing/registered nurse; respiratory care therapy; retailing; small business administration; social sciences; speech communication and rhetoric; sport and fitness administration/management; surgical technology; visual and performing arts; web page, digital/multimedia and information resources design; welding technology.

Academics *Calendar:* semesters. *Degree:* certificates and associate. *Special study options:* academic remediation for entering students, advanced placement credit, cooperative education, distance learning, double majors, English as a second language, honors programs, independent study, internships, part-time degree program, services for LD students, summer session for credit.

Library John F. Kennedy Library plus 1 other. *Books:* 33,604 (physical), 14,281 (digital/electronic); *Serial titles:* 101 (physical); *Databases:* 98. Weekly public service hours: 65.

Student Life *Housing Options:* men-only, women-only. Campus housing is university owned. *Activities and Organizations:* drama/theater group, student-run newspaper, choral group, CKI (Circle K), Honors Club, DragonLAN (Computer/technology club), HutchCC Bigs (Big Brothres/Big Sisters), Collegiate 4-H. *Campus security:* 24-hour emergency response devices and patrols, late-night transport/escort service, controlled dormitory access. *Student services:* health clinic, personal/psychological counseling, veterans affairs office.

Athletics Member NJCAA. *Intercollegiate sports:* baseball M(s), basketball M(s)/W(s), cheerleading M(s)/W(s), cross-country running M(s)/W(s), football M(s), golf M(s), soccer W(s), softball W(s), track and field M(s)/W(s), volleyball W(s). *Intramural sports:* basketball M, football M, soccer M, table tennis M/W, volleyball M.

Applying *Options:* electronic application, early admission, deferred entrance. *Required:* high school transcript. *Required for some:* interview. *Application deadlines:* rolling (freshmen), rolling (transfers). *Notification:* continuous (freshmen), continuous (transfers).

Freshman Application Contact Mr. Corbin Strobel, Director of Admissions, Hutchinson Community College, 1300 North Plum, Hutchinson, KS 67501. *Phone:* 620-665-3536. *Toll-free phone:* 888-GO-HUTCH. *Fax:* 620-665-3301. *E-mail:* strobelc@hutchcc.edu. *Website:* http://www.hutchcc.edu/.

Independence Community College

Independence, Kansas

- **State-supported** 2-year, founded 1925, part of Kansas Board of Regents
- **Rural** 68-acre campus
- **Coed**

Undergraduates 510 full-time, 387 part-time. Students come from 31 states and territories; 6 other countries; 44% are from out of state; 16% Black or African American, non-Hispanic/Latino; 5% Hispanic/Latino; 0.6% Asian, non-Hispanic/Latino; 0.6% Native Hawaiian or other Pacific Islander, non-Hispanic/Latino; 2% American Indian or Alaska Native, non-Hispanic/Latino; 6% Two or more races, non-Hispanic/Latino; 6% Race/ethnicity unknown; 2% international; 3% transferred in. *Retention:* 39% of full-time freshmen returned.

Faculty *Student/faculty ratio:* 12:1.

Academics *Calendar:* semesters. *Degree:* certificates and associate. *Special study options:* academic remediation for entering students, advanced placement credit, cooperative education, distance learning, English as a second language, external degree program, independent study, part-time degree program, services for LD students, summer session for credit.

Library Independence Community College Library plus 1 other.

Student Life *Campus security:* controlled dormitory access, night patrol.

Athletics Member NJCAA.

Applying *Required:* high school transcript. *Required for some:* essay or personal statement, minimum 2.5 GPA, 2 letters of recommendation, interview.

Freshman Application Contact Ms. Brittany Thornton, Admissions Coordinator, Independence Community College, PO Box 708, 1057 W. College Avenue, Independence, KS 673001. *Phone:* 620-332-5495. *Toll-free phone:* 800-842-6063. *Fax:* 620-331-0946. *E-mail:* bthornton@indycc.edu. *Website:* http://www.indycc.edu/.

Johnson County Community College

Overland Park, Kansas

Freshman Application Contact Johnson County Community College, 12345 College Boulevard, Overland Park, KS 66210-1299. *Phone:* 913-469-8500 Ext. 3865. *Website:* http://www.jccc.edu/.

Kansas City Kansas Community College

Kansas City, Kansas

Freshman Application Contact Dr. Denise McDowell, Dean of Enrollment Management/Registrar, Kansas City Kansas Community College, Admissions Office, 7250 State Avenue, Kansas City, KS 66112. *Phone:* 913-288-7694. *Fax:* 913-288-7648. *E-mail:* dmcdowell@kckcc.edu. *Website:* http://www.kckcc.edu/.

Labette Community College

Parsons, Kansas

Freshman Application Contact Ms. Tammy Fuentez, Director of Admission, Labette Community College, 200 South 14th Street, Parsons, KS 67357-4299. *Phone:* 620-421-6700. *Toll-free phone:* 888-522-3883. *Fax:* 620-421-0180. *Website:* http://www.labette.edu/.

Manhattan Area Technical College

Manhattan, Kansas

Freshman Application Contact Mr. Neil Ross, Director of Admissions, Manhattan Area Technical College, 3136 Dickens Avenue, Manhattan, KS 66503. *Phone:* 785-320-4554. *Toll-free phone:* 800-352-7575. *Fax:* 785-587-2804. *E-mail:* neilross@manhattantech.edu. *Website:* http://www.manhattantech.edu/.

Neosho County Community College

Chanute, Kansas

Freshman Application Contact Ms. Lisa Last, Dean of Student Development, Neosho County Community College, 800 West 14th Street, Chanute, KS 66720. *Phone:* 620-431-2820 Ext. 213. *Toll-free phone:* 800-729-6222. *Fax:* 620-431-0082. *E-mail:* llast@neosho.edu. *Website:* http://www.neosho.edu/.

North Central Kansas Technical College
Beloit, Kansas

Freshman Application Contact Ms. Judy Heidrick, Director of Admissions, North Central Kansas Technical College, PO Box 507, 3033 US Highway 24, Beloit, KS 67420. *Toll-free phone:* 800-658-4655. *E-mail:* jheidrick@ ncktc.tec.ks.us. *Website:* http://www.ncktc.edu/.

Northwest Kansas Technical College
Goodland, Kansas

Admissions Office Contact Northwest Kansas Technical College, PO Box 668, 1209 Harrison Street, Goodland, KS 67735. *Toll-free phone:* 800-316-4127. *Website:* http://www.nwktc.edu/.

Pratt Community College
Pratt, Kansas

Freshman Application Contact Ms. Theresa Ziehr, Office Assistant, Student Services, Pratt Community College, 348 Northeast State Road 61, Pratt, KS 67124. *Phone:* 620-450-2217. *Toll-free phone:* 800-794-3091. *Fax:* 620-672-5288. *E-mail:* theresaz@prattcc.edu. *Website:* http://www.prattcc.edu/.

Salina Area Technical College
Salina, Kansas

Freshman Application Contact Mrs. Rebekah Ohlde, Director of Academic Advising, Salina Area Technical College, 2562 Centennial Road, Salina, KS 67401. *Phone:* 785-309-3119. *Fax:* 785-309-3101. *E-mail:* rebekah.ohlde@ salinatech.edu. *Website:* http://www.salinatech.edu/.

Seward County Community College and Area Technical School
Liberal, Kansas

Director of Admissions Dr. Gerald Harris, Dean of Student Services, Seward County Community College and Area Technical School, PO Box 1137, Liberal, KS 67905-1137. *Phone:* 620-624-1951 Ext. 617. *Toll-free phone:* 800-373-9951. *Website:* http://www.sccc.edu/.

Wichita Area Technical College
Wichita, Kansas

Freshman Application Contact Mr. Andy McFayden, Director, Admissions, Wichita Area Technical College, 4004 N. Webb Road, Suite 100, Wichita, KS 67226 . *Phone:* 316-677-9400. *Fax:* 316-677-9555. *E-mail:* info@watc.edu. *Website:* http://www.watc.edu/.

Wichita Technical Institute
Wichita, Kansas

Admissions Office Contact Wichita Technical Institute, 2051 S. Meridian Avenue, Wichita, KS 67213. *Website:* http://www.wti.edu/.

KENTUCKY

American National University
Danville, Kentucky

Director of Admissions James McGuire, Campus Director, American National University, 115 East Lexington Avenue, Danville, KY 40422. *Phone:* 859-236-6991. *Toll-free phone:* 888-9-JOBREADY. *Website:* http://www.an.edu/.

American National University
Florence, Kentucky

Director of Admissions Mr. Terry Kovacs, Campus Director, American National University, 8095 Connector Drive, Florence, KY 41042. *Phone:* 859-525-6510. *Toll-free phone:* 888-9-JOBREADY. *Website:* http://www.an.edu/.

American National University
Lexington, Kentucky

Director of Admissions Kim Thomasson, Campus Director, American National University, 2376 Sir Barton Way, Lexington, KY 40509. *Phone:* 859-253-0621. *Toll-free phone:* 888-9-JOBREADY. *Website:* http://www.an.edu/.

American National University
Louisville, Kentucky

Director of Admissions Vincent C. Tinebra, Campus Director, American National University, 4205 Dixie Highway, Louisville, KY 40216. *Phone:* 502-447-7634. *Toll-free phone:* 888-9-JOBREADY. *Website:* http://www.an.edu/.

American National University
Pikeville, Kentucky

Director of Admissions Tammy Riley, Campus Director, American National University, 50 National College Boulevard, Pikeville, KY 41501. *Phone:* 606-478-7200. *Toll-free phone:* 888-9-JOBREADY. *Website:* http://www.an.edu/.

American National University
Richmond, Kentucky

Director of Admissions Ms. Keeley Gadd, Campus Director, American National University, 125 South Killarney Lane, Richmond, KY 40475. *Phone:* 859-623-8956. *Toll-free phone:* 888-9-JOBREADY. *Website:* http://www.an.edu/.

Ashland Community and Technical College
Ashland, Kentucky

Freshman Application Contact Ashland Community and Technical College, 1400 College Drive, Ashland, KY 41101-3683. *Phone:* 606-326-2008. *Toll-free phone:* 800-928-4256. *Website:* http://www.ashland.kctcs.edu/.

ATA College
Louisville, Kentucky

Freshman Application Contact Admissions Office, ATA College, 10180 Linn Station Road, Suite A200, Louisville, KY 40223. *Phone:* 502-371-8330. *Fax:* 502-371-8598. *Website:* http://www.ata.edu/.

Beckfield College
Florence, Kentucky

Freshman Application Contact Mrs. Leah Boerger, Director of Admissions, Beckfield College, 16 Spiral Drive, Florence, KY 41042. *Phone:* 859-371-9393. *E-mail:* lboerger@beckfield.edu. *Website:* http://www.beckfield.edu/.

Big Sandy Community and Technical College
Prestonsburg, Kentucky

Director of Admissions Jimmy Wright, Director of Admissions, Big Sandy Community and Technical College, One Bert T. Combs Drive, Prestonsburg, KY 41653-1815. *Phone:* 606-886-3863. *Toll-free phone:* 888-641-4132. *E-mail:* jimmy.wright@kctcs.edu. *Website:* http://www.bigsandy.kctcs.edu/.

Bluegrass Community and Technical College
Lexington, Kentucky

Freshman Application Contact Mrs. Shelbie Hugle, Director of Admission Services, Bluegrass Community and Technical College, 470 Cooper Drive, Lexington, KY 40506. *Phone:* 859-246-6216. *Toll-free phone:* 800-744-4872 (in-state); 866-744-4872 (out-of-state). *E-mail:* shelbie.hugle@kctcs.edu. *Website:* http://www.bluegrass.kctcs.edu/.

Daymar College
Bowling Green, Kentucky

Freshman Application Contact Mrs. Traci Henderson, Admissions Director, Daymar College, 2421 Fitzgerald Industrial Drive, Bowling Green, KY 42101. *Phone:* 270-843-6750. *Toll-free phone:* 877-258-7796. *E-mail:* thenderson@daymarcollege.edu. *Website:* http://www.daymarcollege.edu/.

Elizabethtown Community and Technical College
Elizabethtown, Kentucky

Freshman Application Contact Elizabethtown Community and Technical College, 620 College Street Road, Elizabethtown, KY 42701. *Phone:* 270-706-8800. *Toll-free phone:* 877-246-2322. *Website:* http://www.elizabethtown.kctcs.edu/.

Galen College of Nursing
Hazard, Kentucky

Admissions Office Contact Galen College of Nursing, 100 Airport Gardens Drive, Hazard, KY 41701. *Website:* http://www.galencollege.edu/.

Galen College of Nursing
Louisville, Kentucky

Admissions Office Contact Galen College of Nursing, 1031 Zorn Avenue, Suite 400, Louisville, KY 40207. *Toll-free phone:* 877-223-7040. *Website:* http://www.galencollege.edu/.

Gateway Community and Technical College
Florence, Kentucky

- **State-supported** 2-year, founded 1961, part of Kentucky Community and Technical College System
- **Suburban** campus with easy access to Cincinnati
- **Coed**

Undergraduates 5% are from out of state; 7% Black or African American, non-Hispanic/Latino; 4% Hispanic/Latino; 0.7% Asian, non-Hispanic/Latino; 0.2% American Indian or Alaska Native, non-Hispanic/Latino; 2% Two or more races, non-Hispanic/Latino; 2% Race/ethnicity unknown.
Faculty *Student/faculty ratio:* 18:1.
Academics *Calendar:* semesters. *Degree:* certificates, diplomas, and associate. *Special study options:* academic remediation for entering students, cooperative education, distance learning, internships, part-time degree program, services for LD students, summer session for credit.
Library Main Library plus 3 others.
Student Life *Campus security:* 24-hour emergency response devices, campus security during hours of operation.
Standardized Tests *Required:* ACT or SAT; KYOTE (Math); TABE-Advanced (Reading and Writing) (for admission).
Applying *Options:* electronic application, early admission, deferred entrance. *Required:* high school transcript.
Freshman Application Contact Gateway Community and Technical College, 500 Technology Way, Florence, KY 41042. *Phone:* 859-442-4176. *E-mail:* andre.washington@kctcs.edu. *Website:* http://www.gateway.kctcs.edu/.

Hazard Community and Technical College
Hazard, Kentucky

Freshman Application Contact Director of Admissions, Hazard Community and Technical College, 1 Community College Drive, Hazard, KY 41701-2403. *Phone:* 606-487-3102. *Toll-free phone:* 800-246-7521. *Website:* http://www.hazard.kctcs.edu/.

Henderson Community College
Henderson, Kentucky

- **State-supported** 2-year, founded 1963, part of Kentucky Community and Technical College System
- **Small-town** 120-acre campus
- **Coed,** 1,586 undergraduate students, 32% full-time, 68% women, 32% men

Undergraduates 506 full-time, 1,080 part-time. Students come from 9 states and territories; 9% are from out of state; 10% Black or African American, non-Hispanic/Latino; 4% Hispanic/Latino; 0.4% Asian, non-Hispanic/Latino; 0.1% Native Hawaiian or other Pacific Islander, non-Hispanic/Latino; 0.1% American Indian or Alaska Native, non-Hispanic/Latino; 5% Two or more races, non-Hispanic/Latino; 0.5% Race/ethnicity unknown; 3% transferred in. *Retention:* 52% of full-time freshmen returned.
Freshmen *Admission:* 259 enrolled. *Average high school GPA:* 3.0.
Majors Agricultural production; business administration and management; child-care provision; clinical/medical laboratory technology; computer and information sciences; electromechanical technology; liberal arts and sciences/liberal studies; medical/clinical assistant; registered nursing/registered nurse.
Academics *Calendar:* semesters. *Degree:* certificates, diplomas, and associate. *Special study options:* academic remediation for entering students, accelerated degree program, adult/continuing education programs, advanced placement credit, cooperative education, distance learning, double majors, English as a second language, external degree program, independent study, internships, off-campus study, part-time degree program, summer session for credit.
Library Hartfield Learning Resource Center plus 1 other.
Student Life *Housing:* college housing not available. *Activities and Organizations:* drama/theater group, student-run radio station. *Campus security:* 24-hour emergency response devices. *Student services:* personal/psychological counseling.
Applying *Required:* high school transcript. *Required for some:* essay or personal statement, interview. *Application deadline:* 9/1 (transfers).
Freshman Application Contact Mr. Chad Phillips, Registrar/Director of Admissions, Henderson Community College, 2660 Green Street, Henderson, KY 42420. *Phone:* 270-827-1867. *Toll-free phone:* 800-696-9958. *E-mail:* chad.phillips@kctcs.edu.
Website: http://www.henderson.kctcs.edu/.

Hopkinsville Community College
Hopkinsville, Kentucky

- **State-supported** 2-year, founded 1965, part of Kentucky Community and Technical College System
- **Small-town** 69-acre campus with easy access to Nashville
- **Coed**

Undergraduates 1,245 full-time, 1,875 part-time. 22% Black or African American, non-Hispanic/Latino; 9% Hispanic/Latino; 1% Asian, non-Hispanic/Latino; 0.8% Native Hawaiian or other Pacific Islander, non-Hispanic/Latino; 0.5% American Indian or Alaska Native, non-Hispanic/Latino; 4% Two or more races, non-Hispanic/Latino; 2% Race/ethnicity unknown; 0.2% international; 7% transferred in. *Retention:* 43% of full-time freshmen returned.
Faculty *Student/faculty ratio:* 12:1.
Academics *Calendar:* semesters. *Degree:* certificates, diplomas, and associate. *Special study options:* academic remediation for entering students, advanced placement credit, cooperative education, distance learning, honors programs, independent study, part-time degree program, services for LD students, summer session for credit.
Library Learning Resource Center.
Student Life *Campus security:* 24-hour emergency response devices, late-night transport/escort service, security provided by trained security personnel during hours of normal operation.
Financial Aid Of all full-time matriculated undergraduates who enrolled in 2017, 30 Federal Work-Study jobs (averaging $1500). *Financial aid deadline:* 6/30.
Applying *Options:* electronic application, deferred entrance. *Recommended:* high school transcript.
Freshman Application Contact Hopkinsville Community College, KY. *Phone:* 270-707-3811. *Toll-free phone:* 866-534-2224. *Website:* http://hopkinsville.kctcs.edu/.

Interactive College of Technology

Newport, Kentucky

Freshman Application Contact Diana Mamas, Interactive College of Technology, 76 Carothers Road, Newport, KY 41071. *Phone:* 859-282-8989. *Fax:* 859-282-8475. *E-mail:* dmamas@ict.edu. *Website:* http://ict.edu/.

Jefferson Community and Technical College

Louisville, Kentucky

Freshman Application Contact Ms. Melanie Vaughan-Cooke, Admissions Coordinator, Jefferson Community and Technical College, Louisville, KY 40202. *Phone:* 502-213-4000. *Fax:* 502-213-2540. *Website:* http://www.jefferson.kctcs.edu/.

Madisonville Community College

Madisonville, Kentucky

Director of Admissions Mr. Jay Parent, Registrar, Madisonville Community College, 2000 College Drive, Madisonville, KY 42431-9185. *Phone:* 270-821-2250. *Website:* http://www.madisonville.kctcs.edu/.

Maysville Community and Technical College

Maysville, Kentucky

- **State-supported** 2-year, founded 1967, part of Kentucky Community and Technical College System
- **Rural** 12-acre campus
- **Coed**

Undergraduates 1,402 full-time, 2,093 part-time. 2% Black or African American, non-Hispanic/Latino; 2% Hispanic/Latino; 0.2% Asian, non-Hispanic/Latino; 0.1% Native Hawaiian or other Pacific Islander, non-Hispanic/Latino; 0.1% American Indian or Alaska Native, non-Hispanic/Latino; 2% Two or more races, non-Hispanic/Latino; 0.9% Race/ethnicity unknown.
Academics *Calendar:* semesters. *Degree:* certificates, diplomas, and associate. *Special study options:* academic remediation for entering students, adult/continuing education programs, advanced placement credit, cooperative education, distance learning, English as a second language, external degree program, honors programs, independent study, internships, off-campus study, part-time degree program, services for LD students, summer session for credit.
Library Finch Library.
Student Life *Campus security:* 24-hour emergency response devices, student patrols, evening parking lot security.
Financial Aid Of all full-time matriculated undergraduates who enrolled in 2017, 30 Federal Work-Study jobs (averaging $1960).
Applying *Options:* electronic application, early admission. *Required:* high school transcript.
Freshman Application Contact Maysville Community and Technical College, 1755 US 68, Maysville, KY 41056. *Phone:* 606-759-7141 Ext. 66271. *Website:* http://www.maysville.kctcs.edu/.

Maysville Community and Technical College

Morehead, Kentucky

Director of Admissions Patee Massie, Registrar, Maysville Community and Technical College, 609 Viking Drive, Morehead, KY 40351. *Phone:* 606-759-7141 Ext. 66184. *Website:* http://www.maysville.kctcs.edu/.

Owensboro Community and Technical College

Owensboro, Kentucky

- **State-supported** 2-year, founded 1986, part of Kentucky Community and Technical College System
- **Suburban** 102-acre campus
- **Coed,** 3,947 undergraduate students, 38% full-time, 53% women, 47% men

Undergraduates 1,519 full-time, 2,428 part-time. Students come from 31 states and territories; 1 other country; 6% are from out of state; 4% Black or African American, non-Hispanic/Latino; 3% Hispanic/Latino; 1% Asian, non-Hispanic/Latino; 0.1% Native Hawaiian or other Pacific Islander, non-Hispanic/Latino; 0.2% American Indian or Alaska Native, non-Hispanic/Latino; 3% Two or more races, non-Hispanic/Latino; 0.5% Race/ethnicity unknown; 4% transferred in. *Retention:* 61% of full-time freshmen returned.
Freshmen *Admission:* 557 enrolled.
Faculty *Total:* 142, 54% full-time. *Student/faculty ratio:* 24:1.
Majors Agricultural production; automobile/automotive mechanics technology; building/property maintenance; business administration and management; child-care provision; computer and information sciences; criminal justice/law enforcement administration; diesel mechanics technology; dramatic/theater arts; electrical and electronic engineering technologies related; electrician; emergency medical technology (EMT paramedic); executive assistant/executive secretary; fine/studio arts; fire science/firefighting; heating, air conditioning, ventilation and refrigeration maintenance technology; industrial mechanics and maintenance technology; liberal arts and sciences/liberal studies; machine shop technology; medical administrative assistant and medical secretary; medical/clinical assistant; radiologic technology/science; registered nursing/registered nurse; surgical technology; veterinary/animal health technology; welding technology.
Academics *Calendar:* semesters. *Degree:* certificates, diplomas, and associate. *Special study options:* academic remediation for entering students, adult/continuing education programs, advanced placement credit, cooperative education, distance learning, English as a second language, external degree program, honors programs, independent study, off-campus study, part-time degree program, services for LD students, student-designed majors, study abroad, summer session for credit. *ROTC:* Army (b).
Library Main Campus Library plus 1 other. *Books:* 24,843 (physical), 131,593 (digital/electronic); *Serial titles:* 19 (physical); *Databases:* 52. Weekly public service hours: 48.
Student Life *Housing:* college housing not available. *Activities and Organizations:* drama/theater group, choral group, Student Government Association. *Campus security:* 24-hour emergency response devices, late-night transport/escort service. *Student services:* veterans affairs office.
Standardized Tests *Recommended:* SAT or ACT (for admission).
Financial Aid Of all full-time matriculated undergraduates who enrolled in 2016, 2,016 applied for aid, 1,803 were judged to have need, 263 had their need fully met. 31 Federal Work-Study jobs (averaging $4236). In 2016, 21 non-need-based awards were made. *Average financial aid package:* $5700. *Average need-based gift aid:* $3700. *Average non-need-based aid:* $1000. *Financial aid deadline:* 7/1.
Applying *Options:* electronic application. *Required:* high school transcript. *Application deadlines:* rolling (freshmen), rolling (transfers). *Notification:* continuous (freshmen), continuous (transfers).
Freshman Application Contact Ms. Barbara Tipmore, Director of Counseling Services, Owensboro Community and Technical College, 4800 New Hartford Road, Owensboro, KY 42303. *Phone:* 270-686-4530. *Toll-free phone:* 866-755-6282. *E-mail:* barb.tipmore@kctcs.edu. *Website:* http://www.owensboro.kctcs.edu/.

Ross College

Hopkinsville, Kentucky

Freshman Application Contact Ross College, 4001 Fort Cambell Boulevard, Hopkinsville, KY 42240. *Phone:* 270-886-1302. *Toll-free phone:* 866-815-5578. *Website:* http://www.rosseducation.edu/.

Somerset Community College

Somerset, Kentucky

- **State-supported** 2-year, founded 1965, part of Kentucky Community and Technical College System
- **Small-town** 70-acre campus
- **Coed**

Undergraduates *Retention:* 58% of full-time freshmen returned.
Faculty *Student/faculty ratio:* 24:1.
Academics *Calendar:* semesters. *Degree:* certificates, diplomas, and associate. *Special study options:* academic remediation for entering students, adult/continuing education programs, advanced placement credit, distance learning, part-time degree program, services for LD students, summer session for credit.
Library Somerset Community College Library.
Applying *Options:* electronic application, early admission. *Required:* high school transcript.
Freshman Application Contact Director of Admission, Somerset Community College, 808 Monticello Street, Somerset, KY 42501-2973. *Phone:* 606-451-6630. *Toll-free phone:* 877-629-9722. *E-mail:* somerset-admissions@kctcs.edu. *Website:* http://www.somerset.kctcs.edu/.

Southcentral Kentucky Community and Technical College

Bowling Green, Kentucky

- **State-supported** 2-year, founded 1938, part of Kentucky Community and Technical College System
- **Coed**

Academics *Calendar:* semesters. *Degree:* certificates, diplomas, and associate.

Freshman Application Contact Southcentral Kentucky Community and Technical College, 1845 Loop Drive, Bowling Green, KY 42101. *Phone:* 270-901-1114. *Toll-free phone:* 800-790-0990. *Website:* http://southcentral.kctcs.edu/.

Southeast Kentucky Community and Technical College

Cumberland, Kentucky

- **State-supported** 2-year, founded 1960, part of Kentucky Community and Technical College System
- **Rural** 150-acre campus
- **Coed**

Undergraduates 1,480 full-time, 1,645 part-time. Students come from 21 states and territories; 1 other country; 6% are from out of state; 2% Black or African American, non-Hispanic/Latino; 0.5% Hispanic/Latino; 0.2% Asian, non-Hispanic/Latino; 0.3% Native Hawaiian or other Pacific Islander, non-Hispanic/Latino; 0.6% American Indian or Alaska Native, non-Hispanic/Latino; 2% Two or more races, non-Hispanic/Latino; 5% Race/ethnicity unknown; 2% transferred in. *Retention:* 64% of full-time freshmen returned.

Faculty *Student/faculty ratio:* 20:1.

Academics *Calendar:* semesters. *Degree:* certificates, diplomas, and associate. *Special study options:* academic remediation for entering students, accelerated degree program, adult/continuing education programs, advanced placement credit, distance learning, independent study, part-time degree program, study abroad, summer session for credit.

Library Gertrude Dale Library plus 4 others.

Standardized Tests *Recommended:* ACT (for admission).

Financial Aid Of all full-time matriculated undergraduates who enrolled in 2017, 90 Federal Work-Study jobs (averaging $635).

Applying *Required:* high school transcript.

Freshman Application Contact Southeast Kentucky Community and Technical College, 700 College Road, Cumberland, KY 40823-1099. *Phone:* 606-589-2145 Ext. 13018. *Toll-free phone:* 888-274-SECC. *Website:* http://www.southeast.kctcs.edu/.

West Kentucky Community and Technical College

Paducah, Kentucky

- **State-supported** 2-year, founded 1932, part of Kentucky Community and Technical College System
- **Small-town** 117-acre campus
- **Coed,** 6,259 undergraduate students, 33% full-time, 53% women, 44% men

Undergraduates 2,062 full-time, 3,981 part-time. Students come from 25 states and territories; 8% Black or African American, non-Hispanic/Latino; 4% Hispanic/Latino; 0.6% Asian, non-Hispanic/Latino; 0.3% American Indian or Alaska Native, non-Hispanic/Latino; 4% Two or more races, non-Hispanic/Latino; 6% Race/ethnicity unknown; 0.1% international. *Retention:* 57% of full-time freshmen returned.

Faculty *Total:* 121. *Student/faculty ratio:* 18:1.

Majors Animation, interactive technology, video graphics and special effects; automobile/automotive mechanics technology; business administration and management; child-care provision; clinical/medical laboratory technology; computer and information sciences; criminal justice/law enforcement administration; culinary arts; diagnostic medical sonography and ultrasound technology; electrician; emergency medical technology (EMT paramedic); fine/studio arts; fire science/firefighting; health services/allied health/health sciences; homeland security, law enforcement, firefighting and protective services related; industrial mechanics and maintenance technology; liberal arts and sciences/liberal studies; logistics, materials, and supply chain management; machine shop technology; marine transportation related; mechanic and repair technologies related; medical administrative assistant and medical secretary; multi/interdisciplinary studies related; physical therapy technology; registered nursing/registered nurse; surgical technology.

Academics *Calendar:* semesters. *Degree:* certificates, diplomas, and associate. *Special study options:* academic remediation for entering students, accelerated degree program, adult/continuing education programs, cooperative education, distance learning, English as a second language, external degree program, honors programs, independent study, part-time degree program, study abroad, summer session for credit.

Library WKCTC Matheson Library.

Student Life *Housing:* college housing not available. *Campus security:* 24-hour patrols. *Student services:* veterans affairs office.

Athletics *Intramural sports:* basketball M.

Financial Aid Of all full-time matriculated undergraduates who enrolled in 2017, 50 Federal Work-Study jobs (averaging $1650).

Applying *Options:* electronic application, early admission. *Required:* high school transcript. *Application deadlines:* rolling (freshmen), rolling (transfers). *Notification:* continuous (freshmen), continuous (transfers).

Freshman Application Contact Mr. Trent Johnson, Director of Admission, West Kentucky Community and Technical College, 4810 Alben Barkley Drive, Paducah, KY 42001. *E-mail:* trent.johnson@kctcs.edu. *Website:* http://www.westkentucky.kctcs.edu/.

LOUISIANA

Baton Rouge Community College

Baton Rouge, Louisiana

Director of Admissions Nancy Clay, Interim Executive Director for Enrollment Services, Baton Rouge Community College, 201 Community College Drive, Baton Rouge, LA 70806. *Phone:* 225-216-8700. *Toll-free phone:* 800-601-4558. *Website:* http://www.mybrcc.edu/.

Baton Rouge School of Computers

Baton Rouge, Louisiana

Freshman Application Contact Admissions Office, Baton Rouge School of Computers, 9352 Interline Avenue, Baton Rouge, LA 70809. *Phone:* 225-923-2524. *Toll-free phone:* 888-920-2772. *Fax:* 225-923-2979. *E-mail:* admissions@brsc.net. *Website:* http://www.brsc.edu/.

Bossier Parish Community College

Bossier City, Louisiana

- **State-supported** 2-year, founded 1967, part of Louisiana Community and Technical College System
- **Urban** 64-acre campus with easy access to Shreveport
- **Coed**

Undergraduates 2,310 full-time, 3,732 part-time. 3% are from out of state; 42% Black or African American, non-Hispanic/Latino; 1% Hispanic/Latino; 0.7% Asian, non-Hispanic/Latino; 0.2% Native Hawaiian or other Pacific Islander, non-Hispanic/Latino; 1% American Indian or Alaska Native, non-Hispanic/Latino; 3% Two or more races, non-Hispanic/Latino; 3% Race/ethnicity unknown; 0.1% international; 13% transferred in. *Retention:* 42% of full-time freshmen returned.

Faculty *Student/faculty ratio:* 22:1.

Academics *Calendar:* semesters. *Degree:* certificates, diplomas, and associate. *Special study options:* academic remediation for entering students, adult/continuing education programs, advanced placement credit, distance learning, double majors, part-time degree program, services for LD students, summer session for credit.

Library Bossier Parish Community College Library.

Student Life *Campus security:* student patrols.

Athletics Member NJCAA.

Financial Aid Of all full-time matriculated undergraduates who enrolled in 2017, 2,084 applied for aid, 1,908 were judged to have need, 50 had their need fully met. In 2017, 7. *Average percent of need met:* 36. *Average financial aid package:* $10,987. *Average need-based loan:* $1978. *Average need-based gift aid:* $1985. *Average non-need-based aid:* $600.

Applying *Options:* early admission.

Freshman Application Contact Mr. Richard Cockerham, Registrar, Bossier Parish Community College, 6220 East Texas Street, Bossier City, LA 71111. *Phone:* 318-678-6093. *Fax:* 318-678-6390. *Website:* http://www.bpcc.edu/.

Cameron College

New Orleans, Louisiana

Admissions Office Contact Cameron College, 2740 Canal Street, New Orleans, LA 70119. *Website:* http://www.cameroncollege.com/.

Central Louisiana Technical Community College

Alexandria, Louisiana

- **State-supported** 2-year, part of Louisiana Technical Community College System
- **Small-town** campus
- **Endowment** $289,536
- **Coed**

Undergraduates 1,107 full-time, 1,325 part-time. Students come from 3 states and territories; 2% are from out of state; 29% Black or African American, non-Hispanic/Latino; 0.4% Asian, non-Hispanic/Latino; 3% American Indian or Alaska Native, non-Hispanic/Latino; 2% Two or more races, non-Hispanic/Latino; 27% Race/ethnicity unknown; 9% transferred in. *Retention:* 69% of full-time freshmen returned.
Faculty *Student/faculty ratio:* 24:1.
Academics *Calendar:* semesters. *Degree:* certificates, diplomas, and associate. *Special study options:* academic remediation for entering students, advanced placement credit, distance learning, double majors, English as a second language, honors programs, independent study, internships, part-time degree program, services for LD students, summer session for credit.
Library ***Books:*** 1,484 (physical), 5,331 (digital/electronic); *Databases:* 86. Weekly public service hours: 40.
Student Life *Campus security:* 24-hour emergency response devices.
Financial Aid Of all full-time matriculated undergraduates who enrolled in 2017, 1,088 applied for aid, 769 were judged to have need, 692 had their need fully met. 29 Federal Work-Study jobs (averaging $2613). In 2017, 8. *Average percent of need met:* 90. *Average financial aid package:* $22,887. *Average need-based loan:* $13,152. *Average need-based gift aid:* $11,693. *Average non-need-based aid:* $787.
Applying *Options:* electronic application. *Application fee:* $5. *Required:* high school transcript.
Freshman Application Contact Heather Renier, Director of Student Affairs and Services, Central Louisiana Technical Community College, 4311 South MacArthur Drive, Alexandria, LA 71302. *Phone:* 318-487-5443 Ext. 1129. *Fax:* 318-487-5970. *E-mail:* meredithclark@cltcc.edu. *Website:* http://www.cltcc.edu/.

Delgado Community College

New Orleans, Louisiana

Freshman Application Contact Ms. Gwen Boute, Director of Admissions, Delgado Community College, 615 City Park Avenue, New Orleans, LA 70119. *Phone:* 504-671-5010. *Fax:* 504-483-1895. *E-mail:* enroll@dcc.edu. *Website:* http://www.dcc.edu/.

Fletcher Technical Community College

Schriever, Louisiana

Director of Admissions Admissions Office, Fletcher Technical Community College, 1407 Highway 311, Schriever, LA 70395. *Phone:* 985-857-3659. *Website:* http://www.fletcher.edu/.

Fortis College

Baton Rouge, Louisiana

Director of Admissions Ms. Sheri Kirley, Associate Director of Admissions, Fortis College, 9255 Interline Avenue, Baton Rouge, LA 70809. *Phone:* 225-248-1015. *Toll-free phone:* 855-4-FORTIS. *Website:* http://www.fortis.edu/.

ITI Technical College

Baton Rouge, Louisiana

- **Proprietary** 2-year, founded 1973
- **Suburban** 10-acre campus
- **Coed**

Undergraduates 622 full-time. Students come from 2 states and territories; 45% Black or African American, non-Hispanic/Latino; 1% Hispanic/Latino; 0.3% Asian, non-Hispanic/Latino; 0.5% American Indian or Alaska Native, non-Hispanic/Latino; 2% Two or more races, non-Hispanic/Latino; 1% Race/ethnicity unknown.
Academics *Calendar:* quarters. *Degree:* certificates and associate. *Special study options:* internships.
Library ITI Technical College Library.
Student Life *Campus security:* electronic alarm devices during non-business hours, security cameras 24-hours.
Applying *Required:* high school transcript, interview.
Freshman Application Contact Mr. Shawn Norris, Admissions Director, ITI Technical College, 13944 Airline Highway, Baton Rouge, LA 70817. *Phone:* 225-752-4230 Ext. 261. *Toll-free phone:* 888-211-7165. *Fax:* 225-756-0903. *E-mail:* snorris@iticollege.edu. *Website:* http://www.iticollege.edu/.

Louisiana Culinary Institute

Baton Rouge, Louisiana

Admissions Office Contact Louisiana Culinary Institute, 10550 Airline Highway, Baton Rouge, LA 70816. *Toll-free phone:* 877-533-3198. *Website:* http://www.lci.edu/.

Louisiana Delta Community College

Monroe, Louisiana

Freshman Application Contact Ms. Kathy Gardner, Interim Dean of Enrollment Services, Louisiana Delta Community College, 7500 Millhaven Drive, Monroe, LA 71203. *Phone:* 318-345-9261. *Toll-free phone:* 866-500-LDCC. *Website:* http://www.ladelta.edu/.

Louisiana State University at Eunice

Eunice, Louisiana

- **State-supported** 2-year, founded 1967, part of Louisiana State University System
- **Small-town** 199-acre campus
- **Endowment** $2.1 million
- **Coed**

Undergraduates 1,388 full-time, 1,518 part-time. Students come from 16 states and territories; 6 other countries; 2% are from out of state; 25% Black or African American, non-Hispanic/Latino; 2% Hispanic/Latino; 0.7% Asian, non-Hispanic/Latino; 0.5% American Indian or Alaska Native, non-Hispanic/Latino; 2% Two or more races, non-Hispanic/Latino; 1% Race/ethnicity unknown; 0.3% international; 25% transferred in; 6% live on campus.
Faculty *Student/faculty ratio:* 21:1.
Academics *Calendar:* semesters. *Degree:* certificates and associate. *Special study options:* academic remediation for entering students, adult/continuing education programs, advanced placement credit, cooperative education, distance learning, honors programs, off-campus study, part-time degree program, services for LD students, summer session for credit.
Library Arnold LeDoux Library. *Books:* 65,807 (physical), 90 (digital/electronic). Weekly public service hours: 90.
Student Life *Campus security:* 24-hour emergency response devices and patrols, controlled dormitory access.
Athletics Member NJCAA.
Financial Aid Of all full-time matriculated undergraduates who enrolled in 2017, 78 Federal Work-Study jobs (averaging $1525).
Applying *Options:* electronic application, early admission. *Application fee:* $25. *Required:* high school transcript.
Freshman Application Contact Ms. Tasha Naquin, Admissions Counselor, Louisiana State University at Eunice, PO Box 1129, Eunice, LA 70535. *Phone:* 337-550-1329. *Toll-free phone:* 888-367-5783. *E-mail:* admissions@lsue.edu. *Website:* http://www.lsue.edu/.

McCann School of Business & Technology

Monroe, Louisiana

Freshman Application Contact Mrs. Susan Boudreaux, Admissions Office, McCann School of Business & Technology, 2319 Louisville Avenue, Monroe, LA 71201. *Phone:* 318-323-2889. *Toll-free phone:* 866-865-8065. *Fax:* 318-324-9883. *E-mail:* susan.boudreaux@careertc.edu. *Website:* http://www.mccann.edu/.

Northshore Technical Community College

Bogalusa, Louisiana

Director of Admissions Admissions Office, Northshore Technical Community College, 1710 Sullivan Drive, Bogalusa, LA 70427. *Phone:* 985-732-6640. *Website:* http://www.northshorecollege.edu/.

Northwest Louisiana Technical College
Minden, Louisiana

Director of Admissions Ms. Helen Deville, Admissions Office, Northwest Louisiana Technical College, 9500 Industrial Drive, Minden, LA 71055. *Phone:* 318-371-3035. *Toll-free phone:* 800-529-1387. *Fax:* 318-371-3155. *Website:* http://www.nwltc.edu/.

Nunez Community College
Chalmette, Louisiana

- **State-supported** 2-year, founded 1992, part of Louisiana Community and Technical College System
- **Suburban** 20-acre campus with easy access to New Orleans
- **Endowment** $1.2 million
- **Coed**

Undergraduates 986 full-time, 1,613 part-time. Students come from 15 states and territories; 9 other countries; 1% are from out of state; 40% Black or African American, non-Hispanic/Latino; 7% Hispanic/Latino; 2% Asian, non-Hispanic/Latino; 0.2% Native Hawaiian or other Pacific Islander, non-Hispanic/Latino; 0.7% American Indian or Alaska Native, non-Hispanic/Latino; 3% Two or more races, non-Hispanic/Latino; 4% Race/ethnicity unknown; 0.6% international; 16% transferred in.
Faculty *Student/faculty ratio:* 23:1.
Academics *Calendar:* semesters. *Degree:* certificates, diplomas, and associate. *Special study options:* academic remediation for entering students, accelerated degree program, adult/continuing education programs, advanced placement credit, cooperative education, distance learning, double majors, independent study, internships, off-campus study, part-time degree program, services for LD students, student-designed majors, summer session for credit.
Library Nunez Community College Library.
Student Life *Campus security:* late-night transport/escort service, security cameras.
Athletics Member NJCAA.
Financial Aid Of all full-time matriculated undergraduates who enrolled in 2016, 2,599 applied for aid, 2,175 were judged to have need. 37 Federal Work-Study jobs (averaging $2567). *Average financial aid package:* $6229. *Average need-based loan:* $2703. *Average need-based gift aid:* $3526.
Applying *Options:* electronic application, early admission, deferred entrance. *Application fee:* $20. *Required for some:* high school transcript.
Freshman Application Contact Mrs. Becky Maillet, Nunez Community College, 3710 Paris Road, Chalmette, LA 70043. *Phone:* 504-278-6477. *E-mail:* bmaillet@nunez.edu. *Website:* http://www.nunez.edu/.

Remington College–Baton Rouge Campus
Baton Rouge, Louisiana

Director of Admissions Monica Butler-Johnson, Director of Recruitment, Remington College–Baton Rouge Campus, 4520 South Sherwood Forrest Boulevard, Baton Rouge, LA 70816. *Phone:* 225-236-3200. *Toll-free phone:* 800-323-8122. *Fax:* 225-922-3250. *E-mail:* monica.johnson@remingtoncollege.edu. *Website:* http://www.remingtoncollege.edu/.

Remington College–Lafayette Campus
Lafayette, Louisiana

Freshman Application Contact Remington College–Lafayette Campus, 303 Rue Louis XIV, Lafayette, LA 70508. *Phone:* 337-981-4010. *Toll-free phone:* 800-323-8122. *Website:* http://www.remingtoncollege.edu/.

Remington College–Shreveport
Shreveport, Louisiana

Freshman Application Contact Mr. Marc Wright, Remington College–Shreveport, 2106 West Bert Kouns Industrial Loop, Shreveport, LA 71118. *Phone:* 318-671-4000. *Toll-free phone:* 800-323-8122. *Website:* http://www.remingtoncollege.edu/.

River Parishes Community College
Gonzales, Louisiana

Director of Admissions Ms. Allison Dauzat, Dean of Students and Enrollment Management, River Parishes Community College, 925 West Edenborne Parkway, Gonzales, LA 70737. *Phone:* 225-675-8270. *Fax:* 225-675-5478. *E-mail:* adauzat@rpcc.cc.la.us. *Website:* http://www.rpcc.edu/.

South Central Louisiana Technical College
Morgan City, Louisiana

Director of Admissions Ms. Melanie Henry, Admissions Office, South Central Louisiana Technical College, 900 Youngs Road, Morgan City, LA 70380. *Phone:* 504-380-2436. *Fax:* 504-380-2440. *Website:* http://www.scl.edu/.

Southern University at Shreveport
Shreveport, Louisiana

- **State-supported** 2-year, founded 1964, part of Southern University System
- **Urban** 103-acre campus
- **Endowment** $619,644
- **Coed,** 2,651 undergraduate students, 57% full-time, 71% women, 29% men
- 74% of applicants were admitted

Undergraduates 1,511 full-time, 1,140 part-time. Students come from 25 states and territories; 3 other countries; 3% are from out of state; 91% Black or African American, non-Hispanic/Latino; 0.2% Hispanic/Latino; 0.4% Asian, non-Hispanic/Latino; 0.3% American Indian or Alaska Native, non-Hispanic/Latino; 0.3% Two or more races, non-Hispanic/Latino; 3% international; 7% transferred in; 7% live on campus. *Retention:* 41% of full-time freshmen returned.
Freshmen *Admission:* 1 applied, 1,331 admitted, 652 enrolled. *Average high school GPA:* 2.0. *Test scores:* ACT scores over 18: 8%.
Faculty *Total:* 129, 53% full-time, 9% with terminal degrees. *Student/faculty ratio:* 21:1.
Majors Accounting; accounting technology and bookkeeping; avionics maintenance technology; business/commerce; clinical/medical laboratory technology; computer science; criminal justice/law enforcement administration; dental hygiene; general studies; health information/medical records administration; health information/medical records technology; human services; liberal arts and sciences and humanities related; medical radiologic technology; physical therapy technology; radiologic technology/science; registered nursing/registered nurse; respiratory care therapy; surgical technology.
Academics *Calendar:* semesters. *Degree:* certificates and associate. *Special study options:* academic remediation for entering students, adult/continuing education programs, advanced placement credit, cooperative education, distance learning, double majors, English as a second language, honors programs, internships, part-time degree program, services for LD students, student-designed majors, summer session for credit. *ROTC:* Army (c).
Library Library/Learning Resources Center plus 1 other. *Books:* 56,043 (physical), 11,097 (digital/electronic); *Serial titles:* 164 (physical); *Databases:* 86. Students can reserve study rooms.
Student Life *Housing Options:* coed. Campus housing is provided by a third party. *Activities and Organizations:* student-run newspaper, choral group, marching band, Afro-American Society, SUSLA Gospel Choir, Student Center Board, Allied Health, Engineering Club. *Campus security:* 24-hour emergency response devices and patrols, controlled dormitory access. *Student services:* personal/psychological counseling, veterans affairs office.
Athletics Member NJCAA. *Intercollegiate sports:* basketball W(s). *Intramural sports:* basketball M, cheerleading M, soccer M.
Standardized Tests *Required for some:* SAT or ACT (for admission). *Recommended:* ACT (for admission).
Applying *Application fee:* $25. *Recommended:* high school transcript. *Application deadlines:* rolling (freshmen), rolling (transfers).
Freshman Application Contact Ms. Danielle Anderson, Admissions Advisor, Southern University at Shreveport, 3050 Martin Luther King Jr. Drive, Shreveport, LA 71107. *Phone:* 318-670-9211. *Toll-free phone:* 800-458-1472. *Fax:* 318-670-6483. *E-mail:* danderson@susla.edu. *Website:* http://www.susla.edu/.

South Louisiana Community College
Lafayette, Louisiana

Freshman Application Contact Director of Admissions, South Louisiana Community College, 1101 Bertrand Drive, Lafayette, LA 70506. *Phone:* 337-521-8953. *E-mail:* admissions@solacc.edu. *Website:* http://www.solacc.edu/.

Sowela Technical Community College

Lake Charles, Louisiana

- **State-supported** 2-year, founded 1938, part of Louisiana Community and Technical College System
- **Urban** 84-acre campus
- **Endowment** $1.0 million
- **Coed,** 3,459 undergraduate students, 52% full-time, 49% women, 51% men
- 100% of applicants were admitted

Undergraduates 1,796 full-time, 1,663 part-time. Students come from 21 states and territories; 15 other countries; 2% are from out of state; 24% Black or African American, non-Hispanic/Latino; 4% Hispanic/Latino; 0.7% Asian, non-Hispanic/Latino; 0.8% Native Hawaiian or other Pacific Islander, non-Hispanic/Latino; 1% American Indian or Alaska Native, non-Hispanic/Latino; 4% Two or more races, non-Hispanic/Latino; 3% Race/ethnicity unknown; 0.5% international; 12% transferred in. *Retention:* 54% of full-time freshmen returned.

Freshmen *Admission:* 762 applied, 762 admitted, 755 enrolled. *Average high school GPA:* 3.0.

Faculty *Total:* 159, 52% full-time, 14% with terminal degrees. *Student/faculty ratio:* 24:1.

Majors Accounting technology and bookkeeping; administrative assistant and secretarial science; aircraft powerplant technology; business/commerce; chemical technology; commercial and advertising art; computer programming; computer systems networking and telecommunications; criminal justice/safety; culinary arts; drafting and design technology; electrician; general studies; industrial production technologies related; information technology; instrumentation technology; liberal arts and sciences and humanities related; registered nursing/registered nurse.

Academics *Calendar:* semesters. *Degree:* certificates, diplomas, and associate. *Special study options:* academic remediation for entering students, accelerated degree program, adult/continuing education programs, advanced placement credit, distance learning, double majors, external degree program, internships, off-campus study, part-time degree program, services for LD students, summer session for credit.

Library Library and Learning Resource Center plus 3 others. *Books:* 7,767 (physical), 11,150 (digital/electronic); *Serial titles:* 21 (physical), 32,295 (digital/electronic); *Databases:* 64. Weekly public service hours: 50; students can reserve study rooms.

Student Life *Housing:* college housing not available. *Activities and Organizations:* student-run newspaper, choral group, SkillsUSA, Student Government Association (SGA), Graphic Arts, Nursing Association, Phi Theta Kappa. *Campus security:* security guard on duty. *Student services:* personal/psychological counseling, veterans affairs office.

Applying *Options:* electronic application, early admission. *Required:* proof of immunization, proof of Selective Service status. *Required for some:* high school transcript. *Application deadlines:* rolling (freshmen), rolling (transfers). *Notification:* continuous (freshmen), continuous (transfers).

Director of Admissions Allison Dering, Executive Director of Enrollment Services and Student Affairs, Sowela Technical Community College, 3820 Senator J. Bennett Johnston Avenue, Lake Charles, LA 70615. *Phone:* 337-421-6955. *Toll-free phone:* 800-256-0483. *Fax:* 337-491-2443. *E-mail:* allison.dering@sowela.edu. *Website:* http://www.sowela.edu/.

MAINE

Beal College

Bangor, Maine

- **Proprietary** 2-year, founded 1891
- **Small-town** 4-acre campus
- **Coed**

Undergraduates 363 full-time, 101 part-time. Students come from 1 other state; 0.9% Black or African American, non-Hispanic/Latino; 1% Hispanic/Latino; 0.6% Asian, non-Hispanic/Latino; 0.2% Native Hawaiian or other Pacific Islander, non-Hispanic/Latino; 2% American Indian or Alaska Native, non-Hispanic/Latino; 4% Race/ethnicity unknown; 10% transferred in. *Retention:* 60% of full-time freshmen returned.

Faculty *Student/faculty ratio:* 30:1.

Academics *Calendar:* modular. *Degree:* certificates, diplomas, and associate. *Special study options:* accelerated degree program, adult/continuing education programs, advanced placement credit, internships, part-time degree program, summer session for credit.

Library Beal College Library. *Books:* 4,256 (physical); *Serial titles:* 28 (physical). Weekly public service hours: 40.

Standardized Tests *Required:* entrance exam (for admission).

Applying *Options:* deferred entrance. *Application fee:* $30. *Required:* essay or personal statement, high school transcript, 1 letter of recommendation, interview, immunizations.

Freshman Application Contact Tasha Sullivan, Admissions Representative, Beal College, 99 Farm Road, Bangor, ME 04401. *Phone:* 207-947-4591. *Toll-free phone:* 800-660-7351. *Fax:* 207-947-0208. *E-mail:* admissions@bealcollege.edu. *Website:* http://www.bealcollege.edu/.

Central Maine Community College

Auburn, Maine

- **State-supported** 2-year, founded 1964, part of Maine Community College System
- **Small-town** 135-acre campus
- **Endowment** $975,000
- **Coed**

Undergraduates 1,095 full-time, 1,805 part-time. Students come from 12 states and territories; 3 other countries; 5% are from out of state; 8% Black or African American, non-Hispanic/Latino; 2% Hispanic/Latino; 0.7% Asian, non-Hispanic/Latino; 0.1% Native Hawaiian or other Pacific Islander, non-Hispanic/Latino; 0.5% American Indian or Alaska Native, non-Hispanic/Latino; 2% Two or more races, non-Hispanic/Latino; 21% Race/ethnicity unknown; 0.7% international; 7% transferred in; 8% live on campus.

Faculty *Student/faculty ratio:* 17:1.

Academics *Calendar:* semesters. *Degree:* certificates and associate. *Special study options:* academic remediation for entering students, accelerated degree program, adult/continuing education programs, advanced placement credit, cooperative education, distance learning, English as a second language, honors programs, independent study, internships, part-time degree program, services for LD students, summer session for credit.

Library Central Maine Community College Library. *Books:* 7,810 (physical); *Serial titles:* 44 (physical); *Databases:* 92. Weekly public service hours: 53; students can reserve study rooms.

Student Life *Campus security:* 24-hour emergency response devices, student patrols, controlled dormitory access, night patrols by police.

Athletics Member USCAA.

Standardized Tests *Recommended:* SAT and SAT Subject Tests or ACT (for admission).

Financial Aid Of all full-time matriculated undergraduates who enrolled in 2017, 89 Federal Work-Study jobs (averaging $1200). *Financial aid deadline:* 8/1.

Applying *Options:* electronic application, deferred entrance. *Application fee:* $20. *Required:* high school transcript. *Recommended:* essay or personal statement.

Freshman Application Contact Ms. Joan Nichols, Admissions Assistant, Central Maine Community College, 1250 Turner Street, Auburn, ME 04210. *Phone:* 207-755-5273. *Toll-free phone:* 800-891-2002. *Fax:* 207-755-5493. *E-mail:* enroll@cmcc.edu. *Website:* http://www.cmcc.edu/.

Eastern Maine Community College

Bangor, Maine

Freshman Application Contact Mr. W. Gregory Swett, Director of Admissions, Eastern Maine Community College, 354 Hogan Road, Bangor, ME 04401. *Phone:* 207-974-4680. *Toll-free phone:* 800-286-9357. *Fax:* 207-974-4683. *E-mail:* admissions@emcc.edu. *Website:* http://www.emcc.edu/.

Kennebec Valley Community College

Fairfield, Maine

- **State-supported** 2-year, founded 1970, part of Maine Community College System
- **Small-town** campus
- **Endowment** $3.1 million
- **Coed**

Undergraduates 565 full-time, 1,989 part-time. Students come from 13 states and territories; 2% are from out of state; 1% Black or African American, non-Hispanic/Latino; 1% Hispanic/Latino; 0.7% Asian, non-Hispanic/Latino; 0.1% Native Hawaiian or other Pacific Islander, non-Hispanic/Latino; 0.7% American Indian or Alaska Native, non-Hispanic/Latino; 0.9% Two or more races, non-Hispanic/Latino; 9% Race/ethnicity unknown; 0.2% international; 8% transferred in.

Academics *Calendar:* semesters. *Degree:* certificates, diplomas, and associate. *Special study options:* academic remediation for entering students, accelerated degree program, adult/continuing education programs, advanced placement credit, distance learning, external degree program, independent

study, internships, part-time degree program, services for LD students, summer session for credit.
Library Lunder Library plus 2 others.
Student Life *Campus security:* evening security patrol.
Standardized Tests *Required for some:* HESI nursing exam, HOBET for allied health programs, ACCUPLACER. *Recommended:* SAT or ACT (for admission).
Financial Aid Of all full-time matriculated undergraduates who enrolled in 2015, 1,875 applied for aid, 1,627 were judged to have need, 14 had their need fully met. 27 Federal Work-Study jobs (averaging $1338). In 2015, 12. *Average percent of need met:* 52. *Average financial aid package:* $7483. *Average need-based loan:* $3217. *Average need-based gift aid:* $6087. *Average non-need-based aid:* $1214.
Applying *Options:* electronic application, deferred entrance. *Required:* essay or personal statement, high school transcript. *Required for some:* interview.
Freshman Application Contact Mr. Crichton McKenna, Assistant Director of Admissions, Kennebec Valley Community College, 92 Western Avenue, Fairfield, ME 04937-1367. *Phone:* 207-453-5155. *Toll-free phone:* 800-528-5882. *Fax:* 207-453-5011. *E-mail:* admissions@kvcc.me.edu. *Website:* http://www.kvcc.me.edu/.

The Landing School
Arundel, Maine

Freshman Application Contact Kristin Potter, Admissions Representative, The Landing School, 286 River Road, Arundel, ME 04046. *Phone:* 207-985-7976. *E-mail:* info@landingschool.edu. *Website:* http://www.landingschool.edu/.

Maine College of Health Professions
Lewiston, Maine

- **Independent** primarily 2-year, founded 1891
- **Urban** campus
- **Coed**

Undergraduates 44 full-time, 144 part-time. Students come from 1 other state; 2% Black or African American, non-Hispanic/Latino; 1% Hispanic/Latino; 2% Asian, non-Hispanic/Latino; 0.5% American Indian or Alaska Native, non-Hispanic/Latino; 2% Two or more races, non-Hispanic/Latino; 10% Race/ethnicity unknown; 50% transferred in; 4% live on campus.
Faculty *Student/faculty ratio:* 5:1.
Academics *Calendar:* semesters. *Degrees:* certificates, associate, and bachelor's. *Special study options:* advanced placement credit, off-campus study, services for LD students, summer session for credit.
Library Gerrish True Health Sciences Library plus 1 other. *Books:* 2,816 (physical), 172 (digital/electronic); *Databases:* 17. Study areas open 24 hours, 5–7 days a week.
Student Life *Campus security:* 24-hour emergency response devices and patrols, late-night transport/escort service, controlled dormitory access.
Standardized Tests *Required for some:* SAT or ACT (for admission), HESI Entrance Exam for nursing, ACCUPLACER.
Financial Aid Of all full-time matriculated undergraduates who enrolled in 2018, 70 applied for aid, 55 were judged to have need.
Applying *Options:* electronic application. *Application fee:* $50. *Required:* essay or personal statement, high school transcript, high school or college-level algebra, second math, biology, chemistry.
Freshman Application Contact Ms. Erica Watson, Admissions Director, Maine College of Health Professions, 70 Middle Street, Lewiston, ME 04240. *Phone:* 207-795-2843. *Fax:* 207-795-2849. *E-mail:* watsoner@mchp.edu. *Website:* http://www.mchp.edu/.

Northern Maine Community College
Presque Isle, Maine

- **State-supported** 2-year, founded 1963, part of Maine Community College System
- **Small-town** 86-acre campus
- **Coed**

Undergraduates Students come from 4 states and territories; 4% are from out of state; 50% live on campus. *Retention:* 57% of full-time freshmen returned.
Faculty *Student/faculty ratio:* 15:1.
Academics *Calendar:* semesters. *Degree:* certificates and associate. *Special study options:* academic remediation for entering students, adult/continuing education programs, advanced placement credit, cooperative education, double majors, independent study, internships, off-campus study, part-time degree program, services for LD students, summer session for credit.
Library Northern Maine Community College Library. Weekly public service hours: 40; students can reserve study rooms.
Student Life *Campus security:* 24-hour emergency response devices and patrols, controlled dormitory access.
Financial Aid Of all full-time matriculated undergraduates who enrolled in 2012, 664 applied for aid, 612 were judged to have need, 17 had their need fully met. In 2012, 10. *Average percent of need met:* 48. *Average financial aid package:* $6588. *Average need-based loan:* $3072. *Average need-based gift aid:* $4815. *Average non-need-based aid:* $890.
Applying *Options:* electronic application, early admission, deferred entrance. *Application fee:* $20. *Required:* high school transcript, interview. *Recommended:* essay or personal statement, minimum 2.0 GPA.
Freshman Application Contact Ms. Nicole Poulin, Admissions Specialist, Northern Maine Community College, 33 Edgemont Drive, Presque Isle, ME 04769-2016. *Phone:* 207-768-2785. *Toll-free phone:* 800-535-6682. *Fax:* 207-768-2848. *E-mail:* nnpoulin@nmcc.edu. *Website:* http://www.nmcc.edu/.

Southern Maine Community College
South Portland, Maine

- **State-supported** 2-year, founded 1946, part of Maine Community College System
- **Suburban** 80-acre campus
- **Coed,** 8,491 undergraduate students, 40% full-time, 69% women, 31% men

Undergraduates 3,424 full-time, 5,067 part-time. Students come from 15 states and territories; 10 other countries; 7% Black or African American, non-Hispanic/Latino; 4% Hispanic/Latino; 2% Asian, non-Hispanic/Latino; 0.2% Native Hawaiian or other Pacific Islander, non-Hispanic/Latino; 0.3% American Indian or Alaska Native, non-Hispanic/Latino; 3% Two or more races, non-Hispanic/Latino; 3% Race/ethnicity unknown; 0.7% international; 5% live on campus. *Retention:* 55% of full-time freshmen returned.
Freshmen *Admission:* 1,664 enrolled.
Faculty *Total:* 446, 22% full-time. *Student/faculty ratio:* 18:1.
Majors Agroecology and sustainable agriculture; allied health and medical assisting services related; automobile/automotive mechanics technology; biotechnology; building construction technology; business administration and management; cardiovascular technology; computer and information systems security; computer engineering technology; computer science; criminal justice/safety; culinary arts; dietetic technology; digital communication and media/multimedia; drafting and design technology; early childhood education; education; electrical, electronic and communications engineering technology; emergency medical technology (EMT paramedic); engineering; fire science/firefighting; health services/allied health/health sciences; heating, air conditioning, ventilation and refrigeration maintenance technology; human services; liberal arts and sciences and humanities related; liberal arts and sciences/liberal studies; machine tool technology; marine biology and biological oceanography; materials engineering; medical/clinical assistant; network and system administration; plumbing technology; radiologic technology/science; registered nursing/registered nurse; respiratory care therapy; surgical technology.
Academics *Calendar:* semesters. *Degree:* certificates and associate. *Special study options:* academic remediation for entering students, advanced placement credit, distance learning, double majors, English as a second language, honors programs, independent study, internships, off-campus study, part-time degree program, services for LD students, study abroad, summer session for credit.
Library Southern Maine Community College Library. *Books:* 20,586 (physical), 30,783 (digital/electronic); *Serial titles:* 1,026 (physical), 23,074 (digital/electronic); *Databases:* 34. Weekly public service hours: 68; students can reserve study rooms.
Student Life *Housing Options:* coed, men-only. Campus housing is university owned. *Activities and Organizations:* drama/theater group, student-run newspaper, choral group, Student Senate. *Campus security:* 24-hour patrols, student patrols, late-night transport/escort service, controlled dormitory access. *Student services:* personal/psychological counseling.
Athletics Member USCAA. *Intercollegiate sports:* baseball M, basketball M/W, golf M/W, soccer M/W, softball W.
Applying *Options:* electronic application. *Application fee:* $20. *Required:* high school transcript. *Application deadlines:* rolling (freshmen), rolling (out-of-state freshmen), rolling (transfers). *Notification:* continuous (freshmen), continuous (out-of-state freshmen), continuous (transfers).
Freshman Application Contact Amy Lee, Assistant Dean of Enrollment Management, Southern Maine Community College, 2 Fort Road, South Portland, ME 04106. *Phone:* 207-741-5800. *Toll-free phone:* 877-282-2182. *Fax:* 207-741-5760. *E-mail:* alee@smccme.edu. *Website:* http://www.smccme.edu/.

Washington County Community College

Calais, Maine

Freshman Application Contact Washington County Community College, One College Drive, Calais, ME 04619. *Phone:* 207-454-1000. *Toll-free phone:* 800-210-6932. *Website:* http://www.wccc.me.edu/.

York County Community College

Wells, Maine

- **State-supported** 2-year, founded 1994, part of Maine Community College System
- **Small-town** 84-acre campus with easy access to Boston
- **Coed**

Undergraduates 399 full-time, 1,309 part-time. Students come from 8 states and territories; 3% are from out of state; 0.9% Black or African American, non-Hispanic/Latino; 2% Hispanic/Latino; 2% Asian, non-Hispanic/Latino; 0.3% American Indian or Alaska Native, non-Hispanic/Latino; 2% Two or more races, non-Hispanic/Latino; 24% Race/ethnicity unknown; 0.3% international; 14% transferred in. *Retention:* 64% of full-time freshmen returned.
Faculty *Student/faculty ratio:* 13:1.
Academics *Calendar:* semesters. *Degree:* certificates and associate. *Special study options:* academic remediation for entering students, adult/continuing education programs, advanced placement credit, cooperative education, distance learning, internships, off-campus study, part-time degree program, services for LD students, summer session for credit.
Library Library and Learning Resource Center plus 1 other. *Books:* 12,399 (physical); *Serial titles:* 1,625 (physical); *Databases:* 28. Weekly public service hours: 57; students can reserve study rooms.
Student Life *Campus security:* full-time College Safety and Security Manager.
Standardized Tests *Recommended:* SAT or ACT (for admission).
Financial Aid Of all full-time matriculated undergraduates who enrolled in 2017, 321 applied for aid, 364 were judged to have need, 11 had their need fully met. 28 Federal Work-Study jobs (averaging $43,467). 8 state and other part-time jobs (averaging $9039). In 2017, 20. *Average percent of need met:* 39. *Average financial aid package:* $6318. *Average need-based loan:* $2509. *Average need-based gift aid:* $5568. *Average non-need-based aid:* $891.
Applying *Options:* electronic application, deferred entrance. *Application fee:* $20. *Required:* high school transcript. *Recommended:* interview.
Freshman Application Contact Fred Quistgard, Director of Admissions, York County Community College, 112 College Drive, Wells, ME 04090. *Phone:* 207-216-4406. *Toll-free phone:* 800-580-3820. *Fax:* 207-641-0837. *Website:* http://www.yccc.edu/.

MARYLAND

Allegany College of Maryland

Cumberland, Maryland

Freshman Application Contact Ms. Cathy Nolan, Director of Admissions and Registration, Allegany College of Maryland, Cumberland, MD 21502. *Phone:* 301-784-5000 Ext. 5202. *Fax:* 301-784-5220. *E-mail:* cnolan@allegany.edu. *Website:* http://www.allegany.edu/.

Anne Arundel Community College

Arnold, Maryland

- **State and locally supported** 2-year, founded 1961
- **Suburban** 230-acre campus with easy access to Baltimore and Washington, DC
- **Coed**

Undergraduates 3,815 full-time, 9,539 part-time. Students come from 28 states and territories; 87 other countries; 1% are from out of state; 58% Black or African American, non-Hispanic/Latino; 8% Hispanic/Latino; 0.3% Asian, non-Hispanic/Latino; 0.2% Native Hawaiian or other Pacific Islander, non-Hispanic/Latino; 4% American Indian or Alaska Native, non-Hispanic/Latino; 4% Two or more races, non-Hispanic/Latino; 7% Race/ethnicity unknown; 2% international; 29% transferred in. *Retention:* 63% of full-time freshmen returned.
Faculty *Student/faculty ratio:* 12:1.
Academics *Calendar:* semesters. *Degree:* certificates and associate. *Special study options:* academic remediation for entering students, advanced placement credit, cooperative education, distance learning, English as a second language, honors programs, independent study, internships, part-time degree program, services for LD students, summer session for credit. *ROTC:* Army (c), Air Force (c).
Library Andrew G. Truxal Library plus 1 other. *Books:* 152,186 (physical), 114,000 (digital/electronic); *Serial titles:* 135 (physical), 15,000 (digital/electronic); *Databases:* 60. Weekly public service hours: 77.
Student Life *Campus security:* 24-hour emergency response devices and patrols, student patrols, late-night transport/escort service.
Athletics Member NJCAA.
Applying *Options:* electronic application, early admission. *Required:* high school transcript. *Required for some:* letters of recommendation.
Freshman Application Contact Mr. Thomas McGinn, Director of Enrollment Development and Admissions, Anne Arundel Community College, 101 College Parkway, Arnold, MD 21012-1895. *Phone:* 410-777-2240. *Fax:* 410-777-2246. *E-mail:* 4info@aacc.edu. *Website:* http://www.aacc.edu/.

Baltimore City Community College

Baltimore, Maryland

Freshman Application Contact Baltimore City Community College, 2901 Liberty Heights Avenue, Baltimore, MD 21215-7893. *Phone:* 410-462-8311. *Toll-free phone:* 888-203-1261. *Website:* http://www.bccc.edu/.

Carroll Community College

Westminster, Maryland

- **State and locally supported** 2-year, founded 1993, part of Maryland Higher Education Commission
- **Suburban** 80-acre campus with easy access to Baltimore
- **Endowment** $7.7 million
- **Coed**

Undergraduates 997 full-time, 2,023 part-time. Students come from 6 states and territories; 20 other countries; 2% are from out of state; 4% Black or African American, non-Hispanic/Latino; 5% Hispanic/Latino; 3% Asian, non-Hispanic/Latino; 0.1% Native Hawaiian or other Pacific Islander, non-Hispanic/Latino; 0.1% American Indian or Alaska Native, non-Hispanic/Latino; 2% Two or more races, non-Hispanic/Latino; 3% Race/ethnicity unknown; 0.2% international; 7% transferred in.
Faculty *Student/faculty ratio:* 13:1.
Academics *Calendar:* semesters plus winter and summer sessions. *Degree:* certificates and associate. *Special study options:* academic remediation for entering students, advanced placement credit, distance learning, English as a second language, honors programs, independent study, internships, part-time degree program, services for LD students, summer session for credit.
Library Carroll Community College Library. *Books:* 39,451 (physical), 150,490 (digital/electronic); *Serial titles:* 152 (physical), 18,508 (digital/electronic); *Databases:* 42.
Student Life *Campus security:* 24-hour emergency response devices, late night security escort to vehicle in parking lot.
Financial Aid Of all full-time matriculated undergraduates who enrolled in 2016, 32 Federal Work-Study jobs (averaging $2658).
Applying *Options:* electronic application. *Required:* high school transcript.
Freshman Application Contact Ms. Candace Edwards, Director of Admissions, Carroll Community College, 1601 Washington Road, Westminster, MD 21157. *Phone:* 410-386-8405. *Toll-free phone:* 888-221-9748. *Fax:* 410-386-8446. *E-mail:* cedwards@carrollcc.edu. *Website:* http://www.carrollcc.edu/.

Cecil College

North East, Maryland

- **County-supported** primarily 2-year, founded 1968
- **Small-town** 159-acre campus with easy access to Baltimore
- **Coed**

Undergraduates 867 full-time, 1,601 part-time. Students come from 9 states and territories; 21 other countries; 16% are from out of state; 10% Black or African American, non-Hispanic/Latino; 6% Hispanic/Latino; 1% Asian, non-Hispanic/Latino; 0.1% Native Hawaiian or other Pacific Islander, non-Hispanic/Latino; 0.3% American Indian or Alaska Native, non-Hispanic/Latino; 5% Two or more races, non-Hispanic/Latino; 1% Race/ethnicity unknown; 0.6% international; 4% transferred in. *Retention:* 56% of full-time freshmen returned.
Faculty *Student/faculty ratio:* 11:1.
Academics *Calendar:* semesters. *Degrees:* certificates, associate, and bachelor's. *Special study options:* academic remediation for entering students, accelerated degree program, adult/continuing education programs, advanced placement credit, cooperative education, distance learning, double majors, English as a second language, independent study, internships, off-campus study, part-time degree program, services for LD students, summer session for credit.

Library Cecil County Veterans Memorial Library.
Student Life *Campus security:* 24-hour emergency response devices, late-night transport/escort service, armed patrols from 6:30 am-7:00 pm.
Athletics Member NJCAA.
Applying *Options:* electronic application, early admission, deferred entrance. *Required:* high school transcript.
Freshman Application Contact Dr. Christy Dryer, Cecil College, One Seahawk Drive, North East, MD 21901-1999. *Phone:* 410-287-6060. *Fax:* 410-287-1001. *E-mail:* cdryer@cecil.edu. *Website:* http://www.cecil.edu/.

Chesapeake College
Wye Mills, Maryland

- **State and locally supported** 2-year, founded 1965
- **Rural** 170-acre campus with easy access to Baltimore and Washington, DC
- **Coed**

Undergraduates 580 full-time, 1,609 part-time.
Academics *Calendar:* semesters. *Degree:* certificates and associate. *Special study options:* academic remediation for entering students, adult/continuing education programs, advanced placement credit, distance learning, English as a second language, honors programs, independent study, internships, part-time degree program, services for LD students, summer session for credit.
Library Learning Resource Center. *Books:* 44,000 (physical), 300,000 (digital/electronic); *Serial titles:* 38 (physical), 25,500 (digital/electronic); *Databases:* 56. Weekly public service hours: 56.
Student Life *Campus security:* 24-hour emergency response devices.
Athletics Member NJCAA.
Financial Aid Of all full-time matriculated undergraduates who enrolled in 2017, 32 Federal Work-Study jobs (averaging $1482).
Applying *Options:* electronic application. *Required:* high school transcript.
Freshman Application Contact Ms. Angela Denherder, Director of Student Recruitment and Outreach, Chesapeake College, 1000 College Circle, Wye Mills, MD 21679. *Phone:* 410-827-5856. *E-mail:* adenherder@chesapeake.edu. *Website:* http://www.chesapeake.edu/.

College of Southern Maryland
La Plata, Maryland

Freshman Application Contact Admissions Department, College of Southern Maryland, PO Box 910, La Plata, MD 20646-0910. *Phone:* 301-934-2251. *Toll-free phone:* 800-933-9177. *Fax:* 301-934-7698. *E-mail:* askme@csmd.edu. *Website:* http://www.csmd.edu/.

Community College of Baltimore County
Baltimore, Maryland

- **County-supported** 2-year, founded 1957
- **Suburban** 350-acre campus with easy access to Baltimore
- **Coed,** 18,833 undergraduate students, 27% full-time, 62% women, 38% men

Undergraduates 5,081 full-time, 13,752 part-time. 39% Black or African American, non-Hispanic/Latino; 5% Hispanic/Latino; 6% Asian, non-Hispanic/Latino; 0.2% Native Hawaiian or other Pacific Islander, non-Hispanic/Latino; 0.3% American Indian or Alaska Native, non-Hispanic/Latino; 3% Two or more races, non-Hispanic/Latino; 0.9% Race/ethnicity unknown; 6% international.
Freshmen *Admission:* 3,424 enrolled.
Faculty *Total:* 1,132, 37% full-time, 11% with terminal degrees.
Majors Accounting technology and bookkeeping; aeronautics/aviation/aerospace science and technology; airline pilot and flight crew; air traffic control; anesthesiologist assistant; applied horticulture/horticulture operations; architectural drafting and CAD/CADD; automobile/automotive mechanics technology; aviation/airway management; biological and physical sciences; building/construction finishing, management, and inspection related; building/construction site management; business administration and management; business/commerce; chemistry teacher education; child-care and support services management; clinical/medical laboratory technology; commercial and advertising art; communications technologies and support services related; computer and information sciences; computer and information systems security; computer engineering; computer systems networking and telecommunications; criminal justice/police science; deaf studies; dental hygiene; early childhood education; education; electrical and electronics engineering; elementary education; emergency medical technology (EMT paramedic); engineering; engineering technologies and engineering related; English/language arts teacher education; funeral service and mortuary science; health services/allied health/health sciences; heating, ventilation, air conditioning and refrigeration engineering technology; histologic technology/histotechnologist; hydraulics and fluid power technology; legal assistant/paralegal; liberal arts and sciences and humanities related; liberal arts and sciences/liberal studies; management information systems; massage therapy; mathematics teacher education; medical administrative assistant and medical secretary; medical informatics; medical radiologic technology; occupational therapy; parks, recreation, leisure, and fitness studies related; physics teacher education; registered nursing/registered nurse; respiratory care therapy; sign language interpretation and translation; Spanish language teacher education; substance abuse/addiction counseling; transportation/mobility management; veterinary/animal health technology; visual and performing arts.
Academics *Calendar:* semesters. *Degree:* certificates and associate. *Special study options:* academic remediation for entering students, advanced placement credit, cooperative education, distance learning, English as a second language, honors programs, independent study, internships, off-campus study, part-time degree program, services for LD students, study abroad, summer session for credit.
Student Life *Housing:* college housing not available. *Activities and Organizations:* drama/theater group, student-run newspaper, choral group. *Campus security:* 24-hour emergency response devices and patrols, late-night transport/escort service. *Student services:* veterans affairs office.
Athletics Member NJCAA. *Intercollegiate sports:* baseball M(s), basketball M(s)/W(s), cross-country running M(s)/W(s), lacrosse M(s)/W(s), soccer M(s)/W(s), softball W(s), volleyball W(s). *Intramural sports:* bowling M/W.
Applying *Options:* electronic application. *Required:* high school transcript. *Application deadlines:* rolling (freshmen), rolling (transfers).
Freshman Application Contact Ms. Diane Drake, Director of Admissions, Community College of Baltimore County, 7201 Rossville Boulevard, Baltimore, MD 21237-3899. *Phone:* 443-840-4392. *E-mail:* ddrake@ccbcmd.edu.
Website: http://www.ccbcmd.edu/.

Fortis College
Landover, Maryland

Admissions Office Contact Fortis College, 4351 Garden City Drive, Landover, MD 20785. *Toll-free phone:* 855-4-FORTIS. *Website:* http://www.fortis.edu/.

Frederick Community College
Frederick, Maryland

- **State and locally supported** 2-year, founded 1957
- **Small-town** 100-acre campus with easy access to Baltimore and Washington, DC
- **Endowment** $13.8 million
- **Coed**

Undergraduates 2,027 full-time, 4,193 part-time. 15% Black or African American, non-Hispanic/Latino; 13% Hispanic/Latino; 4% Asian, non-Hispanic/Latino; 0.1% Native Hawaiian or other Pacific Islander, non-Hispanic/Latino; 0.2% American Indian or Alaska Native, non-Hispanic/Latino; 5% Two or more races, non-Hispanic/Latino; 0.3% Race/ethnicity unknown; 1% international; 3% transferred in. *Retention:* 46% of full-time freshmen returned.
Faculty *Student/faculty ratio:* 15:1.
Academics *Calendar:* semesters. *Degree:* certificates and associate. *Special study options:* academic remediation for entering students, adult/continuing education programs, advanced placement credit, cooperative education, distance learning, English as a second language, external degree program, freshman honors college, honors programs, independent study, internships, off-campus study, part-time degree program, services for LD students, study abroad, summer session for credit.
Library FCC Library. *Books:* 11,831 (physical), 52,846 (digital/electronic); *Serial titles:* 19 (physical); *Databases:* 25. Students can reserve study rooms.
Student Life *Campus security:* 24-hour emergency response devices and patrols, late-night transport/escort service.
Athletics Member NJCAA.
Financial Aid Of all full-time matriculated undergraduates who enrolled in 2017, 25 Federal Work-Study jobs (averaging $1368). 14 state and other part-time jobs (averaging $2715).
Applying *Options:* electronic application. *Recommended:* high school transcript.
Freshman Application Contact Ms. Lisa A. Freel, Director of Admissions, Frederick Community College, 7932 Opossumtown Pike, Frederick, MD 21702. *Phone:* 301-846-2468. *Fax:* 301-624-2799. *E-mail:* admissions@frederick.edu. *Website:* http://www.frederick.edu/.

Garrett College

McHenry, Maryland

Freshman Application Contact Mrs. Shauna McQuade, Director of Enrollment Management, Garrett College, 687 Mosser Road, McHenry, MD 21541. *Phone:* 301-387-3739. *Toll-free phone:* 866-55-GARRETT. *E-mail:* admissions@garrettcollege.edu. *Website:* http://www.garrettcollege.edu/.

Hagerstown Community College

Hagerstown, Maryland

- **State and locally supported** 2-year, founded 1946
- **Suburban** 319-acre campus with easy access to Baltimore and Washington, DC
- **Coed**

Undergraduates 999 full-time, 3,070 part-time. 10% Black or African American, non-Hispanic/Latino; 6% Hispanic/Latino; 2% Asian, non-Hispanic/Latino; 0.1% Native Hawaiian or other Pacific Islander, non-Hispanic/Latino; 0.3% American Indian or Alaska Native, non-Hispanic/Latino; 4% Two or more races, non-Hispanic/Latino; 2% Race/ethnicity unknown; 1% international; 8% transferred in.

Faculty *Student/faculty ratio:* 17:1.

Academics *Calendar:* semesters. *Degree:* certificates and associate. *Special study options:* academic remediation for entering students, accelerated degree program, adult/continuing education programs, advanced placement credit, cooperative education, distance learning, English as a second language, honors programs, independent study, internships, off-campus study, part-time degree program, services for LD students, summer session for credit.

Library William Brish Library.

Student Life *Campus security:* 24-hour patrols, student patrols.

Athletics Member NJCAA.

Financial Aid Of all full-time matriculated undergraduates who enrolled in 2016, 721 applied for aid, 587 were judged to have need, 31 had their need fully met. 43 Federal Work-Study jobs (averaging $2054). 170 state and other part-time jobs (averaging $2797). In 2016, 23. *Average percent of need met:* 44. *Average financial aid package:* $5889. *Average need-based loan:* $2995. *Average need-based gift aid:* $4473. *Average non-need-based aid:* $964.

Applying *Options:* electronic application, deferred entrance. *Required for some:* high school transcript.

Admissions Office Contact Hagerstown Community College, 11400 Robinwood Drive, Hagerstown, MD 21742. *Website:* http://www.hagerstowncc.edu/.

Harford Community College

Bel Air, Maryland

- **State and locally supported** 2-year, founded 1957
- **Small-town** 352-acre campus with easy access to Baltimore
- **Coed**

Undergraduates 2,183 full-time, 3,917 part-time. Students come from 23 states and territories; 51 other countries; 4% are from out of state; 16% Black or African American, non-Hispanic/Latino; 5% Hispanic/Latino; 2% Asian, non-Hispanic/Latino; 0.2% Native Hawaiian or other Pacific Islander, non-Hispanic/Latino; 0.3% American Indian or Alaska Native, non-Hispanic/Latino; 4% Two or more races, non-Hispanic/Latino; 0.8% Race/ethnicity unknown; 1% international.

Faculty *Student/faculty ratio:* 21:1.

Academics *Calendar:* semesters. *Degree:* certificates, diplomas, and associate. *Special study options:* academic remediation for entering students, adult/continuing education programs, advanced placement credit, cooperative education, distance learning, double majors, English as a second language, honors programs, independent study, internships, part-time degree program, services for LD students, student-designed majors, study abroad, summer session for credit.

Library Harford Community College Library. *Books:* 43,126 (physical), 324,718 (digital/electronic); *Serial titles:* 828 (physical), 75 (digital/electronic); *Databases:* 79.

Student Life *Campus security:* 24-hour patrols, late-night transport/escort service.

Athletics Member NJCAA.

Financial Aid Of all full-time matriculated undergraduates who enrolled in 2016, 1,286 applied for aid, 889 were judged to have need. 57 Federal Work-Study jobs (averaging $1984).

Applying *Options:* electronic application.

Admissions Office Contact Harford Community College, 401 Thomas Run Road, Bel Air, MD 21015-1698. *Website:* http://www.harford.edu/.

Howard Community College

Columbia, Maryland

- **State and locally supported** 2-year, founded 1966
- **Suburban** 122-acre campus with easy access to Baltimore and Washington, DC
- **Coed**

Undergraduates Students come from 13 states and territories; 110 other countries; 0.6% are from out of state; 31% Black or African American, non-Hispanic/Latino; 11% Hispanic/Latino; 13% Asian, non-Hispanic/Latino; 0.3% Native Hawaiian or other Pacific Islander, non-Hispanic/Latino; 0.3% American Indian or Alaska Native, non-Hispanic/Latino; 5% Two or more races, non-Hispanic/Latino; 4% Race/ethnicity unknown.

Faculty *Student/faculty ratio:* 14:1.

Academics *Calendar:* semesters. *Degree:* certificates and associate. *Special study options:* academic remediation for entering students, adult/continuing education programs, advanced placement credit, cooperative education, distance learning, double majors, English as a second language, external degree program, freshman honors college, honors programs, internships, off-campus study, part-time degree program, services for LD students, study abroad, summer session for credit.

Library Howard Community College Library. Students can reserve study rooms.

Student Life *Campus security:* 24-hour emergency response devices and patrols, late-night transport/escort service.

Athletics Member NJCAA.

Standardized Tests *Required for some:* SAT or ACT (for admission).

Financial Aid Of all full-time matriculated undergraduates who enrolled in 2013, 571 applied for aid, 477 were judged to have need. In 2013, 31. *Average percent of need met:* 22. *Average financial aid package:* $3871. *Average need-based loan:* $2525. *Average need-based gift aid:* $4032. *Average non-need-based aid:* $1288.

Applying *Options:* electronic application, early admission, deferred entrance. *Application fee:* $25. *Required for some:* essay or personal statement, high school transcript, minimum 3.2 GPA, 2 letters of recommendation.

Freshman Application Contact Aaron Alder, Assistant Director of Admissions, Howard Community College, 10901 Little Patuxent Parkway, Columbia, MD 21044-3197. *Phone:* 443-518-4599. *Fax:* 443-518-4589. *E-mail:* admissions@howardcc.edu. *Website:* http://www.howardcc.edu/.

Lincoln College of Technology

Columbia, Maryland

Admissions Office Contact Lincoln College of Technology, 9325 Snowden River Parkway, Columbia, MD 21046. *Toll-free phone:* 844-215-1513. *Website:* http://www.lincolntech.edu/.

Montgomery College

Rockville, Maryland

- **State and locally supported** 2-year, founded 1946
- **Suburban** 333-acre campus with easy access to Washington, DC
- **Endowment** $26.1 million
- **Coed**

Undergraduates 8,060 full-time, 14,815 part-time. Students come from 24 states and territories; 163 other countries; 3% are from out of state; 26% Black or African American, non-Hispanic/Latino; 25% Hispanic/Latino; 12% Asian, non-Hispanic/Latino; 0.2% Native Hawaiian or other Pacific Islander, non-Hispanic/Latino; 0.3% American Indian or Alaska Native, non-Hispanic/Latino; 3% Two or more races, non-Hispanic/Latino; 0.1% Race/ethnicity unknown; 10% international; 65% transferred in.

Faculty *Student/faculty ratio:* 17:1.

Academics *Calendar:* semesters. *Degree:* certificates, diplomas, and associate. *Special study options:* academic remediation for entering students, adult/continuing education programs, advanced placement credit, cooperative education, distance learning, double majors, English as a second language, external degree program, honors programs, independent study, internships, off-campus study, part-time degree program, services for LD students, study abroad, summer session for credit. *ROTC:* Air Force (c).

Library Montgomery College Library plus 3 others. *Books:* 211,641 (physical), 57,782 (digital/electronic); *Serial titles:* 9,356 (physical), 104,416 (digital/electronic); *Databases:* 176. Weekly public service hours: 73; students can reserve study rooms.

Student Life *Campus security:* 24-hour emergency response devices and patrols.

Athletics Member NJCAA.

Applying *Options:* electronic application, early admission, deferred entrance. *Application fee:* $25. *Recommended:* high school transcript, interview.
Freshman Application Contact Montgomery College, 51 Mannakee Street, Rockville, MD 20850. *Phone:* 240-567-5036. *Website:* http://www.montgomerycollege.edu/.

Prince George's Community College
Largo, Maryland

Freshman Application Contact Ms. Vera Bagley, Director of Admissions and Records, Prince George's Community College, 301 Largo Road, Largo, MD 20774-2199. *Phone:* 301-322-0801. *Fax:* 301-322-0119. *E-mail:* enrollmentservices@pgcc.edu. *Website:* http://www.pgcc.edu/.

Wor-Wic Community College
Salisbury, Maryland

- **State and locally supported** 2-year, founded 1976
- **Small-town** 202-acre campus
- **Endowment** $19.0 million
- **Coed,** 3,025 undergraduate students, 26% full-time, 64% women, 36% men

Undergraduates 786 full-time, 2,239 part-time. Students come from 11 states and territories; 5 other countries; 3% are from out of state; 28% Black or African American, non-Hispanic/Latino; 6% Hispanic/Latino; 2% Asian, non-Hispanic/Latino; 0.1% Native Hawaiian or other Pacific Islander, non-Hispanic/Latino; 0.4% American Indian or Alaska Native, non-Hispanic/Latino; 4% Two or more races, non-Hispanic/Latino; 2% Race/ethnicity unknown; 0.7% international; 6% transferred in.
Freshmen *Admission:* 943 applied, 943 admitted, 606 enrolled.
Faculty *Total:* 161, 40% full-time, 21% with terminal degrees. *Student/faculty ratio:* 16:1.
Majors Administrative assistant and secretarial science; biology/biological sciences; business administration and management; business/commerce; child-care and support services management; computer and information sciences; computer systems analysis; criminal justice/police science; early childhood education; education; elementary education; emergency medical technology (EMT paramedic); hospitality administration; liberal arts and sciences and humanities related; medical radiologic technology; occupational therapist assistant; physical therapy technology; registered nursing/registered nurse; substance abuse/addiction counseling.
Academics *Calendar:* semesters. *Degree:* certificates and associate. *Special study options:* academic remediation for entering students, accelerated degree program, adult/continuing education programs, advanced placement credit, distance learning, double majors, English as a second language, honors programs, independent study, internships, part-time degree program, services for LD students, summer session for credit.
Library Patricia M. Hazel Resource Center plus 4 others. *Databases:* 55. Weekly public service hours: 70.
Student Life *Housing:* college housing not available. *Activities and Organizations:* Nursing Student Organization, Criminal Justice Club, The Gaming Association, Veterans - Military Association, Phi Theta Kappa (PTK): Alpha Nu Omicron. *Campus security:* 24-hour emergency response devices, late-night transport/escort service. *Student services:* personal/psychological counseling, veterans affairs office.
Applying *Options:* electronic application, early admission. *Recommended:* high school transcript. *Application deadlines:* rolling (freshmen), rolling (transfers).
Freshman Application Contact Ms. Angie N. Hayden, Director of Admissions and Records, Wor-Wic Community College, 32000 Campus Drive, Salisbury, MD 21804. *Phone:* 410-572-8712. *Fax:* 410-334-2954. *E-mail:* admissions@worwic.edu. *Website:* http://www.worwic.edu/.

MASSACHUSETTS

Bay State College
Boston, Massachusetts

Freshman Application Contact Kimberly Odusami, Director of Admissions, Bay State College, 122 Commonwealth Avenue, Boston, MA 02116. *Phone:* 617-217-9186. *Toll-free phone:* 800-81-LEARN. *E-mail:* admissions@baystate.edu. *Website:* http://www.baystate.edu/.

Benjamin Franklin Institute of Technology
Boston, Massachusetts

Freshman Application Contact Ms. Brittainy Johnson, Associate Director of Admissions, Benjamin Franklin Institute of Technology, Boston, MA 02116. *Phone:* 617-423-4630 Ext. 122. *Toll-free phone:* 877-400-BFIT. *Fax:* 617-482-3706. *E-mail:* bjohnson@bfit.edu. *Website:* http://www.bfit.edu/.

Berkshire Community College
Pittsfield, Massachusetts

Freshman Application Contact Ms. Tina Schettini, Senior Admissions Counselor, Berkshire Community College, 1350 West Street, Pittsfield, MA 01201-5786. *Phone:* 413-236-1635. *Toll-free phone:* 800-816-1233. *Fax:* 413-496-9511. *E-mail:* tschetti@berkshirecc.edu. *Website:* http://www.berkshirecc.edu/.

Bristol Community College
Fall River, Massachusetts

- **State-supported** 2-year, founded 1965, part of Massachusetts Community College System
- **Urban** 102-acre campus with easy access to Boston
- **Endowment** $9.5 million
- **Coed**

Undergraduates Students come from 7 other countries; 13% are from out of state; 8% Black or African American, non-Hispanic/Latino; 9% Hispanic/Latino; 2% Asian, non-Hispanic/Latino; 0.1% Native Hawaiian or other Pacific Islander, non-Hispanic/Latino; 0.2% American Indian or Alaska Native, non-Hispanic/Latino; 6% Two or more races, non-Hispanic/Latino; 5% Race/ethnicity unknown.
Faculty *Student/faculty ratio:* 16:1.
Academics *Calendar:* semesters. *Degree:* certificates and associate. *Special study options:* academic remediation for entering students, accelerated degree program, adult/continuing education programs, advanced placement credit, cooperative education, distance learning, English as a second language, honors programs, independent study, internships, off-campus study, part-time degree program, services for LD students, student-designed majors, summer session for credit.
Library Learning Resources Center plus 3 others. *Books:* 53,650 (physical), 47,790 (digital/electronic); *Serial titles:* 98 (physical); *Databases:* 83. Weekly public service hours: 73; students can reserve study rooms.
Student Life *Campus security:* 24-hour emergency response devices and patrols, late-night transport/escort service.
Athletics Member NJCAA.
Applying *Options:* electronic application, deferred entrance. *Application fee:* $10. *Required:* high school transcript.
Freshman Application Contact Dr. John McLaughlin, Dean of Admissions, Bristol Community College, 777 Elsbree Street, Fall River, MA 02720. *Phone:* 508-678-2811 Ext. 2947. *Fax:* 508-730-3265. *E-mail:* john.mclaughlin2@bristolcc.edu. *Website:* http://www.bristolcc.edu/.

Bunker Hill Community College
Boston, Massachusetts

- **State-supported** 2-year, founded 1973
- **Urban** 21-acre campus
- **Endowment** $4.6 million
- **Coed,** 12,657 undergraduate students, 33% full-time, 58% women, 42% men
- 89% of applicants were admitted

Undergraduates 4,185 full-time, 8,472 part-time. 26% Black or African American, non-Hispanic/Latino; 27% Hispanic/Latino; 11% Asian, non-Hispanic/Latino; 0.1% Native Hawaiian or other Pacific Islander, non-Hispanic/Latino; 0.3% American Indian or Alaska Native, non-Hispanic/Latino; 2% Two or more races, non-Hispanic/Latino; 8% Race/ethnicity unknown; 5% international.
Freshmen *Admission:* 7,383 applied, 6,606 admitted, 2,688 enrolled.
Faculty *Total:* 780, 19% full-time. *Student/faculty ratio:* 22:1.
Majors Accounting; art; bioengineering and biomedical engineering; biology/biological sciences; biotechnology; business administration and management; business administration, management and operations related; business operations support and secretarial services related; cardiovascular technology; chemistry; clinical/medical laboratory technology; computer and information sciences and support services related; computer and information systems security; computer/information technology services administration related; computer programming; computer programming (specific

applications); computer science; computer systems networking and telecommunications; criminal justice/law enforcement administration; criminal justice/police science; culinary arts; data entry/microcomputer applications; design and visual communications; diagnostic medical sonography and ultrasound technology; early childhood education; education; electrical/electronics maintenance and repair technology related; emergency medical technology (EMT paramedic); engineering; English; entrepreneurship; finance; fine arts related; fire prevention and safety technology; foreign languages and literatures; general studies; health information/medical records administration; history; hospitality administration; hospitality administration related; human services; international business/trade/commerce; legal assistant/paralegal; mass communication/media; mathematics; medical administrative assistant and medical secretary; medical radiologic technology; music; operations management; physics; psychology; registered nursing/registered nurse; respiratory therapy technician; sociology; speech communication and rhetoric; sport and fitness administration/management; tourism and travel services management; web page, digital/multimedia and information resources design.

Academics *Calendar:* semesters. *Degree:* certificates and associate. *Special study options:* academic remediation for entering students, accelerated degree program, advanced placement credit, cooperative education, distance learning, English as a second language, external degree program, honors programs, independent study, internships, part-time degree program, services for LD students, study abroad, summer session for credit.

Library Bunker Hill Community College Library. *Books:* 40,964 (physical), 80,596 (digital/electronic); *Serial titles:* 92 (physical), 39 (digital/electronic); *Databases:* 105.

Student Life *Housing:* college housing not available. *Activities and Organizations:* drama/theater group, student-run radio station, choral group, Alpha Kappa Mu Honor Society, Asian-Pacific Students Association, Music Club, Latinos Unidos Club, Christian Fellowship. *Campus security:* 24-hour emergency response devices and patrols, late-night transport/escort service. *Student services:* health clinic, personal/psychological counseling, veterans affairs office.

Athletics Member NJCAA. *Intercollegiate sports:* baseball M, basketball M/W, soccer M/W, volleyball W.

Financial Aid Of all full-time matriculated undergraduates who enrolled in 2017, 159 Federal Work-Study jobs (averaging $2712).

Applying *Options:* electronic application. *Required:* high school transcript. *Application deadlines:* rolling (freshmen), rolling (transfers). *Notification:* continuous (freshmen), continuous (transfers).

Director of Admissions Francine S. Kupferman, Director of Admissions and Recruitment, Bunker Hill Community College, 250 New Rutherford Avenue, Boston, MA 02129. *Phone:* 617-228-3398. *Fax:* 617-228-3481. *E-mail:* Admissions@bhcc.mass.edu. *Website:* http://www.bhcc.mass.edu/.

Cape Cod Community College

West Barnstable, Massachusetts

Freshman Application Contact Director of Admissions, Cape Cod Community College, 2240 Iyannough Road, West Barnstable, MA 02668-1599. *Phone:* 508-362-2131 Ext. 4311. *Toll-free phone:* 877-846-3672. *Fax:* 508-375-4089. *E-mail:* admiss@capecod.edu. *Website:* http://www.capecod.edu/.

FINE Mortuary College, LLC

Norwood, Massachusetts

- **Proprietary** 2-year, founded 1996
- **Suburban** campus with easy access to Boston
- **Coed**

Undergraduates 15 full-time, 84 part-time. Students come from 6 states and territories; 23% are from out of state; 8% Black or African American, non-Hispanic/Latino; 4% Hispanic/Latino; 1% American Indian or Alaska Native, non-Hispanic/Latino; 1% Two or more races, non-Hispanic/Latino; 1% transferred in.

Faculty *Student/faculty ratio:* 8:1.

Academics *Calendar:* continuous. *Degree:* associate. *Special study options:* academic remediation for entering students, adult/continuing education programs, cooperative education, distance learning, internships, off-campus study, part-time degree program, summer session for credit.

Library FINE Multimedia Center. *Books:* 550 (physical); *Serial titles:* 3 (physical).

Applying *Application fee:* $75. *Required:* essay or personal statement, high school transcript, 1 letter of recommendation. *Recommended:* interview.

Freshman Application Contact FINE Mortuary College, LLC, 150 Kerry Place, Norwood, MA 02062. *Phone:* 781-762-1211. *Website:* http://www.fmc.edu/.

Greenfield Community College

Greenfield, Massachusetts

Freshman Application Contact Ms. Colleen Kucinski, Assistant Director of Admission, Greenfield Community College, 1 College Drive, Greenfield, MA 01301-9739. *Phone:* 413-775-1000. *Fax:* 413-773-5129. *E-mail:* admission@gcc.mass.edu. *Website:* http://www.gcc.mass.edu/.

Holyoke Community College

Holyoke, Massachusetts

- **State-supported** 2-year, founded 1946, part of Massachusetts Public Higher Education System
- **Small-town** 135-acre campus
- **Endowment** $13.0 million
- **Coed**

Undergraduates 2,506 full-time, 3,059 part-time. Students come from 18 states and territories; 1% are from out of state; 6% Black or African American, non-Hispanic/Latino; 27% Hispanic/Latino; 3% Asian, non-Hispanic/Latino; 0.4% American Indian or Alaska Native, non-Hispanic/Latino; 3% Two or more races, non-Hispanic/Latino; 2% Race/ethnicity unknown; 0.8% international; 7% transferred in.

Faculty *Student/faculty ratio:* 15:1.

Academics *Calendar:* semesters. *Degree:* certificates and associate. *Special study options:* academic remediation for entering students, adult/continuing education programs, advanced placement credit, cooperative education, distance learning, double majors, English as a second language, honors programs, independent study, internships, off-campus study, part-time degree program, services for LD students, student-designed majors, study abroad, summer session for credit. *ROTC:* Army (c), Air Force (c).

Library Holyoke Community College Library plus 1 other. *Books:* 40,127 (physical), 62,355 (digital/electronic); *Serial titles:* 22 (physical), 32,539 (digital/electronic); *Databases:* 183. Weekly public service hours: 65; students can reserve study rooms.

Student Life *Campus security:* 24-hour emergency response devices and patrols, late-night transport/escort service.

Athletics Member NJCAA.

Applying *Options:* electronic application, early admission, deferred entrance. *Required:* high school transcript. *Recommended:* interview.

Freshman Application Contact Ms. Renee Tastad, Director of Admissions and Transfer Affairs, Holyoke Community College, Admission Office, Holyoke, MA 01040. *Phone:* 413-552-2321. *Fax:* 413-552-2045. *E-mail:* admissions@hcc.edu. *Website:* http://www.hcc.edu/.

Labouré College

Milton, Massachusetts

Director of Admissions Ms. Gina M. Morrissette, Director of Admissions, Labouré College, 303 Adams Street, Milton, MA 02186. *Phone:* 617-296-8300. *Website:* http://www.laboure.edu/.

Lawrence Memorial/Regis College

Medford, Massachusetts

Admissions Office Contact Lawrence Memorial/Regis College, 170 Governors Avenue, Medford, MA 02155. *Website:* http://www.lmregis.org/.

Massachusetts Bay Community College

Wellesley Hills, Massachusetts

- **State-supported** 2-year, founded 1961
- **Suburban** 84-acre campus with easy access to Boston
- **Coed,** 4,368 undergraduate students, 34% full-time, 53% women, 47% men

Undergraduates 1,471 full-time, 2,897 part-time. Students come from 10 states and territories; 73 other countries; 1% are from out of state; 16% Black or African American, non-Hispanic/Latino; 21% Hispanic/Latino; 4% Asian, non-Hispanic/Latino; 0.1% Native Hawaiian or other Pacific Islander, non-Hispanic/Latino; 0.4% American Indian or Alaska Native, non-Hispanic/Latino; 2% Two or more races, non-Hispanic/Latino; 5% Race/ethnicity unknown; 2% international; 6% transferred in. *Retention:* 57% of full-time freshmen returned.

Freshmen *Admission:* 2,589 applied, 2,060 admitted, 925 enrolled.

Faculty *Total:* 341, 21% full-time. *Student/faculty ratio:* 17:1.

Majors Accounting; animal physiology; automobile/automotive mechanics technology; bioinformatics; biological and biomedical sciences related; biology/biotechnology laboratory technician; business administration and management; community health and preventive medicine; computer and information sciences and support services related; computer and information systems security; computer/information technology services administration related; computer science; criminal justice/law enforcement administration; early childhood education; electrical and electronic engineering technologies related; electrical, electronic and communications engineering technology; elementary education; engineering technologies and engineering related; engineering technology; English; environmental control technologies related; general studies; hospitality administration; international business/trade/commerce; international/global studies; legal assistant/paralegal; liberal arts and sciences/liberal studies; mathematics; mechanical engineering/mechanical technology; network and system administration; radiologic technology/science; registered nursing/registered nurse; social sciences.

Academics *Calendar:* semesters. *Degree:* certificates and associate. *Special study options:* academic remediation for entering students, adult/continuing education programs, advanced placement credit, cooperative education, distance learning, double majors, English as a second language, honors programs, independent study, internships, part-time degree program, services for LD students, study abroad, summer session for credit.

Library Perkins Library plus 1 other. *Books:* 20,790 (physical), 6,806 (digital/electronic); *Serial titles:* 27 (physical), 322,824 (digital/electronic); *Databases:* 117. Weekly public service hours: 66.

Student Life *Housing:* college housing not available. *Activities and Organizations:* drama/theater group, choral group, Veterans Club, Gamer's Guild, Nursing Club, Student Government Association, International Club. *Campus security:* 24-hour emergency response devices and patrols. *Student services:* personal/psychological counseling, veterans affairs office.

Athletics Member NJCAA. *Intercollegiate sports:* basketball W, cross-country running W, volleyball W. *Intramural sports:* basketball M, soccer M, volleyball M.

Applying *Options:* electronic application, deferred entrance. *Required for some:* high school transcript. *Application deadlines:* rolling (freshmen), rolling (transfers). *Notification:* continuous (freshmen), continuous (transfers).

Freshman Application Contact Ms. Alison McCarty, Director of Admissions, Massachusetts Bay Community College, 50 Oakland Street, Wellesley Hills, MA 02481. *Phone:* 781-239-2506. *E-mail:* amccarty1@massbay.edu.
Website: http://www.massbay.edu/.

Massasoit Community College
Brockton, Massachusetts

Freshman Application Contact Michelle Hughes, Director of Admissions, Massasoit Community College, 1 Massasoit Boulevard, Brockton, MA 02302-3996. *Phone:* 508-588-9100. *Toll-free phone:* 800-CAREERS. *Website:* http://www.massasoit.mass.edu/.

Middlesex Community College
Bedford, Massachusetts

Freshman Application Contact Middlesex Community College, 591 Springs Road, Bedford, MA 01730-1655. *Phone:* 978-656-3211. *Toll-free phone:* 800-818-3434. *Website:* http://www.middlesex.mass.edu/.

Mount Wachusett Community College
Gardner, Massachusetts

- **State-supported** 2-year, founded 1963, part of Massachusetts Public Higher Education System
- **Small-town** 270-acre campus with easy access to Boston
- **Endowment** $399,545
- **Coed**

Undergraduates 1,345 full-time, 2,509 part-time. Students come from 9 states and territories; 7 other countries; 7% Black or African American, non-Hispanic/Latino; 16% Hispanic/Latino; 2% Asian, non-Hispanic/Latino; 0.1% Native Hawaiian or other Pacific Islander, non-Hispanic/Latino; 0.4% American Indian or Alaska Native, non-Hispanic/Latino; 2% Two or more races, non-Hispanic/Latino; 4% Race/ethnicity unknown; 0.3% international; 7% transferred in.

Faculty *Student/faculty ratio:* 12:1.

Academics *Calendar:* semesters. *Degree:* certificates, diplomas, and associate. *Special study options:* academic remediation for entering students, accelerated degree program, adult/continuing education programs, advanced placement credit, cooperative education, distance learning, double majors, English as a second language, honors programs, independent study, internships, part-time degree program, services for LD students, study abroad, summer session for credit. *ROTC:* Army (c).

Library LaChance Library. *Books:* 36,000 (physical), 43,164 (digital/electronic); *Serial titles:* 24 (physical); *Databases:* 67. Weekly public service hours: 57; students can reserve study rooms.

Student Life *Campus security:* 24-hour emergency response devices and patrols, late-night transport/escort service, security cameras, access cards for laboratory access.

Financial Aid Of all full-time matriculated undergraduates who enrolled in 2017, 1,132 applied for aid, 890 were judged to have need, 22 had their need fully met. In 2017, 18. *Average percent of need met:* 97. *Average financial aid package:* $6125. *Average need-based loan:* $1888. *Average need-based gift aid:* $5572. *Average non-need-based aid:* $798.

Applying *Options:* electronic application, early admission. *Required for some:* high school transcript.

Freshman Application Contact Ms. Marcia Rosbury-Henne, Dean of Admissions and Enrollment, Mount Wachusett Community College, 444 Green Street, Gardner, MA 01440-1378. *Phone:* 978-632-6600 Ext. 337. *Fax:* 978-630-9558. *E-mail:* admissions@mwcc.mass.edu. *Website:* http://www.mwcc.edu/.

Northern Essex Community College
Haverhill, Massachusetts

- **State-supported** 2-year, founded 1960
- **Suburban** 106-acre campus with easy access to Boston
- **Endowment** $3.8 million
- **Coed**

Undergraduates 1,943 full-time, 3,783 part-time. Students come from 9 states and territories; 1 other country; 13% are from out of state; 4% Black or African American, non-Hispanic/Latino; 42% Hispanic/Latino; 2% Asian, non-Hispanic/Latino; 0.3% Native Hawaiian or other Pacific Islander, non-Hispanic/Latino; 0.2% American Indian or Alaska Native, non-Hispanic/Latino; 1% Two or more races, non-Hispanic/Latino; 5% Race/ethnicity unknown; 0.6% international; 5% transferred in. *Retention:* 58% of full-time freshmen returned.

Academics *Calendar:* semesters. *Degree:* certificates and associate. *Special study options:* academic remediation for entering students, adult/continuing education programs, advanced placement credit, cooperative education, distance learning, double majors, English as a second language, freshman honors college, honors programs, independent study, internships, off-campus study, part-time degree program, services for LD students, study abroad, summer session for credit. *ROTC:* Air Force (c).

Library Bentley Library. *Books:* 41,604 (physical), 11,287 (digital/electronic); *Serial titles:* 3,440 (physical), 27,741 (digital/electronic); *Databases:* 68.

Student Life *Campus security:* 24-hour emergency response devices and patrols.

Athletics Member NJCAA.

Standardized Tests *Required for some:* Psychological Corporation Aptitude Test for practical nursing.

Financial Aid Of all full-time matriculated undergraduates who enrolled in 2017, 74 Federal Work-Study jobs (averaging $1759).

Applying *Options:* early admission. *Required:* high school transcript.

Freshman Application Contact Northern Essex Community College, 100 Elliott Street, Haverhill, MA 01830. *Phone:* 978-556-3616. *Website:* http://www.necc.mass.edu/.

North Shore Community College
Danvers, Massachusetts

- **State-supported** 2-year, founded 1965
- **Suburban** campus with easy access to Boston
- **Endowment** $7.4 million
- **Coed**

Undergraduates Students come from 14 states and territories; 7 other countries; 2% are from out of state; 10% Black or African American, non-Hispanic/Latino; 24% Hispanic/Latino; 4% Asian, non-Hispanic/Latino; 0.2% Native Hawaiian or other Pacific Islander, non-Hispanic/Latino; 0.1% American Indian or Alaska Native, non-Hispanic/Latino; 3% Two or more races, non-Hispanic/Latino; 1% Race/ethnicity unknown; 0.1% international.

Faculty *Student/faculty ratio:* 17:1.

Academics *Calendar:* semesters. *Degree:* certificates and associate. *Special study options:* academic remediation for entering students, accelerated degree program, adult/continuing education programs, advanced placement credit, cooperative education, distance learning, English as a second language, honors programs, independent study, internships, part-time degree program, services for LD students, summer session for credit.

Library Learning Resource Center plus 2 others.

Student Life *Campus security:* 24-hour emergency response devices and patrols, late-night transport/escort service.

Financial Aid Of all full-time matriculated undergraduates who enrolled in 2009, 1,658 applied for aid, 1,438 were judged to have need, 23 had their need fully met. 123 Federal Work-Study jobs (averaging $1359). In 2009, 11. *Average percent of need met:* 18. *Average financial aid package:* $6856. *Average need-based loan:* $1639. *Average need-based gift aid:* $2522. *Average non-need-based aid:* $614.
Applying *Options:* electronic application, early admission, deferred entrance. *Required for some:* essay or personal statement, high school transcript, interview.
Freshman Application Contact Mrs. Gissel Lopez, Academic Counselor, North Shore Community College, Danvers, MA 01923. *Phone:* 978-762-4000 Ext. 2108. *Fax:* 978-762-4015. *E-mail:* gilopez@northshore.edu. *Website:* http://www.northshore.edu/.

Quincy College
Quincy, Massachusetts

Freshman Application Contact Quincy College, 1250 Hancock Street, Quincy, MA 02169. *Phone:* 617-984-1710. *Toll-free phone:* 800-698-1700. *Website:* http://www.quincycollege.edu/.

Quinsigamond Community College
Worcester, Massachusetts

- **State-supported** 2-year, founded 1963, part of Massachusetts System of Higher Education
- **Urban** 57-acre campus with easy access to Boston
- **Endowment** $473,714
- **Coed,** 7,265 undergraduate students, 35% full-time, 58% women, 42% men

Undergraduates 2,541 full-time, 4,724 part-time. Students come from 19 states and territories; 35 other countries; 1% are from out of state; 13% Black or African American, non-Hispanic/Latino; 20% Hispanic/Latino; 5% Asian, non-Hispanic/Latino; 0.1% Native Hawaiian or other Pacific Islander, non-Hispanic/Latino; 0.4% American Indian or Alaska Native, non-Hispanic/Latino; 3% Two or more races, non-Hispanic/Latino; 5% Race/ethnicity unknown; 0.5% international; 10% transferred in.
Freshmen *Admission:* 4,052 applied, 2,632 admitted, 1,487 enrolled.
Faculty *Total:* 567, 24% full-time, 14% with terminal degrees. *Student/faculty ratio:* 16:1.
Majors Automobile/automotive mechanics technology; biology/biological sciences; biomedical technology; biotechnology; business administration and management; business/commerce; chemistry; computer and information sciences; computer and information systems security; computer engineering technology; computer graphics; computer programming; computer programming (specific applications); computer science; computer support specialist; computer systems analysis; criminal justice/police science; data modeling/warehousing and database administration; deaf studies; dental hygiene; dental services and allied professions related; directing and theatrical production; early childhood education; electrical, electronic and communications engineering technology; elementary education; emergency medical technology (EMT paramedic); energy management and systems technology; English; executive assistant/executive secretary; fire services administration; game and interactive media design; general studies; health information/medical records technology; health services/allied health/health sciences; history; hospitality administration; human services; kindergarten/preschool education; laser and optical technology; liberal arts and sciences/liberal studies; manufacturing engineering technology; medical administrative assistant and medical secretary; music; occupational therapist assistant; pre-engineering; pre-pharmacy studies; psychology; radiologic technology/science; registered nursing/registered nurse; respiratory care therapy; restaurant/food services management; sociology; web page, digital/multimedia and information resources design.
Academics *Calendar:* semesters. *Degree:* certificates and associate. *Special study options:* academic remediation for entering students, accelerated degree program, advanced placement credit, cooperative education, distance learning, double majors, English as a second language, honors programs, independent study, internships, off-campus study, part-time degree program, services for LD students, summer session for credit. *ROTC:* Army (c).
Library Alden Library plus 1 other. *Books:* 43,862 (physical), 83,063 (digital/electronic); *Serial titles:* 12 (physical), 62,000 (digital/electronic); *Databases:* 61. Weekly public service hours: 67; students can reserve study rooms.
Student Life *Housing:* college housing not available. *Activities and Organizations:* drama/theater group, student-run newspaper, Academic-Related Clubs, Phi Theta Kappa, Student Senate, Anime Club, Psi Beta Club. *Campus security:* 24-hour emergency response devices and patrols, late-night transport/escort service. *Student services:* personal/psychological counseling, veterans affairs office.
Athletics Member NJCAA. *Intercollegiate sports:* baseball M, basketball M/W. *Intramural sports:* basketball M/W, cheerleading W(c), soccer M/W, table tennis M/W, ultimate Frisbee M/W, volleyball M/W.
Applying *Options:* electronic application. *Application fee:* $20. *Required:* high school transcript. *Required for some:* interview. *Application deadlines:* rolling (freshmen), rolling (transfers). *Notification:* continuous (freshmen), continuous (transfers).
Director of Admissions Mishawn Davis-Eyene, Director of Admissions, Quinsigamond Community College, 670 West Boylston Street, Worcester, MA 01606-2092. *Phone:* 508-854-4576. *E-mail:* meyene@qcc.mass.edu. *Website:* http://www.qcc.edu/.

Roxbury Community College
Roxbury Crossing, Massachusetts

Director of Admissions Nancy Santos, Director, Admissions, Roxbury Community College, 1234 Columbus Avenue, Roxbury Crossing, MA 02120-3400. *Phone:* 617-541-5310. *Website:* http://www.rcc.mass.edu/.

Salter College
Chicopee, Massachusetts

Admissions Office Contact Salter College, 645 Shawinigan Drive, Chicopee, MA 01020. *Website:* http://www.saltercollege.com/.

Salter College
West Boylston, Massachusetts

Admissions Office Contact Salter College, 184 West Boylston Street, West Boylston, MA 01583. *Website:* http://www.saltercollege.com/.

Springfield Technical Community College
Springfield, Massachusetts

- **State-supported** 2-year, founded 1967
- **Urban** 34-acre campus
- **Coed**

Undergraduates 2,287 full-time, 3,056 part-time. Students come from 16 states and territories; 41 other countries; 2% are from out of state; 16% Black or African American, non-Hispanic/Latino; 29% Hispanic/Latino; 3% Asian, non-Hispanic/Latino; 0.1% Native Hawaiian or other Pacific Islander, non-Hispanic/Latino; 0.3% American Indian or Alaska Native, non-Hispanic/Latino; 3% Two or more races, non-Hispanic/Latino; 6% Race/ethnicity unknown; 6% transferred in. *Retention:* 55% of full-time freshmen returned.
Faculty *Student/faculty ratio:* 15:1.
Academics *Calendar:* semesters. *Degree:* certificates and associate. *Special study options:* academic remediation for entering students, adult/continuing education programs, advanced placement credit, cooperative education, distance learning, English as a second language, honors programs, independent study, internships, off-campus study, part-time degree program, services for LD students, summer session for credit.
Library Springfield Technical Community College Library. *Books:* 45,975 (physical), 9,270 (digital/electronic); *Serial titles:* 159 (physical), 12 (digital/electronic); *Databases:* 93. Weekly public service hours: 61.
Student Life *Campus security:* 24-hour emergency response devices and patrols, late-night transport/escort service.
Athletics Member NJCAA.
Standardized Tests *Required for some:* SAT (for admission).
Applying *Options:* electronic application. *Required:* high school transcript. *Required for some:* interview.
Freshman Application Contact Mr. LaRue Pierce, Dean of Students, Springfield Technical Community College, Springfield, MA 01105. *Phone:* 413-781-7822 Ext. 4078. *E-mail:* lapierce@stcc.edu. *Website:* http://www.stcc.edu/.

Urban College of Boston
Boston, Massachusetts

- **Independent** 2-year, founded 1993
- **Urban** campus with easy access to Boston
- **Coed, primarily women**

Undergraduates 59 full-time, 753 part-time. 0.7% transferred in. *Retention:* 33% of full-time freshmen returned.
Faculty *Student/faculty ratio:* 12:1.

Academics *Calendar:* semesters. *Degree:* certificates and associate. *Special study options:* part-time degree program.
Student Life *Campus security:* 24-hour emergency response devices.
Applying *Application fee:* $10. *Required for some:* high school transcript.
Admissions Office Contact Urban College of Boston, 2 Boylston Street, 2nd Floor, Boston, MA 02116. *Website:* http://www.urbancollege.edu/.

MICHIGAN

Alpena Community College
Alpena, Michigan

Freshman Application Contact Mr. Mike Kollien, Director of Admissions, Alpena Community College, 665 Johnson, Alpena, MI 49707. *Phone:* 989-358-7339. *Toll-free phone:* 888-468-6222. *Fax:* 989-358-7540. *E-mail:* kollienm@alpenacc.edu. *Website:* http://www.alpenacc.edu/.

Bay de Noc Community College
Escanaba, Michigan

Freshman Application Contact Ms. Jessica LeMarch, Director of Admissions, Bay de Noc Community College, 2001 North Lincoln Road, Escanaba, MI 49829. *Phone:* 906-217-4010. *Toll-free phone:* 800-221-2001. *Fax:* 906-217-1714. *E-mail:* jessica.lamarch@baycollege.edu. *Website:* http://www.baycollege.edu/.

Bay Mills Community College
Brimley, Michigan

Freshman Application Contact Ms. Elaine Lehre, Admissions Officer, Bay Mills Community College, 12214 West Lakeshore Drive, Brimley, MI 49715. *Phone:* 906-248-3354. *Toll-free phone:* 800-844-BMCC. *Fax:* 906-248-3351. *Website:* http://www.bmcc.edu/.

Career Quest Learning Center–Jackson
Jackson, Michigan

Admissions Office Contact Career Quest Learning Center–Jackson, 209 East Washington Avenue, Suite 241, Jackson, MI 49201. *Website:* http://www.careerquest.edu/.

Career Quest Learning Center–Lansing
Lansing, Michigan

Admissions Office Contact Career Quest Learning Center–Lansing, 3215 South Pennsylvania Avenue, Lansing, MI 48910. *Website:* http://www.careerquest.edu/.

Career Quest Learning Center–Mt. Pleasant
Mount Pleasant, Michigan

Admissions Office Contact Career Quest Learning Center–Mt. Pleasant, 2116 South Mission Street, Mount Pleasant, MI 48858. *Website:* http://www.careerquest.edu/.

Delta College
University Center, Michigan

Freshman Application Contact Mr. Zachary Ward, Director of Admissions and Recruitment, Delta College, 1961 Delta Road, University Center, MI 48710. *Phone:* 989-686-9590. *Fax:* 989-667-2202. *E-mail:* admit@delta.edu. *Website:* http://www.delta.edu/.

Glen Oaks Community College
Centreville, Michigan

Freshman Application Contact Ms. Beverly M. Andrews, Director of Admissions/Registrar, Glen Oaks Community College, 62249 Shimmel Road, Centreville, MI 49032-9719. *Phone:* 269-294-4249. *Toll-free phone:* 888-994-7818. *Fax:* 269-467-4114. *E-mail:* thowden@glenoaks.edu. *Website:* http://www.glenoaks.edu/.

Gogebic Community College
Ironwood, Michigan

Freshman Application Contact Ms. Kim Zeckovich, Director of Admissions, Marketing, and Public Relations, Gogebic Community College, E. 4946 Jackson Road, Ironwood, MI 49938. *Phone:* 906-932-4231 Ext. 347. *Toll-free phone:* 800-682-5910. *Fax:* 906-932-2339. *E-mail:* jeanneg@gogebic.edu. *Website:* http://www.gogebic.edu/.

Grand Rapids Community College
Grand Rapids, Michigan

- **District-supported** 2-year, founded 1914, part of Michigan Department of Education
- **Urban** 35-acre campus
- **Endowment** $31.2 million
- **Coed,** 13,767 undergraduate students, 30% full-time, 52% women, 48% men

Undergraduates 4,104 full-time, 9,663 part-time. Students come from 3 states and territories; 6 other countries; 1% are from out of state; 9% Black or African American, non-Hispanic/Latino; 14% Hispanic/Latino; 4% Asian, non-Hispanic/Latino; 0.1% Native Hawaiian or other Pacific Islander, non-Hispanic/Latino; 0.5% American Indian or Alaska Native, non-Hispanic/Latino; 3% Two or more races, non-Hispanic/Latino; 8% Race/ethnicity unknown; 0.4% international; 8% transferred in.
Freshmen *Admission:* 8,687 applied, 2,904 enrolled. *Average high school GPA:* 2.9.
Faculty *Total:* 705, 31% full-time. *Student/faculty ratio:* 21:1.
Majors Accounting technology and bookkeeping; architectural technology; architecture; art; automation engineer technology; automobile/automotive mechanics technology; business administration and management; chemical technology; child-care and support services management; commercial and advertising art; computer programming; computer support specialist; computer systems networking and telecommunications; corrections; criminal justice/police science; culinary arts; dental assisting; dental hygiene; electrical, electronic and communications engineering technology; fashion merchandising; fine/studio arts; heating, air conditioning, ventilation and refrigeration maintenance technology; industrial mechanics and maintenance technology; interior design; landscaping and groundskeeping; liberal arts and sciences/liberal studies; manufacturing engineering technology; music; music teacher education; plastics and polymer engineering technology; quality control technology; registered nursing/registered nurse; restaurant, culinary, and catering management; web page, digital/multimedia and information resources design; welding technology.
Academics *Calendar:* semesters. *Degree:* certificates and associate. *Special study options:* academic remediation for entering students, adult/continuing education programs, advanced placement credit, cooperative education, distance learning, English as a second language, honors programs, independent study, internships, off-campus study, part-time degree program, services for LD students, study abroad, summer session for credit.
Library Arthur Andrews Memorial Library. *Books:* 67,050 (physical), 168,882 (digital/electronic); *Serial titles:* 357 (physical), 25,196 (digital/electronic); *Databases:* 100. Students can reserve study rooms.
Student Life *Housing:* college housing not available. *Activities and Organizations:* drama/theater group, student-run newspaper, choral group, Student Alliance, Phi Theta Kappa, Hispanic Student Organization, Student Gamers Association, Foreign Affairs Club. *Campus security:* 24-hour emergency response devices, late-night transport/escort service. *Student services:* personal/psychological counseling, veterans affairs office.
Athletics Member NJCAA. *Intercollegiate sports:* baseball M, basketball M/W, cross-country running M/W, golf M, softball W, volleyball W.
Financial Aid Of all full-time matriculated undergraduates who enrolled in 2008, 6,142 applied for aid, 4,896 were judged to have need, 1,012 had their need fully met. In 2008, 96 non-need-based awards were made. *Average financial aid package:* $4850. *Average need-based loan:* $2764. *Average need-based gift aid:* $3984. *Average non-need-based aid:* $1051.
Applying *Options:* electronic application, deferred entrance. *Required:* high school transcript. *Application deadline:* rolling (transfers). *Notification:* continuous (freshmen), continuous (transfers).
Freshman Application Contact Ms. Lori Cook, Director of Admissions, Grand Rapids Community College, Grand Rapids, MI 49503-3201. *Phone:* 616-234-4100. *Fax:* 616-234-4005. *E-mail:* lcook@grcc.edu. *Website:* http://www.grcc.edu/.

Henry Ford College
Dearborn, Michigan

Freshman Application Contact Admissions Office, Henry Ford College, 5101 Evergreen Road, Dearborn, MI 48128-1495. *Phone:* 313-845-6403. *Toll-free phone:* 800-585-HFCC. *Fax:* 313-845-6464. *E-mail:* enroll@hfcc.edu. *Website:* http://www.hfcc.edu/.

Jackson College
Jackson, Michigan

Freshman Application Contact Mr. Daniel Vainner, Registrar, Jackson College, 2111 Emmons Road, Jackson, MI 49201. *Phone:* 517-796-8425. *Toll-free phone:* 888-522-7344. *Fax:* 517-796-8446. *E-mail:* admissions@jccmi.edu. *Website:* http://www.jccmi.edu/.

Kalamazoo Valley Community College
Kalamazoo, Michigan

Freshman Application Contact Kalamazoo Valley Community College, PO Box 4070, Kalamazoo, MI 49003-4070. *Phone:* 269-488-4207. *Website:* http://www.kvcc.edu/.

Kellogg Community College
Battle Creek, Michigan

- **State and locally supported** 2-year, founded 1956, part of Michigan Department of Education
- **Urban** 120-acre campus
- **Coed**

Undergraduates 1,160 full-time, 3,654 part-time. Students come from 3 other countries; 9% Black or African American, non-Hispanic/Latino; 5% Hispanic/Latino; 2% Asian, non-Hispanic/Latino; 0.1% Native Hawaiian or other Pacific Islander, non-Hispanic/Latino; 1% American Indian or Alaska Native, non-Hispanic/Latino; 4% Two or more races, non-Hispanic/Latino; 9% Race/ethnicity unknown; 0.4% international; 5% transferred in.
Faculty *Student/faculty ratio:* 17:1.
Academics *Calendar:* semesters. *Degree:* certificates and associate. *Special study options:* academic remediation for entering students, accelerated degree program, adult/continuing education programs, advanced placement credit, cooperative education, distance learning, double majors, English as a second language, freshman honors college, honors programs, independent study, internships, off-campus study, part-time degree program, services for LD students, summer session for credit.
Library Emory W. Morris Learning Resource Center. *Books:* 51,629 (physical), 20,975 (digital/electronic); *Serial titles:* 62 (physical), 74,000 (digital/electronic); *Databases:* 67. Weekly public service hours: 81; students can reserve study rooms.
Student Life *Campus security:* 24-hour emergency response devices and patrols, late-night transport/escort service.
Athletics Member NJCAA.
Financial Aid Of all full-time matriculated undergraduates who enrolled in 2017, 41 Federal Work-Study jobs (averaging $2251). 43 state and other part-time jobs (averaging $2058).
Applying *Options:* electronic application, early admission. *Required for some:* high school transcript, minimum 2.0 GPA.
Freshman Application Contact Ms. Nicole Jewell, Director of Admissions, Kellogg Community College, 450 North Avenue, Battle Creek, MI 49017. *Phone:* 269-965-3931. *Fax:* 269-965-4133. *E-mail:* jewelln@kellogg.edu. *Website:* http://www.kellogg.edu/.

Keweenaw Bay Ojibwa Community College
Baraga, Michigan

Freshman Application Contact Ms. Megan Shanahan, Admissions Officer, Keweenaw Bay Ojibwa Community College, 111 Beartown Road, Baraga, MI 49908. *Phone:* 909-353-4600. *E-mail:* megan@kbocc.org. *Website:* http://www.kbocc.edu/.

Kirtland Community College
Roscommon, Michigan

- **District-supported** 2-year, founded 1966
- **Rural** 180-acre campus
- **Coed**

Undergraduates 499 full-time, 1,029 part-time. Students come from 7 states and territories; 1% Black or African American, non-Hispanic/Latino; 2% Hispanic/Latino; 0.7% Asian, non-Hispanic/Latino; 1% American Indian or Alaska Native, non-Hispanic/Latino; 1% Two or more races, non-Hispanic/Latino; 1% Race/ethnicity unknown.
Faculty *Student/faculty ratio:* 17:1.
Academics *Calendar:* semesters. *Degree:* certificates and associate. *Special study options:* academic remediation for entering students, adult/continuing education programs, advanced placement credit, cooperative education, distance learning, honors programs, independent study, internships, part-time degree program, services for LD students, summer session for credit.
Library Kirtland Community College Library plus 1 other. *Books:* 27,089 (physical), 180,843 (digital/electronic); *Serial titles:* 105 (physical); *Databases:* 55. Weekly public service hours: 40; students can reserve study rooms.
Student Life *Campus security:* 24-hour emergency response devices, student patrols, late-night transport/escort service, campus warning siren, uniformed armed police officers, RAVE alert system (text, email, voice).
Athletics Member NJCAA.
Standardized Tests *Recommended:* SAT or ACT (for admission).
Financial Aid Of all full-time matriculated undergraduates who enrolled in 2017, 50 Federal Work-Study jobs (averaging $1253). 28 state and other part-time jobs (averaging $1647).
Applying *Options:* electronic application. *Required:* high school transcript.
Freshman Application Contact Ms. Michelle Vyskocil, Dean of Student Services, Kirtland Community College, 10775 North Saint Helen Road, Roscommon, MI 48653. *Phone:* 989-275-5000 Ext. 248. *Fax:* 989-275-6789. *E-mail:* registrar@kirtland.edu. *Website:* http://www.kirtland.edu/.

Lake Michigan College
Benton Harbor, Michigan

Freshman Application Contact Mr. Louis Thomas, Lead Admissions Specialist, Lake Michigan College, 2755 East Napier Avenue, Benton Harbor, MI 49022-1899. *Phone:* 269-927-6584. *Toll-free phone:* 800-252-1LMC. *Fax:* 269-927-6718. *E-mail:* thomas@lakemichigancollege.edu. *Website:* http://www.lakemichigancollege.edu/.

Lansing Community College
Lansing, Michigan

Freshman Application Contact Ms. Tammy Grossbauer, Director of Admissions/Registrar, Lansing Community College, 1121 Enrollment Services, PO BOX 40010, Lansing, MI 48901. *Phone:* 517-483-1200. *Toll-free phone:* 800-644-4LCC. *Fax:* 517-483-1170. *E-mail:* grossbt@lcc.edu. *Website:* http://www.lcc.edu/.

Macomb Community College
Warren, Michigan

- **District-supported** 2-year, founded 1954, part of Michigan Public Community College System
- **Suburban** 384-acre campus with easy access to Detroit
- **Endowment** $20.4 million
- **Coed**

Undergraduates 6,116 full-time, 14,898 part-time. Students come from 4 states and territories; 11% Black or African American, non-Hispanic/Latino; 3% Hispanic/Latino; 5% Asian, non-Hispanic/Latino; 0.1% Native Hawaiian or other Pacific Islander, non-Hispanic/Latino; 0.5% American Indian or Alaska Native, non-Hispanic/Latino; 2% Two or more races, non-Hispanic/Latino; 7% Race/ethnicity unknown; 2% international. *Retention:* 56% of full-time freshmen returned.
Faculty *Student/faculty ratio:* 24:1.
Academics *Calendar:* semesters. *Degree:* certificates and associate. *Special study options:* academic remediation for entering students, adult/continuing education programs, advanced placement credit, cooperative education, English as a second language, honors programs, internships, off-campus study, part-time degree program, services for LD students, student-designed majors, summer session for credit.
Library Library of South Campus. *Books:* 181,121 (physical), 51,203 (digital/electronic); *Serial titles:* 51,079 (physical), 97,750 (digital/electronic). Students can reserve study rooms.
Student Life *Campus security:* 24-hour emergency response devices and patrols, late-night transport/escort service, security phones in parking lots, surveillance cameras.
Athletics Member NJCAA.
Applying *Options:* early admission, deferred entrance.
Freshman Application Contact Mr. Brian Bouwman, Coordinator of Admissions and Transfer Credit, Macomb Community College, 14500 East 12 Mile Road, Warren, MI 48088-3896. *Phone:* 586-445-7246. *Toll-free phone:* 866-MACOMB1. *Fax:* 586-445-7140. *E-mail:* stevensr@macomb.edu. *Website:* http://www.macomb.edu/.

MIAT College of Technology
Canton, Michigan

Admissions Office Contact MIAT College of Technology, 2955 South Haggerty Road, Canton, MI 48188. *Website:* http://www.miat.edu/.

Mid Michigan Community College
Harrison, Michigan

Freshman Application Contact Jennifer Casebeer, Admissions Specialist, Mid Michigan Community College, 1375 South Clare Avenue, Harrison, MI 48625-9447. *Phone:* 989-386-6661. *E-mail:* apply@midmich.edu. *Website:* http://www.midmich.edu/.

Monroe County Community College
Monroe, Michigan

- **County-supported** 2-year, founded 1964, part of Michigan Department of Education
- **Small-town** 150-acre campus with easy access to Detroit, Toledo
- **Coed**

Undergraduates 954 full-time, 2,190 part-time. Students come from 2 other countries; 4% are from out of state; 3% Black or African American, non-Hispanic/Latino; 3% Hispanic/Latino; 0.8% Asian, non-Hispanic/Latino; 0.1% Native Hawaiian or other Pacific Islander, non-Hispanic/Latino; 0.3% American Indian or Alaska Native, non-Hispanic/Latino; 0.7% Two or more races, non-Hispanic/Latino; 8% Race/ethnicity unknown; 0.1% international.
Academics *Calendar:* semesters. *Degree:* certificates and associate. *Special study options:* academic remediation for entering students, advanced placement credit, distance learning, honors programs, independent study, part-time degree program, services for LD students, study abroad, summer session for credit.
Library Campbell Learning Resource Center.
Student Life *Campus security:* police patrols during open hours.
Standardized Tests *Required:* ACT, ACT Compass, SAT, ACCUPLACER (for admission). *Recommended:* SAT (for admission), ACT (for admission).
Applying *Options:* early admission, deferred entrance. *Required:* high school transcript.
Freshman Application Contact Mr. Mark V. Hall, Director of Admissions and Guidance Services, Monroe County Community College, 1555 South Raisinville Road, Monroe, MI 48161. *Phone:* 734-384-4261. *Toll-free phone:* 877-YES-MCCC. *Fax:* 734-242-9711. *E-mail:* mhall@monroeccc.edu. *Website:* http://www.monroeccc.edu/.

Montcalm Community College
Sidney, Michigan

Freshman Application Contact Ms. Debra Alexander, Associate Dean of Student Services, Montcalm Community College, 2800 College Drive, SW, Sidney, MI 48885. *Phone:* 989-328-1276. *Toll-free phone:* 877-328-2111. *E-mail:* admissions@montcalm.edu. *Website:* http://www.montcalm.edu/.

Mott Community College
Flint, Michigan

- **District-supported** 2-year, founded 1923
- **Urban** 32-acre campus with easy access to Detroit
- **Endowment** $40.1 million
- **Coed**

Undergraduates 2,022 full-time, 5,667 part-time. 16% Black or African American, non-Hispanic/Latino; 5% Hispanic/Latino; 0.6% Asian, non-Hispanic/Latino; 0.1% Native Hawaiian or other Pacific Islander, non-Hispanic/Latino; 0.4% American Indian or Alaska Native, non-Hispanic/Latino; 4% Two or more races, non-Hispanic/Latino; 6% Race/ethnicity unknown; 0.3% international; 2% transferred in.
Faculty *Student/faculty ratio:* 16:1.
Academics *Calendar:* semesters. *Degree:* certificates and associate. *Special study options:* academic remediation for entering students, accelerated degree program, adult/continuing education programs, advanced placement credit, cooperative education, distance learning, double majors, English as a second language, honors programs, independent study, internships, part-time degree program, services for LD students, summer session for credit.
Library Charles Stewart Mott Library. Students can reserve study rooms.
Student Life *Campus security:* 24-hour emergency response devices and patrols, student patrols, late-night transport/escort service, closed-circuit TV surveillance, whistle alert program, 3P Campaign: Prevent, Protect, and Prosecute Violence Against Women.
Athletics Member NJCAA.
Applying *Options:* electronic application, early admission, deferred entrance. *Required:* high school transcript.
Freshman Application Contact Ms. Regina Broomfield, Director, Admissions, Mott Community College, 1401 East Court Street, Flint, MI 48503. *Phone:* 810-762-0358. *Toll-free phone:* 800-852-8614. *Fax:* 810-232-9442. *E-mail:* regina.broomfield@mcc.edu. *Website:* http://www.mcc.edu/.

Muskegon Community College
Muskegon, Michigan

- **State and locally supported** 2-year, founded 1926, part of Michigan Department of Education
- **Small-town** 112-acre campus with easy access to Grand Rapids
- **Coed**

Undergraduates 1,488 full-time, 3,018 part-time. Students come from 4 states and territories; 9% Black or African American, non-Hispanic/Latino; 3% Hispanic/Latino; 0.8% Asian, non-Hispanic/Latino; 0.1% Native Hawaiian or other Pacific Islander, non-Hispanic/Latino; 0.9% American Indian or Alaska Native, non-Hispanic/Latino; 4% Two or more races, non-Hispanic/Latino; 5% Race/ethnicity unknown; 0.4% international. *Retention:* 59% of full-time freshmen returned.
Faculty *Student/faculty ratio:* 19:1.
Academics *Calendar:* semesters. *Degree:* associate. *Special study options:* academic remediation for entering students, adult/continuing education programs, cooperative education, honors programs, part-time degree program, student-designed majors, summer session for credit.
Library Hendrik Meijer and Technology Center.
Student Life *Campus security:* 24-hour emergency response devices, on-campus security officer.
Athletics Member NJCAA.
Financial Aid Of all full-time matriculated undergraduates who enrolled in 2017, 250 Federal Work-Study jobs (averaging $2500). 50 state and other part-time jobs (averaging $2500).
Applying *Options:* electronic application, early admission, deferred entrance. *Required:* high school transcript.
Freshman Application Contact Mr. Johnathon Skidmore, Senior Clerk 1 Admissions, Muskegon Community College, 221 South Quarterline Road, Muskegon, MI 49442-1493. *Phone:* 231-777-0366. *Toll-free phone:* 866-711-4622. *E-mail:* johnathon.skidmore@muskegoncc.edu. *Website:* http://www.muskegoncc.edu/.

North Central Michigan College
Petoskey, Michigan

Director of Admissions Ms. Julieanne Tobin, Director of Enrollment Management, North Central Michigan College, 1515 Howard Street, Petoskey, MI 49770-8717. *Phone:* 231-439-6511. *Toll-free phone:* 888-298-6605. *E-mail:* jtobin@ncmich.edu. *Website:* http://www.ncmich.edu/.

Northwestern Michigan College
Traverse City, Michigan

Freshman Application Contact Catheryn Claerhout, Director of Admissions, Northwestern Michigan College, 1701 E. Front Street, Traverse City, MI 49686. *Phone:* 231-995-1034. *Toll-free phone:* 800-748-0566. *E-mail:* c.claerhout@nmc.edu. *Website:* http://www.nmc.edu/.

Oakland Community College
Bloomfield Hills, Michigan

Freshman Application Contact Stephan M. Linden, Registrar, Oakland Community College, 2480 Opdyke Road, Bloomfield Hills, MI 48304-2266. *Phone:* 248-341-2192. *Fax:* 248-341-2099. *E-mail:* smlinden@oaklandcc.edu. *Website:* http://www.oaklandcc.edu/.

Saginaw Chippewa Tribal College
Mount Pleasant, Michigan

- **Independent** 2-year, founded 1998
- **Small-town** campus
- **Coed**

Undergraduates 36 full-time, 104 part-time. 2% Black or African American, non-Hispanic/Latino; 6% Hispanic/Latino; 72% American Indian or Alaska Native, non-Hispanic/Latino; 2% Two or more races, non-Hispanic/Latino.
Faculty *Student/faculty ratio:* 6:1.
Academics *Calendar:* semesters. *Degree:* associate. *Special study options:* part-time degree program, summer session for credit.

Library Saginaw Chippewa Tribal College Library. *Books:* 2,134 (physical), 12,155 (digital/electronic); *Serial titles:* 4 (physical). Students can reserve study rooms.
Applying *Options:* electronic application. *Required:* high school transcript.
Freshman Application Contact Ms. Amanda Flaugher, Admissions Officer/Registrar/Financial Aid, Saginaw Chippewa Tribal College, 2274 Enterprise Drive, Mount Pleasant, MI 48858. *Phone:* 989-317-4760. *Fax:* 989-317-4781. *E-mail:* aflaugher@sagchip.edu. *Website:* http://www.sagchip.edu/.

St. Clair County Community College
Port Huron, Michigan

Freshman Application Contact St. Clair County Community College, 323 Erie Street, PO Box 5015, Port Huron, MI 48061-5015. *Phone:* 810-989-5501. *Toll-free phone:* 800-553-2427. *Website:* http://www.sc4.edu/.

Schoolcraft College
Livonia, Michigan

- **District-supported** primarily 2-year, founded 1961, part of Michigan Department of Education
- **Suburban** campus with easy access to Detroit
- **Coed**

Undergraduates 2,955 full-time, 7,603 part-time. 14% Black or African American, non-Hispanic/Latino; 5% Hispanic/Latino; 4% Asian, non-Hispanic/Latino; 0.1% Native Hawaiian or other Pacific Islander, non-Hispanic/Latino; 0.6% American Indian or Alaska Native, non-Hispanic/Latino; 3% Two or more races, non-Hispanic/Latino; 7% Race/ethnicity unknown; 2% international; 23% transferred in. *Retention:* 62% of full-time freshmen returned.
Faculty *Student/faculty ratio:* 23:1.
Academics *Calendar:* semesters. *Degrees:* certificates, associate, and bachelor's. *Special study options:* academic remediation for entering students, advanced placement credit, distance learning, English as a second language, honors programs, independent study, internships, part-time degree program, services for LD students, study abroad, summer session for credit.
Library Bradner Library plus 1 other. *Books:* 67,778 (physical), 74,201 (digital/electronic); *Databases:* 147. Students can reserve study rooms.
Student Life *Campus security:* 24-hour emergency response devices and patrols, late-night transport/escort service.
Athletics Member NJCAA.
Financial Aid Of all full-time matriculated undergraduates who enrolled in 2017, 124 Federal Work-Study jobs (averaging $4000).
Applying *Options:* electronic application, early admission, deferred entrance. *Required for some:* high school transcript. *Recommended:* high school transcript.
Freshman Application Contact Ms. Lisa Bushaw, Director of Admissions, Schoolcraft College, 18600 Haggerty Road, Livonia, MI 48152-2696. *Phone:* 734-462-4683. *E-mail:* admissions@schoolcraft.edu. *Website:* http://www.schoolcraft.edu/.

Southwestern Michigan College
Dowagiac, Michigan

- **State and locally supported** 2-year, founded 1964
- **Rural** 240-acre campus
- **Coed,** 2,130 undergraduate students, 41% full-time, 59% women, 41% men

Undergraduates 880 full-time, 1,250 part-time. Students come from 10 states and territories; 1 other country; 18% are from out of state; 12% Black or African American, non-Hispanic/Latino; 5% Hispanic/Latino; 2% Asian, non-Hispanic/Latino; 0.1% Native Hawaiian or other Pacific Islander, non-Hispanic/Latino; 1% American Indian or Alaska Native, non-Hispanic/Latino; 3% Two or more races, non-Hispanic/Latino; 5% Race/ethnicity unknown; 0.1% international; 5% transferred in; 22% live on campus. *Retention:* 48% of full-time freshmen returned.
Freshmen *Admission:* 1,928 applied, 1,927 admitted, 496 enrolled.
Faculty *Total:* 123, 48% full-time, 27% with terminal degrees. *Student/faculty ratio:* 20:1.
Majors Accounting technology and bookkeeping; agricultural production; automation engineer technology; automobile/automotive mechanics technology; business administration and management; carpentry; computer programming; computer systems networking and telecommunications; criminal justice/safety; early childhood education; engineering technology; fire science/firefighting; general studies; graphic design; health information/medical records technology; industrial mechanics and maintenance technology; liberal arts and sciences/liberal studies; medical/clinical assistant; registered nursing/registered nurse; social work; sport and fitness administration/management.
Academics *Calendar:* semesters. *Degree:* certificates and associate. *Special study options:* academic remediation for entering students, accelerated degree program, adult/continuing education programs, advanced placement credit, cooperative education, English as a second language, honors programs, independent study, internships, part-time degree program, services for LD students, summer session for credit.
Library Fred L. Mathews Library. *Books:* 23,473 (physical), 725 (digital/electronic); *Serial titles:* 4 (physical), 37,873 (digital/electronic); *Databases:* 49. Weekly public service hours: 61; students can reserve study rooms.
Student Life *Housing Options:* coed. Campus housing is university owned. *Activities and Organizations:* drama/theater group, choral group, Agriscience Club, Business Club, Criminal Justice Club, Rock Climbing Club, STEM Club. *Campus security:* 24-hour emergency response devices and patrols, controlled dormitory access. *Student services:* personal/psychological counseling.
Athletics *Intramural sports:* basketball M/W, football M/W, racquetball M/W, rock climbing M/W, soccer M/W, softball M/W, ultimate Frisbee M/W, volleyball M/W.
Financial Aid Of all full-time matriculated undergraduates who enrolled in 2017, 125 Federal Work-Study jobs (averaging $1000). 75 state and other part-time jobs (averaging $1000).
Applying *Options:* electronic application, deferred entrance. *Required:* high school transcript. *Required for some:* interview. *Application deadlines:* rolling (freshmen), rolling (out-of-state freshmen), rolling (transfers). *Notification:* continuous (freshmen), continuous (out-of-state freshmen), continuous (transfers).
Freshman Application Contact Dr. Lucian Leone, Director of Admissions, Southwestern Michigan College, Dowagiac, MI 49047. *Phone:* 269-782-1000 Ext. 1238. *Toll-free phone:* 800-456-8675. *Fax:* 269-782-1371. *E-mail:* lleone@swmich.edu.
Website: http://www.swmich.edu/.

Washtenaw Community College
Ann Arbor, Michigan

Freshman Application Contact Washtenaw Community College, 4800 East Huron River Drive, PO Box D-1, Ann Arbor, MI 48106. *Phone:* 734-973-3315. *Website:* http://www.wccnet.edu/.

Wayne County Community College District
Detroit, Michigan

- **State and locally supported** 2-year, founded 1967
- **Urban** campus
- **Coed,** 14,957 undergraduate students, 13% full-time, 65% women, 35% men

Undergraduates 2,005 full-time, 12,952 part-time. 69% Black or African American, non-Hispanic/Latino; 2% Hispanic/Latino; 0.6% Asian, non-Hispanic/Latino; 0.1% Native Hawaiian or other Pacific Islander, non-Hispanic/Latino; 0.2% American Indian or Alaska Native, non-Hispanic/Latino; 5% Two or more races, non-Hispanic/Latino; 6% Race/ethnicity unknown; 0.6% international; 10% transferred in.
Freshmen *Admission:* 2,268 enrolled.
Faculty *Student/faculty ratio:* 17:1.
Majors Accounting technology and bookkeeping; adult development and aging; aircraft powerplant technology; airframe mechanics and aircraft maintenance technology; anesthesiologist assistant; autobody/collision and repair technology; automobile/automotive mechanics technology; biomedical technology; building/property maintenance; business administration and management; CAD/CADD drafting/design technology; child-care and support services management; computer numerically controlled (CNC) machinist technology; computer programming; corrections; criminal justice/police science; data modeling/warehousing and database administration; dental hygiene; digital communication and media/multimedia; e-commerce; electrical, electronic and communications engineering technology; elementary education; emergency medical technology (EMT paramedic); fashion merchandising; fire prevention and safety technology; food service systems administration; game and interactive media design; heating, air conditioning, ventilation and refrigeration maintenance technology; legal assistant/paralegal; liberal arts and sciences/liberal studies; medical office assistant; mortuary science and embalming; office management; pharmacy technician; physician assistant; pre-engineering; psychiatric/mental health services technology; registered nursing/registered nurse; social work; surgical technology; web/multimedia management and webmaster; welding technology.

Academics *Calendar:* semesters. *Degree:* certificates and associate. *Special study options:* academic remediation for entering students, adult/continuing education programs, advanced placement credit, cooperative education, distance learning, English as a second language, honors programs, internships, part-time degree program, services for LD students, study abroad, summer session for credit.
Library Learning Resource Center.
Student Life *Housing:* college housing not available. *Campus security:* 24-hour emergency response devices. *Student services:* veterans affairs office.
Athletics Member NJCAA. *Intercollegiate sports:* basketball M/W, bowling M/W, cross-country running M/W, golf M, volleyball W.
Financial Aid Of all full-time matriculated undergraduates who enrolled in 2017, 239 Federal Work-Study jobs (averaging $2360). 147 state and other part-time jobs (averaging $1200).
Applying *Options:* electronic application, early admission, deferred entrance. *Required:* high school transcript. *Application deadlines:* rolling (freshmen), rolling (transfers).
Freshman Application Contact Mr. Adrian Phillips, District Associate Vice Chancellor of Student Services, Wayne County Community College District, 801 West Fort Street, Detroit, MI 48226-9975. *Phone:* 313-496-2820. *Fax:* 313-962-1643. *E-mail:* aphilli1@wcccd.edu.
Website: http://www.wcccd.edu/.

West Shore Community College
Scottville, Michigan

Freshman Application Contact Wendy Fought, Director of Admissions, West Shore Community College, PO Box 277, 3000 North Stiles Road, Scottville, MI 49454-0277. *Phone:* 231-843-5503. *Fax:* 231-845-3944. *E-mail:* admissions@westshore.edu. *Website:* http://www.westshore.edu/.

MINNESOTA

Alexandria Technical and Community College
Alexandria, Minnesota

- **State-supported** 2-year, founded 1961, part of Minnesota State Colleges and Universities System
- **Small-town** 98-acre campus
- **Coed,** 2,483 undergraduate students, 47% full-time, 51% women, 49% men

Undergraduates 1,165 full-time, 1,318 part-time. Students come from 18 states and territories; 3% are from out of state; 2% Black or African American, non-Hispanic/Latino; 2% Hispanic/Latino; 1% Asian, non-Hispanic/Latino; 2% American Indian or Alaska Native, non-Hispanic/Latino; 5% Race/ethnicity unknown.
Faculty *Total:* 95, 65% full-time, 4% with terminal degrees. *Student/faculty ratio:* 20:1.
Majors Accounting; automation engineer technology; business administration and management; business/commerce; clinical/medical laboratory technology; commercial and advertising art; computer systems networking and telecommunications; criminal justice/police science; diesel mechanics technology; early childhood education; fashion merchandising; human services; information science/studies; interior design; legal administrative assistant/secretary; legal assistant/paralegal; liberal arts and sciences/liberal studies; mechanical drafting and CAD/CADD; medical administrative assistant and medical secretary; multi/interdisciplinary studies related; office management; physical fitness technician; pre-engineering; registered nursing/registered nurse; speech-language pathology assistant.
Academics *Calendar:* semesters. *Degree:* certificates, diplomas, and associate. *Special study options:* academic remediation for entering students, advanced placement credit, distance learning, double majors, independent study, internships, part-time degree program, services for LD students, student-designed majors, summer session for credit.
Library Learning Resource Center. *Books:* 7,582 (physical), 13,367 (digital/electronic); *Serial titles:* 24 (physical); *Databases:* 14. Weekly public service hours: 51; students can reserve study rooms.
Student Life *Housing:* college housing not available. *Activities and Organizations:* Student Senate, Intercultural Club, Trapshooting League, GAT (Gamers of Alex Tech), Book Club. *Campus security:* student patrols, late-night transport/escort service. *Student services:* personal/psychological counseling, veterans affairs office.
Athletics *Intramural sports:* basketball M/W, football M/W, softball M/W, volleyball M/W.
Financial Aid Of all full-time matriculated undergraduates who enrolled in 2017, 94 Federal Work-Study jobs (averaging $1871).
Applying *Options:* electronic application, early admission, deferred entrance. *Application fee:* $20. *Required for some:* high school transcript, interview. *Recommended:* interview. *Application deadlines:* rolling (freshmen), rolling (out-of-state freshmen), rolling (transfers). *Notification:* continuous (freshmen), continuous (out-of-state freshmen), continuous (transfers).
Freshman Application Contact Vicki Sward, Information Center Manager, Alexandria Technical and Community College, 1601 Jefferson Street, Alexandria, MN 56308. *Phone:* 320-762-4600. *Toll-free phone:* 888-234-1222. *Fax:* 320-762-4501. *E-mail:* info@alextech.edu.
Website: http://www.alextech.edu/.

Anoka-Ramsey Community College
Coon Rapids, Minnesota

Freshman Application Contact Admissions Department, Anoka-Ramsey Community College, 11200 Mississippi Boulevard NW, Coon Rapids, MN 55433-3470. *Phone:* 763-433-1300. *Fax:* 763-433-1521. *E-mail:* admissions@anokaramsey.edu. *Website:* http://www.anokaramsey.edu/.

Anoka Technical College
Anoka, Minnesota

Freshman Application Contact Enrollment Services, Anoka Technical College, 1355 West Highway 10, Anoka, MN 55303. *Phone:* 763-576-7710. *E-mail:* enrollmentservices@anokatech.edu. *Website:* http://www.anokatech.edu/.

Central Lakes College
Brainerd, Minnesota

- **State-supported** 2-year, founded 1938, part of Minnesota State Colleges and Universities System
- **Small-town** campus
- **Endowment** $7.3 million
- **Coed**

Undergraduates 1,559 full-time, 2,156 part-time. Students come from 26 states and territories; 2% are from out of state. *Retention:* 58% of full-time freshmen returned.
Faculty *Student/faculty ratio:* 20:1.
Academics *Calendar:* semesters. *Degree:* certificates, diplomas, and associate. *Special study options:* academic remediation for entering students, advanced placement credit, distance learning, English as a second language, external degree program, independent study, internships, off-campus study, part-time degree program, services for LD students, summer session for credit.
Library Learning Resource Center.
Student Life *Campus security:* 24-hour emergency response devices and patrols, student patrols, late-night transport/escort service.
Athletics Member NJCAA.
Applying *Options:* electronic application, deferred entrance. *Application fee:* $20. *Required:* high school transcript.
Freshman Application Contact Ms. Rose Tretter, Central Lakes College, 501 West College Drive, Brainerd, MN 56401-3904. *Phone:* 218-855-8036. *Toll-free phone:* 800-933-0346. *Fax:* 218-855-8220. *E-mail:* rtretter@clcmn.edu. *Website:* http://www.clcmn.edu/.

Century College
White Bear Lake, Minnesota

- **State-supported** 2-year, founded 1970, part of Minnesota State Colleges and Universities System
- **Suburban** 170-acre campus with easy access to Minneapolis-St. Paul
- **Coed**

Undergraduates 3,641 full-time, 4,801 part-time. Students come from 37 states and territories; 50 other countries; 6% are from out of state; 10% Black or African American, non-Hispanic/Latino; 8% Hispanic/Latino; 18% Asian, non-Hispanic/Latino; 0.1% Native Hawaiian or other Pacific Islander, non-Hispanic/Latino; 0.3% American Indian or Alaska Native, non-Hispanic/Latino; 5% Two or more races, non-Hispanic/Latino; 0.8% Race/ethnicity unknown; 2% international; 42% transferred in.
Faculty *Student/faculty ratio:* 22:1.
Academics *Calendar:* semesters. *Degree:* certificates, diplomas, and associate. *Special study options:* academic remediation for entering students, advanced placement credit, distance learning, double majors, English as a second language, honors programs, independent study, internships, part-time degree program, services for LD students, student-designed majors, summer session for credit. *ROTC:* Air Force (c).

Library Century College Library. *Books:* 58,410 (physical), 180,870 (digital/electronic); *Serial titles:* 285 (physical), 39,784 (digital/electronic); *Databases:* 61. Weekly public service hours: 65; students can reserve study rooms.
Student Life *Campus security:* late-night transport/escort service, day patrols.
Athletics Member NJCAA.
Financial Aid Of all full-time matriculated undergraduates who enrolled in 2017, 81 Federal Work-Study jobs (averaging $2763). 85 state and other part-time jobs (averaging $2646).
Applying *Options:* electronic application, deferred entrance. *Application fee:* $20. *Required:* high school transcript.
Freshman Application Contact Robert Beaver, Assistant Admissions Director, Century College, 3300 Century Avenue North, White Bear Lake, MN 55110. *Phone:* 651-779-5744. *Toll-free phone:* 800-228-1978. *Fax:* 651-773-1796. *E-mail:* admissions@century.edu. *Website:* http://www.century.edu/.

Dakota County Technical College
Rosemount, Minnesota

Freshman Application Contact Mr. Patrick Lair, Admissions Director, Dakota County Technical College, 1300 East 145th Street, Rosemount, MN 55068. *Phone:* 651-423-8399. *Toll-free phone:* 877-YES-DCTC. *Fax:* 651-423-8775. *E-mail:* admissions@dctc.mnscu.edu. *Website:* http://www.dctc.edu/.

Dunwoody College of Technology
Minneapolis, Minnesota

- **Independent** primarily 2-year, founded 1914
- **Urban** 11-acre campus with easy access to Minneapolis-St. Paul
- **Endowment** $22.6 million
- **Coed, primarily men,** 1,305 undergraduate students, 81% full-time, 17% women, 83% men

Undergraduates 1,053 full-time, 252 part-time. Students come from 3 other countries; 3% are from out of state; 5% Black or African American, non-Hispanic/Latino; 3% Hispanic/Latino; 7% Asian, non-Hispanic/Latino; 0.3% American Indian or Alaska Native, non-Hispanic/Latino; 6% Two or more races, non-Hispanic/Latino; 9% Race/ethnicity unknown; 0.2% international; 18% transferred in; 1% live on campus. *Retention:* 100% of full-time freshmen returned.
Freshmen *Admission:* 614 applied, 380 admitted, 217 enrolled. *Average high school GPA:* 2.7.
Faculty *Total:* 155, 57% full-time, 17% with terminal degrees. *Student/faculty ratio:* 10:1.
Majors Architectural technology; architecture; autobody/collision and repair technology; automobile/automotive mechanics technology; building/construction site management; business administration and management; CAD/CADD drafting/design technology; civil engineering technology; computer numerically controlled (CNC) machinist technology; computer software engineering; computer systems analysis; computer systems networking and telecommunications; construction management; desktop publishing and digital imaging design; electrical and electronics engineering; electrical, electronic and communications engineering technology; electrical/electronics drafting and CAD/CADD; electrician; graphic design; heating, air conditioning, ventilation and refrigeration maintenance technology; heating, ventilation, air conditioning and refrigeration engineering technology; interior design; manufacturing engineering; mechanical engineering; medical radiologic technology; web page, digital/multimedia and information resources design; welding technology.
Academics *Calendar:* semesters. *Degrees:* certificates, associate, and bachelor's. *Special study options:* academic remediation for entering students, adult/continuing education programs, cooperative education, distance learning, independent study, internships, study abroad, summer session for credit.
Library Learning Resource Center plus 1 other. *Books:* 8,000 (physical), 188,153 (digital/electronic); *Serial titles:* 136 (physical); *Databases:* 26. Weekly public service hours: 55.
Student Life *Housing:* college housing not available. *Options:* coed. *Activities and Organizations:* Phi Theta Kappa, Historic Green, Dunwoody Motorsports Club, Architectural Institute of America Student Chapter, Professional Association for Design. *Campus security:* 24-hour emergency response devices, late-night transport/escort service. *Student services:* women's center.
Standardized Tests *Required for some:* ACT (for admission).
Financial Aid Of all full-time matriculated undergraduates who enrolled in 2017, 1,138 applied for aid, 993 were judged to have need, 45 had their need fully met. 19 Federal Work-Study jobs (averaging $4404). 28 state and other part-time jobs (averaging $5039). In 2017, 31 non-need-based awards were made. *Average percent of need met:* 42%. *Average financial aid package:* $11,383. *Average need-based loan:* $3726. *Average need-based gift aid:* $9228. *Average non-need-based aid:* $1960.
Applying *Options:* electronic application. *Application fee:* $50. *Required:* interview. *Required for some:* 1 letter of recommendation, ACT scores and Resumes. *Recommended:* minimum 2.5 GPA. *Application deadlines:* rolling (freshmen), rolling (transfers). *Notification:* continuous (freshmen), continuous (transfers).
Freshman Application Contact Kelly O'Brien, Director of Admissions, Dunwoody College of Technology, 818 Dunwoody Boulevard, Minneapolis, MN 55403. *Phone:* 612-381-3302. *Toll-free phone:* 800-292-4625. *Fax:* 612-677-3131. *E-mail:* kobrien@dunwoody.edu.
Website: http://www.dunwoody.edu/.

Fond du Lac Tribal and Community College
Cloquet, Minnesota

Freshman Application Contact Kathie Jubie, Admissions Representative, Fond du Lac Tribal and Community College, 2101 14th Street, Cloquet, MN 55720. *Phone:* 218-879-0808. *Toll-free phone:* 800-657-3712. *E-mail:* admissions@fdltcc.edu. *Website:* http://www.fdltcc.edu/.

Hennepin Technical College
Brooklyn Park, Minnesota

Freshman Application Contact Admissions, Hennepin Technical College, 9000 Brooklyn Boulevard, Brooklyn Park, MN 55445. *Phone:* 763-488-2580. *Toll-free phone:* 800-345-4655 (in-state); 800-645-4655 (out-of-state). *Fax:* 763-550-2113. *E-mail:* info@hennepintech.edu. *Website:* http://www.hennepintech.edu/.

Herzing University
Minneapolis, Minnesota

Freshman Application Contact Ms. Shelly Larson, Director of Admissions, Herzing University, 5700 West Broadway, Minneapolis, MN 55428. *Phone:* 763-231-3155. *Toll-free phone:* 800-596-0724. *Fax:* 763-535-9205. *E-mail:* info@mpls.herzing.edu. *Website:* http://www.herzing.edu/minneapolis.

Hibbing Community College
Hibbing, Minnesota

Freshman Application Contact Admissions, Hibbing Community College, 1515 East 25th Street, Hibbing, MN 55746. *Phone:* 218-262-7200. *Toll-free phone:* 800-224-4HCC. *Fax:* 218-262-6717. *E-mail:* admissions@hibbing.edu. *Website:* http://www.hcc.mnscu.edu/.

The Institute of Production and Recording
Minneapolis, Minnesota

Freshman Application Contact The Institute of Production and Recording, 300 North 1st Avenue, Suite 500, Minneapolis, MN 55401. *Website:* http://www.ipr.edu/.

Inver Hills Community College
Inver Grove Heights, Minnesota

Freshman Application Contact Mr. Casey Carmody, Admissions Representative, Inver Hills Community College, 2500 East 80th Street, Inver Grove Heights, MN 55076-3224. *Phone:* 651-450-3589. *Fax:* 651-450-3677. *E-mail:* admissions@inverhills.edu. *Website:* http://www.inverhills.edu/.

Itasca Community College
Grand Rapids, Minnesota

Freshman Application Contact Ms. Candace Perry, Director of Enrollment Services, Itasca Community College, Grand Rapids, MN 55744. *Phone:* 218-322-2340. *Toll-free phone:* 800-996-6422. *Fax:* 218-327-4350. *E-mail:* iccinfo@itascacc.edu. *Website:* http://www.itascacc.edu/.

Lake Superior College
Duluth, Minnesota

- **State-supported** 2-year, founded 1995, part of Minnesota State
- **Urban** 105-acre campus
- **Coed,** 4,690 undergraduate students, 39% full-time, 56% women, 44% men

Undergraduates 1,849 full-time, 2,841 part-time. Students come from 34 states and territories; 13 other countries; 13% are from out of state; 3% Black or African American, non-Hispanic/Latino; 3% Hispanic/Latino; 2% Asian, non-Hispanic/Latino; 0.1% Native Hawaiian or other Pacific Islander, non-Hispanic/Latino; 2% American Indian or Alaska Native, non-Hispanic/Latino; 5% Two or more races, non-Hispanic/Latino; 0.7% Race/ethnicity unknown; 2% international; 34% transferred in.
Freshmen *Admission:* 1,310 applied, 1,310 admitted, 660 enrolled.
Faculty *Total:* 249, 41% full-time, 6% with terminal degrees. *Student/faculty ratio:* 18:1.
Majors Accounting; airframe mechanics and aircraft maintenance technology; airline pilot and flight crew; architectural drafting and CAD/CADD; automobile/automotive mechanics technology; aviation/airway management; building construction technology; business administration and management; business automation/technology/data entry; CAD/CADD drafting/design technology; carpentry; civil engineering technology; clinical/medical laboratory technology; computer numerically controlled (CNC) machinist technology; computer technology/computer systems technology; dental hygiene; electrical, electronic and communications engineering technology; electrician; fine/studio arts; fire prevention and safety technology; fire services administration; health services/allied health/health sciences; legal assistant/paralegal; liberal arts and sciences/liberal studies; management information systems; medical administrative assistant and medical secretary; multi/interdisciplinary studies related; network and system administration; office management; physical therapy technology; radiologic technology/science; registered nursing/registered nurse; respiratory care therapy; sheet metal technology; surgical technology; web page, digital/multimedia and information resources design; welding technology.
Academics *Calendar:* semesters. *Degree:* certificates, diplomas, and associate. *Special study options:* academic remediation for entering students, advanced placement credit, distance learning, double majors, independent study, internships, part-time degree program, services for LD students, study abroad, summer session for credit.
Library Harold P. Erickson Library. Students can reserve study rooms.
Student Life *Housing:* college housing not available. *Activities and Organizations:* choral group. *Campus security:* 24-hour emergency response devices, late-night transport/escort service. *Student services:* personal/psychological counseling, veterans affairs office.
Athletics Member NJCAA. *Intercollegiate sports:* basketball M/W, soccer M/W. *Intramural sports:* rock climbing M/W, ultimate Frisbee M/W, volleyball M/W.
Applying *Options:* electronic application. *Application fee:* $20. *Required:* high school transcript. *Application deadlines:* rolling (freshmen), rolling (transfers). *Notification:* continuous (freshmen), continuous (transfers).
Freshman Application Contact Ms. Sherry Sanchez Tibbetz, Interim Director of Admissions, Lake Superior College, 2101 Trinity Road, Duluth, MN 55811. *Phone:* 218-733-7601. *Toll-free phone:* 800-432-2884. *E-mail:* enroll@lsc.edu.
Website: http://www.lsc.edu/.

Leech Lake Tribal College
Cass Lake, Minnesota

Freshman Application Contact Ms. Shelly Braford, Recruiter, Leech Lake Tribal College, PO Box 180, 6945 Littlewolf Road NW, Cass Lake, MN 56633. *Phone:* 218-335-4200 Ext. 4270. *Fax:* 218-335-4217. *E-mail:* shelly.braford@lltc.edu. *Website:* http://www.lltc.edu/.

Mesabi Range College
Virginia, Minnesota

- **State-supported** 2-year, founded 1918, part of Minnesota State
- **Small-town** 30-acre campus
- **Coed**

Undergraduates 619 full-time, 470 part-time. Students come from 6 states and territories; 2 other countries; 8% Black or African American, non-Hispanic/Latino; 2% Hispanic/Latino; 0.3% Asian, non-Hispanic/Latino; 0.2% Native Hawaiian or other Pacific Islander, non-Hispanic/Latino; 3% American Indian or Alaska Native, non-Hispanic/Latino; 5% Race/ethnicity unknown; 10% live on campus.
Faculty *Student/faculty ratio:* 24:1.
Academics *Calendar:* semesters. *Degree:* certificates, diplomas, and associate. *Special study options:* academic remediation for entering students, adult/continuing education programs, advanced placement credit, cooperative education, distance learning, independent study, internships, off-campus study, part-time degree program, services for LD students, student-designed majors, study abroad, summer session for credit.
Library Mesabi Library.
Athletics Member NJCAA.
Financial Aid Of all full-time matriculated undergraduates who enrolled in 2011, 168 Federal Work-Study jobs (averaging $1227). 82 state and other part-time jobs (averaging $1380).
Applying *Options:* electronic application, early admission, deferred entrance. *Application fee:* $20. *Required:* high school transcript.
Freshman Application Contact Ms. Brenda Kochevar, Enrollment Services Director, Mesabi Range College, Virginia, MN 55792. *Phone:* 218-749-0314. *Toll-free phone:* 800-657-3860. *Fax:* 218-749-0318. *E-mail:* b.kochevar@mesabirange.edu. *Website:* http://www.mesabirange.edu/.

Minneapolis Business College
Roseville, Minnesota

Freshman Application Contact Admissions Office, Minneapolis Business College, 1711 West County Road B, Roseville, MN 55113. *Phone:* 651-636-7406. *Toll-free phone:* 800-279-5200. *Website:* http://www.minneapolisbusinesscollege.edu/.

Minneapolis Community and Technical College
Minneapolis, Minnesota

Freshman Application Contact Minneapolis Community and Technical College, 1501 Hennepin Avenue, Minneapolis, MN 55403. *Phone:* 612-659-6200. *Toll-free phone:* 800-247-0911. *E-mail:* admissions.office@minneapolis.edu. *Website:* http://www.minneapolis.edu/.

Minnesota State College–Southeast Technical
Winona, Minnesota

- **State-supported** 2-year, founded 1992, part of Minnesota State Colleges and Universities System
- **Small-town** 132-acre campus with easy access to Minneapolis-St. Paul
- **Coed,** 1,814 undergraduate students, 39% full-time, 55% women, 45% men

Undergraduates 710 full-time, 1,104 part-time. 26% are from out of state; 4% Black or African American, non-Hispanic/Latino; 4% Hispanic/Latino; 3% Asian, non-Hispanic/Latino; 0.1% Native Hawaiian or other Pacific Islander, non-Hispanic/Latino; 0.5% American Indian or Alaska Native, non-Hispanic/Latino; 4% Two or more races, non-Hispanic/Latino; 0.8% Race/ethnicity unknown; 0.4% international; 10% transferred in.
Freshmen *Admission:* 1,666 applied, 583 admitted, 227 enrolled. *Average high school GPA:* 2.7.
Faculty *Total:* 102, 49% full-time, 5% with terminal degrees. *Student/faculty ratio:* 15:1.
Majors Accounting; accounting technology and bookkeeping; administrative assistant and secretarial science; autobody/collision and repair technology; biomedical technology; business administration and management; CAD/CADD drafting/design technology; carpentry; computer programming; computer systems networking and telecommunications; computer technology/computer systems technology; cosmetology; criminal justice/safety; early childhood education; electrical, electronic and communications engineering technology; heating, air conditioning, ventilation and refrigeration maintenance technology; industrial mechanics and maintenance technology; legal administrative assistant/secretary; massage therapy; medical administrative assistant and medical secretary; multi/interdisciplinary studies related; radiologic technology/science; registered nursing/registered nurse; retailing; selling skills and sales; web page, digital/multimedia and information resources design.
Academics *Calendar:* semesters. *Degree:* certificates, diplomas, and associate. *Special study options:* distance learning, double majors, internships.
Library Learning Resource Center.
Student Life *Housing:* college housing not available. *Activities and Organizations:* student-run newspaper. *Campus security:* 24-hour emergency response devices, late-night transport/escort service.
Financial Aid Of all full-time matriculated undergraduates who enrolled in 2017, 618 applied for aid, 542 were judged to have need, 19 had their need fully met. In 2017, 27 non-need-based awards were made. *Average percent of*

need met: 38%. *Average financial aid package:* $6659. *Average need-based loan:* $3227. *Average need-based gift aid:* $5021. *Average non-need-based aid:* $2012.
Applying *Options:* electronic application. *Application fee:* $20. *Required:* high school transcript. *Recommended:* interview. *Application deadlines:* rolling (freshmen), rolling (transfers). *Notification:* continuous (freshmen), continuous (transfers).
Director of Admissions Tammy Vondrasek, Director of Enrollment Services, Minnesota State College–Southeast Technical, 1250 Homer Road, PO Box 409, Winona, MN 55987. *Phone:* 507-453-2639. *Toll-free phone:* 800-372-8164. *E-mail:* tvondrasek@southeastmn.edu.
Website: http://www.southeastmn.edu/.

Minnesota State Community and Technical College

Fergus Falls, Minnesota

- **State-supported** 2-year, founded 1960, part of Minnesota State Colleges and Universities System
- **Rural** campus
- **Coed**

Undergraduates 2% live on campus.
Academics *Calendar:* semesters. *Degree:* certificates, diplomas, and associate. *Special study options:* academic remediation for entering students, accelerated degree program, advanced placement credit, cooperative education, distance learning, double majors, English as a second language, freshman honors college, honors programs, independent study, internships, off-campus study, part-time degree program, services for LD students, study abroad, summer session for credit.
Library Minnesota State Community and Technical College - Fergus Falls Library plus 4 others.
Student Life *Campus security:* 24-hour emergency response devices, late-night transport/escort service, security for special events.
Financial Aid Of all full-time matriculated undergraduates who enrolled in 2017, 6,298 applied for aid. 95 Federal Work-Study jobs, 103 state and other part-time jobs. *Average financial aid package:* $7816. *Average need-based loan:* $3500. *Average need-based gift aid:* $750. *Financial aid deadline:* 7/1.
Applying *Options:* electronic application, early admission, deferred entrance. *Application fee:* $20.
Admissions Office Contact Minnesota State Community and Technical College, 1414 College Way, Fergus Falls, MN 56537-1009. *Toll-free phone:* 877-450-3322. *Website:* http://www.minnesota.edu/.

Minnesota State Community and Technical College–Detroit Lakes

Detroit Lakes, Minnesota

Freshman Application Contact Minnesota State Community and Technical College–Detroit Lakes, 900 Highway 34, E, Detroit Lakes, MN 56501. *Phone:* 218-846-3777. *Toll-free phone:* 800-492-4836. *Website:* http://www.minnesota.edu/.

Minnesota State Community and Technical College–Moorhead

Moorhead, Minnesota

Freshman Application Contact Minnesota State Community and Technical College–Moorhead, 1900 28th Avenue, South, Moorhead, MN 56560. *Phone:* 218-299-6824. *Toll-free phone:* 800-426-5603. *Website:* http://www.minnesota.edu/.

Minnesota State Community and Technical College–Wadena

Wadena, Minnesota

Freshman Application Contact Minnesota State Community and Technical College–Wadena, 405 Colfax Avenue, SW, PO Box 566, Wadena, MN 56482. *Phone:* 218-631-7818. *Toll-free phone:* 800-247-2007. *Website:* http://www.minnesota.edu/.

Minnesota West Community and Technical College

Pipestone, Minnesota

- **State-supported** 2-year, founded 1967, part of Minnesota State Colleges and Universities System
- **Rural** campus
- **Coed**

Undergraduates 1,153 full-time, 2,029 part-time. 11% are from out of state; 5% Black or African American, non-Hispanic/Latino; 6% Hispanic/Latino; 3% Asian, non-Hispanic/Latino; 0.1% Native Hawaiian or other Pacific Islander, non-Hispanic/Latino; 0.9% American Indian or Alaska Native, non-Hispanic/Latino; 2% Two or more races, non-Hispanic/Latino; 5% Race/ethnicity unknown. *Retention:* 60% of full-time freshmen returned.
Faculty *Student/faculty ratio:* 21:1.
Academics *Calendar:* semesters. *Degrees:* certificates, diplomas, and associate (profile contains information from Canby, Granite Falls, Jackson, and Worthington campuses). *Special study options:* academic remediation for entering students, advanced placement credit, cooperative education, distance learning, double majors, external degree program, honors programs, independent study, internships, part-time degree program, services for LD students, summer session for credit.
Library Library and Academic Resource Center plus 4 others.
Athletics Member NJCAA.
Financial Aid Of all full-time matriculated undergraduates who enrolled in 2017, 1,525 applied for aid, 1,525 were judged to have need. 98 Federal Work-Study jobs (averaging $2508). 90 state and other part-time jobs (averaging $1800).
Applying *Options:* electronic application. *Application fee:* $20. *Required:* high school transcript.
Freshman Application Contact Ms. Crystal Strouth, College Registrar, Minnesota West Community and Technical College, 1450 Collegeway, Worthington, MN 56187. *Phone:* 507-372-3451. *Toll-free phone:* 800-658-2330. *Fax:* 507-372-5803. *E-mail:* crystal.strouth@mnwest.edu. *Website:* http://www.mnwest.edu/.

Normandale Community College

Bloomington, Minnesota

Freshman Application Contact Admissions Office, Normandale Community College, 9700 France Avenue South, Bloomington, MN 55431. *Phone:* 952-358-8201. *Toll-free phone:* 800-481-5412. *Fax:* 952-358-8230. *E-mail:* information@normandale.edu. *Website:* http://www.normandale.edu/.

North Hennepin Community College

Brooklyn Park, Minnesota

- **State-supported** 2-year, founded 1966, part of Minnesota State Colleges and Universities system
- **Suburban** 80-acre campus with easy access to Minneapolis-St. Paul
- **Endowment** $761,415
- **Coed**

Academics *Calendar:* semesters. *Degree:* certificates and associate. *Special study options:* academic remediation for entering students, accelerated degree program, adult/continuing education programs, advanced placement credit, distance learning, double majors, English as a second language, external degree program, honors programs, independent study, internships, off-campus study, part-time degree program, services for LD students, student-designed majors, study abroad, summer session for credit. *ROTC:* Army (c), Navy (c), Air Force (c).
Library Learning Resource Center.
Student Life *Campus security:* 24-hour emergency response devices, student patrols, late-night transport/escort service.
Applying *Options:* electronic application, early admission, deferred entrance. *Application fee:* $20. *Recommended:* high school transcript.
Freshman Application Contact Mr. Sean Olson, Associate Director of Admissions and Outreach, North Hennepin Community College, 7411 85th Avenue North, Brooklyn Park, MN 55445. *Phone:* 763-424-0724. *Toll-free phone:* 800-818-0395. *Fax:* 763-493-0563. *E-mail:* solson2@nhcc.edu. *Website:* http://www.nhcc.edu/.

Northland Community and Technical College

Thief River Falls, Minnesota

- **State-supported** 2-year, founded 1949, part of Minnesota State Colleges and Universities System
- **Small-town** 239-acre campus
- **Coed**

Undergraduates 1,375 full-time, 2,224 part-time. Students come from 24 states and territories; 1 other country; 7% are from out of state; 7% Black or African American, non-Hispanic/Latino; 4% Hispanic/Latino; 3% Asian, non-Hispanic/Latino; 0.1% Native Hawaiian or other Pacific Islander, non-Hispanic/Latino; 2% American Indian or Alaska Native, non-Hispanic/Latino; 4% Two or more races, non-Hispanic/Latino; 5% Race/ethnicity unknown; 0.5% international; 11% transferred in. *Retention:* 56% of full-time freshmen returned.
Faculty *Student/faculty ratio:* 19:1.
Academics *Calendar:* semesters. *Degree:* certificates, diplomas, and associate. *Special study options:* academic remediation for entering students, adult/continuing education programs, advanced placement credit, cooperative education, distance learning, double majors, internships, off-campus study, part-time degree program, services for LD students, summer session for credit.
Library Northland Community and Technical College Library plus 1 other. *Books:* 24,000 (physical), 19,000 (digital/electronic); *Serial titles:* 55 (physical); *Databases:* 47. Weekly public service hours: 82; students can reserve study rooms.
Student Life *Campus security:* student patrols, late-night transport/escort service.
Athletics Member NJCAA.
Financial Aid Of all full-time matriculated undergraduates who enrolled in 2011, 98 Federal Work-Study jobs (averaging $2701). 68 state and other part-time jobs (averaging $2839).
Applying *Options:* electronic application, early admission, deferred entrance. *Application fee:* $20. *Required:* high school transcript.
Freshman Application Contact Mrs. Nicki Carlson, Director of Enrollment Management, Northland Community and Technical College, 1101 Highway One East, Thief River Falls, MN 56701. *Phone:* 218-683-8546. *Toll-free phone:* 800-959-6282. *Fax:* 218-683-8980. *E-mail:* nicki.carlson@northlandcollege.edu. *Website:* http://www.northlandcollege.edu/.

Northwest Technical College

Bemidji, Minnesota

Freshman Application Contact Ms. Kari Kantack-Miller, Diversity and Enrollment Representative, Northwest Technical College, 905 Grant Avenue, Southeast, Bemidji, MN 56601. *Phone:* 218-333-6645. *Toll-free phone:* 800-942-8324. *Fax:* 218-333-6694. *E-mail:* kari.kantack@ntcmn.edu. *Website:* http://www.ntcmn.edu/.

Pine Technical and Community College

Pine City, Minnesota

Freshman Application Contact Pine Technical and Community College, 900 4th Street SE, Pine City, MN 55063. *Phone:* 320-629-5100. *Toll-free phone:* 800-521-7463. *Website:* http://www.pine.edu/.

Rainy River Community College

International Falls, Minnesota

- **State-supported** 2-year, founded 1967, part of Minnesota State Colleges and Universities System
- **Small-town** 80-acre campus
- **Coed**

Undergraduates 203 full-time, 38 part-time. Students come from 16 states and territories; 2 other countries; 19% Black or African American, non-Hispanic/Latino; 9% Hispanic/Latino; 1% Asian, non-Hispanic/Latino; 8% American Indian or Alaska Native, non-Hispanic/Latino; 7% international.
Faculty *Student/faculty ratio:* 15:1.
Academics *Calendar:* semesters. *Degree:* certificates, diplomas, and associate. *Special study options:* academic remediation for entering students, adult/continuing education programs, advanced placement credit, cooperative education, honors programs, independent study, internships, part-time degree program, services for LD students, summer session for credit.
Library Rainy River Community College Library.
Student Life *Campus security:* 24-hour emergency response devices, late-night transport/escort service, controlled dormitory access.
Athletics Member NJCAA.
Applying *Options:* electronic application, early admission, deferred entrance. *Application fee:* $20. *Recommended:* high school transcript.
Freshman Application Contact Ms. Berta Wilcox, Registrar, Rainy River Community College, 1501 Highway 71, International Falls, MN 56649. *Phone:* 218-285-2207. *Toll-free phone:* 800-456-3996. *Fax:* 218-285-2314. *E-mail:* berta.wilcox@rainyriver.edu. *Website:* http://www.rainyriver.edu/.

Ridgewater College

Willmar, Minnesota

- **State-supported** 2-year, founded 1961, part of Minnesota State Colleges and Universities System
- **Small-town** 83-acre campus
- **Coed,** 4,385 students

Faculty *Total:* 186, 59% full-time.
Majors Accounting; administrative assistant and secretarial science; agribusiness; agricultural production; agriculture; agronomy and crop science; animal/livestock husbandry and production; autobody/collision and repair technology; automobile/automotive mechanics technology; biology/biological sciences; business administration and management; carpentry; chemistry; commercial photography; computer programming; computer science; computer systems networking and telecommunications; computer technology/computer systems technology; cosmetology; criminal justice/police science; crop production; dairy husbandry and production; desktop publishing and digital imaging design; digital communication and media/multimedia; electrical, electronic and communications engineering technology; electrician; electromechanical technology; health information/medical records technology; instrumentation technology; legal administrative assistant/secretary; liberal arts and sciences and humanities related; liberal arts and sciences/liberal studies; machine tool technology; marketing/marketing management; mechanical drafting and CAD/CADD; medical administrative assistant and medical secretary; medical/clinical assistant; network and system administration; radiologic technology/science; recording arts technology; registered nursing/registered nurse; sales, distribution, and marketing operations; selling skills and sales; teacher assistant/aide; telecommunications technology; therapeutic recreation; tool and die technology; veterinary/animal health technology; web page, digital/multimedia and information resources design; welding technology.
Academics *Calendar:* semesters. *Degree:* certificates, diplomas, and associate. *Special study options:* academic remediation for entering students, advanced placement credit, cooperative education, distance learning, internships, off-campus study, part-time degree program, services for LD students, student-designed majors, study abroad, summer session for credit.
Student Life *Housing:* college housing not available. *Campus security:* 24-hour emergency response devices. *Student services:* personal/psychological counseling, veterans affairs office.
Athletics Member NJCAA. *Intercollegiate sports:* basketball W, softball W, volleyball W.
Financial Aid Of all full-time matriculated undergraduates who enrolled in 2017, 350 Federal Work-Study jobs (averaging $3000). 133 state and other part-time jobs (averaging $2400).
Applying *Options:* electronic application. *Application fee:* $20. *Required:* high school transcript. *Required for some:* interview.
Freshman Application Contact Ms. Linda Duering, Admissions Assistant, Ridgewater College, 2101 15th Avenue NW, Willmar, MN 56201. *Phone:* 320-222-5976. *Toll-free phone:* 800-722-1151. *E-mail:* linda.duering@ridgewater.edu.
Website: http://www.ridgewater.edu/.

Riverland Community College

Austin, Minnesota

Freshman Application Contact Riverland Community College, 1900 8th Avenue, NW, Austin, MN 55912. *Phone:* 507-433-0600. *Toll-free phone:* 800-247-5039. *Website:* http://www.riverland.edu/.

Rochester Community and Technical College

Rochester, Minnesota

Director of Admissions Mr. Troy Tynsky, Director of Admissions, Rochester Community and Technical College, 851 30th Avenue, SE, Rochester, MN 55904-4999. *Phone:* 507-280-3509. *Website:* http://www.rctc.edu/.

St. Cloud Technical & Community College

St. Cloud, Minnesota

Freshman Application Contact Ms. Jodi Elness, Admissions Office, St. Cloud Technical & Community College, 1540 Northway Drive, St. Cloud, MN 56303. *Phone:* 320-308-5089. *Toll-free phone:* 800-222-1009. *Fax:* 320-308-5981. *E-mail:* jelness@sctcc.edu. *Website:* http://www.sctcc.edu/.

Saint Paul College–A Community & Technical College

St. Paul, Minnesota

Freshman Application Contact Ms. Sarah Carrico, Saint Paul College–A Community & Technical College, 235 Marshall Avenue, Saint Paul, MN 55102. *Phone:* 651-846-1424. *Toll-free phone:* 800-227-6029. *Fax:* 651-846-1703. *E-mail:* admissions@saintpaul.edu. *Website:* http://www.saintpaul.edu/.

South Central College

North Mankato, Minnesota

Freshman Application Contact Ms. Beverly Herda, Director of Admissions, South Central College, 1920 Lee Boulevard, North Mankato, MN 56003. *Phone:* 507-389-7334. *Fax:* 507-388-9951. *Website:* http://southcentral.edu/.

Vermilion Community College

Ely, Minnesota

Freshman Application Contact Mr. Todd Heiman, Director of Enrollment Services, Vermilion Community College, 1900 East Camp Street, Ely, MN 55731-1996. *Phone:* 218-365-7224. *Toll-free phone:* 800-657-3608. *Website:* http://www.vcc.edu/.

White Earth Tribal and Community College

Mahnomen, Minnesota

Admissions Office Contact White Earth Tribal and Community College, 102 3rd Street NE, Mahnomen, MN 56557. *Website:* http://www.wetcc.edu/.

MISSISSIPPI

Antonelli College

Hattiesburg, Mississippi

Freshman Application Contact Mrs. Karen Gautreau, Director, Antonelli College, 1500 North 31st Avenue, Hattiesburg, MS 39401. *Phone:* 601-583-4100. *Fax:* 601-583-0839. *E-mail:* admissionsh@antonellicollege.edu. *Website:* http://www.antonellicollege.edu/.

Antonelli College

Jackson, Mississippi

Freshman Application Contact Antonelli College, 2323 Lakeland Drive, Jackson, MS 39232. *Phone:* 601-362-9991. *Website:* http://www.antonellicollege.edu/.

Coahoma Community College

Clarksdale, Mississippi

Freshman Application Contact Mrs. Wanda Holmes, Director of Admissions and Records, Coahoma Community College, Clarksdale, MS 38614-9799. *Phone:* 662-621-4205. *Toll-free phone:* 866-470-1CCC. *Website:* http://www.coahomacc.edu/.

Concorde Career College

Southaven, Mississippi

Admissions Office Contact Concorde Career College, 7900 Airways Boulevard, Suite 103, Southaven, MS 38671. *Website:* http://www.concorde.edu/.

Copiah-Lincoln Community College

Wesson, Mississippi

- **State and locally supported** 2-year, founded 1928, part of Mississippi Community College Board
- **Rural** 525-acre campus with easy access to Jackson
- **Endowment** $2.5 million
- **Coed**

Undergraduates 2,128 full-time, 972 part-time. Students come from 8 states and territories; 1 other country; 1% are from out of state; 40% Black or African American, non-Hispanic/Latino; 0.9% Hispanic/Latino; 0.1% Asian, non-Hispanic/Latino; 0.5% Two or more races, non-Hispanic/Latino; 3% Race/ethnicity unknown; 5% transferred in; 30% live on campus.

Academics *Calendar:* semesters. *Degree:* certificates and associate. *Special study options:* academic remediation for entering students, accelerated degree program, adult/continuing education programs, advanced placement credit, distance learning, honors programs, part-time degree program, services for LD students, student-designed majors, study abroad, summer session for credit.

Library Oswalt Memorial Library.

Student Life *Campus security:* 24-hour patrols.

Athletics Member NJCAA.

Financial Aid Of all full-time matriculated undergraduates who enrolled in 2017, 125 Federal Work-Study jobs (averaging $1000).

Applying *Options:* early admission. *Required:* high school transcript.

Freshman Application Contact Ms. Gay Langham, Student Records Manager, Copiah-Lincoln Community College, PO Box 649, Wesson, MS 39191-0457. *Phone:* 601-643-8307. *E-mail:* gay.langham@colin.edu. *Website:* http://www.colin.edu/.

East Central Community College

Decatur, Mississippi

Director of Admissions Ms. Donna Luke, Director of Admissions, Records, and Research, East Central Community College, PO Box 129, Decatur, MS 39327-0129. *Phone:* 601-635-2111 Ext. 206. *Toll-free phone:* 877-462-3222. *Website:* http://www.eccc.edu/.

East Mississippi Community College

Scooba, Mississippi

Director of Admissions Ms. Melinda Sciple, Admissions Officer, East Mississippi Community College, PO Box 158, Scooba, MS 39358-0158. *Phone:* 662-476-5041. *Website:* http://www.eastms.edu/.

Hinds Community College

Raymond, Mississippi

- **State and locally supported** 2-year, founded 1917, part of Mississippi Community College Board
- **Small-town** 671-acre campus with easy access to Jackson
- **Coed**

Undergraduates 7,196 full-time, 4,865 part-time. Students come from 23 states and territories; 15 other countries; 3% are from out of state; 56% Black or African American, non-Hispanic/Latino; 2% Hispanic/Latino; 0.9% Asian, non-Hispanic/Latino; 0.2% American Indian or Alaska Native, non-Hispanic/Latino; 3% Two or more races, non-Hispanic/Latino; 2% Race/ethnicity unknown; 8% transferred in. *Retention:* 57% of full-time freshmen returned.

Faculty *Student/faculty ratio:* 17:1.

Academics *Calendar:* semesters. *Degrees:* certificates and associate (profile includes Raymond, Jackson Academic and Technical Center, Jackson Nursing-Allied Health Center, Rankin, Utica, and Vicksburg campus locations). *Special study options:* academic remediation for entering students, accelerated degree program, adult/continuing education programs, advanced placement credit, cooperative education, distance learning, double majors, honors programs, independent study, internships, part-time degree program, services for LD students, study abroad, summer session for credit. *ROTC:* Army (b).

Library McLendon Library plus 5 others. Students can reserve study rooms.

Student Life *Campus security:* 24-hour emergency response devices and patrols, late-night transport/escort service, controlled dormitory access.

Athletics Member NJCAA.

Financial Aid Of all full-time matriculated undergraduates who enrolled in 2017, 300 Federal Work-Study jobs (averaging $1250). 200 state and other part-time jobs (averaging $1000).

Applying *Options:* electronic application.

Freshman Application Contact Hinds Community College, PO Box 1100, Raymond, MS 39154-1100. *Phone:* 601-857-3280. *Toll-free phone:* 800-HINDSCC. *Website:* http://www.hindscc.edu/.

Holmes Community College

Goodman, Mississippi

Director of Admissions Dr. Lynn Wright, Dean of Admissions and Records, Holmes Community College, PO Box 369, Goodman, MS 39079-0369. *Phone:* 601-472-2312 Ext. 1023. *Toll-free phone:* 800-HOLMES-4. *Website:* http://www.holmescc.edu/.

Itawamba Community College

Fulton, Mississippi

Freshman Application Contact Mr. Larry Boggs, Director of Student Recruitment and Scholarships, Itawamba Community College, 602 West Hill Street, Fulton, MS 38843. *Phone:* 601-862-8252. *E-mail:* laboggs@iccms.edu. *Website:* http://www.iccms.edu/.

Jones County Junior College

Ellisville, Mississippi

Director of Admissions Mrs. Dianne Speed, Director of Admissions and Records, Jones County Junior College, 900 South Court Street, Ellisville, MS 39437-3901. *Phone:* 601-477-4025. *Website:* http://www.jcjc.edu/.

Meridian Community College

Meridian, Mississippi

- **State and locally supported** 2-year, founded 1937, part of Mississippi Community College Board
- **Small-town** 91-acre campus
- **Endowment** $12.7 million
- **Coed**

Undergraduates 2,424 full-time, 1,131 part-time. 43% Black or African American, non-Hispanic/Latino; 1% Hispanic/Latino; 0.5% Asian, non-Hispanic/Latino; 2% American Indian or Alaska Native, non-Hispanic/Latino; 0.5% Two or more races, non-Hispanic/Latino; 5% Race/ethnicity unknown; 12% live on campus. *Retention:* 55% of full-time freshmen returned.
Faculty *Student/faculty ratio:* 18:1.
Academics *Calendar:* semesters. *Degree:* certificates and associate. *Special study options:* academic remediation for entering students, accelerated degree program, adult/continuing education programs, advanced placement credit, cooperative education, distance learning, double majors, English as a second language, freshman honors college, honors programs, independent study, internships, part-time degree program, services for LD students, summer session for credit.
Library L.O. Todd-Billy C. Beal Learning Resources Center. *Books:* 49,544 (physical), 174,022 (digital/electronic); *Serial titles:* 207 (physical), 11 (digital/electronic); *Databases:* 13.
Student Life *Campus security:* 24-hour patrols by law enforcement officers.
Athletics Member NJCAA.
Applying *Options:* early admission. *Required:* high school transcript, minimum 2.0 GPA.
Freshman Application Contact Ms. Angela Payne, Director of Admissions, Meridian Community College, 910 Highway 19 North, Meridian, MS 39307. *Phone:* 601-484-8357. *Toll-free phone:* 800-MCC-THE-1. *E-mail:* apayne@meridiancc.edu. *Website:* http://www.meridiancc.edu/.

Mississippi Delta Community College

Moorhead, Mississippi

Freshman Application Contact Mississippi Delta Community College, PO Box 668, Highway 3 and Cherry Street, Moorhead, MS 38761-0668. *Phone:* 662-246-6302. *Website:* http://www.msdelta.edu/.

Mississippi Gulf Coast Community College

Perkinston, Mississippi

Freshman Application Contact Mrs. Nichol Green, Director of Admissions, Mississippi Gulf Coast Community College, PO Box 548, Perkinston, MS 39573. *Phone:* 601-928-6264. *Fax:* 601-928-6345. *Website:* http://www.mgccc.edu/.

Northeast Mississippi Community College

Booneville, Mississippi

Freshman Application Contact Office of Enrollment Services, Northeast Mississippi Community College, 101 Cunningham Boulevard, Booneville, MS 38829. *Phone:* 662-720-7239. *Toll-free phone:* 800-555-2154. *E-mail:* admitme@nemcc.edu. *Website:* http://www.nemcc.edu/.

Northwest Mississippi Community College

Senatobia, Mississippi

- **State and locally supported** 2-year, founded 1927, part of Mississippi State Board for Community and Junior Colleges
- **Rural** 75-acre campus with easy access to Memphis
- **Coed**

Undergraduates *Retention:* 60% of full-time freshmen returned.
Faculty *Student/faculty ratio:* 20:1.
Academics *Calendar:* semesters. *Degree:* associate. *Special study options:* academic remediation for entering students, adult/continuing education programs, distance learning, honors programs, part-time degree program, services for LD students, summer session for credit. *ROTC:* Air Force (b).
Library R. C. Pugh Library. Study areas open 24 hours, 5–7 days a week.
Student Life *Campus security:* 24-hour emergency response devices and patrols, late-night transport/escort service, controlled dormitory access.
Athletics Member NJCAA.
Applying *Options:* electronic application, early admission, deferred entrance. *Required:* high school transcript.
Freshman Application Contact Northwest Mississippi Community College, 4975 Highway 51 North, Senatobia, MS 38668-1701. *Phone:* 662-562-8217. *Website:* http://www.northwestms.edu/.

Pearl River Community College

Poplarville, Mississippi

Freshman Application Contact Mr. J. Dow Ford, Director of Admissions, Pearl River Community College, 101 Highway 11 North, Poplarville, MS 39470. *Phone:* 601-403-1000. *E-mail:* dford@prcc.edu. *Website:* http://www.prcc.edu/.

Southwest Mississippi Community College

Summit, Mississippi

Freshman Application Contact Mr. Matthew Calhoun, Vice President of Admissions and Records, Southwest Mississippi Community College, 1156 College Drive, Summit, MS 39666. *Phone:* 601-276-2001. *Fax:* 601-276-3888. *E-mail:* mattc@smcc.edu. *Website:* http://www.smcc.cc.ms.us/.

MISSOURI

American Trade School

Saint Ann, Missouri

Admissions Office Contact American Trade School, 3925 Industrial Drive, Saint Ann, MO 63074. *Website:* http://www.americantradeschool.edu/.

Bolivar Technical College

Bolivar, Missouri

Admissions Office Contact Bolivar Technical College, 1135 North Oakland Avenue, Bolivar, MO 65613. *Website:* http://www.bolivarcollege.org/.

Concorde Career College

Kansas City, Missouri

Freshman Application Contact Deborah Crow, Director, Concorde Career College, 3239 Broadway Street, Kansas City, MO 64111. *Phone:* 816-531-5223. *Fax:* 816-756-3231. *E-mail:* dcrow@concorde.edu. *Website:* http://www.concorde.edu/.

Cottey College

Nevada, Missouri

- **Independent** primarily 2-year, founded 1884
- **Small-town** 51-acre campus
- **Endowment** $108.8 million
- **Women only**

Undergraduates 260 full-time, 5 part-time. Students come from 32 states and territories; 18 other countries; 85% are from out of state; 5% Black or African American, non-Hispanic/Latino; 8% Hispanic/Latino; 0.4% Asian, non-Hispanic/Latino; 0.4% Native Hawaiian or other Pacific Islander, non-Hispanic/Latino; 2% American Indian or Alaska Native, non-Hispanic/Latino; 5% Two or more races, non-Hispanic/Latino; 15% international; 4% transferred in; 90% live on campus. *Retention:* 70% of full-time freshmen returned.
Faculty *Student/faculty ratio:* 7:1.
Academics *Calendar:* semesters. *Degrees:* associate and bachelor's. *Special study options:* advanced placement credit, distance learning, independent study, internships, part-time degree program, services for LD students, study abroad.
Library Blanche Skiff Ross Memorial Library plus 1 other. Weekly public service hours: 88.
Student Life *Campus security:* 24-hour emergency response devices and patrols, late-night transport/escort service, controlled dormitory access.
Athletics Member NJCAA.
Standardized Tests *Required:* SAT or ACT (for admission). *Required for some:* TOEFL, IELTS.
Financial Aid Of all full-time matriculated undergraduates who enrolled in 2017, 208 applied for aid, 190 were judged to have need, 65 had their need fully met. 26 Federal Work-Study jobs (averaging $1943). 141 state and other part-time jobs (averaging $1913). In 2017, 69. *Average percent of need met:* 84. *Average financial aid package:* $20,618. *Average need-based loan:* $3234. *Average need-based gift aid:* $16,932. *Average non-need-based aid:* $14,736. *Average indebtedness upon graduation:* $20,406.
Applying *Options:* electronic application, early admission, deferred entrance. *Application fee:* $20. *Required:* essay or personal statement, high school transcript, 1 letter of recommendation. *Recommended:* minimum 2.6 GPA, interview.
Freshman Application Contact Mrs. Angela Moore, Enrollment Office, Cottey College, 1000 West Austin Boulevard, Nevada, MO 64772. *Phone:* 417-667-8181. *Toll-free phone:* 888-526-8839. *Fax:* 417-667-8103. *E-mail:* amoore@cottey.edu. *Website:* http://www.cottey.edu/.

Crowder College

Neosho, Missouri

- **State and locally supported** 2-year, founded 1963, part of Missouri Coordinating Board for Higher Education
- **Rural** 608-acre campus
- **Coed**

Undergraduates Students come from 12 states and territories; 6% are from out of state; 1% Black or African American, non-Hispanic/Latino; 9% Hispanic/Latino; 2% Asian, non-Hispanic/Latino; 0.4% Native Hawaiian or other Pacific Islander, non-Hispanic/Latino; 2% American Indian or Alaska Native, non-Hispanic/Latino; 5% Two or more races, non-Hispanic/Latino; 2% Race/ethnicity unknown; 1% international; 10% live on campus. *Retention:* 64% of full-time freshmen returned.
Faculty *Student/faculty ratio:* 11:1.
Academics *Calendar:* semesters. *Degree:* certificates and associate. *Special study options:* academic remediation for entering students, adult/continuing education programs, advanced placement credit, cooperative education, English as a second language, freshman honors college, honors programs, independent study, part-time degree program, student-designed majors, study abroad, summer session for credit.
Library Bill & Margot Lee Library.
Student Life *Campus security:* 24-hour patrols.
Athletics Member NJCAA.
Financial Aid Of all full-time matriculated undergraduates who enrolled in 2017, 150 Federal Work-Study jobs (averaging $1000).
Applying *Application fee:* $25. *Required:* high school transcript.
Freshman Application Contact Mr. James P. Dickey, Admissions Coordinator, Crowder College, Neosho, MO 64850. *Phone:* 417-451-3223 Ext. 5466. *Toll-free phone:* 866-238-7788. *Fax:* 417-455-5731. *E-mail:* jamesdickey@crowder.edu. *Website:* http://www.crowder.edu/.

East Central College

Union, Missouri

- **District-supported** 2-year, founded 1959
- **Rural** 207-acre campus with easy access to St. Louis
- **Coed,** 2,629 undergraduate students, 46% full-time, 60% women, 40% men

Undergraduates 1,219 full-time, 1,410 part-time. 1% Black or African American, non-Hispanic/Latino; 2% Hispanic/Latino; 0.9% Asian, non-Hispanic/Latino; 0.5% American Indian or Alaska Native, non-Hispanic/Latino; 2% Two or more races, non-Hispanic/Latino; 1% Race/ethnicity unknown; 0.5% international.
Freshmen *Admission:* 652 admitted, 652 enrolled.
Majors Accounting technology and bookkeeping; automobile/automotive mechanics technology; biology/biotechnology laboratory technician; business/commerce; child-care and support services management; computer systems networking and telecommunications; construction trades; culinary arts; education; emergency medical technology (EMT paramedic); engineering; fine/studio arts; fire science/firefighting; general studies; health information/medical records technology; heating, air conditioning, ventilation and refrigeration maintenance technology; industrial technology; machine tool technology; medical/clinical assistant; medical radiologic technology; music; occupational therapist assistant; technical teacher education; welding technology.
Academics *Calendar:* semesters. *Degree:* certificates and associate. *Special study options:* academic remediation for entering students, adult/continuing education programs, advanced placement credit, distance learning, English as a second language, honors programs, independent study, internships, off-campus study, part-time degree program, services for LD students, study abroad, summer session for credit.
Library East Central College Library. Students can reserve study rooms.
Student Life *Housing:* college housing not available. *Activities and Organizations:* drama/theater group, student-run newspaper, choral group, Student Nurse Association - Union Campus, Rolla Student Nurse Organization, R&R Club, Art Club, Engineering Club. *Campus security:* 24-hour emergency response devices, late-night transport/escort service. *Student services:* personal/psychological counseling.
Athletics Member NJCAA. *Intercollegiate sports:* softball W(s), volleyball W(s).
Applying *Options:* electronic application, early admission, deferred entrance. *Required:* high school transcript. *Application deadlines:* rolling (freshmen), rolling (transfers).
Freshman Application Contact Mr. JC Crane, Director, Admissions, East Central College, 1964 Prairie Dell Road, Union, MO 63084. *Phone:* 636-584-6552. *E-mail:* jc.crane@eastcentral.edu.
Website: http://www.eastcentral.edu/.

Jefferson College

Hillsboro, Missouri

Freshman Application Contact Dr. Kimberly Harvey, Director of Student Records and Admissions Services, Jefferson College, 1000 Viking Drive, Hillsboro, MO 63050-2441. *Phone:* 636-481-3205 Ext. 3205. *Fax:* 636-789-5103. *E-mail:* admissions@jeffco.edu. *Website:* http://www.jeffco.edu/.

L'Ecole Culinaire–Kansas City

Kansas City, Missouri

Admissions Office Contact L'Ecole Culinaire–Kansas City, 310 Ward Parkway, Kansas City, MO 64112. *Toll-free phone:* 855-549-7577. *Website:* http://www.lecole.edu/kansas-city/kansas-city-culinary-school.asp.

L'Ecole Culinaire–St. Louis

St. Louis, Missouri

Admissions Office Contact L'Ecole Culinaire–St. Louis, 9811 South Forty Drive, St. Louis, MO 63124. *Toll-free phone:* 855-764-0043. *Website:* http://www.lecole.edu/st-louis/st-louis-culinary-school.asp.

Metro Business College

Cape Girardeau, Missouri

Director of Admissions Ms. Kyla Evans, Admissions Director, Metro Business College, 1732 North Kingshighway, Cape Girardeau, MO 63701. *Phone:* 573-334-9181. *Toll-free phone:* 888-206-4545. *Fax:* 573-334-0617. *Website:* http://www.metrobusinesscollege.edu/.

Metro Business College

Jefferson City, Missouri

Freshman Application Contact Ms. Cheri Chockley, Campus Director, Metro Business College, 210 El Mercado Plaza, Jefferson City, MO 65109. *Phone:* 573-635-6600. *Toll-free phone:* 888-206-4545. *Fax:* 573-635-6999. *E-mail:* cheri@metrobusinesscollege.edu. *Website:* http://www.metrobusinesscollege.edu/.

Metro Business College

Rolla, Missouri

Freshman Application Contact Admissions Office, Metro Business College, 1202 East Highway 72, Rolla, MO 65401. *Phone:* 573-364-8464. *Toll-free phone:* 888-206-4545. *Fax:* 573-364-8077. *E-mail:* inforolla@metrobusinesscollege.edu. *Website:* http://www.metrobusinesscollege.edu/.

Metropolitan Community College–Kansas City

Kansas City, Missouri

Freshman Application Contact Dr. Tuesday Stanley, Vice Chancellor of Student Development and Enrollment Services, Metropolitan Community College–Kansas City, 3200 Broadway, Kansas City, MO 64111-2429. *Phone:* 816-604-1253. *E-mail:* tuesday.stanley@mcckc.edu. *Website:* http://www.mcckc.edu/.

Midwest Institute

Fenton, Missouri

Freshman Application Contact Admissions Office, Midwest Institute, 964 South Highway Drive, Fenton, MO 63026. *Toll-free phone:* 800-695-5550. *Website:* http://www.midwestinstitute.com/.

Midwest Institute

St. Louis, Missouri

Freshman Application Contact Admissions Office, Midwest Institute, 4260 Shoreline Drive, St. Louis, MO 63045. *Phone:* 314-344-4440. *Toll-free phone:* 800-695-5550. *Fax:* 314-344-0495. *Website:* http://www.midwestinstitute.com/.

Mineral Area College

Park Hills, Missouri

Freshman Application Contact Pam Reeder, Registrar, Mineral Area College, PO Box 1000, Park Hills, MO 63601-1000. *Phone:* 573-518-2204. *Fax:* 573-518-2166. *E-mail:* preeder@mineralarea.edu. *Website:* http://www.mineralarea.edu/.

Missouri State University–West Plains

West Plains, Missouri

- **State-supported** 2-year, founded 1963, part of Missouri State University
- **Small-town** 20-acre campus
- **Endowment** $8.3 million
- **Coed,** 1,909 undergraduate students, 42% full-time, 65% women, 35% men

Undergraduates 806 full-time, 1,103 part-time. Students come from 18 states and territories; 15 other countries; 3% are from out of state; 1% Black or African American, non-Hispanic/Latino; 3% Hispanic/Latino; 0.1% Asian, non-Hispanic/Latino; 84% Native Hawaiian or other Pacific Islander, non-Hispanic/Latino; 5% American Indian or Alaska Native, non-Hispanic/Latino; 3% Two or more races, non-Hispanic/Latino; 3% Race/ethnicity unknown; 0.7% international; 4% transferred in; 10% live on campus.

Freshmen *Admission:* 947 applied, 370 admitted, 422 enrolled. *Average high school GPA:* 3.2.

Faculty *Total:* 106, 34% full-time, 27% with terminal degrees. *Student/faculty ratio:* 20:1.

Majors Agriculture; animation, interactive technology, video graphics and special effects; business/commerce; criminal justice/police science; elementary education; engineering; food science; general studies; health/medical preparatory programs related; health services/allied health/health sciences; human development and family studies; industrial production technologies related; registered nursing/registered nurse; restaurant, culinary, and catering management; viticulture and enology.

Academics *Calendar:* semesters. *Degree:* certificates and associate. *Special study options:* academic remediation for entering students, adult/continuing education programs, advanced placement credit, cooperative education, distance learning, honors programs, internships, off-campus study, part-time degree program, services for LD students, study abroad, summer session for credit.

Library Garnett Library. *Books:* 42,808 (physical), 234,677 (digital/electronic); *Serial titles:* 118 (physical), 5,877 (digital/electronic); *Databases:* 239. Weekly public service hours: 67.

Student Life *Housing:* on-campus residence required for freshman year. *Options:* coed, special housing for students with disabilities. Campus housing is university owned and is provided by a third party. *Activities and Organizations:* Student Government Association, Student Nurses Association, Student Ambassadors, Christian Campus House, Grizzly Cheer Team. *Campus security:* 24-hour emergency response devices, student patrols, late-night transport/escort service, controlled dormitory access, access only with key, agreement with city police for patrols. *Student services:* personal/psychological counseling, legal services, veterans affairs office.

Athletics Member NJCAA. *Intercollegiate sports:* volleyball W(s).

Financial Aid Of all full-time matriculated undergraduates who enrolled in 2017, 63 Federal Work-Study jobs (averaging $2000).

Applying *Options:* electronic application. *Required for some:* high school transcript. *Application deadlines:* rolling (freshmen), rolling (out-of-state freshmen), rolling (transfers). *Notification:* continuous (freshmen), continuous (out-of-state freshmen), continuous (transfers).

Freshman Application Contact Ms. Melissa Jett, Coordinator of Admissions, Missouri State University–West Plains, 128 Garfield, West Plains, MO 65775. *Phone:* 417-255-7955. *Toll-free phone:* 888-466-7897. *Fax:* 417-255-7959. *E-mail:* melissajett@missouristate.edu. *Website:* http://wp.missouristate.edu/.

Moberly Area Community College

Moberly, Missouri

Freshman Application Contact Dr. James Grant, Dean of Student Services, Moberly Area Community College, Moberly, MO 65270-1304. *Phone:* 660-263-4110 Ext. 235. *Toll-free phone:* 800-622-2070. *Fax:* 660-263-2406. *E-mail:* info@macc.edu. *Website:* http://www.macc.edu/.

North Central Missouri College

Trenton, Missouri

Freshman Application Contact Jamie Cunningham, Admissions Recruiter, North Central Missouri College, Trenton, MO 64683. *Phone:* 660-359-3948 Ext. 1414. *E-mail:* jcunningham@mail.ncmissouri.edu/. *Website:* http://www.ncmissouri.edu/.

Ozarks Technical Community College

Springfield, Missouri

- **District-supported** 2-year, founded 1990, part of Missouri Coordinating Board for Higher Education
- **Urban** campus
- **Endowment** $2.8 million
- **Coed**

Undergraduates 5,826 full-time, 7,434 part-time. Students come from 31 states and territories; 2% are from out of state; 3% Black or African American, non-Hispanic/Latino; 5% Hispanic/Latino; 1% Asian, non-Hispanic/Latino; 0.2% Native Hawaiian or other Pacific Islander, non-Hispanic/Latino; 0.5% American Indian or Alaska Native, non-Hispanic/Latino; 5% Two or more races, non-Hispanic/Latino; 2% Race/ethnicity unknown.

Faculty *Student/faculty ratio:* 21:1.

Academics *Calendar:* semesters. *Degree:* certificates, diplomas, and associate. *Special study options:* academic remediation for entering students, adult/continuing education programs, cooperative education, distance learning, double majors, English as a second language, honors programs, internships, off-campus study, part-time degree program, services for LD students, summer session for credit.

Library Main Library plus 1 other.

Student Life *Campus security:* 24-hour emergency response devices.

Financial Aid Of all full-time matriculated undergraduates who enrolled in 2016, 180 Federal Work-Study jobs (averaging $1533).

Applying *Options:* electronic application. *Required:* high school transcript.

Freshman Application Contact Ozarks Technical Community College, 1001 E. Chestnut Expressway, Springfield, MO 65802. *Website:* http://www.otc.edu/.

Pinnacle Career Institute

Kansas City, Missouri

Director of Admissions Ms. Ruth Matous, Director of Admissions, Pinnacle Career Institute, 10301 Hickman Mills Drive, Kansas City, MO 64137. *Phone:* 816-331-5700 Ext. 212. *Toll-free phone:* 877-241-3097. *Website:* http://www.pcitraining.edu/.

Pinnacle Career Institute

Kansas City, Missouri

Freshman Application Contact Pinnacle Career Institute, 11500 NW Ambassador Drive, Suite 221, Kansas City, MO 64153. *Phone:* 816-331-5700. *Toll-free phone:* 877-241-3097. *Website:* http://www.pcitraining.edu/.

Ranken Technical College

St. Louis, Missouri

Freshman Application Contact Ranken Technical College, 4431 Finney Avenue, St. Louis, MO 63113. *Phone:* 314-371-0233 Ext. 4811. *Toll-free phone:* 866-4-RANKEN. *Website:* http://www.ranken.edu/.

St. Charles Community College

Cottleville, Missouri

- **State-supported** 2-year, founded 1986, part of Missouri Coordinating Board for Higher Education
- **Suburban** 228-acre campus with easy access to St. Louis
- **Endowment** $83,673
- **Coed,** 6,269 undergraduate students, 51% full-time, 57% women, 43% men

Undergraduates 3,167 full-time, 3,102 part-time. Students come from 14 states and territories; 36 other countries; 7% Black or African American, non-Hispanic/Latino; 5% Hispanic/Latino; 2% Asian, non-Hispanic/Latino; 0.1% Native Hawaiian or other Pacific Islander, non-Hispanic/Latino; 0.3% American Indian or Alaska Native, non-Hispanic/Latino; 4% Two or more races, non-Hispanic/Latino; 3% Race/ethnicity unknown; 0.9% international; 6% transferred in.

Freshmen *Admission:* 1,477 applied, 1,522 enrolled.

Faculty *Total:* 374, 29% full-time, 24% with terminal degrees. *Student/faculty ratio:* 20:1.

Majors Accounting technology and bookkeeping; biology/biological sciences; chemistry; child-care and support services management; commercial and advertising art; computer programming; criminal justice/police science; drafting and design technology; education (specific subject areas) related; emergency medical technology (EMT paramedic); environmental health; general studies; health information/medical records technology; human services; industrial technology; liberal arts and sciences/liberal studies; manufacturing engineering technology; marketing/marketing management; music; occupational therapist assistant; office management; precision production related; pre-engineering; pre-pharmacy studies; teacher assistant/aide; welding technology.

Academics *Calendar:* semesters. *Degree:* certificates and associate. *Special study options:* academic remediation for entering students, adult/continuing education programs, advanced placement credit, cooperative education, distance learning, double majors, English as a second language, honors programs, independent study, internships, part-time degree program, services for LD students, study abroad, summer session for credit.

Library Paul and Helen Schnare Library. *Books:* 56,851 (physical), 30,196 (digital/electronic); *Serial titles:* 349 (physical), 348,033 (digital/electronic); *Databases:* 43. Weekly public service hours: 72.

Student Life *Activities and Organizations:* drama/theater group, student-run newspaper, choral group, Phi Theta Kappa, GAMES Club, Student Government Association, Cougar Activities Crew, International Club. *Campus security:* 24-hour emergency response devices and patrols, late-night transport/escort service, campus police officers on duty during normal operating hours. *Student services:* personal/psychological counseling, veterans affairs office.

Athletics Member NJCAA. *Intercollegiate sports:* cross-country running W, soccer W(s), softball W(s), track and field W.

Financial Aid Of all full-time matriculated undergraduates who enrolled in 2017, 20 Federal Work-Study jobs (averaging $2567).

Applying *Options:* electronic application, early admission, deferred entrance. *Application fee:* $10. *Required for some:* high school transcript, minimum 2.5 GPA. *Application deadlines:* rolling (freshmen), rolling (transfers). *Notification:* continuous (freshmen), continuous (transfers).

Freshman Application Contact Ms. Cassie Akins, Director of Enrollment Services/Registrar, St. Charles Community College, 4601 Mid Rivers Mall Drive, Cottleville, MO 63376-0975. *Phone:* 636-922-8436. *Fax:* 636-922-8236. *E-mail:* cakins@stchas.edu. *Website:* http://www.stchas.edu/.

St. Louis College of Health Careers

Fenton, Missouri

Admissions Office Contact St. Louis College of Health Careers, 1297 North Highway Drive, Fenton, MO 63026. *Toll-free phone:* 866-529-2070. *Website:* http://www.slchc.com/.

St. Louis College of Health Careers

St. Louis, Missouri

Freshman Application Contact Admissions Office, St. Louis College of Health Careers, 909 South Taylor Avenue, St. Louis, MO 63110. *Phone:* 314-652-0300. *Toll-free phone:* 866-529-2070. *Fax:* 314-652-4825. *Website:* http://www.slchc.com/.

St. Louis Community College

St. Louis, Missouri

- **Public** 2-year, founded 1962, part of St. Louis Community College
- **Suburban** campus with easy access to St. Louis
- **Coed,** 18,157 undergraduate students, 36% full-time, 61% women, 39% men

Undergraduates 6,580 full-time, 11,577 part-time. Students come from 31 states and territories; 110 other countries; 2% are from out of state; 33% Black or African American, non-Hispanic/Latino; 3% Hispanic/Latino; 3% Asian, non-Hispanic/Latino; 0.1% Native Hawaiian or other Pacific Islander, non-Hispanic/Latino; 0.2% American Indian or Alaska Native, non-Hispanic/Latino; 5% Two or more races, non-Hispanic/Latino; 2% Race/ethnicity unknown; 2% international; 7% transferred in. *Retention:* 58% of full-time freshmen returned.

Freshmen *Admission:* 3,158 enrolled.

Faculty *Total:* 1,209, 28% full-time. *Student/faculty ratio:* 17:1.

Majors Accounting technology and bookkeeping; automobile/automotive mechanics technology; baking and pastry arts; behavioral aspects of health; biology/biotechnology laboratory technician; business/commerce; child development; clinical/medical laboratory technology; computer and information systems security; criminal justice/police science; culinary arts; dental hygiene; diesel mechanics technology; electrical, electronic and communications engineering technology; emergency medical technology (EMT paramedic); fire science/firefighting; funeral service and mortuary science; graphic design; health information/medical records technology; human services; interior design; legal assistant/paralegal; liberal arts and sciences/liberal studies; manufacturing engineering technology; occupational therapist assistant; radiologic technology/science; respiratory care therapy; sign language interpretation and translation; surgical technology.

Academics *Calendar:* semesters. *Degree:* certificates and associate. *Special study options:* academic remediation for entering students, accelerated degree program, adult/continuing education programs, advanced placement credit, distance learning, English as a second language, honors programs, independent study, internships, part-time degree program, services for LD students, study abroad, summer session for credit.

Student Life *Housing:* college housing not available. *Activities and Organizations:* drama/theater group, student-run newspaper. *Campus security:* 24-hour emergency response devices, late-night transport/escort service. *Student services:* personal/psychological counseling, veterans affairs office.

Athletics Member NJCAA. *Intercollegiate sports:* basketball W(s), soccer W(s), softball W(s), volleyball W(s).

Applying *Options:* electronic application. *Required for some:* high school transcript, interview. *Application deadlines:* rolling (freshmen), rolling (transfers). *Notification:* continuous (freshmen), continuous (transfers).

Admissions Office Contact St. Louis Community College, 300 South Broadway, St. Louis, MO 63102. *Website:* http://www.stlcc.edu/.

Southeast Missouri Hospital College of Nursing and Health Sciences

Cape Girardeau, Missouri

Freshman Application Contact Southeast Missouri Hospital College of Nursing and Health Sciences, 2001 William Street, Cape Girardeau, MO 63701. *Phone:* 573-334-6825 Ext. 12. *Website:* http://www.sehcollege.edu/.

State Fair Community College

Sedalia, Missouri

Freshman Application Contact State Fair Community College, 3201 West 16th Street, Sedalia, MO 65301-2199. *Phone:* 660-596-7379. *Toll-free phone:* 877-311-7322. *Website:* http://www.sfccmo.edu/.

State Technical College of Missouri

Linn, Missouri

- **State-supported** 2-year, founded 1961
- **Rural** 350-acre campus
- **Coed, primarily men**

Undergraduates 1,041 full-time, 215 part-time. Students come from 7 states and territories; 3% are from out of state; 1% Black or African American, non-Hispanic/Latino; 2% Hispanic/Latino; 0.2% Asian, non-Hispanic/Latino; 0.3% American Indian or Alaska Native, non-Hispanic/Latino; 0.1% Two or more races, non-Hispanic/Latino; 2% Race/ethnicity unknown; 10% transferred in; 11% live on campus. *Retention:* 86% of full-time freshmen returned.

Faculty *Student/faculty ratio:* 11:1.

Academics *Calendar:* semesters. *Degree:* certificates and associate. *Special study options:* academic remediation for entering students, adult/continuing education programs, advanced placement credit, cooperative education, distance learning, double majors, external degree program, independent study, internships, off-campus study, part-time degree program, services for LD students, summer session for credit.

Library State Technical College of Missouri Library plus 1 other. Weekly public service hours: 64; students can reserve study rooms.

Student Life *Campus security:* 24-hour emergency response devices, student patrols, controlled dormitory access, indoor and outdoor surveillance cameras.

Standardized Tests *Required:* ACCUPLACER (for admission). *Required for some:* ACT (for admission).

Financial Aid Of all full-time matriculated undergraduates who enrolled in 2017, 70 Federal Work-Study jobs (averaging $769).

Applying *Options:* electronic application, early admission, early decision, early action. *Required:* high school transcript. *Required for some:* essay or personal statement, 1 letter of recommendation, interview.

Freshman Application Contact State Technical College of Missouri, One Technology Drive, Linn, MO 65051-9606. *Phone:* 573-897-5196. *Toll-free phone:* 800-743-TECH. *Website:* http://www.statetechmo.edu/.

Texas County Technical College

Houston, Missouri

Admissions Office Contact Texas County Technical College, 6915 S. Hwy 63, Houston, MO 65483. *Website:* http://www.texascountytech.edu/.

Three Rivers College

Poplar Bluff, Missouri

- **State and locally supported** 2-year, founded 1966, part of Missouri Coordinating Board for Higher Education
- **Rural** 80-acre campus
- **Coed**

Undergraduates 1,789 full-time, 1,437 part-time. Students come from 14 states and territories; 1 other country; 3% are from out of state; 10% Black or African American, non-Hispanic/Latino; 2% Hispanic/Latino; 0.5% Asian, non-Hispanic/Latino; 0.1% Native Hawaiian or other Pacific Islander, non-Hispanic/Latino; 0.5% American Indian or Alaska Native, non-Hispanic/Latino; 7% Race/ethnicity unknown; 0.2% international; 2% transferred in; 5% live on campus.

Academics *Calendar:* semesters. *Degree:* certificates and associate. *Special study options:* academic remediation for entering students, adult/continuing education programs, advanced placement credit, cooperative education, distance learning, double majors, English as a second language, external degree program, honors programs, independent study, off-campus study, part-time degree program, services for LD students, summer session for credit.

Library Rutland Library. *Books:* 15,286 (physical), 200,299 (digital/electronic); *Serial titles:* 40 (physical); *Databases:* 53. Weekly public service hours: 57; students can reserve study rooms.

Student Life *Campus security:* 24-hour emergency response devices, 24-hour Mass Notification and Storm Warning System.

Athletics Member NJCAA.

Applying *Options:* electronic application, early admission. *Required for some:* high school transcript. *Recommended:* high school transcript.

Freshman Application Contact Three Rivers College, 2080 Three Rivers Boulevard, Poplar Bluff, MO 63901-2393. *Toll-free phone:* 877-TRY-TRCC. *Website:* http://www.trcc.edu/.

WellSpring School of Allied Health

Kansas City, Missouri

Admissions Office Contact WellSpring School of Allied Health, 9140 Ward Parkway, Suite 100, Kansas City, MO 64114. *Website:* http://www.wellspring.edu/.

MONTANA

Aaniiih Nakoda College

Harlem, Montana

Freshman Application Contact Aaniiih Nakoda College, PO Box 159, Harlem, MT 59526-0159. *Phone:* 406-353-2607 Ext. 233. *Website:* http://www.ancollege.edu/.

Blackfeet Community College

Browning, Montana

Freshman Application Contact Ms. Deana M. McNabb, Registrar and Admissions Officer, Blackfeet Community College, PO Box 819, Browning, MT 59417-0819. *Phone:* 406-338-5421. *Toll-free phone:* 800-549-7457. *Fax:* 406-338-3272. *Website:* http://www.bfcc.edu/.

Chief Dull Knife College

Lame Deer, Montana

Freshman Application Contact Director of Admissions, Chief Dull Knife College, PO Box 98, 1 College Drive, Lame Deer, MT 59043-0098. *Phone:* 406-477-6215. *Website:* http://www.cdkc.edu/.

Dawson Community College

Glendive, Montana

- **State and locally supported** 2-year, founded 1940, part of Montana University System
- **Rural** 300-acre campus
- **Endowment** $3.5 million
- **Coed**

Undergraduates 205 full-time, 124 part-time. Students come from 19 states and territories; 2 other countries; 80% are from out of state; 5% Black or African American, non-Hispanic/Latino; 3% Hispanic/Latino; 0.9% Asian, non-Hispanic/Latino; 0.3% Native Hawaiian or other Pacific Islander, non-Hispanic/Latino; 3% American Indian or Alaska Native, non-Hispanic/Latino; 4% Two or more races, non-Hispanic/Latino; 2% Race/ethnicity unknown; 2% international; 11% transferred in.

Faculty *Student/faculty ratio:* 17:1.

Academics *Calendar:* semesters. *Degree:* certificates and associate. *Special study options:* academic remediation for entering students, adult/continuing education programs, distance learning, independent study, internships, part-time degree program, services for LD students, summer session for credit.

Library Jane Carey Memorial Library plus 1 other. *Books:* 33,477 (physical), 13,359 (digital/electronic); *Serial titles:* 81 (physical); *Databases:* 118. Weekly public service hours: 40; students can reserve study rooms.

Student Life *Campus security:* 24-hour emergency response devices.

Athletics Member NJCAA.

Financial Aid Of all full-time matriculated undergraduates who enrolled in 2016, 158 applied for aid, 158 were judged to have need. 35 Federal Work-Study jobs (averaging $2200). 8 state and other part-time jobs (averaging $2200).

Applying *Options:* electronic application, deferred entrance. *Application fee:* $30. *Required:* high school transcript.

Freshman Application Contact Ms. Julie Brandt, Admissions Specialist, Dawson Community College, 300 College Drive, Glendive, MT 59330. *Phone:* 406-377-9411. *Toll-free phone:* 800-821-8320. *Fax:* 406-377-8132. *E-mail:* jbrandt@dawson.edu. *Website:* http://www.dawson.edu/.

Flathead Valley Community College

Kalispell, Montana

Freshman Application Contact Ms. Marlene C. Stoltz, Admissions/Graduation Coordinator, Flathead Valley Community College, 777 Grandview Drive, Kalispell, MT 59901-2622. *Phone:* 406-756-3846. *Toll-free phone:* 800-313-3822. *E-mail:* mstoltz@fvcc.cc.mt.us. *Website:* http://www.fvcc.edu/.

Fort Peck Community College

Poplar, Montana

Director of Admissions Mr. Robert McAnally, Vice President for Student Services, Fort Peck Community College, PO Box 398, Poplar, MT 59255-0398. *Phone:* 406-768-6329. *Website:* http://www.fpcc.edu/.

Great Falls College Montana State University

Great Falls, Montana

- **State-supported** 2-year, founded 1969, part of Montana University System
- **Small-town** 40-acre campus
- **Endowment** $11,300
- **Coed**

Undergraduates 646 full-time, 1,044 part-time. Students come from 28 states and territories; 2 other countries; 4% are from out of state; 2% Black or African American, non-Hispanic/Latino; 5% Hispanic/Latino; 0.9% Asian, non-Hispanic/Latino; 0.1% Native Hawaiian or other Pacific Islander, non-Hispanic/Latino; 5% American Indian or Alaska Native, non-Hispanic/Latino; 5% Two or more races, non-Hispanic/Latino; 2% Race/ethnicity unknown; 0.1% international; 7% transferred in.

Faculty *Student/faculty ratio:* 15:1.

Academics *Calendar:* semesters. *Degree:* certificates and associate. *Special study options:* academic remediation for entering students, advanced placement credit, distance learning, double majors, independent study, internships, off-campus study, part-time degree program, services for LD students, summer session for credit.

Library Weaver Library plus 1 other. *Books:* 9,239 (physical), 266,102 (digital/electronic); *Serial titles:* 60 (physical), 121,995 (digital/electronic); *Databases:* 55. Students can reserve study rooms.

Student Life *Campus security:* 24-hour emergency response devices, patrol by security personnel.

Financial Aid Of all full-time matriculated undergraduates who enrolled in 2017, 550 applied for aid, 490 were judged to have need, 118 had their need fully met. In 2017, 7. *Average percent of need met:* 77. *Average financial aid package:* $9152. *Average need-based loan:* $5971. *Average need-based gift aid:* $4847. *Average non-need-based aid:* $879.

Applying *Options:* electronic application, early admission. *Application fee:* $30. *Required:* high school transcript, proof of immunization.

Freshman Application Contact Mr. Joe Simonsen, Admissions, Great Falls College Montana State University, 2100 16th Avenue South, Great Falls, MT 59405. *Phone:* 406-771-4309. *Toll-free phone:* 800-446-2698. *Fax:* 406-771-2267. *E-mail:* joe.simonsen@gfcmsu.edu. *Website:* http://www.gfcmsu.edu/.

Helena College University of Montana

Helena, Montana

Freshman Application Contact Mr. Ryan Loomis, Admissions Representative/Recruiter, Helena College University of Montana, 1115 North Roberts Street, Helena, MT 59601. *Phone:* 406-447-6904. *Toll-free phone:* 800-241-4882. *Website:* http://www.umhelena.edu/.

Highlands College of Montana Tech

Butte, Montana

Admissions Office Contact Highlands College of Montana Tech, 25 Basin Creek Road, Butte, MT 59701. *Website:* http://www.mtech.edu/academics/highlands/.

Little Big Horn College

Crow Agency, Montana

Freshman Application Contact Ms. Ann Bullis, Dean of Student Services, Little Big Horn College, Box 370, 1 Forest Lane, Crow Agency, MT 59022-0370. *Phone:* 406-638-2228 Ext. 50. *Website:* http://www.lbhc.edu/.

Miles Community College

Miles City, Montana

Freshman Application Contact Mr. Haley Anderson, Admissions Representative, Miles Community College, 2715 Dickinson Street, Miles City, MT 59301. *Phone:* 406-874-6178. *Toll-free phone:* 800-541-9281. *E-mail:* andersonh@milescc.edu. *Website:* http://www.milescc.edu/.

Pima Medical Institute

Dillon, Montana

Admissions Office Contact Pima Medical Institute, 434 East Poindexter Street, Dillon, MT 59725. *Website:* http://www.pmi.edu/.

Salish Kootenai College

Pablo, Montana

Freshman Application Contact Ms. Jackie Moran, Admissions Officer, Salish Kootenai College, PO Box 70, Pablo, MT 59855-0117. *Phone:* 406-275-4866. *Fax:* 406-275-4810. *E-mail:* jackie_moran@skc.edu. *Website:* http://www.skc.edu/.

Stone Child College

Box Elder, Montana

Director of Admissions Mr. Ted Whitford, Director of Admissions/Registrar, Stone Child College, 8294 Upper Box Elder Road, Box Elder, MT 59521. *Phone:* 406-395-4313 Ext. 110. *E-mail:* uanet337@quest.ocsc.montana.edu. *Website:* http://www.stonechild.edu/.

NEBRASKA

Central Community College–Columbus Campus

Columbus, Nebraska

Freshman Application Contact Ms. Erica Leffler, Admissions/Recruiting Coordinator, Central Community College–Columbus Campus, PO Box 1027, Columbus, NE 68602-1027. *Phone:* 402-562-1296. *Toll-free phone:* 877-CCC-0780. *Fax:* 402-562-1201. *E-mail:* eleffler@cccneb.edu. *Website:* http://www.cccneb.edu/.

Central Community College–Grand Island Campus

Grand Island, Nebraska

Freshman Application Contact Michelle Lubken, Admissions Director, Central Community College–Grand Island Campus, PO Box 4903, Grand Island, NE 68802-4903. *Phone:* 308-398-7406 Ext. 406. *Toll-free phone:* 877-CCC-0780. *Fax:* 308-398-7398. *E-mail:* mlubken@cccneb.edu. *Website:* http://www.cccneb.edu/.

Central Community College–Hastings Campus

Hastings, Nebraska

Freshman Application Contact Mr. Robert Glenn, Admissions and Recruiting Director, Central Community College–Hastings Campus, PO Box 1024, East Highway 6, Hastings, NE 68902-1024. *Phone:* 402-461-2428. *Toll-free phone:* 877-CCC-0780. *E-mail:* rglenn@ccneb.edu. *Website:* http://www.cccneb.edu/.

CHI Health School of Radiologic Technology

Omaha, Nebraska

- **Independent** 2-year
- **Urban** 1-acre campus with easy access to Omaha, NE
- **Coed**

Undergraduates 15 full-time. Students come from 4 states and territories; 20% are from out of state; 7% Black or African American, non-Hispanic/Latino. *Retention:* 9% of full-time freshmen returned.

Faculty *Student/faculty ratio:* 7:1.

Academics *Degree:* associate. *Special study options:* academic remediation for entering students, services for LD students.

Student Life *Campus security:* 24-hour emergency response devices and patrols.

Standardized Tests *Required:* entrance exam (for admission).

Applying *Application fee:* $25. *Required:* essay or personal statement, high school transcript, minimum 2.0 GPA, 3 letters of recommendation, interview. *Required for some:* interview.
Freshman Application Contact CHI Health School of Radiologic Technology, 6911 North 68th Plaza, Omaha, NE 68122. *Phone:* 402-572-3650. *Website:* http://www.chihealth.com/school-of-radiologic-technology.

Little Priest Tribal College
Winnebago, Nebraska

Freshman Application Contact Little Priest Tribal College, PO Box 270, Winnebago, NE 68071. *Phone:* 402-878-2380 Ext. 112. *Website:* http://www.littlepriest.edu/.

Metropolitan Community College
Omaha, Nebraska

Freshman Application Contact Ms. Maria Vazquez, Associate Vice President for Student Affairs, Metropolitan Community College, PO Box 3777, Omaha, NE 69103-0777. *Phone:* 402-457-2430. *Toll-free phone:* 800-228-9553. *Fax:* 402-457-2238. *E-mail:* mvazquez@mccneb.edu. *Website:* http://www.mccneb.edu/.

Mid-Plains Community College
North Platte, Nebraska

- **District-supported** 2-year, founded 1973
- **Small-town** campus
- **Endowment** $6.6 million
- **Coed**

Undergraduates 800 full-time, 1,422 part-time. Students come from 30 states and territories; 13 other countries; 9% are from out of state; 2% Black or African American, non-Hispanic/Latino; 8% Hispanic/Latino; 0.6% Asian, non-Hispanic/Latino; 0.1% Native Hawaiian or other Pacific Islander, non-Hispanic/Latino; 0.5% American Indian or Alaska Native, non-Hispanic/Latino; 2% Two or more races, non-Hispanic/Latino; 2% Race/ethnicity unknown; 2% international; 20% live on campus.
Faculty *Student/faculty ratio:* 8:1.
Academics *Calendar:* semesters. *Degree:* certificates, diplomas, and associate. *Special study options:* academic remediation for entering students, accelerated degree program, adult/continuing education programs, advanced placement credit, cooperative education, distance learning, double majors, English as a second language, external degree program, independent study, internships, part-time degree program, services for LD students, summer session for credit.
Library von Riesen Library plus 1 other. *Books:* 17,993 (physical), 51,889 (digital/electronic); *Serial titles:* 50 (physical); *Databases:* 37. Weekly public service hours: 70; students can reserve study rooms.
Student Life *Campus security:* controlled dormitory access.
Athletics Member NJCAA.
Standardized Tests *Required for some:* ACCUPLACER. *Recommended:* ACT (for admission).
Financial Aid Of all full-time matriculated undergraduates who enrolled in 2017, 569 applied for aid, 454 were judged to have need, 90 had their need fully met. 39 Federal Work-Study jobs (averaging $995). In 2017, 143. *Average percent of need met:* 68. *Average financial aid package:* $7268. *Average need-based loan:* $2586. *Average need-based gift aid:* $6012. *Average non-need-based aid:* $1775.
Applying *Options:* electronic application, deferred entrance. *Required:* high school transcript. *Required for some:* 2 letters of recommendation, interview.
Freshman Application Contact Ms. Sandy Ablard, Admissions Specialist, Mid-Plains Community College, 1101 Halligan Drive, North Platte, NE 69101. *Phone:* 308-535-3609. *Toll-free phone:* 800-658-4308 (in-state); 800-658-4348 (out-of-state). *Fax:* 308-534-5767. *E-mail:* ablards@mpcc.edu. *Website:* http://www.mpcc.edu/.

Myotherapy Institute
Lincoln, Nebraska

Freshman Application Contact Admissions Office, Myotherapy Institute, 4001 Pioneers Woods Drive, Lincoln, NE 68506. *Phone:* 402-421-7410. *Website:* http://www.myotherapy.edu/.

Nebraska College of Technical Agriculture
Curtis, Nebraska

Freshman Application Contact Kevin Martin, Assistant Admissions Coordinator, Nebraska College of Technical Agriculture, 404 East 7th Street, Curtis, NE 69025. *Phone:* 308-367-4124. *Toll-free phone:* 800-3CURTIS. *Website:* http://www.ncta.unl.edu/.

Nebraska Indian Community College
Macy, Nebraska

- **Federally supported** 2-year, founded 1979
- **Rural** 22-acre campus with easy access to Omaha
- **Coed**
- 100% of applicants were admitted

Undergraduates 47 full-time, 133 part-time. Students come from 3 states and territories; 13% are from out of state; 2% transferred in.
Faculty *Student/faculty ratio:* 5:1.
Academics *Calendar:* semesters. *Degree:* certificates and associate. *Special study options:* academic remediation for entering students, adult/continuing education programs, distance learning, double majors, independent study, internships, part-time degree program, services for LD students, study abroad, summer session for credit.
Library Macy Library plus 1 other. *Books:* 17,555 (physical), 370 (digital/electronic). Weekly public service hours: 40.
Applying *Options:* electronic application, early admission. *Required:* high school transcript. *Required for some:* certificate of tribal enrollment.
Freshman Application Contact Troy Munhofen, Registrar, Nebraska Indian Community College, PO Box 428, Macy, NE 68039. *Phone:* 402-241-5922. *Toll-free phone:* 844-440-NICC. *Fax:* 402-837-4183. *E-mail:* tmunhofen@thenicc.edu. *Website:* http://www.thenicc.edu/.

Northeast Community College
Norfolk, Nebraska

- **State and locally supported** 2-year, founded 1973, part of Nebraska Coordinating Commission for Postsecondary Education
- **Small-town** 202-acre campus
- **Coed**

Undergraduates 2,121 full-time, 2,954 part-time. Students come from 12 states and territories; 5% are from out of state; 1% Black or African American, non-Hispanic/Latino; 10% Hispanic/Latino; 0.4% Asian, non-Hispanic/Latino; 1% American Indian or Alaska Native, non-Hispanic/Latino; 2% Two or more races, non-Hispanic/Latino; 4% Race/ethnicity unknown; 1% international; 5% transferred in; 20% live on campus. *Retention:* 70% of full-time freshmen returned.
Faculty *Student/faculty ratio:* 17:1.
Academics *Calendar:* semesters. *Degree:* certificates, diplomas, and associate. *Special study options:* academic remediation for entering students, adult/continuing education programs, advanced placement credit, cooperative education, distance learning, double majors, English as a second language, independent study, internships, off-campus study, part-time degree program, services for LD students, study abroad, summer session for credit.
Library Library Resource Center. *Books:* 20,648 (physical); *Serial titles:* 411 (physical); *Databases:* 70. Weekly public service hours: 78.
Student Life *Campus security:* 24-hour emergency response devices and patrols, controlled dormitory access, building walk-throughs and parking lot patrols, door and dorm checks, armed security.
Athletics Member NJCAA.
Financial Aid Of all full-time matriculated undergraduates who enrolled in 2017, 1,619 applied for aid, 1,301 were judged to have need, 194 had their need fully met. 59 Federal Work-Study jobs (averaging $1205). In 2017, 32. *Average percent of need met:* 66. *Average financial aid package:* $6836. *Average need-based loan:* $3090. *Average need-based gift aid:* $5681. *Average non-need-based aid:* $773. *Average indebtedness upon graduation:* $10,616.
Applying *Options:* electronic application, early admission. *Required for some:* essay or personal statement, high school transcript, 3 letters of recommendation, interview. *Recommended:* high school transcript.
Freshman Application Contact Tiffany Hopper, Admissions Specialist, Northeast Community College, 801 East Benjamin Avenue, PO Box 469, Norfolk, NE 68702-0469. *Phone:* 402-844-7260. *Toll-free phone:* 800-348-9033 Ext. 7260. *E-mail:* admission@northeast.edu. *Website:* http://www.northeast.edu/.

Omaha School of Massage and Healthcare of Herzing University

Omaha, Nebraska

Admissions Office Contact Omaha School of Massage and Healthcare of Herzing University, 9748 Park Drive, Omaha, NE 68127. *Website:* http://www.osmhc.com/.

Southeast Community College, Beatrice Campus

Beatrice, Nebraska

Freshman Application Contact Admissions Office, Southeast Community College, Beatrice Campus, 4771 West Scott Road, Beatrice, NE 68310. *Phone:* 402-228-3468. *Toll-free phone:* 800-233-5027. *Fax:* 402-228-2218. *Website:* http://www.southeast.edu/.

Southeast Community College, Lincoln Campus

Lincoln, Nebraska

Freshman Application Contact Admissions Office, Southeast Community College, Lincoln Campus, 8800 O Street, Lincoln, NE 68520. *Phone:* 402-471-3333. *Toll-free phone:* 800-642-4075. *Fax:* 402-437-2404. *E-mail:* admissions@southeast.edu. *Website:* http://www.southeast.edu/.

Southeast Community College, Milford Campus

Milford, Nebraska

Freshman Application Contact Admissions Office, Southeast Community College, Milford Campus, 600 State Street, Milford, NE 68405. *Phone:* 402-761-2131. *Toll-free phone:* 800-933-7223. *Fax:* 402-761-2324. *E-mail:* admissions@southeast.edu. *Website:* http://www.southeast.edu/.

Universal College of Healing Arts

Omaha, Nebraska

Admissions Office Contact Universal College of Healing Arts, 8702 North 30th Street, Omaha, NE 68112-1810. *Website:* http://www.ucha.edu/.

Western Nebraska Community College

Sidney, Nebraska

Director of Admissions Mr. Troy Archuleta, Admissions and Recruitment Director, Western Nebraska Community College, 371 College Drive, Sidney, NE 69162. *Phone:* 308-635-6015. *Toll-free phone:* 800-222-9682. *E-mail:* rhovey@wncc.net. *Website:* http://www.wncc.net/.

NEVADA

Career College of Northern Nevada

Sparks, Nevada

- **Proprietary** 2-year, founded 1984
- **Urban** 2-acre campus with easy access to Reno, NV
- **Coed**

Undergraduates 342 full-time. Students come from 1 other country; 3% are from out of state.
Faculty *Student/faculty ratio:* 20:1.
Academics *Calendar:* quarters 6-week terms. *Degree:* diplomas and associate. *Special study options:* academic remediation for entering students, accelerated degree program, cooperative education, double majors, internships, summer session for credit.
Library Library. *Books:* 1,200 (physical), 110,000 (digital/electronic). Weekly public service hours: 50.
Student Life *Campus security:* 24-hour emergency response devices.
Standardized Tests *Required:* Wonderlic aptitude test (for admission).
Financial Aid Of all full-time matriculated undergraduates who enrolled in 2017, 6 Federal Work-Study jobs (averaging $3000).
Applying *Application fee:* $25. *Required:* high school transcript, interview.
Freshman Application Contact Ms. Maria Clark, Director of Admissions, Career College of Northern Nevada, 1421 Pullman Dr, Sparks, NV 89434. *Phone:* 775-856-2266. *Fax:* 775-856-0935. *E-mail:* mclark@ccnn4u.com. *Website:* http://www.ccnn.edu/.

Carrington College–Las Vegas

Las Vegas, Nevada

Freshman Application Contact Carrington College–Las Vegas, 5740 South Eastern Avenue, Suite 140, Las Vegas, NV 89119. *Website:* http://www.carrington.edu/.

Carrington College–Reno

Reno, Nevada

Freshman Application Contact Carrington College–Reno, 5580 Kietzke Lane, Reno, NV 89511. *Phone:* 775-335-2900. *Website:* http://www.carrington.edu/.

College of Southern Nevada

Las Vegas, Nevada

Freshman Application Contact Admissions and Records, College of Southern Nevada, 6375 West Charleston Boulevard, Las Vegas, NV 89146. *Phone:* 702-651-4060. *Website:* http://www.csn.edu/.

Great Basin College

Elko, Nevada

Freshman Application Contact Ms. Jan King, Director of Admissions and Registrar, Great Basin College, 1500 College Parkway, Elko, NV 89801. *Phone:* 775-753-2102. *E-mail:* jan.king@gbcnv.edu. *Website:* http://www.gbcnv.edu/.

Northwest Career College

Las Vegas, Nevada

Admissions Office Contact Northwest Career College, 7398 Smoke Ranch Road, Suite 100, Las Vegas, NV 89128. *Website:* http://www.northwestcareercollege.edu/.

Pima Medical Institute

Las Vegas, Nevada

Freshman Application Contact Admissions Office, Pima Medical Institute, 3333 East Flamingo Road, Las Vegas, NV 89121. *Phone:* 702-458-9650 Ext. 202. *Toll-free phone:* 800-477-PIMA. *Website:* http://www.pmi.edu/.

Truckee Meadows Community College

Reno, Nevada

- **State-supported** primarily 2-year, founded 1971, part of Nevada System of Higher Education
- **Suburban** 63-acre campus
- **Endowment** $11.1 million
- **Coed**, 10,861 undergraduate students, 27% full-time, 53% women, 47% men

Undergraduates 2,927 full-time, 7,934 part-time. Students come from 23 states and territories; 20 other countries; 6% are from out of state; 3% Black or African American, non-Hispanic/Latino; 30% Hispanic/Latino; 6% Asian, non-Hispanic/Latino; 1% American Indian or Alaska Native, non-Hispanic/Latino; 4% Two or more races, non-Hispanic/Latino; 2% Race/ethnicity unknown; 0.5% international; 6% transferred in. *Retention:* 63% of full-time freshmen returned.
Freshmen *Admission:* 3,290 applied, 3,290 admitted, 1,562 enrolled.
Faculty *Total:* 716, 22% full-time. *Student/faculty ratio:* 21:1.
Majors Anthropology; architectural drafting and CAD/CADD; architecture; automobile/automotive mechanics technology; biology/biological sciences; business/commerce; chemistry; civil engineering; commercial and advertising art; computer programming (specific applications); computer systems networking and telecommunications; cooking and related culinary arts; criminal justice/police science; criminal justice/safety; crisis/emergency/disaster management; dental assisting; dental hygiene; diesel mechanics technology; dietetics; drafting and design technology; elementary education; energy management and systems technology; engineering; engineering technologies and engineering related; English; entrepreneurial and

small business related; environmental science; fine arts related; fire prevention and safety technology; foods, nutrition, and wellness; general studies; geology/earth science; heating, air conditioning, ventilation and refrigeration maintenance technology; history; kindergarten/preschool education; landscape architecture; legal assistant/paralegal; liberal arts and sciences/liberal studies; logistics, materials, and supply chain management; management information systems and services related; manufacturing engineering technology; mathematics; medical radiologic technology; mental health counseling; music; music performance; natural resources/conservation; philosophy; physics; psychology; registered nursing/registered nurse; science, technology and society; veterinary/animal health technology; welding technology.
Academics *Calendar:* semesters. *Degrees:* certificates, associate, and bachelor's. *Special study options:* academic remediation for entering students, accelerated degree program, adult/continuing education programs, advanced placement credit, cooperative education, distance learning, double majors, English as a second language, independent study, internships, part-time degree program, services for LD students, summer session for credit. *ROTC:* Army (c).
Library Elizabeth Sturm Library plus 2 others. *Books:* 48,770 (physical); *Serial titles:* 36 (physical), 4 (digital/electronic); *Databases:* 93.
Student Life *Housing:* college housing not available. *Activities and Organizations:* drama/theater group, student-run newspaper, Entrepreneurship Club, International Club, Phi Theta Kappa, Student Government Association, Student Media and Broadcasting Club. *Campus security:* 24-hour emergency response devices and patrols, late-night transport/escort service. *Student services:* personal/psychological counseling, veterans affairs office.
Financial Aid Of all full-time matriculated undergraduates who enrolled in 2017, 126 Federal Work-Study jobs (averaging $5000). 368 state and other part-time jobs (averaging $5000).
Applying *Options:* electronic application, early admission. *Application fee:* $10. *Application deadlines:* rolling (freshmen), rolling (transfers). *Notification:* continuous (freshmen), continuous (transfers).
Director of Admissions Mr. Andrew Hughes, Director of Admissions and Records, Truckee Meadows Community College, 7000 Dandini Boulevard, Reno, NV 89512-3901. *Phone:* 775-673-7240. *Fax:* 775-673-7028. *E-mail:* ahughes@tmcc.edu.
Website: http://www.tmcc.edu/.

Western Nevada College
Carson City, Nevada

Freshman Application Contact Admissions and Records, Western Nevada College, 2201 West College Parkway, Carson City, NV 89703. *Phone:* 775-445-2377. *Fax:* 775-445-3147. *E-mail:* wncc_aro@wncc.edu. *Website:* http://www.wnc.edu/.

NEW HAMPSHIRE

Great Bay Community College
Portsmouth, New Hampshire

Freshman Application Contact Mr. Matt Thornton, Admissions Coordinator, Great Bay Community College, 320 Corporate Drive, Portsmouth, NH 03801. *Phone:* 603-427-7605. *Toll-free phone:* 800-522-1194. *E-mail:* askgreatbay@ccsnh.edu. *Website:* http://www.greatbay.edu/.

Lakes Region Community College
Laconia, New Hampshire

- **State-supported** 2-year, part of Community College System of New Hampshire
- **Small-town** campus
- **Coed**

Undergraduates 490 full-time, 689 part-time. Students come from 5 states and territories; 2 other countries; 3% are from out of state; 0.5% Black or African American, non-Hispanic/Latino; 1% Hispanic/Latino; 0.5% Asian, non-Hispanic/Latino; 0.1% Native Hawaiian or other Pacific Islander, non-Hispanic/Latino; 0.5% American Indian or Alaska Native, non-Hispanic/Latino; 0.9% Two or more races, non-Hispanic/Latino; 22% Race/ethnicity unknown.
Faculty *Student/faculty ratio:* 9:1.
Academics *Calendar:* semesters accelerated terms also offered. *Degree:* certificates and associate. *Special study options:* academic remediation for entering students, accelerated degree program, adult/continuing education programs, cooperative education, distance learning, double majors, external degree program, independent study, internships, part-time degree program, services for LD students, student-designed majors, summer session for credit.
Library Hugh Bennett Library plus 1 other. Students can reserve study rooms.
Student Life *Campus security:* 24-hour emergency response devices, late-night transport/escort service, controlled dormitory access, Evening patrols by trained security personnel.
Applying *Options:* electronic application, deferred entrance. *Required:* high school transcript.
Admissions Office Contact Lakes Region Community College, 379 Belmont Road, Laconia, NH 03246. *Toll-free phone:* 800-357-2992. *Website:* http://www.lrcc.edu/.

Manchester Community College
Manchester, New Hampshire

Freshman Application Contact Ms. Jacquie Poirier, Coordinator of Admissions, Manchester Community College, 1066 Front Street, Manchester, NH 03102-8518. *Phone:* 603-668-6706 Ext. 283. *Toll-free phone:* 800-924-3445. *E-mail:* jpoirier@nhctc.edu. *Website:* http://www.mccnh.edu/.

Nashua Community College
Nashua, New Hampshire

Freshman Application Contact Ms. Patricia Goodman, Vice President of Student Services, Nashua Community College, Nashua, NH 03063. *Phone:* 603-882-6923 Ext. 1529. *Fax:* 603-882-8690. *E-mail:* pgoodman@ccsnh.edu. *Website:* http://www.nashuacc.edu/.

NHTI, Concord's Community College
Concord, New Hampshire

Freshman Application Contact NHTI, Concord's Community College, 31 College Drive, Concord, NH 03301-7412. *Toll-free phone:* 800-247-0179. *Website:* http://www.nhti.edu/.

River Valley Community College
Claremont, New Hampshire

Freshman Application Contact River Valley Community College, 1 College Place, Claremont, NH 03743. *Phone:* 603-542-7744 Ext. 5323. *Toll-free phone:* 800-837-0658. *Website:* http://www.rivervalley.edu/.

St. Joseph School of Nursing
Nashua, New Hampshire

- **Independent** 2-year, founded 1964, affiliated with Roman Catholic Church
- **Urban** campus with easy access to Boston, Portland
- **Coed**

Undergraduates 63 full-time, 81 part-time. Students come from 3 states and territories; 9 other countries; 27% are from out of state; 24% transferred in.
Academics *Calendar:* semesters. *Degree:* associate. *Special study options:* academic remediation for entering students, advanced placement credit, services for LD students, summer session for credit.
Student Life *Campus security:* 24-hour emergency response devices and patrols, late-night transport/escort service.
Applying *Options:* electronic application. *Application fee:* $50. *Required:* essay or personal statement, high school transcript, minimum 2.5 GPA, 3 letters of recommendation, interview.
Freshman Application Contact Mrs. L. Nadeau, Admissions, St. Joseph School of Nursing, 5 Woodward Avenue, Nashua, NH 03060. *Toll-free phone:* 800-370-3169. *Website:* http://www.sjson.edu/.

White Mountains Community College
Berlin, New Hampshire

- **State-supported** 2-year, founded 1966, part of Community College System of New Hampshire
- **Rural** 325-acre campus
- **Coed**

Undergraduates 299 full-time, 503 part-time. Students come from 6 states and territories; 13% are from out of state; 0.2% Black or African American, non-Hispanic/Latino; 1% Hispanic/Latino; 0.4% Asian, non-Hispanic/Latino; 0.1% American Indian or Alaska Native, non-Hispanic/Latino; 9% Race/ethnicity unknown; 4% transferred in.
Faculty *Student/faculty ratio:* 8:1.

Academics *Calendar:* semesters. *Degree:* certificates and associate. *Special study options:* academic remediation for entering students, adult/continuing education programs, advanced placement credit, cooperative education, distance learning, double majors, external degree program, independent study, internships, part-time degree program, services for LD students, student-designed majors, summer session for credit.
Library Fortier Library. *Books:* 17,808 (physical); *Serial titles:* 35 (physical); *Databases:* 48. Weekly public service hours: 55; students can reserve study rooms.
Student Life *Campus security:* 24-hour emergency response devices, late-night transport/escort service.
Standardized Tests *Required for some:* TEAS for associate's degree nursing program.
Applying *Options:* electronic application, deferred entrance. *Application fee:* $20. *Required:* high school transcript. *Required for some:* letters of recommendation.
Freshman Application Contact Ms. Amanda Gaeb, Admissions Counselor, White Mountains Community College, 2020 Riverside Drive, Berlin, NH 03570. *Phone:* 603-342-3006. *Toll-free phone:* 800-445-4525. *Fax:* 603-752-6335. *E-mail:* agaeb@ccsnh.edu. *Website:* http://www.wmcc.edu/.

NEW JERSEY

Assumption College for Sisters
Denville, New Jersey

Freshman Application Contact Sr. Gerardine Tantsits, Academic Dean/Registrar, Assumption College for Sisters, 350 Bernardsville Road, Mendham, NJ 07945-2923. *Phone:* 973-543-6528 Ext. 228. *Fax:* 973-543-1738. *E-mail:* deanregistrar@acs350.org. *Website:* http://www.acs350.org/.

Atlantic Cape Community College
Mays Landing, New Jersey

Freshman Application Contact Mrs. Linda McLeod, Assistant Director, Admissions and College Recruitment, Atlantic Cape Community College, 5100 Black Horse Pike, Mays Landing, NJ 08330-2699. *Phone:* 609-343-5009. *Fax:* 609-343-4921. *E-mail:* accadmit@atlantic.edu. *Website:* http://www.atlantic.edu/.

Bergen Community College
Paramus, New Jersey

Freshman Application Contact Admissions Office, Bergen Community College, 400 Paramus Road, Paramus, NJ 07652-1595. *Phone:* 201-447-7195. *E-mail:* admsoffice@bergen.edu. *Website:* http://www.bergen.edu/.

Brookdale Community College
Lincroft, New Jersey

Director of Admissions Ms. Kim Toomey, Registrar, Brookdale Community College, 765 Newman Springs Road, Lincroft, NJ 07738-1597. *Phone:* 732-224-2268. *Website:* http://www.brookdalecc.edu/.

Camden County College
Blackwood, New Jersey

- **State and locally supported** 2-year, founded 1967, part of New Jersey Office of the Secretary of Higher Education
- **Suburban** 320-acre campus with easy access to Philadelphia
- **Coed**

Undergraduates 5,041 full-time, 5,451 part-time. Students come from 21 states and territories; 2% are from out of state; 20% Black or African American, non-Hispanic/Latino; 17% Hispanic/Latino; 6% Asian, non-Hispanic/Latino; 0.3% Native Hawaiian or other Pacific Islander, non-Hispanic/Latino; 1% American Indian or Alaska Native, non-Hispanic/Latino; 0.6% Two or more races, non-Hispanic/Latino; 6% Race/ethnicity unknown; 3% international; 8% transferred in.
Academics *Calendar:* semesters. *Degree:* certificates and associate. *Special study options:* academic remediation for entering students, adult/continuing education programs, advanced placement credit, cooperative education, distance learning, double majors, English as a second language, external degree program, freshman honors college, honors programs, independent study, internships, off-campus study, part-time degree program, services for LD students, study abroad, summer session for credit.
Library Wolverton Center Library.
Student Life *Campus security:* 24-hour emergency response devices and patrols, late-night transport/escort service.
Athletics Member NJCAA.
Financial Aid Of all full-time matriculated undergraduates who enrolled in 2017, 117 Federal Work-Study jobs (averaging $1126).
Applying *Options:* electronic application, early admission. *Required for some:* high school transcript.
Freshman Application Contact Mr. Donald Delaney, Director of Program Outreach, Camden County College, PO Box 200, Blackwood, NJ 08012-0200. *Phone:* 856-227-7200 Ext. 4660. *Fax:* 856-374-4916. *E-mail:* ddelaney@camdencc.edu. *Website:* http://www.camdencc.edu/.

County College of Morris
Randolph, New Jersey

- **County-supported** 2-year, founded 1966
- **Suburban** 218-acre campus with easy access to New York City
- **Endowment** $5.4 million
- **Coed**

Undergraduates 3,819 full-time, 4,130 part-time. Students come from 6 states and territories; 0.4% are from out of state; 5% Black or African American, non-Hispanic/Latino; 21% Hispanic/Latino; 6% Asian, non-Hispanic/Latino; 0.2% Native Hawaiian or other Pacific Islander, non-Hispanic/Latino; 0.4% American Indian or Alaska Native, non-Hispanic/Latino; 2% Two or more races, non-Hispanic/Latino; 6% Race/ethnicity unknown; 2% international; 5% transferred in. *Retention:* 72% of full-time freshmen returned.
Academics *Calendar:* semesters. *Degree:* certificates and associate. *Special study options:* academic remediation for entering students, accelerated degree program, advanced placement credit, cooperative education, distance learning, double majors, English as a second language, independent study, internships, services for LD students, study abroad, summer session for credit.
Library Learning Resource Center plus 1 other. *Books:* 38,594 (physical), 3,508 (digital/electronic); *Serial titles:* 26 (physical), 5 (digital/electronic); *Databases:* 123. Weekly public service hours: 68.
Student Life *Campus security:* 24-hour emergency response devices and patrols, late-night transport/escort service.
Athletics Member NJCAA.
Financial Aid Of all full-time matriculated undergraduates who enrolled in 2017, 588 Federal Work-Study jobs (averaging $1947).
Applying *Options:* electronic application. *Application fee:* $30. *Required:* high school transcript.
Freshman Application Contact County College of Morris, 214 Center Grove Road, Randolph, NJ 07869-2086. *Phone:* 973-328-5096. *Website:* http://www.ccm.edu/.

Cumberland County College
Vineland, New Jersey

Freshman Application Contact Ms. Anne Daly-Eimer, Director of Admissions and Registration, Cumberland County College, 3322 College Drive, Vineland, NJ 08360. *Phone:* 856-691-8600. *Website:* http://www.cccnj.edu/.

Eastern International College
Belleville, New Jersey

- **Proprietary** primarily 2-year
- **Urban** campus with easy access to Manhattan, New York
- **Coed**

Academics *Degrees:* associate and bachelor's.
Freshman Application Contact Eastern International College, 251 Washington Avenue, Belleville, NJ 07109. *Website:* http://www.eicollege.edu/.

Eastern International College
Jersey City, New Jersey

Admissions Office Contact Eastern International College, 684 Newark Avenue, Jersey City, NJ 07306. *Website:* http://www.eicollege.edu/.

Eastwick College
Hackensack, New Jersey

Admissions Office Contact Eastwick College, 250 Moore Street, Hackensack, NJ 07601. *Website:* http://www.eastwickcollege.edu/.

Eastwick College
Nutley, New Jersey

Admissions Office Contact Eastwick College, 103 Park Avenue, Nutley, NJ 07110. *Website:* http://www.eastwickcollege.edu/.

Eastwick College
Ramsey, New Jersey

Admissions Office Contact Eastwick College, 10 South Franklin Turnpike, Ramsey, NJ 07446. *Website:* http://www.eastwickcollege.edu/.

Essex County College
Newark, New Jersey

Freshman Application Contact Ms. Marva Mack, Director of Admissions, Essex County College, 303 University Avenue, Newark, NJ 07102. *Phone:* 973-877-3119. *Fax:* 973-623-6449. *Website:* http://www.essex.edu/.

Hudson County Community College
Jersey City, New Jersey

- **State and locally supported** 2-year, founded 1974
- **Urban** campus with easy access to New York City
- **Coed**

Undergraduates 5,136 full-time, 3,728 part-time. 14% Black or African American, non-Hispanic/Latino; 55% Hispanic/Latino; 8% Asian, non-Hispanic/Latino; 0.5% Native Hawaiian or other Pacific Islander, non-Hispanic/Latino; 0.3% American Indian or Alaska Native, non-Hispanic/Latino; 2% Two or more races, non-Hispanic/Latino; 8% Race/ethnicity unknown; 0.5% international; 4% transferred in. *Retention:* 58% of full-time freshmen returned.
Faculty *Student/faculty ratio:* 35:1.
Academics *Calendar:* semesters. *Degree:* certificates and associate. *Special study options:* academic remediation for entering students, advanced placement credit, distance learning, English as a second language, honors programs, independent study, internships, part-time degree program, services for LD students, summer session for credit.
Library Hudson County Community College Library plus 1 other. *Books:* 49,853 (physical), 2,881 (digital/electronic); *Serial titles:* 1,269 (physical), 750 (digital/electronic); *Databases:* 74. Students can reserve study rooms.
Student Life *Campus security:* 24-hour emergency response devices, late-night transport/escort service.
Financial Aid Of all full-time matriculated undergraduates who enrolled in 2017, 102 Federal Work-Study jobs (averaging $3000).
Applying *Options:* electronic application. *Application fee:* $20.
Freshman Application Contact Hudson County Community College, 70 Sip Avenue, Jersey City, NJ 07306. *Phone:* 201-360-4111. *Website:* http://www.hccc.edu/.

Jersey College
Teterboro, New Jersey

Freshman Application Contact Jersey College, 546 US Highway 46, Teterboro, NJ 07608. *Website:* http://www.jerseycollege.edu/.

Mercer County Community College
Trenton, New Jersey

Freshman Application Contact Dr. L. Campbell, Dean for Student and Academic Services, Mercer County Community College, 1200 Old Trenton Road, PO Box B, Trenton, NJ 08690-1004. *Phone:* 609-586-4800 Ext. 3222. *Toll-free phone:* 800-392-MCCC. *Fax:* 609-586-6944. *E-mail:* admiss@mccc.edu. *Website:* http://www.mccc.edu/.

Middlesex County College
Edison, New Jersey

Freshman Application Contact Middlesex County College, 2600 Woodbridge Avenue, PO Box 3050, Edison, NJ 08818-3050. *Website:* http://www.middlesexcc.edu/.

Ocean County College
Toms River, New Jersey

Freshman Application Contact Ms. Sheenah Hartigan, CRM Communications Administrator, Ocean County College, College Drive, PO Box 2001, Toms River, NJ 08754-2001. *Phone:* 732-255-0400 Ext. 2189. *E-mail:* shartigan@ocean.edu. *Website:* http://www.ocean.edu/.

Passaic County Community College
Paterson, New Jersey

Freshman Application Contact Mr. Patrick Noonan, Director of Admissions, Passaic County Community College, One College Boulevard, Paterson, NJ 07505-1179. *Phone:* 973-684-6304. *Website:* http://www.pccc.cc.nj.us/.

Raritan Valley Community College
Branchburg, New Jersey

- **State and locally supported** 2-year, founded 1965
- **Suburban** 240-acre campus with easy access to New York City, Philadelphia
- **Endowment** $139,462
- **Coed,** 7,887 undergraduate students, 39% full-time, 49% women, 51% men
- 100% of applicants were admitted

Undergraduates 3,089 full-time, 4,798 part-time. Students come from 12 states and territories; 1% are from out of state; 12% Black or African American, non-Hispanic/Latino; 24% Hispanic/Latino; 5% Asian, non-Hispanic/Latino; 0.3% Native Hawaiian or other Pacific Islander, non-Hispanic/Latino; 0.2% American Indian or Alaska Native, non-Hispanic/Latino; 2% Two or more races, non-Hispanic/Latino; 6% Race/ethnicity unknown; 2% international; 5% transferred in. *Retention:* 69% of full-time freshmen returned.
Freshmen *Admission:* 2,306 applied, 2,306 admitted, 1,525 enrolled.
Faculty *Total:* 497, 25% full-time. *Student/faculty ratio:* 20:1.
Majors Accounting related; accounting technology and bookkeeping; administrative assistant and secretarial science; allied health and medical assisting services related; animation, interactive technology, video graphics and special effects; automotive engineering technology; business administration and management; business/commerce; child-care provision; communication and media related; computer and information sciences; computer programming; construction engineering technology; criminal justice/law enforcement administration; crisis/emergency/disaster management; dance; dental hygiene; engineering science; engineering technologies and engineering related; English; fine/studio arts; game and interactive media design; health information/medical records technology; health services/allied health/health sciences; heating, ventilation, air conditioning and refrigeration engineering technology; human computer interaction; human services; information technology; interior design; kindergarten/preschool education; kinesiology and exercise science; legal assistant/paralegal; liberal arts and sciences/liberal studies; lineworker; management information systems; manufacturing engineering technology; medical/clinical assistant; meeting and event planning; modeling, virtual environments and simulation; multi/interdisciplinary studies related; music; occupational therapist assistant; opticianry; optometric technician; registered nursing/registered nurse; rehabilitation and therapeutic professions related; respiratory care therapy; restaurant, culinary, and catering management; small business administration.
Academics *Calendar:* semesters. *Degree:* certificates and associate. *Special study options:* academic remediation for entering students, adult/continuing education programs, advanced placement credit, cooperative education, distance learning, double majors, English as a second language, freshman honors college, honors programs, independent study, internships, off-campus study, part-time degree program, services for LD students, summer session for credit. *ROTC:* Army (c), Air Force (c).
Library Evelyn S. Field Library. *Books:* 64,100 (physical), 130,487 (digital/electronic); *Serial titles:* 109 (physical), 58,888 (digital/electronic); *Databases:* 73.
Student Life *Housing:* college housing not available. *Activities and Organizations:* drama/theater group, student-run newspaper, radio station, choral group, Phi Theta Kappa, Rotaract, Enactus, Health Oriented Peer Educators (HOPE), Orgullo Latino (OLC). *Campus security:* 24-hour emergency response devices and patrols, late-night transport/escort service. *Student services:* personal/psychological counseling.
Athletics Member NJCAA. *Intercollegiate sports:* basketball W(s), cross-country running W, soccer W, volleyball W. *Intramural sports:* basketball M, soccer M.
Financial Aid Of all full-time matriculated undergraduates who enrolled in 2017, 12 Federal Work-Study jobs (averaging $2500).
Applying *Options:* electronic application. *Application fee:* $25. *Application deadlines:* rolling (freshmen), rolling (transfers). *Notification:* continuous (freshmen), continuous (out-of-state freshmen), continuous (transfers).
Freshman Application Contact Mr. John Wheeler, Registrar, Enrollment Services, Raritan Valley Community College, 118 Lamington Road,

Branchburg, NJ 08876. *Phone:* 908-526-1200 Ext. 8339. *Fax:* 908-704-3442. *E-mail:* jwheeler@raritanval.edu. *Website:* http://www.raritanval.edu/.

Rowan College at Burlington County

Pemberton, New Jersey

Freshman Application Contact Rowan College at Burlington County, 601 Pemberton Browns Mills Road, Pemberton, NJ 08068. *Phone:* 609-894-9311 Ext. 1200. *Website:* http://www.rcbc.edu/.

Rowan College at Gloucester County

Sewell, New Jersey

Freshman Application Contact Ms. Judy Atkinson, Registrar/Admissions, Rowan College at Gloucester County, 1400 Tanyard Road, Sewell, NJ 08080. *Phone:* 856-415-2209. *E-mail:* jatkinso@gccnj.edu. *Website:* http://www.rcgc.edu/.

Salem Community College

Carneys Point, New Jersey

Freshman Application Contact Kelly McShay, Director of Retention and Admissions, Salem Community College, 460 Hollywood Avenue, Carneys Point, NJ 08069. *Phone:* 856-351-2919. *E-mail:* kmcshay@salemcc.edu. *Website:* http://www.salemcc.edu/.

Sussex County Community College

Newton, New Jersey

Freshman Application Contact Mr. Todd Poltersdorf, Director of Admissions, Sussex County Community College, 1 College Hill Road, Newton, NJ 07860. *Phone:* 973-300-2253. *E-mail:* tpoltersdorf@sussex.edu. *Website:* http://www.sussex.edu/.

Union County College

Cranford, New Jersey

- **State and locally supported** 2-year, founded 1933
- **Urban** 47-acre campus with easy access to New York City
- **Coed,** 9,412 undergraduate students, 45% full-time, 62% women, 38% men
- 100% of applicants were admitted

Undergraduates 4,223 full-time, 5,189 part-time. 28% Black or African American, non-Hispanic/Latino; 39% Hispanic/Latino; 4% Asian, non-Hispanic/Latino; 0.4% Native Hawaiian or other Pacific Islander, non-Hispanic/Latino; 0.3% American Indian or Alaska Native, non-Hispanic/Latino; 2% Two or more races, non-Hispanic/Latino; 9% Race/ethnicity unknown; 1% international; 8% transferred in.
Freshmen *Admission:* 4,836 applied, 4,836 admitted, 1,866 enrolled.
Majors Accounting technology and bookkeeping; American Sign Language (ASL); automobile/automotive mechanics technology; biology/biological sciences; business administration and management; business/commerce; chemistry; computer and information sciences and support services related; computer science; criminal justice/law enforcement administration; cyber/computer forensics and counterterrorism; diagnostic medical sonography and ultrasound technology; electromechanical technology; emergency medical technology (EMT paramedic); engineering; engineering technologies and engineering related; English; fire prevention and safety technology; health services/allied health/health sciences; history; hospitality administration; human services; information technology; legal assistant/paralegal; liberal arts and sciences/liberal studies; marketing/marketing management; mass communication/media; mathematics; physical therapy technology; radiologic technology/science; registered nursing/registered nurse; rehabilitation and therapeutic professions related; respiratory care therapy; sport and fitness administration/management.
Academics *Calendar:* semesters. *Degree:* certificates and associate. *Special study options:* academic remediation for entering students, adult/continuing education programs, advanced placement credit, distance learning, English as a second language, honors programs, independent study, internships, off-campus study, part-time degree program, services for LD students, summer session for credit. *ROTC:* Air Force (c).
Library MacKay Library plus 2 others. *Books:* 88,960 (physical), 239,464 (digital/electronic); *Serial titles:* 222 (physical), 363,355 (digital/electronic); *Databases:* 96.
Student Life *Housing:* college housing not available. *Activities and Organizations:* drama/theater group, student-run newspaper, radio station. *Campus security:* 24-hour emergency response devices and patrols. *Student services:* personal/psychological counseling, veterans affairs office.
Athletics Member NJCAA. *Intercollegiate sports:* basketball W(s), cross-country running W, golf W, soccer W, track and field W, volleyball W.
Applying *Options:* electronic application. *Required:* high school transcript, Immunization records. *Required for some:* essay or personal statement, interview. *Application deadlines:* rolling (freshmen), rolling (transfers). *Notification:* continuous (freshmen), continuous (transfers).
Freshman Application Contact Ms. Beatriz Rodriguez, Director of Enrollment Services, Union County College, Cranford, NJ 07016. *Phone:* 908-709-7000. *E-mail:* rodriguez@ucc.edu. *Website:* http://www.ucc.edu/.

Warren County Community College

Washington, New Jersey

Freshman Application Contact Shannon Horwath, Associate Director of Admissions, Warren County Community College, 475 Route 57 West, Washington, NJ 07882-9605. *Phone:* 908-835-2300. *E-mail:* shorwath@warren.edu. *Website:* http://www.warren.edu/.

NEW MEXICO

Carrington College–Albuquerque

Albuquerque, New Mexico

Freshman Application Contact Carrington College–Albuquerque, 1001 Menaul Boulevard NE, Albuquerque, NM 87107. *Website:* http://www.carrington.edu/.

Central New Mexico Community College

Albuquerque, New Mexico

- **State-supported** 2-year, founded 1965
- **Urban** 304-acre campus
- **Endowment** $1.9 million
- **Coed,** 23,717 undergraduate students, 28% full-time, 58% women, 42% men

Undergraduates 6,538 full-time, 17,179 part-time. Students come from 18 other countries; 1% are from out of state; 3% Black or African American, non-Hispanic/Latino; 52% Hispanic/Latino; 2% Asian, non-Hispanic/Latino; 0.2% Native Hawaiian or other Pacific Islander, non-Hispanic/Latino; 6% American Indian or Alaska Native, non-Hispanic/Latino; 2% Two or more races, non-Hispanic/Latino; 7% Race/ethnicity unknown; 0.2% international; 4% transferred in.
Freshmen *Admission:* 4,758 applied, 4,758 admitted, 3,665 enrolled.
Faculty *Total:* 959, 34% full-time. *Student/faculty ratio:* 23:1.
Majors Accounting; administrative assistant and secretarial science; airframe mechanics and aircraft maintenance technology; anthropology; architectural drafting and CAD/CADD; art; biology/biological sciences; biotechnology; building construction technology; business administration and management; chemistry; cinematography and film/video production; clinical/medical laboratory technology; communication; computer and information sciences; computer science; construction management; cosmetology; criminal justice/law enforcement administration; criminology; culinary arts; diagnostic medical sonography and ultrasound technology; early childhood education; education (multiple levels); emergency medical technology (EMT paramedic); English; environmental design/architecture; fire science/firefighting; general studies; geographic information science and cartography; geography; health and physical education/fitness; health information/medical records administration; health information/medical records technology; health services/allied health/health sciences; heating, air conditioning, ventilation and refrigeration maintenance technology; history; hospitality administration; human development and family studies; Latin American studies; liberal arts and sciences/liberal studies; machine tool technology; mathematics; physical therapy technology; physics; pre-engineering; pre-law studies; psychology; radiologic technology/science; registered nursing/registered nurse; respiratory care therapy; sociology; surgical technology; surveying engineering; technology/industrial arts teacher education; vehicle maintenance and repair technologies related; veterinary/animal health technology; welding technology.
Academics *Calendar:* trimesters. *Degree:* certificates and associate. *Special study options:* academic remediation for entering students, accelerated degree program, adult/continuing education programs, advanced placement credit, cooperative education, distance learning, English as a second language, honors programs, independent study, internships, off-campus study, part-time degree

program, services for LD students, summer session for credit. *ROTC:* Army (c), Navy (c), Air Force (c).
Library Main Campus Library plus 5 others. *Books:* 37,327 (physical), 246,604 (digital/electronic); *Serial titles:* 173 (physical), 1,511 (digital/electronic); *Databases:* 83.
Student Life *Housing:* college housing not available. *Activities and Organizations:* student-run newspaper. *Campus security:* 24-hour emergency response devices and patrols, late-night transport/escort service. *Student services:* veterans affairs office.
Financial Aid Of all full-time matriculated undergraduates who enrolled in 2017, 4,897 applied for aid, 4,384 were judged to have need. *Average need-based loan:* $2862. *Average need-based gift aid:* $2232.
Applying *Options:* electronic application. *Application deadlines:* rolling (freshmen), rolling (out-of-state freshmen), rolling (transfers). *Notification:* continuous (freshmen), continuous (out-of-state freshmen), continuous (transfers).
Freshman Application Contact Glenn Damiani, Senior Director, Enrollment Services, Central New Mexico Community College, Albuquerque, NM 87106. *Phone:* 505-224-4000 Ext. 1104. *E-mail:* gdamiani@cnm.edu. *Website:* http://www.cnm.edu/.

Clovis Community College

Clovis, New Mexico

Freshman Application Contact Ms. Rosie Corrie, Director of Admissions and Records/Registrar, Clovis Community College, Clovis, NM 88101-8381. *Phone:* 575-769-4962. *Toll-free phone:* 800-769-1409. *Fax:* 575-769-4190. *E-mail:* admissions@clovis.edu. *Website:* http://www.clovis.edu/.

Doña Ana Community College

Las Cruces, New Mexico

Freshman Application Contact Mrs. Ricci Montes, Admissions Advisor, Doña Ana Community College, MSC-3DA, Box 30001, 3400 South Espina Street, Las Cruces, NM 88003-8001. *Phone:* 575-527-7683. *Toll-free phone:* 800-903-7503. *Fax:* 575-527-7515. *Website:* http://dacc.nmsu.edu/.

Eastern New Mexico University–Roswell

Roswell, New Mexico

Freshman Application Contact Eastern New Mexico University–Roswell, PO Box 6000, Roswell, NM 88202-6000. *Phone:* 505-624-7142. *Toll-free phone:* 800-243-6687 (in-state); 800-624-7000 (out-of-state). *Website:* http://www.roswell.enmu.edu/.

IntelliTec College

Albuquerque, New Mexico

Admissions Office Contact IntelliTec College, 5001 Montgomery Boulevard NE, Suite A24, Albuquerque, NM 87109. *Website:* http://www.intelliteccollege.edu/.

Luna Community College

Las Vegas, New Mexico

Freshman Application Contact Ms. Henrietta Griego, Director of Admissions, Recruitment, and Retention, Luna Community College, PO Box 1510, Las Vegas, NM 87701. *Phone:* 505-454-2020. *Toll-free phone:* 800-588-7232. *Fax:* 505-454-2588. *E-mail:* hgriego@luna.cc.nm.us. *Website:* http://www.luna.edu/.

Mesalands Community College

Tucumcari, New Mexico

- **State-supported** 2-year, founded 1979
- **Small-town** campus
- **Coed**

Faculty *Student/faculty ratio:* 18:1.
Academics *Calendar:* semesters. *Degree:* certificates and associate.
Student Life *Campus security:* 24-hour emergency response devices.
Applying *Required:* high school transcript.
Freshman Application Contact Mesalands Community College, 911 South Tenth Street, Tucumcari, NM 88401. *Phone:* 575-461-4413. *Website:* http://www.mesalands.edu/.

New Mexico Junior College

Hobbs, New Mexico

Freshman Application Contact New Mexico Junior College, 5317 Lovington Highway, Hobbs, NM 88240-9123. *Phone:* 575-492-2587. *Toll-free phone:* 800-657-6260. *Website:* http://www.nmjc.edu/.

New Mexico Military Institute

Roswell, New Mexico

Freshman Application Contact New Mexico Military Institute, Roswell, NM 88201-5173. *Phone:* 505-624-8050. *Toll-free phone:* 800-421-5376. *Fax:* 505-624-8058. *E-mail:* admissions@nmmi.edu. *Website:* http://www.nmmi.edu/.

New Mexico State University–Alamogordo

Alamogordo, New Mexico

- **State-supported** 2-year, founded 1958, part of New Mexico State University System
- **Small-town** 540-acre campus
- **Endowment** $147,086
- **Coed**

Undergraduates 425 full-time, 1,285 part-time. Students come from 9 states and territories; 3 other countries; 4% Black or African American, non-Hispanic/Latino; 45% Hispanic/Latino; 1% Asian, non-Hispanic/Latino; 0.4% Native Hawaiian or other Pacific Islander, non-Hispanic/Latino; 4% American Indian or Alaska Native, non-Hispanic/Latino; 3% Two or more races, non-Hispanic/Latino; 2% Race/ethnicity unknown; 2% international; 4% transferred in. *Retention:* 46% of full-time freshmen returned.
Faculty *Student/faculty ratio:* 16:1.
Academics *Calendar:* semesters. *Degree:* certificates and associate. *Special study options:* academic remediation for entering students, adult/continuing education programs, advanced placement credit, distance learning, double majors, independent study, internships, off-campus study, part-time degree program, services for LD students, study abroad, summer session for credit.
Library David H. Townsend Library.
Student Life *Campus security:* late-night transport/escort service.
Financial Aid Of all full-time matriculated undergraduates who enrolled in 2017, 10 Federal Work-Study jobs (averaging $3300). 60 state and other part-time jobs (averaging $3300). *Financial aid deadline:* 5/1.
Applying *Options:* electronic application, early admission, deferred entrance. *Application fee:* $20. *Required:* high school transcript, minimum 2.0 GPA.
Freshman Application Contact Ms. Elma Hernandez, Coordinator of Admissions and Records, New Mexico State University–Alamogordo, 2400 North Scenic Drive, Alamogordo, NM 88311-0477. *Phone:* 575-439-3700. *E-mail:* advisor@nmsu.edu. *Website:* http://nmsua.edu/.

New Mexico State University–Carlsbad

Carlsbad, New Mexico

Freshman Application Contact Ms. Everal Shannon, Records Specialist, New Mexico State University–Carlsbad, 1500 University Drive, Carlsbad, NM 88220. *Phone:* 575-234-9222. *Fax:* 575-885-4951. *E-mail:* eshannon@nmsu.edu. *Website:* http://www.cavern.nmsu.edu/.

New Mexico State University–Grants

Grants, New Mexico

Director of Admissions Ms. Irene Lutz, Campus Student Services Officer, New Mexico State University–Grants, 1500 3rd Street, Grants, NM 87020-2025. *Phone:* 505-287-7981. *Website:* http://grants.nmsu.edu/.

Pima Medical Institute

Albuquerque, New Mexico

Freshman Application Contact Admissions Office, Pima Medical Institute, 4400 Cutler Avenue NE, Albuquerque, NM 87110. *Phone:* 505-881-1234. *Toll-free phone:* 800-477-PIMA. *Fax:* 505-881-5329. *Website:* http://www.pmi.edu/.

San Juan College
Farmington, New Mexico

- **State-supported** 2-year, founded 1958, part of New Mexico Higher Education Department
- **Small-town** 698-acre campus
- **Endowment** $15.7 million
- **Coed,** 4,790 undergraduate students, 46% full-time, 69% women, 31% men

Undergraduates 2,212 full-time, 2,578 part-time. Students come from 52 states and territories; 22 other countries; 30% are from out of state; 1% Black or African American, non-Hispanic/Latino; 16% Hispanic/Latino; 0.8% Asian, non-Hispanic/Latino; 0.2% Native Hawaiian or other Pacific Islander, non-Hispanic/Latino; 34% American Indian or Alaska Native, non-Hispanic/Latino; 2% Two or more races, non-Hispanic/Latino; 4% Race/ethnicity unknown; 1% international; 10% transferred in.
Freshmen *Admission:* 765 admitted, 765 enrolled.
Faculty *Total:* 311, 46% full-time. *Student/faculty ratio:* 20:1.
Majors Accounting technology and bookkeeping; American Indian/Native American studies; autobody/collision and repair technology; automobile/automotive mechanics technology; biology/biological sciences; business administration and management; carpentry; chemistry; child-care provision; clinical/medical laboratory technology; commercial and advertising art; cosmetology; criminal justice/police science; data processing and data processing technology; dental hygiene; diesel mechanics technology; drafting and design technology; electrical, electronic and communications engineering technology; elementary education; emergency medical technology (EMT paramedic); engineering; engineering technology; fire science/firefighting; general studies; health and physical education/fitness; health information/medical records technology; industrial mechanics and maintenance technology; industrial technology; instrumentation technology; legal assistant/paralegal; liberal arts and sciences/liberal studies; mathematics; occupational safety and health technology; occupational therapist assistant; parks, recreation and leisure; physical sciences; physical therapy technology; physics; premedical studies; psychology; registered nursing/registered nurse; respiratory care therapy; secondary education; social work; special education; surgical technology; theater design and technology; veterinary/animal health technology; welding technology.
Academics *Calendar:* semesters. *Degree:* certificates, diplomas, and associate. *Special study options:* academic remediation for entering students, adult/continuing education programs, advanced placement credit, cooperative education, distance learning, double majors, English as a second language, freshman honors college, honors programs, independent study, internships, part-time degree program, services for LD students, summer session for credit.
Library San Juan College Library. *Books:* 78,682 (physical), 208,891 (digital/electronic); *Serial titles:* 247 (physical), 30,188 (digital/electronic); *Databases:* 100. Weekly public service hours: 69.
Student Life *Housing:* college housing not available. *Activities and Organizations:* drama/theater group, choral group, National Society of Leadership and Success (NSLS), Student American Dental Hygienists' Association, Student Nurses Association, Society for Advancement of Chicanos and Native Americans in Science, All Nations Leadership Association, national fraternities, national sororities. *Campus security:* 24-hour emergency response devices and patrols, late-night transport/escort service. *Student services:* personal/psychological counseling, veterans affairs office.
Athletics *Intramural sports:* basketball M/W, volleyball M/W.
Financial Aid Of all full-time matriculated undergraduates who enrolled in 2017, 150 Federal Work-Study jobs (averaging $2500). 175 state and other part-time jobs (averaging $2500).
Applying *Options:* electronic application, early admission, deferred entrance. *Application fee:* $10. *Required:* high school transcript. *Application deadlines:* rolling (freshmen), rolling (transfers). *Notification:* continuous (freshmen), continuous (transfers).
Freshman Application Contact Mrs. Abby Calcote, Director of Admissions & Recruitment, San Juan College, 4601 College Boulevard, Farmington, NM 87402. *Phone:* 505-566-3572. *Fax:* 505-566-3500. *E-mail:* calcotea@sanjuancollege.edu.
Website: http://www.sanjuancollege.edu/.

Santa Fe Community College
Santa Fe, New Mexico

Freshman Application Contact Marcos Maez, Student Recruitment and Outreach Administrator, Santa Fe Community College, 6401 Richards Avenue, Santa Fe, NM 87508. *Phone:* 505-428-1779. *E-mail:* marcos.maez@sfcc.edu. *Website:* http://www.sfcc.edu/.

Southwestern Indian Polytechnic Institute
Albuquerque, New Mexico

- **Federally supported** 2-year, founded 1971
- **Suburban** 144-acre campus with easy access to Albuquerque
- **Coed**

Undergraduates 346 full-time, 56 part-time. Students come from 18 states and territories; 60% live on campus.
Faculty *Student/faculty ratio:* 16:1.
Academics *Calendar:* trimesters. *Degree:* certificates and associate. *Special study options:* academic remediation for entering students, advanced placement credit, cooperative education, distance learning, double majors, internships, part-time degree program, services for LD students, summer session for credit.
Library Southwestern Indian Polytechnic Institute Library.
Student Life *Campus security:* 24-hour emergency response devices and patrols, late-night transport/escort service.
Applying *Required:* high school transcript, Certificate of Indian Blood, physical, immunization records.
Freshman Application Contact Tawna Harrison, First Year Counselor, Southwestern Indian Polytechnic Institute, PO Box 10146, 9169 Coors Road NW, Albuquerque, NM 87184. *Phone:* 505-922-6516. *Toll-free phone:* 800-586-7474. *E-mail:* tawna.harrison@bie.edu. *Website:* http://www.sipi.edu/.

University of New Mexico–Gallup
Gallup, New Mexico

Freshman Application Contact University of New Mexico–Gallup, 705 Gurley Avenue, Gallup, NM 87301. *Phone:* 505-863-7576. *Website:* http://www.gallup.unm.edu/.

University of New Mexico–Los Alamos Branch
Los Alamos, New Mexico

Freshman Application Contact Mrs. Irene K. Martinez, Enrollment Representative, University of New Mexico–Los Alamos Branch, 4000 University Drive, Los Alamos, NM 87544-2233. *Phone:* 505-662-0332. *E-mail:* l65130@unm.edu. *Website:* http://losalamos.unm.edu/.

University of New Mexico–Taos
Taos, New Mexico

Director of Admissions Vickie Alvarez, Student Enrollment Associate, University of New Mexico–Taos, 115 Civic Plaza Drive, Taos, NM 87571. *Phone:* 575-737-6425. *E-mail:* valvarez@unm.edu. *Website:* http://taos.unm.edu/.

University of New Mexico–Valencia Campus
Los Lunas, New Mexico

Director of Admissions Richard M. Hulett, Director of Admissions and Recruitment, University of New Mexico–Valencia Campus, 280 La Entrada, Los Lunas, NM 87031-7633. *Phone:* 505-277-2446. *E-mail:* mhulett@unm.edu. *Website:* http://valencia.unm.edu/.

NEW YORK

Adirondack Community College
Queensbury, New York

- **State and locally supported** 2-year, founded 1960, part of State University of New York System
- **Small-town** 141-acre campus
- **Endowment** $3.9 million
- **Coed**

Undergraduates 2,189 full-time, 1,784 part-time. Students come from 10 states and territories; 19 other countries; 0.9% are from out of state; 3% Black or African American, non-Hispanic/Latino; 3% Hispanic/Latino; 0.9% Asian, non-Hispanic/Latino; 0.5% American Indian or Alaska Native, non-Hispanic/Latino; 2% Two or more races, non-Hispanic/Latino; 13%

Race/ethnicity unknown; 0.2% international; 5% transferred in. *Retention:* 63% of full-time freshmen returned.
Faculty *Student/faculty ratio:* 17:1.
Academics *Calendar:* semesters. *Degree:* certificates and associate. *Special study options:* academic remediation for entering students, accelerated degree program, adult/continuing education programs, advanced placement credit, cooperative education, distance learning, double majors, English as a second language, independent study, internships, part-time degree program, services for LD students, study abroad, summer session for credit.
Library SUNY Adirondack Library.
Student Life *Campus security:* late-night transport/escort service, patrols by trained security personnel 8 am to 10 pm.
Athletics Member NJCAA.
Financial Aid Of all full-time matriculated undergraduates who enrolled in 2017, 98 Federal Work-Study jobs (averaging $462).
Applying *Options:* electronic application. *Application fee:* $35.
Freshman Application Contact Office of Admissions, Adirondack Community College, 640 Bay Road, Queensbury, NY 12804. *Phone:* 518-743-2264. *Toll-free phone:* 888-SUNY-ADK. *Fax:* 518-743-2200. *Website:* http://www.sunyacc.edu/.

American Academy McAllister Institute of Funeral Service

New York, New York

Freshman Application Contact Mr. Norman Provost, Registrar, American Academy McAllister Institute of Funeral Service, 450 West 56th Street, New York, NY 10019-3602. *Phone:* 212-757-1190. *Toll-free phone:* 866-932-2264. *Website:* http://www.funeraleducation.org/.

American Academy of Dramatic Arts–New York

New York, New York

- **Independent** 2-year, founded 1884
- **Urban** campus
- **Coed**

Undergraduates 310 full-time. Students come from 28 states and territories; 25 other countries; 84% are from out of state; 8% Black or African American, non-Hispanic/Latino; 5% Hispanic/Latino; 0.6% Asian, non-Hispanic/Latino; 0.3% American Indian or Alaska Native, non-Hispanic/Latino; 6% Two or more races, non-Hispanic/Latino; 5% Race/ethnicity unknown; 28% international; 53% live on campus. *Retention:* 75% of full-time freshmen returned.
Faculty *Student/faculty ratio:* 8:1.
Academics *Calendar:* semesters. *Degree:* certificates and associate. *Special study options:* academic remediation for entering students, honors programs.
Library Academy/CBS Library.
Student Life *Campus security:* 24-hour emergency response devices and patrols, controlled dormitory access, trained security guard during hours of operation and for campus housing.
Financial Aid Of all full-time matriculated undergraduates who enrolled in 2012, 240 applied for aid, 231 were judged to have need. 50 Federal Work-Study jobs (averaging $900). 50 state and other part-time jobs (averaging $2000). In 2012, 59. *Average percent of need met:* 67. *Average financial aid package:* $18,150. *Average need-based loan:* $4500. *Average need-based gift aid:* $7000. *Average non-need-based aid:* $7000. *Average indebtedness upon graduation:* $15,000. *Financial aid deadline:* 5/15.
Applying *Options:* electronic application, deferred entrance. *Application fee:* $50. *Required:* essay or personal statement, high school transcript, minimum 2.0 GPA, 2 letters of recommendation, interview, audition.
Freshman Application Contact Kerin Reilly, Director of Admissions, American Academy of Dramatic Arts–New York, 120 Madison Avenue, New York, NY 10016. *Phone:* 212-686-9244 Ext. 333. *Toll-free phone:* 800-463-8990. *E-mail:* kreilly@aada.edu. *Website:* http://www.aada.edu/.

ASA College

Brooklyn, New York

Freshman Application Contact Admissions Office, ASA College, 81 Willoughby Street, Brooklyn, NY 11201. *Phone:* 718-522-9073. *Toll-free phone:* 877-679-8772. *Website:* http://www.asa.edu/.

The Belanger School of Nursing

Schenectady, New York

- **Independent** 2-year, founded 1906
- **Urban** campus
- **Coed**

Undergraduates 37 full-time, 77 part-time. Students come from 1 other state; 8% Black or African American, non-Hispanic/Latino; 5% Hispanic/Latino; 15% Asian, non-Hispanic/Latino; 0.9% American Indian or Alaska Native, non-Hispanic/Latino; 0.9% Two or more races, non-Hispanic/Latino; 3% Race/ethnicity unknown.
Faculty *Student/faculty ratio:* 4:1.
Academics *Degree:* associate. *Special study options:* honors programs, part-time degree program, summer session for credit.
Library Ellis Medicine's Health Services Library. *Books:* 2,000 (physical). Weekly public service hours: 40.
Student Life *Campus security:* on-campus security department 24/7.
Standardized Tests *Required:* Kaplan Admission Test (for admission).
Applying *Options:* electronic application. *Application fee:* $70. *Required:* essay or personal statement, high school transcript, minimum 3.0 GPA, 2 letters of recommendation.
Freshman Application Contact Carolyn Lansing, Student Services Manager, The Belanger School of Nursing, 650 McClellan Street, Schenectady, NY 12304. *Phone:* 518-831-8810. *Fax:* 518-243-4470. *E-mail:* lansingc@ellismedicine.org. *Website:* http://www.ellismedicine.org/school-of-nursing/.

Bill and Sandra Pomeroy College of Nursing at Crouse Hospital

Syracuse, New York

Freshman Application Contact Ms. Amy Graham, Enrollment Management Supervisor, Bill and Sandra Pomeroy College of Nursing at Crouse Hospital, 765 Irving Avenue, Syracuse, NY 13210. *Phone:* 315-470-7481. *Fax:* 315-470-7925. *E-mail:* amygraham@crouse.org. *Website:* http://www.crouse.org/nursing/.

Borough of Manhattan Community College of the City University of New York

New York, New York

- **State and locally supported** 2-year, founded 1963, part of City University of New York System
- **Urban** 5-acre campus
- **Coed,** 26,506 undergraduate students, 68% full-time, 58% women, 42% men

Undergraduates 18,076 full-time, 8,430 part-time. 4% are from out of state; 27% Black or African American, non-Hispanic/Latino; 45% Hispanic/Latino; 11% Asian, non-Hispanic/Latino; 0.2% Native Hawaiian or other Pacific Islander, non-Hispanic/Latino; 0.4% American Indian or Alaska Native, non-Hispanic/Latino; 2% Two or more races, non-Hispanic/Latino; 6% international; 7% transferred in.
Freshmen *Admission:* 25,455 applied, 24,994 admitted, 6,795 enrolled. *Test scores:* SAT evidence-based reading and writing scores over 500: 21%; SAT math scores over 500: 12%; SAT evidence-based reading and writing scores over 600: 1%; SAT math scores over 600: 2%.
Faculty *Total:* 1,714, 30% full-time. *Student/faculty ratio:* 24:1.
Majors Accounting; accounting technology and bookkeeping; administrative assistant and secretarial science; animation, interactive technology, video graphics and special effects; art history, criticism and conservation; biotechnology; business administration and management; community organization and advocacy; computer and information sciences; computer science; criminal justice/police science; economics; emergency medical technology (EMT paramedic); engineering; English; ethnic, cultural minority, gender, and group studies related; finance; fine/studio arts; foreign languages and literatures; forensic science and technology; general studies; geographic information science and cartography; gerontology; health information/medical records technology; health services/allied health/health sciences; history; liberal arts and sciences/liberal studies; linguistics; mass communication/media; mathematics; music; physical sciences; psychology; public health; public health education and promotion; radio and television broadcasting technology; registered nursing/registered nurse; respiratory therapy technician; small business administration; sociology; teacher assistant/aide; visual and performing arts; web page, digital/multimedia and information resources design; women's studies.
Academics *Calendar:* semesters. *Degree:* certificates and associate. *Special study options:* academic remediation for entering students, accelerated degree

program, adult/continuing education programs, advanced placement credit, cooperative education, distance learning, English as a second language, honors programs, independent study, internships, off-campus study, part-time degree program, services for LD students, study abroad, summer session for credit.
Library A. Philip Randolph Library plus 1 other. *Books:* 113,472 (physical), 580,303 (digital/electronic); *Serial titles:* 1,061 (physical), 114,687 (digital/electronic); *Databases:* 169. Weekly public service hours: 80; students can reserve study rooms.
Student Life *Activities and Organizations:* drama/theater group, student-run newspaper, choral group, Bangladeshi Student Association, Health Information Technology, Muslim Students Association, Resurgence in Christ, Urban Mentors and Leaders Association. *Campus security:* 24-hour patrols. *Student services:* health clinic, personal/psychological counseling, women's center, veterans affairs office.
Athletics Member NJCAA. *Intercollegiate sports:* basketball W, soccer W, volleyball W.
Standardized Tests *Recommended:* SAT or ACT (for admission).
Financial Aid Of all full-time matriculated undergraduates who enrolled in 2017, 15,958 applied for aid, 15,643 were judged to have need.
Applying *Options:* electronic application, deferred entrance. *Application fee:* $65. *Required:* high school transcript. *Application deadlines:* rolling (freshmen), rolling (transfers). *Notification:* continuous (freshmen), continuous (transfers).
Freshman Application Contact Ms. Lisa Kasper, Director of Enrollment Management, Borough of Manhattan Community College of the City University of New York, 199 Chambers Street, Room S-310, New York, NY 10007. *Phone:* 212-220-1272. *Toll-free phone:* 866-583-5729. *Fax:* 212-220-2366. *E-mail:* admissions@bmcc.cuny.edu.
Website: http://www.bmcc.cuny.edu/.

Bronx Community College of the City University of New York

Bronx, New York

Freshman Application Contact Ms. Patricia A. Ramos, Admissions Officer, Bronx Community College of the City University of New York, 2155 University Avenue, Bronx, NY 10453. *Phone:* 718-289-5888. *E-mail:* admission@bcc.cuny.edu. *Website:* http://www.bcc.cuny.edu/.

Bryant & Stratton College–Albany Campus

Albany, New York

Freshman Application Contact Mr. Robert Ferrell, Director of Admissions, Bryant & Stratton College–Albany Campus, 1259 Central Avenue, Albany, NY 12205. *Phone:* 518-437-1802 Ext. 205. *Fax:* 518-437-1048. *Website:* http://www.bryantstratton.edu/.

Bryant & Stratton College–Amherst Campus

Clarence, New York

Freshman Application Contact Mr. Brian K. Dioguardi, Director of Admissions, Bryant & Stratton College–Amherst Campus, Audubon Business Center, 40 Hazelwood Drive, Amherst, NY 14228. *Phone:* 716-691-0012. *Fax:* 716-691-0012. *E-mail:* bkdioguardi@bryantstratton.edu. *Website:* http://www.bryantstratton.edu/.

Bryant & Stratton College–Buffalo Campus

Buffalo, New York

Freshman Application Contact Mr. Philip J. Struebel, Director of Admissions, Bryant & Stratton College–Buffalo Campus, 465 Main Street, Suite 400, Buffalo, NY 14203. *Phone:* 716-884-9120. *Fax:* 716-884-0091. *E-mail:* pjstruebel@bryantstratton.edu. *Website:* http://www.bryantstratton.edu/.

Bryant & Stratton College–Greece Campus

Rochester, New York

Freshman Application Contact Bryant & Stratton College–Greece Campus, 854 Long Pond Road, Rochester, NY 14612. *Phone:* 585-720-0660. *Website:* http://www.bryantstratton.edu/.

Bryant & Stratton College–Henrietta Campus

Rochester, New York

Freshman Application Contact Bryant & Stratton College–Henrietta Campus, 1225 Jefferson Road, Rochester, NY 14623. *Phone:* 585-292-5627 Ext. 101. *Website:* http://www.bryantstratton.edu/.

Bryant & Stratton College–Orchard Park Campus

Orchard Park, New York

Freshman Application Contact Bryant & Stratton College–Orchard Park Campus, 200 Redtail Road, Orchard Park, NY 14127. *Phone:* 716-677-9500. *Website:* http://www.bryantstratton.edu/.

Bryant & Stratton College–Syracuse Campus

Syracuse, New York

Freshman Application Contact Ms. Dawn Rajkowski, Director of High School Enrollments, Bryant & Stratton College–Syracuse Campus, 953 James Street, Syracuse, NY 13203-2502. *Phone:* 315-472-6603 Ext. 248. *Fax:* 315-474-4383. *Website:* http://www.bryantstratton.edu/.

Bryant & Stratton College–Syracuse North Campus

Liverpool, New York

Freshman Application Contact Ms. Heather Macnik, Director of Admissions, Bryant & Stratton College–Syracuse North Campus, 8687 Carling Road, Liverpool, NY 13090. *Phone:* 315-652-6500. *Website:* http://www.bryantstratton.edu/.

Cayuga County Community College

Auburn, New York

- **State and locally supported** 2-year, founded 1953, part of State University of New York System
- **Small-town** 50-acre campus with easy access to Rochester, Syracuse
- **Endowment** $14.1 million
- **Coed,** 4,921 undergraduate students, 32% full-time, 60% women, 40% men

Undergraduates 1,585 full-time, 3,336 part-time. Students come from 11 states and territories; 10 other countries; 1% are from out of state; 6% Black or African American, non-Hispanic/Latino; 4% Hispanic/Latino; 1% Asian, non-Hispanic/Latino; 0.5% American Indian or Alaska Native, non-Hispanic/Latino; 1% Two or more races, non-Hispanic/Latino; 6% Race/ethnicity unknown; 0.5% international; 4% transferred in. *Retention:* 55% of full-time freshmen returned.
Freshmen *Admission:* 670 applied, 576 enrolled. *Average high school GPA:* 2.6.
Faculty *Total:* 222, 20% full-time. *Student/faculty ratio:* 26:1.
Majors Accounting technology and bookkeeping; art; business administration and management; child-care and support services management; computer and information sciences; computer and information sciences and support services related; corrections; criminal justice/police science; drafting and design technology; education (multiple levels); electrical, electronic and communications engineering technology; fine/studio arts; game and interactive media design; information science/studies; liberal arts and sciences/liberal studies; mechanical engineering/mechanical technology; music related; occupational therapist assistant; radio, television, and digital communication related; registered nursing/registered nurse; sport and fitness administration/management; telecommunications technology; wine steward/sommelier; writing.
Academics *Calendar:* semesters. *Degree:* certificates and associate. *Special study options:* academic remediation for entering students, advanced placement credit, cooperative education, distance learning, honors programs, internships, off-campus study, part-time degree program, services for LD students, study abroad, summer session for credit.
Library Norman F. Bourke Memorial Library plus 2 others. *Books:* 71,419 (physical), 151,020 (digital/electronic); *Serial titles:* 287 (physical), 61,585 (digital/electronic); *Databases:* 118. Weekly public service hours: 61; students can reserve study rooms.
Student Life *Housing:* college housing not available. *Activities and Organizations:* drama/theater group, student-run newspaper, radio and television station, choral group, Student Activity Board, Student Government,

Criminal Justice Club, Tutor Club, Early Childhood Club. *Student services:* health clinic, personal/psychological counseling, veterans affairs office.
Athletics Member NJCAA. *Intercollegiate sports:* basketball W, cross-country running W, golf W, lacrosse W, soccer W, softball W, volleyball W. *Intramural sports:* basketball M, cross-country running M, golf M, soccer M.
Financial Aid Of all full-time matriculated undergraduates who enrolled in 2017, 150 Federal Work-Study jobs (averaging $2000). 200 state and other part-time jobs (averaging $1000).
Applying *Options:* electronic application. *Required:* high school transcript. *Required for some:* specific additional requirements for nursing and occupational therapy programs. *Application deadlines:* rolling (freshmen), rolling (transfers). *Notification:* continuous (freshmen), continuous (transfers).
Director of Admissions Mr. Bruce M. Blodgett, Director of Admissions, Cayuga County Community College, 197 Franklin Street, Auburn, NY 13021-3099. *Phone:* 315-255-1743 Ext. 2244. *Toll-free phone:* 866-598-8883. *Website:* http://www.cayuga-cc.edu/.

Clinton Community College
Plattsburgh, New York

Freshman Application Contact Clinton Community College, 136 Clinton Point Drive, Plattsburgh, NY 12901-9573. *Phone:* 518-562-4171. *Toll-free phone:* 800-552-1160. *Website:* http://www.clinton.edu/.

Cochran School of Nursing
Yonkers, New York

- **Independent** 2-year, founded 1894
- **Urban** campus with easy access to New York City
- **Coed, primarily women**

Undergraduates 27 full-time, 93 part-time. 6% are from out of state; 11% Black or African American, non-Hispanic/Latino; 38% Hispanic/Latino; 2% Asian, non-Hispanic/Latino; 0.8% Two or more races, non-Hispanic/Latino; 42% Race/ethnicity unknown; 0.8% international; 32% transferred in.
Faculty *Student/faculty ratio:* 13:1.
Academics *Calendar:* semesters. *Degree:* associate. *Special study options:* advanced placement credit, part-time degree program.
Library Cochran School of Nursing Library. *Books:* 2,340 (physical), 559 (digital/electronic); *Serial titles:* 29 (physical), 7 (digital/electronic); *Databases:* 13. Weekly public service hours: 24; study areas open 24 hours, 5–7 days a week.
Student Life *Campus security:* 24-hour emergency response devices and patrols, late-night transport/escort service.
Applying *Options:* deferred entrance. *Application fee:* $50. *Required:* high school transcript.
Freshman Application Contact Brandy Haughton, Admissions Counselor, Cochran School of Nursing, 967 North Broadway, Yonkers, NY 10701. *Phone:* 914-964-4606. *Fax:* 914-964-4796. *E-mail:* bhaughton@riversidehealth.org. *Website:* http://www.cochranschoolofnursing.us/.

The College of Westchester
White Plains, New York

- **Proprietary** primarily 2-year, founded 1915
- **Suburban** campus with easy access to New York City
- **Coed**

Undergraduates 721 full-time, 194 part-time. Students come from 5 states and territories; 4% are from out of state; 38% Black or African American, non-Hispanic/Latino; 47% Hispanic/Latino; 2% Asian, non-Hispanic/Latino; 0.2% Native Hawaiian or other Pacific Islander, non-Hispanic/Latino; 0.1% American Indian or Alaska Native, non-Hispanic/Latino; 1% Two or more races, non-Hispanic/Latino; 3% Race/ethnicity unknown; 10% transferred in. *Retention:* 65% of full-time freshmen returned.
Faculty *Student/faculty ratio:* 20:1.
Academics *Calendar:* semesters. *Degrees:* certificates, associate, and bachelor's. *Special study options:* academic remediation for entering students, accelerated degree program, adult/continuing education programs, cooperative education, distance learning, double majors, honors programs, internships, part-time degree program, summer session for credit.
Library Dr. William R. Papallo Library.
Standardized Tests *Recommended:* SAT (for admission).
Applying *Options:* electronic application, deferred entrance. *Application fee:* $40. *Required:* high school transcript, interview. *Required for some:* essay or personal statement.
Freshman Application Contact Mr. Matt Curtis, Vice President, Enrollment Management, The College of Westchester, 325 Central Avenue, PO Box 710, White Plains, NY 10602. *Phone:* 914-948-4442 Ext. 313. *Toll-free phone:* 855-403-7722. *Fax:* 914-948-5441. *E-mail:* admissions@cw.edu. *Website:* http://www.cw.edu/.

Columbia-Greene Community College
Hudson, New York

- **State and locally supported** 2-year, founded 1966, part of State University of New York System
- **Rural** 143-acre campus
- **Coed,** 1,584 undergraduate students, 39% full-time, 63% women, 37% men
- 100% of applicants were admitted

Undergraduates 623 full-time, 961 part-time. Students come from 4 states and territories; 1 other country; 9% Black or African American, non-Hispanic/Latino; 10% Hispanic/Latino; 2% Asian, non-Hispanic/Latino; 0.5% American Indian or Alaska Native, non-Hispanic/Latino; 4% Two or more races, non-Hispanic/Latino; 1% Race/ethnicity unknown; 0.1% international; 6% transferred in. *Retention:* 61% of full-time freshmen returned.
Freshmen *Admission:* 363 applied, 362 admitted, 296 enrolled.
Faculty *Total:* 79, 51% full-time. *Student/faculty ratio:* 15:1.
Majors Accounting technology and bookkeeping; art; automobile/automotive mechanics technology; business administration and management; business/commerce; computer and information sciences; criminal justice/law enforcement administration; cyber/computer forensics and counterterrorism; environmental studies; general studies; humanities; human services; information technology; liberal arts and sciences/liberal studies; medical/clinical assistant; registered nursing/registered nurse.
Academics *Calendar:* semesters. *Degree:* certificates and associate. *Special study options:* academic remediation for entering students, advanced placement credit, cooperative education, distance learning, English as a second language, honors programs, independent study, internships, part-time degree program, services for LD students, summer session for credit.
Library Columbia-Greene Library plus 1 other.
Student Life *Housing:* college housing not available. *Activities and Organizations:* student-run radio station, Criminal Justice Club, Human Services Club, Psychology Club, Student Senate, Animal Advocates. *Campus security:* 24-hour emergency response devices and patrols, student patrols, late-night transport/escort service. *Student services:* personal/psychological counseling, veterans affairs office.
Athletics Member NCAA, NJCAA. All NCAA Division III. *Intercollegiate sports:* track and field W. *Intramural sports:* basketball M.
Applying *Options:* electronic application, deferred entrance. *Required:* high school transcript. *Required for some:* interview. *Application deadlines:* rolling (freshmen), rolling (out-of-state freshmen), rolling (transfers).
Freshman Application Contact Ms. Rachel Kappel, Director of Admissions, Columbia-Greene Community College, 4400 Route 23, Hudson, NY 12534. *Phone:* 518-828-4181 Ext. 3370. *Fax:* 518-822-2015. *E-mail:* rachel.kappel@sunycgcc.edu. *Website:* http://www.sunycgcc.edu/.

Corning Community College
Corning, New York

Freshman Application Contact Corning Community College, One Academic Drive, Corning, NY 14830-3297. *Phone:* 607-962-9540. *Toll-free phone:* 800-358-7171. *Website:* http://www.corning-cc.edu/.

Dutchess Community College
Poughkeepsie, New York

- **State and locally supported** 2-year, founded 1957, part of State University of New York System
- **Suburban** 130-acre campus with easy access to New York City
- **Coed**

Undergraduates 3,839 full-time, 5,222 part-time. 1% are from out of state; 11% Black or African American, non-Hispanic/Latino; 19% Hispanic/Latino; 3% Asian, non-Hispanic/Latino; 0.1% Native Hawaiian or other Pacific Islander, non-Hispanic/Latino; 0.1% American Indian or Alaska Native, non-Hispanic/Latino; 4% Two or more races, non-Hispanic/Latino; 2% Race/ethnicity unknown; 0.9% international; 3% transferred in; 5% live on campus.
Faculty *Student/faculty ratio:* 19:1.
Academics *Calendar:* semesters. *Degree:* certificates and associate. *Special study options:* academic remediation for entering students, adult/continuing education programs, advanced placement credit, distance learning, English as a second language, freshman honors college, honors programs, internships, off-campus study, part-time degree program, services for LD students, summer session for credit.
Library Dutchess Library plus 1 other. *Books:* 89,515 (physical), 159,235 (digital/electronic); *Serial titles:* 128 (physical), 336,174 (digital/electronic); *Databases:* 70. Weekly public service hours: 70.

Student Life *Campus security:* 24-hour emergency response devices and patrols, late-night transport/escort service, controlled dormitory access, Mass Notification System.
Athletics Member NJCAA.
Applying *Options:* electronic application, early admission, deferred entrance. *Required:* high school transcript.
Freshman Application Contact Dutchess Community College, 53 Pendell Road, Poughkeepsie, NY 12601-1595. *Phone:* 845-431-8010. *Website:* http://www.sunydutchess.edu/.

Elim Bible Institute and College
Lima, New York

Admissions Office Contact Elim Bible Institute and College, 7245 College Street, Lima, NY 14485. *Website:* http://www.elim.edu/.

Elmira Business Institute
Elmira, New York

Freshman Application Contact Ms. Lindsay Dull, Director of Student services, Elmira Business Institute, Elmira, NY 14901. *Phone:* 607-733-7177. *Toll-free phone:* 800-843-1812. *E-mail:* info@ebi-college.com. *Website:* http://www.ebi.edu/.

Elyon College
Brooklyn, New York

Admissions Office Contact Elyon College, 1400 West 6th Street, Brooklyn, NY 11204. *Website:* http://www.elyon.edu/.

Erie Community College
Buffalo, New York

- **State and locally supported** 2-year, founded 1971, part of State University of New York System
- **Urban** 1-acre campus
- **Coed**

Undergraduates 1,828 full-time, 589 part-time. Students come from 14 states and territories; 7 other countries; 0.8% are from out of state; 34% Black or African American, non-Hispanic/Latino; 9% Hispanic/Latino; 6% Asian, non-Hispanic/Latino; 0.1% Native Hawaiian or other Pacific Islander, non-Hispanic/Latino; 0.6% American Indian or Alaska Native, non-Hispanic/Latino; 3% Two or more races, non-Hispanic/Latino; 6% Race/ethnicity unknown; 2% international; 7% transferred in.
Faculty *Student/faculty ratio:* 19:1.
Academics *Calendar:* semesters plus summer sessions, winter intersession. *Degree:* certificates, diplomas, and associate. *Special study options:* academic remediation for entering students, adult/continuing education programs, advanced placement credit, cooperative education, distance learning, double majors, English as a second language, honors programs, independent study, internships, part-time degree program, services for LD students, student-designed majors, study abroad, summer session for credit. *ROTC:* Army (c).
Library Leon E. Butler Library. *Books:* 20,998 (physical), 2,579 (digital/electronic); *Serial titles:* 162 (physical), 23 (digital/electronic); *Databases:* 71. Weekly public service hours: 63; students can reserve study rooms.
Student Life *Campus security:* 24-hour emergency response devices and patrols, late-night transport/escort service.
Athletics Member NJCAA.
Applying *Options:* electronic application. *Application fee:* $25. *Required:* high school transcript. *Required for some:* interview.
Freshman Application Contact Erie Community College, 45 Oak Street, Buffalo, NY 14203-2620. *Phone:* 716-851-1155. *Fax:* 716-270-2821. *E-mail:* admissions@ecc.edu. *Website:* http://www.ecc.edu/.

Erie Community College, North Campus
Williamsville, New York

- **State and locally supported** 2-year, founded 1946, part of State University of New York System
- **Suburban** 120-acre campus with easy access to Buffalo
- **Coed**

Undergraduates 3,309 full-time, 1,620 part-time. Students come from 17 states and territories; 26 other countries; 0.7% are from out of state; 13% Black or African American, non-Hispanic/Latino; 5% Hispanic/Latino; 5% Asian, non-Hispanic/Latino; 0.4% American Indian or Alaska Native, non-Hispanic/Latino; 2% Two or more races, non-Hispanic/Latino; 5% Race/ethnicity unknown; 3% international; 11% transferred in.
Faculty *Student/faculty ratio:* 19:1.
Academics *Calendar:* semesters plus summer sessions, winter intersession. *Degree:* certificates, diplomas, and associate. *Special study options:* academic remediation for entering students, adult/continuing education programs, advanced placement credit, cooperative education, distance learning, double majors, English as a second language, honors programs, independent study, internships, part-time degree program, services for LD students, student-designed majors, study abroad, summer session for credit. *ROTC:* Army (c).
Library Richard R. Dry Memorial Library. *Books:* 48,505 (physical), 2,579 (digital/electronic); *Serial titles:* 238 (physical), 23 (digital/electronic); *Databases:* 71. Weekly public service hours: 65.
Student Life *Campus security:* 24-hour emergency response devices and patrols, late-night transport/escort service.
Athletics Member NJCAA.
Applying *Options:* electronic application. *Application fee:* $25. *Required:* high school transcript. *Required for some:* interview.
Freshman Application Contact Erie Community College, North Campus, 6205 Main Street, Williamsville, NY 14221-7095. *Phone:* 716-851-1455. *Fax:* 716-270-2961. *E-mail:* admissions@ecc.edu. *Website:* http://www.ecc.edu/.

Erie Community College, South Campus
Orchard Park, New York

- **State and locally supported** 2-year, founded 1974, part of State University of New York System
- **Suburban** 110-acre campus with easy access to Buffalo
- **Coed**

Undergraduates 2,132 full-time, 1,657 part-time. Students come from 19 states and territories; 5 other countries; 1% are from out of state; 9% Black or African American, non-Hispanic/Latino; 6% Hispanic/Latino; 2% Asian, non-Hispanic/Latino; 0.2% Native Hawaiian or other Pacific Islander, non-Hispanic/Latino; 1% American Indian or Alaska Native, non-Hispanic/Latino; 3% Two or more races, non-Hispanic/Latino; 5% Race/ethnicity unknown; 0.7% international; 6% transferred in.
Faculty *Student/faculty ratio:* 19:1.
Academics *Calendar:* semesters plus summer sessions, winter intersession. *Degree:* certificates, diplomas, and associate. *Special study options:* academic remediation for entering students, adult/continuing education programs, advanced placement credit, cooperative education, distance learning, double majors, English as a second language, honors programs, independent study, internships, part-time degree program, services for LD students, student-designed majors, study abroad, summer session for credit. *ROTC:* Army (c).
Library Library Resource Center. *Books:* 34,131 (physical), 2,579 (digital/electronic); *Serial titles:* 218 (physical), 23 (digital/electronic); *Databases:* 71. Weekly public service hours: 63.
Student Life *Campus security:* 24-hour emergency response devices and patrols, late-night transport/escort service.
Athletics Member NJCAA.
Applying *Options:* electronic application. *Application fee:* $25. *Required:* high school transcript. *Required for some:* interview.
Freshman Application Contact Erie Community College, South Campus, 4041 Southwestern Boulevard, Orchard Park, NY 14127-2199. *Phone:* 716-851-1655. *Fax:* 716-851-1687. *E-mail:* admissions@ecc.edu. *Website:* http://www.ecc.edu/.

Eugenio María de Hostos Community College of the City University of New York
Bronx, New York

Freshman Application Contact Mr. Roland Velez, Director of Admissions, Eugenio María de Hostos Community College of the City University of New York, 120 149th Street, Bronx, NY 10451. *Phone:* 718-319-7968. *Fax:* 718-319-7919. *E-mail:* admissions@hostos.cuny.edu. *Website:* http://www.hostos.cuny.edu/.

Fashion Institute of Technology
New York, New York

- **State and locally supported** comprehensive, founded 1944, part of State University of New York System
- **Urban** 5-acre campus with easy access to New York City
- **Coed, primarily women,** 8,555 undergraduate students, 85% full-time, 83% women, 17% men

Undergraduates 7,246 full-time, 1,309 part-time. 31% are from out of state; 9% Black or African American, non-Hispanic/Latino; 20% Hispanic/Latino;

12% Asian, non-Hispanic/Latino; 0.2% Native Hawaiian or other Pacific Islander, non-Hispanic/Latino; 0.1% American Indian or Alaska Native, non-Hispanic/Latino; 4% Two or more races, non-Hispanic/Latino; 0.4% Race/ethnicity unknown; 11% international; 9% transferred in; 21% live on campus. *Retention:* 89% of full-time freshmen returned.
Freshmen *Admission:* 4,507 applied, 2,374 admitted, 1,342 enrolled. *Average high school GPA:* 3.6.
Faculty *Total:* 1,116, 21% full-time. *Student/faculty ratio:* 15:1.
Majors Advertising; animation, interactive technology, video graphics and special effects; apparel and textile manufacturing; cinematography and film/video production; commercial and advertising art; commercial photography; design and applied arts related; entrepreneurial and small business related; fashion/apparel design; fashion merchandising; fashion modeling; film/cinema/video studies; fine and studio arts management; fine/studio arts; graphic design; illustration; industrial and product design; interior design; international marketing; marketing research; merchandising, sales, and marketing operations related (specialized); metal and jewelry arts; special products marketing.
Academics *Calendar:* semesters. *Degrees:* certificates, associate, bachelor's, and master's. *Special study options:* academic remediation for entering students, advanced placement credit, distance learning, English as a second language, honors programs, independent study, internships, part-time degree program, services for LD students, study abroad, summer session for credit.
Library Gladys Marcus Library.
Student Life *Housing Options:* coed, women-only, special housing for students with disabilities. Campus housing is university owned. Freshman applicants given priority for college housing. *Activities and Organizations:* drama/theater group, student-run newspaper, radio and television station, choral group. *Campus security:* 24-hour emergency response devices and patrols, late-night transport/escort service, controlled dormitory access. *Student services:* health clinic, personal/psychological counseling.
Athletics Member NJCAA.
Financial Aid Of all full-time matriculated undergraduates who enrolled in 2017, 4,604 applied for aid, 3,688 were judged to have need, 1,817 had their need fully met. In 2017, 321 non-need-based awards were made. *Average percent of need met:* 68%. *Average financial aid package:* $12,023. *Average need-based loan:* $3149. *Average need-based gift aid:* $6591. *Average non-need-based aid:* $853. *Average indebtedness upon graduation:* $23,968.
Applying *Options:* electronic application. *Application fee:* $50. *Required:* essay or personal statement, high school transcript. *Required for some:* portfolio for art and design programs. *Application deadlines:* 1/1 (freshmen), 1/1 (transfers). *Notification:* 4/1 (freshmen), 4/1 (transfers).
Freshman Application Contact Ms. Magda Francois, Director of Admissions and Strategic Recruitment, Fashion Institute of Technology, Seventh Avenue at 27th Street, New York, NY 10001-5992. *E-mail:* fitinfo@fitnyc.edu. *Website:* http://www.fitnyc.edu/.

Finger Lakes Community College
Canandaigua, New York

Freshman Application Contact Ms. Bonnie B. Ritts, Director of Admissions, Finger Lakes Community College, 3325 Marvin Sands Drive, Canandaigua, NY 14424-8395. *Phone:* 585-785-1279. *Fax:* 585-785-1734. *E-mail:* admissions@flcc.edu. *Website:* http://www.flcc.edu/.

Finger Lakes Health College of Nursing
Geneva, New York

Admissions Office Contact Finger Lakes Health College of Nursing, 196 North Street, Geneva, NY 14456. *Website:* http://www.flhcon.edu/.

Fiorello H. LaGuardia Community College of the City University of New York
Long Island City, New York

- **State and locally supported** 2-year, founded 1970, part of City University of New York System
- **Urban** 25-acre campus with easy access to New York City
- **Coed**

Undergraduates 10,838 full-time, 8,518 part-time. Students come from 17 states and territories; 148 other countries; 0.4% are from out of state; 17% Black or African American, non-Hispanic/Latino; 48% Hispanic/Latino; 20% Asian, non-Hispanic/Latino; 0.4% Native Hawaiian or other Pacific Islander, non-Hispanic/Latino; 0.6% American Indian or Alaska Native, non-Hispanic/Latino; 4% international; 9% transferred in. *Retention:* 37% of full-time freshmen returned.
Faculty *Student/faculty ratio:* 21:1.
Academics *Calendar:* enhanced semester. *Degree:* certificates and associate. *Special study options:* academic remediation for entering students, accelerated degree program, adult/continuing education programs, advanced placement credit, cooperative education, distance learning, double majors, English as a second language, honors programs, independent study, internships, off-campus study, part-time degree program, services for LD students, student-designed majors, study abroad, summer session for credit.
Library Fiorello H. LaGuardia Community College Library Media Resources Center plus 1 other. *Books:* 89,478 (physical), 545,512 (digital/electronic); *Serial titles:* 491 (physical), 105,706 (digital/electronic); *Databases:* 211,328. Weekly public service hours: 82; students can reserve study rooms.
Student Life *Campus security:* 24-hour emergency response devices and patrols, late-night transport/escort service.
Financial Aid Of all full-time matriculated undergraduates who enrolled in 2017, 8,791 applied for aid, 8,637 were judged to have need, 31 had their need fully met. *Average percent of need met:* 38. *Average financial aid package:* $6571. *Average need-based loan:* $3090. *Average need-based gift aid:* $6262.
Applying *Options:* electronic application, early admission, deferred entrance. *Application fee:* $65. *Required:* high school transcript.
Freshman Application Contact Ms. LaVora Desvigne, Director of Admissions, Fiorello H. LaGuardia Community College of the City University of New York, RM-147, 31-10 Thomson Avenue, Long Island City, NY 11101. *Phone:* 718-482-5114. *Fax:* 718-482-5112. *E-mail:* admissions@lagcc.cuny.edu. *Website:* http://www.lagcc.cuny.edu/.

Fulton-Montgomery Community College
Johnstown, New York

Freshman Application Contact Fulton-Montgomery Community College, 2805 State Highway 67, Johnstown, NY 12095-3790. *Phone:* 518-762-4651 Ext. 8301. *Website:* http://www.fmcc.suny.edu/.

Genesee Community College
Batavia, New York

- **State and locally supported** 2-year, founded 1966, part of State University of New York System
- **Small-town** 256-acre campus with easy access to Buffalo, Rochester
- **Endowment** $5.0 million
- **Coed**

Undergraduates 2,353 full-time, 3,553 part-time. Students come from 25 states and territories; 20 other countries; 2% are from out of state; 6% Black or African American, non-Hispanic/Latino; 4% Hispanic/Latino; 1% Asian, non-Hispanic/Latino; 0.7% American Indian or Alaska Native, non-Hispanic/Latino; 3% Two or more races, non-Hispanic/Latino; 9% Race/ethnicity unknown; 3% international.
Faculty *Student/faculty ratio:* 15:1.
Academics *Calendar:* semesters. *Degree:* certificates and associate. *Special study options:* academic remediation for entering students, adult/continuing education programs, advanced placement credit, cooperative education, distance learning, double majors, English as a second language, honors programs, independent study, internships, part-time degree program, services for LD students, study abroad, summer session for credit. *ROTC:* Army (c).
Library Alfred C. OConnell Library. *Books:* 79,535 (physical), 17,645 (digital/electronic); *Serial titles:* 164 (physical), 67,604 (digital/electronic); *Databases:* 89. Weekly public service hours: 76.
Student Life *Campus security:* 24-hour emergency response devices and patrols, student patrols, late-night transport/escort service, controlled dormitory access.
Athletics Member NJCAA.
Applying *Options:* electronic application. *Required:* high school transcript. *Required for some:* 1 letter of recommendation.
Freshman Application Contact Mrs. Tanya Lane-Martin, Director of Admissions, Genesee Community College, Batavia, NY 14020. *Phone:* 585-343-0055 Ext. 6413. *Toll-free phone:* 866-CALL GCC. *Fax:* 585-345-6892. *E-mail:* tmlanemartin@genesee.edu. *Website:* http://www.genesee.edu/.

Helene Fuld College of Nursing
New York, New York

Freshman Application Contact Helene Fuld College of Nursing, 24 East 120th Street, New York, NY 10035. *Phone:* 212-616-7271. *Website:* http://www.helenefuld.edu/.

Herkimer County Community College

Herkimer, New York

Freshman Application Contact Herkimer County Community College, 100 Reservoir Road, Herkimer, NY 13350. *Phone:* 315-866-0300 Ext. 8278. *Toll-free phone:* 888-464-4222 Ext. 8278. *Website:* http://www.herkimer.edu/.

Hudson Valley Community College

Troy, New York

Freshman Application Contact Ms. Marie Claire Bauer, Director of Admissions, Hudson Valley Community College, 80 Vandenburgh Avenue, Troy, NY 12180-6096. *Phone:* 518-629-7309. *Toll-free phone:* 877-325-HVCC. *Website:* http://www.hvcc.edu/.

Island Drafting and Technical Institute

Amityville, New York

Freshman Application Contact Larry Basile, Island Drafting and Technical Institute, 128 Broadway, Amityville, NY 11701. *Phone:* 631-691-8733 Ext. 114. *Fax:* 631-691-8738. *E-mail:* info@idti.edu. *Website:* http://www.idti.edu/.

Jamestown Business College

Jamestown, New York

Freshman Application Contact Mrs. Brenda Salemme, Director of Admissions, Jamestown Business College, 7 Fairmount Avenue, Box 429, Jamestown, NY 14702-0429. *Phone:* 716-664-5100. *Fax:* 716-664-3144. *E-mail:* brendasalemme@jbc.edu. *Website:* http://www.jbc.edu/.

Jamestown Community College

Jamestown, New York

- **State and locally supported** 2-year, founded 1950, part of State University of New York System
- **Small-town** 107-acre campus
- **Coed**

Undergraduates 2,060 full-time, 2,403 part-time. Students come from 10 states and territories; 18 other countries; 10% are from out of state; 5% Black or African American, non-Hispanic/Latino; 6% Hispanic/Latino; 0.8% Asian, non-Hispanic/Latino; 0.1% Native Hawaiian or other Pacific Islander, non-Hispanic/Latino; 1% American Indian or Alaska Native, non-Hispanic/Latino; 3% Two or more races, non-Hispanic/Latino; 1% Race/ethnicity unknown; 0.9% international; 5% transferred in; 11% live on campus.
Faculty *Student/faculty ratio:* 16:1.
Academics *Calendar:* semesters. *Degree:* certificates and associate. *Special study options:* academic remediation for entering students, adult/continuing education programs, advanced placement credit, distance learning, honors programs, independent study, internships, off-campus study, part-time degree program, services for LD students, study abroad, summer session for credit.
Library Hultquist Library plus 1 other. *Books:* 90,813 (physical), 2,360 (digital/electronic); *Serial titles:* 687 (physical), 14 (digital/electronic); *Databases:* 89. Weekly public service hours: 63.
Student Life *Campus security:* 24-hour emergency response devices, controlled dormitory access.
Athletics Member NJCAA.
Financial Aid Of all full-time matriculated undergraduates who enrolled in 2017, 85 Federal Work-Study jobs (averaging $1500). 85 state and other part-time jobs (averaging $1300).
Applying *Options:* electronic application, deferred entrance. *Required:* high school transcript.
Freshman Application Contact Ms. Wendy Present, Director of Admissions, Jamestown Community College, 525 Falconer Street, PO Box 20, Jamestown, NY 14702-0020. *Phone:* 716-338-1001. *Toll-free phone:* 800-388-8557. *Fax:* 716-338-1450. *E-mail:* admissions@mail.sunyjcc.edu. *Website:* http://www.sunyjcc.edu/.

Jefferson Community College

Watertown, New York

- **State and locally supported** 2-year, founded 1961, part of State University of New York System
- **Small-town** 90-acre campus with easy access to Syracuse
- **Coed**

Undergraduates 2,082 full-time, 1,550 part-time. 7% Black or African American, non-Hispanic/Latino; 10% Hispanic/Latino; 1% Asian, non-Hispanic/Latino; 0.2% Native Hawaiian or other Pacific Islander, non-Hispanic/Latino; 0.6% American Indian or Alaska Native, non-Hispanic/Latino; 3% Two or more races, non-Hispanic/Latino; 3% Race/ethnicity unknown; 0.9% international; 6% transferred in.
Academics *Calendar:* semesters. *Degree:* certificates and associate. *Special study options:* academic remediation for entering students, advanced placement credit, cooperative education, distance learning, double majors, honors programs, independent study, internships, part-time degree program, services for LD students, student-designed majors, summer session for credit.
Library Melvil Dewey Library plus 1 other. Students can reserve study rooms.
Student Life *Campus security:* 24-hour emergency response devices and patrols, late-night transport/escort service, controlled dormitory access.
Athletics Member NJCAA.
Standardized Tests *Recommended:* SAT or ACT (for admission).
Financial Aid Of all full-time matriculated undergraduates who enrolled in 2009, 1,748 applied for aid. 98 Federal Work-Study jobs (averaging $1093).
Applying *Options:* electronic application, early admission, deferred entrance. *Required:* high school transcript. *Required for some:* interview.
Freshman Application Contact Sandra L. Spadoni, Dean for Enrollment, Jefferson Community College, 1220 Coffeen Street, Watertown, NY 13601. *Phone:* 315-786-2437. *Toll-free phone:* 888-435-6522. *Fax:* 315-786-2349. *E-mail:* admissions@sunyjefferson.edu. *Website:* http://www.sunyjefferson.edu/.

Kingsborough Community College of the City University of New York

Brooklyn, New York

- **State and locally supported** 2-year, founded 1963, part of City University of New York System
- **Urban** 72-acre campus with easy access to New York City
- **Coed**

Undergraduates 8,298 full-time, 6,982 part-time. Students come from 13 states and territories; 136 other countries; 1% are from out of state; 29% Black or African American, non-Hispanic/Latino; 17% Hispanic/Latino; 15% Asian, non-Hispanic/Latino; 0.2% American Indian or Alaska Native, non-Hispanic/Latino; 3% international; 4% transferred in. *Retention:* 71% of full-time freshmen returned.
Academics *Calendar:* semesters. *Degree:* certificates and associate. *Special study options:* academic remediation for entering students, accelerated degree program, adult/continuing education programs, advanced placement credit, cooperative education, distance learning, English as a second language, honors programs, independent study, internships, off-campus study, part-time degree program, services for LD students, summer session for credit.
Library Robert J. Kibbee Library. *Books:* 224,727 (physical), 481,635 (digital/electronic); *Serial titles:* 230 (physical), 77,212 (digital/electronic); *Databases:* 140. Weekly public service hours: 79.
Student Life *Campus security:* 24-hour emergency response devices and patrols.
Athletics Member NJCAA.
Applying *Options:* electronic application. *Application fee:* $65. *Required:* high school transcript.
Freshman Application Contact Mr. Javier Morgades, Director of Admissions Information Center, Kingsborough Community College of the City University of New York, 2001 Oriental Boulevard, Brooklyn, NY 11235. *Phone:* 718-368-4600. *E-mail:* info@kbcc.cuny.edu. *Website:* http://www.kbcc.cuny.edu/.

Long Island Business Institute

Flushing, New York

Freshman Application Contact Mr. Keith Robertson, Director of Admissions, Long Island Business Institute, 408 Broadway, 2nd Floor, New York, NY 10013. *Phone:* 212-226-7300. *E-mail:* krobertson@libi.edu. *Website:* http://www.libi.edu/.

Mandl School

New York, New York

Admissions Office Contact Mandl School, 254 West 54th Street, 9th Floor, New York, NY 10019. *Website:* http://www.mandl.edu/.

Memorial College of Nursing

Albany, New York

Freshman Application Contact Admissions Office, Memorial College of Nursing, 600 Northern Boulevard, Albany, NY 12204. *Website:* http://www.nehealth.com/son/.

Mildred Elley–New York City
New York, New York

Admissions Office Contact Mildred Elley–New York City, 25 Broadway, 16th Floor, New York, NY 10004-1010. *Website:* http://www.mildred-elley.edu/.

Mildred Elley School
Albany, New York

Director of Admissions Mr. Michael Cahalan, Enrollment Manager, Mildred Elley School, 855 Central Avenue, Albany, NY 12206. *Phone:* 518-786-3171 Ext. 227. *Toll-free phone:* 800-622-6327. *Website:* http://www.mildred-elley.edu/.

Mohawk Valley Community College
Utica, New York

- **State and locally supported** 2-year, founded 1946, part of State University of New York System
- **Suburban** 80-acre campus
- **Endowment** $4.9 million
- **Coed**

Undergraduates 3,324 full-time, 3,182 part-time. Students come from 16 states and territories; 22 other countries; 41% are from out of state; 11% Black or African American, non-Hispanic/Latino; 8% Hispanic/Latino; 6% Asian, non-Hispanic/Latino; 0.2% Native Hawaiian or other Pacific Islander, non-Hispanic/Latino; 0.3% American Indian or Alaska Native, non-Hispanic/Latino; 3% Two or more races, non-Hispanic/Latino; 0.1% Race/ethnicity unknown; 1% international; 3% transferred in; 7% live on campus.
Faculty *Student/faculty ratio:* 18:1.
Academics *Calendar:* semesters. *Degree:* certificates and associate. *Special study options:* academic remediation for entering students, accelerated degree program, advanced placement credit, distance learning, double majors, English as a second language, honors programs, independent study, internships, off-campus study, part-time degree program, services for LD students, student-designed majors, summer session for credit.
Library Mohawk Valley Community College Library plus 1 other. *Books:* 98,450 (physical), 278,863 (digital/electronic); *Serial titles:* 461 (physical), 105,147 (digital/electronic); *Databases:* 103. Weekly public service hours: 126.
Student Life *Campus security:* 24-hour emergency response devices and patrols, late-night transport/escort service, controlled dormitory access.
Athletics Member NJCAA.
Financial Aid Of all full-time matriculated undergraduates who enrolled in 2017, 229 Federal Work-Study jobs (averaging $1750).
Applying *Options:* electronic application, deferred entrance. *Required for some:* high school transcript. *Recommended:* interview.
Freshman Application Contact Kirsten Edwards, Technical Assistant, Admissions, Mohawk Valley Community College, 1101 Sherman Drive, Utica, NY 13501. *Phone:* 315-792-5640. *Toll-free phone:* 800-SEE-MVCC. *Fax:* 315-792-5527. *E-mail:* kedwards@mvcc.edu. *Website:* http://www.mvcc.edu/.

Monroe Community College
Rochester, New York

- **State and locally supported** 2-year, founded 1961, part of State University of New York System
- **Suburban** 314-acre campus with easy access to Buffalo
- **Coed**

Undergraduates 7,866 full-time, 5,041 part-time. Students come from 40 states and territories; 46 other countries; 1% are from out of state; 20% Black or African American, non-Hispanic/Latino; 10% Hispanic/Latino; 5% Asian, non-Hispanic/Latino; 0.1% Native Hawaiian or other Pacific Islander, non-Hispanic/Latino; 0.5% American Indian or Alaska Native, non-Hispanic/Latino; 4% Two or more races, non-Hispanic/Latino; 0.7% Race/ethnicity unknown; 1% international. *Retention:* 51% of full-time freshmen returned.
Faculty *Student/faculty ratio:* 22:1.
Academics *Calendar:* semesters. *Degree:* certificates and associate. *Special study options:* academic remediation for entering students, accelerated degree program, adult/continuing education programs, advanced placement credit, cooperative education, English as a second language, honors programs, internships, off-campus study, part-time degree program, services for LD students, summer session for credit. *ROTC:* Army (c), Navy (c), Air Force (c).
Library LeRoy V. Good Library. Weekly public service hours: 58; students can reserve study rooms.
Student Life *Campus security:* 24-hour emergency response devices and patrols, late-night transport/escort service, controlled dormitory access.
Athletics Member NCAA, NJCAA. All NCAA Division III.
Applying *Options:* electronic application, early admission. *Required:* high school transcript.
Freshman Application Contact Ms. Sarah Hagreen, Interim Director of Admissions, Monroe Community College, 1000 East Henrietta Road, Rochester, NY 14623. *Phone:* 585-292-2222. *Fax:* 585-292-3860. *E-mail:* admissions@monroecc.edu. *Website:* http://www.monroecc.edu/.

Montefiore School of Nursing
Mount Vernon, New York

Director of Admissions Sandra Farrior, Coordinator of Student Services, Montefiore School of Nursing, 53 Valentine Street, Mount Vernon, NY 10550. *Phone:* 914-361-6472. *E-mail:* hopferadmissions@sshsw.org. *Website:* http://www.montefiorehealthsystem.org/landing.cfm?id=19.

Nassau Community College
Garden City, New York

- **State and locally supported** 2-year, founded 1959, part of State University of New York System
- **Suburban** 225-acre campus with easy access to New York City
- **Coed,** 17,278 undergraduate students, 57% full-time, 51% women, 49% men

Undergraduates 9,844 full-time, 7,434 part-time. Students come from 19 states and territories; 21% Black or African American, non-Hispanic/Latino; 29% Hispanic/Latino; 7% Asian, non-Hispanic/Latino; 0.3% Native Hawaiian or other Pacific Islander, non-Hispanic/Latino; 0.2% American Indian or Alaska Native, non-Hispanic/Latino; 2% Two or more races, non-Hispanic/Latino; 4% Race/ethnicity unknown; 0.8% international.
Freshmen *Admission:* 3,542 enrolled. *Average high school GPA:* 2.5.
Faculty *Total:* 1,528, 27% full-time, 27% with terminal degrees. *Student/faculty ratio:* 21:1.
Majors Accounting; accounting technology and bookkeeping; administrative assistant and secretarial science; African American/Black studies; art; business administration and management; civil engineering technology; clinical/medical laboratory technology; commercial and advertising art; computer and information sciences; computer and information sciences related; computer graphics; computer science; computer systems networking and telecommunications; criminal justice/law enforcement administration; criminal justice/safety; dance; data processing and data processing technology; design and visual communications; dramatic/theater arts; engineering; entrepreneurship; fashion/apparel design; fashion merchandising; funeral service and mortuary science; general studies; hotel/motel administration; instrumentation technology; insurance; interior design; kindergarten/preschool education; legal administrative assistant/secretary; legal assistant/paralegal; liberal arts and sciences/liberal studies; management information systems; marketing/marketing management; mass communication/media; mathematics; medical administrative assistant and medical secretary; medical radiologic technology; music performance; photography; physical therapy technology; real estate; registered nursing/registered nurse; rehabilitation and therapeutic professions related; respiratory care therapy; retailing; speech communication and rhetoric; surgical technology; theater design and technology; transportation and materials moving related; visual and performing arts.
Academics *Calendar:* semesters. *Degree:* certificates and associate. *Special study options:* academic remediation for entering students, adult/continuing education programs, advanced placement credit, cooperative education, distance learning, English as a second language, honors programs, internships, off-campus study, part-time degree program, services for LD students, summer session for credit.
Library A. Holly Patterson Library.
Student Life *Housing:* college housing not available. *Activities and Organizations:* drama/theater group, student-run newspaper, radio station, choral group, Muslim Student Association, Make a Difference Club, Interact Club, Political Science Club, Investment Club. *Campus security:* 24-hour emergency response devices and patrols, late-night transport/escort service. *Student services:* personal/psychological counseling, women's center.
Athletics Member NJCAA. *Intercollegiate sports:* basketball W, cross-country running W, golf W, lacrosse W, soccer W, softball W, tennis W, track and field W, volleyball W. *Intramural sports:* badminton M, baseball M, basketball M, cheerleading M, racquetball M, soccer M, softball M, swimming and diving M, table tennis M, tennis M, volleyball M.
Financial Aid Of all full-time matriculated undergraduates who enrolled in 2017, 400 Federal Work-Study jobs (averaging $3000).

Applying *Options:* electronic application, deferred entrance. *Application fee:* $40. *Required:* high school transcript. *Required for some:* minimum 3.0 GPA, interview. *Recommended:* minimum 2.0 GPA. *Application deadline:* 8/7 (transfers). *Notification:* continuous (freshmen), continuous (transfers).
Director of Admissions David Follick, Dean, Admissions, Nassau Community College, 1 Education Drive, Garden City, NY 11530-6793. *Phone:* 516-572-7345. *E-mail:* david.follick@ncc.edu.
Website: http://www.ncc.edu/.

Niagara County Community College
Sanborn, New York

- **State and locally supported** 2-year, founded 1962, part of State University of New York System
- **Rural** 287-acre campus with easy access to Buffalo
- **Endowment** $10.0 million
- **Coed**

Undergraduates 3,228 full-time, 2,238 part-time. Students come from 17 states and territories; 3 other countries; 1% are from out of state; 11% Black or African American, non-Hispanic/Latino; 4% Hispanic/Latino; 2% Asian, non-Hispanic/Latino; 1% American Indian or Alaska Native, non-Hispanic/Latino; 5% Race/ethnicity unknown; 8% transferred in; 4% live on campus.
Faculty *Student/faculty ratio:* 17:1.
Academics *Calendar:* semesters. *Degree:* certificates and associate. *Special study options:* academic remediation for entering students, adult/continuing education programs, advanced placement credit, cooperative education, distance learning, double majors, honors programs, independent study, internships, off-campus study, part-time degree program, services for LD students, student-designed majors, study abroad, summer session for credit. *ROTC:* Army (c).
Library Henrietta G. Lewis Library. *Books:* 77,511 (physical); *Serial titles:* 290 (physical); *Databases:* 95. Weekly public service hours: 64; students can reserve study rooms.
Student Life *Campus security:* 24-hour emergency response devices and patrols, student patrols, late-night transport/escort service.
Athletics Member NJCAA.
Financial Aid Of all full-time matriculated undergraduates who enrolled in 2017, 5,163 applied for aid, 5,163 were judged to have need. *Average percent of need met:* 85. *Average financial aid package:* $5664. *Average need-based loan:* $3067. *Average need-based gift aid:* $729.
Applying *Options:* electronic application, early admission. *Required:* high school transcript. *Required for some:* minimum 2.0 GPA.
Freshman Application Contact Robert McKeown, Assistant Vice President of Enrollment Management, Niagara County Community College, 3111 Saunders Settlement Road, Sanborn, NY 14132. *Phone:* 716-614-6200. *Fax:* 716-614-6820. *E-mail:* admissions@niagaracc.suny.edu. *Website:* http://www.niagaracc.suny.edu/.

North Country Community College
Saranac Lake, New York

Freshman Application Contact Enrollment Management Assistant, North Country Community College, 23 Santanoni Avenue, PO Box 89, Saranac Lake, NY 12983-0089. *Phone:* 518-891-2915 Ext. 686. *Toll-free phone:* 800-TRY-NCCC (in-state); 888-TRY-NCCC (out-of-state). *Fax:* 518-891-0898. *E-mail:* info@nccc.edu. *Website:* http://www.nccc.edu/.

Onondaga Community College
Syracuse, New York

Freshman Application Contact Mr. Denny Nicholson, Onondaga Community College, 4585 West Seneca Turnpike, Syracuse, NY 13215. *Phone:* 315-488-2912. *Fax:* 315-488-2107. *E-mail:* admissions@sunyocc.edu. *Website:* http://www.sunyocc.edu/.

Orange County Community College
Middletown, New York

Freshman Application Contact Michael Roe, Director of Admissions and Recruitment, Orange County Community College, 115 South Street, Middletown, NY 10940. *Phone:* 845-341-4205. *Fax:* 845-343-1228. *E-mail:* apply@sunyorange.edu. *Website:* http://www.sunyorange.edu/.

Phillips Beth Israel School of Nursing
New York, New York

Freshman Application Contact Mrs. Bernice Pass-Stern, Assistant Dean, Phillips Beth Israel School of Nursing, 776 Sixth Avenue, 4th Floor, New York, NY 10010-6354. *Phone:* 212-614-6176. *Fax:* 212-614-6109. *E-mail:* bstern@chpnet.org. *Website:* http://www.mountsinai.org/locations/beth-israel/pson.

Plaza College
Forest Hills, New York

Freshman Application Contact Dean Vanessa Lopez, Dean of Admissions, Plaza College, 118-33 Queens Boulevard, Forest Hills, NY 11375. *Phone:* 718-779-1430. *E-mail:* info@plazacollege.edu. *Website:* http://www.plazacollege.edu/.

Queensborough Community College of the City University of New York
Bayside, New York

- **State and locally supported** 2-year, founded 1958, part of City University of New York
- **Urban** 37-acre campus with easy access to New York City
- **Coed,** 15,411 undergraduate students, 60% full-time, 53% women, 47% men

Undergraduates 9,232 full-time, 6,179 part-time. Students come from 7 states and territories; 127 other countries; 2% are from out of state; 24% Black or African American, non-Hispanic/Latino; 33% Hispanic/Latino; 22% Asian, non-Hispanic/Latino; 0.7% Native Hawaiian or other Pacific Islander, non-Hispanic/Latino; 1% American Indian or Alaska Native, non-Hispanic/Latino; 2% Two or more races, non-Hispanic/Latino; 6% international; 6% transferred in. *Retention:* 64% of full-time freshmen returned.
Freshmen *Admission:* 12,076 applied, 11,864 admitted, 3,212 enrolled.
Faculty *Total:* 888, 49% full-time, 53% with terminal degrees. *Student/faculty ratio:* 20:1.
Majors Accounting; accounting technology and bookkeeping; administrative assistant and secretarial science; architectural drafting and CAD/CADD; art; biotechnology; business administration and management; chemistry; computer and information sciences; computer engineering technology; criminal justice/law enforcement administration; dance; data processing and data processing technology; digital arts; dramatic/theater arts; electrical, electronic and communications engineering technology; engineering; engineering science; environmental science; forensic science and technology; health services/allied health/health sciences; information technology; liberal arts and sciences/liberal studies; massage therapy; mechanical engineering/mechanical technology; medical/clinical assistant; museum studies; music history, literature, and theory; physical sciences; psychology; public health; recording arts technology; registered nursing/registered nurse; telecommunications technology.
Academics *Calendar:* semesters. *Degree:* certificates and associate. *Special study options:* academic remediation for entering students, accelerated degree program, advanced placement credit, cooperative education, distance learning, double majors, English as a second language, honors programs, independent study, internships, off-campus study, part-time degree program, services for LD students, student-designed majors, study abroad, summer session for credit. *ROTC:* Army (c).
Library The Kurt R. Schmeller Library. *Books:* 109,962 (physical), 581,791 (digital/electronic); *Serial titles:* 1,195 (physical), 103,782 (digital/electronic); *Databases:* 145. Weekly public service hours: 78.
Student Life *Housing:* college housing not available. *Activities and Organizations:* drama/theater group, student-run newspaper, choral group, Phi Theta kappa, Student Organization for Disability Awareness (SODA), ASAP Club, CSTEP Club, Chemistry Club. *Campus security:* 24-hour emergency response devices and patrols. *Student services:* health clinic, personal/psychological counseling, legal services, veterans affairs office.
Athletics Member NJCAA. *Intercollegiate sports:* basketball W, cross-country running W, swimming and diving W, track and field W, volleyball W. *Intramural sports:* badminton M, basketball M, swimming and diving M(c), table tennis M, tennis M, volleyball M, weight lifting M.
Applying *Options:* electronic application, deferred entrance. *Application fee:* $65. *Required:* high school transcript. *Required for some:* A New York State High School Equivalency Diploma (GED/TASC) is required in lieu of high school diploma. *Application deadlines:* 2/1 (freshmen), 2/1 (transfers). *Notification:* continuous (freshmen), continuous (transfers).
Freshman Application Contact Ms. Linda Evangleou, Director of Admissions & Recruitment, Queensborough Community College of the City University of New York, 222-05 56th Avenue, Bayside, NY 11364. *Phone:* 718-281-5000 Ext. 1. *Fax:* 718-281-5189. *E-mail:* admissions@qcc.cuny.edu.
Website: http://www.qcc.cuny.edu/.

Rockland Community College

Suffern, New York

Freshman Application Contact Rockland Community College, 145 College Road, Suffern, NY 10901-3699. *Phone:* 845-574-4484. *Toll-free phone:* 800-722-7666. *Website:* http://www.sunyrockland.edu/.

St. Elizabeth College of Nursing

Utica, New York

Freshman Application Contact Donna Ernst, Director of Recruitment, St. Elizabeth College of Nursing, 2215 Genesee Street, Utica, NY 13501. *Phone:* 315-798-8189. *E-mail:* dernst@secon.edu. *Website:* http://www.secon.edu/.

St. Joseph's College of Nursing

Syracuse, New York

Freshman Application Contact Ms. Felicia Corp, Recruiter, St. Joseph's College of Nursing, 206 Prospect Avenue, Syracuse, NY 13203. *Phone:* 315-448-5040. *Fax:* 315-448-5745. *E-mail:* collegeofnursing@sjhsyr.org. *Website:* http://www.sjhcon.edu/.

St. Paul's School of Nursing

Queens, New York

Director of Admissions Nancy Wolinski, Chairperson of Admissions, St. Paul's School of Nursing, 97-77 Queens Boulevard, Queens, NY 11374. *Phone:* 718-357-0500 Ext. 131. *E-mail:* nwolinski@svcmcny.org. *Website:* http://www.stpaulsschoolofnursing.edu/.

St. Paul's School of Nursing

Staten Island, New York

Admissions Office Contact St. Paul's School of Nursing, Corporate Commons Two, 2 Teleport Drive, Suite 203, Staten Island, NY 10311. *Website:* http://www.stpaulsschoolofnursing.edu/.

Samaritan Hospital School of Nursing

Troy, New York

Director of Admissions Ms. Diane Dyer, Student Services Coordinator, Samaritan Hospital School of Nursing, 1300 Massachusetts Avenue, Troy, NY 12180. *Phone:* 518-271-3734. *Fax:* 518-271-3303. *E-mail:* marronej@nehealth.com. *Website:* http://www.nehealth.com/.

Schenectady County Community College

Schenectady, New York

- **State and locally supported** 2-year, founded 1969, part of State University of New York System
- **Urban** 50-acre campus
- **Coed**

Undergraduates 2,184 full-time, 4,450 part-time. 14% Black or African American, non-Hispanic/Latino; 7% Hispanic/Latino; 7% Asian, non-Hispanic/Latino; 0.4% Native Hawaiian or other Pacific Islander, non-Hispanic/Latino; 0.8% American Indian or Alaska Native, non-Hispanic/Latino; 1% Two or more races, non-Hispanic/Latino; 3% Race/ethnicity unknown; 5% transferred in.

Faculty *Student/faculty ratio:* 21:1.

Academics *Calendar:* semesters. *Degree:* certificates and associate. *Special study options:* academic remediation for entering students, adult/continuing education programs, advanced placement credit, distance learning, double majors, English as a second language, honors programs, internships, off-campus study, part-time degree program, services for LD students, summer session for credit.

Library Begley Library.

Student Life *Campus security:* 24-hour emergency response devices and patrols, late-night transport/escort service.

Athletics Member NJCAA.

Financial Aid Of all full-time matriculated undergraduates who enrolled in 2017, 50 Federal Work-Study jobs (averaging $2400).

Applying *Options:* electronic application, early admission, deferred entrance. *Required:* high school transcript.

Freshman Application Contact Mr. David Sampson, Director of Admissions, Schenectady County Community College, 78 Washington Avenue, Schenectady, NY 12305-2294. *Phone:* 518-381-1370 Ext. 1370. *E-mail:* sampsodg@gw.sunysccc.edu. *Website:* http://www.sunysccc.edu/.

State University of New York Broome Community College

Binghamton, New York

Freshman Application Contact Ms. Jenae Norris, Director of Admissions, State University of New York Broome Community College, PO Box 1017, Upper Front Street, Binghamton, NY 13902. *Phone:* 607-778-5001. *Fax:* 607-778-5394. *E-mail:* admissions@sunybroome.edu. *Website:* http://www.sunybroome.edu/.

State University of New York College of Technology at Alfred

Alfred, New York

- **State-supported** primarily 2-year, founded 1908, part of State University of New York System
- **Rural** 1084-acre campus with easy access to Rochester
- **Endowment** $5.6 million
- **Coed,** 3,737 undergraduate students, 92% full-time, 38% women, 62% men

Undergraduates 3,456 full-time, 281 part-time. Students come from 32 states and territories; 15 other countries; 4% are from out of state; 12% Black or African American, non-Hispanic/Latino; 9% Hispanic/Latino; 1% Asian, non-Hispanic/Latino; 0.1% Native Hawaiian or other Pacific Islander, non-Hispanic/Latino; 0.3% American Indian or Alaska Native, non-Hispanic/Latino; 3% Two or more races, non-Hispanic/Latino; 2% Race/ethnicity unknown; 0.7% international; 8% transferred in; 63% live on campus. *Retention:* 69% of full-time freshmen returned.

Freshmen *Admission:* 7,065 applied, 4,449 admitted, 1,222 enrolled. *Average high school GPA:* ####. *Test scores:* SAT evidence-based reading and writing scores over 500: 66%; SAT math scores over 500: 71%; ACT scores over 18: 85%; SAT evidence-based reading and writing scores over 600: 21%; SAT math scores over 600: 22%; ACT scores over 24: 37%; SAT evidence-based reading and writing scores over 700: 2%; SAT math scores over 700: 3%; ACT scores over 30: 6%.

Faculty *Total:* 262, 65% full-time, 30% with terminal degrees. *Student/faculty ratio:* 18:1.

Majors Accounting technology and bookkeeping; agribusiness; agriculture; animation, interactive technology, video graphics and special effects; architectural engineering technology; architecture; autobody/collision and repair technology; automobile/automotive mechanics technology; biology/biological sciences; business administration and management; business, management, and marketing related; computer and information sciences; computer and information systems security; computer engineering technology; computer programming (specific applications); construction engineering technology; construction management; construction trades related; court reporting; criminology; culinary arts; diagnostic medical sonography and ultrasound technology; diesel mechanics technology; drafting and design technology; electrical, electronic and communications engineering technology; engineering; environmental engineering technology; financial planning and services; forensic science and technology; game and interactive media design; general studies; graphic design; health/health-care administration; health information/medical records technology; health services/allied health/health sciences; heating, air conditioning, ventilation and refrigeration maintenance technology; heavy/industrial equipment maintenance technologies related; humanities; human resources management; human services; information science/studies; interior design; intermedia/multimedia; liberal arts and sciences and humanities related; liberal arts and sciences/liberal studies; machine shop technology; masonry; mechanical engineering/mechanical technology; motorcycle maintenance and repair technology; radiologic technology/science; registered nursing/registered nurse; sales, distribution, and marketing operations; sport and fitness administration/management; surveying technology; system, networking, and LAN/WAN management; vehicle maintenance and repair technologies related; veterinary/animal health technology; web/multimedia management and webmaster; welding technology.

Academics *Calendar:* semesters. *Degrees:* certificates, associate, and bachelor's. *Special study options:* academic remediation for entering students, accelerated degree program, adult/continuing education programs, advanced placement credit, cooperative education, distance learning, double majors, English as a second language, honors programs, independent study, internships, off-campus study, part-time degree program, services for LD students, student-designed majors, study abroad, summer session for credit. *ROTC:* Army (c).

Library Walter C. Hinkle Memorial Library plus 1 other. *Books:* 33,901 (physical), 1,901 (digital/electronic); *Serial titles:* 175 (physical); *Databases:* 214. Weekly public service hours: 88.

Student Life *Housing Options:* coed, men-only, women-only, special housing for students with disabilities. Campus housing is university owned. Freshman campus housing is guaranteed. *Activities and Organizations:* drama/theater group, student-run newspaper, radio station, choral group, Outdoor Recreation Club, Caribbean Student Association, Alfred Programming Board, Pioneer Woodsmen, Disaster Relief Team. *Campus security:* 24-hour emergency response devices and patrols, late-night transport/escort service, controlled dormitory access, residence hall entrance guards. *Student services:* health clinic, personal/psychological counseling, veterans affairs office.

Athletics Member NCAA, USCAA. All Division III. *Intercollegiate sports:* basketball W, cross-country running W, equestrian sports W, soccer W, softball W, swimming and diving W, track and field W, volleyball W. *Intramural sports:* archery M(c), basketball M, cheerleading M(c), equestrian sports M(c), football M, golf M, ice hockey M(c), rock climbing M, soccer M, softball M, swimming and diving M, tennis M, ultimate Frisbee M, volleyball M.

Standardized Tests *Recommended:* SAT or ACT (for admission).

Financial Aid Of all full-time matriculated undergraduates who enrolled in 2017, 3,165 applied for aid, 2,829 were judged to have need, 257 had their need fully met. In 2017, 126 non-need-based awards were made. *Average percent of need met:* 58%. *Average financial aid package:* $11,337. *Average need-based loan:* $3842. *Average need-based gift aid:* $6801. *Average non-need-based aid:* $5855. *Average indebtedness upon graduation:* $32,052.

Applying *Options:* electronic application. *Application fee:* $50. *Required:* high school transcript, minimum 2.0 GPA, Common Application with essay on supplemental application. *Recommended:* essay or personal statement, interview. *Application deadlines:* rolling (freshmen), rolling (transfers). *Notification:* continuous (freshmen), continuous (transfers).

Freshman Application Contact Ms. Betsy Penrose, Vice President for Enrollment Management, State University of New York College of Technology at Alfred, Huntington Administration Building, 10 Upper College Drive, Alfred, NY 14802. *Phone:* 607-587-3945. *Toll-free phone:* 800-4-ALFRED. *Fax:* 607-587-4299. *E-mail:* admissions@alfredstate.edu. *Website:* http://www.alfredstate.edu/.

Stella and Charles Guttman Community College

New York, New York

Admissions Office Contact Stella and Charles Guttman Community College, 50 West 40th Street, New York, NY 10018. *Website:* http://guttman.cuny.edu/.

Suffolk County Community College

Selden, New York

Freshman Application Contact Suffolk County Community College, 533 College Road, Selden, NY 11784-2899. *Phone:* 631-451-4000. *Website:* http://www.sunysuffolk.edu/.

Sullivan County Community College

Loch Sheldrake, New York

- **State and locally supported** 2-year, founded 1962, part of State University of New York System
- **Rural** 405-acre campus
- **Endowment** $921,102
- **Coed**, 1,538 undergraduate students, 51% full-time, 55% women, 45% men

Undergraduates 782 full-time, 756 part-time. Students come from 2 states and territories; 9 other countries; 1% are from out of state; 16% Black or African American, non-Hispanic/Latino; 24% Hispanic/Latino; 2% Asian, non-Hispanic/Latino; 0.1% Native Hawaiian or other Pacific Islander, non-Hispanic/Latino; 0.4% American Indian or Alaska Native, non-Hispanic/Latino; 4% Two or more races, non-Hispanic/Latino; 6% Race/ethnicity unknown; 1% international; 6% transferred in; 16% live on campus.

Freshmen *Admission:* 1,300 applied, 1,293 admitted, 315 enrolled. *Average high school GPA:* 2.3.

Faculty *Total:* 93, 41% full-time, 22% with terminal degrees. *Student/faculty ratio:* 21:1.

Majors Accounting; administrative assistant and secretarial science; baking and pastry arts; business administration and management; commercial and advertising art; computer graphics; computer programming (specific applications); construction engineering technology; consumer merchandising/retailing management; criminal justice/police science; crisis/emergency/disaster management; culinary arts; data entry/microcomputer applications; electrical, electronic and communications engineering technology; elementary education; environmental studies; fire prevention and safety technology; forensic science and technology; hospitality administration; human services; information science/studies; kindergarten/preschool education; legal assistant/paralegal; liberal arts and sciences/liberal studies; marketing/marketing management; mathematics; medical/clinical assistant; parks, recreation and leisure; photography; psychology; radio and television; radio, television, and digital communication related; registered nursing/registered nurse; respiratory care therapy; science technologies related; sport and fitness administration/management; tourism and travel services management.

Academics *Calendar:* semesters. *Degree:* certificates and associate. *Special study options:* academic remediation for entering students, adult/continuing education programs, advanced placement credit, cooperative education, distance learning, double majors, honors programs, independent study, internships, off-campus study, part-time degree program, services for LD students, summer session for credit.

Library Hermann Memorial Library plus 1 other. *Books:* 59,923 (physical), 169,353 (digital/electronic); *Serial titles:* 128 (physical), 3 (digital/electronic); *Databases:* 94. Weekly public service hours: 62.

Student Life *Housing Options:* coed. Campus housing is provided by a third party. Freshman applicants given priority for college housing. *Activities and Organizations:* drama/theater group, Science Alliance, Black Student Union, Gay-Straight Alliance, Dance Club, Honor Society. *Campus security:* 24-hour emergency response devices and patrols, student patrols, controlled dormitory access. *Student services:* health clinic, personal/psychological counseling, legal services.

Athletics Member NJCAA. *Intercollegiate sports:* basketball W, cross-country running W, softball W, volleyball W. *Intramural sports:* baseball M, basketball M, bowling M, cross-country running M, golf M, racquetball M, soccer M, softball M, table tennis M, tennis M, volleyball M, weight lifting M.

Financial Aid Of all full-time matriculated undergraduates who enrolled in 2017, 643 applied for aid, 628 were judged to have need, 628 had their need fully met. 52 Federal Work-Study jobs (averaging $737). 11 state and other part-time jobs (averaging $949). *Average percent of need met:* 100%. *Average financial aid package:* $4327. *Average need-based loan:* $1756. *Average need-based gift aid:* $3706.

Applying *Options:* electronic application, early admission, deferred entrance. *Required:* high school transcript. *Application deadlines:* rolling (freshmen), rolling (transfers). *Notification:* continuous (freshmen), continuous (transfers).

Freshman Application Contact Mr. Steven Alhona, Director of Admissions, Sullivan County Community College, 112 College Road, Loch Sheldrake, NY 12759. *Phone:* 845-434-5750 Ext. 4356. *Toll-free phone:* 800-577-5243. *Fax:* 845-434-4806. *E-mail:* salhona@sunysullivan.edu. *Website:* http://www.sunysullivan.edu/.

Tompkins Cortland Community College

Dryden, New York

- **State and locally supported** 2-year, founded 1968, part of State University of New York System
- **Rural** 300-acre campus
- **Coed**

Undergraduates 1,830 full-time, 802 part-time. Students come from 17 states and territories; 23 other countries; 3% are from out of state; 14% Black or African American, non-Hispanic/Latino; 10% Hispanic/Latino; 2% Asian, non-Hispanic/Latino; 0.2% American Indian or Alaska Native, non-Hispanic/Latino; 4% Two or more races, non-Hispanic/Latino; 5% Race/ethnicity unknown; 3% international; 8% transferred in.

Faculty *Student/faculty ratio:* 18:1.

Academics *Calendar:* semesters. *Degree:* certificates and associate. *Special study options:* academic remediation for entering students, adult/continuing education programs, advanced placement credit, cooperative education, distance learning, double majors, English as a second language, freshman honors college, honors programs, independent study, internships, off-campus study, part-time degree program, services for LD students, study abroad, summer session for credit.

Library Gerald A. Barry Memorial Library plus 1 other.

Student Life *Campus security:* 24-hour patrols, late-night transport/escort service, controlled dormitory access, armed peace officers.

Athletics Member NJCAA.

Financial Aid Of all full-time matriculated undergraduates who enrolled in 2017, 150 Federal Work-Study jobs (averaging $1000). 150 state and other part-time jobs (averaging $1000).

Applying *Options:* electronic application, early admission, deferred entrance. *Required:* high school transcript. *Required for some:* essay or personal statement, interview.

Admissions Office Contact Tompkins Cortland Community College, 170 North Street, PO Box 139, Dryden, NY 13053-0139. *Toll-free phone:* 888-567-8211. *Website:* http://www.tompkinscortland.edu/.

Trocaire College
Buffalo, New York

Freshman Application Contact Trocaire College, 360 Choate Avenue, Buffalo, NY 14220-2094. *Phone:* 716-826-2558. *Website:* http://www.trocaire.edu/.

Ulster County Community College
Stone Ridge, New York

Freshman Application Contact Admissions Office, Ulster County Community College, 491 Cottekill Road, Stone Ridge, NY 12484. *Phone:* 845-687-5022. *Toll-free phone:* 800-724-0833. *E-mail:* admissionsoffice@sunyulster.edu. *Website:* http://www.sunyulster.edu/.

Westchester Community College
Valhalla, New York

- **State and locally supported** 2-year, founded 1946, part of State University of New York System
- **Suburban** 218-acre campus with easy access to New York City
- **Coed,** 11,535 undergraduate students, 53% full-time, 53% women, 47% men

Undergraduates 6,156 full-time, 5,379 part-time. 23% Black or African American, non-Hispanic/Latino; 37% Hispanic/Latino; 4% Asian, non-Hispanic/Latino; 0.3% Native Hawaiian or other Pacific Islander, non-Hispanic/Latino; 1% American Indian or Alaska Native, non-Hispanic/Latino; 3% Two or more races, non-Hispanic/Latino; 3% Race/ethnicity unknown; 1% international; 7% transferred in.

Freshmen *Admission:* 4,378 applied, 4,378 admitted, 2,351 enrolled.

Faculty *Total:* 801, 20% full-time.

Majors Accounting; accounting technology and bookkeeping; administrative assistant and secretarial science; animal sciences; art; business administration and management; child-care and support services management; civil engineering technology; commercial and advertising art; community organization and advocacy; computer and information sciences; computer and information sciences and support services related; computer and information systems security; corrections; design and applied arts related; dietitian assistant; digital arts; digital communication and media/multimedia; drafting and design technology; electrical, electronic and communications engineering technology; emergency medical technology (EMT paramedic); environmental control technologies related; environmental science; environmental studies; food service systems administration; health and physical education/fitness; health information/medical records technology; health professions related; humanities; information science/studies; international business/trade/commerce; journalism; legal assistant/paralegal; liberal arts and sciences and humanities related; liberal arts and sciences/liberal studies; marketing related; mechanical engineering/mechanical technology; medical administrative assistant and medical secretary; medical radiologic technology; merchandising, sales, and marketing operations related (general); practical nursing, vocational nursing and nursing assistants related; registered nursing/registered nurse; respiratory care therapy; restaurant, culinary, and catering management; retailing; small business administration; speech communication and rhetoric; substance abuse/addiction counseling; teacher assistant/aide; visual and performing arts.

Academics *Calendar:* semesters. *Degree:* certificates and associate. *Special study options:* academic remediation for entering students, adult/continuing education programs, advanced placement credit, cooperative education, distance learning, double majors, English as a second language, honors programs, independent study, internships, off-campus study, part-time degree program, services for LD students, study abroad, summer session for credit.

Library Harold L. Drimmer Library.

Student Life *Housing:* college housing not available. *Activities and Organizations:* student-run newspaper, radio station, choral group, Deca Fashion Retail, Future Educators, Respiratory Club, Black Student Union, Diversity Action. *Campus security:* 24-hour emergency response devices and patrols, late-night transport/escort service. *Student services:* health clinic, personal/psychological counseling, women's center, veterans affairs office.

Athletics Member NJCAA. *Intercollegiate sports:* basketball W, bowling W, softball W, volleyball W. *Intramural sports:* badminton M, basketball M, softball M, swimming and diving M, tennis M, volleyball M, weight lifting M.

Financial Aid Of all full-time matriculated undergraduates who enrolled in 2017, 4,846 applied for aid, 3,903 were judged to have need. In 2017, 245 non-need-based awards were made. *Average percent of need met:* 57%. *Average financial aid package:* $3799. *Average need-based loan:* $1810. *Average need-based gift aid:* $3665. *Average non-need-based aid:* $1761.

Applying *Options:* electronic application, early action. *Application fee:* $35. *Required:* high school transcript. *Required for some:* interview. *Application deadline:* rolling (freshmen).

Freshman Application Contact Ms. Gloria De La Paz, Director of Admissions, Westchester Community College, 75 Grasslands Road, Administration Building, Valhalla, NY 10595-1698. *Phone:* 914-606-6735. *Fax:* 914-606-6540. *E-mail:* admissions@sunywcc.edu. *Website:* http://www.sunywcc.edu/.

Yeshiva Sholom Shachna
Brooklyn, New York

Admissions Office Contact Yeshiva Sholom Shachna, 401 Elmwood Avenue, Brooklyn, NY 11230.

NORTH CAROLINA

Alamance Community College
Graham, North Carolina

- **State-supported** 2-year, founded 1958, part of North Carolina Community College System
- **Small-town** 48-acre campus
- **Endowment** $2.9 million
- **Coed,** 4,233 undergraduate students, 61% full-time, 60% women, 40% men

Undergraduates 2,565 full-time, 1,668 part-time. Students come from 7 states and territories; 6 other countries; 1% are from out of state; 21% Black or African American, non-Hispanic/Latino; 9% Hispanic/Latino; 2% Asian, non-Hispanic/Latino; 0.2% Native Hawaiian or other Pacific Islander, non-Hispanic/Latino; 0.4% American Indian or Alaska Native, non-Hispanic/Latino; 2% Two or more races, non-Hispanic/Latino; 0.6% international; 28% transferred in.

Freshmen *Admission:* 448 enrolled.

Faculty *Total:* 435, 26% full-time, 3% with terminal degrees. *Student/faculty ratio:* 20:1.

Majors Accounting technology and bookkeeping; animal sciences; applied horticulture/horticulture operations; automobile/automotive mechanics technology; banking and financial support services; biotechnology; business administration and management; carpentry; clinical/medical laboratory technology; commercial and advertising art; criminal justice/safety; culinary arts; electrical, electronic and communications engineering technology; executive assistant/executive secretary; heating, ventilation, air conditioning and refrigeration engineering technology; information science/studies; kindergarten/preschool education; legal administrative assistant/secretary; liberal arts and sciences/liberal studies; machine tool technology; mechanical engineering/mechanical technology; medical administrative assistant and medical secretary; medical/clinical assistant; office occupations and clerical services; registered nursing/registered nurse; retailing; teacher assistant/aide; welding technology.

Academics *Calendar:* semesters. *Degree:* certificates, diplomas, and associate. *Special study options:* academic remediation for entering students, adult/continuing education programs, cooperative education, distance learning, double majors, English as a second language, independent study, off-campus study, part-time degree program, services for LD students, summer session for credit.

Library Learning Resources Center. Weekly public service hours: 64; students can reserve study rooms.

Student Life *Housing:* college housing not available. *Campus security:* 24-hour emergency response devices and patrols, student patrols, late-night transport/escort service. *Student services:* personal/psychological counseling, veterans affairs office.

Financial Aid Of all full-time matriculated undergraduates who enrolled in 2010, 4,000 applied for aid, 3,000 were judged to have need. 200 Federal Work-Study jobs (averaging $1250). *Average percent of need met:* 30%. *Average financial aid package:* $4500. *Average need-based gift aid:* $4500. *Average indebtedness upon graduation:* $2500.

Applying *Options:* electronic application. *Required:* high school transcript. *Application deadlines:* rolling (freshmen), rolling (transfers). *Notification:* continuous (freshmen), continuous (transfers).

Freshman Application Contact Ms. Elizabeth Brehler, Director for Enrollment Management, Alamance Community College, Graham, NC 27253-8000. *Phone:* 336-506-4120. *Fax:* 336-506-4264. *E-mail:* brehlere@alamancecc.edu. *Website:* http://www.alamancecc.edu/.

Asheville-Buncombe Technical Community College

Asheville, North Carolina

- **State-supported** 2-year, founded 1959, part of North Carolina Community College System
- **Urban** 126-acre campus
- **Coed**

Undergraduates 1% are from out of state.
Faculty *Student/faculty ratio:* 15:1.
Academics *Calendar:* semesters. *Degree:* certificates, diplomas, and associate. *Special study options:* academic remediation for entering students, adult/continuing education programs, advanced placement credit, cooperative education, distance learning, double majors, independent study, internships, part-time degree program, services for LD students, summer session for credit.
Library Locke Learning Resources Center. Students can reserve study rooms.
Student Life *Campus security:* 24-hour emergency response devices and patrols.
Financial Aid Of all full-time matriculated undergraduates who enrolled in 2017, 55 Federal Work-Study jobs (averaging $2000).
Applying *Options:* deferred entrance. *Required:* high school transcript. *Required for some:* interview.
Freshman Application Contact Asheville-Buncombe Technical Community College, 340 Victoria Road, Asheville, NC 28801-4897. *Phone:* 828-398-7900 Ext. 7887. *Website:* http://www.abtech.edu/.

Beaufort County Community College

Washington, North Carolina

Freshman Application Contact Mr. Gary Burbage, Director of Admissions, Beaufort County Community College, PO Box 1069, 5337 US Highway 264 East, Washington, NC 27889-1069. *Phone:* 252-940-6233. *Fax:* 252-940-6393. *E-mail:* garyb@beaufortccc.edu. *Website:* http://www.beaufortccc.edu/.

Bladen Community College

Dublin, North Carolina

Freshman Application Contact Ms. Andrea Fisher, Enrollment Specialist, Bladen Community College, PO Box 266, Dublin, NC 28332. *Phone:* 910-879-5593. *Fax:* 910-879-5564. *E-mail:* acarterfisher@bladencc.edu. *Website:* http://www.bladencc.edu/.

Blue Ridge Community College

Flat Rock, North Carolina

Freshman Application Contact Blue Ridge Community College, 180 West Campus Drive, Flat Rock, NC 28731. *Phone:* 828-694-1810. *Website:* http://www.blueridge.edu/.

Brunswick Community College

Supply, North Carolina

Freshman Application Contact Admissions Counselor, Brunswick Community College, 50 College Road, PO Box 30, Supply, NC 28462-0030. *Phone:* 910-755-7300. *Toll-free phone:* 800-754-1050. *Fax:* 910-754-9609. *E-mail:* admissions@brunswickcc.edu. *Website:* http://www.brunswickcc.edu/.

Caldwell Community College and Technical Institute

Hudson, North Carolina

- **State-supported** 2-year, founded 1964, part of North Carolina Community College System
- **Small-town** 50-acre campus
- **Coed**

Undergraduates 1,240 full-time, 2,274 part-time.
Faculty *Student/faculty ratio:* 18:1.
Academics *Calendar:* semesters. *Degree:* certificates, diplomas, and associate. *Special study options:* academic remediation for entering students, adult/continuing education programs, advanced placement credit, cooperative education, distance learning, double majors, independent study, part-time degree program, services for LD students, summer session for credit.
Library Broyhill Center for Learning Resources. Students can reserve study rooms.
Student Life *Campus security:* trained security personnel during hours of operation.
Athletics Member NJCAA.
Financial Aid Of all full-time matriculated undergraduates who enrolled in 2017, 69 Federal Work-Study jobs (averaging $960).
Applying *Options:* early admission. *Required:* high school transcript.
Freshman Application Contact Patricia Brinkley, Admissions Representative, Caldwell Community College and Technical Institute, 2855 Hickory Boulevard, Hudson, NC 28638. *Phone:* 828-726-2700. *Fax:* 828-726-2709. *E-mail:* pbrinkley@cccti.edu. *Website:* http://www.cccti.edu/.

Cape Fear Community College

Wilmington, North Carolina

Freshman Application Contact Ms. Linda Kasyan, Director of Admissions, Cape Fear Community College, 411 North Front Street, Wilmington, NC 28401-3993. *Phone:* 910-362-7054. *Toll-free phone:* 877-799-2322. *Fax:* 910-362-7080. *E-mail:* admissions@cfcc.edu. *Website:* http://www.cfcc.edu/.

Carolinas College of Health Sciences

Charlotte, North Carolina

Freshman Application Contact Ms. Merritt Newman, Admissions Representative, Carolinas College of Health Sciences, 1200 Blythe Boulevard, Charlotte, NC 28203. *Phone:* 704-355-5583. *Fax:* 704-355-9336. *E-mail:* merritt.newman@carolinascollege.edu. *Website:* http://www.carolinascollege.edu/.

Carteret Community College

Morehead City, North Carolina

- **State-supported** 2-year, founded 1963, part of North Carolina Community College System
- **Small-town** 41-acre campus
- **Endowment** $4.8 million
- **Coed**

Undergraduates 571 full-time, 792 part-time. Students come from 8 states and territories; 1% are from out of state; 9% Black or African American, non-Hispanic/Latino; 4% Hispanic/Latino; 1% Asian, non-Hispanic/Latino; 0.2% Native Hawaiian or other Pacific Islander, non-Hispanic/Latino; 0.7% American Indian or Alaska Native, non-Hispanic/Latino; 3% Two or more races, non-Hispanic/Latino; 2% Race/ethnicity unknown; 11% transferred in.
Faculty *Student/faculty ratio:* 10:1.
Academics *Calendar:* semesters. *Degrees:* certificates, diplomas, associate, and postbachelor's certificates. *Special study options:* academic remediation for entering students, adult/continuing education programs, cooperative education, distance learning, double majors, internships, part-time degree program, services for LD students, summer session for credit.
Library Michael J. Smith Learning Resource Center. *Books:* 18,182 (physical), 173,614 (digital/electronic); *Databases:* 74. Weekly public service hours: 63.
Student Life *Campus security:* late-night transport/escort service, security service from 7 am until 11:30 pm.
Athletics Member NCAA. All Division I.
Applying *Options:* electronic application. *Required for some:* high school transcript.
Admissions Office Contact Carteret Community College, 3505 Arendell Street, Morehead City, NC 28557-2989. *Website:* http://www.carteret.edu/.

Catawba Valley Community College

Hickory, North Carolina

Freshman Application Contact Catawba Valley Community College, 2550 Highway 70 SE, Hickory, NC 28602-9699. *Phone:* 828-327-7000 Ext. 4618. *Website:* http://www.cvcc.edu/.

Central Carolina Community College

Sanford, North Carolina

Freshman Application Contact Mrs. Jamie Tyson Childress, Dean of Enrollment/Registrar, Central Carolina Community College, 1105 Kelly Drive, Sanford, NC 27330-9000. *Phone:* 919-718-7239. *Toll-free phone:* 800-682-8353. *Fax:* 919-718-7380. *Website:* http://www.cccc.edu/.

Central Piedmont Community College

Charlotte, North Carolina

Freshman Application Contact Ms. Linda McComb, Associate Dean, Central Piedmont Community College, PO Box 35009, Charlotte, NC 28235-5009. *Phone:* 704-330-6784. *Fax:* 704-330-6136. *Website:* http://www.cpcc.edu/.

Cleveland Community College

Shelby, North Carolina

- **State-supported** 2-year, founded 1965, part of North Carolina Community College System
- **Small-town** 43-acre campus with easy access to Charlotte
- **Coed**

Undergraduates 990 full-time, 1,710 part-time. 18% Black or African American, non-Hispanic/Latino; 4% Hispanic/Latino; 0.9% Asian, non-Hispanic/Latino; 0.1% Native Hawaiian or other Pacific Islander, non-Hispanic/Latino; 0.5% American Indian or Alaska Native, non-Hispanic/Latino; 3% Two or more races, non-Hispanic/Latino; 2% Race/ethnicity unknown; 0.7% international.

Faculty *Student/faculty ratio:* 11:1.

Academics *Calendar:* semesters. *Degree:* certificates, diplomas, and associate. *Special study options:* academic remediation for entering students, adult/continuing education programs, advanced placement credit, cooperative education, distance learning, double majors, English as a second language, independent study, off-campus study, part-time degree program, summer session for credit.

Library Jim & Patsy Rose Library.

Student Life *Campus security:* security personnel during hours of operation.

Financial Aid Of all full-time matriculated undergraduates who enrolled in 2017, 20 Federal Work-Study jobs.

Applying *Options:* electronic application, deferred entrance. *Required:* high school transcript.

Freshman Application Contact Cleveland Community College, 137 South Post Road, Shelby, NC 28152. *Phone:* 704-669-4321. *Website:* http://www.clevelandcc.edu/.

Coastal Carolina Community College

Jacksonville, North Carolina

Freshman Application Contact Ms. Heather Calihan, Counseling Coordinator, Coastal Carolina Community College, Jacksonville, NC 28546. *Phone:* 910-938-6241. *Fax:* 910-455-2767. *E-mail:* calihanh@coastal.cc.nc.us. *Website:* http://www.coastalcarolina.edu/.

College of The Albemarle

Elizabeth City, North Carolina

- **State-supported** 2-year, founded 1960, part of North Carolina Community College System
- **Small-town** 40-acre campus
- **Coed,** 2,557 undergraduate students, 39% full-time, 65% women, 35% men

Undergraduates 999 full-time, 1,558 part-time. Students come from 5 states and territories; 16% Black or African American, non-Hispanic/Latino; 5% Hispanic/Latino; 1% Asian, non-Hispanic/Latino; 0.3% Native Hawaiian or other Pacific Islander, non-Hispanic/Latino; 0.4% American Indian or Alaska Native, non-Hispanic/Latino; 3% Two or more races, non-Hispanic/Latino; 1% Race/ethnicity unknown; 5% international.

Freshmen *Admission:* 262 enrolled.

Majors Architectural engineering technology; art; aviation/airway management; biotechnology; business administration and management; computer engineering technology; computer programming; computer programming (specific applications); construction trades; crafts, folk art and artisanry; criminal justice/law enforcement administration; culinary arts; data entry/microcomputer applications; drafting/design engineering technologies related; dramatic/theater arts; education; health and physical education/fitness; information science/studies; information technology; liberal arts and sciences/liberal studies; licensed practical/vocational nurse training; medical administrative assistant and medical secretary; metal and jewelry arts; music; phlebotomy technology; registered nursing/registered nurse; teacher assistant/aide.

Academics *Calendar:* semesters. *Degree:* certificates, diplomas, and associate. *Special study options:* academic remediation for entering students, adult/continuing education programs, advanced placement credit, cooperative education, English as a second language, part-time degree program, services for LD students, summer session for credit.

Library Learning Resources Center.

Student Life *Housing:* college housing not available. *Activities and Organizations:* drama/theater group, choral group, Phi Beta Lambda, Phi Theta Kappa. *Campus security:* 24-hour patrols. *Student services:* personal/psychological counseling.

Athletics *Intramural sports:* archery M, baseball M, basketball M, football M, golf M, gymnastics M, sailing M, soccer M(c), softball M, swimming and diving M, table tennis M, tennis M, volleyball M.

Applying *Options:* electronic application, early admission, deferred entrance. *Required:* high school transcript. *Application deadlines:* rolling (freshmen), rolling (transfers). *Notification:* continuous (freshmen), continuous (transfers).

Freshman Application Contact Angie Godfrey-Dawson, Director of Admissions/Financial Aid, College of The Albemarle, PO Box 2327, Elizabeth City, NC 27906-2327. *Phone:* 252-335-0821 Ext. 2360. *Fax:* 252-337-6813. *Website:* http://www.albemarle.edu/.

Craven Community College

New Bern, North Carolina

- **State-supported** 2-year, founded 1965, part of North Carolina Community College System
- **Suburban** 100-acre campus
- **Coed**

Undergraduates 1,126 full-time, 1,895 part-time. 16% Black or African American, non-Hispanic/Latino; 8% Hispanic/Latino; 3% Asian, non-Hispanic/Latino; 0.5% Native Hawaiian or other Pacific Islander, non-Hispanic/Latino; 0.7% American Indian or Alaska Native, non-Hispanic/Latino; 4% Two or more races, non-Hispanic/Latino; 4% Race/ethnicity unknown; 1% international; 13% transferred in.

Faculty *Student/faculty ratio:* 19:1.

Academics *Calendar:* semesters. *Degree:* certificates, diplomas, and associate. *Special study options:* academic remediation for entering students, adult/continuing education programs, advanced placement credit, cooperative education, distance learning, double majors, English as a second language, honors programs, independent study, internships, part-time degree program, services for LD students, study abroad, summer session for credit.

Library R. C. Godwin Memorial Library. *Books:* 17,065 (physical), 240,000 (digital/electronic); *Serial titles:* 27 (physical), 18,759 (digital/electronic); *Databases:* 86. Students can reserve study rooms.

Student Life *Campus security:* 24-hour emergency response devices and patrols.

Applying *Options:* electronic application. *Required:* high school transcript.

Freshman Application Contact Craven Community College, 800 College Court, New Bern, NC 28562. *Phone:* 252-638-4597. *Website:* http://www.cravencc.edu/.

Davidson County Community College

Lexington, North Carolina

Freshman Application Contact Davidson County Community College, PO Box 1287, Lexington, NC 27293-1287. *Phone:* 336-249-8186 Ext. 6715. *Fax:* 336-224-0240. *E-mail:* admissions@davidsonccc.edu. *Website:* http://www.davidsonccc.edu/.

Durham Technical Community College

Durham, North Carolina

Director of Admissions Ms. Penny Augustine, Director of Admissions and Testing, Durham Technical Community College, 1637 Lawson Street, Durham, NC 27703-5023. *Phone:* 919-686-3619. *Website:* http://www.durhamtech.edu/.

Edgecombe Community College

Tarboro, North Carolina

Freshman Application Contact Ms. Jackie Heath, Admissions Officer, Edgecombe Community College, 2009 West Wilson Street, Tarboro, NC 27886-9399. *Phone:* 252-823-5166 Ext. 254. *Website:* http://www.edgecombe.edu/.

Fayetteville Technical Community College

Fayetteville, North Carolina

- **State-supported** 2-year, founded 1961, part of North Carolina Community College System
- **Suburban** 204-acre campus with easy access to Raleigh
- **Endowment** $39,050
- **Coed,** 11,534 undergraduate students, 39% full-time, 59% women, 41% men

Undergraduates 4,509 full-time, 7,025 part-time. Students come from 43 states and territories; 12 other countries; 25% are from out of state; 37% Black or African American, non-Hispanic/Latino; 12% Hispanic/Latino; 2% Asian, non-Hispanic/Latino; 0.4% Native Hawaiian or other Pacific Islander, non-Hispanic/Latino; 2% American Indian or Alaska Native, non-Hispanic/Latino; 5% Two or more races, non-Hispanic/Latino; 4% Race/ethnicity unknown; 0.5% international; 6% transferred in.

Freshmen *Admission:* 4,711 applied, 4,711 admitted, 1,817 enrolled. *Average high school GPA:* 2.6.

Faculty *Total:* 553, 50% full-time, 6% with terminal degrees. *Student/faculty ratio:* 19:1.

Majors Accounting and finance; applied horticulture/horticulture operations; architectural engineering technology; autobody/collision and repair technology; automobile/automotive mechanics technology; building/construction finishing, management, and inspection related; business administration and management; civil engineering technology; commercial and advertising art; cosmetology; criminal justice/safety; crisis/emergency/disaster management; culinary arts; dental hygiene; early childhood education; electrical, electronic and communications engineering technology; electrician; electromechanical and instrumentation and maintenance technologies related; elementary education; emergency medical technology (EMT paramedic); entrepreneurship; fire prevention and safety technology; forensic science and technology; funeral service and mortuary science; game and interactive media design; gunsmithing; health and physical education related; heating, air conditioning, ventilation and refrigeration maintenance technology; hotel, motel, and restaurant management; information technology; intelligence; legal assistant/paralegal; liberal arts and sciences and humanities related; liberal arts and sciences/liberal studies; logistics, materials, and supply chain management; machine shop technology; medical office management; office management; pharmacy technician; physical therapy technology; pre-engineering; radiologic technology/science; registered nursing/registered nurse; respiratory care therapy; speech-language pathology assistant; surgical technology; surveying technology.

Academics *Calendar:* semesters. *Degree:* certificates, diplomas, and associate. *Special study options:* academic remediation for entering students, accelerated degree program, adult/continuing education programs, advanced placement credit, cooperative education, distance learning, double majors, English as a second language, freshman honors college, honors programs, independent study, internships, off-campus study, part-time degree program, services for LD students, summer session for credit. *ROTC:* Air Force (c).

Library Paul H. Thompson Library plus 1 other. *Books:* 35,540 (physical), 275,000 (digital/electronic); *Serial titles:* 53 (physical), 5 (digital/electronic); *Databases:* 200.

Student Life *Housing:* college housing not available. *Activities and Organizations:* choral group, Parents for Higher Education, Phi Theta Kappa, Phi Beta Lambda, Sigma Kappa Delta, Student Veterans of America. *Campus security:* 24-hour emergency response devices and patrols, late-night transport/escort service, campus-wide emergency notification system. *Student services:* personal/psychological counseling, veterans affairs office.

Athletics Member NJCAA. *Intercollegiate sports:* basketball W, softball W, volleyball W. *Intramural sports:* basketball M.

Financial Aid Of all full-time matriculated undergraduates who enrolled in 2017, 75 Federal Work-Study jobs (averaging $2000). *Financial aid deadline:* 6/1.

Applying *Options:* electronic application, deferred entrance. *Required:* high school transcript. *Required for some:* essay or personal statement, interview. *Application deadlines:* rolling (freshmen), rolling (transfers). *Notification:* continuous (freshmen), continuous (transfers).

Freshman Application Contact Dr. Louanna Castleman, Director of Admissions & Counseling, Fayetteville Technical Community College, 2201 Hull Road, PO Box 35236, Fayetteville, NC 28303-0236. *Phone:* 910-678-0141. *Fax:* 910-678-0085. *E-mail:* castleml@faytechcc.edu. *Website:* http://www.faytechcc.edu/.

Forsyth Technical Community College

Winston-Salem, North Carolina

Freshman Application Contact Admissions Office, Forsyth Technical Community College, 2100 Silas Creek Parkway, Winston-Salem, NC 27103-5197. *Phone:* 336-734-7556. *E-mail:* admissions@forsythtech.edu. *Website:* http://www.forsythtech.edu/.

Gaston College

Dallas, North Carolina

Freshman Application Contact Terry Basier, Director of Enrollment Management and Admissions, Gaston College, 201 Highway 321 South, Dallas, NC 28034. *Phone:* 704-922-6214. *Fax:* 704-922-6443. *Website:* http://www.gaston.edu/.

Guilford Technical Community College

Jamestown, North Carolina

Freshman Application Contact Guilford Technical Community College, PO Box 309, Jamestown, NC 27282-0309. *Phone:* 336-334-4822 Ext. 50125. *Website:* http://www.gtcc.edu/.

Halifax Community College

Weldon, North Carolina

- **State and locally supported** 2-year, founded 1967, part of North Carolina Community College System
- **Rural** 109-acre campus
- **Endowment** $1365
- **Coed,** 1,083 undergraduate students, 38% full-time, 63% women, 37% men
- 68% of applicants were admitted

Undergraduates 409 full-time, 674 part-time.

Freshmen *Admission:* 673 applied, 457 admitted, 193 enrolled.

Faculty *Total:* 84, 52% full-time, 8% with terminal degrees. *Student/faculty ratio:* 11:1.

Majors Automobile/automotive mechanics technology; business administration and management; commercial and advertising art; cosmetology; criminal justice/safety; dental hygiene; early childhood education; electromechanical and instrumentation and maintenance technologies related; engineering; human services; industrial mechanics and maintenance technology; information technology; legal assistant/paralegal; liberal arts and sciences and humanities related; liberal arts and sciences/liberal studies; medical administrative assistant and medical secretary; medical office management; mental and social health services and allied professions related; office management; registered nursing/registered nurse; welding technology.

Academics *Calendar:* semesters. *Degree:* certificates, diplomas, and associate. *Special study options:* academic remediation for entering students, cooperative education, distance learning, double majors, English as a second language, independent study, internships, part-time degree program, services for LD students, summer session for credit.

Library Learning Resources Center. *Books:* 23,686 (physical), 202,576 (digital/electronic); *Serial titles:* 86 (physical), 1,382 (digital/electronic); *Databases:* 89. Weekly public service hours: 52.

Student Life *Housing:* college housing not available. *Activities and Organizations:* Phi Theta Kappa, PRIDE, Women of Excellence. *Campus security:* 24-hour emergency response devices, 12-hour patrols by trained security personnel. *Student services:* health clinic, veterans affairs office.

Applying *Required:* high school transcript. *Application deadlines:* rolling (freshmen), rolling (out-of-state freshmen), rolling (transfers). *Notification:* continuous (freshmen), continuous (out-of-state freshmen), continuous (transfers).

Freshman Application Contact Mr. Antonio Squire, Director of Admissions, Halifax Community College, P.O. Drawer 809, 100 College Drive, Weldon, NC 27890. *Phone:* 252-536-7225. *E-mail:* asquire374@halifaxcc.edu. *Website:* http://www.halifaxcc.edu/.

Haywood Community College

Clyde, North Carolina

- **State and locally supported** 2-year, founded 1965, part of North Carolina Community College System
- **Rural** 85-acre campus
- **Endowment** $9.1 million
- **Coed,** 1,627 undergraduate students, 35% full-time, 61% women, 39% men

Undergraduates 574 full-time, 1,053 part-time. Students come from 1 other state; 0.5% are from out of state; 5% Black or African American, non-Hispanic/Latino; 4% Hispanic/Latino; 1% Asian, non-Hispanic/Latino; 0.1% Native Hawaiian or other Pacific Islander, non-Hispanic/Latino; 2% American Indian or Alaska Native, non-Hispanic/Latino; 0.9% Two or more races, non-Hispanic/Latino; 3% Race/ethnicity unknown; 0.1% international; 12% transferred in. *Retention:* 74% of full-time freshmen returned.

Freshmen *Admission:* 110 admitted, 207 enrolled. *Average high school GPA:* 3.0.

Faculty *Total:* 235, 25% full-time, 5% with terminal degrees.
Majors Accounting; accounting technology and bookkeeping; applied horticulture/horticulture operations; autobody/collision and repair technology; automobile/automotive mechanics technology; building/construction finishing, management, and inspection related; business administration and management; child-care and support services management; computer systems networking and telecommunications; cosmetology; crafts, folk art and artisanry; criminal justice/law enforcement administration; criminal justice/safety; early childhood education; electrical, electronic and communications engineering technology; electrician; electromechanical and instrumentation and maintenance technologies related; elementary education; entrepreneurship; fiber, textile and weaving arts; forest technology; information technology; liberal arts and sciences and humanities related; liberal arts and sciences/liberal studies; medical/clinical assistant; medical office management; metal and jewelry arts; pre-engineering; registered nursing/registered nurse; welding technology; wildlife, fish and wildlands science and management.
Academics *Calendar:* semesters. *Degree:* certificates, diplomas, and associate. *Special study options:* academic remediation for entering students, adult/continuing education programs, advanced placement credit, cooperative education, distance learning, double majors, English as a second language, honors programs, independent study, internships, part-time degree program, services for LD students, study abroad, summer session for credit.
Library Freedlander Learning Resource Center. *Books:* 36,213 (physical), 382,812 (digital/electronic); *Serial titles:* 123 (physical), 23,465 (digital/electronic); *Databases:* 91. Weekly public service hours: 47; students can reserve study rooms.
Student Life *Housing:* college housing not available. *Activities and Organizations:* Wildlife Society, Timbersport Forestry Club, Student Association of Medical Assistants (SAMA), HCC Student Nurses Association, HCC Skills USA Club. *Campus security:* Emergency Phone and Patrols while campus is open. *Student services:* veterans affairs office.
Financial Aid Of all full-time matriculated undergraduates who enrolled in 2017, 41 Federal Work-Study jobs (averaging $857).
Applying *Options:* electronic application. *Required:* high school transcript. *Required for some:* interview. *Application deadlines:* rolling (freshmen), rolling (transfers).
Director of Admissions Danielle Harris, Director of Enrollment Management, Haywood Community College, 185 Freedlander Drive, Clyde, NC 28721-9453. *Phone:* 828-627-4507. *Toll-free phone:* 866-GOTOHCC. *E-mail:* ldharris@haywood.edu.
Website: http://www.haywood.edu/.

Isothermal Community College
Spindale, North Carolina

Freshman Application Contact Ms. Vickie Searcy, Enrollment Management Office, Isothermal Community College, PO Box 804, Spindale, NC 28160-0804. *Phone:* 828-286-3636 Ext. 251. *Fax:* 828-286-8109. *E-mail:* vsearcy@isothermal.edu. *Website:* http://www.isothermal.edu/.

James Sprunt Community College
Kenansville, North Carolina

- **State-supported** 2-year, founded 1964, part of North Carolina Community College System
- **Rural** 51-acre campus with easy access to Raleigh, Wilmington
- **Endowment** $1.3 million
- **Coed**

Undergraduates 424 full-time, 795 part-time. Students come from 3 states and territories; 1% are from out of state; 28% Black or African American, non-Hispanic/Latino; 21% Hispanic/Latino; 0.3% Asian, non-Hispanic/Latino; 0.1% Native Hawaiian or other Pacific Islander, non-Hispanic/Latino; 0.4% American Indian or Alaska Native, non-Hispanic/Latino; 2% Two or more races, non-Hispanic/Latino; 2% Race/ethnicity unknown; 0.3% international; 6% transferred in.
Faculty *Student/faculty ratio:* 10:1.
Academics *Calendar:* semesters. *Degree:* certificates, diplomas, and associate. *Special study options:* academic remediation for entering students, accelerated degree program, advanced placement credit, cooperative education, distance learning, double majors, English as a second language, independent study, internships, part-time degree program, services for LD students, summer session for credit.
Library James Sprunt Community College Library. *Books:* 24,762 (physical), 197,656 (digital/electronic); *Serial titles:* 58 (physical), 24,281 (digital/electronic); *Databases:* 92. Weekly public service hours: 46.
Student Life *Campus security:* day, evening, and Saturday trained security personnel.
Financial Aid Of all full-time matriculated undergraduates who enrolled in 2017, 35 Federal Work-Study jobs (averaging $1057).
Applying *Options:* electronic application. *Required:* high school transcript.
Freshman Application Contact Ms. Wanda Edwards, Admissions Specialist, James Sprunt Community College, PO Box 398, 133 James Sprunt Drive, Kenansville, NC 28349. *Phone:* 910-275-6364. *Fax:* 910-296-1222. *E-mail:* wedwards@jamessprunt.edu. *Website:* http://www.jamessprunt.edu/.

Johnston Community College
Smithfield, North Carolina

- **State-supported** 2-year, founded 1969, part of North Carolina Community College System
- **Rural** 100-acre campus
- **Endowment** $6.4 million
- **Coed,** 4,152 undergraduate students, 37% full-time, 64% women, 36% men

Undergraduates 1,546 full-time, 2,606 part-time. 13% Black or African American, non-Hispanic/Latino; 14% Hispanic/Latino; 0.7% Asian, non-Hispanic/Latino; 0.1% Native Hawaiian or other Pacific Islander, non-Hispanic/Latino; 0.6% American Indian or Alaska Native, non-Hispanic/Latino; 2% Two or more races, non-Hispanic/Latino; 7% Race/ethnicity unknown; 1% international.
Freshmen *Admission:* 589 enrolled.
Faculty *Total:* 285, 40% full-time, 6% with terminal degrees.
Majors Accounting; administrative assistant and secretarial science; business administration and management; criminal justice/police science; diesel mechanics technology; early childhood education; heating, air conditioning, ventilation and refrigeration maintenance technology; legal assistant/paralegal; liberal arts and sciences/liberal studies; medical/clinical assistant; medical office management; office management; pre-engineering; registered nursing/registered nurse.
Academics *Calendar:* semesters. *Degree:* certificates, diplomas, and associate. *Special study options:* academic remediation for entering students, adult/continuing education programs, advanced placement credit, cooperative education, distance learning, double majors, honors programs, independent study, part-time degree program, services for LD students, summer session for credit.
Library Johnston Community College Library plus 1 other. *Books:* 27,174 (physical), 202,576 (digital/electronic); *Serial titles:* 64 (physical), 23,465 (digital/electronic); *Databases:* 131. Weekly public service hours: 57; students can reserve study rooms.
Student Life *Housing:* college housing not available. *Campus security:* 24-hour patrols. *Student services:* personal/psychological counseling.
Athletics Member NJCAA. *Intercollegiate sports:* basketball M/W.
Standardized Tests *Required:* NC DAP (for admission). *Recommended:* SAT or ACT (for admission).
Financial Aid Of all full-time matriculated undergraduates who enrolled in 2017, 35 Federal Work-Study jobs (averaging $1853).
Applying *Options:* electronic application. *Required:* high school transcript, interview. *Application deadlines:* rolling (freshmen), rolling (transfers). *Notification:* continuous (freshmen), continuous (transfers).
Freshman Application Contact Megan L. Shaner, Director of Enrollment Management & Retention, Johnston Community College, 245 College Road, PO Box 2350, Smithfield, NC 27577. *Phone:* 919-209-2201. *Fax:* 919-989-7862. *E-mail:* mlshaner@johnstoncc.edu.
Website: http://www.johnstoncc.edu/.

Lenoir Community College
Kinston, North Carolina

- **State-supported** 2-year, founded 1960, part of North Carolina Community College System
- **Small-town** 86-acre campus
- **Coed**

Undergraduates 1,013 full-time, 1,651 part-time. Students come from 27 states and territories; 1 other country; 3% are from out of state; 34% Black or African American, non-Hispanic/Latino; 8% Hispanic/Latino; 0.6% Asian, non-Hispanic/Latino; 0.1% Native Hawaiian or other Pacific Islander, non-Hispanic/Latino; 0.6% American Indian or Alaska Native, non-Hispanic/Latino; 1% Two or more races, non-Hispanic/Latino; 0.1% international; 7% transferred in.
Faculty *Student/faculty ratio:* 15:1.
Academics *Calendar:* semesters. *Degree:* certificates, diplomas, and associate. *Special study options:* academic remediation for entering students, adult/continuing education programs, advanced placement credit, cooperative education, distance learning, double majors, English as a second language, independent study, part-time degree program, summer session for credit.
Library Learning Resources Center plus 1 other. *Books:* 26,338 (physical), 370,363 (digital/electronic); *Serial titles:* 22 (physical), 135,249 (digital/electronic); *Databases:* 139. Students can reserve study rooms.

Student Life *Campus security:* 24-hour emergency response devices and patrols, student patrols.
Athletics Member NJCAA.
Standardized Tests *Recommended:* SAT or ACT (for admission).
Applying *Options:* electronic application, early admission. *Required:* high school transcript.
Freshman Application Contact Mrs. Kim Hill, Director of Admissions, Lenoir Community College, 231 Highway 58 South, Kinston, NC 28502-0188. *Phone:* 252-527-6223 Ext. 301. *Fax:* 252-233-6895. *E-mail:* krhill01@lenoircc.edu. *Website:* http://www.lenoircc.edu/.

Louisburg College

Louisburg, North Carolina

Freshman Application Contact Ms. Stephanie Tolbert, Vice President for Enrollment Management, Louisburg College, 501 North Main Street, Louisburg, NC 27549-2399. *Phone:* 919-497-3233. *Toll-free phone:* 800-775-0208. *Fax:* 919-496-1788. *E-mail:* admissions@louisburg.edu. *Website:* http://www.louisburg.edu/.

Martin Community College

Williamston, North Carolina

Freshman Application Contact Martin Community College, 1161 Kehukee Park Road, Williamston, NC 27892. *Phone:* 252-792-1521 Ext. 244. *Website:* http://www.martincc.edu/.

Mayland Community College

Spruce Pine, North Carolina

Director of Admissions Ms. Cathy Morrison, Director of Admissions, Mayland Community College, PO Box 547, Spruce Pine, NC 28777-0547. *Phone:* 828-765-7351 Ext. 224. *Toll-free phone:* 800-462-9526. *Website:* http://www.mayland.edu/.

McDowell Technical Community College

Marion, North Carolina

Freshman Application Contact Mr. Rick L. Wilson, Director of Admissions, McDowell Technical Community College, 54 College Drive, Marion, NC 28752. *Phone:* 828-652-0632. *Fax:* 828-652-1014. *E-mail:* rickw@mcdowelltech.edu. *Website:* http://www.mcdowelltech.edu/.

Miller-Motte College

Cary, North Carolina

Admissions Office Contact Miller-Motte College, 2205 Walnut Street, Cary, NC 27518. *Toll-free phone:* 800-705-9182. *Website:* http://www.miller-motte.edu/.

Miller-Motte College

Fayetteville, North Carolina

Admissions Office Contact Miller-Motte College, 3725 Ramsey Street, Fayetteville, NC 28311. *Toll-free phone:* 800-705-9182. *Website:* http://www.miller-motte.edu/.

Miller-Motte College

Jacksonville, North Carolina

Admissions Office Contact Miller-Motte College, 1291 Hargett Street, Jacksonville, NC 28540. *Toll-free phone:* 800-705-9182. *Website:* http://www.miller-motte.edu/.

Miller-Motte College

Raleigh, North Carolina

Admissions Office Contact Miller-Motte College, 3901 Capital Boulevard, Suite 151, Raleigh, NC 27604. *Toll-free phone:* 800-705-9182. *Website:* http://www.miller-motte.edu/.

Miller-Motte College

Wilmington, North Carolina

Freshman Application Contact Admissions Office, Miller-Motte College, 5000 Market Street, Wilmington, NC 28405. *Toll-free phone:* 800-705-9182. *Website:* http://www.miller-motte.edu/.

Mitchell Community College

Statesville, North Carolina

- **State-supported** 2-year, founded 1852, part of North Carolina Community College System
- **Small-town** 14-acre campus with easy access to Charlotte
- **Endowment** $18.4 million
- **Coed,** 3,164 undergraduate students, 31% full-time, 60% women, 40% men

Undergraduates 974 full-time, 2,190 part-time. 11% Black or African American, non-Hispanic/Latino; 11% Hispanic/Latino; 2% Asian, non-Hispanic/Latino; 0.1% Native Hawaiian or other Pacific Islander, non-Hispanic/Latino; 0.4% American Indian or Alaska Native, non-Hispanic/Latino; 2% Two or more races, non-Hispanic/Latino; 1% Race/ethnicity unknown; 0.9% international; 6% transferred in. *Retention:* 51% of full-time freshmen returned.
Freshmen *Admission:* 1,679 applied, 1,679 admitted, 398 enrolled.
Faculty *Total:* 170, 51% full-time. *Student/faculty ratio:* 18:1.
Majors Accounting; agribusiness; business administration and management; child-care and support services management; computer programming; computer programming (specific applications); computer systems analysis; cooking and related culinary arts; criminal justice/law enforcement administration; early childhood education; electrical, electronic and communications engineering technology; electrician; electromechanical and instrumentation and maintenance technologies related; elementary education; engineering/industrial management; executive assistant/executive secretary; general studies; health professions related; information science/studies; information technology; kindergarten/preschool education; liberal arts and sciences and humanities related; liberal arts and sciences/liberal studies; machine shop technology; manufacturing engineering technology; mechanical drafting and CAD/CADD; mechanical engineering/mechanical technology; mechatronics, robotics, and automation engineering; medical/clinical assistant; office management; operations management; registered nursing/registered nurse; special education–early childhood; teacher assistant/aide.
Academics *Calendar:* semesters. *Degree:* certificates, diplomas, and associate. *Special study options:* academic remediation for entering students, adult/continuing education programs, advanced placement credit, cooperative education, distance learning, English as a second language, part-time degree program, services for LD students, summer session for credit.
Library Huskins Library. *Books:* 14,669 (physical), 203,337 (digital/electronic); *Serial titles:* 2 (physical), 23,468 (digital/electronic); *Databases:* 93. Students can reserve study rooms.
Student Life *Housing:* college housing not available. *Activities and Organizations:* choral group, Cosmetology Club, Early Childhood Association, Student Nurses Association, Phi Theta Kappa, Student Government Association. *Campus security:* late-night transport/escort service, day and evening security guards. *Student services:* personal/psychological counseling, veterans affairs office.
Financial Aid Of all full-time matriculated undergraduates who enrolled in 2017, 30 Federal Work-Study jobs.
Applying *Options:* electronic application. *Required:* high school transcript. *Application deadlines:* rolling (freshmen), rolling (transfers). *Notification:* continuous (freshmen), continuous (transfers).
Director of Admissions Porter Brannon, Dean of Student Services, Mitchell Community College, 500 West Broad Street, Statesville, NC 28677. *Phone:* 704-878-3281.
Website: http://www.mitchellcc.edu/.

Montgomery Community College

Troy, North Carolina

- **State-supported** 2-year, founded 1967, part of North Carolina Community College System
- **Rural** 159-acre campus
- **Coed**

Undergraduates 314 full-time, 611 part-time. Students come from 11 states and territories; 1% are from out of state; 18% Black or African American, non-Hispanic/Latino; 17% Hispanic/Latino; 2% Asian, non-Hispanic/Latino; 0.1% Native Hawaiian or other Pacific Islander, non-Hispanic/Latino; 1% American Indian or Alaska Native, non-Hispanic/Latino; 2% Two or more races, non-Hispanic/Latino; 0.2% Race/ethnicity unknown; 0.3% international. *Retention:* 70% of full-time freshmen returned.

Faculty *Student/faculty ratio:* 8:1.
Academics *Calendar:* semesters. *Degree:* certificates, diplomas, and associate. *Special study options:* academic remediation for entering students, advanced placement credit, distance learning, English as a second language, part-time degree program, services for LD students, summer session for credit.
Library Montgomery Community College Learning Resource Center. *Books:* 17,572 (physical), 197,546 (digital/electronic); *Serial titles:* 55 (physical), 24,280 (digital/electronic); *Databases:* 104. Weekly public service hours: 55; students can reserve study rooms.
Student Life *Campus security:* 24-hour emergency response devices.
Financial Aid Of all full-time matriculated undergraduates who enrolled in 2017, 24 Federal Work-Study jobs (averaging $500).
Applying *Options:* electronic application, early admission, deferred entrance. *Required:* high school transcript.
Admissions Office Contact Montgomery Community College, 1011 Page Street, Troy, NC 27371. *Toll-free phone:* 877-572-6222. *Website:* http://www.montgomery.edu/.

Nash Community College
Rocky Mount, North Carolina

Freshman Application Contact Ms. Dorothy Gardner, Admissions Officer, Nash Community College, PO Box 7488, Rocky Mount, NC 27804. *Phone:* 252-451-8300. *E-mail:* dgardner@nashcc.edu. *Website:* http://www.nashcc.edu/.

Pamlico Community College
Grantsboro, North Carolina

Director of Admissions Mr. Floyd H. Hardison, Admissions Counselor, Pamlico Community College, PO Box 185, Grantsboro, NC 28529-0185. *Phone:* 252-249-1851 Ext. 28. *Website:* http://www.pamlicocc.edu/.

Piedmont Community College
Roxboro, North Carolina

- **State-supported** 2-year, founded 1970, part of North Carolina Community College System
- **Small-town** 178-acre campus
- **Coed**

Undergraduates 403 full-time, 908 part-time.
Faculty *Student/faculty ratio:* 12:1.
Academics *Calendar:* semesters. *Degree:* certificates, diplomas, and associate. *Special study options:* academic remediation for entering students, adult/continuing education programs, advanced placement credit, cooperative education, distance learning, double majors, English as a second language, off-campus study, part-time degree program, summer session for credit.
Library Learning Resource Center.
Student Life *Campus security:* routine patrols by the local sheriff department.
Applying *Options:* electronic application, early admission, deferred entrance. *Required for some:* high school transcript.
Freshman Application Contact Piedmont Community College, PO Box 1197, Roxboro, NC 27573-1197. *Phone:* 336-599-1181. *Website:* http://www.piedmontcc.edu/.

Pitt Community College
Winterville, North Carolina

Freshman Application Contact Dr. Kimberly Williamson, Interim Coordinator of Counseling, Pitt Community College, PO Drawer 7007, Greenville, NC 27835-7007. *Phone:* 252-493-7217. *Fax:* 252-321-4612. *E-mail:* pittadm@pcc.pitt.cc.nc.us. *Website:* http://www.pittcc.edu/.

Randolph Community College
Asheboro, North Carolina

- **State-supported** 2-year, founded 1962, part of North Carolina Community College System
- **Small-town** 44-acre campus with easy access to Greensboro, Winston-Salem, High Point
- **Endowment** $11.6 million
- **Coed**

Undergraduates 914 full-time, 1,733 part-time. Students come from 2 states and territories; 5% Black or African American, non-Hispanic/Latino; 10% Hispanic/Latino; 0.8% Asian, non-Hispanic/Latino; 0.1% Native Hawaiian or other Pacific Islander, non-Hispanic/Latino; 0.5% American Indian or Alaska Native, non-Hispanic/Latino; 0.8% Two or more races, non-Hispanic/Latino; 23% Race/ethnicity unknown; 0.4% international; 2% transferred in.
Faculty *Student/faculty ratio:* 10:1.
Academics *Calendar:* semesters. *Degree:* certificates, diplomas, and associate. *Special study options:* academic remediation for entering students, adult/continuing education programs, advanced placement credit, cooperative education, distance learning, double majors, English as a second language, independent study, internships, off-campus study, part-time degree program, services for LD students, summer session for credit. *ROTC:* Air Force (c).
Library R. Alton Cox Learning Resources Center. *Books:* 25,000 (physical).
Student Life *Campus security:* 24-hour emergency response devices, security officer during hours of operation.
Applying *Options:* electronic application, deferred entrance.
Freshman Application Contact Ms. Hillary D Pritchard, Director of Admissions, Records and Registration, Randolph Community College, 629 Industrial Park Avenue, Asheboro, NC 27205-7333. *Phone:* 336-633-0122. *Fax:* 336-629-9547. *E-mail:* hdpritchard@randolph.edu. *Website:* http://www.randolph.edu/.

Richmond Community College
Hamlet, North Carolina

- **State-supported** 2-year, founded 1964, part of North Carolina Community College System
- **Rural** 163-acre campus
- **Coed,** 2,555 undergraduate students, 41% full-time, 64% women, 36% men

Undergraduates 1,056 full-time, 1,499 part-time. 0.5% are from out of state; 22% Black or African American, non-Hispanic/Latino; 5% Hispanic/Latino; 1% Asian, non-Hispanic/Latino; 0.1% Native Hawaiian or other Pacific Islander, non-Hispanic/Latino; 8% American Indian or Alaska Native, non-Hispanic/Latino; 2% Two or more races, non-Hispanic/Latino; 28% Race/ethnicity unknown; 0.4% international.
Freshmen *Admission:* 334 enrolled.
Faculty *Student/faculty ratio:* 15:1.
Majors Accounting and finance; business administration and management; computer engineering technology; criminal justice/safety; early childhood education; electrical and power transmission installation; electrical, electronic and communications engineering technology; electromechanical and instrumentation and maintenance technologies related; electromechanical technology; health information/medical records technology; heating, air conditioning, ventilation and refrigeration maintenance technology; information technology; liberal arts and sciences/liberal studies; mechanical engineering/mechanical technology; medical/clinical assistant; medical office management; mental and social health services and allied professions related; office management; pre-engineering; registered nursing/registered nurse; substance abuse/addiction counseling.
Academics *Calendar:* semesters. *Degree:* certificates, diplomas, and associate. *Special study options:* academic remediation for entering students, adult/continuing education programs, advanced placement credit, cooperative education, distance learning, double majors, English as a second language, independent study, internships, part-time degree program, student-designed majors, summer session for credit.
Library Richmond Community College Library.
Student Life *Housing:* college housing not available. *Activities and Organizations:* choral group. *Campus security:* 24-hour emergency response devices. *Student services:* personal/psychological counseling.
Financial Aid Of all full-time matriculated undergraduates who enrolled in 2017, 35 Federal Work-Study jobs (averaging $2000).
Applying *Options:* electronic application, deferred entrance. *Required:* high school transcript. *Application deadlines:* rolling (freshmen), rolling (transfers). *Notification:* continuous (freshmen), continuous (transfers).
Freshman Application Contact Cayce Holmes, Registrar, Richmond Community College, PO Box 1189, 1042 W. Hamlet Avenue, Hamlet, NC 28345. *Phone:* 910-410-1737. *Fax:* 910-582-7102. *E-mail:* ccholmes@richmondcc.edu.
Website: http://www.richmondcc.edu/.

Roanoke-Chowan Community College
Ahoskie, North Carolina

Director of Admissions Miss Sandra Copeland, Director, Counseling Services, Roanoke-Chowan Community College, 109 Community College Road, Ahoskie, NC 27910. *Phone:* 252-862-1225. *Website:* http://www.roanokechowan.edu/.

Robeson Community College
Lumberton, North Carolina

Freshman Application Contact Ms. Patricia Locklear, College Recruiter, Robeson Community College, PO Box 1420, Lumberton, NC 28359. *Phone:* 910-272-3356 Ext. 251. *Fax:* 910-618-5686. *E-mail:* plocklear@robeson.edu. *Website:* http://www.robeson.edu/.

Rockingham Community College
Wentworth, North Carolina

Freshman Application Contact Mr. Derrick Satterfield, Director of Enrollment Services, Rockingham Community College, PO Box 38, Wentworth, NC 27375-0038. *Phone:* 336-342-4261 Ext. 2114. *Fax:* 336-342-1809. *E-mail:* admissions@rockinghamcc.edu. *Website:* http://www.rockinghamcc.edu/.

Rowan-Cabarrus Community College
Salisbury, North Carolina

- **State-supported** 2-year, founded 1963, part of North Carolina Community College System
- **Small-town** 100-acre campus with easy access to Charlotte
- **Coed**

Undergraduates Students come from 11 states and territories; 1% are from out of state; 19% Black or African American, non-Hispanic/Latino; 10% Hispanic/Latino; 2% Asian, non-Hispanic/Latino; 0.1% Native Hawaiian or other Pacific Islander, non-Hispanic/Latino; 0.5% American Indian or Alaska Native, non-Hispanic/Latino; 3% Two or more races, non-Hispanic/Latino; 1% Race/ethnicity unknown; 1% international.
Faculty *Student/faculty ratio:* 15:1.
Academics *Calendar:* semesters. *Degree:* certificates, diplomas, and associate. *Special study options:* academic remediation for entering students, adult/continuing education programs, advanced placement credit, cooperative education, distance learning, English as a second language, internships, part-time degree program, services for LD students, summer session for credit.
Library Learning Resource Center. Students can reserve study rooms.
Student Life *Campus security:* on-campus security during hours of operation.
Applying *Required:* high school transcript.
Freshman Application Contact Rowan-Cabarrus Community College, 1333 Jake Alexander Boulevard South, Salisbury, NC 28146. *Website:* http://www.rccc.edu/.

Sampson Community College
Clinton, North Carolina

Director of Admissions Mr. William R. Jordan, Director of Admissions, Sampson Community College, PO Box 318, 1801 Sunset Avenue, Highway 24 West, Clinton, NC 28329-0318. *Phone:* 910-592-8084 Ext. 2022. *Website:* http://www.sampsoncc.edu/.

Sandhills Community College
Pinehurst, North Carolina

Freshman Application Contact Mr. Isai Robledo, Recruiter, Sandhills Community College, 3395 Airport Road, Pinehurst, NC 28374-8299. *Phone:* 910-246-5365. *Toll-free phone:* 800-338-3944. *Fax:* 910-695-3981. *E-mail:* robledoi@sandhills.edu. *Website:* http://www.sandhills.edu/.

Southeastern Community College
Whiteville, North Carolina

Freshman Application Contact Ms. Sylvia McQueen, Registrar, Southeastern Community College, PO Box 151, Whiteville, NC 28472. *Phone:* 910-642-7141 Ext. 249. *Fax:* 910-642-5658. *Website:* http://www.sccnc.edu/.

South Piedmont Community College
Polkton, North Carolina

Freshman Application Contact Ms. Amanda Secrest, Assistant Director Admissions and Testing, South Piedmont Community College, PO Box 126, Polkton, NC 28135. *Phone:* 704-290-5847. *Toll-free phone:* 800-766-0319. *E-mail:* asecrest@spcc.edu. *Website:* http://www.spcc.edu/.

Southwestern Community College
Sylva, North Carolina

- **State-supported** 2-year, founded 1964, part of North Carolina Community College System
- **Small-town** 77-acre campus
- **Coed,** 2,353 undergraduate students, 35% full-time, 60% women, 40% men

Undergraduates 816 full-time, 1,537 part-time. 2% Black or African American, non-Hispanic/Latino; 9% Hispanic/Latino; 1% Asian, non-Hispanic/Latino; 8% American Indian or Alaska Native, non-Hispanic/Latino; 2% Two or more races, non-Hispanic/Latino; 0.9% Race/ethnicity unknown; 0.8% international.
Freshmen *Admission:* 240 enrolled.
Faculty *Student/faculty ratio:* 16:1.
Majors Accounting; automobile/automotive mechanics technology; business administration and management; child development; clinical/medical laboratory technology; commercial and advertising art; computer engineering technology; cosmetology; criminal justice/police science; culinary arts; electrical, electronic and communications engineering technology; emergency medical technology (EMT paramedic); health information/medical records administration; health information/medical records technology; information science/studies; legal assistant/paralegal; liberal arts and sciences/liberal studies; massage therapy; mechatronics, robotics, and automation engineering; medical office management; medical radiologic technology; mental health counseling; occupational therapist assistant; office management; parks, recreation, leisure, and fitness studies related; physical therapy technology; registered nursing/registered nurse; respiratory care therapy; substance abuse/addiction counseling; system, networking, and LAN/WAN management; trade and industrial teacher education.
Academics *Calendar:* semesters. *Degree:* certificates, diplomas, and associate. *Special study options:* academic remediation for entering students, adult/continuing education programs, advanced placement credit, cooperative education, distance learning, double majors, English as a second language, honors programs, independent study, off-campus study, part-time degree program, services for LD students, summer session for credit.
Library Holt Library.
Student Life *Housing:* college housing not available. *Campus security:* security during hours of operation. *Student services:* personal/psychological counseling, veterans affairs office.
Applying *Required:* high school transcript. *Required for some:* minimum 2.5 GPA, interview.
Freshman Application Contact Mark Ellison, Director of Enrollment Management, Southwestern Community College, 447 College Drive, Sylva, NC 28779. *Phone:* 828-339-4229. *Toll-free phone:* 800-447-4091 (in-state); 800-447-7091 (out-of-state). *E-mail:* m_ellison@southwesterncc.edu. *Website:* http://www.southwesterncc.edu/.

Stanly Community College
Albemarle, North Carolina

Freshman Application Contact Mrs. Denise B. Ross, Associate Dean, Admissions, Stanly Community College, 141 College Drive, Albemarle, NC 28001. *Phone:* 704-982-0121 Ext. 264. *Fax:* 704-982-0255. *E-mail:* dross7926@stanly.edu. *Website:* http://www.stanly.edu/.

Surry Community College
Dobson, North Carolina

Freshman Application Contact Renita Hazelwood, Director of Admissions, Surry Community College, 630 South Main Street, Dobson, NC 27017. *Phone:* 336-386-3392. *Fax:* 336-386-3690. *E-mail:* hazelwoodr@surry.edu. *Website:* http://www.surry.edu/.

Tri-County Community College
Murphy, North Carolina

- **State-supported** 2-year, founded 1964, part of North Carolina Community College System
- **Rural** 40-acre campus
- **Coed**

Faculty *Student/faculty ratio:* 21:1.
Academics *Calendar:* semesters. *Degree:* certificates, diplomas, and associate. *Special study options:* academic remediation for entering students, adult/continuing education programs, distance learning, double majors, internships, part-time degree program, study abroad, summer session for credit.

Standardized Tests *Recommended:* SAT and SAT Subject Tests or ACT (for admission).
Financial Aid Of all full-time matriculated undergraduates who enrolled in 2017, 11 Federal Work-Study jobs.
Applying *Options:* electronic application. *Required:* high school transcript.
Freshman Application Contact Mrs. Samantha Jones, First Year Success Coach and Retention Specialist, Tri-County Community College, 21 Campus Circle, Murphy, NC 28906-7919. *Phone:* 828-837-6810. *Fax:* 828-837-3266. *E-mail:* sjones@tricountycc.edu. *Website:* http://www.tricountycc.edu/.

Vance-Granville Community College

Henderson, North Carolina

Freshman Application Contact Ms. Kathy Kutl, Admissions Officer, Vance-Granville Community College, PO Box 917, State Road 1126, Henderson, NC 27536. *Phone:* 252-492-2061 Ext. 3265. *Fax:* 252-430-0460. *Website:* http://www.vgcc.edu/.

Wake Technical Community College

Raleigh, North Carolina

Director of Admissions Ms. Susan Bloomfield, Director of Admissions, Wake Technical Community College, 9101 Fayetteville Road, Raleigh, NC 27603-5696. *Phone:* 919-866-5452. *E-mail:* srbloomfield@waketech.edu. *Website:* http://www.waketech.edu/.

Wayne Community College

Goldsboro, North Carolina

- **State and locally supported** 2-year, founded 1957, part of North Carolina Community College System
- **Small-town** 175-acre campus with easy access to Raleigh
- **Endowment** $92,408
- **Coed**

Undergraduates 1,813 full-time, 2,024 part-time. 4% are from out of state; 27% Black or African American, non-Hispanic/Latino; 8% Hispanic/Latino; 2% Asian, non-Hispanic/Latino; 0.3% Native Hawaiian or other Pacific Islander, non-Hispanic/Latino; 0.6% American Indian or Alaska Native, non-Hispanic/Latino; 0.8% Two or more races, non-Hispanic/Latino; 2% Race/ethnicity unknown; 0.3% international; 26% transferred in.
Faculty *Student/faculty ratio:* 20:1.
Academics *Calendar:* semesters. *Degree:* certificates, diplomas, and associate. *Special study options:* academic remediation for entering students, adult/continuing education programs, advanced placement credit, cooperative education, distance learning, double majors, English as a second language, external degree program, honors programs, part-time degree program, services for LD students, summer session for credit.
Library Dr. Clyde A. Erwin, Jr. Library.
Student Life *Campus security:* 24-hour emergency response devices and patrols.
Standardized Tests *Required for some:* SAT or ACT (for admission).
Financial Aid Of all full-time matriculated undergraduates who enrolled in 2017, 100 Federal Work-Study jobs (averaging $2000).
Applying *Options:* electronic application. *Required:* high school transcript, interview.
Freshman Application Contact Mrs. Lea Matthews, Associate Director of Admissions and Records, Wayne Community College, PO Box 8002, Goldsboro, NC 27533. *Phone:* 919-735-5151 Ext. 6717. *Fax:* 919-736-9425. *E-mail:* rlmatthews@waynecc.edu. *Website:* http://www.waynecc.edu/.

Western Piedmont Community College

Morganton, North Carolina

Freshman Application Contact Susan Williams, Director of Admissions, Western Piedmont Community College, 1001 Burkemont Avenue, Morganton, NC 28655-4511. *Phone:* 828-438-6051. *Fax:* 828-438-6065. *E-mail:* swilliams@wpcc.edu. *Website:* http://www.wpcc.edu/.

Wilkes Community College

Wilkesboro, North Carolina

Freshman Application Contact Mr. Mac Warren, Director of Admissions, Wilkes Community College, PO Box 120, Wilkesboro, NC 28697. *Phone:* 336-838-6141. *Fax:* 336-838-6547. *E-mail:* mac.warren@wilkescc.edu. *Website:* http://www.wilkescc.edu/.

Wilson Community College

Wilson, North Carolina

Freshman Application Contact Mrs. Maegan Williams, Admissions Technician, Wilson Community College, Wilson, NC 27893-0305. *Phone:* 252-246-1275. *Fax:* 252-243-7148. *E-mail:* mwilliams@wilsoncc.edu. *Website:* http://www.wilsoncc.edu/.

NORTH DAKOTA

Bismarck State College

Bismarck, North Dakota

Freshman Application Contact Karen Erickson, Director of Admissions and Enrollment Services, Bismarck State College, PO Box 5587, Bismarck, ND 58506. *Phone:* 701-224-5424. *Toll-free phone:* 800-445-5073. *Fax:* 701-224-5643. *E-mail:* karen.erickson@bismarckstate.edu. *Website:* http://www.bismarckstate.edu/.

Cankdeska Cikana Community College

Fort Totten, North Dakota

Director of Admissions DeShawn Lawrence, Registrar, Cankdeska Cikana Community College, PO Box 269, Fort Totten, ND 58335-0269. *Phone:* 701-766-1342. *Toll-free phone:* 888-783-1463. *Website:* http://www.littlehoop.edu/.

Dakota College at Bottineau

Bottineau, North Dakota

- **State-supported** 2-year, founded 1906, part of North Dakota University System
- **Rural** 35-acre campus
- **Coed,** 996 undergraduate students

Undergraduates 9% Black or African American, non-Hispanic/Latino; 5% Hispanic/Latino; 0.3% Asian, non-Hispanic/Latino; 0.1% Native Hawaiian or other Pacific Islander, non-Hispanic/Latino; 4% American Indian or Alaska Native, non-Hispanic/Latino; 5% Two or more races, non-Hispanic/Latino; 5% Race/ethnicity unknown.
Faculty *Student/faculty ratio:* 8:1.
Majors Accounting; accounting related; accounting technology and bookkeeping; administrative assistant and secretarial science; adult development and aging; advertising; agriculture; applied horticulture/horticultural business services related; applied horticulture/horticulture operations; biology/biological sciences; business administration and management; business automation/technology/data entry; chemistry; child-care and support services management; child-care provision; computer and information sciences; computer and information sciences and support services related; computer software and media applications related; computer technology/computer systems technology; crop production; education; entrepreneurial and small business related; environmental engineering technology; executive assistant/executive secretary; floriculture/floristry management; general studies; greenhouse management; health and physical education/fitness; health services/allied health/health sciences; history; horticultural science; hospitality and recreation marketing; information science/studies; information technology; landscaping and groundskeeping; land use planning and management; liberal arts and sciences and humanities related; liberal arts and sciences/liberal studies; licensed practical/vocational nurse training; marketing/marketing management; marketing related; mathematics; medical administrative assistant and medical secretary; medical/clinical assistant; medical insurance coding; medical office assistant; natural resources/conservation; network and system administration; office management; office occupations and clerical services; ornamental horticulture; parks, recreation and leisure; parks, recreation and leisure facilities management; parks, recreation, leisure, and fitness studies related; photography; physical sciences; physical sciences related; premedical studies; prenursing studies; pre-veterinary studies; psychology; receptionist; registered nursing/registered nurse; science technologies related; small business administration; social sciences; teacher assistant/aide; urban forestry; wildlife, fish and wildlands science and management; zoology/animal biology.
Academics *Calendar:* semesters. *Degree:* certificates, diplomas, and associate. *Special study options:* academic remediation for entering students, advanced placement credit, cooperative education, distance learning, double majors, off-campus study, part-time degree program, services for LD students, summer session for credit.
Library Dakota College at Bottineau Library plus 1 other.

Student Life *Housing:* on-campus residence required through sophomore year. *Options:* men-only, women-only. Campus housing is university owned. Freshman campus housing is guaranteed. *Activities and Organizations:* drama/theater group, Intramurals, LeaderJacks, Student Senate, LumberActs, Phi Theta Kappa. *Campus security:* controlled dormitory access, security cameras, night security personnel. *Student services:* health clinic, personal/psychological counseling.
Athletics Member NJCAA. *Intercollegiate sports:* basketball W(s), softball W(s), volleyball W(s). *Intramural sports:* badminton M, basketball M, skiing (downhill) M, table tennis M, volleyball M, weight lifting M.
Financial Aid Of all full-time matriculated undergraduates who enrolled in 2015, 296 applied for aid, 246 were judged to have need, 62 had their need fully met. 65 Federal Work-Study jobs (averaging $668). In 2015, 26 non-need-based awards were made. *Average percent of need met:* 70%. *Average financial aid package:* $10,004. *Average need-based loan:* $5400. *Average need-based gift aid:* $5196. *Average non-need-based aid:* $2012. *Average indebtedness upon graduation:* $12,305.
Applying *Options:* electronic application, early admission, deferred entrance. *Application fee:* $35. *Required:* high school transcript, immunization records, previous college official transcripts. *Application deadlines:* rolling (freshmen), rolling (transfers).
Freshman Application Contact Mrs. Heidi Hauf, Admissions Clerk, Dakota College at Bottineau, 105 Simrall Boulevard, Bottineau, ND 58318. *Phone:* 701-228-5487. *Toll-free phone:* 800-542-6866. *Fax:* 701-228-5499. *E-mail:* heidi.hauf@dakotacollege.edu.
Website: http://www.dakotacollege.edu/.

Lake Region State College

Devils Lake, North Dakota

- **State-supported** 2-year, founded 1941, part of North Dakota University System
- **Small-town** 120-acre campus
- **Coed**, 2,072 undergraduate students, 26% full-time, 57% women, 43% men

Undergraduates 538 full-time, 1,534 part-time. Students come from 41 states and territories; 16 other countries; 15% are from out of state; 4% Black or African American, non-Hispanic/Latino; 6% Hispanic/Latino; 0.6% Asian, non-Hispanic/Latino; 0.4% Native Hawaiian or other Pacific Islander, non-Hispanic/Latino; 3% American Indian or Alaska Native, non-Hispanic/Latino; 6% Two or more races, non-Hispanic/Latino; 2% Race/ethnicity unknown; 5% international; 4% transferred in; 12% live on campus. *Retention:* 61% of full-time freshmen returned.
Freshmen *Admission:* 205 enrolled.
Faculty *Total:* 101, 45% full-time, 4% with terminal degrees.
Majors Agricultural business and management; automobile/automotive mechanics technology; business administration and management; child-care provision; computer installation and repair technology; criminal justice/police science; electrical and electronic engineering technologies related; language interpretation and translation; liberal arts and sciences/liberal studies; management information systems; merchandising, sales, and marketing operations related (general); physical fitness technician; registered nursing/registered nurse; speech-language pathology.
Academics *Calendar:* semesters. *Degree:* certificates, diplomas, and associate. *Special study options:* academic remediation for entering students, cooperative education, distance learning, double majors, English as a second language, honors programs, internships, off-campus study, part-time degree program, services for LD students, summer session for credit.
Library Paul Hoghaug Library. *Books:* 11,536 (physical), 75,983 (digital/electronic); *Databases:* 67. Students can reserve study rooms.
Student Life *Housing Options:* coed, men-only, women-only. Campus housing is university owned. *Activities and Organizations:* drama/theater group, Student Senate, Phi Theta Kappa, Delta Epsilon Chi, Phi Theta Lambda, Student Nurse Organization. *Campus security:* 24-hour emergency response devices, controlled dormitory access. *Student services:* personal/psychological counseling.
Athletics Member NJCAA. *Intercollegiate sports:* basketball W(s), softball W(s), volleyball W(s). *Intramural sports:* basketball M, riflery M(c), soccer M, volleyball M, weight lifting M.
Financial Aid Of all full-time matriculated undergraduates who enrolled in 2017, 371 applied for aid, 294 were judged to have need, 109 had their need fully met. In 2017, 105 non-need-based awards were made. *Average percent of need met:* 77%. *Average financial aid package:* $9828. *Average need-based loan:* $5912. *Average need-based gift aid:* $5599. *Average non-need-based aid:* $1062. *Average indebtedness upon graduation:* $15,163.
Applying *Options:* electronic application. *Application fee:* $35. *Required for some:* high school transcript, immunization records, college transcripts. *Application deadlines:* rolling (freshmen), rolling (transfers). *Notification:* continuous (freshmen), continuous (transfers).
Freshman Application Contact Merissa Halvorson, Admissions Associate, Lake Region State College, 1801 College Drive North, Devils Lake, ND 58301. *Phone:* 701-662-1519. *Toll-free phone:* 800-443-1313. *Fax:* 701-662-1581. *E-mail:* merissa.halvorson@lrsc.edu.
Website: http://www.lrsc.edu/.

North Dakota State College of Science

Wahpeton, North Dakota

- **State-supported** 2-year, founded 1903, part of North Dakota University System
- **Rural** 128-acre campus
- **Endowment** $18.4 million
- **Coed**

Undergraduates 1,707 full-time, 1,278 part-time. Students come from 35 states and territories; 7 other countries; 42% are from out of state; 7% Black or African American, non-Hispanic/Latino; 2% Hispanic/Latino; 1% Asian, non-Hispanic/Latino; 0.8% American Indian or Alaska Native, non-Hispanic/Latino; 4% Two or more races, non-Hispanic/Latino; 1% Race/ethnicity unknown; 1% international; 7% transferred in; 58% live on campus.
Faculty *Student/faculty ratio:* 13:1.
Academics *Calendar:* semesters. *Degree:* certificates, diplomas, and associate. *Special study options:* academic remediation for entering students, cooperative education, distance learning, double majors, English as a second language, independent study, internships, part-time degree program, services for LD students, student-designed majors, summer session for credit.
Library Mildred Johnson Library. *Books:* 57,489 (physical), 15,859 (digital/electronic); *Serial titles:* 204 (physical), 23,940 (digital/electronic); *Databases:* 80.
Student Life *Campus security:* 24-hour patrols, late-night transport/escort service, controlled dormitory access.
Athletics Member NJCAA.
Financial Aid Of all full-time matriculated undergraduates who enrolled in 2017, 1,461 applied for aid, 1,066 were judged to have need, 380 had their need fully met. In 2017, 94. *Average percent of need met:* 61. *Average financial aid package:* $10,990. *Average need-based loan:* $5687. *Average need-based gift aid:* $5220. *Average non-need-based aid:* $1145. *Average indebtedness upon graduation:* $18,329.
Applying *Options:* electronic application, early admission. *Application fee:* $35. *Required:* high school transcript.
Freshman Application Contact Mr. Justin Grams, Director of Admissions, North Dakota State College of Science, 800 North 6th Street, Wahpeton, ND 58076. *Phone:* 701-671-2189. *Toll-free phone:* 800-342-4325. *E-mail:* justin.grams@ndscs.edu. *Website:* http://www.ndscs.edu/.

Nueta Hidatsa Sahnish College

New Town, North Dakota

Freshman Application Contact Office of Admissions, Nueta Hidatsa Sahnish College, PO Box 490, 220 8th Avenue North, New Town, ND 58763-0490. *Phone:* 701-627-4738 Ext. 295. *Website:* http://www.nhsc.edu/.

Turtle Mountain Community College

Belcourt, North Dakota

Director of Admissions Ms. Joni LaFontaine, Admissions/Records Officer, Turtle Mountain Community College, Box 340, Belcourt, ND 58316-0340. *Phone:* 701-477-5605 Ext. 217. *E-mail:* jlafontaine@tm.edu. *Website:* http://www.tm.edu/.

United Tribes Technical College

Bismarck, North Dakota

Freshman Application Contact Ms. Vivian Gillette, Director of Admissions, United Tribes Technical College, Bismarck, ND 58504. *Phone:* 701-255-3285 Ext. 1334. *Fax:* 701-530-0640. *E-mail:* vgillette@uttc.edu. *Website:* http://www.uttc.edu/.

Williston State College

Williston, North Dakota

- **State-supported** 2-year, founded 1957, part of North Dakota University System
- **Small-town** 80-acre campus
- **Endowment** $52,232
- **Coed**

Undergraduates 615 full-time, 483 part-time. Students come from 29 states and territories; 7 other countries; 18% are from out of state; 4% Black or African American, non-Hispanic/Latino; 7% Hispanic/Latino; 0.7% Asian, non-Hispanic/Latino; 0.1% Native Hawaiian or other Pacific Islander, non-Hispanic/Latino; 2% American Indian or Alaska Native, non-Hispanic/Latino; 5% Two or more races, non-Hispanic/Latino; 3% Race/ethnicity unknown; 3% international; 15% transferred in. *Retention:* 57% of full-time freshmen returned.
Faculty *Student/faculty ratio:* 30:1.
Academics *Calendar:* semesters. *Degree:* certificates and associate. *Special study options:* academic remediation for entering students, advanced placement credit, cooperative education, distance learning, double majors, English as a second language, independent study, part-time degree program, services for LD students, student-designed majors, study abroad, summer session for credit.
Library Williston State College Learning Commons. *Books:* 8,865 (physical), 6,889 (digital/electronic); *Databases:* 45. Students can reserve study rooms.
Student Life *Campus security:* controlled dormitory access.
Athletics Member NJCAA.
Financial Aid Of all full-time matriculated undergraduates who enrolled in 2017, 530 applied for aid, 337 were judged to have need, 67 had their need fully met. In 2017, 176. *Average percent of need met:* 53. *Average financial aid package:* $8504. *Average need-based loan:* $4888. *Average need-based gift aid:* $5676. *Average non-need-based aid:* $4633. *Average indebtedness upon graduation:* $7902.
Applying *Options:* electronic application, deferred entrance. *Application fee:* $35. *Required:* high school transcript.
Freshman Application Contact Ms. Jamee Robbins, Enrollment Services Associate, Williston State College, 1410 University Avenue, Williston, ND 58801. *Phone:* 701-774-4278. *Toll-free phone:* 888-863-9455. *E-mail:* wsc.admission@willistonstate.edu. *Website:* http://www.willistonstate.edu/.

NORTHERN MARIANA ISLANDS

Northern Marianas College

Saipan, Northern Mariana Islands

Freshman Application Contact Ms. Leilani M. Basa-Alam, Admission Specialist, Northern Marianas College, PO Box 501250, Saipan, MP 96950-1250. *Phone:* 670-234-3690 Ext. 1539. *Fax:* 670-235-4967. *E-mail:* leilanib@nmcnet.edu. *Website:* http://www.marianas.edu/.

OHIO

AIC College of Design

Cincinnati, Ohio

- **Independent** primarily 2-year, founded 1976
- **Urban** 3-acre campus with easy access to Cincinnati
- **Coed**

Undergraduates 30 full-time, 4 part-time. Students come from 3 states and territories; 27% are from out of state; 18% Black or African American, non-Hispanic/Latino. *Retention:* 90% of full-time freshmen returned.
Faculty *Student/faculty ratio:* 5:1.
Academics *Degrees:* associate and bachelor's. *Special study options:* academic remediation for entering students, accelerated degree program, adult/continuing education programs, advanced placement credit, cooperative education, part-time degree program, services for LD students.
Library AIC College of Design Library plus 1 other.
Student Life *Campus security:* 24-hour emergency response devices, SMS.
Standardized Tests *Recommended:* SAT or ACT (for admission).
Applying *Options:* early admission, early decision, deferred entrance. *Application fee:* $100. *Required:* essay or personal statement, high school transcript, interview. *Recommended:* minimum 2.0 GPA, letters of recommendation.
Freshman Application Contact Megan Orsburn, Admissions Assistant, AIC College of Design, 1171 E. Kemper Road, Cincinnati, OH 45246. *Phone:* 513-751-1206. *Website:* http://www.aic-arts.edu/.

American Institute of Alternative Medicine

Columbus, Ohio

Admissions Office Contact American Institute of Alternative Medicine, 6685 Doubletree Avenue, Columbus, OH 43229. *Website:* http://www.aiam.edu/.

American National University

Kettering, Ohio

Director of Admissions Gregory J. Shields, Director, American National University, 1837 Woodman Center Drive, Kettering, OH 45420. *Phone:* 937-299-9450. *Website:* http://www.an.edu/.

American National University

Youngstown, Ohio

Admissions Office Contact American National University, 3487 Belmont Avenue, Youngstown, OH 44505. *Website:* http://www.an.edu/.

Antonelli College

Cincinnati, Ohio

Freshman Application Contact Antonelli College, 124 East Seventh Street, Cincinnati, OH 45202. *Phone:* 513-241-4338. *Toll-free phone:* 877-500-4304. *Website:* http://www.antonellicollege.edu/.

Beckfield College

Cincinnati, Ohio

Freshman Application Contact Beckfield College, 225 Pictoria Drive, Suite 200, Cincinnati, OH 45246. *Website:* http://www.beckfield.edu/.

Belmont College

St. Clairsville, Ohio

Director of Admissions Michael Sterling, Director of Recruitment, Belmont College, 120 Fox Shannon Place, St. Clairsville, OH 43950-9735. *Phone:* 740-695-9500 Ext. 1563. *Toll-free phone:* 800-423-1188. *E-mail:* msterling@btc.edu. *Website:* http://www.belmontcollege.edu/.

Bowling Green State University–Firelands College

Huron, Ohio

- **State-supported** primarily 2-year, founded 1968, part of Bowling Green State University System
- **Rural** 216-acre campus with easy access to Cleveland, Toledo
- **Coed**

Undergraduates 936 full-time, 1,034 part-time. Students come from 6 states and territories; 1 other country; 1% are from out of state; 6% Black or African American, non-Hispanic/Latino; 5% Hispanic/Latino; 0.8% Asian, non-Hispanic/Latino; 0.2% American Indian or Alaska Native, non-Hispanic/Latino; 4% Two or more races, non-Hispanic/Latino; 5% Race/ethnicity unknown; 0.1% international. *Retention:* 53% of full-time freshmen returned.
Faculty *Student/faculty ratio:* 20:1.
Academics *Calendar:* semesters. *Degrees:* certificates, associate, and bachelor's (also offers some upper-level and graduate courses). *Special study options:* academic remediation for entering students, adult/continuing education programs, advanced placement credit, cooperative education, distance learning, double majors, honors programs, independent study, internships, part-time degree program, services for LD students, student-designed majors, study abroad, summer session for credit. *ROTC:* Army (c), Air Force (c).
Library BGSU Firelands College Library.
Student Life *Campus security:* 24-hour emergency response devices, late-night transport/escort service, patrols by trained security personnel.

Applying *Options:* electronic application, early admission, deferred entrance. *Application fee:* $45. *Required:* high school transcript.
Freshman Application Contact Dr. Megan Zahler, Assistant Dean for Strategic Enrollment Planning, Bowling Green State University–Firelands College, One University Drive, Huron, OH 44839-9791. *Phone:* 419-433-5560. *Toll-free phone:* 800-322-4787. *Fax:* 419-372-0604. *E-mail:* mzahler@bgsu.edu. *Website:* http://www.firelands.bgsu.edu/.

Bradford School
Columbus, Ohio

Freshman Application Contact Admissions Office, Bradford School, 2469 Stelzer Road, Columbus, OH 43219. *Phone:* 614-416-6200. *Toll-free phone:* 800-678-7981. *Website:* http://www.bradfordschoolcolumbus.edu/.

Bryant & Stratton College–Eastlake Campus
Eastlake, Ohio

Freshman Application Contact Ms. Melanie Pettit, Director of Admissions, Bryant & Stratton College–Eastlake Campus, 35350 Curtis Boulevard, Eastlake, OH 44095. *Phone:* 440-510-1112. *Website:* http://www.bryantstratton.edu/.

Bryant & Stratton College–Parma Campus
Parma, Ohio

Freshman Application Contact Bryant & Stratton College–Parma Campus, 12955 Snow Road, Parma, OH 44130-1005. *Phone:* 216-265-3151. *Toll-free phone:* 866-948-0571. *Website:* http://www.bryantstratton.edu/.

Central Ohio Technical College
Newark, Ohio

- **State-supported** 2-year, founded 1971, part of Ohio Department of Higher Education
- **Small-town** 177-acre campus with easy access to Columbus
- **Endowment** $3.2 million
- **Coed,** 3,442 undergraduate students, 21% full-time, 67% women, 33% men

Undergraduates 735 full-time, 2,707 part-time. Students come from 44 states and territories; 2% are from out of state; 9% Black or African American, non-Hispanic/Latino; 2% Hispanic/Latino; 2% Asian, non-Hispanic/Latino; 0.1% Native Hawaiian or other Pacific Islander, non-Hispanic/Latino; 0.2% American Indian or Alaska Native, non-Hispanic/Latino; 4% Two or more races, non-Hispanic/Latino; 13% Race/ethnicity unknown; 0.1% international; 7% transferred in. *Retention:* 49% of full-time freshmen returned.
Freshmen *Admission:* 374 applied, 374 admitted, 374 enrolled.
Faculty *Total:* 207, 30% full-time. *Student/faculty ratio:* 11:1.
Majors Accounting; advertising; architectural drafting and CAD/CADD; business administration and management; CAD/CADD drafting/design technology; civil drafting and CAD/CADD; civil engineering technology; computer graphics; computer programming; computer support specialist; criminal justice/law enforcement administration; criminal justice/police science; culinary arts; diagnostic medical sonography and ultrasound technology; early childhood education; electrical, electronic and communications engineering technology; emergency medical technology (EMT paramedic); fire science/firefighting; forensic science and technology; health services/allied health/health sciences; human services; liberal arts and sciences/liberal studies; licensed practical/vocational nurse training; manufacturing engineering technology; radiologic technology/science; registered nursing/registered nurse; surgical technology; web page, digital/multimedia and information resources design.
Academics *Calendar:* semesters. *Degree:* certificates and associate. *Special study options:* academic remediation for entering students, accelerated degree program, adult/continuing education programs, advanced placement credit, cooperative education, distance learning, double majors, internships, off-campus study, part-time degree program, services for LD students, student-designed majors, summer session for credit.
Library Newark Campus Library. *Books:* 45,000 (physical); *Serial titles:* 170 (physical). Students can reserve study rooms.
Student Life *Housing:* college housing not available. *Activities and Organizations:* drama/theater group, choral group, Radiologic Technology Student Organization, Phi Theta Kappa, Society of Engineering Technology, The Human Services Committee, Digital Media Design Coshocton. *Campus security:* 24-hour emergency response devices and patrols, student patrols, late-night transport/escort service. *Student services:* personal/psychological counseling, veterans affairs office.
Athletics *Intramural sports:* badminton M/W, basketball M/W, sand volleyball M/W, soccer M/W, softball M/W, table tennis M/W, ultimate Frisbee M/W, volleyball M/W, weight lifting M/W.
Financial Aid Of all full-time matriculated undergraduates who enrolled in 2017, 43 Federal Work-Study jobs (averaging $4000).
Applying *Options:* electronic application, early admission, deferred entrance. *Required for some:* high school transcript. *Application deadlines:* rolling (freshmen), rolling (transfers).
Freshman Application Contact Melanie Garrabrant, Central Ohio Technical College, 1179 University Drive, Newark, OH 43055. *Phone:* 740-755-7109. *Toll-free phone:* 800-9NEWARK. *E-mail:* garrabrant.34@mail.cotc.edu. *Website:* http://www.cotc.edu/.

Chatfield College
St. Martin, Ohio

Freshman Application Contact Chatfield College, 20918 State Route 251, St. Martin, OH 45118-9705. *Phone:* 513-875-3344 Ext. 138. *Website:* http://www.chatfield.edu/.

The Christ College of Nursing and Health Sciences
Cincinnati, Ohio

Freshman Application Contact Mr. Bradley Jackson, Admissions, The Christ College of Nursing and Health Sciences, 2139 Auburn Avenue, Cincinnati, OH 45219. *Phone:* 513-585-0016. *E-mail:* bradley.jackson@thechristcollege.edu. *Website:* http://www.thechristcollege.edu/.

Cincinnati State Technical and Community College
Cincinnati, Ohio

Freshman Application Contact Ms. Gabriele Boeckermann, Director of Admission, Cincinnati State Technical and Community College, Office of Admissions, 3520 Central Parkway, Cincinnati, OH 45223-2690. *Phone:* 513-569-1550. *Toll-free phone:* 877-569-0115. *Fax:* 513-569-1562. *E-mail:* adm@cincinnatistate.edu. *Website:* http://www.cincinnatistate.edu/.

Clark State Community College
Springfield, Ohio

Freshman Application Contact Admissions Office, Clark State Community College, PO Box 570, Springfield, OH 45501-0570. *Phone:* 937-328-3858. *Fax:* 937-328-6133. *E-mail:* admissions@clarkstate.edu. *Website:* http://www.clarkstate.edu/.

Columbus Culinary Institute at Bradford School
Columbus, Ohio

Freshman Application Contact Admissions Office, Columbus Culinary Institute at Bradford School, 2435 Stelzer Road, Columbus, OH 43219. *Phone:* 614-944-4200. *Toll-free phone:* 877-506-5006. *Website:* http://www.columbusculinary.com/.

Columbus State Community College
Columbus, Ohio

Freshman Application Contact Director of Admissions, Columbus State Community College, 550 E. Spring Street, Columbus, OH 43215. *Phone:* 614-287-2669. *Toll-free phone:* 800-621-6407 Ext. 2669. *Fax:* 614-287-6019. *Website:* http://www.cscc.edu/.

Cuyahoga Community College
Cleveland, Ohio

Freshman Application Contact Mr. Kevin McDaniel, Director of Admissions and Records, Cuyahoga Community College, Cleveland, OH 44115. *Phone:* 216-987-4030. *Toll-free phone:* 800-954-8742. *Fax:* 216-696-2567. *Website:* http://www.tri-c.edu/.

Davis College
Toledo, Ohio

Freshman Application Contact Mr. Timothy Brunner, Davis College, 4747 Monroe Street, Toledo, OH 43623-4307. *Phone:* 419-473-2700. *Toll-free phone:* 800-477-7021. *Fax:* 419-473-2472. *E-mail:* tbrunner@daviscollege.edu. *Website:* http://www.daviscollege.edu/.

Daymar College
Columbus, Ohio

Freshman Application Contact Holly Hankinson, Admissions Office, Daymar College, 2745 Winchester Pike, Columbus, OH 43232. *Phone:* 740-687-6126. *Toll-free phone:* 877-258-7796. *E-mail:* hhankinson@daymarcollege.edu. *Website:* http://www.daymarcollege.edu/.

Eastern Gateway Community College
Steubenville, Ohio

- **State and locally supported** 2-year, founded 1966, part of Ohio Board of Regents
- **Small-town** 83-acre campus with easy access to Pittsburgh
- **Endowment** $448,293
- **Coed**

Undergraduates 1,770 full-time, 6,776 part-time. Students come from 50 states and territories; 1 other country; 53% are from out of state; 19% Black or African American, non-Hispanic/Latino; 9% Hispanic/Latino; 1% Asian, non-Hispanic/Latino; 0.5% Native Hawaiian or other Pacific Islander, non-Hispanic/Latino; 0.5% American Indian or Alaska Native, non-Hispanic/Latino; 4% Two or more races, non-Hispanic/Latino; 1% Race/ethnicity unknown; 0.8% transferred in.
Faculty *Student/faculty ratio:* 23:1.
Academics *Calendar:* semesters. *Degree:* certificates and associate. *Special study options:* academic remediation for entering students, accelerated degree program, adult/continuing education programs, cooperative education, distance learning, double majors, off-campus study, part-time degree program, services for LD students, summer session for credit.
Library Eastern Gateway Community College Library. *Books:* 15,948 (physical); *Serial titles:* 6 (physical), 29,684 (digital/electronic); *Databases:* 142.
Student Life *Campus security:* 24-hour emergency response devices, day and evening security.
Athletics Member NJCAA.
Standardized Tests *Required for some:* SAT or ACT (for admission).
Financial Aid Of all full-time matriculated undergraduates who enrolled in 2017, 30 Federal Work-Study jobs (averaging $1500).
Applying *Options:* electronic application, early admission, deferred entrance. *Application fee:* $20. *Required for some:* high school transcript.
Freshman Application Contact Ms. Marlise Barker, Registrar, Eastern Gateway Community College, 4000 Sunset Boulevard, Steubenville, OH 43952. *Phone:* 740-264-5591 Ext. 1611. *Toll-free phone:* 800-68-COLLEGE. *E-mail:* mbarker@egcc.edu. *Website:* http://www.egcc.edu/.

Edison State Community College
Piqua, Ohio

- **State-supported** 2-year, founded 1973, part of Ohio Board of Regents
- **Small-town** 131-acre campus with easy access to Dayton, Columbus, Cincinnati
- **Coed**

Undergraduates 753 full-time, 2,495 part-time. Students come from 8 states and territories; 12% are from out of state; 5% Black or African American, non-Hispanic/Latino; 2% Hispanic/Latino; 0.9% Asian, non-Hispanic/Latino; 0.3% Native Hawaiian or other Pacific Islander, non-Hispanic/Latino; 0.2% American Indian or Alaska Native, non-Hispanic/Latino; 2% Two or more races, non-Hispanic/Latino; 2% Race/ethnicity unknown; 0.4% transferred in. *Retention:* 83% of full-time freshmen returned.
Faculty *Student/faculty ratio:* 17:1.
Academics *Calendar:* semesters. *Degrees:* certificates, associate, and postbachelor's certificates. *Special study options:* academic remediation for entering students, accelerated degree program, adult/continuing education programs, advanced placement credit, distance learning, double majors, English as a second language, honors programs, independent study, internships, off-campus study, part-time degree program, services for LD students, student-designed majors, summer session for credit.
Library Edison Community College Library. *Books:* 18,825 (physical), 112,623 (digital/electronic); *Serial titles:* 61 (physical), 11,044 (digital/electronic); *Databases:* 149. Weekly public service hours: 50; students can reserve study rooms.
Student Life *Campus security:* late-night transport/escort service, 18-hour patrols by trained security personnel.
Athletics Member NJCAA.
Financial Aid Of all full-time matriculated undergraduates who enrolled in 2017, 42 Federal Work-Study jobs (averaging $3000).
Applying *Options:* electronic application. *Required:* high school transcript.
Freshman Application Contact Dr. Loleta Collins, Director of Student Services, Edison State Community College, 1973 Edison Drive, Piqua, OH 45356. *Phone:* 937-778-7983. *E-mail:* lcollins@edisonohio.edu. *Website:* http://www.edisonohio.edu/.

ETI Technical College of Niles
Niles, Ohio

Freshman Application Contact Ms. Diane Marsteller, Director of Admissions, ETI Technical College of Niles, 2076 Youngstown-Warren Road, Niles, OH 44446-4398. *Phone:* 330-652-9919 Ext. 16. *Fax:* 330-652-4399. *E-mail:* dianemarsteller@eticollege.edu. *Website:* http://eticollege.edu/.

Fortis College
Centerville, Ohio

Freshman Application Contact Fortis College, 555 East Alex Bell Road, Centerville, OH 45459. *Phone:* 937-433-3410. *Toll-free phone:* 855-4-FORTIS. *Website:* http://www.fortis.edu/.

Fortis College
Cincinnati, Ohio

Admissions Office Contact Fortis College, 11499 Chester Road, Suite 200, Cincinnati, OH 45246. *Toll-free phone:* 855-4-FORTIS. *Website:* http://www.fortis.edu/.

Fortis College
Cuyahoga Falls, Ohio

Freshman Application Contact Admissions Office, Fortis College, 2545 Bailey Road, Cuyahoga Falls, OH 44221. *Phone:* 330-923-9959. *Toll-free phone:* 855-4-FORTIS. *Fax:* 330-923-0886. *Website:* http://www.fortis.edu/.

Fortis College
Ravenna, Ohio

Freshman Application Contact Admissions Office, Fortis College, 653 Enterprise Parkway, Ravenna, OH 44266. *Toll-free phone:* 855-4-FORTIS. *Website:* http://www.fortis.edu/.

Fortis College
Westerville, Ohio

Admissions Office Contact Fortis College, 4151 Executive Parkway, Suite 120, Westerville, OH 43081. *Toll-free phone:* 855-4-FORTIS. *Website:* http://www.fortis.edu/.

Good Samaritan College of Nursing and Health Science
Cincinnati, Ohio

Freshman Application Contact Admissions Office, Good Samaritan College of Nursing and Health Science, 375 Dixmyth Avenue, Cincinnati, OH 45220. *Phone:* 513-862-2743. *Fax:* 513-862-3572. *Website:* http://www.gscollege.edu/.

Herzing University
Akron, Ohio

Admissions Office Contact Herzing University, 1600 South Arlington Street, Suite 100, Akron, OH 44306. *Toll-free phone:* 800-596-0724. *Website:* http://www.herzing.edu/akron.

Herzing University
Toledo, Ohio
Admissions Office Contact Herzing University, 5212 Hill Avenue, Toledo, OH 43615. *Toll-free phone:* 800-596-0724. *Website:* http://www.herzing.edu/toledo.

Hocking College
Nelsonville, Ohio
Freshman Application Contact Hocking College, 3301 Hocking Parkway, Nelsonville, OH 45764-9588. *Phone:* 740-753-3591 Ext. 7080. *Website:* http://www.hocking.edu/.

Hondros College
Westerville, Ohio
Director of Admissions Ms. Carol Thomas, Operations Manager, Hondros College, 4140 Executive Parkway, Westerville, OH 43081-3855. *Phone:* 614-508-7244. *Toll-free phone:* 888-HONDROS. *Website:* http://www.hondros.edu/.

International College of Broadcasting
Dayton, Ohio
Freshman Application Contact International College of Broadcasting, 6 South Smithville Road, Dayton, OH 45431-1833. *Phone:* 937-258-8251. *Toll-free phone:* 800-517-7284. *Website:* http://www.icb.edu/.

James A. Rhodes State College
Lima, Ohio
Freshman Application Contact Traci Cox, Director, Office of Admissions, James A. Rhodes State College, Lima, OH 45804-3597. *Phone:* 419-995-8040. *E-mail:* cox.t@rhodesstate.edu. *Website:* http://www.rhodesstate.edu/.

Kent State University at Ashtabula
Ashtabula, Ohio
- **State-supported** primarily 2-year, founded 1958, part of Kent State University System
- **Small-town** 83-acre campus with easy access to Cleveland
- **Coed**

Undergraduates 1,027 full-time, 944 part-time. Students come from 25 states and territories; 3 other countries; 5% are from out of state; 5% Black or African American, non-Hispanic/Latino; 5% Hispanic/Latino; 1% Asian, non-Hispanic/Latino; 0.2% Native Hawaiian or other Pacific Islander, non-Hispanic/Latino; 0.2% American Indian or Alaska Native, non-Hispanic/Latino; 3% Two or more races, non-Hispanic/Latino; 2% Race/ethnicity unknown; 0.4% international; 4% transferred in. *Retention:* 51% of full-time freshmen returned.

Faculty *Student/faculty ratio:* 20:1.

Academics *Calendar:* semesters. *Degrees:* certificates, associate, and bachelor's (also offers some upper-level and graduate courses). *Special study options:* academic remediation for entering students, advanced placement credit, distance learning, double majors, independent study, internships, part-time degree program, services for LD students, student-designed majors, study abroad, summer session for credit. *ROTC:* Army (c), Air Force (c).

Library Kent State at Ashtabula Library. Weekly public service hours: 56.

Student Life *Campus security:* 24-hour emergency response devices.

Standardized Tests *Required for some:* SAT or ACT (for admission). *Recommended:* SAT or ACT (for admission).

Financial Aid Of all full-time matriculated undergraduates who enrolled in 2018, 449 applied for aid, 403 were judged to have need, 24 had their need fully met. 6 Federal Work-Study jobs (averaging $3384). In 2018, 8. *Average percent of need met:* 52. *Average financial aid package:* $7634. *Average need-based loan:* $3631. *Average need-based gift aid:* $5194. *Average non-need-based aid:* $1705.

Applying *Options:* electronic application, deferred entrance. *Application fee:* $40. *Required:* high school transcript.

Freshman Application Contact Megan Krippel, Admissions Coordinator, Kent State University at Ashtabula, 3300 Lake Road West, Ashtabula, OH 44004. *Phone:* 440-964-4277. *Fax:* 440-964-4269. *E-mail:* ashtabula_admissions@kent.edu. *Website:* http://www.ashtabula.kent.edu/.

Kent State University at East Liverpool
East Liverpool, Ohio
- **State-supported** primarily 2-year, founded 1967, part of Kent State University System
- **Small-town** 3-acre campus with easy access to Pittsburgh, Youngstown
- **Coed**

Undergraduates 635 full-time, 539 part-time. Students come from 13 states and territories; 10 other countries; 6% are from out of state; 5% Black or African American, non-Hispanic/Latino; 2% Hispanic/Latino; 0.6% Asian, non-Hispanic/Latino; 0.2% American Indian or Alaska Native, non-Hispanic/Latino; 4% Two or more races, non-Hispanic/Latino; 2% Race/ethnicity unknown; 0.6% international; 4% transferred in. *Retention:* 65% of full-time freshmen returned.

Faculty *Student/faculty ratio:* 25:1.

Academics *Calendar:* semesters. *Degrees:* certificates, associate, and bachelor's. *Special study options:* academic remediation for entering students, accelerated degree program, adult/continuing education programs, advanced placement credit, distance learning, double majors, freshman honors college, honors programs, independent study, internships, part-time degree program, services for LD students, student-designed majors, study abroad, summer session for credit. *ROTC:* Army (c), Air Force (c).

Library Paul Blair Memorial Library. Weekly public service hours: 46.

Student Life *Campus security:* 24-hour emergency response devices, student patrols, late-night transport/escort service.

Standardized Tests *Required for some:* SAT or ACT (for admission). *Recommended:* SAT or ACT (for admission).

Financial Aid Of all full-time matriculated undergraduates who enrolled in 2018, 133 applied for aid, 109 were judged to have need, 7 had their need fully met. In 2018, 11. *Average percent of need met:* 57. *Average financial aid package:* $8279. *Average need-based loan:* $3929. *Average need-based gift aid:* $5196. *Average non-need-based aid:* $1587.

Applying *Options:* electronic application, deferred entrance. *Application fee:* $40. *Required:* high school transcript.

Freshman Application Contact Office of Admissions, Kent State University at East Liverpool, 400 East 4th Street, East Liverpool, OH 43920-3497. *Phone:* 330-385-3805. *Website:* http://www.eliv.kent.edu/.

Kent State University at Salem
Salem, Ohio
- **State-supported** primarily 2-year, founded 1966, part of Kent State University System
- **Rural** 100-acre campus with easy access to Youngstown
- **Coed**

Undergraduates 1,062 full-time, 632 part-time. Students come from 7 states and territories; 2% are from out of state; 4% Black or African American, non-Hispanic/Latino; 2% Hispanic/Latino; 0.9% Asian, non-Hispanic/Latino; 0.1% American Indian or Alaska Native, non-Hispanic/Latino; 2% Two or more races, non-Hispanic/Latino; 3% Race/ethnicity unknown; 0.1% international; 6% transferred in. *Retention:* 53% of full-time freshmen returned.

Faculty *Student/faculty ratio:* 19:1.

Academics *Calendar:* semesters. *Degrees:* certificates, associate, and bachelor's (also offers some upper-level and graduate courses). *Special study options:* academic remediation for entering students, accelerated degree program, adult/continuing education programs, advanced placement credit, cooperative education, distance learning, double majors, freshman honors college, honors programs, independent study, part-time degree program, services for LD students, student-designed majors, study abroad, summer session for credit. *ROTC:* Army (c), Air Force (c).

Library Kent State Salem Library. *Books:* 23,500 (physical); *Serial titles:* 4,500 (physical).

Student Life *Campus security:* 24-hour emergency response devices, late-night transport/escort service.

Standardized Tests *Required for some:* SAT or ACT (for admission). *Recommended:* SAT or ACT (for admission).

Financial Aid Of all full-time matriculated undergraduates who enrolled in 2018, 521 applied for aid, 434 were judged to have need, 37 had their need fully met. 22 Federal Work-Study jobs (averaging $1583). In 2018, 59. *Average percent of need met:* 54. *Average financial aid package:* $7474. *Average need-based loan:* $3825. *Average need-based gift aid:* $5242. *Average non-need-based aid:* $1154.

Applying *Options:* electronic application, deferred entrance. *Application fee:* $40. *Required:* high school transcript. *Required for some:* essay or personal statement.

Freshman Application Contact Office of Admissions, Kent State University at Salem, 2491 State Route 45 South, Salem, OH 44460-9412. *Phone:* 330-332-0361. *Website:* http://www.salem.kent.edu/.

Kent State University at Trumbull

Warren, Ohio

- **State-supported** primarily 2-year, founded 1954, part of Kent State University System
- **Suburban** 438-acre campus with easy access to Akron, Youngstown
- **Coed**

Undergraduates 1,476 full-time, 801 part-time. Students come from 6 states and territories; 3% are from out of state; 8% Black or African American, non-Hispanic/Latino; 3% Hispanic/Latino; 0.9% Asian, non-Hispanic/Latino; 0.1% Native Hawaiian or other Pacific Islander, non-Hispanic/Latino; 0.2% American Indian or Alaska Native, non-Hispanic/Latino; 3% Two or more races, non-Hispanic/Latino; 3% Race/ethnicity unknown; 0.4% international. *Retention:* 60% of full-time freshmen returned.
Faculty *Student/faculty ratio:* 25:1.
Academics *Calendar:* semesters. *Degrees:* associate and bachelor's (also offers some upper-level and graduate courses). *Special study options:* academic remediation for entering students, adult/continuing education programs, advanced placement credit, distance learning, double majors, freshman honors college, honors programs, independent study, internships, part-time degree program, services for LD students, student-designed majors, summer session for credit. *ROTC:* Army (c), Air Force (c).
Library Gelbke Library at Kent State Trumbull. *Books:* 40,000 (physical), 100,000 (digital/electronic); *Serial titles:* 40 (physical); *Databases:* 459. Weekly public service hours: 56.
Student Life *Campus security:* 24-hour emergency response devices, late-night transport/escort service, patrols by trained security personnel during hours of operation.
Standardized Tests *Recommended:* SAT or ACT (for admission).
Financial Aid Of all full-time matriculated undergraduates who enrolled in 2018, 654 applied for aid, 568 were judged to have need, 46 had their need fully met. 12 Federal Work-Study jobs (averaging $1755). In 2018, 42. *Average percent of need met:* 55. *Average financial aid package:* $7669. *Average need-based loan:* $3756. *Average need-based gift aid:* $5144. *Average non-need-based aid:* $3150.
Applying *Options:* electronic application, deferred entrance. *Application fee:* $40. *Required:* high school transcript.
Freshman Application Contact Office of Enrollment Management, Kent State University at Trumbull, 4314 Mahoning Avenue, NW, Warren, OH 44483-1998. *Phone:* 330-675-8860. *E-mail:* trumbullinfo@kent.edu. *Website:* http://www.trumbull.kent.edu/.

Kent State University at Tuscarawas

New Philadelphia, Ohio

- **State-supported** primarily 2-year, founded 1962, part of Kent State University System
- **Small-town** 180-acre campus with easy access to Akron, Canton
- **Coed**

Undergraduates 1,299 full-time, 832 part-time. Students come from 8 states and territories; 3 other countries; 2% are from out of state; 4% Black or African American, non-Hispanic/Latino; 2% Hispanic/Latino; 0.7% Asian, non-Hispanic/Latino; 0.4% American Indian or Alaska Native, non-Hispanic/Latino; 2% Two or more races, non-Hispanic/Latino; 2% Race/ethnicity unknown; 0.5% international; 6% transferred in. *Retention:* 62% of full-time freshmen returned.
Faculty *Student/faculty ratio:* 22:1.
Academics *Calendar:* semesters. *Degrees:* certificates, diplomas, associate, and bachelor's (also offers some upper-level and graduate courses). *Special study options:* academic remediation for entering students, accelerated degree program, adult/continuing education programs, advanced placement credit, distance learning, double majors, freshman honors college, honors programs, independent study, internships, part-time degree program, services for LD students, student-designed majors, study abroad, summer session for credit. *ROTC:* Army (c), Air Force (c).
Library Kent State Tuscarawas Library. *Books:* 52,500 (physical), 12 (digital/electronic); *Serial titles:* 540 (physical).
Student Life *Campus security:* 24-hour emergency response devices.
Athletics Member USCAA.
Standardized Tests *Recommended:* SAT or ACT (for admission).
Financial Aid Of all full-time matriculated undergraduates who enrolled in 2018, 700 applied for aid, 576 were judged to have need, 56 had their need fully met. 8 Federal Work-Study jobs (averaging $2325). In 2018, 75. *Average percent of need met:* 58. *Average financial aid package:* $7531. *Average need-based loan:* $3805. *Average need-based gift aid:* $4608. *Average non-need-based aid:* $2653.
Applying *Options:* electronic application, deferred entrance. *Application fee:* $40. *Required:* high school transcript.
Freshman Application Contact Office of Admissions, Kent State University at Tuscarawas, 330 University Drive NE, New Philadelphia, OH 44663-9403. *Phone:* 330-339-3391. *E-mail:* infotusc@kent.edu. *Website:* http://www.tusc.kent.edu/.

Lakeland Community College

Kirtland, Ohio

- **State and locally supported** 2-year, founded 1967, part of Ohio Department of Higher Education
- **Suburban** 380-acre campus with easy access to Cleveland
- **Endowment** $35,367
- **Coed**

Undergraduates 2,198 full-time, 5,383 part-time. Students come from 5 states and territories; 1 other country; 13% Black or African American, non-Hispanic/Latino; 3% Hispanic/Latino; 1% Asian, non-Hispanic/Latino; 0.2% Native Hawaiian or other Pacific Islander, non-Hispanic/Latino; 0.3% American Indian or Alaska Native, non-Hispanic/Latino; 2% Two or more races, non-Hispanic/Latino; 2% Race/ethnicity unknown; 0.1% international; 5% transferred in.
Faculty *Student/faculty ratio:* 17:1.
Academics *Calendar:* semesters. *Degree:* certificates and associate. *Special study options:* academic remediation for entering students, adult/continuing education programs, advanced placement credit, cooperative education, distance learning, English as a second language, external degree program, independent study, internships, off-campus study, part-time degree program, services for LD students, study abroad, summer session for credit.
Library Lakeland Community College Library.
Student Life *Campus security:* 24-hour emergency response devices and patrols, student patrols, late-night transport/escort service.
Athletics Member NJCAA.
Standardized Tests *Required:* ACT Compass (for admission).
Financial Aid Of all full-time matriculated undergraduates who enrolled in 2015, 3,430 applied for aid, 2,959 were judged to have need, 469 had their need fully met. 63 Federal Work-Study jobs (averaging $3489). *Average percent of need met:* 56. *Average financial aid package:* $7024. *Average need-based loan:* $3232. *Average need-based gift aid:* $5250.
Applying *Options:* electronic application, early admission, deferred entrance. *Application fee:* $15. *Required:* high school transcript.
Freshman Application Contact Lakeland Community College, 7700 Clocktower Drive, Kirtland, OH 44094-5198. *Phone:* 440-525-7230. *Toll-free phone:* 800-589-8520. *Website:* http://www.lakelandcc.edu/.

Lorain County Community College

Elyria, Ohio

- **State and locally supported** 2-year, founded 1963, part of University System of Ohio
- **Suburban** 280-acre campus with easy access to Cleveland
- **Coed**

Undergraduates 2,956 full-time, 8,086 part-time. Students come from 28 states and territories; 29 other countries; 0.6% are from out of state; 9% Black or African American, non-Hispanic/Latino; 10% Hispanic/Latino; 1% Asian, non-Hispanic/Latino; 0.1% Native Hawaiian or other Pacific Islander, non-Hispanic/Latino; 0.4% American Indian or Alaska Native, non-Hispanic/Latino; 4% Two or more races, non-Hispanic/Latino; 1% Race/ethnicity unknown; 0.6% international; 5% transferred in. *Retention:* 63% of full-time freshmen returned.
Academics *Calendar:* semesters. *Degree:* certificates and associate. *Special study options:* academic remediation for entering students, adult/continuing education programs, advanced placement credit, distance learning, double majors, English as a second language, independent study, internships, off-campus study, part-time degree program, services for LD students, student-designed majors, study abroad, summer session for credit.
Library Barbara and Mike Bass Library & Community Resource Center plus 1 other. *Books:* 88,354 (physical), 192,532 (digital/electronic); *Serial titles:* 919 (physical), 132,353 (digital/electronic); *Databases:* 178. Weekly public service hours: 54; students can reserve study rooms.
Student Life *Campus security:* 24-hour emergency response devices and patrols, late-night transport/escort service.
Athletics Member NJCAA.
Financial Aid Of all full-time matriculated undergraduates who enrolled in 2017, 2,256 applied for aid, 1,764 were judged to have need, 106 had their need fully met. 84 Federal Work-Study jobs (averaging $1855). In 2017, 327. *Average percent of need met:* 57. *Average financial aid package:* $5455. *Average need-based loan:* $2987. *Average need-based gift aid:* $4802. *Average non-need-based aid:* $3017.

Applying *Options:* electronic application. *Required for some:* high school transcript.
Freshman Application Contact Lorain County Community College, 1005 Abbe Road, North, Elyria, OH 44035. *Phone:* 440-366-7622. *Toll-free phone:* 800-995-5222 Ext. 4032. *Website:* http://www.lorainccc.edu/.

Marion Technical College
Marion, Ohio

Freshman Application Contact Mr. Joel Liles, Dean of Enrollment Services, Marion Technical College, 1467 Mount Vernon Avenue, Marion, OH 43302. *Phone:* 740-389-4636 Ext. 249. *Fax:* 740-389-6136. *E-mail:* enroll@mtc.edu. *Website:* http://www.mtc.edu/.

The Modern College of Design
Kettering, Ohio

- **Proprietary** 2-year, founded 1983
- **Suburban** 5-acre campus with easy access to Columbus
- **Coed**

Undergraduates 191 full-time, 3 part-time. Students come from 3 states and territories; 9% are from out of state; 6% Black or African American, non-Hispanic/Latino; 4% Hispanic/Latino; 2% Asian, non-Hispanic/Latino; 1% American Indian or Alaska Native, non-Hispanic/Latino; 0.5% Two or more races, non-Hispanic/Latino; 0.5% Race/ethnicity unknown; 5% transferred in. *Retention:* 79% of full-time freshmen returned.
Faculty *Student/faculty ratio:* 14:1.
Academics *Calendar:* semesters. *Degree:* associate.
Library SAA Library. *Books:* 881 (physical), 45,000 (digital/electronic); *Serial titles:* 32 (physical); *Databases:* 2. Weekly public service hours: 60.
Applying *Options:* electronic application. *Required:* high school transcript, minimum 2.0 GPA, interview. *Required for some:* essay or personal statement, 2 letters of recommendation.
Freshman Application Contact Mrs. Mariesa Brewster, Director of Admissions, The Modern College of Design, 1725 E. David Road, Kettering, OH 45440. *Phone:* 937-294-0592. *Toll-free phone:* 877-300-9866. *Fax:* 937-294-5869. *E-mail:* mariesa@saa.edu. *Website:* http://www.themoderncollegeofdesign.com/.

North Central State College
Mansfield, Ohio

Freshman Application Contact Ms. Nikia L. Fletcher, Director of Admissions, North Central State College, 2441 Kenwood Circle, PO Box 698, Mansfield, OH 44901-0698. *Phone:* 419-755-4813. *Toll-free phone:* 888-755-4899. *E-mail:* nfletcher@ncstatecollege.edu. *Website:* http://www.ncstatecollege.edu/.

Northwest State Community College
Archbold, Ohio

Freshman Application Contact Mrs. Amanda Potts, Director of Admissions, Northwest State Community College, 22600 State Route 34, Archbold, OH 43502. *Phone:* 419-267-1364. *Toll-free phone:* 855-267-5511. *Fax:* 419-267-3688. *E-mail:* apotts@northweststate.edu. *Website:* http://www.northweststate.edu/.

Ohio Business College
Sandusky, Ohio

Freshman Application Contact Ohio Business College, 5202 Timber Commons Drive, Sandusky, OH 44870. *Phone:* 419-627-8345. *Toll-free phone:* 888-627-8345. *Website:* http://www.ohiobusinesscollege.edu/.

Ohio Business College
Sheffield Village, Ohio

Freshman Application Contact Ohio Business College, 5095 Waterford Drive, Sheffield Village, OH 44035. *Toll-free phone:* 888-514-3126. *Website:* http://www.ohiobusinesscollege.edu/.

The Ohio State University Agricultural Technical Institute
Wooster, Ohio

- **State-supported** 2-year, founded 1971, part of The Ohio State University
- **Small-town** 1942-acre campus with easy access to Cleveland, Columbus, Akron, Canton
- **Coed**

Undergraduates 707 full-time, 50 part-time. Students come from 9 states and territories; 2% are from out of state; 4% transferred in. *Retention:* 67% of full-time freshmen returned.
Faculty *Student/faculty ratio:* 21:1.
Academics *Calendar:* semesters. *Degree:* certificates, diplomas, and associate. *Special study options:* academic remediation for entering students, accelerated degree program, adult/continuing education programs, advanced placement credit, cooperative education, distance learning, double majors, independent study, internships, off-campus study, part-time degree program, services for LD students, student-designed majors, study abroad. *ROTC:* Army (c), Navy (c), Air Force (c).
Library Agricultural Technical Institute Library plus 1 other.
Student Life *Campus security:* 24-hour emergency response devices and patrols, controlled dormitory access.
Standardized Tests *Required for some:* SAT or ACT (for admission).
Financial Aid Of all full-time matriculated undergraduates who enrolled in 2010, 540 applied for aid, 474 were judged to have need, 25 had their need fully met. 64 Federal Work-Study jobs (averaging $2000). In 2010, 24. *Average percent of need met:* 44. *Average financial aid package:* $6859. *Average need-based loan:* $3826. *Average need-based gift aid:* $4241. *Average non-need-based aid:* $2107.
Applying *Options:* electronic application. *Application fee:* $60. *Required:* high school transcript.
Freshman Application Contact Ms. Julia Morris, Admissions Counselor, The Ohio State University Agricultural Technical Institute, 1328 Dover Road, Wooster, OH 44691. *Phone:* 330-287-1327. *Toll-free phone:* 800-647-8283 Ext. 1327. *Fax:* 330-287-1333. *E-mail:* morris.878@osu.edu. *Website:* http://www.ati.osu.edu/.

Ohio Technical College
Cleveland, Ohio

- **Proprietary** 2-year, founded 1969
- **Urban** 18-acre campus
- **Coed,** 905 undergraduate students, 100% full-time, 7% women, 93% men
- 100% of applicants were admitted

Undergraduates 905 full-time. Students come from 14 states and territories; 2 other countries; 57% are from out of state; 21% Black or African American, non-Hispanic/Latino; 6% Hispanic/Latino; 0.2% Asian, non-Hispanic/Latino; 0.1% Native Hawaiian or other Pacific Islander, non-Hispanic/Latino; 0.4% American Indian or Alaska Native, non-Hispanic/Latino; 2% Two or more races, non-Hispanic/Latino; 0.3% Race/ethnicity unknown; 2% transferred in. *Retention:* 80% of full-time freshmen returned.
Freshmen *Admission:* 226 applied, 226 admitted, 226 enrolled.
Faculty *Total:* 63, 78% full-time. *Student/faculty ratio:* 16:1.
Majors Autobody/collision and repair technology; automobile/automotive mechanics technology; diesel mechanics technology; high performance and custom engine technology; mechanic and repair technologies related; motorcycle maintenance and repair technology; vehicle maintenance and repair technologies; welding technology.
Academics *Degree:* certificates, diplomas, and associate.
Library Ohio Technical College Library Resource Center. *Books:* 3,859 (physical), 21 (digital/electronic); *Databases:* 6. Weekly public service hours: 40.
Student Life *Housing Options:* Campus housing is provided by a third party. *Campus security:* late-night transport/escort service. *Student services:* personal/psychological counseling.
Applying *Options:* electronic application. *Required:* high school transcript, interview. *Application deadlines:* rolling (freshmen), rolling (out-of-state freshmen).
Director of Admissions Ms. Caroline LaBel-smith, Director of Admissions, Ohio Technical College, 1374 East 51st Street, Cleveland, OH 44103. *Phone:* 216-881-1700. *Toll-free phone:* 800-322-7000. *Fax:* 216-881-9145. *E-mail:* csmith@ohiotech.edu.
Website: http://www.ohiotech.edu/.

Ohio Valley College of Technology
East Liverpool, Ohio

Freshman Application Contact Mr. Scott S. Rogers, Director, Ohio Valley College of Technology, 15258 State Route 170, East Liverpool, OH 43920. *Phone:* 330-385-1070. *Website:* http://www.ovct.edu/.

Owens Community College
Toledo, Ohio

Freshman Application Contact Ms. Meghan L. Schmidbauer, Director, Admissions, Owens Community College, PO Box 10000, Toledo, OH 43699. *Phone:* 567-661-2155. *Toll-free phone:* 800-GO-OWENS. *Fax:* 567-661-7734. *E-mail:* meghan_schmidbauer@owens.edu. *Website:* http://www.owens.edu/.

Professional Skills Institute
Maumee, Ohio

Director of Admissions Ms. Hope Finch, Director of Marketing, Professional Skills Institute, 1505 Holland Road, Maumee, OH 43537. *Phone:* 419-531-9610. *Website:* http://www.proskills.edu/.

Remington College–Cleveland Campus
Cleveland, Ohio

Director of Admissions Director of Recruitment, Remington College–Cleveland Campus, 14445 Broadway Avenue, Cleveland, OH 44125. *Phone:* 216-475-7520. *Toll-free phone:* 800-323-8122. *Fax:* 216-475-6055. *Website:* http://www.remingtoncollege.edu/.

Rosedale Bible College
Irwin, Ohio

Freshman Application Contact Rosedale Bible College, 2270 Rosedale Road, Irwin, OH 43029-9501. *Phone:* 740-857-1311. *Website:* http://www.rosedale.edu/.

Ross College
Canton, Ohio

Freshman Application Contact Ross College, 4300 Munson Street NW, Canton, OH 44718. *Phone:* 330-494-1214. *Toll-free phone:* 866-815-5578. *Website:* http://www.rosseducation.edu/.

Ross College
Sylvania, Ohio

Admissions Office Contact Ross College, 5834 Monroe Street, Suite F-J, Sylvania, OH 43560. *Toll-free phone:* 866-815-5578. *Website:* http://www.rosseducation.edu/.

Sinclair Community College
Dayton, Ohio

Freshman Application Contact Ms. Sara Smith, Director and Systems Manager, Outreach Services, Sinclair Community College, 444 West Third Street, Dayton, OH 45402-1460. *Phone:* 937-512-3060. *Toll-free phone:* 800-315-3000. *Fax:* 937-512-2393. *E-mail:* ssmith@sinclair.edu. *Website:* http://www.sinclair.edu/.

Southern State Community College
Hillsboro, Ohio

Freshman Application Contact Ms. Wendy Johnson, Director of Admissions, Southern State Community College, Hillsboro, OH 45133. *Phone:* 937-393-3431 Ext. 2720. *Toll-free phone:* 800-628-7722. *Fax:* 937-393-6682. *E-mail:* wjohnson@sscc.edu. *Website:* http://www.sscc.edu/.

Stark State College
North Canton, Ohio

- **State-related** 2-year, founded 1960, part of University System of Ohio
- **Suburban** 100-acre campus with easy access to Cleveland
- **Endowment** $6.2 million
- **Coed**

Undergraduates 3,090 full-time, 7,938 part-time. Students come from 10 states and territories; 1 other country; 1% are from out of state; 13% Black or African American, non-Hispanic/Latino; 2% Hispanic/Latino; 2% Asian, non-Hispanic/Latino; 0.1% Native Hawaiian or other Pacific Islander, non-Hispanic/Latino; 0.4% American Indian or Alaska Native, non-Hispanic/Latino; 4% Two or more races, non-Hispanic/Latino; 7% Race/ethnicity unknown; 0.1% international; 8% transferred in.

Faculty *Student/faculty ratio:* 21:1.

Academics *Calendar:* semesters. *Degree:* certificates and associate. *Special study options:* academic remediation for entering students, adult/continuing education programs, cooperative education, distance learning, double majors, external degree program, independent study, internships, off-campus study, part-time degree program, services for LD students, student-designed majors, summer session for credit.

Library Learning Resource Center plus 1 other.

Student Life *Campus security:* 24-hour emergency response devices and patrols, student patrols, late-night transport/escort service, patrols by trained security personnel during hours of operation.

Financial Aid Of all full-time matriculated undergraduates who enrolled in 2014, 1,939 applied for aid, 1,697 were judged to have need, 6 had their need fully met. 74 Federal Work-Study jobs (averaging $2306). *Average need-based loan:* $2537. *Average need-based gift aid:* $4317.

Applying *Options:* electronic application. *Required:* high school transcript.

Freshman Application Contact J. P. Cooney, Executive Director to Recruitment, Admissions and Marketing, Stark State College, 6200 Frank Road NE, Canton, OH 44720. *Phone:* 330-494-6170 Ext. 4401. *Toll-free phone:* 800-797-8275. *E-mail:* info@starkstate.edu. *Website:* http://www.starkstate.edu/.

Stautzenberger College
Brecksville, Ohio

Admissions Office Contact Stautzenberger College, 8001 Katherine Boulevard, Brecksville, OH 44141. *Toll-free phone:* 800-437-2997. *Website:* http://www.sctoday.edu/.

Stautzenberger College
Maumee, Ohio

Director of Admissions Ms. Karen Fitzgerald, Director of Admissions and Marketing, Stautzenberger College, 1796 Indian Wood Circle, Maumee, OH 43537. *Phone:* 419-866-0261. *Toll-free phone:* 800-552-5099. *Fax:* 419-867-9821. *E-mail:* klfitzgerald@stautzenberger.com. *Website:* http://www.sctoday.edu/maumee/.

Terra State Community College
Fremont, Ohio

Freshman Application Contact Mr. Heath Martin, Director of Admissions and Enrollment Services, Terra State Community College, 2830 Napoleon Road, Fremont, OH 43420. *Phone:* 419-559-2154. *Toll-free phone:* 866-AT-TERRA. *Fax:* 419-559-2352. *Website:* http://www.terra.edu/.

The University of Akron Wayne College
Orrville, Ohio

Freshman Application Contact Ms. Alicia Broadus, Student Services Counselor, The University of Akron Wayne College, Orrville, OH 44667. *Phone:* 800-221-8308 Ext. 8901. *Toll-free phone:* 800-221-8308. *Fax:* 330-684-8989. *E-mail:* wayneadmissions@uakron.edu. *Website:* http://www.wayne.uakron.edu/.

University of Cincinnati Blue Ash College
Cincinnati, Ohio

Freshman Application Contact University of Cincinnati Blue Ash College, 9555 Plainfield Road, Cincinnati, OH 45236-1007. *Phone:* 513-745-5700. *Website:* http://www.ucblueash.edu/.

University of Cincinnati Clermont College

Batavia, Ohio

Freshman Application Contact Mrs. Jamie Adkins, University Services Associate, University of Cincinnati Clermont College, 4200 Clermont College Drive, Batavia, OH 45103. *Phone:* 513-732-5294. *Toll-free phone:* 866-446-2822. *Fax:* 513-732-5303. *E-mail:* jamie.adkins@uc.edu. *Website:* http://www.ucclermont.edu/.

Valor Christian College

Canal Winchester, Ohio

Admissions Office Contact Valor Christian College, 4595 Gender Road, PO Box 800, Canal Winchester, OH 43110. *Website:* http://www.valorcollege.edu/.

Vet Tech Institute at Bradford School

Columbus, Ohio

Freshman Application Contact Admissions Office, Vet Tech Institute at Bradford School, 2469 Stelzer Road, Columbus, OH 43219. *Phone:* 800-678-7981. *Toll-free phone:* 800-678-7981. *Website:* http://columbus.vettechinstitute.edu/.

Washington State Community College

Marietta, Ohio

Freshman Application Contact Ms. Rebecca Peroni, Director of Admissions, Washington State Community College, 110 Colegate Drive, Marietta, OH 45750. *Phone:* 740-374-8716. *Fax:* 740-376-0257. *E-mail:* rperoni@wscc.edu. *Website:* http://www.wscc.edu/.

Zane State College

Zanesville, Ohio

Director of Admissions Mr. Paul Young, Director of Admissions, Zane State College, 1555 Newark Road, Zanesville, OH 43701-2626. *Phone:* 740-454-2501 Ext. 1225. *Toll-free phone:* 800-686-8324. *E-mail:* pyoung@zanestate.edu. *Website:* http://www.zanestate.edu/.

OKLAHOMA

Carl Albert State College

Poteau, Oklahoma

- **State-supported** 2-year, founded 1934, part of Oklahoma State Regents for Higher Education
- **Small-town** 78-acre campus
- **Coed**

Undergraduates 1,320 full-time, 874 part-time. Students come from 9 states and territories; 3% Black or African American, non-Hispanic/Latino; 7% Hispanic/Latino; 0.3% Asian, non-Hispanic/Latino; 25% American Indian or Alaska Native, non-Hispanic/Latino; 6% Two or more races, non-Hispanic/Latino; 1% Race/ethnicity unknown; 1% international; 12% live on campus.

Faculty *Student/faculty ratio:* 16:1.

Academics *Calendar:* semesters. *Degree:* certificates and associate. *Special study options:* academic remediation for entering students, adult/continuing education programs, cooperative education, part-time degree program.

Library Joe E. White Library.

Student Life *Campus security:* security guards.

Athletics Member NJCAA.

Standardized Tests *Recommended:* SAT or ACT (for admission).

Financial Aid Of all full-time matriculated undergraduates who enrolled in 2017, 112 Federal Work-Study jobs (averaging $2100).

Applying *Required:* high school transcript.

Admissions Office Contact Carl Albert State College, 1507 South McKenna, Poteau, OK 74953-5208. *Website:* http://www.carlalbert.edu/.

Clary Sage College

Tulsa, Oklahoma

Freshman Application Contact Dr. Raye Mahlberg, Campus Director, Clary Sage College, 3131 South Sheridan, Tulsa, OK 74145. *Phone:* 918-298-8200 Ext. 1025. *E-mail:* rmahlberg@clarysagecollege.com. *Website:* http://www.clarysagecollege.com/.

College of the Muscogee Nation

Okmulgee, Oklahoma

Admissions Office Contact College of the Muscogee Nation, 2170 Raven Circle, Okmulgee, OK 74447-0917. *Website:* http://www.cmn.edu/.

Community Care College

Tulsa, Oklahoma

Freshman Application Contact Dr. Kevin Kirk, President, Community Care College, 4242 South Sheridan, Tulsa, OK 74145. *Phone:* 918-610-0027 Ext. 2003. *Fax:* 918-610-0029. *E-mail:* kkirk@communitycarecollege.edu. *Website:* http://www.communitycarecollege.edu/.

Connors State College

Warner, Oklahoma

Freshman Application Contact Ms. Sonya Baker, Registrar, Connors State College, Route 1 Box 1000, Warner, OK 74469-9700. *Phone:* 918-463-6233. *Website:* http://www.connorsstate.edu/.

Eastern Oklahoma State College

Wilburton, Oklahoma

Freshman Application Contact Ms. Leah McLaughlin, Director of Admissions, Eastern Oklahoma State College, 1301 West Main, Wilburton, OK 74578-4999. *Phone:* 918-465-1811. *Toll-free phone:* 855-534-3672. *Fax:* 918-465-2431. *E-mail:* lmiller@eosc.edu. *Website:* http://www.eosc.edu/.

Murray State College

Tishomingo, Oklahoma

Freshman Application Contact Murray State College, One Murray Campus, Tishomingo, OK 73460. *Phone:* 580-371-2371 Ext. 171. *Website:* http://www.mscok.edu/.

Northeastern Oklahoma Agricultural and Mechanical College

Miami, Oklahoma

Freshman Application Contact Amy Ishmael, Vice President for Enrollment Management, Northeastern Oklahoma Agricultural and Mechanical College, 200 I Street, NE, Miami, OK 74354-6434. *Phone:* 918-540-6212. *Toll-free phone:* 800-464-6636. *Fax:* 918-540-6946. *E-mail:* neoadmission@neo.edu. *Website:* http://www.neo.edu/.

Northern Oklahoma College

Tonkawa, Oklahoma

Freshman Application Contact Ms. Sheri Snyder, Director of College Relations, Northern Oklahoma College, 1220 East Grand Avenue, PO Box 310, Tonkawa, OK 74653-0310. *Phone:* 580-628-6290. *Website:* http://www.noc.edu/.

Oklahoma City Community College

Oklahoma City, Oklahoma

- **State-supported** 2-year, founded 1969, part of Oklahoma State Regents for Higher Education
- **Urban** 143-acre campus with easy access to Oklahoma City
- **Endowment** $310,298
- **Coed**

Undergraduates 4,359 full-time, 7,955 part-time. Students come from 22 states and territories; 94 other countries; 5% are from out of state; 10% Black or African American, non-Hispanic/Latino; 17% Hispanic/Latino; 5% Asian, non-Hispanic/Latino; 0.2% Native Hawaiian or other Pacific Islander, non-Hispanic/Latino; 5% American Indian or Alaska Native, non-Hispanic/Latino;

8% Two or more races, non-Hispanic/Latino; 4% Race/ethnicity unknown; 3% international; 29% transferred in.
Faculty *Student/faculty ratio:* 23:1.
Academics *Calendar:* semesters. *Degree:* certificates and associate. *Special study options:* academic remediation for entering students, accelerated degree program, advanced placement credit, cooperative education, distance learning, double majors, honors programs, independent study, internships, part-time degree program, services for LD students, student-designed majors, summer session for credit.
Library Keith Leftwich Memorial Library. *Books:* 85,305 (physical), 19,895 (digital/electronic); *Serial titles:* 101 (physical), 11,707 (digital/electronic); *Databases:* 44. Weekly public service hours: 70.
Student Life *Campus security:* 24-hour emergency response devices and patrols, late-night transport/escort service.
Financial Aid Of all full-time matriculated undergraduates who enrolled in 2016, 108 Federal Work-Study jobs (averaging $2643). 440 state and other part-time jobs (averaging $3211).
Applying *Options:* electronic application. *Application fee:* $30. *Required for some:* high school transcript, college and university transcripts.
Freshman Application Contact Ms. Jillian C. Hibblen, Acting Director of Recruitment and Admissions, Oklahoma City Community College, 7777 South May Avenue, Oklahoma City, OK 73159. *Phone:* 405-682-7743. *Fax:* 405-682-7817. *E-mail:* jhibblen@occc.edu. *Website:* http://www.occc.edu/.

Oklahoma State University Institute of Technology

Okmulgee, Oklahoma

- **State-supported** primarily 2-year, founded 1946, part of Oklahoma State University
- **Small-town** 160-acre campus with easy access to Tulsa
- **Endowment** $7.6 million
- **Coed**

Undergraduates 1,744 full-time, 758 part-time. Students come from 23 states and territories; 10 other countries; 7% are from out of state; 5% Black or African American, non-Hispanic/Latino; 6% Hispanic/Latino; 1% Asian, non-Hispanic/Latino; 12% American Indian or Alaska Native, non-Hispanic/Latino; 11% Two or more races, non-Hispanic/Latino; 12% Race/ethnicity unknown; 0.6% international; 9% transferred in; 25% live on campus. *Retention:* 64% of full-time freshmen returned.
Faculty *Student/faculty ratio:* 15:1.
Academics *Calendar:* trimesters. *Degrees:* associate and bachelor's. *Special study options:* academic remediation for entering students, adult/continuing education programs, advanced placement credit, distance learning, double majors, independent study, internships, part-time degree program, services for LD students, summer session for credit.
Library Oklahoma State University Institute of Technology Library. *Books:* 9,520 (physical), 147,054 (digital/electronic); *Serial titles:* 149 (physical), 70,987 (digital/electronic); *Databases:* 106. Weekly public service hours: 73; students can reserve study rooms.
Student Life *Campus security:* 24-hour emergency response devices and patrols, late-night transport/escort service, controlled dormitory access.
Standardized Tests *Required for some:* SAT or ACT (for admission). *Recommended:* ACT (for admission).
Financial Aid Of all full-time matriculated undergraduates who enrolled in 2018, 1,419 applied for aid, 1,267 were judged to have need, 8 had their need fully met. In 2018, 29. *Average percent of need met:* 53. *Average financial aid package:* $10,027. *Average need-based loan:* $3659. *Average need-based gift aid:* $7229. *Average non-need-based aid:* $1956. *Financial aid deadline:* 6/30.
Applying *Options:* deferred entrance. *Required:* high school transcript.
Freshman Application Contact Kyle Gregorio, Assistant Registrar, Oklahoma State University Institute of Technology, 1801 E. 4th Street, Okmulgee, OK 74447. *Phone:* 918-293-5274. *Toll-free phone:* 800-722-4471. *Fax:* 918-293-4643. *E-mail:* kyleg@okstate.edu. *Website:* http://www.osuit.edu/.

Oklahoma State University–Oklahoma City

Oklahoma City, Oklahoma

- **State-supported** primarily 2-year, founded 1961, part of Oklahoma State University
- **Urban** 110-acre campus with easy access to Oklahoma City
- **Coed**

Undergraduates 1,728 full-time, 4,111 part-time. Students come from 28 states and territories; 12 other countries; 4% are from out of state; 11% Black or African American, non-Hispanic/Latino; 16% Hispanic/Latino; 3% Asian, non-Hispanic/Latino; 0.2% Native Hawaiian or other Pacific Islander, non-Hispanic/Latino; 4% American Indian or Alaska Native, non-Hispanic/Latino; 7% Two or more races, non-Hispanic/Latino; 4% Race/ethnicity unknown; 2% international; 13% transferred in. *Retention:* 51% of full-time freshmen returned.
Faculty *Student/faculty ratio:* 16:1.
Academics *Calendar:* semesters. *Degrees:* certificates, associate, and bachelor's. *Special study options:* academic remediation for entering students, advanced placement credit, distance learning, double majors, honors programs, independent study, internships, part-time degree program, services for LD students, study abroad, summer session for credit.
Library Oklahoma State University, Oklahoma City Library. *Books:* 34,772 (physical), 198,662 (digital/electronic); *Serial titles:* 229 (physical); *Databases:* 72. Weekly public service hours: 75.
Student Life *Campus security:* 24-hour patrols, late-night transport/escort service.
Financial Aid Of all full-time matriculated undergraduates who enrolled in 2017, 1,116 applied for aid, 1,116 were judged to have need, 856 had their need fully met. 192 Federal Work-Study jobs (averaging $275). In 2017, 611. *Average percent of need met:* 81. *Average financial aid package:* $1757. *Average need-based gift aid:* $2293. *Average non-need-based aid:* $1025. *Average indebtedness upon graduation:* $3119.
Applying *Options:* electronic application. *Required for some:* high school transcript.
Freshman Application Contact Mr. Kyle Williams, Senior Director of Enrollment Management, Oklahoma State University–Oklahoma City, 900 North Portland Avenue, AD202, Oklahoma City, OK 73107. *Phone:* 405-945-9152. *Toll-free phone:* 800-560-4099. *E-mail:* wilkylw@osuokc.edu. *Website:* http://www.osuokc.edu/.

Oklahoma Technical College

Tulsa, Oklahoma

Freshman Application Contact Mr. Jeremy Cooper, Campus Director, Oklahoma Technical College, 4444 South Sheridan Road, Tulsa, OK 74145. *Phone:* 918-895-7500 Ext. 3007. *Fax:* 918-895-7885. *E-mail:* jcooper@oklahomatechnicalcollege.com. *Website:* http://www.oklahomatechnicalcollege.com/.

Platt College

Moore, Oklahoma

Admissions Office Contact Platt College, 201 North Eastern Avenue, Moore, OK 73160. *Toll-free phone:* 877-392-6616. *Website:* http://www.plattcolleges.edu/.

Platt College

Oklahoma City, Oklahoma

Admissions Office Contact Platt College, 2727 West Memorial Road, Oklahoma City, OK 73134. *Toll-free phone:* 877-392-6616. *Website:* http://www.plattcolleges.edu/.

Platt College

Tulsa, Oklahoma

Director of Admissions Mrs. Susan Rone, Director, Platt College, 3801 South Sheridan Road, Tulsa, OK 74145. *Phone:* 918-663-9000. *Toll-free phone:* 877-392-6616. *Fax:* 918-622-1240. *E-mail:* susanr@plattcollege.org. *Website:* http://www.plattcolleges.edu/.

Redlands Community College

El Reno, Oklahoma

Freshman Application Contact Redlands Community College, 1300 South Country Club Road, El Reno, OK 73036-5304. *Phone:* 405-262-2552 Ext. 1263. *Toll-free phone:* 866-415-6367. *Website:* http://www.redlandscc.edu/.

Rose State College

Midwest City, Oklahoma

Freshman Application Contact Ms. Mechelle Aitson-Roessler, Registrar and Director of Admissions, Rose State College, 6420 Southeast 15th Street, Midwest City, OK 73110-2799. *Phone:* 405-733-7308. *Toll-free phone:* 866-621-0987. *Fax:* 405-736-0203. *E-mail:* maitson@ms.rose.cc.ok.us. *Website:* http://www.rose.edu/.

Seminole State College
Seminole, Oklahoma

- **State-supported** 2-year, founded 1931, part of Oklahoma State Regents for Higher Education
- **Small-town** 40-acre campus with easy access to Oklahoma City
- **Endowment** $3.1 million
- **Coed**

Undergraduates 967 full-time, 666 part-time. Students come from 9 states and territories; 9 other countries; 1% are from out of state; 6% Black or African American, non-Hispanic/Latino; 2% Hispanic/Latino; 0.6% Asian, non-Hispanic/Latino; 0.2% Native Hawaiian or other Pacific Islander, non-Hispanic/Latino; 26% American Indian or Alaska Native, non-Hispanic/Latino; 1% Two or more races, non-Hispanic/Latino; 3% Race/ethnicity unknown; 1% international; 5% transferred in; 10% live on campus.
Faculty *Student/faculty ratio:* 19:1.
Academics *Calendar:* semesters. *Degree:* certificates, diplomas, and associate. *Special study options:* academic remediation for entering students, adult/continuing education programs, advanced placement credit, cooperative education, distance learning, double majors, English as a second language, independent study, off-campus study, part-time degree program, services for LD students, study abroad, summer session for credit.
Library Boren Library plus 1 other. *Books:* 29,131 (physical); *Serial titles:* 35 (physical), 11 (digital/electronic); *Databases:* 8. Weekly public service hours: 48.
Student Life *Campus security:* 24-hour emergency response devices and patrols, student patrols, late-night transport/escort service, controlled dormitory access, police department staffed with state certified officers.
Athletics Member NJCAA.
Financial Aid Of all full-time matriculated undergraduates who enrolled in 2016, 17 Federal Work-Study jobs (averaging $5600).
Applying *Options:* early admission, deferred entrance. *Application fee:* $15. *Recommended:* high school transcript.
Admissions Office Contact Seminole State College, 2701 Boren Boulevard, PO Box 351, Seminole, OK 74818-0351. *Website:* http://www.sscok.edu/.

Spartan College of Aeronautics and Technology
Tulsa, Oklahoma

Freshman Application Contact Mr. Mark Fowler, Vice President of Student Records and Finance, Spartan College of Aeronautics and Technology, 8820 East Pine Street, Tulsa, OK 74115. *Phone:* 918-836-6886. *Toll-free phone:* 800-331-1204. *Website:* http://www.spartan.edu/.

Tulsa Community College
Tulsa, Oklahoma

- **State-supported** 2-year, founded 1968, part of Oklahoma State Regents for Higher Education
- **Urban** 160-acre campus
- **Coed,** 16,391 undergraduate students, 29% full-time, 63% women, 37% men

Undergraduates 4,820 full-time, 11,571 part-time. 1% are from out of state; 9% Black or African American, non-Hispanic/Latino; 11% Hispanic/Latino; 4% Asian, non-Hispanic/Latino; 0.1% Native Hawaiian or other Pacific Islander, non-Hispanic/Latino; 7% American Indian or Alaska Native, non-Hispanic/Latino; 12% Two or more races, non-Hispanic/Latino; 3% Race/ethnicity unknown; 3% international; 3% transferred in.
Freshmen *Admission:* 6,157 applied, 6,149 admitted, 3,485 enrolled. *Average high school GPA:* 3.1.
Faculty *Total:* 816, 34% full-time. *Student/faculty ratio:* 19:1.
Majors Accounting technology and bookkeeping; aeronautical/aerospace engineering technology; air traffic control; applied horticulture/horticulture operations; biotechnology; business administration and management; business/commerce; business, management, and marketing related; child development; clinical/medical laboratory technology; communication; computer and information sciences and support services related; computer and information sciences related; computer installation and repair technology; computer science; criminal justice/police science; dental hygiene; diagnostic medical sonography and ultrasound technology; digital communication and media/multimedia; dramatic/theater arts; education; electrical, electronic and communications engineering technology; engineering-related technologies; environmental science; fire services administration; foreign languages related; general studies; graphic and printing equipment operation/production; health information/medical records technology; health/medical preparatory programs related; human resources management; interior design; international business/trade/commerce; legal assistant/paralegal; marketing/marketing management; mathematics; medical radiologic technology; multi/interdisciplinary studies related; music; nutrition sciences; occupational therapy; physical sciences; physical therapy technology; pre-engineering; prenursing studies; pre-pharmacy studies; registered nursing/registered nurse; respiratory care therapy; sign language interpretation and translation; social sciences; social work; sport and fitness administration/management; surgical technology; veterinary/animal health technology.
Academics *Calendar:* semesters. *Degree:* certificates and associate. *Special study options:* academic remediation for entering students, accelerated degree program, adult/continuing education programs, advanced placement credit, cooperative education, distance learning, English as a second language, freshman honors college, honors programs, independent study, internships, off-campus study, part-time degree program, services for LD students, student-designed majors, study abroad, summer session for credit.
Student Life *Housing:* college housing not available. *Activities and Organizations:* drama/theater group, student-run newspaper, radio station, choral group. *Campus security:* 24-hour emergency response devices and patrols, student patrols, late-night transport/escort service. *Student services:* health clinic, personal/psychological counseling, women's center.
Athletics *Intramural sports:* basketball M, football M, soccer M, softball M, volleyball M.
Financial Aid Of all full-time matriculated undergraduates who enrolled in 2018, 3,986 applied for aid, 2,872 were judged to have need, 115 had their need fully met. In 2018, 500 non-need-based awards were made. *Average percent of need met:* 66%. *Average financial aid package:* $3503. *Average need-based loan:* $1708. *Average need-based gift aid:* $3174. *Average non-need-based aid:* $1830.
Applying *Options:* electronic application, early admission. *Application fee:* $20. *Required:* high school transcript. *Application deadlines:* rolling (freshmen), rolling (transfers).
Freshman Application Contact Ms. Traci Heck, Dean of Enrollment Management, Tulsa Community College, 6111 East Skelly Drive, Tulsa, OK 74135. *Phone:* 918-595-3411. *E-mail:* traci.heck@tulsacc.edu. *Website:* http://www.tulsacc.edu/.

Tulsa Welding School
Tulsa, Oklahoma

Freshman Application Contact Mrs. Debbie Renee Burke, Vice President/Executive Director, Tulsa Welding School, 2545 East 11th Street, Tulsa, OK 74104. *Phone:* 918-587-6789 Ext. 2258. *Toll-free phone:* 888-765-5555. *Fax:* 918-295-6812. *E-mail:* dburke@twsweld.com. *Website:* http://www.tulsaweldingschool.com/.

Western Oklahoma State College
Altus, Oklahoma

Freshman Application Contact Dean Chad E. Wiginton, Dean of Student Support Services, Western Oklahoma State College, 2801 North Main, Altus, OK 73521. *Phone:* 580-477-7918. *Fax:* 580-477-7716. *E-mail:* chad.wiginton@wosc.edu. *Website:* http://www.wosc.edu/.

OREGON

Blue Mountain Community College
Pendleton, Oregon

Director of Admissions Ms. Theresa Bosworth, Director of Admissions, Blue Mountain Community College, 2411 Northwest Carden Avenue, PO Box 100, Pendleton, OR 97801-1000. *Phone:* 541-278-5774. *E-mail:* tbosworth@bluecc.edu. *Website:* http://www.bluecc.edu/.

Central Oregon Community College
Bend, Oregon

- **District-supported** 2-year, founded 1949, part of Oregon Community College Association
- **Small-town** 193-acre campus
- **Endowment** $21.3 million
- **Coed,** 4,871 undergraduate students, 47% full-time, 53% women, 47% men

Undergraduates 2,303 full-time, 2,568 part-time. 0.6% Black or African American, non-Hispanic/Latino; 12% Hispanic/Latino; 1% Asian, non-Hispanic/Latino; 0.3% Native Hawaiian or other Pacific Islander, non-

Hispanic/Latino; 2% American Indian or Alaska Native, non-Hispanic/Latino; 4% Two or more races, non-Hispanic/Latino; 7% Race/ethnicity unknown; 9% transferred in. *Retention:* 61% of full-time freshmen returned.

Freshmen *Admission:* 979 applied, 979 admitted, 1,139 enrolled.

Faculty *Total:* 341, 38% full-time. *Student/faculty ratio:* 19:1.

Majors Accounting; airline pilot and flight crew; art; automobile/automotive mechanics technology; biological and physical sciences; biology/biological sciences; business administration and management; CAD/CADD drafting/design technology; child-care and support services management; computer and information sciences related; computer science; computer systems networking and telecommunications; cooking and related culinary arts; customer service management; dental assisting; dietetics; drafting and design technology; early childhood education; education; electrical, electronic and communications engineering technology; emergency medical technology (EMT paramedic); engineering; entrepreneurship; fire science/firefighting; foreign languages and literatures; forestry; forest technology; health and physical education/fitness; health information/medical records technology; hotel/motel administration; humanities; industrial technology; kinesiology and exercise science; liberal arts and sciences/liberal studies; licensed practical/vocational nurse training; management information systems; manufacturing engineering technology; marketing/marketing management; massage therapy; mathematics; medical/clinical assistant; natural resources/conservation; physical sciences; physical therapy; polymer/plastics engineering; pre-law studies; premedical studies; pre-pharmacy studies; radiologic technology/science; registered nursing/registered nurse; retailing; social sciences; speech communication and rhetoric; sport and fitness administration/management; substance abuse/addiction counseling.

Academics *Calendar:* quarters. *Degree:* certificates, diplomas, and associate. *Special study options:* academic remediation for entering students, cooperative education, distance learning, double majors, English as a second language, independent study, internships, part-time degree program, services for LD students, student-designed majors, study abroad, summer session for credit. *ROTC:* Army (c).

Library COCC Barber Library plus 1 other. *Books:* 58,892 (physical), 236,191 (digital/electronic); *Serial titles:* 5,544 (physical), 126,380 (digital/electronic); *Databases:* 135. Weekly public service hours: 79.

Student Life *Housing Options:* coed, special housing for students with disabilities. Campus housing is university owned. *Activities and Organizations:* drama/theater group, student-run newspaper, choral group, Club Sports, Student Newspaper, Criminal Justice Club, Aviation Club. *Campus security:* 24-hour emergency response devices and patrols, late-night transport/escort service, controlled dormitory access. *Student services:* personal/psychological counseling, veterans affairs office.

Athletics *Intramural sports:* baseball M, basketball M, cross-country running M, football M, rugby M, skiing (cross-country) M, skiing (downhill) M, soccer M, track and field M, volleyball M, weight lifting M.

Financial Aid Of all full-time matriculated undergraduates who enrolled in 2018, 1,723 applied for aid, 1,414 were judged to have need, 140 had their need fully met. In 2018, 30 non-need-based awards were made. *Average percent of need met:* 68%. *Average financial aid package:* $10,951. *Average need-based loan:* $3320. *Average need-based gift aid:* $6325. *Average non-need-based aid:* $1317.

Applying *Options:* electronic application. *Application fee:* $25. *Application deadlines:* rolling (freshmen), rolling (transfers). *Notification:* continuous (freshmen), continuous (transfers).

Director of Admissions Mr. Tyler Hayes, Director, Admissions, Central Oregon Community College, 2600 Northwest College Way, Bend, OR 97703. *Phone:* 541-383-7500. *E-mail:* welcome@cocc.edu. *Website:* http://www.cocc.edu/.

Chemeketa Community College
Salem, Oregon

Freshman Application Contact Admissions Office, Chemeketa Community College, PO Box 14009, Salem, OR 97309. *Phone:* 503-399-5001. *E-mail:* admissions@chemeketa.edu. *Website:* http://www.chemeketa.edu/.

Clackamas Community College
Oregon City, Oregon

Freshman Application Contact Ms. Tara Sprehe, Registrar, Clackamas Community College, 19600 South Molalla Avenue, Oregon City, OR 97045. *Phone:* 503-657-6958 Ext. 2742. *Fax:* 503-650-6654. *E-mail:* pattyw@clackamas.edu. *Website:* http://www.clackamas.edu/.

Clatsop Community College
Astoria, Oregon

Freshman Application Contact Ms. Monica Van Steenberg, Recruiting Coordinator, Clatsop Community College, 1651 Lexington Avenue, Astoria, OR 97103. *Phone:* 503-338-2417. *Toll-free phone:* 855-252-8767. *Fax:* 503-325-5738. *E-mail:* admissions@clatsopcc.edu. *Website:* http://www.clatsopcc.edu/.

Columbia Gorge Community College
The Dalles, Oregon

Freshman Application Contact Columbia Gorge Community College, 400 East Scenic Drive, The Dalles, OR 97058. *Phone:* 541-506-6025. *Website:* http://www.cgcc.edu/.

Concorde Career College
Portland, Oregon

Admissions Office Contact Concorde Career College, 1425 NE Irving Street, Portland, OR 97232. *Website:* http://www.concorde.edu/.

Klamath Community College
Klamath Falls, Oregon

Freshman Application Contact Tammi Garlock, Retention Coordinator, Klamath Community College, 7390 South 6th Street, Klamath Falls, OR 97603. *Phone:* 541-882-3521. *Fax:* 541-885-7758. *E-mail:* garlock@klamathcc.edu. *Website:* http://www.klamathcc.edu/.

Lane Community College
Eugene, Oregon

Freshman Application Contact Lane Community College, 4000 East 30th Avenue, Eugene, OR 97405-0640. *Phone:* 541-747-4501 Ext. 2686. *Website:* http://www.lanecc.edu/.

Linn-Benton Community College
Albany, Oregon

Freshman Application Contact Ms. Kim Sullivan, Outreach Coordinator, Linn-Benton Community College, 6500 Pacific Boulevard, SW, Albany, OR 97321. *Phone:* 541-917-4847. *Fax:* 541-917-4838. *E-mail:* admissions@linnbenton.edu. *Website:* http://www.linnbenton.edu/.

Mt. Hood Community College
Gresham, Oregon

Director of Admissions Dr. Craig Kolins, Associate Vice President of Enrollment Services, Mt. Hood Community College, 26000 Southeast Stark Street, Gresham, OR 97030-3300. *Phone:* 503-491-7265. *Website:* http://www.mhcc.edu/.

Oregon Coast Community College
Newport, Oregon

Freshman Application Contact Student Services, Oregon Coast Community College, 400 SE College Way, Newport, OR 97366. *Phone:* 541-265-2283. *Fax:* 541-265-3820. *E-mail:* webinfo@occc.cc.or.us. *Website:* http://www.oregoncoastcc.org/.

Pacific Bible College
Medford, Oregon

Admissions Office Contact Pacific Bible College, 28 South Fir Street, Medford, OR 97501. *Website:* http://www.pacificbible.com/.

Pioneer Pacific College
Wilsonville, Oregon

Freshman Application Contact Ms. Juli Lau, Vice President of Admissions, Pioneer Pacific College, 27375 Southwest Parkway Avenue, Wilsonville, OR 97070. *Phone:* 503-682-1862. *Toll-free phone:* 866-PPC-INFO. *Fax:* 503-682-1514. *E-mail:* info@pioneerpacific.edu. *Website:* http://www.pioneerpacific.edu/.

Portland Community College
Portland, Oregon

Freshman Application Contact Admissions and Registration Office, Portland Community College, PO Box 19000, Portland, OR 97280. *Phone:* 503-977-8888. *Toll-free phone:* 866-922-1010. *Website:* http://www.pcc.edu/.

Rogue Community College
Grants Pass, Oregon

Freshman Application Contact Mr. John Duarte, Director of Enrollment Services, Rogue Community College, 3345 Redwood Highway, Grants Pass, OR 97527-9291. *Phone:* 541-956-7176. *Fax:* 541-471-3585. *E-mail:* jduarte@roguecc.edu. *Website:* http://www.roguecc.edu/.

Southwestern Oregon Community College
Coos Bay, Oregon

Freshman Application Contact Ms. Brenda Rogers, Admissions, Southwestern Oregon Community College, 1988 Newmark Avenue, Coos Bay, OR 97420. *Phone:* 541-888-7636. *Toll-free phone:* 800-962-2838. *E-mail:* lwells@socc.edu. *Website:* http://www.socc.edu/.

Sumner College
Portland, Oregon

- **Proprietary** 2-year, founded 1974
- **Urban** campus with easy access to Portland
- **Coed, primarily women,** 261 undergraduate students, 100% full-time, 84% women, 16% men

Undergraduates 261 full-time. 10% are from out of state; 15% Black or African American, non-Hispanic/Latino; 6% Hispanic/Latino; 7% Asian, non-Hispanic/Latino; 0.8% Race/ethnicity unknown.
Freshmen *Admission:* 261 enrolled.
Faculty *Total:* 25, 48% full-time. *Student/faculty ratio:* 15:1.
Majors Registered nursing/registered nurse.
Academics *Calendar:* quarters. *Degree:* diplomas and associate. *Special study options:* academic remediation for entering students, distance learning.
Library Main Library plus 1 other. *Books:* 800 (physical); *Serial titles:* 100 (digital/electronic); *Databases:* 2. Weekly public service hours: 50; students can reserve study rooms.
Student Life *Housing:* college housing not available. *Activities and Organizations:* Medical Club.
Applying *Required:* high school transcript, interview. *Required for some:* essay or personal statement, Entrance exam.
Admissions Office Contact Sumner College, 15115 SW Sequoia Parkway, Suite 200, Portland, OR 97224.
Website: http://www.sumnercollege.edu/.

Tillamook Bay Community College
Tillamook, Oregon

- **District-supported** 2-year, founded 1984
- **Rural** 7-acre campus
- **Endowment** $475,359
- **Coed**

Undergraduates 127 full-time, 134 part-time. Students come from 1 other state; 18% Hispanic/Latino; 2% Asian, non-Hispanic/Latino; 0.4% Native Hawaiian or other Pacific Islander, non-Hispanic/Latino; 2% American Indian or Alaska Native, non-Hispanic/Latino; 3% Race/ethnicity unknown; 4% international; 3% transferred in. *Retention:* 14% of full-time freshmen returned.
Faculty *Student/faculty ratio:* 15:1.
Academics *Calendar:* quarters. *Degree:* certificates and associate. *Special study options:* academic remediation for entering students, advanced placement credit, distance learning, English as a second language, independent study, part-time degree program, services for LD students, summer session for credit.
Library Tillamook Bay Community College Library. *Books:* 3,696 (physical), 172,327 (digital/electronic); *Serial titles:* 27 (physical), 44,286 (digital/electronic). Weekly public service hours: 48; students can reserve study rooms.
Student Life *Campus security:* alarmed exterior doors, classroom door locks.
Applying *Options:* electronic application. *Recommended:* high school transcript.
Freshman Application Contact Rhoda Hanson, Director of Student Services, Tillamook Bay Community College, 4301 Third Street, Tillamook, OR 97224. *Phone:* 503-842-8222 Ext. 1110. *Fax:* 503-842-8334. *E-mail:* rhodahanson@tillamookbaycc.edu. *Website:* http://www.tillamookbaycc.edu/.

Treasure Valley Community College
Ontario, Oregon

- **State and locally supported** 2-year, founded 1962
- **Rural** 90-acre campus with easy access to Boise
- **Endowment** $5.9 million
- **Coed,** 1,866 undergraduate students, 43% full-time, 55% women, 45% men

Undergraduates 807 full-time, 1,059 part-time. Students come from 15 states and territories; 2 other countries; 67% are from out of state; 2% Black or African American, non-Hispanic/Latino; 25% Hispanic/Latino; 0.7% Asian, non-Hispanic/Latino; 0.3% Native Hawaiian or other Pacific Islander, non-Hispanic/Latino; 1% American Indian or Alaska Native, non-Hispanic/Latino; 3% Two or more races, non-Hispanic/Latino; 4% Race/ethnicity unknown; 0.4% international; 6% transferred in; 4% live on campus. *Retention:* 40% of full-time freshmen returned.
Freshmen *Admission:* 2,447 applied, 2,447 admitted, 389 enrolled.
Faculty *Total:* 86, 55% full-time, 79% with terminal degrees. *Student/faculty ratio:* 21:1.
Majors Agricultural business and management; agricultural economics; agriculture; agronomy and crop science; airline pilot and flight crew; animal sciences; business administration and management; carpentry; computer and information sciences; computer science; criminal justice/police science; drafting and design technology; elementary education; farm and ranch management; fire prevention and safety technology; general studies; horse husbandry/equine science and management; horticultural science; industrial technology; liberal arts and sciences/liberal studies; management information systems; medical administrative assistant and medical secretary; medical/clinical assistant; medical transcription; natural resources/conservation; office management; range science and management; registered nursing/registered nurse; soil science and agronomy; solar energy technology; substance abuse/addiction counseling; welding technology; wildlife, fish and wildlands science and management.
Academics *Calendar:* quarters. *Degree:* certificates and associate. *Special study options:* academic remediation for entering students, accelerated degree program, adult/continuing education programs, advanced placement credit, cooperative education, distance learning, English as a second language, honors programs, independent study, internships, off-campus study, part-time degree program, services for LD students, summer session for credit.
Library Treasure Valley Community College Library. *Books:* 26,100 (physical), 1.5 million (digital/electronic); *Serial titles:* 47 (physical), 3 (digital/electronic); *Databases:* 10. Weekly public service hours: 72; students can reserve study rooms.
Student Life *Housing Options:* coed, special housing for students with disabilities. Campus housing is university owned. *Activities and Organizations:* choral group, Phi Theta Kappa, Natural Resources, International Business Club, Circle K International (service organization), Ag Ambassadors. *Campus security:* 24-hour emergency response devices, late-night transport/escort service, controlled dormitory access.
Athletics *Intercollegiate sports:* basketball W(s), cross-country running W(s), soccer W(s), softball W(s), tennis W(s), track and field W(s), volleyball W(s). *Intramural sports:* basketball M, soccer M, softball M, table tennis M, volleyball M.
Financial Aid Of all full-time matriculated undergraduates who enrolled in 2017, 90 Federal Work-Study jobs (averaging $1500).
Applying *Options:* electronic application, early admission, deferred entrance. *Application deadlines:* rolling (freshmen), rolling (transfers). *Notification:* continuous (freshmen), continuous (transfers).
Freshman Application Contact Mr. Travis McFetridge, Director of Admissions and Student Success, Treasure Valley Community College, 650 College Boulevard, Ontario, OR 97914. *Phone:* 541-881-5825. *E-mail:* tmcfetri@tvcc.cc.
Website: http://www.tvcc.cc/.

Umpqua Community College
Roseburg, Oregon

Freshman Application Contact Admissions Office, Umpqua Community College, PO Box 967, Roseburg, OR 97470-0226. *Phone:* 541-440-7743. *Fax:* 541-440-4612. *Website:* http://www.umpqua.edu/.

PENNSYLVANIA

All-State Career School–Essington Campus

Essington, Pennsylvania

Admissions Office Contact All-State Career School–Essington Campus, 50 West Powhattan Ave, Essington, PA 19029. *Website:* http://www.allstatecareer.edu/.

Berks Technical Institute

Wyomissing, Pennsylvania

Freshman Application Contact Mr. Allan Brussolo, Academic Dean, Berks Technical Institute, 2205 Ridgewood Road, Wyomissing, PA 19610-1168. *Phone:* 610-372-1722. *Toll-free phone:* 866-591-8384. *Fax:* 610-376-4684. *E-mail:* abrussolo@berks.edu. *Website:* http://www.berks.edu/.

Bidwell Training Center

Pittsburgh, Pennsylvania

Freshman Application Contact Admissions Office, Bidwell Training Center, 1815 Metropolitan Street, Pittsburgh, PA 15233. *Phone:* 412-322-1773. *Toll-free phone:* 800-516-1800. *E-mail:* admissions@mcg-btc.org. *Website:* http://www.bidwelltraining.edu/.

Bucks County Community College

Newtown, Pennsylvania

- **County-supported** 2-year, founded 1964
- **Suburban** 200-acre campus with easy access to Philadelphia
- **Endowment** $7.1 million
- **Coed,** 7,761 undergraduate students, 37% full-time, 57% women, 43% men

Undergraduates 2,852 full-time, 4,909 part-time. Students come from 18 states and territories; 1% are from out of state; 6% Black or African American, non-Hispanic/Latino; 8% Hispanic/Latino; 4% Asian, non-Hispanic/Latino; 0.2% Native Hawaiian or other Pacific Islander, non-Hispanic/Latino; 0.5% American Indian or Alaska Native, non-Hispanic/Latino; 3% Two or more races, non-Hispanic/Latino; 8% Race/ethnicity unknown; 0.4% international; 72% transferred in. *Retention:* 69% of full-time freshmen returned.

Freshmen *Admission:* 3,742 applied, 3,420 admitted, 1,571 enrolled.

Faculty *Total:* 638, 23% full-time, 21% with terminal degrees. *Student/faculty ratio:* 15:1.

Majors Accounting technology and bookkeeping; art history, criticism and conservation; baking and pastry arts; biology/biotechnology laboratory technician; biology teacher education; business administration and management; business/commerce; cabinetmaking and millwork; chemical technology; child-care provision; cinematography and film/video production; clinical/medical laboratory technology; commercial and advertising art; commercial photography; computer and information sciences; computer and information systems security; computer systems networking and telecommunications; criminal justice/safety; critical infrastructure protection; culinary arts; early childhood education; engineering; engineering technology; English; environmental science; fire services administration; general studies; health professions related; health services/allied health/health sciences; history; history teacher education; hospitality administration; information science/studies; journalism; kinesiology and exercise science; legal professions and studies related; liberal arts and sciences and humanities related; liberal arts and sciences/liberal studies; mathematics; mathematics teacher education; medical/clinical assistant; medical insurance coding; meeting and event planning; multi/interdisciplinary studies related; music; network and system administration; neuroscience; physical education teaching and coaching; psychology; radiologic technology/science; registered nursing/registered nurse; small business administration; social sciences; social work; speech communication and rhetoric; sport and fitness administration/management; visual and performing arts; web page, digital/multimedia and information resources design.

Academics *Calendar:* semesters. *Degree:* certificates and associate. *Special study options:* academic remediation for entering students, adult/continuing education programs, advanced placement credit, cooperative education, distance learning, English as a second language, external degree program, independent study, internships, part-time degree program, services for LD students, student-designed majors, summer session for credit.

Library Bucks County Community College Library. *Books:* 111,025 (physical), 8,473 (digital/electronic); *Serial titles:* 186 (physical), 66 (digital/electronic); *Databases:* 59. Weekly public service hours: 73; students can reserve study rooms.

Student Life *Housing:* college housing not available. *Activities and Organizations:* drama/theater group, student-run newspaper, radio and television station, choral group, Bucks Lemon Club, Kinesiology & Sports Studies Club, NSLS, Bucks Business Association, Bucks County Anthropology Society. *Campus security:* 24-hour emergency response devices and patrols, late-night transport/escort service. *Student services:* personal/psychological counseling, women's center, veterans affairs office.

Athletics Member NJCAA. *Intercollegiate sports:* baseball M, basketball M/W, cross-country running M/W, equestrian sports W, golf M/W, soccer M/W, softball W, tennis M/W, volleyball W. *Intramural sports:* baseball M, basketball M/W, cross-country running M/W, equestrian sports W, football M, skiing (downhill) M(c)/W(c), soccer M/W, table tennis M, tennis M/W, volleyball W.

Financial Aid Of all full-time matriculated undergraduates who enrolled in 2016, 147 Federal Work-Study jobs (averaging $1708).

Applying *Options:* electronic application, early admission. *Required:* high school transcript. *Required for some:* essay or personal statement, interview.

Freshman Application Contact Ms. Marlene Barlow, Director of Admissions, Bucks County Community College, 275 Swamp Rd., Newtown, PA 18940. *Phone:* 215-968-8137. *E-mail:* marlene.barlow@bucks.edu. *Website:* http://www.bucks.edu/.

Butler County Community College

Butler, Pennsylvania

Freshman Application Contact Mr. Robert Morris, Director of Admissions, Butler County Community College, College Drive, PO Box 1205, Butler, PA 16003-1203. *Phone:* 724-287-8711 Ext. 344. *Toll-free phone:* 888-826-2829. *Fax:* 724-287-4961. *E-mail:* robert.morris@bc3.edu. *Website:* http://www.bc3.edu/.

Central Pennsylvania Institute of Science and Technology

Pleasant Gap, Pennsylvania

Admissions Office Contact Central Pennsylvania Institute of Science and Technology, 540 North Harrison Road, Pleasant Gap, PA 16823. *Website:* http://www.cpi.edu/.

Commonwealth Technical Institute

Johnstown, Pennsylvania

Freshman Application Contact Mr. Jason Gies, Admissions Supervisor, Commonwealth Technical Institute, Hiram G. Andrews Center, 727 Goucher Street, Johnstown, PA 15905. *Phone:* 814-255-8200 Ext. 0564. *Toll-free phone:* 800-762-4211. *Fax:* 814-255-8283. *E-mail:* jgies@pa.gov. *Website:* http://www.dli.pa.gov/Individuals/Disability-Services/hgac/Pages/default.aspx.

Community College of Allegheny County

Pittsburgh, Pennsylvania

- **County-supported** 2-year, founded 1966
- **Urban** 242-acre campus
- **Coed,** 16,086 undergraduate students, 33% full-time, 54% women, 46% men

Undergraduates 5,354 full-time, 10,732 part-time. 17% Black or African American, non-Hispanic/Latino; 3% Hispanic/Latino; 3% Asian, non-Hispanic/Latino; 0.1% Native Hawaiian or other Pacific Islander, non-Hispanic/Latino; 0.5% American Indian or Alaska Native, non-Hispanic/Latino; 3% Two or more races, non-Hispanic/Latino; 13% Race/ethnicity unknown.

Freshmen *Admission:* 3,768 enrolled.

Faculty *Student/faculty ratio:* 18:1.

Majors Accounting technology and bookkeeping; administrative assistant and secretarial science; airline pilot and flight crew; applied horticulture/horticulture operations; architectural drafting and CAD/CADD; art; athletic training; automobile/automotive mechanics technology; automotive engineering technology; aviation/airway management; banking and financial support services; biology/biological sciences; biotechnology; building construction technology; building/property maintenance; business administration and management; business automation/technology/data entry; business machine repair; CAD/CADD drafting/design technology; carpentry; chemical technology; chemistry; child-care provision; child development; civil drafting and CAD/CADD; civil engineering technology; clinical/medical laboratory technology; commercial and advertising art; communications

technologies and support services related; community health services counseling; computer and information sciences; computer and information systems security; computer engineering technology; computer programming; computer technology/computer systems technology; construction engineering technology; construction trades; construction trades related; corrections; cosmetology and personal grooming arts related; court reporting; criminal justice/police science; critical infrastructure protection; culinary arts; diagnostic medical sonography and ultrasound technology; dietitian assistant; drafting and design technology; drafting/design engineering technologies related; dramatic/theater arts; education (specific levels and methods) related; education (specific subject areas) related; electrical, electronic and communications engineering technology; electrician; electroneurodiagnostic/electroencephalographic technology; elementary education; emergency medical technology (EMT paramedic); energy management and systems technology; engineering science; engineering technologies and engineering related; English; entrepreneurship; environmental engineering technology; fire prevention and safety technology; food service systems administration; foreign languages and literatures; game and interactive media design; general studies; graphic design; greenhouse management; health and physical education/fitness; health information/medical records technology; health professions related; health unit coordinator/ward clerk; heating, air conditioning, ventilation and refrigeration maintenance technology; hotel/motel administration; housing and human environments related; human development and family studies related; humanities; human resources management; hydraulics and fluid power technology; industrial and product design; industrial technology; insurance; journalism; landscaping and groundskeeping; legal administrative assistant/secretary; legal assistant/paralegal; liberal arts and sciences/liberal studies; licensed practical/vocational nurse training; machine shop technology; management information systems; manufacturing engineering technology; marketing/marketing management; mathematics; mechanical drafting and CAD/CADD; mechanical engineering/mechanical technology; mechatronics, robotics, and automation engineering; medical administrative assistant and medical secretary; medical/clinical assistant; medical radiologic technology; middle school education; music; nanotechnology; nuclear medical technology; nursing assistant/aide and patient care assistant/aide; occupational therapist assistant; office management; ornamental horticulture; painting and wall covering; perioperative/operating room and surgical nursing; pharmacy technician; physical therapy technology; physics; plant nursery management; psychiatric/mental health services technology; psychology; quality control technology; radiologic technology/science; real estate; registered nursing/registered nurse; respiratory care therapy; restaurant, culinary, and catering management; retailing; robotics technology; science technologies related; sheet metal technology; sign language interpretation and translation; social sciences; social work; sociology; solar energy technology; substance abuse/addiction counseling; surgical technology; teacher assistant/aide; therapeutic recreation; tourism promotion; turf and turfgrass management; visual and performing arts related; welding technology.
Academics *Calendar:* semesters. *Degree:* certificates, diplomas, and associate. *Special study options:* academic remediation for entering students, accelerated degree program, distance learning, English as a second language, honors programs, off-campus study, part-time degree program, services for LD students, study abroad, summer session for credit. *ROTC:* Army (c), Navy (c), Air Force (c).
Library Community College of Allegheny County Libraries. *Books:* 121,707 (physical), 59,726 (digital/electronic); *Serial titles:* 509 (physical), 5 (digital/electronic); *Databases:* 114. Weekly public service hours: 12.
Student Life *Housing:* college housing not available. *Activities and Organizations:* drama/theater group, student-run radio and television station, choral group, Art Club, Veterans Club, Computer Science Club, Phi Theta Kappa, Women on a Mission. *Campus security:* 24-hour emergency response devices and patrols, late-night transport/escort service. *Student services:* health clinic, personal/psychological counseling, veterans affairs office.
Athletics Member NJCAA. *Intercollegiate sports:* basketball W, bowling W, cross-country running W, golf W, softball W, table tennis W, tennis W, volleyball W. *Intramural sports:* badminton M, basketball M, bowling M, cross-country running M, football M, golf M, lacrosse M, racquetball M, softball M, table tennis M, tennis M, volleyball M, weight lifting M.
Applying *Recommended:* high school transcript.
Admissions Office Contact Community College of Allegheny County, 800 Allegheny Avenue, Pittsburgh, PA 15233-1894.
Website: http://www.ccac.edu/.

Community College of Beaver County
Monaca, Pennsylvania

Freshman Application Contact Enrollment Management, Community College of Beaver County, One Campus Drive, Monaca, PA 15061-2588. *Phone:* 724-480-3500. *Toll-free phone:* 800-335-0222. *E-mail:* admissions@ccbc.edu. *Website:* http://www.ccbc.edu/.

Community College of Philadelphia
Philadelphia, Pennsylvania

- **State and locally supported** 2-year, founded 1964
- **Urban** 14-acre campus with easy access to Philadelphia
- **Coed**

Undergraduates Students come from 50 other countries.
Academics *Calendar:* semesters. *Degree:* certificates, diplomas, and associate. *Special study options:* academic remediation for entering students, accelerated degree program, adult/continuing education programs, advanced placement credit, cooperative education, distance learning, English as a second language, external degree program, honors programs, independent study, internships, off-campus study, part-time degree program, services for LD students, student-designed majors, study abroad, summer session for credit. *ROTC:* Army (c).
Library Main Campus Library plus 2 others. *Books:* 84,000 (physical); *Databases:* 40. Weekly public service hours: 30; students can reserve study rooms.
Student Life *Campus security:* 24-hour emergency response devices and patrols, late-night transport/escort service, phone/alert systems in classrooms/buildings, electronic messages/alerts, ID required to enter buildings.
Athletics Member NJCAA.
Applying *Options:* electronic application, early admission, deferred entrance. *Required for some:* high school transcript, specific entry requirements for allied health and nursing programs.
Freshman Application Contact Community College of Philadelphia, 1700 Spring Garden Street, Philadelphia, PA 19130-3991. *Phone:* 215-751-8010. *Website:* http://www.ccp.edu/.

Dean Institute of Technology
Pittsburgh, Pennsylvania

Director of Admissions Mr. Nicholas Ali, Admissions Director, Dean Institute of Technology, 1501 West Liberty Avenue, Pittsburgh, PA 15226-1103. *Phone:* 412-531-4433. *Website:* http://www.deantech.edu/.

Delaware County Community College
Media, Pennsylvania

Freshman Application Contact Ms. Hope Diehl, Director of Admissions and Enrollment Services, Delaware County Community College, 901 South Media Line Road, Media, PA 19063-1094. *Phone:* 610-359-5050. *Fax:* 610-723-1530. *E-mail:* admiss@dccc.edu. *Website:* http://www.dccc.edu/.

Douglas Education Center
Monessen, Pennsylvania

Freshman Application Contact Ms. Sherry Lee Walters, Director of Enrollment Services, Douglas Education Center, 130 Seventh Street, Monessen, PA 15062. *Phone:* 724-684-3684 Ext. 2181. *Toll-free phone:* 800-413-6013. *Website:* http://www.dec.edu/.

Erie Institute of Technology
Erie, Pennsylvania

Freshman Application Contact Erie Institute of Technology, 940 Millcreek Mall, Erie, PA 16565. *Phone:* 814-868-9900. *Toll-free phone:* 866-868-3743. *Website:* http://www.erieit.edu/.

Fortis Institute
Erie, Pennsylvania

Director of Admissions Guy M. Euliano, President, Fortis Institute, 5757 West 26th Street, Erie, PA 16506. *Phone:* 814-838-7673. *Toll-free phone:* 855-4-FORTIS. *Fax:* 814-838-8642. *E-mail:* geuliano@tsbi.org. *Website:* http://www.fortis.edu/.

Fortis Institute
Forty Fort, Pennsylvania

Freshman Application Contact Admissions Office, Fortis Institute, 166 Slocum Street, Forty Fort, PA 18704. *Phone:* 570-288-8400. *Toll-free phone:* 855-4-FORTIS. *Website:* http://www.fortis.edu/.

Fortis Institute

Scranton, Pennsylvania

Director of Admissions Ms. Heather Contardi, Director of Admissions, Fortis Institute, 517 Ash Street, Scranton, PA 18509. *Phone:* 570-558-1818. *Toll-free phone:* 855-4-FORTIS. *Fax:* 570-342-4537. *E-mail:* heatherp@markogroup.com. *Website:* http://www.fortis.edu/.

Great Lakes Institute of Technology

Erie, Pennsylvania

Admissions Office Contact Great Lakes Institute of Technology, 5100 Peach Street, Erie, PA 16509. *Website:* http://www.glit.edu/.

Harcum College

Bryn Mawr, Pennsylvania

Freshman Application Contact Office of Enrollment Management, Harcum College, 750 Montgomery Avenue, Bryn Mawr, PA 19010-3476. *Phone:* 610-526-6050. *E-mail:* enroll@harcum.edu. *Website:* http://www.harcum.edu/.

Harrisburg Area Community College

Harrisburg, Pennsylvania

- **State and locally supported** 2-year, founded 1964
- **Urban** 212-acre campus
- **Coed,** 18,081 undergraduate students, 29% full-time, 64% women, 36% men

Undergraduates 5,222 full-time, 12,859 part-time. 3% are from out of state; 10% Black or African American, non-Hispanic/Latino; 12% Hispanic/Latino; 4% Asian, non-Hispanic/Latino; 0.1% Native Hawaiian or other Pacific Islander, non-Hispanic/Latino; 0.2% American Indian or Alaska Native, non-Hispanic/Latino; 3% Two or more races, non-Hispanic/Latino; 2% Race/ethnicity unknown; 2% international; 8% transferred in.
Freshmen *Admission:* 12,698 applied, 12,698 admitted, 2,956 enrolled.
Faculty *Total:* 1,076, 31% full-time, 55% with terminal degrees. *Student/faculty ratio:* 17:1.
Majors Administrative assistant and secretarial science; adult development and aging; architectural engineering technology; automobile/automotive mechanics technology; biology/biological sciences; business administration and management; business/commerce; cardiovascular technology; chemistry; civil engineering technology; clinical/medical laboratory technology; communication and journalism related; computer and information sciences; computer and information systems security; computer science; computer systems networking and telecommunications; construction engineering technology; criminal justice/law enforcement administration; criminal justice/police science; culinary arts; dental hygiene; design and visual communications; dramatic/theater arts; early childhood education; electrical, electronic and communications engineering technology; electrician; engineering; engineering technologies and engineering related; environmental science; fire science/firefighting; general studies; geographic information science and cartography; graphic design; health and physical education/fitness; health/health-care administration; health professions related; health services administration; heating, air conditioning, ventilation and refrigeration maintenance technology; hospitality administration related; human services; international relations and affairs; legal assistant/paralegal; mathematics; mechanical engineering/mechanical technology; mechatronics, robotics, and automation engineering; medical informatics; music management; philosophy; photography; physical sciences; psychology; radiologic technology/science; registered nursing/registered nurse; respiratory care therapy; secondary education; social sciences; social work; structural engineering; surgical technology; visual and performing arts; web page, digital/multimedia and information resources design.
Academics *Calendar:* semesters. *Degree:* certificates, diplomas, and associate. *Special study options:* academic remediation for entering students, adult/continuing education programs, advanced placement credit, distance learning, double majors, English as a second language, honors programs, independent study, internships, part-time degree program, services for LD students, summer session for credit. *ROTC:* Army (b).
Library McCormick Library.
Student Life *Housing:* college housing not available. *Activities and Organizations:* drama/theater group, student-run newspaper, Student Government Association, Phi Theta Kappa, African-American Student Association, Mosiaco Club, Fourth Estate. *Campus security:* 24-hour emergency response devices and patrols, late-night transport/escort service. *Student services:* veterans affairs office.
Athletics *Intercollegiate sports:* basketball W, volleyball W.
Financial Aid Of all full-time matriculated undergraduates who enrolled in 2017, 3,844 applied for aid, 3,049 were judged to have need. *Average financial aid package:* $3080. *Average need-based loan:* $3078. *Average need-based gift aid:* $4736.
Applying *Options:* electronic application, early admission, deferred entrance. *Required for some:* high school transcript, 1 letter of recommendation, interview.
Admissions Office Contact Harrisburg Area Community College, 1 HACC Drive, Harrisburg, PA 17110-2999. *Toll-free phone:* 800-ABC-HACC. *Website:* http://www.hacc.edu/.

JNA Institute of Culinary Arts

Philadelphia, Pennsylvania

Freshman Application Contact Admissions Office, JNA Institute of Culinary Arts, 1212 South Broad Street, Philadelphia, PA 19146. *Website:* http://www.culinaryarts.com/.

Johnson College

Scranton, Pennsylvania

- **Independent** 2-year, founded 1912
- **Urban** 65-acre campus
- **Coed**

Undergraduates 363 full-time, 13 part-time. *Retention:* 69% of full-time freshmen returned.
Faculty *Student/faculty ratio:* 17:1.
Academics *Calendar:* semesters. *Degree:* certificates and associate. *Special study options:* academic remediation for entering students, adult/continuing education programs, internships, part-time degree program, services for LD students, summer session for credit.
Library Johnson College Library.
Student Life *Campus security:* 24-hour emergency response devices.
Standardized Tests *Required for some:* SAT (for admission). *Recommended:* SAT (for admission).
Financial Aid Of all full-time matriculated undergraduates who enrolled in 2017, 40 Federal Work-Study jobs (averaging $800).
Applying *Options:* electronic application, deferred entrance. *Application fee:* $30. *Required:* essay or personal statement, high school transcript. *Required for some:* interview.
Freshman Application Contact Johnson College, 3427 North Main Avenue, Scranton, PA 18508-1495. *Phone:* 570-702-8911. *Toll-free phone:* 800-2WE-WORK. *Website:* http://www.johnson.edu/.

Lackawanna College

Scranton, Pennsylvania

- **Independent** primarily 2-year, founded 1894
- **Urban** 4-acre campus
- **Endowment** $5.7 million
- **Coed**

Undergraduates 1,169 full-time, 435 part-time. Students come from 16 states and territories; 16% Black or African American, non-Hispanic/Latino; 11% Hispanic/Latino; 1% Asian, non-Hispanic/Latino; 0.1% Native Hawaiian or other Pacific Islander, non-Hispanic/Latino; 0.4% American Indian or Alaska Native, non-Hispanic/Latino; 2% Two or more races, non-Hispanic/Latino; 8% Race/ethnicity unknown; 0.4% international; 10% transferred in. *Retention:* 55% of full-time freshmen returned.
Faculty *Student/faculty ratio:* 16:1.
Academics *Calendar:* semesters. *Degrees:* certificates, diplomas, associate, and bachelor's. *Special study options:* academic remediation for entering students, adult/continuing education programs, cooperative education, double majors, English as a second language, internships, part-time degree program, services for LD students, summer session for credit. *ROTC:* Army (c), Air Force (c).
Library Albright Memorial Library plus 1 other. Students can reserve study rooms.
Student Life *Campus security:* 24-hour emergency response devices and patrols, late-night transport/escort service, controlled dormitory access, patrols by college liaison staff.
Athletics Member NJCAA.
Standardized Tests *Recommended:* SAT or ACT (for admission).
Financial Aid Of all full-time matriculated undergraduates who enrolled in 2016, 1,049 applied for aid, 953 were judged to have need, 38 had their need fully met. 80 Federal Work-Study jobs (averaging $779). 21 state and other part-time jobs (averaging $619). In 2016, 18. *Average percent of need met:* 47. *Average financial aid package:* $9537. *Average need-based loan:* $3247. *Average need-based gift aid:* $7272. *Average non-need-based aid:* $4882. *Average indebtedness upon graduation:* $7347.

Applying *Options:* electronic application, early admission, deferred entrance. *Application fee:* $35. *Required:* high school transcript, interview.
Freshman Application Contact Mr. Eddie Perry, Admissions Advisor, Lackawanna College, 501 Vine Street, Scranton, PA 18509. *Phone:* 570-961-7889. *Toll-free phone:* 877-346-3552. *E-mail:* perrye@lackawanna.edu. *Website:* http://www.lackawanna.edu/.

Lancaster County Career and Technology Center
Willow Street, Pennsylvania

Admissions Office Contact Lancaster County Career and Technology Center, 1730 Hans Herr Drive, Willow Street, PA 17584. *Website:* http://www.lancasterctc.edu/.

Lansdale School of Business
North Wales, Pennsylvania

Freshman Application Contact Lansdale School of Business, 290 Wissahickon Avenue, North Wales, PA 19454. *Phone:* 215-699-5700 Ext. 112. *Toll-free phone:* 800-219-0486. *Website:* http://www.lsb.edu/.

Laurel Business Institute
Uniontown, Pennsylvania

Freshman Application Contact Mrs. Lisa Dolan, Laurel Business Institute, 11 East Penn Street, PO Box 877, Uniontown, PA 15401. *Phone:* 724-439-4900 Ext. 158. *Fax:* 724-439-3607. *E-mail:* ldolan@laurel.edu. *Website:* http://www.laurel.edu/locations/uniontown.

Laurel Technical Institute
Sharon, Pennsylvania

Freshman Application Contact Irene Lewis, Laurel Technical Institute, 200 Sterling Avenue, Sharon, PA 16146. *Phone:* 724-983-0700. *Fax:* 724-983-8355. *E-mail:* info@biop.edu. *Website:* http://www.laurel.edu/locations/sharon.

Lehigh Carbon Community College
Schnecksville, Pennsylvania

- **State and locally supported** 2-year, founded 1966
- **Suburban** 254-acre campus with easy access to Philadelphia
- **Endowment** $5.7 million
- **Coed**

Undergraduates 2,476 full-time, 4,477 part-time. Students come from 11 states and territories; 18 other countries; 0.4% are from out of state; 7% Black or African American, non-Hispanic/Latino; 22% Hispanic/Latino; 2% Asian, non-Hispanic/Latino; 0.1% American Indian or Alaska Native, non-Hispanic/Latino; 4% Two or more races, non-Hispanic/Latino; 3% Race/ethnicity unknown; 0.4% international; 53% transferred in.
Faculty *Student/faculty ratio:* 18:1.
Academics *Calendar:* semesters. *Degree:* certificates, diplomas, and associate. *Special study options:* academic remediation for entering students, advanced placement credit, cooperative education, distance learning, English as a second language, external degree program, honors programs, independent study, internships, off-campus study, part-time degree program, services for LD students, summer session for credit. *ROTC:* Army (c).
Library Rothrock Library. *Books:* 48,142 (physical), 68,508 (digital/electronic); *Serial titles:* 220 (physical), 182 (digital/electronic); *Databases:* 46. Weekly public service hours: 71.
Student Life *Campus security:* 24-hour emergency response devices.
Athletics Member NJCAA.
Applying *Options:* electronic application. *Required for some:* essay or personal statement, high school transcript, interview.
Freshman Application Contact Ms. Nancy Kelley, Admission Representative, Lehigh Carbon Community College, 4525 Education Park Drive, Schnecksville, PA 18078. *Phone:* 610-799-1558. *Fax:* 610-799-1527. *E-mail:* admissions@lccc.edu. *Website:* http://www.lccc.edu/.

Lincoln Technical Institute
Allentown, Pennsylvania

Freshman Application Contact Admissions Office, Lincoln Technical Institute, 5151 Tilghman Street, Allentown, PA 18104. *Phone:* 610-398-5301. *Toll-free phone:* 844-215-1513. *Website:* http://www.lincolntech.edu/.

Lincoln Technical Institute
Philadelphia, Pennsylvania

Director of Admissions Mr. James Kuntz, Executive Director, Lincoln Technical Institute, 9191 Torresdale Avenue, Philadelphia, PA 19136. *Phone:* 215-335-0800. *Toll-free phone:* 844-215-1513. *Fax:* 215-335-1443. *E-mail:* jkuntz@lincolntech.com. *Website:* http://www.lincolntech.edu/.

Luzerne County Community College
Nanticoke, Pennsylvania

- **County-supported** 2-year, founded 1966
- **Suburban** 122-acre campus
- **Coed,** 4,984 undergraduate students, 41% full-time, 61% women, 39% men

Undergraduates 2,064 full-time, 2,920 part-time. 5% Black or African American, non-Hispanic/Latino; 15% Hispanic/Latino; 2% Asian, non-Hispanic/Latino; 0.1% Native Hawaiian or other Pacific Islander, non-Hispanic/Latino; 0.3% American Indian or Alaska Native, non-Hispanic/Latino; 2% Two or more races, non-Hispanic/Latino; 10% Race/ethnicity unknown. *Retention:* 56% of full-time freshmen returned.
Freshmen *Admission:* 2,371 applied, 2,371 admitted, 1,067 enrolled.
Faculty *Total:* 446, 24% full-time. *Student/faculty ratio:* 15:1.
Majors Accounting; administrative assistant and secretarial science; architectural engineering; architectural engineering technology; automobile/automotive mechanics technology; baking and pastry arts; banking and financial support services; biological and physical sciences; building/property maintenance; business administration and management; child-care provision; commercial and advertising art; commercial photography; computer and information sciences; computer and information sciences related; computer graphics; computer programming related; computer science; computer systems networking and telecommunications; computer technology/computer systems technology; court reporting; criminal justice/law enforcement administration; culinary arts; data entry/microcomputer applications; data processing and data processing technology; dental hygiene; drafting and design technology; drafting/design engineering technologies related; drawing; early childhood education; education; electrical, electronic and communications engineering technology; electrician; emergency medical technology (EMT paramedic); engineering technology; executive assistant/executive secretary; fire science/firefighting; food technology and processing; funeral service and mortuary science; general studies; graphic and printing equipment operation/production; graphic design; health and physical education/fitness; health/health-care administration; heating, air conditioning, ventilation and refrigeration maintenance technology; hospitality and recreation marketing; hotel/motel administration; humanities; human services; industrial and product design; international business/trade/commerce; journalism; legal assistant/paralegal; liberal arts and sciences and humanities related; liberal arts and sciences/liberal studies; mathematics; medical administrative assistant and medical secretary; painting; photography; physical education teaching and coaching; plumbing technology; pre-pharmacy studies; radio and television broadcasting technology; registered nursing/registered nurse; respiratory care therapy; social sciences; surgical technology.
Academics *Calendar:* semesters. *Degree:* certificates, diplomas, and associate. *Special study options:* academic remediation for entering students, accelerated degree program, advanced placement credit, distance learning, external degree program, internships, part-time degree program, services for LD students, summer session for credit. *ROTC:* Army (c).
Library Learning Resources Center plus 1 other. Students can reserve study rooms.
Student Life *Housing:* college housing not available. *Activities and Organizations:* drama/theater group, student-run radio and television station, choral group, Student Government, Circle K, Nursing Forum, Science Club, SADAH. *Campus security:* 24-hour patrols. *Student services:* veterans affairs office.
Athletics Member NJCAA. *Intercollegiate sports:* basketball W, cross-country running W, softball W, volleyball W. *Intramural sports:* basketball M, bowling M, softball M, volleyball M.
Applying *Options:* electronic application. *Recommended:* high school transcript.
Freshman Application Contact Mr. James Domzalski, Director of Enrollment Management, Luzerne County Community College, 1333 South Prospect Street, Nanticoke, PA 18634. *Phone:* 570-740-0342. *Toll-free phone:* 800-377-5222 Ext. 7337. *Fax:* 570-740-0238. *E-mail:* admissions@luzerne.edu.
Website: http://www.luzerne.edu/.

Manor College

Jenkintown, Pennsylvania

- **Independent Byzantine Catholic** primarily 2-year, founded 1947
- **Suburban** 35-acre campus with easy access to Philadelphia
- **Endowment** $2.8 million
- **Coed,** 740 undergraduate students, 65% full-time, 67% women, 33% men

Undergraduates 480 full-time, 260 part-time. Students come from 6 states and territories; 2 other countries; 3% are from out of state; 34% Black or African American, non-Hispanic/Latino; 14% Hispanic/Latino; 3% Asian, non-Hispanic/Latino; 0.3% Native Hawaiian or other Pacific Islander, non-Hispanic/Latino; 1% American Indian or Alaska Native, non-Hispanic/Latino; 2% Two or more races, non-Hispanic/Latino; 5% Race/ethnicity unknown; 0.3% international; 10% transferred in; 11% live on campus. *Retention:* 58% of full-time freshmen returned.
Freshmen *Admission:* 857 applied, 804 admitted, 215 enrolled. *Average high school GPA:* 2.7. *Test scores:* SAT math scores over 500: 21%; ACT scores over 18: 20%; SAT math scores over 600: 7%; ACT scores over 24: 10%; SAT math scores over 700: 5%.
Faculty *Total:* 68, 54% full-time, 34% with terminal degrees. *Student/faculty ratio:* 10:1.
Majors Accounting; child-care and support services management; child development; communication and media related; computer and information sciences; criminal justice/law enforcement administration; criminal justice/police science; dental assisting; dental hygiene; education (specific levels and methods) related; health and medical administrative services related; health/health-care administration; health professions related; legal assistant/paralegal; liberal arts and sciences/liberal studies; management science; marketing/marketing management; medical office management; psychology; public administration; sport and fitness administration/management; veterinary/animal health technology.
Academics *Calendar:* semesters. *Degrees:* certificates, associate, bachelor's, and postbachelor's certificates. *Special study options:* academic remediation for entering students, accelerated degree program, advanced placement credit, distance learning, double majors, honors programs, independent study, internships, part-time degree program, services for LD students, summer session for credit.
Library Basileiad Library. *Books:* 27,188 (physical), 5,037 (digital/electronic); *Serial titles:* 3 (physical); *Databases:* 14. Weekly public service hours: 65.
Student Life *Housing Options:* coed. Campus housing is university owned. *Activities and Organizations:* choral group, Rotoract (student service organization), Vet Tech Club, Campus Activities Board, Macrinian Yearbook, Phi Theta Kappa (honor society). *Campus security:* 24-hour emergency response devices and patrols, late-night transport/escort service. *Student services:* personal/psychological counseling, veterans affairs office.
Athletics Member NJCAA. *Intercollegiate sports:* baseball M, basketball W, cross-country running M/W, soccer M/W, track and field M/W, volleyball M/W.
Standardized Tests *Recommended:* SAT or ACT (for admission).
Financial Aid Of all full-time matriculated undergraduates who enrolled in 2009, 35 Federal Work-Study jobs (averaging $3000). 10 state and other part-time jobs (averaging $3600).
Applying *Options:* electronic application, deferred entrance. *Required:* high school transcript, minimum 2.0 GPA. *Required for some:* essay or personal statement, interview. *Application deadlines:* rolling (freshmen), rolling (transfers). *Notification:* continuous (freshmen), continuous (transfers).
Freshman Application Contact Angelica Crespo, Admissions Office Manager, Manor College, 700 Fox Chase Road, Jenkintown, PA 19046. *Phone:* 215-885-2216 Ext. 212. *Fax:* 215-576-6564. *E-mail:* swalker@manor.edu.
Website: http://www.manor.edu/.

McCann School of Business & Technology

Allentown, Pennsylvania

Admissions Office Contact McCann School of Business & Technology, 2200 North Irving Street, Allentown, PA 18109. *Website:* http://www.mccann.edu/.

McCann School of Business & Technology

Lewisburg, Pennsylvania

Admissions Office Contact McCann School of Business & Technology, 7495 Westbranch Highway, Lewisburg, PA 17837. *Toll-free phone:* 866-865-8065. *Website:* http://www.mccann.edu/.

Mercyhurst North East

North East, Pennsylvania

Director of Admissions Travis Lindahl, Director of Admissions, Mercyhurst North East, 16 West Division Street, North East, PA 16428. *Phone:* 814-725-6217. *Toll-free phone:* 866-846-6042. *Fax:* 814-725-6251. *E-mail:* neadmiss@mercyhurst.edu. *Website:* http://northeast.mercyhurst.edu/.

Montgomery County Community College

Blue Bell, Pennsylvania

- **County-supported** 2-year, founded 1964
- **Suburban** 186-acre campus with easy access to Philadelphia
- **Coed**

Undergraduates 3,518 full-time, 6,874 part-time. Students come from 7 states and territories; 96 other countries; 1% are from out of state; 15% Black or African American, non-Hispanic/Latino; 8% Hispanic/Latino; 6% Asian, non-Hispanic/Latino; 0.2% Native Hawaiian or other Pacific Islander, non-Hispanic/Latino; 0.3% American Indian or Alaska Native, non-Hispanic/Latino; 3% Two or more races, non-Hispanic/Latino; 7% Race/ethnicity unknown; 2% international. *Retention:* 60% of full-time freshmen returned.
Faculty *Student/faculty ratio:* 18:1.
Academics *Calendar:* semesters plus winter term. *Degree:* certificates and associate. *Special study options:* academic remediation for entering students, accelerated degree program, adult/continuing education programs, advanced placement credit, cooperative education, distance learning, English as a second language, honors programs, independent study, internships, part-time degree program, services for LD students, student-designed majors, study abroad, summer session for credit.
Library The Brendlinger Library. *Books:* 73,691 (physical), 98,911 (digital/electronic); *Serial titles:* 237 (physical), 19,750 (digital/electronic); *Databases:* 37. Weekly public service hours: 76; students can reserve study rooms.
Student Life *Campus security:* 24-hour emergency response devices and patrols, late-night transport/escort service, bicycle patrol.
Athletics Member NJCAA.
Financial Aid Of all full-time matriculated undergraduates who enrolled in 2017, 60 Federal Work-Study jobs (averaging $2500).
Applying *Options:* electronic application, early admission, deferred entrance. *Required:* high school transcript. *Required for some:* interview.
Freshman Application Contact Montgomery County Community College, Blue Bell, PA 19422. *Phone:* 215-641-6551. *Fax:* 215-619-7188. *E-mail:* admrec@admin.mc3.edu. *Website:* http://www.mc3.edu/.

New Castle School of Trades

New Castle, Pennsylvania

- **Independent** 2-year, founded 1945
- **Rural** 20-acre campus with easy access to Pittsburgh
- **Coed, primarily men**

Undergraduates 503 full-time. Students come from 3 states and territories; 1 other country; 14% Black or African American, non-Hispanic/Latino; 3% Hispanic/Latino; 2% Asian, non-Hispanic/Latino; 0.2% international.
Faculty *Student/faculty ratio:* 10:1.
Academics *Calendar:* quarters. *Degree:* diplomas and associate. *Special study options:* part-time degree program.
Library New Castle School of Trades plus 1 other. *Books:* 600 (physical). Weekly public service hours: 60.
Student Life *Campus security:* 24-hour emergency response devices.
Standardized Tests *Required:* Wonderlic aptitude test (for admission).
Applying *Application fee:* $25. *Required:* high school transcript, interview. *Required for some:* essay or personal statement.
Freshman Application Contact Mr. Joe Blazak, Admissions Director, New Castle School of Trades, 4117 Pulaski Road, New Castle, PA 16101. *Phone:* 724-964-8811. *Toll-free phone:* 800-837-8299. *Fax:* 724-964-8177. *Website:* http://www.ncstrades.edu/.

Northampton Community College

Bethlehem, Pennsylvania

- **State and locally supported** 2-year, founded 1967
- **Suburban** 165-acre campus with easy access to Philadelphia
- **Coed,** 9,769 undergraduate students, 44% full-time, 61% women, 39% men

Undergraduates 4,255 full-time, 5,514 part-time. 2% are from out of state; 13% Black or African American, non-Hispanic/Latino; 23% Hispanic/Latino; 2% Asian, non-Hispanic/Latino; 0.2% Native Hawaiian or other Pacific

Islander, non-Hispanic/Latino; 0.2% American Indian or Alaska Native, non-Hispanic/Latino; 3% Two or more races, non-Hispanic/Latino; 1% Race/ethnicity unknown; 1% international; 9% transferred in; 6% live on campus.
Freshmen *Admission:* 5,630 applied, 5,630 admitted, 1,839 enrolled.
Faculty *Total:* 702, 17% full-time, 17% with terminal degrees. *Student/faculty ratio:* 19:1.
Majors Accounting technology and bookkeeping; acting; administrative assistant and secretarial science; applied psychology; architectural engineering technology; athletic training; automobile/automotive mechanics technology; biology/biological sciences; biotechnology; business administration and management; business/commerce; CAD/CADD drafting/design technology; chemistry; computer and information systems security; computer programming; computer science; computer support specialist; computer systems networking and telecommunications; construction management; criminal justice/safety; culinary arts; dental hygiene; diagnostic medical sonography and ultrasound technology; early childhood education; electrician; electromechanical technology; engineering; environmental science; fine/studio arts; fire science/firefighting; fire services administration; funeral service and mortuary science; general studies; graphic design; heating, air conditioning, ventilation and refrigeration maintenance technology; hotel/motel administration; industrial electronics technology; interior design; international/global studies; journalism; legal assistant/paralegal; liberal arts and sciences and humanities related; liberal arts and sciences/liberal studies; marketing/marketing management; mathematics; medical administrative assistant and medical secretary; meeting and event planning; middle school education; physics; public health education and promotion; quality control technology; radio and television broadcasting technology; radiologic technology/science; registered nursing/registered nurse; restaurant/food services management; secondary education; social work; speech communication and rhetoric; sport and fitness administration/management; teacher assistant/aide; veterinary/animal health technology; web page, digital/multimedia and information resources design; welding technology.
Academics *Calendar:* semesters. *Degree:* certificates, diplomas, and associate. *Special study options:* academic remediation for entering students, adult/continuing education programs, advanced placement credit, distance learning, English as a second language, honors programs, independent study, internships, off-campus study, part-time degree program, services for LD students, student-designed majors, study abroad, summer session for credit.
Library Paul & Harriett Mack Library. Weekly public service hours: 83; students can reserve study rooms.
Student Life *Housing Options:* coed. Campus housing is university owned. *Activities and Organizations:* student-run newspaper, radio station, choral group, Phi Theta Kappa, Student Senate, Nursing Student Organization, American Dental Hygiene Association (ADHA), International Student Organization. *Campus security:* 24-hour emergency response devices and patrols, controlled dormitory access. *Student services:* health clinic, personal/psychological counseling, veterans affairs office.
Athletics Member NJCAA. *Intercollegiate sports:* basketball W, cross-country running W, soccer W, softball W, tennis W, volleyball W. *Intramural sports:* basketball M, cheerleading M(c), soccer M, volleyball M.
Financial Aid Of all full-time matriculated undergraduates who enrolled in 2018, 201 Federal Work-Study jobs (averaging $2400). 148 state and other part-time jobs (averaging $2000).
Applying *Options:* electronic application, deferred entrance. *Application fee:* $25. *Required for some:* high school transcript, minimum 2.5 GPA, interview, interview for radiography and veterinary programs. *Application deadlines:* rolling (freshmen), rolling (transfers). *Notification:* continuous (freshmen), continuous (transfers).
Freshman Application Contact Mr. James McCarthy, Director of Admissions, Northampton Community College, 3835 Green Pond Road, Bethlehem, PA 18020-7599. *Phone:* 610-861-5506. *Fax:* 610-861-5551. *E-mail:* jrmccarthy@northampton.edu. *Website:* http://www.northampton.edu/.

Penn Commercial Business and Technical School

Washington, Pennsylvania

Director of Admissions Mr. Michael John Joyce, Director of Admissions, Penn Commercial Business and Technical School, 242 Oak Spring Road, Washington, PA 15301. *Phone:* 724-222-5330 Ext. 1. *Toll-free phone:* 888-309-7484. *E-mail:* mjoyce@penn-commercial.com. *Website:* http://www.penncommercial.edu/.

Pennco Tech

Bristol, Pennsylvania

Freshman Application Contact Pennco Tech, 3815 Otter Street, Bristol, PA 19007-3696. *Phone:* 215-785-0111. *Toll-free phone:* 800-575-9399. *Website:* http://www.penncotech.edu/.

Penn State DuBois

DuBois, Pennsylvania

- **State-related** primarily 2-year, founded 1935, part of Pennsylvania State University
- **Small-town** campus
- **Coed**

Undergraduates 464 full-time, 121 part-time. 3% are from out of state; 2% Black or African American, non-Hispanic/Latino; 2% Hispanic/Latino; 2% Asian, non-Hispanic/Latino; 1% Two or more races, non-Hispanic/Latino; 0.6% Race/ethnicity unknown; 1% international; 4% transferred in. *Retention:* 80% of full-time freshmen returned.
Faculty *Student/faculty ratio:* 12:1.
Academics *Calendar:* semesters. *Degrees:* certificates, associate, and bachelor's. *Special study options:* adult/continuing education programs, external degree program.
Athletics Member NJCAA.
Standardized Tests *Required:* SAT or ACT (for admission).
Financial Aid Of all full-time matriculated undergraduates who enrolled in 2017, 461 applied for aid, 420 were judged to have need, 67 had their need fully met. In 2017, 22. *Average percent of need met:* 57. *Average financial aid package:* $9809. *Average need-based loan:* $3955. *Average need-based gift aid:* $5074. *Average non-need-based aid:* $2528. *Average indebtedness upon graduation:* $36,208.
Applying *Options:* electronic application, early admission, deferred entrance. *Application fee:* $65. *Required:* high school transcript. *Required for some:* interview. *Recommended:* essay or personal statement.
Freshman Application Contact Admissions Office, Penn State DuBois, 1 College Place, DuBois, PA 15801. *Phone:* 814-375-4720. *Toll-free phone:* 800-346-7627. *Fax:* 814-375-4784. *E-mail:* duboisinfo@psi.edu. *Website:* http://www.ds.psu.edu/.

Penn State Fayette, The Eberly Campus

Lemont Furnace, Pennsylvania

- **State-related** primarily 2-year, founded 1934, part of Pennsylvania State University
- **Small-town** campus
- **Coed**

Undergraduates 589 full-time, 63 part-time. 5% are from out of state; 4% Black or African American, non-Hispanic/Latino; 3% Hispanic/Latino; 0.8% Asian, non-Hispanic/Latino; 0.2% Native Hawaiian or other Pacific Islander, non-Hispanic/Latino; 0.3% American Indian or Alaska Native, non-Hispanic/Latino; 4% Two or more races, non-Hispanic/Latino; 0.9% Race/ethnicity unknown; 1% international; 5% transferred in. *Retention:* 78% of full-time freshmen returned.
Faculty *Student/faculty ratio:* 12:1.
Academics *Calendar:* semesters. *Degrees:* certificates, associate, and bachelor's. *Special study options:* adult/continuing education programs, external degree program.
Student Life *Campus security:* student patrols, 8-hour patrols by trained security personnel.
Athletics Member NJCAA.
Standardized Tests *Required:* SAT or ACT (for admission).
Financial Aid Of all full-time matriculated undergraduates who enrolled in 2017, 589 applied for aid, 542 were judged to have need, 78 had their need fully met. In 2017, 44. *Average percent of need met:* 61. *Average financial aid package:* $10,679. *Average need-based loan:* $4040. *Average need-based gift aid:* $5554. *Average non-need-based aid:* $2906. *Average indebtedness upon graduation:* $32,520.
Applying *Options:* electronic application, early admission, deferred entrance. *Application fee:* $65. *Required:* high school transcript. *Required for some:* interview. *Recommended:* essay or personal statement.
Freshman Application Contact Admissions Office, Penn State Fayette, The Eberly Campus, 2201 University Drive, Lemont Furnace, PA 15456. *Phone:* 724-430-4130. *Toll-free phone:* 877-568-4130. *Fax:* 724-430-4175. *E-mail:* feadm@psu.edu. *Website:* http://www.fe.psu.edu/.

Penn State Mont Alto
Mont Alto, Pennsylvania

- **State-related** primarily 2-year, founded 1929, part of Pennsylvania State University
- **Small-town** campus
- **Coed**

Undergraduates 653 full-time, 264 part-time. 15% are from out of state; 5% Black or African American, non-Hispanic/Latino; 8% Hispanic/Latino; 3% Asian, non-Hispanic/Latino; 4% Two or more races, non-Hispanic/Latino; 0.8% Race/ethnicity unknown; 0.5% international; 3% transferred in; 24% live on campus. *Retention:* 83% of full-time freshmen returned.
Faculty *Student/faculty ratio:* 11:1.
Academics *Calendar:* semesters. *Degrees:* certificates, associate, and bachelor's. *Special study options:* adult/continuing education programs, external degree program. *ROTC:* Army (c).
Student Life *Campus security:* 24-hour patrols, controlled dormitory access.
Athletics Member NJCAA.
Standardized Tests *Required:* SAT or ACT (for admission).
Financial Aid Of all full-time matriculated undergraduates who enrolled in 2017, 649 applied for aid, 582 were judged to have need, 116 had their need fully met. In 2017, 55. *Average percent of need met:* 64. *Average financial aid package:* $10,886. *Average need-based loan:* $4220. *Average need-based gift aid:* $4814. *Average non-need-based aid:* $3442. *Average indebtedness upon graduation:* $44,034.
Applying *Options:* electronic application, early admission, deferred entrance. *Application fee:* $65. *Required:* high school transcript. *Required for some:* interview. *Recommended:* essay or personal statement.
Freshman Application Contact Admissions Office, Penn State Mont Alto, 1 Campus Drive, Mont Alto, PA 17237. *Phone:* 717-749-6130. *Toll-free phone:* 800-392-6173. *Fax:* 717-749-6132. *E-mail:* psuma@psu.edu. *Website:* http://www.ma.psu.edu/.

Pennsylvania Highlands Community College
Johnstown, Pennsylvania

- **State and locally supported** 2-year, founded 1994
- **Small-town** campus
- **Coed**

Undergraduates 782 full-time, 2,002 part-time. Students come from 3 states and territories; 1% are from out of state; 5% Black or African American, non-Hispanic/Latino; 2% Hispanic/Latino; 0.7% Asian, non-Hispanic/Latino; 0.1% American Indian or Alaska Native, non-Hispanic/Latino; 3% Two or more races, non-Hispanic/Latino; 4% Race/ethnicity unknown. *Retention:* 48% of full-time freshmen returned.
Faculty *Student/faculty ratio:* 18:1.
Academics *Calendar:* semesters. *Degree:* certificates, diplomas, and associate. *Special study options:* academic remediation for entering students, adult/continuing education programs, advanced placement credit, cooperative education, distance learning, independent study, internships, part-time degree program, services for LD students, summer session for credit.
Library Mangarella Library. *Books:* 1,274 (physical), 2,192 (digital/electronic); *Databases:* 35.
Athletics Member NJCAA.
Financial Aid Of all full-time matriculated undergraduates who enrolled in 2017, 25 Federal Work-Study jobs (averaging $2500).
Applying *Options:* electronic application.
Freshman Application Contact Mr. Jeff Maul, Admissions Officer, Pennsylvania Highlands Community College, 101 Community College Way, Johnstown, PA 15904. *Phone:* 814-262-6431. *Toll-free phone:* 888-385-7325. *Fax:* 814-269-9743. *E-mail:* jmaul@pennhighlands.edu. *Website:* http://www.pennhighlands.edu/.

Pennsylvania Institute of Health and Technology
Mount Braddock, Pennsylvania

Admissions Office Contact Pennsylvania Institute of Health and Technology, 1015 Mount Braddock Road, Mount Braddock, PA 15465. *Website:* http://www.piht.edu/.

Pennsylvania Institute of Technology
Media, Pennsylvania

- **Independent** 2-year, founded 1953
- **Small-town** 12-acre campus with easy access to Philadelphia
- **Coed**

Undergraduates 261 full-time, 186 part-time.
Faculty *Student/faculty ratio:* 11:1.
Academics *Calendar:* 4 terms. *Degree:* certificates and associate. *Special study options:* academic remediation for entering students, adult/continuing education programs, advanced placement credit, cooperative education, distance learning, part-time degree program, summer session for credit.
Library Pennsylvania Institute of Technology Library/Learning Resource Center plus 1 other.
Student Life *Campus security:* 24-hour emergency response devices.
Financial Aid Of all full-time matriculated undergraduates who enrolled in 2017, 15 Federal Work-Study jobs (averaging $1025). *Financial aid deadline:* 8/1.
Applying *Options:* electronic application, deferred entrance. *Application fee:* $25. *Required:* high school transcript, interview. *Recommended:* essay or personal statement.
Freshman Application Contact Mr. Matthew Meyers, Director of Admissions, Pennsylvania Institute of Technology, 800 Manchester Avenue, Media, PA 19063-4036. *Phone:* 610-892-1543. *Toll-free phone:* 800-422-0025. *Fax:* 610-892-1510. *E-mail:* info@pit.edu. *Website:* http://www.pit.edu/.

Pittsburgh Career Institute
Pittsburgh, Pennsylvania

Freshman Application Contact Pittsburgh Career Institute, 421 Seventh Avenue, Pittsburgh, PA 15219-1907. *Phone:* 412-281-2600. *Toll-free phone:* 800-333-6607. *Website:* http://www.pci.edu/.

Pittsburgh Institute of Aeronautics
Pittsburgh, Pennsylvania

Freshman Application Contact Steven D. Sabold, Director of Admissions, Pittsburgh Institute of Aeronautics, PO Box 10897, Pittsburgh, PA 15236-0897. *Phone:* 412-346-2100. *Toll-free phone:* 800-444-1440. *Fax:* 412-466-5013. *E-mail:* admissions@pia.edu. *Website:* http://www.pia.edu/.

Pittsburgh Institute of Mortuary Science, Incorporated
Pittsburgh, Pennsylvania

Freshman Application Contact Ms. Karen Rocco, Registrar, Pittsburgh Institute of Mortuary Science, Incorporated, 5808 Baum Boulevard, Pittsburgh, PA 15206-3706. *Phone:* 412-362-8500 Ext. 105. *Fax:* 412-362-1684. *E-mail:* pims5808@aol.com. *Website:* http://www.pims.edu/.

Pittsburgh Technical College
Oakdale, Pennsylvania

- **Proprietary** primarily 2-year, founded 1946
- **Suburban** 180-acre campus with easy access to Pittsburgh
- **Coed**
- 87% of applicants were admitted

Undergraduates 1,835 full-time. Students come from 17 states and territories; 2 other countries; 17% are from out of state; 7% Black or African American, non-Hispanic/Latino; 0.4% Hispanic/Latino; 0.7% Asian, non-Hispanic/Latino; 0.1% Native Hawaiian or other Pacific Islander, non-Hispanic/Latino; 0.3% American Indian or Alaska Native, non-Hispanic/Latino; 4% Two or more races, non-Hispanic/Latino; 21% Race/ethnicity unknown; 11% transferred in; 44% live on campus. *Retention:* 55% of full-time freshmen returned.
Faculty *Student/faculty ratio:* 12:1.
Academics *Calendar:* quarters. *Degrees:* certificates, associate, and bachelor's. *Special study options:* academic remediation for entering students, adult/continuing education programs, advanced placement credit, cooperative education, distance learning, double majors, internships, services for LD students.
Library Library Resource Center. *Books:* 7,378 (physical), 46,000 (digital/electronic); *Serial titles:* 116 (physical), 6 (digital/electronic); *Databases:* 12. Weekly public service hours: 58.

Student Life *Campus security:* 24-hour emergency response devices and patrols, student patrols, late-night transport/escort service, controlled dormitory access.
Standardized Tests *Required:* entrance exams for practical nursing certificate and nursing and surgical technology Associate degrees (for admission). *Required for some:* SAT or ACT (for admission).
Applying *Options:* electronic application, deferred entrance. *Required:* high school transcript. *Required for some:* essay or personal statement, criminal background check, minimum rank in top 80% of class. *Recommended:* interview.
Freshman Application Contact Ms. Nancy Goodlin, Admissions Office Assistant, Pittsburgh Technical College, 1111 McKee Road, Oakdale, PA 15071. *Phone:* 412-809-5100. *Toll-free phone:* 800-784-9675. *Fax:* 412-809-5351. *E-mail:* goodlin.nancy@ptcollege.edu. *Website:* http://www.ptcollege.edu/.

Reading Area Community College
Reading, Pennsylvania

Freshman Application Contact Ms. Debbie Hettinger, Enrollment Services Coordinator/Communications Specialist, Reading Area Community College, PO Box 1706, Reading, PA 19603-1706. *Phone:* 610-372-4721 Ext. 5130. *E-mail:* dhettinger@racc.edu. *Website:* http://www.racc.edu/.

The Restaurant School at Walnut Hill College
Philadelphia, Pennsylvania

Freshman Application Contact Mr. John English, Director of Admissions, The Restaurant School at Walnut Hill College, 4207 Walnut Street, Philadelphia, PA 19104-3518. *Phone:* 267-295-2353. *Fax:* 215-222-4219. *E-mail:* jenglish@walnuthillcollege.edu. *Website:* http://www.walnuthillcollege.edu/.

Rosedale Technical Institute
Pittsburgh, Pennsylvania

Freshman Application Contact Ms. Debbie Bier, Director of Admissions, Rosedale Technical Institute, 215 Beecham Drive, Suite 2, Pittsburgh, PA 15205-9791. *Phone:* 412-521-6200. *Toll-free phone:* 800-521-6262. *Fax:* 412-521-2520. *E-mail:* admissions@rosedaletech.org. *Website:* http://www.rosedaletech.org/.

South Hills School of Business & Technology
State College, Pennsylvania

Freshman Application Contact Mr. Troy R. Otradovec, Regional Director of Admissions, South Hills School of Business & Technology, 480 Waupelani Drive, State College, PA 16801-4516. *Phone:* 814-234-7755 Ext. 2020. *Toll-free phone:* 888-282-7427. *Fax:* 814-234-0926. *E-mail:* admissions@southhills.edu. *Website:* http://www.southhills.edu/.

Thaddeus Stevens College of Technology
Lancaster, Pennsylvania

- **State-supported** 2-year, founded 1905
- **Urban** 33-acre campus with easy access to Philadelphia
- **Endowment** $696,058
- **Coed**

Undergraduates 1,135 full-time, 7 part-time. Students come from 1 other state; 10% Black or African American, non-Hispanic/Latino; 14% Hispanic/Latino; 1% Asian, non-Hispanic/Latino; 0.6% American Indian or Alaska Native, non-Hispanic/Latino; 4% Two or more races, non-Hispanic/Latino; 0.4% Race/ethnicity unknown; 7% transferred in; 45% live on campus. *Retention:* 69% of full-time freshmen returned.
Faculty *Student/faculty ratio:* 12:1.
Academics *Calendar:* semesters. *Degree:* certificates and associate. *Special study options:* academic remediation for entering students, advanced placement credit, internships, services for LD students.
Library K. W. Schuler Learning Resources Center plus 1 other. *Books:* 59,073 (physical), 1,187 (digital/electronic); *Serial titles:* 21 (physical), 2,823 (digital/electronic); *Databases:* 21. Weekly public service hours: 78; students can reserve study rooms.
Student Life *Campus security:* 24-hour emergency response devices and patrols, controlled dormitory access.
Athletics Member NJCAA.
Standardized Tests *Required:* ACT, SAT, or ACT Compass (for admission).
Applying *Options:* electronic application, deferred entrance. *Application fee:* $45. *Required:* essay or personal statement, high school transcript, minimum 2.0 GPA. *Required for some:* interview.
Freshman Application Contact Ms. Amy Kwiatkowski, Thaddeus Stevens College of Technology, 750 East King Street, Lancaster, PA 17055. *Phone:* 717-391-3540. *Toll-free phone:* 800-842-3832. *E-mail:* kwiatkowski@stevenscollege.edu. *Website:* http://www.stevenscollege.edu/.

Triangle Tech, Bethlehem
Bethlehem, Pennsylvania

Freshman Application Contact Triangle Tech, Bethlehem, 3184 Airport Road, Bethlehem, PA 18017. *Website:* http://www.triangle-tech.edu/.

Triangle Tech, DuBois
Falls Creek, Pennsylvania

Freshman Application Contact Terry Kucic, Director of Admissions, Triangle Tech, DuBois, PO Box 551, DuBois, PA 15801. *Phone:* 814-371-2090. *Toll-free phone:* 800-874-8324. *Fax:* 814-371-9227. *E-mail:* tkucic@triangle-tech.com. *Website:* http://www.triangle-tech.edu/.

Triangle Tech, Erie
Erie, Pennsylvania

Freshman Application Contact Admissions Representative, Triangle Tech, Erie, 2000 Liberty Street, Erie, PA 16502-2594. *Phone:* 814-453-6016. *Toll-free phone:* 800-874-8324 (in-state); 800-TRI-TECH (out-of-state). *Website:* http://www.triangle-tech.edu/.

Triangle Tech, Greensburg
Greensburg, Pennsylvania

Freshman Application Contact Mr. John Mazzarese, Vice President of Admissions, Triangle Tech, Greensburg, 222 East Pittsburgh Street, Greensburg, PA 15601. *Phone:* 412-359-1000. *Toll-free phone:* 800-874-8324. *Website:* http://www.triangle-tech.edu/.

Triangle Tech, Pittsburgh
Pittsburgh, Pennsylvania

Freshman Application Contact Director of Admissions, Triangle Tech, Pittsburgh, 1940 Perrysville Avenue, Pittsburgh, PA 15214-3897. *Phone:* 412-359-1000. *Toll-free phone:* 800-874-8324. *Fax:* 412-359-1012. *E-mail:* info@triangle-tech.edu. *Website:* http://www.triangle-tech.edu/.

Triangle Tech, Sunbury
Sunbury, Pennsylvania

Freshman Application Contact Triangle Tech, Sunbury, 191 Performance Road, Sunbury, PA 17801. *Phone:* 412-359-1000. *Website:* http://www.triangle-tech.edu/.

University of Pittsburgh at Titusville
Titusville, Pennsylvania

Freshman Application Contact Ms. Colleen R. Motter, Admissions Counselor, University of Pittsburgh at Titusville, 504 East Main Street, Titusville, PA 16354. *Phone:* 814-827-4408. *Toll-free phone:* 888-878-0462. *Fax:* 814-827-4519. *E-mail:* motter@pitt.edu. *Website:* http://www.upt.pitt.edu/.

Valley Forge Military College
Wayne, Pennsylvania

Freshman Application Contact Maj. Greg Potts, Dean of Enrollment Management, Valley Forge Military College, 1001 Eagle Road, Wayne, PA 19087-3695. *Phone:* 610-989-1300. *Toll-free phone:* 800-234-8362. *Fax:* 610-688-1545. *E-mail:* admissions@vfmac.edu. *Website:* http://www.vfmac.edu/.

Vet Tech Institute
Pittsburgh, Pennsylvania

Freshman Application Contact Admissions Office, Vet Tech Institute, 125 7th Street, Pittsburgh, PA 15222-3400. *Phone:* 412-391-7021. *Toll-free phone:* 800-570-0693. *Website:* http://pittsburgh.vettechinstitute.edu/.

Westmoreland County Community College

Youngwood, Pennsylvania

Freshman Application Contact Ms. Shawna Little, Admissions Coordinator, Westmoreland County Community College, 145 Pavillon Lane, Youngwood, PA 15697. *Phone:* 724-925-4064. *Toll-free phone:* 800-262-2103. *Fax:* 724-925-4292. *E-mail:* littles@wccc.edu. *Website:* http://www.westmoreland.edu/.

Williamson College of the Trades

Media, Pennsylvania

Freshman Application Contact Mr. Jay Merillat, Dean of Admissions, Williamson College of the Trades, 106 South New Middletown Road, Media, PA 19063. *Phone:* 610-566-1776 Ext. 235. *E-mail:* jmerillat@williamson.edu. *Website:* http://www.williamson.edu/.

The Workforce Institute's City College

Philadelphia, Pennsylvania

Freshman Application Contact Admissions Office, The Workforce Institute's City College, 1231 North Broad Street, Philadelphia, PA 19122. *Phone:* 215-568-7861. *Website:* http://www.wficitycollege.org/.

YTI Career Institute–Altoona

Altoona, Pennsylvania

Admissions Office Contact YTI Career Institute–Altoona, 2900 Fairway Drive, Altoona, PA 16602. *Website:* http://www.yti.edu/.

YTI Career Institute–Lancaster

Lancaster, Pennsylvania

Admissions Office Contact YTI Career Institute–Lancaster, 3050 Hempland Road, Lancaster, PA 17601. *Website:* http://www.yti.edu/.

YTI Career Institute–York

York, Pennsylvania

Freshman Application Contact YTI Career Institute–York, 1405 Williams Road, York, PA 17402-9017. *Phone:* 717-757-1100 Ext. 318. *Toll-free phone:* 800-557-6335. *Website:* http://www.yti.edu/.

PUERTO RICO

The Center of Cinematography, Arts and Television

Bayamon, Puerto Rico

Admissions Office Contact The Center of Cinematography, Arts and Television, 51 Dr. Veve Street, Degetau Street Corner, Bayamon, PR 00960. *Website:* http://ccatmiami.com/.

Centro de Estudios Multidisciplinarios

Mayaguez, Puerto Rico

Admissions Office Contact Centro de Estudios Multidisciplinarios, Calle Cristy #56, Mayaguez, PR 00680. *Website:* http://www.cemcollege.edu/.

Centro de Estudios Multidisciplinarios

Rio Piedras, Puerto Rico

Director of Admissions Admissions Department, Centro de Estudios Multidisciplinarios, Calle 13 #1206, Ext. San Agustin, Rio Piedras, PR 00926. *Phone:* 787-765-4210 Ext. 115. *Toll-free phone:* 877-779-CDEM. *Website:* http://www.cemcollege.edu/.

Dewey University–Bayamón

Bayamón, Puerto Rico

Admissions Office Contact Dewey University–Bayamón, Carr. #2, Km. 15.9, Parque Industrial Corujo, Hato Tejas, Bayamón, PR 00959. *Website:* http://www.dewey.edu/.

Dewey University–Carolina

Carolina, Puerto Rico

Admissions Office Contact Dewey University–Carolina, Carr. #3, Km. 11, Parque Industrial de Carolina, Lote 7, Carolina, PR 00986. *Website:* http://www.dewey.edu/.

Dewey University–Fajardo

Fajardo, Puerto Rico

Admissions Office Contact Dewey University–Fajardo, 267 Calle General Valero, Fajardo, PR 00910. *Website:* http://www.dewey.edu/.

Dewey University–Hato Rey

Hato Rey, Puerto Rico

Admissions Office Contact Dewey University–Hato Rey, 427 Avenida Barbosa, Hato Rey, PR 00923. *Website:* http://www.dewey.edu/.

Dewey University–Juana Diaz

Juana Diaz, Puerto Rico

Admissions Office Contact Dewey University–Juana Diaz, Carr. 149, Km. 55.9, Parque Industrial Lomas, Juana Diaz, PR 00910. *Website:* http://www.dewey.edu/.

Dewey University–Manati

Manati, Puerto Rico

Admissions Office Contact Dewey University–Manati, Carr. 604, Km. 49.1 Barrio Tierras Nuevas, Salientes, Manati, PR 00674. *Toll-free phone:* 866-773-3939. *Website:* http://www.dewey.edu/.

Dewey University–Mayaguez

Mayaguez, Puerto Rico

Admissions Office Contact Dewey University–Mayaguez, Carr. #64 Km 6.6 Barrio Algarrobo, Mayaguez, PR 00682. *Website:* http://www.dewey.edu/.

EDIC College

Caguas, Puerto Rico

Admissions Office Contact EDIC College, Ave. Rafael Cordero Calle Génova Urb. Caguas Norte, Caguas, PR 00726. *Website:* http://www.ediccollege.edu/.

Huertas College

Caguas, Puerto Rico

Director of Admissions Mrs. Barbara Hassim López, Director of Admissions, Huertas College, PO Box 8429, Caguas, PR 00726. *Phone:* 787-743-1242. *Fax:* 787-743-0203. *E-mail:* huertas@huertas.org. *Website:* http://www.huertas.edu/.

Humacao Community College

Humacao, Puerto Rico

- **Independent** primarily 2-year
- **Urban** campus
- **Endowment** $1.3 million
- **Coed**

Undergraduates 359 full-time, 108 part-time. Students come from 1 other state; 100% Hispanic/Latino; 32% transferred in. *Retention:* 54% of full-time freshmen returned.
Faculty *Student/faculty ratio:* 30:1.
Academics *Calendar:* trimesters. *Degrees:* certificates, diplomas, associate, and bachelor's. *Special study options:* academic remediation for entering students, adult/continuing education programs, cooperative education, internships, part-time degree program, services for LD students.

Library Santiago N. Manuez Educational Resources Center plus 1 other. *Books:* 5,320 (physical); *Serial titles:* 43 (physical), 2 (digital/electronic); *Databases:* 5. Weekly public service hours: 56.
Student Life *Campus security:* 24-hour emergency response devices and patrols.
Financial Aid Of all full-time matriculated undergraduates who enrolled in 2017, 64 Federal Work-Study jobs (averaging $546).
Applying *Application fee:* $15. *Required:* high school transcript, interview. *Required for some:* certificate of Immunization for students under 21 years.
Freshman Application Contact Mrs. Arlene Osorio, Recruitment and Promotion Official, Humacao Community College, PO Box 9139, Humacao, PR 00792, Puerto Rico. *Phone:* 787-852-1430 Ext. 225. *Fax:* 787-850-1577. *E-mail:* arlene.osorio@hccpr.edu. *Website:* http://www.hccpr.edu/.

ICPR Junior College–Hato Rey Campus
Hato Rey, Puerto Rico

Freshman Application Contact Admissions Office, ICPR Junior College–Hato Rey Campus, 558 Munoz Rivera Avenue, PO Box 190304, Hato Rey, PR 00919-0304. *Phone:* 787-753-6335. *Website:* http://www.icprjc.edu/.

Ponce Paramedical College
Ponce, Puerto Rico

Admissions Office Contact Ponce Paramedical College, L-15 Acacia Street Villa Flores Urbanizacion, Ponce, PR 00731. *Website:* http://www.popac.edu/.

RHODE ISLAND

Community College of Rhode Island
Warwick, Rhode Island

Freshman Application Contact Community College of Rhode Island, Flanagan Campus, 1762 Louisquisset Pike, Lincoln, RI 02865-4585. *Phone:* 401-333-7490. *Fax:* 401-333-7122. *E-mail:* webadmission@ccri.edu. *Website:* http://www.ccri.edu/.

SOUTH CAROLINA

Aiken Technical College
Graniteville, South Carolina

Freshman Application Contact Jessica Moon, Director of Enrollment Services, Aiken Technical College, 2276 J. Davis Highway, Graniteville, SC 29829. *Phone:* 803-508-7262 Ext. 156. *E-mail:* moonj@atc.edu. *Website:* http://www.atc.edu/.

Central Carolina Technical College
Sumter, South Carolina

Freshman Application Contact Ms. Barbara Wright, Director of Admissions and Counseling, Central Carolina Technical College, 506 North Guignard Drive, Sumter, SC 29150. *Phone:* 803-778-6695. *Toll-free phone:* 800-221-8711. *Fax:* 803-778-6696. *E-mail:* wrightb@cctech.edu. *Website:* http://www.cctech.edu/.

Centura College
Columbia, South Carolina

Admissions Office Contact Centura College, 7500 Two Notch Road, Columbia, SC 29223. *Website:* http://www.centuracollege.edu/.

Clinton College
Rock Hill, South Carolina

Director of Admissions Robert M. Copeland, Vice President for Student Affairs, Clinton College, 1029 Crawford Road, Rock Hill, SC 29730. *Phone:* 803-327-7402. *Toll-free phone:* 877-837-9645. *Fax:* 803-327-3261. *E-mail:* rcopeland@clintonjrcollege.org. *Website:* http://www.clintoncollege.edu/.

Denmark Technical College
Denmark, South Carolina

Freshman Application Contact Ms. Kara Troy, Administrative Specialist II, Denmark Technical College, PO Box 327, 1126 Solomon Blatt Boulevard, Denmark, SC 29042. *Phone:* 803-793-5180. *Fax:* 803-793-5942. *E-mail:* troyk@denmarktech.edu. *Website:* http://www.denmarktech.edu/.

Florence-Darlington Technical College
Florence, South Carolina

Director of Admissions Shelley Fortin, Vice President for Enrollment Management and Student Services, Florence-Darlington Technical College, 2715 West Lucas Street, PO Box 100548, Florence, SC 29501-0548. *Phone:* 843-661-8111 Ext. 117. *Toll-free phone:* 800-228-5745. *E-mail:* shelley.fortin@fdtc.edu. *Website:* http://www.fdtc.edu/.

Forrest College
Anderson, South Carolina

Freshman Application Contact Ms. Janie Turmon, Admissions and Placement Coordinator/Representative, Forrest College, 601 East River Street, Anderson, SC 29624. *Phone:* 864-225-7653. *Fax:* 864-261-7471. *E-mail:* janieturmon@forrestcollege.edu. *Website:* http://www.forrestcollege.edu/.

Fortis College
Columbia, South Carolina

Admissions Office Contact Fortis College, 246 Stoneridge Drive, Suite 101, Columbia, SC 29210. *Toll-free phone:* 855-4-FORTIS. *Website:* http://www.fortis.edu/.

Greenville Technical College
Greenville, South Carolina

- **State-supported** 2-year, founded 1962, part of South Carolina State Board for Technical and Comprehensive Education
- **Urban** 604-acre campus
- **Coed,** 11,745 undergraduate students, 41% full-time, 60% women, 40% men

Undergraduates 4,809 full-time, 6,936 part-time. 1% are from out of state; 22% Black or African American, non-Hispanic/Latino; 10% Hispanic/Latino; 2% Asian, non-Hispanic/Latino; 0.1% Native Hawaiian or other Pacific Islander, non-Hispanic/Latino; 0.3% American Indian or Alaska Native, non-Hispanic/Latino; 3% Two or more races, non-Hispanic/Latino; 2% Race/ethnicity unknown; 0.6% international.
Freshmen *Admission:* 4,922 applied, 4,911 admitted, 2,240 enrolled.
Faculty *Total:* 742, 43% full-time, 11% with terminal degrees. *Student/faculty ratio:* 14:1.
Majors Accounting; administrative assistant and secretarial science; architectural engineering technology; autobody/collision and repair technology; automobile/automotive mechanics technology; business administration and management; child-care and support services management; clinical/medical laboratory technology; computer numerically controlled (CNC) machinist technology; construction engineering technology; criminal justice/safety; culinary arts; data processing and data processing technology; dental hygiene; diagnostic medical sonography and ultrasound technology; drafting and design technology; electrical, electronic and communications engineering technology; electromechanical and instrumentation and maintenance technologies related; emergency medical technology (EMT paramedic); health information/medical records technology; human services; legal assistant/paralegal; liberal arts and sciences/liberal studies; machine tool technology; mechanical engineering/mechanical technology; mechanic and repair technologies related; medical radiologic technology; multi/interdisciplinary studies related; occupational therapist assistant; physical therapy technology; purchasing, procurement/acquisitions and contracts management; registered nursing/registered nurse; respiratory care therapy; sales, distribution, and marketing operations.
Academics *Calendar:* semesters. *Degree:* certificates, diplomas, and associate. *Special study options:* academic remediation for entering students, advanced placement credit, cooperative education, distance learning, double majors, English as a second language, honors programs, independent study, internships, part-time degree program, services for LD students, summer session for credit.
Library J. Verne Smith Library plus 3 others. *Books:* 35,259 (physical), 450,552 (digital/electronic); *Serial titles:* 88 (physical), 28 (digital/electronic); *Databases:* 34. Weekly public service hours: 59.

Student Life *Housing Options:* coed. Campus housing is university owned and is provided by a third party. *Activities and Organizations:* Phi Theta Kappa, Kappa Omega Sigma - Cosmetology Club, Student Government Association (SGA). *Campus security:* 24-hour emergency response devices and patrols, late-night transport/escort service. *Student services:* veterans affairs office.
Athletics *Intramural sports:* basketball M(c), bowling M(c), football M(c), softball M(c), table tennis M(c), tennis M(c), volleyball M(c).
Applying *Options:* electronic application, early admission, deferred entrance. *Required:* high school transcript. *Application deadlines:* rolling (freshmen), rolling (transfers). *Notification:* continuous until 8/18 (freshmen), continuous until 8/18 (transfers).
Director of Admissions Tanisha Latimer, Dean of Enrollment Services, Greenville Technical College, PO Box 5616, Greenville, SC 29606-5616. *Phone:* 864-250-8107. *Toll-free phone:* 800-992-1183 (in-state); 800-723-0673 (out-of-state). *E-mail:* tanisha.latimer@gvltec.edu. *Website:* http://www.gvltec.edu/.

Horry-Georgetown Technical College
Conway, South Carolina

Freshman Application Contact Cynthia Johnston, Assistant Vice President for Enrollment Services, Horry-Georgetown Technical College, 2050 Highway 501 East, PO Box 261966, Conway, SC 29528-6066. *Phone:* 843-349-7835. *Fax:* 843-349-7588. *E-mail:* cynthia.johnston@hgtc.edu. *Website:* http://www.hgtc.edu/.

Midlands Technical College
Columbia, South Carolina

Freshman Application Contact Ms. Sylvia Littlejohn, Director of Admissions, Midlands Technical College, PO Box 2408, Columbia, SC 29202. *Phone:* 803-738-8324. *Toll-free phone:* 800-922-8038. *Fax:* 803-790-7524. *E-mail:* admissions@midlandstech.edu. *Website:* http://www.midlandstech.edu/.

Miller-Motte Technical College
Conway, South Carolina

Admissions Office Contact Miller-Motte Technical College, 2451 Highway 501 East, Conway, SC 29526. *Toll-free phone:* 800-705-9182. *Website:* http://www.miller-motte.edu/.

Miller-Motte Technical College
North Charleston, South Carolina

Freshman Application Contact Ms. Elaine Cue, Campus President, Miller-Motte Technical College, 8085 Rivers Avenue, North Charleston, SC 29406. *Phone:* 843-574-0101. *Toll-free phone:* 800-705-9182. *Fax:* 843-266-3424. *E-mail:* juliasc@miller-mott.net. *Website:* http://www.miller-motte.edu/.

Northeastern Technical College
Cheraw, South Carolina

- **State and locally supported** 2-year, founded 1967, part of South Carolina State Board for Technical and Comprehensive Education
- **Rural** 59-acre campus
- **Endowment** $31,355
- **Coed**

Undergraduates 446 full-time, 530 part-time. Students come from 3 states and territories; 1% are from out of state; 3% transferred in.
Faculty *Student/faculty ratio:* 25:1.
Academics *Calendar:* semesters. *Degree:* certificates, diplomas, and associate. *Special study options:* academic remediation for entering students, adult/continuing education programs, advanced placement credit, distance learning, independent study, part-time degree program, study abroad.
Library Northeastern Technical College Library.
Student Life *Campus security:* 24-hour emergency response devices.
Standardized Tests *Required:* ACT Compass (for admission). *Required for some:* SAT (for admission).
Financial Aid Of all full-time matriculated undergraduates who enrolled in 2017, 26 Federal Work-Study jobs (averaging $2800).
Applying *Options:* electronic application, early admission. *Application fee:* $25. *Required:* high school transcript, interview.
Freshman Application Contact Mrs. Joy L. Hicks, Admissions Administrative Specialist, Northeastern Technical College, 1201 Chesterfield Highway, Cheraw, SC 29520-1007. *Phone:* 843-921-1461. *Toll-free phone:* 800-921-7399. *Fax:* 843-921-1476. *E-mail:* jhicks@netc.edu. *Website:* http://www.netc.edu/.

Orangeburg-Calhoun Technical College
Orangeburg, South Carolina

Freshman Application Contact Mr. Dana Rickards, Director of Recruitment, Orangeburg-Calhoun Technical College, 3250 St Matthews Road, NE, Orangeburg, SC 29118-8299. *Phone:* 803-535-1219. *Toll-free phone:* 800-813-6519. *Website:* http://www.octech.edu/.

Piedmont Technical College
Greenwood, South Carolina

Director of Admissions Mr. Steve Coleman, Director of Admissions, Piedmont Technical College, 620 North Emerald Road, PO Box 1467, Greenwood, SC 29648-1467. *Phone:* 864-941-8603. *Toll-free phone:* 800-868-5528. *Website:* http://www.ptc.edu/.

Spartanburg Community College
Spartanburg, South Carolina

Freshman Application Contact Ms. Sabrina Sims, Admissions Counselor, Spartanburg Community College, PO Box 4386, Spartanburg, SC 29305. *Phone:* 864-592-4816. *Toll-free phone:* 866-591-3700. *Fax:* 864-592-4564. *E-mail:* admissions@sccsc.edu. *Website:* http://www.sccsc.edu/.

Spartanburg Methodist College
Spartanburg, South Carolina

- **Independent Methodist** 2-year, founded 1911
- **Suburban** 110-acre campus with easy access to Charlotte
- **Endowment** $22.0 million
- **Coed**

Undergraduates 784 full-time, 6 part-time. Students come from 16 states and territories; 3 other countries; 9% are from out of state; 38% Black or African American, non-Hispanic/Latino; 8% Hispanic/Latino; 0.9% Asian, non-Hispanic/Latino; 0.3% American Indian or Alaska Native, non-Hispanic/Latino; 3% Two or more races, non-Hispanic/Latino; 0.4% international; 5% transferred in; 67% live on campus.
Faculty *Student/faculty ratio:* 20:1.
Academics *Calendar:* semesters. *Degree:* associate. *Special study options:* academic remediation for entering students, advanced placement credit, English as a second language, honors programs, independent study, part-time degree program, services for LD students, summer session for credit.
Library Marie Blair Burgess Library. *Books:* 46,541 (physical), 155,060 (digital/electronic); *Databases:* 80. Weekly public service hours: 72; students can reserve study rooms.
Student Life *Campus security:* 24-hour emergency response devices and patrols, student patrols, late-night transport/escort service, controlled dormitory access.
Athletics Member NJCAA.
Standardized Tests *Required:* SAT or ACT (for admission).
Financial Aid Of all full-time matriculated undergraduates who enrolled in 2017, 80 Federal Work-Study jobs (averaging $1600). 90 state and other part-time jobs (averaging $1600). *Financial aid deadline:* 8/30.
Applying *Options:* electronic application, deferred entrance. *Application fee:* $25. *Required:* essay or personal statement, high school transcript, minimum 2.0 GPA. *Required for some:* interview. *Recommended:* interview.
Freshman Application Contact Mr. Wells Shepard, Vice President for Enrollment, Spartanburg Methodist College, 1000 Powell Mill Road, Spartanburg, SC 29301-5899. *Phone:* 864-587-4254. *Toll-free phone:* 800-772-7286. *Fax:* 864-587-4355. *E-mail:* admiss@smcsc.edu. *Website:* http://www.smcsc.edu/.

Technical College of the Lowcountry
Beaufort, South Carolina

Freshman Application Contact Rhonda Cole, Admissions Services Manager, Technical College of the Lowcountry, 921 Ribaut Road, PO Box 1288, Beaufort, SC 29901-1288. *Phone:* 843-525-8229. *Fax:* 843-525-8285. *E-mail:* rcole@tcl.edu. *Website:* http://www.tcl.edu/.

Tri-County Technical College
Pendleton, South Carolina

Freshman Application Contact Tri-County Technical College, PO Box 587, 7900 Highway 76, Pendleton, SC 29670-0587. *Phone:* 864-646-1550. *Website:* http://www.tctc.edu/.

Trident Technical College
Charleston, South Carolina

- **State and locally supported** 2-year, founded 1964, part of South Carolina State Board for Technical and Comprehensive Education
- **Urban** campus
- **Coed**

Undergraduates 5,517 full-time, 7,754 part-time. Students come from 85 other countries; 2% are from out of state; 28% Black or African American, non-Hispanic/Latino; 6% Hispanic/Latino; 2% Asian, non-Hispanic/Latino; 0.3% Native Hawaiian or other Pacific Islander, non-Hispanic/Latino; 0.4% American Indian or Alaska Native, non-Hispanic/Latino; 3% Two or more races, non-Hispanic/Latino; 2% Race/ethnicity unknown; 8% transferred in.
Faculty *Student/faculty ratio:* 21:1.
Academics *Calendar:* semesters. *Degree:* certificates, diplomas, and associate. *Special study options:* academic remediation for entering students, advanced placement credit, cooperative education, distance learning, double majors, English as a second language, internships, off-campus study, part-time degree program, services for LD students, study abroad, summer session for credit.
Library Learning Resource Center plus 2 others. Students can reserve study rooms.
Student Life *Campus security:* 24-hour emergency response devices and patrols, late-night transport/escort service.
Applying *Options:* electronic application, early admission. *Application fee:* $30. *Required for some:* high school transcript.
Freshman Application Contact Ms. Clara Martin, Admissions Director, Trident Technical College, Charleston, SC 29423-8067. *Phone:* 843-574-6326. *Fax:* 843-574-6109. *E-mail:* clara.martin@tridenttech.edu. *Website:* http://www.tridenttech.edu/.

University of South Carolina Lancaster
Lancaster, South Carolina

- **State-supported** 2-year, founded 1959, part of University of South Carolina System
- **Small-town** 17-acre campus with easy access to Charlotte
- **Coed**

Undergraduates 794 full-time, 799 part-time. Students come from 10 states and territories; 2 other countries; 1% are from out of state.
Faculty *Student/faculty ratio:* 14:1.
Academics *Calendar:* semesters. *Degree:* associate. *Special study options:* academic remediation for entering students, advanced placement credit, distance learning, honors programs, independent study, internships, part-time degree program, services for LD students.
Library Medford Library.
Athletics Member NJCAA.
Standardized Tests *Required:* SAT or ACT (for admission).
Applying *Options:* electronic application, early admission. *Application fee:* $40. *Required:* high school transcript.
Freshman Application Contact Jennifer Blackmon, Admissions Processor, University of South Carolina Lancaster, PO Box 889, Lancaster, SC 29721. *Phone:* 803-313-7073. *Fax:* 803-313-7116. *E-mail:* jblackmo@mailbox.sc.edu. *Website:* http://usclancaster.sc.edu/.

University of South Carolina Salkehatchie
Allendale, South Carolina

Freshman Application Contact Ms. Carmen Brown, Admissions Coordinator, University of South Carolina Salkehatchie, PO Box 617, Allendale, SC 29810. *Phone:* 803-584-3446. *Toll-free phone:* 800-922-5500. *Fax:* 803-584-3884. *E-mail:* cdbrown@mailbox.sc.edu. *Website:* http://uscsalkehatchie.sc.edu/.

University of South Carolina Sumter
Sumter, South Carolina

Freshman Application Contact Mr. Keith Britton, Director of Admissions, University of South Carolina Sumter, 200 Miller Road, Sumter, SC 29150-2498. *Phone:* 803-938-3882. *Fax:* 803-938-3901. *E-mail:* kbritton@usc.sumter.edu. *Website:* http://www.uscsumter.edu/.

University of South Carolina Union
Union, South Carolina

- **State-supported** primarily 2-year, founded 1965, part of University of South Carolina System
- **Small-town** 7-acre campus with easy access to Charlotte, North Carolina
- **Endowment** $1.2 million
- **Coed,** 905 undergraduate students, 54% full-time, 53% women, 47% men

Undergraduates 487 full-time, 418 part-time. Students come from 3 states and territories; 1 other country; 2% are from out of state; 43% Black or African American, non-Hispanic/Latino; 3% Hispanic/Latino.
Freshmen *Admission:* 1,378 applied, 930 admitted. *Average high school GPA:* 3.3. *Test scores:* ACT scores over 18: 75%; ACT scores over 24: 5%.
Faculty *Total:* 42, 29% full-time. *Student/faculty ratio:* 18:1.
Majors Biological and physical sciences; liberal arts and sciences/liberal studies.
Academics *Calendar:* semesters. *Degrees:* associate and bachelor's. *Special study options:* advanced placement credit, cooperative education, distance learning, double majors, independent study, internships, part-time degree program, study abroad, summer session for credit.
Library Union Carnegie Library plus 1 other. Study areas open 24 hours, 5–7 days a week.
Student Life *Housing:* college housing not available. *Activities and Organizations:* drama/theater group, choral group. *Campus security:* 24-hour emergency response devices. *Student services:* personal/psychological counseling, veterans affairs office.
Athletics Member NJCAA. *Intramural sports:* baseball M, soccer M.
Standardized Tests *Required:* SAT or ACT (for admission).
Financial Aid Of all full-time matriculated undergraduates who enrolled in 2017, 16 Federal Work-Study jobs (averaging $3400).
Applying *Options:* electronic application. *Application fee:* $40. *Required:* high school transcript. *Application deadlines:* rolling (freshmen), rolling (transfers). *Notification:* continuous (freshmen), continuous (transfers).
Freshman Application Contact Mr. Michael B. Greer, Director of Enrollment Services, University of South Carolina Union, PO Drawer 729, Union, SC 29379-0729. *Phone:* 864-424-8039. *E-mail:* greerm@mailbox.sc.edu. *Website:* http://uscunion.sc.edu/.

Williamsburg Technical College
Kingstree, South Carolina

- **State-supported** 2-year, founded 1969, part of South Carolina State Board for Technical and Comprehensive Education
- **Rural** 41-acre campus
- **Coed**

Undergraduates 194 full-time, 538 part-time. Students come from 1 other state; 76% Black or African American, non-Hispanic/Latino; 0.3% Asian, non-Hispanic/Latino; 0.1% American Indian or Alaska Native, non-Hispanic/Latino; 0.4% Race/ethnicity unknown; 4% transferred in. *Retention:* 45% of full-time freshmen returned.
Faculty *Student/faculty ratio:* 12:1.
Academics *Calendar:* semesters. *Degree:* certificates, diplomas, and associate. *Special study options:* academic remediation for entering students, advanced placement credit, distance learning, double majors, independent study, part-time degree program, services for LD students, summer session for credit.
Library Learning Resource Center. *Books:* 18,002 (physical), 391,203 (digital/electronic); *Serial titles:* 91 (physical); *Databases:* 44. Students can reserve study rooms.
Applying *Options:* electronic application, early admission, deferred entrance. *Required:* high school transcript.
Freshman Application Contact Ms. Cheryl DuBose, Director of Admissions, Williamsburg Technical College, 601 MLK Jr. Avenue, Kingstree, SC 29556-4197. *Phone:* 843-355-4165. *Toll-free phone:* 800-768-2021. *Fax:* 843-355-4289. *E-mail:* dubosec@wiltech.edu. *Website:* http://www.wiltech.edu/.

York Technical College
Rock Hill, South Carolina

Freshman Application Contact Mr. Kenny Aldridge, Admissions Department Manager, York Technical College, Rock Hill, SC 29730. *Phone:* 803-327-8008. *Toll-free phone:* 800-922-8324. *Fax:* 803-981-7237. *E-mail:* kaldridge@yorktech.com. *Website:* http://www.yorktech.edu/.

SOUTH DAKOTA

Lake Area Technical Institute

Watertown, South Dakota

- **State-supported** 2-year, founded 1965, part of South Dakota Department of Education
- **Small-town** 40-acre campus
- **Endowment** $2.8 million
- **Coed**

Undergraduates 1,517 full-time, 538 part-time. Students come from 17 states and territories; 4 other countries; 19% are from out of state; 0.7% Black or African American, non-Hispanic/Latino; 2% Hispanic/Latino; 1% Asian, non-Hispanic/Latino; 0.3% Native Hawaiian or other Pacific Islander, non-Hispanic/Latino; 2% American Indian or Alaska Native, non-Hispanic/Latino; 3% Race/ethnicity unknown; 0.3% international; 8% transferred in.
Faculty *Student/faculty ratio:* 17:1.
Academics *Calendar:* semesters. *Degree:* certificates, diplomas, and associate. *Special study options:* academic remediation for entering students, advanced placement credit, cooperative education, distance learning, double majors, English as a second language, independent study, internships, off-campus study, part-time degree program, services for LD students, summer session for credit.
Library Leonard H. Timmerman Library plus 1 other. *Books:* 2,500 (physical), 250,000 (digital/electronic); *Serial titles:* 25 (physical); *Databases:* 40. Weekly public service hours: 58.
Student Life *Campus security:* 24-hour emergency response devices, partnership with local police department.
Standardized Tests *Required for some:* ACCUPLACER, TEAS. *Recommended:* ACT (for admission).
Financial Aid Of all full-time matriculated undergraduates who enrolled in 2017, 1,301 applied for aid, 1,085 were judged to have need, 119 had their need fully met. 127 Federal Work-Study jobs (averaging $1971). In 2017, 54. *Average percent of need met:* 56. *Average financial aid package:* $8520. *Average need-based loan:* $3933. *Average need-based gift aid:* $5465. *Average non-need-based aid:* $1142.
Applying *Options:* electronic application. *Application fee:* $25. *Required:* high school transcript. *Required for some:* essay or personal statement, interview.
Freshman Application Contact Ms. LuAnn Strait, Director of Student Services, Lake Area Technical Institute, 1201 Arrow Avenue, PO Box 730, Watertown, SD 57201. *Phone:* 605-882-5284 Ext. 241. *Toll-free phone:* 800-657-4344. *Fax:* 605-882-6299. *E-mail:* straitl@lakeareatech.edu. *Website:* http://www.lakeareatech.edu/.

Mitchell Technical Institute

Mitchell, South Dakota

- **State-supported** 2-year, founded 1968, part of South Dakota Board of Technical Education
- **Small-town** 90-acre campus
- **Coed,** 1,198 undergraduate students, 70% full-time, 32% women, 68% men

Undergraduates 840 full-time, 358 part-time. Students come from 19 states and territories; 10% are from out of state; 0.8% Black or African American, non-Hispanic/Latino; 2% Hispanic/Latino; 1% Asian, non-Hispanic/Latino; 0.1% Native Hawaiian or other Pacific Islander, non-Hispanic/Latino; 3% American Indian or Alaska Native, non-Hispanic/Latino; 2% Two or more races, non-Hispanic/Latino; 2% Race/ethnicity unknown; 10% transferred in. *Retention:* 81% of full-time freshmen returned.
Freshmen *Admission:* 926 applied, 557 admitted, 358 enrolled. *Average high school GPA:* 2.9. *Test scores:* ACT scores over 18: 67%; ACT scores over 24: 13%; ACT scores over 30: 1%.
Faculty *Total:* 77, 91% full-time, 1% with terminal degrees. *Student/faculty ratio:* 13:1.
Majors Accounting and business/management; agricultural mechanics and equipment technology; agricultural production; automation engineer technology; building construction technology; business automation/technology/data entry; clinical/medical laboratory technology; culinary arts; electrical and power transmission installation; electrician; energy management and systems technology; geographic information science and cartography; heating, air conditioning, ventilation and refrigeration maintenance technology; human services; lineworker; manufacturing engineering technology; medical/clinical assistant; medical office assistant; medical radiologic technology; network and system administration; radiologic technology/science; small engine mechanics and repair technology; speech-language pathology assistant; telecommunications technology; welding engineering technology.
Academics *Calendar:* semesters. *Degree:* certificates, diplomas, and associate. *Special study options:* academic remediation for entering students, advanced placement credit, cooperative education, distance learning, double majors, internships, part-time degree program, services for LD students, summer session for credit.
Library Center for Student Success. *Books:* 187 (physical), 929 (digital/electronic); *Databases:* 17. Weekly public service hours: 45.
Student Life *Housing:* college housing not available. *Activities and Organizations:* Student Representative Board, SkillsUSA, Student Veterans Organization, Rodeo Club, Diversity Club. *Campus security:* 24-hour emergency response devices. *Student services:* personal/psychological counseling.
Athletics *Intramural sports:* basketball M/W, volleyball M/W.
Standardized Tests *Required:* ACCUPLACER (for admission). *Recommended:* ACT (for admission).
Financial Aid Of all full-time matriculated undergraduates who enrolled in 2018, 778 applied for aid, 778 were judged to have need, 155 had their need fully met. In 2018, 51 non-need-based awards were made. *Average percent of need met:* 20%. *Average financial aid package:* $5151. *Average need-based loan:* $3389. *Average need-based gift aid:* $5026. *Average non-need-based aid:* $1081.
Applying *Options:* electronic application. *Required:* high school transcript. *Required for some:* essay or personal statement, interview. *Recommended:* minimum 2.0 GPA. *Application deadlines:* rolling (freshmen), rolling (out-of-state freshmen), rolling (transfers). *Notification:* continuous (freshmen), continuous (out-of-state freshmen), continuous (transfers).
Freshman Application Contact Mr. Clayton Deuter, Dean of Enrollment Services, Mitchell Technical Institute, 1800 East Spruce Street, Mitchell, SD 57301. *Phone:* 605-995-3025. *Toll-free phone:* 800-684-1969. *Fax:* 605-995-3067. *E-mail:* clayton.deuter@mitchelltech.edu.
Website: http://www.mitchelltech.edu/.

Sisseton-Wahpeton College

Sisseton, South Dakota

- **Federally supported** 2-year, founded 1979
- **Rural** 2-acre campus
- **Coed**

Undergraduates 127 full-time, 48 part-time. 14% are from out of state; 5% Black or African American, non-Hispanic/Latino; 3% Hispanic/Latino; 85% American Indian or Alaska Native, non-Hispanic/Latino; 2% transferred in.
Faculty *Student/faculty ratio:* 10:1.
Academics *Calendar:* semesters. *Degree:* certificates and associate. *Special study options:* academic remediation for entering students, adult/continuing education programs, cooperative education, double majors, internships, off-campus study, part-time degree program, summer session for credit.
Library Sisseton-Wahpeton Community College Library.
Student Life *Campus security:* 24-hour emergency response devices.
Standardized Tests *Required:* ACT Compass (for admission).
Financial Aid Of all full-time matriculated undergraduates who enrolled in 2017, 157 applied for aid, 140 were judged to have need, 8 had their need fully met. In 2017, 11. *Average percent of need met:* 56. *Average financial aid package:* $5934. *Average need-based gift aid:* $5934. *Average non-need-based aid:* $2385.
Applying *Required:* high school transcript. *Required for some:* Certificate of Indian Blood for enrolled tribal members. *Recommended:* minimum 2.0 GPA, interview.
Freshman Application Contact Sisseton-Wahpeton College, Old Agency Box 689, Sisseton, SD 57262. *Phone:* 605-698-3966 Ext. 1180. *Website:* http://www.swc.tc/.

Southeast Technical Institute

Sioux Falls, South Dakota

- **State-supported** 2-year, founded 1968
- **Urban** 138-acre campus
- **Coed**

Undergraduates 1,426 full-time, 818 part-time. Students come from 11 states and territories; 10% are from out of state; 2% Black or African American, non-Hispanic/Latino; 4% Hispanic/Latino; 3% Asian, non-Hispanic/Latino; 0.4% American Indian or Alaska Native, non-Hispanic/Latino; 0.8% Two or more races, non-Hispanic/Latino; 5% Race/ethnicity unknown; 17% transferred in; 2% live on campus. *Retention:* 72% of full-time freshmen returned.
Faculty *Student/faculty ratio:* 15:1.
Academics *Calendar:* semesters. *Degree:* certificates, diplomas, and associate. *Special study options:* academic remediation for entering students, advanced placement credit, distance learning, double majors, English as a second language, independent study, internships, part-time degree program, services for LD students, summer session for credit.

Library Southeast Library.
Student Life *Campus security:* 24-hour patrols, late-night transport/escort service, controlled dormitory access.
Standardized Tests *Required for some:* ACT (for admission). *Recommended:* ACT (for admission).
Applying *Options:* electronic application. *Required:* high school transcript, minimum 2.0 GPA. *Required for some:* interview, background check, drug screening.
Freshman Application Contact Mr. Scott Dorman, Recruiter, Southeast Technical Institute, Sioux Falls, SD 57107. *Phone:* 605-367-4458. *Toll-free phone:* 800-247-0789. *Fax:* 605-367-8305. *E-mail:* scott.dorman@southeasttech.edu. *Website:* http://www.southeasttech.edu/.

Western Dakota Technical Institute
Rapid City, South Dakota

- **State-supported** 2-year, founded 1968
- **Small-town** 5-acre campus
- **Endowment** $187,302
- **Coed**

Undergraduates 613 full-time, 436 part-time. Students come from 13 states and territories; 5% are from out of state; 2% Black or African American, non-Hispanic/Latino; 5% Hispanic/Latino; 0.8% Asian, non-Hispanic/Latino; 0.2% Native Hawaiian or other Pacific Islander, non-Hispanic/Latino; 13% American Indian or Alaska Native, non-Hispanic/Latino; 3% Two or more races, non-Hispanic/Latino; 1% Race/ethnicity unknown; 11% transferred in.
Faculty *Student/faculty ratio:* 13:1.
Academics *Calendar:* semesters. *Degree:* certificates, diplomas, and associate. *Special study options:* academic remediation for entering students, advanced placement credit, distance learning, independent study, internships, part-time degree program, services for LD students, summer session for credit.
Library Western Dakota Technical Institute Library plus 1 other. *Books:* 3,500 (physical), 158,080 (digital/electronic); *Databases:* 12. Weekly public service hours: 48.
Student Life *Campus security:* 24-hour video surveillance.
Standardized Tests *Recommended:* SAT or ACT (for admission).
Financial Aid Of all full-time matriculated undergraduates who enrolled in 2018, 517 applied for aid, 475 were judged to have need, 22 had their need fully met. 30 Federal Work-Study jobs (averaging $1780). In 2018, 11. *Average percent of need met:* 73. *Average financial aid package:* $13,619. *Average need-based loan:* $3402. *Average need-based gift aid:* $7093. *Average non-need-based aid:* $1636.
Applying *Options:* electronic application. *Required:* high school transcript. *Required for some:* essay or personal statement, 3 letters of recommendation, interview. *Recommended:* minimum 2.0 GPA.
Freshman Application Contact Ms. Jill Elder, Admissions Coordinator, Western Dakota Technical Institute, 800 Mickelson Drive, Rapid City, SD 57703. *Phone:* 605-718-2411. *Toll-free phone:* 800-544-8765. *Fax:* 605-394-2204. *E-mail:* jill.elder@wdt.edu. *Website:* http://www.wdt.edu/.

TENNESSEE

Chattanooga College–Medical, Dental and Technical Careers
Chattanooga, Tennessee

Freshman Application Contact Chattanooga College–Medical, Dental and Technical Careers, 248 Northgate Mall Drive, Suite 130, Chattanooga, TN 37415. *Phone:* 423-305-7781. *Toll-free phone:* 877-313-2373. *Website:* http://www.chattanoogacollege.edu/.

Chattanooga State Community College
Chattanooga, Tennessee

Freshman Application Contact Brad McCormick, Director of Admissions and Records, Chattanooga State Community College, 4501 Amnicola Highway, Chattanooga, TN 37406. *Phone:* 423-697-4401 Ext. 3264. *Toll-free phone:* 866-547-3733. *Fax:* 423-697-4709. *E-mail:* brad.mccormick@chattanoogastate.edu. *Website:* http://www.chattanoogastate.edu/.

Cleveland State Community College
Cleveland, Tennessee

- **State-supported** 2-year, founded 1967, part of Tennessee Board of Regents
- **Suburban** 83-acre campus
- **Endowment** $8.8 million
- **Coed,** 3,264 undergraduate students, 51% full-time, 57% women, 43% men

Undergraduates 1,656 full-time, 1,608 part-time. Students come from 6 states and territories; 1% are from out of state; 6% Black or African American, non-Hispanic/Latino; 5% Hispanic/Latino; 1% Asian, non-Hispanic/Latino; 0.2% Native Hawaiian or other Pacific Islander, non-Hispanic/Latino; 0.2% American Indian or Alaska Native, non-Hispanic/Latino; 0.3% Two or more races, non-Hispanic/Latino; 3% Race/ethnicity unknown; 0.3% international; 6% transferred in.
Freshmen *Admission:* 1,830 applied, 745 enrolled. *Average high school GPA:* 3.6.
Faculty *Total:* 212, 34% full-time, 18% with terminal degrees. *Student/faculty ratio:* 19:1.
Majors Administrative assistant and secretarial science; business administration and management; child development; computer and information sciences; criminal justice/police science; education; electrical, electronic and communications engineering technology; electromechanical technology; emergency medical technology (EMT paramedic); engineering technology; general studies; health professions related; industrial technology; information technology; liberal arts and sciences/liberal studies; medical/clinical assistant; medical informatics; multi/interdisciplinary studies related; music performance; public administration and social service professions related; registered nursing/registered nurse; science technologies related.
Academics *Calendar:* semesters. *Degree:* certificates and associate. *Special study options:* academic remediation for entering students, adult/continuing education programs, advanced placement credit, cooperative education, distance learning, double majors, external degree program, honors programs, independent study, internships, off-campus study, part-time degree program, services for LD students, summer session for credit.
Library Cleveland State Community College Library plus 1 other. *Books:* 50,426 (physical), 6,533 (digital/electronic); *Serial titles:* 426 (physical); *Databases:* 75.
Student Life *Housing:* college housing not available. *Activities and Organizations:* choral group, Human Services/Social Work, Computer-Aided Design, Phi Theta Kappa, Student Nursing Association, Early Childhood Education. *Campus security:* 24-hour emergency response devices and patrols. *Student services:* personal/psychological counseling.
Athletics Member NJCAA. *Intercollegiate sports:* basketball W(s), cross-country running W(s), softball W(s), volleyball W(s). *Intramural sports:* archery M, basketball M, bowling M, cheerleading M(c), table tennis M, volleyball M.
Financial Aid Of all full-time matriculated undergraduates who enrolled in 2017, 52 Federal Work-Study jobs (averaging $1025).
Applying *Options:* electronic application, early admission, deferred entrance. *Required:* high school transcript. *Application deadline:* 8/15 (out-of-state freshmen). *Notification:* continuous (freshmen).
Freshman Application Contact Mrs. Suzanne Bayne, Director of Admissions, Recruiting, and High School Relations, Cleveland State Community College, PO Box 3570, Cleveland, TN 37320-3570. *Phone:* 423-472-7141 Ext. 280. *Toll-free phone:* 800-604-2722. *Fax:* 423-614-8711. *E-mail:* sbayne@clevelandstatecc.edu.
Website: http://www.clevelandstatecc.edu/.

Columbia State Community College
Columbia, Tennessee

Freshman Application Contact Mr. Joey Scruggs, Coordinator of Recruitment, Columbia State Community College, 1665 Hampshire Pike, Columbia, TN 38401. *Phone:* 931-540-2540. *E-mail:* scruggs@coscc.cc.tn.us. *Website:* http://www.columbiastate.edu/.

Concorde Career College
Memphis, Tennessee

Freshman Application Contact Dee Vickers, Director, Concorde Career College, 5100 Poplar Avenue, Suite 132, Memphis, TN 38137. *Phone:* 901-761-9494. *Fax:* 901-761-3293. *E-mail:* dvickers@concorde.edu. *Website:* http://www.concorde.edu/.

Daymar College
Clarksville, Tennessee

Freshman Application Contact Daymar College, 2691 Trenton Road, Clarksville, TN 37040. *Phone:* 931-552-7600 Ext. 204. *Website:* http://www.daymarcollege.edu/.

Daymar College
Murfreesboro, Tennessee

Admissions Office Contact Daymar College, 415 Golden Bear Court, Murfreesboro, TN 37128. *Website:* http://www.daymarcollege.edu/.

Daymar College
Nashville, Tennessee

Director of Admissions Admissions Office, Daymar College, 560 Royal Parkway, Nashville, TN 37214. *Phone:* 615-361-7555. *Fax:* 615-367-2736. *Website:* http://www.daymarcollege.edu/.

Dyersburg State Community College
Dyersburg, Tennessee

- **State-supported** 2-year, founded 1969, part of Tennessee Board of Regents
- **Small-town** 115-acre campus with easy access to Memphis
- **Endowment** $4.0 million
- **Coed**

Undergraduates 1,253 full-time, 1,563 part-time. Students come from 4 states and territories; 1 other country; 19% Black or African American, non-Hispanic/Latino; 3% Hispanic/Latino; 1% Asian, non-Hispanic/Latino; 0.4% American Indian or Alaska Native, non-Hispanic/Latino; 2% Two or more races, non-Hispanic/Latino; 1% Race/ethnicity unknown; 0.2% international; 5% transferred in. *Retention:* 50% of full-time freshmen returned.
Faculty *Student/faculty ratio:* 21:1.
Academics *Calendar:* semesters. *Degree:* certificates and associate. *Special study options:* academic remediation for entering students, accelerated degree program, adult/continuing education programs, advanced placement credit, cooperative education, distance learning, double majors, honors programs, independent study, internships, off-campus study, part-time degree program, services for LD students, study abroad, summer session for credit.
Library Learning Resource Center plus 2 others. *Books:* 17,817 (physical), 225,400 (digital/electronic); *Serial titles:* 29 (digital/electronic); *Databases:* 121. Weekly public service hours: 66; students can reserve study rooms.
Student Life *Campus security:* 24-hour emergency response devices and patrols.
Athletics Member NJCAA.
Standardized Tests *Required:* SAT or ACT (for admission). *Required for some:* ACT Compass for students who are over 21.
Financial Aid Of all full-time matriculated undergraduates who enrolled in 2016, 34 Federal Work-Study jobs (averaging $1342). 75 state and other part-time jobs (averaging $1360).
Applying *Options:* electronic application. *Required:* high school transcript.
Freshman Application Contact Mrs. Heather Page, Director of Admissions and Records, Dyersburg State Community College, Dyersburg, TN 38024. *Phone:* 731-286-3331. *Fax:* 731-286-3325. *E-mail:* page@dscc.edu. *Website:* http://www.dscc.edu/.

Fortis Institute
Cookeville, Tennessee

Director of Admissions Ms. Sharon Mellott, Director of Admissions, Fortis Institute, 1025 Highway 111, Cookeville, TN 38501. *Phone:* 931-526-3660. *Toll-free phone:* 855-4-FORTIS. *Website:* http://www.fortis.edu/.

Fortis Institute
Nashville, Tennessee

Admissions Office Contact Fortis Institute, 3354 Perimeter Hill Drive, Suite 105, Nashville, TN 37211. *Toll-free phone:* 855-4-FORTIS. *Website:* http://www.fortis.edu/.

Hiwassee College
Madisonville, Tennessee

Director of Admissions Jamie Williamson, Director of Admission, Hiwassee College, 225 Hiwassee College Drive, Madisonville, TN 37354. *Phone:* 423-420-1891. *Toll-free phone:* 800-356-2187. *Website:* http://www.hiwassee.edu/.

Jackson State Community College
Jackson, Tennessee

Freshman Application Contact Ms. Andrea Winchester, Director of High School Initiatives, Jackson State Community College, 2046 North Parkway, Jackson, TN 38301-3797. *Phone:* 731-424-3520 Ext. 50484. *Toll-free phone:* 800-355-5722. *Fax:* 731-425-9559. *E-mail:* awinchester@jscc.edu. *Website:* http://www.jscc.edu/.

John A. Gupton College
Nashville, Tennessee

Freshman Application Contact John A. Gupton College, 1616 Church Street, Nashville, TN 37203-2920. *Phone:* 615-327-3927. *Website:* http://www.guptoncollege.edu/.

L'Ecole Culinaire–Memphis
Cordova, Tennessee

Admissions Office Contact L'Ecole Culinaire–Memphis, 1245 North Germantown Parkway, Cordova, TN 38016. *Toll-free phone:* 888-238-2077. *Website:* http://www.lecole.edu/memphis/.

Lincoln College of Technology
Nashville, Tennessee

Freshman Application Contact Ms. Tanya Smith, Director of Admissions, Lincoln College of Technology, 1524 Gallatin Road, Nashville, TN 37206. *Phone:* 615-226-3990 Ext. 71703. *Toll-free phone:* 844-215-1513. *Fax:* 615-262-8466. *E-mail:* tlegg-smith@lincolntech.com. *Website:* http://www.lincolntech.edu/.

Miller-Motte Technical College
Chattanooga, Tennessee

Admissions Office Contact Miller-Motte Technical College, 6397 Lee Highway, Suite 100, Chattanooga, TN 37421. *Toll-free phone:* 800-705-9182. *Website:* http://www.miller-motte.edu/.

Motlow State Community College
Tullahoma, Tennessee

- **State-supported** 2-year, founded 1969, part of Tennessee Board of Regents
- **Rural** 187-acre campus with easy access to Nashville
- **Endowment** $7.1 million
- **Coed,** 6,886 undergraduate students, 58% full-time, 69% women, 31% men

Undergraduates 4,018 full-time, 2,868 part-time. 1% are from out of state; 12% Black or African American, non-Hispanic/Latino; 9% Hispanic/Latino; 3% Asian, non-Hispanic/Latino; 0.1% Native Hawaiian or other Pacific Islander, non-Hispanic/Latino; 0.3% American Indian or Alaska Native, non-Hispanic/Latino; 3% Two or more races, non-Hispanic/Latino; 0.1% international; 6% transferred in.
Freshmen *Admission:* 4,013 applied, 4,013 admitted, 1,707 enrolled. *Average high school GPA:* 3.1. *Test scores:* ACT scores over 18: 69%; ACT scores over 24: 13%; ACT scores over 30: 1%.
Faculty *Student/faculty ratio:* 18:1.
Majors Business administration and management; child development; clinical/medical laboratory technology; education; electromechanical technology; emergency medical technology (EMT paramedic); interdisciplinary studies; liberal arts and sciences/liberal studies; music performance; registered nursing/registered nurse; web page, digital/multimedia and information resources design.
Academics *Calendar:* semesters. *Degree:* certificates and associate. *Special study options:* academic remediation for entering students, accelerated degree program, adult/continuing education programs, advanced placement credit, cooperative education, distance learning, double majors, honors programs, independent study, part-time degree program, services for LD students, study abroad, summer session for credit.
Library Clayton-Glass Library. *Books:* 63,642 (physical), 419,239 (digital/electronic); *Serial titles:* 94 (physical), 37,886 (digital/electronic); *Databases:* 58. Students can reserve study rooms.
Student Life *Housing:* college housing not available. *Activities and Organizations:* drama/theater group, student-run newspaper, choral group, Phi Theta Kappa, Student Government Association, Baptist Collegiate Ministries, Art Club, Psi Beta. *Campus security:* 24-hour patrols, late-night

transport/escort service. *Student services:* personal/psychological counseling, veterans affairs office.
Athletics Member NJCAA. *Intercollegiate sports:* baseball M(s), basketball M(s)/W(s), soccer W(s), softball W(s).
Standardized Tests *Required:* SAT or ACT (for admission).
Financial Aid Of all full-time matriculated undergraduates who enrolled in 2017, 2,991 applied for aid, 2,294 were judged to have need, 238 had their need fully met. In 2017, 642 non-need-based awards were made. *Average percent of need met:* 55%. *Average financial aid package:* $6067. *Average need-based gift aid:* $5058. *Average non-need-based aid:* $3957.
Applying *Options:* electronic application, early admission, deferred entrance. *Required:* high school transcript. *Notification:* continuous (freshmen), continuous (transfers).
Director of Admissions Mae Sanders, Director of Admissions and Records, Motlow State Community College, PO Box 8500, Lynchburg, TN 37352-8500. *Phone:* 931-393-1530. *Toll-free phone:* 800-654-4877. *Fax:* 931-393-1681. *E-mail:* msanders@mscc.edu.
Website: http://www.mscc.edu/.

Nashville State Community College
Nashville, Tennessee

Freshman Application Contact Mr. Tyler White, Coordinator of Recruitment, Nashville State Community College, 120 White Bridge Road, Nashville, TN 37209-4515. *Phone:* 615-353-3265. *Toll-free phone:* 800-272-7363. *E-mail:* recruiting@nscc.edu. *Website:* http://www.nscc.edu/.

National College
Bristol, Tennessee

Freshman Application Contact National College, 1328 Highway 11 West, Bristol, TN 37620. *Phone:* 423-878-4440. *Toll-free phone:* 888-9-JOBREADY. *Website:* http://www.national-college.edu/.

National College
Nashville, Tennessee

Director of Admissions Jerry Lafferty, Campus Director, National College, 1638 Bell Road, Nashville, TN 37211. *Phone:* 615-333-3344. *Toll-free phone:* 888-9-JOBREADY. *Website:* http://www.national-college.edu/.

North Central Institute
Clarksville, Tennessee

- **Proprietary** 2-year, founded 1988
- **Suburban** 14-acre campus
- **Coed, primarily men**

Undergraduates 29% are from out of state.
Faculty *Student/faculty ratio:* 10:1.
Academics *Calendar:* continuous. *Degree:* associate. *Special study options:* advanced placement credit, external degree program, independent study, part-time degree program, summer session for credit.
Library Media Resource Center.
Student Life *Campus security:* 24-hour emergency response devices.
Applying *Options:* electronic application, early admission. *Application fee:* $35. *Recommended:* high school transcript.
Freshman Application Contact Dale Wood, Director of Admissions, North Central Institute, 168 Jack Miller Boulevard, Clarksville, TN 37042. *Phone:* 931-431-9700. *Toll-free phone:* 800-603-4116. *Fax:* 931-431-9771. *E-mail:* admissions@nci.edu. *Website:* http://www.nci.edu/.

Northeast State Community College
Blountville, Tennessee

- **State-supported** 2-year, founded 1966, part of Tennessee Board of Regents
- **Small-town** 95-acre campus
- **Endowment** $9.9 million
- **Coed**

Undergraduates 3,421 full-time, 2,667 part-time. Students come from 4 states and territories; 5 other countries; 2% are from out of state; 2% Black or African American, non-Hispanic/Latino; 3% Hispanic/Latino; 0.7% Asian, non-Hispanic/Latino; 0.1% Native Hawaiian or other Pacific Islander, non-Hispanic/Latino; 0.3% American Indian or Alaska Native, non-Hispanic/Latino; 3% Two or more races, non-Hispanic/Latino; 1% Race/ethnicity unknown; 0.2% international; 4% transferred in. *Retention:* 61% of full-time freshmen returned.
Faculty *Student/faculty ratio:* 24:1.
Academics *Calendar:* semesters. *Degree:* certificates and associate. *Special study options:* academic remediation for entering students, advanced placement credit, cooperative education, distance learning, double majors, honors programs, part-time degree program, services for LD students, study abroad, summer session for credit.
Library Wayne G. Basler Library plus 1 other. *Books:* 63,647 (physical), 316,562 (digital/electronic); *Serial titles:* 132 (physical), 48,455 (digital/electronic); *Databases:* 93.
Student Life *Campus security:* 24-hour emergency response devices and patrols, late-night transport/escort service, Safe Northeast Program.
Financial Aid Of all full-time matriculated undergraduates who enrolled in 2017, 109 Federal Work-Study jobs (averaging $1318). 35 state and other part-time jobs.
Applying *Options:* electronic application. *Required:* high school transcript.
Freshman Application Contact Mrs. Jennifer G. Starling, Dean of Enrollment Management, Northeast State Community College, PO Box 246, Blountville, TN 37617. *Phone:* 423-279-7635. *Toll-free phone:* 800-836-7822. *Fax:* 423-323-0240. *E-mail:* jgstarling@northeaststate.edu. *Website:* http://www.northeaststate.edu/.

Pellissippi State Community College
Knoxville, Tennessee

Freshman Application Contact Director of Admissions and Records, Pellissippi State Community College, PO Box 22990, Knoxville, TN 37933-0990. *Phone:* 865-694-6400. *Fax:* 865-539-7217. *Website:* http://www.pstcc.edu/.

Remington College–Memphis Campus
Memphis, Tennessee

Director of Admissions Randal Hayes, Director of Recruitment, Remington College–Memphis Campus, 2710 Nonconnah Boulevard, Memphis, TN 38132. *Phone:* 901-345-1000. *Toll-free phone:* 800-323-8122. *Fax:* 901-396-8310. *E-mail:* randal.hayes@remingtoncollege.edu. *Website:* http://www.remingtoncollege.edu/.

Remington College–Nashville Campus
Nashville, Tennessee

Director of Admissions Mr. Frank Vivelo, Campus President, Remington College–Nashville Campus, 441 Donelson Pike, Suite 150, Nashville, TN 37214. *Phone:* 615-889-5520. *Toll-free phone:* 800-323-8122. *Fax:* 615-889-5528. *E-mail:* frank.vivelo@remingtoncollege.edu. *Website:* http://www.remingtoncollege.edu/.

Roane State Community College
Harriman, Tennessee

Freshman Application Contact Admissions Office, Roane State Community College, 276 Patton Lane, Harriman, TN 37748. *Phone:* 865-882-4523. *Toll-free phone:* 866-462-7722 Ext. 4554. *E-mail:* admissionsrecords@roanestate.edu. *Website:* http://www.roanestate.edu/.

SAE Institute Nashville
Nashville, Tennessee

Admissions Office Contact SAE Institute Nashville, 7 Music Circle N, Nashville, TN 37203. *Website:* http://www.sae.edu/.

Southwest Tennessee Community College
Memphis, Tennessee

Freshman Application Contact Mrs. Vanessa Dowdy, Southwest Tennessee Community College, 5983 Macon Cove, Memphis, TN 38134. *Phone:* 901-333-4275. *Toll-free phone:* 877-717-STCC. *E-mail:* vdowdy@southwest.tn.edu. *Website:* http://www.southwest.tn.edu/.

Volunteer State Community College

Gallatin, Tennessee

- **State-supported** 2-year, founded 1970, part of Tennessee Board of Regents
- **Suburban** 110-acre campus with easy access to Nashville
- **Endowment** $4.4 million
- **Coed**

Undergraduates 4,974 full-time, 3,864 part-time. Students come from 14 states and territories; 15 other countries; 1% are from out of state; 10% Black or African American, non-Hispanic/Latino; 6% Hispanic/Latino; 2% Asian, non-Hispanic/Latino; 0.1% Native Hawaiian or other Pacific Islander, non-Hispanic/Latino; 0.4% American Indian or Alaska Native, non-Hispanic/Latino; 3% Two or more races, non-Hispanic/Latino; 2% Race/ethnicity unknown; 0.4% international; 5% transferred in.
Faculty *Student/faculty ratio:* 23:1.
Academics *Calendar:* semesters. *Degree:* certificates and associate. *Special study options:* academic remediation for entering students, accelerated degree program, adult/continuing education programs, advanced placement credit, cooperative education, distance learning, double majors, English as a second language, honors programs, independent study, internships, part-time degree program, services for LD students, study abroad, summer session for credit.
Library Thigpen Library.
Student Life *Campus security:* 24-hour emergency response devices and patrols, late-night transport/escort service.
Athletics Member NJCAA.
Standardized Tests *Required for some:* SAT or ACT (for admission).
Financial Aid Of all full-time matriculated undergraduates who enrolled in 2017, 4,472 applied for aid, 2,967 were judged to have need, 190 had their need fully met. 39 Federal Work-Study jobs (averaging $2304). In 2017, 66. *Average percent of need met:* 55. *Average financial aid package:* $6011. *Average need-based loan:* $2970. *Average need-based gift aid:* $5080. *Average non-need-based aid:* $1603.
Applying *Options:* electronic application, early admission, deferred entrance. *Required:* high school transcript. *Required for some:* minimum 2.0 GPA, interview.
Freshman Application Contact Mr. Tim Amyx, Director of Admissions, Volunteer State Community College, 1480 Nashville Pike, Gallatin, TN 37066-3188. *Phone:* 615-452-8600 Ext. 3614. *Toll-free phone:* 888-335-8722. *Fax:* 615-230-4875. *E-mail:* admissions@volstate.edu. *Website:* http://www.volstate.edu/.

Walters State Community College

Morristown, Tennessee

- **State-supported** 2-year, founded 1970, part of Tennessee Board of Regents
- **Small-town** 100-acre campus
- **Coed**

Undergraduates 3,294 full-time, 2,781 part-time. 1% are from out of state; 3% Black or African American, non-Hispanic/Latino; 4% Hispanic/Latino; 0.7% Asian, non-Hispanic/Latino; 0.1% Native Hawaiian or other Pacific Islander, non-Hispanic/Latino; 0.3% American Indian or Alaska Native, non-Hispanic/Latino; 3% Two or more races, non-Hispanic/Latino; 0.6% international; 4% transferred in.
Faculty *Student/faculty ratio:* 18:1.
Academics *Calendar:* semesters. *Degree:* certificates and associate. *Special study options:* academic remediation for entering students, accelerated degree program, advanced placement credit, cooperative education, distance learning, English as a second language, freshman honors college, honors programs, independent study, internships, off-campus study, part-time degree program, services for LD students, student-designed majors, study abroad, summer session for credit. *ROTC:* Army (c).
Library Walters State Library.
Student Life *Campus security:* 24-hour emergency response devices and patrols, late-night transport/escort service, security cameras.
Athletics Member NJCAA.
Financial Aid Of all full-time matriculated undergraduates who enrolled in 2017, 2,915 applied for aid, 2,556 were judged to have need, 129 had their need fully met. In 2017, 337. *Average percent of need met:* 41. *Average financial aid package:* $6112. *Average need-based gift aid:* $4951. *Average non-need-based aid:* $4673.
Applying *Options:* electronic application, early admission. *Required:* high school transcript.
Freshman Application Contact Mr. Michael Campbell, Assistant Vice President for Student Affairs, Walters State Community College, 500 South Davy Crockett Parkway, Morristown, TN 37813-6899. *Phone:* 423-585-2682. *Toll-free phone:* 800-225-4770. *Fax:* 423-585-6876. *E-mail:* mike.campbell@ws.edu. *Website:* http://www.ws.edu/.

West Tennessee Business College

Jackson, Tennessee

Admissions Office Contact West Tennessee Business College, 1186 Highway 45 Bypass, Jackson, TN 38343. *Website:* http://www.wtbc.edu/.

TEXAS

Alvin Community College

Alvin, Texas

- **State and locally supported** 2-year, founded 1949
- **Suburban** 114-acre campus with easy access to Houston
- **Coed**

Undergraduates 1,411 full-time, 4,374 part-time. Students come from 2 other countries; 15% Black or African American, non-Hispanic/Latino; 40% Hispanic/Latino; 5% Asian, non-Hispanic/Latino; 0.3% Native Hawaiian or other Pacific Islander, non-Hispanic/Latino; 1% American Indian or Alaska Native, non-Hispanic/Latino; 2% Race/ethnicity unknown; 1% international. *Retention:* 62% of full-time freshmen returned.
Faculty *Student/faculty ratio:* 14:1.
Academics *Calendar:* semesters. *Degree:* certificates, diplomas, and associate. *Special study options:* academic remediation for entering students, accelerated degree program, adult/continuing education programs, advanced placement credit, cooperative education, distance learning, double majors, English as a second language, honors programs, independent study, internships, part-time degree program, services for LD students, student-designed majors, study abroad, summer session for credit.
Library Alvin Community College Library. *Books:* 11,000 (physical), 30,000 (digital/electronic); *Databases:* 80. Weekly public service hours: 67; students can reserve study rooms.
Student Life *Campus security:* 24-hour patrols, late-night transport/escort service, Vehicle Assist, emergency messages.
Athletics Member NJCAA.
Applying *Required for some:* high school transcript.
Freshman Application Contact Alvin Community College, 3110 Mustang Road, Alvin, TX 77511-4898. *Phone:* 281-756-3527. *Website:* http://www.alvincollege.edu/.

Amarillo College

Amarillo, Texas

- **State and locally supported** 2-year, founded 1929
- **Urban** 1542-acre campus
- **Endowment** $40.0 million
- **Coed**

Undergraduates 5% Black or African American, non-Hispanic/Latino; 39% Hispanic/Latino; 3% Asian, non-Hispanic/Latino; 0.1% Native Hawaiian or other Pacific Islander, non-Hispanic/Latino; 0.5% American Indian or Alaska Native, non-Hispanic/Latino; 2% Two or more races, non-Hispanic/Latino; 1% Race/ethnicity unknown. *Retention:* 52% of full-time freshmen returned.
Academics *Calendar:* semesters. *Degree:* certificates and associate. *Special study options:* academic remediation for entering students, adult/continuing education programs, advanced placement credit, cooperative education, distance learning, English as a second language, freshman honors college, honors programs, part-time degree program, services for LD students, summer session for credit.
Library Lynn Library Learning Center plus 2 others.
Student Life *Campus security:* 24-hour emergency response devices, late-night transport/escort service, campus police patrol Monday through Saturday 7 am-11 pm.
Financial Aid Of all full-time matriculated undergraduates who enrolled in 2017, 100 Federal Work-Study jobs (averaging $3000).
Applying *Options:* early admission, deferred entrance. *Required:* high school transcript.
Freshman Application Contact Amarillo College, PO Box 447, Amarillo, TX 79178-0001. *Phone:* 806-371-5000. *Toll-free phone:* 800-227-8784. *Fax:* 806-371-5497. *E-mail:* askac@actx.edu. *Website:* http://www.actx.edu/.

Angelina College

Lufkin, Texas

Freshman Application Contact Angelina College, PO Box 1768, Lufkin, TX 75902-1768. *Phone:* 936-633-5213. *Website:* http://www.angelina.edu/.

Auguste Escoffier School of Culinary Arts
Austin, Texas

Admissions Office Contact Auguste Escoffier School of Culinary Arts, 6020-B Dillard, Austin, TX 78752. *Website:* http://www.escoffier.edu/.

Austin Community College District
Austin, Texas

- **State and locally supported** primarily 2-year, founded 1972
- **Urban** campus with easy access to Austin
- **Endowment** $5.9 million
- **Coed,** 40,799 undergraduate students, 22% full-time, 56% women, 44% men

Undergraduates 8,983 full-time, 31,816 part-time. Students come from 52 states and territories; 94 other countries; 2% are from out of state; 7% Black or African American, non-Hispanic/Latino; 37% Hispanic/Latino; 5% Asian, non-Hispanic/Latino; 0.2% Native Hawaiian or other Pacific Islander, non-Hispanic/Latino; 0.7% American Indian or Alaska Native, non-Hispanic/Latino; 4% Two or more races, non-Hispanic/Latino; 0.8% Race/ethnicity unknown; 1% international.
Faculty *Total:* 1,856, 31% full-time, 23% with terminal degrees. *Student/faculty ratio:* 20:1.
Majors Accounting; accounting technology and bookkeeping; administrative assistant and secretarial science; animation, interactive technology, video graphics and special effects; anthropology; Arabic; archeology; art; autobody/collision and repair technology; automobile/automotive mechanics technology; biology/biological sciences; biology/biotechnology laboratory technician; biomedical technology; business administration and management; business/commerce; carpentry; chemistry; child development; Chinese; civil engineering; clinical/medical laboratory technology; commercial photography; computer and information sciences; computer programming; computer systems networking and telecommunications; corrections; creative writing; criminal justice/police science; crisis/emergency/disaster management; culinary arts; dance; dental hygiene; design and visual communications; diagnostic medical sonography and ultrasound technology; digital arts; drafting and design technology; dramatic/theater arts; early childhood education; economics; electrical, electronic and communications engineering technology; emergency medical technology (EMT paramedic); engineering; English; entrepreneurship; environmental engineering technology; environmental science; fire prevention and safety technology; French; general studies; geographic information science and cartography; geography; geology/earth science; German; health and physical education/fitness; health information/medical records technology; heating, ventilation, air conditioning and refrigeration engineering technology; history; hospitality administration; hotel/motel administration; international business/trade/commerce; Italian; Japanese; journalism; kinesiology and exercise science; Latin; legal assistant/paralegal; logistics, materials, and supply chain management; marketing/marketing management; mathematics; mental health counseling; middle school education; multi/interdisciplinary studies related; music; music management; occupational therapist assistant; pharmacy technician; philosophy; photographic and film/video technology; physical therapy technology; physics; political science and government; premedical studies; professional, technical, business, and scientific writing; psychology; radio and television; radiologic technology/science; real estate; registered nursing/registered nurse; rhetoric and composition; Russian; secondary education; sign language interpretation and translation; social work; sociology; Spanish; substance abuse/addiction counseling; surgical technology; surveying technology; therapeutic recreation; tourism and travel services management; veterinary/animal health technology; watchmaking and jewelrymaking; welding technology.
Academics *Calendar:* semesters. *Degrees:* certificates, associate, bachelor's, and postbachelor's certificates. *Special study options:* academic remediation for entering students, accelerated degree program, adult/continuing education programs, advanced placement credit, cooperative education, distance learning, English as a second language, honors programs, independent study, internships, part-time degree program, services for LD students, summer session for credit. *ROTC:* Army (c), Air Force (c).
Library Main Library plus 11 others. *Books:* 158,142 (physical), 50,957 (digital/electronic); *Serial titles:* 394 (physical), 83,559 (digital/electronic); *Databases:* 110. Weekly public service hours: 83; students can reserve study rooms.
Student Life *Housing:* college housing not available. *Activities and Organizations:* Intramurals, Students for Environmental Outreach, Phi Theta Kappa (PTK), National Society of Collegiate Scholars, Students for Community Involvement. *Campus security:* 24-hour emergency response devices, late-night transport/escort service. *Student services:* personal/psychological counseling, veterans affairs office.
Athletics *Intramural sports:* basketball M/W, soccer M/W, volleyball W.
Financial Aid Of all full-time matriculated undergraduates who enrolled in 2018, 4,879 applied for aid, 4,091 were judged to have need. 270 Federal Work-Study jobs (averaging $2407). 27 state and other part-time jobs (averaging $2479). *Average need-based loan:* $3326. *Average need-based gift aid:* $4225.
Applying *Options:* electronic application. *Required:* high school transcript. *Application deadlines:* rolling (freshmen), rolling (transfers).
Freshman Application Contact Mrs. Linda Terry, Executive Director, Admissions and Records, Austin Community College District, 5930 Middle Fiskville Road, Austin, TX 78752. *Phone:* 512-223-7503. *Fax:* 512-223-7963. *E-mail:* admission@austincc.edu.
Website: http://www.austincc.edu/.

Blinn College
Brenham, Texas

Freshman Application Contact Ms. Jennifer Bynum, Director Prospective Student Relations/Community Outreach, Blinn College, PO Box 6030, Bryan, TX 77805-6030. *Phone:* 979-209-7640. *E-mail:* jennifer.bynum@blinn.edu. *Website:* http://www.blinn.edu/.

Brazosport College
Lake Jackson, Texas

Freshman Application Contact Brazosport College, 500 College Drive, Lake Jackson, TX 77566-3199. *Phone:* 979-230-3020. *Website:* http://www.brazosport.edu/.

Brookhaven College
Farmers Branch, Texas

- **County-supported** 2-year, founded 1978, part of Dallas County Community College District System
- **Suburban** 200-acre campus with easy access to Dallas-Fort Worth
- **Coed**

Undergraduates 2,257 full-time, 11,027 part-time. Students come from 35 states and territories; 88 other countries; 3% are from out of state; 14% Black or African American, non-Hispanic/Latino; 31% Hispanic/Latino; 12% Asian, non-Hispanic/Latino; 0.2% Native Hawaiian or other Pacific Islander, non-Hispanic/Latino; 2% American Indian or Alaska Native, non-Hispanic/Latino; 4% Two or more races, non-Hispanic/Latino; 5% Race/ethnicity unknown; 2% international; 9% transferred in.
Faculty *Student/faculty ratio:* 21:1.
Academics *Calendar:* semesters. *Degree:* certificates and associate. *Special study options:* academic remediation for entering students, adult/continuing education programs, advanced placement credit, cooperative education, distance learning, English as a second language, honors programs, independent study, internships, off-campus study, part-time degree program, services for LD students, student-designed majors, study abroad, summer session for credit.
Library Brookhaven College Learning Resources Center plus 1 other. *Books:* 55,595 (physical); *Serial titles:* 80 (physical).
Student Life *Campus security:* 24-hour emergency response devices and patrols, late-night transport/escort service.
Athletics Member NJCAA.
Applying *Options:* electronic application, early admission, deferred entrance. *Required:* high school transcript. *Required for some:* HESI score, minimum GPA in prerequisite courses, completion of support courses for nursing program.
Freshman Application Contact Admissions Office, Brookhaven College, 3939 Valley View Lane, Farmers Branch, TX 75244-4997. *Phone:* 972-860-4883. *Fax:* 972-860-4886. *E-mail:* bhcadmissions@dcccd.edu. *Website:* http://www.brookhavencollege.edu/.

Carrington College–Mesquite
Mesquite, Texas

Admissions Office Contact Carrington College–Mesquite, 3733 West Emporium Circle, Mesquite, TX 75150-6509. *Website:* http://www.carrington.edu/.

Cedar Valley College
Lancaster, Texas

- **State-supported** 2-year, founded 1977, part of Dallas County Community College District System
- **Suburban** 353-acre campus with easy access to Dallas-Fort Worth
- **Coed**
- 100% of applicants were admitted

Undergraduates Students come from 49 states and territories; 6 other countries; 15% are from out of state; 44% Black or African American, non-Hispanic/Latino; 29% Hispanic/Latino; 3% Asian, non-Hispanic/Latino; 0.1% Native Hawaiian or other Pacific Islander, non-Hispanic/Latino; 0.4% American Indian or Alaska Native, non-Hispanic/Latino; 3% Race/ethnicity unknown; 0.2% international. *Retention:* 17% of full-time freshmen returned.
Faculty *Student/faculty ratio:* 24:1.
Academics *Calendar:* semesters. *Degree:* certificates and associate. *Special study options:* academic remediation for entering students, advanced placement credit, cooperative education, distance learning, double majors, English as a second language, internships, off-campus study, part-time degree program, services for LD students, summer session for credit.
Library Cedar Valley College Library plus 1 other.
Student Life *Campus security:* 24-hour emergency response devices and patrols, late-night transport/escort service.
Athletics Member NJCAA.
Standardized Tests *Required:* SAT or ACT (for admission), TSI (for admission). *Required for some:* SAT and SAT Subject Tests or ACT (for admission).
Applying *Options:* electronic application. *Required:* high school transcript, minimum 2.0 GPA.
Freshman Application Contact Admissions Office, Cedar Valley College, Lancaster, TX 75134-3799. *Phone:* 972-860-8206. *Fax:* 972-860-8207. *Website:* http://www.cedarvalleycollege.edu/.

Center for Advanced Legal Studies
Houston, Texas

Freshman Application Contact Mr. James Scheffer, Center for Advanced Legal Studies, 3910 Kirby, Suite 200, Houston, TX 77098. *Phone:* 713-529-2778. *Toll-free phone:* 800-446-6931. *Fax:* 713-523-2715. *E-mail:* james.scheffer@paralegal.edu. *Website:* http://www.paralegal.edu/.

Central Texas College
Killeen, Texas

- **State and locally supported** 2-year, founded 1967
- **Suburban** 500-acre campus with easy access to Austin
- **Endowment** $8.2 million
- **Coed,** 16,073 undergraduate students, 27% full-time, 52% women, 48% men

Undergraduates 4,355 full-time, 11,718 part-time. Students come from 54 states and territories; 31% are from out of state; 27% Black or African American, non-Hispanic/Latino; 25% Hispanic/Latino; 3% Asian, non-Hispanic/Latino; 1% Native Hawaiian or other Pacific Islander, non-Hispanic/Latino; 0.6% American Indian or Alaska Native, non-Hispanic/Latino; 5% Two or more races, non-Hispanic/Latino; 3% Race/ethnicity unknown; 0.4% international; 7% transferred in; 1% live on campus. *Retention:* 52% of full-time freshmen returned.
Freshmen *Admission:* 2,136 enrolled.
Faculty *Total:* 1,145, 18% full-time. *Student/faculty ratio:* 17:1.
Majors Administrative assistant and secretarial science; agriculture; airline pilot and flight crew; autobody/collision and repair technology; automobile/automotive mechanics technology; biology/biological sciences; building/property maintenance; business administration and management; business/commerce; chemistry; clinical/medical laboratory technology; clinical/medical social work; commercial and advertising art; computer and information systems security; computer programming; computer technology/computer systems technology; criminal justice/safety; diesel mechanics technology; drafting and design technology; dramatic/theater arts; early childhood education; emergency medical technology (EMT paramedic); engineering; environmental science; farm and ranch management; fine/studio arts; fire services administration; foreign languages and literatures; general studies; geology/earth science; graphic and printing equipment operation/production; heating, air conditioning, ventilation and refrigeration maintenance technology; hospitality administration; journalism; kinesiology and exercise science; legal assistant/paralegal; liberal arts and sciences/liberal studies; licensed practical/vocational nurse training; mathematics; medical administrative assistant and medical secretary; medical insurance coding; music; public administration; radio and television; registered nursing/registered nurse; restaurant/food services management; social sciences; welding technology.
Academics *Calendar:* semesters. *Degree:* certificates and associate. *Special study options:* academic remediation for entering students, accelerated degree program, adult/continuing education programs, advanced placement credit, cooperative education, distance learning, English as a second language, external degree program, internships, part-time degree program, services for LD students, student-designed majors, summer session for credit. *ROTC:* Army (b).
Library Oveta Culp Hobby Memorial Library. *Books:* 37,738 (physical), 279,575 (digital/electronic); *Serial titles:* 126 (physical); *Databases:* 82. Weekly public service hours: 85; students can reserve study rooms.
Student Life *Housing Options:* coed. Campus housing is university owned. *Activities and Organizations:* drama/theater group, International Student Association, Phi Theta Kappa, Net Impact, Student Nurses Association, Student Veterans Organization. *Campus security:* 24-hour emergency response devices and patrols. *Student services:* veterans affairs office.
Athletics *Intramural sports:* basketball M, football M, soccer M, softball M, volleyball M.
Standardized Tests *Required for some:* TSI Assessment required for those that are not TSI exempt or waived.
Financial Aid Of all full-time matriculated undergraduates who enrolled in 2017, 68 Federal Work-Study jobs (averaging $3658).
Applying *Options:* electronic application, early admission, deferred entrance. *Required:* high school transcript. *Application deadlines:* rolling (freshmen), rolling (transfers).
Director of Admissions Shannon Bralley, Director, Admissions and Recruitment, Central Texas College, PO Box 1800, Killeen, TX 76540-1800. *Phone:* 254-526-1934. *Toll-free phone:* 800-223-4760 (in-state); 800-792-3348 (out-of-state). *E-mail:* shannon.bralley@ctcd.edu. *Website:* http://www.ctcd.edu/.

Cisco College
Cisco, Texas

Freshman Application Contact Mr. Olin O. Odom III, Dean of Admission/Registrar, Cisco College, 101 College Heights, Cisco, TX 76437-9321. *Phone:* 254-442-2567 Ext. 5130. *E-mail:* oodom@cjc.edu. *Website:* http://www.cisco.edu/.

Clarendon College
Clarendon, Texas

Freshman Application Contact Ms. Martha Smith, Admissions Director, Clarendon College, PO Box 968, Clarendon, TX 79226. *Phone:* 806-874-3571 Ext. 106. *Toll-free phone:* 800-687-9737. *Fax:* 806-874-3201. *E-mail:* martha.smith@clarendoncollege.edu. *Website:* http://www.clarendoncollege.edu/.

Coastal Bend College
Beeville, Texas

Freshman Application Contact Mrs. Tammy Adams, Director of Admissions/Registrar, Coastal Bend College, Beeville, TX 78102-2197. *Phone:* 361-354-2245. *Toll-free phone:* 866-722-2838 (in-state); 866-262-2838 (out-of-state). *Fax:* 361-354-2254. *E-mail:* tadams@coastalbend.edu. *Website:* http://www.coastalbend.edu/.

The College of Health Care Professions
Austin, Texas

Admissions Office Contact The College of Health Care Professions, 6505 Airport Boulevard, Austin, TX 78752. *Website:* http://www.chcp.edu/.

The College of Health Care Professions
Fort Worth, Texas

Admissions Office Contact The College of Health Care Professions, 4248 North Freeway, Fort Worth, TX 76137-5021. *Website:* http://www.chcp.edu/.

The College of Health Care Professions
Houston, Texas

Freshman Application Contact Admissions Office, The College of Health Care Professions, 240 Northwest Mall Boulevard, Houston, TX 77092. *Phone:* 713-425-3100. *Toll-free phone:* 800-487-6728. *Fax:* 713-425-3193. *Website:* http://www.chcp.edu/.

The College of Health Care Professions
McAllen, Texas

Admissions Office Contact The College of Health Care Professions, 1917 Nolana Avenue, Suite 100, McAllen, TX 78504. *Website:* http://www.chcp.edu/.

The College of Health Care Professions
San Antonio, Texas

Admissions Office Contact The College of Health Care Professions, 4738 NW Loop 410, San Antonio, TX 78229. *Website:* http://www.chcp.edu/.

College of the Mainland
Texas City, Texas

Freshman Application Contact Mr. Martin Perez, Director of Admissions/International Affairs, College of the Mainland, 1200 Amburn Road, Texas City, TX 77591. *Phone:* 409-933-8653. *Toll-free phone:* 888-258-8859 Ext. 8264. *E-mail:* mperez@com.edu. *Website:* http://www.com.edu/.

Collin County Community College District
McKinney, Texas

- **State and locally supported** 2-year, founded 1985
- **Suburban** 277-acre campus with easy access to Dallas-Fort Worth
- **Endowment** $9.5 million
- **Coed**

Undergraduates 10,231 full-time, 21,388 part-time. Students come from 51 states and territories; 99 other countries; 5% are from out of state; 12% Black or African American, non-Hispanic/Latino; 20% Hispanic/Latino; 10% Asian, non-Hispanic/Latino; 0.2% Native Hawaiian or other Pacific Islander, non-Hispanic/Latino; 0.4% American Indian or Alaska Native, non-Hispanic/Latino; 4% Two or more races, non-Hispanic/Latino; 1% Race/ethnicity unknown; 3% international; 6% transferred in. *Retention:* 66% of full-time freshmen returned.
Faculty *Student/faculty ratio:* 24:1.
Academics *Calendar:* semesters. *Degree:* certificates and associate. *Special study options:* academic remediation for entering students, adult/continuing education programs, advanced placement credit, cooperative education, distance learning, English as a second language, honors programs, internships, part-time degree program, services for LD students, summer session for credit. *ROTC:* Air Force (c).
Library Collin College Library. *Books:* 229,978 (physical), 36,785 (digital/electronic); *Serial titles:* 841 (physical), 94 (digital/electronic); *Databases:* 120. Students can reserve study rooms.
Student Life *Campus security:* 24-hour emergency response devices and patrols, late-night transport/escort service.
Athletics Member NJCAA.
Financial Aid Of all full-time matriculated undergraduates who enrolled in 2017, 4,693 applied for aid, 3,684 were judged to have need, 17 had their need fully met. In 2017, 207. *Average financial aid package:* $5896. *Average need-based loan:* $2741. *Average need-based gift aid:* $5112. *Average non-need-based aid:* $1185.
Applying *Options:* electronic application. *Required for some:* high school transcript.
Freshman Application Contact Mr. Todd E. Fields, Director of Admissions/Registrar, Collin County Community College District, 2800 E. Spring Creek Parkway, Plano, TX 75074. *Phone:* 972-881-5174. *Fax:* 972-881-5175. *E-mail:* tfields@collin.edu. *Website:* http://www.collin.edu/.

Commonwealth Institute of Funeral Service
Houston, Texas

Freshman Application Contact Ms. Patricia Moreno, Registrar, Commonwealth Institute of Funeral Service, 415 Barren Springs Drive, Houston, TX 77090. *Phone:* 281-873-0262. *Toll-free phone:* 800-628-1580. *Fax:* 281-873-5232. *E-mail:* p.moreno@commonwealth.edu. *Website:* http://www.commonwealth.edu/.

Concorde Career College
Dallas, Texas

Admissions Office Contact Concorde Career College, 12606 Greenville Avenue, Suite 130, Dallas, TX 75243. *Website:* http://www.concorde.edu/.

Concorde Career College
Grand Prairie, Texas

Admissions Office Contact Concorde Career College, 3015 West Interstate 20, Grand Prairie, TX 75052. *Toll-free phone:* 800-693-7010. *Website:* http://www.concorde.edu/.

Concorde Career College
San Antonio, Texas

Admissions Office Contact Concorde Career College, 4803 NW Loop 410, Suite 200, San Antonio, TX 78229. *Website:* http://www.concorde.edu/.

Culinary Institute LeNotre
Houston, Texas

- **Proprietary** 2-year, founded 1998
- **Urban** campus with easy access to Houston
- **Coed**

Undergraduates Students come from 6 other countries.
Faculty *Student/faculty ratio:* 12:1.
Academics *Degree:* certificates, diplomas, and associate. *Special study options:* academic remediation for entering students, adult/continuing education programs, cooperative education, internships, part-time degree program.
Library Learning Resource Center.
Student Life *Campus security:* late-night transport/escort service, security personnel patrol during class hours.
Standardized Tests *Required:* ACCUPLACER (for admission).
Applying *Options:* electronic application. *Application fee:* $50. *Required:* high school transcript, interview.
Freshman Application Contact Ellen Hogaboom, Admissions Manager, Culinary Institute LeNotre, 7070 Allensby Street, Houston, TX 77022. *Phone:* 713-692-0077. *Toll-free phone:* 888-LENOTRE. *Fax:* 713-692-7399. *E-mail:* ehogaboom@ciaml.com. *Website:* http://www.culinaryinstitute.edu/.

Dallas Institute of Funeral Service
Dallas, Texas

- **Independent** 2-year, founded 1945, part of Pierce Mortuary Colleges, Inc.
- **Urban** 4-acre campus with easy access to Dallas-Fort Worth
- **Coed**

Undergraduates 95 full-time. Students come from 6 states and territories; 12% are from out of state; 35% Black or African American, non-Hispanic/Latino; 23% Hispanic/Latino; 3% Asian, non-Hispanic/Latino; 42% transferred in.
Faculty *Student/faculty ratio:* 15:1.
Academics *Calendar:* quarters. *Degree:* certificates and associate. *Special study options:* advanced placement credit, cooperative education, distance learning, services for LD students.
Library J. Frank Pierce Library. *Books:* 2,223 (physical).
Student Life *Campus security:* 24-hour emergency response devices, electronically locked doors.
Applying *Options:* electronic application. *Application fee:* $50. *Required:* high school transcript.
Freshman Application Contact Olga Retana, Admissions Representative, Dallas Institute of Funeral Service, 3909 South Buckner Boulevard, Dallas, TX 75227. *Phone:* 214-388-5466 Ext. 817. *Toll-free phone:* 800-235-5444. *Fax:* 214-388-0316. *E-mail:* oretana@dallasinstitute.edu. *Website:* http://www.dallasinstitute.edu/.

Dallas Nursing Institute
Dallas, Texas

Admissions Office Contact Dallas Nursing Institute, 12170 N. Abrams Road, Suite 200, Dallas, TX 75243. *Website:* http://www.dni.edu/.

Del Mar College
Corpus Christi, Texas

- **State and locally supported** 2-year, founded 1935
- **Urban** 159-acre campus
- **Coed**

Undergraduates 2,671 full-time, 9,162 part-time. Students come from 41 states and territories; 30 other countries; 2% are from out of state; 3% Black or African American, non-Hispanic/Latino; 67% Hispanic/Latino; 2% Asian, non-Hispanic/Latino; 0.2% Native Hawaiian or other Pacific Islander, non-Hispanic/Latino; 0.2% American Indian or Alaska Native, non-Hispanic/Latino; 3% Two or more races, non-Hispanic/Latino; 0.4% Race/ethnicity unknown; 0.2% international; 6% transferred in. *Retention:* 56% of full-time freshmen returned.
Faculty *Student/faculty ratio:* 18:1.
Academics *Calendar:* semesters. *Degree:* certificates and associate. *Special study options:* academic remediation for entering students, accelerated degree program, adult/continuing education programs, advanced placement credit, cooperative education, distance learning, double majors, English as a second language, freshman honors college, honors programs, internships, off-campus study, part-time degree program, services for LD students, summer session for credit. *ROTC:* Army (b).
Library White Library plus 1 other. *Books:* 145,107 (physical), 192,073 (digital/electronic); *Serial titles:* 1,635 (physical), 74,730 (digital/electronic); *Databases:* 172.
Student Life *Campus security:* 24-hour emergency response devices and patrols.
Financial Aid Of all full-time matriculated undergraduates who enrolled in 2017, 259 Federal Work-Study jobs (averaging $960). 449 state and other part-time jobs (averaging $1082).
Applying *Options:* electronic application, early admission, deferred entrance. *Required:* high school transcript.
Freshman Application Contact Del Mar College, 101 Baldwin Boulevard, Corpus Christi, TX 78404-3897. *Phone:* 361-698-1248. *Toll-free phone:* 800-652-3357. *Website:* http://www.delmar.edu/.

Eastfield College
Mesquite, Texas

Freshman Application Contact Ms. Glynis Miller, Director of Admissions/Registrar, Eastfield College, 3737 Motley Drive, Mesquite, TX 75150-2099. *Phone:* 972-860-7010. *Fax:* 972-860-8306. *E-mail:* efc@dcccd.edu. *Website:* http://www.eastfieldcollege.edu/.

El Centro College
Dallas, Texas

Freshman Application Contact Ms. Rebecca Garza, Director of Admissions and Registrar, El Centro College, Dallas, TX 75202. *Phone:* 214-860-2618. *Fax:* 214-860-2233. *E-mail:* rgarza@dcccd.edu. *Website:* http://www.elcentrocollege.edu/.

El Paso Community College
El Paso, Texas

- **County-supported** 2-year, founded 1969
- **Urban** campus
- **Endowment** $742,942
- **Coed**

Undergraduates 8,710 full-time, 20,040 part-time. Students come from 49 states and territories; 34 other countries; 3% are from out of state; 2% Black or African American, non-Hispanic/Latino; 85% Hispanic/Latino; 0.7% Asian, non-Hispanic/Latino; 0.1% Native Hawaiian or other Pacific Islander, non-Hispanic/Latino; 0.2% American Indian or Alaska Native, non-Hispanic/Latino; 0.2% Two or more races, non-Hispanic/Latino; 2% Race/ethnicity unknown; 2% international; 4% transferred in.
Faculty *Student/faculty ratio:* 13:1.
Academics *Calendar:* semesters. *Degree:* certificates and associate. *Special study options:* academic remediation for entering students, adult/continuing education programs, advanced placement credit, cooperative education, distance learning, English as a second language, external degree program, honors programs, independent study, internships, off-campus study, part-time degree program, services for LD students, summer session for credit. *ROTC:* Army (c).
Library El Paso Community College Learning Resource Center plus 4 others. *Books:* 140,571 (physical), 149,708 (digital/electronic); *Serial titles:* 231 (physical), 56 (digital/electronic); *Databases:* 90. Weekly public service hours: 80.
Student Life *Campus security:* 24-hour patrols, late-night transport/escort service.
Athletics Member NJCAA.
Applying *Options:* electronic application, early admission, deferred entrance. *Application fee:* $10.
Freshman Application Contact Cassandra Lachica-Chavez, Executive Director Admission and Registrar, El Paso Community College, PO Box 20500, El Paso, TX 79998. *Phone:* 915-831-2580. *E-mail:* clachica@epcc.edu. *Website:* http://www.epcc.edu/.

Florida Career College
Houston, Texas

Admissions Office Contact Florida Career College, 70-A Farm to Market Road 1960 West, Houston, TX 77090. *Website:* http://www.floridacareercollege.edu/.

Fortis College
Grand Prairie, Texas

Admissions Office Contact Fortis College, 401 East Palace Parkway, Suite 100, Grand Prairie, TX 75050. *Toll-free phone:* 855-4-FORTIS. *Website:* http://www.fortis.edu/.

Fortis College
Houston, Texas

Admissions Office Contact Fortis College, 1201 West Oaks Mall, Houston, TX 77082. *Toll-free phone:* 855-4-FORTIS. *Website:* http://www.fortis.edu/.

Frank Phillips College
Borger, Texas

Freshman Application Contact Ms. Michele Stevens, Director of Enrollment Management, Frank Phillips College, PO Box 5118, Borger, TX 79008-5118. *Phone:* 806-457-4200 Ext. 707. *Fax:* 806-457-4225. *E-mail:* mstevens@fpctx.edu. *Website:* http://www.fpctx.edu/.

Galen College of Nursing
San Antonio, Texas

Admissions Office Contact Galen College of Nursing, 7411 John Smith Drive, Suite 1400, San Antonio, TX 78229. *Toll-free phone:* 877-223-7040. *Website:* http://www.galencollege.edu/.

Galveston College
Galveston, Texas

- **State and locally supported** 2-year, founded 1967
- **Urban** 11-acre campus with easy access to Houston
- **Coed**

Undergraduates 584 full-time, 1,624 part-time. 16% Black or African American, non-Hispanic/Latino; 38% Hispanic/Latino; 3% Asian, non-Hispanic/Latino; 0.2% Native Hawaiian or other Pacific Islander, non-Hispanic/Latino; 0.3% American Indian or Alaska Native, non-Hispanic/Latino; 1% Two or more races, non-Hispanic/Latino; 2% Race/ethnicity unknown; 1% international; 12% transferred in. *Retention:* 53% of full-time freshmen returned.
Faculty *Student/faculty ratio:* 16:1.
Academics *Calendar:* semesters. *Degree:* certificates and associate. *Special study options:* adult/continuing education programs, advanced placement credit, cooperative education, distance learning, internships, off-campus study, part-time degree program, services for LD students, summer session for credit.
Library David Glenn Hunt Memorial Library. *Books:* 48,028 (physical), 91,209 (digital/electronic); *Serial titles:* 73 (physical); *Databases:* 68. Students can reserve study rooms.
Student Life *Campus security:* 24-hour emergency response devices and patrols, late-night transport/escort service.
Athletics Member NJCAA.
Standardized Tests *Required:* TSI or exemption test scores and documentation (for admission).
Financial Aid Of all full-time matriculated undergraduates who enrolled in 2016, 27 Federal Work-Study jobs (averaging $3000). 3 state and other part-time jobs (averaging $3000).

Applying *Options:* electronic application. *Required for some:* high school transcript.
Freshman Application Contact Galveston College, 4015 Avenue Q, Galveston, TX 77550. *Phone:* 409-944-1216. *Website:* http://www.gc.edu/.

Grayson College
Denison, Texas

Freshman Application Contact Charles Leslie, Enrollment Advisor, Grayson College, 6101Grayson Drive, Denison, TX 75020. *Phone:* 903-415-2532. *Fax:* 903-463-5284. *E-mail:* lesliec@grayson.edu. *Website:* http://www.grayson.edu/.

Hill College
Hillsboro, Texas

- **District-supported** 2-year, founded 1923
- **Small-town** 80-acre campus with easy access to Dallas-Fort Worth
- **Coed**

Undergraduates 5% Black or African American, non-Hispanic/Latino; 23% Hispanic/Latino; 0.7% Asian, non-Hispanic/Latino; 0.3% Native Hawaiian or other Pacific Islander, non-Hispanic/Latino; 0.6% American Indian or Alaska Native, non-Hispanic/Latino; 3% Two or more races, non-Hispanic/Latino; 0.9% Race/ethnicity unknown; 1% international. *Retention:* 53% of full-time freshmen returned.
Faculty *Student/faculty ratio:* 17:1.
Academics *Calendar:* semesters. *Degree:* certificates and associate. *Special study options:* academic remediation for entering students, advanced placement credit, cooperative education, distance learning, services for LD students, summer session for credit.
Library Hill College Library plus 1 other. *Books:* 55,000 (physical), 203 (digital/electronic); *Serial titles:* 75 (physical); *Databases:* 105. Weekly public service hours: 65.
Student Life *Campus security:* 24-hour emergency response devices, late-night transport/escort service, security officers.
Athletics Member NJCAA.
Financial Aid Of all full-time matriculated undergraduates who enrolled in 2017, 51 Federal Work-Study jobs (averaging $858). 20 state and other part-time jobs (averaging $230).
Applying *Options:* electronic application, early admission. *Required:* high school transcript.
Freshman Application Contact Enrollment Management, Hill College, 112 Lamar Drive, Hillsboro, TX 76645. *Phone:* 254-659-7600. *Fax:* 254-582-7591. *E-mail:* enrollmentinfo@hillcollege.edu. *Website:* http://www.hillcollege.edu/.

Houston Community College
Houston, Texas

- **State and locally supported** 2-year, founded 1971
- **Urban** campus with easy access to Houston
- **Coed**

Undergraduates 17,226 full-time, 39,894 part-time. Students come from 30 states and territories; 145 other countries; 28% Black or African American, non-Hispanic/Latino; 34% Hispanic/Latino; 10% Asian, non-Hispanic/Latino; 0.2% Native Hawaiian or other Pacific Islander, non-Hispanic/Latino; 0.2% American Indian or Alaska Native, non-Hispanic/Latino; 2% Two or more races, non-Hispanic/Latino; 2% Race/ethnicity unknown; 12% international; 7% transferred in.
Faculty *Student/faculty ratio:* 24:1.
Academics *Calendar:* semesters. *Degree:* certificates and associate. *Special study options:* academic remediation for entering students, advanced placement credit, cooperative education, distance learning, English as a second language, honors programs, internships, part-time degree program, services for LD students, study abroad, summer session for credit. *ROTC:* Army (c), Air Force (c).
Library Houston Community College Libraries. Students can reserve study rooms.
Student Life *Campus security:* 24-hour emergency response devices and patrols, late-night transport/escort service, crime prevention services.
Financial Aid Of all full-time matriculated undergraduates who enrolled in 2018, 302 Federal Work-Study jobs (averaging $3602). 284 state and other part-time jobs (averaging $4251).
Applying *Options:* electronic application. *Required for some:* high school transcript, interview.
Freshman Application Contact Ms. Mary Lemburg, Registrar, Houston Community College, 3100 Main Street, PO Box 667517, Houston, TX 77266-7517. *Phone:* 713-718-2000. *Toll-free phone:* 877-422-6111. *Fax:* 713-718-2111. *E-mail:* student.info@hccs.edu. *Website:* http://www.hccs.edu/.

Howard College
Big Spring, Texas

Freshman Application Contact Ms. TaNeal Richardson, Assistant Registrar, Howard College, 1001 Birdwell Lane, Big Spring, TX 79720-3702. *Phone:* 432-264-5105. *Toll-free phone:* 866-HC-HAWKS. *Fax:* 432-264-5604. *E-mail:* trichardson@howardcollege.edu. *Website:* http://www.howardcollege.edu/.

Interactive College of Technology
Houston, Texas

Freshman Application Contact Interactive College of Technology, 4473 I-45 N. Freeway, Airline Plaza, Houston, TX 77022. *Website:* http://ict.edu/.

Interactive College of Technology
Houston, Texas

Freshman Application Contact Interactive College of Technology, 6200 Hillcroft Avenue, Suite 200, Houston, TX 77081. *Website:* http://ict.edu/.

Interactive College of Technology
Pasadena, Texas

Freshman Application Contact Interactive College of Technology, 213 West Southmore Street, Suite 101, Pasadena, TX 77502. *Website:* http://ict.edu/.

International Business College
El Paso, Texas

Admissions Office Contact International Business College, 1155 North Zaragosa Road, El Paso, TX 79907. *Website:* http://www.ibcelpaso.edu/.

International Business College
El Paso, Texas

Admissions Office Contact International Business College, 1156 Barranca Drive, El Paso, TX 79935. *Website:* http://www.ibcelpaso.edu/.

Jacksonville College
Jacksonville, Texas

Freshman Application Contact Danny Morris, Director of Admissions, Jacksonville College, 105 B.J. Albritton Drive, Jacksonville, TX 75766. *Phone:* 903-589-7110. *Toll-free phone:* 800-256-8522. *E-mail:* admissions@jacksonville-college.org. *Website:* http://www.jacksonville-college.edu/.

KD Conservatory College of Film and Dramatic Arts
Dallas, Texas

- **Proprietary** 2-year, founded 1979
- **Urban** campus
- **Coed**

Undergraduates 236 full-time. Students come from 11 states and territories; 1 other country; 5% are from out of state. *Retention:* 69% of full-time freshmen returned.
Faculty *Student/faculty ratio:* 12:1.
Academics *Calendar:* semesters. *Degree:* associate.
Library KD Studio Library.
Student Life *Campus security:* 24-hour emergency response devices and patrols.
Applying *Options:* electronic application, deferred entrance. *Required:* essay or personal statement, high school transcript, interview, audition and/or interview with Program Chair or Director of School.
Freshman Application Contact Mr. Michael Schraeder, Director of Education and Acting Program Chair, KD Conservatory College of Film and Dramatic Arts, 2600 Stemmons Freeway, Suite 117, Dallas, TX 75207. *Phone:* 214-638-0484. *Toll-free phone:* 877-278-2283. *Fax:* 214-630-5140. *E-mail:* mschraeder@kdstudio.com. *Website:* http://www.kdstudio.com/.

Kilgore College
Kilgore, Texas

Freshman Application Contact Kilgore College, 1100 Broadway Boulevard, Kilgore, TX 75662-3299. *Phone:* 903-983-8200. *E-mail:* register@kilgore.cc.tx.us. *Website:* http://www.kilgore.edu/.

Lamar Institute of Technology
Beaumont, Texas

- **State-supported** 2-year, founded 1995
- **Urban** 11-acre campus
- **Coed,** 3,565 undergraduate students, 38% full-time, 55% women, 45% men

Undergraduates 1,365 full-time, 2,200 part-time. Students come from 3 states and territories; 27% Black or African American, non-Hispanic/Latino; 19% Hispanic/Latino; 3% Asian, non-Hispanic/Latino; 0.1% Native Hawaiian or other Pacific Islander, non-Hispanic/Latino; 0.7% American Indian or Alaska Native, non-Hispanic/Latino; 2% Two or more races, non-Hispanic/Latino.
Freshmen *Admission:* 743 enrolled.
Faculty *Total:* 171, 51% full-time, 18% with terminal degrees.
Majors Accounting technology and bookkeeping; administrative assistant and secretarial science; business administration, management and operations related; chemical technology; child-care and support services management; child-care provision; computer and information sciences related; computer technology/computer systems technology; dental hygiene; diagnostic medical sonography and ultrasound technology; diesel mechanics technology; drafting and design technology; emergency medical technology (EMT paramedic); fire prevention and safety technology; health information/medical records technology; heating, ventilation, air conditioning and refrigeration engineering technology; industrial mechanics and maintenance technology; institutional food workers; instrumentation technology; machine tool technology; medical radiologic technology; occupational safety and health technology; public administration; real estate; welding technology.
Academics *Calendar:* semesters. *Degree:* certificates and associate.
Library The Mary and John Gray Library. *Books:* 621,094 (physical), 71,446 (digital/electronic); *Serial titles:* 19,735 (physical), 46,546 (digital/electronic); *Databases:* 127. Weekly public service hours: 93.
Student Life *Housing Options:* Campus housing is university owned. *Activities and Organizations:* Operating Process Technology Club, Radiologic Technology Student Organization, Student Government Association, Phi Theta Kappa. *Campus security:* 24-hour emergency response devices and patrols, late-night transport/escort service, controlled dormitory access.
Athletics *Intramural sports:* archery M(c), baseball M(c), basketball M(c), football M(c).
Financial Aid ***Financial aid deadline:*** 4/1.
Freshman Application Contact Julie Pitts, Student Services Assistant, Lamar Institute of Technology, 855 East Lavaca, Beaumont, TX 77705. *Phone:* 409-880-8858. *Toll-free phone:* 800-950-6989. *Fax:* 409-880-1711. *E-mail:* jrpitts@lit.edu.
Website: http://www.lit.edu/.

Lamar State College–Orange
Orange, Texas

Freshman Application Contact Kerry Olson, Director of Admissions and Financial Aid, Lamar State College–Orange, 410 Front Street, Orange, TX 77632. *Phone:* 409-882-3362. *Fax:* 409-882-3374. *Website:* http://www.lsco.edu/.

Lamar State College–Port Arthur
Port Arthur, Texas

Freshman Application Contact Ms. Connie Nicholas, Registrar, Lamar State College–Port Arthur, PO Box 310, Port Arthur, TX 77641-0310. *Phone:* 409-984-6165. *Toll-free phone:* 800-477-5872. *Fax:* 409-984-6025. *E-mail:* nichoca@lamarpa.edu. *Website:* http://www.lamarpa.edu/.

Laredo College
Laredo, Texas

Freshman Application Contact Ms. Josie Soliz, Admissions Records Supervisor, Laredo College, Laredo, TX 78040-4395. *Phone:* 956-721-5177. *Fax:* 956-721-5493. *Website:* http://www.laredo.edu/.

Lee College
Baytown, Texas

Director of Admissions Ms. Becki Griffith, Registrar, Lee College, PO Box 818, Baytown, TX 77522-0818. *Phone:* 281-425-6399. *E-mail:* bgriffit@lee.edu. *Website:* http://www.lee.edu/.

Lincoln College of Technology
Grand Prairie, Texas

Admissions Office Contact Lincoln College of Technology, 2915 Alouette Drive, Grand Prairie, TX 75052. *Toll-free phone:* 844-215-1513. *Website:* http://www.lincolntech.edu/.

Lone Star College–CyFair
Cypress, Texas

Freshman Application Contact Admissions Office, Lone Star College–CyFair, 9191 Barker Cypress Road, Cypress, TX 77433-1383. *Phone:* 281-290-3200. *E-mail:* cfc.info@lonestar.edu. *Website:* http://www.lonestar.edu/cyfair.

Lone Star College–Kingwood
Kingwood, Texas

Freshman Application Contact Admissions Office, Lone Star College–Kingwood, 20000 Kingwood Drive, Kingwood, TX 77339. *Phone:* 281-312-1525. *Fax:* 281-312-1477. *E-mail:* kingwoodadvising@lonestar.edu. *Website:* http://www.lonestar.edu/kingwood.htm.

Lone Star College–Montgomery
Conroe, Texas

Freshman Application Contact Lone Star College–Montgomery, 3200 College Park Drive, Conroe, TX 77384. *Phone:* 281-290-2721. *Website:* http://www.lonestar.edu/montgomery.

Lone Star College–North Harris
Houston, Texas

Freshman Application Contact Admissions Office, Lone Star College–North Harris, 2700 W. W. Thorne Drive, Houston, TX 77073-3499. *Phone:* 281-618-5410. *E-mail:* nhcounselor@lonestar.edu. *Website:* http://www.lonestar.edu/northharris.

Lone Star College–Tomball
Tomball, Texas

Freshman Application Contact Admissions Office, Lone Star College–Tomball, 30555 Tomball Parkway, Tomball, TX 77375-4036. *Phone:* 281-351-3310. *E-mail:* tcinfo@lonestar.edu. *Website:* http://www.lonestar.edu/tomball.

Lone Star College–University Park
Houston, Texas

Freshman Application Contact Lone Star College–University Park, 20515 SH 249, Houston, TX 77070. *Phone:* 281-290-2721. *Website:* http://www.lonestar.edu/universitypark.

McLennan Community College
Waco, Texas

- **County-supported** 2-year, founded 1965
- **Urban** 200-acre campus
- **Endowment** $15.3 million
- **Coed**

Undergraduates Students come from 17 states and territories; 2% are from out of state; 12% Black or African American, non-Hispanic/Latino; 30% Hispanic/Latino; 1% Asian, non-Hispanic/Latino; 0.4% American Indian or Alaska Native, non-Hispanic/Latino; 3% Two or more races, non-Hispanic/Latino; 1% Race/ethnicity unknown.
Faculty *Student/faculty ratio:* 17:1.
Academics *Calendar:* semesters. *Degree:* certificates and associate. *Special study options:* academic remediation for entering students, adult/continuing education programs, advanced placement credit, cooperative education, distance learning, honors programs, internships, off-campus study, part-time degree program, services for LD students, study abroad, summer session for credit. *ROTC:* Air Force (c).
Library McLennan Community College Library. *Books:* 69,255 (physical), 237,879 (digital/electronic); *Serial titles:* 290 (physical), 61 (digital/electronic); *Databases:* 134. Students can reserve study rooms.
Student Life *Campus security:* 24-hour emergency response devices and patrols.

Athletics Member NCAA, NJCAA. All NCAA Division I.
Financial Aid Of all full-time matriculated undergraduates who enrolled in 2017, 265 Federal Work-Study jobs (averaging $850). 35 state and other part-time jobs (averaging $1000).
Applying *Options:* electronic application, early admission. *Required:* high school transcript.
Freshman Application Contact Amanda Straten, Coordinator of Student Admissions, McLennan Community College, 1400 College Drive, Waco, TX 76708. *Phone:* 254-299-8657. *Fax:* 254-299-8694. *E-mail:* astraten@mclennan.edu. *Website:* http://www.mclennan.edu/.

MediaTech Institute
Dallas, Texas

Admissions Office Contact MediaTech Institute, 13300 Branch View Lane, Dallas, TX 75234. *Toll-free phone:* 866-498-1122. *Website:* http://www.mediatech.edu/.

Mountain View College
Dallas, Texas

Freshman Application Contact Ms. Glenda Hall, Director of Admissions, Mountain View College, 4849 West Illinois Avenue, Dallas, TX 75211-6599. *Phone:* 214-860-8666. *Fax:* 214-860-8570. *E-mail:* ghall@dcccd.edu. *Website:* http://www.mountainviewcollege.edu/.

Navarro College
Corsicana, Texas

- **State and locally supported** 2-year, founded 1946
- **Small-town** 275-acre campus with easy access to Dallas-Fort Worth
- **Coed**

Undergraduates 3,057 full-time, 5,911 part-time. Students come from 39 other countries; 2% are from out of state; 18% Black or African American, non-Hispanic/Latino; 22% Hispanic/Latino; 1% Asian, non-Hispanic/Latino; 0.3% Native Hawaiian or other Pacific Islander, non-Hispanic/Latino; 0.6% American Indian or Alaska Native, non-Hispanic/Latino; 2% Two or more races, non-Hispanic/Latino; 0.7% Race/ethnicity unknown; 1% international; 25% live on campus.
Faculty *Student/faculty ratio:* 16:1.
Academics *Calendar:* semesters. *Degree:* certificates, diplomas, and associate. *Special study options:* academic remediation for entering students, adult/continuing education programs, advanced placement credit, cooperative education, distance learning, freshman honors college, honors programs, part-time degree program, services for LD students, student-designed majors, summer session for credit.
Library Richard M. Sanchez Library.
Student Life *Campus security:* 24-hour emergency response devices.
Athletics Member NJCAA.
Applying *Options:* electronic application, early admission. *Required:* high school transcript.
Freshman Application Contact Tammy Adams, Registrar, Navarro College, 3200 West 7th Avenue, Corsicana, TX 75110-4899. *Phone:* 903-875-7348. *Toll-free phone:* 800-NAVARRO (in-state); 800-628-2776 (out-of-state). *Fax:* 903-875-7353. *E-mail:* tammy.adams@navarrocollege.edu. *Website:* http://www.navarrocollege.edu/.

North Central Texas College
Gainesville, Texas

- **State and locally supported** 2-year, founded 1924
- **Suburban** 132-acre campus with easy access to Dallas-Fort Worth
- **Endowment** $4.3 million
- **Coed**

Undergraduates 2,693 full-time, 7,634 part-time. Students come from 28 states and territories; 15 other countries; 0.9% are from out of state; 9% Black or African American, non-Hispanic/Latino; 23% Hispanic/Latino; 3% Asian, non-Hispanic/Latino; 0.1% Native Hawaiian or other Pacific Islander, non-Hispanic/Latino; 0.7% American Indian or Alaska Native, non-Hispanic/Latino; 3% Two or more races, non-Hispanic/Latino; 1% Race/ethnicity unknown; 2% international; 8% transferred in; 1% live on campus. *Retention:* 99% of full-time freshmen returned.
Faculty *Student/faculty ratio:* 16:1.
Academics *Calendar:* semesters. *Degree:* certificates, diplomas, and associate. *Special study options:* academic remediation for entering students, adult/continuing education programs, advanced placement credit, cooperative education, distance learning, internships, part-time degree program, services for LD students, summer session for credit. *ROTC:* Army (c).
Library North Central Texas College Library plus 1 other.
Student Life *Campus security:* late-night transport/escort service, controlled dormitory access, security cameras.
Athletics Member NJCAA.
Financial Aid Of all full-time matriculated undergraduates who enrolled in 2017, 108 Federal Work-Study jobs (averaging $1253). 29 state and other part-time jobs (averaging $392).
Applying *Options:* electronic application, early admission. *Required:* high school transcript.
Freshman Application Contact Melinda Carroll, Director of Admissions/Registrar, North Central Texas College, 1525 West California, Gainesville, TX 76240-4699. *Phone:* 940-668-7731. *Fax:* 940-668-7075. *E-mail:* mcarroll@nctc.edu. *Website:* http://www.nctc.edu/.

Northeast Lakeview College
Universal City, Texas

Admissions Office Contact Northeast Lakeview College, 1201 Kitty Hawk Road, Universal City, TX 78145. *Website:* http://www.alamo.edu/.

Northeast Texas Community College
Mount Pleasant, Texas

Freshman Application Contact Linda Bond, Admissions Specialist, Northeast Texas Community College, PO Box 1307, Mount Pleasant, TX 75456-1307. *Phone:* 903-434-8140. *Toll-free phone:* 800-870-0142. *E-mail:* lbond@ntcc.edu. *Website:* http://www.ntcc.edu/.

North Lake College
Irving, Texas

Freshman Application Contact Admissions/Registration Office, North Lake College, 5001 North MacArthur Boulevard, Irving, TX 75038. *Phone:* 972-273-3183. *Website:* http://www.northlakecollege.edu/.

Northwest Vista College
San Antonio, Texas

- **District-supported** 2-year, founded 1995, part of Alamo Community College District System
- **Urban** 137-acre campus with easy access to San Antonio
- **Coed**

Undergraduates 4,043 full-time, 9,072 part-time. 6% Black or African American, non-Hispanic/Latino; 65% Hispanic/Latino; 3% Asian, non-Hispanic/Latino; 0.2% Native Hawaiian or other Pacific Islander, non-Hispanic/Latino; 0.2% American Indian or Alaska Native, non-Hispanic/Latino; 4% Two or more races, non-Hispanic/Latino; 0.5% Race/ethnicity unknown; 0.3% international; 7% transferred in.
Faculty *Student/faculty ratio:* 25:1.
Academics *Calendar:* semesters. *Degree:* certificates and associate. *Special study options:* academic remediation for entering students, advanced placement credit, cooperative education, distance learning, double majors, English as a second language, independent study, internships, off-campus study, part-time degree program, services for LD students, study abroad, summer session for credit. *ROTC:* Army (c).
Library Redbud Learning Center. *Books:* 19,338 (physical), 233,202 (digital/electronic); *Serial titles:* 48 (physical), 33,000 (digital/electronic); *Databases:* 133. Weekly public service hours: 67.
Student Life *Campus security:* 24-hour emergency response devices, student patrols, late-night transport/escort service.
Applying *Options:* electronic application, early admission. *Required:* high school transcript.
Freshman Application Contact Ms. Robin Sandberg, Director of Enrollment Management, Northwest Vista College, 3535 North Ellison Drive, San Antonio, TX 78251. *Phone:* 210-486-4134. *Fax:* 210-486-9091. *E-mail:* rsandberg@alamo.edu. *Website:* http://www.alamo.edu/nvc/.

Odessa College
Odessa, Texas

- **State and locally supported** 2-year, founded 1946
- **Urban** 87-acre campus
- **Coed**

Undergraduates 2,243 full-time, 4,065 part-time. Students come from 24 states and territories; 4 other countries; 6% are from out of state; 5% Black or African American, non-Hispanic/Latino; 63% Hispanic/Latino; 1% Asian, non-Hispanic/Latino; 0.1% Native Hawaiian or other Pacific Islander, non-

Hispanic/Latino; 0.5% American Indian or Alaska Native, non-Hispanic/Latino; 0.7% Race/ethnicity unknown; 1% international.
Academics *Calendar:* semesters. *Degree:* certificates and associate. *Special study options:* academic remediation for entering students, adult/continuing education programs, advanced placement credit, cooperative education, distance learning, independent study, internships, part-time degree program, services for LD students, summer session for credit.
Library Murry H. Fly Learning Resources Center plus 1 other.
Student Life *Campus security:* 24-hour emergency response devices and patrols, late-night transport/escort service, controlled dormitory access.
Athletics Member NJCAA.
Applying *Options:* electronic application, early admission, deferred entrance.
Freshman Application Contact Ms. Tracy Avery, Director of Recruitment, Odessa College, 201 West University Avenue, Odessa, TX 79764. *Phone:* 432-335-6765. *Fax:* 432-335-6303. *E-mail:* tavery@odessa.edu. *Website:* http://www.odessa.edu/.

Palo Alto College

San Antonio, Texas

Freshman Application Contact Ms. Elizabeth Aguilar-Villarreal, Director of Enrollment Management, Palo Alto College, 1400 West Villaret Boulevard, San Antonio, TX 78224. *Phone:* 210-486-3713. *E-mail:* eaguilar-villarr@alamo.edu. *Website:* http://www.alamo.edu/pac/.

Panola College

Carthage, Texas

- **State and locally supported** 2-year, founded 1947
- **Small-town** 35-acre campus
- **Coed**

Undergraduates 1,334 full-time, 1,312 part-time. Students come from 10 states and territories; 10 other countries; 8% are from out of state; 23% Black or African American, non-Hispanic/Latino; 11% Hispanic/Latino; 0.6% Asian, non-Hispanic/Latino; 0.4% American Indian or Alaska Native, non-Hispanic/Latino; 1% Two or more races, non-Hispanic/Latino; 2% international; 11% transferred in.
Faculty *Student/faculty ratio:* 18:1.
Academics *Calendar:* semesters. *Degree:* certificates and associate. *Special study options:* academic remediation for entering students, advanced placement credit, cooperative education, distance learning, English as a second language, part-time degree program, services for LD students, summer session for credit.
Library M. P. Baker Library. *Books:* 27,616 (physical), 651,787 (digital/electronic); *Serial titles:* 42 (physical), 15 (digital/electronic); *Databases:* 72. Weekly public service hours: 64; students can reserve study rooms.
Student Life *Campus security:* controlled dormitory access, 24-hour campus police department.
Athletics Member NJCAA.
Financial Aid Of all full-time matriculated undergraduates who enrolled in 2016, 960 applied for aid, 729 were judged to have need. 26 Federal Work-Study jobs (averaging $1354). 16 state and other part-time jobs (averaging $990). *Average percent of need met:* 50. *Average financial aid package:* $7588. *Average need-based loan:* $10,743. *Average need-based gift aid:* $7692.
Applying *Options:* electronic application. *Required for some:* high school transcript. *Recommended:* high school transcript.
Freshman Application Contact Mr. Jeremy Dorman, Registrar/Director of Admissions, Panola College, 1109 West Panola Street, Carthage, TX 75633-2397. *Phone:* 903-693-2009. *Fax:* 903-693-2031. *E-mail:* bsimpson@panola.edu. *Website:* http://www.panola.edu/.

Paris Junior College

Paris, Texas

- **State and locally supported** 2-year, founded 1924
- **Rural** 54-acre campus with easy access to Dallas-Fort Worth
- **Endowment** $22.0 million
- **Coed**

Undergraduates 1,829 full-time, 3,006 part-time. Students come from 21 states and territories; 5 other countries; 3% are from out of state; 11% Black or African American, non-Hispanic/Latino; 17% Hispanic/Latino; 1% Asian, non-Hispanic/Latino; 0.2% Native Hawaiian or other Pacific Islander, non-Hispanic/Latino; 1% American Indian or Alaska Native, non-Hispanic/Latino; 2% Two or more races, non-Hispanic/Latino; 0.2% Race/ethnicity unknown; 0.2% international; 3% transferred in; 6% live on campus.
Academics *Calendar:* semesters. *Degree:* certificates, diplomas, and associate. *Special study options:* academic remediation for entering students, adult/continuing education programs, advanced placement credit, cooperative education, distance learning, double majors, part-time degree program, services for LD students, summer session for credit.
Library Mike Rheudasil Learning Center.
Student Life *Campus security:* 24-hour emergency response devices and patrols, late-night transport/escort service, controlled dormitory access.
Athletics Member NJCAA.
Financial Aid Of all full-time matriculated undergraduates who enrolled in 2017, 62 Federal Work-Study jobs (averaging $3600). 11 state and other part-time jobs (averaging $3600).
Applying *Options:* electronic application, early admission. *Required:* high school transcript.
Freshman Application Contact Paris Junior College, 2400 Clarksville Street, Paris, TX 75460-6298. *Phone:* 903-782-0211. *Toll-free phone:* 800-232-5804. *Website:* http://www.parisjc.edu/.

Pima Medical Institute

El Paso, Texas

Admissions Office Contact Pima Medical Institute, 6926 Gateway Boulevard East, El Paso, TX 79915. *Website:* http://www.pmi.edu/.

Pima Medical Institute

Houston, Texas

Freshman Application Contact Mr. Christopher Luebke, Corporate Director of Admissions, Pima Medical Institute, 2160 South Power Road, Mesa, AZ 85209. *Phone:* 480-610-6063. *Toll-free phone:* 800-477-PIMA. *E-mail:* cluebke@pmi.edu. *Website:* http://www.pmi.edu/.

Quest College

San Antonio, Texas

Admissions Office Contact Quest College, 5430 Fredericksburg Road, Suite 310, San Antonio, TX 78229. *Website:* http://www.questcollege.edu/.

Ranger College

Ranger, Texas

Freshman Application Contact Dr. Jim Davis, Dean of Students, Ranger College, 1100 College Circle, Ranger, TX 76470. *Phone:* 254-647-3234 Ext. 110. *Website:* http://www.rangercollege.edu/.

Remington College–Dallas Campus

Garland, Texas

Director of Admissions Ms. Shonda Wisenhunt, Remington College–Dallas Campus, 1800 Eastgate Drive, Garland, TX 75041. *Phone:* 972-686-7878. *Toll-free phone:* 800-323-8122. *Fax:* 972-686-5116. *E-mail:* shonda.wisenhunt@remingtoncollege.edu. *Website:* http://www.remingtoncollege.edu/.

Remington College–Fort Worth Campus

Fort Worth, Texas

Director of Admissions Marcia Kline, Director of Recruitment, Remington College–Fort Worth Campus, 300 East Loop 820, Fort Worth, TX 76112. *Phone:* 817-451-0017. *Toll-free phone:* 800-323-8122. *Fax:* 817-496-1257. *E-mail:* marcia.kline@remingtoncollege.edu. *Website:* http://www.remingtoncollege.edu/.

Remington College–Houston Southeast Campus

Webster, Texas

Director of Admissions Lori Minor, Director of Recruitment, Remington College–Houston Southeast Campus, 20985 Gulf Freeway, Webster, TX 77598. *Phone:* 281-554-1700. *Toll-free phone:* 800-323-8122. *Fax:* 281-554-1765. *E-mail:* lori.minor@remingtoncollege.edu. *Website:* http://www.remingtoncollege.edu/.

Remington College–North Houston Campus
Houston, Texas

Director of Admissions Edmund Flores, Director of Recruitment, Remington College–North Houston Campus, 11310 Greens Crossing Boulevard, Suite 300, Houston, TX 77067. *Phone:* 281-885-4450. *Toll-free phone:* 800-323-8122. *Fax:* 281-875-9964. *E-mail:* edmund.flores@remingtoncollege.edu. *Website:* http://www.remingtoncollege.edu/.

Richland College
Dallas, Texas

- **State and locally supported** 2-year, founded 1972, part of Dallas County Community College District System
- **Suburban** 250-acre campus
- **Coed**

Undergraduates Students come from 24 states and territories; 21 other countries; 19% Black or African American, non-Hispanic/Latino; 34% Hispanic/Latino; 16% Asian, non-Hispanic/Latino; 0.7% Two or more races, non-Hispanic/Latino; 6% Race/ethnicity unknown.
Academics *Calendar:* semesters. *Degree:* certificates and associate. *Special study options:* academic remediation for entering students, adult/continuing education programs, advanced placement credit, cooperative education, distance learning, English as a second language, freshman honors college, honors programs, off-campus study, part-time degree program, services for LD students, study abroad, summer session for credit.
Library Richland College Library.
Student Life *Campus security:* 24-hour emergency response devices and patrols, late-night transport/escort service, emergency call boxes.
Athletics Member NJCAA.
Financial Aid Of all full-time matriculated undergraduates who enrolled in 2017, 123 Federal Work-Study jobs (averaging $2000).
Applying *Options:* electronic application. *Required for some:* high school transcript.
Freshman Application Contact Richland College, 12800 Abrams Road, Dallas, TX 75243. *Phone:* 972-328-6948. *E-mail:* rlcadmissions@dcccd.edu. *Website:* http://www.richlandcollege.edu/.

St. Philip's College
San Antonio, Texas

- **District-supported** 2-year, founded 1898, part of Alamo Community College District System
- **Urban** 68-acre campus with easy access to San Antonio
- **Coed**

Undergraduates 1,601 full-time, 10,449 part-time. 1% are from out of state; 9% Black or African American, non-Hispanic/Latino; 57% Hispanic/Latino; 2% Asian, non-Hispanic/Latino; 0.1% Native Hawaiian or other Pacific Islander, non-Hispanic/Latino; 0.4% American Indian or Alaska Native, non-Hispanic/Latino; 4% Two or more races, non-Hispanic/Latino; 2% Race/ethnicity unknown; 0.2% international; 5% transferred in.
Faculty *Student/faculty ratio:* 19:1.
Academics *Calendar:* semesters. *Degree:* certificates, diplomas, and associate. *Special study options:* academic remediation for entering students, adult/continuing education programs, advanced placement credit, cooperative education, distance learning, double majors, English as a second language, honors programs, independent study, internships, off-campus study, part-time degree program, services for LD students, study abroad, summer session for credit. *ROTC:* Army (c).
Library St. Philip's College Library. *Books:* 63,136 (physical), 56,724 (digital/electronic); *Serial titles:* 53 (physical), 72,126 (digital/electronic); *Databases:* 118. Weekly public service hours: 68.
Student Life *Campus security:* 24-hour emergency response devices and patrols, late-night transport/escort service.
Applying *Options:* electronic application, early admission. *Required:* high school transcript.
Freshman Application Contact Ms. Angela Molina, Coordinator, Student Success, St. Philip's College, 1801 Martin Luther King Drive, San Antonio, TX 78203-2098. *Phone:* 210-486-2403. *Fax:* 210-486-2103. *E-mail:* amolina@alamo.edu. *Website:* http://www.alamo.edu/spc/.

San Antonio College
San Antonio, Texas

Director of Admissions Mr. J. Martin Ortega, Director of Admissions and Records, San Antonio College, 1819 North Main Avenue, San Antonio, TX 78212-3941. *Phone:* 210-733-2582. *Toll-free phone:* 844-202-5266. *Website:* http://www.alamo.edu/sac/.

San Jacinto College District
Pasadena, Texas

- **State and locally supported** 2-year, founded 1961
- **Suburban** 483-acre campus with easy access to Houston
- **Endowment** $7.0 million
- **Coed,** 32,137 undergraduate students, 23% full-time, 58% women, 42% men

Undergraduates 7,348 full-time, 24,789 part-time. Students come from 44 states and territories; 66 other countries; 1% are from out of state; 9% Black or African American, non-Hispanic/Latino; 60% Hispanic/Latino; 5% Asian, non-Hispanic/Latino; 0.1% Native Hawaiian or other Pacific Islander, non-Hispanic/Latino; 0.2% American Indian or Alaska Native, non-Hispanic/Latino; 2% Two or more races, non-Hispanic/Latino; 1% Race/ethnicity unknown; 1% international; 5% transferred in. *Retention:* 61% of full-time freshmen returned.
Freshmen *Admission:* 13,410 applied, 7,585 admitted, 5,940 enrolled.
Faculty *Total:* 1,136, 41% full-time, 8% with terminal degrees. *Student/faculty ratio:* 21:1.
Majors Accounting; administrative assistant and secretarial science; agribusiness; agriculture; art; autobody/collision and repair technology; automobile/automotive mechanics technology; baking and pastry arts; behavioral sciences; biology/biological sciences; business administration and management; business/commerce; cardiovascular technology; chemical technology; chemistry; child development; clinical/medical laboratory technology; commercial and advertising art; computer and information sciences; construction engineering technology; cosmetology; cosmetology, barber/styling, and nail instruction; criminal justice/police science; culinary arts; dance; diagnostic medical sonography and ultrasound technology; diesel mechanics technology; digital communication and media/multimedia; drafting and design technology; dramatic/theater arts; electrical and power transmission installation; electrical, electronic and communications engineering technology; emergency medical technology (EMT paramedic); engineering; English; environmental science; fire science/firefighting; foreign languages and literatures; general studies; geology/earth science; health and physical education/fitness; health information/medical records technology; heating, air conditioning, ventilation and refrigeration maintenance technology; Hispanic-American, Puerto Rican, and Mexican-American/Chicano studies; history; instrumentation technology; interior design; international business/trade/commerce; journalism; kinesiology and exercise science; legal assistant/paralegal; management information systems; marine science/merchant marine officer; mathematics; medical/clinical assistant; music; occupational safety and health technology; occupational therapy; optometric technician; pharmacy technician; philosophy; physical sciences; physical therapy technology; physics; political science and government; psychiatric/mental health services technology; psychology; radio and television broadcasting technology; radiologic technology/science; real estate; registered nursing/registered nurse; respiratory care therapy; restaurant, culinary, and catering management; rhetoric and composition; science teacher education; secondary education; social sciences; sociology; surgical technology; welding technology.
Academics *Calendar:* semesters. *Degree:* certificates, diplomas, and associate. *Special study options:* academic remediation for entering students, accelerated degree program, adult/continuing education programs, advanced placement credit, cooperative education, distance learning, double majors, English as a second language, honors programs, part-time degree program, services for LD students, student-designed majors, study abroad, summer session for credit. *ROTC:* Army (c), Air Force (c).
Library Lee Davis Library(Central),Edwin E. Lehr(North),Parker Williams(South). *Books:* 363,626 (physical), 15,541 (digital/electronic); *Serial titles:* 1,234 (physical); *Databases:* 152. Weekly public service hours: 68; students can reserve study rooms.
Student Life *Housing:* college housing not available. *Activities and Organizations:* drama/theater group, student-run newspaper, choral group, Phi Theta Kappa honor society, Phi Beta Lambda, Student Government Association, Nurses Association, Men of Honor. *Campus security:* 24-hour emergency response devices and patrols, late-night transport/escort service. *Student services:* personal/psychological counseling, veterans affairs office.
Athletics Member NJCAA. *Intercollegiate sports:* basketball W, softball W(s). *Intramural sports:* soccer M, softball M, tennis M, ultimate Frisbee M, volleyball M, weight lifting M.
Applying *Options:* electronic application, early admission. *Required:* high school transcript. *Required for some:* interview. *Recommended:* interview for nursing and EMT programs. *Application deadlines:* rolling (freshmen), rolling (out-of-state freshmen), rolling (transfers). *Notification:* continuous (freshmen), continuous (out-of-state freshmen), continuous (transfers).
Director of Admissions Kevin McKisson, Registrar and Dean of Records Management, San Jacinto College District, 4624 Fairmont Parkway, Pasadena, TX 77504-3323. *Phone:* 281-998-6150. *E-mail:* Kevin.McKisson@sjcd.edu. *Website:* http://www.sanjac.edu/.

School of Automotive Machinists & Technology
Houston, Texas

Admissions Office Contact School of Automotive Machinists & Technology, 1911 Antoine Drive, Houston, TX 77055. *Website:* http://www.samtech.edu/.

South Plains College
Levelland, Texas

Freshman Application Contact Mrs. Andrea Rangel, Dean of Admissions and Records, South Plains College, 1401 College Avenue, Levelland, TX 78336. *Phone:* 806-894-9611 Ext. 2370. *Fax:* 806-897-3167. *E-mail:* arangel@southplainscollege.edu. *Website:* http://www.southplainscollege.edu/.

South Texas College
McAllen, Texas

Freshman Application Contact Mr. Matthew Hebbard, Director of Enrollment Services and Registrar, South Texas College, 3201 West Pecan, McAllen, TX 78501. *Phone:* 956-872-2147. *Toll-free phone:* 800-742-7822. *E-mail:* mshebbar@southtexascollege.edu. *Website:* http://www.southtexascollege.edu/.

Southwest Texas Junior College
Uvalde, Texas

- **State and locally supported** 2-year, founded 1946
- **Small-town** 97-acre campus with easy access to San Antonio
- **Coed**

Undergraduates Students come from 8 states and territories; 3 other countries; 1% Black or African American, non-Hispanic/Latino; 85% Hispanic/Latino; 0.2% Asian, non-Hispanic/Latino; 0.8% American Indian or Alaska Native, non-Hispanic/Latino; 0.4% Two or more races, non-Hispanic/Latino; 0.8% Race/ethnicity unknown; 9% live on campus.
Academics *Calendar:* semesters. *Degree:* certificates and associate. *Special study options:* academic remediation for entering students, adult/continuing education programs, advanced placement credit, distance learning, English as a second language, external degree program, part-time degree program, summer session for credit.
Library Will C. Miller Memorial Library.
Student Life *Campus security:* 24-hour patrols, controlled dormitory access.
Financial Aid Of all full-time matriculated undergraduates who enrolled in 2017, 150 Federal Work-Study jobs (averaging $1250). 75 state and other part-time jobs (averaging $1250).
Applying *Options:* electronic application, early admission, deferred entrance. *Required:* high school transcript.
Freshman Application Contact Southwest Texas Junior College, 2401 Garner Field Road, Uvalde, TX 78801-6297. *Phone:* 830-278-4401 Ext. 7280. *Website:* http://www.swtjc.edu/.

Tarrant County College District
Fort Worth, Texas

- **County-supported** 2-year, founded 1967
- **Urban** 667-acre campus with easy access to Dallas-Fort Worth
- **Endowment** $5.8 million
- **Coed**

Undergraduates 14,922 full-time, 36,428 part-time. Students come from 40 states and territories; 64 other countries; 17% Black or African American, non-Hispanic/Latino; 32% Hispanic/Latino; 6% Asian, non-Hispanic/Latino; 0.2% Native Hawaiian or other Pacific Islander, non-Hispanic/Latino; 0.4% American Indian or Alaska Native, non-Hispanic/Latino; 3% Two or more races, non-Hispanic/Latino; 1% Race/ethnicity unknown; 0.9% international; 4% transferred in.
Faculty *Student/faculty ratio:* 25:1.
Academics *Calendar:* semesters. *Degree:* certificates and associate. *Special study options:* academic remediation for entering students, adult/continuing education programs, advanced placement credit, distance learning, English as a second language, honors programs, part-time degree program, services for LD students, summer session for credit. *ROTC:* Army (c), Air Force (c).
Library Main Library plus 5 others. *Books:* 200,377 (physical), 197,576 (digital/electronic); *Serial titles:* 496 (physical), 63,698 (digital/electronic); *Databases:* 155.
Student Life *Campus security:* 24-hour emergency response devices and patrols, late-night transport/escort service.
Financial Aid Of all full-time matriculated undergraduates who enrolled in 2016, 7,182 applied for aid, 6,589 were judged to have need. 296 Federal Work-Study jobs (averaging $1624). 75 state and other part-time jobs (averaging $2677). In 2016, 56. *Average need-based loan:* $985. *Average need-based gift aid:* $5032. *Average non-need-based aid:* $1413.
Applying *Options:* electronic application.
Freshman Application Contact Ms. Nichole Mancone, District Director of Admissions and Records, Tarrant County College District, 300 Trinity Campus Circle, Fort Worth, TX 76102-6599. *Phone:* 817-515-1581. *E-mail:* nichole.mancone@tccd.edu. *Website:* http://www.tccd.edu/.

Temple College
Temple, Texas

Freshman Application Contact Ms. Toni Cuellar, Director of Admissions and Records, Temple College, 2600 South First Street, Temple, TX 76504. *Phone:* 254-298-8303. *Toll-free phone:* 800-460-4636. *E-mail:* carey.rose@templejc.edu. *Website:* http://www.templejc.edu/.

Texarkana College
Texarkana, Texas

- **State and locally supported** 2-year, founded 1927
- **Urban** 105-acre campus
- **Coed,** 4,239 undergraduate students, 36% full-time, 63% women, 37% men

Undergraduates 1,516 full-time, 2,723 part-time. 22% Black or African American, non-Hispanic/Latino; 8% Hispanic/Latino; 1% Asian, non-Hispanic/Latino; 0.1% Native Hawaiian or other Pacific Islander, non-Hispanic/Latino; 0.9% American Indian or Alaska Native, non-Hispanic/Latino; 5% Two or more races, non-Hispanic/Latino; 2% Race/ethnicity unknown; 0.9% international; 20% transferred in; 1% live on campus.
Freshmen *Admission:* 528 enrolled.
Faculty *Total:* 129, 71% full-time. *Student/faculty ratio:* 22:1.
Majors Administrative assistant and secretarial science; agriculture; art; automobile/automotive mechanics technology; biology/biological sciences; business administration and management; business/commerce; chemistry; child-care and support services management; child development; computer and information sciences; cosmetology; criminal justice/law enforcement administration; criminal justice/safety; culinary arts; diesel mechanics technology; drafting and design technology; dramatic/theater arts; electrical, electronic and communications engineering technology; emergency medical technology (EMT paramedic); engineering; foreign languages and literatures; health aide; heating, air conditioning, ventilation and refrigeration maintenance technology; humanities; industrial mechanics and maintenance technology; journalism; liberal arts and sciences/liberal studies; licensed practical/vocational nurse training; marketing/marketing management; mathematics; music; pharmacy technician; physics; political science and government; registered nursing/registered nurse; social sciences; substance abuse/addiction counseling; welding technology.
Academics *Calendar:* semesters. *Degree:* certificates and associate. *Special study options:* academic remediation for entering students, adult/continuing education programs, advanced placement credit, cooperative education, distance learning, freshman honors college, honors programs, independent study, internships, part-time degree program, services for LD students, study abroad, summer session for credit.
Library Palmer Memorial Library. *Books:* 46,602 (physical), 28,549 (digital/electronic); *Serial titles:* 143 (physical), 2 (digital/electronic); *Databases:* 101.
Student Life *Housing Options:* coed. Campus housing is university owned. *Activities and Organizations:* drama/theater group, student-run newspaper, choral group, Black Student Association, Earth Club, Culinary Arts Club, Cultural Awareness Student Association, Cosmetology Club. *Campus security:* 24-hour patrols. *Student services:* personal/psychological counseling, veterans affairs office.
Athletics *Intramural sports:* basketball M/W, racquetball M/W, soccer M/W, tennis M/W, volleyball M/W.
Financial Aid Of all full-time matriculated undergraduates who enrolled in 2017, 30 Federal Work-Study jobs (averaging $3090).
Applying *Options:* electronic application, early admission, deferred entrance. *Required:* high school transcript. *Recommended:* interview for nursing program, meningitis vaccine. *Application deadlines:* rolling (freshmen), rolling (transfers).
Freshman Application Contact Mr. Lee Williams, Director of Admissions, Texarkana College, 2500 North Robison Road, Texarkana, TX 75599-0001. *Phone:* 903-823-3016. *Fax:* 903-823-3451. *E-mail:* lee.williams@texarkanacollege.edu. *Website:* http://www.texarkanacollege.edu/.

Texas Southmost College
Brownsville, Texas

Freshman Application Contact New Student Relations, Texas Southmost College, 80 Fort Brown, Brownsville, TX 78520-4991. *Phone:* 956-882-8860. *Toll-free phone:* 877-882-8721. *Fax:* 956-882-8959. *Website:* http://www.utb.edu/.

Texas State Technical College
Waco, Texas

- **State-supported** 2-year, founded 1965
- **Suburban** 200-acre campus
- **Coed**

Undergraduates 4,931 full-time, 7,786 part-time. Students come from 35 states and territories; 6% Black or African American, non-Hispanic/Latino; 55% Hispanic/Latino; 0.6% Asian, non-Hispanic/Latino; 0.1% Native Hawaiian or other Pacific Islander, non-Hispanic/Latino; 0.3% American Indian or Alaska Native, non-Hispanic/Latino; 0.9% Two or more races, non-Hispanic/Latino; 5% Race/ethnicity unknown; 8% transferred in.
Faculty *Student/faculty ratio:* 13:1.
Academics *Calendar:* trimesters. *Degree:* certificates and associate. *Special study options:* academic remediation for entering students, adult/continuing education programs, cooperative education, distance learning, internships, part-time degree program, services for LD students, summer session for credit.
Library Texas State Technical College-Waco Campus Library.
Student Life *Campus security:* 24-hour emergency response devices and patrols, late-night transport/escort service, controlled dormitory access.
Standardized Tests *Required:* Texas Success Initiative assessment (for admission).
Financial Aid Of all full-time matriculated undergraduates who enrolled in 2016, 4,274 applied for aid, 4,247 were judged to have need, 320 had their need fully met. 129 Federal Work-Study jobs (averaging $1480). 27 state and other part-time jobs (averaging $955). In 2016, 5. *Average percent of need met:* 32. *Average financial aid package:* $2787. *Average need-based loan:* $1246. *Average need-based gift aid:* $2787. *Average non-need-based aid:* $250.
Applying *Options:* electronic application, early admission. *Required:* high school transcript. *Required for some:* interview.
Freshman Application Contact Mrs. Paula Arredondo, Registrar/Director of Admission and Records, Texas State Technical College, 3801 Campus Drive, Waco, TX 76705. *Phone:* 254-867-3363. *Toll-free phone:* 800-792-8784 Ext. 2362. *E-mail:* mary.daniel@tstc.edu. *Website:* http://www.tstc.edu/.

Trinity Valley Community College
Athens, Texas

- **State and locally supported** 2-year, founded 1946
- **Rural** 65-acre campus with easy access to Dallas-Fort Worth
- **Coed,** 4,449 undergraduate students, 44% full-time, 58% women, 42% men

Undergraduates 1,950 full-time, 2,499 part-time. Students come from 28 states and territories; 15 other countries; 1% are from out of state; 17% Black or African American, non-Hispanic/Latino; 2% Hispanic/Latino; 0.5% Asian, non-Hispanic/Latino; 0.1% Native Hawaiian or other Pacific Islander, non-Hispanic/Latino; 0.2% American Indian or Alaska Native, non-Hispanic/Latino; 21% Two or more races, non-Hispanic/Latino; 1% Race/ethnicity unknown; 0.0% international; 6% live on campus.
Faculty *Total:* 247, 66% full-time. *Student/faculty ratio:* 19:1.
Majors Accounting; agricultural teacher education; animal sciences; art; automobile/automotive mechanics technology; biology/biological sciences; business administration and management; business teacher education; chemistry; child development; commercial photography; computer science; corrections; cosmetology; criminal justice/law enforcement administration; criminal justice/police science; dance; data processing and data processing technology; developmental and child psychology; drafting and design technology; dramatic/theater arts; education; elementary education; emergency medical technology (EMT paramedic); farm and ranch management; fashion merchandising; finance; geology/earth science; heating, air conditioning, ventilation and refrigeration maintenance technology; history; horticultural science; insurance; journalism; kindergarten/preschool education; legal administrative assistant/secretary; liberal arts and sciences/liberal studies; licensed practical/vocational nurse training; marketing/marketing management; mathematics; music; physical education teaching and coaching; physical sciences; political science and government; pre-engineering; psychology; range science and management; real estate; registered nursing/registered nurse; religious studies; rhetoric and composition; sociology; Spanish; surgical technology; welding technology.
Academics *Calendar:* semesters. *Degree:* certificates, diplomas, and associate. *Special study options:* academic remediation for entering students, adult/continuing education programs, advanced placement credit, cooperative education, distance learning, double majors, English as a second language, honors programs, independent study, internships, part-time degree program, services for LD students, summer session for credit.
Library Ginger Murchison Learning Resource Center plus 3 others. *Books:* 47,948 (physical), 49,908 (digital/electronic); *Serial titles:* 124 (physical), 3 (digital/electronic); *Databases:* 68.
Student Life *Housing Options:* coed, men-only, women-only. Campus housing is university owned. *Activities and Organizations:* drama/theater group, student-run newspaper, choral group, marching band, Student Senate, Phi Theta Kappa, Delta Epsilon Chi. *Campus security:* 24-hour emergency response devices and patrols, controlled dormitory access. *Student services:* personal/psychological counseling.
Athletics Member NJCAA. *Intercollegiate sports:* basketball W(s), cheerleading W(s), softball W(s), volleyball W(s). *Intramural sports:* basketball M, football M, table tennis M, volleyball M.
Financial Aid Of all full-time matriculated undergraduates who enrolled in 2014, 90 Federal Work-Study jobs (averaging $1176). 56 state and other part-time jobs (averaging $660).
Applying *Options:* electronic application, early admission. *Required:* high school transcript. *Application deadlines:* rolling (freshmen), rolling (transfers). *Notification:* continuous (freshmen), continuous (transfers).
Freshman Application Contact Ms. Tammy Denney, Registrar, Trinity Valley Community College, 100 Cardinal Drive, Athens, TX 75751. *Phone:* 903-675-6209 Ext. 209.
Website: http://www.tvcc.edu/.

Tyler Junior College
Tyler, Texas

- **State and locally supported** primarily 2-year, founded 1926
- **Suburban** 137-acre campus
- **Endowment** $42.2 million
- **Coed,** 10,106 undergraduate students, 60% full-time, 62% women, 38% men

Undergraduates 6,026 full-time, 4,080 part-time. Students come from 27 states and territories; 31 other countries; 3% are from out of state; 21% Black or African American, non-Hispanic/Latino; 26% Hispanic/Latino; 2% Asian, non-Hispanic/Latino; 0.1% Native Hawaiian or other Pacific Islander, non-Hispanic/Latino; 0.9% American Indian or Alaska Native, non-Hispanic/Latino; 0.5% Two or more races, non-Hispanic/Latino; 0.7% Race/ethnicity unknown; 0.4% international; 6% transferred in; 11% live on campus. *Retention:* 54% of full-time freshmen returned.
Freshmen *Admission:* 10,778 applied, 10,778 admitted, 3,296 enrolled.
Faculty *Total:* 559, 56% full-time, 9% with terminal degrees. *Student/faculty ratio:* 20:1.
Majors Animation, interactive technology, video graphics and special effects; art; athletic training; automobile/automotive mechanics technology; biology/biological sciences; business administration and management; business/commerce; chemistry; child development; clinical/medical laboratory technology; computer science; computer systems networking and telecommunications; criminalistics and criminal science; criminal justice/safety; dance; dental hygiene; diagnostic medical sonography and ultrasound technology; drafting and design technology; dramatic/theater arts; economics; education (multiple levels); electromechanical technology; emergency medical technology (EMT paramedic); engineering; fire prevention and safety technology; foreign languages and literatures; forest/forest resources management; general studies; geology/earth science; graphic design; health and physical education/fitness; health/health-care administration; health information/medical records technology; heating, air conditioning, ventilation and refrigeration maintenance technology; history; industrial electronics technology; journalism; legal assistant/paralegal; literature; mathematics; medical administrative assistant and medical secretary; middle school education; music; natural sciences; occupational therapist assistant; physical education teaching and coaching; physical therapy technology; physics; political science and government; psychology; public administration; radio and television; radiologic technology/science; registered nursing/registered nurse; respiratory care therapy; secondary education; sign language interpretation and translation; social work; sociology; speech communication and rhetoric; substance abuse/addiction counseling; surgical technology; surveying technology; system, networking, and LAN/WAN management; veterinary/animal health technology; welding technology.
Academics *Calendar:* semesters. *Degrees:* certificates, diplomas, associate, and bachelor's. *Special study options:* academic remediation for entering students, accelerated degree program, adult/continuing education programs, advanced placement credit, distance learning, freshman honors college, honors programs, part-time degree program, services for LD students, study abroad, summer session for credit.

Library Vaughn Library and Learning Resource Center. *Books:* 85,418 (physical), 135,816 (digital/electronic); *Databases:* 100. Weekly public service hours: 74.
Student Life *Housing Options:* coed, men-only, women-only. Campus housing is university owned and is provided by a third party. *Activities and Organizations:* drama/theater group, student-run newspaper, choral group, marching band, Student Government, Religious Affiliation Clubs, Phi Theta Kappa, national sororities. *Campus security:* 24-hour emergency response devices and patrols, controlled dormitory access. *Student services:* health clinic, personal/psychological counseling, veterans affairs office.
Athletics Member NJCAA. *Intercollegiate sports:* basketball W(s), cheerleading W(s), soccer W(s), softball W(s), tennis W(s), volleyball W(s). *Intramural sports:* basketball M, racquetball M, volleyball M, weight lifting M.
Financial Aid ***Average indebtedness upon graduation:*** $14,743. *Financial aid deadline:* 6/1.
Applying *Options:* electronic application, early admission. *Required:* high school transcript. *Application deadlines:* rolling (freshmen), rolling (transfers). *Notification:* continuous (freshmen), continuous (transfers).
Admissions Office Contact Tyler Junior College, PO Box 9020, Tyler, TX 75711-9020. *Toll-free phone:* 800-687-5680.
Website: http://www.tjc.edu/.

Vernon College
Vernon, Texas

Director of Admissions Mr. Joe Hite, Dean of Admissions/Registrar, Vernon College, 4400 College Drive, Vernon, TX 76384-4092. *Phone:* 940-552-6291 Ext. 2204. *Website:* http://www.vernoncollege.edu/.

Vet Tech Institute of Houston
Houston, Texas

Freshman Application Contact Admissions Office, Vet Tech Institute of Houston, 4669 Southwest Freeway, Suite 100, Houston, TX 77027. *Phone:* 800-275-2736. *Toll-free phone:* 800-275-2736. *Website:* http://houston.vettechinstitute.edu/.

Victoria College
Victoria, Texas

- **County-supported** 2-year, founded 1925
- **Rural** 80-acre campus
- **Coed**

Undergraduates 1,053 full-time, 2,947 part-time. Students come from 5 states and territories; 0.1% are from out of state; 6% Black or African American, non-Hispanic/Latino; 48% Hispanic/Latino; 2% Asian, non-Hispanic/Latino; 0.1% Native Hawaiian or other Pacific Islander, non-Hispanic/Latino; 0.2% American Indian or Alaska Native, non-Hispanic/Latino; 1% Two or more races, non-Hispanic/Latino; 0.5% Race/ethnicity unknown; 6% transferred in.
Faculty *Student/faculty ratio:* 17:1.
Academics *Calendar:* semesters. *Degree:* certificates and associate. *Special study options:* academic remediation for entering students, advanced placement credit, distance learning, English as a second language, off-campus study, part-time degree program, services for LD students, summer session for credit.
Library Victoria College/University of Houston-Victoria Library. *Books:* 118,781 (physical), 119,216 (digital/electronic); *Serial titles:* 133 (physical), 81,953 (digital/electronic); *Databases:* 137. Weekly public service hours: 76; students can reserve study rooms.
Student Life *Campus security:* 24-hour emergency response devices.
Applying *Options:* electronic application, early admission. *Required:* high school transcript.
Freshman Application Contact Madelyne Tolliver, Registrar, Victoria College, 2200 E. Red River, Victoria, TX 77901. *Phone:* 361-572-6400. *Toll-free phone:* 877-843-4369. *Fax:* 361-582-2525. *E-mail:* registrar@victoriacollege.edu. *Website:* http://www.victoriacollege.edu/.

Vista College
El Paso, Texas

Director of Admissions Ms. Sarah Hernandez, Registrar, Vista College, 6101 Montana Avenue, El Paso, TX 79925. *Phone:* 915-779-8031. *Toll-free phone:* 866-442-4197. *Website:* http://www.vistacollege.edu/.

Vista College–Online Campus
Richardson, Texas

Admissions Office Contact Vista College–Online Campus, 300 North Coit Road, Suite 300, Richardson, TX 75080. *Website:* http://www.vistacollege.edu/.

Wade College
Dallas, Texas

- **Proprietary** primarily 2-year, founded 1965
- **Urban** 175-acre campus with easy access to Dallas Fort Worth
- **Coed**

Undergraduates Students come from 4 other countries; 10% are from out of state. *Retention:* 60% of full-time freshmen returned.
Faculty *Student/faculty ratio:* 12:1.
Academics *Calendar:* trimesters. *Degrees:* associate and bachelor's. *Special study options:* academic remediation for entering students, advanced placement credit, internships, part-time degree program, services for LD students, summer session for credit.
Library College Library. *Books:* 8,500 (physical), 45,000 (digital/electronic); *Databases:* 10.
Student Life *Campus security:* 24-hour emergency response devices and patrols, late-night transport/escort service, controlled dormitory access.
Applying *Options:* electronic application. *Required:* high school transcript, interview.
Freshman Application Contact Wade College, Infomart, 1950 North Stemmons Freeway, Suite 4080, LB 562, Dallas, TX 75207. *Phone:* 214-637-3530. *Toll-free phone:* 800-624-4850. *Website:* http://www.wadecollege.edu/.

Weatherford College
Weatherford, Texas

Freshman Application Contact Mr. Ralph Willingham, Director of Admissions, Weatherford College, 225 College Park Drive, Weatherford, TX 76086-5699. *Phone:* 817-598-6248. *Toll-free phone:* 800-287-5471. *Fax:* 817-598-6205. *E-mail:* rwillingham@wc.edu. *Website:* http://www.wc.edu/.

Western Technical College
El Paso, Texas

Freshman Application Contact Ms. Laura Pena, Director of Admissions, Western Technical College, 9451 Diana Drive, El Paso, TX 79930-2610. *Phone:* 915-566-9621. *Toll-free phone:* 800-201-9232. *E-mail:* lpena@westerntech.edu. *Website:* http://www.westerntech.edu/.

Western Technical College
El Paso, Texas

Freshman Application Contact Mr. Bill Terrell, Chief Admissions Officer, Western Technical College, 9624 Plaza Circle, El Paso, TX 79927. *Phone:* 915-532-3737 Ext. 117. *Fax:* 915-532-6946. *E-mail:* bterrell@wtc-ep.edu. *Website:* http://www.westerntech.edu/.

Western Texas College
Snyder, Texas

- **State and locally supported** 2-year, founded 1969
- **Small-town** 165-acre campus
- **Coed**

Undergraduates 579 full-time, 1,671 part-time. Students come from 30 states and territories; 17 other countries; 4% are from out of state; 9% Black or African American, non-Hispanic/Latino; 42% Hispanic/Latino; 1% Asian, non-Hispanic/Latino; 0.1% Native Hawaiian or other Pacific Islander, non-Hispanic/Latino; 0.8% American Indian or Alaska Native, non-Hispanic/Latino; 2% Two or more races, non-Hispanic/Latino; 6% international; 3% transferred in; 50% live on campus.
Faculty *Student/faculty ratio:* 22:1.
Academics *Calendar:* semesters. *Degree:* certificates and associate. *Special study options:* academic remediation for entering students, adult/continuing education programs, advanced placement credit, distance learning, honors programs, independent study, internships, part-time degree program, services for LD students, student-designed majors, summer session for credit.
Library Western Texas College Resource Center. *Books:* 31,884 (physical), 29,077 (digital/electronic); *Serial titles:* 97 (physical); *Databases:* 25. Weekly public service hours: 56.
Student Life *Campus security:* 24-hour emergency response devices and patrols, late-night transport/escort service.

Athletics Member NCAA, NJCAA. All NCAA Division I.
Applying *Options:* electronic application, early admission, deferred entrance. *Required:* high school transcript.
Freshman Application Contact Donna Morris, Registrar, Western Texas College, 6200 S. College Avenue, Snyder, TX 79549. *Phone:* 325-573-8511. *Toll-free phone:* 888-GO-TO-WTC. *Fax:* 325-573-9321. *E-mail:* dmorris@wtc.edu. *Website:* http://www.wtc.edu/.

Wharton County Junior College
Wharton, Texas

Freshman Application Contact Mr. Albert Barnes, Dean of Admissions and Registration, Wharton County Junior College, 911 Boling Highway, Wharton, TX 77488-3298. *Phone:* 979-532-6381. *E-mail:* albertb@wcjc.edu. *Website:* http://www.wcjc.edu/.

UTAH

Ameritech College of Healthcare
Draper, Utah

Admissions Office Contact Ameritech College of Healthcare, 12257 South Business Park Drive, Suite 108, Draper, UT 84020-6545. *Website:* http://www.ameritech.edu/.

Fortis College
Salt Lake City, Utah

Admissions Office Contact Fortis College, 3949 South 700 East, Suite 150, Salt Lake City, UT 84107. *Toll-free phone:* 855-4-FORTIS. *Website:* http://www.fortis.edu/.

LDS Business College
Salt Lake City, Utah

- **Independent** 2-year, founded 1886, affiliated with The Church of Jesus Christ of Latter-day Saints, part of The Church Educational System (CES) of The Church of Jesus Christ of Latter-day Saints
- **Urban** 2-acre campus with easy access to Salt Lake City
- **Coed**

Undergraduates 2% Black or African American, non-Hispanic/Latino; 14% Hispanic/Latino; 1% Asian, non-Hispanic/Latino; 2% Native Hawaiian or other Pacific Islander, non-Hispanic/Latino; 0.4% American Indian or Alaska Native, non-Hispanic/Latino; 3% Two or more races, non-Hispanic/Latino; 1% Race/ethnicity unknown; 22% international.
Faculty *Student/faculty ratio:* 25:1.
Academics *Calendar:* semesters. *Degree:* certificates and associate. *Special study options:* academic remediation for entering students, adult/continuing education programs, advanced placement credit, distance learning, double majors, English as a second language, internships, part-time degree program, services for LD students, summer session for credit. *ROTC:* Army (c), Air Force (c).
Library LDS Business College Library. Weekly public service hours: 74; students can reserve study rooms.
Student Life *Campus security:* 24-hour emergency response devices and patrols.
Standardized Tests *Recommended:* SAT or ACT (for admission).
Applying *Options:* electronic application, deferred entrance. *Application fee:* $35.
Freshman Application Contact Kristen Whittaker, Director of Enrollment Management, LDS Business College, 95 North 300 West, Salt Lake City, UT 84101-3500. *Phone:* 801-524-8145. *Toll-free phone:* 800-999-5767. *E-mail:* admissions@ldsbc.edu. *Website:* http://www.ldsbc.edu/.

Nightingale College
Ogden, Utah

Freshman Application Contact Nightingale College, 4155 Harrison Boulevard #100, Ogden, UT 84403. *Website:* http://www.nightingale.edu/.

Provo College
Provo, Utah

Director of Admissions Mr. Gordon Peters, College Director, Provo College, 1450 West 820 North, Provo, UT 84601. *Phone:* 801-375-1861. *Toll-free phone:* 877-777-5886. *Fax:* 801-375-9728. *E-mail:* gordonp@provocollege.org. *Website:* http://www.provocollege.edu/.

Salt Lake Community College
Salt Lake City, Utah

- **State-supported** 2-year, founded 1948, part of Utah System of Higher Education
- **Urban** 114-acre campus with easy access to Salt Lake City
- **Endowment** $837,612
- **Coed**

Undergraduates 7,811 full-time, 21,809 part-time. 2% Black or African American, non-Hispanic/Latino; 18% Hispanic/Latino; 4% Asian, non-Hispanic/Latino; 1% Native Hawaiian or other Pacific Islander, non-Hispanic/Latino; 0.8% American Indian or Alaska Native, non-Hispanic/Latino; 3% Two or more races, non-Hispanic/Latino; 2% Race/ethnicity unknown; 1% international; 7% transferred in.
Faculty *Student/faculty ratio:* 17:1.
Academics *Calendar:* semesters. *Degree:* certificates, diplomas, and associate. *Special study options:* academic remediation for entering students, advanced placement credit, cooperative education, distance learning, double majors, English as a second language, internships, part-time degree program, services for LD students, student-designed majors, study abroad, summer session for credit. *ROTC:* Army (c), Air Force (c).
Library Markosian Library plus 2 others.
Student Life *Campus security:* 24-hour emergency response devices and patrols, late-night transport/escort service.
Athletics Member NJCAA.
Applying *Options:* electronic application, early admission. *Application fee:* $40.
Admissions Office Contact Salt Lake Community College, PO Box 30808, Salt Lake City, UT 84130-0808. *Website:* http://www.slcc.edu/.

Snow College
Ephraim, Utah

- **State-supported** 2-year, founded 1888, part of Utah System of Higher Education
- **Rural** 50-acre campus
- **Endowment** $8.9 million
- **Coed,** 5,574 undergraduate students, 58% full-time, 55% women, 45% men
- 100% of applicants were admitted

Undergraduates 3,227 full-time, 2,347 part-time. Students come from 35 states and territories; 42 other countries; 5% are from out of state; 0.6% Black or African American, non-Hispanic/Latino; 7% Hispanic/Latino; 0.4% Asian, non-Hispanic/Latino; 2% Native Hawaiian or other Pacific Islander, non-Hispanic/Latino; 1% American Indian or Alaska Native, non-Hispanic/Latino; 0.4% Two or more races, non-Hispanic/Latino; 0.2% Race/ethnicity unknown; 3% international; 0.6% transferred in; 20% live on campus. *Retention:* 46% of full-time freshmen returned.
Freshmen *Admission:* 7,676 applied, 7,676 admitted, 1,519 enrolled. *Average high school GPA:* 3.4. *Test scores:* ACT scores over 18: 76%; ACT scores over 24: 29%; ACT scores over 30: 2%.
Faculty *Total:* 281, 55% full-time, 7% with terminal degrees. *Student/faculty ratio:* 21:1.
Majors Accounting; administrative assistant and secretarial science; agricultural business and management; agriculture; animal sciences; art; automobile/automotive mechanics technology; biology/biological sciences; botany/plant biology; building/construction finishing, management, and inspection related; business administration and management; business teacher education; chemistry; child development; computer engineering; computer science; construction engineering technology; criminal justice/law enforcement administration; dance; dramatic/theater arts; economics; education; elementary education; family and community services; family and consumer sciences/human sciences; foods, nutrition, and wellness; forestry; French; geography; geology/earth science; history; humanities; industrial mechanics and maintenance technology; industrial technology; information science/studies; Japanese; kindergarten/preschool education; liberal arts and sciences/liberal studies; mass communication/media; mathematics; music; music history, literature, and theory; music teacher education; natural resources and conservation related; philosophy; physical education teaching and coaching; physical sciences; physics; political science and government; pre-engineering; range science and management; registered nursing/registered nurse; science teacher education; sociology; soil science and agronomy; Spanish; zoology/animal biology.
Academics *Calendar:* semesters. *Degree:* certificates, diplomas, and associate. *Special study options:* academic remediation for entering students, adult/continuing education programs, advanced placement credit, cooperative education, distance learning, English as a second language, external degree program, honors programs, independent study, part-time degree program, services for LD students, summer session for credit.

Library Karen Huntsman Library plus 1 other. *Books:* 57,726 (physical); *Serial titles:* 775 (physical); *Databases:* 85. Weekly public service hours: 66.
Student Life *Housing Options:* coed, men-only, women-only, special housing for students with disabilities. Campus housing is university owned. *Activities and Organizations:* drama/theater group, student-run newspaper, radio and television station, choral group, Phi Beta Lambda & DECA (Business Club), Latter Day Saints Student Association, International Student Society, Western Swing Club, Dead Cats Society (Life Science Club). *Campus security:* 24-hour emergency response devices and patrols, student patrols, late-night transport/escort service, controlled dormitory access. *Student services:* personal/psychological counseling.
Athletics Member NJCAA. *Intercollegiate sports:* basketball W(s), cheerleading W(s), soccer W(s), softball W(s), volleyball W(s). *Intramural sports:* badminton M, basketball M, bowling M, football M, golf M, lacrosse M, racquetball M, rock climbing M(c), rugby M, sand volleyball M, soccer M, softball M, tennis M, ultimate Frisbee M, volleyball M, water polo M, wrestling M.
Standardized Tests *Recommended:* SAT or ACT (for admission).
Financial Aid ***Average financial aid package:*** $2351. *Average need-based loan:* $2903. *Average need-based gift aid:* $2395.
Applying *Options:* electronic application, early admission. *Application fee:* $30. *Required:* high school transcript. *Application deadline:* 6/1 (transfers). *Notification:* continuous (freshmen), continuous (transfers).
Freshman Application Contact Rachel Wade, Admissions Advisor, Snow College, 150 East College Avenue, Ephraim, UT 84627. *Phone:* 435-283-7159. *Fax:* 435-283-7157. *E-mail:* rachel.wade@snow.edu. *Website:* http://www.snow.edu/.

VERMONT

Community College of Vermont
Montpelier, Vermont

Freshman Application Contact Community College of Vermont, 660 Elm Street, Montpelier, VT 05602. *Phone:* 802-654-0505. *Toll-free phone:* 800-CCV-6686. *Website:* http://www.ccv.edu/.

Landmark College
Putney, Vermont

Freshman Application Contact Admissions Main Desk, Landmark College, Admissions Office, River Road South, Putney, VT 05346. *Phone:* 802-387-6718. *Fax:* 802-387-6868. *E-mail:* admissions@landmark.edu. *Website:* http://www.landmark.edu/.

New England Culinary Institute
Montpelier, Vermont

Freshman Application Contact Adonica Williams, New England Culinary Institute, 7 School Street, Montpelier, VT 05602-3115. *Phone:* 802-225-3210. *Toll-free phone:* 877-223-6324. *Fax:* 802-225-3280. *E-mail:* admissions@neci.edu. *Website:* http://www.neci.edu/.

VIRGINIA

Advanced Technology Institute
Virginia Beach, Virginia

Freshman Application Contact Admissions Office, Advanced Technology Institute, 5700 Southern Boulevard, Suite 100, Virginia Beach, VA 23462. *Phone:* 757-490-1241. *Toll-free phone:* 888-468-1093. *Website:* http://www.auto.edu/.

American National University
Charlottesville, Virginia

Director of Admissions Kimberly Moore, Campus Director, American National University, 3926 Seminole Trail, Charlottesville, VA 22911. *Phone:* 434-295-0136. *Toll-free phone:* 888-9-JOBREADY. *Fax:* 434-979-8061. *Website:* http://www.an.edu/.

American National University
Danville, Virginia

Freshman Application Contact Admissions Office, American National University, 336 Old Riverside Drive, Danville, VA 24541. *Phone:* 434-793-6822. *Toll-free phone:* 888-9-JOBREADY. *Website:* http://www.an.edu/.

American National University
Harrisonburg, Virginia

Director of Admissions Jack Evey, Campus Director, American National University, 1515 Country Club Road, Harrisonburg, VA 22802. *Phone:* 540-432-0943. *Toll-free phone:* 888-9-JOBREADY. *Website:* http://www.an.edu/.

American National University
Lynchburg, Virginia

Freshman Application Contact Admissions Representative, American National University, 104 Candlewood Court, Lynchburg, VA 24502. *Phone:* 804-239-3500. *Toll-free phone:* 888-9-JOBREADY. *Website:* http://www.an.edu/.

Blue Ridge Community College
Weyers Cave, Virginia

Freshman Application Contact Blue Ridge Community College, PO Box 80, Weyers Cave, VA 24486-0080. *Phone:* 540-453-2217. *Toll-free phone:* 888-750-2722. *Website:* http://www.brcc.edu/.

Bryant & Stratton College–Richmond Campus
Richmond, Virginia

Freshman Application Contact Mr. David K. Mayle, Director of Admissions, Bryant & Stratton College–Richmond Campus, 8141 Hull Street Road, Richmond, VA 23235-6411. *Phone:* 804-745-2444. *Fax:* 804-745-6884. *E-mail:* tlawson@bryanstratton.edu. *Website:* http://www.bryantstratton.edu/.

Bryant & Stratton College–Virginia Beach Campus
Virginia Beach, Virginia

Freshman Application Contact Bryant & Stratton College–Virginia Beach Campus, 301 Centre Pointe Drive, Virginia Beach, VA 23462. *Phone:* 757-499-7900 Ext. 173. *Website:* http://www.bryantstratton.edu/.

Centra College of Nursing
Lynchburg, Virginia

Admissions Office Contact Centra College of Nursing, 905 Lakeside Drive, Suite A, Lynchburg, VA 24501. *Website:* http://www.centrahealth.com/facilities/centra-college-nursing/.

Central Virginia Community College
Lynchburg, Virginia

- **State-supported** 2-year, founded 1966, part of Virginia Community College System
- **Suburban** 104-acre campus
- **Coed**

Undergraduates 1,269 full-time, 2,859 part-time. Students come from 12 states and territories; 1% are from out of state; 18% Black or African American, non-Hispanic/Latino; 3% Hispanic/Latino; 3% Asian, non-Hispanic/Latino; 0.1% Native Hawaiian or other Pacific Islander, non-Hispanic/Latino; 0.4% American Indian or Alaska Native, non-Hispanic/Latino; 5% Two or more races, non-Hispanic/Latino; 0.8% Race/ethnicity unknown.
Faculty *Student/faculty ratio:* 18:1.
Academics *Calendar:* semesters. *Degree:* certificates, diplomas, and associate. *Special study options:* academic remediation for entering students, advanced placement credit, cooperative education, distance learning, independent study, internships, part-time degree program, services for LD students, summer session for credit.
Library Bedford Learning Resources Center.
Student Life *Campus security:* 24-hour emergency response devices.

Financial Aid Of all full-time matriculated undergraduates who enrolled in 2017, 65 Federal Work-Study jobs (averaging $2700).
Applying *Options:* electronic application, early admission, deferred entrance.
Freshman Application Contact Admissions Office, Central Virginia Community College, 3506 Wards Road, Lynchburg, VA 24502. *Phone:* 434-832-7633. *Toll-free phone:* 800-562-3060. *Fax:* 434-832-7793. *Website:* http://www.centralvirginia.edu/.

Centura College
Chesapeake, Virginia

Director of Admissions Director of Admissions, Centura College, 932 Ventures Way, Chesapeake, VA 23320. *Phone:* 757-549-2121. *Toll-free phone:* 877-575-5627. *Fax:* 575-549-1196. *Website:* http://www.centuracollege.edu/.

Centura College
Newport News, Virginia

Director of Admissions Victoria Whitehead, Director of Admissions, Centura College, 616 Denbigh Boulevard, Newport News, VA 23608. *Phone:* 757-874-2121. *Toll-free phone:* 877-575-5627. *Fax:* 757-874-3857. *E-mail:* admdircpen@centura.edu. *Website:* http://www.centuracollege.edu/.

Centura College
Norfolk, Virginia

Director of Admissions Director of Admissions, Centura College, 7020 North Military Highway, Norfolk, VA 23518. *Phone:* 757-853-2121. *Toll-free phone:* 877-575-5627. *Fax:* 757-852-9017. *Website:* http://www.centuracollege.edu/.

Centura College
North Chesterfield, Virginia

Freshman Application Contact Admissions Office, Centura College, 7914 Midlothian Turnpike, North Chesterfield, VA 23235-5230. *Phone:* 804-330-0111. *Toll-free phone:* 877-575-5627. *Fax:* 804-330-3809. *Website:* http://www.centuracollege.edu/.

Centura College
Virginia Beach, Virginia

Freshman Application Contact Admissions Office, Centura College, 2697 Dean Drive, Suite 100, Virginia Beach, VA 23452. *Phone:* 757-340-2121. *Toll-free phone:* 877-575-5627. *Fax:* 757-340-9704. *Website:* http://www.centuracollege.edu/.

Chester Career College
Chester, Virginia

Admissions Office Contact Chester Career College, 751 West Hundred Road, Chester, VA 23836. *Website:* http://www.chestercareercollege.edu/.

Columbia College
Vienna, Virginia

Admissions Office Contact Columbia College, 8620 Westwood Center Drive, Vienna, VA 22182. *Website:* http://www.ccdc.edu/.

Dabney S. Lancaster Community College
Clifton Forge, Virginia

- **State-supported** 2-year, founded 1964, part of Virginia Community College System
- **Rural** 117-acre campus
- **Endowment** $6.6 million
- **Coed**

Undergraduates 428 full-time, 758 part-time. Students come from 3 states and territories; 4% are from out of state; 4% Black or African American, non-Hispanic/Latino; 2% Hispanic/Latino; 0.6% Asian, non-Hispanic/Latino; 0.7% American Indian or Alaska Native, non-Hispanic/Latino; 4% Two or more races, non-Hispanic/Latino; 0.6% Race/ethnicity unknown; 0.1% international; 29% transferred in.
Faculty *Student/faculty ratio:* 10:1.
Academics *Calendar:* semesters. *Degree:* certificates and associate. *Special study options:* academic remediation for entering students, adult/continuing education programs, advanced placement credit, cooperative education, distance learning, double majors, independent study, internships, off-campus study, part-time degree program, services for LD students, summer session for credit.
Library DSLCC Library. *Books:* 35,154 (physical), 74,281 (digital/electronic); *Serial titles:* 5 (physical), 95,157 (digital/electronic); *Databases:* 117. Weekly public service hours: 60; students can reserve study rooms.
Student Life *Campus security:* 24-hour emergency response devices, Security Cameras at Rockbridge Regional Center.
Standardized Tests *Required for some:* SAT and SAT Subject Tests or ACT (for admission).
Applying *Options:* electronic application. *Recommended:* high school transcript.
Freshman Application Contact Ms. Suzanne Ostling, Admissions Officer, Dabney S. Lancaster Community College, 1000 Dabney Drive, Clifton Forge, VA 24422. *Phone:* 540-863-2826. *Toll-free phone:* 877-73-DSLCC. *Fax:* 540-863-2915. *E-mail:* sostling@dslcc.edu. *Website:* http://www.dslcc.edu/.

Danville Community College
Danville, Virginia

Freshman Application Contact Cathy Pulliam, Coordinator of Student Recruitment and Enrollment, Danville Community College, 1008 South Main Street, Danville, VA 24541-4088. *Phone:* 434-797-8538. *Toll-free phone:* 800-560-4291. *E-mail:* cpulliam@dcc.vccs.edu. *Website:* http://www.dcc.vccs.edu/.

Eastern Shore Community College
Melfa, Virginia

- **State-supported** 2-year, founded 1971, part of Virginia Community College System
- **Rural** 117-acre campus with easy access to Hampton Roads/Virginia Beach, Norfolk
- **Coed**

Undergraduates 264 full-time, 593 part-time. 1% are from out of state; 39% Black or African American, non-Hispanic/Latino; 6% Hispanic/Latino; 1% Asian, non-Hispanic/Latino; 0.2% American Indian or Alaska Native, non-Hispanic/Latino; 0.8% Race/ethnicity unknown.
Faculty *Student/faculty ratio:* 13:1.
Academics *Calendar:* semesters. *Degree:* certificates and associate. *Special study options:* academic remediation for entering students, adult/continuing education programs, distance learning, internships, off-campus study, part-time degree program, services for LD students, summer session for credit.
Library Learning Resources Center plus 1 other.
Student Life *Campus security:* security guards, day and night during classes when the college is in session.
Financial Aid Of all full-time matriculated undergraduates who enrolled in 2017, 11 Federal Work-Study jobs.
Applying *Options:* electronic application. *Required:* high school transcript.
Freshman Application Contact Ms. Cheryll Mills, Coordinator of Student Services, Eastern Shore Community College, 29300 Lankford Highway, Melfa, VA 23410. *Phone:* 757-789-1730. *Toll-free phone:* 877-871-8455. *Fax:* 757-789-1737. *E-mail:* cmills@es.vccs.edu. *Website:* http://www.es.vccs.edu/.

Eastern Virginia Career College
Fredericksburg, Virginia

Admissions Office Contact Eastern Virginia Career College, 10304 Spotsylvania Avenue, Suite 400, Fredericksburg, VA 22408. *Website:* http://www.evcc.edu/.

Fortis College
Norfolk, Virginia

Admissions Office Contact Fortis College, 6300 Center Drive, Suite 100, Norfolk, VA 23502. *Toll-free phone:* 855-4-FORTIS. *Website:* http://www.fortis.edu/.

Fortis College
Richmond, Virginia

Admissions Office Contact Fortis College, 2000 Westmoreland Street, Suite A, Richmond, VA 23230. *Toll-free phone:* 855-4-FORTIS. *Website:* http://www.fortis.edu/.

Germanna Community College
Locust Grove, Virginia

Freshman Application Contact Ms. Rita Dunston, Registrar, Germanna Community College, 10000 Germanna Point Drive, Fredericksburg, VA 22408. *Phone:* 540-891-3020. *Fax:* 540-891-3092. *Website:* http://www.germanna.edu/.

John Tyler Community College
Chester, Virginia

- **State-supported** 2-year, founded 1967, part of Virginia Community College System
- **Suburban** 160-acre campus with easy access to Richmond
- **Coed,** 10,144 undergraduate students, 24% full-time, 57% women, 43% men

Undergraduates 2,431 full-time, 7,713 part-time. 3% are from out of state; 22% Black or African American, non-Hispanic/Latino; 10% Hispanic/Latino; 3% Asian, non-Hispanic/Latino; 0.2% Native Hawaiian or other Pacific Islander, non-Hispanic/Latino; 0.4% American Indian or Alaska Native, non-Hispanic/Latino; 5% Two or more races, non-Hispanic/Latino; 1% Race/ethnicity unknown.
Freshmen *Admission:* 1,468 enrolled.
Faculty *Total:* 420, 26% full-time. *Student/faculty ratio:* 20:1.
Majors Accounting related; architectural technology; business administration and management; business administration, management and operations related; child-care provision; computer and information sciences; criminal justice/law enforcement administration; electrician; emergency medical technology (EMT paramedic); engineering; funeral service and mortuary science; general studies; humanities; industrial technology; information technology; manufacturing engineering technology; mechanical engineering technologies related; mental and social health services and allied professions related; registered nursing/registered nurse; visual and performing arts related.
Academics *Calendar:* semesters. *Degree:* certificates and associate. *Special study options:* academic remediation for entering students, adult/continuing education programs, advanced placement credit, distance learning, external degree program, honors programs, off-campus study, part-time degree program, services for LD students, study abroad, summer session for credit. *ROTC:* Army (c).
Library John Tyler Community College Learning Resource and Technology Center.
Student Life *Housing:* college housing not available. *Activities and Organizations:* drama/theater group, choral group, Phi Theta Kappa, Human Services Club, Future Teachers Club, Student Nurses'; Association, Student Veteran's Organization. *Campus security:* 24-hour emergency response devices and patrols. *Student services:* veterans affairs office.
Athletics *Intramural sports:* basketball M(c), soccer M(c), ultimate Frisbee M(c).
Financial Aid Of all full-time matriculated undergraduates who enrolled in 2017, 40 Federal Work-Study jobs (averaging $2610).
Applying *Options:* electronic application, early admission, deferred entrance. *Recommended:* high school transcript. *Application deadline:* rolling (freshmen). *Notification:* continuous (freshmen).
Freshman Application Contact Mr. Leigh Baxter, Director Admissions and Records and Registrar, John Tyler Community College, Office of Admissions and Records, 800 Charter Colony Parkway, Midlothian, VA 23831. *Phone:* 804-594-1549. *Toll-free phone:* 800-552-3490. *Fax:* 804-594-1543. *E-mail:* lbaxter@jtcc.edu.
Website: http://www.jtcc.edu/.

J. Sargeant Reynolds Community College
Richmond, Virginia

- **State-supported** 2-year, founded 1972, part of Virginia Community College System
- **Suburban** 207-acre campus with easy access to Richmond
- **Endowment** $10.0 million
- **Coed**

Undergraduates 2,567 full-time, 6,767 part-time. Students come from 21 states and territories; 16 other countries; 1% are from out of state; 33% Black or African American, non-Hispanic/Latino; 3% Hispanic/Latino; 6% Asian, non-Hispanic/Latino; 0.2% Native Hawaiian or other Pacific Islander, non-Hispanic/Latino; 0.4% American Indian or Alaska Native, non-Hispanic/Latino; 8% Two or more races, non-Hispanic/Latino; 1% Race/ethnicity unknown; 5% transferred in. *Retention:* 51% of full-time freshmen returned.
Faculty *Student/faculty ratio:* 17:1.
Academics *Calendar:* semesters. *Degree:* certificates and associate. *Special study options:* academic remediation for entering students, adult/continuing education programs, advanced placement credit, distance learning, double majors, English as a second language, honors programs, independent study, internships, off-campus study, part-time degree program, services for LD students, summer session for credit.
Library J. Sargeant Reynolds Community College Library plus 2 others. *Books:* 85,000 (physical), 62,000 (digital/electronic); *Serial titles:* 225 (physical), 52,000 (digital/electronic); *Databases:* 145. Weekly public service hours: 66.
Student Life *Campus security:* 24-hour emergency response devices and patrols, late-night transport/escort service, security during hours of operation.
Financial Aid Of all full-time matriculated undergraduates who enrolled in 2017, 2,608 applied for aid, 1,395 were judged to have need. 31 Federal Work-Study jobs (averaging $1803). *Average financial aid package:* $3408. *Average need-based gift aid:* $2726.
Applying *Options:* electronic application. *Required:* high school transcript. *Required for some:* interview, interview, criminal background check and/or drug screening, physical standard minimum.
Admissions Office Contact J. Sargeant Reynolds Community College, PO Box 85622, Richmond, VA 23285-5622. *Website:* http://www.reynolds.edu/.

Lord Fairfax Community College
Middletown, Virginia

Freshman Application Contact Karen Bucher, Director of Enrollment Management, Lord Fairfax Community College, 173 Skirmisher Lane, Middletown, VA 22645. *Phone:* 540-868-7132. *Toll-free phone:* 800-906-LFCC. *Fax:* 540-868-7005. *E-mail:* kbucher@lfcc.edu. *Website:* http://www.lfcc.edu/.

Mountain Empire Community College
Big Stone Gap, Virginia

Freshman Application Contact Mountain Empire Community College, 3441 Mountain Empire Road, Big Stone Gap, VA 24219. *Phone:* 276-523-2400 Ext. 219. *Website:* http://www.mecc.edu/.

New River Community College
Dublin, Virginia

- **State-supported** 2-year, founded 1969, part of Virginia Community College System
- **Rural** 100-acre campus
- **Coed**

Academics *Calendar:* semesters. *Degree:* certificates, diplomas, and associate. *Special study options:* academic remediation for entering students, adult/continuing education programs, advanced placement credit, cooperative education, distance learning, double majors, independent study, internships, part-time degree program, services for LD students, summer session for credit.
Library New River Community College Library plus 1 other.
Student Life *Campus security:* 24-hour patrols.
Applying *Options:* electronic application, early admission. *Required for some:* high school transcript. *Recommended:* high school transcript.
Freshman Application Contact Mrs. Tammy L. Smith, Coordinator, Admissions and Records, New River Community College, 5251 College Drive, Dublin, VA 24084. *Phone:* 540-674-3600 Ext. 4203. *Toll-free phone:* 866-462-6722. *Fax:* 540-674-3644. *E-mail:* tsmith@nr.edu. *Website:* http://www.nr.edu/.

Northern Virginia Community College
Annandale, Virginia

Freshman Application Contact Northern Virginia Community College, 8333 Little River Turnpike, Annandale, VA 22003. *Phone:* 703-323-3195. *Website:* http://www.nvcc.edu/.

Patrick Henry Community College
Martinsville, Virginia

Freshman Application Contact Mr. Travis Tisdale, Coordinator, Admissions and Records, Patrick Henry Community College, 645 Patriot Avenue, Martinsville, VA 24112. *Phone:* 276-656-0311. *Toll-free phone:* 800-232-7997. *Fax:* 276-656-0352. *Website:* http://www.patrickhenry.edu/.

Paul D. Camp Community College
Franklin, Virginia

Freshman Application Contact Mrs. Trina Jones, Dean Student Services, Paul D. Camp Community College, PO Box 737, 100 N. College Drive, Franklin, VA 23851. *Phone:* 757-569-6720. *E-mail:* tjones@pdc.edu. *Website:* http://www.pdc.edu/.

Piedmont Virginia Community College
Charlottesville, Virginia

- **State-supported** 2-year, founded 1972, part of Virginia Community College System
- **Suburban** 114-acre campus with easy access to Richmond
- **Endowment** $6.8 million
- **Coed**

Undergraduates 1,257 full-time, 4,351 part-time. 13% Black or African American, non-Hispanic/Latino; 7% Hispanic/Latino; 5% Asian, non-Hispanic/Latino; 0.2% Native Hawaiian or other Pacific Islander, non-Hispanic/Latino; 0.3% American Indian or Alaska Native, non-Hispanic/Latino; 5% Two or more races, non-Hispanic/Latino; 1% Race/ethnicity unknown.
Academics *Calendar:* semesters. *Degree:* certificates and associate. *Special study options:* academic remediation for entering students, adult/continuing education programs, advanced placement credit, cooperative education, distance learning, English as a second language, honors programs, independent study, internships, part-time degree program, services for LD students, summer session for credit. *ROTC:* Army (c), Air Force (c).
Library Jessup Library.
Student Life *Campus security:* 24-hour emergency response devices and patrols, late-night transport/escort service, establishment of Campus Police.
Financial Aid ***Average indebtedness upon graduation:*** $4069.
Applying *Options:* electronic application, early admission, deferred entrance. *Required for some:* high school transcript, prerequisite courses for nursing, practical nursing, radiography, sonography, surgical technology, emergency medical services, health information management, and patient admissions coordination.
Freshman Application Contact Ms. Mary Lee Walsh, Dean of Student Services, Piedmont Virginia Community College, 501 College Drive, Charlottesville, VA 22902-7589. *Phone:* 434-961-6540. *Fax:* 434-961-5425. *E-mail:* mwalsh@pvcc.edu. *Website:* http://www.pvcc.edu/.

Rappahannock Community College
Glenns, Virginia

- **State and locally supported** 2-year, founded 1970, part of Virginia Community College System
- **Rural** campus
- **Coed**

Undergraduates 793 full-time, 2,670 part-time.
Academics *Calendar:* semesters. *Degree:* certificates and associate. *Special study options:* academic remediation for entering students, adult/continuing education programs, distance learning, honors programs, internships, off-campus study, part-time degree program, services for LD students, summer session for credit.
Financial Aid Of all full-time matriculated undergraduates who enrolled in 2017, 40 Federal Work-Study jobs (averaging $1015).
Applying *Options:* electronic application, early admission.
Freshman Application Contact Ms. Felicia Packett, Admissions and Records Officer, Rappahannock Community College, 12745 College Drive, Glenns, VA 23149-0287. *Phone:* 804-758-6740. *Toll-free phone:* 800-836-9381. *Website:* http://www.rappahannock.edu/.

Richard Bland College of The College of William and Mary
Petersburg, Virginia

Freshman Application Contact Office of Admissions, Richard Bland College of The College of William and Mary, 8311 Halifax Road, Petersburg, VA 23805. *Phone:* 804-862-6100 Ext. 6249. *E-mail:* apply@rbc.edu. *Website:* http://www.rbc.edu/.

Riverside College of Health Careers
Newport News, Virginia

Admissions Office Contact Riverside College of Health Careers, 316 Main Street, Newport News, VA 23601. *Website:* http://www.riverside.edu/.

Saint Michael College of Allied Health
Alexandria, Virginia

Admissions Office Contact Saint Michael College of Allied Health, 8305 Richmond Highway, Alexandria, VA 22309. *Website:* http://www.stmichaelcollegeva.edu/.

Southside Regional Medical Center Professional Schools
Colonial Heights, Virginia

Admissions Office Contact Southside Regional Medical Center Professional Schools, 430 Clairmont Court, Suite 200, Colonial Heights, VA 23834. *Website:* http://www.srmconline.com/Southside-Regional-Medical-Center/nursingeducation.aspx.

Southside Virginia Community College
Alberta, Virginia

Freshman Application Contact Mr. Brent Richey, Dean of Enrollment Management, Southside Virginia Community College, 109 Campus Drive, Alberta, VA 23821. *Phone:* 434-949-1012. *Fax:* 434-949-7863. *E-mail:* rhina.jones@sv.vccs.edu. *Website:* http://www.southside.edu/.

Southwest Virginia Community College
Richlands, Virginia

- **State-supported** 2-year, founded 1968, part of Virginia Community College System
- **Rural** 100-acre campus
- **Endowment** $20.0 million
- **Coed**

Undergraduates Students come from 7 states and territories; 1 other country; 3% are from out of state; 3% Black or African American, non-Hispanic/Latino; 0.7% Hispanic/Latino; 0.4% Asian, non-Hispanic/Latino; 0.4% American Indian or Alaska Native, non-Hispanic/Latino; 1% Two or more races, non-Hispanic/Latino; 0.3% Race/ethnicity unknown. *Retention:* 55% of full-time freshmen returned.
Faculty *Student/faculty ratio:* 24:1.
Academics *Calendar:* semesters. *Degree:* certificates, diplomas, and associate. *Special study options:* academic remediation for entering students, accelerated degree program, adult/continuing education programs, advanced placement credit, distance learning, double majors, honors programs, internships, off-campus study, part-time degree program, summer session for credit.
Library Southwest Virginia Community College Library. *Books:* 42,207 (physical), 62,566 (digital/electronic); *Serial titles:* 275 (physical), 118,007 (digital/electronic); *Databases:* 118. Students can reserve study rooms.
Student Life *Campus security:* 24-hour emergency response devices and patrols, student patrols, extensive security camera system.
Standardized Tests *Required:* VCCS Math and English Assessments (for admission).
Financial Aid Of all full-time matriculated undergraduates who enrolled in 2017, 150 Federal Work-Study jobs (averaging $1140).
Applying *Options:* electronic application, early admission, deferred entrance. *Required:* high school transcript, interview.
Freshman Application Contact Ms. Dionne Cook, Admissions Counselor, Southwest Virginia Community College, Box SVCC, Richlands, VA 24641. *Phone:* 276-964-7301. *Toll-free phone:* 800-822-7822. *Fax:* 276-964-7716. *E-mail:* dionne.cook@sw.edu. *Website:* http://www.sw.edu/.

Sovah Health School of Health Professions
Danville, Virginia

Admissions Office Contact Sovah Health School of Health Professions, 142 South Main Street, Danville, VA 24541. *Website:* http://www.danvilleregional.com/for-healthcare-professionals/radiologic-technology-program.

Standard Healthcare Services, College of Nursing

Falls Church, Virginia

Admissions Office Contact Standard Healthcare Services, College of Nursing, 7704 Leesburg Pike, Suite 1000, Falls Church, VA 22043. *Website:* http://www.standardcollege.edu/.

Thomas Nelson Community College

Hampton, Virginia

Freshman Application Contact Ms. Geraldine Newson, Senior Admission Specialist, Thomas Nelson Community College, PO Box 9407, Hampton, VA 23670-0407. *Phone:* 757-825-2800. *Fax:* 757-825-2763. *E-mail:* admissions@tncc.edu. *Website:* http://www.tncc.edu/.

Tidewater Community College

Norfolk, Virginia

- **State-supported** 2-year, founded 1968, part of Virginia Community College System
- **Suburban** 520-acre campus
- **Endowment** $7.1 million
- **Coed,** 20,941 undergraduate students, 35% full-time, 60% women, 40% men

Undergraduates 7,375 full-time, 13,566 part-time. 17% are from out of state; 30% Black or African American, non-Hispanic/Latino; 9% Hispanic/Latino; 4% Asian, non-Hispanic/Latino; 0.5% Native Hawaiian or other Pacific Islander, non-Hispanic/Latino; 0.4% American Indian or Alaska Native, non-Hispanic/Latino; 6% Two or more races, non-Hispanic/Latino; 1% Race/ethnicity unknown; 0.7% international. *Retention:* 54% of full-time freshmen returned.

Faculty *Total:* 1,141, 27% full-time. *Student/faculty ratio:* 20:1.

Majors Accounting; administrative assistant and secretarial science; advertising; automobile/automotive mechanics technology; biological and physical sciences; business administration and management; civil engineering; commercial and advertising art; computer programming; drafting and design technology; education; electrical, electronic and communications engineering technology; engineering; finance; fine/studio arts; graphic design; horticultural science; information technology; interior design; kindergarten/preschool education; legal assistant/paralegal; liberal arts and sciences/liberal studies; marketing/marketing management; music; registered nursing/registered nurse.

Academics *Calendar:* semesters. *Degree:* certificates and associate. *Special study options:* academic remediation for entering students, accelerated degree program, adult/continuing education programs, advanced placement credit, cooperative education, distance learning, English as a second language, honors programs, independent study, internships, off-campus study, part-time degree program, services for LD students, summer session for credit.

Library Main Library plus 5 others.

Student Life *Housing:* college housing not available. *Activities and Organizations:* drama/theater group, student-run newspaper. *Campus security:* 24-hour patrols. *Student services:* personal/psychological counseling, women's center.

Financial Aid Of all full-time matriculated undergraduates who enrolled in 2017, 64 Federal Work-Study jobs (averaging $2000).

Applying *Options:* electronic application, early admission, deferred entrance. *Application deadlines:* rolling (freshmen), rolling (transfers). *Notification:* continuous (freshmen), continuous (transfers).

Admissions Office Contact Tidewater Community College, 121 College Place, Norfolk, VA 23510.
Website: http://www.tcc.edu/.

Virginia Highlands Community College

Abingdon, Virginia

Freshman Application Contact Karen Cheers, Acting Director of Admissions, Records, and Financial Aid, Virginia Highlands Community College, PO Box 828, 100 VHCC Drive Abingdon, Abingdon, VA 24212. *Phone:* 276-739-2490. *Toll-free phone:* 877-207-6115. *E-mail:* kcheers@vhcc.edu. *Website:* http://www.vhcc.edu/.

Virginia Western Community College

Roanoke, Virginia

Freshman Application Contact Admissions Office, Virginia Western Community College, PO Box 14007, Roanoke, VA 24038. *Phone:* 540-857-7231. *Website:* http://www.virginiawestern.edu/.

Wave Leadership College

Virginia Beach, Virginia

Admissions Office Contact Wave Leadership College, 1000 North Great Neck Road, Virginia Beach, VA 23454. *Website:* http://www.wavecollege.com/.

Wytheville Community College

Wytheville, Virginia

- **State-supported** 2-year, founded 1963, part of Virginia Community College System
- **Rural** 141-acre campus
- **Coed**

Undergraduates 940 full-time, 1,805 part-time. Students come from 9 states and territories; 2% are from out of state; 4% Black or African American, non-Hispanic/Latino; 2% Hispanic/Latino; 0.8% Asian, non-Hispanic/Latino; 0.1% Native Hawaiian or other Pacific Islander, non-Hispanic/Latino; 0.4% American Indian or Alaska Native, non-Hispanic/Latino; 4% Two or more races, non-Hispanic/Latino; 0.2% Race/ethnicity unknown. *Retention:* 62% of full-time freshmen returned.

Faculty *Student/faculty ratio:* 23:1.

Academics *Calendar:* semesters. *Degree:* certificates, diplomas, and associate. *Special study options:* academic remediation for entering students, adult/continuing education programs, advanced placement credit, distance learning, external degree program, independent study, part-time degree program, services for LD students, summer session for credit.

Library Wytheville Community College Library. *Books:* 33,041 (physical), 51,770 (digital/electronic); *Serial titles:* 3,319 (physical), 3,418 (digital/electronic); *Databases:* 101. Students can reserve study rooms.

Student Life *Campus security:* 24-hour emergency response devices and patrols.

Financial Aid Of all full-time matriculated undergraduates who enrolled in 2017, 125 Federal Work-Study jobs (averaging $2592).

Applying *Options:* electronic application, early admission. *Required:* high school transcript. *Required for some:* interview.

Freshman Application Contact Wytheville Community College, 1000 East Main Street, Wytheville, VA 24382-3308. *Phone:* 276-223-4701. *Toll-free phone:* 800-468-1195. *Website:* http://www.wcc.vccs.edu/.

WASHINGTON

Bates Technical College

Tacoma, Washington

Director of Admissions Director of Admissions, Bates Technical College, 1101 South Yakima Avenue, Tacoma, WA 98405-4895. *Phone:* 253-680-7000. *E-mail:* registration@bates.ctc.edu. *Website:* http://www.bates.ctc.edu/.

Bellevue College

Bellevue, Washington

Freshman Application Contact Morenika Jacobs, Associate Dean of Enrollment Services, Bellevue College, 3000 Landerholm Circle, SE, Bellevue, WA 98007-6484. *Phone:* 425-564-2205. *Fax:* 425-564-4065. *Website:* http://www.bellevuecollege.edu/.

Bellingham Technical College

Bellingham, Washington

Freshman Application Contact Bellingham Technical College, 3028 Lindbergh Avenue, Bellingham, WA 98225. *Phone:* 360-752-8324. *Website:* http://www.btc.edu/.

Big Bend Community College

Moses Lake, Washington

Freshman Application Contact Candis Lacher, Associate Vice President of Student Services, Big Bend Community College, 7662 Chanute Street NE, Moses Lake, WA 98837. *Phone:* 509-793-2061. *Toll-free phone:* 877-745-1212. *Fax:* 509-793-6243. *E-mail:* admissions@bigbend.edu. *Website:* http://www.bigbend.edu/.

Carrington College–Spokane

Spokane, Washington

Freshman Application Contact Carrington College–Spokane, 10102 East Knox Avenue, Suite 200, Spokane, WA 99206. *Website:* http://www.carrington.edu/.

Cascadia College

Bothell, Washington

Freshman Application Contact Ms. Erin Blakeney, Dean for Student Success, Cascadia College, 18345 Campus Way, NE, Bothell, WA 98011. *Phone:* 425-352-8000. *Fax:* 425-352-8137. *E-mail:* admissions@cascadia.edu. *Website:* http://www.cascadia.edu/.

Centralia College

Centralia, Washington

Freshman Application Contact Admissions Office, Centralia College, Centralia, WA 98531. *Phone:* 360-736-9391 Ext. 221. *Fax:* 360-330-7503. *E-mail:* admissions@centralia.edu. *Website:* http://www.centralia.edu/.

Clark College

Vancouver, Washington

- **State-supported** primarily 2-year, founded 1933, part of Washington State Board for Community and Technical Colleges
- **Urban** 101-acre campus with easy access to Portland
- **Endowment** $61.0 million
- **Coed**

Undergraduates 5,035 full-time, 5,442 part-time. 4% are from out of state; 2% Black or African American, non-Hispanic/Latino; 9% Hispanic/Latino; 4% Asian, non-Hispanic/Latino; 0.1% Native Hawaiian or other Pacific Islander, non-Hispanic/Latino; 0.6% American Indian or Alaska Native, non-Hispanic/Latino; 8% Two or more races, non-Hispanic/Latino; 6% Race/ethnicity unknown; 1% international; 3% transferred in.
Faculty *Student/faculty ratio:* 24:1.
Academics *Calendar:* quarters. *Degrees:* certificates, diplomas, associate, and bachelor's. *Special study options:* academic remediation for entering students, adult/continuing education programs, cooperative education, distance learning, English as a second language, honors programs, internships, part-time degree program, services for LD students, summer session for credit. *ROTC:* Army (c), Air Force (c).
Library Lewis D. Cannell Library. Students can reserve study rooms.
Student Life *Campus security:* 24-hour patrols, late-night transport/escort service, security staff during hours of operation.
Applying *Options:* electronic application, early admission, deferred entrance. *Application fee:* $25.
Freshman Application Contact Ms. Vanessa Watkins, Associate Director of Entry Services, Clark College, Vancouver, WA 98663. *Phone:* 360-992-2308. *Fax:* 360-992-2867. *E-mail:* admissions@clark.edu. *Website:* http://www.clark.edu/.

Clover Park Technical College

Lakewood, Washington

Director of Admissions Ms. Judy Richardson, Registrar, Clover Park Technical College, 4500 Steilacoom Boulevard, SW, Lakewood, WA 98499. *Phone:* 253-589-5570. *Website:* http://www.cptc.edu/.

Columbia Basin College

Pasco, Washington

Freshman Application Contact Admissions Department, Columbia Basin College, 2600 North 20th Avenue, Pasco, WA 99301-3397. *Phone:* 509-542-4524. *Fax:* 509-544-2023. *E-mail:* admissions@columbiabasin.edu. *Website:* http://www.columbiabasin.edu/.

Edmonds Community College

Lynnwood, Washington

Freshman Application Contact Ms. Nancy Froemming, Enrollment Services Office Manager, Edmonds Community College, 20000 68th Avenue West, Lynwood, WA 98036-5999. *Phone:* 425-640-1853. *Fax:* 425-640-1159. *E-mail:* nanci.froemming@edcc.edu. *Website:* http://www.edcc.edu/.

Everett Community College

Everett, Washington

Freshman Application Contact Ms. Linda Baca, Entry Services Manager, Everett Community College, 2000 Tower Street, Everett, WA 98201-1327. *Phone:* 425-388-9219. *Fax:* 425-388-9173. *E-mail:* admissions@everettcc.edu. *Website:* http://www.everettcc.edu/.

Grays Harbor College

Aberdeen, Washington

Freshman Application Contact Ms. Brenda Dell, Admissions Officer, Grays Harbor College, 1620 Edward P. Smith Drive, Aberdeen, WA 98520. *Phone:* 360-532-4216. *Toll-free phone:* 800-562-4830. *Website:* http://www.ghc.edu/.

Green River College

Auburn, Washington

Freshman Application Contact Ms. Peggy Morgan, Program Support Supervisor, Green River College, 12401 Southeast 320th Street, Auburn, WA 98092-3699. *Phone:* 253-833-9111. *Fax:* 253-288-3454. *Website:* http://www.greenriver.edu/.

Highline College

Des Moines, Washington

Freshman Application Contact Ms. Michelle Kuwasaki, Director of Admissions, Highline College, 2400 South 240th Street, Des Moines, WA 98198-9800. *Phone:* 206-878-3710 Ext. 9800. *Website:* http://www.highline.edu/.

Lake Washington Institute of Technology

Kirkland, Washington

Freshman Application Contact Shawn Miller, Registrar, Enrollment Services, Lake Washington Institute of Technology, 11605 132nd Avenue NE, Kirkland, WA 98034-8506. *Phone:* 425-739-8104. *E-mail:* info@lwtc.edu. *Website:* http://www.lwtech.edu/.

Lower Columbia College

Longview, Washington

Freshman Application Contact Ms. Nichole Seroshek, Director of Registration, Lower Columbia College, 1600 Maple Street, Longview, WA 98632. *Phone:* 360-442-2372. *Toll-free phone:* 866-900-2311. *Fax:* 360-442-2379. *E-mail:* registration@lowercolumbia.edu. *Website:* http://www.lowercolumbia.edu/.

North Seattle College

Seattle, Washington

Freshman Application Contact Ms. Betsy Abts, Registrar, North Seattle College, Seattle, WA 98103-3599. *Phone:* 206-934-3663. *Fax:* 206-934-3671. *E-mail:* arrc@seattlecolleges.edu. *Website:* http://www.northseattle.edu/.

Northwest Indian College

Bellingham, Washington

Freshman Application Contact Office of Admissions, Northwest Indian College, 2522 Kwina Road, Bellingham, WA 98226. *Phone:* 360-676-2772. *Toll-free phone:* 866-676-2772. *Fax:* 360-392-4333. *E-mail:* admissions@nwic.edu. *Website:* http://www.nwic.edu/.

Northwest School of Wooden Boatbuilding

Port Hadlock, Washington

Freshman Application Contact Northwest School of Wooden Boatbuilding, 42 North Water Street, Port Hadlock, WA 98339. *Phone:* 360-385-4948 Ext. 305. *Website:* http://www.nwswb.edu/.

Olympic College
Bremerton, Washington

Freshman Application Contact Ms. Nora Downard, Program Manager, Olympic College, 1600 Chester Avenue, Bremerton, WA 98337-1699. *Phone:* 360-475-7445. *Toll-free phone:* 800-259-6718. *Fax:* 360-475-7202. *E-mail:* ndownard@olympic.edu. *Website:* http://www.olympic.edu/.

Peninsula College
Port Angeles, Washington

Freshman Application Contact Ms. Pauline Marvin, Peninsula College, 1502 East Lauridsen Boulevard, Port Angeles, WA 98362. *Phone:* 360-417-6596. *Toll-free phone:* 877-452-9277. *Fax:* 360-457-8100. *E-mail:* admissions@pencol.edu. *Website:* http://www.pencol.edu/.

Perry Technical Institute
Yakima, Washington

Admissions Office Contact Perry Technical Institute, 2011 West Washington Avenue, Yakima, WA 98903-1296. *Website:* http://www.perrytech.edu/.

Pierce College Fort Steilacoom
Lakewood, Washington

Freshman Application Contact Admissions Office, Pierce College Fort Steilacoom, 9401 Farwest Drive SW, Lakewood, WA 98498. *Phone:* 253-964-6501. *E-mail:* admiss1@pierce.ctc.edu. *Website:* http://www.pierce.ctc.edu/.

Pierce College Puyallup
Puyallup, Washington

Freshman Application Contact Pierce College Puyallup, 1601 39th Avenue Southeast, Puyallup, WA 98374. *Phone:* 253-840-8400. *Website:* http://www.pierce.ctc.edu/.

Pima Medical Institute
Renton, Washington

Freshman Application Contact Pima Medical Institute, 555 South Renton Village Place, Renton, WA 98057. *Phone:* 425-228-9600. *Toll-free phone:* 800-477-PIMA. *Website:* http://www.pmi.edu/.

Pima Medical Institute
Seattle, Washington

Freshman Application Contact Admissions Office, Pima Medical Institute, 9709 Third Avenue NE, Suite 400, Seattle, WA 98115. *Phone:* 206-322-6100. *Toll-free phone:* 800-477-PIMA. *Website:* http://www.pmi.edu/.

Renton Technical College
Renton, Washington

- **State-supported** primarily 2-year, founded 1942, part of Washington State Board for Community and Technical Colleges
- **Suburban** 30-acre campus with easy access to Seattle
- **Endowment** $837,103
- **Coed,** 3,546 undergraduate students, 35% full-time, 33% women, 67% men

Undergraduates 1,245 full-time, 2,301 part-time. 16% Black or African American, non-Hispanic/Latino; 13% Hispanic/Latino; 19% Asian, non-Hispanic/Latino; 1% Native Hawaiian or other Pacific Islander, non-Hispanic/Latino; 0.5% American Indian or Alaska Native, non-Hispanic/Latino; 6% Two or more races, non-Hispanic/Latino; 6% Race/ethnicity unknown; 0.9% international.

Faculty *Total:* 242, 29% full-time. *Student/faculty ratio:* 16:1.

Majors Accounting and business/management; anesthesiologist assistant; appliance installation and repair technology; autobody/collision and repair technology; automobile/automotive mechanics technology; building/property maintenance; business automation/technology/data entry; civil drafting and CAD/CADD; computer science; computer systems networking and telecommunications; construction management; culinary arts; dental assisting; drafting and design technology; early childhood education; heating, air conditioning, ventilation and refrigeration maintenance technology; industrial mechanics and maintenance technology; legal administrative assistant/secretary; machine tool technology; massage therapy; medical administrative assistant and medical secretary; medical/clinical assistant; medical insurance coding; musical instrument fabrication and repair; ophthalmic technology; pharmacy technician; registered nursing/registered nurse; surgical technology; surveying technology; welding technology.

Academics *Calendar:* quarters. *Degrees:* certificates, diplomas, associate, and bachelor's. *Special study options:* academic remediation for entering students, adult/continuing education programs, advanced placement credit, cooperative education, distance learning, English as a second language, internships, off-campus study, part-time degree program, services for LD students, summer session for credit.

Library Renton Technical College Library. *Books:* 24,464 (physical), 64,437 (digital/electronic); *Serial titles:* 354 (physical), 19,981 (digital/electronic); *Databases:* 22. Weekly public service hours: 62.

Student Life *Housing:* college housing not available. *Campus security:* patrols by security, security system. *Student services:* personal/psychological counseling, veterans affairs office.

Standardized Tests *Required for some:* ACT ASSET, CLEP, ACCUPLACER, DSP.

Applying *Options:* electronic application, early admission. *Application fee:* $30. *Required for some:* essay or personal statement, high school transcript, interview. *Application deadlines:* rolling (freshmen), rolling (transfers). *Notification:* continuous (freshmen), continuous (transfers).

Director of Admissions Patrick Brown, Director of Enrollment Services/Registrar, Renton Technical College, 3000 NE Fourth Street, Renton, WA 98056. *Phone:* 425-2352352 Ext. 5537. *E-mail:* pbrown@rtc.edu. *Website:* http://www.rtc.edu/.

Seattle Central College
Seattle, Washington

Freshman Application Contact Admissions Office, Seattle Central College, 1701 Broadway, Seattle, WA 98122-2400. *Phone:* 206-587-5450. *Website:* http://www.seattlecentral.edu/.

Shoreline Community College
Shoreline, Washington

Freshman Application Contact Shoreline Community College, 16101 Greenwood Avenue North, Shoreline, WA 98133-5696. *Phone:* 206-546-4613. *Website:* http://www.shoreline.edu/.

Skagit Valley College
Mount Vernon, Washington

Freshman Application Contact Ms. Karen Marie Bade, Admissions and Recruitment Coordinator, Skagit Valley College, 2405 College Way, Mount Vernon, WA 98273-5899. *Phone:* 360-416-7620. *E-mail:* karenmarie.bade@skagit.edu. *Website:* http://www.skagit.edu/.

South Puget Sound Community College
Olympia, Washington

Freshman Application Contact Ms. Heidi Dearborn, South Puget Sound Community College, 2011 Mottman Road, SW, Olympia, WA 98512-6292. *Phone:* 360-754-7711 Ext. 5358. *E-mail:* hdearborn@spcc.edu. *Website:* http://www.spscc.edu/.

South Seattle College
Seattle, Washington

Director of Admissions Ms. Kim Manderbach, Dean of Student Services/Registration, South Seattle College, 6000 16th Avenue, SW, Seattle, WA 98106-1499. *Phone:* 206-764-5378. *Fax:* 206-764-7947. *E-mail:* kimmanderb@sccd.ctc.edu. *Website:* http://southseattle.edu/.

Spokane Community College
Spokane, Washington

Freshman Application Contact Ann Hightower-Chavez, Researcher, District Institutional Research, Spokane Community College, Spokane, WA 99217-5399. *Phone:* 509-434-5242. *Toll-free phone:* 800-248-5644. *Fax:* 509-434-5249. *E-mail:* mlee@ccs.spokane.edu. *Website:* http://www.scc.spokane.edu/.

Spokane Falls Community College

Spokane, Washington

Freshman Application Contact Admissions Office, Spokane Falls Community College, Admissions MS 3011, 3410 West Fort George Wright Drive, Spokane, WA 99224. *Phone:* 509-533-3401. *Toll-free phone:* 888-509-7944. *Fax:* 509-533-3852. *Website:* http://www.spokanefalls.edu/.

Tacoma Community College

Tacoma, Washington

Freshman Application Contact Enrollment Services, Tacoma Community College, 6501 South 19th Street, Tacoma, WA 98466. *Phone:* 253-566-5325. *Fax:* 253-566-6034. *Website:* http://www.tacomacc.edu/.

Walla Walla Community College

Walla Walla, Washington

Freshman Application Contact Walla Walla Community College, 500 Tausick Way, Walla Walla, WA 99362-9267. *Phone:* 509-522-2500. *Toll-free phone:* 877-992-9922. *Website:* http://www.wwcc.edu/.

Wenatchee Valley College

Wenatchee, Washington

Freshman Application Contact Wenatchee Valley College, 1300 Fifth Street, Wenatchee, WA 98801-1799. *Phone:* 509-682-6835. *Toll-free phone:* 877-982-4968. *Website:* http://www.wvc.edu/.

Whatcom Community College

Bellingham, Washington

Freshman Application Contact Entry and Advising Center, Whatcom Community College, 237 West Kellogg Road, Bellingham, WA 98226-8003. *Phone:* 360-676-2170. *Fax:* 360-676-2171. *E-mail:* admit@whatcom.ctc.edu. *Website:* http://www.whatcom.ctc.edu/.

Yakima Valley Community College

Yakima, Washington

Freshman Application Contact Ms. Denise Anderson, Registrar and Director for Enrollment Services, Yakima Valley Community College, PO Box 1647, Yakima, WA 98907-1647. *Phone:* 509-574-4702. *Fax:* 509-574-6879. *E-mail:* admis@yvcc.edu. *Website:* http://www.yvcc.edu/.

WEST VIRGINIA

Blue Ridge Community and Technical College

Martinsburg, West Virginia

- **State-supported** 2-year, founded 1974, part of Community and Technical College System of West Virginia
- **Small-town** 46-acre campus
- **Coed,** 6,273 undergraduate students, 18% full-time, 64% women, 36% men

Undergraduates 1,113 full-time, 5,160 part-time. 10% are from out of state; 6% Black or African American, non-Hispanic/Latino; 2% Hispanic/Latino; 2% Asian, non-Hispanic/Latino; 0.3% Native Hawaiian or other Pacific Islander, non-Hispanic/Latino; 0.3% American Indian or Alaska Native, non-Hispanic/Latino; 2% Two or more races, non-Hispanic/Latino; 0.2% Race/ethnicity unknown.

Freshmen *Admission:* 371 enrolled.

Faculty *Total:* 200, 42% full-time, 12% with terminal degrees. *Student/faculty ratio:* 22:1.

Majors Accounting; allied health and medical assisting services related; automation engineer technology; baking and pastry arts; business administration and management; business administration, management and operations related; clinical/medical laboratory technology; computer and information systems security; criminal justice/safety; culinary arts; data entry/microcomputer applications related; electrical and electronic engineering technologies related; emergency medical technology (EMT paramedic); general studies; information technology; legal assistant/paralegal; liberal arts and sciences/liberal studies; medical/clinical assistant; multi/interdisciplinary studies related; operations management; physical therapy technology; registered nursing/registered nurse; restaurant, culinary, and catering management; science technologies related.

Academics *Calendar:* semesters. *Degree:* certificates and associate. *Special study options:* academic remediation for entering students, accelerated degree program, adult/continuing education programs, advanced placement credit, double majors, English as a second language, independent study, internships, part-time degree program, services for LD students.

Student Life *Housing:* college housing not available. *Activities and Organizations:* drama/theater group, Student Leadership Academy, Drama Club, Phi Theta Kappa, Phi Beta Lambda, Student Nurses Association. *Campus security:* late-night transport/escort service. *Student services:* personal/psychological counseling.

Standardized Tests *Recommended:* SAT and SAT Subject Tests or ACT (for admission).

Applying *Options:* electronic application, deferred entrance. *Application fee:* $25. *Required:* high school transcript. *Required for some:* interview.

Freshman Application Contact Brenda K. Neal, Dean of Students, Blue Ridge Community and Technical College, 13650 Apple Harvest Drive, Martinsburg, WV 25403. *Phone:* 304-260-4380 Ext. 2109. *Fax:* 304-260-4376. *E-mail:* bneal@blueridgectc.edu. *Website:* http://www.blueridgectc.edu/.

BridgeValley Community and Technical College

Montgomery, West Virginia

Director of Admissions Ms. Lisa Graham, Director of Admissions, BridgeValley Community and Technical College, 619 2nd Avenue, Montgomery, WV 25136. *Phone:* 304-442-3167. *Website:* http://www.bridgevalley.edu/.

BridgeValley Community and Technical College

South Charleston, West Virginia

Freshman Application Contact Mr. Bryce Casto, Vice President, Student Affairs, BridgeValley Community and Technical College, 2001 Union Carbide Drive, South Charleston, WV 25303. *Phone:* 304-766-3140. *Fax:* 304-766-4158. *E-mail:* castosb@wvstateu.edu. *Website:* http://www.bridgevalley.edu/.

Eastern West Virginia Community and Technical College

Moorefield, West Virginia

Freshman Application Contact Learner Support Services, Eastern West Virginia Community and Technical College, HC 65 Box 402, Moorefield, WV 26836. *Phone:* 304-434-8000. *Toll-free phone:* 877-982-2322. *Fax:* 304-434-7000. *E-mail:* askeast@eastern.wvnet.edu. *Website:* http://www.eastern.wvnet.edu/.

Huntington Junior College

Huntington, West Virginia

Director of Admissions Mr. James Garrett, Educational Services Director, Huntington Junior College, 900 Fifth Avenue, Huntington, WV 25701-2004. *Phone:* 304-697-7550. *Toll-free phone:* 800-344-4522. *Website:* http://www.huntingtonjuniorcollege.com/.

Martinsburg College

Martinsburg, West Virginia

Admissions Office Contact Martinsburg College, 341 Aikens Center, Martinsburg, WV 25404. *Website:* http://www.martinsburgcollege.edu/.

Mountain State College

Parkersburg, West Virginia

Freshman Application Contact Ms. Judith Sutton, President, Mountain State College, 1508 Spring Street, Parkersburg, WV 26101-3993. *Phone:* 304-485-5487. *Toll-free phone:* 800-841-0201. *Fax:* 304-485-3524. *E-mail:* jsutton@msc.edu. *Website:* http://www.msc.edu/.

Mountwest Community & Technical College

Huntington, West Virginia

Freshman Application Contact Dr. Tammy Johnson, Admissions Director, Mountwest Community & Technical College, 1 John Marshall Drive, Huntington, WV 25755. *Phone:* 304-696-3160. *Toll-free phone:* 866-676-5533. *Fax:* 304-696-3135. *E-mail:* admissions@marshall.edu. *Website:* http://www.mctc.edu/.

New River Community and Technical College

Beaver, West Virginia

Director of Admissions Dr. Allen B. Withers, Vice President, Student Services, New River Community and Technical College, 280 University Drive, Beaver, WV 25813. *Phone:* 304-929-5011. *Toll-free phone:* 866-349-3739. *E-mail:* awithers@newriver.edu. *Website:* http://www.newriver.edu/.

Pierpont Community & Technical College

Fairmont, West Virginia

Freshman Application Contact Mr. Steve Leadman, Director of Admissions and Recruiting, Pierpont Community & Technical College, 1201 Locust Avenue, Fairmont, WV 26554. *Phone:* 304-367-4892. *Toll-free phone:* 800-641-5678. *Fax:* 304-367-4789. *Website:* http://www.pierpont.edu/.

Potomac State College of West Virginia University

Keyser, West Virginia

- **State-supported** primarily 2-year, founded 1901, part of West Virginia Higher Education Policy Commission
- **Small-town** 18-acre campus
- **Coed,** 1,340 undergraduate students, 76% full-time, 56% women, 44% men

Undergraduates 1,018 full-time, 322 part-time. 20% are from out of state; 8% Black or African American, non-Hispanic/Latino; 3% Hispanic/Latino; 1% Asian, non-Hispanic/Latino; 0.1% Native Hawaiian or other Pacific Islander, non-Hispanic/Latino; 0.2% American Indian or Alaska Native, non-Hispanic/Latino; 4% Two or more races, non-Hispanic/Latino; 1% Race/ethnicity unknown; 0.4% international; 4% transferred in; 52% live on campus. *Retention:* 39% of full-time freshmen returned.

Freshmen *Admission:* 2,284 applied, 1,726 admitted, 537 enrolled. *Average high school GPA:* 3.1.

Faculty *Total:* 80, 61% full-time, 25% with terminal degrees. *Student/faculty ratio:* 22:1.

Majors Administrative assistant and secretarial science; agricultural and extension education; agricultural business and management; agriculture; agriculture and agriculture operations related; agronomy and crop science; animal sciences; biology/biological sciences; business administration and management; business automation/technology/data entry; chemistry; civil engineering; communication; computer and information sciences; criminal justice/safety; criminology; data entry/microcomputer applications related; early childhood education; economics; electrical and electronics engineering; elementary education; English; forensic science and technology; forest resources production and management; geology/earth science; history; horse husbandry/equine science and management; horticultural science; hospitality administration; journalism; liberal arts and sciences/liberal studies; mathematics; mechanical engineering; medical/clinical assistant; modern languages; parks, recreation and leisure facilities management; physical education teaching and coaching; physics; political science and government; pre-dentistry studies; pre-law studies; premedical studies; prenursing studies; pre-occupational therapy; pre-pharmacy studies; pre-physical therapy; pre-veterinary studies; psychology; registered nursing/registered nurse; secondary education; social work; sociology; wildlife, fish and wildlands science and management; wood science and wood products/pulp and paper technology.

Academics *Calendar:* semesters. *Degrees:* associate and bachelor's. *Special study options:* academic remediation for entering students, adult/continuing education programs, advanced placement credit, cooperative education, distance learning, double majors, honors programs, independent study, internships, part-time degree program, services for LD students, study abroad, summer session for credit.

Library Mary F. Shipper Library. *Books:* 7,011 (physical), 617,383 (digital/electronic); *Serial titles:* 19 (physical), 93,783 (digital/electronic); *Databases:* 687.

Student Life *Housing:* on-campus residence required through sophomore year. *Options:* coed. Campus housing is university owned. Freshman applicants given priority for college housing. *Activities and Organizations:* drama/theater group, student-run newspaper, choral group, Agriculture and Forestry Club, Black Student Alliance, Gamers and Geeks Club, Campus and Community Ministries. *Campus security:* 24-hour patrols, late-night transport/escort service, controlled dormitory access. *Student services:* health clinic, personal/psychological counseling, veterans affairs office.

Athletics Member NJCAA. *Intercollegiate sports:* basketball W(s), cross-country running W(s), lacrosse W(s), soccer W, softball W(s), volleyball W(s). *Intramural sports:* basketball M, football M, soccer M, softball M, table tennis M, ultimate Frisbee M, volleyball M.

Financial Aid Of all full-time matriculated undergraduates who enrolled in 2017, 1,059 applied for aid, 843 were judged to have need, 73 had their need fully met. In 2017, 57 non-need-based awards were made. *Average percent of need met:* 65%. *Average financial aid package:* $4355. *Average need-based loan:* $3039. *Average need-based gift aid:* $3418. *Average non-need-based aid:* $1907. *Average indebtedness upon graduation:* $18,208.

Applying *Options:* electronic application. *Required:* high school transcript. *Application deadlines:* rolling (freshmen), rolling (transfers).

Freshman Application Contact Ms. Beth Little, Director of Enrollment Services, Potomac State College of West Virginia University, 75 Arnold Street, Keyser, WV 26726. *Phone:* 304-788-6820. *Toll-free phone:* 800-262-7332 Ext. 6820. *Fax:* 304-788-6939. *E-mail:* go2psc@mail.wvu.edu. *Website:* http://www.potomacstatecollege.edu/.

Southern West Virginia Community and Technical College

Mount Gay, West Virginia

Freshman Application Contact Mr. Roy Simmons, Registrar, Southern West Virginia Community and Technical College, PO Box 2900, Mt. Gay, WV 25637. *Phone:* 304-792-7160 Ext. 120. *Fax:* 304-792-7096. *E-mail:* admissions@southern.wvnet.edu. *Website:* http://southernwv.edu/.

Valley College

Martinsburg, West Virginia

Freshman Application Contact Ms. Gail Kennedy, Admissions Director, Valley College, 287 Aikens Center, Martinsburg, WV 25404. *Phone:* 304-263-0878. *Fax:* 304-263-2413. *E-mail:* gkennedy@vct.edu. *Website:* http://www.valley.edu/.

West Virginia Junior College–Bridgeport

Bridgeport, West Virginia

Freshman Application Contact Ms. Kristen Kirk, High School Admissions Representative, West Virginia Junior College–Bridgeport, 176 Thompson Drive, Bridgeport, WV 26330. *Phone:* 304-842-4007. *Toll-free phone:* 800-470-5627. *Fax:* 304-842-8191. *E-mail:* kkirk@wvjc.edu. *Website:* http://www.wvjc.edu/.

West Virginia Junior College–Charleston

Charleston, West Virginia

Freshman Application Contact West Virginia Junior College–Charleston, 1000 Virginia Street East, Charleston, WV 25301-2817. *Phone:* 304-345-2820. *Toll-free phone:* 800-924-5208. *Website:* http://www.wvjc.edu/.

West Virginia Junior College–Morgantown

Morgantown, West Virginia

Freshman Application Contact Admissions Office, West Virginia Junior College–Morgantown, 148 Willey Street, Morgantown, WV 26505-5521. *Phone:* 304-296-8282. *Website:* http://www.wvjcmorgantown.edu/.

West Virginia Northern Community College

Wheeling, West Virginia

Freshman Application Contact Mrs. Janet Fike, Vice President of Student Services, West Virginia Northern Community College, 1704 Market Street, Wheeling, WV 26003. *Phone:* 304-214-8837. *E-mail:* jfike@northern.wvnet.edu. *Website:* http://www.wvncc.edu/.

West Virginia University at Parkersburg

Parkersburg, West Virginia

Freshman Application Contact Christine Post, Associate Dean of Enrollment Management, West Virginia University at Parkersburg, 300 Campus Drive, Parkersburg, WV 26104. *Phone:* 304-424-8223 Ext. 223. *Toll-free phone:* 800-WVA-WVUP. *Fax:* 304-424-8332. *E-mail:* christine.post@mail.wvu.edu. *Website:* http://www.wvup.edu/.

WISCONSIN

Blackhawk Technical College

Janesville, Wisconsin

Freshman Application Contact Blackhawk Technical College, 6004 South County Road G, Janesville, WI 53546-9458. *Phone:* 608-757-7713. *Website:* http://www.blackhawk.edu/.

Bryant & Stratton College–Bayshore Campus

Glendale, Wisconsin

Admissions Office Contact Bryant & Stratton College–Bayshore Campus, 500 West Silver Spring Drive, Bayshore Town Center, Suite K340, Glendale, WI 53217. *Website:* http://www.bryantstratton.edu/.

Bryant & Stratton College–Milwaukee Campus

Milwaukee, Wisconsin

Freshman Application Contact Mr. Dan Basile, Director of Admissions, Bryant & Stratton College–Milwaukee Campus, 310 West Wisconsin Avenue, Suite 500 East, Milwaukee, WI 53203-2214. *Phone:* 414-276-5200. *Website:* http://www.bryantstratton.edu/.

Chippewa Valley Technical College

Eau Claire, Wisconsin

- **District-supported** 2-year, founded 1912, part of Wisconsin Technical College System
- **Suburban** 255-acre campus
- **Coed**

Undergraduates 2,129 full-time, 5,005 part-time. 1% Black or African American, non-Hispanic/Latino; 2% Hispanic/Latino; 4% Asian, non-Hispanic/Latino; 0.2% Native Hawaiian or other Pacific Islander, non-Hispanic/Latino; 0.7% American Indian or Alaska Native, non-Hispanic/Latino; 2% Two or more races, non-Hispanic/Latino; 5% Race/ethnicity unknown; 5% transferred in. *Retention:* 60% of full-time freshmen returned.

Faculty *Student/faculty ratio:* 13:1.

Academics *Calendar:* semesters. *Degree:* certificates, diplomas, and associate. *Special study options:* academic remediation for entering students, accelerated degree program, adult/continuing education programs, advanced placement credit, cooperative education, distance learning, double majors, English as a second language, honors programs, independent study, internships, part-time degree program, services for LD students, student-designed majors, summer session for credit.

Library The Learning Center. *Books:* 10,758 (physical), 158,463 (digital/electronic); *Serial titles:* 110 (physical), 3,589 (digital/electronic); *Databases:* 116. Weekly public service hours: 66; students can reserve study rooms.

Student Life *Campus security:* 24-hour emergency response devices, late-night transport/escort service, security cameras.

Financial Aid Of all full-time matriculated undergraduates who enrolled in 2017, 218 Federal Work-Study jobs (averaging $875).

Applying *Options:* electronic application, early admission, deferred entrance. *Application fee:* $30.

Freshman Application Contact Admissions Office, Chippewa Valley Technical College, 620 W. Clairemont Avenue, Eau Claire, WI 54701. *Phone:* 715-833-6200. *Toll-free phone:* 800-547-2882. *Fax:* 715-833-6470. *E-mail:* infocenter@cvtc.edu. *Website:* http://www.cvtc.edu/.

College of Menominee Nation

Keshena, Wisconsin

Director of Admissions Tessa James, Admissions Coordinator, College of Menominee Nation, PO Box 1179, Keshena, WI 54135. *Phone:* 715-799-5600 Ext. 3053. *Toll-free phone:* 800-567-2344. *E-mail:* tjames@menominee.edu. *Website:* http://www.menominee.edu/.

Fox Valley Technical College

Appleton, Wisconsin

- **State and locally supported** 2-year, founded 1967, part of Wisconsin Technical College System
- **Suburban** 100-acre campus
- **Endowment** $3.8 million
- **Coed**
- 69% of applicants were admitted

Undergraduates 2,186 full-time, 9,472 part-time. Students come from 13 states and territories; 5 other countries; 0.7% are from out of state; 2% Black or African American, non-Hispanic/Latino; 4% Hispanic/Latino; 4% Asian, non-Hispanic/Latino; 0.2% Native Hawaiian or other Pacific Islander, non-Hispanic/Latino; 0.9% American Indian or Alaska Native, non-Hispanic/Latino; 1% Two or more races, non-Hispanic/Latino; 12% Race/ethnicity unknown; 0.6% international.

Faculty *Student/faculty ratio:* 11:1.

Academics *Calendar:* semesters. *Degree:* certificates, diplomas, and associate. *Special study options:* academic remediation for entering students, accelerated degree program, advanced placement credit, cooperative education, distance learning, double majors, English as a second language, independent study, internships, off-campus study, part-time degree program, services for LD students, student-designed majors, study abroad, summer session for credit.

Library Student Success Center Library. *Books:* 9,016 (physical), 354,485 (digital/electronic); *Serial titles:* 35 (physical), 31,678 (digital/electronic); *Databases:* 111. Weekly public service hours: 65; students can reserve study rooms.

Student Life *Campus security:* 24-hour emergency response devices, late-night transport/escort service, trained security personnel patrol during hours of operation.

Standardized Tests *Required for some:* ACT or ACCUPLACER, TEAS, Bennett Mechanical Comprehension Test.

Applying *Options:* electronic application. *Application fee:* $30. *Required for some:* high school transcript, interview.

Freshman Application Contact Admissions Center, Fox Valley Technical College, 1825 North Bluemound Drive, PO Box 2277, Appleton, WI 54912-2277. *Phone:* 920-735-5643. *Toll-free phone:* 800-735-3882. *Fax:* 920-735-2582. *Website:* http://www.fvtc.edu/.

Gateway Technical College

Kenosha, Wisconsin

- **State and locally supported** 2-year, founded 1911, part of Wisconsin Technical College System
- **Urban** 10-acre campus with easy access to Chicago, Milwaukee
- **Endowment** $5.7 million
- **Coed**

Undergraduates 1,379 full-time, 7,343 part-time. Students come from 5 states and territories; 2% are from out of state; 10% Black or African American, non-Hispanic/Latino; 15% Hispanic/Latino; 1% Asian, non-Hispanic/Latino; 0.1% Native Hawaiian or other Pacific Islander, non-Hispanic/Latino; 0.5% American Indian or Alaska Native, non-Hispanic/Latino; 3% Two or more races, non-Hispanic/Latino; 7% Race/ethnicity unknown; 10% transferred in. *Retention:* 57% of full-time freshmen returned.

Faculty *Student/faculty ratio:* 10:1.

Academics *Calendar:* semesters. *Degree:* certificates, diplomas, and associate. *Special study options:* academic remediation for entering students, advanced placement credit, cooperative education, distance learning, double majors, English as a second language, independent study, internships, off-campus study, part-time degree program, services for LD students, student-designed majors, summer session for credit.

Library Library/Learning Resources Center plus 2 others. *Books:* 23,575 (physical), 4,369 (digital/electronic); *Serial titles:* 131 (physical); *Databases:* 41. Weekly public service hours: 59; students can reserve study rooms.

Student Life *Campus security:* 24-hour emergency response devices, late-night transport/escort service, patrols by trained security when open, locked/alarmed when closed.

Applying *Options:* electronic application, early admission, deferred entrance. *Application fee:* $30. *Required:* high school transcript. *Required for some:* interview.
Freshman Application Contact Admissions, Gateway Technical College, 3520 30th Avenue, Kenosha, WI 53144-1690. *Phone:* 262-564-2300. *Fax:* 262-564-2301. *E-mail:* admissions@gtc.edu. *Website:* http://www.gtc.edu/.

Lac Courte Oreilles Ojibwa Community College
Hayward, Wisconsin

Freshman Application Contact Ms. Annette Wiggins, Registrar, Lac Courte Oreilles Ojibwa Community College, 13466 West Trepania Road, Hayward, WI 54843-2181. *Phone:* 715-634-4790 Ext. 104. *Toll-free phone:* 888-526-6221. *Website:* http://www.lco.edu/.

Lakeshore Technical College
Cleveland, Wisconsin

- **State and locally supported** 2-year, founded 1967, part of Wisconsin Technical College System
- **Rural** 160-acre campus with easy access to Milwaukee
- **Coed**

Undergraduates Students come from 5 states and territories; 1% are from out of state.
Faculty *Student/faculty ratio:* 14:1.
Academics *Calendar:* semesters. *Degree:* certificates, diplomas, and associate. *Special study options:* academic remediation for entering students, accelerated degree program, adult/continuing education programs, advanced placement credit, cooperative education, distance learning, double majors, English as a second language, external degree program, independent study, internships, part-time degree program, services for LD students, student-designed majors, summer session for credit.
Student Life *Campus security:* 24-hour patrols, student patrols, late-night transport/escort service.
Standardized Tests *Recommended:* SAT or ACT (for admission), ACCUPLACER/ACT ASSET.
Applying *Options:* electronic application, early admission, deferred entrance. *Application fee:* $30. *Required for some:* high school transcript, interview.
Freshman Application Contact Lakeshore Technical College, 1290 North Avenue, Cleveland, WI 53015. *Phone:* 920-693-1339. *Toll-free phone:* 888-GO TO LTC. *Fax:* 920-693-3561. *Website:* http://www.gotoltc.edu/.

Madison Area Technical College
Madison, Wisconsin

Freshman Application Contact Ms. Lori Sebranek, Dean, Enrollment Services, Madison Area Technical College, 1701 Wright Street, Madison, WI 53704. *Phone:* 608-243-4185. *Toll-free phone:* 800-322-6282. *Fax:* 608-243-4353. *E-mail:* enrollmentservices@madisoncollege.edu. *Website:* http://madisoncollege.edu/.

Madison Media Institute
Madison, Wisconsin

Freshman Application Contact Mr. Chris K. Hutchings, President/Director, Madison Media Institute, 2702 Agriculture Drive, Madison, WI 53718. *Phone:* 608-237-8301. *Toll-free phone:* 800-236-4997. *Website:* http://www.mediainstitute.edu/.

Mid-State Technical College
Wisconsin Rapids, Wisconsin

- **State and locally supported** 2-year, founded 1917, part of Wisconsin Technical College System
- **Small-town** 155-acre campus
- **Endowment** $1.2 million
- **Coed**

Undergraduates 950 full-time, 1,686 part-time. 1% Black or African American, non-Hispanic/Latino; 1% Hispanic/Latino; 3% Asian, non-Hispanic/Latino; 0.1% Native Hawaiian or other Pacific Islander, non-Hispanic/Latino; 1% American Indian or Alaska Native, non-Hispanic/Latino; 2% Two or more races, non-Hispanic/Latino; 2% Race/ethnicity unknown; 3% transferred in.
Faculty *Student/faculty ratio:* 12:1.
Academics *Calendar:* semesters. *Degree:* certificates, diplomas, and associate. *Special study options:* academic remediation for entering students, adult/continuing education programs, cooperative education, distance learning, double majors, English as a second language, independent study, internships, part-time degree program, services for LD students, summer session for credit.
Library Mid-State Technical College Library.
Athletics Member NJCAA.
Financial Aid Of all full-time matriculated undergraduates who enrolled in 2009, 1,426 applied for aid, 1,426 were judged to have need. 352 Federal Work-Study jobs (averaging $1000).
Applying *Options:* electronic application, early admission, deferred entrance. *Application fee:* $30. *Required:* high school transcript.
Freshman Application Contact Ms. Carole Prochnow, Admissions Assistant, Mid-State Technical College, 500 32nd Street North, Wisconsin Rapids, WI 54494-5599. *Phone:* 715-422-5444. *Website:* http://www.mstc.edu/.

Milwaukee Area Technical College
Milwaukee, Wisconsin

Freshman Application Contact Sarah Adams, Director, Enrollment Services, Milwaukee Area Technical College, 700 West State Street, Milwaukee, WI 53233-1443. *Phone:* 414-297-6595. *Fax:* 414-297-7800. *E-mail:* adamss4@matc.edu. *Website:* http://www.matc.edu/.

Milwaukee Career College
Milwaukee, Wisconsin

Admissions Office Contact Milwaukee Career College, 3077 N. Mayfair Road, Suite 300, Milwaukee, WI 53222. *Website:* http://www.mkecc.edu/.

Moraine Park Technical College
Fond du Lac, Wisconsin

Freshman Application Contact Karen Jarvis, Student Services, Moraine Park Technical College, 235 North National Avenue, Fond du Lac, WI 54935. *Phone:* 920-924-3200. *Toll-free phone:* 800-472-4554. *Fax:* 920-924-3421. *E-mail:* kjarvis@morainepark.edu. *Website:* http://www.morainepark.edu/.

Nicolet Area Technical College
Rhinelander, Wisconsin

Freshman Application Contact Ms. Susan Kordula, Director of Admissions, Nicolet Area Technical College, PO Box 518, Rhinelander, WI 54501. *Phone:* 715-365-4451. *Toll-free phone:* 800-544-3039. *E-mail:* inquire@nicoletcollege.edu. *Website:* http://www.nicoletcollege.edu/.

Northcentral Technical College
Wausau, Wisconsin

- **District-supported** 2-year, founded 1912, part of Wisconsin Technical College System
- **Rural** 96-acre campus
- **Coed**

Undergraduates 1,361 full-time, 3,806 part-time. Students come from 24 states and territories; 0.9% Black or African American, non-Hispanic/Latino; 2% Hispanic/Latino; 5% Asian, non-Hispanic/Latino; 0.1% Native Hawaiian or other Pacific Islander, non-Hispanic/Latino; 0.8% American Indian or Alaska Native, non-Hispanic/Latino; 0.9% Two or more races, non-Hispanic/Latino; 25% Race/ethnicity unknown.
Faculty *Student/faculty ratio:* 23:1.
Academics *Calendar:* semesters. *Degree:* certificates, diplomas, and associate. *Special study options:* academic remediation for entering students, accelerated degree program, adult/continuing education programs, advanced placement credit, cooperative education, distance learning, double majors, English as a second language, independent study, internships, off-campus study, part-time degree program, services for LD students, student-designed majors, summer session for credit.
Library Northcentral Technical College, Wausau Campus Library.
Student Life *Campus security:* 24-hour emergency response devices, student patrols, late-night transport/escort service.
Financial Aid Of all full-time matriculated undergraduates who enrolled in 2017, 1,389 applied for aid, 1,211 were judged to have need, 98 had their need fully met. In 2017, 23. *Average financial aid package:* $5791. *Average need-based loan:* $3031. *Average need-based gift aid:* $4073. *Average non-need-based aid:* $760.
Applying *Options:* electronic application, early admission, deferred entrance. *Application fee:* $30. *Required for some:* high school transcript, interview.
Freshman Application Contact Northcentral Technical College, 1000 West Campus Drive, Wausau, WI 54401-1899. *Phone:* 715-675-3331. *Website:* http://www.ntc.edu/.

Northeast Wisconsin Technical College

Green Bay, Wisconsin

Freshman Application Contact Christine Lemerande, Program Enrollment Supervisor, Northeast Wisconsin Technical College, 2740 W Mason Street, PO Box 19042, Green Bay, WI 54307-9042. *Phone:* 920-498-5444. *Toll-free phone:* 888-385-6982. *Fax:* 920-498-6882. *Website:* http://www.nwtc.edu/.

Southwest Wisconsin Technical College

Fennimore, Wisconsin

- **State and locally supported** 2-year, founded 1967, part of Wisconsin Technical College System
- **Rural** 53-acre campus
- **Endowment** $2.7 million
- **Coed,** 2,009 undergraduate students, 36% full-time, 58% women, 42% men

Undergraduates 730 full-time, 1,279 part-time. Students come from 20 states and territories; 10% are from out of state; 2% Black or African American, non-Hispanic/Latino; 2% Hispanic/Latino; 0.6% Asian, non-Hispanic/Latino; 0.4% American Indian or Alaska Native, non-Hispanic/Latino; 3% Two or more races, non-Hispanic/Latino; 0.8% Race/ethnicity unknown; 23% transferred in; 7% live on campus.

Freshmen *Admission:* 813 applied, 734 admitted, 416 enrolled.

Faculty *Total:* 125, 62% full-time. *Student/faculty ratio:* 18:1.

Majors Accounting; agribusiness; agricultural/farm supplies retailing and wholesaling; agronomy and crop science; animal/livestock husbandry and production; computer systems networking and telecommunications; criminal justice/police science; criminal justice/safety; culinary arts; direct entry midwifery; early childhood education; electromechanical technology; golf course operation and grounds management; health information/medical records technology; instrumentation technology; interdisciplinary studies; registered nursing/registered nurse; restaurant, culinary, and catering management; web page, digital/multimedia and information resources design.

Academics *Calendar:* semesters. *Degree:* certificates, diplomas, and associate. *Special study options:* academic remediation for entering students, advanced placement credit, distance learning, double majors, English as a second language, independent study, internships, off-campus study, part-time degree program, services for LD students, student-designed majors, summer session for credit.

Library Knox Learning Center. *Books:* 8,867 (physical), 180,598 (digital/electronic); *Serial titles:* 109 (physical); *Databases:* 42. Weekly public service hours: 58.

Student Life *Housing Options:* coed, special housing for students with disabilities. Campus housing is provided by a third party. *Activities and Organizations:* Student Senate, Student Ambassadors, Phi Theta Kappa. *Campus security:* 24-hour emergency response devices. *Student services:* personal/psychological counseling.

Athletics Member NJCAA. *Intramural sports:* basketball M/W, volleyball M/W.

Standardized Tests *Required for some:* TABE, HESI for nursing students.

Applying *Options:* electronic application, early admission. *Application fee:* $30. *Required:* high school transcript, interview. *Application deadlines:* rolling (freshmen), rolling (out-of-state freshmen), rolling (transfers). *Notification:* continuous (freshmen), continuous (out-of-state freshmen), continuous (transfers).

Director of Admissions Dr. Katie Garrity Ph.D., Chief Academic Officer, Southwest Wisconsin Technical College, 1800 Bronson Boulevard, Fennimore, WI 53809-9778. *Phone:* 608-8222471 Ext. 2471. *Toll-free phone:* 800-362-3322. *E-mail:* kgarrity@swtc.edu. *Website:* http://www.swtc.edu/.

University of Wisconsin–Baraboo/Sauk County

Baraboo, Wisconsin

- **State-supported** primarily 2-year, founded 1968, part of University of Wisconsin System
- **Small-town** 68-acre campus with easy access to Madison
- **Coed**

Faculty *Student/faculty ratio:* 16:1.

Academics *Calendar:* semesters. *Degrees:* certificates, associate, and bachelor's. *Special study options:* academic remediation for entering students, advanced placement credit, distance learning, external degree program, honors programs, independent study, internships, off-campus study, part-time degree program, services for LD students, student-designed majors, study abroad, summer session for credit.

Library T. N. Savides Library plus 1 other.

Athletics Member NJCAA.

Standardized Tests *Required:* ACT (for admission).

Applying *Options:* electronic application. *Application fee:* $50. *Required:* high school transcript.

Freshman Application Contact University of Wisconsin–Baraboo/Sauk County, 1006 Connie Road, Baraboo, WI 53913. *Website:* http://www.baraboo.uwc.edu/.

University of Wisconsin–Barron County

Rice Lake, Wisconsin

- **State-supported** primarily 2-year, founded 1968, part of University of Wisconsin System
- **Small-town** 110-acre campus
- **Coed**

Faculty *Student/faculty ratio:* 12:1.

Academics *Calendar:* semesters. *Degrees:* associate and bachelor's. *Special study options:* academic remediation for entering students, adult/continuing education programs, advanced placement credit, distance learning, independent study, internships, off-campus study, part-time degree program, services for LD students, study abroad, summer session for credit.

Library UW Barron County Library plus 1 other.

Standardized Tests *Required:* ACT (for admission).

Applying *Options:* electronic application, deferred entrance. *Application fee:* $50. *Required:* high school transcript.

Freshman Application Contact University of Wisconsin–Barron County, 1800 College Drive, Rice Lake, WI 54868. *Website:* http://www.barron.uwc.edu/.

University of Wisconsin Colleges Online

Madison, Wisconsin

Admissions Office Contact University of Wisconsin Colleges Online, 34 Schroeder Court, Suite 200, Madison, WI 53711. *Toll-free phone:* 877-449-1877. *Website:* http://www.online.uwc.edu/.

University of Wisconsin–Fond du Lac

Fond du Lac, Wisconsin

- **State-supported** 2-year, founded 1972, part of University of Wisconsin System
- **Small-town** 183-acre campus with easy access to Milwaukee
- **Coed**

Undergraduates 1% are from out of state.

Faculty *Student/faculty ratio:* 15:1.

Academics *Calendar:* semesters. *Degree:* certificates and associate. *Special study options:* academic remediation for entering students, accelerated degree program, advanced placement credit, cooperative education, distance learning, external degree program, independent study, off-campus study, part-time degree program, services for LD students, study abroad, summer session for credit.

Library UW-Fond du Lac Library plus 1 other.

Student Life *Campus security:* 24-hour emergency response devices.

Athletics Member NJCAA.

Standardized Tests *Required:* ACT (for admission).

Applying *Options:* electronic application. *Application fee:* $50. *Required:* high school transcript.

Freshman Application Contact University of Wisconsin–Fond du Lac, 400 University Drive, Fond du Lac, WI 54935. *Website:* http://www.fdl.uwc.edu/.

University of Wisconsin–Fox Valley

Menasha, Wisconsin

- **State-supported** 2-year, founded 1960, part of University of Wisconsin System
- **Small-town** 45-acre campus
- **Coed**

Faculty *Student/faculty ratio:* 17:1.

Academics *Calendar:* semesters. *Degree:* certificates and associate. *Special study options:* academic remediation for entering students, accelerated degree program, advanced placement credit, cooperative education, distance learning, external degree program, honors programs, independent study, internships, off-campus study, part-time degree program, services for LD students, study abroad, summer session for credit.

Library UW-Fox Valley Library plus 1 other. Students can reserve study rooms.

Student Life *Campus security:* 24-hour emergency response devices, late-night transport/escort service.

Athletics Member NJCAA.
Standardized Tests *Required:* ACT (for admission).
Applying *Options:* electronic application. *Application fee:* $50. *Required:* high school transcript.
Freshman Application Contact University of Wisconsin–Fox Valley, 1478 Midway Road, Menasha, WI 54952. *Website:* http://www.uwfox.uwc.edu/.

University of Wisconsin–Manitowoc

Manitowoc, Wisconsin

- **State-supported** 2-year, founded 1962, part of University of Wisconsin System
- **Small-town** 40-acre campus with easy access to Milwaukee
- **Coed**
- 100% of applicants were admitted

Faculty *Student/faculty ratio:* 14:1.
Academics *Calendar:* semesters. *Degree:* certificates and associate. *Special study options:* academic remediation for entering students, advanced placement credit, cooperative education, distance learning, external degree program, internships, off-campus study, part-time degree program, services for LD students, student-designed majors, study abroad.
Library UW-Manitowoc Library plus 1 other.
Standardized Tests *Required:* SAT or ACT (for admission).
Applying *Options:* electronic application, early admission, deferred entrance. *Application fee:* $50. *Required:* high school transcript.
Freshman Application Contact University of Wisconsin–Manitowoc, 705 Viebahn Street, Manitowoc, WI 54220. *Website:* http://www.manitowoc.uwc.edu/.

University of Wisconsin–Marathon County

Wausau, Wisconsin

- **State-supported** 2-year, founded 1997, part of University of Wisconsin System
- **Small-town** 7-acre campus
- **Coed**

Faculty *Student/faculty ratio:* 17:1.
Academics *Calendar:* semesters. *Degree:* certificates and associate. *Special study options:* academic remediation for entering students, advanced placement credit, external degree program, honors programs, off-campus study, part-time degree program, student-designed majors, study abroad, summer session for credit. *ROTC:* Army (c).
Library UW-Marathon County Library plus 1 other.
Student Life *Campus security:* 24-hour emergency response devices, controlled dormitory access.
Standardized Tests *Required:* ACT (for admission).
Applying *Options:* electronic application, early admission, deferred entrance. *Application fee:* $50. *Required:* high school transcript.
Freshman Application Contact University of Wisconsin–Marathon County, 518 South 7th Avenue, Wausau, WI 54401. *Toll-free phone:* 888-367-8962. *Website:* http://www.uwmc.uwc.edu/.

University of Wisconsin–Marinette

Marinette, Wisconsin

- **State-supported** 2-year, founded 1972, part of University of Wisconsin System
- **Small-town** 36-acre campus
- **Coed**

Faculty *Student/faculty ratio:* 10:1.
Academics *Calendar:* semesters. *Degree:* certificates and associate. *Special study options:* academic remediation for entering students, advanced placement credit, cooperative education, distance learning, English as a second language, external degree program, independent study, internships, off-campus study, part-time degree program, services for LD students, summer session for credit.
Library UW-Marinette Library plus 1 other.
Standardized Tests *Required:* ACT (for admission).
Applying *Options:* electronic application. *Application fee:* $50. *Required:* high school transcript.
Freshman Application Contact University of Wisconsin–Marinette, 750 West Bay Shore, Marinette, WI 54143. *Website:* http://www.marinette.uwc.edu/.

University of Wisconsin–Marshfield/Wood County

Marshfield, Wisconsin

- **State-supported** primarily 2-year, founded 1963, part of University of Wisconsin System
- **Small-town** 114-acre campus
- **Coed**

Faculty *Student/faculty ratio:* 15:1.
Academics *Calendar:* semesters. *Degrees:* certificates, associate, and bachelor's. *Special study options:* academic remediation for entering students, accelerated degree program, advanced placement credit, distance learning, external degree program, independent study, off-campus study, part-time degree program, services for LD students, study abroad, summer session for credit. *ROTC:* Army (c).
Library Hamilton Roddis Memorial Library plus 1 other.
Student Life *Campus security:* 24-hour patrols, patrols by city police.
Standardized Tests *Required:* ACT (for admission).
Applying *Options:* electronic application, early admission, deferred entrance. *Application fee:* $50. *Required:* high school transcript.
Freshman Application Contact University of Wisconsin–Marshfield/Wood County, 2000 West 5th Street, Marshfield, WI 54449. *Website:* http://marshfield.uwc.edu/.

University of Wisconsin–Richland

Richland Center, Wisconsin

- **State-supported** primarily 2-year, founded 1967, part of University of Wisconsin System
- **Small-town** 135-acre campus
- **Coed**

Faculty *Student/faculty ratio:* 8:1.
Academics *Calendar:* semesters. *Degrees:* certificates, associate, and bachelor's. *Special study options:* academic remediation for entering students, advanced placement credit, distance learning, external degree program, independent study, off-campus study, part-time degree program, services for LD students, study abroad, summer session for credit.
Library Miller Memorial Library plus 1 other.
Standardized Tests *Required:* ACT (for admission).
Applying *Options:* electronic application. *Application fee:* $50. *Required:* high school transcript.
Freshman Application Contact University of Wisconsin–Richland, 1200 Highway 14 West, Richland Center, WI 53581. *Website:* http://richland.uwc.edu/.

University of Wisconsin–Rock County

Janesville, Wisconsin

- **State-supported** primarily 2-year, founded 1966, part of University of Wisconsin System
- **Small-town** 50-acre campus with easy access to Milwaukee
- **Coed**

Faculty *Student/faculty ratio:* 16:1.
Academics *Calendar:* semesters. *Degrees:* certificates, associate, and bachelor's. *Special study options:* academic remediation for entering students, advanced placement credit, distance learning, external degree program, off-campus study, part-time degree program, services for LD students, summer session for credit.
Library Gary J. Lenox Library plus 1 other.
Standardized Tests *Required:* ACT (for admission).
Applying *Options:* electronic application, deferred entrance. *Application fee:* $50. *Required:* high school transcript.
Freshman Application Contact University of Wisconsin–Rock County, 2909 Kellogg Avenue, Janesville, WI 53546. *Toll-free phone:* 888-INFO-UWC. *Website:* http://rock.uwc.edu/.

University of Wisconsin–Sheboygan

Sheboygan, Wisconsin

- **State-supported** 2-year, founded 1933, part of University of Wisconsin System
- **Small-town** 70-acre campus with easy access to Milwaukee
- **Coed**

Faculty *Student/faculty ratio:* 14:1.
Academics *Calendar:* semesters. *Degree:* certificates and associate. *Special study options:* academic remediation for entering students, advanced placement credit, cooperative education, distance learning, English as a second

language, external degree program, independent study, off-campus study, part-time degree program, services for LD students, summer session for credit.
Library University Library plus 1 other.
Student Life *Campus security:* 24-hour patrols by city police.
Standardized Tests *Required:* ACT (for admission).
Applying *Options:* electronic application. *Application fee:* $50. *Required:* high school transcript.
Freshman Application Contact University of Wisconsin–Sheboygan, One University Drive, Sheboygan, WI 53081. *Website:* http://www.sheboygan.uwc.edu/.

University of Wisconsin–Washington County

West Bend, Wisconsin

- **State-supported** 2-year, founded 1968, part of University of Wisconsin System
- **Small-town** 87-acre campus with easy access to Milwaukee
- **Coed**

Faculty *Student/faculty ratio:* 17:1.
Academics *Calendar:* semesters. *Degree:* certificates and associate. *Special study options:* academic remediation for entering students, advanced placement credit, distance learning, double majors, external degree program, honors programs, independent study, off-campus study, part-time degree program, services for LD students, summer session for credit.
Library UW-Washington County Library plus 1 other.
Athletics Member NAIA.
Standardized Tests *Required:* ACT (for admission).
Applying *Options:* electronic application, deferred entrance. *Application fee:* $50. *Required:* high school transcript.
Freshman Application Contact University of Wisconsin–Washington County, 400 University Drive, West Bend, WI 53095. *Website:* http://www.washington.uwc.edu/.

University of Wisconsin–Waukesha

Waukesha, Wisconsin

- **State-supported** primarily 2-year, founded 1966, part of University of Wisconsin System
- **Small-town** 86-acre campus with easy access to Milwaukee
- **Coed**

Faculty *Student/faculty ratio:* 17:1.
Academics *Calendar:* semesters. *Degrees:* associate and bachelor's. *Special study options:* academic remediation for entering students, accelerated degree program, advanced placement credit, distance learning, external degree program, honors programs, internships, off-campus study, part-time degree program, services for LD students, study abroad, summer session for credit.
Library University of Wisconsin-Waukesha Library plus 1 other.
Student Life *Campus security:* late-night transport/escort service, part-time patrols by trained security personnel.
Athletics Member NJCAA.
Standardized Tests *Required:* ACT (for admission).
Applying *Options:* electronic application, early admission, deferred entrance. *Application fee:* $50. *Required:* high school transcript.
Freshman Application Contact University of Wisconsin–Waukesha, 1500 North University Drive, Waukesha, WI 53188. *Website:* http://www.waukesha.uwc.edu/.

Waukesha County Technical College

Pewaukee, Wisconsin

- **State and locally supported** 2-year, founded 1923, part of Wisconsin Technical College System
- **Suburban** 137-acre campus with easy access to Milwaukee
- **Coed**

Undergraduates 1,565 full-time, 6,131 part-time. 6% Black or African American, non-Hispanic/Latino; 8% Hispanic/Latino; 3% Asian, non-Hispanic/Latino; 0.2% Native Hawaiian or other Pacific Islander, non-Hispanic/Latino; 0.3% American Indian or Alaska Native, non-Hispanic/Latino; 2% Two or more races, non-Hispanic/Latino; 3% Race/ethnicity unknown; 0.1% international.
Faculty *Student/faculty ratio:* 17:1.
Academics *Calendar:* semesters. *Degree:* certificates, diplomas, and associate. *Special study options:* academic remediation for entering students, accelerated degree program, adult/continuing education programs, advanced placement credit, cooperative education, distance learning, double majors, English as a second language, independent study, internships, part-time degree program, services for LD students, student-designed majors, study abroad, summer session for credit.
Student Life *Campus security:* patrols by police officers 8 am to 10 pm.
Financial Aid Of all full-time matriculated undergraduates who enrolled in 2016, 180 Federal Work-Study jobs (averaging $2709).
Applying *Options:* electronic application. *Application fee:* $30. *Required:* high school transcript. *Required for some:* interview.
Freshman Application Contact Waukesha County Technical College, 800 Main Street, Pewaukee, WI 53072-4601. *Phone:* 262-691-5464. *Website:* http://www.wctc.edu/.

Western Technical College

La Crosse, Wisconsin

Freshman Application Contact Ms. Jane Wells, Manager of Admissions, Registration, and Records, Western Technical College, PO Box 908, La Crosse, WI 54602-0908. *Phone:* 608-785-9158. *Toll-free phone:* 800-322-9982. *Fax:* 608-785-9094. *E-mail:* mildes@wwtc.edu. *Website:* http://www.westerntc.edu/.

Wisconsin Indianhead Technical College

Shell Lake, Wisconsin

- **District-supported** 2-year, founded 1912, part of Wisconsin Technical College System
- **Suburban** 118-acre campus with easy access to Minneapolis-St Paul Metro Area
- **Endowment** $4.7 million
- **Coed**

Undergraduates 1,086 full-time, 1,935 part-time. Students come from 6 states and territories; 9% are from out of state; 0.6% Black or African American, non-Hispanic/Latino; 0.5% Hispanic/Latino; 1% Asian, non-Hispanic/Latino; 0.1% Native Hawaiian or other Pacific Islander, non-Hispanic/Latino; 2% American Indian or Alaska Native, non-Hispanic/Latino; 2% Two or more races, non-Hispanic/Latino; 1% Race/ethnicity unknown.
Faculty *Student/faculty ratio:* 9:1.
Academics *Calendar:* semesters. *Degree:* certificates, diplomas, and associate. *Special study options:* academic remediation for entering students, adult/continuing education programs, advanced placement credit, distance learning, double majors, English as a second language, external degree program, independent study, internships, off-campus study, part-time degree program, services for LD students, summer session for credit.
Library ***Books:*** 5,569 (physical), 50,557 (digital/electronic); *Serial titles:* 89 (physical), 35,291 (digital/electronic); *Databases:* 85. Students can reserve study rooms.
Student Life *Campus security:* 24-hour emergency response devices.
Applying *Options:* electronic application, early admission, deferred entrance. *Application fee:* $30. *Required:* interview. *Required for some:* high school transcript.
Freshman Application Contact Mr. Steve Bitzer, Vice President, Student Affairs and Campus Administrator, Wisconsin Indianhead Technical College, 2100 Beaser Avenue, Ashland, WI 54806. *Phone:* 715-468-2815 Ext. 3149. *Toll-free phone:* 800-243-9482. *Fax:* 715-468-2819. *E-mail:* steve.bitzer@witc.edu. *Website:* http://www.witc.edu/.

WYOMING

Casper College

Casper, Wyoming

Freshman Application Contact Ms. Kyla Foltz, Director of Admissions Services, Casper College, 125 College Drive, Casper, WY 82601. *Phone:* 307-268-2111. *Toll-free phone:* 800-442-2963. *Fax:* 307-268-2611. *E-mail:* kfoltz@caspercollege.edu. *Website:* http://www.caspercollege.edu/.

★ Central Wyoming College

Riverton, Wyoming

Freshman Application Contact Mr. Patrick Edwards, Director of Admissions, Central Wyoming College, 2660 Peck Avenue, Riverton, WY 82501-2273. *Phone:* 307-855-2022. *Toll-free phone:* 800-735-8418. *Fax:* 307-855-2065. *E-mail:* pedwards@cwc.edu. *Website:* http://www.cwc.edu/.

Eastern Wyoming College
Torrington, Wyoming

Freshman Application Contact Dr. Rex Cogdill, Vice President for Students Services, Eastern Wyoming College, 3200 West C Street, Torrington, WY 82240. *Phone:* 307-532-8257. *Toll-free phone:* 866-327-8996. *Fax:* 307-532-8222. *E-mail:* rex.cogdill@ewc.wy.edu. *Website:* http://www.ewc.wy.edu/.

Laramie County Community College
Cheyenne, Wyoming

- **District-supported** 2-year, founded 1968, part of Wyoming Community College Commission
- **Small-town** 271-acre campus
- **Coed**

Undergraduates 1,634 full-time, 2,592 part-time. 14% are from out of state; 2% Black or African American, non-Hispanic/Latino; 15% Hispanic/Latino; 0.9% Asian, non-Hispanic/Latino; 0.5% Native Hawaiian or other Pacific Islander, non-Hispanic/Latino; 0.9% American Indian or Alaska Native, non-Hispanic/Latino; 3% Two or more races, non-Hispanic/Latino; 7% Race/ethnicity unknown; 1% international; 4% transferred in; 13% live on campus.
Faculty *Student/faculty ratio:* 15:1.
Academics *Calendar:* semesters. *Degree:* certificates, diplomas, and associate. *Special study options:* academic remediation for entering students, adult/continuing education programs, advanced placement credit, cooperative education, distance learning, double majors, English as a second language, honors programs, independent study, internships, off-campus study, part-time degree program, services for LD students, summer session for credit. *ROTC:* Army (c), Air Force (c).
Library Ludden Library.
Student Life *Campus security:* 24-hour emergency response devices and patrols, late-night transport/escort service, controlled dormitory access.
Athletics Member NJCAA.
Financial Aid Of all full-time matriculated undergraduates who enrolled in 2016, 1,287 applied for aid, 938 were judged to have need, 146 had their need fully met. In 2016, 510. *Average percent of need met:* 70. *Average financial aid package:* $6631. *Average need-based loan:* $3150. *Average need-based gift aid:* $1851. *Average non-need-based aid:* $1417.
Applying *Options:* electronic application, deferred entrance. *Required for some:* high school transcript, interview.
Admissions Office Contact Laramie County Community College, 1400 East College Drive, Cheyenne, WY 82007-3299. *Toll-free phone:* 800-522-2993 Ext. 1357. *Website:* http://www.lccc.wy.edu/.

Northwest College
Powell, Wyoming

- **State and locally supported** 2-year, founded 1946, part of Wyoming Community College System
- **Rural** 132-acre campus
- **Endowment** $35.0 million
- **Coed**

Undergraduates 953 full-time, 701 part-time. Students come from 34 states and territories; 28 other countries; 24% are from out of state; 1% Black or African American, non-Hispanic/Latino; 7% Hispanic/Latino; 0.4% Asian, non-Hispanic/Latino; 0.3% Native Hawaiian or other Pacific Islander, non-Hispanic/Latino; 0.3% American Indian or Alaska Native, non-Hispanic/Latino; 4% Two or more races, non-Hispanic/Latino; 5% international; 46% live on campus. *Retention:* 61% of full-time freshmen returned.
Faculty *Student/faculty ratio:* 12:1.
Academics *Calendar:* semesters. *Degree:* certificates and associate. *Special study options:* academic remediation for entering students, adult/continuing education programs, advanced placement credit, cooperative education, distance learning, double majors, English as a second language, external degree program, independent study, internships, off-campus study, part-time degree program, services for LD students, study abroad, summer session for credit.
Library John Taggart Hinckley Library.
Student Life *Campus security:* 24-hour emergency response devices and patrols, late-night transport/escort service, controlled dormitory access.
Athletics Member NJCAA.
Financial Aid Of all full-time matriculated undergraduates who enrolled in 2017, 115 Federal Work-Study jobs (averaging $2700). 215 state and other part-time jobs (averaging $2700).
Applying *Options:* electronic application. *Required:* high school transcript. *Required for some:* minimum 2.0 GPA. *Recommended:* minimum 2.0 GPA.
Freshman Application Contact Mr. West Hernandez, Admissions Manager, Northwest College, 231 W. 6th Street, Orendorff Building 1, Powell, WY 82435-1898. *Phone:* 307-754-6103. *Toll-free phone:* 800-560-4692. *Fax:* 307-754-6249. *E-mail:* west.hernandez@nwc.edu. *Website:* http://www.nwc.edu/.

Sheridan College
Sheridan, Wyoming

Freshman Application Contact Mr. Matt Adams, Admissions Coordinator, Sheridan College, PO Box 1500, Sheridan, WY 82801-1500. *Phone:* 307-674-6446 Ext. 2005. *Toll-free phone:* 800-913-9139 Ext. 2002. *Fax:* 307-674-3373. *E-mail:* madams@sheridan.edu. *Website:* http://www.sheridan.edu/.

Western Wyoming Community College
Rock Springs, Wyoming

- **State and locally supported** 2-year, founded 1959
- **Small-town** 342-acre campus
- **Endowment** $23.7 million
- **Coed,** 3,183 undergraduate students, 34% full-time, 54% women, 46% men

Undergraduates 1,096 full-time, 2,087 part-time. Students come from 15 states and territories; 16 other countries; 16% are from out of state; 2% Black or African American, non-Hispanic/Latino; 12% Hispanic/Latino; 0.9% Asian, non-Hispanic/Latino; 0.1% Native Hawaiian or other Pacific Islander, non-Hispanic/Latino; 0.6% American Indian or Alaska Native, non-Hispanic/Latino; 3% Two or more races, non-Hispanic/Latino; 0.8% Race/ethnicity unknown; 2% international; 10% live on campus.
Freshmen *Admission:* 1,889 applied, 1,123 admitted, 517 enrolled.
Faculty *Total:* 307, 26% full-time, 7% with terminal degrees. *Student/faculty ratio:* 11:1.
Majors Accounting; administrative assistant and secretarial science; anthropology; archeology; art; automobile/automotive mechanics technology; biological and physical sciences; biology/biological sciences; business administration and management; chemistry; computer and information sciences; computer programming (specific applications); computer science; criminal justice/law enforcement administration; criminology; dance; data entry/microcomputer applications; data processing and data processing technology; diesel mechanics technology; dramatic/theater arts; early childhood education; economics; education; education (multiple levels); electrical/electronics equipment installation and repair; electrician; elementary education; engineering technology; English; environmental science; forestry; general studies; geology/earth science; health/medical preparatory programs related; health professions related; health services/allied health/health sciences; heavy equipment maintenance technology; history; humanities; human services; industrial electronics technology; industrial mechanics and maintenance technology; information science/studies; information technology; instrumentation technology; journalism; kinesiology and exercise science; legal administrative assistant/secretary; liberal arts and sciences/liberal studies; licensed practical/vocational nurse training; marketing/marketing management; mathematics; mechanics and repair; medical administrative assistant and medical secretary; medical/clinical assistant; medical office assistant; medical office computer specialist; mining technology; music; nursing assistant/aide and patient care assistant/aide; photography; political science and government; pre-dentistry studies; pre-engineering; pre-law studies; premedical studies; prenursing studies; pre-pharmacy studies; pre-veterinary studies; psychology; secondary education; social sciences; social work; sociology; Spanish; speech communication and rhetoric; theater design and technology; visual and performing arts; web/multimedia management and webmaster; web page, digital/multimedia and information resources design; welding technology; wildlife, fish and wildlands science and management; word processing.
Academics *Calendar:* semesters. *Degree:* certificates, diplomas, and associate. *Special study options:* academic remediation for entering students, advanced placement credit, cooperative education, distance learning, English as a second language, honors programs, independent study, internships, part-time degree program, services for LD students, summer session for credit.
Library Hay Library. *Books:* 93,144 (physical), 747,995 (digital/electronic); *Serial titles:* 136 (physical), 63,272 (digital/electronic); *Databases:* 412. Weekly public service hours: 81; students can reserve study rooms.
Student Life *Housing Options:* coed, special housing for students with disabilities. Campus housing is university owned. *Activities and Organizations:* drama/theater group, student-run newspaper, radio station, choral group, Association of Non-Traditional Students (ANTS), Spanish Club, Residence Hall Association, International Club, Veteran's Club. *Campus security:* 24-hour emergency response devices and patrols, late-night

transport/escort service, controlled dormitory access. *Student services:* personal/psychological counseling, veterans affairs office.
Athletics Member NJCAA. *Intercollegiate sports:* basketball W(s), soccer W(s), volleyball W(s).
Financial Aid Of all full-time matriculated undergraduates who enrolled in 2017, 20 Federal Work-Study jobs (averaging $1500).
Applying *Options:* electronic application, early admission, deferred entrance. *Recommended:* high school transcript. *Application deadlines:* rolling (freshmen), rolling (transfers).
Freshman Application Contact Mr. Kurtis Wilkinson, Director of Admissions, Western Wyoming Community College, 2500 College Drive, Rock Springs, WY 82901. *Phone:* 307-382-1647. *Toll-free phone:* 800-226-1181. *Fax:* 307-382-1636. *E-mail:* admissions@westernwyoming.edu. *Website:* http://www.westernwyoming.edu/.

CANADA

CANADA

Southern Alberta Institute of Technology

Calgary, Alberta, Canada

Freshman Application Contact Southern Alberta Institute of Technology, 1301 16th Avenue NW, Calgary, AB T2M 0L4, Canada. *Phone:* 403-284-8857. *Toll-free phone:* 877-284-SAIT. *Website:* http://www.sait.ca/.

INTERNATIONAL

BERMUDA

Bermuda College

Paget, Bermuda

Admissions Office Contact Bermuda College, 21 Stonington Avenue, South Road, Paget PG 04, Bermuda. *Website:* http://www.college.bm/.

MARSHALL ISLANDS

College of the Marshall Islands

Majuro, Marshall Islands

Freshman Application Contact Ms. Jomi Monica Capelle, Director of Admissions and Records, College of the Marshall Islands, PO Box 1258, Majuro 96960, Marshall Islands. *Phone:* 692-625-6823. *Fax:* 692-625-7203. *E-mail:* cmiadmissions@cmi.edu. *Website:* http://www.cmi.edu/.

MICRONESIA

College of Micronesia–FSM

Kolonia Pohnpei, Micronesia

Freshman Application Contact Rita Hinga, Student Services Specialist, College of Micronesia–FSM, PO Box 159, Kolonia Pohnpei, FM 96941, Micronesia. *Phone:* 691-320-3795 Ext. 15. *E-mail:* rhinga@comfsm.fm. *Website:* http://www.comfsm.fm/.

PALAU

Palau Community College

Koror, Palau

Freshman Application Contact Ms. Dahlia Katosang, Director of Admissions and Financial Aid, Palau Community College, PO Box 9, Koror 96940-0009, Palau. *Phone:* 680-488-2471 Ext. 233. *Fax:* 680-488-4468. *E-mail:* dahliapcc@palaunet.com. *Website:* http://www.palau.edu/.

Indexes

Associate Degree Programs at Two-Year Colleges

ACCOUNTING
Alexandria Tech and Comm Coll (MN)
Austin Comm Coll District (TX)
Black Hawk Coll, Moline (IL)
Blue Ridge Comm and Tech Coll (WV)
Borough of Manhattan Comm Coll of the City U of New York (NY)
Bunker Hill Comm Coll (MA)
Central New Mexico Comm Coll (NM)
Central Ohio Tech Coll (OH)
Central Oregon Comm Coll (OR)
Colorado Northwestern Comm Coll (CO)
Dakota Coll at Bottineau (ND)
Greenville Tech Coll (SC)
Harper Coll (IL)
Hawkeye Comm Coll (IA)
Haywood Comm Coll (NC)
Johnston Comm Coll (NC)
Kaskaskia Coll (IL)
Lake Superior Coll (MN)
Luzerne County Comm Coll (PA)
Manchester Comm Coll (CT)
Manor Coll (PA)
Massachusetts Bay Comm Coll (MA)
McHenry County Coll (IL)
Minnesota State Coll–Southeast Tech (MN)
Mitchell Comm Coll (NC)
Mohave Comm Coll (AZ)
Nassau Comm Coll (NY)
Queensborough Comm Coll of the City U of New York (NY)
Ridgewater Coll (MN)
Rock Valley Coll (IL)
San Jacinto Coll District (TX)
Sierra Coll (CA)
Snow Coll (UT)
Southern U at Shreveport (LA)
Southwestern Comm Coll (NC)
Southwest Wisconsin Tech Coll (WI)
Sullivan County Comm Coll (NY)
Tidewater Comm Coll (VA)
Trinity Valley Comm Coll (TX)
Westchester Comm Coll (NY)
Western Wyoming Comm Coll (WY)

ACCOUNTING AND BUSINESS/ MANAGEMENT
Mitchell Tech Inst (SD)
Renton Tech Coll (WA)

ACCOUNTING AND FINANCE
Fayetteville Tech Comm Coll (NC)
Richmond Comm Coll (NC)

ACCOUNTING RELATED
Dakota Coll at Bottineau (ND)
John Tyler Comm Coll (VA)
Raritan Valley Comm Coll (NJ)

ACCOUNTING TECHNOLOGY AND BOOKKEEPING
Alamance Comm Coll (NC)
Arapahoe Comm Coll (CO)
Austin Comm Coll District (TX)
Borough of Manhattan Comm Coll of the City U of New York (NY)
Bucks County Comm Coll (PA)
Cayuga County Comm Coll (NY)
Coll of Central Florida (FL)
Coll of Marin (CA)
Coll of the Canyons (CA)
Columbia-Greene Comm Coll (NY)
Comm Coll of Allegheny County (PA)
Comm Coll of Aurora (CO)
Comm Coll of Baltimore County (MD)
Comm Coll of Denver (CO)
Dakota Coll at Bottineau (ND)
Daytona State Coll (FL)
East Central Coll (MO)
Front Range Comm Coll (CO)
Grand Rapids Comm Coll (MI)
Haywood Comm Coll (NC)
Hutchinson Comm Coll (KS)
Lamar Inst of Technology (TX)
Minnesota State Coll–Southeast Tech (MN)
Nassau Comm Coll (NY)
Northampton Comm Coll (PA)
Oakton Comm Coll (IL)
Pueblo Comm Coll (CO)
Queensborough Comm Coll of the City U of New York (NY)
Raritan Valley Comm Coll (NJ)
St. Charles Comm Coll (MO)
St. Louis Comm Coll (MO)
San Juan Coll (NM)
Southern U at Shreveport (LA)
Southwestern Comm Coll (IA)
Southwestern Michigan Coll (MI)
Sowela Tech Comm Coll (LA)
State U of New York Coll of Technology at Alfred (NY)
Tulsa Comm Coll (OK)
Union County Coll (NJ)
Vincennes U (IN)
Wayne County Comm Coll District (MI)
Westchester Comm Coll (NY)

ACTING
Northampton Comm Coll (PA)

ADMINISTRATIVE ASSISTANT AND SECRETARIAL SCIENCE
Austin Comm Coll District (TX)
Black Hawk Coll, Moline (IL)
Borough of Manhattan Comm Coll of the City U of New York (NY)
Central New Mexico Comm Coll (NM)
Central Texas Coll (TX)
Cleveland State Comm Coll (TN)
Coll of the Canyons (CA)
Comm Coll of Allegheny County (PA)
Comm Coll of Denver (CO)
Dakota Coll at Bottineau (ND)
Greenville Tech Coll (SC)
Harper Coll (IL)
Harrisburg Area Comm Coll (PA)
Heartland Comm Coll (IL)
Hutchinson Comm Coll (KS)
Johnston Comm Coll (NC)
Lamar Inst of Technology (TX)
Lurleen B. Wallace Comm Coll (AL)
Luzerne County Comm Coll (PA)
Manchester Comm Coll (CT)
McHenry County Coll (IL)
Minnesota State Coll–Southeast Tech (MN)
Nassau Comm Coll (NY)
Northampton Comm Coll (PA)
Oakton Comm Coll (IL)
Potomac State Coll of West Virginia U (WV)
Queensborough Comm Coll of the City U of New York (NY)
Raritan Valley Comm Coll (NJ)
Rend Lake Coll (IL)
Ridgewater Coll (MN)
Rock Valley Coll (IL)
San Jacinto Coll District (TX)
Sierra Coll (CA)
Snow Coll (UT)
Sowela Tech Comm Coll (LA)
Sullivan County Comm Coll (NY)
Texarkana Coll (TX)
Tidewater Comm Coll (VA)
Westchester Comm Coll (NY)
Western Wyoming Comm Coll (WY)
Wor-Wic Comm Coll (MD)

ADULT DEVELOPMENT AND AGING
Dakota Coll at Bottineau (ND)
Harrisburg Area Comm Coll (PA)
Wayne County Comm Coll District (MI)

ADVERTISING
Central Ohio Tech Coll (OH)
Coll of Central Florida (FL)
Dakota Coll at Bottineau (ND)
Tidewater Comm Coll (VA)

AERONAUTICAL/AEROSPACE ENGINEERING TECHNOLOGY
Daytona State Coll (FL)
Tulsa Comm Coll (OK)

AERONAUTICS/AVIATION/ AEROSPACE SCIENCE AND TECHNOLOGY
Comm Coll of Baltimore County (MD)

AFRICAN AMERICAN/BLACK STUDIES
Nassau Comm Coll (NY)

AGRIBUSINESS
Coll of Central Florida (FL)
Mitchell Comm Coll (NC)
Ridgewater Coll (MN)
San Jacinto Coll District (TX)
Southwestern Comm Coll (IA)
Southwest Wisconsin Tech Coll (WI)
State U of New York Coll of Technology at Alfred (NY)

AGRICULTURAL AND EXTENSION EDUCATION
Potomac State Coll of West Virginia U (WV)

AGRICULTURAL BUSINESS AND MANAGEMENT
Black Hawk Coll, Moline (IL)
Lake Region State Coll (ND)
Potomac State Coll of West Virginia U (WV)
Rend Lake Coll (IL)
Snow Coll (UT)
Treasure Valley Comm Coll (OR)
Vincennes U (IN)

AGRICULTURAL ECONOMICS
Treasure Valley Comm Coll (OR)

AGRICULTURAL/FARM SUPPLIES RETAILING AND WHOLESALING
Hawkeye Comm Coll (IA)
Southwest Wisconsin Tech Coll (WI)

AGRICULTURAL MECHANICS AND EQUIPMENT TECHNOLOGY
Black Hawk Coll, Moline (IL)
Hutchinson Comm Coll (KS)
Mitchell Tech Inst (SD)
Rend Lake Coll (IL)

AGRICULTURAL MECHANIZATION
Rend Lake Coll (IL)

AGRICULTURAL POWER MACHINERY OPERATION
Hawkeye Comm Coll (IA)

AGRICULTURAL PRODUCTION
Black Hawk Coll, Moline (IL)
Henderson Comm Coll (KY)
Mitchell Tech Inst (SD)
Owensboro Comm and Tech Coll (KY)
Rend Lake Coll (IL)
Ridgewater Coll (MN)
Southwestern Michigan Coll (MI)

AGRICULTURAL TEACHER EDUCATION
Trinity Valley Comm Coll (TX)

AGRICULTURE
Black Hawk Coll, Moline (IL)
Central Texas Coll (TX)
Coll of Central Florida (FL)
Dakota Coll at Bottineau (ND)
Hutchinson Comm Coll (KS)
Kaskaskia Coll (IL)
Missouri State U–West Plains (MO)
Potomac State Coll of West Virginia U (WV)
Ridgewater Coll (MN)
San Jacinto Coll District (TX)
Sierra Coll (CA)
Snow Coll (UT)
State U of New York Coll of Technology at Alfred (NY)
Texarkana Coll (TX)
Treasure Valley Comm Coll (OR)

AGRICULTURE AND AGRICULTURE OPERATIONS RELATED
Arkansas State U–Newport (AR)
Potomac State Coll of West Virginia U (WV)

AGROECOLOGY AND SUSTAINABLE AGRICULTURE
Southern Maine Comm Coll (ME)

AGRONOMY AND CROP SCIENCE
Potomac State Coll of West Virginia U (WV)
Ridgewater Coll (MN)
Southwest Wisconsin Tech Coll (WI)
Treasure Valley Comm Coll (OR)

AIR AND SPACE OPERATIONS TECHNOLOGY
Mohave Comm Coll (AZ)

AIRCRAFT POWERPLANT TECHNOLOGY
Colorado Northwestern Comm Coll (CO)
Sowela Tech Comm Coll (LA)
Vincennes U (IN)
Wayne County Comm Coll District (MI)

AIRFRAME MECHANICS AND AIRCRAFT MAINTENANCE TECHNOLOGY
Arkansas State U Mid-South (AR)
Central New Mexico Comm Coll (NM)
Lake Superior Coll (MN)
Wayne County Comm Coll District (MI)

AIRLINE PILOT AND FLIGHT CREW
Central Oregon Comm Coll (OR)
Central Texas Coll (TX)
Colorado Northwestern Comm Coll (CO)
Comm Coll of Allegheny County (PA)
Comm Coll of Baltimore County (MD)
Lake Superior Coll (MN)
Treasure Valley Comm Coll (OR)
Vincennes U (IN)

AIR TRAFFIC CONTROL
Comm Coll of Baltimore County (MD)
Tulsa Comm Coll (OK)

ALLIED HEALTH AND MEDICAL ASSISTING SERVICES RELATED
Blue Ridge Comm and Tech Coll (WV)
Raritan Valley Comm Coll (NJ)
Southern Maine Comm Coll (ME)

AMERICAN INDIAN/NATIVE AMERICAN STUDIES
San Juan Coll (NM)

AMERICAN SIGN LANGUAGE (ASL)
Sierra Coll (CA)
Union County Coll (NJ)
Vincennes U (IN)

ANESTHESIOLOGIST ASSISTANT
Comm Coll of Baltimore County (MD)
Renton Tech Coll (WA)
Wayne County Comm Coll District (MI)

ANIMAL/LIVESTOCK HUSBANDRY AND PRODUCTION
Hawkeye Comm Coll (IA)
Ridgewater Coll (MN)
Sierra Coll (CA)
Southwest Wisconsin Tech Coll (WI)

ANIMAL PHYSIOLOGY
Massachusetts Bay Comm Coll (MA)

ANIMAL SCIENCES
Alamance Comm Coll (NC)
Coll of Central Florida (FL)
Kaskaskia Coll (IL)
Potomac State Coll of West Virginia U (WV)
Snow Coll (UT)
Treasure Valley Comm Coll (OR)
Trinity Valley Comm Coll (TX)
Westchester Comm Coll (NY)

ANIMATION, INTERACTIVE TECHNOLOGY, VIDEO GRAPHICS AND SPECIAL EFFECTS
Austin Comm Coll District (TX)
Borough of Manhattan Comm Coll of the City U of New York (NY)
Coll of Marin (CA)
Coll of the Canyons (CA)
Front Range Comm Coll (CO)
McHenry County Coll (IL)
Missouri State U–West Plains (MO)

Pueblo Comm Coll (CO)
Raritan Valley Comm Coll (NJ)
State U of New York Coll of Technology at Alfred (NY)
Tyler Jr Coll (TX)
West Kentucky Comm and Tech Coll (KY)

ANTHROPOLOGY
Austin Comm Coll District (TX)
Central New Mexico Comm Coll (NM)
Truckee Meadows Comm Coll (NV)
Western Wyoming Comm Coll (WY)

APPAREL AND TEXTILE MANUFACTURING
Sierra Coll (CA)

APPAREL AND TEXTILE MARKETING MANAGEMENT
Sierra Coll (CA)

APPLIANCE INSTALLATION AND REPAIR TECHNOLOGY
Renton Tech Coll (WA)

APPLIED HORTICULTURE/ HORTICULTURAL BUSINESS SERVICES RELATED
Dakota Coll at Bottineau (ND)

APPLIED HORTICULTURE/ HORTICULTURE OPERATIONS
Alamance Comm Coll (NC)
Black Hawk Coll, Moline (IL)
Comm Coll of Allegheny County (PA)
Comm Coll of Baltimore County (MD)
Dakota Coll at Bottineau (ND)
Fayetteville Tech Comm Coll (NC)
Front Range Comm Coll (CO)
Haywood Comm Coll (NC)
Kaskaskia Coll (IL)
McHenry County Coll (IL)
Sierra Coll (CA)
Tulsa Comm Coll (OK)
Vincennes U (IN)

APPLIED PSYCHOLOGY
Northampton Comm Coll (PA)

ARABIC
Austin Comm Coll District (TX)

ARCHEOLOGY
Austin Comm Coll District (TX)
Western Wyoming Comm Coll (WY)

ARCHITECTURAL DRAFTING AND CAD/CADD
Central New Mexico Comm Coll (NM)
Central Ohio Tech Coll (OH)
Coll of the Canyons (CA)
Comm Coll of Allegheny County (PA)
Comm Coll of Baltimore County (MD)
Harper Coll (IL)
Hutchinson Comm Coll (KS)
Kaskaskia Coll (IL)
Lake Superior Coll (MN)
Oakton Comm Coll (IL)
Queensborough Comm Coll of the City U of New York (NY)
Rend Lake Coll (IL)
Sierra Coll (CA)
Truckee Meadows Comm Coll (NV)
Vincennes U (IN)

ARCHITECTURAL ENGINEERING
Luzerne County Comm Coll (PA)

ARCHITECTURAL ENGINEERING TECHNOLOGY
Arapahoe Comm Coll (CO)
Coll of The Albemarle (NC)
Fayetteville Tech Comm Coll (NC)
Front Range Comm Coll (CO)
Greenville Tech Coll (SC)
Harper Coll (IL)
Harrisburg Area Comm Coll (PA)
Luzerne County Comm Coll (PA)
Northampton Comm Coll (PA)
State U of New York Coll of Technology at Alfred (NY)

ARCHITECTURAL TECHNOLOGY
Coll of Marin (CA)
Dunwoody Coll of Technology (MN)
Grand Rapids Comm Coll (MI)
John Tyler Comm Coll (VA)

ARCHITECTURE
Coll of Central Florida (FL)
Grand Rapids Comm Coll (MI)
Truckee Meadows Comm Coll (NV)

ART
Austin Comm Coll District (TX)
Black Hawk Coll, Moline (IL)
Bunker Hill Comm Coll (MA)
Cayuga County Comm Coll (NY)
Central New Mexico Comm Coll (NM)
Central Oregon Comm Coll (OR)
Coll of Central Florida (FL)
Coll of Marin (CA)
Coll of The Albemarle (NC)
Coll of the Canyons (CA)
Columbia-Greene Comm Coll (NY)
Comm Coll of Allegheny County (PA)
Grand Rapids Comm Coll (MI)
Harper Coll (IL)
Mohave Comm Coll (AZ)
Nassau Comm Coll (NY)
Queensborough Comm Coll of the City U of New York (NY)
San Jacinto Coll District (TX)
Sierra Coll (CA)
Snow Coll (UT)
Texarkana Coll (TX)
Trinity Valley Comm Coll (TX)
Tyler Jr Coll (TX)
Vincennes U (IN)
Westchester Comm Coll (NY)
Western Wyoming Comm Coll (WY)

ART HISTORY, CRITICISM AND CONSERVATION
Borough of Manhattan Comm Coll of the City U of New York (NY)
Bucks County Comm Coll (PA)

ART TEACHER EDUCATION
Vincennes U (IN)

ATHLETIC TRAINING
Coll of the Canyons (CA)
Comm Coll of Allegheny County (PA)
Northampton Comm Coll (PA)
Tyler Jr Coll (TX)

AUTOBODY/COLLISION AND REPAIR TECHNOLOGY
Arkansas State U–Newport (AR)
Austin Comm Coll District (TX)
Central Texas Coll (TX)
Coll of Marin (CA)
Dunwoody Coll of Technology (MN)
Fayetteville Tech Comm Coll (NC)
Greenville Tech Coll (SC)
Hawkeye Comm Coll (IA)
Haywood Comm Coll (NC)
Hutchinson Comm Coll (KS)
Minnesota State Coll–Southeast Tech (MN)
Ohio Tech Coll (OH)
Pueblo Comm Coll (CO)
Renton Tech Coll (WA)
Ridgewater Coll (MN)
San Jacinto Coll District (TX)
San Juan Coll (NM)
Southwestern Comm Coll (IA)
State U of New York Coll of Technology at Alfred (NY)
U of Arkansas Comm Coll at Morrilton (AR)
Vincennes U (IN)
Wayne County Comm Coll District (MI)

AUTOMATION ENGINEER TECHNOLOGY
Alexandria Tech and Comm Coll (MN)
Blue Ridge Comm and Tech Coll (WV)
Front Range Comm Coll (CO)
Grand Rapids Comm Coll (MI)
Hawkeye Comm Coll (IA)
Hutchinson Comm Coll (KS)
Mitchell Tech Inst (SD)
Southwestern Michigan Coll (MI)
Vincennes U (IN)

AUTOMOBILE/AUTOMOTIVE MECHANICS TECHNOLOGY
Alamance Comm Coll (NC)
Arapahoe Comm Coll (CO)
Arkansas State U–Newport (AR)
Austin Comm Coll District (TX)
Black Hawk Coll, Moline (IL)
Central Oregon Comm Coll (OR)
Central Texas Coll (TX)
Coll of Marin (CA)
Coll of the Canyons (CA)
Colorado Northwestern Comm Coll (CO)
Columbia-Greene Comm Coll (NY)
Comm Coll of Allegheny County (PA)
Comm Coll of Baltimore County (MD)
Dunwoody Coll of Technology (MN)
East Central Coll (MO)
Fayetteville Tech Comm Coll (NC)
Front Range Comm Coll (CO)
Grand Rapids Comm Coll (MI)
Greenville Tech Coll (SC)
Halifax Comm Coll (NC)
Harrisburg Area Comm Coll (PA)
Hawkeye Comm Coll (IA)
Haywood Comm Coll (NC)
Hutchinson Comm Coll (KS)
Kaskaskia Coll (IL)
Lake Region State Coll (ND)
Lake Superior Coll (MN)
Luzerne County Comm Coll (PA)
Massachusetts Bay Comm Coll (MA)
Mohave Comm Coll (AZ)
Northampton Comm Coll (PA)
Oakton Comm Coll (IL)
Ohio Tech Coll (OH)
Owensboro Comm and Tech Coll (KY)
Pueblo Comm Coll (CO)
Quinsigamond Comm Coll (MA)
Rend Lake Coll (IL)
Renton Tech Coll (WA)
Ridgewater Coll (MN)
Rock Valley Coll (IL)
St. Louis Comm Coll (MO)
San Jacinto Coll District (TX)
San Juan Coll (NM)
Sierra Coll (CA)
Snow Coll (UT)
Southern Maine Comm Coll (ME)
Southwestern Comm Coll (IA)
Southwestern Comm Coll (NC)
Southwestern Michigan Coll (MI)
State U of New York Coll of Technology at Alfred (NY)
Texarkana Coll (TX)
Tidewater Comm Coll (VA)
Trinity Valley Comm Coll (TX)
Truckee Meadows Comm Coll (NV)
Tyler Jr Coll (TX)
Union County Coll (NJ)
U of Arkansas Comm Coll at Morrilton (AR)
Vincennes U (IN)
Wayne County Comm Coll District (MI)
Western Wyoming Comm Coll (WY)
West Kentucky Comm and Tech Coll (KY)

AUTOMOTIVE ENGINEERING TECHNOLOGY
Comm Coll of Allegheny County (PA)
Raritan Valley Comm Coll (NJ)

AVIATION/AIRWAY MANAGEMENT
Coll of The Albemarle (NC)
Comm Coll of Allegheny County (PA)
Comm Coll of Baltimore County (MD)
Lake Superior Coll (MN)

AVIONICS MAINTENANCE TECHNOLOGY
Rock Valley Coll (IL)
Southern U at Shreveport (LA)

BAKING AND PASTRY ARTS
Blue Ridge Comm and Tech Coll (WV)
Bucks County Comm Coll (PA)
Luzerne County Comm Coll (PA)
St. Louis Comm Coll (MO)
San Jacinto Coll District (TX)
Sullivan County Comm Coll (NY)

BANKING AND FINANCIAL SUPPORT SERVICES
Alamance Comm Coll (NC)
Comm Coll of Allegheny County (PA)
Harper Coll (IL)
Luzerne County Comm Coll (PA)
Oakton Comm Coll (IL)

BARBERING
Rend Lake Coll (IL)

BEHAVIORAL ASPECTS OF HEALTH
St. Louis Comm Coll (MO)

BEHAVIORAL SCIENCES
Mohave Comm Coll (AZ)
San Jacinto Coll District (TX)
Vincennes U (IN)

BIOENGINEERING AND BIOMEDICAL ENGINEERING
Bunker Hill Comm Coll (MA)

BIOINFORMATICS
Massachusetts Bay Comm Coll (MA)

BIOLOGICAL AND BIOMEDICAL SCIENCES RELATED
Massachusetts Bay Comm Coll (MA)
Vincennes U (IN)

BIOLOGICAL AND PHYSICAL SCIENCES
Black Hawk Coll, Moline (IL)
Central Oregon Comm Coll (OR)
Coll of Marin (CA)
Coll of the Canyons (CA)
Comm Coll of Baltimore County (MD)
Heartland Comm Coll (IL)
Kaskaskia Coll (IL)
Luzerne County Comm Coll (PA)
McHenry County Coll (IL)
Oakton Comm Coll (IL)
Rend Lake Coll (IL)
Sierra Coll (CA)
Tidewater Comm Coll (VA)
U of South Carolina Union (SC)
Western Wyoming Comm Coll (WY)

BIOLOGY/BIOLOGICAL SCIENCES
Austin Comm Coll District (TX)
Bunker Hill Comm Coll (MA)
Central New Mexico Comm Coll (NM)
Central Oregon Comm Coll (OR)
Central Texas Coll (TX)
Coll of Central Florida (FL)
Coll of Marin (CA)
Comm Coll of Allegheny County (PA)
Dakota Coll at Bottineau (ND)
Harper Coll (IL)
Harrisburg Area Comm Coll (PA)
Hutchinson Comm Coll (KS)
Northampton Comm Coll (PA)
Potomac State Coll of West Virginia U (WV)
Quinsigamond Comm Coll (MA)
Ridgewater Coll (MN)
St. Charles Comm Coll (MO)
San Jacinto Coll District (TX)
San Juan Coll (NM)
Sierra Coll (CA)
Snow Coll (UT)
State U of New York Coll of Technology at Alfred (NY)
Texarkana Coll (TX)
Tohono O'odham Comm Coll (AZ)
Trinity Valley Comm Coll (TX)
Truckee Meadows Comm Coll (NV)
Tyler Jr Coll (TX)
Union County Coll (NJ)
Western Wyoming Comm Coll (WY)
Wor-Wic Comm Coll (MD)

BIOLOGY/BIOTECHNOLOGY LABORATORY TECHNICIAN
Austin Comm Coll District (TX)
Bucks County Comm Coll (PA)
East Central Coll (MO)
Massachusetts Bay Comm Coll (MA)
St. Louis Comm Coll (MO)

BIOLOGY TEACHER EDUCATION
Bucks County Comm Coll (PA)

BIOMEDICAL TECHNOLOGY
Austin Comm Coll District (TX)
Minnesota State Coll–Southeast Tech (MN)
Quinsigamond Comm Coll (MA)
Rend Lake Coll (IL)
Wayne County Comm Coll District (MI)

BIOTECHNOLOGY
Alamance Comm Coll (NC)
Borough of Manhattan Comm Coll of the City U of New York (NY)
Bunker Hill Comm Coll (MA)
Central New Mexico Comm Coll (NM)
Coll of The Albemarle (NC)
Comm Coll of Allegheny County (PA)
Northampton Comm Coll (PA)
Queensborough Comm Coll of the City U of New York (NY)
Quinsigamond Comm Coll (MA)
Southern Maine Comm Coll (ME)
Tulsa Comm Coll (OK)

BOTANY/PLANT BIOLOGY
Snow Coll (UT)

BUILDING/CONSTRUCTION FINISHING, MANAGEMENT, AND INSPECTION RELATED
Comm Coll of Baltimore County (MD)
Fayetteville Tech Comm Coll (NC)
Haywood Comm Coll (NC)
Oakton Comm Coll (IL)
Snow Coll (UT)
Vincennes U (IN)

BUILDING/CONSTRUCTION SITE MANAGEMENT
Arapahoe Comm Coll (CO)
Coll of the Canyons (CA)
Comm Coll of Baltimore County (MD)
Dunwoody Coll of Technology (MN)

BUILDING CONSTRUCTION TECHNOLOGY
Central New Mexico Comm Coll (NM)
Coll of the Canyons (CA)
Comm Coll of Allegheny County (PA)
Lake Superior Coll (MN)
Mitchell Tech Inst (SD)
Southern Maine Comm Coll (ME)

BUILDING/PROPERTY MAINTENANCE
Central Texas Coll (TX)
Comm Coll of Allegheny County (PA)
Luzerne County Comm Coll (PA)
Owensboro Comm and Tech Coll (KY)
Renton Tech Coll (WA)
Wayne County Comm Coll District (MI)

BUSINESS ADMINISTRATION AND MANAGEMENT
Alamance Comm Coll (NC)
Alexandria Tech and Comm Coll (MN)
Arapahoe Comm Coll (CO)
Arkansas State U Mid-South (AR)
Austin Comm Coll District (TX)
Blue Ridge Comm and Tech Coll (WV)
Borough of Manhattan Comm Coll of the City U of New York (NY)
Bucks County Comm Coll (PA)
Bunker Hill Comm Coll (MA)
Cayuga County Comm Coll (NY)
Central New Mexico Comm Coll (NM)
Central Ohio Tech Coll (OH)
Central Oregon Comm Coll (OR)
Central Texas Coll (TX)
Cleveland State Comm Coll (TN)
Coll of Central Florida (FL)
Coll of Marin (CA)
Coll of The Albemarle (NC)
Coll of the Canyons (CA)
Columbia-Greene Comm Coll (NY)
Comm Coll of Allegheny County (PA)
Comm Coll of Baltimore County (MD)
Comm Coll of Denver (CO)
Dakota Coll at Bottineau (ND)
Daytona State Coll (FL)
Fayetteville Tech Comm Coll (NC)
Front Range Comm Coll (CO)
Grand Rapids Comm Coll (MI)
Greenville Tech Coll (SC)
Halifax Comm Coll (NC)
Harper Coll (IL)
Harrisburg Area Comm Coll (PA)

Haywood Comm Coll (NC)
Henderson Comm Coll (KY)
Johnston Comm Coll (NC)
John Tyler Comm Coll (VA)
Lake Region State Coll (ND)
Lake Superior Coll (MN)
Luzerne County Comm Coll (PA)
Manchester Comm Coll (CT)
Massachusetts Bay Comm Coll (MA)
McHenry County Coll (IL)
Minnesota State Coll–Southeast Tech (MN)
Mitchell Comm Coll (NC)
Motlow State Comm Coll (TN)
Nassau Comm Coll (NY)
Northampton Comm Coll (PA)
Owensboro Comm and Tech Coll (KY)
Potomac State Coll of West Virginia U (WV)
Pueblo Comm Coll (CO)
Queensborough Comm Coll of the City U of New York (NY)
Quinsigamond Comm Coll (MA)
Raritan Valley Comm Coll (NJ)
Richmond Comm Coll (NC)
Ridgewater Coll (MN)
Rock Valley Coll (IL)
San Jacinto Coll District (TX)
San Juan Coll (NM)
Sierra Coll (CA)
Snow Coll (UT)
Southern Maine Comm Coll (ME)
Southwestern Comm Coll (IA)
Southwestern Comm Coll (NC)
Southwestern Michigan Coll (MI)
State U of New York Coll of Technology at Alfred (NY)
Sullivan County Comm Coll (NY)
Texarkana Coll (TX)
Tidewater Comm Coll (VA)
Tohono O'odham Comm Coll (AZ)
Treasure Valley Comm Coll (OR)
Trinity Valley Comm Coll (TX)
Tulsa Comm Coll (OK)
Tyler Jr Coll (TX)
Union County Coll (NJ)
Vincennes U (IN)
Wayne County Comm Coll District (MI)
Westchester Comm Coll (NY)
Western Wyoming Comm Coll (WY)
West Kentucky Comm and Tech Coll (KY)
Wor-Wic Comm Coll (MD)

BUSINESS ADMINISTRATION, MANAGEMENT AND OPERATIONS RELATED
Blue Ridge Comm and Tech Coll (WV)
Bunker Hill Comm Coll (MA)
Coll of Central Florida (FL)
John Tyler Comm Coll (VA)
Lamar Inst of Technology (TX)

BUSINESS AND PERSONAL/ FINANCIAL SERVICES MARKETING
Hutchinson Comm Coll (KS)

BUSINESS AUTOMATION/ TECHNOLOGY/DATA ENTRY
Comm Coll of Allegheny County (PA)
Dakota Coll at Bottineau (ND)
Kaskaskia Coll (IL)
Lake Superior Coll (MN)
Mitchell Tech Inst (SD)
Potomac State Coll of West Virginia U (WV)
Pueblo Comm Coll (CO)
Renton Tech Coll (WA)

BUSINESS/COMMERCE
Alexandria Tech and Comm Coll (MN)
Arkansas State U Mid-South (AR)
Arkansas State U–Newport (AR)
Austin Comm Coll District (TX)
Bucks County Comm Coll (PA)
Central Texas Coll (TX)
Coll of Central Florida (FL)
Coll of Marin (CA)
Colorado Northwestern Comm Coll (CO)
Columbia-Greene Comm Coll (NY)
Comm Coll of Baltimore County (MD)
East Central Coll (MO)
Harrisburg Area Comm Coll (PA)
Hutchinson Comm Coll (KS)
Kaskaskia Coll (IL)
Missouri State U–West Plains (MO)
Northampton Comm Coll (PA)
Quinsigamond Comm Coll (MA)
Raritan Valley Comm Coll (NJ)
Rend Lake Coll (IL)
St. Louis Comm Coll (MO)
San Jacinto Coll District (TX)
Sierra Coll (CA)
Southern U at Shreveport (LA)
Sowela Tech Comm Coll (LA)
Texarkana Coll (TX)
Truckee Meadows Comm Coll (NV)
Tulsa Comm Coll (OK)
Tyler Jr Coll (TX)
Union County Coll (NJ)
U of Arkansas Comm Coll at Morrilton (AR)
Vincennes U (IN)
Wor-Wic Comm Coll (MD)

BUSINESS MACHINE REPAIR
Comm Coll of Allegheny County (PA)

BUSINESS, MANAGEMENT, AND MARKETING RELATED
Tulsa Comm Coll (OK)

BUSINESS OPERATIONS SUPPORT AND SECRETARIAL SERVICES RELATED
Bunker Hill Comm Coll (MA)

BUSINESS TEACHER EDUCATION
Snow Coll (UT)
Trinity Valley Comm Coll (TX)
Vincennes U (IN)

CABINETMAKING AND MILLWORK
Bucks County Comm Coll (PA)
Sierra Coll (CA)

CAD/CADD DRAFTING/DESIGN TECHNOLOGY
Central Ohio Tech Coll (OH)
Central Oregon Comm Coll (OR)
Comm Coll of Allegheny County (PA)
Dunwoody Coll of Technology (MN)
Front Range Comm Coll (CO)
Lake Superior Coll (MN)
Minnesota State Coll–Southeast Tech (MN)
Northampton Comm Coll (PA)
Wayne County Comm Coll District (MI)

CARDIOVASCULAR TECHNOLOGY
Bunker Hill Comm Coll (MA)
Harper Coll (IL)
Harrisburg Area Comm Coll (PA)
San Jacinto Coll District (TX)
Southern Maine Comm Coll (ME)

CARPENTRY
Alamance Comm Coll (NC)
Austin Comm Coll District (TX)
Comm Coll of Allegheny County (PA)
Hawkeye Comm Coll (IA)
Hutchinson Comm Coll (KS)
Kaskaskia Coll (IL)
Lake Superior Coll (MN)
Minnesota State Coll–Southeast Tech (MN)
Ridgewater Coll (MN)
San Juan Coll (NM)
Southwestern Comm Coll (IA)
Southwestern Michigan Coll (MI)
Tohono O'odham Comm Coll (AZ)
Treasure Valley Comm Coll (OR)
Vincennes U (IN)

CHEMICAL TECHNOLOGY
Bucks County Comm Coll (PA)
Comm Coll of Allegheny County (PA)
Grand Rapids Comm Coll (MI)
Lamar Inst of Technology (TX)
San Jacinto Coll District (TX)
Sowela Tech Comm Coll (LA)

CHEMISTRY
Austin Comm Coll District (TX)
Bunker Hill Comm Coll (MA)
Central New Mexico Comm Coll (NM)
Central Texas Coll (TX)
Coll of Central Florida (FL)
Coll of Marin (CA)
Comm Coll of Allegheny County (PA)
Dakota Coll at Bottineau (ND)
Harper Coll (IL)
Harrisburg Area Comm Coll (PA)
Mohave Comm Coll (AZ)
Northampton Comm Coll (PA)
Potomac State Coll of West Virginia U (WV)
Queensborough Comm Coll of the City U of New York (NY)
Quinsigamond Comm Coll (MA)
Ridgewater Coll (MN)
St. Charles Comm Coll (MO)
San Jacinto Coll District (TX)
San Juan Coll (NM)
Sierra Coll (CA)
Snow Coll (UT)
Texarkana Coll (TX)
Trinity Valley Comm Coll (TX)
Truckee Meadows Comm Coll (NV)
Tyler Jr Coll (TX)
Union County Coll (NJ)
Western Wyoming Comm Coll (WY)

CHEMISTRY RELATED
Vincennes U (IN)

CHEMISTRY TEACHER EDUCATION
Comm Coll of Baltimore County (MD)
Daytona State Coll (FL)
Vincennes U (IN)

CHILD-CARE AND SUPPORT SERVICES MANAGEMENT
Cayuga County Comm Coll (NY)
Central Oregon Comm Coll (OR)
Comm Coll of Baltimore County (MD)
Dakota Coll at Bottineau (ND)
East Central Coll (MO)
Grand Rapids Comm Coll (MI)
Greenville Tech Coll (SC)
Haywood Comm Coll (NC)
Hutchinson Comm Coll (KS)
Lamar Inst of Technology (TX)
Lurleen B. Wallace Comm Coll (AL)
Mitchell Comm Coll (NC)
St. Charles Comm Coll (MO)
Texarkana Coll (TX)
Vincennes U (IN)
Wayne County Comm Coll District (MI)
Westchester Comm Coll (NY)
Wor-Wic Comm Coll (MD)

CHILD-CARE PROVISION
Black Hawk Coll, Moline (IL)
Bucks County Comm Coll (PA)
Coll of Marin (CA)
Coll of the Canyons (CA)
Comm Coll of Allegheny County (PA)
Dakota Coll at Bottineau (ND)
Harper Coll (IL)
Hawkeye Comm Coll (IA)
Heartland Comm Coll (IL)
Henderson Comm Coll (KY)
John Tyler Comm Coll (VA)
Kaskaskia Coll (IL)
Lake Region State Coll (ND)
Lamar Inst of Technology (TX)
Luzerne County Comm Coll (PA)
McHenry County Coll (IL)
Oakton Comm Coll (IL)
Owensboro Comm and Tech Coll (KY)
Raritan Valley Comm Coll (NJ)
Rend Lake Coll (IL)
San Juan Coll (NM)
West Kentucky Comm and Tech Coll (KY)

CHILD DEVELOPMENT
Austin Comm Coll District (TX)
Cleveland State Comm Coll (TN)
Comm Coll of Allegheny County (PA)
Motlow State Comm Coll (TN)
Rock Valley Coll (IL)
St. Louis Comm Coll (MO)
San Jacinto Coll District (TX)
Sierra Coll (CA)
Snow Coll (UT)
Southwestern Comm Coll (NC)
Texarkana Coll (TX)
Trinity Valley Comm Coll (TX)
Tulsa Comm Coll (OK)
Tyler Jr Coll (TX)
U of Arkansas Comm Coll at Morrilton (AR)

CHINESE
Austin Comm Coll District (TX)

CINEMATOGRAPHY AND FILM/ VIDEO PRODUCTION
Bucks County Comm Coll (PA)
Central New Mexico Comm Coll (NM)
Coll of Marin (CA)
Coll of the Canyons (CA)
Comm Coll of Aurora (CO)

CIVIL DRAFTING AND CAD/ CADD
Central Ohio Tech Coll (OH)
Comm Coll of Allegheny County (PA)
Renton Tech Coll (WA)

CIVIL ENGINEERING
Austin Comm Coll District (TX)
Potomac State Coll of West Virginia U (WV)
Tidewater Comm Coll (VA)
Truckee Meadows Comm Coll (NV)

CIVIL ENGINEERING TECHNOLOGY
Central Ohio Tech Coll (OH)
Comm Coll of Allegheny County (PA)
Dunwoody Coll of Technology (MN)
Fayetteville Tech Comm Coll (NC)
Harrisburg Area Comm Coll (PA)
Hawkeye Comm Coll (IA)
Lake Superior Coll (MN)
Nassau Comm Coll (NY)
Westchester Comm Coll (NY)

CLINICAL LABORATORY SCIENCE/MEDICAL TECHNOLOGY
Coll of Central Florida (FL)

CLINICAL/MEDICAL LABORATORY TECHNOLOGY
Alamance Comm Coll (NC)
Alexandria Tech and Comm Coll (MN)
Arapahoe Comm Coll (CO)
Austin Comm Coll District (TX)
Blue Ridge Comm and Tech Coll (WV)
Bucks County Comm Coll (PA)
Bunker Hill Comm Coll (MA)
Central New Mexico Comm Coll (NM)
Central Texas Coll (TX)
Coll of the Canyons (CA)
Comm Coll of Allegheny County (PA)
Comm Coll of Baltimore County (MD)
Greenville Tech Coll (SC)
Harrisburg Area Comm Coll (PA)
Hawkeye Comm Coll (IA)
Henderson Comm Coll (KY)
Hutchinson Comm Coll (KS)
Kaskaskia Coll (IL)
Lake Superior Coll (MN)
Manchester Comm Coll (CT)
Mitchell Tech Inst (SD)
Motlow State Comm Coll (TN)
Nassau Comm Coll (NY)
Oakton Comm Coll (IL)
St. Louis Comm Coll (MO)
San Jacinto Coll District (TX)
San Juan Coll (NM)
Southern U at Shreveport (LA)
Southwestern Comm Coll (NC)
Tulsa Comm Coll (OK)
Tyler Jr Coll (TX)
West Kentucky Comm and Tech Coll (KY)

CLINICAL/MEDICAL SOCIAL WORK
Central Texas Coll (TX)

COMMERCIAL AND ADVERTISING ART
Alamance Comm Coll (NC)
Alexandria Tech and Comm Coll (MN)
Bucks County Comm Coll (PA)
Central Texas Coll (TX)
Comm Coll of Allegheny County (PA)
Comm Coll of Baltimore County (MD)
Fayetteville Tech Comm Coll (NC)
Grand Rapids Comm Coll (MI)
Halifax Comm Coll (NC)
Luzerne County Comm Coll (PA)
Manchester Comm Coll (CT)
Nassau Comm Coll (NY)
St. Charles Comm Coll (MO)
San Jacinto Coll District (TX)
San Juan Coll (NM)
Southwestern Comm Coll (NC)
Sowela Tech Comm Coll (LA)
Sullivan County Comm Coll (NY)
Tidewater Comm Coll (VA)
Truckee Meadows Comm Coll (NV)
Vincennes U (IN)
Westchester Comm Coll (NY)

COMMERCIAL PHOTOGRAPHY
Arapahoe Comm Coll (CO)
Austin Comm Coll District (TX)
Bucks County Comm Coll (PA)
Hawkeye Comm Coll (IA)
Luzerne County Comm Coll (PA)
McHenry County Coll (IL)
Ridgewater Coll (MN)
Sierra Coll (CA)
Trinity Valley Comm Coll (TX)

COMMUNICATION
Central New Mexico Comm Coll (NM)
Potomac State Coll of West Virginia U (WV)
Tulsa Comm Coll (OK)

COMMUNICATION AND JOURNALISM RELATED
Harrisburg Area Comm Coll (PA)

COMMUNICATION AND MEDIA RELATED
Manor Coll (PA)
Raritan Valley Comm Coll (NJ)

COMMUNICATIONS TECHNOLOGIES AND SUPPORT SERVICES RELATED
Comm Coll of Allegheny County (PA)
Comm Coll of Baltimore County (MD)
Vincennes U (IN)

COMMUNICATIONS TECHNOLOGY
Hutchinson Comm Coll (KS)
Pueblo Comm Coll (CO)

COMMUNITY HEALTH AND PREVENTIVE MEDICINE
Massachusetts Bay Comm Coll (MA)

COMMUNITY HEALTH SERVICES COUNSELING
Comm Coll of Allegheny County (PA)
Daytona State Coll (FL)

COMMUNITY ORGANIZATION AND ADVOCACY
Borough of Manhattan Comm Coll of the City U of New York (NY)
Westchester Comm Coll (NY)

COMPUTER AND INFORMATION SCIENCES
Arapahoe Comm Coll (CO)
Arkansas State U Mid-South (AR)
Austin Comm Coll District (TX)
Borough of Manhattan Comm Coll of the City U of New York (NY)
Bucks County Comm Coll (PA)
Cayuga County Comm Coll (NY)
Central New Mexico Comm Coll (NM)
Cleveland State Comm Coll (TN)
Coll of Central Florida (FL)
Columbia-Greene Comm Coll (NY)
Comm Coll of Allegheny County (PA)
Comm Coll of Aurora (CO)
Comm Coll of Baltimore County (MD)
Comm Coll of Denver (CO)
Dakota Coll at Bottineau (ND)
Front Range Comm Coll (CO)
Harper Coll (IL)
Harrisburg Area Comm Coll (PA)
Henderson Comm Coll (KY)
Hutchinson Comm Coll (KS)
John Tyler Comm Coll (VA)
Lurleen B. Wallace Comm Coll (AL)
Luzerne County Comm Coll (PA)
Manor Coll (PA)
Mohave Comm Coll (AZ)
Nassau Comm Coll (NY)
Owensboro Comm and Tech Coll (KY)
Potomac State Coll of West Virginia U (WV)
Pueblo Comm Coll (CO)
Queensborough Comm Coll of the City U of New York (NY)
Quinsigamond Comm Coll (MA)
Raritan Valley Comm Coll (NJ)
San Jacinto Coll District (TX)
State U of New York Coll of Technology at Alfred (NY)
Texarkana Coll (TX)
Treasure Valley Comm Coll (OR)
U of Arkansas Comm Coll at Morrilton (AR)
Westchester Comm Coll (NY)
Western Wyoming Comm Coll (WY)
West Kentucky Comm and Tech Coll (KY)

Wor-Wic Comm Coll (MD)

COMPUTER AND INFORMATION SCIENCES AND SUPPORT SERVICES RELATED
Bunker Hill Comm Coll (MA)
Cayuga County Comm Coll (NY)
Dakota Coll at Bottineau (ND)
Massachusetts Bay Comm Coll (MA)
Sierra Coll (CA)
Tulsa Comm Coll (OK)
Union County Coll (NJ)
Westchester Comm Coll (NY)

COMPUTER AND INFORMATION SCIENCES RELATED
Central Oregon Comm Coll (OR)
Lamar Inst of Technology (TX)
Luzerne County Comm Coll (PA)
Nassau Comm Coll (NY)
Tulsa Comm Coll (OK)

COMPUTER AND INFORMATION SYSTEMS SECURITY
Blue Ridge Comm and Tech Coll (WV)
Bucks County Comm Coll (PA)
Bunker Hill Comm Coll (MA)
Central Texas Coll (TX)
Comm Coll of Allegheny County (PA)
Comm Coll of Baltimore County (MD)
Harrisburg Area Comm Coll (PA)
Massachusetts Bay Comm Coll (MA)
Northampton Comm Coll (PA)
Quinsigamond Comm Coll (MA)
Rend Lake Coll (IL)
St. Louis Comm Coll (MO)
Southern Maine Comm Coll (ME)
Westchester Comm Coll (NY)

COMPUTER ENGINEERING
Comm Coll of Baltimore County (MD)
Snow Coll (UT)

COMPUTER ENGINEERING TECHNOLOGY
Coll of The Albemarle (NC)
Comm Coll of Allegheny County (PA)
Daytona State Coll (FL)
Queensborough Comm Coll of the City U of New York (NY)
Quinsigamond Comm Coll (MA)
Richmond Comm Coll (NC)
Rock Valley Coll (IL)
Southern Maine Comm Coll (ME)
Southwestern Comm Coll (NC)
State U of New York Coll of Technology at Alfred (NY)

COMPUTER GRAPHICS
Central Ohio Tech Coll (OH)
Luzerne County Comm Coll (PA)
Nassau Comm Coll (NY)
Quinsigamond Comm Coll (MA)
Sullivan County Comm Coll (NY)

COMPUTER/INFORMATION TECHNOLOGY SERVICES ADMINISTRATION RELATED
Bunker Hill Comm Coll (MA)
Hawkeye Comm Coll (IA)
Massachusetts Bay Comm Coll (MA)
Vincennes U (IN)

COMPUTER INSTALLATION AND REPAIR TECHNOLOGY
Lake Region State Coll (ND)
Sierra Coll (CA)
Tulsa Comm Coll (OK)

COMPUTER NUMERICALLY CONTROLLED (CNC) MACHINIST TECHNOLOGY
Dunwoody Coll of Technology (MN)
Greenville Tech Coll (SC)
Lake Superior Coll (MN)
Wayne County Comm Coll District (MI)

COMPUTER PROGRAMMING
Austin Comm Coll District (TX)
Bunker Hill Comm Coll (MA)
Central Ohio Tech Coll (OH)
Central Texas Coll (TX)
Coll of The Albemarle (NC)
Comm Coll of Allegheny County (PA)
Daytona State Coll (FL)
Grand Rapids Comm Coll (MI)
Harper Coll (IL)
Minnesota State Coll–Southeast Tech (MN)
Mitchell Comm Coll (NC)
Northampton Comm Coll (PA)
Oakton Comm Coll (IL)
Quinsigamond Comm Coll (MA)
Raritan Valley Comm Coll (NJ)
Rend Lake Coll (IL)
Ridgewater Coll (MN)
St. Charles Comm Coll (MO)
Sierra Coll (CA)
Southwestern Michigan Coll (MI)
Sowela Tech Comm Coll (LA)
Tidewater Comm Coll (VA)
Vincennes U (IN)
Wayne County Comm Coll District (MI)

COMPUTER PROGRAMMING RELATED
Luzerne County Comm Coll (PA)

COMPUTER PROGRAMMING (SPECIFIC APPLICATIONS)
Bunker Hill Comm Coll (MA)
Coll of The Albemarle (NC)
Daytona State Coll (FL)
Harper Coll (IL)
Mitchell Comm Coll (NC)
Quinsigamond Comm Coll (MA)
Sullivan County Comm Coll (NY)
Truckee Meadows Comm Coll (NV)
Western Wyoming Comm Coll (WY)

COMPUTER SCIENCE
Borough of Manhattan Comm Coll of the City U of New York (NY)
Bunker Hill Comm Coll (MA)
Central New Mexico Comm Coll (NM)
Central Oregon Comm Coll (OR)
Coll of Marin (CA)
Coll of the Canyons (CA)
Harper Coll (IL)
Harrisburg Area Comm Coll (PA)
Luzerne County Comm Coll (PA)
Massachusetts Bay Comm Coll (MA)
Mohave Comm Coll (AZ)
Nassau Comm Coll (NY)
Northampton Comm Coll (PA)
Quinsigamond Comm Coll (MA)
Renton Tech Coll (WA)
Ridgewater Coll (MN)
Rock Valley Coll (IL)
Snow Coll (UT)
Southern Maine Comm Coll (ME)
Southern U at Shreveport (LA)
Treasure Valley Comm Coll (OR)
Trinity Valley Comm Coll (TX)
Tulsa Comm Coll (OK)
Tyler Jr Coll (TX)
Union County Coll (NJ)
Western Wyoming Comm Coll (WY)

COMPUTER SOFTWARE AND MEDIA APPLICATIONS RELATED
Dakota Coll at Bottineau (ND)

COMPUTER SUPPORT SPECIALIST
Central Ohio Tech Coll (OH)
Grand Rapids Comm Coll (MI)
Hutchinson Comm Coll (KS)
Northampton Comm Coll (PA)
Quinsigamond Comm Coll (MA)

COMPUTER SYSTEMS ANALYSIS
Hutchinson Comm Coll (KS)
Mitchell Comm Coll (NC)
Quinsigamond Comm Coll (MA)
Wor-Wic Comm Coll (MD)

COMPUTER SYSTEMS NETWORKING AND TELECOMMUNICATIONS
Alexandria Tech and Comm Coll (MN)
Arapahoe Comm Coll (CO)
Austin Comm Coll District (TX)
Bucks County Comm Coll (PA)
Bunker Hill Comm Coll (MA)
Central Oregon Comm Coll (OR)
Coll of Marin (CA)
Coll of the Canyons (CA)
Comm Coll of Aurora (CO)
Comm Coll of Baltimore County (MD)
Dunwoody Coll of Technology (MN)
East Central Coll (MO)
Front Range Comm Coll (CO)
Grand Rapids Comm Coll (MI)
Harrisburg Area Comm Coll (PA)
Hawkeye Comm Coll (IA)
Haywood Comm Coll (NC)
Heartland Comm Coll (IL)
Hutchinson Comm Coll (KS)
Luzerne County Comm Coll (PA)
McHenry County Coll (IL)
Minnesota State Coll–Southeast Tech (MN)
Nassau Comm Coll (NY)
Northampton Comm Coll (PA)
Renton Tech Coll (WA)
Ridgewater Coll (MN)
Rock Valley Coll (IL)
Sierra Coll (CA)
Southwestern Comm Coll (IA)
Southwestern Michigan Coll (MI)
Southwest Wisconsin Tech Coll (WI)
Sowela Tech Comm Coll (LA)
Truckee Meadows Comm Coll (NV)
Tyler Jr Coll (TX)
Vincennes U (IN)

COMPUTER TECHNOLOGY/ COMPUTER SYSTEMS TECHNOLOGY
Arkansas State U–Newport (AR)
Central Texas Coll (TX)
Comm Coll of Allegheny County (PA)
Dakota Coll at Bottineau (ND)
Lake Superior Coll (MN)
Lamar Inst of Technology (TX)
Luzerne County Comm Coll (PA)
Minnesota State Coll–Southeast Tech (MN)
Rend Lake Coll (IL)
Ridgewater Coll (MN)
U of Arkansas Comm Coll at Morrilton (AR)

CONSTRUCTION ENGINEERING TECHNOLOGY
Coll of Central Florida (FL)
Comm Coll of Allegheny County (PA)
Daytona State Coll (FL)
Greenville Tech Coll (SC)
Harrisburg Area Comm Coll (PA)
Raritan Valley Comm Coll (NJ)
Rock Valley Coll (IL)
San Jacinto Coll District (TX)
Snow Coll (UT)
State U of New York Coll of Technology at Alfred (NY)
Sullivan County Comm Coll (NY)

CONSTRUCTION MANAGEMENT
Central New Mexico Comm Coll (NM)
Kaskaskia Coll (IL)
McHenry County Coll (IL)
Northampton Comm Coll (PA)
Renton Tech Coll (WA)

CONSTRUCTION TRADES
Coll of The Albemarle (NC)
Comm Coll of Allegheny County (PA)
East Central Coll (MO)
Sierra Coll (CA)

CONSTRUCTION TRADES RELATED
Comm Coll of Allegheny County (PA)
State U of New York Coll of Technology at Alfred (NY)

CONSUMER MERCHANDISING/ RETAILING MANAGEMENT
Sullivan County Comm Coll (NY)

COOKING AND RELATED CULINARY ARTS
Central Oregon Comm Coll (OR)
Mitchell Comm Coll (NC)
Pueblo Comm Coll (CO)
Truckee Meadows Comm Coll (NV)

CORRECTIONS
Austin Comm Coll District (TX)
Cayuga County Comm Coll (NY)
Comm Coll of Allegheny County (PA)
Grand Rapids Comm Coll (MI)
Trinity Valley Comm Coll (TX)
Wayne County Comm Coll District (MI)
Westchester Comm Coll (NY)

COSMETOLOGY
Arapahoe Comm Coll (CO)
Central New Mexico Comm Coll (NM)
Colorado Northwestern Comm Coll (CO)
Fayetteville Tech Comm Coll (NC)
Halifax Comm Coll (NC)
Haywood Comm Coll (NC)
Hutchinson Comm Coll (KS)
Kaskaskia Coll (IL)
Minnesota State Coll–Southeast Tech (MN)
Pueblo Comm Coll (CO)
Rend Lake Coll (IL)
Ridgewater Coll (MN)
San Jacinto Coll District (TX)
San Juan Coll (NM)
Southwestern Comm Coll (NC)
Texarkana Coll (TX)
Trinity Valley Comm Coll (TX)
Vincennes U (IN)

COSMETOLOGY AND PERSONAL GROOMING ARTS RELATED
Comm Coll of Allegheny County (PA)

COSMETOLOGY, BARBER/ STYLING, AND NAIL INSTRUCTION
San Jacinto Coll District (TX)

COURT REPORTING
Coll of Marin (CA)
Comm Coll of Allegheny County (PA)
Luzerne County Comm Coll (PA)
State U of New York Coll of Technology at Alfred (NY)

CRAFTS, FOLK ART AND ARTISANRY
Coll of The Albemarle (NC)
Haywood Comm Coll (NC)

CREATIVE WRITING
Austin Comm Coll District (TX)

CRIMINALISTICS AND CRIMINAL SCIENCE
Tyler Jr Coll (TX)

CRIMINAL JUSTICE/LAW ENFORCEMENT ADMINISTRATION
Arapahoe Comm Coll (CO)
Arkansas State U–Newport (AR)
Bunker Hill Comm Coll (MA)
Central New Mexico Comm Coll (NM)
Central Ohio Tech Coll (OH)
Coll of Central Florida (FL)
Coll of The Albemarle (NC)
Columbia-Greene Comm Coll (NY)
Comm Coll of Aurora (CO)
Daytona State Coll (FL)
Harper Coll (IL)
Harrisburg Area Comm Coll (PA)
Haywood Comm Coll (NC)
John Tyler Comm Coll (VA)
Kaskaskia Coll (IL)
Luzerne County Comm Coll (PA)
Manchester Comm Coll (CT)
Manor Coll (PA)
Massachusetts Bay Comm Coll (MA)
Mitchell Comm Coll (NC)
Nassau Comm Coll (NY)
Owensboro Comm and Tech Coll (KY)
Pueblo Comm Coll (CO)
Queensborough Comm Coll of the City U of New York (NY)
Raritan Valley Comm Coll (NJ)
Rock Valley Coll (IL)
Snow Coll (UT)
Southern U at Shreveport (LA)
Texarkana Coll (TX)
Trinity Valley Comm Coll (TX)
Union County Coll (NJ)
U of Arkansas Comm Coll at Morrilton (AR)
Western Wyoming Comm Coll (WY)
West Kentucky Comm and Tech Coll (KY)

CRIMINAL JUSTICE/POLICE SCIENCE
Alexandria Tech and Comm Coll (MN)
Austin Comm Coll District (TX)
Black Hawk Coll, Moline (IL)
Borough of Manhattan Comm Coll of the City U of New York (NY)
Bunker Hill Comm Coll (MA)
Cayuga County Comm Coll (NY)
Central Ohio Tech Coll (OH)
Cleveland State Comm Coll (TN)
Coll of Marin (CA)
Coll of the Canyons (CA)
Comm Coll of Allegheny County (PA)
Comm Coll of Baltimore County (MD)
Front Range Comm Coll (CO)
Grand Rapids Comm Coll (MI)
Harrisburg Area Comm Coll (PA)
Hawkeye Comm Coll (IA)
Hutchinson Comm Coll (KS)
Johnston Comm Coll (NC)
Lake Region State Coll (ND)
McHenry County Coll (IL)
Missouri State U–West Plains (MO)
Mohave Comm Coll (AZ)
Oakton Comm Coll (IL)
Quinsigamond Comm Coll (MA)
Rend Lake Coll (IL)
Ridgewater Coll (MN)
St. Charles Comm Coll (MO)
St. Louis Comm Coll (MO)
San Jacinto Coll District (TX)
San Juan Coll (NM)
Sierra Coll (CA)
Southwestern Comm Coll (NC)
Southwest Wisconsin Tech Coll (WI)
Sullivan County Comm Coll (NY)
Treasure Valley Comm Coll (OR)
Trinity Valley Comm Coll (TX)
Truckee Meadows Comm Coll (NV)
Tulsa Comm Coll (OK)
Vincennes U (IN)
Wayne County Comm Coll District (MI)
Wor-Wic Comm Coll (MD)

CRIMINAL JUSTICE/SAFETY
Alamance Comm Coll (NC)
Blue Ridge Comm and Tech Coll (WV)
Bucks County Comm Coll (PA)
Central Texas Coll (TX)
Fayetteville Tech Comm Coll (NC)
Greenville Tech Coll (SC)
Halifax Comm Coll (NC)
Haywood Comm Coll (NC)
Minnesota State Coll–Southeast Tech (MN)
Mohave Comm Coll (AZ)
Nassau Comm Coll (NY)
Northampton Comm Coll (PA)
Potomac State Coll of West Virginia U (WV)
Richmond Comm Coll (NC)
Southern Maine Comm Coll (ME)
Southwestern Michigan Coll (MI)
Southwest Wisconsin Tech Coll (WI)
Sowela Tech Comm Coll (LA)
Texarkana Coll (TX)
Truckee Meadows Comm Coll (NV)
Tyler Jr Coll (TX)

CRIMINOLOGY
Central New Mexico Comm Coll (NM)
Coll of Central Florida (FL)
Potomac State Coll of West Virginia U (WV)
State U of New York Coll of Technology at Alfred (NY)
Western Wyoming Comm Coll (WY)

CRISIS/EMERGENCY/DISASTER MANAGEMENT
Austin Comm Coll District (TX)
Fayetteville Tech Comm Coll (NC)
Raritan Valley Comm Coll (NJ)
Sullivan County Comm Coll (NY)

CRITICAL INFRASTRUCTURE PROTECTION
Bucks County Comm Coll (PA)
Comm Coll of Allegheny County (PA)

CROP PRODUCTION
Black Hawk Coll, Moline (IL)
Dakota Coll at Bottineau (ND)
Ridgewater Coll (MN)

CULINARY ARTS
Alamance Comm Coll (NC)
Austin Comm Coll District (TX)
Blue Ridge Comm and Tech Coll (WV)

Bucks County Comm Coll (PA)
Bunker Hill Comm Coll (MA)
Central New Mexico Comm Coll (NM)
Central Ohio Tech Coll (OH)
Coll of The Albemarle (NC)
Comm Coll of Allegheny County (PA)
East Central Coll (MO)
Fayetteville Tech Comm Coll (NC)
Grand Rapids Comm Coll (MI)
Greenville Tech Coll (SC)
Harrisburg Area Comm Coll (PA)
Kaskaskia Coll (IL)
Luzerne County Comm Coll (PA)
Mitchell Tech Inst (SD)
Mohave Comm Coll (AZ)
Northampton Comm Coll (PA)
Rend Lake Coll (IL)
Renton Tech Coll (WA)
St. Louis Comm Coll (MO)
San Jacinto Coll District (TX)
Southern Maine Comm Coll (ME)
Southwestern Comm Coll (NC)
Southwest Wisconsin Tech Coll (WI)
Sowela Tech Comm Coll (LA)
State U of New York Coll of Technology at Alfred (NY)
Sullivan County Comm Coll (NY)
Texarkana Coll (TX)
Vincennes U (IN)
West Kentucky Comm and Tech Coll (KY)

CUSTOMER SERVICE MANAGEMENT
Central Oregon Comm Coll (OR)

CYBER/COMPUTER FORENSICS AND COUNTERTERRORISM
Columbia-Greene Comm Coll (NY)
Harper Coll (IL)
Union County Coll (NJ)

DAIRY HUSBANDRY AND PRODUCTION
Ridgewater Coll (MN)

DANCE
Austin Comm Coll District (TX)
Coll of Marin (CA)
Nassau Comm Coll (NY)
Queensborough Comm Coll of the City U of New York (NY)
Raritan Valley Comm Coll (NJ)
San Jacinto Coll District (TX)
Snow Coll (UT)
Trinity Valley Comm Coll (TX)
Tyler Jr Coll (TX)
Western Wyoming Comm Coll (WY)

DATA ENTRY/ MICROCOMPUTER APPLICATIONS
Bunker Hill Comm Coll (MA)
Coll of The Albemarle (NC)
Luzerne County Comm Coll (PA)
Sierra Coll (CA)
Sullivan County Comm Coll (NY)
Western Wyoming Comm Coll (WY)

DATA ENTRY/ MICROCOMPUTER APPLICATIONS RELATED
Blue Ridge Comm and Tech Coll (WV)
Potomac State Coll of West Virginia U (WV)

DATA MODELING/ WAREHOUSING AND DATABASE ADMINISTRATION
Coll of Marin (CA)
Quinsigamond Comm Coll (MA)
Wayne County Comm Coll District (MI)

DATA PROCESSING AND DATA PROCESSING TECHNOLOGY
Greenville Tech Coll (SC)
Luzerne County Comm Coll (PA)
Nassau Comm Coll (NY)
Queensborough Comm Coll of the City U of New York (NY)
San Juan Coll (NM)
Trinity Valley Comm Coll (TX)
Western Wyoming Comm Coll (WY)

DEAF STUDIES
Comm Coll of Baltimore County (MD)
Quinsigamond Comm Coll (MA)

DENTAL ASSISTING
Central Oregon Comm Coll (OR)
Coll of Central Florida (FL)
Coll of Marin (CA)
Grand Rapids Comm Coll (MI)
Kaskaskia Coll (IL)
Manor Coll (PA)
Mohave Comm Coll (AZ)
Pueblo Comm Coll (CO)
Renton Tech Coll (WA)
Truckee Meadows Comm Coll (NV)

DENTAL HYGIENE
Austin Comm Coll District (TX)
Colorado Northwestern Comm Coll (CO)
Comm Coll of Baltimore County (MD)
Comm Coll of Denver (CO)
Daytona State Coll (FL)
Fayetteville Tech Comm Coll (NC)
Georgia Highlands Coll (GA)
Grand Rapids Comm Coll (MI)
Greenville Tech Coll (SC)
Halifax Comm Coll (NC)
Harper Coll (IL)
Harrisburg Area Comm Coll (PA)
Hawkeye Comm Coll (IA)
Lake Superior Coll (MN)
Lamar Inst of Technology (TX)
Luzerne County Comm Coll (PA)
Manor Coll (PA)
Mohave Comm Coll (AZ)
Northampton Comm Coll (PA)
Pueblo Comm Coll (CO)
Quinsigamond Comm Coll (MA)
Raritan Valley Comm Coll (NJ)
Rock Valley Coll (IL)
St. Louis Comm Coll (MO)
San Juan Coll (NM)
Southern U at Shreveport (LA)
Truckee Meadows Comm Coll (NV)
Tulsa Comm Coll (OK)
Tyler Jr Coll (TX)
Wayne County Comm Coll District (MI)

DENTAL SERVICES AND ALLIED PROFESSIONS RELATED
Quinsigamond Comm Coll (MA)

DESIGN AND APPLIED ARTS RELATED
Vincennes U (IN)
Westchester Comm Coll (NY)

DESIGN AND VISUAL COMMUNICATIONS
Austin Comm Coll District (TX)
Black Hawk Coll, Moline (IL)
Bunker Hill Comm Coll (MA)
Coll of Marin (CA)
Harrisburg Area Comm Coll (PA)
Hutchinson Comm Coll (KS)
Nassau Comm Coll (NY)

DESKTOP PUBLISHING AND DIGITAL IMAGING DESIGN
Dunwoody Coll of Technology (MN)
Hawkeye Comm Coll (IA)
Ridgewater Coll (MN)

DEVELOPMENTAL AND CHILD PSYCHOLOGY
Trinity Valley Comm Coll (TX)

DIAGNOSTIC MEDICAL SONOGRAPHY AND ULTRASOUND TECHNOLOGY
Austin Comm Coll District (TX)
Bunker Hill Comm Coll (MA)
Central New Mexico Comm Coll (NM)
Central Ohio Tech Coll (OH)
Comm Coll of Allegheny County (PA)
Greenville Tech Coll (SC)
Harper Coll (IL)
Lamar Inst of Technology (TX)
Lurleen B. Wallace Comm Coll (AL)
Northampton Comm Coll (PA)
San Jacinto Coll District (TX)
State U of New York Coll of Technology at Alfred (NY)
Tulsa Comm Coll (OK)
Tyler Jr Coll (TX)
Union County Coll (NJ)
West Kentucky Comm and Tech Coll (KY)

DIESEL MECHANICS TECHNOLOGY
Alexandria Tech and Comm Coll (MN)
Central Texas Coll (TX)
Hawkeye Comm Coll (IA)
Johnston Comm Coll (NC)
Lamar Inst of Technology (TX)
Lurleen B. Wallace Comm Coll (AL)
Ohio Tech Coll (OH)
Owensboro Comm and Tech Coll (KY)
St. Louis Comm Coll (MO)
San Jacinto Coll District (TX)
San Juan Coll (NM)
State U of New York Coll of Technology at Alfred (NY)
Texarkana Coll (TX)
Truckee Meadows Comm Coll (NV)
Vincennes U (IN)
Western Wyoming Comm Coll (WY)

DIETETICS
Central Oregon Comm Coll (OR)
Harper Coll (IL)
Truckee Meadows Comm Coll (NV)
Vincennes U (IN)

DIETETIC TECHNOLOGY
Harper Coll (IL)
Southern Maine Comm Coll (ME)

DIETITIAN ASSISTANT
Comm Coll of Allegheny County (PA)
Westchester Comm Coll (NY)

DIGITAL ARTS
Austin Comm Coll District (TX)
Queensborough Comm Coll of the City U of New York (NY)
Westchester Comm Coll (NY)

DIGITAL COMMUNICATION AND MEDIA/MULTIMEDIA
Arkansas State U Mid-South (AR)
Daytona State Coll (FL)
Hawkeye Comm Coll (IA)
Ridgewater Coll (MN)
San Jacinto Coll District (TX)
Sierra Coll (CA)
Southern Maine Comm Coll (ME)
Tulsa Comm Coll (OK)
Wayne County Comm Coll District (MI)
Westchester Comm Coll (NY)

DIRECT ENTRY MIDWIFERY
Southwest Wisconsin Tech Coll (WI)

DIRECTING AND THEATRICAL PRODUCTION
Quinsigamond Comm Coll (MA)

DRAFTING AND DESIGN TECHNOLOGY
Austin Comm Coll District (TX)
Cayuga County Comm Coll (NY)
Central Oregon Comm Coll (OR)
Central Texas Coll (TX)
Coll of Central Florida (FL)
Comm Coll of Allegheny County (PA)
Comm Coll of Denver (CO)
Daytona State Coll (FL)
Greenville Tech Coll (SC)
Lamar Inst of Technology (TX)
Luzerne County Comm Coll (PA)
Renton Tech Coll (WA)
St. Charles Comm Coll (MO)
San Jacinto Coll District (TX)
San Juan Coll (NM)
Southern Maine Comm Coll (ME)
Sowela Tech Comm Coll (LA)
State U of New York Coll of Technology at Alfred (NY)
Texarkana Coll (TX)
Tidewater Comm Coll (VA)
Treasure Valley Comm Coll (OR)
Trinity Valley Comm Coll (TX)
Truckee Meadows Comm Coll (NV)
Tyler Jr Coll (TX)
U of Arkansas Comm Coll at Morrilton (AR)
Westchester Comm Coll (NY)

DRAFTING/DESIGN ENGINEERING TECHNOLOGIES RELATED
Coll of The Albemarle (NC)
Comm Coll of Allegheny County (PA)
Luzerne County Comm Coll (PA)
Rock Valley Coll (IL)

DRAMATIC/THEATER ARTS
Austin Comm Coll District (TX)
Central Texas Coll (TX)
Coll of Central Florida (FL)
Coll of Marin (CA)
Coll of The Albemarle (NC)
Coll of the Canyons (CA)
Comm Coll of Allegheny County (PA)
Harrisburg Area Comm Coll (PA)
Manchester Comm Coll (CT)
Nassau Comm Coll (NY)
Owensboro Comm and Tech Coll (KY)
Queensborough Comm Coll of the City U of New York (NY)
San Jacinto Coll District (TX)
Snow Coll (UT)
Texarkana Coll (TX)
Trinity Valley Comm Coll (TX)
Tulsa Comm Coll (OK)
Tyler Jr Coll (TX)
Vincennes U (IN)
Western Wyoming Comm Coll (WY)

DRAWING
Luzerne County Comm Coll (PA)

EARLY CHILDHOOD EDUCATION
Alexandria Tech and Comm Coll (MN)
Austin Comm Coll District (TX)
Bucks County Comm Coll (PA)
Bunker Hill Comm Coll (MA)
Central New Mexico Comm Coll (NM)
Central Ohio Tech Coll (OH)
Central Oregon Comm Coll (OR)
Central Texas Coll (TX)
Coll of Central Florida (FL)
Colorado Northwestern Comm Coll (CO)
Comm Coll of Baltimore County (MD)
Daytona State Coll (FL)
Fayetteville Tech Comm Coll (NC)
Front Range Comm Coll (CO)
Halifax Comm Coll (NC)
Harper Coll (IL)
Harrisburg Area Comm Coll (PA)
Haywood Comm Coll (NC)
Johnston Comm Coll (NC)
Luzerne County Comm Coll (PA)
Massachusetts Bay Comm Coll (MA)
Minnesota State Coll–Southeast Tech (MN)
Mitchell Comm Coll (NC)
Northampton Comm Coll (PA)
Potomac State Coll of West Virginia U (WV)
Pueblo Comm Coll (CO)
Quinsigamond Comm Coll (MA)
Renton Tech Coll (WA)
Richmond Comm Coll (NC)
Southern Maine Comm Coll (ME)
Southwestern Michigan Coll (MI)
Southwest Wisconsin Tech Coll (WI)
Tohono O'odham Comm Coll (AZ)
Vincennes U (IN)
Western Wyoming Comm Coll (WY)
Wor-Wic Comm Coll (MD)

E-COMMERCE
Wayne County Comm Coll District (MI)

ECONOMICS
Austin Comm Coll District (TX)
Borough of Manhattan Comm Coll of the City U of New York (NY)
Coll of Central Florida (FL)
Potomac State Coll of West Virginia U (WV)
Snow Coll (UT)
Tyler Jr Coll (TX)
Western Wyoming Comm Coll (WY)

EDUCATION
Bunker Hill Comm Coll (MA)
Central Oregon Comm Coll (OR)
Cleveland State Comm Coll (TN)
Coll of The Albemarle (NC)
Comm Coll of Baltimore County (MD)
Dakota Coll at Bottineau (ND)
East Central Coll (MO)
Hutchinson Comm Coll (KS)
Luzerne County Comm Coll (PA)
Mohave Comm Coll (AZ)
Motlow State Comm Coll (TN)
Snow Coll (UT)
Southern Maine Comm Coll (ME)
Tidewater Comm Coll (VA)
Trinity Valley Comm Coll (TX)
Tulsa Comm Coll (OK)
Western Wyoming Comm Coll (WY)
Wor-Wic Comm Coll (MD)

EDUCATION (MULTIPLE LEVELS)
Cayuga County Comm Coll (NY)
Central New Mexico Comm Coll (NM)
Tyler Jr Coll (TX)
Western Wyoming Comm Coll (WY)

EDUCATION (SPECIFIC LEVELS AND METHODS) RELATED
Comm Coll of Allegheny County (PA)
Manor Coll (PA)

EDUCATION (SPECIFIC SUBJECT AREAS) RELATED
Comm Coll of Allegheny County (PA)
St. Charles Comm Coll (MO)

ELECTRICAL AND ELECTRONIC ENGINEERING TECHNOLOGIES RELATED
Blue Ridge Comm and Tech Coll (WV)
Lake Region State Coll (ND)
Massachusetts Bay Comm Coll (MA)
Owensboro Comm and Tech Coll (KY)

ELECTRICAL AND ELECTRONICS ENGINEERING
Comm Coll of Baltimore County (MD)
Potomac State Coll of West Virginia U (WV)

ELECTRICAL AND POWER TRANSMISSION INSTALLATION
Mitchell Tech Inst (SD)
Richmond Comm Coll (NC)
San Jacinto Coll District (TX)

ELECTRICAL AND POWER TRANSMISSION INSTALLATION RELATED
Vincennes U (IN)

ELECTRICAL, ELECTRONIC AND COMMUNICATIONS ENGINEERING TECHNOLOGY
Alamance Comm Coll (NC)
Austin Comm Coll District (TX)
Cayuga County Comm Coll (NY)
Central Ohio Tech Coll (OH)
Central Oregon Comm Coll (OR)
Cleveland State Comm Coll (TN)
Comm Coll of Allegheny County (PA)
Daytona State Coll (FL)
Dunwoody Coll of Technology (MN)
Fayetteville Tech Comm Coll (NC)
Front Range Comm Coll (CO)
Grand Rapids Comm Coll (MI)
Greenville Tech Coll (SC)
Harper Coll (IL)
Harrisburg Area Comm Coll (PA)
Hawkeye Comm Coll (IA)
Haywood Comm Coll (NC)
Kaskaskia Coll (IL)
Lake Superior Coll (MN)
Luzerne County Comm Coll (PA)
Massachusetts Bay Comm Coll (MA)
Minnesota State Coll–Southeast Tech (MN)
Mitchell Comm Coll (NC)
Oakton Comm Coll (IL)
Pueblo Comm Coll (CO)
Queensborough Comm Coll of the City U of New York (NY)
Quinsigamond Comm Coll (MA)
Richmond Comm Coll (NC)
Ridgewater Coll (MN)
Rock Valley Coll (IL)
St. Louis Comm Coll (MO)
San Jacinto Coll District (TX)
San Juan Coll (NM)
Southern Maine Comm Coll (ME)
Southwestern Comm Coll (NC)
State U of New York Coll of Technology at Alfred (NY)
Sullivan County Comm Coll (NY)
Texarkana Coll (TX)
Tidewater Comm Coll (VA)
Tulsa Comm Coll (OK)
Vincennes U (IN)
Wayne County Comm Coll District (MI)
Westchester Comm Coll (NY)

ELECTRICAL/ELECTRONICS DRAFTING AND CAD/CADD
Dunwoody Coll of Technology (MN)

ELECTRICAL/ELECTRONICS EQUIPMENT INSTALLATION AND REPAIR
Hutchinson Comm Coll (KS)
Sierra Coll (CA)
Western Wyoming Comm Coll (WY)

ELECTRICAL/ELECTRONICS MAINTENANCE AND REPAIR TECHNOLOGY RELATED
Bunker Hill Comm Coll (MA)

ELECTRICIAN
Comm Coll of Allegheny County (PA)
Dunwoody Coll of Technology (MN)
Fayetteville Tech Comm Coll (NC)
Harrisburg Area Comm Coll (PA)
Haywood Comm Coll (NC)
Hutchinson Comm Coll (KS)
John Tyler Comm Coll (VA)
Lake Superior Coll (MN)
Luzerne County Comm Coll (PA)
Mitchell Comm Coll (NC)
Mitchell Tech Inst (SD)
Northampton Comm Coll (PA)
Owensboro Comm and Tech Coll (KY)
Ridgewater Coll (MN)
Rock Valley Coll (IL)
Southwestern Comm Coll (IA)
Sowela Tech Comm Coll (LA)
Tohono O'odham Comm Coll (AZ)
Vincennes U (IN)
Western Wyoming Comm Coll (WY)
West Kentucky Comm and Tech Coll (KY)

ELECTROMECHANICAL AND INSTRUMENTATION AND MAINTENANCE TECHNOLOGIES RELATED
Fayetteville Tech Comm Coll (NC)
Greenville Tech Coll (SC)
Halifax Comm Coll (NC)
Haywood Comm Coll (NC)
Mitchell Comm Coll (NC)
Pueblo Comm Coll (CO)
Richmond Comm Coll (NC)

ELECTROMECHANICAL TECHNOLOGY
Cleveland State Comm Coll (TN)
Henderson Comm Coll (KY)
Motlow State Comm Coll (TN)
Northampton Comm Coll (PA)
Richmond Comm Coll (NC)
Ridgewater Coll (MN)
Southwest Wisconsin Tech Coll (WI)
Tyler Jr Coll (TX)
Union County Coll (NJ)

ELECTRONEURODIAGNOSTIC/ ELECTROENCEPHALOGRAPHIC TECHNOLOGY
Comm Coll of Allegheny County (PA)
Comm Coll of Denver (CO)

ELEMENTARY EDUCATION
Coll of Central Florida (FL)
Comm Coll of Allegheny County (PA)
Comm Coll of Baltimore County (MD)
Fayetteville Tech Comm Coll (NC)
Harper Coll (IL)
Haywood Comm Coll (NC)
Massachusetts Bay Comm Coll (MA)
Missouri State U–West Plains (MO)
Mitchell Comm Coll (NC)
Potomac State Coll of West Virginia U (WV)
Quinsigamond Comm Coll (MA)
San Juan Coll (NM)
Snow Coll (UT)
Sullivan County Comm Coll (NY)
Tohono O'odham Comm Coll (AZ)
Treasure Valley Comm Coll (OR)
Trinity Valley Comm Coll (TX)
Truckee Meadows Comm Coll (NV)
Vincennes U (IN)
Wayne County Comm Coll District (MI)
Western Wyoming Comm Coll (WY)
Wor-Wic Comm Coll (MD)

EMERGENCY MEDICAL TECHNOLOGY (EMT PARAMEDIC)
Arapahoe Comm Coll (CO)
Arkansas State U–Newport (AR)
Austin Comm Coll District (TX)
Black Hawk Coll, Moline (IL)
Blue Ridge Comm and Tech Coll (WV)
Borough of Manhattan Comm Coll of the City U of New York (NY)
Bunker Hill Comm Coll (MA)
Central New Mexico Comm Coll (NM)
Central Ohio Tech Coll (OH)
Central Oregon Comm Coll (OR)
Central Texas Coll (TX)
Cleveland State Comm Coll (TN)
Coll of Central Florida (FL)
Colorado Northwestern Comm Coll (CO)
Comm Coll of Allegheny County (PA)
Comm Coll of Aurora (CO)
Comm Coll of Baltimore County (MD)
Daytona State Coll (FL)
East Central Coll (MO)
Fayetteville Tech Comm Coll (NC)
Greenville Tech Coll (SC)
Hawkeye Comm Coll (IA)
Hutchinson Comm Coll (KS)
John Tyler Comm Coll (VA)
Kaskaskia Coll (IL)
Lamar Inst of Technology (TX)
Lurleen B. Wallace Comm Coll (AL)
Luzerne County Comm Coll (PA)
McHenry County Coll (IL)
Motlow State Comm Coll (TN)
Owensboro Comm and Tech Coll (KY)
Pueblo Comm Coll (CO)
Quinsigamond Comm Coll (MA)
Rend Lake Coll (IL)
St. Charles Comm Coll (MO)
St. Louis Comm Coll (MO)
San Jacinto Coll District (TX)
San Juan Coll (NM)
Southern Maine Comm Coll (ME)
Southwestern Comm Coll (NC)
Texarkana Coll (TX)
Trinity Valley Comm Coll (TX)
Tyler Jr Coll (TX)
Union County Coll (NJ)
Wayne County Comm Coll District (MI)
Westchester Comm Coll (NY)
West Kentucky Comm and Tech Coll (KY)
Wor-Wic Comm Coll (MD)

ENERGY MANAGEMENT AND SYSTEMS TECHNOLOGY
Comm Coll of Allegheny County (PA)
Front Range Comm Coll (CO)
Mitchell Tech Inst (SD)
Quinsigamond Comm Coll (MA)
Rock Valley Coll (IL)
Truckee Meadows Comm Coll (NV)

ENGINEERING
Austin Comm Coll District (TX)
Borough of Manhattan Comm Coll of the City U of New York (NY)
Bucks County Comm Coll (PA)
Bunker Hill Comm Coll (MA)
Central Oregon Comm Coll (OR)
Central Texas Coll (TX)
Coll of Marin (CA)
Comm Coll of Baltimore County (MD)
East Central Coll (MO)
Halifax Comm Coll (NC)
Harper Coll (IL)
Harrisburg Area Comm Coll (PA)
Heartland Comm Coll (IL)
Hutchinson Comm Coll (KS)
John Tyler Comm Coll (VA)
Kaskaskia Coll (IL)
McHenry County Coll (IL)
Missouri State U–West Plains (MO)
Mohave Comm Coll (AZ)
Nassau Comm Coll (NY)
Northampton Comm Coll (PA)
Oakton Comm Coll (IL)
Queensborough Comm Coll of the City U of New York (NY)
Rend Lake Coll (IL)
San Jacinto Coll District (TX)
San Juan Coll (NM)
Sierra Coll (CA)
Southern Maine Comm Coll (ME)
State U of New York Coll of Technology at Alfred (NY)
Texarkana Coll (TX)
Tidewater Comm Coll (VA)
Truckee Meadows Comm Coll (NV)
Tyler Jr Coll (TX)
Union County Coll (NJ)

ENGINEERING/INDUSTRIAL MANAGEMENT
Mitchell Comm Coll (NC)

ENGINEERING-RELATED TECHNOLOGIES
Tulsa Comm Coll (OK)

ENGINEERING SCIENCE
Comm Coll of Allegheny County (PA)
Manchester Comm Coll (CT)
Queensborough Comm Coll of the City U of New York (NY)
Raritan Valley Comm Coll (NJ)
Vincennes U (IN)

ENGINEERING TECHNOLOGIES AND ENGINEERING RELATED
Comm Coll of Allegheny County (PA)
Comm Coll of Baltimore County (MD)
Harrisburg Area Comm Coll (PA)
Massachusetts Bay Comm Coll (MA)
Raritan Valley Comm Coll (NJ)
Truckee Meadows Comm Coll (NV)
Union County Coll (NJ)

ENGINEERING TECHNOLOGY
Bucks County Comm Coll (PA)
Cleveland State Comm Coll (TN)
Coll of Central Florida (FL)
Coll of Marin (CA)
Luzerne County Comm Coll (PA)
Massachusetts Bay Comm Coll (MA)
Pueblo Comm Coll (CO)
San Juan Coll (NM)
Southwestern Michigan Coll (MI)
Western Wyoming Comm Coll (WY)

ENGLISH
Austin Comm Coll District (TX)
Borough of Manhattan Comm Coll of the City U of New York (NY)
Bucks County Comm Coll (PA)
Bunker Hill Comm Coll (MA)
Central New Mexico Comm Coll (NM)
Coll of Central Florida (FL)
Coll of the Canyons (CA)
Comm Coll of Allegheny County (PA)
Harper Coll (IL)
Hutchinson Comm Coll (KS)
Massachusetts Bay Comm Coll (MA)
Mohave Comm Coll (AZ)
Potomac State Coll of West Virginia U (WV)
Quinsigamond Comm Coll (MA)
Raritan Valley Comm Coll (NJ)
San Jacinto Coll District (TX)
Sierra Coll (CA)
Truckee Meadows Comm Coll (NV)
Union County Coll (NJ)
Vincennes U (IN)
Western Wyoming Comm Coll (WY)

ENGLISH/LANGUAGE ARTS TEACHER EDUCATION
Comm Coll of Baltimore County (MD)

ENTREPRENEURIAL AND SMALL BUSINESS RELATED
Dakota Coll at Bottineau (ND)
Truckee Meadows Comm Coll (NV)

ENTREPRENEURSHIP
Austin Comm Coll District (TX)
Bunker Hill Comm Coll (MA)
Central Oregon Comm Coll (OR)
Comm Coll of Allegheny County (PA)
Fayetteville Tech Comm Coll (NC)
Haywood Comm Coll (NC)
Nassau Comm Coll (NY)

ENVIRONMENTAL CONTROL TECHNOLOGIES RELATED
Massachusetts Bay Comm Coll (MA)
Westchester Comm Coll (NY)

ENVIRONMENTAL DESIGN/ ARCHITECTURE
Central New Mexico Comm Coll (NM)

ENVIRONMENTAL ENGINEERING TECHNOLOGY
Austin Comm Coll District (TX)
Comm Coll of Allegheny County (PA)
Dakota Coll at Bottineau (ND)
State U of New York Coll of Technology at Alfred (NY)

ENVIRONMENTAL HEALTH
St. Charles Comm Coll (MO)

ENVIRONMENTAL SCIENCE
Austin Comm Coll District (TX)
Bucks County Comm Coll (PA)
Central Texas Coll (TX)
Coll of the Canyons (CA)
Daytona State Coll (FL)
Harrisburg Area Comm Coll (PA)
Northampton Comm Coll (PA)
Queensborough Comm Coll of the City U of New York (NY)
San Jacinto Coll District (TX)
Truckee Meadows Comm Coll (NV)
Tulsa Comm Coll (OK)
Westchester Comm Coll (NY)
Western Wyoming Comm Coll (WY)

ENVIRONMENTAL STUDIES
Coll of Central Florida (FL)
Columbia-Greene Comm Coll (NY)
Harper Coll (IL)
Sullivan County Comm Coll (NY)
Vincennes U (IN)
Westchester Comm Coll (NY)

EQUESTRIAN STUDIES
Black Hawk Coll, Moline (IL)
Coll of Central Florida (FL)
Colorado Northwestern Comm Coll (CO)
Sierra Coll (CA)

ETHNIC, CULTURAL MINORITY, GENDER, AND GROUP STUDIES RELATED
Borough of Manhattan Comm Coll of the City U of New York (NY)
Coll of Marin (CA)

EXECUTIVE ASSISTANT/ EXECUTIVE SECRETARY
Alamance Comm Coll (NC)
Dakota Coll at Bottineau (ND)
Kaskaskia Coll (IL)
Luzerne County Comm Coll (PA)
Mitchell Comm Coll (NC)
Owensboro Comm and Tech Coll (KY)
Quinsigamond Comm Coll (MA)

FAMILY AND COMMUNITY SERVICES
Snow Coll (UT)

FAMILY AND CONSUMER SCIENCES/HOME ECONOMICS TEACHER EDUCATION
Vincennes U (IN)

FAMILY AND CONSUMER SCIENCES/HUMAN SCIENCES
Coll of Central Florida (FL)
Hutchinson Comm Coll (KS)
Snow Coll (UT)
Vincennes U (IN)

FARM AND RANCH MANAGEMENT
Central Texas Coll (TX)
Hutchinson Comm Coll (KS)
Treasure Valley Comm Coll (OR)
Trinity Valley Comm Coll (TX)

FASHION AND FABRIC CONSULTING
Harper Coll (IL)

FASHION/APPAREL DESIGN
Harper Coll (IL)
Nassau Comm Coll (NY)

FASHION MERCHANDISING
Alexandria Tech and Comm Coll (MN)
Grand Rapids Comm Coll (MI)
Harper Coll (IL)
Nassau Comm Coll (NY)
Trinity Valley Comm Coll (TX)
Vincennes U (IN)
Wayne County Comm Coll District (MI)

FIBER, TEXTILE AND WEAVING ARTS
Haywood Comm Coll (NC)

FILM/CINEMA/VIDEO STUDIES
Coll of Marin (CA)

FINANCE
Borough of Manhattan Comm Coll of the City U of New York (NY)
Bunker Hill Comm Coll (MA)
Harper Coll (IL)
Tidewater Comm Coll (VA)
Trinity Valley Comm Coll (TX)

FINE ARTS RELATED
Bunker Hill Comm Coll (MA)
Truckee Meadows Comm Coll (NV)

FINE/STUDIO ARTS
Borough of Manhattan Comm Coll of the City U of New York (NY)
Cayuga County Comm Coll (NY)
Central Texas Coll (TX)
East Central Coll (MO)
Grand Rapids Comm Coll (MI)
Harper Coll (IL)
Lake Superior Coll (MN)
Manchester Comm Coll (CT)
McHenry County Coll (IL)
Northampton Comm Coll (PA)
Owensboro Comm and Tech Coll (KY)
Raritan Valley Comm Coll (NJ)
Rend Lake Coll (IL)
Tidewater Comm Coll (VA)
Tohono O'odham Comm Coll (AZ)
West Kentucky Comm and Tech Coll (KY)

FIRE PREVENTION AND SAFETY TECHNOLOGY
Austin Comm Coll District (TX)
Bunker Hill Comm Coll (MA)
Coll of the Canyons (CA)
Comm Coll of Allegheny County (PA)
Daytona State Coll (FL)
Fayetteville Tech Comm Coll (NC)
Lake Superior Coll (MN)
Lamar Inst of Technology (TX)
Sullivan County Comm Coll (NY)
Treasure Valley Comm Coll (OR)
Truckee Meadows Comm Coll (NV)
Tyler Jr Coll (TX)
Union County Coll (NJ)
Wayne County Comm Coll District (MI)

FIRE SCIENCE/FIREFIGHTING
Central New Mexico Comm Coll (NM)
Central Ohio Tech Coll (OH)
Central Oregon Comm Coll (OR)
Coll of Central Florida (FL)
Comm Coll of Aurora (CO)
East Central Coll (MO)
Harper Coll (IL)
Harrisburg Area Comm Coll (PA)
Hutchinson Comm Coll (KS)
Luzerne County Comm Coll (PA)
McHenry County Coll (IL)
Mohave Comm Coll (AZ)
Northampton Comm Coll (PA)
Oakton Comm Coll (IL)
Owensboro Comm and Tech Coll (KY)
Pueblo Comm Coll (CO)
Rock Valley Coll (IL)
St. Louis Comm Coll (MO)
San Jacinto Coll District (TX)
San Juan Coll (NM)
Sierra Coll (CA)
Southern Maine Comm Coll (ME)
Southwestern Michigan Coll (MI)
Vincennes U (IN)
West Kentucky Comm and Tech Coll (KY)

FIRE SERVICES ADMINISTRATION
Black Hawk Coll, Moline (IL)
Bucks County Comm Coll (PA)
Central Texas Coll (TX)
Lake Superior Coll (MN)
Northampton Comm Coll (PA)
Quinsigamond Comm Coll (MA)
Tulsa Comm Coll (OK)

FLORICULTURE/FLORISTRY MANAGEMENT
Dakota Coll at Bottineau (ND)

FOOD SCIENCE
Missouri State U–West Plains (MO)

FOOD SERVICE AND DINING ROOM MANAGEMENT
Kaskaskia Coll (IL)

FOOD SERVICE SYSTEMS ADMINISTRATION
Comm Coll of Allegheny County (PA)
Harper Coll (IL)
Wayne County Comm Coll District (MI)
Westchester Comm Coll (NY)

FOODS, NUTRITION, AND WELLNESS
Snow Coll (UT)
Truckee Meadows Comm Coll (NV)

FOOD TECHNOLOGY AND PROCESSING
Luzerne County Comm Coll (PA)

FOREIGN LANGUAGES AND LITERATURES
Borough of Manhattan Comm Coll of the City U of New York (NY)
Bunker Hill Comm Coll (MA)
Central Oregon Comm Coll (OR)
Central Texas Coll (TX)
Coll of Central Florida (FL)
Coll of Marin (CA)
Comm Coll of Allegheny County (PA)
Hutchinson Comm Coll (KS)
San Jacinto Coll District (TX)
Texarkana Coll (TX)
Tyler Jr Coll (TX)
Vincennes U (IN)

FOREIGN LANGUAGES RELATED
Tulsa Comm Coll (OK)

FORENSIC SCIENCE AND TECHNOLOGY
Arkansas State U–Newport (AR)
Borough of Manhattan Comm Coll of the City U of New York (NY)
Central Ohio Tech Coll (OH)
Fayetteville Tech Comm Coll (NC)
Potomac State Coll of West Virginia U (WV)
Queensborough Comm Coll of the City U of New York (NY)
Sullivan County Comm Coll (NY)
U of Arkansas Comm Coll at Morrilton (AR)

FOREST/FOREST RESOURCES MANAGEMENT
Tyler Jr Coll (TX)

FOREST RESOURCES PRODUCTION AND MANAGEMENT
Potomac State Coll of West Virginia U (WV)

FORESTRY
Central Oregon Comm Coll (OR)
Coll of Central Florida (FL)
Sierra Coll (CA)
Snow Coll (UT)
Western Wyoming Comm Coll (WY)

FOREST TECHNOLOGY
Central Oregon Comm Coll (OR)
Haywood Comm Coll (NC)
Lurleen B. Wallace Comm Coll (AL)

FRENCH
Austin Comm Coll District (TX)
Coll of Marin (CA)
Coll of the Canyons (CA)
Snow Coll (UT)

FUNERAL SERVICE AND MORTUARY SCIENCE
Arapahoe Comm Coll (CO)
Comm Coll of Baltimore County (MD)
Fayetteville Tech Comm Coll (NC)
John Tyler Comm Coll (VA)
Luzerne County Comm Coll (PA)
Nassau Comm Coll (NY)
Northampton Comm Coll (PA)
St. Louis Comm Coll (MO)
Vincennes U (IN)

GAME AND INTERACTIVE MEDIA DESIGN
Arapahoe Comm Coll (CO)
Cayuga County Comm Coll (NY)
Comm Coll of Allegheny County (PA)
Fayetteville Tech Comm Coll (NC)
Quinsigamond Comm Coll (MA)
Raritan Valley Comm Coll (NJ)
State U of New York Coll of Technology at Alfred (NY)
Wayne County Comm Coll District (MI)

GENERAL STUDIES
Arapahoe Comm Coll (CO)
Arkansas State U–Newport (AR)
Austin Comm Coll District (TX)
Black Hawk Coll, Moline (IL)
Blue Ridge Comm and Tech Coll (WV)
Borough of Manhattan Comm Coll of the City U of New York (NY)
Bucks County Comm Coll (PA)
Bunker Hill Comm Coll (MA)
Central New Mexico Comm Coll (NM)
Central Texas Coll (TX)
Cleveland State Comm Coll (TN)
Colorado Northwestern Comm Coll (CO)
Columbia-Greene Comm Coll (NY)
Comm Coll of Allegheny County (PA)
Comm Coll of Aurora (CO)
Comm Coll of Denver (CO)
Dakota Coll at Bottineau (ND)
East Central Coll (MO)
Front Range Comm Coll (CO)
Harrisburg Area Comm Coll (PA)
John Tyler Comm Coll (VA)
Kaskaskia Coll (IL)
Lurleen B. Wallace Comm Coll (AL)
Luzerne County Comm Coll (PA)
Manchester Comm Coll (CT)
Massachusetts Bay Comm Coll (MA)
McHenry County Coll (IL)
Missouri State U–West Plains (MO)
Mitchell Comm Coll (NC)
Nassau Comm Coll (NY)
Northampton Comm Coll (PA)
Pueblo Comm Coll (CO)
Quinsigamond Comm Coll (MA)
St. Charles Comm Coll (MO)
San Jacinto Coll District (TX)
San Juan Coll (NM)
Sierra Coll (CA)
Southern U at Shreveport (LA)
Southwestern Michigan Coll (MI)
Sowela Tech Comm Coll (LA)
State U of New York Coll of Technology at Alfred (NY)
Treasure Valley Comm Coll (OR)
Truckee Meadows Comm Coll (NV)
Tulsa Comm Coll (OK)
Tyler Jr Coll (TX)
U of Arkansas Comm Coll at Morrilton (AR)
Western Wyoming Comm Coll (WY)

GEOGRAPHIC INFORMATION SCIENCE AND CARTOGRAPHY
Austin Comm Coll District (TX)
Borough of Manhattan Comm Coll of the City U of New York (NY)
Central New Mexico Comm Coll (NM)
Front Range Comm Coll (CO)
Harrisburg Area Comm Coll (PA)
Mitchell Tech Inst (SD)

GEOGRAPHY
Austin Comm Coll District (TX)
Central New Mexico Comm Coll (NM)
Coll of Marin (CA)
Coll of the Canyons (CA)
Snow Coll (UT)

GEOLOGY/EARTH SCIENCE
Austin Comm Coll District (TX)
Central Texas Coll (TX)
Coll of Marin (CA)
Coll of the Canyons (CA)
Mohave Comm Coll (AZ)
Potomac State Coll of West Virginia U (WV)
San Jacinto Coll District (TX)
Sierra Coll (CA)
Snow Coll (UT)
Trinity Valley Comm Coll (TX)
Truckee Meadows Comm Coll (NV)
Tyler Jr Coll (TX)
Western Wyoming Comm Coll (WY)

GERMAN
Austin Comm Coll District (TX)

GERONTOLOGY
Borough of Manhattan Comm Coll of the City U of New York (NY)

GOLF COURSE OPERATION AND GROUNDS MANAGEMENT
Hawkeye Comm Coll (IA)
Southwest Wisconsin Tech Coll (WI)

GRAPHIC AND PRINTING EQUIPMENT OPERATION/ PRODUCTION
Central Texas Coll (TX)
Luzerne County Comm Coll (PA)
Rock Valley Coll (IL)
Tulsa Comm Coll (OK)

GRAPHIC COMMUNICATIONS
Hutchinson Comm Coll (KS)

GRAPHIC DESIGN
Arapahoe Comm Coll (CO)
Coll of the Canyons (CA)
Comm Coll of Allegheny County (PA)
Comm Coll of Denver (CO)
Dunwoody Coll of Technology (MN)
Harrisburg Area Comm Coll (PA)
Luzerne County Comm Coll (PA)
Northampton Comm Coll (PA)
Oakton Comm Coll (IL)
Rend Lake Coll (IL)
St. Louis Comm Coll (MO)
Sierra Coll (CA)
Southwestern Michigan Coll (MI)
State U of New York Coll of Technology at Alfred (NY)
Tidewater Comm Coll (VA)
Tyler Jr Coll (TX)

GREENHOUSE MANAGEMENT
Comm Coll of Allegheny County (PA)
Dakota Coll at Bottineau (ND)

GUNSMITHING
Fayetteville Tech Comm Coll (NC)

HAZARDOUS MATERIALS MANAGEMENT AND WASTE TECHNOLOGY
Sierra Coll (CA)

HEALTH AIDE
Texarkana Coll (TX)

HEALTH AND PHYSICAL EDUCATION/FITNESS
Arapahoe Comm Coll (CO)
Austin Comm Coll District (TX)
Central New Mexico Comm Coll (NM)
Central Oregon Comm Coll (OR)
Coll of Marin (CA)
Coll of The Albemarle (NC)
Coll of the Canyons (CA)
Comm Coll of Allegheny County (PA)
Dakota Coll at Bottineau (ND)
Harrisburg Area Comm Coll (PA)
Luzerne County Comm Coll (PA)
McHenry County Coll (IL)
San Jacinto Coll District (TX)
San Juan Coll (NM)
Sierra Coll (CA)
Tyler Jr Coll (TX)
Vincennes U (IN)
Westchester Comm Coll (NY)

HEALTH AND PHYSICAL EDUCATION RELATED
Fayetteville Tech Comm Coll (NC)

HEALTH/HEALTH-CARE ADMINISTRATION
Harrisburg Area Comm Coll (PA)
Luzerne County Comm Coll (PA)
Manor Coll (PA)

HEALTH INFORMATION/ MEDICAL RECORDS ADMINISTRATION
Bunker Hill Comm Coll (MA)
Central New Mexico Comm Coll (NM)
Oakton Comm Coll (IL)
Southern U at Shreveport (LA)
Southwestern Comm Coll (NC)

HEALTH INFORMATION/ MEDICAL RECORDS TECHNOLOGY
Arapahoe Comm Coll (CO)
Austin Comm Coll District (TX)
Black Hawk Coll, Moline (IL)
Borough of Manhattan Comm Coll of the City U of New York (NY)
Central New Mexico Comm Coll (NM)
Central Oregon Comm Coll (OR)
Coll of Central Florida (FL)
Comm Coll of Allegheny County (PA)
Daytona State Coll (FL)
East Central Coll (MO)
Front Range Comm Coll (CO)
Greenville Tech Coll (SC)
Hutchinson Comm Coll (KS)
Kaskaskia Coll (IL)
Lamar Inst of Technology (TX)
Quinsigamond Comm Coll (MA)
Raritan Valley Comm Coll (NJ)
Rend Lake Coll (IL)
Richmond Comm Coll (NC)
Ridgewater Coll (MN)
St. Charles Comm Coll (MO)
St. Louis Comm Coll (MO)
San Jacinto Coll District (TX)
San Juan Coll (NM)
Southern U at Shreveport (LA)
Southwestern Comm Coll (NC)
Southwestern Michigan Coll (MI)
Southwest Wisconsin Tech Coll (WI)
State U of New York Coll of Technology at Alfred (NY)
Tulsa Comm Coll (OK)
Tyler Jr Coll (TX)
Vincennes U (IN)
Westchester Comm Coll (NY)

HEALTH/MEDICAL PREPARATORY PROGRAMS RELATED
Coll of Central Florida (FL)
Missouri State U–West Plains (MO)
Tulsa Comm Coll (OK)
Western Wyoming Comm Coll (WY)

HEALTH PROFESSIONS RELATED
Bucks County Comm Coll (PA)
Cleveland State Comm Coll (TN)
Comm Coll of Allegheny County (PA)
Harrisburg Area Comm Coll (PA)
Manor Coll (PA)
Mitchell Comm Coll (NC)
Westchester Comm Coll (NY)
Western Wyoming Comm Coll (WY)

HEALTH SERVICES ADMINISTRATION
Harrisburg Area Comm Coll (PA)

HEALTH SERVICES/ALLIED HEALTH/HEALTH SCIENCES
Borough of Manhattan Comm Coll of the City U of New York (NY)
Bucks County Comm Coll (PA)
Central New Mexico Comm Coll (NM)
Central Ohio Tech Coll (OH)
Coll of Central Florida (FL)
Comm Coll of Baltimore County (MD)
Dakota Coll at Bottineau (ND)
Lake Superior Coll (MN)
Missouri State U–West Plains (MO)
Queensborough Comm Coll of the City U of New York (NY)
Quinsigamond Comm Coll (MA)
Raritan Valley Comm Coll (NJ)
Southern Maine Comm Coll (ME)
Tohono O'odham Comm Coll (AZ)
Union County Coll (NJ)
Western Wyoming Comm Coll (WY)
West Kentucky Comm and Tech Coll (KY)

HEALTH TEACHER EDUCATION
Harper Coll (IL)
Vincennes U (IN)

HEALTH UNIT COORDINATOR/ WARD CLERK
Comm Coll of Allegheny County (PA)

HEATING, AIR CONDITIONING, VENTILATION AND REFRIGERATION MAINTENANCE TECHNOLOGY
Arkansas State U–Newport (AR)
Central New Mexico Comm Coll (NM)
Central Texas Coll (TX)
Comm Coll of Allegheny County (PA)
Dunwoody Coll of Technology (MN)
East Central Coll (MO)
Fayetteville Tech Comm Coll (NC)
Grand Rapids Comm Coll (MI)
Harper Coll (IL)
Harrisburg Area Comm Coll (PA)
Johnston Comm Coll (NC)
Kaskaskia Coll (IL)
Luzerne County Comm Coll (PA)
Minnesota State Coll–Southeast Tech (MN)
Mitchell Tech Inst (SD)
Mohave Comm Coll (AZ)
Northampton Comm Coll (PA)
Owensboro Comm and Tech Coll (KY)
Renton Tech Coll (WA)
Richmond Comm Coll (NC)
San Jacinto Coll District (TX)
Southern Maine Comm Coll (ME)
State U of New York Coll of Technology at Alfred (NY)
Texarkana Coll (TX)
Trinity Valley Comm Coll (TX)
Truckee Meadows Comm Coll (NV)
Tyler Jr Coll (TX)
U of Arkansas Comm Coll at Morrilton (AR)
Vincennes U (IN)
Wayne County Comm Coll District (MI)

HEATING, VENTILATION, AIR CONDITIONING AND REFRIGERATION ENGINEERING TECHNOLOGY
Alamance Comm Coll (NC)
Austin Comm Coll District (TX)
Comm Coll of Baltimore County (MD)
Dunwoody Coll of Technology (MN)
Front Range Comm Coll (CO)
Lamar Inst of Technology (TX)
Oakton Comm Coll (IL)
Raritan Valley Comm Coll (NJ)

HEAVY EQUIPMENT MAINTENANCE TECHNOLOGY
Comm Coll of Aurora (CO)
Rend Lake Coll (IL)
Western Wyoming Comm Coll (WY)

HEAVY/INDUSTRIAL EQUIPMENT MAINTENANCE TECHNOLOGIES RELATED
State U of New York Coll of Technology at Alfred (NY)

HIGH PERFORMANCE AND CUSTOM ENGINE TECHNOLOGY
Ohio Tech Coll (OH)

HISPANIC-AMERICAN, PUERTO RICAN, AND MEXICAN-AMERICAN/CHICANO STUDIES
San Jacinto Coll District (TX)

HISTOLOGIC TECHNOLOGY/ HISTOTECHNOLOGIST
Comm Coll of Baltimore County (MD)

HISTORY
Austin Comm Coll District (TX)
Borough of Manhattan Comm Coll of the City U of New York (NY)
Bucks County Comm Coll (PA)
Bunker Hill Comm Coll (MA)
Central New Mexico Comm Coll (NM)
Coll of Central Florida (FL)
Coll of Marin (CA)
Coll of the Canyons (CA)
Dakota Coll at Bottineau (ND)
Harper Coll (IL)
Potomac State Coll of West Virginia U (WV)
Quinsigamond Comm Coll (MA)
San Jacinto Coll District (TX)
Snow Coll (UT)
Trinity Valley Comm Coll (TX)
Truckee Meadows Comm Coll (NV)
Tyler Jr Coll (TX)
Union County Coll (NJ)
Vincennes U (IN)
Western Wyoming Comm Coll (WY)

HISTORY RELATED
Mohave Comm Coll (AZ)

HISTORY TEACHER EDUCATION
Bucks County Comm Coll (PA)

HOLISTIC HEALTH
Front Range Comm Coll (CO)

HOMELAND SECURITY
Harper Coll (IL)

HOMELAND SECURITY, LAW ENFORCEMENT, FIREFIGHTING AND PROTECTIVE SERVICES RELATED
Mohave Comm Coll (AZ)
West Kentucky Comm and Tech Coll (KY)

HORSE HUSBANDRY/EQUINE SCIENCE AND MANAGEMENT
Black Hawk Coll, Moline (IL)
Potomac State Coll of West Virginia U (WV)
Treasure Valley Comm Coll (OR)

HORTICULTURAL SCIENCE
Dakota Coll at Bottineau (ND)
Potomac State Coll of West Virginia U (WV)
Tidewater Comm Coll (VA)
Treasure Valley Comm Coll (OR)
Trinity Valley Comm Coll (TX)

HOSPITALITY ADMINISTRATION
Arkansas State U Mid-South (AR)
Austin Comm Coll District (TX)
Bucks County Comm Coll (PA)
Bunker Hill Comm Coll (MA)
Central New Mexico Comm Coll (NM)
Central Texas Coll (TX)
Daytona State Coll (FL)
Front Range Comm Coll (CO)
Harper Coll (IL)
Hawkeye Comm Coll (IA)
Massachusetts Bay Comm Coll (MA)
Potomac State Coll of West Virginia U (WV)
Quinsigamond Comm Coll (MA)
Sullivan County Comm Coll (NY)
Union County Coll (NJ)
Wor-Wic Comm Coll (MD)

HOSPITALITY ADMINISTRATION RELATED
Bunker Hill Comm Coll (MA)
Harrisburg Area Comm Coll (PA)

HOSPITALITY AND RECREATION MARKETING
Dakota Coll at Bottineau (ND)
Luzerne County Comm Coll (PA)

HOTEL/MOTEL ADMINISTRATION
Austin Comm Coll District (TX)
Central Oregon Comm Coll (OR)
Coll of the Canyons (CA)
Comm Coll of Allegheny County (PA)
Luzerne County Comm Coll (PA)
Manchester Comm Coll (CT)
Nassau Comm Coll (NY)
Northampton Comm Coll (PA)
Vincennes U (IN)

HOTEL, MOTEL, AND RESTAURANT MANAGEMENT
Fayetteville Tech Comm Coll (NC)

HOUSING AND HUMAN ENVIRONMENTS RELATED
Comm Coll of Allegheny County (PA)

HUMAN COMPUTER INTERACTION
Raritan Valley Comm Coll (NJ)

HUMAN DEVELOPMENT AND FAMILY STUDIES
Central New Mexico Comm Coll (NM)
Missouri State U–West Plains (MO)

HUMAN DEVELOPMENT AND FAMILY STUDIES RELATED
Comm Coll of Allegheny County (PA)

HUMANITIES
Central Oregon Comm Coll (OR)
Coll of Central Florida (FL)
Coll of Marin (CA)
Coll of the Canyons (CA)
Columbia-Greene Comm Coll (NY)
Comm Coll of Allegheny County (PA)
Harper Coll (IL)
John Tyler Comm Coll (VA)
Luzerne County Comm Coll (PA)
Snow Coll (UT)
State U of New York Coll of Technology at Alfred (NY)
Texarkana Coll (TX)
Westchester Comm Coll (NY)
Western Wyoming Comm Coll (WY)

HUMAN RESOURCES MANAGEMENT
Comm Coll of Allegheny County (PA)
Hawkeye Comm Coll (IA)
Tulsa Comm Coll (OK)

HUMAN SERVICES
Alexandria Tech and Comm Coll (MN)
Bunker Hill Comm Coll (MA)
Central Ohio Tech Coll (OH)
Coll of Central Florida (FL)
Columbia-Greene Comm Coll (NY)
Comm Coll of Denver (CO)
Georgia Highlands Coll (GA)
Greenville Tech Coll (SC)
Halifax Comm Coll (NC)
Harper Coll (IL)
Harrisburg Area Comm Coll (PA)
Luzerne County Comm Coll (PA)
Manchester Comm Coll (CT)
Mitchell Tech Inst (SD)
Quinsigamond Comm Coll (MA)
Raritan Valley Comm Coll (NJ)
Rock Valley Coll (IL)
St. Charles Comm Coll (MO)
St. Louis Comm Coll (MO)
Southern Maine Comm Coll (ME)
Southern U at Shreveport (LA)
State U of New York Coll of Technology at Alfred (NY)
Sullivan County Comm Coll (NY)
Union County Coll (NJ)
Western Wyoming Comm Coll (WY)

HYDRAULICS AND FLUID POWER TECHNOLOGY
Comm Coll of Allegheny County (PA)
Comm Coll of Baltimore County (MD)

INDUSTRIAL AND PRODUCT DESIGN
Comm Coll of Allegheny County (PA)
Luzerne County Comm Coll (PA)
Rock Valley Coll (IL)

INDUSTRIAL ELECTRONICS TECHNOLOGY
Lurleen B. Wallace Comm Coll (AL)
Northampton Comm Coll (PA)
Sierra Coll (CA)
Tyler Jr Coll (TX)
Western Wyoming Comm Coll (WY)

INDUSTRIAL ENGINEERING
Manchester Comm Coll (CT)

INDUSTRIAL MECHANICS AND MAINTENANCE TECHNOLOGY
Grand Rapids Comm Coll (MI)
Halifax Comm Coll (NC)
Kaskaskia Coll (IL)
Lamar Inst of Technology (TX)
Minnesota State Coll–Southeast Tech (MN)
Owensboro Comm and Tech Coll (KY)
Rend Lake Coll (IL)
Renton Tech Coll (WA)
San Juan Coll (NM)
Snow Coll (UT)
Southwestern Comm Coll (IA)
Southwestern Michigan Coll (MI)
Texarkana Coll (TX)
U of Arkansas Comm Coll at Morrilton (AR)
Western Wyoming Comm Coll (WY)
West Kentucky Comm and Tech Coll (KY)

INDUSTRIAL PRODUCTION TECHNOLOGIES RELATED
Missouri State U–West Plains (MO)
Sowela Tech Comm Coll (LA)

INDUSTRIAL TECHNOLOGY
Central Oregon Comm Coll (OR)
Cleveland State Comm Coll (TN)
Comm Coll of Allegheny County (PA)
East Central Coll (MO)
Heartland Comm Coll (IL)
John Tyler Comm Coll (VA)
Manchester Comm Coll (CT)
Rock Valley Coll (IL)
St. Charles Comm Coll (MO)
San Juan Coll (NM)
Snow Coll (UT)
Treasure Valley Comm Coll (OR)

INFORMATION SCIENCE/STUDIES
Alamance Comm Coll (NC)
Alexandria Tech and Comm Coll (MN)
Bucks County Comm Coll (PA)
Cayuga County Comm Coll (NY)
Coll of The Albemarle (NC)
Dakota Coll at Bottineau (ND)
Manchester Comm Coll (CT)
Mitchell Comm Coll (NC)
Snow Coll (UT)
Southwestern Comm Coll (NC)
State U of New York Coll of Technology at Alfred (NY)
Sullivan County Comm Coll (NY)
Westchester Comm Coll (NY)
Western Wyoming Comm Coll (WY)

INFORMATION TECHNOLOGY
Black Hawk Coll, Moline (IL)
Blue Ridge Comm and Tech Coll (WV)
Cleveland State Comm Coll (TN)
Coll of Central Florida (FL)
Coll of The Albemarle (NC)
Columbia-Greene Comm Coll (NY)
Dakota Coll at Bottineau (ND)
Daytona State Coll (FL)
Fayetteville Tech Comm Coll (NC)
Halifax Comm Coll (NC)
Haywood Comm Coll (NC)
John Tyler Comm Coll (VA)
McHenry County Coll (IL)
Mitchell Comm Coll (NC)
Oakton Comm Coll (IL)
Queensborough Comm Coll of the City U of New York (NY)
Raritan Valley Comm Coll (NJ)
Richmond Comm Coll (NC)
Sierra Coll (CA)
Sowela Tech Comm Coll (LA)
Tidewater Comm Coll (VA)
Union County Coll (NJ)
Vincennes U (IN)
Western Wyoming Comm Coll (WY)

INSTITUTIONAL FOOD WORKERS
Lamar Inst of Technology (TX)

INSTRUMENTATION TECHNOLOGY
Lamar Inst of Technology (TX)
Nassau Comm Coll (NY)
Ridgewater Coll (MN)
San Jacinto Coll District (TX)
San Juan Coll (NM)
Southwest Wisconsin Tech Coll (WI)
Sowela Tech Comm Coll (LA)
Western Wyoming Comm Coll (WY)

INSURANCE
Comm Coll of Allegheny County (PA)
Nassau Comm Coll (NY)
Trinity Valley Comm Coll (TX)

INTELLIGENCE
Fayetteville Tech Comm Coll (NC)

INTERDISCIPLINARY STUDIES
Mohave Comm Coll (AZ)
Motlow State Comm Coll (TN)
Southwest Wisconsin Tech Coll (WI)
Tohono O'odham Comm Coll (AZ)

INTERIOR ARCHITECTURE
Coll of Central Florida (FL)

INTERIOR DESIGN
Alexandria Tech and Comm Coll (MN)
Arapahoe Comm Coll (CO)
Coll of Marin (CA)
Coll of the Canyons (CA)
Daytona State Coll (FL)
Front Range Comm Coll (CO)
Grand Rapids Comm Coll (MI)
Harper Coll (IL)
Nassau Comm Coll (NY)
Northampton Comm Coll (PA)
Raritan Valley Comm Coll (NJ)
St. Louis Comm Coll (MO)
San Jacinto Coll District (TX)
State U of New York Coll of Technology at Alfred (NY)
Tidewater Comm Coll (VA)
Tulsa Comm Coll (OK)

INTERNATIONAL BUSINESS/TRADE/COMMERCE
Austin Comm Coll District (TX)
Bunker Hill Comm Coll (MA)
Harper Coll (IL)
Luzerne County Comm Coll (PA)
Massachusetts Bay Comm Coll (MA)
San Jacinto Coll District (TX)
Tulsa Comm Coll (OK)
Westchester Comm Coll (NY)

INTERNATIONAL/GLOBAL STUDIES
Massachusetts Bay Comm Coll (MA)
Northampton Comm Coll (PA)

INTERNATIONAL RELATIONS AND AFFAIRS
Coll of Marin (CA)
Harrisburg Area Comm Coll (PA)

ITALIAN
Austin Comm Coll District (TX)

JAPANESE
Austin Comm Coll District (TX)
Snow Coll (UT)

JOURNALISM
Arapahoe Comm Coll (CO)
Austin Comm Coll District (TX)
Bucks County Comm Coll (PA)
Central Texas Coll (TX)
Coll of Central Florida (FL)
Coll of the Canyons (CA)
Comm Coll of Allegheny County (PA)
Luzerne County Comm Coll (PA)
Manchester Comm Coll (CT)
Northampton Comm Coll (PA)
Potomac State Coll of West Virginia U (WV)
San Jacinto Coll District (TX)
Texarkana Coll (TX)
Trinity Valley Comm Coll (TX)
Tyler Jr Coll (TX)
Vincennes U (IN)
Westchester Comm Coll (NY)
Western Wyoming Comm Coll (WY)

JUVENILE CORRECTIONS
Kaskaskia Coll (IL)

KINDERGARTEN/PRESCHOOL EDUCATION
Alamance Comm Coll (NC)
Manchester Comm Coll (CT)
Mitchell Comm Coll (NC)
Nassau Comm Coll (NY)
Quinsigamond Comm Coll (MA)
Raritan Valley Comm Coll (NJ)
Snow Coll (UT)
Sullivan County Comm Coll (NY)
Tidewater Comm Coll (VA)
Trinity Valley Comm Coll (TX)
Truckee Meadows Comm Coll (NV)

KINESIOLOGY AND EXERCISE SCIENCE
Austin Comm Coll District (TX)
Bucks County Comm Coll (PA)
Central Oregon Comm Coll (OR)
Central Texas Coll (TX)
Coll of the Canyons (CA)
Raritan Valley Comm Coll (NJ)
San Jacinto Coll District (TX)
Western Wyoming Comm Coll (WY)

LANDSCAPE ARCHITECTURE
Truckee Meadows Comm Coll (NV)

LANDSCAPING AND GROUNDSKEEPING
Coll of Central Florida (FL)
Coll of Marin (CA)
Comm Coll of Allegheny County (PA)
Dakota Coll at Bottineau (ND)
Grand Rapids Comm Coll (MI)
Hawkeye Comm Coll (IA)

LAND USE PLANNING AND MANAGEMENT
Dakota Coll at Bottineau (ND)

LANGUAGE INTERPRETATION AND TRANSLATION
Lake Region State Coll (ND)

LASER AND OPTICAL TECHNOLOGY
Quinsigamond Comm Coll (MA)

LATIN
Austin Comm Coll District (TX)

LATIN AMERICAN STUDIES
Central New Mexico Comm Coll (NM)

LEGAL ADMINISTRATIVE ASSISTANT/SECRETARY
Alamance Comm Coll (NC)
Alexandria Tech and Comm Coll (MN)
Comm Coll of Allegheny County (PA)
Harper Coll (IL)
Manchester Comm Coll (CT)
Minnesota State Coll–Southeast Tech (MN)
Nassau Comm Coll (NY)
Renton Tech Coll (WA)
Ridgewater Coll (MN)
Trinity Valley Comm Coll (TX)
Western Wyoming Comm Coll (WY)

LEGAL ASSISTANT/PARALEGAL
Alexandria Tech and Comm Coll (MN)
Arapahoe Comm Coll (CO)
Austin Comm Coll District (TX)
Blue Ridge Comm and Tech Coll (WV)
Bunker Hill Comm Coll (MA)
Central Texas Coll (TX)
Coll of Central Florida (FL)
Coll of the Canyons (CA)
Comm Coll of Allegheny County (PA)
Comm Coll of Baltimore County (MD)
Comm Coll of Denver (CO)
Daytona State Coll (FL)
Fayetteville Tech Comm Coll (NC)
Front Range Comm Coll (CO)
Greenville Tech Coll (SC)
Halifax Comm Coll (NC)
Harper Coll (IL)
Harrisburg Area Comm Coll (PA)
Hutchinson Comm Coll (KS)
Johnston Comm Coll (NC)
Lake Superior Coll (MN)
Luzerne County Comm Coll (PA)
Manchester Comm Coll (CT)
Manor Coll (PA)
Massachusetts Bay Comm Coll (MA)
Mohave Comm Coll (AZ)
Nassau Comm Coll (NY)
Northampton Comm Coll (PA)
Raritan Valley Comm Coll (NJ)
St. Louis Comm Coll (MO)
San Jacinto Coll District (TX)
San Juan Coll (NM)
Southwestern Comm Coll (NC)
Sullivan County Comm Coll (NY)
Tidewater Comm Coll (VA)
Truckee Meadows Comm Coll (NV)
Tulsa Comm Coll (OK)
Tyler Jr Coll (TX)
Union County Coll (NJ)
Vincennes U (IN)
Wayne County Comm Coll District (MI)
Westchester Comm Coll (NY)

LEGAL PROFESSIONS AND STUDIES RELATED
Bucks County Comm Coll (PA)

LIBERAL ARTS AND SCIENCES AND HUMANITIES RELATED
Arapahoe Comm Coll (CO)
Bucks County Comm Coll (PA)
Coll of Central Florida (FL)
Colorado Northwestern Comm Coll (CO)
Comm Coll of Aurora (CO)
Comm Coll of Baltimore County (MD)
Dakota Coll at Bottineau (ND)
Fayetteville Tech Comm Coll (NC)
Front Range Comm Coll (CO)
Georgia Highlands Coll (GA)
Halifax Comm Coll (NC)
Haywood Comm Coll (NC)
Luzerne County Comm Coll (PA)
Mitchell Comm Coll (NC)
Northampton Comm Coll (PA)
Pueblo Comm Coll (CO)
Ridgewater Coll (MN)
Southern Maine Comm Coll (ME)
Southern U at Shreveport (LA)
Sowela Tech Comm Coll (LA)
State U of New York Coll of Technology at Alfred (NY)
Vincennes U (IN)
Westchester Comm Coll (NY)
Wor-Wic Comm Coll (MD)

LIBERAL ARTS AND SCIENCES/LIBERAL STUDIES
Alamance Comm Coll (NC)
Alexandria Tech and Comm Coll (MN)
Arapahoe Comm Coll (CO)
Arkansas State U Mid-South (AR)
Arkansas State U–Newport (AR)
Black Hawk Coll, Moline (IL)

Blue Ridge Comm and Tech Coll (WV)
Borough of Manhattan Comm Coll of the City U of New York (NY)
Bucks County Comm Coll (PA)
Cayuga County Comm Coll (NY)
Central New Mexico Comm Coll (NM)
Central Ohio Tech Coll (OH)
Central Oregon Comm Coll (OR)
Central Texas Coll (TX)
Cleveland State Comm Coll (TN)
Coastline Comm Coll (CA)
Coll of Central Florida (FL)
Coll of Marin (CA)
Coll of The Albemarle (NC)
Coll of the Canyons (CA)
Colorado Northwestern Comm Coll (CO)
Columbia-Greene Comm Coll (NY)
Comm Coll of Allegheny County (PA)
Comm Coll of Aurora (CO)
Comm Coll of Baltimore County (MD)
Comm Coll of Denver (CO)
Dakota Coll at Bottineau (ND)
Daytona State Coll (FL)
Fayetteville Tech Comm Coll (NC)
Front Range Comm Coll (CO)
Grand Rapids Comm Coll (MI)
Greenville Tech Coll (SC)
Halifax Comm Coll (NC)
Harper Coll (IL)
Hawkeye Comm Coll (IA)
Haywood Comm Coll (NC)
Heartland Comm Coll (IL)
Henderson Comm Coll (KY)
Hutchinson Comm Coll (KS)
Johnston Comm Coll (NC)
Kaskaskia Coll (IL)
Lake Region State Coll (ND)
Lake Superior Coll (MN)
Lurleen B. Wallace Comm Coll (AL)
Luzerne County Comm Coll (PA)
Manchester Comm Coll (CT)
Manor Coll (PA)
Massachusetts Bay Comm Coll (MA)
McHenry County Coll (IL)
Mitchell Comm Coll (NC)
Mohave Comm Coll (AZ)
Motlow State Comm Coll (TN)
Nassau Comm Coll (NY)
Northampton Comm Coll (PA)
Oakton Comm Coll (IL)
Owensboro Comm and Tech Coll (KY)
Potomac State Coll of West Virginia U (WV)
Pueblo Comm Coll (CO)
Queensborough Comm Coll of the City U of New York (NY)
Quinsigamond Comm Coll (MA)
Raritan Valley Comm Coll (NJ)
Rend Lake Coll (IL)
Richmond Comm Coll (NC)
Ridgewater Coll (MN)
Rock Valley Coll (IL)
St. Charles Comm Coll (MO)
St. Louis Comm Coll (MO)
San Juan Coll (NM)
Sierra Coll (CA)
Snow Coll (UT)
Southern Maine Comm Coll (ME)
Southwestern Comm Coll (IA)
Southwestern Comm Coll (NC)
Southwestern Michigan Coll (MI)
State U of New York Coll of Technology at Alfred (NY)
Sullivan County Comm Coll (NY)
Texarkana Coll (TX)
Tidewater Comm Coll (VA)
Tohono O'odham Comm Coll (AZ)
Treasure Valley Comm Coll (OR)
Trinity Valley Comm Coll (TX)
Truckee Meadows Comm Coll (NV)
Union County Coll (NJ)
U of Arkansas Comm Coll at Morrilton (AR)
U of South Carolina Union (SC)
Vincennes U (IN)
Wayne County Comm Coll District (MI)
Westchester Comm Coll (NY)
Western Wyoming Comm Coll (WY)
West Kentucky Comm and Tech Coll (KY)

LIBRARY AND ARCHIVES ASSISTING
Coll of the Canyons (CA)
Kaskaskia Coll (IL)
Pueblo Comm Coll (CO)

LIBRARY AND INFORMATION SCIENCE
Coll of Central Florida (FL)
Southwestern Comm Coll (IA)

LICENSED PRACTICAL/ VOCATIONAL NURSE TRAINING
Central Ohio Tech Coll (OH)
Central Oregon Comm Coll (OR)
Central Texas Coll (TX)
Coll of The Albemarle (NC)
Comm Coll of Allegheny County (PA)
Comm Coll of Denver (CO)
Dakota Coll at Bottineau (ND)
Sierra Coll (CA)
Texarkana Coll (TX)
Trinity Valley Comm Coll (TX)
Western Wyoming Comm Coll (WY)

LINEWORKER
Mitchell Tech Inst (SD)
Raritan Valley Comm Coll (NJ)
Vincennes U (IN)

LINGUISTICS
Borough of Manhattan Comm Coll of the City U of New York (NY)

LITERATURE
Tyler Jr Coll (TX)

LOGISTICS, MATERIALS, AND SUPPLY CHAIN MANAGEMENT
Austin Comm Coll District (TX)
Fayetteville Tech Comm Coll (NC)
Vincennes U (IN)
West Kentucky Comm and Tech Coll (KY)

MACHINE SHOP TECHNOLOGY
Comm Coll of Allegheny County (PA)
Comm Coll of Denver (CO)
Fayetteville Tech Comm Coll (NC)
Mitchell Comm Coll (NC)
Owensboro Comm and Tech Coll (KY)
Pueblo Comm Coll (CO)
State U of New York Coll of Technology at Alfred (NY)
U of Arkansas Comm Coll at Morrilton (AR)
West Kentucky Comm and Tech Coll (KY)

MACHINE TOOL TECHNOLOGY
Alamance Comm Coll (NC)
Central New Mexico Comm Coll (NM)
Coll of Marin (CA)
East Central Coll (MO)
Greenville Tech Coll (SC)
Hawkeye Comm Coll (IA)
Hutchinson Comm Coll (KS)
Lamar Inst of Technology (TX)
Renton Tech Coll (WA)
Ridgewater Coll (MN)
Southern Maine Comm Coll (ME)

MANAGEMENT INFORMATION SYSTEMS
Central Oregon Comm Coll (OR)
Comm Coll of Allegheny County (PA)
Comm Coll of Baltimore County (MD)
Comm Coll of Denver (CO)
Lake Region State Coll (ND)
Lake Superior Coll (MN)
Manchester Comm Coll (CT)
Nassau Comm Coll (NY)
Raritan Valley Comm Coll (NJ)
San Jacinto Coll District (TX)
Treasure Valley Comm Coll (OR)

MANAGEMENT INFORMATION SYSTEMS AND SERVICES RELATED
Truckee Meadows Comm Coll (NV)

MANUFACTURING ENGINEERING TECHNOLOGY
Black Hawk Coll, Moline (IL)
Central Ohio Tech Coll (OH)
Central Oregon Comm Coll (OR)
Comm Coll of Allegheny County (PA)
Grand Rapids Comm Coll (MI)
Hutchinson Comm Coll (KS)
John Tyler Comm Coll (VA)
Mitchell Comm Coll (NC)
Mitchell Tech Inst (SD)
Oakton Comm Coll (IL)
Quinsigamond Comm Coll (MA)
Raritan Valley Comm Coll (NJ)
Rend Lake Coll (IL)
St. Charles Comm Coll (MO)
St. Louis Comm Coll (MO)
Sierra Coll (CA)
Truckee Meadows Comm Coll (NV)
Vincennes U (IN)

MARINE BIOLOGY AND BIOLOGICAL OCEANOGRAPHY
Southern Maine Comm Coll (ME)

MARINE SCIENCE/MERCHANT MARINE OFFICER
San Jacinto Coll District (TX)

MARINE TRANSPORTATION RELATED
West Kentucky Comm and Tech Coll (KY)

MARKETING/MARKETING MANAGEMENT
Austin Comm Coll District (TX)
Central Oregon Comm Coll (OR)
Coll of Central Florida (FL)
Comm Coll of Allegheny County (PA)
Dakota Coll at Bottineau (ND)
Harper Coll (IL)
Manchester Comm Coll (CT)
Manor Coll (PA)
Nassau Comm Coll (NY)
Northampton Comm Coll (PA)
Oakton Comm Coll (IL)
Ridgewater Coll (MN)
Rock Valley Coll (IL)
St. Charles Comm Coll (MO)
Sullivan County Comm Coll (NY)
Texarkana Coll (TX)
Tidewater Comm Coll (VA)
Trinity Valley Comm Coll (TX)
Tulsa Comm Coll (OK)
Union County Coll (NJ)
Western Wyoming Comm Coll (WY)

MARKETING RELATED
Dakota Coll at Bottineau (ND)
Westchester Comm Coll (NY)

MASONRY
State U of New York Coll of Technology at Alfred (NY)

MASSAGE THERAPY
Central Oregon Comm Coll (OR)
Comm Coll of Baltimore County (MD)
Minnesota State Coll–Southeast Tech (MN)
Queensborough Comm Coll of the City U of New York (NY)
Renton Tech Coll (WA)
Southwestern Comm Coll (NC)

MASS COMMUNICATION/ MEDIA
Borough of Manhattan Comm Coll of the City U of New York (NY)
Bunker Hill Comm Coll (MA)
Coll of Marin (CA)
Nassau Comm Coll (NY)
Snow Coll (UT)
Union County Coll (NJ)

MATERIALS ENGINEERING
Southern Maine Comm Coll (ME)

MATHEMATICS
Austin Comm Coll District (TX)
Borough of Manhattan Comm Coll of the City U of New York (NY)
Bucks County Comm Coll (PA)
Bunker Hill Comm Coll (MA)
Central New Mexico Comm Coll (NM)
Central Oregon Comm Coll (OR)
Central Texas Coll (TX)
Coll of Central Florida (FL)
Coll of Marin (CA)
Coll of the Canyons (CA)
Comm Coll of Allegheny County (PA)
Dakota Coll at Bottineau (ND)
Harper Coll (IL)
Harrisburg Area Comm Coll (PA)
Hutchinson Comm Coll (KS)
Luzerne County Comm Coll (PA)
Massachusetts Bay Comm Coll (MA)
Mohave Comm Coll (AZ)
Nassau Comm Coll (NY)
Northampton Comm Coll (PA)
Potomac State Coll of West Virginia U (WV)
San Jacinto Coll District (TX)
San Juan Coll (NM)
Sierra Coll (CA)
Snow Coll (UT)
Sullivan County Comm Coll (NY)
Texarkana Coll (TX)
Trinity Valley Comm Coll (TX)
Truckee Meadows Comm Coll (NV)
Tulsa Comm Coll (OK)
Tyler Jr Coll (TX)
Union County Coll (NJ)
Western Wyoming Comm Coll (WY)

MATHEMATICS TEACHER EDUCATION
Bucks County Comm Coll (PA)
Comm Coll of Baltimore County (MD)
Vincennes U (IN)

MECHANICAL DRAFTING AND CAD/CADD
Alexandria Tech and Comm Coll (MN)
Comm Coll of Allegheny County (PA)
Hutchinson Comm Coll (KS)
Mitchell Comm Coll (NC)
Ridgewater Coll (MN)
Sierra Coll (CA)
Vincennes U (IN)

MECHANICAL ENGINEERING
Potomac State Coll of West Virginia U (WV)

MECHANICAL ENGINEERING/ MECHANICAL TECHNOLOGY
Alamance Comm Coll (NC)
Arapahoe Comm Coll (CO)
Cayuga County Comm Coll (NY)
Comm Coll of Allegheny County (PA)
Greenville Tech Coll (SC)
Harrisburg Area Comm Coll (PA)
Massachusetts Bay Comm Coll (MA)
Mitchell Comm Coll (NC)
Oakton Comm Coll (IL)
Queensborough Comm Coll of the City U of New York (NY)
Richmond Comm Coll (NC)
State U of New York Coll of Technology at Alfred (NY)
Westchester Comm Coll (NY)

MECHANICAL ENGINEERING TECHNOLOGIES RELATED
John Tyler Comm Coll (VA)

MECHANIC AND REPAIR TECHNOLOGIES RELATED
Greenville Tech Coll (SC)
Ohio Tech Coll (OH)
West Kentucky Comm and Tech Coll (KY)

MECHANICS AND REPAIR
Western Wyoming Comm Coll (WY)

MECHATRONICS, ROBOTICS, AND AUTOMATION ENGINEERING
Comm Coll of Allegheny County (PA)
Harrisburg Area Comm Coll (PA)
Mitchell Comm Coll (NC)
Southwestern Comm Coll (NC)

MEDICAL ADMINISTRATIVE ASSISTANT AND MEDICAL SECRETARY
Alamance Comm Coll (NC)
Alexandria Tech and Comm Coll (MN)
Bunker Hill Comm Coll (MA)
Central Texas Coll (TX)
Coll of Marin (CA)
Coll of The Albemarle (NC)
Comm Coll of Allegheny County (PA)
Comm Coll of Baltimore County (MD)
Dakota Coll at Bottineau (ND)
Halifax Comm Coll (NC)
Harper Coll (IL)
Hawkeye Comm Coll (IA)
Lake Superior Coll (MN)
Luzerne County Comm Coll (PA)
Manchester Comm Coll (CT)
Minnesota State Coll–Southeast Tech (MN)
Nassau Comm Coll (NY)
Northampton Comm Coll (PA)
Owensboro Comm and Tech Coll (KY)
Quinsigamond Comm Coll (MA)
Renton Tech Coll (WA)
Ridgewater Coll (MN)
Treasure Valley Comm Coll (OR)
Tyler Jr Coll (TX)
Westchester Comm Coll (NY)
Western Wyoming Comm Coll (WY)
West Kentucky Comm and Tech Coll (KY)

MEDICAL/CLINICAL ASSISTANT
Alamance Comm Coll (NC)
Arkansas State U Mid-South (AR)
Blue Ridge Comm and Tech Coll (WV)
Bucks County Comm Coll (PA)
Central Oregon Comm Coll (OR)
Cleveland State Comm Coll (TN)
Coll of Marin (CA)
Colorado Northwestern Comm Coll (CO)
Columbia-Greene Comm Coll (NY)
Comm Coll of Allegheny County (PA)
Dakota Coll at Bottineau (ND)
East Central Coll (MO)
Harper Coll (IL)
Haywood Comm Coll (NC)
Henderson Comm Coll (KY)
Johnston Comm Coll (NC)
Mitchell Comm Coll (NC)
Mitchell Tech Inst (SD)
Owensboro Comm and Tech Coll (KY)
Potomac State Coll of West Virginia U (WV)
Queensborough Comm Coll of the City U of New York (NY)
Raritan Valley Comm Coll (NJ)
Rend Lake Coll (IL)
Renton Tech Coll (WA)
Richmond Comm Coll (NC)
Ridgewater Coll (MN)
San Jacinto Coll District (TX)
Southern Maine Comm Coll (ME)
Southwestern Michigan Coll (MI)
Sullivan County Comm Coll (NY)
Treasure Valley Comm Coll (OR)
Western Wyoming Comm Coll (WY)

MEDICAL INFORMATICS
Cleveland State Comm Coll (TN)
Comm Coll of Baltimore County (MD)
Harrisburg Area Comm Coll (PA)

MEDICAL INSURANCE CODING
Bucks County Comm Coll (PA)
Central Texas Coll (TX)
Dakota Coll at Bottineau (ND)
Hawkeye Comm Coll (IA)
Renton Tech Coll (WA)

MEDICAL OFFICE ASSISTANT
Dakota Coll at Bottineau (ND)
Front Range Comm Coll (CO)
Mitchell Tech Inst (SD)
Wayne County Comm Coll District (MI)
Western Wyoming Comm Coll (WY)

MEDICAL OFFICE COMPUTER SPECIALIST
Western Wyoming Comm Coll (WY)

MEDICAL OFFICE MANAGEMENT
Fayetteville Tech Comm Coll (NC)
Halifax Comm Coll (NC)
Haywood Comm Coll (NC)
Johnston Comm Coll (NC)
Pueblo Comm Coll (CO)
Richmond Comm Coll (NC)
Southwestern Comm Coll (NC)

MEDICAL RADIOLOGIC TECHNOLOGY
Bunker Hill Comm Coll (MA)
Coll of Central Florida (FL)
Comm Coll of Allegheny County (PA)
Comm Coll of Baltimore County (MD)
Daytona State Coll (FL)
Dunwoody Coll of Technology (MN)
East Central Coll (MO)
Greenville Tech Coll (SC)
Lamar Inst of Technology (TX)
Mitchell Tech Inst (SD)
Nassau Comm Coll (NY)
Rend Lake Coll (IL)
Southern U at Shreveport (LA)
Southwestern Comm Coll (NC)
Truckee Meadows Comm Coll (NV)
Tulsa Comm Coll (OK)
Vincennes U (IN)
Westchester Comm Coll (NY)
Wor-Wic Comm Coll (MD)

MEDICAL STAFF SERVICES TECHNOLOGY
Rend Lake Coll (IL)

MEDICAL TRANSCRIPTION
Treasure Valley Comm Coll (OR)

MEETING AND EVENT PLANNING
Bucks County Comm Coll (PA)
Northampton Comm Coll (PA)
Raritan Valley Comm Coll (NJ)

MENTAL AND SOCIAL HEALTH SERVICES AND ALLIED PROFESSIONS RELATED
Halifax Comm Coll (NC)
John Tyler Comm Coll (VA)
Richmond Comm Coll (NC)

MENTAL HEALTH COUNSELING
Austin Comm Coll District (TX)
Southwestern Comm Coll (NC)
Truckee Meadows Comm Coll (NV)

MERCHANDISING, SALES, AND MARKETING OPERATIONS RELATED (GENERAL)
Lake Region State Coll (ND)
Westchester Comm Coll (NY)

METAL AND JEWELRY ARTS
Coll of The Albemarle (NC)
Haywood Comm Coll (NC)

MIDDLE SCHOOL EDUCATION
Arkansas State U–Newport (AR)
Austin Comm Coll District (TX)
Comm Coll of Allegheny County (PA)
Northampton Comm Coll (PA)
Tyler Jr Coll (TX)
U of Arkansas Comm Coll at Morrilton (AR)

MINING TECHNOLOGY
Vincennes U (IN)
Western Wyoming Comm Coll (WY)

MODELING, VIRTUAL ENVIRONMENTS AND SIMULATION
Raritan Valley Comm Coll (NJ)

MODERN LANGUAGES
Potomac State Coll of West Virginia U (WV)

MORTUARY SCIENCE AND EMBALMING
Wayne County Comm Coll District (MI)

MOTORCYCLE MAINTENANCE AND REPAIR TECHNOLOGY
Ohio Tech Coll (OH)
State U of New York Coll of Technology at Alfred (NY)

MULTI/INTERDISCIPLINARY STUDIES RELATED
Alexandria Tech and Comm Coll (MN)
Arkansas State U Mid-South (AR)
Arkansas State U–Newport (AR)
Austin Comm Coll District (TX)
Blue Ridge Comm and Tech Coll (WV)
Bucks County Comm Coll (PA)
Cleveland State Comm Coll (TN)
Greenville Tech Coll (SC)
Hawkeye Comm Coll (IA)
Lake Superior Coll (MN)
Minnesota State Coll–Southeast Tech (MN)
Raritan Valley Comm Coll (NJ)
Tulsa Comm Coll (OK)
West Kentucky Comm and Tech Coll (KY)

MUSEUM STUDIES
Queensborough Comm Coll of the City U of New York (NY)

MUSIC
Austin Comm Coll District (TX)
Borough of Manhattan Comm Coll of the City U of New York (NY)
Bucks County Comm Coll (PA)
Bunker Hill Comm Coll (MA)
Central Texas Coll (TX)
Coll of Central Florida (FL)
Coll of Marin (CA)
Coll of The Albemarle (NC)
Coll of the Canyons (CA)
Comm Coll of Allegheny County (PA)
East Central Coll (MO)
Grand Rapids Comm Coll (MI)
Harper Coll (IL)
Kaskaskia Coll (IL)
Manchester Comm Coll (CT)
McHenry County Coll (IL)
Oakton Comm Coll (IL)
Quinsigamond Comm Coll (MA)
Raritan Valley Comm Coll (NJ)
Rend Lake Coll (IL)
St. Charles Comm Coll (MO)
San Jacinto Coll District (TX)
Sierra Coll (CA)
Snow Coll (UT)
Southwestern Comm Coll (IA)
Texarkana Coll (TX)
Tidewater Comm Coll (VA)
Trinity Valley Comm Coll (TX)
Truckee Meadows Comm Coll (NV)
Tulsa Comm Coll (OK)
Tyler Jr Coll (TX)
Vincennes U (IN)
Western Wyoming Comm Coll (WY)

MUSICAL INSTRUMENT FABRICATION AND REPAIR
Renton Tech Coll (WA)

MUSICAL THEATER
Coll of the Canyons (CA)

MUSIC HISTORY, LITERATURE, AND THEORY
Queensborough Comm Coll of the City U of New York (NY)
Snow Coll (UT)

MUSIC MANAGEMENT
Austin Comm Coll District (TX)
Harrisburg Area Comm Coll (PA)

MUSIC PERFORMANCE
Cleveland State Comm Coll (TN)
Motlow State Comm Coll (TN)
Nassau Comm Coll (NY)
Truckee Meadows Comm Coll (NV)

MUSIC RELATED
Cayuga County Comm Coll (NY)

MUSIC TEACHER EDUCATION
Coll of Central Florida (FL)
Grand Rapids Comm Coll (MI)
Snow Coll (UT)

MUSIC TECHNOLOGY
Arapahoe Comm Coll (CO)
Daytona State Coll (FL)

NANOTECHNOLOGY
Comm Coll of Allegheny County (PA)
Harper Coll (IL)

NATURAL RESOURCES AND CONSERVATION RELATED
Snow Coll (UT)

NATURAL RESOURCES/ CONSERVATION
Central Oregon Comm Coll (OR)
Dakota Coll at Bottineau (ND)
Treasure Valley Comm Coll (OR)
Truckee Meadows Comm Coll (NV)
Vincennes U (IN)

NATURAL RESOURCES MANAGEMENT AND POLICY
Hawkeye Comm Coll (IA)
Hutchinson Comm Coll (KS)

NATURAL SCIENCES
Arkansas State U–Newport (AR)
Tyler Jr Coll (TX)

NETWORK AND SYSTEM ADMINISTRATION
Bucks County Comm Coll (PA)
Dakota Coll at Bottineau (ND)
Daytona State Coll (FL)
Kaskaskia Coll (IL)
Lake Superior Coll (MN)
Massachusetts Bay Comm Coll (MA)
Mitchell Tech Inst (SD)
Ridgewater Coll (MN)
Sierra Coll (CA)
Southern Maine Comm Coll (ME)

NEUROSCIENCE
Bucks County Comm Coll (PA)

NUCLEAR MEDICAL TECHNOLOGY
Comm Coll of Allegheny County (PA)

NURSING ASSISTANT/AIDE AND PATIENT CARE ASSISTANT/AIDE
Comm Coll of Allegheny County (PA)
Western Wyoming Comm Coll (WY)

NUTRITION SCIENCES
Tulsa Comm Coll (OK)

OCCUPATIONAL SAFETY AND HEALTH TECHNOLOGY
Lamar Inst of Technology (TX)
San Jacinto Coll District (TX)
San Juan Coll (NM)

OCCUPATIONAL THERAPIST ASSISTANT
Austin Comm Coll District (TX)
Cayuga County Comm Coll (NY)
Comm Coll of Allegheny County (PA)
Daytona State Coll (FL)
East Central Coll (MO)
Greenville Tech Coll (SC)
Hawkeye Comm Coll (IA)
Kaskaskia Coll (IL)
Manchester Comm Coll (CT)
McHenry County Coll (IL)
Pueblo Comm Coll (CO)
Quinsigamond Comm Coll (MA)
Raritan Valley Comm Coll (NJ)
St. Charles Comm Coll (MO)
St. Louis Comm Coll (MO)
San Juan Coll (NM)
Southwestern Comm Coll (NC)
Tyler Jr Coll (TX)
Wor-Wic Comm Coll (MD)

OCCUPATIONAL THERAPY
Coll of Central Florida (FL)
Comm Coll of Baltimore County (MD)
San Jacinto Coll District (TX)
Tulsa Comm Coll (OK)
Vincennes U (IN)

OFFICE MANAGEMENT
Alexandria Tech and Comm Coll (MN)
Coll of Central Florida (FL)
Coll of Marin (CA)
Comm Coll of Allegheny County (PA)
Comm Coll of Denver (CO)
Dakota Coll at Bottineau (ND)
Daytona State Coll (FL)
Fayetteville Tech Comm Coll (NC)
Halifax Comm Coll (NC)
Johnston Comm Coll (NC)
Lake Superior Coll (MN)
Mitchell Comm Coll (NC)
Richmond Comm Coll (NC)
St. Charles Comm Coll (MO)
Southwestern Comm Coll (NC)
Treasure Valley Comm Coll (OR)
Wayne County Comm Coll District (MI)

OFFICE OCCUPATIONS AND CLERICAL SERVICES
Alamance Comm Coll (NC)
Dakota Coll at Bottineau (ND)

OPERATIONS MANAGEMENT
Blue Ridge Comm and Tech Coll (WV)
Bunker Hill Comm Coll (MA)
Daytona State Coll (FL)
McHenry County Coll (IL)
Mitchell Comm Coll (NC)
Oakton Comm Coll (IL)

OPHTHALMIC TECHNOLOGY
Renton Tech Coll (WA)

OPTICIANRY
Raritan Valley Comm Coll (NJ)

OPTOMETRIC TECHNICIAN
Raritan Valley Comm Coll (NJ)
San Jacinto Coll District (TX)

ORNAMENTAL HORTICULTURE
Comm Coll of Allegheny County (PA)
Dakota Coll at Bottineau (ND)

PAINTING
Luzerne County Comm Coll (PA)

PAINTING AND WALL COVERING
Comm Coll of Allegheny County (PA)
Tohono O'odham Comm Coll (AZ)

PARKS, RECREATION AND LEISURE
Coll of Central Florida (FL)
Coll of the Canyons (CA)
Dakota Coll at Bottineau (ND)
San Juan Coll (NM)
Sierra Coll (CA)
Sullivan County Comm Coll (NY)

PARKS, RECREATION AND LEISURE FACILITIES MANAGEMENT
Dakota Coll at Bottineau (ND)
Potomac State Coll of West Virginia U (WV)

PARKS, RECREATION, LEISURE, AND FITNESS STUDIES RELATED
Coll of the Canyons (CA)
Comm Coll of Baltimore County (MD)
Dakota Coll at Bottineau (ND)
Southwestern Comm Coll (NC)

PERIOPERATIVE/OPERATING ROOM AND SURGICAL NURSING
Comm Coll of Allegheny County (PA)

PHARMACY TECHNICIAN
Austin Comm Coll District (TX)
Comm Coll of Allegheny County (PA)
Fayetteville Tech Comm Coll (NC)
Hutchinson Comm Coll (KS)
Renton Tech Coll (WA)
San Jacinto Coll District (TX)
Texarkana Coll (TX)
Vincennes U (IN)
Wayne County Comm Coll District (MI)

PHILOSOPHY
Austin Comm Coll District (TX)
Coll of Central Florida (FL)
Coll of the Canyons (CA)
Harper Coll (IL)
Harrisburg Area Comm Coll (PA)
San Jacinto Coll District (TX)
Sierra Coll (CA)
Snow Coll (UT)
Truckee Meadows Comm Coll (NV)
Vincennes U (IN)

PHLEBOTOMY TECHNOLOGY
Coll of The Albemarle (NC)

PHOTOGRAPHIC AND FILM/ VIDEO TECHNOLOGY
Austin Comm Coll District (TX)
Daytona State Coll (FL)

PHOTOGRAPHY
Coll of the Canyons (CA)
Dakota Coll at Bottineau (ND)
Daytona State Coll (FL)
Harrisburg Area Comm Coll (PA)
Luzerne County Comm Coll (PA)
Nassau Comm Coll (NY)
Sullivan County Comm Coll (NY)
Western Wyoming Comm Coll (WY)

PHOTOJOURNALISM
Vincennes U (IN)

PHYSICAL EDUCATION TEACHING AND COACHING
Bucks County Comm Coll (PA)
Coll of Central Florida (FL)
Harper Coll (IL)
Luzerne County Comm Coll (PA)
Potomac State Coll of West Virginia U (WV)
Snow Coll (UT)
Trinity Valley Comm Coll (TX)
Tyler Jr Coll (TX)
Vincennes U (IN)

PHYSICAL FITNESS TECHNICIAN
Alexandria Tech and Comm Coll (MN)
Lake Region State Coll (ND)

PHYSICAL SCIENCES
Borough of Manhattan Comm Coll of the City U of New York (NY)
Central Oregon Comm Coll (OR)
Coll of Marin (CA)
Dakota Coll at Bottineau (ND)
Harper Coll (IL)
Harrisburg Area Comm Coll (PA)
Hutchinson Comm Coll (KS)
Queensborough Comm Coll of the City U of New York (NY)
San Jacinto Coll District (TX)
San Juan Coll (NM)
Snow Coll (UT)
Trinity Valley Comm Coll (TX)
Tulsa Comm Coll (OK)

PHYSICAL SCIENCES RELATED
Dakota Coll at Bottineau (ND)

PHYSICAL THERAPY
Central Oregon Comm Coll (OR)
Coll of Central Florida (FL)

PHYSICAL THERAPY TECHNOLOGY
Austin Comm Coll District (TX)
Black Hawk Coll, Moline (IL)
Blue Ridge Comm and Tech Coll (WV)
Central New Mexico Comm Coll (NM)
Coll of Central Florida (FL)
Comm Coll of Allegheny County (PA)
Daytona State Coll (FL)
Fayetteville Tech Comm Coll (NC)
Greenville Tech Coll (SC)
Hawkeye Comm Coll (IA)
Heartland Comm Coll (IL)
Hutchinson Comm Coll (KS)
Kaskaskia Coll (IL)
Lake Superior Coll (MN)
Manchester Comm Coll (CT)
Mohave Comm Coll (AZ)
Nassau Comm Coll (NY)
Pueblo Comm Coll (CO)
San Jacinto Coll District (TX)
San Juan Coll (NM)
Southern U at Shreveport (LA)
Southwestern Comm Coll (NC)
Tulsa Comm Coll (OK)
Tyler Jr Coll (TX)
Union County Coll (NJ)
Vincennes U (IN)
West Kentucky Comm and Tech Coll (KY)
Wor-Wic Comm Coll (MD)

PHYSICIAN ASSISTANT
Wayne County Comm Coll District (MI)

PHYSICS
Austin Comm Coll District (TX)
Bunker Hill Comm Coll (MA)
Central New Mexico Comm Coll (NM)
Coll of Central Florida (FL)
Coll of Marin (CA)
Coll of the Canyons (CA)
Comm Coll of Allegheny County (PA)
Northampton Comm Coll (PA)
Potomac State Coll of West Virginia U (WV)
San Jacinto Coll District (TX)
San Juan Coll (NM)
Sierra Coll (CA)
Snow Coll (UT)
Texarkana Coll (TX)
Truckee Meadows Comm Coll (NV)
Tyler Jr Coll (TX)

PHYSICS TEACHER EDUCATION
Comm Coll of Baltimore County (MD)

PIPEFITTING AND SPRINKLER FITTING
Vincennes U (IN)

PLANT NURSERY MANAGEMENT
Coll of Marin (CA)
Comm Coll of Allegheny County (PA)

PLASTICS AND POLYMER ENGINEERING TECHNOLOGY
Grand Rapids Comm Coll (MI)

PLUMBING TECHNOLOGY
Luzerne County Comm Coll (PA)
Southern Maine Comm Coll (ME)
Tohono O'odham Comm Coll (AZ)
Vincennes U (IN)

POLITICAL SCIENCE AND GOVERNMENT
Austin Comm Coll District (TX)
Coll of Marin (CA)
Coll of the Canyons (CA)
Potomac State Coll of West Virginia U (WV)
San Jacinto Coll District (TX)
Snow Coll (UT)
Texarkana Coll (TX)
Trinity Valley Comm Coll (TX)
Tyler Jr Coll (TX)
Western Wyoming Comm Coll (WY)

POLYMER/PLASTICS ENGINEERING
Central Oregon Comm Coll (OR)

PRACTICAL NURSING, VOCATIONAL NURSING AND NURSING ASSISTANTS RELATED
Westchester Comm Coll (NY)

PRECISION PRODUCTION RELATED
St. Charles Comm Coll (MO)

PRE-DENTISTRY STUDIES
Potomac State Coll of West Virginia U (WV)
Western Wyoming Comm Coll (WY)

PRE-ENGINEERING
Alexandria Tech and Comm Coll (MN)
Central New Mexico Comm Coll (NM)
Coll of the Canyons (CA)
Fayetteville Tech Comm Coll (NC)
Haywood Comm Coll (NC)
Johnston Comm Coll (NC)
Quinsigamond Comm Coll (MA)
Richmond Comm Coll (NC)
Rock Valley Coll (IL)
St. Charles Comm Coll (MO)
Snow Coll (UT)
Trinity Valley Comm Coll (TX)
Tulsa Comm Coll (OK)
Wayne County Comm Coll District (MI)
Western Wyoming Comm Coll (WY)

PRE-LAW STUDIES
Central New Mexico Comm Coll (NM)
Central Oregon Comm Coll (OR)
Coll of Central Florida (FL)
Potomac State Coll of West Virginia U (WV)
Vincennes U (IN)
Western Wyoming Comm Coll (WY)

PREMEDICAL STUDIES
Austin Comm Coll District (TX)
Central Oregon Comm Coll (OR)
Coll of Central Florida (FL)
Dakota Coll at Bottineau (ND)
Potomac State Coll of West Virginia U (WV)
San Juan Coll (NM)
Western Wyoming Comm Coll (WY)

PRENURSING STUDIES
Dakota Coll at Bottineau (ND)
Potomac State Coll of West Virginia U (WV)
Tulsa Comm Coll (OK)
Western Wyoming Comm Coll (WY)

PRE-OCCUPATIONAL THERAPY
Potomac State Coll of West Virginia U (WV)

PRE-PHARMACY STUDIES
Central Oregon Comm Coll (OR)
Coll of Central Florida (FL)
Luzerne County Comm Coll (PA)
Potomac State Coll of West Virginia U (WV)
Quinsigamond Comm Coll (MA)
St. Charles Comm Coll (MO)
Tulsa Comm Coll (OK)
Western Wyoming Comm Coll (WY)

PRE-PHYSICAL THERAPY
Potomac State Coll of West Virginia U (WV)

PRE-VETERINARY STUDIES
Coll of Central Florida (FL)
Dakota Coll at Bottineau (ND)
Potomac State Coll of West Virginia U (WV)
Western Wyoming Comm Coll (WY)

PROFESSIONAL, TECHNICAL, BUSINESS, AND SCIENTIFIC WRITING
Austin Comm Coll District (TX)

PSYCHIATRIC/MENTAL HEALTH SERVICES TECHNOLOGY
Comm Coll of Allegheny County (PA)
Pueblo Comm Coll (CO)
San Jacinto Coll District (TX)
Wayne County Comm Coll District (MI)

PSYCHOLOGY
Austin Comm Coll District (TX)
Borough of Manhattan Comm Coll of the City U of New York (NY)
Bucks County Comm Coll (PA)
Bunker Hill Comm Coll (MA)
Central New Mexico Comm Coll (NM)
Coll of Central Florida (FL)
Coll of Marin (CA)
Coll of the Canyons (CA)
Comm Coll of Allegheny County (PA)
Dakota Coll at Bottineau (ND)
Harper Coll (IL)
Harrisburg Area Comm Coll (PA)
Hutchinson Comm Coll (KS)
Manor Coll (PA)
Potomac State Coll of West Virginia U (WV)
Queensborough Comm Coll of the City U of New York (NY)
Quinsigamond Comm Coll (MA)
San Jacinto Coll District (TX)
San Juan Coll (NM)
Sierra Coll (CA)
Sullivan County Comm Coll (NY)
Trinity Valley Comm Coll (TX)
Truckee Meadows Comm Coll (NV)
Tyler Jr Coll (TX)
Western Wyoming Comm Coll (WY)

PUBLIC ADMINISTRATION
Central Texas Coll (TX)
Lamar Inst of Technology (TX)
Tyler Jr Coll (TX)

PUBLIC ADMINISTRATION AND SOCIAL SERVICE PROFESSIONS RELATED
Cleveland State Comm Coll (TN)

PUBLIC HEALTH
Borough of Manhattan Comm Coll of the City U of New York (NY)
Queensborough Comm Coll of the City U of New York (NY)

PUBLIC HEALTH EDUCATION AND PROMOTION
Borough of Manhattan Comm Coll of the City U of New York (NY)
Northampton Comm Coll (PA)

PUBLIC RELATIONS, ADVERTISING, AND APPLIED COMMUNICATION RELATED
Harper Coll (IL)

PUBLIC RELATIONS/IMAGE MANAGEMENT
Vincennes U (IN)

PURCHASING, PROCUREMENT/ ACQUISITIONS AND CONTRACTS MANAGEMENT
Greenville Tech Coll (SC)

QUALITY CONTROL AND SAFETY TECHNOLOGIES RELATED
Comm Coll of Denver (CO)

QUALITY CONTROL TECHNOLOGY
Comm Coll of Allegheny County (PA)
Grand Rapids Comm Coll (MI)
Northampton Comm Coll (PA)

RADIO AND TELEVISION
Austin Comm Coll District (TX)
Central Texas Coll (TX)
Sullivan County Comm Coll (NY)
Tyler Jr Coll (TX)

RADIO AND TELEVISION BROADCASTING TECHNOLOGY
Borough of Manhattan Comm Coll of the City U of New York (NY)
Hutchinson Comm Coll (KS)
Luzerne County Comm Coll (PA)
Northampton Comm Coll (PA)
San Jacinto Coll District (TX)
Vincennes U (IN)

RADIOLOGIC TECHNOLOGY/ SCIENCE
Austin Comm Coll District (TX)
Black Hawk Coll, Moline (IL)
Bucks County Comm Coll (PA)
Central New Mexico Comm Coll (NM)
Central Ohio Tech Coll (OH)
Central Oregon Comm Coll (OR)
Comm Coll of Allegheny County (PA)
Comm Coll of Denver (CO)
Fayetteville Tech Comm Coll (NC)
Harper Coll (IL)
Harrisburg Area Comm Coll (PA)
Heartland Comm Coll (IL)
Hutchinson Comm Coll (KS)
Kaskaskia Coll (IL)
Lake Superior Coll (MN)
Massachusetts Bay Comm Coll (MA)
Minnesota State Coll–Southeast Tech (MN)
Mitchell Tech Inst (SD)
Northampton Comm Coll (PA)
Owensboro Comm and Tech Coll (KY)
Pueblo Comm Coll (CO)
Quinsigamond Comm Coll (MA)
Ridgewater Coll (MN)
St. Louis Comm Coll (MO)
St. Luke's Coll (IA)
San Jacinto Coll District (TX)
Southern Maine Comm Coll (ME)
Southern U at Shreveport (LA)
State U of New York Coll of Technology at Alfred (NY)
Tyler Jr Coll (TX)
Union County Coll (NJ)

RADIO, TELEVISION, AND DIGITAL COMMUNICATION RELATED
Cayuga County Comm Coll (NY)
Sullivan County Comm Coll (NY)

RANGE SCIENCE AND MANAGEMENT
Snow Coll (UT)
Treasure Valley Comm Coll (OR)
Trinity Valley Comm Coll (TX)

REAL ESTATE
Austin Comm Coll District (TX)
Coll of Marin (CA)
Coll of the Canyons (CA)
Comm Coll of Allegheny County (PA)
Lamar Inst of Technology (TX)
Nassau Comm Coll (NY)
Oakton Comm Coll (IL)
San Jacinto Coll District (TX)
Sierra Coll (CA)
Trinity Valley Comm Coll (TX)

RECEPTIONIST
Dakota Coll at Bottineau (ND)

RECORDING ARTS TECHNOLOGY
Front Range Comm Coll (CO)
Queensborough Comm Coll of the City U of New York (NY)
Ridgewater Coll (MN)
Vincennes U (IN)

REGISTERED NURSING/ REGISTERED NURSE
Alamance Comm Coll (NC)
Alexandria Tech and Comm Coll (MN)
Arapahoe Comm Coll (CO)
Arkansas State U–Newport (AR)
Austin Comm Coll District (TX)
Blue Ridge Comm and Tech Coll (WV)
Borough of Manhattan Comm Coll of the City U of New York (NY)
Bucks County Comm Coll (PA)
Bunker Hill Comm Coll (MA)
Cayuga County Comm Coll (NY)
Central New Mexico Comm Coll (NM)
Central Ohio Tech Coll (OH)
Central Oregon Comm Coll (OR)
Central Texas Coll (TX)
Cleveland State Comm Coll (TN)
Coll of Central Florida (FL)
Coll of Marin (CA)
Coll of The Albemarle (NC)
Coll of the Canyons (CA)
Colorado Northwestern Comm Coll (CO)
Columbia-Greene Comm Coll (NY)
Comm Coll of Allegheny County (PA)
Comm Coll of Baltimore County (MD)
Dakota Coll at Bottineau (ND)
Daytona State Coll (FL)
Fayetteville Tech Comm Coll (NC)
Front Range Comm Coll (CO)
Georgia Highlands Coll (GA)
Grand Rapids Comm Coll (MI)
Greenville Tech Coll (SC)
Halifax Comm Coll (NC)
Harper Coll (IL)
Harrisburg Area Comm Coll (PA)
Hawkeye Comm Coll (IA)
Haywood Comm Coll (NC)
Heartland Comm Coll (IL)
Henderson Comm Coll (KY)
Hutchinson Comm Coll (KS)
Johnston Comm Coll (NC)
John Tyler Comm Coll (VA)
Kaskaskia Coll (IL)
Lake Region State Coll (ND)
Lake Superior Coll (MN)
Lurleen B. Wallace Comm Coll (AL)
Luzerne County Comm Coll (PA)
Massachusetts Bay Comm Coll (MA)
McHenry County Coll (IL)
Minnesota State Coll–Southeast Tech (MN)
Missouri State U–West Plains (MO)
Mitchell Comm Coll (NC)
Mohave Comm Coll (AZ)
Motlow State Comm Coll (TN)
Nassau Comm Coll (NY)
Northampton Comm Coll (PA)
Oakton Comm Coll (IL)
Owensboro Comm and Tech Coll (KY)
Pueblo Comm Coll (CO)
Queensborough Comm Coll of the City U of New York (NY)
Quinsigamond Comm Coll (MA)
Raritan Valley Comm Coll (NJ)
Rend Lake Coll (IL)
Renton Tech Coll (WA)
Richmond Comm Coll (NC)
Ridgewater Coll (MN)
Rock Valley Coll (IL)
St. Luke's Coll (IA)
San Jacinto Coll District (TX)
San Juan Coll (NM)
Sierra Coll (CA)
Snow Coll (UT)
Southern Maine Comm Coll (ME)
Southern U at Shreveport (LA)
Southwestern Comm Coll (IA)
Southwestern Comm Coll (NC)
Southwestern Michigan Coll (MI)
Southwest Wisconsin Tech Coll (WI)
Sowela Tech Comm Coll (LA)
State U of New York Coll of Technology at Alfred (NY)
Sullivan County Comm Coll (NY)
Sumner Coll (OR)
Texarkana Coll (TX)
Tidewater Comm Coll (VA)
Treasure Valley Comm Coll (OR)
Trinity Valley Comm Coll (TX)
Truckee Meadows Comm Coll (NV)
Tulsa Comm Coll (OK)
Tyler Jr Coll (TX)
Union County Coll (NJ)
U of Arkansas Comm Coll at Morrilton (AR)
Vincennes U (IN)
Wayne County Comm Coll District (MI)
Westchester Comm Coll (NY)
West Kentucky Comm and Tech Coll (KY)
Wor-Wic Comm Coll (MD)

REHABILITATION AND THERAPEUTIC PROFESSIONS RELATED
Nassau Comm Coll (NY)
Raritan Valley Comm Coll (NJ)
Union County Coll (NJ)

RELIGIOUS STUDIES
Coll of Central Florida (FL)
Trinity Valley Comm Coll (TX)

RESPIRATORY CARE THERAPY
Arkansas State U Mid-South (AR)
Central New Mexico Comm Coll (NM)
Comm Coll of Allegheny County (PA)
Comm Coll of Aurora (CO)
Comm Coll of Baltimore County (MD)
Daytona State Coll (FL)
Fayetteville Tech Comm Coll (NC)
Greenville Tech Coll (SC)
Harrisburg Area Comm Coll (PA)
Hawkeye Comm Coll (IA)
Hutchinson Comm Coll (KS)
Kaskaskia Coll (IL)
Lake Superior Coll (MN)
Luzerne County Comm Coll (PA)
Manchester Comm Coll (CT)
Nassau Comm Coll (NY)
Pueblo Comm Coll (CO)
Quinsigamond Comm Coll (MA)
Raritan Valley Comm Coll (NJ)
Rock Valley Coll (IL)
St. Louis Comm Coll (MO)
St. Luke's Coll (IA)
San Jacinto Coll District (TX)
San Juan Coll (NM)
Southern Maine Comm Coll (ME)
Southern U at Shreveport (LA)
Southwestern Comm Coll (NC)
Sullivan County Comm Coll (NY)
Tulsa Comm Coll (OK)
Tyler Jr Coll (TX)
Union County Coll (NJ)
Westchester Comm Coll (NY)

RESPIRATORY THERAPY TECHNICIAN
Borough of Manhattan Comm Coll of the City U of New York (NY)
Bunker Hill Comm Coll (MA)

RESTAURANT, CULINARY, AND CATERING MANAGEMENT
Blue Ridge Comm and Tech Coll (WV)
Coll of Central Florida (FL)
Coll of the Canyons (CA)
Comm Coll of Allegheny County (PA)
Daytona State Coll (FL)
Grand Rapids Comm Coll (MI)
McHenry County Coll (IL)
Missouri State U–West Plains (MO)
Raritan Valley Comm Coll (NJ)
San Jacinto Coll District (TX)
Southwest Wisconsin Tech Coll (WI)
Vincennes U (IN)
Westchester Comm Coll (NY)

RESTAURANT/FOOD SERVICES MANAGEMENT
Central Texas Coll (TX)
Northampton Comm Coll (PA)
Quinsigamond Comm Coll (MA)

RETAILING
Alamance Comm Coll (NC)
Arapahoe Comm Coll (CO)
Black Hawk Coll, Moline (IL)
Central Oregon Comm Coll (OR)
Comm Coll of Allegheny County (PA)
Hutchinson Comm Coll (KS)
Minnesota State Coll–Southeast Tech (MN)
Nassau Comm Coll (NY)
Westchester Comm Coll (NY)

RHETORIC AND COMPOSITION
Austin Comm Coll District (TX)
San Jacinto Coll District (TX)
Sierra Coll (CA)
Trinity Valley Comm Coll (TX)

ROBOTICS TECHNOLOGY
Comm Coll of Allegheny County (PA)
Kaskaskia Coll (IL)

RUSSIAN
Austin Comm Coll District (TX)

SALES, DISTRIBUTION, AND MARKETING OPERATIONS
Coll of the Canyons (CA)
Greenville Tech Coll (SC)
Harper Coll (IL)
Hawkeye Comm Coll (IA)
Oakton Comm Coll (IL)
Ridgewater Coll (MN)
Sierra Coll (CA)
State U of New York Coll of Technology at Alfred (NY)

SCIENCE TEACHER EDUCATION
San Jacinto Coll District (TX)
Snow Coll (UT)
Vincennes U (IN)

SCIENCE TECHNOLOGIES RELATED
Arapahoe Comm Coll (CO)
Blue Ridge Comm and Tech Coll (WV)
Cleveland State Comm Coll (TN)
Comm Coll of Allegheny County (PA)
Comm Coll of Aurora (CO)
Comm Coll of Denver (CO)
Dakota Coll at Bottineau (ND)
Front Range Comm Coll (CO)
Pueblo Comm Coll (CO)
Sullivan County Comm Coll (NY)

SCIENCE, TECHNOLOGY AND SOCIETY
Truckee Meadows Comm Coll (NV)

SECONDARY EDUCATION
Austin Comm Coll District (TX)
Coll of Central Florida (FL)
Harrisburg Area Comm Coll (PA)
Northampton Comm Coll (PA)
Potomac State Coll of West Virginia U (WV)
San Jacinto Coll District (TX)
San Juan Coll (NM)
Tyler Jr Coll (TX)
Vincennes U (IN)
Western Wyoming Comm Coll (WY)

SELLING SKILLS AND SALES
McHenry County Coll (IL)
Minnesota State Coll–Southeast Tech (MN)
Ridgewater Coll (MN)

SHEET METAL TECHNOLOGY
Comm Coll of Allegheny County (PA)
Lake Superior Coll (MN)
Rock Valley Coll (IL)
Vincennes U (IN)

SIGN LANGUAGE INTERPRETATION AND TRANSLATION
Austin Comm Coll District (TX)
Coll of the Canyons (CA)
Comm Coll of Allegheny County (PA)
Comm Coll of Baltimore County (MD)
Front Range Comm Coll (CO)
St. Louis Comm Coll (MO)
Tulsa Comm Coll (OK)
Tyler Jr Coll (TX)

SMALL BUSINESS ADMINISTRATION
Black Hawk Coll, Moline (IL)
Borough of Manhattan Comm Coll of the City U of New York (NY)
Bucks County Comm Coll (PA)
Coll of the Canyons (CA)
Colorado Northwestern Comm Coll (CO)
Dakota Coll at Bottineau (ND)
Harper Coll (IL)
Hutchinson Comm Coll (KS)
Raritan Valley Comm Coll (NJ)
Sierra Coll (CA)
Westchester Comm Coll (NY)

SMALL ENGINE MECHANICS AND REPAIR TECHNOLOGY
Mitchell Tech Inst (SD)

SOCIAL SCIENCES
Bucks County Comm Coll (PA)
Central Oregon Comm Coll (OR)
Central Texas Coll (TX)
Coll of Central Florida (FL)
Coll of Marin (CA)
Coll of the Canyons (CA)
Comm Coll of Allegheny County (PA)
Dakota Coll at Bottineau (ND)
Harrisburg Area Comm Coll (PA)
Hutchinson Comm Coll (KS)
Luzerne County Comm Coll (PA)
Massachusetts Bay Comm Coll (MA)
San Jacinto Coll District (TX)
Sierra Coll (CA)
Texarkana Coll (TX)
Tohono O'odham Comm Coll (AZ)
Tulsa Comm Coll (OK)
Western Wyoming Comm Coll (WY)

SOCIAL SCIENCES RELATED
Coll of the Canyons (CA)

SOCIAL WORK
Austin Comm Coll District (TX)
Bucks County Comm Coll (PA)
Coll of Central Florida (FL)
Comm Coll of Allegheny County (PA)
Harrisburg Area Comm Coll (PA)
Manchester Comm Coll (CT)
Northampton Comm Coll (PA)
Oakton Comm Coll (IL)
Potomac State Coll of West Virginia U (WV)
San Juan Coll (NM)
Southwestern Michigan Coll (MI)
Tulsa Comm Coll (OK)
Tyler Jr Coll (TX)
Vincennes U (IN)
Wayne County Comm Coll District (MI)
Western Wyoming Comm Coll (WY)

SOCIOLOGY
Austin Comm Coll District (TX)
Borough of Manhattan Comm Coll of the City U of New York (NY)
Bunker Hill Comm Coll (MA)
Central New Mexico Comm Coll (NM)
Coll of Central Florida (FL)
Coll of the Canyons (CA)
Comm Coll of Allegheny County (PA)
Potomac State Coll of West Virginia U (WV)
Quinsigamond Comm Coll (MA)
San Jacinto Coll District (TX)
Snow Coll (UT)
Trinity Valley Comm Coll (TX)
Tyler Jr Coll (TX)
Western Wyoming Comm Coll (WY)

SOCIOLOGY AND ANTHROPOLOGY
Harper Coll (IL)

SOIL SCIENCE AND AGRONOMY
Snow Coll (UT)
Treasure Valley Comm Coll (OR)

SOLAR ENERGY TECHNOLOGY
Comm Coll of Allegheny County (PA)
Treasure Valley Comm Coll (OR)

SPANISH
Austin Comm Coll District (TX)
Coll of Marin (CA)
Coll of the Canyons (CA)
Snow Coll (UT)
Trinity Valley Comm Coll (TX)
Western Wyoming Comm Coll (WY)

SPANISH LANGUAGE TEACHER EDUCATION
Comm Coll of Baltimore County (MD)

SPECIAL EDUCATION
Coll of Central Florida (FL)
McHenry County Coll (IL)
San Juan Coll (NM)
Vincennes U (IN)

SPECIAL EDUCATION–EARLY CHILDHOOD
Mitchell Comm Coll (NC)

SPEECH COMMUNICATION AND RHETORIC
Bucks County Comm Coll (PA)
Bunker Hill Comm Coll (MA)
Central Oregon Comm Coll (OR)
Coll of Marin (CA)
Coll of the Canyons (CA)
Harper Coll (IL)
Hutchinson Comm Coll (KS)
Manchester Comm Coll (CT)
Nassau Comm Coll (NY)
Northampton Comm Coll (PA)
Tyler Jr Coll (TX)
Westchester Comm Coll (NY)
Western Wyoming Comm Coll (WY)

SPEECH-LANGUAGE PATHOLOGY
Lake Region State Coll (ND)

SPEECH-LANGUAGE PATHOLOGY ASSISTANT
Alexandria Tech and Comm Coll (MN)
Fayetteville Tech Comm Coll (NC)
Mitchell Tech Inst (SD)

SPORT AND FITNESS ADMINISTRATION/ MANAGEMENT
Bucks County Comm Coll (PA)
Bunker Hill Comm Coll (MA)
Cayuga County Comm Coll (NY)
Central Oregon Comm Coll (OR)
Hutchinson Comm Coll (KS)
Manor Coll (PA)
Northampton Comm Coll (PA)
Rock Valley Coll (IL)
Southwestern Michigan Coll (MI)
State U of New York Coll of Technology at Alfred (NY)
Sullivan County Comm Coll (NY)
Tulsa Comm Coll (OK)
Union County Coll (NJ)

STATISTICS
Coll of Central Florida (FL)

STRUCTURAL ENGINEERING
Harrisburg Area Comm Coll (PA)

SUBSTANCE ABUSE/ ADDICTION COUNSELING
Austin Comm Coll District (TX)
Central Oregon Comm Coll (OR)
Comm Coll of Allegheny County (PA)
Comm Coll of Baltimore County (MD)
Mohave Comm Coll (AZ)
Oakton Comm Coll (IL)
Richmond Comm Coll (NC)
Southwestern Comm Coll (NC)
Texarkana Coll (TX)
Treasure Valley Comm Coll (OR)
Tyler Jr Coll (TX)
Westchester Comm Coll (NY)
Wor-Wic Comm Coll (MD)

SURGICAL TECHNOLOGY
Arkansas State U–Newport (AR)
Austin Comm Coll District (TX)
Black Hawk Coll, Moline (IL)
Central New Mexico Comm Coll (NM)
Central Ohio Tech Coll (OH)
Comm Coll of Allegheny County (PA)
Fayetteville Tech Comm Coll (NC)
Front Range Comm Coll (CO)
Harrisburg Area Comm Coll (PA)
Hutchinson Comm Coll (KS)
Lake Superior Coll (MN)
Luzerne County Comm Coll (PA)
Manchester Comm Coll (CT)
Mohave Comm Coll (AZ)
Nassau Comm Coll (NY)
Owensboro Comm and Tech Coll (KY)
Pueblo Comm Coll (CO)
Renton Tech Coll (WA)
Rock Valley Coll (IL)
St. Louis Comm Coll (MO)
San Jacinto Coll District (TX)
San Juan Coll (NM)
Southern Maine Comm Coll (ME)
Southern U at Shreveport (LA)
Trinity Valley Comm Coll (TX)
Tulsa Comm Coll (OK)
Tyler Jr Coll (TX)
Vincennes U (IN)
Wayne County Comm Coll District (MI)
West Kentucky Comm and Tech Coll (KY)

SURVEYING ENGINEERING
Central New Mexico Comm Coll (NM)

SURVEYING TECHNOLOGY
Austin Comm Coll District (TX)
Coll of the Canyons (CA)
Fayetteville Tech Comm Coll (NC)
Renton Tech Coll (WA)
State U of New York Coll of Technology at Alfred (NY)
Tyler Jr Coll (TX)
U of Arkansas Comm Coll at Morrilton (AR)
Vincennes U (IN)

SYSTEM, NETWORKING, AND LAN/WAN MANAGEMENT
Southwestern Comm Coll (NC)
Tyler Jr Coll (TX)

TEACHER ASSISTANT/AIDE
Alamance Comm Coll (NC)
Borough of Manhattan Comm Coll of the City U of New York (NY)
Coll of The Albemarle (NC)
Comm Coll of Allegheny County (PA)
Dakota Coll at Bottineau (ND)
Kaskaskia Coll (IL)
Manchester Comm Coll (CT)
Mitchell Comm Coll (NC)
Northampton Comm Coll (PA)
Ridgewater Coll (MN)
St. Charles Comm Coll (MO)
Westchester Comm Coll (NY)

TECHNICAL TEACHER EDUCATION
East Central Coll (MO)

TECHNOLOGY/INDUSTRIAL ARTS TEACHER EDUCATION
Central New Mexico Comm Coll (NM)
Vincennes U (IN)

TELECOMMUNICATIONS TECHNOLOGY
Arapahoe Comm Coll (CO)
Cayuga County Comm Coll (NY)
Mitchell Tech Inst (SD)
Queensborough Comm Coll of the City U of New York (NY)
Ridgewater Coll (MN)

THEATER DESIGN AND TECHNOLOGY
Coll of the Canyons (CA)
Nassau Comm Coll (NY)
San Juan Coll (NM)
Western Wyoming Comm Coll (WY)

THEATER/THEATER ARTS MANAGEMENT
Harper Coll (IL)

THERAPEUTIC RECREATION
Austin Comm Coll District (TX)
Comm Coll of Allegheny County (PA)
Ridgewater Coll (MN)

TOOL AND DIE TECHNOLOGY
Ridgewater Coll (MN)
Rock Valley Coll (IL)
Vincennes U (IN)

TOURISM AND TRAVEL SERVICES MANAGEMENT
Austin Comm Coll District (TX)
Bunker Hill Comm Coll (MA)
Sullivan County Comm Coll (NY)

TOURISM PROMOTION
Comm Coll of Allegheny County (PA)

TRADE AND INDUSTRIAL TEACHER EDUCATION
Southwestern Comm Coll (NC)

TRANSPORTATION AND MATERIALS MOVING RELATED
Nassau Comm Coll (NY)

TRANSPORTATION/MOBILITY MANAGEMENT
Comm Coll of Baltimore County (MD)

TRUCK AND BUS DRIVER/ COMMERCIAL VEHICLE OPERATION/INSTRUCTION
Mohave Comm Coll (AZ)

TURF AND TURFGRASS MANAGEMENT
Comm Coll of Allegheny County (PA)

URBAN FORESTRY
Dakota Coll at Bottineau (ND)

VEHICLE MAINTENANCE AND REPAIR TECHNOLOGIES
Ohio Tech Coll (OH)

VEHICLE MAINTENANCE AND REPAIR TECHNOLOGIES RELATED
Central New Mexico Comm Coll (NM)
State U of New York Coll of Technology at Alfred (NY)

VETERINARY/ANIMAL HEALTH TECHNOLOGY
Austin Comm Coll District (TX)
Black Hawk Coll, Moline (IL)
Central New Mexico Comm Coll (NM)
Coll of Central Florida (FL)
Comm Coll of Baltimore County (MD)
Comm Coll of Denver (CO)
Front Range Comm Coll (CO)
Kaskaskia Coll (IL)
Manor Coll (PA)
Northampton Comm Coll (PA)
Owensboro Comm and Tech Coll (KY)
Ridgewater Coll (MN)
San Juan Coll (NM)
State U of New York Coll of Technology at Alfred (NY)
Truckee Meadows Comm Coll (NV)
Tulsa Comm Coll (OK)
Tyler Jr Coll (TX)

VISUAL AND PERFORMING ARTS
Borough of Manhattan Comm Coll of the City U of New York (NY)
Bucks County Comm Coll (PA)
Comm Coll of Baltimore County (MD)
Harrisburg Area Comm Coll (PA)
Hutchinson Comm Coll (KS)
Nassau Comm Coll (NY)
Sierra Coll (CA)
Westchester Comm Coll (NY)
Western Wyoming Comm Coll (WY)

VISUAL AND PERFORMING ARTS RELATED
Comm Coll of Allegheny County (PA)
John Tyler Comm Coll (VA)

VITICULTURE AND ENOLOGY
Missouri State U–West Plains (MO)

WATCHMAKING AND JEWELRYMAKING
Austin Comm Coll District (TX)

WATER QUALITY AND WASTEWATER TREATMENT MANAGEMENT AND RECYCLING TECHNOLOGY
Coll of the Canyons (CA)

WEB/MULTIMEDIA MANAGEMENT AND WEBMASTER
Kaskaskia Coll (IL)
Wayne County Comm Coll District (MI)
Western Wyoming Comm Coll (WY)

WEB PAGE, DIGITAL/ MULTIMEDIA AND INFORMATION RESOURCES DESIGN
Borough of Manhattan Comm Coll of the City U of New York (NY)
Bucks County Comm Coll (PA)
Bunker Hill Comm Coll (MA)
Central Ohio Tech Coll (OH)
Coll of the Canyons (CA)
Comm Coll of Aurora (CO)
Daytona State Coll (FL)
Dunwoody Coll of Technology (MN)
Grand Rapids Comm Coll (MI)
Harper Coll (IL)
Harrisburg Area Comm Coll (PA)
Hawkeye Comm Coll (IA)
Heartland Comm Coll (IL)
Hutchinson Comm Coll (KS)
Lake Superior Coll (MN)
Minnesota State Coll–Southeast Tech (MN)
Motlow State Comm Coll (TN)
Northampton Comm Coll (PA)
Pueblo Comm Coll (CO)
Quinsigamond Comm Coll (MA)
Ridgewater Coll (MN)
Sierra Coll (CA)
Southwestern Comm Coll (IA)
Southwest Wisconsin Tech Coll (WI)
Western Wyoming Comm Coll (WY)

WELDING ENGINEERING TECHNOLOGY
Mitchell Tech Inst (SD)

WELDING TECHNOLOGY
Alamance Comm Coll (NC)
Austin Comm Coll District (TX)

Central New Mexico Comm Coll (NM)
Central Texas Coll (TX)
Coll of the Canyons (CA)
Comm Coll of Allegheny County (PA)
Comm Coll of Denver (CO)
Dunwoody Coll of Technology (MN)
East Central Coll (MO)
Front Range Comm Coll (CO)
Grand Rapids Comm Coll (MI)
Halifax Comm Coll (NC)
Hawkeye Comm Coll (IA)
Haywood Comm Coll (NC)
Hutchinson Comm Coll (KS)
Kaskaskia Coll (IL)
Lake Superior Coll (MN)
Lamar Inst of Technology (TX)
Mohave Comm Coll (AZ)
Northampton Comm Coll (PA)
Ohio Tech Coll (OH)
Owensboro Comm and Tech Coll (KY)
Pueblo Comm Coll (CO)
Rend Lake Coll (IL)
Renton Tech Coll (WA)
Ridgewater Coll (MN)
Rock Valley Coll (IL)
St. Charles Comm Coll (MO)
San Jacinto Coll District (TX)
San Juan Coll (NM)
Southwestern Comm Coll (IA)
State U of New York Coll of Technology at Alfred (NY)
Texarkana Coll (TX)
Treasure Valley Comm Coll (OR)
Trinity Valley Comm Coll (TX)
Truckee Meadows Comm Coll (NV)
Tyler Jr Coll (TX)
Vincennes U (IN)
Wayne County Comm Coll District (MI)
Western Wyoming Comm Coll (WY)

WILDLIFE, FISH AND WILDLANDS SCIENCE AND MANAGEMENT

Dakota Coll at Bottineau (ND)
Front Range Comm Coll (CO)
Haywood Comm Coll (NC)
Potomac State Coll of West Virginia U (WV)
Treasure Valley Comm Coll (OR)
Western Wyoming Comm Coll (WY)

WINE STEWARD/SOMMELIER

Cayuga County Comm Coll (NY)

WOMEN'S STUDIES

Borough of Manhattan Comm Coll of the City U of New York (NY)
Sierra Coll (CA)

WOOD SCIENCE AND WOOD PRODUCTS/PULP AND PAPER TECHNOLOGY

Potomac State Coll of West Virginia U (WV)

WORD PROCESSING

Western Wyoming Comm Coll (WY)

WRITING

Cayuga County Comm Coll (NY)

ZOOLOGY/ANIMAL BIOLOGY

Dakota Coll at Bottineau (ND)
Snow Coll (UT)

Associate Degree Programs at Four-Year Colleges

ACCOUNTING
Berkeley Coll–New York City Campus (NY)
California U of Pennsylvania (PA)
Calumet Coll of Saint Joseph (IN)
Campbellsville U (KY)
Champlain Coll (VT)
Davenport U, Grand Rapids (MI)
Immaculata U (PA)
Inter American U of Puerto Rico, Aguadilla Campus (PR)
Inter American U of Puerto Rico, Barranquitas Campus (PR)
Inter American U of Puerto Rico, Bayamón Campus (PR)
Inter American U of Puerto Rico, Fajardo Campus (PR)
Inter American U of Puerto Rico, San Germán Campus (PR)
Liberty U (VA)
Mount Marty Coll (SD)
Oakland City U (IN)
The U of Findlay (OH)
U of Northwestern–St. Paul (MN)
Utah Valley U (UT)
Youngstown State U (OH)

ACCOUNTING TECHNOLOGY AND BOOKKEEPING
American Public U System (WV)
State U of New York Coll of Technology at Delhi (NY)
Sullivan U (KY)
The U of Toledo (OH)

ACTING
Academy of Art U (CA)

ADMINISTRATIVE ASSISTANT AND SECRETARIAL SCIENCE
Arkansas Tech U (AR)
Clarion U of Pennsylvania (PA)
Columbia Central U, Caguas (PR)
Idaho State U (ID)
Inter American U of Puerto Rico, San Germán Campus (PR)
Weber State U (UT)

ADULT DEVELOPMENT AND AGING
Madonna U (MI)

ADVERTISING
Academy of Art U (CA)
Fashion Inst of Technology (NY)

AERONAUTICAL/AEROSPACE ENGINEERING TECHNOLOGY
American Public U System (WV)
Idaho State U (ID)
Vaughn Coll of Aeronautics and Technology (NY)

AERONAUTICS/AVIATION/ AEROSPACE SCIENCE AND TECHNOLOGY
Embry-Riddle Aeronautical U–Daytona (FL)
Embry-Riddle Aeronautical U–Worldwide (FL)
LeTourneau U (TX)
Ohio U (OH)
Vaughn Coll of Aeronautics and Technology (NY)

AEROSPACE, AERONAUTICAL AND ASTRONAUTICAL/SPACE ENGINEERING
Embry-Riddle Aeronautical U–Worldwide (FL)

AGRIBUSINESS
Southern Arkansas U–Magnolia (AR)
Vermont Tech Coll (VT)

AGRICULTURAL BUSINESS AND MANAGEMENT
North Carolina State U (NC)
U of New Hampshire (NH)

AGRICULTURAL PRODUCTION
Western Kentucky U (KY)

AGRICULTURE
North Carolina State U (NC)

AGRICULTURE AND AGRICULTURE OPERATIONS RELATED
Murray State U (KY)

AIRCRAFT POWERPLANT TECHNOLOGY
Embry-Riddle Aeronautical U–Worldwide (FL)
Idaho State U (ID)
Liberty U (VA)

AIRFRAME MECHANICS AND AIRCRAFT MAINTENANCE TECHNOLOGY
Vaughn Coll of Aeronautics and Technology (NY)

AIRLINE FLIGHT ATTENDANT
Liberty U (VA)

AIRLINE PILOT AND FLIGHT CREW
Southern Illinois U Carbondale (IL)
Utah Valley U (UT)
Valparaiso U (IN)

AIR TRAFFIC CONTROL
LeTourneau U (TX)

ALLIED HEALTH AND MEDICAL ASSISTING SERVICES RELATED
Clarion U of Pennsylvania (PA)
Eastern U (PA)
Widener U (PA)

ALLIED HEALTH DIAGNOSTIC, INTERVENTION, AND TREATMENT PROFESSIONS RELATED
Cameron U (OK)

AMERICAN NATIVE/NATIVE AMERICAN LANGUAGES
Idaho State U (ID)

AMERICAN SIGN LANGUAGE (ASL)
Idaho State U (ID)
Madonna U (MI)
Weber State U (UT)

ANIMAL/LIVESTOCK HUSBANDRY AND PRODUCTION
North Carolina State U (NC)

ANIMAL SCIENCES
U of New Hampshire (NH)

ANIMATION, INTERACTIVE TECHNOLOGY, VIDEO GRAPHICS AND SPECIAL EFFECTS
Academy of Art U (CA)

New England Inst of Technology (RI)

APPAREL AND TEXTILE MANUFACTURING
Academy of Art U (CA)
Fashion Inst of Technology (NY)
FIDM/Fashion Inst of Design & Merchandising, Los Angeles Campus (CA)

APPAREL AND TEXTILE MARKETING MANAGEMENT
Academy of Art U (CA)

APPAREL AND TEXTILES
Academy of Art U (CA)

APPLIED HORTICULTURE/ HORTICULTURAL BUSINESS SERVICES RELATED
U of Massachusetts Amherst (MA)

APPLIED HORTICULTURE/ HORTICULTURE OPERATIONS
State U of New York Coll of Technology at Delhi (NY)
U of Massachusetts Amherst (MA)
U of New Hampshire (NH)

APPLIED LINGUISTICS
Johnson U Florida (FL)

APPLIED PSYCHOLOGY
Christian Brothers U (TN)

ARCHEOLOGY
Weber State U (UT)

ARCHITECTURAL DRAFTING AND CAD/CADD
Academy of Art U (CA)
Sullivan U (KY)

ARCHITECTURAL ENGINEERING TECHNOLOGY
New England Inst of Technology (RI)
Northern Kentucky U (KY)
State U of New York Coll of Technology at Delhi (NY)
Vermont Tech Coll (VT)

ARCHITECTURE
U of Detroit Mercy (MI)

ART
Oakland City U (IN)
Weber State U (UT)

ART HISTORY, CRITICISM AND CONSERVATION
John Cabot U (Italy)

ATHLETIC TRAINING
Dean Coll (MA)
Limestone Coll (SC)

AUTOBODY/COLLISION AND REPAIR TECHNOLOGY
Academy of Art U (CA)
Arkansas Tech U (AR)
Idaho State U (ID)
New England Inst of Technology (RI)
Utah Valley U (UT)

AUTOMATION ENGINEER TECHNOLOGY
Weber State U (UT)

AUTOMOBILE/AUTOMOTIVE MECHANICS TECHNOLOGY
Arkansas Tech U (AR)
Idaho State U (ID)
New England Inst of Technology (RI)
State U of New York Coll of Technology at Delhi (NY)
Utah Valley U (UT)
Weber State U (UT)

AUTOMOTIVE ENGINEERING TECHNOLOGY
Farmingdale State Coll (NY)
The U of West Alabama (AL)
Vermont Tech Coll (VT)

AVIATION/AIRWAY MANAGEMENT
Embry-Riddle Aeronautical U–Worldwide (FL)
Vaughn Coll of Aeronautics and Technology (NY)

AVIONICS MAINTENANCE TECHNOLOGY
Vaughn Coll of Aeronautics and Technology (NY)

BAKING AND PASTRY ARTS
Sullivan U (KY)

BANKING AND FINANCIAL SUPPORT SERVICES
Arkansas Tech U (AR)
Northern State U (SD)

BEHAVIORAL ASPECTS OF HEALTH
Point U (GA)

BEHAVIORAL SCIENCES
Granite State Coll (NH)
Loyola U Chicago (IL)

BIBLICAL STUDIES
Amridge U (AL)
Carson-Newman U (TN)
Covenant Coll (GA)
Dallas Baptist U (TX)
Eastern Mennonite U (VA)
Johnson U Florida (FL)
Kuyper Coll (MI)
Lancaster Bible Coll (PA)
Lincoln Christian U (IL)
Point U (GA)

BIOLOGICAL AND PHYSICAL SCIENCES
Valparaiso U (IN)

BIOLOGY/BIOLOGICAL SCIENCES
Bryn Athyn Coll of the New Church (PA)
Capilano U (BC, Canada)
Dallas Baptist U (TX)
Dean Coll (MA)
Immaculata U (PA)
New York U (NY)
Utah Valley U (UT)
Wright State U–Lake Campus (OH)

BIOLOGY/BIOTECHNOLOGY LABORATORY TECHNICIAN
Weber State U (UT)

BIOMEDICAL SCIENCES
Lubbock Christian U (TX)

BIOMEDICAL TECHNOLOGY
Indiana U–Purdue U Indianapolis (IN)

BIOTECHNOLOGY
Inter American U of Puerto Rico, Barranquitas Campus (PR)
Northern State U (SD)

BUILDING/HOME/ CONSTRUCTION INSPECTION
Utah Valley U (UT)

BUILDING/PROPERTY MAINTENANCE
Utah Valley U (UT)

BUSINESS ADMINISTRATION AND MANAGEMENT
Amridge U (AL)
Arkansas Tech U (AR)
Austin Peay State U (TN)
Benedictine U (IL)
Berkeley Coll–New York City Campus (NY)
Berkeley Coll–White Plains Campus (NY)
Berkeley Coll–Woodland Park Campus (NJ)
Calumet Coll of Saint Joseph (IN)
Cameron U (OK)
Campbellsville U (KY)
Coll of Saint Mary (NE)
Columbia Southern U (AL)
Dakota State U (SD)
Dallas Baptist U (TX)
Dallas Christian Coll (TX)
Dean Coll (MA)
Eastern Mennonite U (VA)
Embry-Riddle Aeronautical U–Worldwide (FL)
Endicott Coll (MA)
Excelsior Coll (NY)
Franklin Pierce U (NH)
Geneva Coll (PA)
Granite State Coll (NH)
Gwynedd Mercy U (PA)
Immaculata U (PA)
Inter American U of Puerto Rico, Aguadilla Campus (PR)
Inter American U of Puerto Rico, Barranquitas Campus (PR)
Inter American U of Puerto Rico, Bayamón Campus (PR)
Inter American U of Puerto Rico, Fajardo Campus (PR)
Inter American U of Puerto Rico, San Germán Campus (PR)
John Cabot U (Italy)
Lancaster Bible Coll (PA)
Lock Haven U of Pennsylvania (PA)
Loyola U Chicago (IL)
Madonna U (MI)
Marian U (IN)
Miami U Hamilton (OH)
Missouri Baptist U (MO)
Mount Marty Coll (SD)
National U (CA)
New England Coll (NH)
New England Inst of Technology (RI)
Northern State U (SD)
Northwood U, Michigan Campus (MI)
Oakland City U (IN)
Ohio Dominican U (OH)
Point U (GA)
Providence Coll (RI)
Regent U (VA)
Reinhardt U (GA)
Saint Francis U (PA)
Saint Joseph's U (PA)
Saint Leo U (FL)
State U of New York Coll of Technology at Delhi (NY)
Sullivan U (KY)

Taylor U (IN)
Toccoa Falls Coll (GA)
Trevecca Nazarene U (TN)
U of Maine at Presque Isle (ME)
U of New Haven (CT)
U of Pennsylvania (PA)
U of Sioux Falls (SD)
U of Southern Indiana (IN)
U of the Incarnate Word (TX)
Utah Valley U (UT)
Vermont Tech Coll (VT)
Western Kentucky U (KY)
Wright State U–Lake Campus (OH)
Youngstown State U (OH)

BUSINESS ADMINISTRATION, MANAGEMENT AND OPERATIONS RELATED
Eastern Oregon U (OR)
Embry-Riddle Aeronautical U–Worldwide (FL)

BUSINESS AUTOMATION/TECHNOLOGY/DATA ENTRY
Utah Valley U (UT)

BUSINESS/COMMERCE
Adams State U (CO)
American Public U System (WV)
Bryn Athyn Coll of the New Church (PA)
Champlain Coll (VT)
Christian Brothers U (TN)
Coll of Staten Island of the City U of New York (NY)
Columbia Coll (MO)
Davenport U, Grand Rapids (MI)
Delaware Valley U (PA)
Idaho State U (ID)
Indiana U of Pennsylvania (PA)
Indiana U Southeast (IN)
Liberty U (VA)
Limestone Coll (SC)
Murray State U (KY)
New York U (NY)
Nichols Coll (MA)
Northern Kentucky U (KY)
Southeastern U (FL)
Southern Arkansas U–Magnolia (AR)
Southwest Baptist U (MO)
Tabor Coll (KS)
U of Massachusetts Lowell (MA)
The U of Toledo (OH)
Youngstown State U (OH)

BUSINESS/MANAGERIAL ECONOMICS
Weber State U (UT)

CABINETMAKING AND MILLWORK
Utah Valley U (UT)

CAD/CADD DRAFTING/DESIGN TECHNOLOGY
Academy of Art U (CA)
Idaho State U (ID)
State U of New York Coll of Technology at Delhi (NY)

CARDIOPULMONARY TECHNOLOGY
Inter American U of Puerto Rico, Barranquitas Campus (PR)

CARDIOVASCULAR TECHNOLOGY
Arkansas Tech U (AR)
Gwynedd Mercy U (PA)
Molloy Coll (NY)

CARPENTRY
New England Inst of Technology (RI)
State U of New York Coll of Technology at Delhi (NY)

CELL BIOLOGY AND ANATOMICAL SCIENCES RELATED
National U (CA)

CHEMICAL TECHNOLOGY
Lawrence Technological U (MI)
U of South Dakota (SD)
Weber State U (UT)

CHEMISTRY
Ohio Dominican U (OH)

Southern Arkansas U–Magnolia (AR)
U of Saint Francis (IN)
Utah Valley U (UT)
Wright State U–Lake Campus (OH)

CHILD-CARE AND SUPPORT SERVICES MANAGEMENT
Idaho State U (ID)
Southeast Missouri State U (MO)
Youngstown State U (OH)

CHILD-CARE PROVISION
American Public U System (WV)

CHILD DEVELOPMENT
Arkansas Tech U (AR)
Kuyper Coll (MI)
Madonna U (MI)
Ohio U (OH)
Point U (GA)
Youngstown State U (OH)

CHINESE
Weber State U (UT)

CHRISTIAN STUDIES
Messenger Coll (TX)
Oklahoma Baptist U (OK)
Ouachita Baptist U (AR)
Regent U (VA)

CINEMATOGRAPHY AND FILM/VIDEO PRODUCTION
Academy of Art U (CA)
FIDM/Fashion Inst of Design & Merchandising, Los Angeles Campus (CA)
New England Inst of Technology (RI)

CIVIL ENGINEERING TECHNOLOGY
Idaho State U (ID)
Murray State U (KY)
New England Inst of Technology (RI)
U of Massachusetts Lowell (MA)
U of New Hampshire (NH)
U of Puerto Rico–Bayamón (PR)
Vermont Tech Coll (VT)
Youngstown State U (OH)

CLASSICS AND CLASSICAL LANGUAGES
John Cabot U (Italy)

CLINICAL LABORATORY SCIENCE/MEDICAL TECHNOLOGY
New England Inst of Technology (RI)

CLINICAL/MEDICAL LABORATORY ASSISTANT
New England Inst of Technology (RI)
U of Maine at Presque Isle (ME)

CLINICAL/MEDICAL LABORATORY TECHNOLOGY
Farmingdale State Coll (NY)
Marshall U (WV)
Sullivan U (KY)
U of Maine at Presque Isle (ME)
U of Saint Francis (IN)
Weber State U (UT)
Youngstown State U (OH)

COMMERCIAL AND ADVERTISING ART
Academy of Art U (CA)
California U of Pennsylvania (PA)
Fashion Inst of Technology (NY)

COMMERCIAL PHOTOGRAPHY
Fashion Inst of Technology (NY)

COMMUNICATION
John Cabot U (Italy)

COMMUNICATION AND JOURNALISM RELATED
Immaculata U (PA)
Madonna U (MI)
Valparaiso U (IN)

COMMUNICATION AND MEDIA RELATED
Cameron U (OK)

COMMUNICATION DISORDERS SCIENCES AND SERVICES RELATED
Granite State Coll (NH)

COMMUNITY HEALTH AND PREVENTIVE MEDICINE
Utah Valley U (UT)

COMMUNITY HEALTH SERVICES COUNSELING
Johnson U Florida (FL)

COMMUNITY ORGANIZATION AND ADVOCACY
New York U (NY)
Wright State U–Lake Campus (OH)

COMPUTER AND INFORMATION SCIENCES
Inter American U of Puerto Rico, Fajardo Campus (PR)
Manchester U (IN)
New England Inst of Technology (RI)
The U of Toledo (OH)
Utah Valley U (UT)
Youngstown State U (OH)

COMPUTER AND INFORMATION SCIENCES AND SUPPORT SERVICES RELATED
Amridge U (AL)
New York U (NY)
Pace U (NY)
Pace U, Pleasantville Campus (NY)

COMPUTER AND INFORMATION SCIENCES RELATED
Limestone Coll (SC)

COMPUTER AND INFORMATION SYSTEMS SECURITY
Arkansas Tech U (AR)
Davenport U, Grand Rapids (MI)
Saint Leo U (FL)
Sullivan U (KY)

COMPUTER ENGINEERING TECHNOLOGY
California U of Pennsylvania (PA)
Sullivan U (KY)
Vermont Tech Coll (VT)

COMPUTER GRAPHICS
Academy of Art U (CA)

COMPUTER/INFORMATION TECHNOLOGY SERVICES ADMINISTRATION RELATED
Berkeley Coll–New York City Campus (NY)
Berkeley Coll–Woodland Park Campus (NJ)
Limestone Coll (SC)

COMPUTER INSTALLATION AND REPAIR TECHNOLOGY
Inter American U of Puerto Rico, Bayamón Campus (PR)

COMPUTER PROGRAMMING
Champlain Coll (VT)
Coll of Staten Island of the City U of New York (NY)
Columbia Central U, Caguas (PR)
Limestone Coll (SC)
New England Inst of Technology (RI)
The U of Toledo (OH)
Youngstown State U (OH)

COMPUTER PROGRAMMING (SPECIFIC APPLICATIONS)
Academy of Art U (CA)

COMPUTER SCIENCE
Creighton U (NE)
Endicott Coll (MA)
Inter American U of Puerto Rico, Aguadilla Campus (PR)
Inter American U of Puerto Rico, Barranquitas Campus (PR)
Inter American U of Puerto Rico, Bayamón Campus (PR)
Inter American U of Puerto Rico, San Germán Campus (PR)
Madonna U (MI)
New England Inst of Technology (RI)
Southwest Baptist U (MO)
The U of Findlay (OH)
Utah Valley U (UT)
Weber State U (UT)

COMPUTER SOFTWARE AND MEDIA APPLICATIONS RELATED
Academy of Art U (CA)
Champlain Coll (VT)
Pace U (NY)
Pace U, Pleasantville Campus (NY)

COMPUTER SOFTWARE ENGINEERING
Vermont Tech Coll (VT)

COMPUTER SUPPORT SPECIALIST
Sullivan U (KY)

COMPUTER SYSTEMS ANALYSIS
Davenport U, Grand Rapids (MI)

COMPUTER SYSTEMS NETWORKING AND TELECOMMUNICATIONS
Davenport U, Grand Rapids (MI)
Idaho State U (ID)
Inter American U of Puerto Rico, Aguadilla Campus (PR)
Pace U (NY)
Pace U, Pleasantville Campus (NY)
Weber State U (UT)

COMPUTER TECHNOLOGY/COMPUTER SYSTEMS TECHNOLOGY
Excelsior Coll (NY)
New England Inst of Technology (RI)

CONSTRUCTION ENGINEERING TECHNOLOGY
Lawrence Technological U (MI)
State U of New York Coll of Technology at Delhi (NY)
Vermont Tech Coll (VT)

CONSTRUCTION MANAGEMENT
Vermont Tech Coll (VT)
Weber State U (UT)

CONSTRUCTION TRADES
Liberty U (VA)

CONSUMER MERCHANDISING/RETAILING MANAGEMENT
Academy of Art U (CA)

CORRECTIONS
Youngstown State U (OH)

CORRECTIONS AND CRIMINAL JUSTICE RELATED
Cameron U (OK)
Inter American U of Puerto Rico, Aguadilla Campus (PR)

COSMETOLOGY
Arkansas Tech U (AR)

COSTUME DESIGN
FIDM/Fashion Inst of Design & Merchandising, Los Angeles Campus (CA)

CREATIVE WRITING
Capilano U (BC, Canada)
John Cabot U (Italy)
Liberty U (VA)
Trevecca Nazarene U (TN)

CRIMINAL JUSTICE/LAW ENFORCEMENT ADMINISTRATION
Arkansas Tech U (AR)
Campbellsville U (KY)
Clarion U of Pennsylvania (PA)
Columbia Coll (MO)
Excelsior Coll (NY)
Franklin Pierce U (NH)
Inter American U of Puerto Rico, Barranquitas Campus (PR)
Lock Haven U of Pennsylvania (PA)
Mansfield U of Pennsylvania (PA)
New England Coll (NH)
New England Inst of Technology (RI)
Regent U (VA)
Reinhardt U (GA)
Salve Regina U (RI)
Tiffin U (OH)
Toccoa Falls Coll (GA)
Trevecca Nazarene U (TN)
U of Maine at Presque Isle (ME)

Utah Valley U (UT)
Youngstown State U (OH)

CRIMINAL JUSTICE/POLICE SCIENCE
Berkeley Coll–New York City Campus (NY)
Berkeley Coll–White Plains Campus (NY)
Berkeley Coll–Woodland Park Campus (NJ)
Columbia Southern U (AL)
Farmingdale State Coll (NY)
Idaho State U (ID)
Inter American U of Puerto Rico, Barranquitas Campus (PR)
Sullivan U (KY)
U of New Haven (CT)
Youngstown State U (OH)

CRIMINAL JUSTICE/SAFETY
American Public U System (WV)
Amridge U (AL)
Arkansas Tech U (AR)
Calumet Coll of Saint Joseph (IN)
Dean Coll (MA)
Endicott Coll (MA)
Inter American U of Puerto Rico, Aguadilla Campus (PR)
Inter American U of Puerto Rico, Fajardo Campus (PR)
Kansas Wesleyan U (KS)
Liberty U (VA)
Madonna U (MI)
Manchester U (IN)
Mount Marty Coll (SD)
Northern State U (SD)
Oakland City U (IN)
Point U (GA)
Saint Leo U (FL)
State U of New York Coll of Technology at Delhi (NY)
U of Saint Francis (IN)
Weber State U (UT)
Youngstown State U (OH)

CRIMINOLOGY
LeTourneau U (TX)

CRITICAL INFRASTRUCTURE PROTECTION
Idaho State U (ID)

CROP PRODUCTION
North Carolina State U (NC)
U of Massachusetts Amherst (MA)

CULINARY ARTS
Coll of Coastal Georgia (GA)
Indiana U of Pennsylvania (PA)
Inter American U of Puerto Rico, Barranquitas Campus (PR)
State U of New York Coll of Technology at Delhi (NY)
Sullivan U (KY)
Utah Valley U (UT)

CULINARY ARTS RELATED
U of New Hampshire (NH)

CYBER/COMPUTER FORENSICS AND COUNTERTERRORISM
Sullivan U (KY)

DAIRY SCIENCE
Vermont Tech Coll (VT)

DANCE
Dean Coll (MA)
U of Saint Francis (IN)
Utah Valley U (UT)

DATA ENTRY/MICROCOMPUTER APPLICATIONS
Davenport U, Grand Rapids (MI)

DATA MODELING/WAREHOUSING AND DATABASE ADMINISTRATION
American Public U System (WV)
Limestone Coll (SC)

DATA PROCESSING AND DATA PROCESSING TECHNOLOGY
American Public U System (WV)
Campbellsville U (KY)
Pace U, Pleasantville Campus (NY)
Youngstown State U (OH)

DENTAL ASSISTING
U of Southern Indiana (IN)

DENTAL HYGIENE
Farmingdale State Coll (NY)
Indiana U–Purdue U Indianapolis (IN)
New York U (NY)
U of New Haven (CT)
U of Pittsburgh (PA)
Utah Valley U (UT)
Vermont Tech Coll (VT)
Weber State U (UT)
Western Kentucky U (KY)

DESIGN AND APPLIED ARTS RELATED
U of Maine at Presque Isle (ME)

DESIGN AND VISUAL COMMUNICATIONS
FIDM/Fashion Inst of Design & Merchandising, Los Angeles Campus (CA)
U of Saint Francis (IN)
Utah Valley U (UT)

DESKTOP PUBLISHING AND DIGITAL IMAGING DESIGN
New England Inst of Technology (RI)

DIAGNOSTIC MEDICAL SONOGRAPHY AND ULTRASOUND TECHNOLOGY
AdventHealth U (FL)
Nebraska Methodist Coll (NE)
The U of Findlay (OH)

DIESEL MECHANICS TECHNOLOGY
Idaho State U (ID)
Utah Valley U (UT)
Vermont Tech Coll (VT)
Weber State U (UT)

DIETETICS
Northwest Missouri State U (MO)

DIETETIC TECHNOLOGY
Youngstown State U (OH)

DIETITIAN ASSISTANT
Youngstown State U (OH)

DIGITAL ARTS
Academy of Art U (CA)
Oakland City U (IN)

DIGITAL COMMUNICATION AND MEDIA/MULTIMEDIA
Vaughn Coll of Aeronautics and Technology (NY)

DISPUTE RESOLUTION
Life U (GA)

DIVINITY/MINISTRY
Johnson U Florida (FL)
Messenger Coll (TX)
Southeastern U (FL)

DRAFTING AND DESIGN TECHNOLOGY
Academy of Art U (CA)
California U of Pennsylvania (PA)
Utah Valley U (UT)
Youngstown State U (OH)

DRAFTING/DESIGN ENGINEERING TECHNOLOGIES RELATED
Weber State U (UT)

DRAMATIC/THEATER ARTS
Adams State U (CO)
Dean Coll (MA)
Utah Valley U (UT)

EARLY CHILDHOOD EDUCATION
Adams State U (CO)
Clarion U of Pennsylvania (PA)
Coll of Saint Mary (NE)
Dean Coll (MA)
Granite State Coll (NH)
Liberty U (VA)
Manchester U (IN)
Oakland City U (IN)
U of Providence (MT)
Utah Valley U (UT)
Western Kentucky U (KY)

ECONOMICS
John Cabot U (Italy)

EDUCATION
Eastern Oregon U (OR)
LeTourneau U (TX)
Lincoln Christian U (IL)
Saint Francis U (PA)
Union Coll (KY)

EDUCATION RELATED
Liberty U (VA)
Weber State U (UT)

EDUCATION (SPECIFIC LEVELS AND METHODS) RELATED
Immaculata U (PA)

EDUCATION (SPECIFIC SUBJECT AREAS) RELATED
U of New Hampshire (NH)

ELECTRICAL AND ELECTRONIC ENGINEERING TECHNOLOGIES RELATED
Miami U Hamilton (OH)
Rochester Inst of Technology (NY)
Vaughn Coll of Aeronautics and Technology (NY)
Youngstown State U (OH)

ELECTRICAL AND ELECTRONICS ENGINEERING
New England Inst of Technology (RI)

ELECTRICAL AND POWER TRANSMISSION INSTALLATION
State U of New York Coll of Technology at Delhi (NY)

ELECTRICAL, ELECTRONIC AND COMMUNICATIONS ENGINEERING TECHNOLOGY
California U of Pennsylvania (PA)
Coll of Staten Island of the City U of New York (NY)
Idaho State U (ID)
Inter American U of Puerto Rico, Aguadilla Campus (PR)
Inter American U of Puerto Rico, San Germán Campus (PR)
New England Inst of Technology (RI)
State U of New York Coll of Technology at Delhi (NY)
U of Massachusetts Lowell (MA)
Vaughn Coll of Aeronautics and Technology (NY)
Vermont Tech Coll (VT)
Weber State U (UT)
Youngstown State U (OH)

ELECTRICAL/ELECTRONICS EQUIPMENT INSTALLATION AND REPAIR
New England Inst of Technology (RI)

ELECTRICIAN
Weber State U (UT)

ELECTROMECHANICAL AND INSTRUMENTATION AND MAINTENANCE TECHNOLOGIES RELATED
Excelsior Coll (NY)

ELECTROMECHANICAL TECHNOLOGY
Excelsior Coll (NY)
State U of New York Coll of Technology at Delhi (NY)

ELEMENTARY EDUCATION
Adams State U (CO)
Brenau U (GA)
Bryn Athyn Coll of the New Church (PA)
LeTourneau U (TX)
Reinhardt U (GA)
Vanguard U of Southern California (CA)

EMERGENCY MEDICAL TECHNOLOGY (EMT PARAMEDIC)
Arkansas Tech U (AR)
Creighton U (NE)
Idaho State U (ID)
Indiana U–Purdue U Indianapolis (IN)
New England Inst of Technology (RI)
Purdue U Northwest (IN)
Southwest Baptist U (MO)
U of New Haven (CT)
U of Sioux Falls (SD)
The U of West Alabama (AL)
Weber State U (UT)
Youngstown State U (OH)

ENERGY MANAGEMENT AND SYSTEMS TECHNOLOGY
Idaho State U (ID)

ENGINEERING
Cameron U (OK)
Coll of Staten Island of the City U of New York (NY)
Geneva Coll (PA)
Weber State U (UT)

ENGINEERING SCIENCE
Rochester Inst of Technology (NY)

ENGINEERING TECHNOLOGIES AND ENGINEERING RELATED
Excelsior Coll (NY)
State U of New York Maritime Coll (NY)
U of Puerto Rico–Bayamón (PR)

ENGINEERING TECHNOLOGY
Austin Peay State U (TN)
Lawrence Technological U (MI)
The U of Toledo (OH)
The U of West Alabama (AL)
Wright State U–Lake Campus (OH)
Youngstown State U (OH)

ENGLISH
Bryn Athyn Coll of the New Church (PA)
Calumet Coll of Saint Joseph (IN)
Capilano U (BC, Canada)
Dean Coll (MA)
Immaculata U (PA)
Madonna U (MI)
Utah Valley U (UT)

ENGLISH LANGUAGE AND LITERATURE RELATED
John Cabot U (Italy)

ENTREPRENEURSHIP
Inter American U of Puerto Rico, Barranquitas Campus (PR)
John Cabot U (Italy)
The U of Findlay (OH)
U of Maine at Machias (ME)

ENVIRONMENTAL SCIENCE
Madonna U (MI)
U of Saint Francis (IN)

EQUESTRIAN STUDIES
Delaware Valley U (PA)
The U of Findlay (OH)

EXPLOSIVE ORDINANCE/BOMB DISPOSAL
American Public U System (WV)

FASHION/APPAREL DESIGN
Academy of Art U (CA)
Fashion Inst of Technology (NY)
FIDM/Fashion Inst of Design & Merchandising, Los Angeles Campus (CA)

FASHION MERCHANDISING
Academy of Art U (CA)
Berkeley Coll–New York City Campus (NY)
Berkeley Coll–White Plains Campus (NY)
Berkeley Coll–Woodland Park Campus (NJ)
Fashion Inst of Technology (NY)
FIDM/Fashion Inst of Design & Merchandising, Los Angeles Campus (CA)
Immaculata U (PA)
LIM Coll (NY)

FASHION MODELING
Fashion Inst of Technology (NY)

FILM/CINEMA/VIDEO STUDIES
Fashion Inst of Technology (NY)
Southeastern U (FL)

FINANCE
Davenport U, Grand Rapids (MI)
The U of Findlay (OH)
Youngstown State U (OH)

FINANCIAL PLANNING AND SERVICES
Berkeley Coll–New York City Campus (NY)
Berkeley Coll–Woodland Park Campus (NJ)

FINE ARTS RELATED
Academy of Art U (CA)
Bryn Athyn Coll of the New Church (PA)

FINE/STUDIO ARTS
Academy of Art U (CA)
Adams State U (CO)
Bryn Athyn Coll of the New Church (PA)
Fashion Inst of Technology (NY)
U of Saint Francis (IN)

FIRE PREVENTION AND SAFETY TECHNOLOGY
U of New Haven (CT)

FIRE SCIENCE/FIREFIGHTING
American Public U System (WV)
Columbia Southern U (AL)
Idaho State U (ID)
Madonna U (MI)
Utah Valley U (UT)

FOOD SERVICE SYSTEMS ADMINISTRATION
Inter American U of Puerto Rico, Aguadilla Campus (PR)
Wright State U–Lake Campus (OH)

FOODS, NUTRITION, AND WELLNESS
Madonna U (MI)
Youngstown State U (OH)

FOREIGN LANGUAGES AND LITERATURES
Bryn Athyn Coll of the New Church (PA)

FOREST TECHNOLOGY
State U of New York Coll of Environmental Science and Forestry (NY)
U of New Hampshire (NH)

FRENCH
Weber State U (UT)

GAME AND INTERACTIVE MEDIA DESIGN
Academy of Art U (CA)
New England Inst of Technology (RI)

GENERAL STUDIES
AdventHealth U (FL)
Alverno Coll (WI)
American Public U System (WV)
Arkansas Tech U (AR)
Austin Peay State U (TN)
Brandman U (CA)
Brenau U (GA)
Cameron U (OK)
Carson-Newman U (TN)
Christian Brothers U (TN)
Clarion U of Pennsylvania (PA)
Columbia Coll (MO)
Columbia Southern U (AL)
Dakota State U (SD)
Dean Coll (MA)
Eastern Mennonite U (VA)
Geneva Coll (PA)
Granite State Coll (NH)
Idaho State U (ID)
Immaculata U (PA)
King U (TN)
Lawrence Technological U (MI)
Lincoln Christian U (IL)
Lipscomb U (TN)
Madonna U (MI)
McNeese State U (LA)
Mercy Coll of Ohio (OH)
Miami U Hamilton (OH)
Mount Marty Coll (SD)
National U (CA)
Northern State U (SD)
Northwest Christian U (OR)
Oakland City U (IN)
The Ohio State U at Lima (OH)
The Ohio State U at Mansfield (OH)
The Ohio State U at Marion (OH)
The Ohio State U at Newark (OH)
Ouachita Baptist U (AR)
Pace U (NY)
Pace U, Pleasantville Campus (NY)
Point U (GA)
Regent U (VA)
Rider U (NJ)
Sacred Heart U (CT)
Southeastern U (FL)
Southern Arkansas U–Magnolia (AR)
State U of New York Coll of Technology at Delhi (NY)
Toccoa Falls Coll (GA)
Trevecca Nazarene U (TN)
U of Central Arkansas (AR)
U of La Verne (CA)
U of Saint Francis (IN)
U of South Florida Sarasota-Manatee (FL)
U of the Incarnate Word (TX)
The U of Toledo (OH)
U of Wisconsin–Superior (WI)
Utah State U (UT)
Utah Valley U (UT)
Weber State U (UT)
Western Kentucky U (KY)
Widener U (PA)

GEOGRAPHY
Wright State U–Lake Campus (OH)

GEOGRAPHY RELATED
Adams State U (CO)

GEOLOGY/EARTH SCIENCE
Wright State U–Lake Campus (OH)

GERMAN
Weber State U (UT)

GERONTOLOGY
Madonna U (MI)
Manchester U (IN)
Ohio Dominican U (OH)

GRAPHIC COMMUNICATIONS
New England Inst of Technology (RI)

GRAPHIC DESIGN
Academy of Art U (CA)
Columbia Central U, Caguas (PR)
Creative Center (NE)
FIDM/Fashion Inst of Design & Merchandising, Los Angeles Campus (CA)
Inter American U of Puerto Rico, San Germán Campus (PR)
Madonna U (MI)
Northern State U (SD)
Southeastern U (FL)
U of Sioux Falls (SD)
U of South Dakota (SD)
Wright State U–Lake Campus (OH)

HEALTH AND PHYSICAL EDUCATION/FITNESS
State U of New York Coll of Technology at Delhi (NY)
Utah Valley U (UT)

HEALTH AND PHYSICAL EDUCATION RELATED
Dean Coll (MA)

HEALTH AND WELLNESS
Dean Coll (MA)

HEALTH/HEALTH-CARE ADMINISTRATION
Berkeley Coll–New York City Campus (NY)
Berkeley Coll–White Plains Campus (NY)
Berkeley Coll–Woodland Park Campus (NJ)
Columbia Southern U (AL)
LeTourneau U (TX)
Point U (GA)
Regent U (VA)

HEALTH INFORMATION/ MEDICAL RECORDS TECHNOLOGY
Berkeley Coll–New York City Campus (NY)
Berkeley Coll–White Plains Campus (NY)
Berkeley Coll–Woodland Park Campus (NJ)
Dakota State U (SD)
Davenport U, Grand Rapids (MI)
Gwynedd Mercy U (PA)
Idaho State U (ID)
Indiana U Northwest (IN)
Mercy Coll of Ohio (OH)
Sullivan U (KY)
Weber State U (UT)
Western Kentucky U (KY)

HEALTH PROFESSIONS RELATED
American Public U System (WV)
Life U (GA)

Lock Haven U of Pennsylvania (PA)
New York U (NY)

HEALTH SERVICES/ALLIED HEALTH/HEALTH SCIENCES
Berkeley Coll–Woodland Park Campus (NJ)
Cameron U (OK)
Excelsior Coll (NY)
Mercy Coll of Ohio (OH)
Nebraska Methodist Coll (NE)
Ohio Dominican U (OH)
U of the Incarnate Word (TX)
Weber State U (UT)

HEATING, AIR CONDITIONING, VENTILATION AND REFRIGERATION MAINTENANCE TECHNOLOGY
Arkansas Tech U (AR)
State U of New York Coll of Technology at Delhi (NY)

HEATING, VENTILATION, AIR CONDITIONING AND REFRIGERATION ENGINEERING TECHNOLOGY
Sullivan U (KY)

HISTOLOGIC TECHNICIAN
Indiana U–Purdue U Indianapolis (IN)

HISTORY
American Public U System (WV)
Bryn Athyn Coll of the New Church (PA)
Dean Coll (MA)
Immaculata U (PA)
John Cabot U (Italy)
Regent U (VA)
Utah Valley U (UT)
Wright State U–Lake Campus (OH)

HOMELAND SECURITY, LAW ENFORCEMENT, FIREFIGHTING AND PROTECTIVE SERVICES RELATED
Idaho State U (ID)

HORTICULTURAL SCIENCE
Temple U (PA)

HOSPITALITY ADMINISTRATION
Coll of Coastal Georgia (GA)
Endicott Coll (MA)
Indiana U of Pennsylvania (PA)
Utah Valley U (UT)
Youngstown State U (OH)

HOTEL, MOTEL, AND RESTAURANT MANAGEMENT
Sullivan U (KY)

HUMAN DEVELOPMENT AND FAMILY STUDIES
Amridge U (AL)

HUMAN DEVELOPMENT AND FAMILY STUDIES RELATED
Utah State U (UT)

HUMANITIES
Bryn Athyn Coll of the New Church (PA)
John Cabot U (Italy)
Ohio U (OH)
State U of New York Coll of Technology at Delhi (NY)
Utah Valley U (UT)
Valparaiso U (IN)

HUMAN NUTRITION
Huntington U of Health Sciences (TN)

HUMAN RESOURCES MANAGEMENT
Amridge U (AL)
Madonna U (MI)
The U of Findlay (OH)

HUMAN RESOURCES MANAGEMENT AND SERVICES RELATED
Oakland City U (IN)

HUMAN SERVICES
Arkansas Tech U (AR)
Calumet Coll of Saint Joseph (IN)
The Catholic U of America (DC)
Columbia Coll (MO)
Excelsior Coll (NY)
Geneva Coll (PA)

ILLUSTRATION
Academy of Art U (CA)
Fashion Inst of Technology (NY)

INDUSTRIAL AND PRODUCT DESIGN
Academy of Art U (CA)

INDUSTRIAL PRODUCTION TECHNOLOGIES RELATED
California U of Pennsylvania (PA)
Clarion U of Pennsylvania (PA)

INDUSTRIAL RADIOLOGIC TECHNOLOGY
Widener U (PA)

INDUSTRIAL TECHNOLOGY
Arkansas Tech U (AR)
Millersville U of Pennsylvania (PA)
Murray State U (KY)
Southeastern Louisiana U (LA)
U of Puerto Rico–Bayamón (PR)

INFORMATION SCIENCE/STUDIES
Dakota State U (SD)
Immaculata U (PA)
U of Massachusetts Lowell (MA)
U of Pittsburgh at Bradford (PA)

INFORMATION TECHNOLOGY
Arkansas Tech U (AR)
Cameron U (OK)
Life U (GA)
Limestone Coll (SC)
New England Inst of Technology (RI)
Point U (GA)
Purdue U (IN)
Regent U (VA)
Saint Leo U (FL)
Trevecca Nazarene U (TN)
U of the Incarnate Word (TX)
Vermont Tech Coll (VT)
Youngstown State U (OH)

INSTRUMENTATION TECHNOLOGY
Idaho State U (ID)
U of Puerto Rico–Bayamón (PR)

INTERDISCIPLINARY STUDIES
Lesley U (MA)
Ohio Dominican U (OH)
U of North Florida (FL)
U of Sioux Falls (SD)

INTERIOR DESIGN
Academy of Art U (CA)
Berkeley Coll–Woodland Park Campus (NJ)
Fashion Inst of Technology (NY)
FIDM/Fashion Inst of Design & Merchandising, Los Angeles Campus (CA)
Indiana U–Purdue U Indianapolis (IN)
New England Inst of Technology (RI)
Weber State U (UT)

INTERNATIONAL BUSINESS/TRADE/COMMERCE
Berkeley Coll–New York City Campus (NY)
Berkeley Coll–Woodland Park Campus (NJ)
John Cabot U (Italy)

INTERNATIONAL/GLOBAL STUDIES
Capilano U (BC, Canada)
Sacred Heart U (CT)

INTERNATIONAL RELATIONS AND AFFAIRS
John Cabot U (Italy)

ITALIAN STUDIES
John Cabot U (Italy)

JAPANESE
Weber State U (UT)

JOURNALISM
Academy of Art U (CA)
Manchester U (IN)

JOURNALISM RELATED
Adams State U (CO)

KINDERGARTEN/PRESCHOOL EDUCATION
California U of Pennsylvania (PA)

KINESIOLOGY AND EXERCISE SCIENCE
Dean Coll (MA)

LABOR STUDIES
Indiana U Bloomington (IN)
Indiana U Northwest (IN)
Indiana U–Purdue U Indianapolis (IN)

LANDSCAPE ARCHITECTURE
Academy of Art U (CA)

LANDSCAPING AND GROUNDSKEEPING
State U of New York Coll of Technology at Delhi (NY)
U of Massachusetts Amherst (MA)
Vermont Tech Coll (VT)

LAY MINISTRY
Theological U of the Caribbean (PR)
U of Saint Francis (IN)

LEGAL ASSISTANT/PARALEGAL
American Public U System (WV)
Coll of Saint Mary (NE)
Excelsior Coll (NY)
Idaho State U (ID)
Liberty U (VA)
Madonna U (MI)
Marian U (IN)
McNeese State U (LA)
National Paralegal Coll (AZ)
National U (CA)
Sullivan U (KY)
U of Louisville (KY)
The U of Toledo (OH)
Utah Valley U (UT)
Western Kentucky U (KY)
Widener U (PA)

LEGAL PROFESSIONS AND STUDIES RELATED
Berkeley Coll–New York City Campus (NY)
Berkeley Coll–Woodland Park Campus (NJ)

LEGAL STUDIES
U of New Haven (CT)

LIBERAL ARTS AND SCIENCES AND HUMANITIES RELATED
Adams State U (CO)
Coll of Saint Mary (NE)
Marymount California U (CA)
New York U (NY)
State U of New York Coll of Technology at Delhi (NY)
Taylor U (IN)
U of Maryland U Coll (MD)
U of Wisconsin–La Crosse (WI)
U of Wisconsin–River Falls (WI)

LIBERAL ARTS AND SCIENCES/LIBERAL STUDIES
Adams State U (CO)
Adelphi U (NY)
American U (DC)
Amridge U (AL)
Averett U (VA)
Bethel U (MN)
Brenau U (GA)
California U of Pennsylvania (PA)
Carson-Newman U (TN)
Coll of Coastal Georgia (GA)
Coll of Staten Island of the City U of New York (NY)
Concordia U Irvine (CA)
Dean Coll (MA)
Eastern U (PA)
Emmanuel Coll (GA)
Endicott Coll (MA)
Excelsior Coll (NY)
Farmingdale State Coll (NY)
Florida Atlantic U (FL)
Florida Coll (FL)
Georgia Southern U (GA)
Holy Apostles Coll and Seminary (CT)
Indiana U of Pennsylvania (PA)
Judson U (IL)
Kuyper Coll (MI)
Limestone Coll (SC)
Loyola U Chicago (IL)
Mansfield U of Pennsylvania (PA)
Maria Coll (NY)
Marian U (IN)
Marymount California U (CA)
Mercy Coll (NY)
Minnesota State U Moorhead (MN)
Molloy Coll (NY)
Mount Marty Coll (SD)
Murray State U (KY)
National U (CA)
New England Coll (NH)
New York U (NY)
Northern Kentucky U (KY)
The Ohio State U at Mansfield (OH)
The Ohio State U at Marion (OH)
The Ohio State U at Newark (OH)
Ohio U (OH)
Providence Coll (RI)
Reinhardt U (GA)
Rochester Coll (MI)
Rocky Mountain Coll (MT)
Saint Joseph's U (PA)
Saint Leo U (FL)
Salve Regina U (RI)
Shiloh U (IA)
State U of New York Coll of Technology at Delhi (NY)
Syracuse U (NY)
Tabor Coll (KS)
U of Maine at Presque Isle (ME)
U of Northwestern–St. Paul (MN)
U of Pittsburgh at Bradford (PA)
U of Saint Francis (IN)
U of South Dakota (SD)
U of the Incarnate Word (TX)
U of Wisconsin–Eau Claire (WI)
U of Wisconsin–Superior (WI)
Western Connecticut State U (CT)
Youngstown State U (OH)

LICENSED PRACTICAL/VOCATIONAL NURSE TRAINING
Arkansas Tech U (AR)
Inter American U of Puerto Rico, Aguadilla Campus (PR)
Inter American U of Puerto Rico, Barranquitas Campus (PR)
Inter American U of Puerto Rico, Bayamón Campus (PR)
Inter American U of Puerto Rico, San Germán Campus (PR)
Maria Coll (NY)

LOGISTICS, MATERIALS, AND SUPPLY CHAIN MANAGEMENT
American Public U System (WV)
Arkansas Tech U (AR)
Embry-Riddle Aeronautical U–Worldwide (FL)
FIDM/Fashion Inst of Design & Merchandising, Los Angeles Campus (CA)
Sullivan U (KY)

MACHINE TOOL TECHNOLOGY
Idaho State U (ID)

MANAGEMENT INFORMATION SYSTEMS
Liberty U (VA)
Miami U Hamilton (OH)
The U of Findlay (OH)
U of the Incarnate Word (TX)
Weber State U (UT)
Wright State U–Lake Campus (OH)

MANAGEMENT INFORMATION SYSTEMS AND SERVICES RELATED
Amridge U (AL)

MANUFACTURING ENGINEERING TECHNOLOGY
Idaho State U (ID)
Lawrence Technological U (MI)
New England Inst of Technology (RI)
Sullivan U (KY)
Weber State U (UT)

MARINE MAINTENANCE AND SHIP REPAIR TECHNOLOGY
New England Inst of Technology (RI)

MARKETING/MARKETING MANAGEMENT
Berkeley Coll–New York City Campus (NY)
Berkeley Coll–White Plains Campus (NY)
Berkeley Coll–Woodland Park Campus (NJ)
FIDM/Fashion Inst of Design & Merchandising, Los Angeles Campus (CA)
John Cabot U (Italy)
Madonna U (MI)
Miami U Hamilton (OH)
Youngstown State U (OH)

MARKETING RELATED
Point U (GA)

MASSAGE THERAPY
Columbia Central U, Caguas (PR)
Idaho State U (ID)

MASS COMMUNICATION/MEDIA
Adams State U (CO)
Dean Coll (MA)
Johnson U Florida (FL)
U of Sioux Falls (SD)
Wright State U–Lake Campus (OH)

MATHEMATICS
Bryn Athyn Coll of the New Church (PA)
Creighton U (NE)
Dean Coll (MA)
Idaho State U (ID)
Taylor U (IN)
Trevecca Nazarene U (TN)
Utah Valley U (UT)
Weber State U (UT)

MECHANICAL ENGINEERING
New England Inst of Technology (RI)

MECHANICAL ENGINEERING/MECHANICAL TECHNOLOGY
Farmingdale State Coll (NY)
Idaho State U (ID)
Lawrence Technological U (MI)
Miami U Hamilton (OH)
Vermont Tech Coll (VT)
Weber State U (UT)
Youngstown State U (OH)

MECHANICAL ENGINEERING TECHNOLOGIES RELATED
U of Massachusetts Lowell (MA)

MECHANICS AND REPAIR
Idaho State U (ID)
Utah Valley U (UT)
Weber State U (UT)

MECHATRONICS, ROBOTICS, AND AUTOMATION ENGINEERING
Utah Valley U (UT)

MEDICAL ADMINISTRATIVE ASSISTANT AND MEDICAL SECRETARY
Arkansas Tech U (AR)

MEDICAL/CLINICAL ASSISTANT
Arkansas Tech U (AR)
Berkeley Coll–Woodland Park Campus (NJ)
Davenport U, Grand Rapids (MI)
Idaho State U (ID)
New England Inst of Technology (RI)
Sullivan U (KY)
Youngstown State U (OH)

MEDICAL INSURANCE CODING
Columbia Southern U (AL)
Davenport U, Grand Rapids (MI)

MEDICAL OFFICE ASSISTANT
Liberty U (VA)

MEDICAL RADIOLOGIC TECHNOLOGY
Cameron U (OK)
Inter American U of Puerto Rico, San Germán Campus (PR)
U of Sioux Falls (SD)

MEETING AND EVENT PLANNING
Sullivan U (KY)

MENTAL AND SOCIAL HEALTH SERVICES AND ALLIED PROFESSIONS RELATED
Clarion U of Pennsylvania (PA)
New England Inst of Technology (RI)

MERCHANDISING, SALES, AND MARKETING OPERATIONS RELATED (GENERAL)
State U of New York Coll of Technology at Delhi (NY)

METAL AND JEWELRY ARTS
Academy of Art U (CA)
Fashion Inst of Technology (NY)
FIDM/Fashion Inst of Design & Merchandising, Los Angeles Campus (CA)

MICROBIOLOGY
Weber State U (UT)

MILITARY HISTORY
American Public U System (WV)

MISSIONARY STUDIES AND MISSIOLOGY
Southeastern U (FL)
Theological U of the Caribbean (PR)

MULTI/INTERDISCIPLINARY STUDIES RELATED
Arkansas Tech U (AR)
Dallas Baptist U (TX)
Dallas Christian Coll (TX)
Liberty U (VA)
Ohio U (OH)
Utah Valley U (UT)
Wright State U–Lake Campus (OH)

MUSEUM STUDIES
U of Saint Francis (IN)

MUSIC
Marian U (IN)
Utah Valley U (UT)

MUSICAL INSTRUMENT FABRICATION AND REPAIR
Indiana U Bloomington (IN)

MUSICAL THEATER
Dean Coll (MA)

MUSIC PERFORMANCE
Trevecca Nazarene U (TN)

MUSIC RELATED
Academy of Art U (CA)
Alverno Coll (WI)
Trevecca Nazarene U (TN)

MUSIC TECHNOLOGY
U of Saint Francis (IN)

NANOTECHNOLOGY
Lock Haven U of Pennsylvania (PA)

NATURAL RESOURCE RECREATION AND TOURISM
State U of New York Coll of Technology at Delhi (NY)

NATURAL RESOURCES/ CONSERVATION
State U of New York Coll of Environmental Science and Forestry (NY)

NATURAL SCIENCES
Gwynedd Mercy U (PA)
Madonna U (MI)

NUCLEAR ENGINEERING TECHNOLOGY
Arkansas Tech U (AR)
Idaho State U (ID)

NUCLEAR MEDICAL TECHNOLOGY
Molloy Coll (NY)
The U of Findlay (OH)

NUCLEAR/NUCLEAR POWER TECHNOLOGY
Excelsior Coll (NY)

NURSING SCIENCE
Inter American U of Puerto Rico, Barranquitas Campus (PR)

NUTRITION SCIENCES
U of the Incarnate Word (TX)

OCCUPATIONAL SAFETY AND HEALTH TECHNOLOGY
Columbia Southern U (AL)

OCCUPATIONAL THERAPIST ASSISTANT
AdventHealth U (FL)
Arkansas Tech U (AR)
Idaho State U (ID)
Maria Coll (NY)
Mercy Coll (NY)
New England Inst of Technology (RI)
U of Southern Indiana (IN)

OFFICE MANAGEMENT
Columbia Central U, Caguas (PR)
Emmanuel Coll (GA)
Inter American U of Puerto Rico, Aguadilla Campus (PR)
Inter American U of Puerto Rico, Barranquitas Campus (PR)
Inter American U of Puerto Rico, Bayamón Campus (PR)
Inter American U of Puerto Rico, Fajardo Campus (PR)
Inter American U of Puerto Rico, San Germán Campus (PR)

OPTOMETRIC TECHNICIAN
Indiana U Bloomington (IN)

ORGANIZATIONAL BEHAVIOR
Concordia U Chicago (IL)
Johnson U Florida (FL)

ORGANIZATIONAL COMMUNICATION
Creighton U (NE)

ORGANIZATIONAL LEADERSHIP
Point U (GA)
Southeastern U (FL)

ORNAMENTAL HORTICULTURE
Farmingdale State Coll (NY)
Vermont Tech Coll (VT)

PALLIATIVE CARE NURSING
Madonna U (MI)

PARKS, RECREATION AND LEISURE
Dean Coll (MA)

PARKS, RECREATION AND LEISURE FACILITIES MANAGEMENT
State U of New York Coll of Technology at Delhi (NY)
U of Maine at Machias (ME)

PETROLEUM TECHNOLOGY
Mansfield U of Pennsylvania (PA)
U of Pittsburgh at Bradford (PA)

PHARMACY TECHNICIAN
Columbia Central U, Caguas (PR)
Inter American U of Puerto Rico, Aguadilla Campus (PR)
Sullivan U (KY)

PHILOSOPHY
John Cabot U (Italy)
Utah Valley U (UT)

PHILOSOPHY AND RELIGIOUS STUDIES
Bryn Athyn Coll of the New Church (PA)

PHOTOGRAPHY
Inter American U of Puerto Rico, Bayamón Campus (PR)

PHYSICAL FITNESS TECHNICIAN
The U of Findlay (OH)

PHYSICAL SCIENCES
Coll of Staten Island of the City U of New York (NY)
Utah Valley U (UT)

PHYSICAL THERAPY
Louisiana Coll (LA)

PHYSICAL THERAPY TECHNOLOGY
Arkansas Tech U (AR)
California U of Pennsylvania (PA)
Idaho State U (ID)
Nebraska Methodist Coll (NE)
New England Inst of Technology (RI)
Southern Illinois U Carbondale (IL)
U of Maine at Presque Isle (ME)
U of Saint Francis (IN)

PHYSICS
Idaho State U (ID)
Utah Valley U (UT)

PIPEFITTING AND SPRINKLER FITTING
New England Inst of Technology (RI)
State U of New York Coll of Technology at Delhi (NY)

POLITICAL SCIENCE AND GOVERNMENT
John Cabot U (Italy)
Liberty U (VA)

PRE-ENGINEERING
Columbia Coll (MO)
Utah Valley U (UT)

PRENURSING STUDIES
Dean Coll (MA)
Lincoln Christian U (IL)
Missouri Baptist U (MO)

PRE-PHARMACY STUDIES
Madonna U (MI)

PRE-THEOLOGY/PRE-MINISTERIAL STUDIES
Eastern Mennonite U (VA)
Tabor Coll (KS)
Theological U of the Caribbean (PR)

PSYCHOLOGY
Bryn Athyn Coll of the New Church (PA)
Calumet Coll of Saint Joseph (IN)
Capilano U (BC, Canada)
Dean Coll (MA)
John Cabot U (Italy)
Liberty U (VA)
Life U (GA)
Marian U (IN)
New England Coll (NH)
Point U (GA)
Regent U (VA)
Utah Valley U (UT)
Wright State U–Lake Campus (OH)

PUBLIC ADMINISTRATION AND SOCIAL SERVICE PROFESSIONS RELATED
Trevecca Nazarene U (TN)

PUBLIC HEALTH
American Public U System (WV)
Point U (GA)

PUBLIC RELATIONS, ADVERTISING, AND APPLIED COMMUNICATION RELATED
U of Maine at Presque Isle (ME)

PURCHASING, PROCUREMENT/ ACQUISITIONS AND CONTRACTS MANAGEMENT
Miami U Hamilton (OH)
Trevecca Nazarene U (TN)

QUALITY CONTROL AND SAFETY TECHNOLOGIES RELATED
Madonna U (MI)

RADIO AND TELEVISION
Lawrence Technological U (MI)
U of Northwestern–St. Paul (MN)

RADIO AND TELEVISION BROADCASTING TECHNOLOGY
New England Inst of Technology (RI)

RADIOLOGIC TECHNOLOGY/ SCIENCE
AdventHealth U (FL)
Allen Coll (IA)
Coll of Coastal Georgia (GA)
Indiana U Kokomo (IN)
Indiana U Northwest (IN)
Indiana U–Purdue U Indianapolis (IN)
Indiana U South Bend (IN)
Inter American U of Puerto Rico, Aguadilla Campus (PR)
Inter American U of Puerto Rico, Barranquitas Campus (PR)
Mansfield U of Pennsylvania (PA)
Mercy Coll of Ohio (OH)
Missouri Baptist U (MO)
Nebraska Methodist Coll (NE)
Sacred Heart U (CT)
Sullivan U (KY)
U of Saint Francis (IN)
Vermont Tech Coll (VT)
Weber State U (UT)
Widener U (PA)

RADIO, TELEVISION, AND DIGITAL COMMUNICATION RELATED
Madonna U (MI)

REAL ESTATE
American Public U System (WV)
Miami U Hamilton (OH)

RECORDING ARTS TECHNOLOGY
Academy of Art U (CA)
Columbia Central U, Caguas (PR)
Indiana U Bloomington (IN)
New England Inst of Technology (RI)

REGIONAL STUDIES
Arkansas Tech U (AR)

REGISTERED NURSING/ REGISTERED NURSE
Arkansas Tech U (AR)
California U of Pennsylvania (PA)
Campbellsville U (KY)
Clarion U of Pennsylvania (PA)
Coll of Coastal Georgia (GA)
Coll of Staten Island of the City U of New York (NY)
Columbia Central U, Caguas (PR)
Columbia Coll (MO)
Excelsior Coll (NY)
Gwynedd Mercy U (PA)
Idaho State U (ID)
Inter American U of Puerto Rico, Barranquitas Campus (PR)
Lock Haven U of Pennsylvania (PA)
Maria Coll (NY)
Marshall U (WV)
Mercy Coll of Ohio (OH)
New England Inst of Technology (RI)
Sacred Heart U (CT)
Southern Arkansas U–Magnolia (AR)
Southwest Baptist U (MO)
State U of New York Coll of Technology at Delhi (NY)
U of Pittsburgh at Bradford (PA)
U of Saint Francis (IN)
U of South Dakota (SD)
The U of West Alabama (AL)
Utah Valley U (UT)
Vermont Tech Coll (VT)
Weber State U (UT)
Western Kentucky U (KY)

RELIGIOUS EDUCATION
Dallas Baptist U (TX)
Kuyper Coll (MI)
Marian U (IN)

RELIGIOUS/SACRED MUSIC
Southeastern U (FL)
Trevecca Nazarene U (TN)

RELIGIOUS STUDIES
Bryn Athyn Coll of the New Church (PA)
Campbellsville U (KY)
Holy Apostles Coll and Seminary (CT)
Liberty U (VA)
Madonna U (MI)
Mount Marty Coll (SD)
Oakland City U (IN)

RESORT MANAGEMENT
State U of New York Coll of Technology at Delhi (NY)

RESPIRATORY CARE THERAPY
Clarion U of Pennsylvania (PA)
Dakota State U (SD)
Gwynedd Mercy U (PA)
Idaho State U (ID)
Mansfield U of Pennsylvania (PA)
Molloy Coll (NY)
Nebraska Methodist Coll (NE)
New England Inst of Technology (RI)
Sullivan U (KY)
U of Southern Indiana (IN)
Vermont Tech Coll (VT)
Weber State U (UT)

RESPIRATORY THERAPY TECHNICIAN
U of the Incarnate Word (TX)

RESTAURANT, CULINARY, AND CATERING MANAGEMENT
State U of New York Coll of Technology at Delhi (NY)

RESTAURANT/FOOD SERVICES MANAGEMENT
American Public U System (WV)

RETAILING
American Public U System (WV)
The U of Findlay (OH)
Weber State U (UT)

ROBOTICS TECHNOLOGY
Idaho State U (ID)
Utah Valley U (UT)

RUSSIAN
Idaho State U (ID)

SALES, DISTRIBUTION, AND MARKETING OPERATIONS
Inter American U of Puerto Rico, Aguadilla Campus (PR)
Sullivan U (KY)

SCIENCE TEACHER EDUCATION
Wright State U–Lake Campus (OH)

SCIENCE TECHNOLOGIES RELATED
Madonna U (MI)
Maria Coll (NY)

SELLING SKILLS AND SALES
Inter American U of Puerto Rico, San Germán Campus (PR)

SOCIAL SCIENCES
Campbellsville U (KY)
Marymount Manhattan Coll (NY)
U of Sioux Falls (SD)
U of Southern Indiana (IN)
Valparaiso U (IN)

SOCIAL WORK
Youngstown State U (OH)

SOCIOLOGY
Dean Coll (MA)
New England Coll (NH)
Wright State U–Lake Campus (OH)

SPANISH
Weber State U (UT)

SPECIAL EDUCATION
U of Maine at Presque Isle (ME)

SPEECH COMMUNICATION AND RHETORIC
American Public U System (WV)
Dean Coll (MA)
Trevecca Nazarene U (TN)
Utah Valley U (UT)
Weber State U (UT)
Wright State U–Lake Campus (OH)

SPORT AND FITNESS ADMINISTRATION/ MANAGEMENT
Dean Coll (MA)
State U of New York Coll of Technology at Delhi (NY)

SUBSTANCE ABUSE/ ADDICTION COUNSELING
National U (CA)
U of Providence (MT)

SURGICAL TECHNOLOGY
Berkeley Coll–Woodland Park Campus (NJ)
Nebraska Methodist Coll (NE)
New England Inst of Technology (RI)
Sullivan U (KY)
U of Providence (MT)
U of Saint Francis (IN)

SURVEYING TECHNOLOGY
State U of New York Coll of Environmental Science and Forestry (NY)
Utah Valley U (UT)

SUSTAINABILITY STUDIES
Lock Haven U of Pennsylvania (PA)

SYSTEM, NETWORKING, AND LAN/WAN MANAGEMENT
Dakota State U (SD)

TEACHER ASSISTANT/AIDE
Alverno Coll (WI)
Eastern Mennonite U (VA)
U of Maine at Presque Isle (ME)
Valparaiso U (IN)

TELECOMMUNICATIONS TECHNOLOGY
Pace U (NY)

TERRORISM AND COUNTERTERRORISM OPERATIONS
American Public U System (WV)

THEATER DESIGN AND TECHNOLOGY
Utah Valley U (UT)

THEOLOGICAL AND MINISTERIAL STUDIES RELATED
Lincoln Christian U (IL)

THEOLOGY
Creighton U (NE)
Holy Apostles Coll and Seminary (CT)
Immaculata U (PA)
Ohio Dominican U (OH)

THEOLOGY AND RELIGIOUS VOCATIONS RELATED
Missouri Baptist U (MO)
Trevecca Nazarene U (TN)

TOURISM AND TRAVEL SERVICES MARKETING
State U of New York Coll of Technology at Delhi (NY)

TRADE AND INDUSTRIAL TEACHER EDUCATION
Murray State U (KY)

TURF AND TURFGRASS MANAGEMENT
North Carolina State U (NC)
State U of New York Coll of Technology at Delhi (NY)
U of Massachusetts Amherst (MA)

URBAN MINISTRY
Tabor Coll (KS)

VETERINARY/ANIMAL HEALTH TECHNOLOGY
New England Inst of Technology (RI)
Purdue U (IN)
State U of New York Coll of Technology at Delhi (NY)
U of New Hampshire (NH)
Vermont Tech Coll (VT)

WEAPONS OF MASS DESTRUCTION
American Public U System (WV)

WEB/MULTIMEDIA MANAGEMENT AND WEBMASTER
American Public U System (WV)

WEB PAGE, DIGITAL/ MULTIMEDIA AND INFORMATION RESOURCES DESIGN
Academy of Art U (CA)
Amridge U (AL)
Dakota State U (SD)
Limestone Coll (SC)
New England Inst of Technology (RI)
Utah Valley U (UT)
Weber State U (UT)

WELDING ENGINEERING TECHNOLOGY
New England Inst of Technology (RI)

WELDING TECHNOLOGY
Arkansas Tech U (AR)
Idaho State U (ID)
State U of New York Coll of Technology at Delhi (NY)

YOUTH MINISTRY
Johnson U Florida (FL)

Alphabetical Listing of Two-Year Colleges

NOTES

NOTES

NOTES

NOTES

NOTES

NOTES

NOTES

NOTES

NOTES

NOTES

NOTES

NOTES

NOTES

NOTES

NOTES

NOTES

NOTES

NOTES

NOTES

NOTES

NOTES

NOTES